Lecture Notes in Computer Science 14643

The series Lecture Notes in Computer Science (LNCS), including its subseries Lecture Notes in Artificial Intelligence (LNAI) and Lecture Notes in Bioinformatics (LNBI), has established itself as a medium for the publication of new developments in computer science and information technology research, teaching, and education.

LNCS enjoys close cooperation with the computer science R & D community, the series counts many renowned academics among its volume editors and paper authors, and collaborates with prestigious societies. Its mission is to serve this international community by providing an invaluable service, mainly focused on the publication of conference and workshop proceedings and postproceedings. LNCS commenced publication in 1973.

Elisabeth Oswald
Editor

Topics in Cryptology – CT-RSA 2024

Cryptographers' Track at the RSA Conference 2024
San Francisco, CA, USA, May 6–9, 2024
Proceedings

Editor
Elisabeth Oswald
University of Klagenfurt
Klagenfurt, Austria

ISSN 0302-9743 ISSN 1611-3349 (electronic)
Lecture Notes in Computer Science
ISBN 978-3-031-58867-9 ISBN 978-3-031-58868-6 (eBook)
https://doi.org/10.1007/978-3-031-58868-6

This Springer imprint is published by the registered company Springer Nature Switzerland AG
The registered company address is: Gewerbestrasse 11, 6330 Cham, Switzerland

Paper in this product is recyclable.

Preface

The RSA Conference has been the premiere trade show for the security industry since 1991, hosting over 40,000 attendees each year from industry, government, and academia. The Cryptographers' Track (CT-RSA) is RSAC's venue for scientific papers on cryptography. This volume represents the proceedings of the 2024 edition of the Cryptographers' Track at the RSA Conference, which took place in San Francisco, California, USA during May 6–9, 2024.

We received 47 submissions. One submission was later withdrawn. The remaining 46 papers were each assigned three reviewers. Papers that included a program committee member as author were assigned an additional reviewer. The reviewing process was double-blind, and carried out using the HotCRP conference management system. We followed the IACR policy for conflicts of interest.

The review process concluded by selecting 18 papers for acceptance, some of which were assigned a shepherd; these papers comprise the final scientific program. The acceptance rate thus was $18/46 = 39\%$.

CT-RSA would not have been possible without the valuable contributions of many volunteers. My sincere thanks go out to all program committee members, as well as the external reviewers, for their constructive reviews, and for actively participating in the discussions during the selection process.

Special thanks are due to:

- the committee members who acted as shepherds;
- Richard Newell for help organizing the panel discussion;
- Mike Rosulek (CT-RSA 2023 program chair) for kindly sharing knowledge about the role of program chair;
- the RSA Conference team, in particular Britta Glade and Christie Ross, for their support with scheduling and procedural matters.

March 2024 Elisabeth Oswald

Organization

Program Committee Chair

Elisabeth Oswald	University of Klagenfurt, Austria, and University of Birmingham, UK

Program Committee

Masayuki Abe	NTT Social Informatics Laboratories, Japan
Paulo Barreto	University of Washington - Tacoma, USA
Rishiraj Bhattacharyya	University of Birmingham, UK
Alex Biryukov	University of Luxembourg, Luxembourg
Olivier Blazy	Ecole Polytechnique, France
Andreas Erwig	Technische Universität Darmstadt, Germany
Luca De Feo	IBM Research, Switzerland
Georgios Fotiadis	University of Luxembourg, Luxembourg
Benjamin Fuller	University of Connecticut, USA
Steven Galbraith	University of Auckland, New Zealand
Marylin George	Mongo DB, USA
Sylvain Guilley	Secure-IC, France
Mike Hamburg	Rambus Labs, USA
Helena Handschuh	Rambus, USA
Martha Norberg Hovd	Simula UiB, Norway
James Howe	SandboxAQ, UK
Mike Rosulek	Oregon State University, USA
Loic Masure	LIRMM Université de Montpellier, France
Lenka Marekova	ETH Zurich, Switzerland
Amir Moradi	University of Darmstadt, Germany
Arpita Patra	IICS Bangalore, India
Bart Preneel	KU Leuven, Belgium
Arnab Roy	University of Innsbruck, Austria
Yu Sasaki	NTT Social Informatics Laboratories, NIST Associate, Japan
Erkay Savas	Sabanci University, Turkey
Tobias Schneider	NXP Semiconductors, Austria
Sujoy Sinha Roy	TU Graz, Austria
Nigel Smart	KU Leuven and Zama, Belgium

Marloes Venema University of Wuppertal, Germany
Srinivas Vivek IIIT Bangalore, India

Additional Reviewers

Ajith Suresh
Anand Kumar
Bertram Poettering
Deirdre Connolly
Giacomo Borin
Ismail Afia
Lukas Stennes
Marius Lombard-Platet
Matthias Johann Steiner
Melih Rumi Pelen
Nicolas Gama
Nina Bindel
Sikhar Patranabis

Contents

Public Key Cryptography

A Public Key Identity-Based Revocation Scheme:: Fully Attribute-Hiding and Function Private 3
Olivier Blazy and Sayantan Mukherjee

Computational Security Analysis of the Full EDHOC Protocol 25
Loïc Ferreira

Symmetric Cryptography

The Multi-user Security of MACs via Universal Hashing in the Ideal Cipher Model 51
Yusuke Naito

Automated-Based Rebound Attacks on ACE Permutation 78
Jiali Shi, Guoqiang Liu, Chao Li, and Yingxin Li

The Exact Multi-user Security of 2-Key Triple DES 112
Yusuke Naito, Yu Sasaki, and Takeshi Sugawara

Improved Meet-in-the-Middle Attacks on Nine Rounds of the AES-192 Block Cipher 136
Jiqiang Lu and Wenchang Zhou

Signatures

Batch Signatures, Revisited 163
Carlos Aguilar-Melchor, Martin R. Albrecht, Thomas Bailleux, Nina Bindel, James Howe, Andreas Hülsing, David Joseph, and Marc Manzano

History-Free Sequential Aggregation of Hash-and-Sign Signatures 187
Alessio Meneghetti and Edoardo Signorini

Attribute-Based Signatures with Advanced Delegation, and Tracing 224
Cécile Delerablée, Lénaïck Gouriou, and David Pointcheval

Lattice-Based Threshold, Accountable, and Private Signature 249
Yingfei Yan, Yongjun Zhao, Wen Gao, and Baocang Wang

Homomorphic Encryption

TFHE Public-Key Encryption Revisited 277
Marc Joye

Differential Privacy for Free? Harnessing the Noise in Approximate Homomorphic Encryption 292
Tabitha Ogilvie

Identity-Based Encryption

Identity-Based Encryption from LWE with More Compact Master Public Key 319
Parhat Abla

Towards Compact Identity-Based Encryption on Ideal Lattices 354
Huiwen Jia, Yupu Hu, Chunming Tang, and Lin Wang

Constructions

ASCON MAC, PRF, and Short-Input PRF: Lightweight, Fast, and Efficient Pseudorandom Functions 381
Christoph Dobraunig, Maria Eichlseder, Florian Mendel, and Martin Schläffer

Interactive Oracle Arguments in the QROM and Applications to Succinct Verification of Quantum Computation 404
Islam Faisal

Threshold Signatures and Fault Attacks

SoK: Parameterization of Fault Adversary Models Connecting Theory and Practice 433
Dilara Toprakhisar, Svetla Nikova, and Ventzislav Nikov

Cutting the GRASS: Threshold GRoup Action Signature Schemes 460
Michele Battagliola, Giacomo Borin, Alessio Meneghetti, and Edoardo Persichetti

Author Index 491

Public Key Cryptography

A Public Key Identity-Based Revocation Scheme:
Fully Attribute-Hiding and Function Private

Olivier Blazy[1] and Sayantan Mukherjee[2](✉)

[1] Ecole Polytechnique, Paris, France
olivier.blazy@polytechnique.edu
[2] Indian Institute of Technology Jammu, Jammu, India
csayantan.mukherjee@gmail.com

Abstract. Multi-Recipient Encryption allows users to send secure messages to any chosen set of registered users. In ACISP'21, Blazy et al. proposed a multi-recipient encryption with attribute-hiding revocation where ciphertexts do not reveal any information about the users that have been revoked. However, their work only achieved secret key instantiations of multi-recipient encryption with attribute-hiding revocation.

Our work gives the first public-key Identity-Based Revocation with fully attribute-hiding security and computational function privacy. For this purpose, we construct the first fully attribute-hiding Non-zero Inner-Product Encryption (NIPE) with computational function privacy. Toward this goal, we also study the relationship between Zero Inner-Product Encryption (ZIPE) and Non-Zero Inner-Product Encryption (NIPE). We propose a compiler to convert a fully attribute-hiding secure ZIPE into a fully attribute-hiding secure NIPE. We then construct the ZIPE with the necessary security properties. This construction along with the compiler produces the first NIPE with the said full attribute-hiding security. We also argue that this NIPE construction achieves computational function privacy due to a falsifiable assumption. A variation of Attrapadung and Libert's transformation (PKC'11) on our NIPE thus achieves the first attribute-hiding identity-based revocation (IBR) scheme in the standard model. We further show that our IBR construction achieves function privacy under another novel assumption which we show to be falsifiable.

1 Introduction

Identity-based cryptosystem [10,34] has been an essential object in the new paradigm of cloud-based cryptosystems. In the last two decades, *identity-based encryption* (IBE) has been studied extensively in different forms. Katz *et al.* [24] introduced *predicate encryption* (PE) as a framework that generalizes IBE and related offshoots. PE is typically defined for an arbitrary predicate f where the decryption of a ciphertext is decided based on the evaluation of f on the encrypted attribute value. For a PE defined for a predicate f, a secret key sk

E. Oswald (Ed.): CT-RSA 2024, LNCS 14643, pp. 3–24, 2024.
https://doi.org/10.1007/978-3-031-58868-6_1

on *key-attribute* x decrypts a ciphertext Ct defined on *data-attribute* y if $f(x, y)$ takes a particular fixed value. In such an event, we often say that x *matches* y (or x *is authorized for* y). Security of a PE (for a predicate f) requires that sk does not leak any new information about Ct if x *does not match* y (or x *is not authorized for* y). PEs have been studied for a long time through the lens of different security requirements:

1. Confidentiality or Message-Hiding Security (MH): Given Ct encoding $m^{[\mathfrak{b}]}$ for $\mathfrak{b} \leftarrow \{0,1\}$ for adversarially chosen messages $m^{[0]}, m^{[1]}$, no ppt adversary can guess $\mathfrak{b}$ if all secret keys sk it queried are unauthorized.
2. Weak Anonymity or Weakly Attribute-Hiding Security (WAH): Given Ct encoding $y^{[\mathfrak{b}]}$ for $\mathfrak{b} \leftarrow \{0,1\}$ for adversarially chosen attributes $y^{[0]}, y^{[1]}$, no ppt adversary can guess $\mathfrak{b}$ if all secret keys sk it queried are unauthorized.
3. Full Anonymity or Fully Attribute-Hiding Security (FAH): Given Ct encoding $y^{[\mathfrak{b}]}$ for $\mathfrak{b} \leftarrow \{0,1\}$ for adversarially chosen attributes $y^{[0]}, y^{[1]}$, no ppt adversary can guess $\mathfrak{b}$ even if some secret keys sk it queried are authorized and some are unauthorized.
4. Predicate Privacy or Function Privacy (FPriv): Given sk encoding $x^{[\mathfrak{b}]}$ for $\mathfrak{b} \leftarrow \{0,1\}$ for adversarially chosen attributes $x^{[0]}, x^{[1]}$, no ppt adversary can guess $\mathfrak{b}$.

In this work, we focus on two PEs, namely, *inner-product encryptions* (IPE) and *identity-based multi-recipient encryptions* (IBMRE). As the names suggest, the decryption of an IPE depends on the inner-product of key and data-attribute vectors. In contrast, identity-based multi-recipient encryption's decryption depends on the membership relation of key and data attributes. In the literature, two variants of both IPE and IBMRE have been studied:

IPE	Zero Inner-Product Encryption (ZIPE) [24]: Ct corresponding to $\mathbf{y}$ is decrypted by sk corresponding to $\mathbf{x}$ if $\langle \mathbf{x}, \mathbf{y} \rangle = 0$
	Non-zero Inner-Product Encryption (NIPE) [5]: Ct corresponding to $\mathbf{y}$ is decrypted by sk corresponding to $\mathbf{x}$ if $\langle \mathbf{x}, \mathbf{y} \rangle \neq 0$
IBMRE	Identity-based Broadcast Encryption (IBBE) [16]: Ct corresponding to S is decrypted by sk corresponding to id if $\mathsf{id} \in \mathsf{S}$
	Identity-based Revocation (IBR) [9]: Ct corresponding to S is decrypted by sk corresponding to id if $\mathsf{id} \notin \mathsf{S}$

Generic Transformations Towards Fully Anonymous and Function Private IBR? Attrapadung and Libert [5] generically transformed IPE to IBMRE (i.e., ZIPE to IBBE and NIPE to IBR). They showed this transformation to be only confidentiality preserving, as they converted a ZIPE (resp. NIPE) with message-hiding security into an IBBE (resp. IBR) with the same security. Ramanna [33] converted a weakly anonymous ZIPE to a weakly anonymous IBBE in a similar path. We note that the proof technique of Ramanna [33] naturally applies to the fully anonymous setting (i.e. fully anonymous ZIPE to fully anonymous IBBE and fully anonymous NIPE to fully anonymous IBR). But we lack a candidate for fully anonymous NIPE even after having many fully anonymous ZIPEs [15,31]. We further report that there is not even a single fully anonymous NIPE that does not require unrealistically restrictive security models [23,32] (See Sect. 1.4). On top of this, although [32] constructed a function private NIPE, falsifiability of their entropy-based assumptions was not provided, which is highly troublesome after the attacks in auxiliary settings [7,26]. Looking ahead, the transformation of [5] off-the-shelf does not respect function privacy. Thus, even if we had a function private NIPE (resp. a function private ZIPE), just plugging it in the transformation of [5] does not get a function private IBR (resp. a function private IBBE). In this work, therefore, we thus study two very pertinent questions:

1. Can we design a fully attribute-hiding public key NIPE with function privacy?
2. Can we design a fully attribute-hiding public key IBR with function privacy?

Our Motivations. As we look more closely at the literature, let us make our motivations more transparent. Theoretically, these are critical questions as IBR (and NIPE) have been the *lesser attended sibling.* We substantiate this claim with an example: notions like *outsider-anonymous security* [19] and *fully anonymous security* [37] were introduced to capture attribute-hiding security in the multi-recipient encryptions but were studied only in the broadcast encryption setting. Therefore, the study of full attribute-hiding security of IBR (and NIPE) is highly timely. On the other hand, it is well-known that achieving, nay defining function-privacy in the public key setting is quite tricky since, in the public key setting, the adversary can create several ciphertexts and test to win the distinguishing game. A series of works, starting from [11], developed the min-entropy-based definitions and the tools for achieving function privacy in the public key setting. We see the question of function privacy in public key IBR (and in public key NIPE) as a part of the natural progression to the series of works started from [11]. Anonymity (or Attribute-hiding) has been studied for a long time, and only recently, notions like function-privacy, function-hiding, and obfuscation are getting to the centre stage. The function privacy notion of IBR (and NIPE) is highly timely. Incidentally, the function privacy of NIPE (or, in general, SNME [32]) has been explored. In this work, we consider the question of a function private IBR as part of the natural progression. To push it further, [4,13] merged multi-recipient encryption (MRE) with a keyword searching mechanism where the MRE was used as an access control mechanism. Thus, a fully attribute-hiding and function-private IBR replacing the existing MRE might result in more realistic searchable encryption, unlike the present situation where both the ciphertext and the secret keys might leak user identities.

1.1 Related Works

Only recently, Blazy *et al.* [8] explored the question of attribute-hiding in IBR schemes. This brought some balance to the long sequence of works that dealt with the attribute-hiding of receivers in broadcast encryption [6,17,19,28,29]. Blazy *et al.* [8] cleverly modified the IBR construction of [1] to achieve the first attribute-hiding IBR. However, they [8] achieved attribute-hiding security only in the restricted bounded collusion model [21] where the number of keys queried is specified by a constant fixed at the system setup. Furthermore, their construction is in the secret key setting, and this restriction is a proof artefact. Last but not least, they did not address the question of function privacy.

Wee [36] presented an IPE construction (ZIPE, to be precise) that achieves full attribute-hiding security in a non-adaptive simulation-based security model. In the following work, Chen *et al.* [15] constructed a ZIPE with full attribute-hiding security in the adaptive settings, thus closing a long-standing open problem. Patranabis *et al.* [32] lifted this ZIPE to achieve computational *function privacy* as well. However, they did not provide proof of the Min-Entropy MDDH assumption they introduced.

Patranabis *et al.* [32] also looked at the question of attribute-hiding security of NIPE. They proposed a weak attribute-hiding NIPE that too in the restrictive bounded collusion model. This limitation is because they used the proof technique from [2], which argued the security of inner-product functional encryption in the bounded collusion model. An independent work by Katsumata and Yamada [23] also constructed NIPE scheme with weak attribute-hiding security in the bounded collusion model where $\mathbf{x} \in (\mathbf{y}^{[1]} - \mathbf{y}^{[0]})^{\perp}$ for key extraction queries done on $\mathbf{x} \in \mathbb{Z}_p^{\ell}$ and the challenge vectors are $\mathbf{y}^{[0]}, \mathbf{y}^{[1]} \in \mathbb{Z}_p^{\ell}$. They formally presented a generic technique to do the same from the inner-product functional encryption of [2], and thus they could achieve NIPE from DDH, LWE, and DCR assumptions.

Heavy-weight tools like lockable obfuscation [22] can be used to achieve weak-attribute hiding NIPE generically. However, they neither achieve full-attribute hiding nor function privacy. Moreover, the cost seems too high for such a simple primitive. In this work, we primarily focus on pairing-based construction to achieve NIPE and IBR with full attribute-hiding and function privacy.

To summarise, for the existing efficient solutions, we do not know how to restrict an adversary from getting secret keys more than the constant fixed at setup. Therefore, existing efficient NIPEs should never be deployed in any realistic setting.

1.2 Our Contributions

In this paper, we answer both the two questions above in the affirmative. As we give an efficient public key NIPE scheme and an IBR scheme in the pairing-based setting that achieve full attribute-hiding security and computational function privacy. In the process, we bring the siblings closer, i.e., we show a direct transformation from ZIPE to NIPE (which we believe also works for IBBE to IBR). Before this work, NIPE and ZIPE have always been treated separately in the literature despite being heavily related to each other as per their functionality. We list all our achievements in this paper next and provide a graphical representations of our achievements in Fig. 1. Throughout this work, we use PO-ZIPE and PO-NIPE to denote ZIPE and NIPE restricted to the *predicate-only settings* [24] respectively. For a fixed $n \in \mathbb{N}$, we also use n-PO-ZIPE and n-PO-NIPE to denote PO-ZIPE and PO-NIPE, which encrypt n vectors, respectively.

1. We construct an n-PO-ZIPE scheme n-$\mathsf{PO\text{-}ZIPE}$ in the bilinear groups,
   - n-$\mathsf{PO\text{-}ZIPE}$ is fully attribute-hiding under a standard assumption,
   - n-$\mathsf{PO\text{-}ZIPE}$ is computationally function-private under a new assumption,
   - $\mathsf{DDH\text{-}II}$ assumption ([12]) implies the new assumption.
2. We construct a compiler that converts any n-PO-ZIPE scheme into an NIPE scheme,
   - n-$\mathsf{PO\text{-}ZIPE}$ is fully attribute-hiding $\Rightarrow$ NIPE is message-hiding and fully attribute-hiding.
   - n-$\mathsf{PO\text{-}ZIPE}$ is computationally function-private $\Rightarrow$ NIPE is computationally function-private.
3. We modify the generic IPE $\Rightarrow$ IBMRE compiler of [5] to construct IBR from NIPE,
   - NIPE is message-hiding $\Rightarrow$ IBR is message-hiding.
   - NIPE is fully attribute-hiding $\Rightarrow$ IBR is fully attribute-hiding.
   - IBR is computationally function-private under a new min-entropy-based assumption,
   - We further prove that the new min-entropy-based assumption is falsifiable [20].

On a side note, the attribute-hiding security of an IBMRE typically requires that the adversarially chosen sets $S^{[0]}, S^{[1]} \subseteq \mathcal{ID}$ have to be of equal size where $\mathcal{ID}$ is the identity space for users. We observe that such restrictions are no longer necessary if one gets an IBMRE via our transformation (and also the transformation of [5]). This observation and our above contribution result in an IBR scheme IBR that achieves full attribute-hiding security in the strongest model (adaptively secure in the standard model without restriction based on the cardinality of adversarially chosen sets) and computational function privacy.

Despite being linear encoding-based predicate encryptions, neither our NIPE construction (NIPE) nor our IBR construction (IBR) use a blinding factor from $\mathbb{G}_{\mathrm{T}}$ to hide the message. More precisely, both NIPE and IBR use linear encoding-based structures such as pair-encoding [3], predicate-encoding [35] but could avoid adding $g_{\mathrm{T}}^{\alpha s}$ in the ciphertext. This new way of looking at linear encoding-based predicate encryptions should be explored further.

1.3 Technical Overview

One might wonder that even after having so many ZIPE constructions [5,15,24, 30,31,36] with (fully) attribute-hiding security, why do we not even have a single standard model NIPE construction achieveing weakly attribute-hiding security in the pairing-based setting. As per our understanding, we next try to shed some light on the reason assuming a ciphertext Ct encrypts the data-attribute vector

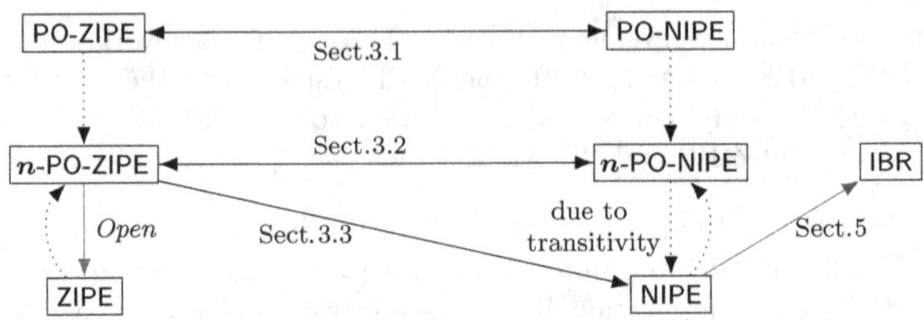

Fig. 1. PO-ZIPE (resp. PO-NIPE) is the predicate-only version of ZIPE (resp. NIPE). n-PO-ZIPE (resp. n-PO-NIPE) is the predicate-only version of ZIPE (resp. NIPE) where n vectors are encrypted simultaneously. IBR is identity-based revocation scheme we propose. The dotted lines stand for generic trivial transformations. The black lines stand for the novel generic transformations. The blue line denotes that our novel transformation only achieved fully attribute-hiding IBR and the function privacy of the IBR uses arguments independent to the function privacy arguments of NIPE. The red line on the other hand poses an open question. In this work, all the primitives mentioned above have been shown to achieve full attribute-hiding and function privacy. (Color figure online)

$\mathbf{y} \in \mathbb{Z}_p^\ell$ and the secret key sk corresponding to the key-attribute vector $\mathbf{x} \in \mathbb{Z}_p^\ell$. Most of the standard ZIPE constructions in pairing-based setting use some form of linear encoding techniques (e.g., pair encoding [3], predicate encoding [35], tag-based encoding [25]) to get a linear secret sharing. We can take an overview of the decryption to understand the overall strategy for secret sharing assuming $e : \mathbb{G}_1 \times \mathbb{G}_2 \rightarrow \mathbb{G}_\mathrm{T}$ is a bilinear pairing where g_s generates $\mathbb{G}_s$. Informally speaking,

1. the decryption [14] computes $g_\mathrm{T}^{\beta+\delta\langle\mathbf{x},\mathbf{y}\rangle}$ where g_T^β is the blinding factor used to hide the message M and δ is some arbitrary random quantity.
2. the decryption [33] computes $(g_\mathrm{T}^{\beta+\gamma}, g_\mathrm{T}^{-\gamma\kappa+\delta\langle\mathbf{x},\mathbf{y}\rangle}, \kappa)$ where g_T^β is the blinding factor used to encrypt the message M and γ, δ, κ are some arbitrary random quantities s.t. $\kappa \neq 0$.

Observe that, in both the cases, for $\langle\mathbf{x},\mathbf{y}\rangle = 0$, the decryption recovers g_2^β, and thus gets back the message M.

NIPE, as a primitive, however, demands that the decryption recover the message M if $\langle\mathbf{x},\mathbf{y}\rangle \neq 0$. We now take an overview of the decryption to understand the overall secret-sharing strategy in NIPE schemes properly. Informally speaking,

1. the decryption computes $g_\mathrm{T}^{\delta\langle\mathbf{x},\mathbf{y}\rangle}$ where g_T^δ is the blinding factor used to hide M.
2. the decryption computes $(g_\mathrm{T}^{\beta+\delta}, g_\mathrm{T}^{\delta\langle\mathbf{x},\mathbf{y}\rangle})$ where g_T^β is the blinding factor used to encrypt M and δ is an arbitrary random quantity with the restriction $\delta \neq 0$.

Observe that, in both the cases, for $z = \langle \mathbf{x}, \mathbf{y} \rangle \neq 0$, the decryption recovers the message M by exponentiating $g_T^{\delta \langle \mathbf{x}, \mathbf{y} \rangle}$ with z^{-1}. Now, computation of z on the fly during the decryption requires that both $\mathbf{x}$ and $\mathbf{y}$ are provided in plain. This is where the chance of achieving any amount of attribute-hiding fails. Moreover, these constructions fail to achieve the function privacy security that demands the secret key sk corresponding to $\mathbf{x}$ hides it for the same reason. Thus, we need a different way of encoding $\mathbf{x}$ and $\mathbf{y}$ so that decryption does not need to compute $z = \langle \mathbf{x}, \mathbf{y} \rangle$ in plain.

We formalize the encoding from [8]. NIPE demands that if $\langle \mathbf{x}, \mathbf{y} \rangle \neq 0$ then we retrive m which is the correctness requirement. For security, NIPE demands that if $\langle \mathbf{x}, \mathbf{y} \rangle = 0$ then we retrive m with only negligible probability. Considering m to be a single bit, we observe that the decryption needs to behave like a bit-wise AND i.e. $(m \text{ AND } (\langle \mathbf{x}, \mathbf{y} \rangle \stackrel{?}{\neq} 0))$. Informally speaking, if $\langle \mathbf{x}, \mathbf{y} \rangle \neq 0$, decryption returns $(m \text{ AND } 1) = m$. More importantly, if $\langle \mathbf{x}, \mathbf{y} \rangle = 0$, decryption returns $(m \text{ AND } 0) = 0$ irrespective of the value of m.

Thus, a secret key sk corresponding to $\mathbf{x} \in \mathbb{Z}_p^\ell$ decrypts a ciphertext Ct corresponding to $m \cdot \mathbf{y} \in \mathbb{Z}_p^\ell$ and retrieves $m \in \{0, 1\}$ correctly if $\langle \mathbf{x}, \mathbf{y} \rangle \neq 0$ which is essentially NIPE. More importantly, decryption can just evaluate $\langle \mathbf{x}, m \cdot \mathbf{y} \rangle$ from Ct and sk; no longer explicitly requires the description of $\mathbf{x}$ or $\mathbf{y}$. Based on this observation, we translate the (message, data-attribute) pair $(m, \mathbf{y})$ that is input to $\mathsf{Encrypt}$ of NIPE, into a vector $m \cdot \mathbf{y}$ that is the input for underlying ZIPE (in predicate-only setting [24]). To consider n-bit message $\mathbf{m} = (m_1, \ldots, m_n) \in \{0, 1\}^n$, we translate $(\mathbf{m}, \mathbf{y})$ into an n-tuple $(m_1 \cdot \mathbf{y}, \ldots, m_n \cdot \mathbf{y})$. Each vector in such a tuple of vectors is then encrypted separately. If we consider the predicate-only settings, ZIPE and NIPE (and their multi-vectors version) are equivalent. More formally, predicate-only ZIPE ($\mathsf{PO\text{-}ZIPE}$) and predicate-only NIPE ($\mathsf{PO\text{-}NIPE}$) are equivalent in the fully attribute-hiding security model. Our work deviates significantly from [8], who modified IPFE to get an attribute-hiding IBR. In particular, to translate user identities to vectors that will be input to the IPFE, [8] used a random map. As their proof required the vectors to be random-looking, and $\mathsf{Encrypt}$ needed these vectors to be easily recalled, [8] had to use a form of table lookup. This restricted their construction to a symmetric-key setting which could be proven secure only in a weaker model with limited challenges. We, on the other hand, make fully attribute-hiding IBR in two steps:

1. Make NIPE from $\mathsf{PO\text{-}ZIPE}$: We propose a fully attribute-hiding predicate-only ZIPE scheme n-$\mathsf{PO\text{-}ZIPE}$ for n-bit messages. Then, we transform this n-$\mathsf{PO\text{-}ZIPE}$ to a fully attribute-hiding NIPE (NIPE) for n-bit message.
2. Make IBR from NIPE: To encode the user identities id to vectors, we could try to encode it into $(1, \mathsf{id}, \mathsf{id}^2, \ldots, \mathsf{id}^q)$ unlike [8] who used a random vector. The basic intuition is that id^i is linearly independent of id^j for all $j < i$, so it will behave as a random vector in the proof but can be computed on the fly knowing only id. Use of this encoding results in fully attribute-hiding IBR scheme IBR. However, looking ahead, all but one entry of the encoding vector are functions of the same id and therefore need more justification for function

privacy. Even if we assume id is coming from a well-spread distribution chosen by the adversary, it needs to be analyzed if the entropy is sufficient.

Next, we look at the above two steps from the lens of function privacy. We achieve the function privacy of NIPE and IBR by formulating novel arguments.

1. Make NIPE from PO-ZIPE: The matrix version of standard DDH ensures $g^{\mathbf{a}\otimes\mathbf{b}}$ is random-looking even given $g^{\mathbf{a}}$ and $g^{\mathbf{b}}$ where $\mathbf{a}, \mathbf{b}$ are random vectors of appropriate size. We introduce a min-entropy variant of this (where $\mathbf{a}$ is a vector from an adversarially chosen well-spread distribution) and argue its security from the well-studied DDH-II assumption [12]. Looking ahead, this assumption directly gives the function privacy as we use $\mathbf{a}$ to simulate the key-attribute vector $\mathbf{x}$ and $\mathbf{b}$ to simulate $\mathbf{u}$ in the keys.
2. Make IBR from NIPE: For function privacy, we modify the encoding to $(\mathsf{id}, \mathsf{id}^2, \ldots, \mathsf{id}^{n+1})$ for a given user identity $\mathsf{id} \hookleftarrow \mathcal{D}_\lambda$ where $\mathcal{D}_\lambda$ has min-entropy $\omega(\log\ \lambda)$. Observe that this modification neither hampers the correctness nor the attribute-hiding security property. Rather, it opens up an opportunity of replacing $(g_s^{\mathsf{id}}, g_s^{\mathsf{id}^2}, \ldots, g_s^{\mathsf{id}^{n+1}})$ for a given user identity $\mathsf{id} \hookleftarrow \mathcal{D}_\lambda$ with $(g_s^{\tilde{\mathsf{id}}}, g_s^{\tilde{\mathsf{id}}^2}, \ldots, g_s^{\tilde{\mathsf{id}}^{n+1}})$ for a uniformly random $\tilde{\mathsf{id}} \leftarrow \mathbb{Z}_p$. The problem is Bartusek *et al.* [7] already has shown that such a replacement can be distinguished for fixed generator settings. In this work, we propose a novel argument in the random generator setting where we replace $(g_s^r, g_s^{r\cdot\mathsf{id}}, g_s^{r\cdot\mathsf{id}^2}, \ldots, g_s^{r\cdot\mathsf{id}^{n+1}})$ for a given user identity $\mathsf{id} \hookleftarrow \mathcal{D}_\lambda$ with $(g_s^r, g_s^{r\cdot\tilde{\mathsf{id}}}, g_s^{r\cdot\tilde{\mathsf{id}}^2}, \ldots, g_s^{r\cdot\tilde{\mathsf{id}}^{n+1}})$ for uniformly random quantities $r, \tilde{\mathsf{id}} \leftarrow \mathbb{Z}_p$. We argue that this replacement is indistinguishable in the generic group model. Since $\tilde{\mathsf{id}}$ is chosen uniformly at random, we reach at the decision that our IBR construction IBR achieves function privacy.

1.4 Comparison with Existing Pairing-Based Schemes

The first step, where we make NIPE from PO-ZIPE, makes the ciphertext $\mathcal{O}(n\ell)$-sized for n-bit messages and ℓ-dimensional vector space. Note that, in typical public key settings, we would use this scheme to send 128 or 256-bit session keys or a stream. In this case, the level of security, particularly anonymity, would be more important than the value of $n = 128$ or $n = 256$. We now compare our constructions with existing schemes to show a clear tradeoff between security and efficiency. For this purpose, we first recall the deficiencies of existing attribute-hiding NIPEs ([23,32]) and attribute-hiding IBRs ([8]). Then we provide the comparisons in Fig. 2.

Existing Attribute-Hiding NIPEs ([23,32]*).* All available attribute-hiding NIPE schemes are constructed from IPFE (in particular ALS-IPFE [2]). Therefore, they suffer from two unnatural restrictions:

1. Both restricted queried key vectors should be orthogonal to the difference of the challenge. This means for challenge $\mathbf{y}^{[0]}$ and $\mathbf{y}^{[1]}$, $\langle\mathbf{x}, \mathbf{y}^{[0]}\rangle = \langle\mathbf{x}, \mathbf{y}^{[1]}\rangle$ for all key queries on $\mathbf{x}$.

2. Both achieve only *weak* attribute-hiding security in the bounded collusion model. This model requires that for the vector space of dimension ℓ, a ppt adversary is allowed to make at most $(\ell - 1)$ queries.

Existing Attribute-Hiding IBR ([8]*).* Only available attribute-hiding IBR scheme is also constructed from IPFE (in particular ALS-IPFE [2]). The symmetric-key IBR of [8] also suffers from some unnatural restrictions:

(i) Although [8] allows both authorized and unauthorized queries, they achieved security in the monotonic anonymity model where users can only be added to the revoked users list as time progresses. Deletion of a user from the challenge revoked list was not allowed.
(ii) It achieves attribute-hiding security in the restrictive bounded collusion model only.

	Schemes	mpk	sk	Ct	Security
NIPE Schemes	[32,23]	$2(\ell+2)$	$\ell+4$	4ℓ	Unnatural restrictions 1. and 2.
	Ours	$3n(\ell+1)$	$n(3\ell+2)$	$3n\ell+2$	Full attribute-hiding + Function Privacy
IBR Schemes	[8]	1	$n^2\ell$	$2n\ell$	Unnatural restrictions (i) and (ii)
	Ours	$3n(\ell+1)$	$n(3\ell+2)$	$3n\ell+2$	Full attribute-hiding + Function Privacy

Fig. 2. Encryption takes a n-bit message and an ℓ-lengthed Vector (NIPE)/Set (IBR). The parameter sizes are presented for the case of SXDH.

1.5 Organization of the Paper

In Sect. 2, we present the required definitions and the mathematical tools. In Sect. 3, we show that PO-NIPE is equivalent to PO-ZIPE and make NIPE from a variant of PO-ZIPE. We then give a construction of predicate-only ZIPE for n-bit messages in Sect. 4. Following this, we construct IBR in Sect. 5 and conclude the paper in Sect. 6.

2 Mathematical Tools and Preliminaries

For $a, b \in \mathbb{N}$ such that $a \leq b$, we denote $[a, b] = \{a, \ldots, b\}$ and write $[b] := [1, b]$. For a distribution D, we write $x \leftarrow D$ to say that x is sampled uniformly at random from D. For a well-spread distribution D (with min-entropy $\omega(\log\ \lambda)$), we write $x \hookleftarrow D$ to say that x is sampled according to the distribution D. The ppt abbreviation stands for probabilistic polynomial time. We often use small-case bold letters like $\mathbf{s} = (s_1, \ldots, s_n)^\top$ to denote a column-vector and large-case bold letters like $\mathbf{S} = \left(s_{ij}\right)_{(i,j)\in I\times J}$ to denote a matrix of appropriate dimension. For a $\mathcal{G} = (p, \mathbb{G}_1, \mathbb{G}_2, \mathbb{G}_\mathrm{T}, g_1, g_2, e : \mathbb{G}_1 \times \mathbb{G}_2 \to \mathbb{G}_\mathrm{T})$ type-III prime-order bilinear pairing group description, we use Escala's [18] additive-group notation to denote g_s^a by $[\![a]\!]_s$ for any $a \in \mathbb{Z}_p$ and $s \in \{1, 2, \mathrm{T}\}$. By $\mathbf{M} \leftarrow \mathcal{D}_{m,k}$, we denote a matrix $\mathbf{M} \in \mathbb{Z}_p^{m\times k}$ is sampled for $m > k \geq 1$. Thus, $[\![\mathbf{M}]\!]_s = \left(g_s^{M_{i,j}}\right)_{(i,j)\in[m]\times[k]}$. Matrix Diffie-Hellman Assumption states that guessing if a random $[\![\mathbf{t}]\!]_s$ is in span of $[\![\mathbf{M}]\!]_s$ is hard even when $[\![\mathbf{M}]\!]_s$ is given. More details can be found in the full version.

2.1 Predicate Encryption

A predicate encryption w.r.t a predicate R allows a secret key sk w.r.t a key-attribute x to decrypt a ciphertext Ct computed w.r.t a data-attribute y and a message m, if $\mathsf{R}(\mathsf{x},\mathsf{y}) = 1$. We provide a brief overview here and defer the formal descriptions to the full version. In the literature, primarily three security notions of predicate encryption have been considered:

1. Message-Hiding (MH) captures $\mathsf{Ct} \leftarrow \mathsf{Encrypt}(\mathsf{mpk},\mathsf{y},m_{\mathfrak{b}})$ hides $\mathfrak{b}$.
2. Attribute-Hiding (FAH) captures $\mathsf{Ct} \leftarrow \mathsf{Encrypt}(\mathsf{mpk},\mathsf{y}_{\mathfrak{b}},m)$ hides $\mathfrak{b}$. There are two variants of this security notion: (i) Weakly Attribute-Hiding: Adversary gets to query x s.t. $\mathsf{R}(\mathsf{x},\mathsf{y}_0) = \mathsf{R}(\mathsf{x},\mathsf{y}_1) = 0$, and (ii) Fully Attribute-Hiding: Adversary gets to query x s.t. $\mathsf{R}(\mathsf{x},\mathsf{y}_0) = \mathsf{R}(\mathsf{x},\mathsf{y}_1)$.
3. Function-Privacy (FPriv) captures sk does not leak x.

In this work, we deal with two predicate encryptions (i) Inner-Product Encryption (IPE) and (ii) Identity-based Multi-recipient Encryption (IBMRE).

- Inner-Product Encryption (IPE): $\mathsf{Decrypt}(\mathsf{KeyGen}(\mathsf{msk},\mathbf{x}),\mathsf{Encrypt}(\mathsf{mpk},\mathbf{y},m)) \rightarrow m$ if $\mathsf{R}(\mathbf{x},\mathbf{y}) = 1$ where $\mathbf{x},\mathbf{y} \in \mathbb{Z}_p^\ell$. In this work, we consider two IPEs: (i) Zero IPE (ZIPE): $\langle \mathbf{x},\mathbf{y}\rangle = 0 \Rightarrow \mathsf{R}(\mathbf{x},\mathbf{y}) = 1$, (ii) Non-zero IPE (NIPE): $\langle \mathbf{x},\mathbf{y}\rangle \neq 0 \Rightarrow \mathsf{R}(\mathbf{x},\mathbf{y}) = 1$.
- Identity-based Multi-recipient Encryption (MRE): $\mathsf{Decrypt}(\mathsf{KeyGen}(\mathsf{msk},\mathsf{id}),\mathsf{Encrypt}(\mathsf{mpk},\mathsf{S},m)) \rightarrow m$ if $\mathsf{R}(\mathsf{id},\mathsf{S}) = 1$ where $\mathsf{id} \in \mathbb{Z}_p, \mathsf{S} \subset \mathbb{Z}_p$. In this work, we consider two IBMREs: (i) ID-based Broadcast Encryption (BE): $\mathsf{id} \in \mathsf{S} \Rightarrow \mathsf{R}(\mathsf{id},\mathsf{S}) = 1$, (ii) ID-based Revocation: $\mathsf{id} \notin \mathsf{S} \Rightarrow \mathsf{R}(\mathsf{id},\mathsf{S}) = 1$.

2.1.1 Predicate-Only Inner-Product Encryption

We define a predicate-only inner-product encryption scheme (PO-IPE) here for $\mathcal{CT}_{po}$ and $\mathcal{SK}_{po}$ denote ciphertext space and secret key space respectively.

- Setup: It takes the security parameter 1^λ and the system description 1^ℓ. It outputs a master secret key msk and the corresponding public key mpk.
- KeyGen: It takes mpk, msk and a key-attribute vector $\mathbf{x} \in \mathcal{X}$ as input. It generates a secret key $\mathsf{sk} \in \mathcal{SK}_{po}$ corresponding to the key-attribute vector $\mathbf{x}$.
- $\mathsf{Encrypt}$: It takes mpk and a data-attribute vector $\mathbf{y} \in \mathcal{Y}$ to output a ciphertext $\mathsf{Ct} \in \mathcal{CT}_{po}$.
- Test: It takes mpk, sk and Ct as input. It outputs 1 or 0.

Correctness. For $(\mathsf{mpk},\mathsf{msk}) \leftarrow \mathsf{Setup}(1^\lambda, 1^\ell)$, all key-attribute vectors $\mathbf{x} \in \mathcal{X}$, all data-attribute vectors $\mathbf{y} \in \mathcal{Y}$, $\mathsf{sk} \leftarrow \mathsf{KeyGen}(\mathsf{msk},\mathbf{x})$, $\mathsf{Ct} \leftarrow \mathsf{Encrypt}(\mathsf{mpk},\mathbf{y})$, $\mathsf{Test}(\mathsf{mpk},\mathsf{sk},\mathsf{Ct}) = \mathsf{R}_i(\mathbf{x},\mathbf{y})$. Clearly, $\mathsf{R}_z(\mathbf{x},\mathbf{y}) = 1 \oplus \mathsf{R}_n(\mathbf{x},\mathbf{y})$ where R_z and R_n are respectively zero and non-zero IPE predicates.

Security.

- fAH: Attribute-hiding security for predicate-only IPE schemes naturally captures hiding data-attribute vectors. To separate it from the attribute-hiding security (FAH) of standard IPE, we use a different name and call it fAH security. We model fAH as a security game between a challenger $\mathcal{C}$ and an adversary $\mathcal{A}$.
  - **Setup**: $\mathcal{C}$ runs Setup to give out mpk and keeps msk as secret.
  - **Key Queries**: Given a key-attribute vector $\mathbf{x} \in \mathcal{X}$, $\mathcal{C}$ returns $\mathsf{sk} \leftarrow \mathsf{KeyGen}(\mathsf{msk}, \mathbf{x})$.
  - **Challenge**: $\mathcal{A}$ provides challenge data-attribute vectors $\mathbf{y}^{[0]}, \mathbf{y}^{[1]} \in \mathcal{Y}$. $\mathcal{C}$ returns $\mathsf{Ct}^{[\mathfrak{b}]} \leftarrow \mathsf{Encrypt}(\mathsf{mpk}, \mathbf{y}^{[\mathfrak{b}]})$ for $\mathfrak{b} \leftarrow \{0,1\}$.
  - **Key Queries**: Given a key-attribute $\mathbf{x} \in \mathcal{X}$, $\mathcal{C}$ returns $\mathsf{sk} \leftarrow \mathsf{KeyGen}(\mathsf{msk}, \mathbf{x})$.
  - **Guess**: $\mathcal{A}$ outputs its guess $\mathfrak{b}' \in \{0,1\}$ and wins if $\mathfrak{b} = \mathfrak{b}'$.

  For any adversary $\mathcal{A}$ with the following restrictions:
  1. Some $\mathbf{x}$ queried are authorized for both challenge vectors: $\mathsf{R}_i(\mathbf{x}, \mathbf{y}^{[0]}) = \mathsf{R}_i(\mathbf{x}, \mathbf{y}^{[1]}) = 1$,
  2. Rest of the $\mathbf{x}$ queried are unauthorized for both challenge vectors: $\mathsf{R}_i(\mathbf{x}, \mathbf{y}^{[0]}) = \mathsf{R}_i(\mathbf{x}, \mathbf{y}^{[1]}) = 0$,

  The advantage of such $\mathcal{A}$ is, $\mathbf{Adv}^{\mathsf{fAH}}_{\mathcal{A},\mathsf{PO\text{-}IPE}}(\lambda) = |\Pr[\mathfrak{b} = \mathfrak{b}'] - 1/2|$. A predicate-only inner-product encryption scheme PO-IPE is said to be fAH secure if for all ppt adversary $\mathcal{A}$, $\mathbf{Adv}^{\mathsf{fAH}}_{\mathcal{A},\mathsf{PO\text{-}IPE}}(\lambda) \leq \mathrm{neg}(\lambda)$.
- FPriv: Function privacy of predicate-only inner-product encryption is modeled as a security game between a challenger $\mathcal{C}$ and an adversary $\mathcal{A}$. This definition is taken from [32].
  - **Setup**: $\mathcal{C}$ runs Setup to give out mpk and keeps msk as secret.
  - **Key Queries**: $\mathcal{A}$ adaptively makes key extraction query on key-attribute $\mathbf{x} \in \mathcal{X}$. $\mathcal{C}$ returns a secret-key $\mathsf{sk} \leftarrow \mathsf{KeyGen}(\mathsf{msk}, \mathbf{x})$.
  - **Challenge**: $\mathcal{A}$ provides two circuits of the form: $\mathcal{X}_0 = [X_j^0]_{j \in [\ell]}$, $\mathcal{X}_1 = [X_j^1]_{j \in [\ell]}$ representing joint distributions over $\mathbb{Z}_p^\ell$, with the following restrictions:
    1. For $j \in [\ell]$, $b \in \{0,1\}$, X_j^b represents an $\omega(\log\ \lambda)$ source over $\mathbb{Z}_p$.
    2. For $i, j \in [\ell]$, $b \in \{0,1\}$, X_i^b and X_j^b represent mutually independent distributions.

    $\mathcal{C}$ samples $\mathbf{x} \leftarrow \mathcal{X}_\mathfrak{b}$ and responds to $\mathcal{A}$ with a secret-key $\mathsf{sk} \leftarrow \mathsf{KeyGen}(\mathsf{msk}, \mathbf{x})$.
  - **Key Queries**: $\mathcal{A}$ can adaptively make key extraction query on key-attribute $\mathbf{x} \in \mathcal{X}$. $\mathcal{C}$ returns a secret-key $\mathsf{sk} \leftarrow \mathsf{KeyGen}(\mathsf{msk}, \mathbf{x})$ to $\mathcal{A}$.
  - **Guess**: $\mathcal{A}$ outputs its guess $\mathfrak{b}' \in \{0,1\}$ and wins if $\mathfrak{b} = \mathfrak{b}'$.

  For any adversary $\mathcal{A}$ the advantage is, $\mathbf{Adv}^{\mathsf{FPriv}}_{\mathcal{A},\mathsf{IPE}}(\lambda) = |\Pr[\mathfrak{b} = \mathfrak{b}'] - 1/2|$. An inner-product encryption scheme IPE is said to be FPriv secure if for all ppt adversary $\mathcal{A}$, $\mathbf{Adv}^{\mathsf{FPriv}}_{\mathcal{A},\mathsf{IPE}}(\lambda) \leq \mathrm{neg}(\lambda)$.

2.1.2 PO-IPE for n Data-Attribute Vectors

We define predicate-only inner-product encryption for n data-attribute vectors scheme next where $\mathcal{CT}_{po}$ and $\mathcal{SK}_{po}$ denote ciphertext space and secret key space respectively. Note that, this scheme supports a fixed number of vectors as data-attributes.

- Setup: It takes the security parameter 1^λ and the system description 1^ℓ and 1^n. It outputs a master secret key msk and the corresponding public key mpk.
- KeyGen: It takes mpk, msk and a key-attribute vector $\mathbf{x} \in \mathcal{X}$ as input. It generates a secret key $\mathsf{sk} \in \mathcal{SK}_{po}$ corresponding to the key-attribute vector $\mathbf{x}$.
- Encrypt: It takes mpk and n data-attribute vectors $\mathbf{Y} = (\mathbf{y}_1, \ldots, \mathbf{y}_n)^\top \in \mathcal{Y}^n$ as input. It outputs a ciphertext Ct.
- Test: It takes mpk, sk and Ct as input. It outputs $(b_1, \ldots, b_n) \in \{0,1\}^n$.

Correctness. For $(\mathsf{mpk}, \mathsf{msk}) \leftarrow \mathsf{Setup}(1^\lambda)$, all key-attribute vectors $\mathbf{x} \in \mathcal{X}$, all data-attribute vectors $\mathbf{Y} \in \mathcal{Y}^n$, $\mathsf{Test}(\mathsf{mpk}, \mathsf{KeyGen}(\mathsf{msk}, \mathbf{x}), \mathsf{Encrypt}(\mathsf{mpk}, \mathbf{Y})) = (\mathsf{R}_i(\mathbf{x}, \mathbf{y}_1), \ldots, \mathsf{R}_i(\mathbf{x}, \mathbf{y}_n))$.

Lifting PO-IPE to Support n Data-Vectors. A PO-IPE for n data-vectors can be constructed as n-PO-IPE by running n parallel instances of PO-IPE scheme PO-IPE. More precisely, in the resulting n-PO-IPE, $\mathsf{msk} = (\mathsf{msk}_1, \ldots, \mathsf{msk}_n)$ and $\mathsf{mpk} = (\mathsf{mpk}_1, \ldots, \mathsf{mpk}_n)$ where $(\mathsf{mpk}_i, \mathsf{msk}_i) \leftarrow \mathsf{PO\text{-}IPE.Setup}(1^\lambda)$ is the key pair of the ith instance. Naturally, a secret key in n-PO-IPE is $\mathsf{sk} = (\mathsf{sk}_1, \ldots, \mathsf{sk}_n)$ where $\mathsf{sk}_i \leftarrow (\mathsf{msk}_i, \mathbf{x})$ is a secret key of the ith instance. The correctness, fAH, and FPriv security of this scheme follow from that of PO-IPE. Indeed, the full attribute-hiding security of PO-IPE ensures key extraction queries $\mathbf{x}$ that might be unauthorized for certain rows of $\mathbf{Y}^{[0]}$ and $\mathbf{Y}^{[1]}$ and authorized for the rest of the rows. We however do not take this route as we will see in Sect. 4.

2.2 Min-Entropy Computational Assumptions

We first introduce an assumption called *Min-Entropy Multi-DDH* (n-mE-DDH) and argue its hardness from well-studied DDH-II ([12]). Then we state the random generator strong power-DDH assumption (n-rSpDDH) and prove its security in the generic group model. We provide proof sketches for the both here and defer the formal arguments to the full version.

2.2.1 Min-Entropy Multi-DDH

In this work, we introduce Min-Entropy Multi-DDH (α, β)-mE-DDH. For all adversary $\mathcal{A}$, the advantage function is defined as $\mathsf{Adv}^{(\alpha,\beta)\text{-mE-DDH}}_{\mathcal{A},\mathbb{G}_s}(\lambda) = |\Pr[\mathcal{A}([\![\mathbf{a}]\!]_s, [\![\mathbf{b} \otimes \mathbf{a}]\!]_s) = 1] - \Pr[\mathcal{A}([\![\mathbf{a}]\!]_s, [\![\mathbf{C}]\!]_s) = 1]|$ where $[\![w]\!]_s = g_s^w$ for $s \in \{0,1\}$, $\mathbf{a} \hookleftarrow \mathcal{F}_\beta$,[1] $\mathbf{b} \leftarrow \mathbb{Z}_p^\alpha$ and $\mathbf{C} \leftarrow \mathbb{Z}_p^{\alpha\times\beta}$ for $\mathcal{F}$ provided by $\mathcal{A}$. The (α, β)-mE-DDH assumption states that $\mathsf{Adv}^{(\alpha,\beta)\text{-mE-DDH}}_{\mathcal{A},\mathbb{G}_s}(\lambda)$ is negligible in λ for all ppt adversary $\mathcal{A}$.

[1] $\mathcal{F}_\beta$ denotes β-independent samples from the well-spread distribution $\mathcal{F}$ (i.e. min-entropy $\omega(\log\lambda)$ for λ being security parameter). Thus, $\mathbf{a} = (a_1, \ldots, a_\beta) \hookleftarrow \mathcal{F}_\beta$ are β elements from the well-spread distribution $\mathcal{F}$.

Lemma 1. *If Min-Entropy DDH* (DDH-II) *holds in* $\mathbb{G}_2$*, the assumption Min-Entropy Multi-DDH* (α, β)-mE-DDH *holds. In particular, for any* ppt *adversary* $\mathcal{A}$ *against* (α, β)-mE-DDH*, there exists adversary* $\mathcal{B}$ *such that,* $\mathsf{Adv}^{(\alpha,\beta)\text{-mE-DDH}}_{\mathcal{A},\mathbb{G}_s}(\lambda) \leq \alpha \cdot \mathsf{Adv}^{\mathsf{DDH\text{-}II}}_{\mathcal{B},\mathbb{G}_s}(\lambda)$.

Proof Sketch. This is argued in two steps: DDH-II in $\mathbb{G}_2$ argues that $[\![ab]\!]_2$ is indistinguishable to $[\![r]\!]_2$ given $([\![1]\!]_2, [\![b]\!]_2, [\![a]\!]_2)$ for $b, r \leftarrow \mathbb{Z}_p$ and $a \hookleftarrow \mathcal{F}$. We first show that $([\![a_1 b]\!]_2, \ldots, [\![a_n b]\!]_2)$ is indistinguishable to $([\![r_1]\!]_2, \ldots, [\![r_n]\!]_2)$ given $([\![1]\!]_2, [\![b]\!]_2, [\![a_1]\!]_2, \ldots, [\![a_n]\!]_2)$ for $b, r_1, \ldots, r_n \leftarrow \mathbb{Z}_p$ and $a_1, \ldots, a_n \hookleftarrow \mathcal{F}$. Random self-reducibility then completes the proof. □

2.2.2 Strong Power-DDH

This assumption was introduced in [27]. By current nomenclature [7], such an assumption will be called fixed-generator strong power-DDH. We state both the fixed-generator strong power-DDH (n-fSpDDH) and random-generator strong power-DDH (n-rSpDDH) next.

- n-fSpDDH: Given $([\![\mathfrak{b}x + (1-\mathfrak{b})s]\!]_\mu, \ldots, [\![\mathfrak{b}x^n + (1-\mathfrak{b})s^n]\!]_\mu)$ determine $\mathfrak{b}$ where $x \hookleftarrow \mathcal{F}$, $s \leftarrow \mathbb{Z}_p$, $\mathfrak{b} \leftarrow \{0,1\}$, $\mu \in \{0,1\}$ where $\mathcal{A}$ provides $\mathcal{F}$.
- n-rSpDDH: Given $([\![r]\!]_\mu, [\![\mathfrak{b}rx + (1-\mathfrak{b})rs]\!]_\mu, \ldots, [\![\mathfrak{b}rx^n + (1-\mathfrak{b})rs^n]\!]_\mu)$ determine $\mathfrak{b}$ where $x \hookleftarrow \mathcal{F}$, $r \leftarrow \mathbb{Z}_p^*$, $s \leftarrow \mathbb{Z}_p$, $\mathfrak{b} \leftarrow \{0,1\}$, $\mu \in \{0,1\}$ where $\mathcal{A}$ provides $\mathcal{F}$.

Bartusek *et al.* [7] showed that the fixed generator variant n-fSpDDH assumption is false for any $n \geq 1$ even in the generic group model. In this work, we introduce the random generator variant n-rSpDDH assumption and prove its security in the generic group model like [7].

Lemma 2. (n-rSpDDH) *Let* $\mathsf{ABSGen}(1^\lambda) \to (p, \mathbb{G}_1, \mathbb{G}_2, \mathbb{G}_T, g_1, g_2, e)$ *where* $2^{\lambda-1} < p < 2^\lambda$*. Let* $\{\mathcal{D}_\lambda\}$ *be a family of well-spread distributions where the domain of* $\mathcal{D}_\lambda$ *is* $\mathbb{Z}_p$*. Then for any* $n = poly(\lambda)$*, for any* ppt *adversary* $\mathcal{A}$*,*

$$\mathsf{Adv}^{n\text{-rSpDDH}}_{\mathcal{A},\mathbb{G}}(\lambda) = |\Pr[\mathcal{A}([\![1]\!]_1, [\![1]\!]_2, [\![r]\!]_2, \{[\![rx^i]\!]_2\}_{i\in[n]}) = 1] - \Pr[\mathcal{A}([\![1]\!]_1, [\![1]\!]_2, [\![r]\!]_2, \{[\![rs^i]\!]_2\}_{i\in[n]}) = 1]|$$

where $x \hookleftarrow \mathcal{D}_\lambda$*,* $r \leftarrow \mathbb{Z}_p^*$ *and* $s \leftarrow \mathbb{Z}_p$*. The* n-rSpDDH *assumption states that* $\mathsf{Adv}^{n\text{-rSpDDH}}_{\mathcal{A},\mathbb{G}_s}(\lambda)$ *is negligible in* λ *for all* ppt *adversary* $\mathcal{A}$.

Proof Sketch. This is argued via a hybrid argument. We first switch to a bit-fixing labeling σ'. Then we replace the randomness with formal variables. Then, we assign σ' randomly on the fly except the bits that are already fixed. Thus, except the bits that are fixed, we have a random labeling which allows us to upper bound the advantage. The overall proof technique takes inspiration from to the proof of DDH-II provided in [7]. □

3 Generic Transformations Between IPEs

Here, we discuss the generic transformations. We first show n-PO-ZIPE and n-PO-NIPE are equivalent for all n. Then we transform n-PO-ZIPE generically to NIPE for n-bit messages.

3.1 Transformation Between PO-IPEs

Given a PO-IPE scheme $\mathsf{P}_1 = (\mathsf{P}_1.\mathsf{Setup}, \mathsf{P}_1.\mathsf{KeyGen}, \mathsf{P}_1.\mathsf{Encrypt}, \mathsf{P}_1.\mathsf{Test})$, we create the *opposite* PO-IPE scheme P_2 as following. To be precise, if P_1 is a PO-ZIPE scheme, P_2 is a PO-NIPE scheme and vice versa. Note that, this equivalence relation naturally extends to PO-ZIPE for n data-vectors and PO-NIPE for n data-vectors.

- $\mathsf{Setup}(1^\lambda, 1^\ell)$: Outputs $(\mathsf{mpk}, \mathsf{msk}) \leftarrow \mathsf{P}_1.\mathsf{Setup}(1^\lambda, 1^\ell)$.
- $\mathsf{KeyGen}(\mathsf{msk}, \mathbf{x})$: Outputs $\mathsf{sk} \leftarrow \mathsf{P}_1.\mathsf{KeyGen}(\mathsf{msk}, \mathbf{x})$.
- $\mathsf{Encrypt}(\mathsf{mpk}, \mathbf{y})$: Outputs $\mathsf{Ct} \leftarrow \mathsf{P}_1.\mathsf{Encrypt}(\mathsf{mpk}, \mathbf{y})$.
- $\mathsf{Test}(\mathsf{mpk}, \mathsf{sk}, \mathsf{Ct})$: Outputs $1 \oplus \mathsf{P}_1.\mathsf{Test}(\mathsf{mpk}, \mathsf{sk}, \mathsf{Ct})$.

Due to space limitation, we defer the proof of correctness and security to the full version. Nevertheless, we mention the security theorems next.

Theorem 1. *If* P_1 *is* fAH*-secure, then* P_2 *is* fAH*-secure.*

Proof Sketch. The reduction essentially behaves as a transparent middle-man between the fAH adversary $\mathcal{A}$ breaking P_2 and the fAH challenger $\mathcal{C}$ of P_1. Since, $\mathsf{R}_z(\mathbf{x}, \mathbf{y}) \oplus \mathsf{R}_n(\mathbf{x}, \mathbf{y}) = 1$, the natural restrictions are naturally related. □

Theorem 2. *If* P_1 *is* FPriv*-secure, then* P_2 *is* FPriv*-secure.*

Proof Sketch. The security holds canonically where every key query by P_2 is forwarded as corresponding key query by P_1. Moreover, the challenge circuits by P_2 are also forwarded in a similar manner. Thus, if P_2 can distinguish between the two circuits, P_1 does the same with exactly same probability. □

3.2 Extending Transformation for PO-IPEs n Data-Attribute Vectors

Given a n-PO-IPE scheme $\mathsf{P}_1 = (\mathsf{P}_1.\mathsf{Setup}, \mathsf{P}_1.\mathsf{KeyGen}, \mathsf{P}_1.\mathsf{Encrypt}, \mathsf{P}_1.\mathsf{Test})$, we create an (opposite) n-PO-IPE scheme P_2 as following. To be precise, if P_1 is n-PO-ZIPE, P_2 is n-PO-NIPE and vice versa.

- $\mathsf{Setup}(1^\lambda, 1^\ell)$: Outputs $(\mathsf{mpk}, \mathsf{msk}) \leftarrow \mathsf{P}_1.\mathsf{Setup}(1^\lambda, 1^\ell)$.
- $\mathsf{KeyGen}(\mathsf{msk}, \mathbf{x})$: Outputs $\mathsf{sk} \leftarrow \mathsf{P}_1.\mathsf{KeyGen}(\mathsf{msk}, \mathbf{x})$.
- $\mathsf{Encrypt}(\mathsf{mpk}, \mathbf{Y})$: Outputs $\mathsf{Ct} \leftarrow \mathsf{P}_1.\mathsf{Encrypt}(\mathsf{mpk}, \mathbf{Y})$.
- $\mathsf{Test}(\mathsf{mpk}, \mathsf{sk}, \mathsf{Ct})$: Outputs $(1, 1, \ldots, 1) \oplus \mathsf{P}_1.\mathsf{Test}(\mathsf{mpk}, \mathsf{sk}, \mathsf{Ct})$.

The correctness of this transformation follows from that of the transformation in Sect. 3.1. The fAH and FPriv security of P_2 follow from those of P_1 just like for the transformation in Sect. 3.1.

3.3 Transformation Between n-PO-ZIPE and NIPE

We construct an NIPE scheme NIPE for the message space $\mathcal{M} = \{0,1\}^n$. Given an n-PO-ZIPE scheme $\mathsf{P}_1 = (\mathsf{P}_1.\mathsf{Setup}, \mathsf{P}_1.\mathsf{KeyGen}, \mathsf{P}_1.\mathsf{Encrypt}, \mathsf{P}_1.\mathsf{Test})$, we create P_2 is an NIPE scheme for $\mathcal{M} = \{0,1\}^n$ as following.

- $\mathsf{Setup}(1^\lambda, 1^\ell, 1^n)$: Outputs $(\mathsf{mpk}, \mathsf{msk}) \leftarrow \mathsf{P}_1.\mathsf{Setup}(1^\lambda, 1^\ell, 1^n)$.
- $\mathsf{KeyGen}(\mathsf{msk}, \mathbf{x})$: Outputs $\mathsf{sk} \leftarrow \mathsf{P}_1.\mathsf{KeyGen}(\mathsf{msk}, \mathbf{x})$.
- $\mathsf{Encrypt}(\mathsf{mpk}, \mathbf{y}, \mathbf{m})$: Defines $\mathbf{y}_\iota = m_\iota \cdot \mathbf{y}$ for all $\iota \in [n]$ to construct a $n \times \ell$ matrix $\mathbf{Y} = \begin{pmatrix}\mathbf{y}_1 \dots \mathbf{y}_n\end{pmatrix}^\top$. Outputs $\mathsf{Ct} \leftarrow \mathsf{P}_1.\mathsf{Encrypt}(\mathsf{mpk}, \mathbf{Y})$.
- $\mathsf{Decrypt}(\mathsf{mpk}, \mathsf{sk}, \mathsf{Ct})$: Outputs $\mathbf{m}' \leftarrow (1, 1, \dots, 1) \oplus \mathsf{P}_1.\mathsf{Test}(\mathsf{mpk}, \mathsf{sk}, \mathsf{Ct})$.

Due to space limitation, we defer the proof of correctness and security to the full version. Nevertheless, we state the security theorems next.

Theorem 3. *If* P_1 *is* fAH*-secure, then* P_2 *is* MH*-secure.*

Proof Sketch. The reduction is devised as a middle-man between fAH challenger of P_1 and MH adversary of P_2. Given two challenge messages $\mathbf{m}^{[0]}, \mathbf{m}^{[1]} \in \mathcal{M}$ and one vector $\mathbf{y} \in \mathcal{Y}$, the reduction devises $\mathbf{Y}^{[0]} = \mathbf{m}^{[0]} \otimes \mathbf{y}$ and $\mathbf{Y}^{[1]} = \mathbf{m}^{[1]} \otimes \mathbf{y}$ as its challenge. The natural restrictions are naturally related. □

Theorem 4. *If* P_1 *is* fAH*-secure, then* P_2 *is* FAH*-secure.*

Proof Sketch. The reduction is devised as a middle-man between fAH challenger of P_1 and MH adversary of P_2. Given a challenge message $\mathbf{m} \in \mathcal{M}$ and two vectors $\mathbf{y}^{[0]}, \mathbf{y}^{[1]} \in \mathcal{Y}$, the reduction devises $\mathbf{Y}^{[0]} = \mathbf{m} \otimes \mathbf{y}^{[0]}$ and $\mathbf{Y}^{[1]} = \mathbf{m} \otimes \mathbf{y}^{[1]}$ as its challenge. The natural restrictions are naturally related. □

Theorem 5. *If* P_1 *is* FPriv*-secure, then* P_2 *is* FPriv*-secure.*

Proof Sketch. The security holds canonically where every key query by P_2 is forwarded as corresponding key query by P_1. Moreover, the challenge circuits given by P_2 are also forwarded in a similar manner. Thus, if P_2 can distinguish between the two circuits, P_1 does the same with exactly same probability. □

4 Constructing a PO-ZIPE Scheme for n Data-Vectors

Till this section, we have seen that PO-ZIPE and PO-NIPE are essentially equivalent. Moreover, this result naturally extends to the equivalence of n-PO-ZIPE and n-PO-NIPE for any $n \in \mathbb{N}$. In Sect. 3.3, we have shown that a n-PO-ZIPE scheme n-$\mathsf{PO\text{-}ZIPE}$ can be used to construct an NIPE scheme (NIPE) with attribute-hiding security for the message space $\mathcal{M} = \{0,1\}^n$. In this section, we construct an fAH-secure n-PO-ZIPE scheme (n-$\mathsf{PO\text{-}ZIPE}$) which automatically gives attribute-hiding NIPE for the message space $\mathcal{M} = \{0,1\}^n$. Then we show that our n-$\mathsf{PO\text{-}ZIPE}$ is FPriv secure which ensures NIPE is also FPriv secure due to the generic transformation in Sect. 3.3.

4.1 Instantiating n-PO-ZIPE

$\underline{\mathsf{Setup}(1^\lambda, 1^{\ell \times n})}$:

$\mathcal{G} = (p, \mathbb{G}_1, \mathbb{G}_2, \mathbb{G}_T, g_1, g_2, e) \leftarrow \mathsf{ABSGen}(1^\lambda)$.

$\mathbf{A} \leftarrow \mathcal{D}_k$ and $\mathbf{B}_1 \leftarrow \mathcal{D}_{2k+1,k}$.

$\mathbf{V}_i, \ldots, \mathbf{V}_n \leftarrow \mathbb{Z}_p^{(k+1)\times(2k+1)}$.

$\mathbf{W}_{1,1}, \ldots, \mathbf{W}_{1,\ell}, \ldots, \mathbf{W}_{n,1}, \ldots, \mathbf{W}_{n,\ell} \leftarrow \mathbb{Z}_p^{(k+1)\times(2k+1)}$.

$\mathsf{msk} = (\mathbf{W}_{1,1}, \ldots, \mathbf{W}_{1,\ell}, \ldots, \mathbf{W}_{n,1}, \ldots, \mathbf{W}_{n,\ell}, \mathbf{B}_1)$.

$\mathsf{mpk} = \left(\mathcal{G}, [\![\mathbf{A}^\top]\!]_1, ([\![\mathbf{A}^\top \mathbf{V}_i]\!]_1)_{i\in[n]}, ([\![\mathbf{A}^\top \mathbf{W}_{i,j}]\!]_1)_{i\in[n], j\in[\ell]}\right)$.

$\underline{\mathsf{Encrypt}(\mathsf{mpk}, \mathbf{Y} = (\mathbf{y}_1, \ldots, \mathbf{y}_n)^\top)}$:

Let $\mathbf{y}_i = (\mathsf{y}_{i,1}, \ldots, \mathsf{y}_{i,\ell}) \in \mathbb{Z}_p^{1\times\ell}$.

$\mathbf{s} \leftarrow \mathbb{Z}_p^k$.

$\mathsf{ct}_0 = [\![\mathbf{s}^\top \mathbf{A}^\top]\!]_1, (\mathsf{ct}_{i,j} = [\![\mathbf{s}^\top \mathbf{A}^\top (\mathsf{y}_{i,j} \mathbf{V}_i + \mathbf{W}_{i,j})]\!]_1)_{i\in[n], j\in[\ell]}$.

$\mathsf{Ct} = (\mathsf{ct}_0, \mathsf{ct}_{1,1}, \ldots, \mathsf{ct}_{1,\ell}, \ldots, \mathsf{ct}_{n,1}, \ldots, \mathsf{ct}_{n,\ell})$.

$\underline{\mathsf{KeyGen}(\mathsf{msk}, \mathbf{x})}$:

Let $\mathbf{x} = (\mathsf{x}_1, \ldots, \mathsf{x}_\ell) \in \mathbb{Z}_p^{1\times\ell}$.

$\mathbf{r} \leftarrow \mathbb{Z}_p^k$, $\mathbf{u} = (u_1, \ldots, u_n) \leftarrow (\mathbb{Z}_p^*)^n$.

$\mathsf{sk} = (K_{i,j})_{i\in[n], j\in[0,\ell]}$.

$$K_{i,j} = \begin{cases} [\![u_i(\mathsf{x}_1 \mathbf{W}_{i,1} + \ldots + \mathsf{x}_\ell \mathbf{W}_{i,\ell})\mathbf{B}_1 \mathbf{r}]\!]_2 & \text{if } j = 0 \\ [\![u_i \mathsf{x}_j \mathbf{B}_1 \mathbf{r}]\!]_2 & \forall j \in [\ell] \end{cases}.$$

$\underline{\mathsf{Test}(\mathsf{mpk}, \mathsf{sk}, \mathsf{Ct})}$:

Let $\mathsf{Ct} = (\mathsf{ct}_0, \mathsf{ct}_{1,1}, \ldots, \mathsf{ct}_{1,\ell}, \ldots, \mathsf{ct}_{n,1}, \ldots, \mathsf{ct}_{n,\ell})$.

Let $\mathsf{sk} = (K_{i,j})_{i\in[n], j\in[0,\ell]}$.

Output $\mathbf{m} = (m_1, \ldots, m_n)$ where

$$m_i = \begin{cases} 1 & \text{if } e(\mathsf{ct}_0, K_{i,0}) = \prod_{j\in[\ell]} e(\mathsf{ct}_{i,j}, K_{i,j}) \\ 0 & \text{otherwise} \end{cases}.$$

Fig. 3. Our n-PO-ZIPE construction $\mathcal{P}$

Due to space limitation, we defer the formal argument of correctness and security to the full version. Nevertheless, we mention the security theorems next and provide proof sketches.

Theorem 6. *If the $\mathcal{D}_k$-Matrix Diffie-Hellman assumption ($\mathcal{D}_k$-matDH) holds in $\mathbb{G}_1$ and $\mathcal{D}_{2k,k}$-Matrix Diffie-Hellman assumption ($\mathcal{D}_{2k,k}$-matDH) holds in $\mathbb{G}_2$, our n-PO-ZIPE construction $\mathcal{P}$ (in Fig. 3) achieves fully attribute-hiding security (i.e. secure in the FAH security model). Precisely, for any ppt adversary $\mathcal{A}$ against $\mathcal{P}$ in the FAH security model that makes at most q secret key queries,*

$$\mathrm{Adv}_{\mathcal{A},\mathcal{P}}^{\mathsf{FAH}}(\lambda) \le \mathrm{Adv}_{\mathcal{B},\mathbb{G}_1}^{\mathcal{D}_k\text{-}\mathsf{matDH}}(\lambda) + 3q \cdot \mathrm{Adv}_{\mathcal{B},\mathbb{G}_2}^{\mathcal{D}_{2k,k}\text{-}\mathsf{matDH}}(\lambda).$$

Proof Sketch. The security proof is given via dual system proof. First, we use the MDDH problem to introduce randomness in the ciphertext and make it so-called semi-functional. Then we analyze the key and ciphertext pair using the lens of Wee [36]. In particular, following Wee [36], we implicitly divide the existing msk into two parts: normal and semi-functional. We further introduce more randomness in the semi-functional part of the secret keys by employing the MDDH assumption. We divide the space $\mathbb{Z}_p^{2k+1}$ into a three tuple dual-basis system $((\mathbf{B}_1, \mathbf{B}_2, \mathbf{B}_3), (\mathbf{B}_1^*, \mathbf{B}_2^*, \mathbf{B}_3^*))$ where,

$$\mathbf{B}_i^* \mathbf{B}_j = \begin{cases} \mathbf{I}_i & \text{if } j = i \\ \mathbf{0} & \text{otherwise.} \end{cases}$$

We aim to convert all the keys present in the span of $\mathbf{B}_1$ to the span of $\mathbf{B}_1$ and $\mathbf{B}_2$ together. To this goal, we consider keys one at a time and utilize $\mathbf{B}_3$. More precisely, for every key, we first change $\mathsf{span}(\mathbf{B}_1)$ to $\mathsf{span}(\mathbf{B}_1, \mathbf{B}_3)$; then $\mathsf{span}(\mathbf{B}_1, \mathbf{B}_3)$ to $\mathsf{span}(\mathbf{B}_1, \mathbf{B}_2, \mathbf{B}_3)$ and finally $\mathsf{span}(\mathbf{B}_1, \mathbf{B}_2, \mathbf{B}_3)$ to $\mathsf{span}(\mathbf{B}_1, \mathbf{B}_2)$. Once the keys are all from the span of $\mathsf{span}(\mathbf{B}_1, \mathbf{B}_2)$, we change the ciphertext generation process. In particular, the ciphertext now encodes a random linear combination of the challenge data-attribute matrices. This step requires a basis change and an information-theoretic argument. This precise step is the reason our public key size is $\mathcal{O}(n\ell)$. Since the ciphertext encodes a random linear combination of the challenge data-attribute matrices, no information about $\mathfrak{b} \leftarrow \{0,1\}$ is leaked from the ciphertext. We defer the details of the proof to the full version due to space limitation. □

Theorem 7. *If the (n,ℓ)-min-Entropy Multi-DDH assumption ((n,ℓ)-*mE-DDH*) holds in $\mathbb{G}_2$, our n-PO-ZIPE construction $\mathcal{P}$ achieves function privacy in the* FPriv *security model. Precisely, for any* ppt *adversary $\mathcal{A}$ of the above construction in the* FPriv *security model that makes at most q secret key queries and a challenge secret key query in an interleaved manner, there exists adversary $\mathcal{B}$ such that,* $\mathrm{Adv}_{\mathcal{A},\mathcal{P}}^{\mathsf{FPriv}}(\lambda) \leq \mathrm{Adv}_{\mathcal{B}}^{(n,\ell)\text{-}\mathsf{mE\text{-}DDH}}(\lambda)$.

Proof Sketch. The security proof is given via a hybrid argument. Game_0 is the real security game where $\mathsf{x}^* = (\mathsf{x}_1^*, \ldots, \mathsf{x}_\ell^*) \leftarrow \mathcal{X}_\mathfrak{b}$ for $\mathfrak{b} \leftarrow \{0,1\}$ is encoded in the secret key. In game Game_1, we replace $[\![u_i \mathsf{x}_j^*]\!]_2$ with a uniformly random quantity $[\![z_{i,j}]\!]_2$. We show that, this replacement is invisible to all ppt adversary due to min-entropy Multi-DDH assumption that we introduced and also have shown to be hard in the GGM due to DDH-II [12]. Finally, since $z_{i,j}$ does not contain any information about identity that is encoded in the secret key, the secret keys leak no information about it. We defer the formal argument to the full version due to space limitation. □

5 Constructing an IBR Scheme

We apply a variant of the transformation from Attrapadung and Libert's seminal work [5] on our fully attribute-hiding and function-hiding NIPE. Compared to [8], the IBR here is a public key scheme, keys are function private and the construction can support polynomial number of key queries ([8] argued security in bounded collision model). Note that IBR in Fig. 4 is basically n-PO-ZIPE of Fig. 3:

- KeyGen takes an identity id and runs KeyGen of n-PO-ZIPE on the key-attribute vector $\mathbf{x} = (\mathsf{id}, \mathsf{id}^2, \ldots, \mathsf{id}^{(m+1)})$.
- Encrypt takes a set S and runs Encrypt of n-PO-ZIPE on $\mathbf{y} = (a_0, \ldots, a_m)$ where $P_\mathsf{S}(z) = \prod_{\mathsf{id} \in \mathsf{S}} (z - \mathsf{id}) = a_0 + a_1 z + \ldots + a_\mathfrak{k} z^\mathfrak{k}$.
- Decrypt takes the mpk, a secret key sk and a ciphertext Ct and runs Test of n-PO-ZIPE on (mpk, sk, Ct).

5.1 Instantiating IBR

$\mathsf{Setup}(1^\lambda, 1^\ell, \mathcal{M} = \{0,1\}^n)$:

$\mathcal{G} = (p, \mathbb{G}_1, \mathbb{G}_2, \mathbb{G}_T, g_1, g_2, e) \leftarrow \mathsf{ABSGen}(1^\lambda)$.

$\mathbf{A} \leftarrow \mathcal{D}_k$ and $\mathbf{B}_1 \leftarrow \mathcal{D}_{2k+1,k}$.

$\mathbf{V}_1, \ldots, \mathbf{V}_n \leftarrow \mathbb{Z}_p^{(k+1)\times(2k+1)}$.

$\mathbf{W}_{1,1}, \ldots, \mathbf{W}_{1,\ell}, \ldots, \mathbf{W}_{n,1}, \ldots, \mathbf{W}_{n,\ell} \leftarrow \mathbb{Z}_p^{(k+1)\times(2k+1)}$.

$\mathsf{msk} = (\mathbf{W}_{1,1}, \ldots, \mathbf{W}_{1,\ell}, \ldots, \mathbf{W}_{n,1}, \ldots, \mathbf{W}_{n,\ell}, \mathbf{B}_1)$.

$\mathsf{mpk} = \left(\mathcal{G}, [\![\mathbf{A}^\top]\!]_1, ([\![\mathbf{A}^\top \mathbf{V}_i]\!]_1)_{i\in[n]}, ([\![\mathbf{A}^\top \mathbf{W}_{i,j}]\!]_1)_{i\in[n], j\in[\ell]}\right)$.

$\mathsf{Encrypt}(\mathsf{mpk}, \mathsf{S}, \mathbf{M} = (M_1, \ldots, M_n) \in \mathcal{M})$:

$P_{\mathsf{S}}(z) = \prod_{\mathsf{id}\in\mathsf{S}} (z - \mathsf{id}) = a_0 + a_1 z + \ldots + a_{\hbar} z^{\hbar}$ where $\hbar \leq \ell$.

Let $\mathbf{y} = (a_0, \ldots, a_{\hbar}, 0, \ldots, 0) \in \mathbb{Z}_p^{1\times\ell}$.

Let $\mathbf{Y} = (\mathbf{y}_1, \ldots, \mathbf{y}_n)^\top$ where $\mathbf{y}_i = (\mathsf{y}_{i,1}, \ldots, \mathsf{y}_{i,\ell}) = M_i \cdot \mathbf{y}$.

$\mathbf{s} \leftarrow \mathbb{Z}_p^k$.

$\mathsf{ct}_0 = [\![\mathbf{s}^\top \mathbf{A}^\top]\!]_1, (\mathsf{ct}_{i,j} = [\![\mathbf{s}^\top \mathbf{A}^\top (\mathsf{y}_{i,j} \mathbf{V}_i + \mathbf{W}_{i,j})]\!]_1)_{i\in[n], j\in[\ell]}$.

$\mathsf{Ct} = (\mathsf{ct}_0, \mathsf{ct}_{1,1}, \ldots, \mathsf{ct}_{1,\ell}, \ldots, \mathsf{ct}_{n,1}, \ldots, \mathsf{ct}_{n,\ell})$.

$\mathsf{KeyGen}(\mathsf{msk}, \mathsf{id})$:

Encode $\mathbf{x} = (\mathsf{id}, \ldots, \mathsf{id}^\ell) \in (\mathbb{Z}_p^*)^{1\times\ell}$.

$\mathbf{r} \leftarrow \mathbb{Z}_p^k$, $\mathbf{u} = (u_1, \ldots, u_n) \leftarrow (\mathbb{Z}_p^*)^n$.

$\mathsf{sk} = (K_{i,j})_{i\in[n], j\in[0,\ell]}$ where

$$K_{i,j} = \begin{cases} [\![u_i(\mathsf{id}\mathbf{W}_{i,1} + \ldots + \mathsf{id}^\ell \mathbf{W}_{i,\ell})\mathbf{B}_1\mathbf{r}]\!]_2 & \text{if } j = 0 \\ [\![u_i \mathsf{id}^j \mathbf{B}_1 \mathbf{r}]\!]_2 & \forall j \in [\ell] \end{cases}.$$

$\mathsf{Decrypt}(\mathsf{mpk}, \mathsf{sk}, \mathsf{Ct})$:

Let $\mathsf{Ct} = (\mathsf{ct}_0, \mathsf{ct}_{1,1}, \ldots, \mathsf{ct}_{1,\ell}, \ldots, \mathsf{ct}_{n,1}, \ldots, \mathsf{ct}_{n,\ell})$.

Let $\mathsf{sk} = (K_{i,j})_{i\in[n], j\in[0,\ell]}$.

Output $\mathbf{m} = (m_1, \ldots, m_n)$ where

$$m_i = \begin{cases} 1 & \text{if } e(\mathsf{ct}_0, K_{i,0}) = \prod_{j\in[\ell]} e(\mathsf{ct}_{i,j}, K_{i,j}) \\ 0 & \text{otherwise} \end{cases}.$$

Fig. 4. Our IBR construction IBR

Intuitively, $\langle \mathbf{x}, \mathbf{y} \rangle \neq 0 \iff \mathsf{id}(a_0 + a_1\mathsf{id} + \ldots + a_m\mathsf{id}^m) \neq 0 \Rightarrow \mathsf{id} \notin \mathsf{S}$. This naturally ensures that IBR is correct. Due to space limitation, we defer the formal argument of correctness and security to the full version.

Theorem 8. *If $\mathcal{P}$ is* MH *secure, then* IBR *is* MH *secure.*

Proof Sketch. Very much similar to the security arguments of [5,33]. □

Theorem 9. *If $\mathcal{P}$ is* FAH *secure, then* IBR *is* FAH *secure.*

Proof Sketch. As the encodings of id and S are public, the security arguments of [5,33] work. □

Theorem 10. *If both the random generator ℓ-Strong Power DDH (ℓ-*rSpDDH*) assumption holds in $\mathbb{G}_2$, then our construction* IBR *achieves function privacy in the* FPriv *security model. Precisely, for any* ppt *adversary $\mathcal{A}$ of the above construction in the* FPriv *security model that makes at most q secret key queries and a challenge secret key query in an interleaved manner, there exists adversary $\mathcal{B}_1, \mathcal{B}_2$ such that,* $\mathrm{Adv}^{\mathsf{FPriv}}_{\mathcal{A},\mathsf{IBR}}(\lambda) \leq \mathrm{Adv}^{\ell\text{-}\mathsf{rSpDDH}}_{\mathcal{B}_1}(\lambda)$.

Proof Sketch. The security proof is also given via a hybrid argument. Game_0 is the real security game where $\tilde{\mathsf{id}} \leftarrow X_{\mathfrak{b}}$ for $\mathfrak{b} \leftarrow \{0,1\}$ is encoded in the secret key. In game Game_1, we replace $\tilde{\mathsf{id}}$ with a uniformly random identity id. We show that, this replacement is invisible to all ppt adversary due to random generator ℓ-strong power-DDH assumption that we introduced and also have shown to be hard in the GGM. Finally, since id does not contain any information about $\mathfrak{b}$, the secret keys leak no information about it. The formal argument is deferred to the full version. □

6 Conclusion

In this paper, we solve a long-standing open problem to relate ZIPE to NIPE. We give an efficient and easy transformation between ZIPE and NIPE in the predicate-only settings. We then give a compiler that converts a predicate-only ZIPE to a standard NIPE, and follow this with a ZIPE instantiation for n data-vectors in the predicate-only settings. Applying this ZIPE on the compiler gives the first fully attribute-hiding secure NIPE construction that also achieves function privacy. We then convert this NIPE to construct the first fully attribute-hiding IBR with function privacy. However, the NIPE construction we propose here is moderately efficient, and we think improving such could be an interesting open problem. We suggest construction of ZIPE from NIPE to be a useful problem for future.

References

1. Agrawal, S., Bhattacherjee, S., Phan, D.H., Stehlé, D., Yamada, S.: Efficient public trace and revoke from standard assumptions: Extended abstract. In: Thuraisingham, B.M., Evans, D., Malkin, T., Xu, D. (eds.) ACM CCS 2017, pp. 2277–2293. ACM Press (2017). https://doi.org/10.1145/3133956.3134041
2. Agrawal, S., Libert, B., Stehlé, D.: Fully secure functional encryption for inner products, from standard assumptions. In: Robshaw, M., Katz, J. (eds.) CRYPTO 2016. LNCS, vol. 9816, pp. 333–362. Springer, Heidelberg (2016). https://doi.org/10.1007/978-3-662-53015-3_12
3. Attrapadung, N.: Dual system encryption via doubly selective security: framework, fully secure functional encryption for regular languages, and more. In: Nguyen, P.Q., Oswald, E. (eds.) EUROCRYPT 2014. LNCS, vol. 8441, pp. 557–577. Springer, Heidelberg (2014). https://doi.org/10.1007/978-3-642-55220-5_31
4. Attrapadung, N., Furukawa, J., Imai, H.: Forward-secure and searchable broadcast encryption with short ciphertexts and private keys. In: Lai, X., Chen, K. (eds.) ASIACRYPT 2006. LNCS, vol. 4284, pp. 161–177. Springer, Heidelberg (2006). https://doi.org/10.1007/11935230_11
5. Attrapadung, N., Libert, B.: Functional Encryption for inner product: achieving constant-size ciphertexts with adaptive security or support for negation. In: Nguyen, P.Q., Pointcheval, D. (eds.) PKC 2010. LNCS, vol. 6056, pp. 384–402. Springer, Heidelberg (2010). https://doi.org/10.1007/978-3-642-13013-7_23
6. Barth, A., Boneh, D., Waters, B.: Privacy in encrypted content distribution using private broadcast encryption. In: Di Crescenzo, G., Rubin, A. (eds.) FC 2006. LNCS, vol. 4107, pp. 52–64. Springer, Heidelberg (2006). https://doi.org/10.1007/11889663_4
7. Bartusek, J., Ma, F., Zhandry, M.: The distinction between fixed and random generators in group-based assumptions. In: Boldyreva, A., Micciancio, D. (eds.) CRYPTO 2019, Part II. LNCS, vol. 11693, pp. 801–830. Springer, Cham (2019). https://doi.org/10.1007/978-3-030-26951-7_27
8. Blazy, O., Mukherjee, S., Nguyen, H., Phan, D.H., Stehlé, D.: An anonymous trace-and-revoke broadcast encryption scheme. In: Baek, J., Ruj, S. (eds.) ACISP 2021. LNCS, vol. 13083, pp. 214–233. Springer, Cham (2021). https://doi.org/10.1007/978-3-030-90567-5_11

9. Boldyreva, A., Goyal, V., Kumar, V.: Identity-based encryption with efficient revocation. In: Ning, P., Syverson, P.F., Jha, S. (eds.) ACM CCS 2008, pp. 417–426. ACM Press (2008). https://doi.org/10.1145/1455770.1455823
10. Boneh, D., Franklin, M.: Identity-based encryption from the Weil pairing. In: Kilian, J. (ed.) CRYPTO 2001. LNCS, vol. 2139, pp. 213–229. Springer, Heidelberg (2001). https://doi.org/10.1007/3-540-44647-8_13
11. Boneh, D., Raghunathan, A., Segev, G.: Function-private identity-based encryption: hiding the function in functional encryption. In: Canetti, R., Garay, J.A. (eds.) CRYPTO 2013. LNCS, vol. 8043, pp. 461–478. Springer, Heidelberg (2013). https://doi.org/10.1007/978-3-642-40084-1_26
12. Canetti, R.: Towards realizing random oracles: hash functions that hide all partial information. In: Kaliski, B.S. (ed.) CRYPTO 1997. LNCS, vol. 1294, pp. 455–469. Springer, Heidelberg (1997). https://doi.org/10.1007/BFb0052255
13. Chatterjee, S., Mukherjee, S.: Keyword search meets membership testing: adaptive security from SXDH. In: Chakraborty, D., Iwata, T. (eds.) INDOCRYPT 2018. LNCS, vol. 11356, pp. 21–43. Springer, Cham (2018). https://doi.org/10.1007/978-3-030-05378-9_2
14. Chen, J., Gay, R., Wee, H.: Improved dual system Abe in prime-order groups via predicate encodings. In: Oswald, E., Fischlin, M. (eds.) EUROCRYPT 2015, Part II. LNCS, vol. 9057, pp. 595–624. Springer, Heidelberg (2015). https://doi.org/10.1007/978-3-662-46803-6_20
15. Chen, J., Gong, J., Wee, H.: Improved inner-product encryption with adaptive security and full attribute-hiding. In: Peyrin, T., Galbraith, S. (eds.) ASIACRYPT 2018, Part II. LNCS, vol. 11273, pp. 673–702. Springer, Cham (2018). https://doi.org/10.1007/978-3-030-03329-3_23
16. Delerablée, C.: Identity-based broadcast encryption with constant size ciphertexts and private keys. In: Kurosawa, K. (ed.) ASIACRYPT 2007. LNCS, vol. 4833, pp. 200–215. Springer, Heidelberg (2007). https://doi.org/10.1007/978-3-540-76900-2_12
17. Do, X.T., Phan, D.H., Yung, M.: A concise bounded anonymous broadcast yielding combinatorial trace-and-revoke schemes. In: Conti, M., Zhou, J., Casalicchio, E., Spognardi, A. (eds.) ACNS 2020, Part II. LNCS, vol. 12147, pp. 145–164. Springer, Cham (2020). https://doi.org/10.1007/978-3-030-57878-7_8
18. Escala, A., Herold, G., Kiltz, E., Ràfols, C., Villar, J.: An algebraic framework for Diffie-Hellman assumptions. In: Canetti, R., Garay, J.A. (eds.) CRYPTO 2013. LNCS, vol. 8043, pp. 129–147. Springer, Heidelberg (2013). https://doi.org/10.1007/978-3-642-40084-1_8
19. Fazio, N., Perera, I.M.: Outsider-anonymous broadcast encryption with sublinear ciphertexts. In: Fischlin, M., Buchmann, J., Manulis, M. (eds.) PKC 2012. LNCS, vol. 7293, pp. 225–242. Springer, Heidelberg (2012). https://doi.org/10.1007/978-3-642-30057-8_14
20. Goldwasser, S., Tauman Kalai, Y.: Cryptographic assumptions: a position paper. In: Kushilevitz, E., Malkin, T. (eds.) TCC 2016, Part I. LNCS, vol. 9562, pp. 505–522. Springer, Heidelberg (2016). https://doi.org/10.1007/978-3-662-49096-9_21
21. Goldwasser, S., Lewko, A., Wilson, D.A.: Bounded-collusion IBE from key homomorphism. In: Cramer, R. (ed.) TCC 2012. LNCS, vol. 7194, pp. 564–581. Springer, Heidelberg (2012). https://doi.org/10.1007/978-3-642-28914-9_32
22. Goyal, R., Koppula, V., Waters, B.: Lockable obfuscation. In: Umans, C. (ed.) 58th FOCS. pp. 612–621. IEEE Computer Society Press (2017). https://doi.org/10.1109/FOCS.2017.62

23. Katsumata, S., Yamada, S.: Non-zero inner product encryption schemes from various assumptions: LWE, DDH and DCR. In: Lin, D., Sako, K. (eds.) PKC 2019, Part II. LNCS, vol. 11443, pp. 158–188. Springer, Cham (2019). https://doi.org/10.1007/978-3-030-17259-6_6
24. Katz, J., Sahai, A., Waters, B.: Predicate encryption supporting disjunctions, polynomial equations, and inner products. In: Smart, N. (ed.) EUROCRYPT 2008. LNCS, vol. 4965, pp. 146–162. Springer, Heidelberg (2008). https://doi.org/10.1007/978-3-540-78967-3_9
25. Kim, J., Susilo, W., Guo, F., Au, M.H.: A tag based encoding: an efficient encoding for predicate encryption in prime order groups. In: Zikas, V., De Prisco, R. (eds.) SCN 2016. LNCS, vol. 9841, pp. 3–22. Springer, Cham (2016). https://doi.org/10.1007/978-3-319-44618-9_1
26. Komargodski, I., Yogev, E.: Another step towards realizing random oracles: non-malleable point obfuscation. Cryptology ePrint Archive, Report 2018/149, Version 20190226:074205, posted 26 February 2019 (2018). https://eprint.iacr.org/2018/149/20190226:074205
27. Komargodski, I., Yogev, E.: On distributional collision resistant hashing. In: Shacham, H., Boldyreva, A. (eds.) CRYPTO 2018. LNCS, vol. 10992, pp. 303–327. Springer, Cham (2018). https://doi.org/10.1007/978-3-319-96881-0_11
28. Li, J., Gong, J.: Improved anonymous broadcast encryptions. In: Preneel, B., Vercauteren, F. (eds.) ACNS 2018. LNCS, vol. 10892, pp. 497–515. Springer, Cham (2018). https://doi.org/10.1007/978-3-319-93387-0_26
29. Libert, B., Paterson, K.G., Quaglia, E.A.: Anonymous broadcast encryption: adaptive security and efficient constructions in the standard model. In: Fischlin, M., Buchmann, J., Manulis, M. (eds.) PKC 2012. LNCS, vol. 7293, pp. 206–224. Springer, Heidelberg (2012). https://doi.org/10.1007/978-3-642-30057-8_13
30. Okamoto, T., Takashima, K.: Fully secure functional encryption with general relations from the decisional linear assumption. In: Rabin, T. (ed.) CRYPTO 2010. LNCS, vol. 6223, pp. 191–208. Springer, Heidelberg (2010). https://doi.org/10.1007/978-3-642-14623-7_11
31. Okamoto, T., Takashima, K.: Adaptively attribute-hiding (hierarchical) inner product encryption. In: Pointcheval, D., Johansson, T. (eds.) EUROCRYPT 2012. LNCS, vol. 7237, pp. 591–608. Springer, Heidelberg (2012). https://doi.org/10.1007/978-3-642-29011-4_35
32. Patranabis, S., Mukhopadhyay, D., Ramanna, S.C.: Function private predicate encryption for low min-entropy predicates. In: Lin, D., Sako, K. (eds.) PKC 2019, Part II. LNCS, vol. 11443, pp. 189–219. Springer, Cham (2019). https://doi.org/10.1007/978-3-030-17259-6_7
33. Ramanna, S.C.: More efficient constructions for inner-product encryption. In: Manulis, M., Sadeghi, A.-R., Schneider, S. (eds.) ACNS 2016. LNCS, vol. 9696, pp. 231–248. Springer, Cham (2016). https://doi.org/10.1007/978-3-319-39555-5_13
34. Shamir, A.: Identity-based cryptosystems and signature schemes. In: Blakley, G.R., Chaum, D. (eds.) CRYPTO 1984. LNCS, vol. 196, pp. 47–53. Springer, Heidelberg (1985). https://doi.org/10.1007/3-540-39568-7_5
35. Wee, H.: Dual system encryption via predicate encodings. In: Lindell, Y. (ed.) TCC 2014. LNCS, vol. 8349, pp. 616–637. Springer, Heidelberg (2014). https://doi.org/10.1007/978-3-642-54242-8_26

36. Wee, H.: Attribute-hiding predicate encryption in bilinear groups, revisited. In: Kalai, Y., Reyzin, L. (eds.) TCC 2017, Part I. LNCS, vol. 10677, pp. 206–233. Springer, Cham (2017). https://doi.org/10.1007/978-3-319-70500-2_8
37. Zhang, M., Takagi, T.: Efficient constructions of anonymous multireceiver encryption protocol and their deployment in group e-mail systems with privacy preservation. IEEE Syst. J. **7**(3), 410–419 (2013). https://doi.org/10.1109/JSYST.2012.2221893

Computational Security Analysis of the Full EDHOC Protocol

Loïc Ferreira(✉)

Orange Innovation, Applied Crypto Group, Caen, France
loic.ferreira@orange.com

Abstract. Ephemeral Diffie-Hellman Over COSE (EDHOC) is designed to be a compact and lightweight authenticated key exchange protocol, providing mutual authentication, forward secrecy, and identity protection. EDHOC aims at being suitable for low-power networks such as cellular IoT, 6TiSCH, and LoRaWAN. In this paper, we perform a security analysis of the last draft of EDHOC (draft 23). We analyse the full protocol including its four different authentication methods. Our results show that the security of the authenticated key exchange in EDHOC depends essentially on that of the authenticated encryption algorithm used during that phase. Finally, we provide more precise estimates of the computational security bounds for all authentication methods in EDHOC so that meaningful choices of quantitative parameters can be done to instantiate the protocol securely.

Keywords: EDHOC · Authenticated Key Exchange · Multi-user Security · Concrete Security · IoT

1 Introduction

1.1 Context

With the rise of the Internet of Things (IoT), the number of active devices in 2030 is expected to be around 30 billion [39]. Such connections are established by devices with constrained resources in terms of computation, memory, energy. Appropriate cryptographic protocols must therefore be implemented in order to take into account these stringent constraints, and several mechanisms have been designed and deployed such as Zigbee [7], LoRaWAN [36,37], Sigfox [35] or OSCORE [31] to name a few. The aforementioned protocols are based on symmetric-key algorithms, but, whereas the first ones make use of static symmetric keys, the last one, designed by the Constrained RESTful Environments (CORE) working group, within the Internet Engineering Task Force (IETF), is compatible with key exchange protocols in order to establish its symmetric keys.

Such protocols must fulfil the small message size and the restricted code and memory requirements implied by the constrained IoT devices. The Lightweight Authenticated Key Exchange (LAKE) working group, in charge of devising

E. Oswald (Ed.): CT-RSA 2024, LNCS 14643, pp. 25–48, 2024.
https://doi.org/10.1007/978-3-031-58868-6_2

such a mechanism, has released the draft 23 of its proposal called Ephemeral Diffie-Hellman Over COSE (EDHOC) [32]. Built on the SIGMA [24] paradigm, EDHOC is a set of four authenticated key exchange protocols (which differ on the used authentication method) that achieves low bandwidth and is 3 to 7 times more efficient compared to possible alternatives such as Compact TLS [28] and DTLS 1.3 [29].

The LAKE working group has solicited analysis of EDHOC in order to incorporate feedbacks from the cryptographic community [40]. So far, only the single-user setting has been considered and all computational analyses focused on only one (distinct) authentication method out of four.

1.2 Related Work

Preliminary drafts of the EDHOC protocol are analysed with formal methods (ProVerif, BAN-Logic, AVISPA, SAPIC+) by Bruni, Jørgensen, Petersen and Schürmann [5], Kim, Duguma, Lee, Kim, Lim and You [22], Norrman, Sundararajan and Bruni [26], and Cheval, Jacomme, Kremer and Künnemann [6].

Jacomme, Klein, Kremer and Racouchot [20] use the SAPIC+ platform to provide a formal analysis of all four authentication methods in EDHOC draft 12. The weaknesses they found have been acknowledged by the EDHOC authors and the proposed mitigations included in draft 14.

Cottier and Pointcheval [8] make a computational analysis of EDHOC draft 15 in the Bellare and Rogaway model [3]. They consider the so-called Stat-Stat authentication method based on static DH keys. They propose improvements (at no additional cost for some of them) in order to achieve 128-bit security instead of 64-bit, for all the security properties they consider in their security model (key indistinguishability, forward secrecy, mutual authentication, identity protection). In particular, they suggest to increase from 64 to 128 bits the MAC tag carried in the third message of the Stat-Stat method, and to compensate by removing the 64-bit tag related to the authentication encryption scheme. They propose also to compute the first main key (PRK_2) based on a session context which makes the reduction cost of the key indistinguishability experiment independent of the number of sessions. The latter is incorporated in the last EDHOC draft. In contrast to Cottier and Pointcheval, we make clear the contribution of the symmetric-key functions involved in the protocol (Cottier and Pointcheval do not incorporate the fourth message of the protocol in their analysis, necessary to guarantee the binding between the session key and the two parties involved in the protocol run). In the same way as Cottier and Poincheval, we incorporate identity protection into our security model but we analyse the four authentication methods (instead of one only) corresponding to the latest draft of the protocol.

Günther and Mukendi [15,16] consider the EDHOC draft 17. They generalise the Bellare and Rogaway security model [2] to capture multi-stage key exchange security [14] and analyse the Sig-Sig authentication method based on signatures. They show that this draft achieves session key indistinguishability, forward secrecy and user authentication even in a strong model where the adversary can register malicious keys with colliding identifiers (which is allowed in EDHOC) given that the employed signature scheme provides so-called "exclusive ownership". They also observe that including the verification key in the signed data (which is done in EDHOC) is enough to thwart such an attack (provided there are no "weak keys"). They propose several improvements, now included in EDHOC draft 23, such as separating the computation of the final session key from the other keys derived during the handshake and binding public keys to the identities when computing the transcript hashes (in order to mitigate "exclusive ownership" attacks where an adversary creates a public key under which an (honestly generated) message-signature pair verifies). In addition to entity authentication, key indistinguishability and forward secrecy, our security model captures also identity privacy.

1.3 Contributions

We provide a computational analysis of the last EDHOC draft [32] in a Bellare and Rogaway [2] security model style, following the approach of Davis and Günther [9]. Our security model captures mutual (explicit) authentication, soundness, key indistinguishability, forward secrecy and identity privacy. The previous analyses concern older drafts (12, 15, 17) of the protocol and lead to modifications independently suggested that, for some of them, are now incorporated in the latest draft (23). We provide an analysis of this version, hence jointly covering all these changes. In addition and in contrast with most of these previous works (in particular all computational ones), we analyse the four authentication methods of the EDHOC protocol. Furthermore, the security bounds we provide rely upon previous results in the multi-user setting for the underlying primitives of the protocol. This allows us to give more precise estimates of the computational bounds for EDHOC (and its four authentication methods) so that meaningful choices of quantitative parameters can be done to instantiate the protocol securely.

Our results show in particular that the ciphersuites allowed in EDHOC are not all equivalent in terms of security. More specifically, although both ChaCha20-Poly1305 and AES 256 GCM are recommended in the EDHOC draft for "*high security applications such as government use and financial applications*" [32, Section 3.6], AES 256 GCM appears to be more suitable.

2 Security Model

2.1 Overview

We analyse the EDHOC protocol in a Bellare and Rogaway [2] security model style, following the approach of Davis and Günther [9]. Our model captures mutual (explicit) authentication, soundness, key indistinguishability, forward secrecy and identity privacy. In order to define the identity privacy property, we borrow the concept of "virtual identity" from Ouafi and Phan [27] and Hermans, Pashalidis, Vercauteren and Preneel [17], which allows hiding the identity of the party the adversary is interacting with. We follow also the paradigm proposed by Schäge, Schwenk and Lauer [30], and incorporate the identity privacy property together with the other security properties. This approach guarantees that the different security properties are independent of each other. That is, any security property holds in the presence of attacks targetting another security property. This leads to a stronger security model where security properties are considered separately and not all the adversarial queries are available in all the experiments.

Our adversary is active, controls all communication and can forward, alter, drop any message exchanged by honest parties, or insert new messages. It is also able to corrupt long-term public keys and reveal session keys. The goal of the adversary is to (i) distinguish the real session key from a value of same size uniformly drawn at random (key indistinguishability), (ii) make an instance accept without a unique partner (authentication), or (iii) distinguish which party out of two is active during a protocol run (identity privacy).

2.2 Execution Environment

In this section we present the security model for authenticated key exchange (AKE) protocols. The corresponding security experiment is depicted by Fig. 1.

Parties. A two-party protocol is carried out by a set of parties. Each party u has an associated pair of long-term public and private keys (pk_u, sk_u). The algorithm Kgen generates a new pair of long-term keys. The public keys pk_u are registered in a list $list_{pk}$. When the long-term private key sk_u of party u is corrupted at time time, then corr_u is set to time.[1]

Instance. Each party can take part in multiple parallel executions of the protocol. Each run of the protocol is called a session. To each session of a party u, an instance π_u^i is associated which embodies this session's execution of the protocol and maintains the following state specific to the session:

- $\mathsf{role} \in \{\mathtt{initiator}, \mathtt{responder}\}$: the role of the instance in the protocol execution, being either the initiator or the responder.
- parent: the party u which an instance π_u^i is associated to.
- pid: the identity of the intended communication partner party of the instance.
- sid: the identifier of the session.
- $\mathsf{status} \in \{\bot, \mathtt{running}, \mathtt{accepted}, \mathtt{rejected}\}$: the status of the instance, initialised to $\bot$.
- $\mathsf{t_{acc}}$: the time time when the instance accepts.
- sk: the session key computed by the instance.
- $\mathsf{revealed} \in \{\mathtt{false}, \mathtt{true}\}$: indicates whether the session key is revealed, initialised to $\mathtt{false}$.

[1] Note that our model does not give the adversary the ability to register its own (malicious) keys, contrary to [15,16].

$G^{\mathsf{AKE}}_{\Pi,\mathcal{A}}$

```
INITIALISE
time ← 0
n ← 0
𝒯 ← ∅
𝒱 ← ∅
b_key ←$ {0,1}
b_id ←$ {0,1}

NEWPARTY
n ← n + 1
(pk_n, sk_n) ← Kgen()
corr_n ← +∞
list_pk[n] ← pk_n
return pk_n

SEND(u, i, m)
if π_u^i = ⊥ then
   role ← m
   (π_u^i, m') ←$ Activate(u, sk_u, list_pk, role)
   π_u^i.t_acc ← 0
else
   (π_u^i, m') ←$ Run(u, sk_u, π_u^i, list_pk, m)
if π_u^i.status = accepted then
   time ← time + 1
   π_u^i.t_acc ← time
return m'

CORRUPT(u)
time ← time + 1
corr_u ← time
return sk_u

REVEALKEY(u, i)
if (π_u^i = ⊥  ∨ π_u^i.status ≠ accepted) then
   return ⊥
π_u^i.revealed ← true
return π_u^i.sk

TEST(u, i)
if (π_u^i = ⊥  ∨
      π_u^i.status ≠ accepted ∨
      π_u^i.tested) then
   return ⊥
π_u^i.tested ← true
𝒯 ← 𝒯 ∪ {π_u^i}
k_0 ← π_u^i.sk
k_1 ←$ {0,1}^|k_0|
return k_{b_key}

DRAWVID(u, v)
vid ← (u, v)
𝒱 ← 𝒱 ∪ {vid}
return vid

FREEVID(vid)
time ← time + 1
free_vid ← time
∀ π_u^i
   if ((π_u^i.parent = realvid(vid) ∨
          π_u^i.pid = realvid(vid)) ∧
         π_u^i.status = running) then
        π_u^i.status ← rejected

FINALISE(x, b*)
if ¬Sound then
   return 1
if ¬ExplicitAuth then
   return 1
if (x = KEY) then
   b' ← b_key
   if ¬FreshKey then
      b* ← 0
if (x = ID) then
   b' ← b_id
   if ¬FreshIdentity then
      b* ← 0
return [[b' = b*]]
```

Fig. 1. Security experiment for the AKE protocol

FreshKey

```
∀ π_u^i ∈ T
   if π_u^i.revealed then
      return false
   if ∃ π_v^j ≠ π_u^i | (π_v^j.sid = π_u^i.sid ∧
         (π_v^j.tested ∨ π_v^j.revealed)) then
      return false
   if corr_{π_u^i.pid} < π_u^i.t_acc then
      return false
return true
```

FreshIdentity

```
∀ vid ∈ V
   w ← realvid(vid)
   if ∃ i | (corr_{π_w^i.pid} < π_w^i.t_acc ∧
               corr_{π_w^i.pid} < free_vid) then
      return false
   if ∃ i | (π_w^i.role = responder ∧
               π_w^i.status ≠ accepted) then
      return false
return true
```

Sound

```
if ∃ distinct π_u^i, π_v^j, π_w^k |
         π_u^i.sid = π_v^j.sid = π_w^k.sid ≠⊥ then
   return false
if ∃ π_u^i, π_v^j | (π_u^i.status = π_v^j.status
                        = accepted ∧
                  π_u^i.sid = π_v^j.sid ∧
                  π_u^i.pid = v ∧
                  π_v^j.pid = u ∧
                  π_u^i.role ≠ π_v^j.role) then
   if π_u^i.sk ≠ π_v^j.sk then
      return false
return true
```

ExplicitAuth

```
return [[∀ π_u^i (π_u^i.status = accepted ∧
                    π_u^i.t_acc < corr_{π_u^i.pid})
   ⇒ ∃ π_v^j | (π_u^i.pid = v ∧
                  π_u^i.sid = π_v^j.sid ∧
                  π_u^i.role ≠ π_v^j.role ∧
                  (π_v^j.status = accepted
                   ⇒ π_v^j.pid = u))]]
```

Fig. 1. (*continued*)

- tested $\in \{\texttt{false}, \texttt{true}\}$: indicates whether the instance is tested, initialised to false.

The algorithm Activate initiates a new session and generates in particular the corresponding instance. The algorithm Run delivers the next incoming protocol message, resulting in particular in an updated instance and a response message.

Partnership. The notion of partnership between two instances is based on the session identifier sid. Two instances are partnered if they share the same sid.

Virtual Identity. We use the notion of virtual identity [17,27] to define the identity privacy security experiment. The privacy property guarantees that the identity of a party remains confidential and that two different protocol runs are unlinkable.

A virtual identity $vid = (u, v)$ designates one out of two possible parties u and v. The goal of the adversary in the identity privacy experiment is to guess which party lies behind vid. The real involved party hidden under $vid = (u, v)$ is designated by realvid(vid), depending on the secret identity bit $b_{\mathsf{id}} \in \{0, 1\}$. This bit is sampled at the initialisation of the security experiment. If $b_{\mathsf{id}} = 0$ then realvid(vid) $= u$, otherwise realvid(vid) $= v$.

The adversary uses the oracles DrawVid and FreeVid respectively to create and release a virtual identifier. When a virtual identifier vid is released at time time, then free_{vid} is set to time. Further, we say that a virtual identifier $vid = (u, v)$ is corrupted if either party u or party v is corrupted.

The following predicates are used to determine if the adversary wins the AKE security experiment.

Soundness. The soundness predicate Sound is used to guarantee that only two session identifiers can be equal, and that two instances ending in accepting state which share the same session identifier mutually agree on their partner's identity, have opposite roles, and compute the same session key.

Explicit Authentication. When the explicit authentication predicate ExplicitAuth is true, then all instances accepting with an uncorrupted peer, are partnered (i.e., share the same session identifier as another instance), such that the instance and its partner have opposite role, and they mutually agree on their partner's identity (upon acceptance). Our model captures also key-compromise impersonation attacks [4] by allowing the parent party of the tested instance to be corrupted at any point in time.

Identity Freshness. The identity freshness predicate FreshIdentity aims at excluding trivial attacks. A first trivial attack is the following one: an adversary corrupts a party and then successfully completes a protocol run (as initiator or responder) with an honest vid. Hence the adversary learns straightforwardly the real identity of its peer. Therefore if, for any party vid, there exists an instance such that its partner is corrupted before acceptance, then FreshIdentity is false. We exclude the corruption of a peer only before the time $\mathsf{realvid}(vid)$ is involved in vid, but not after (hence the condition "$\mathsf{corr}_{\pi_w^i.\mathsf{pid}} < \mathsf{free}_{vid}$" where $w = \mathsf{realvid}(vid)$), in order to narrow the rule to relevant cases.

In a second trivial attack, the adversary merely initiates a protocol run (as initiator). Then (upon reception of message msg_2), it learns the real identity of the peer (which behaves as responder). The adversary does not need to corrupt any party, nor to make the peer accept. This trivial attack is also excluded in FreshIdentity (through the second "if" condition). This attack is due to the fact that, in a two-party protocol, the first party that authenticates cannot hide its identity to an active adversary, even if this identity is sent encrypted [24]. However such protocols can protect the identity of both communicating parties from a passive adversary.

In other words, these trivial attacks are *not* attacks in the sense of our security definition for the identity privacy property because either the honest instance aborts eventually, or it accepts because its partner was corrupted beforehand.

Key Freshness. The key freshness predicate FreshKey aims also at excluding trivial attacks during the session key indistinguishability experiment. More specifically, if a session key is revealed or a party is corrupted, then the adversary can straightforwardly win the experiment. Likewise, if, among two partnered instances, one is tested, then the adversary can correctly answer the TEST-challenge.

The forward secrecy property is incorporated by allowing the adversary to corrupt any party as long as all tested sessions accept prior to corrupting their respective intended peer.

Finally we define the AKE security (Definition 1).

Definition 1 (Authenticated key exchange security). *Let* Π *be an authenticated key exchange protocol and* $G^{\mathsf{AKE}}_{\Pi,\mathcal{A}}$ *be the* AKE *security experiment defined in Fig. 1. We define*

$$\mathsf{adv}^{\mathsf{AKE}}_{\Pi}(t, q_{\mathrm{N}}, q_{\mathrm{S}}, q_{\mathrm{C}}, q_{\mathrm{R}}, q_{\mathrm{T}}) = \max_{\mathcal{A}} \Pr\left[G^{\mathsf{AKE}}_{\Pi,\mathcal{A}} \Rightarrow 1\right] - \frac{1}{2}$$

where the maximum is taken over all adversaries, denoted $(t, q_{\mathrm{N}}, q_{\mathrm{S}}, q_{\mathrm{C}}, q_{\mathrm{R}}, q_{\mathrm{T}})$*-*AKE*-adversaries, running in time at most* t*, and making at most* q_{N}, q_{S}, q_{C}, q_{R}, *and* q_{T} *queries to the oracles* NEWPARTY, SEND, CORRUPT, REVEALKEY, *and* TEST *respectively.*

2.3 Assumptions and Building Blocks

Our security proofs lean upon several assumptions and blocks. More specifically, key indistinguishability (and forward secrecy) relies upon the Strong (SDH) and Gap (GDH) DH assumptions, and on the PRF-security of the Expand function (used to compute in particular some intermediary and session keys). Authentication depends on the unforgeability of the signature scheme or the MAC function (depending on the authentication method), as well as on the collision resistance of the hash functions. Identity privacy relies upon the ciphertext indistinguishability of the symmetric-key encryption functions. The unforgeability of authenticated encryption functions may also contribute to the soundness property.

Due to lack of space, we provide the corresponding definitions in the full version of the paper [13].

3 Description of the EDHOC Protocol

The EDHOC protocol aims at establishing a secure channel between two devices. It is dedicated to constrained devices. That is, devices with narrowed computational capabilities, low throughput, reduced memory. EDHOC provides mainly mutual authentication, indistinguishability of the session key, forward secrecy and identity protection (against passive adversaries for both communicating parties and against active adversaries for the initiator).

The protocol offers four methods for the parties to authenticate. While the key exchange phase is essentially based on the Diffie-Hellman (DH) protocol [12], authentication of the parties can be done by means of a static public DH key (from which a MAC tag is computed) or a signature. Consequently, an execution

Initiator | Responder

Initiator:

$\underline{\mathsf{InitMsg0}(\hat{I}, sk_I, \pi_I)}$
Choose $suites$, mth
$x \xleftarrow{\$} (\mathbb{Z}/p\mathbb{Z})^*$, $X \leftarrow g^x$
Generate ci_I
$msg_1 \leftarrow (mth, suites, X, ci_I, [data_1])$

$\xrightarrow{msg_1}$

Responder:

$\underline{\mathsf{RespMsg1}(\hat{R}, sk_R, \pi_R, list_{pk}, msg_1)}$
If $suites$ not valid then abort.
$y \xleftarrow{\$} (\mathbb{Z}/p\mathbb{Z})^*$, $Y \leftarrow g^y$
Generate ci_R
$\mathsf{sid} \leftarrow (X, Y, *)$
$h_2 \leftarrow \mathsf{H}(Y \| \mathsf{H}(msg_1))$
$PRK_2 \leftarrow \mathsf{Extract}(h_2, X^y)$, $PRK_3 \leftarrow PRK_2$
$ctx_2 \leftarrow ci_R \| id_R \| h_2 \| cr_R \| [data_2]$
$\tau_2 \leftarrow \mathsf{Expand}(PRK_3, 2 \| ctx_2 \| \ell_\tau, \ell_\tau)$
$\sigma_R \leftarrow \mathsf{Sig.Sign}(sk_R, ctx_2 \| \tau_2)$
$p_2 \leftarrow ci_R \| id_R \| \sigma_R \| [data_2]$
$ks_2 \leftarrow \mathsf{Expand}(PRK_2, 0 \| h_2 \| \ell_{pt}, \ell_{pt})$
$c_2 \leftarrow ks_2 \oplus p_2$
$msg_2 \leftarrow (Y, c_2)$

$\xleftarrow{msg_2}$

Initiator:

$\underline{\mathsf{InitMsg2}(\hat{I}, sk_I, \pi_I, list_{pk}, msg_2)}$
$\mathsf{sid} \leftarrow (X, Y, I)$
$h_2 \leftarrow \mathsf{H}(Y \| \mathsf{H}(msg_1))$
$PRK_2 \leftarrow \mathsf{Extract}(h_2, Y^x)$, $PRK_3 \leftarrow PRK_2$
$ks_2 \leftarrow \mathsf{Expand}(PRK_2, 0 \| h_2 \| \ell_{pt}, \ell_{pt})$
$p_2 \leftarrow c_2 \oplus ks_2$
If responder's identity not valid then abort.
$ctx_2 \leftarrow ci_R \| id_R \| h_2 \| cr_R \| [data_2]$
$\tau_2 \leftarrow \mathsf{Expand}(PRK_3, 2 \| ctx_2 \| \ell_\tau, \ell_\tau)$
If $\mathsf{Sig.Vrfy}(pk_R, ctx_2 \| \tau_2, \sigma_R) = \mathtt{false}$ then abort.
$\mathsf{pid} \leftarrow \hat{R}$

$h_3 \leftarrow \mathsf{H}(h_2 \| p_2 \| cr_R)$
$SLT_4 \leftarrow \mathsf{Expand}(PRK_3, 5 \| h_3 \| \ell_h, \ell_h)$
$PRK_4 \leftarrow \mathsf{Extract}(SLT_4, Y^i)$
$ctx_3 \leftarrow id_I \| h_3 \| cr_I \| [data_3]$
$\tau_3 \leftarrow \mathsf{Expand}(PRK_4, 6 \| ctx_3 \| \ell_\tau, \ell_\tau)$
$K_3 \leftarrow \mathsf{Expand}(PRK_3, 3 \| h_3 \| \ell_k, \ell_k)$
$IV_3 \leftarrow \mathsf{Expand}(PRK_3, 4 \| h_3 \| \ell_{iv}, \ell_{iv})$
$p_3 \leftarrow id_I \| \tau_3 \| [data_3]$
$c_3 \leftarrow \mathsf{AEAD}(K_3, IV_3, h_3, p_3)$
$msg_3 \leftarrow c_3$

$\xrightarrow{msg_3}$

Responder:

$\underline{\mathsf{RespMsg3}(\hat{R}, sk_R, \pi_R, list_{pk}, msg_3)}$
$h_3 \leftarrow \mathsf{H}(h_2 \| p_2 \| cr_R)$
$K_3 \leftarrow \mathsf{Expand}(PRK_3, 3 \| h_3 \| \ell_k, \ell_k)$
$IV_3 \leftarrow \mathsf{Expand}(PRK_3, 4 \| h_3 \| \ell_{iv}, \ell_{iv})$
$p_3 \leftarrow \mathsf{AEAD}^{-1}(K_3, IV_3, h_3, c_3)$
If $p_3 = \perp$ then abort.
If initiator's identity not valid then abort.
$\mathsf{sid} \leftarrow (X, Y, I)$
$SLT_4 \leftarrow \mathsf{Expand}(PRK_3, 5 \| h_3 \| \ell_h, \ell_h)$
$PRK_4 \leftarrow \mathsf{Extract}(SLT_4, I^y)$
$ctx_3 \leftarrow id_I \| h_3 \| cr_I \| [data_3]$
$\tau_3' \leftarrow \mathsf{Expand}(PRK_4, 6 \| ctx_3 \| \ell_\tau, \ell_\tau)$
If $\tau_3' \neq \tau_3$ then abort.
$\mathsf{status} \leftarrow \mathsf{accepted}$, $\mathsf{pid} \leftarrow \hat{I}$

$h_4 \leftarrow \mathsf{H}(h_3 \| p_3 \| cr_I)$
$K_4 \leftarrow \mathsf{Expand}(PRK_4, 8 \| h_4 \| \ell_k, \ell_k)$
$IV_4 \leftarrow \mathsf{Expand}(PRK_4, 9 \| h_4 \| \ell_{iv}, \ell_{iv})$
$c_4 \leftarrow \mathsf{AEAD}(K_4, IV_4, h_4, [data_4])$
$PRK_{out} \leftarrow \mathsf{Expand}(PRK_4, 7 \| h_4 \| \ell_h, \ell_h)$
$msg_4 \leftarrow c_4$

$\xleftarrow{msg_4}$

Initiator:

$\underline{\mathsf{InitMsg4}(\hat{I}, sk_i, \pi_I, list_{pk}, msg_4)}$
$h_4 \leftarrow \mathsf{H}(h_3 \| p_3 \| cr_I)$
$K_4 \leftarrow \mathsf{Expand}(PRK_4, 8 \| h_4 \| \ell_k, \ell_k)$
$IV_4 \leftarrow \mathsf{Expand}(PRK_4, 9 \| h_4 \| \ell_{iv}, \ell_{iv})$
$[data_4] \leftarrow \mathsf{AEAD}^{-1}(K_4, IV_4, h_4, c_4)$
If $[data_4] = \perp$ then abort.
$\mathsf{status} \leftarrow \mathsf{accepted}$
$PRK_{out} \leftarrow \mathsf{Expand}(PRK_4, 7 \| h_4 \| \ell_h, \ell_h)$

Fig. 2. EDHOC protocol with authentication method Stat-Sig. Values surrounded with brackets are optional.

```
Activate(id, sk, list_pk, role)
π.role ← role
π.status ← running
if role = initiator then
   (π, m) ← InitMsg0(id, sk, π)
else
   m ←⊥
return (π, m)
```

```
// EDHOC-0 and EDHOC-1
Run(id, sk, π, list_pk, m)
if π.status ≠ running then
   return ⊥
if π.role = initiator then
   (π, m) ← InitMsg2(id, sk, π, list_pk, m)
else if π.sid =⊥ then
   (π, m) ← RespMsg1(id, sk, π, list_pk, m)
else
   (π, m) ← RespMsg3(id, sk, π, list_pk, m)
return (π, m)
```

```
// EDHOC-2 and EDHOC-3
Run(id, sk, π, list_pk, m)
if π.status ≠ running then
   return ⊥
if π.role = initiator then
   if π.sid =⊥ then
      (π, m) ← InitMsg2(id, sk, π, list_pk, m)
   else
      (π, m) ← InitMsg4(id, sk, π, list_pk, m)
else if π.sid =⊥ then
   (π, m) ← RespMsg1(id, sk, π, list_pk, m)
else
   (π, m) ← RespMsg3(id, sk, π, list_pk, m)
return (π, m)
```

Fig. 3. Definition of the Activate and Run algorithms in EDHOC

of the protocol is made of three (msg_1, msg_2, msg_3) or four messages (msg_4) depending on the authentication method (mth).

With the two first messages, the two communicating parties agree on the authentication method and on cryptographic components that will be used to compute the subsequent messages of the protocol run. These messages transport also ephemeral DH shares (X, Y) for the key exchange. The second and third messages transport the identities and are used to authenticate the involved parties. The different messages are encrypted and integrity-protected by symmetric-key functions which keys are computed from the successive shared DH secrets that are exchanged during the execution.

More specifically, the session key output by each new protocol execution is denoted PRK_{out}. Prior to the computation of the session key, intermediary keys (PRK_2, PRK_3, PRK_4) are used to compute authentication tags (τ_2, τ_3), derive encryption material (ks_2, K_3 and IV_3, K_4 and IV_4), and eventually encrypt data. Transcripts of the plaintext data (h_2, h_3, h_4) are also involved in the computation of the authentication tags, encryption material, and the session key. Among optional additional plaintext data ($data_2$, $data_3$), an identifier of the responder's (resp. initiator's) credential is transported (encrypted) in msg_2 (resp. msg_3). This identifier (id_I, id_R) allows retrieving the credential (cr_I, cr_R) of the corresponding party, containing in particular the authentication public key in the form of either a signature key or a static DH key (depending on the authentication method). Optionally, this identifier can embed the credential itself.

The intermediary keys PRK_2, PRK_3, PRK_4 are output by the Extract function (that we model as a random oracle) keyed with either transcripts of data (h_2) or salt values (SLT_3, SLT_4) and using shared secret DH values as input. The salt values, the encryption material and the authentication tags are output by the Expand function keyed with one of the PRK keys using as input a distinct label and either transcripts of data or plaintext data, credentials and identifiers. The two or three last messages (depending on the authentication method) are encrypted either with a one-time pad scheme or with an AEAD scheme keyed with one of the encryption keys (ks_2, K_3, K_4).

Figure 2 depicts the protocol execution with the authentication methods Stat-Sig (the other methods are depicted in the full version of this paper [13]), where ℓ_{pt} corresponds to the size of the plaintext p_2.

4 Security Proofs

In this section, we prove that the four authentication methods in EDHOC correspond to secure AKE protocols according to Definition 1.

4.1 Security Bounds

Theorem 1. *Let EDHOC-*0 *(Sig-Sig), EDHOC-*1 *(Sig-Stat), EDHOC-*2 *(Stat-Sig), EDHOC-*3 *(Stat-Stat) be the four EDHOC protocols (EDHOC-*2 *is described by Figs. 2 and 3). Let* $\mathbb{G}$ *be a group of prime order* p*,* H *a hash function,* Sign *a signature scheme,* AEAD *an authenticated encryption scheme,* Expand *a pseudo-random function, and* Extract *be modelled as a random oracle. For any* $(t, q_N, q_S, q_C, q_R, q_T)$-AKE*-adversary* $\mathcal{A}$ *against EDHOC-*i*,* $i \in \{0, 1, 2, 3\}$*, running in time at most* t*, and making at most* q_N*,* q_S*,* q_C*,* q_R*, and* q_T *queries to the oracles* NewParty*,* Send*,* Corrupt*,* RevealKey*, and* Test *respectively, and making at most* q_{RO} *queries to* Extract*, with* ℓ_τ *the size of* τ_2 *and* τ_3

$$
\begin{aligned}
&\mathsf{adv}^{\mathsf{AKE}}_{EDHOC\text{-}0}(t, q_{\mathrm{N}}, q_{\mathrm{S}}, q_{\mathrm{C}}, q_{\mathrm{R}}, q_{\mathrm{T}}) \le \frac{q_{\mathrm{S}}^2}{p} + \mathsf{adv}^{\mathsf{CR}}_{\mathsf{H}}(t_{\mathcal{A}}) \\
&\quad + \mathsf{adv}^{\mathsf{SDH}}_{\mathbb{G},\mathsf{Extract}}(t_{\mathcal{A}} + 2q_{\mathrm{RO}}\log_2(p), q_{\mathrm{RO}}) + \mathsf{adv}^{\mathsf{mu\text{-}PRF}}_{\mathsf{Expand}}(t_{\mathcal{A}}, q_{\mathrm{S}}, 6q_{\mathrm{S}}, 6) \\
&\quad + \mathsf{adv}^{\mathsf{mu\text{-}IND\text{-}CCA}}_{\mathsf{AEAD}}(t_{\mathcal{A}}, q_{\mathrm{S}}, q_{\mathrm{S}}, 1, q_{\mathrm{S}}, 1) + \mathsf{adv}^{\mathsf{mu\text{-}EUF\text{-}CMA}}_{\mathsf{Sig}}(t_{\mathcal{A}}, q_{\mathrm{N}}, q_{\mathrm{S}}, q_{\mathrm{S}}, q_{\mathrm{C}}) \\
&\mathsf{adv}^{\mathsf{AKE}}_{EDHOC\text{-}1}(t, q_{\mathrm{N}}, q_{\mathrm{S}}, q_{\mathrm{C}}, q_{\mathrm{R}}, q_{\mathrm{T}}) \le \frac{q_{\mathrm{S}}^2}{p} + \frac{q_{\mathrm{S}}}{2^{\ell_\tau}} + \mathsf{adv}^{\mathsf{CR}}_{\mathsf{H}}(t_{\mathcal{A}}) \\
&\quad + \mathsf{adv}^{\mathsf{SDH}}_{\mathbb{G},\mathsf{Extract}}(t_{\mathcal{A}} + 2q_{\mathrm{RO}}\log_2(p), q_{\mathrm{RO}}) + q_{\mathrm{N}} \cdot \mathsf{adv}^{\mathsf{GDH}}_{\mathbb{G},\mathsf{Extract}}(t_{\mathcal{A}}, q_{\mathrm{RO}}) \\
&\quad + \mathsf{adv}^{\mathsf{mu\text{-}PRF}}_{\mathsf{Expand}}(t_{\mathcal{A}}, q_{\mathrm{S}}, 2q_{\mathrm{S}}, 2) + \mathsf{adv}^{\mathsf{mu\text{-}PRF}}_{\mathsf{Expand}}(t_{\mathcal{A}}, q_{\mathrm{S}}, 5q_{\mathrm{S}}, 5) \\
&\quad + \mathsf{adv}^{\mathsf{mu\text{-}IND\text{-}CCA}}_{\mathsf{AEAD}}(t_{\mathcal{A}}, q_{\mathrm{S}}, q_{\mathrm{S}}, 1, q_{\mathrm{S}}, 1) + \mathsf{adv}^{\mathsf{mu\text{-}EUF\text{-}CMA}}_{\mathsf{Sig}}(t_{\mathcal{A}}, q_{\mathrm{N}}, q_{\mathrm{S}}, q_{\mathrm{S}}, q_{\mathrm{C}}) \\
&\mathsf{adv}^{\mathsf{AKE}}_{EDHOC\text{-}2}(t, q_{\mathrm{N}}, q_{\mathrm{S}}, q_{\mathrm{C}}, q_{\mathrm{R}}, q_{\mathrm{T}}) \le \frac{q_{\mathrm{S}}^2}{p} + \frac{q_{\mathrm{S}}}{2^{\ell_\tau}} + \mathsf{adv}^{\mathsf{CR}}_{\mathsf{H}}(t_{\mathcal{A}}) \\
&\quad + (1 + q_{\mathrm{N}}) \cdot \mathsf{adv}^{\mathsf{SDH}}_{\mathbb{G},\mathsf{Extract}}(t_{\mathcal{A}} + 2q_{\mathrm{RO}}\log_2(p), q_{\mathrm{RO}}) + \mathsf{adv}^{\mathsf{mu\text{-}PRF}}_{\mathsf{Expand}}(t_{\mathcal{A}}, q_{\mathrm{S}}, 5q_{\mathrm{S}}, 5) \\
&\quad + \mathsf{adv}^{\mathsf{mu\text{-}PRF}}_{\mathsf{Expand}}(t_{\mathcal{A}}, q_{\mathrm{S}}, 4q_{\mathrm{S}}, 4) + 2 \cdot \mathsf{adv}^{\mathsf{mu\text{-}IND\text{-}CCA}}_{\mathsf{AEAD}}(t_{\mathcal{A}}, q_{\mathrm{S}}, q_{\mathrm{S}}, 1, q_{\mathrm{S}}, 1) \\
&\quad + \mathsf{adv}^{\mathsf{mu\text{-}INT\text{-}CTXT}}_{\mathsf{AEAD}}(t_{\mathcal{A}}, q_{\mathrm{S}}, q_{\mathrm{S}}, 1, q_{\mathrm{S}}, 1) + \mathsf{adv}^{\mathsf{mu\text{-}EUF\text{-}CMA}}_{\mathsf{Sig}}(t_{\mathcal{A}}, q_{\mathrm{N}}, q_{\mathrm{S}}, q_{\mathrm{S}}, q_{\mathrm{C}}) \\
&\mathsf{adv}^{\mathsf{AKE}}_{EDHOC\text{-}3}(t, q_{\mathrm{N}}, q_{\mathrm{S}}, q_{\mathrm{C}}, q_{\mathrm{R}}, q_{\mathrm{T}}) \le \frac{q_{\mathrm{S}}^2}{p} + \mathsf{adv}^{\mathsf{CR}}_{\mathsf{H}}(t_{\mathcal{A}}) + \frac{q_{\mathrm{S}}}{2^{\ell_\tau - 1}} \\
&\quad + (1 + q_{\mathrm{N}}) \cdot \mathsf{adv}^{\mathsf{SDH}}_{\mathbb{G},\mathsf{Extract}}(t_{\mathcal{A}} + 2q_{\mathrm{RO}}\log_2(p), q_{\mathrm{RO}}) + q_{\mathrm{N}} \cdot \mathsf{adv}^{\mathsf{GDH}}_{\mathbb{G},\mathsf{Extract}}(t_{\mathcal{A}}, q_{\mathrm{RO}}) \\
&\quad + \mathsf{adv}^{\mathsf{mu\text{-}PRF}}_{\mathsf{Expand}}(t_{\mathcal{A}}, q_{\mathrm{S}}, 2q_{\mathrm{S}}, 2) + 2 \cdot \mathsf{adv}^{\mathsf{mu\text{-}PRF}}_{\mathsf{Expand}}(t_{\mathcal{A}}, q_{\mathrm{S}}, 4q_{\mathrm{S}}, 4) \\
&\quad + 2 \cdot \mathsf{adv}^{\mathsf{mu\text{-}IND\text{-}CCA}}_{\mathsf{AEAD}}(t_{\mathcal{A}}, q_{\mathrm{S}}, q_{\mathrm{S}}, 1, q_{\mathrm{S}}, 1) + \mathsf{adv}^{\mathsf{mu\text{-}INT\text{-}CTXT}}_{\mathsf{AEAD}}(t_{\mathcal{A}}, q_{\mathrm{S}}, q_{\mathrm{S}}, 1, q_{\mathrm{S}}, 1)
\end{aligned}
$$

4.2 Sketch of Proof

In this Section, we present a sketch of the proof for EDHOC with authentication method Stat-Sig. Complete proofs for all authentication methods are given in the full version of this paper [13]. We choose to focus here on the Stat-Sig method because the security notions it builds its security upon are also used in our other proofs. Moreover no other security analysis provides a result for that method. We proceed through a sequence of games [3,34].

Game 0. This game corresponds to the AKE security experiment described in Sect. 2.2 applied to EDHOC with authentication method Stat-Sig.

Game 1. In this game, the challenger aborts if two ephemeral DH shares collide among honest instances. This implies a collision term equal to q_{S}^2/p.

Game 2. In this game, we want to avoid any collision on h_2 and in any other output of H. Therefore the challenger aborts the experiment if such a collision occurs. This reduces straightforwardly to the collision resistance of H. Hence a loss equal to $\mathsf{adv}^{\mathsf{CR}}_{\mathsf{H}}(t_{\mathcal{A}})$.

Games 3–4. Here, any honest responder instance that receives a first message msg_1 from an honest initiator instance stops computing PRK_2 with the $\mathsf{Extract}$ function and samples the key uniformly at random. Therefore PRK_2 does not depend anymore on the DH exchange X, Y. We bound the probability that $\mathcal{A}$

detects such a change with the probability to solve the SDH problem in the DH group $\mathbb{G}$. Hence a loss equal to $\mathsf{adv}^{\mathsf{SDH}}_{\mathbb{G},\mathsf{Extract}}(t_{\mathcal{A}} + 2q_{\mathrm{RO}} \log_2(p), q_{\mathrm{RO}})$.

Game 5. In this game, any responder instance that receives a first message from an honest initiator instance replaces the PRF function Expand keyed with PRK_2 with a random function $\mathsf{RF}_{\mathsf{Expand}(\mathsf{PRK}_2,\cdot)}$. Likewise, any instance that keys Expand with PRK_2 uses $\mathsf{RF}_{\mathsf{Expand}(\mathsf{PRK}_2,\cdot)}$ from now on. Since the key PRK_2 is sampled independently of the random oracle $\mathsf{Extract}$ and the rest of the game, this reduces straightforwardly to the multi-user PRF-security of Expand. Hence a loss equal to $\mathsf{adv}^{\mathsf{mu\text{-}PRF}}_{\mathsf{Expand}}(t_{\mathcal{A}}, q_{\mathrm{S}}, 5q_{\mathrm{S}}, 5)$.

Games 6–7. Here, any honest responder instance that receives a first message msg_1 from an honest initiator instance samples the value c_2 uniformly at random. Due to Game 5, ks_2 is sampled randomly. Therefore ks_2 acts as a one-time pad in the computation of c_2. Consequently, the change is indistinguishable to the adversary.

Games 8–9. Here, any honest initiator instance samples the value c_3 uniformly at random. Therefore this reduces straightforwardly to the multi-user security of the symmetric-key encryption function AEAD (the encryption key is $PRK_3 = PRK_2$). Hence a loss equal to $\mathsf{adv}^{\mathsf{mu\text{-}IND\text{-}CCA}}_{\mathsf{AEAD}}(t_{\mathcal{A}}, q_{\mathrm{S}}, q_{\mathrm{S}}, 1, q_{\mathrm{S}}, 1)$.

Games 10–11. Here, any honest responder instance that receives a valid message msg_3 from an honest initiator instance stops computing PRK_4 and samples the key uniformly at random. Therefore PRK_4 does not depend anymore on the DH exchange Y, I. We bound the probability that $\mathcal{A}$ detects such a change with the probability to solve the SDH problem in the DH group $\mathbb{G}$. Taking into account that there is at most q_{N} parties (i.e., as many choices for the initiator party), this implies a loss equal to $q_{\mathrm{N}} \cdot \mathsf{adv}^{\mathsf{SDH}}_{\mathbb{G},\mathsf{Extract}}(t_{\mathcal{A}} + 2q_{\mathrm{RO}} \log_2(p), q_{\mathrm{RO}})$.

Game 12. Any responder instance that receives a valid message msg_3 from an honest initiator instance replaces the PRF function Expand keyed with PRK_4 with a random function $\mathsf{RF}_{\mathsf{Expand}(\mathsf{PRK}_4,\cdot)}$. Likewise, any instance that keys Expand with PRK_4 uses $\mathsf{RF}_{\mathsf{Expand}(\mathsf{PRK}_4,\cdot)}$ from now on. Since the key PRK_4 is sampled independently of the rest of the game, this reduces straightforwardly to the multi-user PRF-security of Expand. Hence a loss equal to $\mathsf{adv}^{\mathsf{mu\text{-}PRF}}_{\mathsf{Expand}}(t_{\mathcal{A}}, q_{\mathrm{S}}, 4q_{\mathrm{S}}, 4)$.

Game 13. In this game, the experiment aborts if an honest responder receives a valid tag τ_3 but no honest instance has computed τ_3. Due to Game 12, τ_3 is output by a random function. Therefore an adversary computes a valid tag τ_3 with probability $1/2^{\ell_\tau}$. Taking into account the maximum number of sessions, this implies a loss equal to $q_{\mathrm{S}}/2^{\ell_\tau}$.

Game 14. In this game, the challenger aborts the experiment if an instance receives a valid ciphertext c_4 but no honest instance has computed c_4. Due to Game 12, K_4 (and IV_4) is randomly sampled. Therefore this reduces to the ability to break the forgery resistance of the function AEAD in the multi-user setting. Hence a loss equal to $\mathsf{adv}^{\mathsf{mu\text{-}INT\text{-}CTXT}}_{\mathsf{AEAD}}(t_{\mathcal{A}}, q_{\mathrm{S}}, q_{\mathrm{S}}, 1, q_{\mathrm{S}}, 1)$.

Games 15–16. Here, any honest responder instance samples the value c_4 uniformly at random. This change is indistinguishable to $\mathcal{A}$ unless it detects whether

c_4 is a "real" ciphertext or is sampled at random. Due to Game 12, K_4 (and IV_4) is sampled randomly. Therefore this reduces straightforwardly to the multi-user security (in the indistinguishability sense) of the symmetric-key encryption function AEAD. Hence a loss equal to $\mathsf{adv}_{\mathsf{AEAD}}^{\mathsf{mu\text{-}IND\text{-}CCA}}(t_{\mathcal{A}}, q_S, q_S, 1, q_S, 1)$.

Game 17. In this game, the experiment aborts if the adversary $\mathcal{A}$ produces a valid signature under an uncorrupted signature key for a message that was not output by an honest instance. This reduces straightforwardly to the multi-user security of the signature scheme Sig. Hence a loss equal to $\mathsf{adv}_{\mathsf{Sig}}^{\mathsf{mu\text{-}EUF\text{-}CMA}}(t_{\mathcal{A}}, q_N, q_S, q_S, q_C)$.

Reasoning. The uniqueness of the DH shares guarantees that of the session identifiers among two honest instances. The tag τ_3 and the authenticated ciphertext c_4 allows both instances to check that they share the same key PRK_4 used to compute the session key PRK_{out}. Moreover the validity of the tag τ_3 and the unforgeability of the (encrypted) responder signature scheme prove that both instances share the same inputs used to compute the session key PRK_{out}. In addition, this validates the two identities. Hence the predicate Sound is true in Game 17.

With the same reasoning as above we can conclude that a session identifier is shared by two instances only. Moreover the tag τ_3 and the signature σ_R can be used to differentiate the roles of initiator and responder. They also validate the respective identities. Therefore, the predicate $\mathsf{ExplicitAuth}$ is true in Game 17.

In Game 17, $\mathsf{ExplicitAuth}$ and Sound are true. Therefore, two honest partnered instances share the same session key PRK_{out}. If $\mathsf{FreshKey}$ is true, then the adversary can do no better than guessing the challenge key bit b_{key}, which corresponds to a probability equal to 1/2 and an advantage equal to 0 in the session key indistinguishability experiment.

Regarding the identity privacy experiment, $\mathsf{ExplicitAuth}$ and Sound are true in Game 17, and c_2, c_3 and c_4 are indistinguable from random strings. Furthermore, if $\mathsf{FreshIdentity}$ is true, then the party partner is not corrupted. Assuming that the data sent in plaintext ($suites$, mth, $data_1$, ci_I) or the length of encrypted data (id_I, id_R, $data_2$, $data_3$, $data_4$) do not allow identifying a party, an adversary (passive towards a responder party) can do no better than guessing the challenge identity bit b_{id}. This corresponds to a probability equal to 1/2 and an advantage equal to 0 in the identity privacy experiment.

This concludes the sketch of proof.

5 Concrete Evaluation

In this section, we apply the security bounds from Sect. 4 to obtain concrete figures for EDHOC.

5.1 Bounds for Multi-user Security

In order to get concrete figures from the advantages presented in Theorem 1, we use the following inequalities.

PRF. If a random oracle RO is used as PRF with key length ℓ_k, then

$$\mathsf{adv}_{\mathsf{RO}}^{\mathsf{mu\text{-}PRF}}(t, q_{\mathrm{Nw}}, q_{\mathrm{Fc}}, q_{\mathrm{Fc/U}}, q_{\mathrm{RO}}) \leq \frac{q_{\mathrm{Nw}} \cdot q_{\mathrm{RO}}}{2^{\ell_k}}$$

where q_{RO} is the number of queries issued to RO.

Moreover, if the PRF corresponds (as it is the case in EDHOC for some ciphersuites) to HKDF-Expand [23,25] (with fixed output length), then Diemert and Jager [11, Corollary 2] show that

$$\mathsf{adv}_{\mathrm{HKDF\text{-}Expand}}^{\mathsf{mu\text{-}PRF}}(t, q_{\mathrm{Nw}}, q_{\mathrm{Fc}}, q_{\mathrm{Fc/U}}, q_{\mathrm{RO}}) \leq \frac{q_{\mathrm{Nw}}^2 + 2q_{\mathrm{Nw}}}{2^{\ell_k - 1}} + \frac{q_{\mathrm{RO}}^2}{2^{\ell_h - 1}}$$

where the underlying hash function is modelled as a random oracle RO with output length ℓ_h, and q_{RO} is the number of queries issued to RO.

In EDHOC, the key length of the PRF is equal to the output length of the underlying hash function (i.e., $\ell_k = \ell_h$ in the above two inequalities).

Authenticated Encryption. Jonsson [21] provides security bounds in the single-user setting for CCM. In turn, Hoang, Tessaro and Thiruvengadam [18] provide a tight bound for the multi-user security of GCM. Degabriele, Govinden, Günther and Paterson [10] do the same for ChaCha20-Poly1305 (and improve that of GCM), such that a practical comparison can be done between the bounds corresponding to the two latter AEAD schemes.

AES CCM. Jonsson [21, Theorems 1 and 2] show that the advantages of breaking CCM's IND-CPA and INT-CTXT security (in the single-user setting) are respectively bounded by

$$\frac{(2B \cdot q_e)^2}{2^{\ell_b}} \text{ and } \frac{q_d}{2^{\ell_\tau}} + \frac{(2B(q_e + q_d))^2}{2^{\ell_b}}$$

where ℓ_b is the block length, ℓ_τ is the MAC length, B is a bound on the number of blocks encrypted, and q_e and q_d are bounds on the encryption and decryption queries respectively.

In order to provide bounds for CCM in the multi-user setting we use the generic reduction to single-user security, with a loss depending on the number of keys. That is

$$\begin{aligned}&\mathsf{adv}_{\mathsf{AEAD}}^{\mathsf{mu\text{-}INT\text{-}CTXT}}(t, q_{\mathrm{Nw}}, q_{\mathrm{E}}, q_{\mathrm{E/U}}, q_{\mathrm{D}}, q_{\mathrm{D/U}})\\ \leq\, & q_{\mathrm{Nw}} \cdot \mathsf{adv}_{\mathsf{AEAD}}^{\mathsf{mu\text{-}INT\text{-}CTXT}}(t', 1, q_{\mathrm{E/U}}, q_{\mathrm{E/U}}, q_{\mathrm{D/U}}, q_{\mathrm{D/U}})\end{aligned}$$

and

$$\begin{aligned}&\mathsf{adv}_{\mathsf{AEAD}}^{\mathsf{mu\text{-}IND\text{-}CCA}}(t, q_{\mathrm{Nw}}, q_{\mathrm{E}}, q_{\mathrm{E/U}}, q_{\mathrm{D}}, q_{\mathrm{D/U}})\\ \leq\, & q_{\mathrm{Nw}} \cdot \mathsf{adv}_{\mathsf{AEAD}}^{\mathsf{mu\text{-}IND\text{-}CCA}}(t', 1, q_{\mathrm{E/U}}, q_{\mathrm{E/U}}, q_{\mathrm{D/U}}, q_{\mathrm{D/U}})\\ \leq\, & q_{\mathrm{Nw}} \cdot \left(\mathsf{adv}_{\mathsf{AEAD}}^{\mathsf{IND\text{-}CPA}}(t'', q_{\mathrm{E/U}}, 0) + 2 \cdot \mathsf{adv}_{\mathsf{AEAD}}^{\mathsf{INT\text{-}CTXT}}(t''', q_{\mathrm{E/U}}, q_{\mathrm{D/U}})\right)\end{aligned}$$

with $t \simeq t'$, $t \simeq t''$, and $t \simeq t'''$. The last inequality can be easily proven (see for instance Bellare and Namprempre [1, Theorem 3.2] adapted to our setting).

ChaCha20-Poly1305. Degabriele et al. [10, Theorem 7.8] show that the advantage of breaking ChaCha20-Poly1305's AE security in the multi-user setting is bounded by

$$\frac{q_v(c \cdot B' + 3)}{2^{\ell_\tau}} + \frac{d(q_\pi + q_e)}{2^{\ell_k}} + \frac{2q_\pi(\ell_b - \ell_k)}{2^{\ell_k}} + \frac{2q_v(\ell_b - \ell_k + 4\ell_\tau)}{2^{\ell_k}} + \frac{(\sigma_e + q_e)^2}{2^{\ell_b+1}} + \frac{1}{2^{2\ell_\tau-2}} + \frac{1}{2^{\ell_b-\ell_k-2}} + \frac{1}{2^{\delta\ell_r}}$$

where ℓ_k, ℓ_b and ℓ_r are the key, block and nonce length respectively, B' is the maximum size in ℓ_τ-bit blocks (including associated data) that the adversary is allowed to query to its encryption and verification oracles, $c \simeq 2^{25}$, q_π is the number of ideal permutation queries (i.e., offline adversary work), q_e is the number of encryption queries totalling σ_e encrypted blocks, q_v is the number of verification queries, $0 \leq \delta \leq \ell_\tau/\ell_r \times 2^{2\ell_\tau-1}$, and $d = \left\lceil \frac{(\delta+1)\ell_r}{\max(1, \ell_r - \log_2(q_e))} \right\rceil$.

δ can be chosen such that $1/2^{\delta\ell_\tau}$ is non-dominant. Furthermore, considering the ChaCha20-Poly1305 parameters ($\ell_k = 256$, $\ell_b = 512$), the dominant term in the above advantage is $q_v \cdot c \cdot B'/2^{\ell_\tau}$.

AES GCM. Hoang et al. [18, Theorem 4.3] show that the advantage of breaking GCM's AE security in the multi-user setting is bounded by

$$\frac{d(q_\pi + q_{e,v}) + \ell_b(q_\pi + q_{e,v} + \sigma_{e,v})}{2^{\ell_k}} + \frac{\sigma_{e,v}(2B + c \cdot \ell_b + 2)}{2^{\ell_b}} + \frac{2q_{e,v} + 1}{2^{2\ell_b}} + \frac{\sigma_{e,v}(\sigma_{e,v} + \ell_b \cdot c \cdot d) + 2q_{e,v}q_\pi}{2^{\ell_k+\ell_b}} + \frac{1}{2^{\ell_r/2}}$$

where ℓ_k, ℓ_b and ℓ_r are the key, block and nonce length respectively, B is a bound on the number of blocks encrypted per user, q_π is the number of ideal cipher queries (i.e., offline adversary work), $q_{e,v}$ is a bound on the encryption/verification queries of total block length at most $\sigma_{e,v}$ with $q_{e,v} \leq 2^{(1-\epsilon)\ell_r}$, $0 < \epsilon < 1$, $d = \lceil 1.5/\epsilon \rceil - 1$, and $c = 1.5$.

Degabriele et al. [10] improve the latter advantage such that its last term depending on the nonce length ℓ_r becomes non-dominant. Furthermore, considering the AES GCM parameters ($\ell_k \in \{128, 256\}$, $\ell_b = 128$), the dominant term in the above advantage is either $\sigma_{e,v} \cdot B/2^{\ell_b-1}$ (if $\ell_k = 256$) or the latter augmented with $(d(q_\pi + q_{e,v}) + \ell_b(q_\pi + q_{e,v} + \sigma_{e,v}))/2^{\ell_k}$.

Moreover, we can bound $\mathsf{adv}^{\text{mu-INT-CTXT}}_{\mathsf{AEAD}}$ and $\mathsf{adv}^{\text{mu-IND-CCA}}_{\mathsf{AEAD}}$ both with $\mathsf{adv}^{\text{mu-AE}}_{\mathsf{AEAD}}$ (see [13]):

$$\begin{aligned}
\mathsf{adv}^{\text{mu-IND-CCA}}_{\mathsf{AEAD}}(t, q_{\mathrm{Nw}}, q_{\mathrm{E}}, q_{\mathrm{E/U}}, q_{\mathrm{D}}, q_{\mathrm{D/U}}) &\leq \mathsf{adv}^{\text{mu-AE}}_{\mathsf{AEAD}}(t', q_{\mathrm{Nw}}, q_{\mathrm{E}}, q_{\mathrm{E/U}}, q_{\mathrm{V}}, q_{\mathrm{V/U}}) \\
&\quad + 2 \cdot \mathsf{adv}^{\text{mu-INT-CTXT}}_{\mathsf{AEAD}}(t'', q_{\mathrm{Nw}}, q_{\mathrm{E}}, q_{\mathrm{E/U}}, q_{\mathrm{D}}, q_{\mathrm{D/U}}) \\
\mathsf{adv}^{\text{mu-INT-CTXT}}_{\mathsf{AEAD}}(t, q_{\mathrm{Nw}}, q_{\mathrm{E}}, q_{\mathrm{E/U}}, q_{\mathrm{D}}, q_{\mathrm{D/U}}) &\leq 2 \cdot \mathsf{adv}^{\text{mu-AE}}_{\mathsf{AEAD}}(t', q_{\mathrm{Nw}}, q_{\mathrm{E}}, q_{\mathrm{E/U}}, q_{\mathrm{V}}, q_{\mathrm{V/U}})
\end{aligned}$$

with $t \simeq t'$ and $t \simeq t''$. Therefore

$$\mathsf{adv}^{\text{mu-IND-CCA}}_{\mathsf{AEAD}}(t, q_{\mathrm{Nw}}, q_{\mathrm{E}}, q_{\mathrm{E/U}}, q_{\mathrm{D}}, q_{\mathrm{D/U}}) \leq 5 \cdot \mathsf{adv}^{\text{mu-AE}}_{\mathsf{AEAD}}(t', q_{\mathrm{Nw}}, q_{\mathrm{E}}, q_{\mathrm{E/U}}, q_{\mathrm{V}}, q_{\mathrm{V/U}})$$

Signature. As in [9], we consider the signature unforgeability (in the single-user setting) as equally hard as the corresponding discrete logarithm problem. That is

$$\mathsf{adv}_{\mathsf{Sig}}^{\mathsf{mu\text{-}EUF\text{-}CMA}}(t, q_{\mathrm{NW}}, q_{\mathrm{SG}}, q_{\mathrm{SG/U}}, q_{\mathrm{C}}) \leq q_{\mathrm{NW}} \cdot t'^2/p$$

with $t \simeq t'$.

Hash Function. If a random oracle RO is used as hash function H, then by the birthday bound

$$\mathsf{adv}_{\mathsf{RO}}^{\mathsf{CR}}(t, q_{\mathrm{RO}}) \leq \frac{q_{\mathrm{RO}}^2}{2^{\ell_h+1}} + \frac{1}{2^{\ell_h}}$$

Strong Diffie-Hellman. In EDHOC, all Diffie-Hellman groups are built upon elliptic curves. This allows applying the bounds found in the generic group model for the Strong DH problem by Davis et al. [9, Theorem 3.3]. The latter state that the Strong DH problem is essentially as hard as solving the corresponding discrete logarithm problem. That is, in the generic group model,

$$\mathsf{adv}_{\mathbb{G}}^{\mathsf{SDH}}(t, q_{\mathrm{SDH}}) \leq 4t^2/p$$

Gap Diffie-Hellman. We consider this problem as equally hard as the Strong Diffie-Hellman problem.

5.2 Parameters and Concrete Advantages

Parameters. EDHOC draft 23 defines nine different ciphersuites [32, Section 10.2] that we describe in Table 1. We recall that ℓ_k, ℓ_b, ℓ_r and ℓ_τ correspond to the bit length of respectively the key, block, nonce and authentication tag for the corresponding AEAD algorithm. Let p be the group order related to the elliptic curve, ℓ_h the bit length of the hash output and ℓ_σ the bit length of the signature.

In order to provide concrete bounds, we use the following parameters based on the specificities of the different authentication methods for the EDHOC protocol (Sect. 3) and the results of the security analysis (Sect. 4.1):

Table 1. Ciphersuites and parameters in EDHOC

Id.	AEAD algorithm	Hash alg.	Elliptic curve	Signature alg.	p ($\simeq$)	ℓ_τ	ℓ_k	ℓ_b	ℓ_r	ℓ_h	ℓ_σ
0	AES-CCM-16-64-128	SHA-256	X25519	EdDSA	2^{252}	64	128	128	104	256	512
1	AES-CCM-16-128-128	SHA-256	X25519	EdDSA	2^{252}	128	128	128	104	256	512
2	AES-CCM-16-64-128	SHA-256	P-256	ECDSA	2^{256}	64	128	128	104	256	512
3	AES-CCM-16-128-128	SHA-256	P-256	ECDSA	2^{256}	128	128	128	104	256	512
4	ChaCha20-Poly1305	SHA-256	X25519	EdDSA	2^{252}	128	256	512	96	256	512
5	ChaCha20-Poly1305	SHA-256	P-256	ECDSA	2^{256}	128	256	512	96	256	512
6	AES 128 GCM	SHA-256	X25519	ECDSA	2^{252}	128	128	128	96	256	512
24	AES 256 GCM	SHA-384	P-384	ECDSA	2^{384}	128	256	128	96	384	768
25	ChaCha20-Poly1305	SHAKE256	X448	EdDSA	2^{446}	128	256	512	96	512	912

- $q_e = q_v = q_d = q_E = q_V = q_D = q_S$
- $q_{e,v} = q_e + q_v = 2q_S$
- $q_{Nw} = q_S$
- $\sigma_e = q_e \cdot B = q_S \cdot B$
- $\sigma_{e,v} = q_{e,v} \cdot B = 2q_S \cdot B$
- We choose B as the largest message (in ℓ_b-bit blocks) encrypted in EDHOC with the AEAD algorithm. This corresponds to the message $p_3 = id_I \| x \| [data_3]$ with $x \in \{\sigma_I, \tau_3\}$ depending on the authentication method (Sig-{Sig, Stat} or Stat-{Sig, Stat}). Omitting the optional $data_3$, we have $B = (|id_I| + \ell_x)/\ell_b$ with $\ell_x \in \{\ell_\sigma, \ell_\tau\}$. Based on the test vectors from [33], the maximum length for p_3 is 471 bytes (including the byte string encoding used in EDHOC which adds a few supplementary bytes).
- We choose B' the same way as B supplemented with the associated data h_3. That is, $B' = (|id_I| + \ell_x + \ell_h)/\ell_\tau$. Based on [33], the maximum length for $p_3 \| h_3$ is 599 bytes.
- For AES GCM, we choose $q_{e,v}$ as equal to $2^{(1-\epsilon)\ell_r}$ and express $d = \lceil 1.5/\epsilon \rceil$ from the latter: $d = \left\lceil \dfrac{1.5\ell_r}{\ell_r - \log_2(q_{e,v})} \right\rceil$.

EDHOC is designed to be suitable for low-power networks such as cellular IoT, 6TiSCH [19], and LoRaWAN [36,37]. The number of LPWAN devices deployed in 2023 is around 4 billion and the number of IoT connections in 2030 is expected to be around 30 billion [38,39]. Therefore we consider the number of parties as $q_N \in \{2^{30}, 2^{40}\}$. We consider the number of sessions that an adversary can interact with as $q_S \in \{2^{30}, 2^{40}, 2^{50}\}$ depending on its capabilities (small to global-scale attacker). Likewise, we consider a runtime corresponding to $t \in \{2^{40}, 2^{60}, 2^{80}\}$. We fix the number of random oracle queries q_{RO} and ideal cipher queries q_π as a fraction of the runtime t, following [9]. That is, $q_{RO} = q_\pi = t/2^{10}$.

Concrete Advantages. The security of EDHOC depends mainly on the authenticated encryption schemes used during the key exchange. In turn, given the ciphersuites allowed in EDHOC, the security of these AEAD schemes is mainly influenced by the number of protocol runs q_S and the offline adversary work q_π. Therefore, in Table 2, we display only the latter parameters.

As we can see in Table 2, the ciphersuites based on ChaCha20-Poly1305 (id. 4, 5, 25) and AES GCM (id. 6, 24) provide the lowest advantages. This is due to the fact that they depend (linearly) on the number of sessions, and on the authentication tag size (ChaCha20-Poly1305) or on the block and key length (AES GCM).

On the contrary, the ciphersuites based on AES CCM provide the lowest security level. The figures we get likely come from the fact that the security bounds are non-tight due to the generic reduction that we use from multi-user to single-user security. The advantages related to AES CCM in the single-user setting depend quadratically on the number of sessions and on the block and authentication tag size. Furthermore, the latter can be as low as 64 bits (instead

Table 2. Concrete security bounds for EDHOC

Adv. resources			Ciphersuites								
t	q_S	q_π	0	1	2	3	4	5	6	24	25
2^{40}	2^{30}	2^{30}	2^{-2}	2^{-22}	2^{-2}	2^{-22}	2^{-66}	2^{-66}	2^{-83}	2^{-85}	2^{-66}
2^{40}	2^{40}	2^{30}	1	1	1	1	2^{-56}	2^{-56}	2^{-73}	2^{-75}	2^{-56}
2^{40}	2^{50}	2^{30}	1	1	1	1	2^{-46}	2^{-46}	2^{-63}	2^{-65}	2^{-46}
2^{60}	2^{30}	2^{50}	2^{-2}	2^{-22}	2^{-2}	2^{-22}	2^{-66}	2^{-66}	2^{-69}	2^{-85}	2^{-66}
2^{60}	2^{40}	2^{50}	1	1	1	1	2^{-56}	2^{-56}	2^{-69}	2^{-75}	2^{-56}
2^{60}	2^{50}	2^{50}	1	1	1	1	2^{-46}	2^{-46}	2^{-63}	2^{-65}	2^{-46}
2^{80}	2^{30}	2^{70}	2^{-2}	2^{-22}	2^{-2}	2^{-22}	2^{-66}	2^{-66}	2^{-49}	2^{-85}	2^{-66}
2^{80}	2^{40}	2^{70}	1	1	1	1	2^{-56}	2^{-56}	2^{-49}	2^{-75}	2^{-56}
2^{80}	2^{50}	2^{70}	1	1	1	1	2^{-46}	2^{-46}	2^{-49}	2^{-65}	2^{-46}

(a) With authentication methods Sig-{Sig, Stat}

Adv. resources			Ciphersuites								
t	q_S	q_π	0	1	2	3	4	5	6	24	25
2^{40}	2^{30}	2^{30}	2^{-1}	2^{-21}	2^{-1}	2^{-21}	2^{-65}	2^{-65}	2^{-82}	2^{-84}	2^{-65}
2^{40}	2^{40}	2^{30}	1	1	1	1	2^{-55}	2^{-55}	2^{-72}	2^{-74}	2^{-55}
2^{40}	2^{50}	2^{30}	1	1	1	1	2^{-45}	2^{-45}	2^{-62}	2^{-64}	2^{-45}
2^{60}	2^{30}	2^{50}	2^{-1}	2^{-21}	2^{-1}	2^{-21}	2^{-65}	2^{-65}	2^{-67}	2^{-84}	2^{-65}
2^{60}	2^{40}	2^{50}	1	1	1	1	2^{-55}	2^{-55}	2^{-67}	2^{-74}	2^{-55}
2^{60}	2^{50}	2^{50}	1	1	1	1	2^{-45}	2^{-45}	2^{-62}	2^{-64}	2^{-45}
2^{80}	2^{30}	2^{70}	2^{-1}	2^{-21}	2^{-1}	2^{-21}	2^{-65}	2^{-65}	2^{-47}	2^{-84}	2^{-65}
2^{80}	2^{40}	2^{70}	1	1	1	1	2^{-55}	2^{-55}	2^{-47}	2^{-74}	2^{-55}
2^{80}	2^{50}	2^{70}	1	1	1	1	2^{-45}	2^{-45}	2^{-47}	2^{-64}	2^{-45}

(b) With authentication methods Stat-{Sig, Stat}

of 128 bits) for some AES CCM ciphersuites (0, 2) which contribute to an augmented advantage.

Our results suggest that a preferable choice with respect to security corresponds to ciphersuites based on AES GCM (in particular with 256-bit key), unless the tag size of the ChaCha20-Poly1305 ciphersuites be increased (see Degabriele et al. [10, Section 7.4]). The EDHOC draft [32, Section 3.6] indicates that ciphersuites 24 and 25 (respectively AES 256 GCM with 384-bit elliptic curve and ChaCha20-Poly1305 with 448-bit elliptic curve) are intended for "*high security applications such as government use and financial applications*". Our results show that ciphersuite 25 is similar, with respect to the security bounds, to the other ones based on ChaCha20-Poly1305 (recommended for "*less constrained applications*"). Regarding ciphersuite 6 based on AES 128 GCM (also recommended for "*less constrained applications*"), the corresponding advantage is in fact as low as that of ciphersuite 24 as long as the amount of offline adversary work is not too high ($q_\pi \leq 2^{30}$).

Note that the (low) figures we get for the different security bounds come mainly from identity privacy (through the confidentiality guaranteed in the different ciphertexts) and also soundness properties (through the authenticity of the ciphertext c_4). Regarding the authentication and key indistinguishability security, the adversary's advantage depends mainly on the tag length ℓ_τ (τ_2, τ_3) but for the authentication method Sig-Sig where the dominant term corresponds to the resistance to signature forgery.

6 Observations

Authenticity in msg_3. The authenticity protection provided by c_3 appears to be useless. Firstly the data protected by the ciphertext is also protected by τ_3. Secondly, the latter is computed with the key PRK_4 which depends on the shared secret DH value corresponding to the exchanged X, Y. Moreover τ_3 protects not only all the data integrity-protected by c_3 but also cr_I (which identifies the initiator). Further, τ_3 is either sent in message msg_3 or involved in the computation of the initiator's signature σ_I. This is why our security proofs do no rely on the authenticity protection provided by the AEAD scheme to c_3.

Confidentiality in msg_4. In the proof of the identity privacy experiment for the authentication methods Stat-Sig and Stat-Stat, we choose to be conservative. That is, we rely on the confidentiality of c_4 in order to guarantee that $data_4$ does not leak any information on the responder's identity. Yet, since $data_4$ is optional (and is supposed to be opaque to EDHOC [32, Section 3.8]), we can relax this requirement. This removes one component $\mathsf{adv}^{\mathsf{mu\text{-}IND\text{-}CCA}}_{\mathsf{AEAD}}(t_{\mathcal{A}}, q_{\mathrm{S}}, q_{\mathrm{S}}, 1, q_{\mathrm{S}}, 1)$ in the advantages related to EDHOC-2 (Stat-Sig) and EDHOC-3 (Stat-Stat) in Theorem 1 and does not change notably the figures in Table 2.

Fourth Message. A fourth message is necessary only when the initiator authenticates by means of a static DH key (i.e., authentication methods Stat-Sig and Stat-Stat), as also noted by Norrman et al. [26]. With methods Stat-Sig and Stat-Stat, this fourth message is authenticated with the key PRK_4 from which the session key PRK_{out} is computed (and $PRK_4 \neq PRK_3$). In contrast, with authentication methods Sig-Sig and Sig-Stat τ_2 is computed with $PRK_3 = PRK_4$. Therefore, with methods Stat-Sig and Stat-Stat, this fourth message proves to the initiator that the responder shares the same key PRK_4 which is necessary to guarantee the "consistency" of the scheme[2], as shown in our proofs of soundness. (In the opposite direction, τ_3, computed with PRK_4, fulfils the same purpose.) This message proves also to the initiator that the responder shares the same session identifier, which is needed in the proof of explicit authentication.

Identity Privacy Assumptions. In the identity privacy experiment we use an assumption regarding the (un)ability of an adversary to identify an honest party based on the parameters sent in plaintext (mth, $suites$, ci_I), or on the length of other (encrypted) parameters (e.g., id_I, id_R). This can be achieved if padding, which can be optionally added to the plaintext ($data_2$, $data_3$, $data_4$) before encryption, is systematically leveraged in order to hide the size of the data. Yet, this contradicts the goal for EDHOC to incur minimal bandwidth.

Passing Data to the Security Application. The EDHOC draft states correctly that the data transported in messages msg_1 and msg_2 is not protected (against respectively a passive and an active adversary), contrary to the data transported in messages msg_3 and msg_4. However the draft indicates also that the data (in particular $data_2$ and $data_3$ respectively in messages msg_2 and msg_3) is sent to the security application before the sender be authenticated. That is, without any guarantee regarding the origin of the data. As indicated in the EDHOC draft [32, Section 3.8], this kind of data is not any regular application data and deserves a special treatment. However we see no reason why $data_2$ and $data_3$ would be reliable when it is sent by an illegitimate party. Therefore, according to us, $data_2$ and $data_3$ should be sent to the security application only once the sender is authenticated by the receiver.

7 Conclusion

In this paper, we perform a security analysis of the last version of the EDHOC protocol, considering its four different authentication methods. Our security model captures security properties (identity protection) not considered by previous analyses of EDHOC for several authentication methods. The security proofs we provide uncover asymptotic complexities that appear in other analyses. Our security bounds leverage previous results in the multi-user setting for the underlying primitives of the protocol. This allows us to give more precise estimates of the computational bounds for EDHOC (and its four authentication methods) so that meaningful choices of quantitative parameters can be done to instantiate the protocol securely.

We show that security in EDHOC depends essentially on that of the authenticated encryption algorithm used during the key exchange phase. Our results indicate also that the ciphersuite based on AES 256 GCM is preferable for high

[2] Informally, the "consistency" (defined by Krawczyk in [24]) guarantees a binding between a session key and the two parties involved in the protocol run. In the security model we use, the Sound predicate guarantees (when true) this property.

security applications (in contrast with ChaCha20-Poly1305 also recommended in the EDHOC draft for the same kind of applications).

Although it is still unclear when (or even if) a quantum processor efficient enough to break current asymmetric cryptographic algorithms will exist, a future area of research is to devise post-quantum variants of EDHOC. As indicated in the last draft, EDHOC supports post-quantum signatures, and a post-quantum key encapsulation mechanism can be used in place of DH with method Sig-Sig. Yet, a challenging avenue of future work is to design, implement and test post-quantum variants of EDHOC with all authentication methods, in stand-alone or hybrid mode (i.e., combining classical and post-quantum algorithms), such that the stringent constraints of the IoT networks and end-devices are fulfilled.

Acknowledgements. The author thanks the reviewers for their valuable remarks. This work was partly supported by the French ANR MobiS5 project (ANR18-CE-39-0019-02).

References

1. Bellare, M., Namprempre, C.: Authenticated encryption: relations among notions and analysis of the generic composition paradigm. In: Okamoto, T. (ed.) ASIACRYPT 2000. LNCS, vol. 1976, pp. 531–545. Springer, Heidelberg (2000). https://doi.org/10.1007/3-540-44448-3_41
2. Bellare, M., Rogaway, P.: Entity authentication and key distribution. In: Stinson, D.R. (ed.) CRYPTO 1993. LNCS, vol. 773, pp. 232–249. Springer, Heidelberg (1994). https://doi.org/10.1007/3-540-48329-2_21
3. Bellare, M., Rogaway, P.: The security of triple encryption and a framework for code-based game-playing proofs. In: Vaudenay, S. (ed.) EUROCRYPT 2006. LNCS, vol. 4004, pp. 409–426. Springer, Heidelberg (2006). https://doi.org/10.1007/11761679_25
4. Blake-Wilson, S., Johnson, D., Menezes, A.: Key agreement protocols and their security analysis. In: Darnell, M. (ed.) Cryptography and Coding 1997. LNCS, vol. 1355, pp. 30–45. Springer, Heidelberg (1997). https://doi.org/10.1007/BFb0024447
5. Bruni, A., Sahl Jørgensen, T., Grønbech Petersen, T., Schürmann, C.: Formal verification of ephemeral diffie-hellman over cose (edhoc). In: Cremers, C., Lehmann, A. (eds.) Security Standardisation Research, pp. 21–36 (2018)
6. Cheval, V., Jacomme, C., Kremer, S., Künnemann, R.: SAPIC+: protocol verifiers of the world, unite! In: Butler, K.R.B., Thomas, K. (eds.) USENIX Security 2022, pp. 3935–3952. USENIX Association (2022)
7. Connectivity Standards Alliance: Zigbee specification
8. Cottier, B., Pointcheval, D.: Security analysis of the EDHOC protocol (2022). https://doi.org/10.48550/arXiv.2209.03599
9. Davis, H., Günther, F.: Tighter proofs for the SIGMA and TLS 1.3 key exchange protocols. In: Sako, K., Tippenhauer, N.O. (eds.) ACNS 2021. LNCS, vol. 12727, pp. 448–479. Springer, Cham (2021). https://doi.org/10.1007/978-3-030-78375-4_18
10. Degabriele, J.P., Govinden, J., Günther, F., Paterson, K.G.: The security of ChaCha20-Poly1305 in the multi-user setting. In: Vigna, G., Shi, E. (eds.) ACM CCS 2021, pp. 1981–2003. ACM Press (2021)

11. Diemert, D., Jager, T.: On the tight security of TLS 1.3: theoretically sound cryptographic parameters for real-world deployments. J. Cryptol. **34**(3), 30 (2021)
12. Diffie, W., Hellman, M.E.: New directions in cryptography. IEEE Trans. Inf. Theory **22**(6), 644–654 (1976). https://doi.org/10.1109/TIT.1976.1055638
13. Ferreira, L.: Computational security analysis of the full EDHOC protocol. Cryptology ePrint Archive (2024)
14. Fischlin, M., Günther, F.: Multi-stage key exchange and the case of Google's QUIC protocol. In: Ahn, G.J., Yung, M., Li, N. (eds.) ACM CCS 2014, pp. 1193–1204. ACM Press (2014)
15. Günther, F., Mukendi, M.I.T.: Careful with MAc-then-SIGn: a computational analysis of the EDHOC lightweight authenticated key exchange protocol. Cryptology ePrint Archive, Report 2022/1705 (2022)
16. Günther, F., Mukendi, M.I.T.: Careful with MAc-then-SIGn: A computational analysis of the EDHOC lightweight authenticated key exchange protocol. In: 8th IEEE European Symposium on Security and Privacy, EuroS&P 2023 (2023)
17. Hermans, J., Pashalidis, A., Vercauteren, F., Preneel, B.: A new RFID privacy model. In: Atluri, V., Díaz, C. (eds.) ESORICS 2011. LNCS, vol. 6879, pp. 568–587. Springer, Heidelberg (2011). https://doi.org/10.1007/978-3-642-23822-2_31
18. Hoang, V.T., Tessaro, S., Thiruvengadam, A.: The multi-user security of GCM, revisited: tight bounds for nonce randomization. In: Lie, D., Mannan, M., Backes, M., Wang, X. (eds.) ACM CCS 2018, pp. 1429–1440. ACM Press (2018)
19. IETF: IPv6 over the TSCH mode of IEEE 802.15.4e (6tisch) (2021)
20. Jacomme, C., Kremer, S., Künnemann, R.: A comprehensive, formal and automated analysis of the EDHOC protocol. In: 32nd USENIX Security Symposium (USENIX Security 23) (2023)
21. Jonsson, J.: On the security of CTR + CBC-MAC. In: Nyberg, K., Heys, H.M. (eds.) SAC 2002. LNCS, vol. 2595, pp. 76–93. Springer, Heidelberg (2003). https://doi.org/10.1007/3-540-36492-7_7
22. Kim, J., et al.: Scrutinizing the vulnerability of ephemeral Diffie-Hellman over COSE (EDHOC) for IoT environment using formal approaches. Mob. Inf. Syst. **2021**, 1–18 (2021)
23. Krawczyk, H., Eronen, P.: HMAC-based Extract-and-Expand Key Derivation Function (HKDF) (2010). RFC 5869
24. Krawczyk, H.: SIGMA: the 'SIGn-and-MAc' approach to authenticated Diffie-Hellman and its use in the IKE protocols. In: Boneh, D. (ed.) CRYPTO 2003. LNCS, vol. 2729, pp. 400–425. Springer, Heidelberg (2003). https://doi.org/10.1007/978-3-540-45146-4_24
25. Krawczyk, H.: Cryptographic extraction and key derivation: the HKDF scheme. In: Rabin, T. (ed.) CRYPTO 2010. LNCS, vol. 6223, pp. 631–648. Springer, Heidelberg (2010). https://doi.org/10.1007/978-3-642-14623-7_34
26. Norrman, K., Sundararajan, V., Bruni, A.: Formal analysis of EDHOC key establishment for constrained IoT devices. In: di Vimercati, S.D.C., Samarati, P. (eds.) Proceedings of the 18th International Conference on Security and Cryptography, SECRYPT 2021, pp. 210–221. SCITEPRESS (2021)
27. Ouafi, K., Phan, R.C.W.: Traceable privacy of recent provably-secure RFID protocols. In: Bellovin, S.M., Gennaro, R., Keromytis, A.D., Yung, M. (eds.) ACNS 2008. LNCS, vol. 5037, pp. 479–489. Springer, Heidelberg (2008). https://doi.org/10.1007/978-3-540-68914-0_29
28. Rescorla, E., Barnes, R., Tschofenig, H.: Compact TLS 1.3 (2023)
29. Rescorla, E., Tschofenig, H., Modadugu, N.: The Datagram Transport Layer Security (DTLS) Protocol Version 1.3 (2022)

30. Schäge, S., Schwenk, J., Lauer, S.: Privacy-preserving authenticated key exchange and the case of IKEv2. In: Kiayias, A., Kohlweiss, M., Wallden, P., Zikas, V. (eds.) PKC 2020. LNCS, vol. 12111, pp. 567–596. Springer, Heidelberg (2020). https://doi.org/10.1007/978-3-030-45388-6_20
31. Selander, G., Mattsson, J., Palombini, F., Seitz, L.: Object Security for Constrained RESTful Environments (OSCORE) (2019). RFC 8613
32. Selander, G., Preuß Mattsson, J., Palombini, F.: Ephemeral Diffie-Hellman Over COSE (EDHOC) – draft-ietf-lake-edhoc-23 (2024)
33. Selander, G., Preuß Mattsson, J., Serafin, L., Tiloca, M., Vučinić, M.: Traces of EDHOC (2023)
34. Shoup, V.: Sequences of games: a tool for taming complexity in security proofs. Cryptology ePrint Archive, Report 2004/332 (2004)
35. Sigfox: Sigfox connected objects: Radio specifications (2023). rev. 1.7
36. Sornin, N.: LoRaWAN 1.1 Specification (2017). LoRa Alliance, version 1.1
37. Sornin, N., Luis, M., Eirich, T., Kramp, T.: LoRaWAN Specification (2016). LoRa Alliance, version 1.0
38. Transforma Insights: IoT connections in 2030: 4 billion LPWA, 468 million 5G (non-mMTC), and 4% of cellular using private networks (2021)
39. Transforma Insights: Global IoT connections to hit 29.4 billion in 2030 (2022)
40. Vucinic, M., Selander, G., Mattsson, J.P., Watteyne, T.: Lightweight authenticated key exchange with EDHOC. Computer **55**(4), 94–100 (2022)

Symmetric Cryptography

The Multi-user Security of MACs via Universal Hashing in the Ideal Cipher Model

Yusuke Naito(✉)

Mitsubishi Electric Corporation, Kamakura, Kanagawa, Japan
Naito.Yusuke@ce.MitsubishiElectric.co.jp

Abstract. The security of block-cipher-based hash-then-encrypt-type message authentication codes (MACs) has been proven with universal hash functions. Thus, the security of the underlying hash functions has been evaluated with the pseudo-random-permutation assumption, i.e., the block ciphers are replaced with random permutations to which an adversary cannot directly access. Due to a hybrid argument, this replacement offers tight multi-user bounds regarding online security. However, it degrades its offline security depending on the number of users u: from k bits (key size) to $k - \log_2 u$ bits.

We thus revise the definitions of universal hashing, ϵ_1-regular and ϵ_2-almost XOR universal, by involving ideal cipher, and show that multi-user security of several hash-then-encrypt-type MACs does not degrade from the single-user security.

- Using the revised definitions, we evaluate the multi-user security of the following MAC, called HtE: $\mathsf{HtE}_{K,L}(M) = E_K(H_L^E(M))$ where M is a message, E_K is an n-bit ideal cipher with a k-bit key K, and H_L^E is an ideal-cipher-based hash function with a key L. We derive the multi-user-bound $O\left(q_u q\epsilon_2 + q\epsilon_1 + \frac{p+\ell q}{2^k}\right)$ where p (resp. q) is the number of primitive (resp. construction) queries, and q_u is the maximum number of construction queries within one user.
- We next evaluate the multi-user security of another hash-then-encrypt-type MAC, called HtXE. HtXE is a generalization of XCBC and TMAC where a single-key block cipher is used and another key is applied to the state before the last block-cipher call of HtXE. We show that HtXE achieves the same level of security as HtE.
- Finally, we show regular and almost-XOR-universal bounds of CBC. Combining the bounds with those of HtE and of HtXE, we obtain the bound $O\left(\frac{\ell q_u q}{2^n} + \frac{p}{2^k}\right)$ for HtE or HtXE with CBC, including EMAC, XCBC, and TMAC. If $q_u \ll 2^{n/2}$, then they achieve beyond-birthday-bound security.

Keywords: Deterministic MAC · Hash-then-Encrypt · Multi-User Setting · PRF Security · Universal Hashing · Ideal Cipher · CBC

1 Introduction

Message authentication codes (MACs) are the core algorithms in symmetric-key cryptography. They protect the authenticity and integrity of the communication

E. Oswald (Ed.): CT-RSA 2024, LNCS 14643, pp. 51–77, 2024.
https://doi.org/10.1007/978-3-031-58868-6_3

between two parties. Block cipher is one of the important primitives for MAC, and many block-cipher-based MACs have been designed, such as the NIST standard CMAC [14,15] and the ISO/IEC 9797-1 constructions [20].

Hereafter, we use the following definitions. A query from an adversary to a MAC (resp. an ideal cipher (or idealized block cipher)) is called a "construction (resp. primitive) query." Let p (resp. q) be the number of primitive (resp. construction) queries. Let ℓ be the maximum block-length of construction queries. Let σ be the total number of block-cipher calls by construction queries. Security for construction (resp. primitive) queries is called "online (resp. offline) security."

Many block-cipher-based MACs, e.g., [7,9,14,15,23], follow hash-then-encrypt-type design called HtE. The design ensures design simplicity, efficiency regarding speed or memory size, and simplicity of proofs. Let H_L be an n-bit hash function with a key L. Let E be a block cipher with k-bit keys and n-bit blocks, and E_K a block cipher with a key $K \in \{0,1\}^k$. Then, for a message M, the tag of HtE is defined as $\mathsf{HtE}_{K,L}(M) = E_K(H_L(M))$. The block cipher E_K performed after the hash function is called "outer function." Note that if H_L is based on a block cipher E, we denote the hash function by H_L^E.

The security of HtE-based MACs has mainly been proven in the sense of pseudo-random-function (PRF) security in the single-user setting. In this setting, an adversary has access to either a single instantiation of the target MAC or a random function by construction queries and tries to distinguish between them, where the keys of the MAC are randomly chosen. If K and L are independent, the block cipher is a secure pseudo-random permutation (PRP), and the hash function is ϵ-almost universal [34],[1] then HtE is a secure PRF up to the birthday bound $O\left(q^2\epsilon + \frac{q^2}{2^n}\right)$. The HtE design enables us to focus on designing an almost-universal hash function.

Multi-user security, initially proposed by Bellare et al. [3] for public key encryption, has gathered attention in the research of symmetric-key cryptography and the multi-user security of symmetric-key algorithms [2,6,8,11,17–19,24,25,32] have been actively researched. The multi-user setting captures real-world attack scenarios wherein an adversary targets a particular service rather than a particular user. The multi-user adversary can access to either multiple instantiations of the target MAC or independent random functions, where the user's keys are independently chosen.

Regarding parameters of the multi-user setting, let u be the number of users, B the maximum number of blocks per user in construction queries, and q_u the maximum number of queries to one user.

A hybrid argument is a generic method that provides a multi-user bound from a single-user bound, where the multi-user bound can be derived by multiplying the number of users u with the single-user bound. Regarding HtE, a hybrid

[1] H_L is ϵ-almost universal if for any distinct messages M, M' and a random key L that is chosen independently of M, $\Pr[H_L(M) = H_L(M')] \le \epsilon$.

argument provides the multi-user-PRF bound $O\left(uq^2\epsilon + \frac{uq^2}{2^n}\right) + u \cdot \mathbf{Adv}_{\mathsf{HtE}}^{\mathsf{prp}}$[2] where $\mathbf{Adv}_{\mathsf{HtE}}^{\mathsf{prp}}$ is a PRP-advantage of the underlying block cipher. The bound shows that the online (resp. offline) security degrades from $\frac{n}{2}$ bits (resp. k bits) to $\frac{n}{2} - \log_2 u$ bits (resp. $k - \log_2 u$ bits), assuming the optimal probability $\epsilon = \frac{1}{2^n}$.[3]

Meanwhile, several works showed that important schemes, e.g., (randomized) AES-GCM [19,25], Even-Mansour [26], double encryption [18], and triple encryption [28], keep the security even when switching from the single-user setting to the multi-user setting. These proofs are given in the ideal-cipher model that ensures security against generic attacks. In the ideal-cipher model, a block cipher is chosen uniformly at random from the set of all block ciphers. Then, an adversary is allowed to make primitive queries to the ideal cipher as well as construction ones. Note that proving that the security of HtE-type MACs in the ideal-cipher model does not degrade is not trivial, since several HtE-type MACs such as HtE with $K = L$ are essentially degraded. In the multi-user setting of the HtE, there are u keys, and an adversary wins if one of the keys is recovered. The number of primitive queries to recover one of the keys is at most $2^k/u$ [6], meaning the offline security is at most $k - \log_2 u$ bits.

Bose et al. [8] designed GMAC^+, an HtE-type MAC, and evaluated the multi-user-PRF security in the ideal-cipher model assuming that the hash function is almost XOR universal (AXU).[4,5,6] For an input pair (N, M) such that all values for N in construction queries are distinct, the output of GMAC^+ is defined as $\mathsf{GMAC}^+_{K,L}(N, M) = E_K(0\|\mathsf{lsb}_{n-1}((0\|N) \oplus H_L(M)))$, where K and L are independent and lsb_{n-1} returns the least significant $(n-1)$ bits of the n-bit input. They proved that the multi-user-PRF bound is $O\left(\frac{qB}{2^n} + \frac{pqB}{2^{n+k}}\right)$. For adversaries making queries with the maximum number of blocks $B = \ell q$, the bound is $O\left(\frac{\ell q^2}{2^n} + \frac{\ell q^2 p}{2^{n+k}}\right)$, meaning the security of GMAC^+ does not degrade even when switching the single-user setting to the multi-user setting. If B can be limited to $B \ll 2^{n/2}$, then GMAC^+ achieves beyond-birthday-bound online security.

1.1 Mu-PRF Security of HtE

Research Challenge. The multi-user security of GMAC^+ does not degrade from the single-user setting if the hash function is AXU. However, the AXU assumption does not support primitive queries. Thus, the assumption for the

[2] Let Time be the running time of the PRP adversary in the single-user bound. Then, by the hybrid argument, the running time of the PRP adversary in the multi-user bound is $\mathsf{Time} + O(\sigma)$, where σ is the total number of block-cipher calls by construction queries.

[3] In the ideal-cipher model and the single-user setting, the PRP-security advantage is $\frac{p}{2^k}$. In the multi-user setting, the bound becomes $\frac{u(p+\sigma)}{2^k}$. Note that the key collision probability $\frac{u^2}{2^k}$ is taken into account by the term $\frac{u(p+\sigma)}{2^k}$.

[4] Note that the ideal-cipher assumption is only for the block cipher in the outer function and not for the hash function.

[5] GMAC^+ is designed as a KDF of the authenticated encryption AES-GCM-SIV.

[6] H_L is ϵ_2-AXU if for any M and Y, $\Pr[H_L(M) \oplus H_L(M') = Y] \le \epsilon_2$ where L is chosen randomly and independently of M and Y.

block cipher in the hash function must not contain primitive queries, i.e., the PRP assumption, which degrades the offline security by u as mentioned above. Hence, a research challenge from GMAC^+ is to find if the security of HtE degrades when using a block-cipher-based hash function.

Our Result. We define security notions for hash functions in the ideal-cipher model, prove the multi-user-PRF security of HtE with the security notions, and confirm if the multi-user security does not degrade from the single-user security when using the important block-cipher-based hash function CBC [30]. The attacks by Biham [6] and by Chatterjee et al. [11] show that HtE requires at least two block-cipher keys in order to avoid security degradation. We thus consider HtE such that K and L are independent, which includes EMAC [9].

We first define security notions for hash functions in the ideal-cipher model. In order to cover ideal-cipher-based n-bit hash functions H_L^E, we revise the notions of regular hashing[7] and AXU hashing (See footnote 6) by involving primitive queries, that is, the adversary makes primitive queries to an ideal cipher (E, E^{-1}) and returns a message (M, Y) for regular hashing; (M, M', Y) for AXU hashing.

- H_L^E is (ϵ_1, p)-regular in the ideal-cipher model if for any adversary $\mathbf{A}$ making p primitive queries, $\Pr[H_L^E(M) = Y : (M, Y) \leftarrow \mathbf{A}^{E, E^{-1}}] \leq \epsilon_1$, where an ideal cipher E is chosen before the first $\mathbf{A}$'s query and L is randomly chosen after $\mathbf{A}$ outputs (M, Y).
- H_L^E is (ϵ_2, p)-AXU in the ideal-cipher model if for any adversary $\mathbf{A}$ making p primitive queries, $\Pr[H_L^E(M) \oplus H_L(M') = Y : (M, M', Y) \leftarrow \mathbf{A}^{E, E^{-1}}] \leq \epsilon_2$, where an ideal cipher E is chosen before the first $\mathbf{A}$'s query and L is randomly chosen after $\mathbf{A}$ outputs (M, Y).

With the revised notions, we derive the multi-user-PRF bound of HtE in the ideal-cipher model, $O\left(q_u q \epsilon_2 + q\epsilon_1 + \frac{p + \ell q}{2^k}\right)$.

We next show the following regular and AXU bounds for CBC [30]: $\epsilon_1 = \epsilon_2 = O\left(\frac{\ell}{2^{\min\{n,k\}}} + (\frac{p}{2^k})^{\ell \max\{k,n\}}\right)$. By combining the bounds with the one of HtE and assuming $n \leq k$, we obtain the bound $O\left(\frac{\ell q_u q}{2^n} + \frac{p}{2^k}\right)$ for the multi-user-PRF security of HtE with CBC (i.e., EMAC). The bound shows that the offline security of EMAC does not degrade. Moreover, if $q_u \ll 2^{n/2}$, then EMAC achieves beyond-birthday-bound online security.

1.2 Mu-PRF Security of XCBC/TMAC-Type HtE

Research Challenge. HtE uses (at least) two block-cipher keys, thus performing the key schedule twice and requiring memory to keep the two (tuples of sub) keys. This motivates us to design an HtE-based MAC with a single-block-cipher key to improve the efficiency regarding memory size and speed. The topic was initially studied in the single-user setting for the CBC-type MACs XCBC [7] and

[7] H_L is ϵ_1-regular if for any M and Y, $\Pr[H_L(M) = Y] \leq \epsilon_1$ where L is chosen randomly and independently of M and Y.

TMAC [23]. Extending the topic to the multi-user setting is a natural extension of the previous researches.

Our Result. We consider HtXE, a variant of HtE and a generalization of the CBC-based MACs XCBC and TMAC. In these MACs, the current state is updated by using the additional key before processing the last message block. We thus define HtXE by following the design: For a message $M = M_{\mathsf{pf}} \| M_{\mathsf{sf}}$ where $|M_{\mathsf{sf}}| = n$ and $|M|$ is a multiple of n, the output is defined as $\mathsf{HtXE}_{K,L}(M) = E_K(H^{E_K}(M_{\mathsf{pf}}) \oplus L \oplus M_{\mathsf{sf}})$, where K is the block-cipher's key, L is additional key, and H^{E_K} is an n-bit hash function with a block cipher E_K. To avoid the offline-security degradation by the generic attacks in [6,11], we assume that K and L are independent. Note that this construction is a simplified version of HtXE, and the full one is defined in Sect. 4, where input lengths are variable, and the masking function is a universal hash function instead of L.

We next prove that the multi-user-PRF bound of HtXE in the ideal-cipher model is $O\left(q_u q \epsilon_2 + \frac{\ell q_u q}{2^n} + \frac{p}{2^k}\right)$ as long as the hash function is (ϵ_2, p)-AXU. Hence, HtXE achieves the same level of security as HtE. By combining the bound of CBC with the one of HtXE, and assuming $n \leq k$, we obtain the bound $O\left(\frac{\ell q_u q}{2^n} + \frac{p}{2^k}\right)$ for the multi-user-PRF security of HtXE with CBC, i.e., XCBC and TMAC. Hence, the offline security of these HtXE-type MACs does not degrade.

1.3 Related Works

The security of CBC-type MACs has mainly been evaluated in the single-user setting and the standard PRP assumption, e.g., [4,5,7,10,12,21–23,29]. The first bounds of CBC are the birthday bounds $O\left(\frac{(\ell q)^2}{2^n}\right)$ and $O\left(\frac{\sigma^2}{2^n}\right)$, where σ is the total number of block-cipher calls by all queries [4,7,21,23]. The bounds have been improved to weaken query-length influences [5,10,12,22,29]. Finally, several works proved the length-free bound $O\left(\frac{q^2}{2^n}\right)$ for CBC-type MACs [12,22].

Shen et al. [32,33] proved mu-PRF security bounds of double-block-hash-then-sum-type MACs in the ideal-cipher model such as SUM-ECB [35], PMAC_Plus [36], LightMAC_Plus [27], and their variants. However, several flaws in the proofs were pointed out by Guo and Wang [16] and Datta et al. [13]. Datta et al. [13] proved a multi-user-PRF bound of the double-block-hash-then-sum MAC, which achieves beyond-birthday-bound security. The assumption for the hash function is a standard universal hashing that does not support offline queries.

1.4 Comparison

In Table 1, we compare the existing works with our results for the CBC-type MACs. The existing works on the first line showed the length-free bound $O\left(\frac{q^2}{2^n}\right)$ but considered only the single-user setting. The security of GMAC^+ is given in the multi-user setting, and the bound is similar to our bounds. However, the AXU assumption of the GMAC^+'s hash function covers only PRP-based hash

Table 1. Comparison of Security Bonds of HtE-type MACs. p (resp. q) is the number of primitive (resp. construction) queries. ℓ is the maximum block-length of construction queries. B is the maximum number of blocks per user in construction queries. q_u is the maximum number of queries to one user.

Scheme	Bound	Hash's Model	Outer's Model	User's PModel	Ref.
CBC-type MACs	$O\left(\frac{q^2}{2^n}\right)$	PRP	PRP	Single User	[12,22]
GMAC$^+$	$O\left(\frac{qB}{2^n} + \frac{pqB}{2^{n+k}}\right)$	AXU	IC	Multi User	[8]
EMAC, XCBC, TMAC	$O\left(\frac{\ell q_u q}{2^n} + \frac{p}{2^k}\right)$	IC	IC	Multi User	**Ours**

functions (and polynomial hash functions); thus, the offline security degrades. Finally, we note that our bounds include the query length ℓ, and removing the query length is an open problem in this paper.

1.5 Organization

We begin by giving basic notations and definitions in Section. 2. In Sect. 3, we revise regular and AXU notions, show the multi-user-PRF bound of HtE, and give an intuition of the multi-user-PRF security. In Sect. 4, we show the multi-user-PRF bound of HtXE, and give an intuition of the multi-user-PRF security. In Sect. 5, we show the regular and AXU bounds of CBC in the ideal-cipher model, combine the bounds with the bounds of HtE and HtXE, and outline the proofs. In Sect. 6, we prove the multi-user-PRF security of HtE. In Sect. 7, we prove the regular and AXU bounds of CBC in the ideal-cipher model.

2 Preliminaries

2.1 Notations

For an integer $n \geq 0$ and a bit string X, let $|X|$ be the bit length of X. Let ε be an empty string, $\emptyset$ an empty set, and $\{0,1\}^*$ be the set of all bit strings. For an integer $n \geq 0$, let $\{0,1\}^n$ be the set of all n-bit strings, $\{0,1\}^0 := \{\varepsilon\}$, and $\{0,1\}^{n*} := \{X \in \{0,1\}^* \mid |X| \bmod n = 0\}$. Let 0^i be the bit string of i-bit zeros. For integers $0 \leq i \leq j$, let $[i,j] := \{i, i+1, \ldots, j\}$, and $[j] := [1,j]$. If $i > j$, then $[i,j] := \emptyset$. For a non-empty set $\mathcal{T}$, $T \xleftarrow{\$} \mathcal{T}$ means that an element is chosen uniformly at random from $\mathcal{T}$ and assigned to T. The concatenation of two bit strings X and Y is written as $X \| Y$ or XY when no confusion is possible.

A block cipher (BC) is a set of permutations indexed by a key. Throughout this paper, the block and key lengths of BC are respectively denoted by n and k. An encryption of BC: $\{0,1\}^k \times \{0,1\}^n \rightarrow \{0,1\}^n$ is denoted by E, and its decryption: $\{0,1\}^k \times \{0,1\}^n \rightarrow \{0,1\}^n$ is denoted by E^{-1}. E (resp. E^{-1}) with a key K is denoted by E_K or $E(K,\cdot)$ (resp. E_K^{-1} or $E^{-1}(K,\cdot)$). Let **BC** be the set of all k-bit key and n-bit BC encryptions.

Init_R	Init_I
$E \xleftarrow{\$} \mathbf{BC}$; **for** $i = 1, \ldots, u$ **do** $K_i \xleftarrow{\$} \mathcal{K}$	$E \xleftarrow{\$} \mathbf{BC}$; **for** $i = 1, \ldots, u$ **do** $\mathcal{F}_i \xleftarrow{\$} \mathsf{Func}$
$\mathsf{Cons}_R(\nu, M)$	$\mathsf{Cons}_I(\nu, M)$
return $\Pi^E_{K_\nu}(M)$	return $\mathcal{F}_\nu(M)$
$\mathsf{Prim}_R(x, W, X)$	$\mathsf{Prim}_I(x, W, X)$
if $x = +$ then return $E(W, X)$	if $x = +$ then return $E(W, X)$
if $x = -$ then return $E^{-1}(W, Y)$	if $x = -$ then return $E^{-1}(W, Y)$

Fig. 1. Real-world (left) and ideal-world (right) oracles.

2.2 Multi-user PRF Security in the Ideal-Cipher (IC) Model

Let $\Pi^E_K : \{0,1\}^* \rightarrow \{0,1\}^t$ be a MAC having a key $K \in \mathcal{K}$ and using a BC $E \in \mathbf{BC}$, where $t > 0$ is a tag size and $\mathcal{K}$ is a key space. Let u be the number of users. Let Func be the set of all functions with the same domain and range of Π^E_K.

In the mu-PRF-security game, an adversary $\mathbf{A}$ has access to either real-world oracles $(\mathsf{Cons}_R, \mathsf{Prim}_R)$ or ideal-world ones $(\mathsf{Cons}_I, \mathsf{Prim}_I)$ defined in Fig. 1. Before making the first query by $\mathbf{A}$, the initialization Init_R in the real world (resp. Init_I in the ideal world) is performed, where an IC E and user's keys K_i (resp. random functions $\mathcal{F}_i$) are defined. For a query (ν, M), which is a pair of a user number and a message, an oracle Cons returns the output $\Pi^E_{K_\nu}(M)$ (resp. $\mathcal{F}_\nu(M)$) in the real (resp. ideal) world. An oracle Prim returns an IC's output. At the end of this game, the adversary $\mathbf{A}$ returns a decision bit. Let $\mathbf{A}^{\mathsf{Cons},\mathsf{Prim}}$ be an output of $\mathbf{A}$ with access to oracles $(\mathsf{Cons}, \mathsf{Prim})$. Then, the mu-PRF-security advantage function of $\mathbf{A}$ is defined as

$$\mathbf{Adv}^{\mathsf{mu\text{-}prf}}_{\Pi}(\mathbf{A}) := \Pr\left[\mathbf{A}^{\mathsf{Cons}_R,\mathsf{Prim}_R} = 1\right] - \Pr\left[\mathbf{A}^{\mathsf{Cons}_I,\mathsf{Prim}_I} = 1\right].$$

We refer to the particular queries as follows: primitive queries: queries to Prim; forward queries: queries to Prim with the symbol $+$; inverse queries: queries to Prim with the symbol $-$; and construction queries: queries to $\mathsf{Cons}_R/\mathsf{Cons}_I$.

2.3 Mu-PRF Bound with Coefficient H Technique

Let T_R be a transcript in the real world obtained by random samplings such as sampling of user's keys and an IC. Let T_I be a transcript in the ideal world obtained by random samplings such as random functions and an IC. For a transcript τ, which is an adversary's view (or information obtained) in the security game, we call τ a valid transcript if $\Pr[\mathsf{T}_I = \tau] > 0$. Let $\mathbf{T}$ be the set of all valid transcripts such that $\forall \tau \in \mathbf{T} : \Pr[\mathsf{T}_R = \tau] \leq \Pr[\mathsf{T}_I = \tau]$. Then, the advantage function $\mathbf{Adv}^{\mathsf{mu\text{-}prf}}_{\Pi}(\mathbf{A})$ is upper-bounded by the statistical distance $\mathsf{SD}(\mathsf{T}_R, \mathsf{T}_I)$ as follows: $\mathbf{Adv}^{\mathsf{mu\text{-}prf}}_{\Pi}(\mathbf{A}) \leq \mathsf{SD}(\mathsf{T}_R, \mathsf{T}_I) = \sum_{\tau \in \mathbf{T}} (\Pr[\mathsf{T}_I = \tau] - \Pr[\mathsf{T}_R = \tau])$.

We prove the security of HtE and HtXE using the coefficient H technique [31].

Lemma 1. *Let $\mathbf{T}_{\mathsf{good}}$ and $\mathbf{T}_{\mathsf{bad}}$ be respectively sets of good transcripts and of bad ones into which $\mathbf{T}$ is partitioned. If $\forall \tau \in \mathbf{T}_{\mathsf{good}} : \frac{\Pr[\mathsf{T}_R = \tau]}{\Pr[\mathsf{T}_I = \tau]} \geq 1 - \varepsilon$ s.t. $0 \leq \varepsilon \leq 1$, then $\mathsf{SD}(\mathsf{T}_R, \mathsf{T}_I) \leq \Pr[\mathsf{T}_I \in \mathbf{T}_{\mathsf{bad}}] + \varepsilon$.*

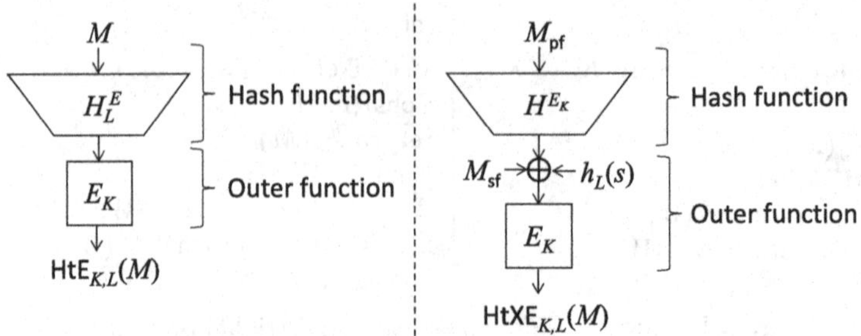

Fig. 2. HtE (left) and HtXE (right).

In our proofs, we (1) partition $\mathbf{T}$ into $\mathbf{T}_{\mathsf{good}}$ and $\mathbf{T}_{\mathsf{bad}}$; (2) upper-bound $\Pr[\mathsf{T}_I \in \mathbf{T}_{\mathsf{bad}}]$; and (3) lower-bound $\frac{\Pr[\mathsf{T}_R=\tau]}{\Pr[\mathsf{T}_I=\tau]}$ for any $\tau \in \mathbf{T}_{\mathsf{good}}$. Then, we obtain mu-PRF bounds via the lemma.

3 Multi-user Security of HtE

In this section, we revise the notions for regular and AXU hash functions by using IC. We then show an mu-PRF bound of HtE with the updated notions.

3.1 Security Notions for Keyed Hash Functions in the IC Model

Regarding HtE with a (standard) regular and AXU hash function, if the hash function uses BCs, the offline security degrades depending on the number of construction queries due to the reduction of pseudo-random permutations. We thus revisit these notions to involve IC queries, i.e., an adversary $\mathbf{A}$ makes p primitive queries to the IC (E, E^{-1}) and then returns a message (M, Y) for regular hashing; (M, M', Y) for AXU hashing. The definitions are given below.

Definition 1 (Regular Hashing in the IC Model). *Let $\epsilon > 0$. H is said to be (ϵ, p)-regular in the IC model if for an IC E and any adversary $\mathbf{A}$ making at most p primitive queries such that* $\Pr[H_L^E(M) = Y \wedge M \neq \varepsilon : E \xleftarrow{\$} \mathbf{BC}; (M, Y) \leftarrow \mathbf{A}^{E,E^{-1}}; L \xleftarrow{\$} \mathcal{L}] \leq \epsilon$.

Definition 2 (AXU Hashing in the IC Model). *Let $\epsilon > 0$. H is said to be (ϵ, p)-AXU in the IC model if for an IC E and any adversary $\mathbf{A}$ making at most p primitive queries such that* $\Pr[H_L^E(M) \oplus H_L^E(M') = Y \wedge M \neq M' : E \xleftarrow{\$} \mathbf{BC}; (M, M', Y) \leftarrow \mathbf{A}^{E,E^{-1}}; L \xleftarrow{\$} \mathcal{L}] \leq \epsilon$.

3.2 Specification of HtE

Let $\mathcal{L}$ be a set of hash keys, $L \in \mathcal{L}$ a hash key, and $H_L^E : \{0,1\}^* \to \{0,1\}^n$ a hash function using a BC E and having a key $L \in \mathcal{L}$. Let K be a BC's key in the outer function of HtE. Then, for a message $M \in \{0,1\}^*$, the tag of HtE is defined as $\mathsf{HtE}_{K,L}(M) = E_K(H_L^E(M))$. Figure 2-(left) shows the structure of HtE.

3.3 Security of HtE in the IC Model

Using the revised notions, we prove the following mu-PRF security bound of HtE in the IC model.

Theorem 1. *Let $C_n := \frac{n}{\log_2 n}$ and $D_n := \log_2 n$. Assume that the keys K and L of* HtE *are independently chosen. Let* **A** *be an adversary making p primitive and q construction queries such that the number of construction queries to each user is at most q_u and the maximum number of BC calls in the hash function is at most ℓ. Assume that H is (ϵ_1, p)-regular and (ϵ_2, p)-AXU in the IC model. Then, we have*

$$\mathbf{Adv}^{\text{mu-prf}}_{\text{HtE}}(\mathbf{A}) \leq q_u q \epsilon_2 + \frac{(pq + \ell q^2)\epsilon_1 + C_n(p + \ell q)}{2^k} + \left(\frac{eD_n \cdot q}{2^n}\right)^{C_n}.$$

An intuition of the mu-PRF security of HtE is given below. The full proof is given in Sect. 6.

We study the bound in Theorem 1. We assume that $p \leq 2^k$, $n \leq k$, $\ell q \leq 2^n$, and $\ell q \leq p$. Then, the second term becomes $2q\epsilon_1 + \frac{2C_n p}{2^k} = O\left(q\epsilon_1 + \frac{p}{2^k}\right)$, ignoring the negligible factor C_n. The third term is $O\left(\frac{q}{2^n}\right)$, ignoring the negligible factor D_n. Then, the bound is $O\left(q_u q \epsilon_2 + q\epsilon_1 + \frac{p}{2^k}\right)$. Assuming the optimal probabilities $\epsilon_1 = \epsilon_2 = 2^{-n}$, the bound shows that HtE achieves $(n - \log_2 q_u)$-bit online security and k-bit offline security. If $q \ll 2^{n/2}$, HtE achieves beyond-birthday-bound online security.

We next discuss the tightness of the bound. For the sake of simplicity, we assume that $\epsilon_1 \approx \epsilon_2$. Then, the bound becomes $O\left(q_u q \epsilon_2 + \frac{p}{2^k}\right)$. There are two generic attacks on HtE.

- The first attack is based on a collision of the hash function in some user. The hash collision yields a tag collision, thus leading to a distinguishing attack to the user. We consider an adversary that accesses $\frac{q}{q_u}$ users and makes q_u construction queries to each user. By the birthday analysis, the hash-collision probability is $O\left(q_u^2 \epsilon_2\right)$, offering the success probability $O\left(q_u^2 \epsilon_2 \cdot \frac{q}{q_u}\right) = O\left(q_u q \epsilon_2\right)$. Hence, the first term $q_u q \epsilon_2$ is tight.
- The second attack is the simple meet-in-the-middle attack, where for a construction query-response pair (M, T) of some user, an adversary guesses the user's keys, K' and L', and check the equality $H^E_{L'}(M) \stackrel{?}{=} E^{-1}_{K'}(T)$, where K' and L' are the guessed keys. The adversary can confirm if the guessed keys are valid by using the check. Assuming that the number of BC calls in $H^E_{L'}(M)$ is a small constant, the attack complexity is about $2^{\max\{k, |L|\}}$. If $|L| \leq k$, the second term $\frac{p}{2^k}$ is tight.

These attacks ensure that our bound is tight.

3.4 Intuition of the mu-PRF Security of HtE

Assume that H^E_L is (ϵ_1, p)-regular and (ϵ_2, p)-AXU in the IC model. Let u be the number of users. For $\nu \in [u]$, let q_ν be the number of construction queries to the ν-th user.

We explain intuition by using two additional worlds as well as the real and ideal worlds. The first-world oracles consist of an IC and u instantiations of a variant of HtE where the outer function is a random function. The second-world oracles consist of an IC and u instantiations of a variant of HtE where the outer function is a random permutation.

Firstly, we consider the difference between the ideal and first worlds. The ideal-world oracles are an IC and u random functions. For the first world, if no hash collision occurs for each of u instantiations, then all outputs of HtE are random, and there is no difference between these worlds. The collision probability is at most $\sum_{\nu \in [u]} 0.5 q_\nu^2 \epsilon_2 \leq 0.5 q_u q \epsilon_2$.

Secondly, we consider the difference between the first and second worlds from the outer functions. By the PRF-PRP switching, the probability that the difference occurs is at most $\sum_{\nu \in [u]} \frac{0.5 q_\nu^2}{2^n} \leq \frac{0.5 q_u q}{2^n}$.

Finally, we consider the difference between the second and real worlds. For $\nu \in [u]$, let $\mathcal{Q}_{\mathsf{hash}}[\nu]$ be the set of input-output tuples of IC defined by the hash function of the ν-th user, $\mathcal{Q}_{\mathsf{outer}}[\nu]$ the set of input-output tuples of the outer function of the ν-th user, and $\mathcal{Q}_{\mathsf{prim}}$ the set of input-output tuples of an IC defined by primitive queries. In the real world, there might exist the same input-output tuples of IC among $\mathcal{Q}_{\mathsf{outer}}[1], \ldots, \mathcal{Q}_{\mathsf{outer}}[\nu]$, $\mathcal{Q}_{\mathsf{hash}}[1], \ldots, \mathcal{Q}_{\mathsf{hash}}[\nu]$, and $\mathcal{Q}_{\mathsf{prim}}$. On the other hand, in the second world, the outer functions are independent of each other and are independent of an IC. Hence, if for each $\nu \in [u]$, each element of $\mathcal{Q}_{\mathsf{outer}}[\nu]$ is distinct from $\mathcal{Q}_{\mathsf{outer}}[i]$ for $i \in [1, \nu - 1] \cup [\nu + 1, u]$, $\mathcal{Q}_{\mathsf{hash}}[1], \ldots, \mathcal{Q}_{\mathsf{hash}}[\nu]$, and $\mathcal{Q}_{\mathsf{prim}}$, then we can ensure the independence in the real world as the second one, and there is no difference between these worlds. We thus evaluate the collision probability between $\mathcal{Q}_{\mathsf{outer}}[\nu]$ and other sets. Regarding a collision with pairs of key and input block in $\mathcal{Q}_{\mathsf{outer}}[\nu]$, since the keys are k-bit random values and the input blocks are defined by regular and AXU hash functions, the collision probability can be at most $O(\frac{(q^2 + \ell q^2)\epsilon_1}{2^k} + \frac{pq\epsilon_1}{2^k})$. Regarding a collision with pairs of a key and an output block in $\mathcal{Q}_{\mathsf{outer}}[\nu]$, we evaluate the collision probability using a multi-collision technique for outputs of HtE and the randomness of keys. Then, the collision probability is at most $O(\frac{C_n(p+\ell q))}{2^k} + (\frac{D_n q}{2^n})^{C_n})$.

Combining the above bounds, we obtain the mu-PRF bound of HtE: $O(q_u q \epsilon_2 + \frac{(pq + \ell q^2)\epsilon_1}{2^k} + \frac{C_n(p+\ell q)}{2^k} + (\frac{D_n q}{2^n})^{C_n})$.

4 Multi-user Security of XCBC/TMAC-Type HtE

In this section, we evaluate mu-PRF security of HtXE, a generalization of XCBC [7] and TMAC [23], which are single-key-BC-based MACs. In HtXE, a state before the last BC call is updated by using a key that is independent of the BC's key.

4.1 Specification of HtXE

Let $K \in \{0,1\}^k$ be a BC's key. Let $H^{E_K} : \{0,1\}^{*n} \rightarrow \{0,1\}^n$ be a hash function using a BC E_K such that $H^{E_K}(\varepsilon) = 0^n$. Let $\mathcal{L}$ be a set of hash keys, $L \in \mathcal{L}$

a hash key, and $h_L : \{1,2\} \to \{0,1\}^n$ be a hash function. Let $\mathsf{ozp} : \{0,1\}^* \to \{0,1\}^{n*}$ be a one-zero padding function where for an input $M \in \{0,1\}^*$, it returns $M\|10^{n-1-(|M| \bmod n)}$ if $M = \varepsilon$ or $(|M| \bmod n) > 0$; it returns M otherwise. Then, for a message M, the output of HtXE, denoted by $\mathsf{HtXE}_{K,L}(M)$, is defined as follows. Figure 2-(right) shows the structure of HtXE.

1. Partition $\mathsf{ozp}(M)$ into n-bit blocks $M_1, \cdots, M_m$ // $\mathsf{ozp}(M) = M_1\|\cdots\|M_m$
2. $M_{\mathsf{sf}} \leftarrow M_m$; **if** $m > 1$ **then** $M_{\mathsf{pf}} := M_1\|\cdots\|M_{m-1}$; **if** $m = 1$ **then** $M_{\mathsf{pf}} := \varepsilon$
3. **if** $M = \varepsilon$ or $|M| \bmod n \neq 0$ **then** $s = 1$; **else** $s = 2$ **end if**
4. $\mathsf{HtXE}_{K,L}(M) \leftarrow E_K(h_L(s) \oplus M_{\mathsf{sf}} \oplus H^{E_K}(M_{\mathsf{pf}}))$

4.2 Security of HtXE

Using the revised notions in defined Sect. 3.1, we prove the following mu-PRF bound of HtXE in the IC model.

Theorem 2. *Let $C_n := \frac{n}{\log_2 n}$ and $D_n := \log_2 n$. Assume that the keys K and L of* HtXE *are independently chosen. Let* **A** *be an adversary making p primitive and q construction queries such that the number of construction queries to each user is at most q_u and the number of IC calls in each construction query is at most ℓ. Assume that H is (ϵ_1, p)-AXU in the IC model, and h is ϵ_2-regular and ϵ_3-AXU. Then,*

$$\mathbf{Adv}^{\mathsf{mu\text{-}prf}}_{\mathsf{HtXE}}(\mathbf{A}) \leq q_u q \max\{\epsilon_1, \epsilon_3\} + 2\ell q \epsilon_2 + \frac{\ell q_u q}{2^n} + \frac{1.5\ell q^2 \epsilon_2}{2^k} + \frac{C_n \cdot p}{2^k} + \left(\frac{eD_n \cdot q}{2^n}\right)^{C_n}.$$

An intuition of the security of HtXE is given in Subsect. 4.3.

We study the bound in Theorem 2. We assume that $\epsilon_2 = \epsilon_3 = \frac{1}{2^n}$, $n \leq k$, $\ell q \leq 2^n$, and $\ell q \leq p$. Then, the first three terms become $O\left(q_u q \epsilon_1 + \frac{\ell q_u q}{2^n}\right)$, and the last three terms become $O\left(\frac{q}{2^k} + \frac{p}{2^k}\right)$, ignoring the negligible factors C_n. The third term is $O\left(\frac{q}{2^n}\right)$, ignoring the negligible factors C_n and D_n. Then, the bound is $O\left(q_u q \epsilon_1 + \frac{\ell q_u q}{2^n} + \frac{p}{2^k}\right)$. Assuming the optimal probabilities $\epsilon_1 = 2^{-n}$ and the query length ℓ is a small constant, the bound shows that HtXE achieves $(n - \log_2 q_u)$-bit online security and k-bit offline security. If $q \ll 2^{n/2}$, HtE achieves beyond-birthday-bound online security.

Regarding the tightness of the bound, the first and last terms are tight by the same discussion as in Subsect. 3.3. On the other hand, the second term could be improved since there is no attack that makes use of the length ℓ, except for attacks with a hash collision.

4.3 Intuition of the Security of HtXE in Theorem 2

The security proof of HtXE is almost the same as that of HtE. The difference between these proofs comes from the structural difference between HtXE and

HtE, i.e., the difference between the outer functions. Regarding HtE, for each user, the IC's key in the outer function is independent of the IC's key in the hash function. Regarding HtXE, for each user, the IC's keys in the outer function and in the hash function are the same, but an input block of the outer function is defined by using a regular and AXU hash function h_L. Hence, if, for each user, no collision occurs between IC's input-output tuples in the hash function and in the outer function, then we can ensure that the outer function is independent of the hash function as HtE. Regarding the collision, using the regular and AXU properties of h, the collision probability can be upper-bounded by $O(\ell q\epsilon_2 + \frac{\ell q^2 \epsilon_2}{2^k} + (\frac{D_n q}{2^n})^{C_n})$. If no collision occurs, the proof is similar to that of HtE, offering the mu-PRF bound $O(q_u q \max\{\epsilon_1, \epsilon_3\} + \frac{\ell q^2 \epsilon_2}{2^k} + \frac{C_n p}{2^k})$. Hence, we obtain the mu-PRF bound $O(q_u q \max\{\epsilon_1, \epsilon_3\} + \ell q \epsilon_2 + \frac{\ell q^2 \epsilon_2}{2^k} + \frac{C_n p}{2^k} + (\frac{D_n q}{2^n})^{C_n})$.

5 Regular and AXU Bounds for CBC and Applications

In this section, we show regular and AXU bounds of CBC in the IC model. We then combine the bounds with the mu-PRF ones in Theorems 1 and 2, and obtain mu-PRF bounds of HtE and HtXE with CBC, which include EMAC [9], XCBC [7], and TMAC [23].

5.1 Specification of CBC

For the sake of simplicity, we consider messages in $\{0,1\}^{n*}$. Let L be a BC's key of CBC. Then, for an input message $M \in \{0,1\}^{n*}$, the output of $\mathsf{CBC}[E_L](M)$ is defined as follows.

1. Partition $M \in \{0,1\}^{n*}$ into n-bit blocks $M_1, \cdots, M_m$ // $M = M_1 \| \cdots \| M_m$
2. $V_0 \leftarrow 0^n$
3. **for** $i = 1, \ldots, m$ **do** $U_i \leftarrow V_{i-1} \oplus M_i; V_i \leftarrow E_L(U_i)$ **end for**
4. $\mathsf{CBC}[E_L](M) \leftarrow V_m$

5.2 Regular and AXU Bounds of CBC in the IC Model

Theorem 3. *Let ℓ be the maximum block-length of messages. Assume that $\ell \leq \min\{2^{n/3}, 2^{n-2}\}$ and $p \leq 2^k$. CBC is (ϵ_1, p)-regular and (ϵ_2, p)-AXU in the IC model where*

$$\epsilon_1 = \epsilon_2 = \frac{16\ell}{2^n} + \frac{3\max\{k,n\} \cdot (\ell+1)}{2^{\min\{n,k\}}} + \left(\frac{4}{\ell+1} \cdot \frac{p}{2^k}\right)^{\max\{k,n\}(\ell+1)}.$$

An outline of the proof is given in Subsect. 5.5. The full proof is given in Sect. 7.

5.3 Mu-Security of HtE with CBC (EMAC)

Combining the regular and AXU bounds in Theorem 3 with the mu-PRF bound in Theorem 1, we obtain the following mu-PRF bound of HtE with CBC, i.e. EMAC.

Corollary 1. *Assume that $n \leq k$, and the keys K and L of* EMAC *are independently chosen. Let* $\mathbf{A}$ *be an adversary making p primitive and q construction queries such that the number of construction queries to each user is at most q_u and the maximum block-length of messages is ℓ such that $\ell \leq \min\{2^{n/3}, 2^{n-2}\}$. Then, we have*

$$\mathbf{Adv}_{\mathsf{EMAC}}^{\mathsf{mu\text{-}prf}}(\mathbf{A}) \leq \frac{(6k+32)\cdot(\ell+1)(q_u+1)q}{2^n} + \frac{n}{\log_2 n}\cdot\frac{p}{2^k} + \left(\frac{8}{\ell+1}\cdot\frac{p}{2^k}\right)^{k(\ell+1)}.$$

The bound is roughly $O(\frac{\ell q_u q}{2^n} + \frac{p}{2^k})$. Thus, EMAC achieves birthday-bound online security and k-bit offline security. If $q_u \ll 2^{n/2}$, then EMAC achieves beyond-birthday-bound online security.

5.4 Mu-Security of HtXE with CBC (XCBC and TMAC)

XCBC and TMAC are HtXE-type MACs with CBC. XCBC uses two n-bit keys L_1 and L_2 of h. The function h_L of XCBC is defined as $h_L(1) = L_1$; $h_L(2) = L_2$. TMAC uses an n-bit key L of h. The function h_L of TMAC is defined as $h_L(1) = L$ and $h_L(2) = 2 \cdot L$ where the multiplication is done over $GF(2^n)^*$, a primitive polynomial is fixed, and 2 is a generator of $GF(2^n)^*$. When these keys are chosen uniformly at random from $\{0,1\}^n$, the regular and AXU bounds for XCBC and TMAC become $\frac{1}{2^n}$.

Then, combining the regular and AXU bounds in Theorem 3 with the mu-PRF bound in Theorem 2, we obtain the following mu-PRF bounds of XCBC and TMAC in the IC model.

Corollary 2. *Let $\Pi \in \{\mathsf{XCBC}, \mathsf{TMAC}\}$. Assume that $n \leq k$, and and the keys K and L of Π are independently chosen. Let* $\mathbf{A}$ *be an adversary making p primitive and q construction queries such that the number of construction queries to each user is at most q_u and the maximum block-length of construction queries is ℓ such that $\ell \leq \min\{2^{n/3}, 2^{n-2}\}$. Then, we have*

$$\mathbf{Adv}_{\Pi}^{\mathsf{mu\text{-}prf}}(\mathbf{A}) \leq \frac{(3k+20)\cdot(\ell+1)(q_u+1)q}{2^n} + \frac{n}{\log_2 n}\cdot\frac{p}{2^k} + \left(\frac{8}{\ell+1}\cdot\frac{p}{2^k}\right)^{k(\ell+1)}.$$

The bound is roughly $O(\frac{\ell q_u q}{2^n} + \frac{p}{2^k})$. Thus, XCBC and TMAC achieve the same level of security as EMAC.

5.5 Outline of the Proof of Theorem 3

Since $\mathsf{CBC}[E_L](M) = Y \Leftrightarrow \mathsf{CBC}[E_L](M) \oplus \mathsf{CBC}[E_L](\varepsilon) = Y$, $\epsilon_1 \leq \epsilon_2$ is satisfied. Hence, we evaluate an AXU bound ϵ_2.

For a pair of distinct messages $(M^{(1)}, M^{(2)})$ and $Z \in \{0,1\}^n$ defined after making p primitive queries, we evaluate the probability that the following event occurs:

- coll : $\left(L \xleftarrow{\$} \{0,1\}^k; \mathsf{CBC}[E_L](M^{(1)}) \oplus \mathsf{CBC}[E_L](M^{(2)}) = Z\right)$.

For $i \in [2]$, let m_i be the block length of $M^{(i)}$ and $M_j^{(i)}$ be the j-th block of $M^{(i)}$. Let $\mathcal{Q}_{\mathsf{prim}}$ be the set of primitive query-response tuples. For $L^* \in \{0,1\}^k$, let $f(L^*) := \mathsf{CBC}[E_{L^*}](M^{(1)}) \oplus \mathsf{CBC}[E_{L^*}](M^{(2)}) \oplus Z$.

We then consider the following cases.

- E_1: $\exists i \in [2]$ s.t. the last block of $\mathsf{CBC}[E_L](M^{(i)})$ is fresh (not in $\mathcal{Q}_{\mathsf{prim}}$).
- E_2: $\exists i \in [2], j \in [m_i - 1]$ s.t. the j-th block is fresh and the next block is not fresh (in $\mathcal{Q}_{\mathsf{prim}}$).
- E_3: $\forall i \in [2]$: All blocks defined in $\mathsf{CBC}[E_L](M^{(i)})$ are not fresh.

In the case E_1, there exist $i \in [2]$ and $j \in [m_i - 1]$ such that input-output tuples from j-th to m_i blocks are all fresh, i.e., the IC processes of these blocks can be seen as RPs, and thus we can make use of the existing AXU bounds of CBC in the RP model, e.g., [5,22]. Using the bound, we have $\Pr[\mathsf{coll} \wedge \mathsf{E}_1] \leq O(\frac{\ell}{2^n})$.

In the case E_2, there exists a query-response tuple in $\mathcal{Q}_{\mathsf{prim}}$ such that the key element is equal to L and the input block is equal to some fresh output of E_L defined in the CBC evaluation (and not in $\mathcal{Q}_{\mathsf{prim}}$). Since L is a k-bit random value and the output of E_L is an (almost) n-bit random value, we have $\Pr[\mathsf{E}_2] \leq O(\frac{\ell p}{2^{k+n}}) \leq O(\frac{\ell}{2^n})$, assuming $p \leq 2^k$.

In the case E_3, we consider the number of key candidates L^* such that $f(L^*) = 0^n$ and all input-output blocks of E in the evaluation are not fresh since coll with E_3 implies that L equals one of the key candidates. Let N_L be the number of the key candidates. Let μ be a threshold for the number of key candidates. Then, assuming that the number of keys is less than μ, the probability that coll occurs is bounded by the probability that one of the (at most) $\mu - 1$ keys collides with L, which is $\frac{\mu-1}{2^k}$. By choosing μ so that the probabilities $\frac{\mu-1}{2^k}$ and $\Pr[N_L \geq \mu]$ are balanced, we have $\Pr[\mathsf{coll} \wedge \mathsf{E}_3] \leq O(\frac{\ell}{2^{\min\{n,k\}}} + (\frac{p}{2^k})^{\max\{k,n\}(\ell+1)})$.

By the above bounds, we obtain the bound $O(\frac{\ell}{2^{\min\{n,k\}}} + (\frac{p}{2^k})^{\max\{k,n\}(\ell+1)})$.

6 Proof of Theorem 1 (Proof for HtE)

Without loss of generality, an adversary is deterministic and makes no repeated query to the same user. We prove the mu-PRF security of HtE using the coefficient-H technique.

6.1 Overview

In Subsect. 6.2, we define notations for this proof.

In Subsect. 6.3, we define an **A**'s view as a set of query-response tuples and additional values. This proof permits **A** to obtain all the user's keys and all hash values after outputting a decision bit. The view includes all input-output tuples of E in the outer function by the additional setting.

In Subsect. 6.4, we define bad events that are collision events within the input-output tuples of the outer function and between the input-output tuples of the outer function and the other input-output tuples of E. Bad transcripts $\mathbf{T}_{\mathsf{bad}}$ are defined so that the bad events are satisfied. Good transcripts $\mathbf{T}_{\mathsf{good}}$ are defined to be the other transcripts.

In Subsect. 6.5, we upper-bound $\Pr[\mathsf{T}_I \in \mathbf{T}_{\mathsf{bad}}]$, the probability that one of bad events occurs in the ideal world. Each bad event is for a collision with the input-output tuples of E in the outer function. For the collision events for pairs of an input block and a key of the outer function, we bound the probabilities by using the randomnesses of the user's keys and regular or AXU properties of the hash function. For the collision events with pairs of an output block and a key, we bound the probabilities by using the randomnesses of the user's keys and the multi-collision technique for random functions that define the outputs of the outer functions.

In Subsect. 6.6, we lower-bound the ratio $\frac{\Pr[\mathsf{T}_R=\tau]}{\Pr[\mathsf{T}_I=\tau]}$ for any $\tau \in \mathbf{T}_{\mathsf{good}}$. $\mathbf{T}_{\mathsf{good}}$ is defined so that no collision corresponding with the outer functions occurs. The definition ensures that all outputs of HtE are independently defined. Using this fact, we lower-bound the ratio by 1.

6.2 Definition

Let u be the number of users. For $\nu \in [u]$, let q_ν be the number of construction queries to the ν-th user. Let K_ν (resp. L_ν) be the BC (resp. hash) key of the ν-th user. For $\alpha \in [p]$, the α-th primitive query-response tuple is denoted by $(W^{(\alpha)}, X^{(\alpha)}, Y^{(\alpha)})$, where $Y^{(\alpha)} = E(W^{(\alpha)}, X^{(\alpha)})$ if the query is a forward one and $X^{(\alpha)} = E^{-1}(W^{(\alpha)}, Y^{(\alpha)})$ if the query is an inverse one. For $\alpha \in [q]$, values (including the user's key) in the α-th construction query is denoted by using the symbol (α), e.g. $M^{(\alpha)}$, $T^{(\alpha)}$, etc. The user number of the α-th construction query is denoted by ν_α, and $V^{(\alpha)} := H^E_{L^{(\alpha)}}(M^{(\alpha)})$. Note that $K^{(\alpha)} = K_{\nu_\alpha}$ and $L^{(\alpha)} = L_{\nu_\alpha}$. For $\alpha \in [q]$, let $\mathcal{H}^{(\alpha)}$ the set of input-output tuples of E defined in the process of $H^E_{L^{(\alpha)}}(M^{(\alpha)})$. Let $\mathcal{H} := \cup_{\alpha \in [q]} \mathcal{H}^{(\alpha)}$.

The stage that an adversary makes queries is called "query stage", and the stage after the query stage "decision stage".

6.3 Adversary's View

This proof permits an adversary to obtain user's keys $\{(K_\nu, L_\nu) \mid \nu \in [u]\}$, hash values $\{V^{(\alpha)} \mid \alpha \in [q]\}$, and IC's input-output tuples in $\mathcal{H}$ in the decision stage.

In the ideal world, for each $\nu \in [u]$, the user's keys are defined as $(K_\nu, L_\nu) \xleftarrow{\$} \{0,1\}^k \times \mathcal{L}$ in the decision stage. Using the user's keys, hash values are defined as $V^{(\alpha)} := H^E_{L^{(\alpha)}}(M^{(\alpha)})$. Hence, an adversary obtains the following tuples before outputting a decision bit:

- primitive query-response tuples $\{(W^{(\alpha)}, X^{(\alpha)}, Y^{(\alpha)}) \mid \alpha \in [p]\}$,
- construction query-response tuples $\{(M^{(\alpha)}, T^{(\alpha)}) \mid \alpha \in [q]\}$,
- user's keys $\{(K_\nu, L_\nu) \mid \nu \in [u]\}$,
- $\mathcal{H}$: all input-output tuples of E defined in the processes of the hash function, and
- hash values $\{V^{(\alpha)} \mid \alpha \in [q]\}$.

6.4 Good and Bad Transcripts

We define bad events below.

- bad_1: $\exists \alpha, \beta \in [q]$ s.t. $\alpha \neq \beta \wedge (K^{(\alpha)}, V^{(\alpha)}) = (K^{(\beta)}, V^{(\beta)})$.
  This event defines a collision in pairs of key and input block of E in the outer function.
- bad_2: $\exists \alpha, \beta \in [q]$ s.t. $\alpha \neq \beta \wedge (K^{(\alpha)}, T^{(\alpha)}) = (K^{(\beta)}, T^{(\beta)})$.
  This event defines a collision in pairs of key and output block of E in the outer function.
- bad_3: $\exists \alpha \in [q], Z \in \{0,1\}^n$ s.t. $(K^{(\alpha)}, V^{(\alpha)}, Z) \in \mathcal{H} \vee (K^{(\alpha)}, Z, T^{(\alpha)}) \in \mathcal{H}$.
  This event considers collisions in pairs of key and input/output block between the hash function and the outer one.
- bad_4: $\exists \alpha \in [q], \beta \in [p]$ s.t. $(K^{(\alpha)}, V^{(\alpha)}) = (W^{(\beta)}, X^{(\beta)})$.
  This event defines a collision between pairs of key and input block of E defined by the outer function and by primitive queries.
- bad_5: $\exists \alpha \in [q], \beta \in [p]$ s.t. $(K^{(\alpha)}, T^{(\alpha)}) = (W^{(\beta)}, Y^{(\beta)})$.
  This event defines a collision between pairs of key and output block of E defined by the outer function and by primitive queries.

Let $\mathsf{bad} := \vee_{i \in [5]} \mathsf{bad}_i$.

Then, $\mathbf{T}_{\mathsf{bad}}$ is a set of transcripts that satisfy bad, and $\mathbf{T}_{\mathsf{good}} := \mathbf{T} \backslash \mathbf{T}_{\mathsf{bad}}$.

6.5 Upper-Bounding $\Pr[\mathsf{T}_I \in \mathbf{T}_{\mathsf{bad}}]$

In this analysis, we use the following μ-multi-collision event for tags.

- bad_6: $\exists \alpha_1, \ldots, \alpha_\mu \in [q]$ s.t. $\alpha_1, \ldots, \alpha_\mu$ are all distinct and $T^{(\alpha_1)} = \cdots = T^{(\alpha_\mu)}$.

Fixing $\alpha_1, \ldots, \alpha_\mu \in [q]$, each of μ outputs $T^{(\alpha_1)}, \ldots, T^{(\alpha_\mu)}$ is chosen uniformly at random from $\{0,1\}^n$, and we have $\Pr[T^{(\alpha_1)} = \cdots = T^{(\alpha_\mu)}] \leq \left(\frac{1}{2^n}\right)^{\mu-1}$. Hence, we have $\Pr[\mathsf{bad}_6] \leq \binom{q}{\mu}\left(\frac{1}{2^n}\right)^{\mu-1} \leq 2^n \left(\frac{eq}{\mu 2^n}\right)^\mu$ by Stirling's approximation ($\mu! \geq (\mu/e)^\mu$ for any μ).

For each $i \in [5]$, we upper-bound $\Pr[\mathsf{bad}_i]$, the probability that bad_i occurs in the ideal world under the assumption that other bad events (including bad_6) do not occur. These probabilities are evaluated below, and the upper-bounds are given in Eqs. (2), (3), (4), (5), and (6). Using the bounds, we have

$$\Pr[\mathsf{T}_I \in \mathbf{T}_{\mathsf{bad}}] \leq \sum_{i \in [6]} \Pr[\mathsf{bad}_i] \leq \frac{0.5q^2\epsilon_1}{2^k} + 0.5q_u q\epsilon_2 + \frac{0.5q^2}{2^{n+k}} + \frac{0.5qq_u}{2^n} + \frac{0.5\ell q^2\epsilon_1 + \mu\ell q}{2^k} + \frac{pq\epsilon_1}{2^k} + \frac{(\mu-1)p}{2^k} + 2^n\left(\frac{eq}{\mu 2^n}\right)^{\mu}.$$

Choosing the parameter $\mu = C_n (= \frac{n}{\log_2 n})$, and assuming $\epsilon_1, \epsilon_2 \geq 1/2^n$ and $p \leq 2^k$, we have

$$\Pr[\mathsf{T}_I \in \mathbf{T}_{\mathsf{bad}}] \leq q_u q\epsilon_2 + \frac{C_n(p+\ell q) + (pq + \ell q^2)\epsilon_1}{2^k} + \left(\frac{eD_n q}{2^n}\right)^{C_n}. \tag{1}$$

Upper-Bounding Pr[bad₁]. The bad event bad_1 implies that $\exists \alpha, \beta \in [q]$ s.t. $\alpha \neq \beta \wedge (K^{(\alpha)}, V^{(\alpha)}) = (K^{(\beta)}, V^{(\beta)})$.

- For each $\alpha, \beta \in [q]$ such that $\alpha \neq \beta$ and $\nu_\alpha \neq \nu_\beta$, the collision $V^{(\alpha)} = V^{(\beta)}$ implies that the regular property is broken, and the key collision probability is at most $\frac{1}{2^k}$. We thus have $\Pr[(K^{(\alpha)}, V^{(\alpha)}) = (K^{(\beta)}, V^{(\beta)})] \leq \frac{\epsilon_1}{2^k}$.
- For each $\alpha, \beta \in [q]$ such that $\alpha \neq \beta$ and $\nu_\alpha = \nu_\beta$, the collision $V^{(\alpha)} = V^{(\beta)}$ implies that the AXU property is broken, and thus we have $\Pr[(K^{(\alpha)}, V^{(\alpha)}) = (K^{(\beta)}, V^{(\beta)})] \leq \epsilon_2$.

Using these bounds,[8] we have

$$\Pr[\mathsf{bad}_1] = \Pr[\mathsf{bad}_1 \wedge \nu_\alpha \neq \nu_\beta] + \Pr[\mathsf{bad}_1 \wedge \nu_\alpha = \nu_\beta] \leq \binom{q}{2} \cdot \frac{\epsilon_1}{2^k} + \sum_{\nu \in [u]} \binom{q_\nu}{2} \cdot \epsilon_2$$

$$\leq \frac{0.5q^2\epsilon_1}{2^k} + \sum_{\nu \in [u]} 0.5q_\nu^2\epsilon_2 \leq \frac{0.5q^2\epsilon_1}{2^k} + 0.5q_u q\epsilon_2. \tag{2}$$

Upper-Bounding Pr[bad₂]. For each $\alpha, \beta \in [q]$ such that $\alpha < \beta$,

- if $\nu_\alpha = \nu_\beta$, then we have $\Pr[(K^{(\alpha)}, T^{(\alpha)}) = (K^{(\beta)}, T^{(\beta)})] \leq \frac{1}{2^n}$, and
- if $\nu_\alpha \neq \nu_\beta$, then we have $\Pr[(K^{(\alpha)}, T^{(\alpha)}) = (K^{(\beta)}, T^{(\beta)})] \leq \frac{1}{2^{n+k}}$.

Using the bounds, we have

$$\Pr[\mathsf{bad}_2] \leq \binom{q}{2} \cdot \frac{1}{2^{n+k}} + \sum_{\nu \in [u]} \binom{q_\nu}{2} \cdot \frac{1}{2^n} \frac{0.5q^2}{2^{n+k}} + \frac{0.5q_u q}{2^n}. \tag{3}$$

[8] We can derive the bounds of $\Pr[\mathsf{bad}_1 \wedge \nu_\alpha \neq \nu_\beta]$ and of $\Pr[\mathsf{bad}_1 \wedge \nu_\alpha = \nu_\beta]$ by another way that is a reduction from bad_1 to the (IC-based) AXU or regular property.

Upper-Bounding Pr[bad_3]. In this evaluation, we consider the following events, where $\mathsf{bad}_3 = \mathsf{bad}_{3,1} \vee \mathsf{bad}_{3,2} \vee \mathsf{bad}_{3,3}$.

- $\mathsf{bad}_{3,1} := \Big(\exists \alpha, \beta \in [q], Z \in \{0,1\}^n \text{ s.t. } (\nu_\alpha = \nu_\beta) \wedge \big((K^{(\alpha)}, V^{(\alpha)}, Z) \in \mathcal{H}^{(\beta)} \vee (K^{(\alpha)}, Z, T^{(\alpha)}) \in \mathcal{H}^{(\beta)}\big)\Big)$,
- $\mathsf{bad}_{3,2} := \Big(\exists \alpha, \beta \in [q], Z \in \{0,1\}^n \text{ s.t. } (\nu_\alpha \neq \nu_\beta) \wedge \big((K^{(\alpha)}, V^{(\alpha)}, Z) \in \mathcal{H}^{(\beta)}\big)\Big)$, and
- $\mathsf{bad}_{3,3} := \Big(\exists \alpha, \beta \in [q], Z \in \{0,1\}^n \text{ s.t. } (\nu_\alpha \neq \nu_\beta) \wedge \big((K^{(\alpha)}, Z, T^{(\alpha)}) \in \mathcal{H}^{(\beta)}\big)\Big)$.

We evaluate $\Pr[\mathsf{bad}_{3,1}]$, $\Pr[\mathsf{bad}_{3,2}]$, and $\Pr[\mathsf{bad}_{3,3}]$ below.

Firstly, we evaluate $\Pr[\mathsf{bad}_{3,1}]$. If the event occurs, for some user number $\nu \in [u]$, K_ν is equal to one of the IC's keys in L_ν. The number of the IC's keys is at most ℓ. Thus, the collision probability is at most $\frac{\ell}{2^k}$, and we have $\Pr[\mathsf{bad}_{3,1}] \leq \frac{\ell u}{2^k}$.

Secondly, we evaluate $\Pr[\mathsf{bad}_{3,2}]$. If $\mathsf{bad}_{3,2}$ occurs, some hash value $V^{(\alpha)}$ collides with some value in $\mathcal{H}^{(\beta)}$, and thus the regular property of the hash function H is broken. For each distinct values $\alpha, \beta \in [q]$, the probability that $K^{(\alpha)}$ is equal to one of the keys elements in $\mathcal{H}^{(\beta)}$ is at most $\frac{\ell}{2^k}$, as $|\mathcal{H}^{(\beta)}| \leq \ell$. We thus have $\Pr[\mathsf{bad}_{3,2}] \leq \binom{q}{2} \frac{\ell}{2^k} \cdot \epsilon_1 \leq \frac{0.5\ell q^2 \epsilon_1}{2^k}$.[9]

Thirdly, we evaluate $\Pr[\mathsf{bad}_{3,3}]$. For each element $(K^*, X^*, Y^*) \in \mathcal{H}$, the number of tags that equal Y^* is at most $\mu - 1$ by $\neg\mathsf{bad}_6$, and thus there are at most $\mu - 1$ keys of the outer function whose tags are equal to Y^*. Since $|\mathcal{H}| \leq \ell q$, we have $\Pr[\mathsf{bad}_{3,3}] \leq \frac{\ell q(\mu-1)}{2^k}$.

Using these bounds, we have

$$\Pr[\mathsf{bad}_3] \leq \frac{\ell u + 0.5\ell q^2 \epsilon_1 + (\mu - 1)\ell q}{2^k} \leq \frac{0.5\ell q^2 \epsilon_1 + \mu \ell q}{2^k}. \quad (4)$$

Upper-Bound of Pr[bad_4]. Recall the bad event bad_4: $\exists \alpha \in [q], \beta \in [p]$ s.t. $(K^{(\alpha)}, V^{(\alpha)}) = (W^{(\beta)}, X^{(\beta)})$. The collision $V^{(\alpha)} = X^{(\beta)}$ implies that the regular property is broken.[10] The probability that the key collision $K^{(\alpha)} = W^{(\beta)}$ occurs is at most $\frac{1}{2^k}$. We thus have

$$\Pr[\mathsf{bad}_4] \leq \frac{pq\epsilon_1}{2^k}. \quad (5)$$

Upper-Bound of Pr[bad_5]. First, we fix $\beta \in [p]$. By $\neg\mathsf{bad}_6$, for each primitive query-response tuple $(W^{(\beta)}, X^{(\beta)}, Y^{(\beta)})$, the number of construction query-response tuples whose tags are equal to $Y^{(\beta)}$ is at most $\mu - 1$. Thus, the number of keys with the tag $Y^{(\beta)}$ is at most $\mu - 1$, and the probability that $W^{(\beta)}$ is equal to one of the $(\mu - 1)$ user's keys is at most $\frac{\mu-1}{2^k}$.

[9] As the evaluation of $\Pr[\mathsf{bad}_1]$, we can derive the bound of $\Pr[\mathsf{bad}_{3,2}]$ by a reduction from $\mathsf{bad}_{3,2}$ to the (IC-based) regular property.

[10] As the evaluation of $\Pr[\mathsf{bad}_1]$, we can derive the bound of $\Pr[\mathsf{bad}_4]$ by a reduction from bad_4 to the (IC-based) regular property.

Summing the bound for each β, we have

$$\Pr[\mathsf{bad}_5] \le \frac{(\mu-1)p}{2^k}. \tag{6}$$

6.6 Lower-Bounding $\Pr[\mathsf{T}_R = \tau]/\Pr[\mathsf{T}_I = \tau]$ for $\tau \in \mathbf{T}_{\mathsf{good}}$

Fix a good transcript $\tau \in \mathbf{T}_{\mathsf{good}}$, which consists of the set of user's keys τ_K, the set of primitive query-response tuples τ_{prim}, the set of IC's input-output tuples defined in the hash function τ_H, the set of hash values τ_V, and the set of construction query-response tuples τ_{const}. For a set τ', let $\mathsf{T}_R \vdash \tau'$ (resp. $\mathsf{T}_I \vdash \tau'$) be an event that T_R (resp. T_I) satisfies all elements in τ'.

Firstly, we evaluate the probabilities for τ_K, $\Pr[\mathsf{T}_R \vdash \tau_K]$ and $\Pr[\mathsf{T}_I \vdash \tau_K]$. In both worlds, for each $\nu \in [u]$, the ν-th user's keys K_ν and L_ν are chosen uniformly at random from $\{0,1\}^k$ and $\mathcal{L}$, respectively. Hence, we have $\Pr[\mathsf{T}_R \vdash \tau_K] = \Pr[\mathsf{T}_I \vdash \tau_K]$. Hereafter, we assume that $\mathsf{T}_R \vdash \tau_K$ and $\mathsf{T}_I \vdash \tau_K$ are satisfied.

Secondly, we evaluate the probabilities for τ_{prim}, $\Pr[\mathsf{T}_R \vdash \tau_{\mathsf{prim}}]$ and $\Pr[\mathsf{T}_I \vdash \tau_{\mathsf{prim}}]$. In both worlds, responses to the primitive queries are chosen by an IC. Hence, we have $\Pr[\mathsf{T}_R \vdash \tau_{\mathsf{prim}}] = \Pr[\mathsf{T}_I \vdash \tau_{\mathsf{prim}}]$. Hereafter, we assume that $\mathsf{T}_R \vdash \tau_{\mathsf{prim}}$ and $\mathsf{T}_I \vdash \tau_{\mathsf{prim}}$ are satisfied.

Thirdly, we evaluate the probabilities for τ_H, $\Pr[\mathsf{T}_R \vdash \tau_H]$ and $\Pr[\mathsf{T}_I \vdash \tau_H]$. In both worlds, output blocks defined in the hash function are chosen by an IC. Hence, we have $\Pr[\mathsf{T}_R \vdash \tau_H] = \Pr[\mathsf{T}_I \vdash \tau_H]$. Hereafter, we assume that $\mathsf{T}_R \vdash \tau_H$ and $\mathsf{T}_I \vdash \tau_H$ are satisfied.

Fourthly, we evaluate the probabilities for τ_V, $\Pr[\mathsf{T}_R \vdash \tau_V]$ and $\Pr[\mathsf{T}_I \vdash \tau_V]$. In both worlds, by $\mathsf{T}_R \vdash \tau_{\mathcal{H}}$ and $\mathsf{T}_I \vdash \tau_{\mathcal{H}}$, we have $\Pr[\mathsf{T}_R \vdash \tau_V] = \Pr[\mathsf{T}_I \vdash \tau_V]$. Hereafter, we assume that $\mathsf{T}_R \vdash \tau_V$ and $\mathsf{T}_I \vdash \tau_V$ are satisfied.

Fifthly, we evaluate the probabilities for τ_{const}, $\Pr[\mathsf{T}_R \vdash \tau_{\mathsf{const}}]$ and $\Pr[\mathsf{T}_I \vdash \tau_{\mathsf{const}}]$. By $\neg\mathsf{bad}_2$, for each user, the tags are all distinct. In the ideal world, for each $\alpha \in [q]$, the response to the α-th construction query is chosen uniformly at random from $\{0,1\}^n$. In the real world, for each $\alpha \in [q]$, by $\neg\mathsf{bad}$, the input $(K^{(\alpha)}, V^{(\alpha)})$ is new, and thus the output $T^{(\alpha)}$ is chosen from $\{0,1\}^n$ excluding the previous outputs of E with the key $K^{(\alpha)}$. Hence, we have $\Pr[\mathsf{T}_R \vdash \tau_{\mathsf{const}}] \ge \Pr[\mathsf{T}_I \vdash \tau_{\mathsf{const}}]$.

Finally, we have

$$\begin{aligned}
&\frac{\Pr[\mathsf{T}_R = \tau]}{\Pr[\mathsf{T}_I = \tau]} \\
&= \frac{\Pr[\mathsf{T}_R \vdash \tau_K] \cdot \Pr[\mathsf{T}_R \vdash \tau_{\mathsf{prim}}] \cdot \Pr[\mathsf{T}_R \vdash \tau_H] \cdot \Pr[\mathsf{T}_R \vdash \tau_V] \cdot \Pr[\mathsf{T}_R \vdash \tau_{\mathsf{const}}]}{\Pr[\mathsf{T}_I \vdash \tau_K] \cdot \Pr[\mathsf{T}_I \vdash \tau_{\mathsf{prim}}] \cdot \Pr[\mathsf{T}_I \vdash \tau_H] \cdot \Pr[\mathsf{T}_I \vdash \tau_V] \cdot \Pr[\mathsf{T}_I \vdash \tau_{\mathsf{const}}]} \\
&\ge 1.
\end{aligned} \tag{7}$$

6.7 Conclusion of the Proof

By using the bounds in Eqs. (1) and (7), we obtain the bound in Theorem 1.

7 Proof of Theorem 3 (Proof for CBC)

In the following proof, we evaluate an AXU bound ϵ_2. Since $\epsilon_1 \leq \epsilon_2$, we can obtain the regular bound ϵ_1 from the AXU bound. The bound comes from the relation $\mathsf{CBC}[E_L](M) = Y \Leftrightarrow \mathsf{CBC}[E_L](M\|0^n) \oplus \mathsf{CBC}[E_L](Y) = 0^n$.

7.1 Notations

Let $(M^{(1)}, M^{(2)}, Z)$ be an **A**'s output. Without loss of generality, we assume that $|M^{(1)}| \geq |M^{(2)}|$ and if $M^{(2)} \neq \varepsilon$ then $M^{(2)}$ is not a suffix of $M^{(1)}$.[11] Values corresponding with $M^{(1)}$ (resp. $M^{(2)}$) are denoted by using the symbol (1) (resp. (2)), and the length m is denoted by m_1 (resp. m_2). Hence, $M^{(\alpha)} = M_1^{(\alpha)}\|\cdots\|M_{m_\alpha}^{(\alpha)}$ for $\alpha \in [2]$, and $(L, U_i^{(\alpha)}, V_i^{(\alpha)})$ is the i-th input-output tuple in the process of $\mathsf{CBC}[E_L](M^{(\alpha)})$. For $i \leq j$ and $\alpha \in [2]$, let $M_{i,j}^{(\alpha)} := M_i^{(\alpha)}\|M_{i+1}^{(\alpha)}\|\cdots\|M_j^{(\alpha)}$. For convenience, if $i > j$, $M_{i,j}^{(\alpha)} := \varepsilon$. Let $\mathcal{Q}_{\mathsf{prim}}^F$ (resp. $\mathcal{Q}_{\mathsf{prim}}^I$) be the set of forward (resp. inverse) query-response tuples. Let $\mathcal{Q}_{\mathsf{prim}} := \mathcal{Q}_{\mathsf{prim}}^F \cup \mathcal{Q}_{\mathsf{prim}}^I$ be the set of primitive query-response tuples. We denote a primitive query-response tuple by (W, X, Y) (with some indexes), where $Y = E(W, X)$ if the query is a forward one; $X = E^{-1}(W, Y)$ if the query is an inverse one. Let $p_1 := |\mathcal{Q}_{\mathsf{prim}}^F|$ and $p_2 := |\mathcal{Q}_{\mathsf{prim}}^I|$.

7.2 Super Query

In the this proof, we use the technique given in [1], which allows an adversary to make additional queries called super queries. The super queries ensure the randomnesses of IC's outputs.

Definition 3 (Super queries). *For a key element W of an IC, after* **A** *makes 2^{n-1} queries with W to E or E^{-1}, we permit an adversary* **A** *to obtain the remaining input-output tuples of E with W, i.e.,* **A** *obtains all input-output tuples with W. The additional queries, which we call super queries.*

The super queries ensure that the outputs of E or E^{-1} are chosen uniformly at random from 2^{n-1} elements in $\{0,1\}^n$. Specifically, fixing Y^*, for a super query (W, X), the probability that the output Y is equal to Y^* is $\frac{(2^{n-1}-1)!}{(2^{n-1})!} = \frac{1}{2^{n-1}}$. Without loss of generality, super queries are forward ones. By the super queries, we have $|\mathcal{Q}_{\mathsf{prim}}| \leq 2p$.

[11] If $M^{(2)}$ is a suffix of $M^{(1)}$ and $Z = 0^n$, then the condition that **A** wins becomes $\mathsf{CBC}[E_L](M_1^{(1)}\|\cdots\|M_{m_1-m_2}^{(1)}) \oplus \mathsf{CBC}[E_L](\varepsilon) = 0^n$.

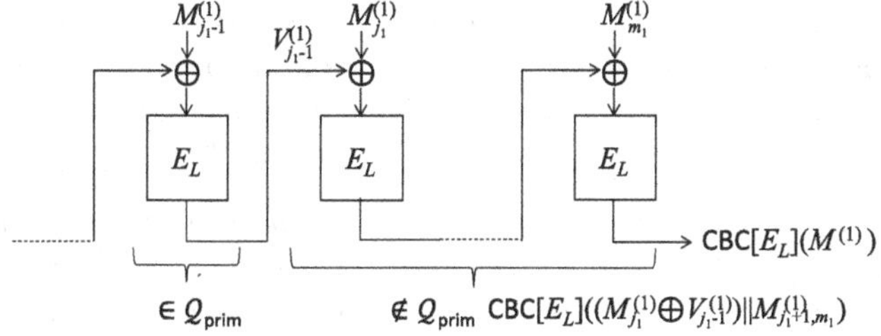

Fig. 3. Structure of $\mathsf{CBC}[E_L]((M_{j_1}^{(1)} \oplus V_{j_1-1}^{(1)}) \| M_{j_1+1,m_1}^{(1)})$.

7.3 The Upper-Bound ϵ_2

We use the following events. The first event is that **A** breaks the AXU property of CBC. The second one is that in the CBC evaluations, one of the last blocks is fresh. The third event is that some output block in the CBC evaluations connects with some primitive query with the key L. The last event is that all blocks of the CBC evaluations are not fresh.

- coll : $\mathsf{CBC}[E_L](M^{(1)}) \oplus \mathsf{CBC}[E_L](M^{(2)}) = Z$.
- **E1**: $(L, U_{m_1}^{(1)}, V_{m_1}^{(1)}) \notin \mathcal{Q}_{\mathsf{prim}} \vee (L, U_{m_2}^{(2)}, V_{m_2}^{(2)}) \notin \mathcal{Q}_{\mathsf{prim}}$.
- **E2**: $\exists \alpha \in [2], i \in [m_\alpha - 1]$ s.t. $(L, U_i^{(\alpha)}, V_i^{(\alpha)}) \notin \mathcal{Q}_{\mathsf{prim}} \wedge (L, U_{i+1}^{(\alpha)}, V_{i+1}^{(\alpha)}) \in \mathcal{Q}_{\mathsf{prim}}$.
- **E3**: $\forall i \in [m_1] : (L, U_i^{(1)}, V_i^{(1)}) \in \mathcal{Q}_{\mathsf{prim}} \wedge \forall i \in [m_2] : (L, U_i^{(2)}, V_i^{(2)}) \in \mathcal{Q}_{\mathsf{prim}}$.

Since coll $=$ coll $\wedge$ (**E1** $\vee$ **E2** $\vee$ **E3**), we have

$$\Pr[\mathsf{coll}] \leq \Pr[\mathsf{coll} \mid \mathbf{E1}] + \Pr[\mathbf{E2}] + \Pr[\mathsf{coll} \wedge \mathbf{E3}].$$

These probabilities are evaluated in Sects. 7.4, 7.5, and 7.6. The bounds are given in Eqs. (9), (10) and (11). Using the bounds, for any $\mu > 0$, we have

$$\Pr[\mathsf{coll}] \leq \frac{16\ell}{2^n} + \frac{\mu - 1}{2^k} + 2^{n-1}(2p)^{2(\ell+1)} \left(\frac{2ep}{\mu 2^n}\right)^{\mu}.$$

By using the parameter $\mu = 3\lceil 2^{k-n} \rceil \cdot \max\{k, n\} \cdot (\ell + 1)$ and assuming $p \leq 2^k$, we have

$$\epsilon_2 = \frac{16\ell}{2^n} + \frac{3\max\{k,n\} \cdot (\ell+1)}{2^{\min\{n,k\}}} + \left(\frac{4}{\ell+1} \cdot \frac{p}{2^k}\right)^{\max\{k,n\}(\ell+1)}.$$

7.4 Upper-Bounding Pr[coll | E1]

We first evaluate the probability $\Pr[\mathsf{coll} \wedge (L, U_{m_1}^{(1)}, V_{m_1}^{(1)}) \notin \mathcal{Q}_{\mathsf{prim}}]$. Let $j_1 := \max\left\{j \in [2, m_1] \mid (L, U_{j-1}^{(1)}, V_{j-1}^{(1)}) \in \mathcal{Q}_{\mathsf{prim}} \wedge (L, U_j^{(1)}, V_j^{(i)}) \notin \mathcal{Q}_{\mathsf{prim}}\right\}$. If $\forall i \in [m_1] : (L, U_i^{(1)}, V_i^{(1)}) \notin \mathcal{Q}_{\mathsf{prim}}$, then $j_1 := 1$. Using the parameter, we have

$$\mathsf{coll} \Leftrightarrow \mathsf{CBC}[E_L]((M_{j_1}^{(1)} \oplus V_{j_1-1}^{(1)}) \| M_{j_1+1,m_1}^{(1)}) \oplus \mathsf{CBC}[E_L](M_{1,m_2}^{(2)}) = Z. \quad (8)$$

The process of $\mathsf{CBC}[E_L]((M^{(1)}_{j_1} \oplus V^{(1)}_{j_1-1}) \| M^{(1)}_{j_1+1,m_1})$ is given in Fig. 3. Hence, we can use the following AXU bound of CBC in the random permutation model. Several works such as [5,22] showed the same AXU bounds (except for constants). The following bound can be obtained by the same proof.

Lemma 2. *Let π be an n-bit permutation such that each output is chosen uniformly at random from $\mathbf{N} \subseteq \{0,1\}^n$ without replacement. For any $Z \in \{0,1\}^n$ and any pair of distinct messages $(M^{(1)}, M^{(1)})$ of length at most ℓ blocks, we have* $\Pr[\mathsf{CBC}[\pi](M^{(1)}) \oplus \mathsf{CBC}[\pi](M^{(2)}) = Z] \leq \frac{2(\ell-1)}{|\mathbf{N}|-2\ell} + \frac{\ell(\ell-1)(\ell-2)^2}{6(|\mathbf{N}|-2\ell)^2}$.

The input-output pairs in the process of $\mathsf{CBC}[E_L]((M^{(1)}_{j_1} \oplus V^{(1)}_{j_1-1}) \| M^{(1)}_{j_1+1,m_1})$ are not in $\mathcal{Q}_{\mathsf{prim}}$, and thus are defined by non-super queries. Hence, these outputs are respectively chosen uniformly at random from at least $2^{n-1} - 2\ell \geq 2^{n-2}$ elements, assuming $\ell \leq 2^{n-3}$. We also assume that $\ell \leq 2^{n/3}$. We then have

$$\Pr[\mathsf{coll} \mid (L, U^{(1)}_{m_1}, V^{(1)}_{m_1}) \notin \mathcal{Q}_{\mathsf{prim}}] \leq \frac{4\ell}{2^n}.$$

Regarding $\Pr[\mathsf{coll} \mid (L, U^{(2)}_{m_2}, V^{(2)}_{m_2}) \notin \mathcal{Q}_{\mathsf{prim}}]$, the evaluation is the same as the above one. We thus have

$$\Pr[\mathsf{coll} \mid (L, U^{(2)}_{m_2}, V^{(2)}_{m_2}) \notin \mathcal{Q}_{\mathsf{prim}}] \leq \frac{4\ell}{2^n}.$$

Using these bounds, we have

$$\Pr[\mathsf{coll} \mid \mathbf{E1}] \leq \frac{8\ell}{2^n}. \tag{9}$$

7.5 Upper-Bounding Pr[E2]

We consider the following events **E21** and **E22** such that $\mathbf{E2} = \mathbf{E21} \vee \mathbf{E22}$.

- **E21**: $\exists i \in [m_1 - 1]$ s.t. $(L, U^{(1)}_i, V^{(1)}_i) \notin \mathcal{Q}_{\mathsf{prim}} \wedge (L, U^{(1)}_{i+1}, V^{(1)}_{i+1}) \in \mathcal{Q}_{\mathsf{prim}}$.
- **E22**: $\exists i \in [m_2 - 1]$ s.t. $(L, U^{(2)}_i, V^{(2)}_i) \notin \mathcal{Q}_{\mathsf{prim}} \wedge (L, U^{(2)}_{i+1}, V^{(2)}_{i+1}) \in \mathcal{Q}_{\mathsf{prim}}$.

We first evaluate $\Pr[\mathbf{E21}]$. Fix $(W, X, Y) \in \mathcal{Q}_{\mathsf{prim}}$ and $i \in [m_1 - 1]$ such that $(L, U^{(1)}_i, V^{(1)}_i) \notin \mathcal{Q}_{\mathsf{prim}}$ (hence, the query for $(L, U^{(1)}_i, V^{(1)}_i)$ is not a super-query). We then consider the collision $(L, U^{(1)}_{i+1}, V^{(1)}_{i+1}) = (W, X, Y)$. By the randomnesses of L and $V^{(1)}_i$, we have $\Pr[W = L] \leq \frac{1}{2^k}$ and $\Pr[V^{(1)}_i \oplus M^{(1)}_{i+1} = X] \leq \frac{2}{2^n}$. These bounds give $\Pr\left[(L, U^{(1)}_{i+1}, V^{(1)}_{i+1}) = (W, X, Y)\right] \leq \frac{2}{2^{n+k}}$. Summing the bound $\frac{2}{2^{n+k}}$ for each i and (W, X, Y), we have

$$\Pr[\mathbf{E21}] \leq \frac{2\ell(2p)}{2^{n+k}} \leq \frac{4\ell}{2^n}, \text{ assuming } p \leq 2^k.$$

The evaluation of $\Pr[\mathbf{E22}]$ is the same as that of $\Pr[\mathbf{E21}]$, and thus we have

$$\Pr[\mathbf{E2}] \leq \frac{8\ell}{2^n}. \tag{10}$$

7.6 Upper-Bounding Pr[coll $\wedge$ E3]

Let $\mathcal{ML} \subseteq \{0,1\}^* \times \{0,1\}^k$ be the set of all possible pairs of message and key of CBC obtained from $\mathcal{Q}_{\mathsf{prim}}$, i.e., for any $(M', L') \in \mathcal{ML}$, all input-output tuples in the process of $\mathsf{CBC}[E_{L'}](M')$ are defined in $\mathcal{Q}_{\mathsf{prim}}$. Let $\mathcal{L} := \{L' \mid (M', L') \in \mathcal{ML}\}$ be all possible keys obtained from $\mathcal{Q}_{\mathsf{prim}}$. Let $\mathcal{M}^2\mathcal{L} := \{(M', M^*, L^*) \mid (M', L^*), (M^*, L^*) \in \mathcal{ML} \text{ s.t. } M' \neq M^*\}$. For $Z^* \in \{0,1\}^n$, and two distinct messages $M', M^* \in \{0,1\}^*$, we define a function $f_{M',M^*,Z^*} : \{0,1\}^k \to (\{0,1\}^n \cup \{\varepsilon\})$. For $L^* \in \{0,1\}^k$,

- if $(M', M^*, L^*) \in \mathcal{M}^2\mathcal{L}$, then $f_{M',M^*,Z^*}(L^*) := \mathsf{CBC}[E_{L^*}](M') \oplus \mathsf{CBC}[E_{L^*}](M^*) \oplus Z^*$, and
- otherwise $f_{M',M^*,Z^*}(L^*) := \varepsilon$.

Then, the event coll $\wedge$ **E3** implies that for the **A**'s output tuple $(M^{(1)}, M^{(2)}, Z)$, there exists $L^* \in \{0,1\}^k$ such that $(M^{(1)}, M^{(2)}, L^*) \in \mathcal{M}^2\mathcal{L}$, $f_{M^{(1)},M^{(2)},Z}(L^*) = 0^n$, and $L^* = L$.

We next introduce a threshold μ regarding the number of tuples (M', M^*, L_1^*, Z^*), $(M', M^*, L_2^*, Z^*), \ldots$, and consider the following event.

- μ-keys : $\exists L_1^*, \ldots, L_\mu^* \in \mathcal{L}, Z^* \in \{0,1\}^n$, $M', M^* \in \mathcal{M}$ s.t. $L_1^*, \ldots, L_\mu^*$ are all distinct, $M' \neq M^*$, and $\forall i \in [\mu] : f_{M',M^*,Z^*}(L_i^*) = 0^n$.

Using the event, we have Pr[coll$\wedge$**E3**] $\leq$ Pr[coll$\wedge$**E3** | $\neg\mu$-keys]+Pr[μ-keys]. These probabilities are evaluated below, and the upper-bounds are given in Eqs. (12) and (13). Using the bounds, we have

$$\Pr[\mathsf{coll} \wedge \mathbf{E3}] \leq \frac{\mu - 1}{2^k} + 2^{n-1}(2p)^{2(\ell+1)} \left(\frac{2ep}{\mu 2^n}\right)^{\mu}. \tag{11}$$

Evaluating Pr[coll $\wedge$ E3 | $\neg\mu$-keys]. Assuming that μ-keys does not occur, one can ensure that for any tuple (M', M^*, Z^*), the number of key candidates L_i^* such that $f_{M',M^*,Z^*}(L_i^*) = 0^n$ is at most $\mu - 1$. Then, coll $\wedge$ **E3** implies that for the **A**'s output tuple $(M^{(1)}, M^{(2)}, Z)$, there exists $(M^{(1)}, M^{(2)}, L^*) \in \mathcal{M}^2\mathcal{L}$ such that $f_{M^{(1)},M^{(2)},Z}(L^*) = 0^n$ and $L^* = L$. Hence, we have

$$\Pr[\mathsf{coll} \wedge \mathbf{E3} \mid \neg\mu\text{-keys}] \leq \frac{\mu - 1}{2^k}. \tag{12}$$

Evaluating Pr[μ-keys]. We first fix $(M', M^*, L_1^*) \in \mathcal{M}^2\mathcal{L}$ and other $(\mu - 1)$ key elements $L_2^*, \ldots, L_\mu^* \in \mathcal{L}$ such that $f_{M',M^*,Z^*}(L_1^*) = 0^n$, and evaluate the probability $\Pr[\forall i \in [2, \mu] : f_{M',M^*,Z^*}(L_i^*) = 0^n]$ where $Z^* = \mathsf{CBC}[E_{L_1^*}](M') \oplus \mathsf{CBC}[E_{L_1^*}](M^*)$. Let (L_i^*, U_j', V_j') and (L_i^*, U_j^*, V_j^*) be respectively the j-th input-output tuples of $\mathsf{CBC}[E_{L_i^*}](M')$ and of $\mathsf{CBC}[E_{L_i^*}](M^*)$, and m' and m^* respectively the block-lengths of M' and of M^*.

For each key candidate L_i^* where $i \in [2, \mu]$, if $f_{M',M^*,Z^*}(L_i^*) = 0^n$ is satisfied, then the internal values satisfy one of the following conditions.

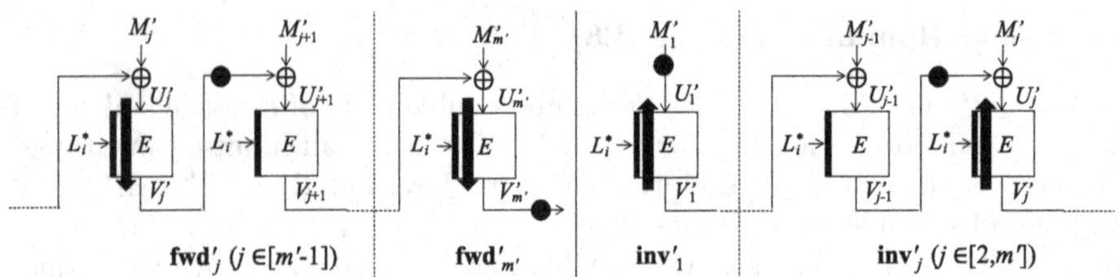

Fig. 4. Conditions $\mathbf{fwd}_j'$ ($j \in [m']$) (left) and $\mathbf{inv}_j'$ ($j \in [m']$) (right). The mark "•" shows the target value for each condition. The up (resp. down) arrows show that the outputs are defined by inverse (resp. forward) queries. When replacing the prime symbol with the asterisk symbol, the figure shows the conditions $\mathbf{fwd}_j^*$ ($j \in [m^*]$) (left) and $\mathbf{inv}_j^*$ ($j \in [m^*]$)s (right).

- $\mathbf{fwd}_j'$ (resp. $\mathbf{fwd}_j^*$) for $j \in [m']$: The j-th input-output tuple (L_i^*, U_j', V_j') (resp. (L_i^*, U_j^*, V_j^*)) is defined by a forward query before the other tuples used in the process of $f_{M',M^*,Z^*}(L_i^*)$ are defined.
- $\mathbf{inv}_j'$ (resp. $\mathbf{inv}_j^*$) for $j \in [m']$: The j-th input-output tuple (L_i^*, U_j', V_j') (resp. (L_i^*, U_j^*, V_j^*)) is defined by an inverse query before the other tuples used in the process of $f_{M',M^*,Z^*}(L_i^*)$ are defined.

Figure 4 shows these conditions.

For each key candidate L_i^* where $i \in [2, \mu]$ and each condition, we evaluate the probability that $f_{M',M^*,Z^*}(L_i^*) = 0^n$ is satisfied under the condition.

- Fixing $j \in [m']$, we evaluate the probability that $f_{M',M^*,Z^*}(L_i^*) = 0^n$ is satisfied under the condition that $\mathbf{fwd}_j'$ or $\mathbf{inv}_j'$ is satisfied. Since M', M^*, Z^*, and L_i^* are fixed,[12] the target value of V_j' (resp. U_j') is uniquely fixed before the j-th tuple is defined under the condition $\mathbf{fwd}_j'$ (resp. $\mathbf{inv}_j'$). Hence, the probability that V_j' (resp. U_j') is equal to the target value is at most $\frac{2}{2^n}$.
- Similarly, the probability that $f_{M',M^*,Z^*}(L_i^*) = 0^n$ is satisfied under the condition that $\mathbf{fwd}_j^*$ (resp. $\mathbf{inv}_j^*$) is at most $\frac{2}{2^n}$ (resp. $\frac{2}{2^n}$).

By the above bounds, we have $\Pr[\forall i \in [\mu] : f_{M',M^*,Z^*}(L_i^*) = 0^n] \le \left(\frac{2}{2^n}\right)^{\mu-1}$. Since $|\mathcal{M}^2\mathcal{L}| \le \left(\sum_{i\in[\ell]}(2p)^i\right)^2 \le (2p)^{2(\ell+1)}$,[13] and $|\mathcal{L}| \le p$, we have

$$\Pr[\mu\text{-}\mathsf{keys}] \le (2p)^{2(\ell+1)} \binom{p}{\mu} \left(\frac{2}{2^n}\right)^{\mu-1} \le 2^{n-1}(2p)^{2(\ell+1)} \left(\frac{2ep}{\mu 2^n}\right)^{\mu}, \qquad (13)$$

using Stirling's approximation ($x! \ge (x/e)^x$ for any x).

---

[12] When deriving the bound of $\Pr[\mu\text{-}\mathsf{keys}]$ in Eq. (13), all possible tuples for M', M^*, Z^*, and L_i^* are taken into account.

[13] The block lengths of M' and M' are respectively at most ℓ, and each input-output tuple is defined by forward or inverse query.

References

1. Armknecht, F., Fleischmann, E., Krause, M., Lee, J., Stam, M., Steinberger, J.: The preimage security of double-block-length compression functions. In: Lee, D.H., Wang, X. (eds.) ASIACRYPT 2011. LNCS, vol. 7073, pp. 233–251. Springer, Heidelberg (2011). https://doi.org/10.1007/978-3-642-25385-0_13
2. Bellare, M., Bernstein, D.J., Tessaro, S.: Hash-function based PRFs: AMAC and its multi-user security. In: Fischlin, M., Coron, J.-S. (eds.) EUROCRYPT 2016. LNCS, vol. 9665, pp. 566–595. Springer, Heidelberg (2016). https://doi.org/10.1007/978-3-662-49890-3_22
3. Bellare, M., Boldyreva, A., Micali, S.: Public-key encryption in a multi-user setting: security proofs and improvements. In: Preneel, B. (ed.) EUROCRYPT 2000. LNCS, vol. 1807, pp. 259–274. Springer, Heidelberg (2000). https://doi.org/10.1007/3-540-45539-6_18
4. Bellare, M., Kilian, J., Rogaway, P.: The security of cipher block chaining. In: Desmedt, Y.G. (ed.) CRYPTO 1994. LNCS, vol. 839, pp. 341–358. Springer, Heidelberg (1994). https://doi.org/10.1007/3-540-48658-5_32
5. Bellare, M., Pietrzak, K., Rogaway, P.: Improved security analyses for CBC MACs. In: Shoup, V. (ed.) CRYPTO 2005. LNCS, vol. 3621, pp. 527–545. Springer, Heidelberg (2005). https://doi.org/10.1007/11535218_32
6. Biham, E.: How to decrypt or even substitute DES-encrypted messages in 2^{28} steps. Inf. Process. Lett. **84**(3), 117–124 (2002)
7. Black, J., Rogaway, P.: CBC MACs for arbitrary-length messages: the three-key constructions. In: Bellare, M. (ed.) CRYPTO 2000. LNCS, vol. 1880, pp. 197–215. Springer, Heidelberg (2000). https://doi.org/10.1007/3-540-44598-6_12
8. Bose, P., Hoang, V.T., Tessaro, S.: Revisiting AES-GCM-SIV: multi-user security, faster key derivation, and better bounds. In: Nielsen, J.B., Rijmen, V. (eds.) EUROCRYPT 2018. LNCS, vol. 10820, pp. 468–499. Springer, Cham (2018). https://doi.org/10.1007/978-3-319-78381-9_18
9. Bosselaers, A., Preneel, B. (eds.): Integrity Primitives for Secure Information Systems. LNCS, vol. 1007. Springer, Heidelberg (1995). https://doi.org/10.1007/3-540-60640-8
10. Chakraborty, B., Chattopadhyay, S., Jha, A., Nandi, M.: On length independent security bounds for the PMAC family. IACR Trans. Symmetric Cryptol. **2021**(2), 423–445 (2021)
11. Chatterjee, S., Menezes, A., Sarkar, P.: Another look at tightness. In: Miri, A., Vaudenay, S. (eds.) SAC 2011. LNCS, vol. 7118, pp. 293–319. Springer, Heidelberg (2012). https://doi.org/10.1007/978-3-642-28496-0_18
12. Chattopadhyay, S., Jha, A., Nandi, M.: Towards tight security bounds for OMAC, XCBC and TMAC. In: Agrawal, S., Lin, D. (eds.) Advances in Cryptology – ASIACRYPT 2022. ASIACRYPT 2022. LNCS, vol. 13791, pp. 348–378. Springer, Cham (2022). https://doi.org/10.1007/978-3-031-22963-3_12
13. Datta, N., Dutta, A., Nandi, M., Talnikar, S.: Tight multi-user security bound of DbHtS. IACR Trans. Symmetric Cryptol. **2023**(1), 192–223 (2023)
14. Dworkin, M.J.: Recommendation for Block Cipher Modes of Operation: the CMAC Mode for Authentication. SP 800-38B (2005)
15. Dworkin, M.J.: Recommendation for block cipher modes of operation: the CMAC mode for authentication. Technical report, NIST, 2016. Supersedes SP 800-38B (2016)

16. Guo, T., Wang, P.: A note on the security framework of two-key dbhts macs. Cryptology ePrint Archive, Report 2022/375 (2022). https://ia.cr/2022/375
17. Hoang, V.T., Tessaro, S.: Key-alternating ciphers and key-length extension: exact bounds and multi-user security. In: Robshaw, M., Katz, J. (eds.) CRYPTO 2016. LNCS, vol. 9814, pp. 3–32. Springer, Heidelberg (2016). https://doi.org/10.1007/978-3-662-53018-4_1
18. Hoang, V.T., Tessaro, S.: The multi-user security of double encryption. In: Coron, J.-S., Nielsen, J.B. (eds.) EUROCRYPT 2017. LNCS, vol. 10211, pp. 381–411. Springer, Cham (2017). https://doi.org/10.1007/978-3-319-56614-6_13
19. Hoang, V.T., Tessaro, S., Thiruvengadam, A.: The multi-user security of GCM, revisited: tight bounds for nonce randomization. In: CCS 2018, pp. 1429–1440. ACM (2018)
20. ISO/IEC: Information Technology - Security Techniques - Message Authentication Codes (MACs) - Part 1: Mechanisms Using a Block Cipher. Technical report, ISO/IEC (2011)
21. Iwata, T., Kurosawa, K.: OMAC: one-key CBC MAC. In: Johansson, T. (ed.) FSE 2003. LNCS, vol. 2887, pp. 129–153. Springer, Heidelberg (2003). https://doi.org/10.1007/978-3-540-39887-5_11
22. Jha, A., Nandi, M.: Revisiting structure graphs: applications to CBC-MAC and EMAC. J. Math. Cryptol. **10**(3–4), 157–180 (2016)
23. Kurosawa, K., Iwata, T.: TMAC: two-key CBC MAC. In: Joye, M. (ed.) CT-RSA 2003. LNCS, vol. 2612, pp. 33–49. Springer, Heidelberg (2003). https://doi.org/10.1007/3-540-36563-X_3
24. Luykx, A., Mennink, B., Paterson, K.G.: Analyzing multi-key security degradation. In: Takagi, T., Peyrin, T. (eds.) ASIACRYPT 2017. LNCS, vol. 10625, pp. 575–605. Springer, Cham (2017). https://doi.org/10.1007/978-3-319-70697-9_20
25. Bellare, M., Tackmann, B.: The multi-user security of authenticated encryption: AES-GCM in TLS 1.3. In: Robshaw, M., Katz, J. (eds.) CRYPTO 2016. LNCS, vol. 9814, pp. 247–276. Springer, Heidelberg (2016). https://doi.org/10.1007/978-3-662-53018-4_10
26. Mouha, N., Luykx, A.: Multi-key security: the Even-Mansour construction revisited. In: Gennaro, R., Robshaw, M. (eds.) CRYPTO 2015. LNCS, vol. 9215, pp. 209–223. Springer, Heidelberg (2015). https://doi.org/10.1007/978-3-662-47989-6_10
27. Naito, Y.: Blockcipher-based MACs: beyond the birthday bound without message length. In: Takagi, T., Peyrin, T. (eds.) ASIACRYPT 2017. LNCS, vol. 10626, pp. 446–470. Springer, Cham (2017). https://doi.org/10.1007/978-3-319-70700-6_16
28. Naito, Y., Sasaki, Y., Sugawara, T., Yasuda, K.: The multi-user security of triple encryption, revisited: exact security, strengthening, and application to TDES. In: CCS 2022, pp. 2323–2336 (2022)
29. Nandi, M.: Improved security analysis for OMAC as a pseudorandom function. J. Math. Cryptol. **3**(2), 133–148 (2009)
30. NIST: FIPS 113, Computer data authentication. Federal Information Processing Standards Publication 113, U. S. Department of Commerce/National Bureau of Standards, National Technical Information Service, Springfield, Virginia (1985)
31. Patarin, J.: The coefficients H technique. In: Avanzi, R.M., Keliher, L., Sica, F. (eds.) SAC 2008. LNCS, vol. 5381, pp. 328–345. Springer, Heidelberg (2009). https://doi.org/10.1007/978-3-642-04159-4_21

32. Shen, Y., Wang, L., Gu, D., Weng, J.: Revisiting the security of DbHtS MACs: beyond-birthday-bound in the multi-user setting. In: Malkin, T., Peikert, C. (eds.) CRYPTO 2021. LNCS, vol. 12827, pp. 309–336. Springer, Cham (2021). https://doi.org/10.1007/978-3-030-84252-9_11
33. Shen, Y., Wang, L., Weng, J.: Revisiting the Security of DbHtS MACs: Beyond-Birthday-Bound in the Multi-User Setting. IACR Cryptol. ePrint Arch., p. 1523 (2020)
34. Wegman, M.N., Carter, L.: New hash functions and their use in authentication and set equality. J. Comput. Syst. Sci. **22**(3), 265–279 (1981)
35. Yasuda, K.: The sum of CBC MACs is a secure PRF. In: Pieprzyk, J. (ed.) CT-RSA 2010. LNCS, vol. 5985, pp. 366–381. Springer, Heidelberg (2010). https://doi.org/10.1007/978-3-642-11925-5_25
36. Yasuda, K.: A new variant of PMAC: beyond the birthday bound. In: Rogaway, P. (ed.) CRYPTO 2011. LNCS, vol. 6841, pp. 596–609. Springer, Heidelberg (2011). https://doi.org/10.1007/978-3-642-22792-9_34

Automated-Based Rebound Attacks on ACE Permutation

Jiali Shi[1(✉)], Guoqiang Liu[1(✉)], Chao Li[1], and Yingxin Li[2]

[1] College of Science, National University of Defense Technology, Changsha, China
jiali00@126.com, liuguoqiang87@hotmail.com
[2] Shanghai Key Laboratory of Trustworthy Computing,
East China Normal University, Shanghai, China

Abstract. ACE, a second-round candidate of the NIST Lightweight Cryptography Standardization project, is a 16-step iterative permutation that operates on a 320-bit state. It aims to optimize the software efficiency and hardware cost for authentication encryption (AE) mode and a hashing mode based on sufficient security margins. However, the security of such permutation has not been studied well so far. In this paper, an algorithm is used for searching rebound distinguishers of ACE permutation. By applying this algorithm, we obtained the first 14-step rebound attack on ACE permutation. The nonlinear function (ordinary represented as Sbox) of ACE permutation is based on 8 rounds unkeyed Simeck-64 abbreviated as SB-64. By constructing an SMT model, the lower bound on the number of active SB-64s for the differential characteristics of ACE has been verified. Then, by making use of SB-64's iterative differentials, we construct 128 11-step/13-step rebound distinguishers and 9 14-step rebound distinguishers for ACE permutation, the complexity of these rebound attacks was also discussed. All these attacks are the best ones so far, and this reduces the security margin of ACE permutation to 12.5%.

Keywords: NIST Lightweight cryptography · ACE permutation · Rebound Attack · SAT/SMT Model

1 Introduction

In the second round of the Lightweight Cryptography (LWC) Standardization project held by the NIST, sLiSCP [2], sLiSCP-light [3], and ACE [1] are designed based on the unkeyed Simeck to support both authenticated encryptions and hash functions. Simeck [30] is a family of lightweight block ciphers which combine the good design components from both Simon and Speck [4] to devise even more compact and efficient block ciphers. This type of permutation has a large state size and complicated step functions, making it difficult to crytanalysis. For example, 18-step sLiSCP-192/sLiSCP-256 permutation can be equivalent to 216/288 rounds of Simeck-48/Simeck-64. In SAC 2018, Liu *et al.* [17] attempted

E. Oswald (Ed.): CT-RSA 2024, LNCS 14643, pp. 78–111, 2024.
https://doi.org/10.1007/978-3-031-58868-6_4

to use MILP to find the 6-step differential characteristics of sLiSCP-192, but after 2,000,000 s, the solver has not yet completed the solution. However, ACE permutation supports 320 bits, and the total number of rounds of Simeck-64 used in the 16-step ACE permutation is as high as 384, which is more complex than sLiSCP permutation. There are difficulties in analyzing the security of ACE, and providing security analysis for the second round candidates of NIST LWC is also very significant.

Rebound attack, introduced by Mendel *et al.* [20] at FSE 2009, is a variant of differential attack. It is one of the most effective tools for the cryptanalysis of block cipher-based and permutations-based constructions. The idea of the rebound attack is to divide an attack into two phases: the inbound phase and the outbound phase. In the inbound phase, degrees of freedom are used to realize part of the differential deterministically. The remainder of the differentials in the outbound phase is fulfilled in a probabilistic manner. Following the target of the rebound attacks, Gilbert and Peyrin introduced Limited brithday distinguishers (LBD) to distinguish AES-like permutations from the ideal permutation in the known-key setting [8]. Subsequently, the understanding of LBD for the permutation continued to deepen [7,10,24]. Thanks to the framework of LBD, these studies [9,17] have applied rebound attacks on sLiSCP and sLiSCP-Light permutations. Since sLiSCP and sLiSCP-Light permutations are based on a Type-II generalized Feistel-like structure [5,25], which makes it easy to track the relationship between input and output differences, Liu *et al.* applied the iterative differentials of Simeck to construct the rebound distinguishers of sLiSCP permutation [17]. To improve these attacks, Hosoyamada *et al.* [9] reduced the complexity of the 15-step rebound attack for sLiSCP and provided the 16-step rebound attack for sLiSCP-256 with time complexity $2^{154.6}$, which cover one more step by improving the procedure for the inbound phase. In summary, according to the permutation's structure, it is fully possible to utilize the iterative differentials of Simeck to construct the rebound distinguishers of sLiSCP and sLiSCP-Light permutations. These methods can't be directly applied to ACE permutation, and how to construct a rebound distinguisher for ACE remains to be studied.

The designers provided various cryptanalysis on ACE permutation. They evaluated a lower bound of the number of active SB-64s without considering the internal information of SB-64, and provided 8-step integral distinguishers [1]. Shortly after, Liu *et al.* used the method of the characteristic matrix [27] to find 8-step impossible distinguishers and provided that there is no impossible differential distinguisher cover 9-step [16]. For a variant structure of ACE permutation, Ye *et al.* found 12-step word-oriented impossible differential distinguishers and integral distinguishers cover 12-step [31]. Therefore, the security evaluation of ACE permutation needs further improvement.

Our Contributions. In this paper, we proposed an algorithm to derive the rebound distinguisher for ACE permutation and found the first 14 steps rebound attack on ACE permutation. In a nutshell, our contributions are as follows.

- By adding the internal information of SB-64, we verified the lower bound on the number of active SB-64s with the help of the SMT/SAT model. In

Table 1. A summary of attacks on ACE

Type of Attack	Steps	Num	Data	Time	Memory	Ref
Integral attack	8	–	–	–	–	[1]
	12⋆	–	–	–	–	[31]
Impossible differential attack	8	–	–	–	–	[16]
	12⋆	–	–	–	–	[31]
Rebound attack	11 (1+3+7)	128	N/A	$2^{167.80}$	2^{64}	Sect. 5
	13 (2+4+7)	128	N/A	$2^{134.17}$	2^{64}	Sect. 5
	14 (3+4+7)	9	N/A	$2^{152.36}$	2^{64}	Sect. 5

⋆ The permutation analyzed in the paper is a variant structure of ACE permutation.

addition, we provide the optimal probability of the first 5-step differential characteristics.

- Based on the found differential characteristics, a new algorithm proposed is used to search for the rebound distinguisher of ACE permutation. This algorithm was applied to ACE permutation and found 128 11-step, 128 13-step, and 9 14-step rebound distinguishers.
- The 11-step, 13-step, and 14-step rebound attacks were applied to ACE permutation. The lowest time complexities of the 11-step, 13-step and 14-step rebound attacks are about $2^{167.80}$, $2^{134.17}$ and $2^{152.36}$. The memory complexity of these attacks is 2^{64} words. The comparison of the attack complexities is given in Table 1. As far as we know, these are the best results for ACE permutation.

Outline. The brief description of ACE permutation and rebound attack is introduced in Sect. 2. The SMT/SAT automatic model provided in Sect. 3 is used to search for characteristics with the minimum number of active SB-64s or optimal probability. Section 4 gives an algorithm applied to search for the rebound distinguishers of ACE. The 11-step, 13-step, and 14-step rebound attack was applied to ACE permutation in Sect. 5. We summarize and conclude our work in Sect. 6.

2 Preliminaries

2.1 The ACE Permutation

ACE permutation operates on a 320-bit state and iterates a step function 16 times [1]. The step function is shown in Fig. 1. For ACE permutation, there are three operations performed in the step function: nonlinear layer (SB-64), linear layer (π-permutation), and constant addition. The input state is viewed as five 64-bit subblocks written as $(A^i, B^i, C^i, D^i, E^i)$, $i \in \{0, 1, \ldots, 15\}$. The state is updated by performing the step function as follows.

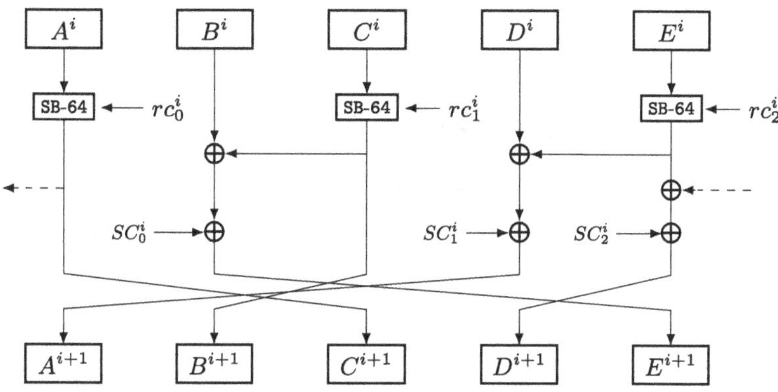

Fig. 1. The structure of ACE

$$\begin{cases} A^{i+1} \leftarrow D^i \oplus \texttt{SB-64}(E^i, rc_2^i) \oplus SC_1^i, \\ B^{i+1} \leftarrow \texttt{SB-64}(C^i, rc_1^i), \\ C^{i+1} \leftarrow \texttt{SB-64}(A^i, rc_0^i), \\ D^{i+1} \leftarrow \texttt{SB-64}(E^i, rc_2^i) \oplus \texttt{SB-64}(A^i, rc_0^i) \oplus SC_2^i, \\ E^{i+1} \leftarrow B^i \oplus \texttt{SB-64}(C^i, rc_1^i) \oplus SC_0^i. \end{cases}$$

Nonlinear Layer (SB-64). SB-64 is an unkeyed 64-bit permutation that is constructed by using 8-round Simeck-64 [30] with round constant addition $\tau^r = 1^{31}||q^r$, where $q^r \in \{0,1\}$ and $0 \leq r \leq 7$. Let $X^{r+1}||X^r$ and $X^{r+2}||X^{r+1}$ denote the input and output states of the i-th round, respectively. The round function of Simeck-64 is shown in Fig. 2 and the description of SB-64 is given by

$$(X^9, X^8) \leftarrow \texttt{SB-64}(X^1||X^0, rc)$$

where $X^r \leftarrow f_{(5,0,1)}(X^{r-1}) \oplus X^{r-2} \oplus \tau^{r-2}$, $2 \leq r \leq 9$. and $f_{(5,0,1)}$ is a function of 32-bit mapped to 32-bit, that is,

$$f_{(5,0,1)}(x) = (x \lll 5) \odot x \oplus (x \lll 1)$$

Linear Layer (π permutation). ACE permutation applies the shuffle operation π:

$$(A, B, C, D, E) \leftarrow (D, C, A, E, B)$$

to the five 64-bit subblocks.

Constant Addition. The round constant (rc_0^i, rc_1^i, rc_2^i) and step constant (SC_0^i, SC_1^i, SC_2^i) are used in the SB-64 and the subblocks B, D and E, respectively.

Note that the round constant rc_0^i, rc_1^i and rc_2^i used by SB-64 in each step corresponds to the round constant τ^r in each round. For specific details, please refer to [1]. Moreover, the round constants rc_j^i and step constants RC_j^i are omitted since they don't impact to differential attack, where $j \in \{0,1,2\}$.

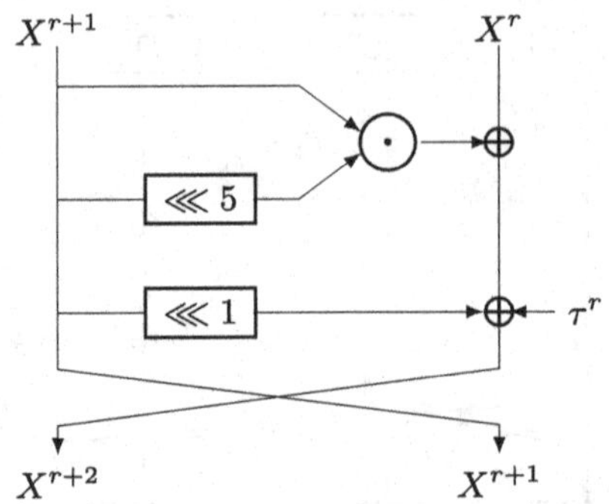

Fig. 2. The round function of Simeck

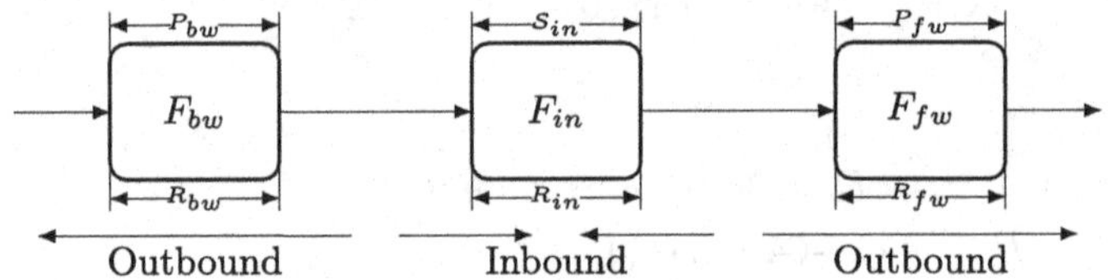

Fig. 3. The rebound attack

2.2 Rebound Attack

The rebound attack is a method proposed by Mendel *et al.* [20] against AES-like hashing and is currently widely used to analyze permutation-based constructions. Let F be a permutation-based construction, which can be split into three sub-permutations $F = F_{fw} \circ F_{in} \circ F_{bw}$. The idea of the rebound attack shown in Fig. 3 is to divide an attack into the following two phases.

- **Inbound phase.** The attacker generates a lot of matched pairs conforming to the middle of the R_{in}-round differential characteristic by utilizing the meet-in-the-middle technique. These matched pairs acted as the starting points that can lead to efficient matches of the differential characteristics in the outbound phase.
- **Outbound phase.** For each starting point obtained during the inbound phase propagates forward and backward to the outbound phase, detecting whether it matches the R_{out}-round differential propagation with probability P_{out} of the outbound phase, where $R_{out} = R_{bw} + R_{fw}$, $P_{out} = P_{bw} \cdot P_{fw}$.

In order to construct effective attacks, the starting points are generated during the inbound phase which is used to conform to the differential in the inbound phase. Suppose the probability of the outbound phase is $P_{out} = P_{bw} \cdot P_{fw}$, then we have to prepare S_{in} starting points in the inbound phase to expect one pair conforming to the differential of the outbound phase, that is $S_{in} > \frac{1}{P_{out}}$. Otherwise, the round-reduced differential characteristics in the inbound and outbound phases are repeatedly searched for to construct the rebound distinguisher.

The rebound attack is based on differential characteristics used to detect non-ideal behavior for a permutation. The goal of rebound attack is to find a tuple (x, x', y, y') that confirm both of the input and output differences Δx, Δy for the n-bit permutation F, where $F(x) = y$, $F(x') = y'$, $x \oplus x' = \Delta x$ and $y \oplus y' = \Delta y$. If the complexity of finding such a tuple is lower than the random permutation, then the target permutation is regarded as non-ideal, LBD is used to solve this problem. LBD on an n-bit permutation is claimed to be a valid attack when its time complexity is less than

$$\frac{2^{n+1}}{\mid \Delta In \mid \cdot \mid \Delta Out \mid}.$$

where ΔIn and ΔOut are closed sets of input and output differences, $\Delta x \in \Delta In$ and $\Delta y \in \Delta Out$.

3 SMT/SAT-Based Automatic Model

In this section, we provide the SMT/SAT model to search the lower bound of the active SB-64s and the optimal probability of the differential characteristics for ACE permutation.

For ACE permutation, an 8-round unkeyed Simeck-64 is used to provide diffusion, and five 64-bit words shuffled in a fixed order provide confusion. These operations are designed to come up with a judicious mix of components that will give a secure permutation. In fact, AND is the only nonlinear transformation of the cipher. At CRYPTO 2015, Kölbl *et al.* derived the expression used to describe the exact differential behavior of Simeck-like round functions [11]. For such round function $f(x) = (x \lll a) \odot (x \lll b) \oplus (x \lll c)$ with input and output differences Δ_0, Δ_1, the probability that Δ_0 maps to Δ_1 is as follows.

$$P(\Delta_0 \to \Delta_1) = \begin{cases} 2^{n-1}, & if\ \Delta_0 = 1,\ wt(\Delta_m) \equiv 0 \mod 2, \\ 2^{-wt(\text{var}+\text{dou})}, & if\ \Delta_0 \neq 1, \Delta_m \odot \overline{\text{var}} = 0, \\ & (\Delta_m \oplus (\Delta_m \lll (a-b))) \odot \text{dou} = 0, \\ 0, & else. \end{cases} \quad (1)$$

where $\gcd(n, a-b) = 1$, $n \mod 2 = 0$ and $a > b$, and

$$\begin{cases} \text{var} = & (\Delta_0 \lll a) \vee (\Delta_0 \lll b), \\ \text{dou} = & (\Delta_0 \lll b) \odot \overline{(\Delta_0 \lll a)} \odot (\Delta_0 \lll (2a-b)), \\ \Delta_m = & \Delta_1 \oplus (\Delta_0 \lll c). \end{cases}$$

Using the Eq. (1), we can describe the differential propagation of the Simeck-like round function and calculate its probability.

The Boolean satisfiability problem (SAT) is the problem of determining whether there exists an evaluation for the binary variables such that the value of the given Boolean formula equals "True". An extension of the SAT problem is the satisfiability modulo theories (SMT) problem. The problem of deciding the satisfiability of propositional formulas (SAT/SMT) not only lies at the heart of the most important open problem in complexity theory (P vs. NP), but it is also at the basis of many practical applications in such areas as Electronic Design Automation, Verification, Artificial Intelligence, and Operations Research. Thanks to recent advances in SAT/SMT-solving technology, these solvers are becoming the tool of choice for tackling more and more cryptographic tasks, such as finding cryptographic keys [19], a collision attack [21], preimage attack [22], differential cryptanalysis [23,28] and so on.

SMT model supports CVC (Cooperating Validity Checker) language as its input and aims to solve constraints of bit vectors and arrays. The advantage of SMT is that it can directly depict logical operations such as AND, OR, NOT, XOR, and it also supports conditional terms, i.e., the statement "IF a then b ELSE c ENDIF", where a is a boolean term, and b and c are bit vector terms. Therefore, the SMT model makes it easier to describe cryptographic problems, and here, the SMT model is used to search for characteristics with minimum active SB-64s for ACE permutation. For SAT models, CNF (Conjunctive Normal Form) converted by any boolean formula is used as input language. Some research shows that the SAT model is faster to solve. Here, the SAT model is used to solve the differential characteristics with optimal probability. Then, the SMT/SAT-based automatic model is introduced to search for differential characteristics and solved using the CryptoMiniSat5 [12] solver.

3.1 SMT-Based Model for Searching Differential Characteristics with the Minimum Number of Active SB-64s

Since SB-64 is designed by 8-round unkeyed Simeck-64, there are many studies on the differential probability of Simeck [15,18]. Therefore, when evaluating the bounds for differential probability of ACE permutation, SB-64 is considered as a whole. Therefore, in the step function of ACE permutation, basic operations consist of Copy, XOR, and SB-64. We will provide the statements in CVC format to describe the differential propagation of these operations.

Copy. Let Δx denote the input difference, and $(\Delta y_0, \Delta y_1, \ldots, \Delta y_{m-1})$ represent the m-bit output difference. For the Copy function, the relationship between its input and output differences is $(\Delta y_0, \Delta y_1, \ldots, \Delta y_{m-1}) = (\Delta x, \Delta x, \ldots, \Delta x)$. The statements of the Copy operation are as follows.

$$ASSERT(\Delta y_j = \Delta x);$$

where $0 \leq j \leq m-1$.

XOR. Let $\Delta x_0, \Delta x_1$ denote 2-bit input differences, and Δy indicate 1-bit output difference. The output of the XOR operation is calculated as $\Delta y = \Delta x_0 \oplus \Delta x_1$. The corresponding statement is below.

$$ASSERT(\Delta y = BVXOR(\Delta x_0, \Delta x_1));$$

Algorithm 1: SMT-based model describing the activeness of SB-64

Input: The input differences of i-th round Simeck-64 $\Delta X^{i+1}||\Delta X^{i}$, where $0 \leq i \leq 7$. The output differences of AND operation in the i-th round are written as ΔX_m^i. The variable $flag$ is used to denote the activeness of SB-64.

Output: The statements used to describe the activeness of SB-64.

ASSERT(IF $\Delta X^1||\Delta X^0$= 0hex0000 0000 0000 0000 THEN $flag$ = 0hex000 ELSE $flag$= 0hex001 ENDIF) ;"

for $i = 0$ *to* 7 **do**

/* Output the statements about Equations (1) without calculating probability to represent the activeness of SB-64. */

ASSERT(var^i = $(\Delta X^{i+1}[26:0]@\Delta X^{i+1}[31:27])|(\Delta X^{i+1})$) ;

ASSERT(dou^i = ΔX^{i+1} & $(\sim(\Delta X^{i+1}[26:0]@\Delta X^{i+1}[31:27]))$ & $(\Delta X^{i+1}[21:0]@\Delta X^{i+1}[31:22])$) ;

ASSERT($\Delta X_m^i = \Delta X^{i+2} \oplus (\Delta X^{i+1}[30:0]@\Delta X^{i+1}[31:31])$) ;

ASSERT(ΔX_m^i & $(\sim$ var$^i)$ = 0hex0000 0000) ;

ASSERT($\Delta X_m^i \oplus (\Delta X_m^i[26:0]@\Delta X_m^i[31:27])$ & dou^i =0hex0000 0000) ;

end

The Activeness of SB-64. Let $\Delta_{in} = \Delta X^1||\Delta X^0$, $\Delta_{out} = \Delta X^9||\Delta X^8$ be 64-bit input and output differences, and $flag$ indicate the activeness of SB-64, where $\Delta_{out} \leftarrow$ SB-64(Δ_{in}) and $\Delta X^i = \Delta x_0^i||\Delta x_1^i||\ldots||\Delta x_{31}^i$, $0 \leq i \leq 9$. For 8-round Simeck, $\Delta X^{i+1}||\Delta X^i$ is the input for the i-th round, and its output is $\Delta X^{i+2}||\Delta X^{i+1}$. In this case, Eq. (1) in CVC format is used to describe the effective differential of SB-64. Meanwhile, if $\Delta X_{in} = 0$, then SB-64 is considered inactive and $flag$ = 0hex000. In other cases, setting $flag$ = 0hex001 indicates that SB-64 is active. "0hex" is the hexadecimal representation in CVC language. Finally, the statements generated by Algorithm 1 model to describe the activeness of SB-64.

3.2 SAT-Based Model for Searching Differential Characteristics with the Optimal Probability

CNF, the standard input format of SAT solvers, written as $\bigwedge_{i=0}^{n}(\bigvee_{j=0}^{n_i} a_j^i)$, where $a_{i,j}$ is a boolean variable or constant or the negation of a boolean variable. Each disjunction $(\bigvee_{j=0}^{n_i} a_j^i)$ is called a clause. The search problem about differential characteristics with optimal probability is generally transformed into a mathematical solution problem. Any Boolean function can be transformed into CNF format, so similarly, the differential propagation of these operations such as Copy, XOR, and SB-64 are also described in CNF. The objective function of such a problem can be abstracted as the Boolean cardinality constraints $\sum_{i=0}^{n-1} x_i \leq k$, where x_i are Boolean variables, and k is a non-negative integer. The SAT model uses clauses to describe the differential propagation of ACE and uses sequences coding methods [26] to convert the Boolean cardinality constraint $\sum_{i=0}^{n-1} x_i \leq k$ into CNF formulas. The CNF model for searching the differential propagation of these basic operations can be found in [28,29].

The SAT model abbreviated as $\mathcal{M}_0$ is used to search the differential characteristics with the optimal probability of ACE permutation. The clustering effect of characteristics can improve the probability of distinguishers. If an adversary wants to construct a distinguisher, he actually does not care about any intermediate differences and is only interested in the probability of the differential [13]. In this case, the adversary can collect all differential characteristics sharing the same input and output differences to get a better estimate. Therefore, on the basis of solving the SAT model of differential characteristics for SB-64, by adding a negative proposition in CNF format for each known differential characteristic, it can be used to enumerate the differential characteristics that contribute to the differential with the same input and output differences.

4 Application to ACE Permutation

The SMT/SAT-based automatic model given in Sect. 3 is exploited for the differential characteristics for ACE permutation. The characteristics with minimum active SB-64s or optimal probabilities are illustrated in Sect. 4.1. Based on the properties of these characteristics and the iterative differentials of SB-64, an algorithm provided in Sect. 4.2 is proposed to construct the rebound distinguisher for ACE permutation.

4.1 Differential Characteristics of ACE Permutation

In this section, using the SMT/SAT-based automatic model, we verified the lower bound on the number of active SB-64s for the differential characteristics of ACE[1]. In addition, some differential characteristics with optimal probability for reduced step ACE permutation are presented. The results are shown in Table 2, where "#SB-64" refers to the number of active SB-64s and the optimal probability of characteristics for ACE permutation is written as "P".

In the design document, regarding the SB-64 as a black box, the designers used the MILP model to find that the minimum active SB-64s of 16-step characteristics for ACE is 21 [1]. It is known that the optimal probability of the differential of SB-64 is $2^{-15.8}$ [2], and thus the upper bound on the probability of the 16-step characteristics is estimated to be $2^{-331.8}$. As shown in Table 2, it can be seen that the lower bounds on the number of the active SB-64s are re-evaluated in this paper. For example, there are at least 4 active SB-64s for 5-step differential characteristics illustrated in Table 7 of Appendix A. Table 3 illustrates a 16-step differential characteristic with 19 active SB-64s. Therefore, the upper bound on the probability of the characteristic for ACE permutation is $2^{-300.2}$, which is higher than the probability 2^{-320} of a random permutation, rather than the designer's claimed upper bound on the probability $2^{-331.8}$. Moreover, the minimum active SB-64s of 17-step differential characteristics shown in Table 4 for ACE permutation is 21.

[1] ACE Team. https://csrc.nist.gov/CSRC/media/Projects/lightweight-cryptography/documents/round-2/official-comments/ace-round2-official-comment.pdf.

Table 2. Experimental results of ACE permutation

Step		1	2	3	4	5	6	7	8	9
#SB-64	[1]	0	1	2	3	5	7	8	9	11
	Sect. 4.1	0	1	2	3	4	6	7	8	10
P	Sect. 4.1	1	2^{-18}	2^{-36}	2^{-62}	2^{-80}	2^{-124}†	2^{-148}†	-	-
Step		10	11	12	13	14	15	16	17	
#SB-64	[1]	12	13	15	16	17	19	21	-	
	Sect. 4.1	11	13	14	15	16	18	19	21	

The symbol "†" indicates that the probability has not been verified to be the optimal probability.

Table 3. The 16-step characteristic of ACE permutation with 19 active SB-64s

Step	ΔA	ΔB	ΔC	ΔD	ΔE
0	0x0000 0000 0000 0000	0xE976 3F28 FF7F FEAE	0x6998 B1CC 140A 9442	0x0000 0000 0000 0000	0x0000 0000 0000 0000
1	0x0000 0000 0000 0000	0xE976 3F28 FF7F FEAE	0x0000 0000 0000 0000	0x0000 0000 0000 0000	0x0000 0000 0000 0000
2	0x0000 0000 0000 0000	0x0000 0000 0000 0000	0x0000 0000 0000 0000	0x0000 0000 0000 0000	0xE976 3F28 FF7F FEAE
3	0xFFFF FFFF FFFF FFFA	0x0000 0000 0000 0000	0x0000 0000 0000 0000	0xFFFF FFFF FFFF FFFA	0x0000 0000 0000 0000
4	0xFFFF FFFF FFFF FFFA	0x0000 0000 0000 0000	0xFFF7 BFFF FFFF FFFF	0xFFF7 BFFF FFFF FFFF	0x0000 0000 0000 0000
5	0xFFF7 BFFF FFFF FFFF	0xFFFF FFFF FFFF FFFF	0xFFFF FFFF FFF7 FFFD	0xFFFF FFFF FFF7 FFFD	0xFFFF FFFF FFFF FFFF
6	0x0000 0000 0000 0000	0xFFFF FFFF FFFF FFFF	0xFFFF FFFF FFF7 FFFD	0x0000 0000 0000 0000	0x0000 0000 0000 0000
7	0x0000 0000 0000 0000	0xFFFF FFFF FFFF FFFF	0x0000 0000 0000 0000	0x0000 0000 0000 0000	0x0000 0000 0000 0000
8	0x0000 0000 0000 0000	0x0000 0000 0000 0000	0x0000 0000 0000 0000	0x0000 0000 0000 0000	0xFFFF FFFF FFFF FFFF
9	0xFFFF FFFF FFFF FFFF	0x0000 0000 0000 0000	0x0000 0000 0000 0000	0xFFFF FFFF FFFF FFFF	0x0000 0000 0000 0000
10	0xFFFF FFFF FFFF FFFF	0x0000 0000 0000 0000	0xFFFF FFFF FFFF FFFF	0xFFFF FFFF FFFF FFFF	0x0000 0000 0000 0000
11	0xFFFF FFFF FFFF FFFF	0xFFFF FFFF FFFF FFFF	0xFFFF FFFF FFFF FFFF	0xFFFF FFFF FFFF FFFF	0xFFFF FFFF FFFF FFFF
12	0x0000 0000 0000 0000	0xFFFF FFFF FFFF FFFF	0xFFFF FFFF FFFF FFFF	0x0000 0000 0000 0000	0x0000 0000 0000 0000
13	0x0000 0000 0000 0000	0xFFFF FFFF FFFF FFFF	0x0000 0000 0000 0000	0x0000 0000 0000 0000	0x0000 0000 0000 0000
14	0x0000 0000 0000 0000	0x0000 0000 0000 0000	0x0000 0000 0000 0000	0x0000 0000 0000 0000	0xFFFF FFFF FFFF FFFF
15	0xFFFF FFFF FFFF FFFF	0x0000 0000 0000 0000	0x0000 0000 0000 0000	0xFFFF FFFF FFFF FFFF	0x0000 0000 0000 0000
16	0xFFFF FFFF FFFF FFFF	0x0000 0000 0000 0000	0x429A 0961 7F76 966A	0x429A 0961 7F76 966A	0x0000 0000 0000 0000

In Table 2, we obtained the differential characteristics with the optimal probability of the first 5 steps. For instance, the optimal probability of the 5-step characteristic for ACE permutation in Table 8 of Appendix A is 2^{-80}. As shown in Table 5, the probability of finding the 7-step differential characteristic is 2^{-148}. Additionally, the SAT model found a 6-step and 7-step differential characteristic Ω_c^6 and Ω_c^7 with good properties, but we do not confirm that the probability of 6-step and 7-step characteristics is optimal. The differential propagation pattern of the 6-step characteristic

$$(\alpha, \alpha, 0, 0, 0) \mapsto (0, 0, \alpha, \alpha, 0)$$

is shown in Fig. 4. By observing the relationship between the input and output differences of each active SB-64, it is found that such characteristics can be constructed by the iterative differentials $\alpha \rightleftharpoons \beta$ of SB-64, where α and β is the input or output differences of the active SB-64. The output difference corresponding to extending the 6-step characteristics to the 7-step characteristics is $(\alpha, \beta, 0, 0, \beta)$, that is,

$$(\alpha, \alpha, 0, 0, 0) \mapsto (\alpha, \beta, 0, 0, \beta).$$

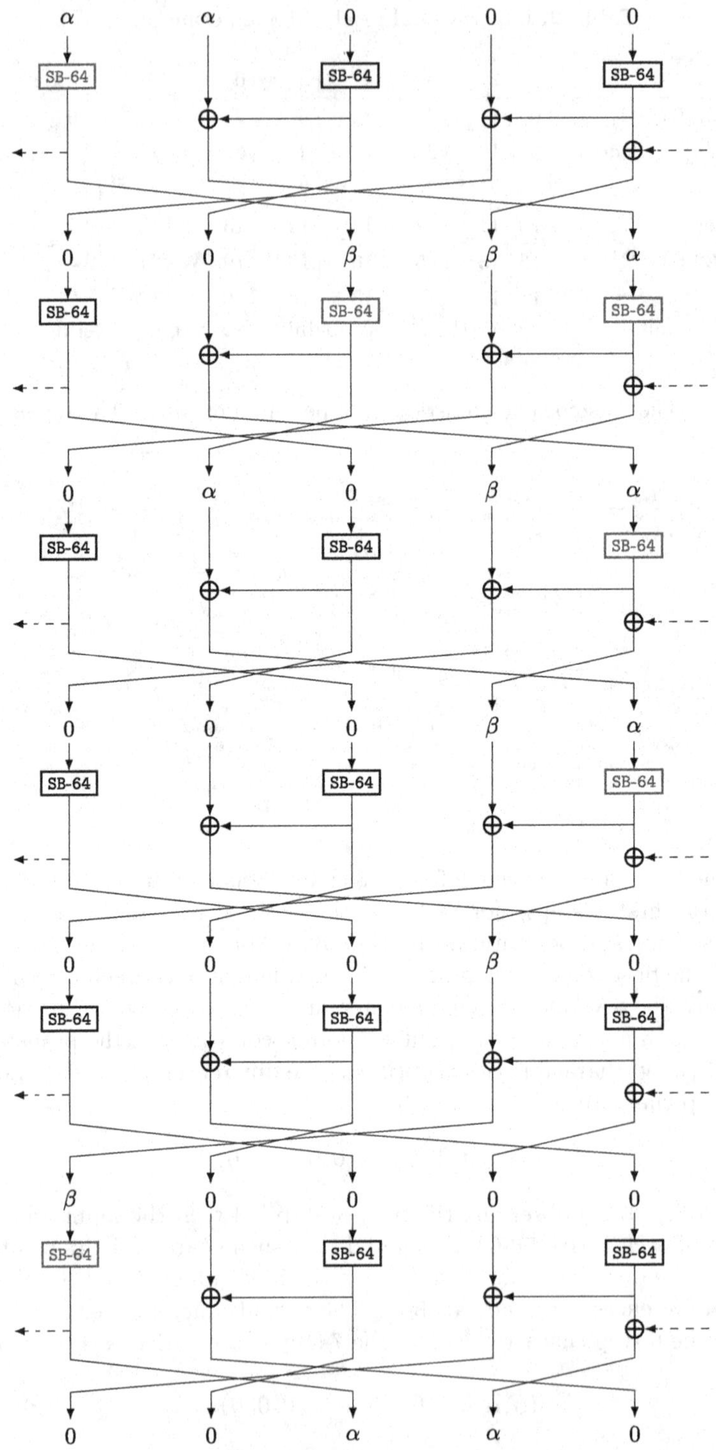

Fig. 4. 6-step differential characteristic Ω_c^6 of ACE permutation

Table 4. The 17-step characteristic of ACE permutation with 21 active SB-64s

Step	ΔA	ΔB	ΔC	ΔD	ΔE
0	0x4B2F 3299 90E2 2502	0x0000 0000 0010 0000	0x0190 8A00 8000 1000	0x0000 0000 0000 0000	0x0000 0000 0000 0000
1	0x0000 0000 0000 0000	0x0000 0000 0010 0000	0x5F00 ABA0 0E01 0284	0x5F00 ABA0 0E01 0284	0x0000 0000 0000 0000
2	0x5F00 ABA0 0E01 0284	0x0000 0000 0010 0000	0x0000 0000 0000 0000	0x0000 0000 0000 0000	0x0000 0000 0000 0000
3	0x0000 0000 0000 0000	0x0000 0000 0000 0000	0x0AE0 0000 01F0 0000	0x0AE0 0000 01F0 0000	0x0000 0000 0010 0000
4	0x0000 0000 0000 0000	0x00A0 0008 0101 9082	0x0000 0000 0000 0000	0x0AE0 0000 01F0 0000	0x00A0 0008 0101 9082
5	0x0000 0000 0000 0000	0x0000 0000 0000 0000	0x0000 0000 0000 0000	0x0AE0 0000 01F0 0000	0x00A0 0008 0101 9082
6	0x0000 0000 0000 0000	0x0000 0000 0000 0000	0x0000 0000 0000 0000	0x0AE0 0000 01F0 0000	0x0000 0000 0000 0000
7	0x0AE0 0000 01F0 0000	0x0000 0000 0000 0000	0x0000 0000 0000 0000	0x0000 0000 0000 0000	0x0000 0000 0000 0000
8	0x0000 0000 0000 0000	0x0000 0000 0000 0000	0x1136 10E0 04D9 4740	0x1136 10E0 04D9 4740	0x0000 0000 0000 0000
9	0x1136 10E0 04D9 4740	0x0807 8B73 C144 0210	0x0000 0000 0000 0000	0x0000 0000 0000 0000	0x0807 8B73 C144 0210
10	0x0840 8001 0000 0040	0x0000 0000 0000 0000	0x12C8 2011 A806 4001	0x1A88 A010 A806 4041	0x0807 8B73 C144 0210
11	0x0000 0000 0000 0000	0xD376 F8B4 3D7B A0D9	0x4AE1 F380 C965 64A0	0x5069 5390 6163 24E1	0xD376 F8B4 3D7B A0D9
12	0x0000 0000 0000 0000	0x632B A292 AB68 34DD	0x0000 0000 0000 0000	0x5069 5390 6163 24E1	0xB05D 5A26 9613 9404
13	0x0000 0000 0000 0000	0x0000 0000 0000 0000	0x0000 0000 0000 0000	0x5069 5390 6163 24E1	0x632B A292 AB68 34DD
14	0x0000 0000 0000 0000	0x0000 0000 0000 0000	0x0000 0000 0000 0000	0x5069 5390 6163 24E1	0x0000 0000 0000 0000
15	0x5069 5390 6163 24E1	0x0000 0000 0000 0000	0x0000 0000 0000 0000	0x0000 0000 0000 0000	0x0000 0000 0000 0000
16	0x0000 0000 0000 0000	0x0000 0000 0000 0000	0x0000 2022 0000 5014	0x0000 2022 0000 5014	0x0000 0000 0000 0000
17	0x0000 2022 0000 5014	0x0000 0512 0000 0004	0x0000 0000 0000 0000	0x0000 0000 0000 0000	0x0000 0512 0000 0004

Table 5. The 7-step characteristic Ω_c^7 of ACE permutation with probability 2^{-148}

Step	ΔA	ΔB	ΔC	ΔD	ΔE
0	0x0000 8000 0001 5800	0x0000 8000 0001 5800	0x0000 0000 0000 0000	0x0000 0000 0000 0000	0x0000 0000 0000 0000
1	0x0000 0000 0000 0000	0x0000 0000 0000 0000	0x0000 2800 0000 1000	0x0000 2800 0000 1000	0x0000 8000 0001 5800
2	0x0000 0000 0000 0000	0x0000 A800 0000 1000	0x0000 0000 0000 0000	0x0000 2800 0000 1000	0x0000 A800 0000 1000
3	0x0000 0000 0000 0000	0x0000 0000 0000 0000	0x0000 0000 0000 0000	0x0000 2800 0000 1000	0x0000 A800 0000 1000
4	0x0000 0000 0000 0000	0x0000 0000 0000 0000	0x0000 0000 0000 0000	0x0000 2800 0000 1000	0x0000 0000 0000 0000
5	0x0000 2800 0000 1000	0x0000 0000 0000 0000	0x0000 0000 0000 0000	0x0000 0000 0000 0000	0x0000 0000 0000 0000
6	0x0000 0000 0000 0000	0x0000 0000 0000 0000	0x0000 A800 0000 1000	0x0000 A800 0000 1000	0x0000 0000 0000 0000
7	0x0000 A800 0000 1000	0x0000 2800 0000 1000	0x0000 0000 0000 0000	0x0000 0000 0000 0000	0x0000 2800 0000 1000

4.2 The Algorithm for Searching Rebound Distinguisher of ACE Permutation

The state of ACE permutation is large and the step function is complex, making it difficult to directly search the rebound distinguisher using a model. Unlike the start-from-the-middle attacks used in most work [6,8,14], we adopt the start-from-the-bottom strategy to explore rebound distinguishers. Therefore, we provide a three-step search method displayed in Algorithm 2 for finding the rebound distinguisher of ACE, including the differential in the F_{fw}, F_{in} and F_{bw} sub-permutations. This method can also be used for other ciphers. Next, we will provide a detailed explanation of the process.

- Step 1. Construct 128 7-step differentials with better probability P_{fw}^7 of the F_{fw} sub-permutation for ACE permutation.
  Firstly, for the 7-step differential characteristic Ω_c^7, fixed its input and output differences for each active SB-64, utilizing the clustering effect of the characteristics of SB-64, the probability of the differential

$$(0x0000\ 8000\ 0001\ 5800, 0x0000\ 8000\ 0001\ 5800, 0, 0, 0) \mapsto$$
$$(0x0000\ A800\ 0000\ 1000, 0x0000\ 2800\ 0000\ 1000, 0, 0, 0x0000\ 2800\ 0000\ 1000)$$

Algorithm 2: The algorithm used to search for the rebound distinguisher of ACE permutation

/* **Step 1: Construct 128 7-step differentials in F_{fw} part.** */

Get 128 7-step characteristics in F_{fw} part by using the iterative characteristics $\alpha_i \rightleftharpoons \beta_i$ of SB-64.

The probability $P^7_{fw,j}$ of the 128 7-step differential $\Omega^7_{fw,j}$ domainted by these characteristics can be improved to $2^{-130.83}$ by considering the clustering effect of characteristics of SB-64, where $0 \leq j \leq 127$.

Store these input and output differences and their probability of these differential in the set $\mathcal{D}^7_{fw}$.

/* **Step 2: Search for the optimal differential in F_{in} phase.** */

for *j from 0 to 127* **do**

  The output difference of the model $\mathcal{M}_0$ is fixed as the input difference of characheristics $\Omega^7_{fw,j}$ in the set $\mathcal{D}^7_{fw}$.

  The 3-step and 4-step differential characteristics with optimal probability are returned by the Cryptominisat5 solver.

  Store these input and output differences and their probability $P^3_{in,j}/P^3_{in,j}$ of these 3/4-step differential in the set $\mathcal{D}^3_{in}/\mathcal{D}^3_{in}$.

end

/* **Step 3: Determine the rebound distinguisher.** */

if *128 3/4-step differential $\Omega^3_{in,j}/\Omega^4_{in,j}$ in F_{in} phase are used as candidates* **then**

  for *j from 0 to 127* **do**

    The output difference of the model $\mathcal{M}_0$ is fixed as the input difference of characheristics $\Omega^3_{in,j}/\Omega^4_{in,j}$ and solved by the solver.

    Store these input and output differences and their probability $P^1_{bw,j}$ of the obtained 128 1-step/2-step/3-step differential in the set $\mathcal{D}^1_{bw}/\mathcal{D}^2_{bw}/\mathcal{D}^3_{bw}$.

    if *the complexity is lower than random permutation* **then**

      Return the 11-step/13-step/14-step rebound distinguishers.

    end

  end

end

is improved from 2^{-148} to $2^{-135.94}$. Based on the observed 6-step and 7-step differential characteristics Ω^6_C and Ω^7_c, their properties were found to be able to construct 7-step characteristics using the iterative differentials of SB-64. Meanwhile, utilizing the clustering effect of the SB-64's characteristics, the probability of the differential

$$(\alpha, \alpha, 0, 0, 0) \mapsto (\alpha, \beta, 0, 0, \beta)$$

can be improved from 2^{-154} to $2^{-130.83}$, which is higher than $2^{-135.94}$. Secondly, for each 128 iterative differentials $\alpha \rightleftharpoons \beta$ of SB-64 displayed in Table 9 of Appendix A, by utilizing the clustering effect of differential characteristics, we collected 49880 characteristics to improve the probability of the differential from 2^{-22} to $2^{-18.69}$. The distribution of these characteristics is shown in Table 10 of Appendix A, where "$\#DC$" represents the number of characteristics with the probability "P_{DC}". Finally, we can construct 128 7-step differentials with better probability $2^{-130.83}$. Store the input and output differences of 128 candidate differentials in set $\mathcal{D}^7_{fw}$.

- Step 2. Search the optimal differential for the F_{in} sub-permutation.
For each candidate differential in the F_{fw} phase, model M_{in} is utilized to search for the optimal characteristics in the inbound phase. Firstly, the output difference of the model $\mathcal{M}_0$ is fixed as the input difference in the set $\mathcal{D}^7_{fw}$, and the solver returns corresponding 128 3-step and 4-step characteristics with optimal probability. Subsequently, the clustering effect of characteristics is utilized to improve the probability of 3-step and 4-step differentials. Subsequently, the clustering effect of differential characteristics is utilized to further improve the probability of 3-step and 4-step differentials. The results show that the range of probability P^3_{in} for the 3-step differential in the inbound phase is $\{2^{-131}, 2^{-136}, 2^{-142}\}$ increased to $2^{-115.93} \sim 2^{-122.18}$ by the clustering effect of characteristics. That is $\max\{P^3_{in}\} = 2^{-115.93}$, $\min\{P^3_{in}\} = 2^{-122.18}$. The range of probability P^4_{in} for the 4-step differential characteristics is $\{2^{-176}, 2^{-177}, 2^{-180}\}$ which can be improved to around $2^{-146.71} \sim 2^{-157.66}$. Namely, $\max\{P^4_{in}\} = 2^{-146.71}$, $\min\{P^4_{in}\} = 2^{-157.66}$. The input and output differences of the above 128 3-step and 4-step differentials are stored in the set $\mathcal{D}^3_{in}$ and $\mathcal{D}^4_{in}$, respectively.
- Step 3. Determine the rebound distinguisher of ACE permutation by observing the differential behavior for the F_{bw}, F_{in} and F_{fw} sub-permutation.
  - When selecting 128 3-step differentials in the F_{in} phase as candidates, that is, the output difference of the characteristic in the F_{bw} phase is fixed as the input difference in the set $\mathcal{D}^3_{in}$. At this point, the range of the optimal probability for the corresponding 128 1-step characteristics in the F_{bw} stage is

$$\{2^{-64}, 2^{-66}, 2^{-68}, 2^{-70}, 2^{-71}, 2^{-72}, 2^{-74}, 2^{-84}, 2^{-87}\}$$

    which can be increased to $2^{-53.90} \sim 2^{-75.82}$, *i.e.* $\max\{P^1_{bw}\} = 2^{-53.90}$, $\min\{P^1_{bw}\} = 2^{-75.82}$. According to the complexity of the rebound attack, there are 128 11-step rebound distinguishers constructed by 1-step in the F_{bw}, 3-step in the F_{in} and 7-step in the F_{fw} phase. The 11-step rebound attack on ACE permutation in Sect. 5.1.
  - The 128 4-step candidate differentials are used as the distinguishers in the inbound phase, then, the input difference in set $\mathcal{D}^4_{in}$ is used as the output difference of the characteristics in F_{bw} phase. Next, use the solver to search for characteristics with optimal probability in the F_{bw} phase. As result, the range of these optimal probabilities of the obtained 128 2-step characteristics in the F_{bw} phase is

$$\{2^{-24}, 2^{-28}, 2^{-46}, 2^{-48}, 2^{-50}, 2^{-51}, 2^{-52}, 2^{-53}, 2^{-54}, 2^{-60}\}.$$

    The probability of these differentials can be improved to $2^{-22.04} \sim 2^{-51.54}$, *i.e.* $\max\{P^2_{bw}\} = 2^{-22.04}$, $\min\{P^2_{bw}\} = 2^{-51.54}$. After analyzing these distinguishers, 15 of them can be directly used for rebound attacks.

Among the 128 2-step characteristics of F_{bw} sub-permutation, there are eight characteristics with optimal probability 2^{-24} and a characteristic with optimal probability 2^{-28}. Then, we attempted to extend it to 3-step, and the results showed that the optimal probability of the 9 3-step characteristics is 2^{-44}. The probabilities of such a 3-step differential were increased to $2^{-40.33}$, *i.e.* $P^3_{bw} = 2^{-40.33}$. Therefore, 9 14-step rebound distinguishers were constructed and consisted of 7 steps differential in F_{fw} phase, 4 steps differential in F_{in} phase, and 3 steps differential in F_{bw} phase. These 14-step rebound attacks of ACE permutation will be explained in Sect. 5.2.

5 Rebound Attacks on ACE Permutation

For ACE permutation, according to the new search algorithm, Sect. 4.2 shows that many rebound distinguishers have been found. Referring to the attack strategy in [9,17], we introduce the complexity analysis of rebound attacks on 11-step, 13-step, and 14-step in this section.

5.1 11-Step Rebound Attacks Against ACE Permutation

In Sect. 4.2, for ACE permutation, 128 11-step rebound distinguishers were found, among which 2 11-step rebound distinguishers are shown in Table 6. Actually, by directly using these distinguishers for rebound attacks, only 123 distinguishers were able to initiate effective rebound attacks, while the other 5 rebound distinguishers failed due to insufficient starting points in the inbound phase. By relaxing the input or output states of the distinguisher, all 128 distinguishers can perform effective rebound attacks. From a complexity perspective, three rebound distinguishers Ω^{11}_j are used to explain the complexity of these 11-step rebound attacks, where $0 \le j \le 2$. Next, we will introduce the attack process taking the 11-step distinguisher Ω^{11}_0 depicted in Fig. 5 with the lowest complexity as an example.

The 11-step rebound distinguisher Ω^{11}_0 consists of 1-step characteristics in F_{bw}, the 3-step differential in F_{in} and 7-step differential in F_{fw}. The distinguisher Ω^{11} directly initiates a rebound attack, with the following input and output differences

$$\begin{aligned}&(\text{0x0008 0000 0050 0000}, \text{0x0008 0000 0118 0000}, \text{0x0008 0000 0008 0000},\\ &\text{0x0000 0000 0050 0000}, \text{0x0008 0000 0158 0000}) \mapsto\\ &(\text{0x0088 0000 0000 0000}, \text{0x0008 0000 0000 0000}, 0, 0, \text{0x0008 0000 0000 0000}).\end{aligned}$$

The rebound attack process includes two steps: In the inbound phase, the available degrees of freedom (in terms of actual values of the state) are used to guarantee that the differential in F_{in} phase holds; The differential in the outbound phase is supposed to have a relatively high probability. The specific process is as follows:

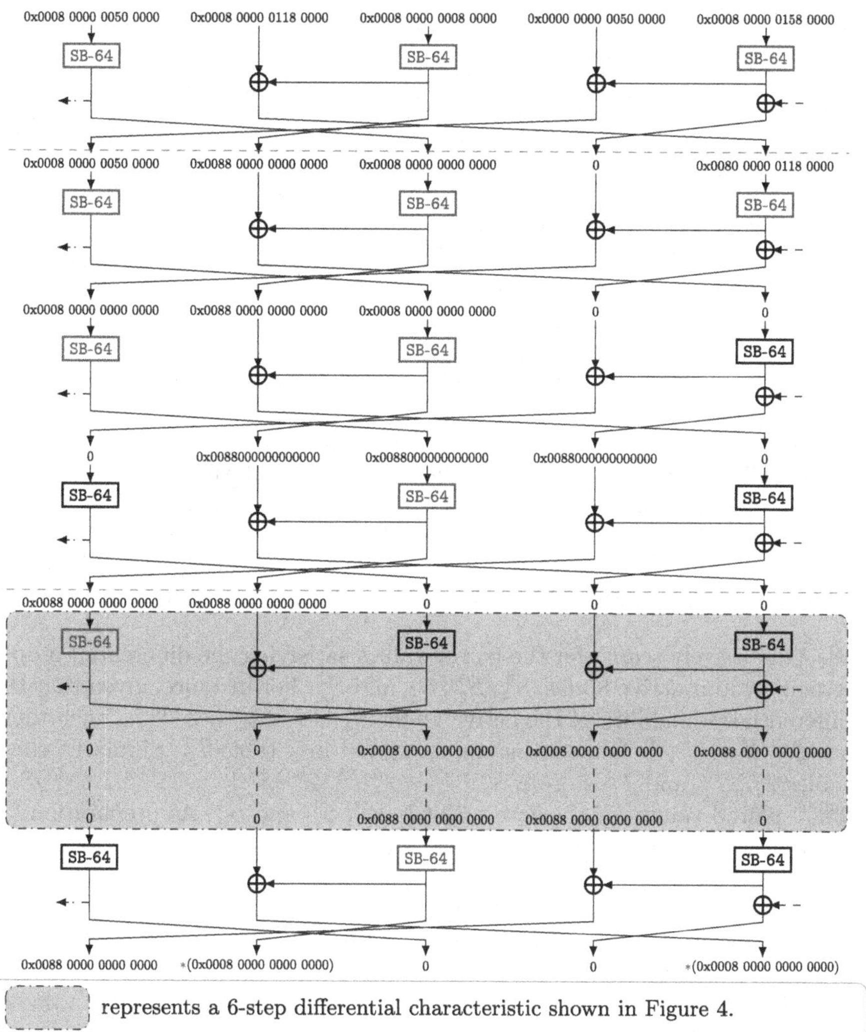

Fig. 5. 11-step rebound distinguisher Ω_0^{11} of ACE permutation

Table 6. 11-step rebound distinguishers of ACE permutation

ID	Step	$(\Delta A, \Delta B, \Delta C, \Delta D, \Delta E)$
Ω_1^{11}	0	(0x0000 0000 4000 0000, 0x4000 0000 C000 0000, 0x4000 0004 8000 0004, 0x0000 0000 0000 0004, 0x4000 0000 8000 0000)
	1	(0x4000 0000 8000 0000, 0x4000 0000 C000 0000, 0x0000 0000 4000 0004, 0x4000 0000 C000 0000, 0x0000 0000 0000 0000)
	2	(0x4000 0000 C000 0000, 0x0000 0000 4000 0000, 0x4000 0004 8000 0000, 0x4000 0004 8000 0000, 0x4000 0000 8000 0000)
	3	(0x0000 0000 0000 0000, 0x0000 0000 4000 0000, 0x4000 0004 C000 0000, 0x0000 0000 4000 0000, 0x0000 0000 0000 0000)
	4	(0x0000 0000 4000 0000, 0x0000 0000 4000 0000, 0x0000 0000 0000 0000, 0x0000 0000 0000 0000, 0x0000 0000 0000 0000)
	⋮	⋮
	11	(0x0000 0000 4000 0000, ∗(0x0000 0000 4000 0004), 0x0000 0000 0000 0000, 0x0000 0000 0000 0000, ∗(0x0000 0000 4000 0004))
Ω_2^{11}	0	(0x0000 0000 0000 0C00, 0x0000 2400 0000 5400, 0x0000 2000 0000 1400, 0x0000 6400 0000 B000, 0x0000 0400 0000 0800)
	1	(0x0000 2000 0000 5400, 0x0000 2400 0000 5400, 0x0000 4400 0000 8000, 0x0000 0000 0000 6400, 0x0000 0000 0000 0000)
	2	(0x0000 0000 0000 6400, 0x0000 0400 0000 0000, 0x0000 2000 0000 1400, 0x0000 2000 0000 1400, 0x0000 2000 0000 5400)
	3	(0x0000 0000 0000 0000, 0x0000 0400 0000 0000, 0x0000 2400 0000 1400, 0x0000 0400 0000 0000, 0x0000 0000 0000 0000)
	4	(0x0000 0400 0000 0000, 0x0000 0400 0000 0000, 0x0000 0000 0000 0000, 0x0000 0000 0000 0000, 0x0000 0000 0000 0000)
	⋮	⋮
	11	(0x0000 0400 0000 0000, ∗(0x0000 4400 0000 0000), 0x0000 0000 0000 0000, 0x0000 0000 0000 0000, ∗(0x0000 4400 0000 0000))

Inbound Phase. The active SB-64 in the A-branch of i-th step is denoted as S_A^i, and the probability of the differential for the active S_A^i is expressed as $P(S_A^i)$, where $0 \leq i \leq 15$. Similarly, the active SB-64 in the C-branch or E-branch is also represented in this way. Next, we will discuss how to utilize the divide-and-conquer approach to obtain the starting points during the inbound phase.

1) We exhaustively search for the paired values satisfying the differential propagation for four active SB-64s S_A^1, S_C^1, S_E^1 and S_A^2. For instance, given that the differential probability of the active SB-64 S_A^1 is $P(S_A^1) = 2^{-18.35}$, then there are $2^{64-18.35} = 2^{45.65}$ matching values stored in a table T_A^1. Similarly, these tables T_C^1, T_E^2 and T_A^2 store $2^{64-18.95} = 2^{45.05}$, $2^{64-19.31} = 2^{44.69}$,$2^{64-18.95} = 2^{45.05}$ paired values for the active SB-64s S_C^1, S_E^1 and S_A^2. As preparation for Step 3), we also search for the paired values for the input of the B-branch in the second step.
2) The active SB-64 S_C^2 requires testing $2^{45.65}$ values in the table T_A^1. Due to the filtering probability of S_C^2 being $P(S_C^2) = 2^{-18.95}$, $2^{45.65-18.95} = 2^{26.7}$ solutions were obtained.
3) Test $2^{45.05}$ paired values in the table T_A^2 to determine the matching value of the active SB-64 S_C^3. The filtering probability of S_C^3 is $P(S_C^3) = 2^{-24.52}$, and the number of solutions obtained for S_C^3 is $2^{45.05-24.52} = 2^{20.53}$.
4) Any combination of the obtained paired values $2^{45.05} \times 2^{44.69} \times 2^{26.7} \times 2^{20.53} = 2^{136.97}$ and the precomputed 2^{64} solutions of B-branch will fix the entire state. Therefore, we can produce at most $2^{136.97} \times 2^{64} = 2^{200.97}$ values that follow the differential in the inbound phase. In other words, up to $2^{200.97}$ starting points propagate to the outbound phase to satisfy the differential.

Outbound Phase. In the outbound phase, the 4-step differential in the inbound phase extends forward by 2-step and backward by 7-step, respectively. By fixing the $2^{200.97}$ paired values in the inbound phase, all 320-bit states can be fixed. Propagated these values to F_{bw} and F_{fw} parts, used to check if the differential in the outbound phase is a match. The probabilities of F_{bw} and F_{fw} part are known to be $P_{bw} = 2^{-55.66}$ and $P_{fw} = 2^{-130.83}$, that is, the total probability in the outbound phase is $2^{-186.49}$. Therefore, the degree of freedom fully satisfies the 11-step rebound distinguisher.

Complexity Evaluation. Time complexity in the inbound phase.

$$4 \times 2^{64} + 2^{45.65} + 2^{45.05} + 2^{64} \approx 2^{66.32}.$$

Memory complexity:

$$2^{45.65} + 2^{45.05} + 2^{44.69} + 2^{45.05} + 2^{64} \approx 2^{64}.$$

The outbound phase requires $2^{186.49}$ computations to satisfy differential propagation. In summary, the attack complexity is calculated at $2^{186.49}$ and stored at 2^{64} words.

In this case, usually, the complexity of finding the same pair for a random permutation is higher. If the subspace of the input difference is fixed with a choice of $\mid x \mid= 1$, and the subspace of the output difference satisfies $\mid y \mid= 1$, then the attack complexity is $\frac{2^{320+1}}{1} = 2^{321}$, which is higher than the rebound attack. For these 123 valid rebound distinguishers, the attack complexity launched by the 11-step distinguisher Ω_1^{11} is highest. The output difference of the distinguisher Ω_1^{11} is as follows.

$$(\text{0x0000 0000 4000 0000}, \text{0x0000 0000 4000 0004}, 0, 0, \text{0x0000 0000 4000 0004}).$$

The probability of the distinguisher of F_{bw}, F_{in} and F_{fw} sub-permutation for rebound distinguisher Ω_1^{11} are $2^{-65.09}$, $2^{-121.44}$ and $2^{-130.83}$, respectively. Similarly, when using distinguisher Ω_1^{11} for rebound attacks, the time complexity is $2^{195.92}$, the memory complexity is approximately 2^{64}.

In another case, where the input or output difference of the distinguisher is relaxed, all 128 11-step distinguishers can implement a rebound attack. At this point, for a random permutation, if the subspace of the input difference is fixed with a choice of $\mid x \mid= 1$, and the subspace of the output difference satisfies $\mid y \mid= 2^{128}$, then the attack complexity is $\frac{2^{320+1}}{1 \cdot 2^{128}} = 2^{192}$, which enables all 128 distinguishers to perform effective rebound attacks.

By relaxing the output difference of the active S_C^{10}, the attack complexity of the distinguisher Ω_0^{11} with the following output difference

$$(\text{0x0088 0000 0000 0000}, *, 0, 0, *)$$

is improved, namely time complexity $2^{167.80}$. In addition, the form of the relaxed output difference of the distinguisher Ω_2^{11} is as follows.

$$(\text{0x0000 0400 0000 0000}, *, 0, 0, *).$$

The probability of the distinguisher of F_{bw}, F_{in} and F_{fw} sub-permutation for rebound distinguisher Ω_2^{11} are $2^{-75.83}$, $2^{-123.06}$ and $2^{-130.83+18.69} = 2^{-112.14}$. Therefore, the time complexity of the 11-step rebound attack launched by the distinguisher Ω_2^{11} is about $2^{187.97}$.

5.2 14-Step Rebound Attacks Against ACE Permutation

As shown in the analysis of the new algorithm given in Sect. 4.2, there are 9 valid rebound distinguishers illustrated in Fig. 6 and Table 12 of Appendix A. The 14-step rebound distinguisher is composed of a 4-step differential in the inbound phase, which extends forward by two steps and backward by seven steps in the outbound phase. After analysis, it was found that the attack complexity of distinguisher $\Omega_0^{14} \sim \Omega_7^{14}$ was similar, while distinguisher Ω_8^{14} initiating the rebound attack with the highest complexity. Next, we will first introduce the complexity analysis of Ω_0^{14} illustrated in Fig. 6. The distribution of characteristics of the active SB-64 which is based on unkeyed 8-round Simeck-64 is shown in Table 13, 14, 15, 16, 17, 18 and 19 of Appendix A. The relaxed output difference of the 14-step rebound attack Ω_0^{14} is as follows.

$$(0x4000\ 0000\ 0000\ 0000, *, 0, 0, *)$$

Then, we will introduce the attack process.

Inbound Phase

1) For these active SB-64s S_A^3, S_A^4, S_A^5, we exhaustively determine all solutions that satisfy their differential propagation. Test 2^{64} inputs for these active SB-64s, because $P(S_A^3) = 2^{-18.28}$, $P(S_A^4) = 2^{-18.28}$, and $P(S_A^5) = 2^{-26.44}$, the solutions of these active SB-64s S_A^3, S_A^4, S_A^5 are stored in the table T_A^3, T_A^4 and T_A^5, respectively, namely $2^{64-18.28} = 2^{45.72}$, $2^{64-18.28} = 2^{45.72}$ and $2^{64-26.44} = 2^{37.56}$. The time complexity of these operations is $3 \times 2^{64} = 2^{65.58}$ computations, and $2^{45.72} + 2^{45.72} + 2^{37.56} = 2^{46.72}$ words need to be stored.
2) For the active SB-64 S_C^4, requires testing $2^{45.72}$ solutions in the table T_A^3. The filtering probability of S_C^4 is $P(S_C^4) = 2^{-21.46}$, so the number of solutions for the active SB-64 S_C^4 is $2^{45.72-21.46} = 2^{23.96}$. The time complexity of this step is $2^{45.72}$, and $2^{23.96}$ words are stored.
3) Test $2^{45.72}$ solutions in the table T_A^4 to determine the matching value of active SB-64. The filtering probability of S_C^5 is $P(S_C^5) = 2^{-21.54}$, and the number of solutions obtained for S_C^5 is $2^{45.72-21.54} = 2^{24.18}$. Therefore, the time complexity is $2^{45.72}$, and the memory complexity is $2^{24.18}$ words.
4) For the active SB-64 S_E^5, the value of matching differential propagation is obtained through an exhaustive search. It is required to test 2^{64} inputs, and its differential probability is known to be $P(S_E^5) = 2^{-25.72}$. Therefore, a total of $2^{64-25.72} = 2^{38.28}$ solutions are stored in the table T_E^5. The time complexity is 2^{64}, and memory complexity is $2^{38.28}$ words.
5) For the active SB-64 S_C^6, the value of matching differential propagation needs to be determined by testing $2^{37.56}$ values in the table T_A^5. Given the filtering probability $P(S_C^6) = 2^{-20.7}$, the solution of the active SB-64 is $2^{37.56-20.7} = 2^{16.86}$. The time complexity is $2^{37.56}$, and the memory complexity is $2^{16.86}$ words.
6) The combination of the $2^{23.96} \times 2^{24.18} \times 2^{38.28} \times 2^{16.86} = 2^{103.28}$ solutions obtained above and any value of the precomputed in B-branch (i.e. 64 solutions) will fix the entire state. Among them, the time complexity of the pre-calculation process is 2^{64}, and the memory complexity is 2^{64}. Therefore, up

to $2^{103.28} \times 2^{64} = 2^{167.28}$ starting points can be generated from the 4-step distinguisher in the inbound phase. Then, propagate each starting point to the outbound phase to match the differential propagation of the 14-step rebound distinguisher.

Outbound Phase. Fixed $2^{167.28}$ solutions in the inbound phase, all 320-bit state values can be determined. Propagate the values to F_{bw} and F_{fw}, and check if the outbound phase is satisfied. The probability of the 2-step differential in the F_{bw} phase is known to be $P^2_{bw} = 2^{-40.22}$, and the probability of the 7-step differential in the F_{fw} phase is $2^{-130.83}$, that is, the total probability of the differentials in the outbound phase is $2^{-40.22-130.83} = 2^{-171.05}$. Therefore, the degree of freedom cannot fully satisfy the 14-step distinguisher. In order to implement the 14-step rebound attack for ACE permutation, relax the output difference of the active SB-64 S^{13}_C in the 14th step, so that the output difference of S^{13}_C takes any value. The form of the output difference of the 14-step distinguisher is

$$(0x4000000000000000, *, 0, 0, *).$$

This enables the total probability of the differentials in the outbound phase to be improved to $2^{-152.36}$, obtaining $2^{167.28}$ starting points based on the distinguishers.

Complexity Evaluation. The time complexity of the 14-step rebound attack launched by the distinguisher Ω^{14}_0 in the inbound phase is as follows.

$$2^{65.58} + 2^{45.72} + 2^{45.71} + 2^{64} + 2^{37.56} + 2^{64} \approx 2^{66.32}$$

A memory to store

$$2^{46.72} + 2^{23.96} + 2^{24.17} + 2^{38.29} + 2^{16.86} + 2^{64} \approx 2^{64}$$

words in the inbound phase. For the outbound phase, $2^{152.36}$ computations are required to satisfy differential propagation. In summary, the time complexity of the rebound attack is about $2^{152.36}$ computations, and the memory complexity is approximately 2^{64}.

In addition, for distinguisher Ω^{14}_8, the differential probabilities of distinguisher in F_{bw}, F_{in} and F_{fw} phase are $2^{-42.82}$, $2^{-153.81}$ and $2^{-130.83}$, respectively. By relaxing the output differences of S^{13}_C, that is, its output difference of the distinguisher Ω^{14}_8 is

$$(0x0000\ 2000\ 0000\ 0000, *, 0, 0, *).$$

The probability P^7_{fw} of the differential in the F_{fw} phase can be increased to $2^{-112.14}$. Therefore, the time complexity is $2^{-154.96}$.

5.3 13-Step Rebound Attacks Against ACE Permutation

The 128 13-step rebound distinguishers mentioned in Sect. 4.2 are constructed by 2-step, 4-step and 7-step distinguishers for F_{bw}, F_{in} and F_{fw} sub-permutation, respectively. Table 11 lists 16 13-step rebound distinguishers. After analyzing these distinguishers, 15 of them can be directly used for rebound attacks. At this point, the distinguishers Ω_i^{13} ($P_{bw}^2 = 2^{-22.04}$, $P_{in}^4 = 2^{-153.81}$ and $P_{fw}^7 = 2^{-130.83}$) with the lowest attack complexity $2^{152.86}$ and the distinguishers Ω_5^{13} ($P_{bw}^2 = 2^{-40.04}$, $P_{in}^4 = 2^{-148.97}$ and $P_{fw}^7 = 2^{-130.83}$) with the highest time complexity $2^{-170.87}$, where $i \in \{2, 3, 4, 6, 7, 8, 14\}$. However, when the input difference or output difference is relaxed, all 128 13-step distinguishers can execute rebound attacks, and the attack complexity $2^{134.17}$ launched by the distinguishers Ω_i^{13} ($P_{bw}^2 = 2^{-22.04}$, $P_{in}^4 = 2^{-153.81}$ and $P_{fw}^7 = 2^{-112.14}$) remains the lowest, while the attack with the highest complexity $2^{161.07}$ is based on the distinguishers Ω_{15}^{13} ($P_{bw}^2 = 2^{-48.93}$, $P_{in}^4 = 2^{-156.85}$ and $P_{fw}^7 = 2^{-112.14}$).

6 Conclusions

In this paper, we propose an algorithm to search for the rebound distinguishers of ACE permutation and this search strategy can also be used for other permutations. Firstly, we verified the lower bound on the number of active SB-64s for ACE permutation. Then, combined with Simeck-64's iterative differential and the clustering effect of characteristics, the probability of the differentials is improved. The new algorithm constructs many rebound distinguishers based on these differentials. As a consequence, the first 14-step rebound attack was launched for ACE permutation.

Acknowledgements. The authors would like to thank the reviewers for their valuable comments. This work is supported by the National Natural Science Foundation of China (No. 61702537, No. 62172427).

A The Experimental Results on ACE

Table 7. The 5-round characteristic of ACE permutation with 4 active SB-64s

Step	ΔA	ΔB	ΔC	ΔD	ΔE
0	0x0000 0000 0000 0000	0x4800 00BC 9100 0080	0x0000 0000 0000 0000	0x0000 0000 0100 0000	0x1100 0000 0000 0000
1	0x0000 0000 0000 0000	0x0000 0000 0000 0000	0x0000 0000 0000 0000	0x0000 0000 0100 0000	0x4800 00BC 9100 0080
2	0x0000 0000 0000 0000	0x0000 0000 0000 0000	0x0000 0000 0000 0000	0x0000 0000 0100 0000	0x0000 0000 0000 0000
3	0x0000 0000 0100 0000	0x0000 0000 0000 0000	0x0000 0000 0000 0000	0x0000 0000 0000 0000	0x0000 0000 0000 0000
4	0x0000 0000 0000 0000	0x0000 0000 0000 0000	0x8000 0000 5100 0000	0x8000 0000 5100 0000	0x0000 0000 0000 0000
5	0x8000 0000 5100 0000	0x8A00 0000 5100 0000	0x0000 0000 0000 0000	0x0000 0000 0000 0000	0x8A00 0000 5100 0000

Table 8. The 5-step characteristic of ACE permutation with optimal probability 2^{-80}

Step	ΔA	ΔB	ΔC	ΔD	ΔE
0	0x0000 0000 0000 0000	0x0000 0050 0000 0080	0x0000 0000 0000 0000	0x0000 0150 0000 0080	0x0000 0050 0000 0080
1	0x0000 0000 0000 0000	0x0000 0000 0000 0000	0x0000 0000 0000 0000	0x0000 0150 0000 0080	0x0000 0050 0000 0080
2	0x0000 0000 0000 0000	0x0000 0000 0000 0000	0x0000 0000 0000 0000	0x0000 0150 0000 0080	0x0000 0000 0000 0000
3	0x0000 0150 0000 0080	0x0000 0000 0000 0000	0x0000 0000 0000 0000	0x0000 0000 0000 0000	0x0000 0000 0000 0000
4	0x0000 0000 0000 0000	0x0000 0000 0000 0000	0x0000 0050 0000 0080	0x0000 0050 0000 0080	0x0000 0000 0000 0000
5	0x0000 0050 0000 0080	0x0000 0150 0000 0080	0x0000 0000 0000 0000	0x0000 0000 0000 0000	0x0000 0150 0000 0080

Table 9. The iterative differentials of SB-64

ID	$\alpha \rightleftharpoons \beta$	ID	$\alpha \rightleftharpoons \beta$
0	0x1100 0000 0000 0000⇌0x0100 0000 0000 0000	32	0x0004 0000 0000 0000⇌0x0044 0000 0000 0000
1	0x0088 0000 0000 0000⇌0x0008 0000 0000 0000	33	0x0000 0000 0001 1000⇌0x0000 0000 0000 1000
2	0x0000 0000 0000 0002⇌0x0000 0000 0000 0022	34	0x2000 0000 0000 0000⇌0x2000 0002 0000 0000
3	0x0000 0000 0000 0004⇌0x0000 0000 0000 0044	35	0x0000 0000 0110 0000⇌0x0000 0000 0010 0000
4	0x0000 0000 8000 0000⇌0x0000 0000 8000 0008	36	0x0000 0044 0000 0000⇌0x0000 0004 0000 0000
5	0x0800 0000 0000 0000⇌0x8800 0000 0000 0000	37	0x0200 0000 0000 0000⇌0x2200 0000 0000 0000
6	0x0000 0000 0020 0000⇌0x0000 0000 0220 0000	38	0x0000 0000 0008 0000⇌0x0000 0000 0088 0000
7	0x0000 0000 0400 0000⇌0x0000 0000 4400 0000	39	0x0000 0000 0002 2000⇌0x0000 0000 0000 2000
8	0x0002 0000 0000 0000⇌0x0022 0000 0000 0000	40	0x0000 0000 1100 0000⇌0x0000 0000 0100 0000
9	0x0040 0000 0000 0000⇌0x0440 0000 0000 0000	41	0x0000 0000 1000 0000⇌0x0000 0000 1000 0001
10	0x0020 0000 0000 0000⇌0x0220 0000 0000 0000	42	0x0000 0000 0000 8800⇌0x0000 0000 0000 0800
11	0x0002 2000 0000 0000⇌0x0000 2000 0000 0000	43	0x0000 0220 0000 0000⇌0x0000 0020 0000 0000
12	0x0000 0000 0000 0100⇌0x0000 0000 0000 1100	44	0x0000 0000 0008 8000⇌0x0000 0000 0000 8000
13	0x4400 0000 0000 0000⇌0x0400 0000 0000 0000	45	0x0000 0200 0000 0000⇌0x0000 2200 0000 0000
14	0x4000 0004 0000 0000⇌0x4000 0000 0000 0000	46	0x0000 0000 0004 4000⇌0x0000 0000 0000 4000
15	0x8000 0008 0000 0000⇌0x8000 0000 0000 0000	47	0x0000 0880 0000 0000⇌0x0000 0080 0000 0000
16	0x0000 0000 0000 0088⇌0x0000 0000 0000 0008	48	0x0000 0000 0000 2200⇌0x0000 0000 0000 0200
17	0x0000 0000 0000 0080⇌0x0000 0000 0000 0880	49	0x0000 0000 0040 0000⇌0x0000 0000 0440 0000
18	0x0000 1000 0000 0000⇌0x0001 1000 0000 0000	50	0x0000 8000 0000 0000⇌0x0008 8000 0000 0000
19	0x0000 0000 0000 4400⇌0x0000 0000 0000 0400	51	0x0000 0000 0880 0000⇌0x0000 0000 0080 0000
20	0x0000 0000 2000 0002⇌0x0000 0000 2000 0000	52	0x0000 1100 0000 0000⇌0x0000 0100 0000 0000
21	0x0000 0000 0000 0011⇌0x0000 0000 0000 0001	53	0x0000 0040 0000 0000⇌0x0000 0440 0000 0000
22	0x0080 0000 0000 0000⇌0x0880 0000 0000 0000	54	0x0000 0022 0000 0000⇌0x0000 0002 0000 0000
23	0x1000 0001 0000 0000⇌0x1000 0000 0000 0000	55	0x0000 0000 0000 0040⇌0x0000 0000 0000 0440
24	0x0000 0000 0002 0000⇌0x0000 0000 0022 0000	56	0x0000 0001 0000 0000⇌0x0000 0011 0000 0000
25	0x0110 0000 0000 0000⇌0x0010 0000 0000 0000	57	0x0000 0000 0000 0010⇌0x0000 0000 0000 0110
26	0x0000 4000 0000 0000⇌0x0004 4000 0000 0000	58	0x0000 0800 0000 0000⇌0x0000 8800 0000 0000
27	0x0000 0000 8800 0000⇌0x0000 0000 0800 0000	59	0x0000 0000 0004 0000⇌0x0000 0000 0044 0000
28	0x0000 0000 4000 0000⇌0x0000 0000 4000 0004	60	0x0000 0000 0011 0000⇌0x0000 0000 0001 0000
29	0x0000 0000 0200 0000⇌0x0000 0000 2200 0000	61	0x0000 4400 0000 0000⇌0x0000 0400 0000 0000
30	0x0000 0088 0000 0000⇌0x0000 0008 0000 0000	62	0x0000 0010 0000 0000⇌0x0000 0110 0000 0000
31	0x0001 0000 0000 0000⇌0x0011 0000 0000 0000	63	0x0000 0000 0000 0020⇌0x0000 0000 0000 0220

Table 10. The distribution of characteristics in the iterative differentials $\alpha \rightleftharpoons \beta$ with probability $2^{-18.69}$ of SB-64

P_{DC}	2^{-22}	2^{-23}	2^{-24}	2^{-25}	2^{-26}	2^{-27}	2^{-28}	2^{-29}	2^{-30}	2^{-31}
#DC	1	0	6	3	22	16	70	80	180	305
P_{DC}	2^{-32}	2^{-33}	2^{-34}	2^{-35}	2^{-36}	2^{-37}	2^{-38}	2^{-39}	2^{-40}	2^{-41}
#DC	511	854	1427	2143	3279	4725	6364	8210	10074	11610

Table 11. 13-step rebound distinguishers of ACE permutation

ID	Step	$(\Delta A, \Delta B, \Delta C, \Delta D, \Delta E)$
Ω_0^{13}	0	(0x0000 0000 0000 0000,0x0200 0000 0100 0000,0x0000 0000 0000 0000,0x0200 0000 0000 0000,0x0200 0000 1600 0000)
	1	(0x0000 0000 0000 0000,0x0000 0000 0000 0000,0x0000 0000 0000 0000,0x0200 0000 0000 0000,0x0200 0000 0100 0000)
	2	(0x0000 0000 1100 0000,0x0000 0000 0000 0000,0x0000 0000 0000 0000,0x0200 0000 1100 0000,0x0000 0000 0000 0000)
	3	(0x0200 0000 1100 0000,0x0000 0000 0000 0000,0x0100 0000 0100 0000,0x0100 0000 0100 0000,0x0000 0000 0000 0000)
	4	(0x0100 0000 0100 0000,0x1100 0000 0000 0000,0x0200 0000 0100 0000,0x0200 0000 0100 0000,0x1100 0000 0000 0000)
	5	(0x0000 0000 0000 0000,0x1100 0000 0000 0000,0x1300 0000 0100 0000,0x1100 0000 0000 0000,0x0000 0000 0000 0000)
	6	(0x1100 0000 0000 0000,0x1100 0000 0000 0000,0x0000 0000 0000 0000,0x0000 0000 0000 0000,0x0000 0000 0000 0000)
	⋮	⋮
	13	(0x1100 0000 0000 0000,*(0x0100 0000 0000 0000),0x0000 0000 0000 0000,0x0000 0000 0000 0000,*(0x0100 0000 0000 0000))
Ω_1^{13}	0	(0x0000 0000 0000 0000,0x0000 4000 0000 2000,0x0000 0000 0000 0000,0x0000 4000 0000 0000,0x0000 4000 0002 8000)
	1	(0x0000 0000 0000 0000,0x0000 0000 0000 0000,0x0000 0000 0000 0000,0x0000 4000 0000 0000,0x0000 4000 0000 2000)
	2	(0x0000 00000 0022 000,0x0000 0000 0000 0000,0x0000 0000 0000 0000,0x0000 4000 0002 2000,0x0000 0000 0000 0000)
	3	(0x0000 4000 0002 2000,0x0000 0000 0000 0000,0x0000 2000 0000 2000,0x0000 2000 0000 2000,0x0000 0000 0000 0000)
	4	(0x0000 2000 0000 2000,0x0002 2000 0000 0000,0x0000 4000 0000 2000,0x0000 4000 0000 2000,0x0002 2000 0000 0000)
	5	(0x0000 0000 0000 0000,0x0002 2000 0000 0000,0x0002 6000 0000 2000,0x0002 2000 0000 0000,0x0000 0000 0000 0000)
	6	(0x0002 2000 0000 0000,0x0002 2000 0000 0000,0x0000 0000 0000 0000,0x0000 0000 0000 0000,0x0000 0000 0000 0000)
	⋮	⋮
	13	(0x0002 2000 0000 0000,*(0x0000 2000 0000 0000),0x0000 0000 0000 0000,0x0000 0000 0000 0000,*(0x0000 2000 0000 0000))
Ω_2^{13}	0	(0x0000 0000 0000 0000,0x8000 0000 C000 0005,0x0000 0000 0000 0000,0x0000 0000 0000 0000,0x0000 0000 0000 0000)
	1	(0x0000 0000 0000 0000,0x0000 0000 0000 0000,0x0000 0000 0000 0000,0x0000 0000 0000 0000,0x8000 0000 C000 0005)
	2	(0x8000 0000 4000 0001,0x0000 0000 0000 0000,0x0000 0000 0000 0000,0x8000 0000 4000 0001,0x0000 0000 0000 0000)
	3	(0x8000 0000 4000 0001,0x0000 0000 0000 0000,0x8000 0000 4000 0005,0x8000 0000 4000 0005,0x0000 0000 0000 0000)
	4	(0x8000 0000 4000 0005,0x4000 0000 0000 0000,0x8000 0004 4000 0005,0x8000 0004 4000 0005,0x4000 0000 0000 0000)
	5	(0x0000 0000 0000 0000,0x4000 0000 0000 0000,0xC000 0004 4000 0005,0x4000 0000 0000 0000,0x0000 0000 0000 0000)
	6	(0x4000 0000 0000 0000,0x4000 0000 0000 0000,0x0000 0000 0000 0000,0x0000 0000 0000 0000,0x0000 0000 0000 0000)
	⋮	⋮
	13	(0x4000 0000 0000 0000,*(0x4000 0004 0000 0000),0x0000 0000 0000 0000,0x0000 0000 0000 0000,*(0x4000 0004 0000 0000))
Ω_3^{13}	0	(0x0000 0000 0000 0000,0x01000 0000 B800 000,0x0000 0000 0000 0000,0x0000 0000 0000 0000,0x0000 0000 0000 0000)
	1	(0x0000 0000 0000 0000,0x0000 0000 0000 0000,0x0000 0000 0000 0000,0x0000 0000 0000 0000,0x0100 0000 0B80 0000)
	2	(0x0100 0000 0280 0000,0x0000 0000 0000 0000,0x0000 0000 0000 0000,0x0100 0000 0280 0000,0x0000 0000 0000 0000)
	3	(0x0100 0000 0280 0000,0x0000 0000 0000 0000,0x0100 0000 0A80 0000,0x0100 0000 0A80 0000,0x0000 0000 0000 0000)
	4	(0x0100 0000 0A80 0000,0x0080 0000 0000 0000,0x0900 0000 0A80 0000,0x0900 0000 0A80 0000,0x0080 0000 0000 0000)
	5	(0x0000 0000 0000 0000,0x0080 0000 0000 0000,0x0980 0000 0A80 0000,0x0080 0000 0000 0000,0x0000 0000 0000 0000)
	6	(0x0080 0000 0000 0000,0x0080 0000 0000 0000,0x0000 0000 0000 0000,0x0000 0000 0000 0000,0x0000 0000 0000 0000)
	⋮	⋮
	13	(0x0080 0000 0000 0000,*(0x0880 0000 0000 0000),0x0000 0000 0000 0000,0x0000 0000 0000 0000,*(0x0880 0000 0000 0000))

(continued)

Table 11. (*continued*)

ID	Step	$(\Delta A, \Delta B, \Delta C, \Delta D, \Delta E)$
Ω_4^{13}	0	(0x0000 0000 0000 0000,0x0000 8000 0005 4000,0x0000 0000 0000 0000,0x0000 0000 0000 0000,0x0000 0000 0000 0000)
	1	(0x0000 0000 0000 0000,0x0000 0000 0000 0000,0x0000 0000 0000 0000,0x0000 0000 0000 0000,0x0000 8000 0005 4000)
	2	(0x0000 8000 0001 4000,0x0000 0000 0000 0000,0x0000 0000 0000 0000,0x0000 8000 0001 4000,0x0000 0000 0000 0000)
	3	(0x0000 8000 0001 4000,0x0000 0000 0000 0000,0x0000 8000 0005 4000,0x0000 8000 0005 4000,0x0000 0000 0000 0000)
	4	(0x0000 8000 0005 4000,0x0000 4000 0000 0000,0x0004 8000 0005 4000,0x0004 8000 0005 4000,0x0000 4000 0000 0000)
	5	(0x0000 0000 0000 0000,0x0000 4000 0000 0000,0x0004 C000 0005 4000,0x0000 4000 0000 0000,0x0000 0000 0000 0000)
	6	(0x0000 4000 0000 0000,0x0000 4000 0000 0000,0x0000 0000 0000 0000,0x0000 0000 0000 0000,0x0000 0000 0000 0000)
	⋮	⋮
	13	(0x0000 4000 0000 0000,∗(0x0004 4000 0000 0000),0x0000 0000 0000 0000,0x0000 0000 0000 0000,∗(0x0004 4000 0000 0000))
Ω_5^{13}	0	(0x0000 0000 0000 0000, 0x0000 0010 0000 0018, 0x0000 0000 0000 0000, 0x0000 0010 0000 0000, 0x0000 0010 0000 00a0)
	1	(0x0000 0000 0000 0000, 0x0000 0000 0000 0000, 0x0000 0000 0000 0000, 0x0000 0010 0000 0000, 0x0000 0010 0000 0018)
	2	(0x0000 0000 0000 0088, 0x0000 0000 0000 0000, 0x0000 0000 0000 0000, 0x0000 0010 0000 0088, 0x0000 0000 0000 0000)
	3	(0x0000 0010 0000 0088, 0x0000 0000 0000 0000, 0x0000 0008 0000 0008, 0x0000 0008 0000 0008, 0x0000 0000 0000 0000)
	4	(0x0000 0008 0000 0008, 0x0000 0088 0000 0000, 0x0000 0010 0000 0008, 0x0000 0010 0000 0008, 0x0000 0088 0000 0000)
	5	(0x0000 0000 0000 0000, 0x0000 0088 0000 0000, 0x0000 0098 0000 0008, 0x0000 0088 0000 0000, 0x0000 0000 0000 0000)
	6	(0x0000 0088 0000 0000, 0x0000 0088 0000 0000, 0x0000 0000 0000 0000, 0x0000 0000 0000 0000, 0x0000 0000 0000 0000)
	⋮	⋮
	13	(0x0000 0088 0000 0000, ∗(0x0000 0008 0000 0000), 0x0000 0000 0000 0000, 0x0000 0000 0000 0000, ∗(0x0000 0008 0000 0000))
Ω_6^{13}	0	(0x0000 0000 0000 0000,0x4000 0000 E000 0002,0x0000 0000 0000 0000,0x0000 0000 0000 0000,0x0000 0000 0000 0000)
	1	(0x0000 0000 0000 0000,0x0000 0000 0000 0000,0x0000 0000 0000 0000,0x0000 0000 0000 0000,0x4000 0000 E000 0002)
	2	(0x4000 0000 A000 0000,0x0000 0000 0000 0000,0x0000 0000 0000 0000,0x4000 0000 A000 0000,0x0000 0000 0000 0000)
	3	(0x4000 0000 A000 0000,0x0000 0000 0000 0000,0x4000 0000 A000 0002,0x4000 0000 A000 0002,0x0000 0000 0000 0000)
	4	(0x4000 0000 A000 0002,0x2000 0000 0000 0000,0x4000 0002 A000 0002,0x4000 0002 A000 0002,0x2000 0000 0000 0000)
	5	(0x0000 0000 0000 0000,0x2000 0000 0000 0000,0x6000 0002 A000 0002,0x2000 0000 0000 0000,0x0000 0000 0000 0000)
	6	(0x2000 0000 0000 0000,0x2000 0000 0000 0000,0x0000 0000 0000 0000,0x0000 0000 0000 0000,0x0000 0000 0000 0000)
	⋮	⋮
	13	(0x2000 0000 0000 0000,∗(0x2000 0002 0000 0000),0x0000 0000 0000 0000,0x0000 0000 0000 0000,∗(0x2000 0002 0000 0000))
Ω_7^{13}	0	(0x0000 0000 0000 0000,0x2000 0000 5000 0001,0x0000 0000 0000 0000,0x0000 0000 0000 0000,0x0000 0000 0000 0000)
	1	(0x0000 0000 0000 0000,0x0000 0000 0000 0000,0x0000 0000 0000 0000,0x0000 0000 0000 0000,0x2000 0000 5000 0001)
	2	(0x2000 0000 5000 0000,0x0000 0000 0000 0000,0x0000 0000 0000 0000,0x2000 0000 5000 0000,0x0000 0000 0000 0000)
	3	(0x2000 0000 5000 0000,0x0000 0000 0000 0000,0x2000 0000 5000 0001,0x2000 0000 5000 0001,0x0000 0000 0000 0000)
	4	(0x2000 0000 5000 0001,0x1000 0000 0000 0000,0x3000 0001 5000 0001,0x3000 0001 5000 0001,0x1000 0000 0000 0000)
	5	(0x0000 0000 0000 0000,0x1000 0000 0000 0000,0x2000 0001 5000 0001,0x1000 0000 0000 0000,0x0000 0000 0000 0000)
	6	(0x1000 0000 0000 0000,0x1000 0000 0000 0000,0x0000 0000 0000 0000,0x0000 0000 0000 0000,0x0000 0000 0000 0000)
	⋮	⋮
	13	(0x1000 0000 0000 0000,∗(0x0000 0000 8000 0000),0x0000 0000 0000 0000,0x0000 0000 0000 0000,∗(0x0000 0000 8000 0000))

(*continued*)

Table 11. (*continued*)

ID	Step	$(\Delta A, \Delta B, \Delta C, \Delta D, \Delta E)$
Ω_8^{13}	0	(0x0000 0000 0000 0000,0x0800 0000 5400 0000,0x0000 0000 0000 0000,0x0000 0000 0000 0000,0x0000 0000 0000 0000)
	1	(0x0000 0000 0000 0000,0x0000 0000 0000 0000,0x0000 0000 0000 0000,0x0000 0000 0000 0000,0x0800 0000 5400 0000)
	2	(0x0800 0000 1400 0000,0x0000 0000 0000 0000,0x0000 0000 0000 0000,0x0800 0000 1400 0000,0x0000 0000 0000 0000)
	3	(0x0800 0000 1400 0000,0x0000 0000 0000 0000,0x0800 0000 5400 0000,0x0800 0000 5400 0000,0x0000 0000 0000 0000)
	4	(0x0800 0000 5400 0000,0x0400 0000 0000 0000,0x4C00 0000 5400 0000,0x4C00 0000 5400 0000,0x0400 0000 0000 0000)
	5	(0x0000 0000 0000 0000,0x0400 0000 0000 0000,0x4800 0000 5400 0000,0x0400 0000 0000 0000,0x0000 0000 0000 0000)
	6	(0x0400 0000 0000 0000,0x0400 0000 0000 0000,0x0000 0000 0000 0000,0x0000 0000 0000 0000,0x0000 0000 0000 0000)
	⋮	⋮
	13	(0x0400 0000 0000 0000,*(0x4400 0000 0000 0000),0x0000 0000 0000 0000,0x0000 0000 0000 0000,*(0x4400 0000 0000 0000))
Ω_9^{13}	0	(0x0000 0000 0000 0000,0x0000 0000 0000 2000,0x0000 0000 0000 0000,0x0000 0000 0000 0000,0x0000 0000 0000 0000)
	1	(0x0000 0000 0000 0000,0x0000 0000 0000 0000,0x0000 0000 0000 0000,0x0000 0000 0000 0000,0x0000 0000 0000 2000)
	2	(0x0000 4000 0000 E000,0x0000 0000 0000 0000,0x0000 0000 0000 0000,0x0000 4000 0000 E000,0x0000 0000 0000 0000)
	3	(0x0000 4000 0000 E000,0x0000 0000 0000 0000,0x0000 4000 0002 A000,0x0000 4000 0002 A000,0x0000 0000 0000 0000)
	4	(0x0000 4000 0002 A000,0x0000 2000 0000 0000,0x0002 6000 0002 A000,0x0002 6000 0002 A000,0x0000 2000 0000 0000)
	5	(0x0000 0000 0000 0000,0x0000 2000 0000 0000,0x0002 4000 0002 A000,0x0000 2000 0000 0000,0x0000 0000 0000 0000)
	6	(0x0000 2000 0000 0000,0x0000 2000 0000 0000,0x0000 0000 0000 0000,0x0000 0000 0000 0000,0x0000 0000 0000 0000)
	⋮	⋮
	13	(0x0000 2000 0000 0000,*(0x0002 2000 0000 0000),0x0000 0000 0000 0000,0x0000 0000 0000 0000,*(0x0002 2000 0000 0000))
Ω_{10}^{13}	0	(0x0000 0000 0000 0000,,0x0000 0000 0000 0000,0x0000 8000 0000 0000,0x0000 8000 0005 0000)
	1	(0x0000 0000 0000 0000,0x0000 0000 0000 0000,0x0000 0000 0000 0000,0x0000 8000 0000 0000,0x0000 8000 0000 4000)
	2	(0x0000 0000 0004 4000,0x0000 0000 0000 0000,0x0000 0000 0000 0000,0x0000 8000 0004 4000,0x0000 0000 0000 0000)
	3	(0x0000 8000 0004 4000,0x0000 0000 0000 0000,0x0000 4000 0000 4000,0x0000 4000 0000 4000,0x0000 0000 0000 0000)
	4	(0x0000 4000 0000 4000,0x0004 4000 0000 0000,0x0000 8000 0000 4000,0x0000 8000 0000 4000,0x0004 4000 0000 0000)
	5	(0x0000 0000 0000 0000,0x0004 4000 0000 0000,0x0004 C000 0000 4000,0x0004 4000 0000 0000,0x0000 0000 0000 0000)
	6	(0x0004 4000 0000 0000,0x0004 4000 0000 0000,0x0000 0000 0000 0000,0x0000 0000 0000 0000,0x0000 0000 0000 0000)
	⋮	⋮
	13	(0x0004 4000 0000 0000,*(0x0000 4000 0000 0000),0x0000 0000 0000 0000,0x0000 0000 0000 0000,*(0x0000 4000 0000 0000))
Ω_{11}^{13}	0	(0x0000 0000 0000 0000,0x0004 0000 0002 0000,0x0000 0000 0000 0000,0x0004 0000 0000 0000,0x0004 0000 002C 0000)
	1	(0x0000 0000 0000 0000,0x0000 0000 0000 0000,0x0000 0000 0000 0000,0x0004 0000 0000 0000,0x0004 0000 0002 0000)
	2	(0x0000 0000 0022 0000,0x0000 0000 0000 0000,0x0000 0000 0000 0000,0x0004 0000 0022 0000,0x0000 0000 0000 0000)
	3	(0x0004 0000 0022 0000,0x0000 0000 0000 0000,0x0002 0000 0002 0000,0x0002 0000 0002 0000,0x0000 0000 0000 0000)
	4	(0x0002 0000 0002 0000,0x0022 0000 0000 0000,0x0004 0000 0002 0000,0x0004 0000 0002 0000,0x0022 0000 0000 0000)
	5	(0x0000 0000 0000 0000,0x0022 0000 0000 0000,0x0026 0000 0002 0000,0x0022 0000 0000 0000,0x0000 0000 0000 0000)
	6	(0x0022 0000 0000 0000,0x0022 0000 0000 0000,0x0000 0000 0000 0000,0x0000 0000 0000 0000,0x0000 0000 0000 0000)
	⋮	⋮
	13	(0x0022 0000 0000 0000,*(0x0002 0000 0000 0000),0x0000 0000 0000 0000,0x0000 0000 0000 0000,*(0x0002 0000 0000 0000))

(*continued*)

Table 11. (*continued*)

ID	Step	$(\Delta A, \Delta B, \Delta C, \Delta D, \Delta E)$
Ω^{13}_{12}	0	(0x0000 0000 0000 0000,0x0000 0200 0000 1500,0x0000 0000 0000 0000,0x0000 0000 0000 0000,0x0000 0000 0000 0000)
	1	(0x0000 0000 0000 0000,0x0000 0000 0000 0000,0x0000 0000 0000 0000,0x0000 0000 0000 0000,0x0000 0200 0000 1500)
	2	(0x0000 0200 0000 0500,0x0000 0000 0000 0000,0x0000 0000 0000 0000,0x0000 0200 0000 0500,0x0000 0000 0000 0000)
	3	(0x0000 0200 0000 0500,0x0000 0000 0000 0000,0x0000 0200 0000 1500,0x0000 0200 0000 1500,0x0000 0000 0000 0000)
	4	(0x0000 0200 0000 1500,0x0000 0100 0000 0000,0x0000 1300 0000 1500,0x0000 1300 0000 1500,0x0000 0100 0000 0000)
	5	(0x0000 0000 0000 0000,0x0000 0100 0000 0000,0x0000 1200 0000 1500,0x0000 0100 0000 0000,0x0000 0000 0000 0000)
	6	(0x0000 0100 0000 0000,0x0000 0100 0000 0000,0x0000 0000 0000 0000,0x0000 0000 0000 0000,0x0000 0000 0000 0000)
	⋮	⋮
	13	(0x0000 0100 0000 0000,*(0x0000 1100 0000 0000),0x0000 0000 0000 0000,0x0000 0000 0000 0000,*(0x0000 1100 0000 0000))
Ω^{13}_{13}	0	(0x0000 0000 0000 0000,0x0000 0800 0000 0400,0x0000 0000 0000 0000,0x0000 0800 0000 0000,0x0000 8000 0001 1800)
	1	(0x0000 0000 0000 0000,0x0000 0000 0000 0000,0x0000 0000 0000 0000,0x0000 0800 0000 0000,0x0000 0800 0000 0400)
	2	(0x0000 0000 0000 4400,0x0000 0000 0000 0000,0x0000 0000 0000 0000,0x0000 0800 0000 4400,0x0000 0000 0000 0000)
	3	(0x0000 0800 0000 4400,0x0000 0000 0000 0000,0x0000 0400 0000 0400,0x0000 0400 0000 0400,0x0000 0000 0000 0000)
	4	(0x0000 0400 0000 0400,0x0000 4400 0000 0000,0x0000 0800 0000 0400,0x0000 0800 0000 0400,0x0000 4400 0000 0000)
	5	(0x0000 0000 0000 0000,0x0000 4400 0000 0000,0x0000 4C00 0000 0400,0x0000 4400 0000 0000,0x0000 0000 0000 0000)
	6	(0x0000 4400 0000 0000,0x0000 4400 0000 0000,0x0000 0000 0000 0000,0x0000 0000 0000 0000,0x0000 0000 0000 0000)
	⋮	⋮
	13	(0x0000 4400 0000 0000,*(0x0000 0400 0000 0000),0x0000 0000 0000 0000,0x0000 0000 0000 0000,*(0x0000 0400 0000 0000))
Ω^{13}_{14}	0	(0x0000 0000 0000 0000,0x0000 0010 0000 00A8,0x0000 0000 0000 0000,0x0000 0000 0000 0000,0x0000 0000 0000 0000)
	1	(0x0000 0000 0000 0000,0x0000 0000 0000 0000,0x0000 0000 0000 0000,0x0000 0000 0000 0000,0x0000 0010 0000 00A8)
	2	(0x0000 0010 0000 0028,0x0000 0000 0000 0000,0x0000 0000 0000 0000,0x0000 0010 0000 0028,0x0000 0000 0000 0000)
	3	(0x0000 0010 0000 0028,0x0000 0000 0000 0000,0x0000 0010 0000 00A8,0x0000 0010 0000 00A8,0x0000 0000 0000 0000)
	4	(0x0000 0010 0000 00A8,0x0000 0008 0000 0000,0x0000 0090 0000 00A8,0x0000 0090 0000 00A8,0x0000 0008 0000 0000)
	5	(0x0000 0000 0000 0000,0x0000 0008 0000 0000,0x0000 0098 0000 00A8,0x0000 0008 0000 0000,0x0000 0000 0000 0000)
	6	(0x0000 0008 0000 0000,0x0000 0008 0000 0000,0x0000 0000 0000 0000,0x0000 0000 0000 0000,0x0000 0000 0000 0000)
	⋮	⋮
	13	(0x0000 0008 0000 0000,*(0x0000 0088 0000 0000),0x0000 0000 0000 0000,0x0000 0000 0000 0000,*(0x0000 0088 0000 0000))
Ω^{13}_{15}	0	(0x0000 0000 0000 0000, 0x0000 0020 0000 0058, 0x0000 0000 0000 0000, 0x0000 0088 0000 01F8, 0x0000 0010 0000 0038)
	1	(0x0000 0000 0000 0000, 0x0000 0000 0000 0000, 0x0000 0000 0000 0000, 0x0000 0088 0000 01F8, 0x0000 0020 0000 0058)
	2	(0x0000 0000 0000 0088, 0x0000 0000 0000 0000, 0x0000 0000 0000 0000, 0x0000 0088 0000 0170, 0x0000 0000 0000 0000)
	3	(0x0000 0088 0000 0170, 0x0000 0000 0000 0000, 0x0000 0000 0000 0008, 0x0000 0000 0000 0008, 0x0000 0000 0000 0000)
	4	(0x0000 0000 0000 0008, 0x0000 0000 0000 0088, 0x0000 0028 0000 0010, 0x0000 0028 0000 0010, 0x0000 0000 0000 0088)
	5	(0x0000 0000 0000 0000, 0x0000 0000 0000 0088, 0x0000 0028 0000 0098, 0x0000 0000 0000 0088, 0x0000 0000 0000 0000)
	6	(0x0000 0000 0000 0088, 0x0000 0000 0000 0088, 0x0000 0000 0000 0000, 0x0000 0000 0000 0000, 0x0000 0000 0000 0000)
	⋮	⋮
	13	(0x0000 0000 0000 0088, *(0x0000 0000 0000 0008), 0x0000 0000 0000 0000, 0x0000 0000 0000 0000, *(0x0000 0000 0000 0008))

Table 12. 14-step rebound distinguishers of ACE permutation

ID	Step	$(\Delta A, \Delta B, \Delta C, \Delta D, \Delta E)$
Ω_1^{14}	0	(0x0000 0000 0000 0000, 0x0100 0000 0A80 0000, 0x0100 0000 0380 0000, 0x0000 0000 0000 0000, 0x0000 0000 0000 0000)
	1	(0x0000 0000 0000 0000, 0x0100 0000 0A80 0000, 0x0000 0000 0000 0000, 0x0000 0000 0000 0000, 0x0000 0000 0000 0000)
	2	(0x0000 0000 0000 0000, 0x0000 0000 0000 0000, 0x0000 0000 0000 0000, 0x0000 0000 0000 0000, 0x0100 0000 0A80 0000)
	3	(0x0100 0000 0280 0000, 0x0000 0000 0000 0000, 0x0000 0000 0000 0000, 0x0100 0000 0280 0000, 0x0000 0000 0000 0000)
	4	(0x0100 0000 0280 0000, 0x0000 0000 0000 0000, 0x0100 0000 0A80 0000, 0x0100 0000 0A80 0000, 0x0000 0000 0000 0000)
	5	(0x0100 0000 0A80 0000, 0x0080 0000 0000 0000, 0x0900 0000 0A80 0000, 0x0900 0000 0A80 0000, 0x0080 0000 0000 0000)
	6	(0x0000 0000 0000 0000, 0x0080 0000 0000 0000, 0x0980 0000 0A80 0000, 0x0080 0000 0000 0000, 0x0000 0000 0000 0000)
	7	(0x0080 0000 0000 0000, 0x0080 0000 0000 0000, 0x0000 0000 0000 0000, 0x0000 0000 0000 0000, 0x0000 0000 0000 0000)
	⋮	⋮
	14	(0x0080 0000 0000 0000, *(0x0880 0000 0000 0000), 0x0000 0000 0000 0000, 0x0000 0000 0000 0000, *(0x0880 0000 0000 0000))
Ω_2^{14}	0	(0x0000 0000 0000 0000, 0x0000 8000 0005 4000, 0x0000 8000 0001 4000, 0x0000 0000 0000 0000, 0x0000 0000 0000 0000)
	1	(0x0000 0000 0000 0000, 0x0000 8000 0005 4000, 0x0000 0000 0000 0000, 0x0000 0000 0000 0000, 0x0000 0000 0000 0000)
	2	(0x0000 0000 0000 0000, 0x0000 0000 0000 0000, 0x0000 0000 0000 0000, 0x0000 0000 0000 0000, 0x0000 8000 0005 4000)
	3	(0x0000 8000 0001 4000, 0x0000 0000 0000 0000, 0x0000 0000 0000 0000, 0x0000 8000 0001 4000, 0x0000 0000 0000 0000)
	4	(0x0000 8000 0001 4000, 0x0000 0000 0000 0000, 0x0000 8000 0005 4000, 0x0000 8000 0005 4000, 0x0000 0000 0000 0000)
	5	(0x0000 8000 0005 4000, 0x0000 4000 0000 0000, 0x0004 8000 0005 4000, 0x0004 8000 0005 4000, 0x0000 4000 0000 0000)
	6	(0x0000 0000 0000 0000, 0x0000 4000 0000 0000, 0x0004 c000 0005 4000, 0x0000 4000 0000 0000, 0x0000 0000 0000 0000)
	7	(0x0000 4000 0000 0000, 0x0000 4000 0000 0000, 0x0000 0000 0000 0000, 0x0000 0000 0000 0000, 0x0000 0000 0000 0000)
	⋮	⋮
	14	(0x0000 4000 0000 0000, *(0x0004 4000 0000 0000), 0x0000 0000 0000 0000, 0x0000 0000 0000 0000, *(0x0004 4000 0000 0000))
Ω_3^{14}	0	(0x0000 0000 0000 0000, 0x4000 0000 A000 0002, 0x4000 0000 A000 0000, 0x0000 0000 0000 0000, 0x0000 0000 0000 0000)
	1	(0x0000 0000 0000 0000, 0x4000 0000 a000 0002, 0x0000 0000 0000 0000, 0x0000 0000 0000 0000, 0x0000 0000 0000 0000)
	2	(0x0000 0000 0000 0000, 0x0000 0000 0000 0000, 0x0000 0000 0000 0000, 0x0000 0000 0000 0000, 0x4000 0000 A000 0002)
	3	(0x4000 0000 A000 0000, 0x0000 0000 0000 0000, 0x0000 0000 0000 0000, 0x4000 0000 A000 0000, 0x0000 0000 0000 0000)
	4	(0x4000 0000 A000 0000, 0x0000 0000 0000 0000, 0x4000 0000 A000 0002, 0x4000 0000 A000 0002, 0x0000 0000 0000 0000)
	5	(0x4000 0000 A000 0002, 0x2000 0000 0000 0000, 0x4000 0002 A000 0002, 0x4000 0002 A000 0002, 0x2000 0000 0000 0000)
	6	(0x0000 0000 0000 0000, 0x2000 0000 0000 0000, 0x6000 0002 A000 0002, 0x2000 0000 0000 0000, 0x0000 0000 0000 0000)
	7	(0x2000 0000 0000 0000, 0x2000 0000 0000 0000, 0x0000 0000 0000 0000, 0x0000 0000 0000 0000, 0x0000 0000 0000 0000)
	⋮	⋮
	14	(0x2000 0000 0000 0000, *(0x2000 0002 0000 0000), 0x0000 0000 0000 0000, 0x0000 0000 0000 0000, *(0x2000 0002 0000 0000))
Ω_4^{14}	0	(0x0000 0000 0000 0000, 0x2000 0000 5000 0001, 0x2000 0000 5000 0000, 0x0000 0000 0000 0000, 0x0000 0000 0000 0000)
	1	(0x0000 0000 0000 0000, 0x2000 0000 5000 0001, 0x0000 0000 0000 0000, 0x0000 0000 0000 0000, 0x0000 0000 0000 0000)
	2	(0x0000 0000 0000 0000, 0x0000 0000 0000 0000, 0x0000 0000 0000 0000, 0x0000 0000 0000 0000, 0x2000 0000 5000 0001)

(continued)

Table 12. (*continued*)

ID	Step	$(\Delta A, \Delta B, \Delta C, \Delta D, \Delta E)$
	3	(0x2000 0000 5000 0000, 0x0000 0000 0000 0000, 0x0000 0000 0000 0000, 0x2000 0000 5000 0000, 0x0000 0000 0000 0000)
	4	(0x2000 0000 5000 0000, 0x0000 0000 0000 0000, 0x2000 0000 5000 0001, 0x2000 0000 5000 0001, 0x0000 0000 0000 0000)
	5	(0x2000 0000 5000 0001, 0x1000 0000 0000 0000, 0x3000 0001 5000 0001, 0x3000 0001 5000 0001, 0x1000 0000 0000 0000)
	6	(0x0000 0000 0000 0000, 0x1000 0000 0000 0000, 0x2000 0001 5000 0001, 0x1000 0000 0000 0000, 0x0000 0000 0000 0000)
	7	(0x1000 0000 0000 0000, 0x1000 0000 0000 0000, 0x0000 0000 0000 0000, 0x0000 0000 0000 0000, 0x0000 0000 0000 0000)
	⋮	⋮
	14	(0x1000 0000 0000 0000, ∗(0x1000 0001 0000 0000), 0x0000 0000 0000 0000, 0x0000 0000 0000 0000, ∗(0x1000 0001 0000 0000))
Ω_5^{14}	0	(0x0000 0000 0000 0000, 0x080 0000 05400 0000, 0x0800 0000 1400 0000, 0x0000 0000 0000 0000, 0x0000 0000 0000 0000)
	1	(0x0000 0000 0000 0000, 0x0800 0000 5400 0000, 0x0000 0000 0000 0000, 0x0000 0000 0000 0000, 0x0000 0000 0000 0000)
	2	(0x0000 0000 0000 0000, 0x0000 0000 0000 0000, 0x0000 0000 0000 0000, 0x0000 0000 0000 0000, 0x0800 0000 5400 0000)
	3	(0x0800 0000 1400 0000, 0x0000 0000 0000 0000, 0x0000 0000 0000 0000, 0x0800 0000 1400 0000, 0x0000 0000 0000 0000)
	4	(0x0800 0000 1400 0000, 0x0000 0000 0000 0000, 0x0800 0000 5400 0000, 0x0800 0000 5400 0000, 0x0000 0000 0000 0000)
	5	(0x0800 0000 5400 0000, 0x0400 0000 0000 0000, 0x4C00 0000 5400 0000, 0x4C00 0000 5400 0000, 0x0400 0000 0000 0000)
	6	(0x0000 0000 0000 0000, 0x0400 0000 0000 0000, 0x4800 0000 5400 0000, 0x0400 0000 0000 0000, 0x0000 0000 0000 0000)
	7	(0x0400 0000 0000 0000, 0x0400 0000 0000 0000, 0x0000 0000 0000 0000, 0x0000 0000 0000 0000, 0x0000 0000 0000 0000)
	⋮	⋮
	14	(0x0400 0000 0000 0000, ∗(0x4400 0000 0000 0000), 0x0000 0000 0000 0000, 0x0000 0000 0000 0000, ∗(0x4400 0000 0000 0000))
Ω_6^{14}	0	(0x0000 0000 0000 0000, 0x0000 0200 0000 1500, 0x0000 0200 0000 0500, 0x0000 0000 0000 0000, 0x0000 0000 0000 0000)
	1	(0x0000 0000 0000 0000, 0x0000 0200 0000 1500, 0x0000 0000 0000 0000, 0x0000 0000 0000 0000, 0x0000 0000 0000 0000)
	2	(0x0000 0000 0000 0000, 0x0000 0000 0000 0000, 0x0000 0000 0000 0000, 0x0000 0000 0000 0000, 0x0000 0200 0000 1500)
	3	(0x0000 0200 0000 0500, 0x0000 0000 0000 0000, 0x0000 0000 0000 0000, 0x0000 0200 0000 0500, 0x0000 0000 0000 0000)
	4	(0x0000 0200 0000 0500, 0x0000 0000 0000 0000, 0x0000 0200 0000 1500, 0x0000 0200 0000 1500, 0x0000 0000 0000 0000)
	5	(0x0000 0200 0000 1500, 0x0000 0100 0000 0000, 0x0000 1300 0000 1500, 0x0000 1300 0000 1500, 0x0000 0100 0000 0000)
	6	(0x0000 0000 0000 0000, 0x0000 0100 0000 0000, 0x0000 1200 0000 1500, 0x0000 0100 0000 0000, 0x0000 0000 0000 0000)
	7	(0x0000 0100 0000 0000, 0x0000 0100 0000 0000, 0x0000 0000 0000 0000, 0x0000 0000 0000 0000, 0x0000 0000 0000 0000)
	⋮	⋮
	14	(0x0000 0100 0000 0000, ∗(0x0000 1100 0000 0000), 0x0000 0000 0000 0000, 0x0000 0000 0000 0000, ∗(0x0000 1100 0000 0000))
Ω_7^{14}	0	(0x0000 0000 0000 0000, 0x0000 0010 0000 00A8, 0x0000 0010 0000 0028, 0x0000 0000 0000 0000, 0x0000 0000 0000 0000)
	1	(0x0000 0000 0000 0000, 0x0000 0010 0000 00A8, 0x0000 0000 0000 0000, 0x0000 0000 0000 0000, 0x0000 0000 0000 0000)
	2	(0x0000 0000 0000 0000, 0x0000 0000 0000 0000, 0x0000 0000 0000 0000, 0x0000 0000 0000 0000, 0x0000 0010 0000 00A8)
	3	(0x0000 0010 0000 0028, 0x0000 0000 0000 0000, 0x0000 0000 0000 0000, 0x0000 0010 0000 0028, 0x0000 0000 0000 0000)
	4	(0x0000 0010 0000 0028, 0x0000 0000 0000 0000, 0x0000 0010 0000 00A8, 0x0000 0010 0000 00A8, 0x0000 0000 0000 0000)
	5	(0x0000 0010 0000 00A8, 0x0000 0008 0000 0000, 0x0000 0090 0000 00A8, 0x0000 0090 0000 00A8, 0x0000 0008 0000 0000)

(*continued*)

Table 12. (*continued*)

ID	Step	$(\Delta A, \Delta B, \Delta C, \Delta D, \Delta E)$
	6	(0x0000 0000 0000 0000, 0x0000 0008 0000 0000, 0x0000 0098 0000 00A8, 0x0000 0008 0000 0000, 0x0000 0000 0000 0000)
	7	(0x0000 0008 0000 0000, 0x0000 0008 0000 0000, 0x0000 0000 0000 0000, 0x0000 0000 0000 0000, 0x0000 0000 0000 0000)
	⋮	⋮
	14	(0x0000 0008 0000 0000, *(0x0000 0088 0000 0000), 0x0000 0000 0000 0000, 0x0000 0000 0000 0000, *(0x0000 0088 0000 0000))
Ω_8^{14}	0	(0x0000 0000 0000 0000, 0x0000 4000 0002 A000, 0x0000 4000 0000 A000, 0x0000 0000 0000 0000, 0x0000 0000 0000 0000)
	1	(0x0000 0000 0000 0000, 0x0000 4000 0002 A000, 0x0000 0000 0000 0000, 0x0000 0000 0000 0000, 0x0000 0000 0000 0000)
	2	(0x0000 0000 0000 0000, 0x0000 0000 0000 0000, 0x0000 0000 0000 0000, 0x0000 0000 0000 0000, 0x0000 4000 0002 A000)
	3	(0x0000 4000 0000 E000, 0x0000 0000 0000 0000, 0x0000 0000 0000 0000, 0x0000 4000 0000 E000, 0x0000 0000 0000 0000)
	4	(0x0000 4000 0000 E000, 0x0000 0000 0000 0000, 0x0000 4000 0002 A000, 0x0000 4000 0002 A000, 0x0000 0000 0000 0000)
	5	(0x0000 4000 0002 A000, 0x0000 2000 0000 0000, 0x0002 6000 0002 A000, 0x0002 6000 0002 A000, 0x0000 2000 0000 0000)
	6	(0x0000 0000 0000 0000, 0x0000 2000 0000 0000, 0x0002 4000 0002 A000, 0x0000 2000 0000 0000, 0x0000 0000 0000 0000)
	7	(0x0000 2000 0000 0000, 0x0000 2000 0000 0000, 0x0000 0000 0000 0000, 0x0000 0000 0000 0000, 0x0000 0000 0000 0000)
	⋮	⋮
	14	(0x0000 2000 0000 0000, *(0x0002 2000 0000 0000), 0x0000 0000 0000 0000, 0x0000 0000 0000 0000, *(0x0002 2000 0000 0000))

Table 13. The distribution of characteristics in S_C^0, S_A^3 and S_A^4 with probabilities $2^{-18.28}$ for the 14-step rebound distinguisher Ω_0^{14}

P_{DC}	2^{-20}	2^{-21}	2^{-22}	2^{-23}	2^{-24}	2^{-25}	2^{-26}	2^{-27}	2^{-28}	2^{-29}	2^{-30}
#DC	1	0	4	2	7	4	13	12	19	31	27
P_{DC}	2^{-31}	2^{-32}	2^{-33}	2^{-34}	2^{-35}	2^{-36}	2^{-37}	2^{-38}	2^{-39}	2^{-40}	2^{-41}
#DC	22	19	9	29	44	112	192	386	624	1114	1881

Table 14. The distribution of characteristics in S_E^2 with probability $2^{-21.94}$ for the 14-step rebound distinguisher Ω_0^{14}

P_{DC}	2^{-24}	2^{-25}	2^{-26}	2^{-27}	2^{-28}	2^{-29}	2^{-30}	2^{-31}	2^{-32}	2^{-33}	2^{-34}
#DC	1	0	4	2	9	8	19	25	38	57	87
P_{DC}	2^{-35}	2^{-36}	2^{-37}	2^{-38}	2^{-39}	2^{-40}	2^{-41}	2^{-42}	2^{-43}	2^{-44}	2^{-45}
#DC	117	187	253	453	743	1390	2154	3690	6984	12189	25068

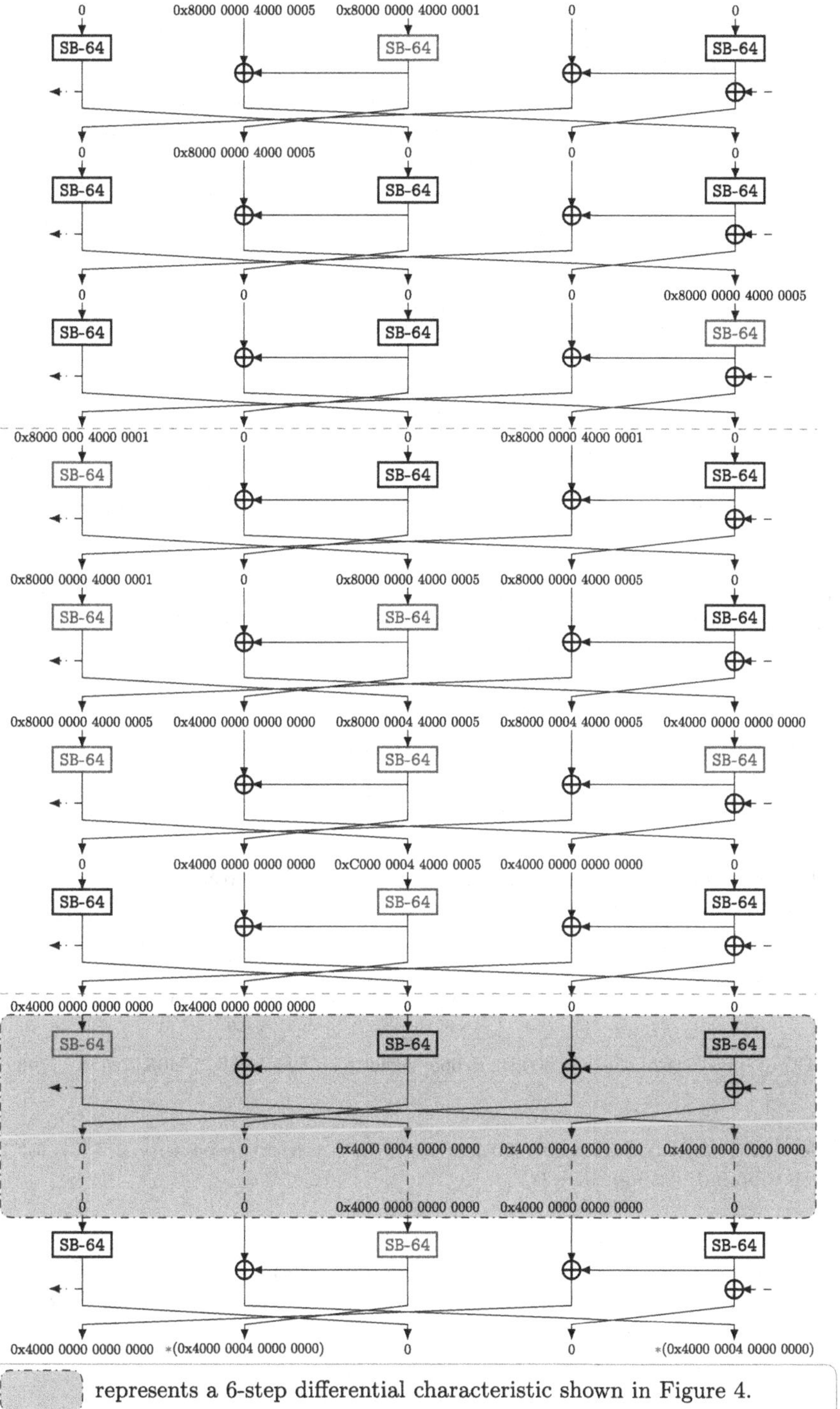

Fig. 6. 14-step rebound distinguisher Ω_0^{14} of ACE permutation

Table 15. The distribution of characteristics in S_C^4 with probability $2^{-21.46}$ for the 14-step rebound distinguisher Ω_0^{14}

P_{DC}	2^{-24}	2^{-25}	2^{-26}	2^{-27}	2^{-28}	2^{-29}	2^{-30}	2^{-31}	2^{-32}	2^{-33}	2^{-34}
#DC	1	0	4	2	13	7	41	48	95	166	268
P_{DC}	2^{-35}	2^{-36}	2^{-37}	2^{-38}	2^{-39}	2^{-40}	2^{-41}	2^{-42}	2^{-43}	2^{-44}	2^{-45}
#DC	400	603	829	1004	1068	988	780	512	279	123	42

Table 16. The distribution of characteristics in S_A^5 with probability $2^{-26.44}$ for the 14-step rebound distinguisher Ω_0^{14}

P_{DC}	2^{-32}	2^{-33}	2^{-34}	2^{-35}	2^{-36}	2^{-37}	2^{-38}	2^{-39}	2^{-40}	2^{-41}	2^{-42}
#DC	3	4	22	45	92	167	270	396	644	914	1569
P_{DC}	2^{-43}	2^{-44}	2^{-45}	2^{-46}	2^{-47}	2^{-48}	2^{-49}	2^{-50}	2^{-51}	2^{-52}	2^{-53}
#DC	2655	4771	8668	15900	29277	47453	55906	62924	59370	60059	52015

Table 17. The distribution of characteristics in S_C^5 with probability $2^{-21.54}$ for the 14-step rebound distinguisher Ω_0^{14}

P_{DC}	2^{-25}	2^{-26}	2^{-27}	2^{-28}	2^{-29}	2^{-30}	2^{-31}	2^{-32}	2^{-33}	2^{-34}	2^{-35}
#DC	1	0	7	3	27	19	82	94	207	354	572
P_{DC}	2^{-36}	2^{-37}	2^{-38}	2^{-39}	2^{-40}	2^{-41}	2^{-42}	2^{-43}	2^{-44}	2^{-45}	2^{-46}
#DC	927	1444	2059	2820	3709	4553	5196	5586	5559	5023	4038

Table 18. The distribution of characteristics in S_E^5 with probability $2^{-25.72}$ for the 14-step rebound distinguisher Ω_0^{14}

P_{DC}	2^{-32}	2^{-33}	2^{-34}	2^{-35}	2^{-36}	2^{-37}	2^{-38}	2^{-39}	2^{-40}	2^{-41}	2^{-42}
#DC	2	0	21	13	115	142	467	819	1747	3400	6332
P_{DC}	2^{-43}	2^{-44}	2^{-45}	2^{-46}	2^{-47}	2^{-48}	2^{-49}	2^{-50}	2^{-51}	2^{-52}	2^{-53}
#DC	11998	21829	38769	60094	67665	62560	71689	71418	75465	73118	73633

Table 19. The distribution of characteristics in S_C^6 with probability $2^{-20.70}$ for the 14-step rebound distinguisher Ω_0^{14}

P_{DC}	2^{-24}	2^{-25}	2^{-26}	2^{-27}	2^{-28}	2^{-29}	2^{-30}	2^{-31}	2^{-32}	2^{-33}	2^{-34}
#DC	1	0	6	3	22	16	70	80	180	305	511
P_{DC}	2^{-35}	2^{-36}	2^{-37}	2^{-38}	2^{-39}	2^{-40}	2^{-41}	2^{-42}	2^{-43}	2^{-44}	2^{-45}
#DC	854	1427	2143	3279	4725	6364	8210	10074	11610	1258	12923

References

1. Aagaard, M., AlTawy, R., Gong, G., Mandal, K., Rohit, R.: ACE: an authenticated encryption and hash algorithm. Submission to NIST-LWC (Round 2) (2019). https://csrc.nist.gov/CSRC/media/Projects/lightweight-cryptography/documents/round-2/spec-doc-rnd2/ace-spec-round2.pdf
2. AlTawy, R., Rohit, R., He, M., Mandal, K., Yang, G., Gong, G.: sLiSCP: simeck-based permutations for lightweight sponge cryptographic primitives. In: Adams, C., Camenisch, J. (eds.) SAC 2017. LNCS, vol. 10719, pp. 129–150. Springer, Cham (2018). https://doi.org/10.1007/978-3-319-72565-9_7
3. AlTawy, R., Rohit, R., He, M., Mandal, K., Yang, G., Gong, G.: Sliscp-light: towards hardware optimized sponge-specific cryptographic permutations. ACM Trans. Embed. Comput. Syst. **17**(4), 81:1–81:26 (2018). https://doi.org/10.1145/3233245
4. Beaulieu, R., Shors, D., Smith, J., Treatman-Clark, S., Weeks, B., Wingers, L.: The SIMON and SPECK families of lightweight block ciphers. IACR Cryptology ePrint Archive, p. 404 (2013). http://eprint.iacr.org/2013/404
5. Bogdanov, A., Shibutani, K.: Generalized Feistel networks revisited. Des. Codes Cryptogr. **66**(1–3), 75–97 (2013). https://doi.org/10.1007/s10623-012-9660-z
6. Dong, X., Guo, J., Li, S., Pham, P.: Triangulating rebound attack on AES-like hashing. In: Dodis, Y., Shrimpton, T. (eds.) CRYPTO 2022, Part I. LNCS, vol. 13507, pp. 94–124. Springer, Cham (2022). https://doi.org/10.1007/978-3-031-15802-5_4
7. Dong, X., Li, S., Pham, P.: Chosen-key distinguishing attacks on full AES-192, AES-256, Kiasu-BC, and more. IACR Cryptology ePrint Archive, p. 1095 (2023). https://eprint.iacr.org/2023/1095
8. Gilbert, H., Peyrin, T.: Super-Sbox cryptanalysis: improved attacks for AES-like permutations. In: Hong, S., Iwata, T. (eds.) FSE 2010. LNCS, vol. 6147, pp. 365–383. Springer, Heidelberg (2010). https://doi.org/10.1007/978-3-642-13858-4_21
9. Hosoyamada, A., Naya-Plasencia, M., Sasaki, Y.: Improved attacks on sLiSCP permutation and tight bound of limited birthday distinguishers. IACR Trans. Symmetric Cryptol. **2020**(4), 147–172 (2020). https://doi.org/10.46586/tosc.v2020.i4.147-172
10. Iwamoto, M., Peyrin, T., Sasaki, Yu.: Limited-birthday distinguishers for hash functions. In: Sako, K., Sarkar, P. (eds.) ASIACRYPT 2013, Part II. LNCS, vol. 8270, pp. 504–523. Springer, Heidelberg (2013). https://doi.org/10.1007/978-3-642-42045-0_26
11. Kölbl, S., Leander, G., Tiessen, T.: Observations on the SIMON block cipher family. In: Gennaro, R., Robshaw, M. (eds.) CRYPTO 2015, Part I. LNCS, vol. 9215, pp. 161–185. Springer, Heidelberg (2015). https://doi.org/10.1007/978-3-662-47989-6_8
12. Kullmann, O. (ed.): SAT 2009. LNCS, vol. 5584. Springer, Heidelberg (2009). https://doi.org/10.1007/978-3-642-02777-2
13. Lai, X., Massey, J.L., Murphy, S.: Markov ciphers and differential cryptanalysis. In: Davies, D.W. (ed.) EUROCRYPT 1991. LNCS, vol. 547, pp. 17–38. Springer, Heidelberg (1991). https://doi.org/10.1007/3-540-46416-6_2
14. Lamberger, M., Mendel, F., Schläffer, M., Rechberger, C., Rijmen, V.: The rebound attack and subspace distinguishers: application to whirlpool. J. Cryptol. **28**(2), 257–296 (2015). https://doi.org/10.1007/s00145-013-9166-5

15. Leurent, G., Pernot, C., Schrottenloher, A.: Clustering effect in SIMON and SIMECK. In: Tibouchi, M., Wang, H. (eds.) ASIACRYPT 2021, Part I. LNCS, vol. 13090, pp. 272–302. Springer, Cham (2021). https://doi.org/10.1007/978-3-030-92062-3_10
16. Liu, J., Liu, G., Qu, L.: A new automatic tool searching for impossible differential of NIST candidate ACE. Mathematics **8**(9), 1576 (2020). Number: 9 Publisher: Multidisciplinary Digital Publishing Institute
17. Liu, Y., Sasaki, Y., Song, L., Wang, G.: Cryptanalysis of reduced sLiSCP permutation in sponge-hash and duplex-AE modes. In: Cid, C., Jacobson, M., Jr. (eds.) SAC 2018. LNCS, vol. 11349, pp. 92–114. Springer, Cham (2018). https://doi.org/10.1007/978-3-030-10970-7_5
18. Liu, Z., Li, Y., Wang, M.: Optimal differential trails in Simon-like ciphers. IACR Trans. Symmetric Cryptol. **2017**(1), 358–379 (2017). https://doi.org/10.13154/tosc.v2017.i1.358-379
19. Massacci, F., Marraro, L.: Logical cryptanalysis as a SAT problem. J. Autom. Reason. **24**(1/2), 165–203 (2000). https://doi.org/10.1023/A:1006326723002
20. Mendel, F., Rechberger, C., Schläffer, M., Thomsen, S.S.: The rebound attack: cryptanalysis of reduced whirlpool and. In: Dunkelman, O. (ed.) FSE 2009. LNCS, vol. 5665, pp. 260–276. Springer, Heidelberg (2009). https://doi.org/10.1007/978-3-642-03317-9_16
21. Mironov, I., Zhang, L.: Applications of SAT solvers to cryptanalysis of hash functions. In: Biere, A., Gomes, C.P. (eds.) SAT 2006. LNCS, vol. 4121, pp. 102–115. Springer, Heidelberg (2006). https://doi.org/10.1007/11814948_13
22. Morawiecki, P., Srebrny, M.: A SAT-based preimage analysis of reduced Keccak hash functions. Inf. Process. Lett. **113**(10–11), 392–397 (2013). https://doi.org/10.1016/j.ipl.2013.03.004
23. Nieuwenhuis, R., Oliveras, A., Tinelli, C.: Solving SAT and SAT modulo theories: From an abstract Davis-Putnam-Logemann-Loveland procedure to DPLL(T). J. ACM **53**(6), 937–977 (2006). https://doi.org/10.1145/1217856.1217859
24. Nikolić, I., Pieprzyk, J., Sokołowski, P., Steinfeld, R.: Known and chosen key differential distinguishers for block ciphers. In: Rhee, K.-H., Nyang, D.H. (eds.) ICISC 2010. LNCS, vol. 6829, pp. 29–48. Springer, Heidelberg (2011). https://doi.org/10.1007/978-3-642-24209-0_3
25. Nyberg, K.: Generalized Feistel networks. In: Kim, K., Matsumoto, T. (eds.) ASIACRYPT 1996. LNCS, vol. 1163, pp. 91–104. Springer, Heidelberg (1996). https://doi.org/10.1007/BFb0034838
26. Sinz, C.: Towards an optimal CNF encoding of Boolean cardinality constraints. In: van Beek, P. (ed.) CP 2005. LNCS, vol. 3709, pp. 827–831. Springer, Heidelberg (2005). https://doi.org/10.1007/11564751_73
27. Sun, B., Liu, M., Guo, J., Rijmen, V., Li, R.: Provable security evaluation of structures against impossible differential and zero correlation linear cryptanalysis. In: Fischlin, M., Coron, J.-S. (eds.) EUROCRYPT 2016. LNCS, vol. 9665, pp. 196–213. Springer, Heidelberg (2016). https://doi.org/10.1007/978-3-662-49890-3_8
28. Sun, L., Wang, W., Wang M.: Accelerating the search of differential and linear characteristics with the SAT method. IACR Trans. Symmetric Cryptol. **2021**(1), 269–315 (2021). https://doi.org/10.46586/tosc.v2021.i1.269-315
29. Wang, S., Feng, D., Hu, B., Guan, J., Shi, T., Zhang, K.: The simplest SAT model of combining Matsui's bounding conditions with sequential encoding method. IACR Cryptology ePrint Archive, p. 626 (2022). https://eprint.iacr.org/2022/626

30. Yang, G., Zhu, B., Suder, V., Aagaard, M.D., Gong, G.: The Simeck family of lightweight block ciphers. In: Güneysu, T., Handschuh, H. (eds.) CHES 2015. LNCS, vol. 9293, pp. 307–329. Springer, Heidelberg (2015). https://doi.org/10.1007/978-3-662-48324-4_16
31. Ye, T., Wei, Y., Li, L., Pasalic, E.: Impossible differential cryptanalysis and integral cryptanalysis of the ACE-class permutation. In: Deng, R., et al. (eds.) ISPEC 2021. LNCS, vol. 13107, pp. 306–326. Springer, Cham (2021). https://doi.org/10.1007/978-3-030-93206-0_19

The Exact Multi-user Security of 2-Key Triple DES

Yusuke Naito[1(✉)], Yu Sasaki[2], and Takeshi Sugawara[3]

[1] Mitsubishi Electric Corporation, Kamakura, Kanagawa, Japan
Naito.Yusuke@ce.MitsubishiElectric.co.jp

[2] NTT Social Informatics Laboratories, Tokyo, Japan
yusk.sasaki@ntt.com

[3] The University of Electro-Communications, Tokyo, Japan
sugawara@uec.ac.jp

Abstract. We study the tight multi-user (mu) security of 2-key triple encryption (2kTE) with its application to 2-key TDES. With an n-bit block and k-bit key primitive block cipher, our new mu lower bound regarding the number of primitive queries is $2^{\min\{2k,k+n\}}/q$ with q construction queries, which matches the previous best attacks and is tight. The bound ensures $(112 - \log_2 q)$-bit security with 2-key TDES, and this can be used to evaluate and predict the security of systems supporting 2-key TDES for legacy use. We finally show that the FX construction does not efficiently improve the mu security with 2kTE, unlike the previous result with 3-key triple encryption appeared in CCS 2022. We show a concrete key-recovery attack with $O(2^{n+k}/q)$ primitive queries.

Keywords: 2-key Triple DES · 2-key Triple Encryption · Multi-User Security · Strengthening · FX Construction · Tight Bound

1 Introduction

Block ciphers are fundamental primitives for modern cryptographic protocols and products. Block ciphers' security is determined by the key size, so the key-length extension is an important topic. Cascade encryption (CE) constructs a block cipher with a longer key by repeating a primitive block cipher with a shorter key. Triple encryption (TE) is the cascade encryption with three rounds, and we refer to the variants with 2 and 3 keys as 2kTE and 3kTE, respectively. They are practically important because their realizations, namely 2-key and 3-key Triple DES (TDES), have been standards for a long time [2,20]. The security of 2kTE and 2-key TDES is the main focus of this paper.

The security of 2kTE needs particular care because of the previous attacks. In this paper, we refer to the bit lengths of the message block and key as n and k, e.g., $n = 64$ and $k = 56$ in DES. In 1977, Diffie and Hellman showed the key-recovery attack with 2^k chosen-plaintext queries, 2^k memory, and 2^k offline computation for a $2k$-bit key [9]. This corresponds to k-bit security in

E. Oswald (Ed.): CT-RSA 2024, LNCS 14643, pp. 112–135, 2024.
https://doi.org/10.1007/978-3-031-58868-6_5

the bit-security paradigm, which considers the maximum of the data, time, and memory complexities, and thus there is no security improvement from a single DES[1]. Meanwhile, making 2^k chosen-plaintext queries is considered more challenging compared to 2^k offline computation. Then, van Oorschot and Wiener extended the attack to the known-plaintext setting by introducing the data-time trade-off in 1990 [21]. With q known-plaintext queries, the attack succeeds with $2^{n+k}/q$ offline computation and q memory. Finally, in 2015, Gazi, Lee, Seurin, Steinberger, and Tessaro proved the optimality of the attack under $q \leq 2^k$ [11][2].

2-key TDES is considered weak because of the above attacks and is being depreciated, but many systems still need to support it. NIST already disallowed 2-key TDES in 2015 but still accepts decryption for legacy use [3,4]. The other standards are more conservative, and ISO/TR 14742:2010 [15], the ISO standard for financial services, still recommends 2-key TDES. More recently, EMVCo announced in August 2021 that they continue to use 2-key TDES [26].

ISO/TR 14742:2010 evaluates 2-key TDES' security in the single-user (su) setting, which is 80–112 bits depending on the number of plaintext-ciphertext pairs for the *same* key. However, protecting a particular key is sometimes not enough, and researchers are revisiting the security of cryptographic schemes in the multi-user (mu) setting [5,8,13,17,19] wherein an adversary can send queries to multiple users with distinct keys and is challenged to break one of the keys. The mu security captures the reality of a system with multiple users, and the practical internet protocols [23–25] now determine the AES-GCM's rekeying frequencies based on the mu-security bound [5,13,17].

Figure 1 summarizes 2kTE's state-of-the-art mu/su security bounds regarding p primitive and q construction queries, i.e., p offline and q online computations. We discuss the security of 2kTE in the ideal cipher model by following the previous works. Mitchell [18] showed in the known-plaintext setting that 2kTE's mu upper bound is the same as its su upper bound [21]. In the mu-setting, an adversary can distribute q queries to multiple users as desired. The number of queries each user receives is not fixed in advance. Cryptographic schemes should be evaluated in a worst case. Hence, we evaluate security including the following worst case: each of q users is queried only once. Furthermore, we consider a stronger adversary who makes chosen-plaintext (cf. known-plaintext) queries. In such a worst case, Biham's attack [6], which recovers one of q user's keys with $2^{2k}/q$ primitive queries, outperforms Mitchell's attack [18], as shown in Fig. 1.

On the other hand, 2kTE's mu lower bound is unknown. It is still possible to derive a mu lower bound by applying a hybrid argument (or a generic reduction) to the conventional best single-user bound. However, the bound derived in this way has an additional multiplicative factor u from the su-security bound, where u is an upper bound on the number of users, which is further upper bounded by q. This multiplicative factor q can be too big to be ignored. In fact, adopting the hybrid argument to the su bound of Gazi et al. [11], the obtained lower bound and Biham's upper bound have a large gap.

---

[1] The security of the single encryption is k bits by an exhaustive key search.

[2] [9] is better with $k < n$, e.g., DES, but it is out of the scope of [11] because $q = 2^k$.

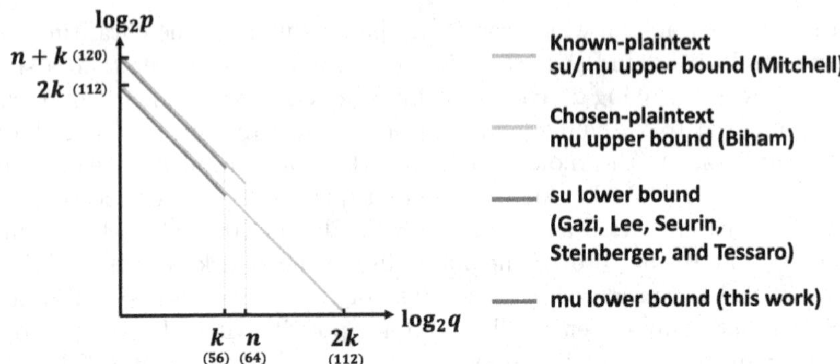

Fig. 1. Conventional mu upper and lower bounds of 2kTE. The numbers represent the bit security when the underlying cipher is DES, i.e., 2-key TDES.

Besides 2kTE, Naito, Sasaki, Sugawara, and Yasuda [19] recently solved the same problem regarding 3kTE, providing a tight bound with 3kTE. Additionally, they proposed to strengthen 3kTE with the FX construction [16], which can efficiently improve the mu security [19] while maintaining backward compatibility with legacy hardware accelerators using standard modes of operation such as CBC [10,14].

In summary, finding a tight mu-security bound for 2kTE is an open problem and is practically important for evaluating the security of 2-key TDES in legacy systems. Evaluating the effectiveness of 2kTE with the FX construction is also important for strengthening the legacy systems.

1.1 Contributions

We study tight mu security of 2kTE and provide the following key contributions.

Tight Mu Lower Bound in 2kTE for $q \leq 2^k$ (Sects. 3 and 5). We show a new mu lower bound of 2kTE. The new bound $p = 2^{\min\{2k,k+n\}}/q$ in $q \leq 2^k$ matches with the previous best attack and is tight (see Fig. 1). The lower and upper bounds show that the tight security bound of 2kTE is $\min\{2k, k+n\} - \log_2 q$ bits. The bound ensures that 2-key TDES has $(112 - \log_2 q)$-bit security.

Inefficiency of the FX Construction with 2kTE (Sect. 6). Strengthening using the FX construction is inefficient with 2kTE, unlike the previous result with 3kTE [19]. Namely, even by adding two n-bit keys L and L' to 2kTE, the construction can be attacked only with $p = 2^{n+k}/q$ in the chosen-plaintext setting. Compared to the $(112 - \log_2 q)$-bit security of 2-key TDES, the bit security of 2kTE-FX is at most $(120 - \log_2 q)$ bits. We show a concrete information-theoretic key-recovery attack with $p = O(2^{n+k}/q)$ primitive queries.

Implications for the Real-World Legacy Systems. Our result has several implications for the security of 2-key TDES in legacy systems. System operators can evaluate the bit security of the target system by assigning the total number of queries q to the bound, i.e., $112 - \log_2 q$. q is static for systems maintained for legacy use only that accepts no new encryption, e.g., the systems compliant with NIST SP800 [3,4]. The other systems can decide when to stop new encryption by considering the rate of consuming q and the acceptable level of security.

1.2 Organization

We begin by giving basic notations in Sect. 2. Section 3 gives basic definitions and the main theorem. Section 4 shows an overview of the proof and explain the coefficient H technique and the re-sampling method that are the tools used in the proof. Section 5 provides the complete proof. By showing a concrete attack, we finally show that the FX construction is inefficient in salvaging 2kTE, unlike 3kTE in Sect. 6. Section 7 is the conclusion.

2 Basic Notation

Let ε be an empty string and $\emptyset$ an empty set. For an integer $i \geq 0$, let $\{0,1\}^i$ be the set of all i-bit strings and $\{0,1\}^0 := \{\varepsilon\}$. For integers $0 \leq i \leq j$, let $[i,j] := \{i, i+1, \ldots, j\}$, $(j] := [0,j]$, and $[j] := [1,j]$. Note that for $[i,j]$, if $j < i$ then $[i,j] := \emptyset$. For a non-empty set $\mathcal{T}$, $T \xleftarrow{\$} \mathcal{T}$ means that an element is chosen uniformly at random from $\mathcal{T}$ and assigned to T. For integers s, t, "$i \in \overrightarrow{[s,t]}$ (resp. $i \in \overleftarrow{[s,t]}$)" means that in a for statement, i is chosen from $[s,t]$ in ascending (resp. descending) order from s (resp. from t). Regarding $i \in \overrightarrow{[s,t]}$ (resp. $i \in \overleftarrow{[s,t]}$), if $s > t$ (resp. $s < t$), then there is no choice for i.

3 Mu-Security of 2kTE

In this section, we first give the specification of 2kTE. Secondly, we define the notion of mu-SPRP security in the ideal cipher mode. Thirdly, we give a bound of the mu-SPRP security of 2kTE. Fourthly, we explain the coefficient H technique [22] that is a method for proving the mu-SPRP security of 2kTE. Finally, we explain the re-sampling method for 3kTE by Naito et al. [19], and then show how to apply the method to 2kTE.

3.1 Specification of 2kTE

Let $E : \{0,1\}^k \times \{0,1\}^n \to \{0,1\}^n$ be a block cipher (BC) with k-bit keys and n-bit blocks that is a set of n-bit permutations indexed by key. Let E^{-1} : $\{0,1\}^k \times \{0,1\}^n \to \{0,1\}^n$ be the decryption of E. Let $\mathcal{K} := \{0,1\}^{2k}$ be the key space of 2kTE (Triple Encryption), $K_1 \in \{0,1\}^k$ the 1st and 3rd round key, and K_2 the 2nd round key. The encryption of 2kTE is defined as follows. For a key $K \in \mathcal{K}$ and a plaintext $M \in \{0,1\}^n$,

$$\mathsf{2kTE}_K[E](M) = E_{K_1} \circ E_{K_2} \circ E_{K_1}(M).$$

• Initialization	**• Initialization**
$E \xleftarrow{\$} \mathcal{BC}$; **for** $\nu \in \overrightarrow{[q]}$ **do** $K^{(\nu)} \xleftarrow{\$} \mathcal{K}$	$E \xleftarrow{\$} \mathcal{BC}$; **for** $\nu \in \overrightarrow{[q]}$ **do** $\Pi_\nu \xleftarrow{\$} \mathsf{Perm}$
• Construction query $\mathbf{\Sigma}(\nu, a, D)$	**• Construction query** $\mathbf{\Pi}(\nu, a, D)$
if $a = +$ **then return** $\mathsf{2kTE}_{K^{(\nu)}}[E](D)$	**if** $a = +$ **then return** $\Pi_\nu(D)$
if $a = -$ **then return** $\mathsf{2kTE}^{-1}_{K^{(\nu)}}[E^{-1}](D)$	**if** $a = -$ **then return** $\Pi_\nu^{-1}(D)$
• Primitive query $E^{\pm}(a, W, X)$	**• Primitive query** $E^{\pm}(a, W, X)$
if $a = +$ **then return** $E(W, X)$	**if** $a = +$ **then return** $E(W, X)$
if $a = -$ **then return** $E^{-1}(W, Y)$	**if** $a = -$ **then return** $E^{-1}(W, Y)$

Fig. 2. Real-world (left) and ideal-world (right) oracles.

Let $Z_0 := M$, $Z_1 := E_{K_1}(M)$, $Z_2 := E_{K_2} \circ E_{K_1}(M)$, and $Z_3 := \mathsf{2kTE}_K[E^{\pm}](M)$. Let $\mathsf{2kTE}_K^{-1}[E^{-1}]$ be the decryption of TE with a key K.

3.2 Security Definition: Mu-SPRP Security in Ideal Cipher Model

We analyze muti-user (mu) SPRP (strong-pseudo-random-permutation) security of $\mathsf{2kTE}$ in the ideal cipher (IC) model. Let $\mathcal{BC}$ be the set of all BCs with the key space $\{0,1\}^k$ and the input/output block space $\{0,1\}^n$. Let Perm be the set of all n-bit permutations. In the security game, an adversary $\mathbf{A}$ tries to distinguish between the target BC scheme (in the real world) and random permutations (in the ideal world), where the underlying BC is ideal. Oracles in this game are defined in Fig. 2. Firstly, the initialization is performed, where in the real (resp. ideal) world, user's keys $K^{(\nu)}$ (resp. random permutations $\Pi_\nu^{\pm}$) and an ideal cipher E are defined. Then, $\mathbf{A}$ has access to an ideal cipher and each user via the interfaces $E^{\pm}$ and $\mathbf{\Sigma}/\mathbf{\Pi}$, respectively. Finally, $\mathbf{A}$ returns a decision bit. The advantage function of $\mathbf{A}$ is defined as

$$\mathbf{Adv}^{\mathsf{mu\text{-}sprp}}_{\mathsf{2kTE}}(\mathbf{A}) = \Pr[\mathbf{A}^{\mathbf{\Sigma}, E^{\pm}} = 1] - \Pr[\mathbf{A}^{\mathbf{\Pi}, E^{\pm}} = 1],$$

where $\mathbf{A}^{\mathbf{\Sigma}, E^{\pm}} \in \{0,1\}$ (resp. $\mathbf{A}^{\mathbf{\Pi}, E^{\pm}} \in \{0,1\}$) is an output of $\mathbf{A}$ in the real (resp. ideal) world, and the probabilities are taken over $\mathbf{A}$, $K^{(1)}, \ldots, K^{(u)}$, and E in the real world and $\mathbf{A}$, $\Pi_1, \ldots, \Pi_u$, and E in the ideal world. We refer the particular queries to as follows:

- Primitive (resp. construction) queries: queries to $E^{\pm}$ (resp. $\mathbf{\Sigma}/\mathbf{\Pi}$).
- Forward (resp. inverse) queries: primitive queries with $+$ (resp. $-$).
- Encryption (resp. decryption) queries: construction queries with $+$ (resp. $-$).

3.3 Mu-SPRP Security of 2kTE

The following theorem shows the mu-SPRP security bound of 2kTE.

Theorem 1 (Mu-SPRP Security of 2kTE). *Let* **A** *be an adversary that makes at most p primitive queries and q construction queries such that* $q \leq 2^{n-3}$. *Let* $Q := 2p + 3q$. *Then, for any value* $\omega > 0$, *we have*

$$\mathbf{Adv}^{\mathsf{mu\text{-}sprp}}_{\mathsf{2kTE}}(\mathbf{A}) \leq \max\left\{\left(\frac{8n \cdot qQ}{2^{n+k}}\right)^{\frac{1}{2}}, \frac{\frac{2n}{\log_2 n} \cdot qQ}{2^{2k}}\right\} + \frac{(8n+8) \cdot qQ}{2^{n+k}} + \frac{q}{2^k} + \frac{2q}{2^n}.$$

The above bound ensures that 2kTE is mu-SPRP secure up to about $\frac{2^{k+\min\{k,n\}}}{q}$ primitive queries, ignoring the coefficients and assuming that the last two terms are negligible. The security level is $(k + \min\{k, n/2\})$ bits.

4 Overview and Tool for Proof of Theorem 1

In our proof, we derive the mu-SPRP bound in Theorem 1 by using the coefficient H technique [22] and the re-sampling method [19]. In Subsect. 4.1, we give an overview of the proof of Theorem 1. In Subsect. 4.2, we define the coefficient H technique. In Subsect. 4.3, we explain the re-sampling method.

4.1 Proof Overview

In the coefficient H technique, bad events are analyzed in the ideal world. For cases where bad events do not occur, the ratio of the real and ideal worlds is derived. Then, the mu-SPRP bound is obtained by combining the probabilities for the bad events with the ratio. In order to derive the tight bound, we make use of the re-sampling method. Hence, we derive the mu-SPRP bound by the following steps.

1. We perform the following steps that make the re-sampling method available to the proof based on the coefficient H technique.
   (a) Modify the game where at the end of the game the adversary obtains all keys and internal state values of 2kTE in addition to query-response pairs.
   (b) Define an algorithm that derives the internal state values by using the idea of the re-sampling method.
2. We perform the following steps that are based on the coefficient H technique.
   (a) Define bad events.
   (b) Evaluate the probabilities for the bad events.
   (c) Evaluate the ratio of the real and ideal worlds for cases where bad events do not occur.
3. We obtain the mu-SPRP bound by combining the probabilities for the bad events with the ratio.

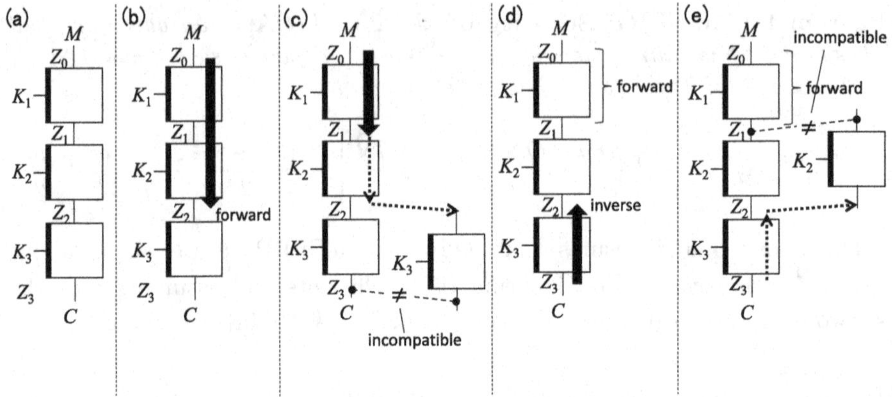

Fig. 3. (a) Structure of 3kTE. (b) Forward sampling. (c) Bad event for the forward sampling. (d) Inverse sampling. (e) Bad event for the inverse sampling.

4.2 Methodology for Proving the Mu-SPRP Security

Let T_R be a transcript in the real world obtained by samplings of keys and an ideal cipher in the real world. Let T_I be a transcript in the ideal world obtained by samplings of random permutations and an ideal cipher in the ideal world. For a transcript τ which is an adversary's view (or information obtained) in the security game, we call a transcript τ *valid* if $\Pr[\mathsf{T}_I = \tau] > 0$. Let $\mathcal{T}$ be all valid transcripts such that $\forall \tau \in \mathcal{T} : \Pr[\mathsf{T}_R = \tau] \leq \Pr[\mathsf{T}_I = \tau]$. Then, we have

$$\mathbf{Adv}^{\mathsf{mu\text{-}sprp}}_{\mathsf{2kTE}}(\mathbf{A}) \leq \mathsf{SD}(\mathsf{T}_R, \mathsf{T}_I) = \sum_{\tau \in \mathcal{T}} (\Pr[\mathsf{T}_I = \tau] - \Pr[\mathsf{T}_R = \tau]).$$

We derive an mu-SPRP bound using the coefficient H technique [22]. Here, $\mathcal{T}$ is partitioned into two transcripts: good transcripts $\mathcal{T}_{\mathsf{good}}$ and bad ones $\mathcal{T}_{\mathsf{bad}}$.

Lemma 1. *For good transcripts* $\mathcal{T}_{\mathsf{good}}$ *and bad transcripts* $\mathcal{T}_{\mathsf{bad}}$*, if* $\forall \tau \in \mathcal{T}_{\mathsf{good}}$: $\frac{\Pr[\mathsf{T}_R=\tau]}{\Pr[\mathsf{T}_I=\tau]} \geq 1 - \varepsilon$ *s.t.* $0 \leq \varepsilon \leq 1$*, then* $\mathsf{SD}(\mathsf{T}_R, \mathsf{T}_I) \leq \Pr[\mathsf{T}_I \in \mathcal{T}_{\mathsf{bad}}] + \varepsilon$.

We thus show the following three points: (1) define good and bad transcripts; (2) upper-bound $\Pr[\mathsf{T}_I \in \mathcal{T}_{\mathsf{bad}}]$; (3) lower-bound $\frac{\Pr[\mathsf{T}_R=\tau]}{\Pr[\mathsf{T}_I=\tau]}$. Then, putting these bounds into the above lemma, we obtain an upper-bound of $\mathbf{Adv}^{\mathsf{mu\text{-}sprp}}_{\mathsf{2kTE}}(\mathbf{A})$.

4.3 Re-sampling Method

Our proof makes use of the re-sampling method for 3kTE. The re-sampling method offers a tight bound on 3kTE. The evaluation of 3kTE is for three keys whereas 2kTE is a two-key scheme. We thus update the evaluation with the re-sampling method to the two-key scheme 2kTE.

Re-sampling Method for 3kTE. We first recall the re-sampling method for 3kTE [19] in the su-setting. The security proof uses the coefficient-H technique. In the proof, a dummy key is defined in the ideal world. Then, in both worlds, a (dummy) key is revealed to an adversary after finishing all queries.

The re-sampling method defines dummy internal values in the ideal world in a novel way, and the dummy internal values are revealed to an adversary in addition to a dummy key. This method makes good-transcript analysis easier than the existing proofs for 3kTE. Existing proofs such as [7,12] do not define dummy internal values in the ideal world (thus do not reveal internal values to an adversary). Hence, this setting makes the analysis of good transcripts complex since one needs to count the number of solutions of the internal values with a huge number of cases.

A naive method for defining dummy internal values is to define all internal values only by the forward sampling (See Fig. 3(b)). This method can avoid such a heavy counting step but cannot offer a tight bound. The bad event for this method is that some internal value is connected with some primitive query-response tuple with the user's key, which yields an incompatible internal value for the next round (See Fig. 3(c)).[3] If the forward sampling fails, then we cannot obtain compatible internal values anymore. Let p (resp. q) be the number of primitive (resp. construction) queries. Then, the probability that the naive method fails to define a dummy internal value is roughly $O(\frac{p}{2^{k+n}})$, since the key (resp. the internal value) is chosen uniformly at random from 2^k (resp. about 2^n) elements. As the number of dummy internal values is at most $3q$, the probability that the naive method fails is at most $O(\frac{qp}{2^{k+n}})$. When making a full codebook construction queries, i.e., $q = O(2^n)$, the naive method yields the $O(2^k)$ security regarding primitive queries, which is not tight for the triple encryption.

The re-sampling method avoids the non-tight bound by introducing an inverse sampling. Thus, for each construction query-response pair (M, C), dummy internal values are defined by E from the first round to the last round (forward sampling). If the forward sampling fails, then the remaining internal values, including the (incompatible) internal value, are (re)defined by E^{-1} from the last round. This step is called the inverse sampling. Figure 3(d) exemplifies the inverse sampling. In this example, the internal value Z_1 is defined by the forward sampling; the internal value Z_2 by the forward sampling becomes an incompatible internal value; the internal value Z_2 is (re)defined by the inverse sampling. By the re-sampling method, internal values that are compatible with construction query-response pairs can be defined up to the tight bound.

Regarding the bad event for the re-sampling method, the inverse sampling fails if some internal value is connected with some primitive query-response tuple with the user's key. For example, if the value Z_2 in Fig. 3(e) connects with some primitive query-response tuple with the user's key K_2, then the re-sampling method fails to define compatible internal values. The probability that the bad event occurs is upper-bounded by the probability that forward and inverse

[3] This is because in the ideal world, a random permutation and the underlying ideal cipher are independently defined.

samplings fail for the same construction query-response pair. For each construction query, the probability that an internal value by the forward (resp. inverse) sampling is connected with some primitive query-response tuple with the user's key is roughly $p/2^{n+k}$ (resp. $p/2^{n+k}$). Hence, the probability that the bad event occurs is at most roughly $q(p/2^{n+k})^2$. The bound is tight as long as $q \le 2^n$ (the bound becomes $p^2/2^{2k+n}$).

Regarding the evaluation for good transcripts τ, as transcripts include all internal values, we can avoid the heavy counting step. In the evaluation, we need to evaluate $\frac{\Pr[\mathsf{T}_R=\tau]}{\Pr[\mathsf{T}_I=\tau]}$, the ratio of the real-world and ideal-world probabilities. In the real world, all input-output tuples are defined by an ideal cipher E. On the other hand, in the ideal world, responses to construction queries are defined by a random permutation, and responses to primitive queries are defined by an ideal cipher E, which is independent of the random permutation. Hence, the ratio $\frac{\Pr[\mathsf{T}_R=\tau]}{\Pr[\mathsf{T}_I=\tau]}$ is greater than or equal to 1, since the output space of the ideal world is larger than that of the real world. Regarding the evaluation with the re-sampling method, we need to take into account the inverse sampling, which increases the number of chances to satisfy the target good transcript. Naito et al. [19] proved that regarding 3kTE, the influence of the increase can be canceled out by using the budget of the output space of the ideal world, and the ratio can be greater than or equal to 1.

Security Proof with Re-sampling Method for 2kTE. The difference between 2kTE and 3kTE is the 3rd-round key. The three-round key of 3kTE is independent from 1st-round and 2nd-round keys whereas that of 2kTE is the same as the 1st-round key. We thus update the evaluation with the re-sampling method by involving the equivalence between the 1st-round and 3rd-round keys.

Regarding the bad events of the re-sampling method for 2kTE, 1st-round (resp. 3rd-round) input-output tuples must be involved in the bad event of the forward (resp. inverse) sampling. These involvements are not considered in 3kTE. Besides, other bad events must be updated by taking into account the equivalence between the 1st-round and 3rd-round keys.

For each construction query, we can ensure the independence between the 1st-round and 3rd-round evaluations by using the randomness of the 2nd-round internal value Z_2. The input to the ideal cipher at the 1st round is the plaintext and is under the control of an adversary, but the 2nd-round internal value is not. Thus, by using the randomnesses of the Z_2 values and user's keys, we can ensure the independence up to roughly $\frac{qp}{2^{k+\min\{k,n\}}}$.

5 Proof of Theorem 1

Without loss of generality, we assume that an adversary is deterministic, makes no repeated construction query to the same user, and makes no repeated primitive query.

5.1 Definitions

For $\nu \in [q]$, let q_ν be the number of construction queries to the ν-th user. Let $K^{(\nu)} = K_1^{(\nu)} \| K_2^{(\nu)}$ be the key of the ν-th user, where $K_1^{(\nu)}$ is the 1st-round and 3rd-round key and $K_2^{(\nu)}$ is the 2nd-round key. For convenience, the 3rd-round round key is denoted by $K_3^{(\nu)}$. Note that $K_3^{(\nu)} = K_1^{(\nu)}$. For $\nu \in [q]$ and $i \le j$, let $K_{i,j}^{(\nu)} := K_i^{(\nu)} \| \cdots \| K_j^{(\nu)}$.

For $\alpha \in [p]$, the α-th primitive query-response tuple is denoted by $(W^{(\alpha)}, X^{(\alpha)}, Y^{(\alpha)})$, where $Y^{(\alpha)} = E(W^{(\alpha)}, X^{(\alpha)})$ if the query is a forward one and $X^{(\alpha)} = E^{-1}(W^{(\alpha)}, Y^{(\alpha)})$ if the query is an inverse one. For $\nu \in [q]$ and $\alpha \in [q_\nu]$, the α-th construction query-response pair to the ν-th user is denoted by $(M^{(\nu,\alpha)}, C^{(\nu,\alpha)})$, where in the real (resp. ideal) world, $C^{(\nu,\alpha)} = \mathsf{2kTE}_{K^{(\nu)}}[E](M^{(\nu,\alpha)})$ (resp. $C^{(\nu,\alpha)} = \Pi_\nu(M^{(\nu,\alpha)})$) if the query is an encryption one, and $M^{(\nu,\alpha)} = \mathsf{2kTE}^{-1}_{K^{(\nu)}}[E^{-1}](C^{(\nu,\alpha)})$ (resp. $M^{(\nu,\alpha)} = \Pi_\nu^{-1}(C^{(\nu,\alpha)})$) if the query is a decryption one. For $\nu \in [q]$, $\alpha \in [q_\nu]$, and $i \in [2]$, let $Z_i^{(\nu,\alpha)}$ be the i-th round internal value for the α-th construction query to the ν-th user, $Z_0^{(\nu,\alpha)} := M^{(\nu,\alpha)}$, and $Z_3^{(\nu,\alpha)} := C^{(\nu,\alpha)}$.

We next define the following sets.

- $\mathcal{MC}^{(\nu)} := \{(M^{(\nu,\alpha)}, C^{(\nu,\alpha)}) \mid \alpha \in [q_\nu]\}$.
- $\mathcal{MC} := \cup_{\nu \in [q]} \mathcal{MC}^{(\nu)}$.
- $\mathcal{Z}^{(\nu,\alpha)} := \{(K_i^{(\nu)}, Z_{i-1}^{(\nu,\alpha)}, Z_i^{(\nu,\alpha)}) \mid i \in [3]\}$.
- $\mathcal{Z} := \bigcup_{\nu \in [q]} \bigcup_{\alpha \in [q_\nu]} \mathcal{Z}^{(\nu,\alpha)}$.
- $\mathcal{P} := \{(W^{(\alpha)}, X^{(\alpha)}, Y^{(\alpha)}) \mid \alpha \in [p]\}$.
- $\mathcal{L}^{(\nu,<\alpha)} := \bigcup_{\beta \in [\alpha-1]} \mathcal{Z}^{(\nu,\beta)}$.
- $\mathcal{L}^{(<\nu,\alpha)} := \mathcal{P} \cup \left(\bigcup_{\nu \in [\nu-1]} \bigcup_{\beta \in [q_\nu]} \mathcal{Z}^{(\nu,\beta)}\right) \cup \mathcal{L}^{(\nu,<\alpha)}$.
- $\mathcal{L} := \mathcal{L}^{(<q+1,1)}$.

The stage that an adversary makes queries is called "query stage", and the stage after the query stage "decision stage".

We next define chains constructed from input-output tuples in $\mathcal{L}^{(<\nu,\alpha)}$ with respect to the α-th construction query to the ν-th user.

Definition 1 (Chains from $\mathcal{L}^{(<\nu,\alpha)}$ for the ν-th user). *For $\ell \in [3]$, a sequence of ℓ tuples $(W_1, X_1, Y_1), \ldots, (W_\ell, X_\ell, Y_\ell) \in \mathcal{L}^{(<\nu,\alpha)}$ is an ℓ-chain from $\mathcal{L}^{(<\nu,\alpha)}$ if $Y_j = X_{j+1}$ for each $j \in [\ell - 1]$. X_1 (resp. Y_ℓ) is called a head (resp. tail) of the chain. The concatenation $W_1 \| \ldots \| W_\ell$ is called a key of the chain. Note that 1-chains are equal to $\mathcal{L}^{(<\nu,\alpha)}$. Let $\ell\text{-ChainH}^H[\mathcal{L}^{(<\nu,\alpha)}, K^*]$ be an ℓ-chain from $\mathcal{L}^{(<\nu,\alpha)}$ whose key and head are respectively equal to K^* and H. If there does not exist such chain or $\ell \le 0$, then $\ell\text{-ChainH}^H[\mathcal{L}^{(<\nu,\alpha)}, K^*] := \varepsilon$. Let $\ell\text{-ChainT}_T[\mathcal{L}^{(<\nu,\alpha)}, K^*]$ be an ℓ-chain from $\mathcal{L}^{(<\nu,\alpha)}$ whose key and tail are respectively equal to K^* and T. If there does not exist such chain or $\ell \le 0$, then $\ell\text{-ChainT}_T[\mathcal{L}^{(<\nu,\alpha)}, K^*] := \varepsilon$.*

Algorithm 1. Procedure to define internal values in the ideal world

1: $\mathsf{fail}_{\mathsf{sample}} \leftarrow \mathsf{false}$
2: **for** $\nu = 1$ to q **do**
3: $K^{(\nu)} \xleftarrow{\$} \{0,1\}^{2k}$
4: **for** $\alpha \in \overrightarrow{[q_\nu]}$ **do**
5: $m \leftarrow \max\left(\left\{i \mid i \in [3] \wedge i\text{-ChainH}^{M^{(\nu,\alpha)}}[\mathcal{L}^{(<\nu,\alpha)}, K_{1,i}^{(\nu)}] \neq \varepsilon\right\} \cup \{0\}\right)$
6: $c \leftarrow \min\left(\left\{i \mid i \in [3] \wedge (4-i)\text{-ChainT}_{C^{(\nu,\alpha)}}[\mathcal{L}^{(<\nu,\alpha)}, K_{i,3}^{(\nu)}] \neq \varepsilon\right\} \cup \{4\}\right)$
7: $u \leftarrow m$; $Z_0^{(\nu,\alpha)} \leftarrow M^{(\nu,\alpha)}$; $Z_3^{(\nu,\alpha)} \leftarrow C^{(\nu,\alpha)}$
8: **for** $i = \overrightarrow{[m]}$ **do** $Z_i^{(\nu,\alpha)} \leftarrow E(K_i^{(\nu)}, Z_{i-1}^{(\nu,\alpha)})$
9: **for** $i \in \overleftarrow{[c,3]}$ **do** $Z_{i-1}^{(\nu,\alpha)} \leftarrow E^{-1}(K_i^{(\nu)}, Z_i^{(\nu,\alpha)})$
10: **for** $i \in \overrightarrow{[m+1, c-2]}$ **do** ▷ Forward sampling
11: $T_i^{(\nu,\alpha)} \leftarrow E(K_i^{(\nu)}, Z_{i-1}^{(\nu,\alpha)})$
12: **if** $\exists Z^* \in \{0,1\}^n$ s.t. $(K_{i+1}^{(\nu)}, T_i^{(\nu,\alpha)}, Z^*) \in \mathcal{E}$ **then**
13: $\mathcal{E} \leftarrow \mathcal{E} \backslash \{(K_i^{(\nu)}, Z_{i-1}^{(\nu,\alpha)}, T_i^{(\nu,\alpha)})\}$ ▷ Delete the tuple from the table $\mathcal{E}$
14: **goto step** 18
15: **end if**
16: $Z_i^{(\nu,\alpha)} \leftarrow T_i^{(\nu,\alpha)}$; $\mathcal{E} \xleftarrow{\cup} (K_i^{(\nu)}, Z_{i-1}^{(\nu,\alpha)}, Z_i^{(\nu,\alpha)})$; $u \leftarrow i$
17: **end for**
18: **for** $i \in \overleftarrow{[u+2, c-1]}$ **do** ▷ Inverse sampling
19: $Z_{i-1}^{(\nu,\alpha)} \leftarrow E^{-1}(K_i^{(\nu)}, Z_i^{(\nu,\alpha)})$
20: **if** $\exists Z^* \in \{0,1\}^n$ s.t. $(K_{i-1}, Z^*, Z_{i-1}^{(\nu,\alpha)}) \in \mathcal{E}$ **then** $\mathsf{fail}_{\mathsf{sample}} \leftarrow \mathsf{true}$
21: **end for**
22: $\mathcal{E} \xleftarrow{\cup} (K^{(\nu)}, Z_u^{(\nu,\alpha)}, Z_{u+1}^{(\nu,\alpha)})$
23: **end for**
24: **end for**

5.2 Lazy Sampled Ideal Cipher

In this proof, an ideal cipher E is realized by lazy sampling. Let $\mathcal{E}$ be a table that is initially empty and keeps query-response tuples of the ideal cipher. Let $\mathcal{E}_W^+ := \{Y \mid (W, X, Y) \in \mathcal{E}\}$ (resp. $\mathcal{E}_W^- := \{X \mid (W, X, Y) \in \mathcal{E}\}$) be a set that keeps ciphertext (resp. plaintext) blocks. For a forward query (W, X), the response is defined as $Y \xleftarrow{\$} \{0,1\}^n \backslash \mathcal{E}_W^+$, and (W, X, Y) is added to $\mathcal{E}$. For an inverse query (W, Y), the response is defined as $X \xleftarrow{\$} \{0,1\}^n \backslash \mathcal{E}_W^-$, and (W, X, Y) is added to $\mathcal{E}$.

5.3 Adversary's View

In this proof, Algorithm 1 is performed in the decision stage of the ideal world. The algorithm defines (dummy) internal values $Z_i^{(\nu,\alpha)}$ and (dummy) keys $K^{(\nu)}$ in the ideal world, where $\nu \in [q]$, $\alpha \in [q_\nu]$, and $i \in (3]$. Regarding the α-th construction query to the ν-th user, the internal values $Z_i^{(\nu,\alpha)}$ with $i \in [m] \cup [c-1, 2]$ were defined previously, and are set in the steps 8 and 9. The procedure of the step 10–17 are called forward sampling, which freshly define the internal values $Z_{m+1}^{(\nu,\alpha)}, \ldots, Z_u^{(\nu,\alpha)}$ by E. In the forward sampling, an ideal-cipher's output is firstly kept as a temporary value $T_i^{(\nu,\alpha)}$. If the forward sampling does not fail, then $T_i^{(\nu,\alpha)}$ is assigned to the internal value $Z_i^{(\nu,\alpha)}$. The procedure of the steps 18–21 is called inverse sampling, which freshly define the internal values $Z_{u+1}^{(\nu,\alpha)}, \ldots, Z_{c-1}^{(\nu,\alpha)}$ by E^{-1}. u is the round number such that internal values are defined by the forward sampling up to the u-th round. $\mathsf{fail}_{\mathsf{sample}}$ is a flag for a bad event of the re-sampling method where the forward and inverse samplings fail for some ν, α. Note that tuples $(K^{(\nu)}, Z_u^{(\nu,\alpha)}, Z_{u+1}^{(\nu,\alpha)})$ are defined from the results of the forward and inverse samplings and are not defined by the ideal cipher. To ensure the compatibility with the ideal cipher, the tuples are stored in the ideal-cipher's table $\mathcal{E}$ at the step 22. For convenience, we assume that these tuples are defined by E.

This proof permits an adversary $\mathbf{A}$ to obtain user's keys and all internal values after finishing all queries by $\mathbf{A}$ but before returning a decision bit. Hence, before outputting a decision bit, $\mathbf{A}$ obtains a transcript τ which consists of (dummy) user's keys $\tau_K = \{K^{(\nu)} \mid \nu \in [q]\}$, primitive query-response tuples $\mathcal{P}$, construction query-response tuples $\mathcal{MC}$, and (dummy) internal input-output tuples $\mathcal{Z}$. As $\mathcal{MC}$ can be obtained from τ_K and $\mathcal{Z}$, $\mathcal{MC}$ can be omitted from τ.

5.4 Good and Bad Transcripts

We define bad events below.

- $\mathsf{2ChainH}$: $\exists \nu \in [q], \alpha \in [q_\nu]$ s.t. $\text{2-ChainH}^{M^{(\nu,\alpha)}}[\mathcal{L}^{(<\nu,\alpha)}, K_{1,2}^{(\nu,\alpha)}] \neq \varepsilon$.
- $\mathsf{2ChainT}$: $\exists \nu \in [q], \alpha \in [q_\nu]$ s.t. $\text{2-ChainT}_{C^{(\nu,\alpha)}}[\mathcal{L}^{(<\nu,\alpha)}, K_{2,3}^{(\nu,\alpha)}] \neq \varepsilon$.
- KColl: $\exists \nu \in [q]$ s.t. $K_1^{(\nu)} = K_2^{(\nu)}$.
- MCColl: $\exists \nu \in [q], \alpha \in [q_\nu]$ s.t. $T_1^{(\nu,\alpha)} = C^{(\nu,\alpha)} \vee Z_2^{(\nu,\alpha)} = M^{(\nu,\alpha)}$.
- $\mathsf{fail}_{\mathsf{sample}}$: the flag becomes true in Algorithm 1.
- mcoll: $\exists (W_1, X_1, Y_1), \ldots, (W_\omega, X_\omega, Y_\omega) \in \mathcal{L}$
  s.t. $W_1, \ldots, W_\omega$ are all distinct and $(X_1, Y_1) = \ldots = (X_\omega, Y_\omega)$.

Let $\mathsf{bad} = \mathsf{2ChainH} \vee \mathsf{2ChainT} \vee \mathsf{KColl} \vee \mathsf{MCColl} \vee \mathsf{fail}_{\mathsf{sample}} \vee \mathsf{mcoll}$. Then, $\mathcal{T}_{\mathsf{bad}}$ is a set of transcripts that satisfy bad, and $\mathcal{T}_{\mathsf{good}} := \mathcal{T} \backslash \mathcal{T}_{\mathsf{bad}}$.

$\mathsf{2ChainH}$ and $\mathsf{2ChainT}$ consider events that all internal values at some construction query are recovered, i.e., the user's key is recovered. KColl considers a collision between round keys of some user. MCColl considers an event that some 1st-round input-output tuple appears at the 3rd round or some 3rd-round input-output tuple appears at the 1st round, i.e., the event takes into account the influence of the equivalence between the 1st-round and 3rd-round keys. $\mathsf{fail}_{\mathsf{sample}}$ is an event that the re-sampling method fails. Note that $\mathsf{fail}_{\mathsf{sample}}$ is satisfied in only the ideal world. Finally, mcoll is a multi-collision event for ideal-cipher's input-output tuples, and is used to analyze the events $\mathsf{2ChainH}$ and $\mathsf{2ChainT}$.

5.5 Upper-Bounding $\Pr[\mathsf{T}_I \in \mathcal{T}_{\mathsf{bad}}]$

Without loss of generality, we assume that **A** aborts just after one of the bad events occurs. Hence, for each event ev, $\Pr[\mathsf{ev}]$ is the probability that ev occurs under the condition that other bad events do not occur.

We upper-bound the ideal-world probabilities $\Pr[\mathsf{2ChainH}]$, $\Pr[\mathsf{2ChainT}]$, $\Pr[\mathsf{KColl}]$, $\Pr[\mathsf{MCColl}]$, $\Pr[\mathsf{fail}_{\mathsf{sample}}]$, and $\Pr[\mathsf{mcoll}]$. Since $\Pr[\mathsf{T}_I \in \mathcal{T}_{\mathsf{bad}}] = \Pr[\mathsf{bad}]$ is satisfied, $\Pr[\mathsf{bad}]$ can be upper-bounded by summing upper-bounds of the ideal-world probabilities. The upper-bounds are given below. We define the parameter in the event mcoll as $\omega := \max\left\{\left(2n \cdot \frac{2^{3k-n}}{qQ}\right)^{1/2}, \frac{2n}{\log_2 n}\right\}$, and then have

$$\Pr[\mathsf{T}_I \in \mathcal{T}_{\mathsf{bad}}] \leq \max\left\{\left(\frac{8n \cdot qQ}{2^{n+k}}\right)^{\frac{1}{2}}, \frac{\frac{2n}{\log_2 n} \cdot qQ}{2^{2k}}\right\} + \frac{(8n+8)\cdot qQ}{2^{n+k}} + \frac{q}{2^k} + \frac{2q}{2^n}.$$

In the following evaluations, to ensure the randomnesses of outputs of E and E^{-1}, we use the technique given in [1]: For any key element W of E, if **A** makes 2^{n-1} primitive queries with the key W, then **A** obtains all other 2^{n-1} input-output tuples of E with the key W. The additional queries are called super queries. Without loss of generality, the super queries are forward ones. Introducing the super queries ensures that responses of non-super queries are chosen uniformly at random from at least 2^{n-1} elements in $\{0,1\}^n$. Regarding super queries, fixing Y^*, for a super query (W, X), the probability that the output Y is equal to Y^* is at most $(2^n/2-1)!/(2^n/2)! = 2/2^n$.

Upper-Bounding $\Pr[\mathsf{2ChainH}]$. Regarding the 2-chain in the definition of $\mathsf{2ChainH}$, let $\text{2-ChainH}^{M^{(\nu,\alpha)}}[\mathcal{L}^{(<\nu,\alpha)}, K_{1,2}^{(\nu,\alpha)}] := ((W_1, X_1, Y_1), (W_2, X_2, Y_2))$.[4] As $\mathcal{L}^{(<\nu,\alpha)} = \mathcal{L}^{(<\nu,1)} \cup \mathcal{L}^{(\nu,<\alpha)}$ and $\mathsf{2ChainH} = \mathsf{2ChainH}_1 \vee \mathsf{2ChainH}_2$ (defined below), we evaluate the probabilities $\Pr[\mathsf{2ChainH}_1]$ and $\Pr[\mathsf{2ChainH}_2]$. Note that $(W_2, X_2, Y_2) \in \mathcal{L}^{(<\nu,1)}$ must be satisfied.[5]

- $\mathsf{2ChainH}_1$: $\mathsf{2ChainH} \wedge \big((W_1, X_1, Y_1), (W_2, X_2, Y_2)\big) \in \mathcal{L}^{(<\nu,1)} \times \mathcal{L}^{(<\nu,1)}$.
- $\mathsf{2ChainH}_2$: $\mathsf{2ChainH} \wedge \big((W_1, X_1, Y_1), (W_2, X_2, Y_2)\big) \in \mathcal{L}^{(\nu,<\alpha)} \times \mathcal{L}^{(<\nu,1)}$.

We evaluate $\Pr[\mathsf{2ChainH}_1]$ using the following cases. We fix $\nu \in [q]$ and $\alpha \in [q_\nu]$. The number of 2nd elements (W_2, X_2, Y_2) is at most Q. For each 2nd element (W_2, X_2, Y_2), the number of the 1st elements (W_1, X_1, Y_1) such that $X_1 = M^{(\nu,\alpha)}$ and $Y_1 = X_2$ is at most ω by the assumption that mcoll does not occur. Thus, the number of 2-chains from $\mathcal{L}^{(<\nu,1)}$ whose head is $M^{(\nu,\alpha)}$ is at most ωQ. We thus have

$$\Pr[\mathsf{2ChainH}_1] \leq \sum_{\nu \in [q], \alpha \in [q_\nu]} \frac{\omega Q}{2^{2k}} = \frac{\omega q Q}{2^{2k}}.$$

---

[4] Thus $X^{(\alpha_1)} = M^{(\nu,\alpha)}$, $W^{(\alpha_1)} = K_1^{(\nu)}$, and $W^{(\alpha_2)} = K_2^{(\nu)}$.

[5] This is because for each $\nu \in [u]$, $K_2^{(\nu)}$ is used at only the 2nd round.

We next evaluate $\Pr[\mathsf{2ChainH}_2]$. As $(W_1, X_1, Y_1) \in \mathcal{L}^{(\nu,<\alpha)}$, the tuple (W_1, X_1, Y_1) must be defined by some β-th construction query to the ν-th user such that $\beta < \alpha$. As an adversary makes no repeated query to the same user, the tuple must be defined at the 3rd round of the β-th construction query. Then, we can use the randomness of X_1, since it is not a plaintext. For each $(W_1, X_1, Y_1) \in \mathcal{L}^{(\nu,<\alpha)}$, we have $\Pr[X_1 = M^{(\nu,\alpha)}] \leq \frac{2}{2^n}$. For each $(W_2, X_2, Y_2) \in \mathcal{L}^{(<\nu,1)}$, we have $\Pr[W_2 = K_2^{(\nu)}] \leq \frac{1}{2^k}$. We thus have

$$\Pr[\mathsf{2ChainH}_2] \leq \sum_{\nu \in [q]} q_\nu Q \cdot \frac{2}{2^{n+k}} = \frac{2qQ}{2^{n+k}}.$$

Using these bounds, we have

$$\Pr[\mathsf{2ChainH}] \leq \frac{\omega q Q}{2^{2k}} + \frac{2qQ}{2^{n+k}}.$$

Upper-Bounding Pr[2ChainH]. The evaluation is the same as that of $\Pr[\mathsf{2ChainH}]$, since 2-chains considered in 2ChainH and in 2ChainT are symmetric. We thus have

$$\Pr[\mathsf{2ChainT}] \leq \frac{\omega q Q}{2^{2k}} + \frac{2qQ}{2^{n+k}}.$$

Upper-Bounding Pr[KColl]. For each $\nu \in [q]$, we have $\Pr[K_1^{(\nu)} = K_2^{(\nu)}] \leq \frac{1}{2^k}$. We thus have

$$\Pr[\mathsf{KColl}] \leq \sum_{\nu \in [q]} \frac{1}{2^k} \leq \frac{q}{2^k}.$$

Upper-Bounding Pr[MCColl]. For each $\nu \in [q]$ and $\alpha \in [q_\nu]$, we have $\Pr[T_1^{(\nu,\alpha)} = C^{(\nu,\alpha)}] \leq \frac{2}{2^n}$ and $\Pr[Z_2^{(\nu,\alpha)} = M^{(\nu,\alpha)}] \leq \frac{2}{2^n}$ by super queries. Hence, we have

$$\Pr[\mathsf{MCColl}] \leq \sum_{\nu \in [q], \alpha \in [q_\nu]} \frac{2}{2^n} \leq \frac{2q}{2^n}.$$

Upper-Bounding Pr[$\mathsf{fail}_{\mathsf{sample}}$]. The values m and c at the α-th loop of the ν-th user in Algorithm 1 are denoted by $m_{\nu,\alpha}$ and $c_{\nu,\alpha}$, respectively. Since 2ChainH and 2ChainT do not occur, $\forall \nu \in [q], \alpha \in [q_\nu] : m_{\nu,\alpha} < c_{\nu,\alpha} - 1$ is satisfied. For $\nu \in [q], \alpha \in [q_\nu]$, let $\mathsf{fail}_{\mathsf{sample}}[\nu, \alpha]$ be an event that $\mathsf{fail}_{\mathsf{sample}}$ occurs a the α-th loop of the ν-th user in Algorithm 1.

First, we fix $\nu \in [q], \alpha \in [q_\nu]$ and upper-bound the probability $\Pr[\mathsf{fail}_{\mathsf{sample}}[\nu, \alpha]]$. If $\mathsf{fail}_{\mathsf{sample}}[\nu, \alpha]$ occurs, then the conditions of the steps 12 and 20 in Algorithm 1 are satisfied. Let i_F (resp. i_I) be a round number such that the forward (resp. inverse) sampling fails, i.e., the condition on the step 12 (resp. step 20) is satisfied. As $i_F < i_I$ is satisfied, $(i_F, i_I) = (1, 2)$, $(i_F, i_I) = (1, 3)$, or $(i_F, i_I) = (2, 3)$ is satisfied. Hence, we consider two cases $i_F = 1$; $i_I = 3$.

- $i_F = 1$: This case is that there exists $(W, X, Y) \in \mathcal{L}^{(<\nu,\alpha)}$ such that $W = K_2^{(\nu)}$ and the internal value $T_1^{(\nu,\alpha)}$ defined by the forward sampling is equal to X. Since $T_1^{(\nu,\alpha)}$ must be distinct from the previous 1st-round internal values of the ν-th user $\{Z_1^{(\nu,\beta)} \mid \beta \in [\alpha-1]\}$ and KColl does not occur, we have only to consider the condition $(W, X, Y) \in \mathcal{L}^{(<\nu,1)}$. As for each $(W, X, Y) \in \mathcal{L}^{(<\nu,1)}$, $K_2^{(\nu)}$ is defined independently of W, and we have $\Pr[K_2^{(\nu)} = W] \le \frac{1}{2^k}$. Using the randomness of $T_1^{(\nu,\alpha)}$, we have $\Pr[T_1^{(\nu,\alpha)} = X] \le \frac{2}{2^n}$. As $|\mathcal{L}^{(<\nu,1)}| \le Q$, the probability that $i_F = 1$ is satisfied is at most $\frac{2Q}{2^{n+k}}$.
- $i_I = 3$: This case is that there exists $(W, X, Y) \in \mathcal{L}^{(<\nu,\alpha)}$ such that $W = K_2^{(\nu)}$ and the internal value $Z_2^{(\nu,\alpha)}$ defined by the inverse sampling is equal to Y. This evaluation is the same as that of $i_F = 1$. Thus, the probability that $i_I = 3$ is satisfied is at most $\frac{2Q}{2^{n+k}}$.

Using these bounds, we have

$$\Pr[\mathsf{fail}_{\mathsf{sample}}[\nu, \alpha]] \le \frac{4Q}{2^{n+k}}.$$

Summing the bound for each ν, α, we have

$$\Pr[\mathsf{fail}_{\mathsf{sample}}] \le \frac{4qQ}{2^{n+k}}.$$

Upper-Bounding Pr[mcoll]. Fix X_0 and Y_0. For a tuple $(W', X', Y') \in \mathcal{L}$ such that $X' = X_0$ and the tuple is defined by E, we have $\Pr[Y' = Y_0] \le \frac{2}{2^n}$. For a tuple $(W^*, X^*, Y^*) \in \mathcal{L}$ such that $Y^* = Y_0$ and the tuple is defined by E^{-1}, we have $\Pr[X^* = X_0] \le \frac{2}{2^n}$. Fixing X_0, Y_0, and $(W_1, X_1, Y_1), \ldots, (W_\omega, X_\omega, Y_\omega) \in \mathcal{L}$ such that $W_1, \ldots, W_\omega$ are all distinct, we have $\Pr[(X_1, Y_1) = \cdots = (X_\mu, Y_\omega)] \le \left(\frac{2}{2^n}\right)^\omega$. We thus have

$$\Pr[\mathsf{mcoll}] \le 2^n \cdot 2^n \cdot \binom{2^k}{\omega} \left(\frac{2}{2^n}\right)^\omega \le 2^{2n} \cdot \left(\frac{2e}{\omega 2^{n-k}}\right)^\omega,$$

using Stirling's approximation ($x! \ge (x/e)^x$ for any x).

5.6 Overview of Deriving the Lower-Bound of $\frac{\Pr[\mathsf{T}_R = \tau]}{\Pr[\mathsf{T}_I = \tau]}$

We give an overview of the evaluation, and the detail is given in Subsect. 5.7.

We fix a good transcript $\tau \in \mathcal{T}_{\mathsf{good}}$. Since each key is randomly chosen uniformly at random from $\{0,1\}^{2k}$ in the real and ideal worlds, the real-world and ideal-world probabilities that the keys satisfy τ are the same. For primitive query-response tuples, since the responses are chosen by an ideal cipher in both worlds, the real-world and ideal-world probabilities that the responses satisfy τ are the same. Hence, $\Pr[\mathsf{T}_R = \tau]/\Pr[\mathsf{T}_I = \tau]$ is lower-bounded by the ratio of the real-world probability to the ideal-world one for tuples of internal values $(Z_0^{(\nu,\alpha)}, Z_1^{(\nu,\alpha)}, Z_2^{(\nu,\alpha)}, Z_3^{(\nu,\alpha)})$ for $\nu \in [q]$ and $\alpha \in [q_\nu]$.

We fix $\nu \in [u]$ and $\alpha \in [q_\nu]$. Since τ does not satisfy 2ChainH and 2ChainT, we obtain the condition $c - m \geq 2$. Hence, at least two of the internal values are freshly sampled in both worlds. In both worlds, $Z_0^{(\nu,\alpha)}$ is the plaintext $M^{(\alpha)}$. In the real world, we sample the remaining internal values $Z_1^{(\nu,\alpha)}, Z_2^{(\nu,\alpha)}, Z_3^{(\nu,\alpha)}$ by E. In the ideal world, the internal value $Z_3^{(\nu,\alpha)}$ $(= C^{(\nu,\alpha)})$ is defined by a random permutation Π_ν, and the remaining internal values $Z_1^{(\nu,\alpha)}, Z_2^{(\nu,\alpha)}$ are defined by $E^{\pm}$ via Algorithm 1. Hence, in the real world, each internal value is chosen from $\{0,1\}^n$ excluding the output blocks with the same key previously defined by primitive and construction queries. In the real world, each of the internal values $Z_1^{(\nu,\alpha)}, Z_2^{(\nu,\alpha)}$ is chosen by the same way, but the internal value $Z_3^{(\nu,\alpha)}$ is chosen from $\{0,1\}^n$ excluding the output blocks with the same key previously defined by construction queries. Hence, in the ideal world, $Z_3^{(\nu,\alpha)}$ is chosen from the larger space than the real world. By using the difference, though the inverse sampling in the ideal world enhances the ideal-world probability, we can show that the real-world probability that the internal values satisfy τ is less than or equal to the real-world one.

Hence, we have $\frac{\Pr[\mathsf{T}_R=\tau]}{\Pr[\mathsf{T}_I=\tau]} \geq 1$ for any $\tau \in \mathcal{T}_{\mathsf{good}}$.

5.7 Lower-Bounding $\frac{\Pr[\mathsf{T}_R=\tau]}{\Pr[\mathsf{T}_I=\tau]}$

Fix a good transcript τ which consists of τ_K, $\mathcal{P}$, and $\mathcal{Z}$. For a set τ', let $\mathsf{T}_R \vdash \tau'$ (resp. $\mathsf{T}_I \vdash \tau'$) be an event that T_R (resp. T_I) satisfies all elements in τ'. For $W \in \{R, I\}$ and a value V defined by the sampling of T_W, the corresponding element in τ is denoted by V^*. Hence, $\mathsf{T}_W \vdash \tau'$ means that for any value V defined by the sampling of T_W and $V^* \in \tau'$, $V = V^*$ is satisfied. For each $\nu \in [q]$ and $\alpha \in [q_\alpha]$, let $\mu_{2,3}^{(\nu,\alpha)}$ be the number of 2-chains from $\mathcal{L}^{(<\nu,\alpha)}$ whose keys are equal to $K_{2,3}^{(\nu)}$. For each $\nu \in [q]$, $\alpha \in [q_\alpha]$, and $i \in [3]$, let $\mu_i^{(\nu,\alpha)}$ be elements in $\mathcal{L}^{(<\nu,\alpha)}$ whose keys are equal to $K_i^{(\nu)}$. Note that $\mu_1^{(\nu,\alpha)} = \mu_3^{(\nu,\alpha)}$. For $\alpha \in [q]$ and $i, j \in [3]$ with $i \leq j$, $Z_{i,j}^{(\nu,\alpha)} := (Z_i^{(\nu,\alpha)}, \ldots, Z_j^{(\nu,\alpha)})$, and $Z_{i,j}^{(\nu,\alpha)*} := (Z_i^{(\nu,\alpha)*}, \ldots, Z_j^{(\nu,\alpha)*})$. Let $(Z_{i,j}^{(\nu,\alpha)})_R$ (resp. $(Z_{i,j}^{(\nu,\alpha)})_I$) be the values $Z_{i,j}^{(\nu,\alpha)}$ in the real (resp. ideal) world. If the target world is clear from context, we omit the symbols "R" and "I".

Evaluating $\Pr[\mathsf{T}_W \vdash \tau_K]$ for $W \in \{R, I\}$. In both worlds, for each $\nu \in [q]$, the key $K^{(\nu)}$ is chosen uniformly at random from $\{0,1\}^{2k}$, we have $\Pr[\mathsf{T}_R \vdash \tau_K] = \Pr[\mathsf{T}_I \vdash \tau_K]$. Hereafter, we assume that $\mathsf{T}_R \vdash \tau_K$ and $\mathsf{T}_I \vdash \tau_K$ are satisfied.

Evaluating $\Pr[\mathsf{T}_W \vdash \mathcal{P}]$ for $W \in \{R, I\}$. In both worlds, responses to primitive queries are defined by an ideal cipher. We thus have $\Pr[\mathsf{T}_R \vdash \mathcal{P}] = \Pr[\mathsf{T}_I \vdash \mathcal{P}]$. Hereafter, we assume that $\mathsf{T}_R \vdash \mathcal{P}$ and $\mathsf{T}_I \vdash \mathcal{P}$ are satisfied.

Evaluating $\Pr[\mathsf{T}_W \vdash \mathcal{Z}]$ for $W \in \{R, I\}$. We first fix $\nu \in [q]$ and $\alpha \in [q_\nu]$, and lower-bound $\frac{\Pr[(Z_{1,3}^{(\nu,\alpha)})_R = Z_{1,3}^{(\nu,\alpha)*}]}{\Pr[(Z_{1,3}^{(\nu,\alpha)})_I = Z_{1,3}^{(\nu,\alpha)*}]}$. Regarding the values m and c defined at the α-th loop of the ν-th user in Algorithm 1, by $\neg$2ChainH and $\neg$2ChainT, $c - m \geq 2$ is satisfied. Hence, we consider the three cases: (a) $c-m=4$; (b) $c-m=3 \wedge c=4$; (c) $c-m=3 \wedge c=3$; (d) $c-m=2$.

The following evaluations show that $\frac{\Pr[(Z_{1,3}^{(\nu,\alpha)})_R = Z_{1,3}^{(\nu,\alpha)*}]}{\Pr[(Z_{1,3}^{(\nu,\alpha)})_I = Z_{1,3}^{(\nu,\alpha)*}]} \geq 1$. We thus have

$$\frac{\Pr[\mathsf{T}_R \vdash \mathcal{Z}]}{\Pr[\mathsf{T}_I \vdash \mathcal{Z}]} = \prod_{\nu \in [q]} \prod_{\alpha \in [q_\nu]} \frac{\Pr[(Z_{1,3}^{(\nu,\alpha)})_R = Z_{1,3}^{(\nu,\alpha)*}]}{\Pr[(Z_{1,3}^{(\nu,\alpha)})_I = Z_{1,3}^{(\nu,\alpha)*}]} \geq 1.$$

(a): $c-m=4$. In this case, $Z_{1,3}^{(\nu,\alpha)}$ are not fixed before the α-th construction query of the ν-th user (the α-th loop of the ν-th user in Algorithm 1 in the ideal world).

- In the real world, we sample $Z_{1,3}^{(\nu,\alpha)}$ by E. Then, for each $i \in [2]$, $Z_i^{(\nu,\alpha)}$ is chosen uniformly at random from $2^n - \mu_i^{(\nu,\alpha)}$ elements in $\{0,1\}^n$, and $Z_3^{(\nu,\alpha)}$ is chosen uniformly at random from $2^n - \mu_1^{(\nu,\alpha)} - 1$ elements in $\{0,1\}^n$. We thus have

$$\Pr[(Z_{1,3}^{(\nu,\alpha)})_R = Z_{1,3}^{(\nu,\alpha)*} \mid (a)] = \frac{1}{2^n - \mu_1^{(\nu,\alpha)}} \cdot \frac{1}{2^n - \mu_2^{(\nu,\alpha)}} \cdot \frac{1}{2^n - \mu_1^{(\nu,\alpha)} - 1}.$$

- In the ideal world, there are three cases that $Z_{1,3}^{(\nu,\alpha)} = Z_{1,3}^{(\nu,\alpha)*}$ is satisfied. Note that $Z_3^{(\nu,\alpha)} = C^{(\nu,\alpha)}$ is satisfied. We sample the value $Z_3^{(\nu,\alpha)}$ by Π_ν. Then, we have

$$\Pr[Z_3^{(\nu,\alpha)} = Z_3^{(\nu,\alpha)*}] = \frac{1}{2^n - (\alpha - 1)}.$$

1. The 1st case is that the values $Z_{1,2}^{(\nu,\alpha)}$ are defined by E. Then, we have

$$\Pr[Z_{1,3}^{(\nu,\alpha)} = Z_{1,3}^{(\nu,\alpha)*} \wedge (1) \mid (a)] = \frac{1}{2^n - (\alpha - 1)} \cdot \frac{1}{2^n - \mu_1^{(\nu,\alpha)}} \cdot \frac{1}{2^n - \mu_2^{(\nu,\alpha)}}.$$

2. The 2nd case is that the value $Z_1^{(\nu,\alpha)}$ (resp. $Z_2^{(\nu,\alpha)}$) is defined by E (resp. E^{-1}). Then, we have $\Pr[Z_{1,2}^{(\nu,\alpha)} = Z_{1,2}^{(\nu,\alpha)*}] = \frac{1}{2^n - \mu_1^{(\nu,\alpha)}} \cdot \frac{1}{2^n - \mu_1^{(\nu,\alpha)} - 1}$. In this case, when $T_2^{(\nu,\alpha)}$ is defined by E in the forward sampling, $T_2^{(\nu,\alpha)} \neq Z_2^{(\nu,\alpha)*}$ is satisfied and the condition in the step 12 in Algorithm 1 is satisfied, i.e., $T_2^{(\nu,\alpha)}$ collides with some input block of $(\mu_1^{(\nu,\alpha)} - \mu_{2,3}^{(\nu,\alpha)})$ elements with the key $K_1^{(\nu)}$ in $\mathcal{L}^{(<\nu,\alpha)}$. The collision probability is $\frac{\mu_1^{(\nu,\alpha)} - \mu_{2,3}^{(\nu,\alpha)}}{2^n - \mu_2^{(\nu,\alpha)}}$. Hence, we have

$$\begin{aligned} &\Pr[(Z_{1,3}^{(\nu,\alpha)} = Z_{1,3}^{(\nu,\alpha)*} \wedge (2) \mid (a)] \\ &= \frac{1}{2^n - (\alpha - 1)} \cdot \left(\frac{1}{2^n - \mu_1^{(\nu,\alpha)}} \cdot \frac{1}{2^n - \mu_1^{(\nu,\alpha)} - 1} \right) \cdot \frac{\mu_1^{(\nu,\alpha)} - \mu_{2,3}^{(\nu,\alpha)}}{2^n - \mu_2^{(\nu,\alpha)}}. \end{aligned}$$

3. The 3rd case is that the values $Z_{1,2}^{(\nu,\alpha)}$ are defined by E^{-1}. Then, we have $\Pr[Z_{1,2}^{(\nu,\alpha)} = Z_{1,2}^{(\nu,\alpha)*}] = \frac{1}{2^n - \mu_1^{(\nu,\alpha)}} \cdot \frac{1}{2^n - \mu_2^{(\nu,\alpha)}}$. In this case, when $T_1^{(\nu,\alpha)}$ is defined by E in the forward sampling, $T_1^{(\nu,\alpha)} \neq Z_1^{(\nu,\alpha)*}$ is satisfied and the condition in the step 12 in Algorithm 1 is satisfied, i.e., $T_1^{(\nu,\alpha)}$ collides with a head of some 2-chain with the key $K_{2,3}^{(\nu)}$ from $\mathcal{L}^{(<\nu,\alpha)}$. Note that in $\mu_{2,3}^{(\nu,\alpha)}$ 2-chains, $T_1^{(\nu,\alpha)}$ must not collide with at least $(\alpha-1)$ 2-chains, since the $(\alpha-1)$ 2-chains are constructed from pairs of 2nd-round and 3rd-round input-output tuples defined by construction queries to the ν-th user and an adversary does not a repeated construction query to the same user. Thus, the collision probability is at most $\frac{\mu_{2,3}^{(\nu,\alpha)} - (\alpha-1)}{2^n - \mu_1^{(\nu,\alpha)}}$. Hence, we have

$$\begin{aligned}&\Pr[Z_{1,3}^{(\nu,\alpha)} = Z_{1,3}^{(\nu,\alpha)*} \wedge (3) \mid (a)]\\&= \frac{1}{2^n - (\alpha-1)} \cdot \left(\frac{1}{2^n - \mu_1^{(\nu,\alpha)}} \cdot \frac{1}{2^n - \mu_2^{(\nu,\alpha)}}\right) \cdot \frac{\mu_{2,3}^{(\nu,\alpha)} - (\alpha-1)}{2^n - \mu_1^{(\nu,\alpha)}}.\end{aligned}$$

Hence, we have

$$\begin{aligned}&\Pr[Z_{1,3}^{(\nu,\alpha)} = Z_{1,3}^{(\nu,\alpha)*} \mid (a)]\\&\le \frac{1}{2^n - (\alpha-1)} \cdot \frac{1}{2^n - \mu_1^{(\nu,\alpha)}} \cdot \frac{1}{2^n - \mu_2^{(\nu,\alpha)}}\\&+ \frac{1}{2^n - (\alpha-1)} \cdot \left(\frac{1}{2^n - \mu_1^{(\nu,\alpha)}} \cdot \frac{1}{2^n - \mu_1^{(\nu,\alpha)} - 1}\right) \cdot \frac{\mu_1^{(\nu,\alpha)} - \mu_{2,3}^{(\nu,\alpha)}}{2^n - \mu_2^{(\nu,\alpha)}}\\&+ \frac{1}{2^n - (\alpha-1)} \cdot \left(\frac{1}{2^n - \mu_1^{(\nu,\alpha)}} \cdot \frac{1}{2^n - \mu_2^{(\nu,\alpha)}}\right) \cdot \frac{\mu_{2,3}^{(\nu,\alpha)} - (\alpha-1)}{2^n - \mu_1^{(\nu,\alpha)}}.\end{aligned}$$

Using the above probabilities, we have

$$\begin{aligned}&\frac{\Pr[(Z_{1,3}^{(\nu,\alpha)})_R = Z_{1,3}^{(\nu,\alpha)*} \mid (a)]}{\Pr[(Z_{1,3}^{(\nu,\alpha)})_I = Z_{1,3}^{(\nu,\alpha)*} \mid (a)]}\\&= \left(\frac{2^n - (\mu_1^{(\nu,\alpha)} + 1)}{2^n - (\alpha-1)} + \frac{\mu_1^{(\nu,\alpha)} - \mu_{2,3}^{(\nu,\alpha)}}{2^n - (\alpha-1)} + \frac{(\mu_{2,3}^{(\nu,\alpha)} - (\alpha-1))(2^n - (\mu_1^{(\nu,\alpha)} + 1))}{(2^n - (\alpha-1))(2^n - \mu_1^{(\nu,\alpha)})}\right)^{-1}\\&\ge 1.\end{aligned}$$

<u>$(b)\, c - m = 3 \wedge c = 4$.</u> In this case, $m = 1$ is satisfied, and thus $Z_1^{(\nu,\alpha)}$ is fixed but $Z_2^{(\nu,\alpha)}$ is not fixed before the α-th construction query to the ν-th user (the α-th loop of the ν-th user in Algorithm 1 in the ideal world).

- In the real world, we sample $Z_i^{(\nu,\alpha)}$ for $i \in [2,3]$ by E, and then $Z_2^{(\nu,\alpha)}$ (resp. $Z_3^{(\nu,\alpha)}$) is chosen uniformly at random from $2^n - \mu_2^{(\nu,\alpha)}$ (resp. $2^n - \mu_1^{(\nu,\alpha)}$) elements in $\{0,1\}^n$. Hence, we have

$$\Pr[(Z_{1,3}^{(\nu,\alpha)})_R = Z_{1,3}^{(\nu,\alpha)*} \mid (b)] = \frac{1}{2^n - \mu_1^{(\nu,\alpha)}} \cdot \frac{1}{2^n - \mu_2^{(\nu,\alpha)}}.$$

- In the ideal world, there are two cases that $Z_{1,3}^{(\nu,\alpha)} = Z_{1,3}^{(\nu,\alpha)*}$ is satisfied. Note that $Z_3^{(\nu,\alpha)} = C^{(\nu,\alpha)}$ is satisfied. We sample the value $Z_3^{(\nu,\alpha)}$ by Π_ν. Then, we have
$$\Pr[Z_3^{(\nu,\alpha)} = Z_3^{(\nu,\alpha)*}] = \frac{1}{2^n - (\alpha - 1)}.$$

1. The 1st case is that $Z_2^{(\nu,\alpha)}$ is defined by E. Then, we have
$$\Pr[Z_2^{(\nu,\alpha)} = Z_2^{(\nu,\alpha)*} \wedge (1)] = \frac{1}{2^n - \mu_2^{(\nu,\alpha)}}.$$

2. The 2nd case is that $Z_2^{(\nu,\alpha)}$ is defined by E^{-1}. Then, we have $\Pr[Z_2^{(\nu,\alpha)} = Z_2^{(\nu,\alpha)*}] = \frac{1}{2^n - \mu_1^{(\nu,\alpha)}}$. In this case, when $T_2^{(\nu,\alpha)}$ is defined by E in the forward sampling, $T_2^{(\nu,\alpha)} \neq Z_2^{(\nu,\alpha)*}$ and the condition in the step 1 in Algorithm 1 is satisfied, i.e., $T_2^{(\nu,\alpha)}$ collides with some input block of $(\mu_1^{(\nu,\alpha)} - (\alpha - 1))$ elements with the key $K_3^{(\nu)}$ $(= K_1^{(\nu)})$ in $\mathcal{L}^{(<\nu,\alpha)}$. Note that the $(\alpha - 1)$ elements are the 3rd-round input-output tuples defined by the construction queries to the ν-th user. The collision probability is $\frac{\mu_1^{(\nu,\alpha)} - (\alpha-1)}{2^n - \mu_2^{(\nu,\alpha)}}$. Hence, we have

$$\Pr[Z_2^{(\nu,\alpha)} = Z_2^{(\nu,\alpha)*} \wedge (2)] = \frac{1}{2^n - \mu_1^{(\nu,\alpha)}} \cdot \frac{\mu_1^{(\nu,\alpha)} - (\alpha - 1)}{2^n - \mu_2^{(\nu,\alpha)}}.$$

By the above probabilities, we have

$$\Pr[(Z_{1,3}^{(\nu,\alpha)})_I = Z_{1,3}^{(\nu,\alpha)*} \mid (b)]$$
$$= \frac{1}{2^n - (\alpha - 1)} \cdot \frac{1}{2^n - \mu_2^{(\nu,\alpha)}} + \frac{1}{2^n - (\alpha - 1)} \cdot \left(\frac{1}{2^n - \mu_1^{(\nu,\alpha)}} \cdot \frac{\mu_1^{(\nu,\alpha)} - (\alpha - 1)}{2^n - \mu_2^{(\nu,\alpha)}} \right).$$

Using the above probabilities, we have

$$\frac{\Pr[(Z_{1,3}^{(\nu,\alpha)})_R = Z_{1,3}^{(\nu,\alpha)*} \mid (b)]}{\Pr[(Z_{1,3}^{(\nu,\alpha)})_I = Z_{1,3}^{(\nu,\alpha)*} \mid (b)]} \geq \left(\frac{2^n - \mu_1^{(\nu,\alpha)}}{2^n - (\alpha - 1)} + \frac{\mu_1^{(\nu,\alpha)} - (\alpha - 1)}{2^n - (\alpha - 1)} \right)^{-1} = 1.$$

<u>(c) $c - m = 3 \wedge c = 3$.</u> In this case, $m = 0$ is satisfied, and thus $Z_1^{(\nu,\alpha)}$ is not fixed but $Z_2^{(\nu,\alpha)}$ is fixed before the α-th construction query to the ν-th user (the α-th loop of the ν-th user in Algorithm 1 in the ideal world). This evaluation is the same as the evaluation of the case (b), since this case and the case (b) are symmetric. Thus, we have

$$\frac{\Pr[(Z_{1,3}^{(\nu,\alpha)})_R = Z_{1,3}^{(\nu,\alpha)*} \mid (c)]}{\Pr[(Z_{1,3}^{(\nu,\alpha)})_I = Z_{1,3}^{(\nu,\alpha)*} \mid (c)]} \geq 1$$

(d) $c - m = 2$. We consider the three cases: (1): $m = 2 \wedge c = 4$; (2): $m = 1 \wedge c = 3$; and (3): $m = 0 \wedge c = 2$.

We first consider the case (1). In this case, before the α-th construction query to the ν-th user (the α-th loop of the ν-th user in Algorithm 1 in the ideal world), the values $Z_{1,2}^{(\nu,\alpha)}$ are fixed but $Z_3^{(\nu,\alpha)}$ is not fixed.

In the real world, we sample $Z_3^{(\nu,\alpha)}$ by E. Then, we have $\Pr[(Z_{1,3}^{(\nu,\alpha)})_R = Z_{1,3}^{(\nu,\alpha)*} \mid (d) \wedge (1)] = \frac{1}{2^n - \mu_1^{(\nu,\alpha)}}$. In the ideal world, we define $Z_3^{(\nu,\alpha)}$ by Π_ν. Then, we have $\Pr[(Z_{1,3}^{(\nu,\alpha)})_I = Z_{1,3}^{(\nu,\alpha)*} \mid (d) \wedge (1)] = \frac{1}{2^n - (\alpha - 1)}$. As $\alpha - 1 \leq \mu_1^{(\nu,\alpha)}$, we have

$$\frac{\Pr[(Z_{1,3}^{(\nu,\alpha)})_R = Z_{1,3}^{(\nu,\alpha)*} \mid (d) \wedge (1)]}{\Pr[(Z_{1,3}^{(\nu,\alpha)})_I = Z_{1,3}^{(\nu,\alpha)*} \mid (d) \wedge (1)]} \geq 1.$$

For other cases, these evaluations are the same as the case (1). We thus have

$$\frac{\Pr[(Z_{1,3}^{(\nu,\alpha)})_R = Z_{1,3}^{(\nu,\alpha)*} \mid (d) \wedge (i)]}{\Pr[(Z_{1,3}^{(\nu,\alpha)})_I = Z_{1,3}^{(\nu,\alpha)*} \mid (d) \wedge (i)]} \geq 1 \text{ for each } i \in [2, 3].$$

Hence, we have

$$\frac{\Pr[(Z_{1,3}^{(\nu,\alpha)})_R = Z_{1,3}^{(\nu,\alpha)*} \mid (d)]}{\Pr[(Z_{1,3}^{(\nu,\alpha)})_I = Z_{1,3}^{(\nu,\alpha)*} \mid (d)]} \geq 1.$$

Conclusion of the Evaluation. By the above evaluations, for any good transcript τ, we have

$$\frac{\Pr[\mathsf{T}_R = \tau]}{\Pr[\mathsf{T}_I = \tau]} \geq 1.$$

6 Limited Security Enhancement by FX with 2kTE

Naito et al. [19] showed that the mu-security of the 3kTE and 3-key TDES can be efficiently enhanced by further applying the FX-construction [16]. Then, the natural question is whether the same applies to 2kTE and 2-key TDES. In this section, we show that the security enhancement of the FX-construction is very limited with 2kTE and 2-key TDES by demonstrating the information-theoretic attack having the cost of $p = 2^{n+k}/q$.

6.1 Attacks on 2kTE-FX

Given a 2kTE scheme $E_{K_1} \circ E_{K_2} \circ E_{K_1}$, a 2kTE-FX scheme computes a ciphertext C of a plaintext P by using n-bit keys L and L' as $C = E_{K_1} \circ E_{K_2} \circ E_{K_1}(P \oplus L) \oplus L'$. The structure is depicted in Fig. 4.

The attack overview is as follows. L and L' can be recovered by making $2^n/X$ construction queries and by collecting X input and output pairs of 2k-TE generated under the right values of (K_1, K_2). The adversary first makes q

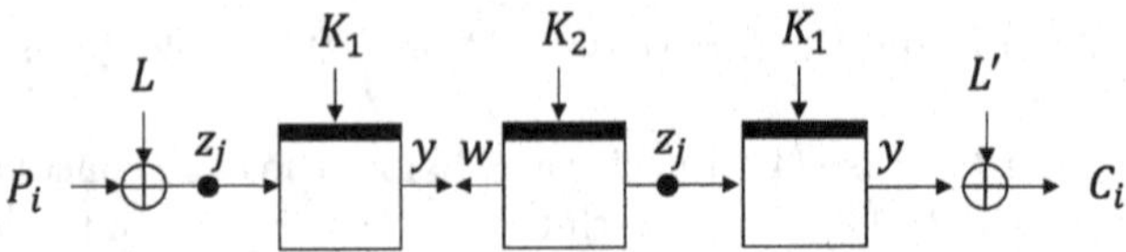

Fig. 4. 2kTE-FX Structure and Attack Configuration.

construction queries in the known-plaintext setting to obtain q distinct plaintext-ciphertext pairs. Then, the adversary collects $2^n/q$ input-output pairs of 2kTE for all (K_1, K_2) only by making $2^{n+k}/q$ primitive queries. The attack procedure is as follows, where its algorithmic description is given in Algorithm 2.

Online. An adversary accesses to q users. For each user i, $i = 1, \ldots, q$, the adversary makes 3 construction queries P_i, P'_i, and P''_i to get the ciphertexts C_i, C'_i, and C''_i. Then $(P_i, C_i, P'_i, C'_i, P''_i, C''_i)$ are stored in a table T_{on}.

Offline. The adversary chooses $2^n/q$ distinct n-bit state values denoted by z_j for $j = 1, \ldots, 2^n/q$. For each z_j, the following procedure is executed.

- The state value at the input of 2kTE, i.e. the value of $P \oplus L$ for the 2kTE-FX, is fixed to z_j. The state value between the second and the third block cipher invocations is also fixed to z_j.
- The adversary exhaustively guesses K_1 denoted by g_1 and compute $y = E_{g_1}(z_j)$. The generated 2^k pairs of (g_1, y) are stored in a table T_1.
- The adversary exhaustively guesses K_2 denoted by g_2 and compute $w = E^{-1}_{g_2}(z_j)$. The generated 2^k pairs of (g_2, w) are stored in a table T_2.
- The adversary finds a match of y in T_1 and w in T_2. The output of the third block cipher is $E_{g_1}(z_j)$, which is y. Hence, each matched pair suggests that (z_j, y) is a valid input and output pair of 2kTE under the guessed key values g_1 and g_2. The tuples of (z_j, y, g_1, g_2) for all the matched pairs are stored in a table T_{off}.
- For all the combinations of the entries in T_{on} associated with $(P_i, C_i, P'_i, C'_i, P''_i, C''_i)$ and T_{off} associated with (z_j, y, g_1, g_2), the adversary computes L and L' by $P_i \oplus z_j$ and $y \oplus C_i$, respectively. Then, the adversary checks whether $C'_i = E_{K_1} \circ E_{K_2} \circ E_{K_1}(P'_i \oplus L) \oplus L'$ and $C''_i = E_{K_1} \circ E_{K_2} \circ E_{K_1}(P''_i \oplus L) \oplus L'$ are satisfied. If both are satisfied, the corresponding g_1, g_2, L, L' are the keys of user i.

In this attack, the number of construction queries is $3q$. The primitive queries is 2^k for $y = E_{g_1}(z_j)$ and $w = E^{-1}_{g_2}(z_j)$ for all the $2^n/q$ choices of z_j. Hence, the number of offline queries, p, is $2^{n+k+1}/q$ and can be simplified to $2^{n+k}/q$ if the constant factor is ignored.

Recall that the security of 2kTE without FX was $\min\{2k, k+n\} - \log_2 q$ bits. In particular, in the chosen-plaintext setting with $k < n$ like DES, the attack by Biham works with $p = 2^{2k}/q$. Compared to this, the attack cost of 2kTE-FX is $p = 2^{n+k}/q$. With $k < n$, this is higher than $p = 2^{2k}/q$ by a factor of at most $n-k$ bits, i.e. 8 bits in DES. For the case of 3-keys, Naito et al. [19] showed that the security of 3-key TDES is $79 - (1/2) \cdot \log_2 u$ bits while the one of 3kTE-FX

Algorithm 2. Attack on 2kTE-FX.

Make 3 construction queries P_i, P'_i, and P''_i to get the ciphertexts C_i, C'_i, and C''_i for $i = 1, \ldots, u$ and store $(P_i, C_i, P'_i, C'_i, P''_i, C''_i)$ in a table T_{on}.
Choose $2^n/q$ distinct values and set them to z_j for $j = 1, \ldots, 2^n/q$.
for all $j = 1, \ldots, 2^n/q$ **do**
  for all $g_1 = 0, \ldots, 2^k - 1$, **do**
    Compute $y = E_{g_1}(z_j)$ to store (g_1, y) in a table T_1.
  end for
  for all $g_2 = 0, \ldots, 2^k - 1$, **do**
    Compute $w = E^{-1}_{g_2}(z_j)$ to store (g_2, w) in a table T_2.
  end for
  for all (g_1, y) in T_1 and (g_2, w) in T_2 satisfying $y = w$ **do**
    (z_j, y, g_1, g_2) are stored in a table T_{off}.
    for all $(P_i, C_i, P'_i, C'_i, P''_i, C''_i)$ in T_{on} and (z_j, y, g_1, g_2) in T_{off} **do**
      Compute $L \leftarrow P_i \oplus z_j$ and $L' \leftarrow y \oplus C_i$.
      if $C'_i = E_{g_1} \circ E_{g_2} \circ E_{g_1}(P'_i \oplus L) \oplus L'$ **then**
        if $C''_i = E_{g_1} \circ E_{g_2} \circ E_{g_1}(P''_i \oplus L) \oplus L'$ **then**
          Set $K_1 \leftarrow g_1$ and $K_2 \leftarrow g_2$.
          return K_1, K_2, L, L' as the key for user i.
        end if
      end if
    end for
  end for
end for

is $114 - (1/2) \cdot \log_2 q$ bits, thus the security is enhanced by a factor of 35 bits. Comparing to it, we conclude that using FX with 2kTE is not a good idea.

7 Conclusion

This paper gives a new multi-user (mu) bound of 2-key triple encryption (2kTE). With an n-bit block and k-bit key primitive block cipher, our new mu lower bound regarding the number of primitive queries is $2^{\min\{2k,k+n\}}/q$ with q construction queries, which matches the previous best attack and is tight. The bound ensures $(112 - \log_2 q)$-bit security with 2-key TDES. We also show that strengthening of TE with the FX construction, originally proposed for 3kTE, is inefficient with 2kTE by showing the attack which strengthens the security on by a factor of $n - k$ bits, i.e. 8 bits for TDES.

References

1. Armknecht, F., Fleischmann, E., Krause, M., Lee, J., Stam, M., Steinberger, J.: The preimage security of double-block-length compression functions. In: Lee, D.H., Wang, X. (eds.) ASIACRYPT 2011. LNCS, vol. 7073, pp. 233–251. Springer, Heidelberg (2011). https://doi.org/10.1007/978-3-642-25385-0_13

2. Barker, E., Mouha, N.: NIST special publication 800-67 rev. 2: recommendation for the triple data encryption algorithm (TDEA) block cipher (2017)
3. Barker, E., Roginsky, A.: NIST special publication 800-131A: transitioning the use of cryptographic algorithms and key lengths (2011)
4. Barker, E., Roginsky, A.: NIST special publication 800-131A revision 2: transitioning the use of cryptographic algorithms and key lengths (2019)
5. Bellare, M., Tackmann, B.: The multi-user security of authenticated encryption: AES-GCM in TLS 1.3. In: Robshaw, M., Katz, J. (eds.) CRYPTO 2016. LNCS, vol. 9814, pp. 247–276. Springer, Heidelberg (2016). https://doi.org/10.1007/978-3-662-53018-4_10
6. Biham, E.: How to decrypt or even substitute DES-encrypted messages in 2^{28} steps. Inf. Process. Lett. **84**(3), 117–124 (2002)
7. Chen, S., Lampe, R., Lee, J., Seurin, Y., Steinberger, J.: Minimizing the two-round even-Mansour cipher. In: Garay, J.A., Gennaro, R. (eds.) CRYPTO 2014. LNCS, vol. 8616, pp. 39–56. Springer, Heidelberg (2014). https://doi.org/10.1007/978-3-662-44371-2_3
8. Degabriele, J.P., Govinden, J., Günther, F., Paterson, K.G.: The security of ChaCha20-Poly1305 in the multi-user setting. In: CCS 2021, pp. 1981–2003 (2021)
9. Diffie, W., Hellman, M.E.: Special feature exhaustive cryptanalysis of the NBS data encryption standard. Computer **10**(6), 74–84 (1977)
10. EMVCo: EMV integrated circuit card specifications for payment systems, book2, security and key management version 4.3 (2011)
11. Gazi, P., Lee, J., Seurin, Y., Steinberger, J.P., Tessaro, S.: Relaxing full-codebook security: a refined analysis of key-length extension schemes. In: FSE 2015, vol. 9054, pp. 319–341 (2015)
12. Hoang, V.T., Tessaro, S.: Key-alternating ciphers and key-length extension: exact bounds and multi-user security. In: Robshaw, M., Katz, J. (eds.) CRYPTO 2016. LNCS, vol. 9814, pp. 3–32. Springer, Heidelberg (2016). https://doi.org/10.1007/978-3-662-53018-4_1
13. Hoang, V.T., Tessaro, S., Thiruvengadam, A.: The multi-user security of GCM, revisited: tight bounds for nonce randomization. In: CCS 2018, pp. 1429–1440 (2018)
14. ISO: ISO/TR 19038:2005 banking and related financial services—triple DEA—modes of operation—implementation guidelines (2005)
15. ISO: ISO/TR 14742:2010 financial services—recommendations on cryptographic algorithms and their use (2010)
16. Kilian, J., Rogaway, P.: How to protect DES against exhaustive key search (an analysis of DESX). J. Cryptol. **14**(1), 17–35 (2001)
17. Luykx, A., Mennink, B., Paterson, K.G.: Analyzing multi-key security degradation. In: Takagi, T., Peyrin, T. (eds.) ASIACRYPT 2017. LNCS, vol. 10625, pp. 575–605. Springer, Cham (2017). https://doi.org/10.1007/978-3-319-70697-9_20
18. Mitchell, C.J.: On the security of 2-key triple DES. IEEE Trans. Inf. Theory **62**(11), 6260–6267 (2016)
19. Naito, Y., Sasaki, Y., Sugawara, T., Yasuda, K.: The multi-user security of triple encryption, revisited: exact security, strengthening, and application to TDES. In: CCS 2022 (2022)
20. NIST: FIPS pub. 46-3: Data encryption standard (1999)
21. van Oorschot, P.C., Wiener, M.J.: A known-plaintext attack on two-key triple encryption. In: Damgård, I.B. (ed.) EUROCRYPT 1990. LNCS, vol. 473, pp. 318–325. Springer, Heidelberg (1991). https://doi.org/10.1007/3-540-46877-3_29

22. Patarin, J.: The "coefficients H" technique. In: Avanzi, R.M., Keliher, L., Sica, F. (eds.) SAC 2008. LNCS, vol. 5381, pp. 328–345. Springer, Heidelberg (2009). https://doi.org/10.1007/978-3-642-04159-4_21
23. Rescorla, E.: RFC 8446: the transport layer security (TLS) protocol version 1.3 (2018)
24. Rescorla, E., Tschofenig, H., Modadugu, N.: The datagram transport layer security (DTLS) protocol version 1.3 (2021)
25. Thomson, M., Turner, S.: Using TLS to secure QUIC. RFC **9001**, 1–52 (2021)
26. Ward, M.: How EMVCo is supporting card data encryption advancements for card personalisation (2021). https://www.emvco.com/emv_insights_post/how-emvco-is-supporting-card-data-encryption-advancements-for-card-personalisation. Accessed 15 Oct 2022

Improved Meet-in-the-Middle Attacks on Nine Rounds of the AES-192 Block Cipher

Jiqiang Lu[1,2,3(✉)] and Wenchang Zhou[1,3]

[1] School of Cyber Science and Technology, Beihang University, Beijing 100083, China
{lvjiqiang,wenchangzhou}@buaa.edu.cn
[2] State Key Laboratory of Cryptology, P. O. Box 5159, Beijing 100878, China
[3] HangZhou Innovation Institute, Beihang University, Hangzhou 310051, China

Abstract. In the single-key attack scenario, meet-in-the-middle (MitM) attack method has led to the best currently published cryptanalytic results on the AES block cipher, except biclique attack. Particularly, for AES with a 192-bit key (AES-192), Li et al. published 5-round MitM distinguishers and 9-round MitM attacks in 2014, by introducing the key-dependent sieve technique to reduce the number of unknown constants for a MitM distinguisher and using a so-called weak-key approach to reduce the memory complexity of an ordinary MitM attack, and their final main result is an attack on the first 9 rounds of AES-192 with a data complexity of 2^{121} chosen plaintexts, a memory complexity of 2^{181} bytes and a time complexity of $2^{187.7}$ encryptions. In this paper, we observe that Li et al. used a wrong direction for the rotation operation of the AES-192 key schedule, which causes all their distinguishers and attacks to be seriously flawed, but fortunately we exploit a correct 5-round distinguisher with different active input and output byte positions, so that the resulting 9-round AES-192 attacks with/without Li et al.'s weak-key approach have the same complexities as Li et al.'s (flawed) attacks. Further, we give a trick to exploit two complicated additional one-byte linear relations (between the round keys of precomputation phase and the round keys of online phase) to further reduce memory complexity, and finally we make an attack on the 9-round AES-192 with a data complexity of 2^{121} chosen plaintexts, a memory complexity of $2^{172.3}$ bytes and a time complexity of $2^{187.6}$ encryptions. Besides, we show that the 5-round MitM distinguisher can be extended to a 6-round MitM distinguisher, which can also attack the 9-round AES-192 with the same complexity. Our work corrects and improves Li et al.'s work, and the trick can potentially be used for MitM attacks on other block ciphers.

Keywords: Block cipher · AES · Meet-in-the-middle attack · Differential cryptanalysis

1 Introduction

The AES (Advanced Encryption Standard) [18] block cipher has a 128-bit block size and a user key of 128, 192 or 256 bits, with a total of 10 rounds for a

E. Oswald (Ed.): CT-RSA 2024, LNCS 14643, pp. 136–159, 2024.
https://doi.org/10.1007/978-3-031-58868-6_6

128-bit key, 12 rounds for a 192-bit key and 14 rounds for a 256-bit key. We are concerned with AES with a 192-bit key in this paper, which we denote by AES-192 below.

In the single-key attack scenario, many cryptanalytic results on AES have been published [2,5–8,10–12,15–17], and the best non-trivial results are due to meet-in-the-middle (MitM) [9] attack method. Specifically, the main MitM attack advances on AES-192 are as follows. In 2008, building on Gilbert and Minier's work [12], Demirci and Selçuk [5] presented a 4-round MitM distinguisher with 25 (or 24 if considering the difference between a pair) unknown byte parameters, and attacked the first 7 rounds of AES-192 with a time-memory tradeoff. In 2010, Dunkelman et al. [10] introduced the differential enumeration technique to reduce the possible values for the (unknown) byte parameters of Demirci and Selçuk's 4-round MitM distinguisher to be only 2^{127} by using a 4-round truncated differential [1,14] of AES, and attacked the first 8 rounds of AES-192. In 2013, Derbez et al. [8] used a rebound-like tabulation way to reduce the 24 byte parameters to 10 byte parameters for Dunkelman et al.'s 4-round MitM distinguisher, then attacked the first 8 rounds of AES-192 with a less data and memory complexity than Dunkelman et al.'s 8-round AES-192 attack, and they gave a 5-round MitM distinguisher with 26 byte parameters. In 2014, Li et al. [15] observed that some round key relations can be used to reduce the possible values for the byte parameters of a MitM distinguisher (which they called the key-dependent sieve technique), gave a 5-round MitM distinguisher with only 2^{192} possible values and attacked the first 9 rounds of AES-192, and finally they used one or more relations between the round keys of the precomputational phase and the round keys of the online key recovery phase to divide the whole key space into a number of smaller subspaces, so that the attack was transformed into a series of so-called weak-key attacks under the subspaces with a reduced memory complexity; besides, Li et al. also gave similar attacks on Rounds 3 to 11 of AES-192 with a less complexity. Li et al.'s 9-round MitM attacks are the best currently published cryptanalytic results on AES-192 in the single-key attack scenario, except biclique attack [2] that is generally treated as a kind of exhaustive key search.[1]

In this paper, we observe that Li et al. used a wrong direction for the rotation operation of the AES key schedule in all their 9-round AES-192 attacks [15], which causes the actual numbers of byte parameters of their 5-round distinguishers to be more than they claimed and thus causes their attacks to either have a larger complexity or be no longer valid. Then, we follow Li et al.'s key-dependent sieve idea to find a correct 5-round MitM distinguisher on AES-192 with 2^{192} possible values by using different active input and output bytes, so that the resulting attacks on the first 9 rounds of AES-192 with/without their weak-key approach have the same complexities as their (flawed) attacks. Further, we find

[1] We note that in [19,20] Wang and Zhu gave a 5-round MitM distinguisher on AES-192 with 22 byte parameters and presented a 9-round AES-192 attack with a different complexity compared with Li et al.'s 9-round AES-192 attacks. However, we point out their attack is seriously flawed and invalid in the full version of this paper.

Table 1. Main cryptanalytic results on AES-192 in the single-key attack scenario

Attack Method	Rounds	Data (CP)	Memory (Bytes)	Time (Enc.)	Source
Square	8	$2^{127.997}$	2^{132}	2^{188}	[11]
MitM	8	2^{113}	2^{133}	2^{172}	[10]
	8	2^{113}	2^{86}	2^{172}	[6]
	8	2^{107}	2^{100}	2^{172}	[6]
	$9^{\dagger}$	2^{121}	2^{189}	$2^{187.7}$	[15]
	$9^{\dagger}$	2^{121}	2^{181}	$2^{187.7}$	[15]
	9	2^{121}	2^{189}	$2^{187.7}$	Section 4.2
	9	2^{121}	2^{181}	$2^{187.7}$	Section 4.3
	9	2^{121}	$2^{172.3}$	$2^{187.6}$	Section 5.1
Biclique	full	2^{80}	2^{8}	$2^{189.4}$	[2]

†: The attack is seriously flawed, see Sect. 3 of this paper.

a trick to exploit two complicated additional one-byte linear relations between the round keys of precomputation phase and the round keys of online phase to further reduce memory complexity without affecting data and time complexity, which builds a precomputation table that links ciphertext, the last round's SubBytes output and a few round key bytes, and finally we make a MitM attack on the first 9 rounds of AES-192 with a data complexity of 2^{121} chosen plaintexts, a memory complexity of $2^{172.3}$ bytes and a time complexity of $2^{187.6}$ 9-round AES-192 encryptions, where the memory complexity is due to the precomputation table of the trick, instead of the sequences of the MitM distinguisher under a key subspace. At last, we show that the 5-round distinguisher can be extended to a 6-round distinguisher by using a simple linear relation as Derbez and Fouque did in [6], and it can also be used to attack the 9-round AES-192 with the same complexity. We have also checked similar MitM attacks on different series of intermediate 9 rounds, including Rounds 3–11, but did not get a better cryptanalytic result. Table 1 summarises previous and our main cryptanalytic results on AES-192 in the single-key attack scenario, where CP represents the number of required chosen plaintexts.

The remainder of the paper is organised as follows. We describe the notation, the AES block cipher and a few definitions and properties about AES in the next section, and present our results in Sects. 3 to 5. Section 6 concludes this paper.

2 Preliminaries

In this section, we give the notation and briefly introduce the AES block cipher and several definitions and properties about AES.

2.1 Notation

In all descriptions we assume that a number without a prefix is in decimal notation, and a number with prefix $0x$ is in hexadecimal notation. We use the following notation throughout this paper.

$||$ bit string concatenation
$\oplus$ bitwise logical exclusive XOR
$\otimes$ polynomial multiplication modulo $x^8 + x^4 + x^3 + x + 1$ in GF(2^8)
$\lll$ left rotation of a bit string
$\circ$ functional composition

2.2 The AES Block Cipher

AES [3] has a 128-bit block size, a user key of 128, 192 or 256 bits, and a total number of 10, 12 or 14 rounds, respectively. Its plaintext, ciphertext and intermediate states are represented each as a 4×4 byte array, and the 16 bytes of a 4×4 byte array are numbered from top to bottom from left to right, starting with 0. AES is made up of the following four elementary operations:

- SubBytes (SB): SubBytes operation is a nonlinear transformation, which applies the same 8×8-bit bijective S-box (denoted below by $\mathbf{S}$) 16 times in parallel to a 4×4 byte array.
- ShiftRows (SR): ShiftRows operation is a linear transformation, which cyclically shifts the i-th row of a 4×4 byte array to the left by i bytes, $(0 \leq i \leq 3)$.
- MixColumns (MC): Mixlolumns operation is a linear transformation, which pre-multiplies a 4×4 byte array by the following fixed 4×4 byte matrix $\mathbf{M}$. The matrix $\mathbf{M}$ and its inverse $\mathbf{M}^{-1}$ are as follows.

$$\mathbf{M} = \begin{pmatrix} 0x02 & 0x03 & 0x01 & 0x01 \\ 0x01 & 0x02 & 0x03 & 0x01 \\ 0x01 & 0x01 & 0x02 & 0x03 \\ 0x03 & 0x01 & 0x01 & 0x02 \end{pmatrix}, \quad \mathbf{M}^{-1} = \begin{pmatrix} 0x0e & 0x0b & 0x0d & 0x09 \\ 0x09 & 0x0e & 0x0b & 0x0d \\ 0x0d & 0x09 & 0x0e & 0x0b \\ 0x0b & 0x0d & 0x09 & 0x0e \end{pmatrix}.$$

- AddRoundKey (ARK): AddRoundKey operation is a linear transformation, which XORs a 4×4 byte array with a 16-byte subkey.

AES-192 uses a total of thirteen 128-bit round keys K_i, $(0 \leq i \leq 12)$, all derived from a 192-bit user key by the following key schedule, where $Rcon[\cdot]$ are 32-bit public constants with only the first byte being nonzero each.

- Represent the 192-bit user key as six 32-bit words $(W_0, W_1, \cdots, W_5)$;
- For $j = 6, 7, \cdots, 51$, do:
  - If $j \bmod 6 = 0$, then $W[j] = W[j-6] \oplus \mathrm{SB}(W[j-1] \lll 8) \oplus Rcon[\frac{j}{6}]$;
  - Else $W[j] = W[j-6] \oplus W[j-1]$.
- $K_i = (W[4i], W[4i+1], W[4i+2], W[4i+3])$.

The encryption procedure of AES-192 is as follows, where P is a 128-bit plaintext block, and $x_l, y_l, z_l, w_l, x_{13}$ are 16-byte variables ($1 \leq l \leq 12$).

1. $x_1 = \text{ARK}(P, K_0)$.
2. For $i = 1$ to 11:
   $y_i = \text{SB}(x_i)$,
   $z_i = \text{SR}(y_i)$,
   $w_i = \text{MC}(z_i)$,
   $x_{i+1} = \text{ARK}(w_i, K_i)$.
3. $y_{12} = \text{SB}(x_{12}), z_{12} = \text{SR}(y_{12})$.
4. Ciphertext $= x_{13} = \text{ARK}(z_{12}, K_{12})$.

Besides, an equivalent encryption procedure can be derived by reversing the order of the MC and ARK operations of a round, and we define $\widehat{K}_i = \text{MC}^{-1}(K_i)$ and $\widehat{w}_i = z_i \oplus \widehat{K}_i$. Note that SB, SR, MC and ARK are sometimes abused to represent a column of their above formal representations.

2.3 Definitions and Properties About AES

We use the following two definitions on Super-Sbox and δ-Set and two properties about the (Super-)Sbox and MixColumns operations of AES in this paper, that are extensively used in previous cryptanalysis of AES, e.g. [3,4,8,10,15–17].

Definition 1 (Super-Sbox [4]). *An AES super-sbox maps a 4-byte input $a = [a_0, a_1, a_2, a_3]$ into a 4-byte output $b = [b_0, b_1, b_2, b_3]$ under a 4-byte key value K, which is defined as*

$$b = SB \circ ARK \circ MC \circ SB(a) = SB(MC(SB(a)) \oplus K),$$

where SB, MC and ARK are abused to represent a column of their formal representations given in Sect. 2.

Definition 2 (δ-Set [3,10]). *A δ-set is a set of 256 AES states with one byte traversing all possible values (the active byte) and the other 15 bytes being fixed to be constant.*

Property 1 ((Super-)Sbox [10,13,17]). *Given a randomly chosen pair of input and output differences (Δ_i, Δ_o), the equation $\mathbf{S}(x) \oplus \mathbf{S}(x \oplus \Delta_i) = \Delta_o$ has one solution on input x on average. It holds similarly for an AES super-sbox.*

Property 2 (MixColumns [3,4]). *If the values (or differences) in any four out of the eight input/output bytes of a column of the MixColumns operation are known, the values (or differences) in the remaining four bytes can be determined uniquely.*

We have the following key relations on AES-192 from its key schedule.

Property 3. *For AES-192, the following key relations hold:*

(1) $K_0[7] = K_4[11] \oplus K_4[15] \oplus \mathbf{S}(K_4[0] \oplus K_4[4])$;
(2) $K_1[11] = K_4[11] \oplus \mathbf{S}(K_4[4]) \oplus \mathbf{S}(K_4[0] \oplus K_4[4])$;
(3) $K_2[12, 13, 14, 15] = K_4[0, 1, 2, 3] \oplus K_4[4, 5, 6, 7]$;
(4) $\widehat{K}_3[3] = 0x0b \otimes (K_4[8] \oplus \mathbf{S}(K_4[5]) \oplus Rcon[3][0]) \oplus 0x0d \otimes (K_4[9] \oplus \mathbf{S}(K_4[6])) \oplus 0x09 \otimes (K_4[10] \oplus \mathbf{S}(K_4[7])) \oplus 0x0e \otimes (K_4[11] \oplus \mathbf{S}(K_4[4]))$;
(5) $\widehat{K}_3[6] = 0x0d \otimes (K_4[12] \oplus K_4[8]) \oplus 0x09 \otimes (K_4[13] \oplus K_4[9]) \oplus 0x0e \otimes (K_4[14] \oplus K_4[10]) \oplus 0x0b \otimes (K_4[15] \oplus K_4[11])$;
(6) $K_6[1] = K_4[9] \oplus \mathbf{S}(K_5[10] \oplus K_4[6])$;
(7) $K_7[12, 13, 14, 15] = K_9[0, 1, 2, 3] \oplus K_9[4, 5, 6, 7]$;
(8) $\widehat{K}_8[3] = 0x0b \otimes (K_9[4] \oplus K_9[8]) \oplus 0x0d \otimes (K_9[5] \oplus K_9[9]) \oplus 0x09 \otimes (K_9[6] \oplus K_9[10]) \oplus 0x0e \otimes (K_9[7] \oplus K_9[11])$;
(9) $\widehat{K}_8[6] = 0x0d \otimes (K_9[8] \oplus K_9[12]) \oplus 0x09 \otimes (K_9[9] \oplus K_9[13]) \oplus 0x0e \otimes (K_9[10] \oplus K_9[14]) \oplus 0x0b \otimes (K_9[11] \oplus K_9[15])$;
(10) $\widehat{K}_8[9] = 0x09 \otimes (K_4[0] \oplus K_9[0] \oplus K_9[12]) \oplus 0x0e \otimes (K_4[1] \oplus K_9[1] \oplus K_9[13]) \oplus 0x0b \otimes (K_4[2] \oplus K_9[2] \oplus K_9[14]) \oplus 0x0d \otimes (K_4[3] \oplus K_9[3] \oplus K_9[15])$;
(11) $\widehat{K}_8[12] = 0x0e \otimes (K_4[0] \oplus K_4[4] \oplus K_9[0] \oplus K_9[4]) \oplus 0x0b \otimes (K_4[1] \oplus K_4[5] \oplus K_9[1] \oplus K_9[5]) \oplus 0x0d \otimes (K_4[2] \oplus K_4[6] \oplus K_9[2] \oplus K_9[6]) \oplus 0x09 \otimes (K_4[3] \oplus K_4[7] \oplus K_9[3] \oplus K_9[7])$;
(12) $K_0[13] = K_9[5] \oplus K_9[13] \oplus \mathbf{S}(K_4[2] \oplus K_4[6] \oplus K_9[2] \oplus K_9[6] \oplus K_9[10] \oplus K_9[14])$;
(13) $K_5[5] = K_9[1] \oplus K_9[5] \oplus K_9[9] \oplus K_9[13]$.

Proof. By the key schedule of AES-192, we have

$$\begin{aligned}
K_0[7] &= K_1[15] \oplus K_1[11] = K_3[7] \oplus \mathbf{S}(K_2[12]) \\
&= K_4[15] \oplus K_4[11] \oplus \mathbf{S}(K_4[0] \oplus K_4[4]); \\
K_1[11] &= K_3[3] \oplus \mathbf{S}(K_2[12]) = K_4[11] \oplus \mathbf{S}(K_4[4]) \oplus \mathbf{S}(K_4[0] \oplus K_4[4]); \\
K_4[4,5,6,7] &= K_4[0,1,2,3] \oplus K_2[12,13,14,15]; \\
K_3[0,1,2,3] &= K_4[8,9,10,11] \oplus \mathbf{S}(K_4[5,6,7,4]) \oplus Rcon[3]; \\
K_3[4,5,6,7] &= K_4[8,9,10,11] \oplus K_4[12,13,14,15]; \\
K_6[1] &= K_4[9] \oplus \mathbf{S}(K_5[14]) = K_4[9] \oplus \mathbf{S}(K_4[6] \oplus K_5[10]); \\
K_9[4,5,6,7] &= K_9[0,1,2,3] \oplus K_7[12,13,14,15]; \\
K_8[0,1,2,3] &= K_9[8,9,10,11] \oplus K_9[4,5,6,7]; \\
K_8[4,5,6,7] &= K_9[12,13,14,15] \oplus K_9[8,9,10,11]; \\
K_8[8,9,10,11] &= K_8[4,5,6,7] \oplus K_7[0,1,2,3] \\
&= K_8[4,5,6,7] \oplus K_5[8,9,10,11] \oplus K_6[12,13,14,15] \\
&= K_8[4,5,6,7] \oplus (K_4[0,1,2,3] \oplus K_5[4,5,6,7]) \oplus \\
&\quad (K_5[4,5,6,7] \oplus K_6[8,9,10,11]) \\
&= K_8[4,5,6,7] \oplus K_4[0,1,2,3] \oplus K_7[12,13,14,15] \oplus K_8[0,1,2,3] \\
&= K_8[4,5,6,7] \oplus K_4[0,1,2,3] \oplus (K_9[0,1,2,3] \oplus K_9[4,5,6,7]) \oplus \\
&\quad (K_9[4,5,6,7] \oplus K_9[8,9,10,11]) \\
&= K_9[12,13,14,15] \oplus K_4[0,1,2,3] \oplus K_9[0,1,2,3];
\end{aligned}$$

$$\begin{aligned}
K_8[12,13,14,15] &= K_8[8,9,10,11] \oplus K_7[4,5,6,7] \\
&= (K_9[12,13,14,15] \oplus K_4[0,1,2,3] \oplus K_9[0,1,2,3]) \oplus \\
&\quad K_7[4,5,6,7] \\
&= (K_9[12,13,14,15] \oplus K_4[0,1,2,3] \oplus K_9[0,1,2,3]) \oplus \\
&\quad (K_7[0,1,2,3] \oplus K_5[12,13,14,15]) \\
&= (K_9[12,13,14,15] \oplus K_4[0,1,2,3] \oplus K_9[0,1,2,3]) \oplus \\
&\quad (K_6[12,13,14,15] \oplus K_5[8,9,10,11] \oplus K_5[12,13,14,15]) \\
&= (K_9[12,13,14,15] \oplus K_4[0,1,2,3] \oplus K_9[0,1,2,3]) \oplus \\
&\quad (K_6[12,13,14,15] \oplus K_4[4,5,6,7]) \\
&= (K_9[12,13,14,15] \oplus K_4[0,1,2,3] \oplus K_9[0,1,2,3]) \oplus \\
&\quad (K_8[0,1,2,3] \oplus K_8[4,5,6,7] \oplus K_4[4,5,6,7]) \\
&= (K_9[12,13,14,15] \oplus K_4[0,1,2,3] \oplus K_9[0,1,2,3]) \oplus \\
&\quad (K_9[4,5,6,7] \oplus K_9[12,13,14,15] \oplus K_4[4,5,6,7]) \\
&= K_4[0,1,2,3] \oplus K_9[0,1,2,3] \oplus K_9[4,5,6,7] \oplus K_4[4,5,6,7]; \\
K_0[13] &= K_2[5] \oplus K_2[1] = (K_3[9] \oplus K_3[13]) \oplus (K_3[5] \oplus K_3[9]) \\
&= (K_5[5] \oplus K_5[1]) \oplus (K_4[13] \oplus K_4[9]) \\
&= (K_6[13] \oplus K_6[9] \oplus K_6[9] \oplus K_6[5]) \oplus (K_4[13] \oplus K_4[9]) \\
&= (K_8[1] \oplus K_8[5]) \oplus (K_6[1] \oplus K_4[13]) \oplus (K_4[13] \oplus K_4[9]) \\
&= (K_9[5] \oplus K_9[13]) \oplus \mathbf{S}(K_5[14]) \\
&= K_9[5] \oplus K_9[13] \oplus \mathbf{S}(K_4[6] \oplus K_5[10]) \\
&= K_9[5] \oplus K_9[13] \oplus \mathbf{S}(K_4[6] \oplus K_5[6] \oplus K_4[2]) \\
&= K_9[5] \oplus K_9[13] \oplus \mathbf{S}(K_4[6] \oplus (K_6[14] \oplus K_6[10]) \oplus K_4[2]) \\
&= K_9[5] \oplus K_9[13] \oplus \mathbf{S}(K_4[6] \oplus (K_8[6] \oplus K_7[14]) \oplus K_4[2]) \\
&= K_9[5] \oplus K_9[13] \oplus \mathbf{S}(K_4[2] \oplus K_4[6] \oplus K_9[2] \oplus K_9[6] \oplus \\
&\quad K_9[10] \oplus K_9[14]); \\
K_5[5] &= K_6[9] \oplus K_6[13] = K_7[13] \oplus K_8[5] = K_9[1] \oplus K_9[5] \oplus K_9[9] \oplus \\
&\quad K_9[13].
\end{aligned}$$

As a result, Property 3 follows from these equations, where Properties 3-(4), 3-(5), 3-(8), 3-(9), 3-(10) and 3-(11) are obtained by applying MC^{-1} to the corresponding equations, respectively.

3 Flaws in Li et al.'s MitM Attacks on 9-Round AES-192

In this section, we describe flaws in Li et al.'s MitM attacks on 9-round AES-192, and briefly discuss the correct complexities based on corrected byte parameters for their 5-round MitM distinguishers under the correct AES-192 key schedule. Note that when describing Li et al.'s work below, we change their notation to ours, particularly the numbers of rounds start with 1, and the round keys start with K_0.

Li et al. [15] first gave a 5-round MitM distinguisher with 26 (secret) byte parameters (taking 2^{192} possible values due to two key byte conditions) from (the output of the MixColumns operation of) Round 1 to (the output of the AddRoundKey operation of) Round 6 and attacked Rounds 1–9 (see Fig. 1), then they gave a 5-round distinguisher on Rounds 4–9 with 25 byte parameters (taking 2^{184} possible values) and attacked Rounds 3–11 with a reduced attack complexity, and finally they improved these attacks by transforming them into a series of so-called weak-key attacks. Unfortunately, we observe that several round key relations in Li et al.'s attacks are not correct, and as a consequence their 5-round distinguishers should involve one more byte parameter and thus the resulting attacks should have a larger complexity. As described in [18] or Sect. 2.2, the keyword $W[j]$ for $j \bmod 6 = 0$ is generated as $W[j] = W[j-6] \oplus \text{SB}(W[j-1] \lll 8) \oplus Rcon[\frac{j}{6}]$, where the $\lll 8$ operation (i.e. the **RotWord**() function in [18]) takes a (4-byte) word $[a_0, a_1, a_2, a_3]$ as input and returns the word $[a_1, a_2, a_3, a_0]$. Note that the direction of the left rotation is from a larger subscript to a smaller subscript. Taking this into Li et al.'s attacks, we observe that Li et al. mistakenly used an inverse direction, more specifically:

- Li et al. thought $K_6[6] = K_6[2] \oplus K_4[14] = K_4[10] \oplus \mathbf{S}(K_5[13]) \oplus K_4[14]$ in their attacks on Rounds 1–9 without using weak-key approach (see partially their Fig. 4 [15]), and since K_4 and $K_5[13]$ appeared earlier (either guessed or deduced), $K_6[6]$ could be deduced and there was no need to guess it. However, by [18] and our above explanations, the fact should be that $K_6[6] = K_6[2] \oplus K_4[14] = K_4[10] \oplus \mathbf{S}(K_5[15]) \oplus K_4[14]$, but $K_5[15]$ does not appear earlier (that is unknown), so $K_6[6]$ cannot be deduced from those known key bytes and should be additionally guessed in order to compute $x_7[6]$, which means that this 5-round distinguisher should involve 27 byte parameters taking 2^{200} possible values, instead of 26 byte parameters with 2^{192} possible values as they proved.
- A similar flaw exists in Li et al.'s attacks on Rounds 3–11 without using weak-key approach. Li et al. claimed that when moving the 5-round distinguisher from Rounds 1–6 to Rounds 4–9, the number of involved byte parameters could be reduced from 26 to 25, taking 2^{184} possible values, since they thought $K_6[1] = K_7[9] \oplus \mathbf{S}(K_7[4]) \oplus Rcon[4][1]$ and $K_7[4]$ could be deduced by the already known $K_6[1]$ and $K_7[9]$ (see their Fig. 6 and the third equation on page 15 in their paper [15]). However, by [18] and our above explanations, the fact is that $K_6[1] = K_7[9] \oplus \mathbf{S}(K_7[6]) \oplus Rcon[4][1]$. Thus, the required $K_7[4]$ cannot be deduced, and this is contrary to what Li et al. claimed on page 14 of their paper. So this 5-round distinguisher should involve 26 byte parameters taking 2^{192} possible values.
- A few similar flaws exist in Li et al.'s attacks on Rounds 1–9 and Rounds 3–11 under weak-key approach. First, these attacks are the counterparts of the above-mentioned attacks, so the above-mentioned flaws also exist in these weak-key cases. Besides, there are other similar flaws, specifically,

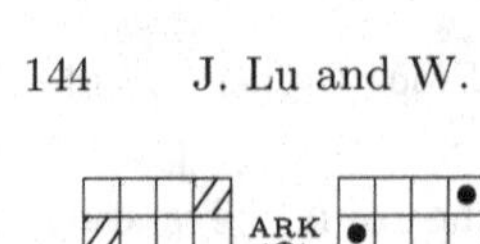

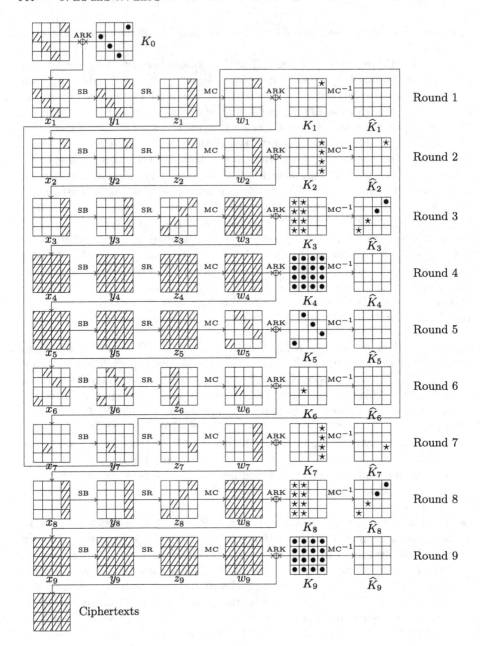

Fig. 1. Li et al.'s 5-round distinguisher and 9-round attack on AES-192

for the attacks on Rounds 1–9, Li et al. used a one-byte key relation $K_0[6] = \mathbf{S}(K_4[1] \oplus K_4[5]) \oplus K_4[10] \oplus K_4[14] \oplus Rcon[2][2]$ to split the space of K_4 into 2^8 subspaces (so as to conduct a series of so-called weak-key attacks under a smaller memory complexity). However, this key relation is not correct, and it should be $K_0[6] = \mathbf{S}(K_4[3] \oplus K_4[7]) \oplus K_4[10] \oplus K_4[14] \oplus Rcon[2][2]$ by [18] or our above explanations. For the attacks on Rounds 3–11, Li et al. used two one-byte key relations $K_2[6] = K_6[2] \oplus K_6[6] \oplus K_6[14]$ and $K_2[11] = K_6[7] \oplus K_6[11] \oplus K_7[3]$ to split the space of K_4 into 2^{16} subspaces. However, the two key relations are not correct, either, and they should be $K_2[6] = K_6[2] \oplus K_6[6] \oplus K_6[14] \oplus K_6[10]$ and $K_2[11] = K_6[7] \oplus K_6[11] \oplus K_7[3] \oplus K_6[15]$, respectively.

As a consequence, we have checked the resulting attack complexities based on the corrected parameters for Li et al.'s 5-round distinguishers, as follows:

- Their straightforward attack on Rounds 1–9 without using weak-key approach should have a memory complexity of $2^{193} \times 2^8 \times 16 = 2^{205}$ bytes and a time complexity of $2^{194.8} \times 2^8 = 2^{202.8}$ 9-round AES encryptions in the precomputation phase and have a time complexity of $2^{178.4}$ 9-round AES encryptions in the online phase, under 2^{113} chosen plaintexts. Now, it is infeasible to reduce the overall time complexity below 2^{192} by a data-memory-time tradeoff that precomputes a fraction 2^8 of possible sequences and uses 2^8 times of chosen plaintexts as Li et al. did. The best data-memory-time tradeoff, that precomputes a fraction $2^{-12.2}$ of possible sequences and uses $2^{12.2} \times 2^{113} = 2^{125.2}$ chosen plaintexts, has a memory complexity of $2^{205-12.2} = 2^{192.8}$ bytes and a total time complexity of $2^{202.8-12.2} + 2^{178.4+12.2} = 2^{191.6}$ 9-round AES encryptions, but its success probability is about $1 - \binom{2^{156.2}}{0}(2^{-144} \times 2^{-12.2})^0(1 - 2^{-144} \times 2^{-12.2})^{2^{156.2}} = 1 - (1 - 2^{-156.2})^{2^{156.2}} \approx 63\%$. This is worse than exhaustive key search with $2^{191.6}$ encryptions, which has a success probability 75%. Hence, this way is not feasible.
- Their straightforward attack on Rounds 3–11 without using weak-key approach should have a memory complexity of $2^{185} \times 2^8 \times 16 = 2^{197}$ bytes and a time complexity of $2^{186.8} \times 2^8 = 2^{194.8}$ 9-round AES encryptions in the precomputation phase and have a time complexity of $2^{178.4}$ 9-round AES encryptions in the online phase, under 2^{113} chosen plaintexts. A data-memory-time tradeoff that precomputes a fraction 2^{-8} of possible sequences and uses $2^8 \times 2^{113} = 2^{121}$ chosen plaintexts has a memory complexity of $2^{197-8} = 2^{189}$ bytes and a total time complexity of $2^{194.8-8} + 2^{178.4+8} \approx 2^{187.6}$ 9-round AES encryptions.
- Their straightforward attack on Rounds 1–9 under weak-key approach should have a memory complexity of $2^{205-8} = 2^{197}$ bytes and a time complexity of $2^8 \times 2^{194.8} = 2^{202.8}$ 9-round AES encryptions in the precomputation phase, and have a time complexity of $2^8 \times 2^{170.4} = 2^{178.4}$ 9-round AES encryptions in the online phase, under 2^{113} chosen plaintexts. As discussed above, this way is not feasible and its trade-offs are not better than exhaustive key search, either.
- Their straightforward attack on Rounds 3–11 under weak-key approach should have a memory complexity of $2^{120} \times 2^{40} \times 2^{16} \times 1 \times 32 = 2^{181}$ bytes and a time complexity of $2^{16} \times (2^{120} \times 2^{64} \times \frac{2}{9} + 2^{120} \times 2^{40} \times 2^{16} \times 1 \times 32 \times \frac{2}{9}) = 2^{198}$

9-round AES encryptions in the precomputation phase, and have a time complexity of $2^{178.4}$ 9-round AES encryptions in the online phase, under 2^{113} chosen plaintexts. A data-memory-time tradeoff that precomputes a fraction 2^{-8} of possible sequences and uses $2^8 \times 2^{113} = 2^{121}$ chosen plaintexts has a memory complexity of $2^{181-8} = 2^{173}$ bytes and a total time complexity of $2^{198-8} + 2^{178.4+8} \approx 2^{190.1}$ 9-round AES encryptions. Besides, a data-memory-time tradeoff that precomputes a fraction $2^{-9.8}$ of possible sequences and uses $2^{9.8} \times 2^{113} = 2^{122.8}$ chosen plaintexts has a memory complexity of $2^{181-9.8} = 2^{171.2}$ bytes and a total time complexity of $2^{198-9.8} + 2^{178.4+9.8} \approx 2^{189.2}$ 9-round AES encryptions.

Of course, these time complexities may be reduced by half with a slightly more memory complexity, as Li et al. did in [15]. Anyway, in the next section, we give better cryptanalytic results in another correction direction, by applying Li et al.'s key-dependent sieve technique and weak-key approach to obtain correct 5-round AES-192 distinguisher with different active input and output byte positions and 9-round AES-192 attacks.

4 Correcting Li et al.'s 9-Round AES-192 Attacks Under Their Ideas

In this section, we show that a 5-round MitM distinguisher and 9-round MitM attacks on AES-192 (with/without weak-key approach) that have the same complexity numbers as Li et al. claimed [15] can be obtained under their ideas (i.e., key-dependent sieve technique and weak-key approach), by changing the positions of the active input and output bytes of Li et al.'s 5-round distinguisher. In the other words, these attacks correct Li et al.'s attacks by following their ideas, and thus they can be seen as correct counterparts of Li et al.'s attacks.

4.1 Corrected 5-Round MitM Distinguisher on AES-192

We follow Li et al.'s idea to find the following 5-round AES-192 distinguisher on Rounds 1–6 with 26 byte parameters taking 2^{192} values, where the input active byte is $w_1[11]$ and the output active byte is $x_7[1]$, which avoids guessing a key byte by the key relations $K_6[1] = K_4[9] \oplus \mathbf{S}(K_5[14])$ and $K_5[14] = K_5[10] \oplus K_4[6]$.

Proposition 1 (A 5-Round MitM Distinguisher on AES-192). *Encrypt the first 32 values $\{w_1^0, w_1^1, \cdots, w_1^{31}\}$ of a δ-set with byte (11) being active, through the 5-round AES-192 from the ARK operation of Round 1 to the SB operation of Round 7. In case that a pair from the δ-set conforms to the 5-round truncated differential characteristic depicted in Fig. 2, the 256-bit ordered sequence $(y_7^0[1], y_7^1[1], \cdots, y_7^{31}[1])$ takes at most 2^{192} values (out of 2^{256} values theoretically).*

Proof. Consider a general pair (w_1, w_1^*) from the δ-set, and denote $w_1 \oplus w_1^*$ by Δw_1. First, we show that the sequence $(y_7^0[1], y_7^1[1], \cdots, y_7^{31}[1])$ is decided by the 43 bytes $(w_1[11] \| x_2[11] \| x_3[12,13,14,15] \| x_4 \| K_4 \| K_5[0,5,10,15] \| K_6[1])$. Since $\Delta x_2[11] = \Delta w_1[11] = w_1[11] \oplus w_1^*[11]$, we can use $(x_2[11], \Delta x_2[11])$ to compute $\Delta y_2^*[11] = \mathbf{S}(x_2[11]) \oplus \mathbf{S}(x_2[11] \oplus \Delta x_2[11])$, and then obtain $\Delta x_3[12,13,14,15]$. Similarly, we use $(x_3[12,13,14,15], \Delta x_3[12,13,14,15])$ to compute $\Delta y_3^*[12,13,14,15] = \mathrm{SB}(x_3[12,13,14,15]) \oplus \mathrm{SB}(x_3[12,13,14,15] \oplus \Delta x_3[12,13,14,15])$, and we can obtain Δx_4. Then, we use x_4 to obtain $y_4^* = \mathrm{SB}(x_4 \oplus \Delta x_4)$ and $\Delta y_4 = y_4^* \oplus \mathrm{SB}(x_4)$. Since K_4 is known, we can obtain $w_5^* = \mathrm{MC} \circ \mathrm{SR} \circ \mathrm{SB} \circ \mathrm{ARK} \circ \mathrm{MC} \circ \mathrm{SR}(y_4^*)$ and $\Delta w_5 = w_5^* \oplus \mathrm{MC} \circ \mathrm{SR} \circ \mathrm{SB} \circ \mathrm{ARK} \circ \mathrm{MC} \circ \mathrm{SR}(y_4^* \oplus \Delta y_4)$, and then we can obtain $\Delta x_6[0,5,10,15] = \Delta w_5[0,5,10,15]$. Since $K_5[0,5,10,15]$ is known, we can obtain $x_6^*[0,5,10,15] = w_5^*[0,5,10,15] \oplus K_5[0,5,10,15]$, and then we can compute $y_6^*[0,5,10,15] = \mathrm{SB}(x_6^*[0,5,10,15])$ and $\Delta y_6[0,5,10,15] = y_6^*[0,5,10,15] \oplus \mathrm{SB}(x_6^*[0,5,10,15] \oplus \Delta x_6[0,5,10,15])$, and get $w_6^*[1]$ and $\Delta x_7[1]$. Since $K_6[1]$ is known, we can obtain $x_7^*[1] = w_6^*[1] \oplus K_6[1]$ and $y_7^*[1] = \mathrm{SB}(x_7^*[1])$. Thus, by letting w_1^* be w_1^i $(i = 0, 1, \cdots, 31)$, we can generate the sequence $(y_7^0[1], y_7^1[1], \cdots, y_7^{31}[1])$.

Next, we show that in case that (w_1, w_1^*) conforms to the 5-round truncated differential characteristic depicted in Fig. 2, the above 43 bytes are determined by the following 26 bytes $(\Delta z_2[15] \| x_3[12,13,14,15] \| y_5 \| y_6[0,5,10,15] \| \Delta w_6[1])$. Since $\Delta z_2[15]$ is known and the other bytes of Δz_2 are zero, we can compute $\Delta x_3[12,13,14,15]$. Since $x_3[12,13,14,15]$ is known, we can get $y_3[12,13,14,15] = \mathrm{SB}(x_3[12,13,14,15])$ and $y_3^*[12,13,14,15] = \mathrm{SB}(x_3[12,13,14,15] \oplus \Delta x_3^*[12,13,14,15])$, and thus we can get $\Delta y_3[12,13,14,15] = y_3[12,13,14,15] \oplus y_3^*[12,13,14,15]$ and then get Δx_4. On the other hand, in the decryption direction, since $\Delta w_6[1]$ is known and the other bytes of Δw_6 are zero, we can compute $\Delta y_6[0,5,10,15]$. Since $y_6[12,13,14,15]$ is known, we can compute $x_6[0,5,10,15] = \mathrm{SB}^{-1}(y_6[0,5,10,15])$ and $x_6^*[0,5,10,15] = \mathrm{SB}^{-1}(y_6[0,5,10,15] \oplus \Delta y_6^*[0,5,10,15])$, and thus we can get $\Delta x_6[0,5,10,15] = x_6[0,5,10,15] \oplus x_6^*[0,5,10,15]$ and then get $\Delta w_5[0,5,10,15]$ and Δy_5. We can use y_5 to compute $x_5 = \mathrm{SB}^{-1}(y_5)$ and $x_5^* = \mathrm{SB}^{-1}(y_5 \oplus \Delta y_5)$, and thus get $\Delta x_5 = x_5 \oplus x_5^*$ and Δy_4. It is expected that there exists one (x_4^*, y_4^*) under $(\Delta x_4, \Delta y_4)$ by Property 1. Subsequently, we can use (y_4^*, x_5^*) to recover K_4, use $(y_5, x_6[0,5,10,15])$ to recover $K_5[0,5,10,15]$, and use $(y_3[12,13,14,15], x_4)$ to recover $\widehat{K}_3[3,6,9,15]$. We can get $(K_2[12,13,14,15], K_1[11])$ from K_4 by Properties 3-(2) and 3-(3), and get $K_6[1]$ from $(K_4, K_5[10])$ by Property 3-(6). Finally, we can decrypt $x_3[12,13,14,15]$ with $K_2[12,13,14,15]$ to get $x_2[11]$, and further decrypt $x_2[11]$ with $K_1[11]$ to obtain $w_1[11]$. Hence, the 43 bytes $(w_1[11] \| x_2[11] \| x_3[12,13,14,15] \| x_4 \| K_4 \| K_5[0,5,10,15] \| K_6[1])$ can be determined by the 26 bytes $(\Delta z_2[15] \| x_3[12,13,14,15] \| y_5 \| y_6[0,5,10,15] \| \Delta w_6[1])$.

Finally, on the other hand we can also get $\widehat{K}_3[3,6]$ from K_4 by Properties 3-(4) and 3-(5), which poses a 2-byte filtering condition on the above 26 bytes. Therefore, there are at most $2^{26 \times 8 - 2 \times 8} = 2^{192}$ possible values for the 26 bytes, and the sequence $(y_7^0[1], y_7^1[1], \cdots, y_7^{31}[1])$ has at most 2^{192} possible values.

Note that the 43 bytes $(w_1[11]\|x_2[11]\|x_3[12,13,14,15]\|x_4\|K_4\|K_5[0,5,10,15]\|K_6[1])$ are also determined by the 26 bytes $(\Delta z_2[15]\|x_3[12,13,14,15]\|K_4\|y_6[0,5,10,15]\|\Delta w_6[1])$ equivalently, since we can compute Δx_4 from $(\Delta z_2[15], x_3[12,13,14,15])$, compute Δy_5 from $(y_6[0,5,10,15], \Delta w_6[1])$, then get (x_4, y_5) for $(\Delta x_4, \Delta y_5)$ under K_4 by Property 1, and the rest of the proof is similar to the above proof.

At last, we would like to mention that the number of byte parameters for the 5-round distinguisher can be reduced from 26 to 25 by making use of MixColumns' property, but still taking 2^{192} values: the 43 bytes $(w_1[11]\|x_2[11]\|x_3[12, 13,14,15]\|x_4\|K_4\|K_5[0,5,10,15]\|K_6[1])$ are also determined by the 25 bytes $(\Delta y_3[12,13,14,15]\|K_4\|y_6[0,5,10,15]\|\Delta w_6[1])$ equivalently, and the main reason is as follows. Compute Δx_4 with $\Delta y_3[12,13,14,15]$, compute Δy_5 with $(y_6[0,5,10,15], \Delta w_6[1])$, get (x_4, y_5) for $(\Delta x_4, \Delta y_5)$ under K_4 by Property 1, compute $(y_3[14,15], x_3[14,15], \Delta x_3[14,15])$ with $(x_4, \Delta y_3[14,15], \widehat{K}_3[3,6])$, which produces an 8-bit filtering condition due to the fact that there are at most 255 possible values for $\Delta x_3[12,13,14,15]$ under the 255 possible values for $\Delta z_2[15]$. Then, under a possible $(\Delta x_3[12,13,14,15], \Delta y_3[12,13,14,15])$, get a value for $(x_3[12,13,14,15], y_3[12,13,14,15])$ by Property 1, and get $\widehat{K}_3[9,12]$ with $(y_3[12, 13,14,15], x_4)$. The rest of the proof is similar to the above proof. Due to the above 8-bit filtering condition, the 25 bytes take at most $2^{25\times 8-8} = 2^{192}$ possible values.

4.2 Corrected Basic 9-Round AES-192 Attack

Similar to Li et al.'s attack procedure, we can apply the above 5-round MitM distinguisher to attack 9-round AES-192 by appending one round forwards and three rounds backwards, as follows.

Precomputation Phase. In this phase, we generate a hash table $\mathcal{H}$ that contains all possible values of the sequence $(y_7^0[1], y_7^1[1], \cdots, y_7^{31}[1])$, as follows, as illustrated in Fig. 2.

1. For every possible 40-bit $(y_6[0,5,10,15], \Delta w_6[1])$, compute $(x_6[0,5,10,15], \Delta x_6[0,5,10,15])$, where $\Delta w_6[0,2,3] = 0$. Store $x_6[0,5,10,15]$ in a hash table $\mathcal{T}_1$, indexed by $\Delta x_6[0,5,10,15]$. It is expected that there are on average about $\frac{2^8\times 2^{32}}{2^{32}} = 2^8$ values for $x_6[0,5,10,15]$ under every index $\Delta x_6[0,5,10,15]$.
2. For every possible K_4:
   (a) Compute $K_1[11]$, $K_2[12,13,14,15]$ and $\widehat{K}_3[3,6]$ from K_4 by Properties 3-(2)–3-(5).
   (b) For every possible 64-bit $(\Delta y_3[12,13,14,15], \Delta x_6[0,5,10,15])$, compute $(\Delta x_4,\ \Delta y_5)$, get (x_4, y_5) under $(\Delta x_4, \Delta y_5)$ by Property 1, and compute $w_5[0,5,10,15]$ from y_5, and compute $y_3[14,15]$ from x_4 with $\widehat{K}_3[3,6]$. Store $(\Delta x_6[0,5,10,15], x_4,\ w_5[0,5,10,15])$ in a hash table $\mathcal{T}_2$, indexed by $(\Delta y_3[12,13,14,15], y_3[14,15])$. It is expected that there are on average about $\frac{2^{64}}{2^{48}} = 2^{16}$ values for $(\Delta x_6[0,5,10,15], x_4,\ w_5[0,5,10,15])$ under every index $(\Delta y_3[12,13,14,15], y_3[14,15])$.

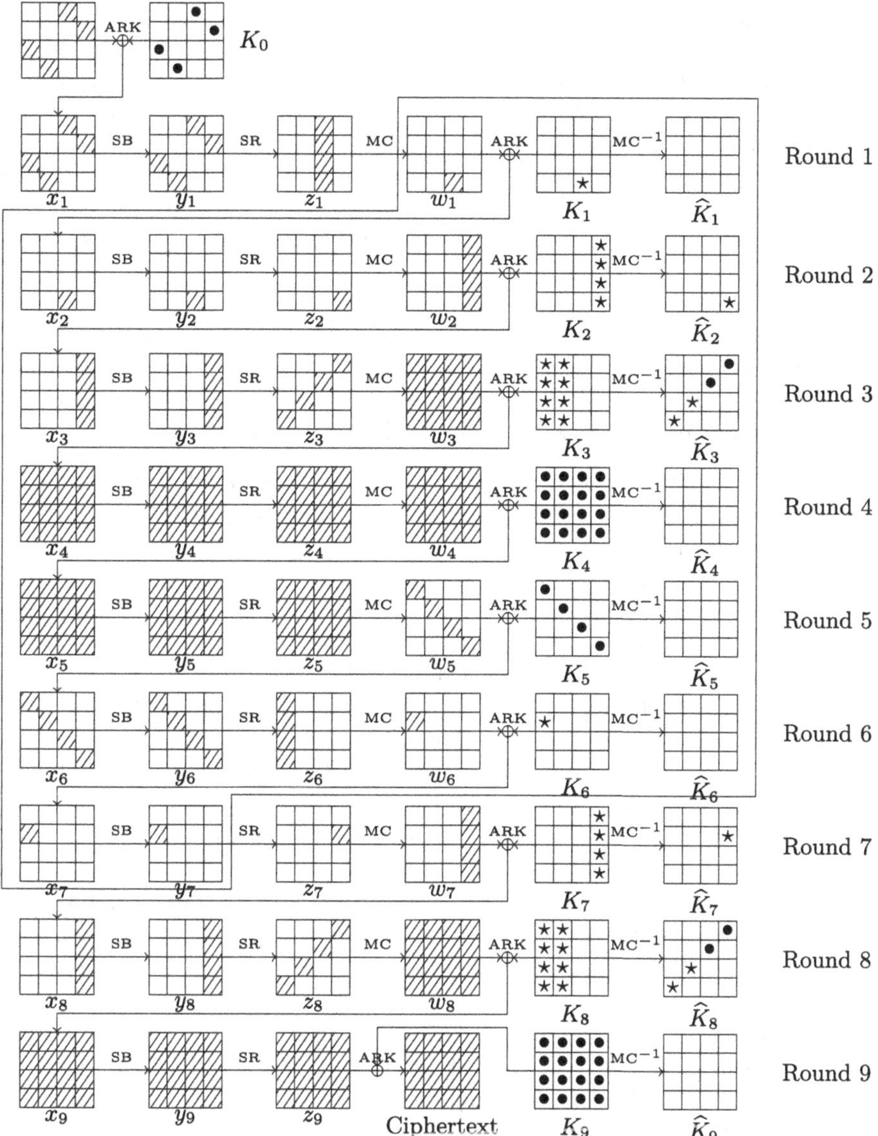

Fig. 2. Our 5-round distinguisher and 9-round attack on AES-192

(c) For every possible 40-bit $(\Delta z_2[15], x_3[12, 13, 14, 15])$:
  (i) Compute $(x_2[11], w_1[11])$ with $(x_3[12, 13, 14, 15], K_1[11], K_2[12, 13, 14, 15])$, and compute $(y_3[12, 13, 14, 15], \Delta y_3[12, 13, 14, 15])$ with $(\Delta z_2[15], x_3[12, 13, 14, 15])$.
  (ii) Access the $\mathcal{T}_2$ table by $(\Delta y_3[12, 13, 14, 15], y_3[14, 15])$ to get $(\Delta x_6[0, 5, 10, 15], x_4, w_5[0, 5, 10, 15])$, whose number is expected to be 2^{16}. Note

that we can get $\widehat{K}_3[9,12]$ from $(y_3[12,13], x_4)$. For every $(\Delta x_6[0,5,10,15], x_4, w_5[0,5,10,15])$, access the $\mathcal{T}_1$ table by $\Delta x_6[0,5,10,15]$ to get $x_6[0,5,10,15]$, whose number is expected to be 2^8. For every $x_6[0,5,10,15]$, compute $K_5[0,5,10,15] = w_5[0,5,10,15] \oplus x_6[0,5,10,15]$, and compute $K_6[1]$ from $(K_4, K_5[10])$ by Property 3-(6). Thus, we obtain the 43 bytes $(w_1[11] \| x_2[11] \| x_3[12,13,14,15] \| x_4 \| K_4 \| K_5[0,5,10,15] \| K_6[1])$. At last, generate the sequence $(y_7^0[1], y_7^1[1], \cdots, y_7^{31}[1])$, and store it in the hash table $\mathcal{H}$. The total number of possible sequences in $\mathcal{H}$ is 2^{192} at most.

Online Phase: In this phase, to recover the user key, we first generate some message pairs, then for each message pair, we construct a δ-set, generate a sequence $(y_7^0[1], y_7^1[1], \cdots, y_7^{31}[1])$, and finally check whether the sequence exists in the $\mathcal{H}$ table. The attack procedure is as follows, as illustrated in Fig. 2.

1. Choose 2^{81} structures, where a structure is defined to be a set of 2^{32} plaintexts with bytes $(2,7,8,13)$ taking all the possible values and the other 12 bytes being fixed. Each structure can generate $\binom{2^{32}}{2} \approx 2^{63}$ plaintext pairs, and thus the 2^{81} structures can produce a total of $2^{81} \times 2^{63} = 2^{144}$ plaintext pairs. It is expected that there is about $2^{144} \times 2^{-(3+12+3)\times 8} = 1$ plaintext pair producing the truncated differential characteristic of Fig. 2.
2. For each of the 2^{144} plaintext pairs, do as follows:
   (a) Guess $\Delta y_8[12,13,14,15]$, and then compute Δx_9. Obtain Δy_9 from the corresponding ciphertext pair. Then, get (x_9, y_9) for each $(\Delta x_9, \Delta y_9)$ by Property 1, and compute $K_9 = x_{10} \oplus \mathrm{SR}(y_9)$, where x_{10} is a ciphertext. Compute $\widehat{K}_8[3,6]$ from K_9 by Properties 3-(8) and 3-(9), and get $(y_8[14,15], \Delta y_8[14,15], \Delta x_8[14,15])$ with $(x_9, \widehat{K}_8[3,6])$.
   (b) Guess $\Delta x_8[12,13]$ such that $\Delta z_7[12,14,15] = 0$ together with $\Delta x_8[14,15]$. For every satisfying $(\Delta y_8[12,13,14,15], \Delta x_8[12,13,14,15])$, obtain $(y_8[12,13,14,15], x_8[12,13,14,15])$ by Property 1, and get $\widehat{K}_8[9,12]$ with $(x_9, y_8[12,13])$. It is expected that there are $2^{4\times 8+2\times 8-3\times 8} = 2^{24}$ satisfying values for $(\Delta y_8[12,13,14,15], \Delta x_8[12,13])$.
   (c) Guess $\Delta w_1[11]$, compute $\Delta y_1[2,7,8,13]$, get $\Delta x_1[2,7,8,13]$ from the plaintext pair, get $x_1[2,7,8,13]$ for $(\Delta x_1[2,7,8,13], \Delta y_1[2,7,8,13])$ by Property 1, and compute $K_0[2,7,8,13]$. Compute $K_7[12,13,14,15] = K_9[0,1,2,3] \oplus K_9[4,5,6,7]$ by Property 3-(7) to get $\widehat{K}_7[13]$.
   (d) Change $w_1[11]$ to be $\{0,1,\cdots,31\}$, generate a sequence $(y_7^0[1], y_7^1[1], \cdots, y_7^{31}[1])$, and check whether it exists in the $\mathcal{H}$ table; if not, discard this $(K_9, \widehat{K}_8[9,12], K_0[2,7,8,13])$.
3. Exhaustively search $\widehat{K}_8[8,10,11,13,14,15]$ under every remaining $(K_9, \widehat{K}_8[9,12])$ after Step 2 to determine the whole 192-bit user key. It is expected that there remain $2^{144} \times 2^{24} \times 2^8 \times \frac{2^{192}}{2^{256}} = 2^{112}$ guesses for $(K_9, \widehat{K}_8[9,12])$ after Step 2.

The attack requires $2^{81} \times 2^{32} = 2^{113}$ chosen plaintexts. The precomputation phase has a memory complexity of about $2^{192} \times 32 = 2^{197}$ bytes and a time complexity of about $2^{104} \times 2^{64} \times \frac{2}{9} + 2^{128} \times 2^{40} \times 2^{16} \times 2^{8} \times 32 \times \frac{2}{9} \approx 2^{194.8}$ 9-round AES encryptions, by approximating each $y_7^m[1]$ value of the δ-set as a 2-round AES encryption. The online phase has a time complexity of about $2^{144} \times 2^{24} \times 2^{8} \times 32 \times \frac{1.5}{9} \approx 2^{178.4}$ 9-round AES encryptions. Note that $\mathcal{T}_2$ takes a time complexity of $2^{128} \times 2^{64} = 2^{192}$ table lookups, which is $\frac{2^{192}}{144} \approx 2^{184.8}$ 9-round AES-192 encryptions if a single 9-round AES-192 encryption is treated as $9 \times 16 = 144$ table lookups under a usual approximation that a one-round AES encryption is equivalent to 16 table lookups.

There are data-memory-time tradeoffs to the above attack, for example, by precomputing only a fraction of 2^{-8} of all possible sequences and executing the online phase with $2^{81} \times 2^{8} = 2^{89}$ structures of plaintexts, the precomputation phase has a memory complexity of $2^{197} \times 2^{-8} = 2^{189}$ bytes and a time complexity of about $2^{194.8} \times 2^{-8} + 2^{184.8} \approx 2^{187.1}$ 9-round AES encryptions, and the online phase has a time complexity of about $2^{178.4} \times 2^{8} = 2^{186.4}$ 9-round AES encryptions, that is, a total time complexity of $2^{187.1} + 2^{186.4} \approx 2^{187.7}$ 9-round AES encryptions.

These complexity numbers are identical to Li et al.'s in [15], except that Li et al. did not take the complexity $2^{184.8}$ of $\mathcal{T}_2$ (that is T_0 in [15]) into consideration, that is, the time complexity for Li et al.'s attacks should also be $2^{187.7}$ 9-round AES encryptions.

4.3 Corrected 9-Round AES-192 Attack Under Their Weak-Key Approach

In [15], Li et al. observed that there were a few relations between the keys of precomputation phase and the keys of online phase, and they suggested using linear relations to save storage. For their attack on Rounds 1–9, they exploited a one-byte linear relation between a few round key bytes (i.e., $K_4[1,5,10,14]$) of precomputation phase and a round key byte (i.e., $K_0[6]$) of online phase, then according to this one-byte linear relation they divided the whole key space into 2^8 key subspaces, which they called weak key classes, and conducted a series of 2^8 sub-attacks for the 2^8 key subspaces sequentially in a streaming mode, where each sub-attack should only precompute and store a fraction $\frac{1}{2^8}$ of the total 2^{192} possible sequences of the whole key space case, and this storage was reused from one key subspace to another, thus decreasing the total memory complexity by a factor of 2^8 compared with the single attack for the whole key space case. (Note that this key relation is not correct, as mentioned in Sect. 3.)

In our above 9-round AES-192 attack, there is a similar one-byte linear relation between a round key of the precomputation phase and a round key byte of the online phase, that is $K_0[7] = K_4[15] \oplus K_4[11] \oplus \mathbf{S}(K_4[4] \oplus K_4[0])$ given as Property 3-(1). Thus, as Li et al. did in [15] under their weak-key approach, we can use this one-byte key relation to reduce the memory complexity of the 9-round AES-192 attack of Sect. 4.2 by a factor of 2^8, without changing its data and time complexity, that is, a data complexity of 2^{121} chosen plaintexts, a memory complexity of $2^{189} \times 2^{-8} = 2^{181}$ bytes and a time complexity of about $2^{187.7}$ 9-round AES encryptions.

4.4 A Remark

Li et al. [15] observed that the 5-round MitM distinguisher on Rounds 4–9 took only 2^{184} possible values due to their (wrong) AES-192 key schedule, 2^8 less than the possible values of their 5-round MitM distinguisher on Rounds 1–6, and they applied it to attack Rounds 3–11 with/without weak-key approach, with a less complexity than their attack on Rounds 1–9. However, we have checked that this 5-round MitM distinguisher on Rounds 4–9 does not have advantage over the 5-round MitM distinguisher of Proposition 1 under the original AES-192 key schedule, and neither does the resulting 9-round attack with/without weak-key approach.

5 Improved 9-Round AES-192 Attacks with a New Trick

In this section, we improve the above 9-round attack under weak-key approach by using a new trick to exploit more complicated key relations to further reduce memory. The trick lies in building a novel precomputation table that links ciphertext, the last round's SubBytes output and a few round key bytes. This attack can also be seen as an improved version of Li et al.'s attack.

5.1 A 9-Round AES-192 Attack Using 4-Byte Key Relations

In [15], Li et al. mentioned that there were many intersecting key bits between the keys of precomputation phase and the keys of online phase in their attacks, but finally they used only a one-byte linear key relation for a reduced memory complexity in their 9-round AES-192 attack on Rounds 1–9 under so-called weak-key approach. This case also holds for our 9-round AES-192 attack of Sect. 4.2, as given in Sect. 4.3. Specifically, in our 9-round AES-192 attack of Sect. 4.2, the precomputation phase involves explicitly or implicitly a total of 30 (equivalent) round key bytes $(K_4, K_5[0,5,10,15], K_1[11], K_2[12,13,14,15], \widehat{K}_3[3,6,9,12], K_6[1])$, and the online phase involves explicitly or implicitly a total of 28 (equivalent) round key bytes $(K_9, \widehat{K}_8[3,6,9,12], K_7[12,13,14,15], K_0[2,7,8,13])$, and there is a similar one-byte linear relation $K_0[7] = K_4[15] \oplus K_4[11] \oplus \mathbf{S}(K_4[4] \oplus K_4[0])$ that can be easily used to reduce memory complexity, like Li et al.'s way.

It is easy to get the many key relations between the keys of precomputation phase and the keys of online phase, but the challenging problem is how to use them to reduce memory complexity under weak-key approach. The way that the above-mentioned one-byte key relation is used in Li et al.'s 9-round attack or our 9-round attack of Sect. 4.3 is easy and straightforward, but it is tough to use the remaining key relations, although some of them are also linear, for example, there exist the following three linear relations $K_5[5] = K_9[1] \oplus K_9[5] \oplus K_9[9] \oplus K_9[13]$, $K_5[10] = K_9[14] \oplus K_9[10] \oplus K_9[6] \oplus K_9[2] \oplus K_4[2]$ and $K_5[15] = K_9[3] \oplus K_9[7] \oplus K_9[11] \oplus K_9[15] \oplus K_4[3] \oplus K_4[7]$, but when we would like to use one or more of them to further reduce memory together with the above-mentioned one-byte linear relation $K_0[7] = K_4[15] \oplus K_4[11] \oplus \mathbf{S}(K_4[4] \oplus K_4[0])$, a delicate investigation reveals that it did not much sense. Nevertheless, among the many remaining key relations (between the round keys of the precomputation phase and the round keys of the online phase), we observe that there are two complicated one-byte linear relations, namely Properties 3-(10) and 3-(11), so that we find a trick for exploiting them through a novel precomputation table (i.e. $\mathcal{T}_4$ below) to further reduce the memory complexity of the 9-round AES-192 attack of Sect. 4.3 while keeping its data and time complexity unchanged. Even more, we observe that another one-byte key relation Property 3-(12) can be used to slightly further reduce memory, although this reduction can be somewhat negligible overall (Note that Property 3-(12) is nonlinear by Li et al.'s concept, but it can be transformed into linear). The final attack is as follows, where we assume without loss of generality that there is no MixColumns operation in the last round to simplify our descriptions, and we will explain why the $\mathcal{T}_4$ table is generated that way at the end of this section.

1. According to Properties 3-(1), 3-(10), 3-(11) and 3-(12), define the following four byte parameters Θ_1, Θ_2, Θ_3 and Θ_4:

$$\Theta_1 = K_4[15] \oplus K_4[11] \oplus \mathbf{S}(K_4[0] \oplus K_4[4]) = K_0[7]; \quad (1)$$

$$\begin{aligned}\Theta_2 &= 0x09 \otimes K_4[0] \oplus 0x0e \otimes K_4[1] \oplus 0x0b \otimes K_4[2] \oplus 0x0d \otimes K_4[3] \\ &= \widehat{K}_8[9] \oplus 0x09 \otimes (K_9[0] \oplus K_9[12]) \oplus 0x0e \otimes (K_9[1] \oplus K_9[13]) \oplus \\ &\quad 0x0b \otimes (K_9[2] \oplus K_9[14]) \oplus 0x0d \otimes (K_9[3] \oplus K_9[15]); \quad (2)\end{aligned}$$

$$\begin{aligned}\Theta_3 &= 0x0e \otimes (K_4[0] \oplus K_4[4]) \oplus 0x0b \otimes (K_4[1] \oplus K_4[5]) \oplus \\ &\quad 0x0d \otimes (K_4[2] \oplus K_4[6]) \oplus 0x09 \otimes (K_4[3] \oplus K_4[7]) \\ &= \widehat{K}_8[12] \oplus 0x0e \otimes (K_9[0] \oplus K_9[4]) \oplus 0x0b \otimes (K_9[1] \oplus K_9[5]) \oplus \\ &\quad 0x0d \otimes (K_9[2] \oplus K_9[6]) \oplus 0x09 \otimes (K_9[3] \oplus K_9[7]); \quad (3)\end{aligned}$$

$$\begin{aligned}\Theta_4 &= K_4[2] \oplus K_4[6] \\ &= \mathbf{S}^{-1}(K_0[13] \oplus K_9[5] \oplus K_9[13]) \oplus K_9[2] \oplus K_9[6] \oplus K_9[10] \oplus K_9[14]. \quad (4)\end{aligned}$$

Then, divide the space of K_4 into 2^{32} subspaces $\mathcal{K}_\Theta = \{K_4 | Eqs.\ (1){-}(4)\}$ according to the values of $\Theta = (\Theta_1, \Theta_2, \Theta_3, \Theta_4)$. Every $\mathcal{K}_\Theta$ contains $\frac{2^{128}}{2^{32}} = 2^{96}$ values of K_4.

2. Construct a precomputation table $\mathcal{T}_3$, as follows. For every possible $(\Delta w_6[1], y_6[0,5,10,15])$, compute $(x_6[0,5,10,15], \Delta x_6[0,5,10,15])$, and store $x_6[0,5,10,15]$ into the hash table $\mathcal{T}_3$, indexed by $\Delta x_6[0,5,10,15]$. It is expected that there are on average about $\frac{2^{32} \times 2^8}{2^{32}} = 2^8$ value for $x_6[0,5,10,15]$ under every index $\Delta x_6[0,5,10,15]$.
3. Construct a precomputation table $\mathcal{T}_4$, as follows. For every possible $(\Delta z_7[13], x_8[12,13,14,15])$ and every possible ciphertext difference denoted by ΔX_{10}:
   (a) Compute $(y_8[12,13,14,15], \Delta y_8[12,13,14,15], \Delta x_9)$ with $(\Delta z_7[13], x_8[12,13,14,15])$, deduce Δy_9 from ΔX_{10}, and obtain (x_9, y_9) under $(\Delta x_9, \Delta y_9)$ by Property 1.
   (b) Compute $(\widehat{w}_7[13], \widehat{K}_8[3,6,9,12])$ with $(y_8[12,13,14,15], x_9)$. Store $(y_9, \widehat{K}_8[9,12], \widehat{w}_7[13], \Delta z_7[13])$ into the hash table $\mathcal{T}_4$, indexed by the 160-bit

value $(\Delta X_{10}, \widehat{K}_8[3]\oplus 0x0b\otimes(y_9[8]\oplus y_9[4])\oplus 0x0d\otimes(y_9[13]\oplus y_9[9])\oplus 0x09\otimes(y_9[14]\oplus y_9[2])\oplus 0x0e\otimes(y_9[3]\oplus y_9[7]), \widehat{K}_8[6]\oplus 0x0d\otimes(y_9[8]\oplus y_9[12])\oplus 0x09\otimes(y_9[13]\oplus y_9[1])\oplus 0x0e\otimes(y_9[2]\oplus y_9[6])\oplus 0x0b\otimes(y_9[7]\oplus y_9[11]), \widehat{K}_8[9]\oplus 0x09\otimes(y_9[0]\oplus y_9[12])\oplus 0x0e\otimes(y_9[5]\oplus y_9[1])\oplus 0x0b\otimes(y_9[10]\oplus y_9[6])\oplus 0x0d\otimes(y_9[15]\oplus y_9[11], \widehat{K}_8[12]\oplus 0x0e\otimes(y_9[0]\oplus y_9[4])\oplus 0x0b\otimes(y_9[5]\oplus y_9[9])\oplus 0x0d\otimes(y_9[10]\oplus y_9[14])\oplus 0x09\otimes(y_9[15]\oplus y_9[3])]))$. (How the index is generated will be explained later.) It is expected that there are on average about $\frac{2^8\times 2^{32}\times 2^{128}}{2^{128}\times(2^8)^4} = 2^8$ values for $(y_9, \widehat{K}_8[9,12], \widehat{w}_7[13], \Delta z_7[13])$ under every 160-bit index.

4. Choose 2^{81} structures $\mathcal{S}_i$, where a structure $\mathcal{S}_i$ is defined to be a set of 2^{32} plaintexts $P_{i,j}$ with bytes $(2,7,8,13)$ taking all the possible values and the other 12 bytes being fixed $(i=0,1,\cdots,2^{81}-1, j=0,1,\cdots,2^{32}-1)$. Obtain their ciphertexts $C_{i,j}$ in a chosen-plaintext attack scenario. The 2^{81} structures can produce approximately $2^{81}\times 2^{63} = 2^{144}$ plaintext pairs (P_{i,j_0}, P_{i,j_1}), and we denote their ciphertext pairs by (C_{i,j_0}, C_{i,j_1}), where $0\le j_0\ne j_1\le 2^{32}-1$.
5. Construct a hash table $\mathcal{H}^*$ for $\mathcal{K}_\Theta$, as follows. For every possible K_4 in $\mathcal{K}_\Theta$:
   (a) Compute $K_1[11]$, $K_2[12,13,14,15]$ and $\widehat{K}_3[3,6]$ from K_4 by Properties 3-(2)–3-(5). Note that $K_0[7]=\Theta_1$ by Eq. (1).
   (b) For every possible 64-bit $(\Delta y_3[12,13,14,15], \Delta w_5[0,5,10,15])$, do as follows.
      (i) Compute $(\Delta x_4, \Delta y_5)$, obtain (x_4, y_5) under $(\Delta x_4, \Delta y_5)$ by Property 1, compute $w_5[0,5,10,15]$ from y_5, compute $y_3[14,15]$ from x_4 with $\widehat{K}_3[3,6]$, and compute $(x_3[14,15], \Delta x_3[14,\ 15])$ with $(y_3[14,15], \Delta y_3[14,15])$.
      (ii) Given that $\Delta z_2[12,13,14] = 0$ and $\Delta w_2[15] = \Delta x_3[15]$, determine uniquely a value for $(\Delta z_2[15], \Delta x_3[12,13,14] = \Delta w_2[12,13,14])$ by Property 2, and we denote the value of $\Delta x_3[12,13,14]$ by $\Delta\overline{x}_3[12,13,14]$, and keep only $\Delta\overline{x}_3[12,13,14]$ such that $\Delta\overline{x}_3[14]$ is equal to the $\Delta x_3[14]$ value obtained in Step 5-(i), which produces an 8-bit filtering condition. Now, $\Delta\overline{x}_3[12,13,14]$ is actually $\Delta x_3[12,13,14]$, and we have $(\Delta x_3[12,13,14,15], \Delta y_3[12,13,14,15])$.
      (iii) Obtain $(x_3[12,13,14,15], y_3[12,13,14,15])$ under $(\Delta x_3[12,13,14,15], \Delta y_3[12,13,14,15])$ by Property 1, and compute $(x_2[11], w_1[11])$ from $x_3[12,13,14,15]$ with $(K_2[12,13,14,15], K_1[11])$. It is expected that there are on average approximately $\frac{2^{64}\times 2^{-8}}{2^{32}} = 2^{24}$ values for $(w_1[11], x_2[11], x_3[12,13,14,15], x_4, w_5[0,5,10,15])$ under every index $\Delta w_5[0,5,10,15]$.
      (iv) For every $\Delta x_6[0,5,10,15] = \Delta w_5[0,5,10,15]$, access the $\mathcal{T}_3$ table to get the corresponding 2^8 values for $x_6[0,5,10,15]$, and for every possible $(w_5[0,5,10,15], x_6[0,5,10,15])$, compute $K_5[0,5,10,15] = x_6[0,5,10,15]\oplus w_5[0,5,10,15]$, compute $K_6[1]$ from $(K_4, K_5[10])$ by Property 3-(6), and thus we get the 43 bytes $(w_1[11]\|x_2[11]\|x_3[12,13,14,15]\|x_4\|K_4\|K_5[0,5,10,15]\|K_6[1])$, and we can generate a 256-bit ordered sequence $(y_7^0[1], y_7^1[1],\cdots,y_7^{31}[1])$ and store it in the hash

table $\mathcal{H}^*$. There are a total of $2^{96} \times 2^{32} \times 2^{24} \times 2^8 = 2^{160}$ possible sequences in $\mathcal{H}^*$ at most.

6. Check whether the 192-bit user key exists under the $\mathcal{H}^*$ table for $\mathcal{K}_\Theta$, as follows. Guess $K_0[2, 8, 13]$:
   (a) For every structure $\mathcal{S}_i$, partially encrypt a plaintext with $K_0[2, 7, 8, 13]$ to get $y_1[2, 7, 8, 13]$, XOR $y_1[2, 7, 8, 13]$ with all the 255 possible values of $\Delta y_1[2, 7, 8, 13]$ such that $\Delta w_1[8, 9, 10] = 0$, and partially decrypt them to get their corresponding plaintexts, where $K_0[7] = \Theta_1$. By this way, we can efficiently get all the $\frac{2^{32}}{2} \times 2^8 = 2^{39}$ plaintext pairs (P_{i,j_0}, P_{i,j_1}) with $\Delta w_1[8, 9, 10] = 0$ under $K_0[2, 7, 8, 13]$ in $\mathcal{S}_i$, and the 2^{81} structures produce a total of approximately $2^{81} \times 2^{39} = 2^{120}$ such plaintext pairs under every $K_0[2, 7, 8, 13]$.
   (b) For every ciphertext pair (C_{i,j_0}, C_{i,j_1}), access the $\mathcal{T}_4$ table with index $(C_{i,j_0} \oplus C_{i,j_1}, 0x0b \otimes (C[8] \oplus C[4]) \oplus 0x0d \otimes (C[9] \oplus C[5]) \oplus 0x09 \otimes (C[6] \oplus C[10]) \oplus 0x0e \otimes (C[7] \oplus C[11]), 0x0d \otimes (C[8] \oplus C[12]) \oplus 0x09 \otimes (C[9] \oplus C[13]) \oplus 0x0e \otimes (C[10] \oplus C[14]) \oplus 0x0b \otimes (C[11] \oplus C[15]), \Theta_2 \oplus 0x09 \otimes (C[0] \oplus C[12]) \oplus 0x0e \otimes (C[1] \oplus C[13]) \oplus 0x0b \otimes (C[2] \oplus C[14]) \oplus 0x0d \otimes (C[3] \oplus C[15]), \Theta_3 \oplus 0x0e \otimes (C[0] \oplus C[4]) \oplus 0x0b \otimes (C[1] \oplus C[5]) \oplus 0x0d \otimes (C[2] \oplus C[6]) \oplus 0x09 \otimes (C[3] \oplus C[7]))$ to get 2^8 values for $(y_9, \widehat{K}_8[9, 12], \widehat{w}_7[13], \Delta z_7[13])$, where $C \in \{C_{i,j_0}, C_{i,j_1}\}$. Then, for each $(y_9, \widehat{K}_8[9, 12], \widehat{w}_7[13], \Delta z_7[13])$, compute K_9 with (y_9, C), and check whether it satisfies $\Theta_4 = \mathbf{S}^{-1}(K_0[13] \oplus K_9[13] \oplus K_9[5]) \oplus K_9[2] \oplus K_9[6] \oplus K_9[10] \oplus K_9[14]$ by Eq. (4), which produces an 8-bit filtering condition on K_9. Next, compute $\widehat{K}_7[13]$ from K_9 by Property 3-(7) and get $y_7[1]$ with $\widehat{w}_7[13]$. Finally, we can generate a sequence and check whether it is in the $\mathcal{H}^*$ table; if yes, exhaustively search $\widehat{K}_8[8, 10, 11, 13, 14, 15]$ under $(K_9, \widehat{K}_8[9, 12])$ to determine the whole 192-bit user key. For $\mathcal{K}_\Theta$ it is expected that there are $2^{24} \times 2^{120} \times 2^8 \times 2^{-8} \times \frac{2^{160}}{2^{256}} = 2^{48}$ remaining $(K_0[2, 8, 13], K_9, \widehat{K}_8[9, 12])$.

The attack requires $2^{81} \times 2^{32} = 2^{113}$ chosen plaintexts. In Step 3, $\mathcal{T}_4$ takes a time complexity of approximately $2^{128} \times 2^{32} \times 2^8 \times \frac{1.5}{9} \approx 2^{165.4}$ 9-round AES encryptions and a memory of $2^{128} \times 2^{32} \times 2^8 \times 20 \approx 2^{172.3}$ bytes. For a given subspace $\mathcal{K}_\Theta$, Step 5 has a time complexity of approximately $2^{96} \times 2^{32} \times 2^{32} \times \frac{2}{9} + 2^{96} \times 2^{32} \times 2^{24} \times 2^8 \times 32 \times \frac{2}{9} \approx 2^{162.8}$ 9-round AES encryptions and a memory complexity of $2^{160} \times 32 = 2^{165}$ bytes, and Step 6 has a time complexity of about $2^{24} \times 2^{81} \times 2^{31} \times 255 \times \frac{0.25}{9} + 2^{24} \times 2^{120} \times 2^8 \times 2^{-8} \times 32 \times \frac{1.5}{9} \approx 2^{146.4}$ 9-round AES encryptions. Therefore, the precomputational phase (Steps 2, 3 and 5) has a memory complexity of $2^{172.3} + 2^{165} \approx 2^{172.3}$ bytes and a time complexity of $2^{165.4} + 2^{32} \times 2^{162.8} \approx 2^{194.8}$ 9-round AES encryptions, and the online phase (Steps 4 and 6) has a time complexity of $2^{32} \times 2^{146.4} \approx 2^{178.4}$ 9-round AES encryptions. (Note that strictly speaking, the $\mathcal{H}^*$ table should not be treated as a precomputation table, for building the next $\mathcal{H}^*$ (if any) has to wait after the online phase for the current $\mathcal{K}_\Theta$ completes, but we treat it as this for simplicity.)

There are data-memory-time tradeoffs, for example, by precomputing only a fraction 2^{-8} of all possible sequences and executing the online phase with

$2^{113+8} = 2^{121}$ plaintexts, the precomputational phase has a memory complexity of $2^{172.3} + 2^{165} \times 2^{-8} \approx 2^{172.3}$ bytes and a time complexity of $2^{194.8} \times 2^{-8} = 2^{186.8}$ 9-round AES encryptions, and the online phase has a time complexity of $2^{178.4} \times 2^{8} = 2^{186.4}$ 9-round AES encryptions, that is, the total time complexity is $2^{186.8} + 2^{186.4} \approx 2^{187.6}$ 9-round AES encryptions. Note that Property 3-(12) is used to reduce memory and is also used as a filtering condition in the last key-recovery phase, but its contribution to reducing memory can be neglected compared with the memory of $\mathcal{T}_4$, that is, the overall complexity is almost the same without using Property 3-(12). Also note that data-memory-time tradeoffs can be made by precomputing a fraction of $\mathcal{T}_4$, for a reduced memory complexity.

Explaining the Trick Exploiting Properties 3-(10) and 3-(11). A critical trick for our above attack is owing to the construction of $\mathcal{T}_4$. Below we briefly explain how the index for the $\mathcal{T}_4$ table is generated and how $\mathcal{T}_4$ exploits the two one-byte linear relations Properties 3-(10) and 3-(11). Recall that it is assumed that there is no MixColumns operation in the last round, without loss of generality. Given a ciphertext C, we have

$$\begin{array}{lll}
K_9[0] = y_9[0] \oplus C[0], & K_9[1] = y_9[5] \oplus C[1], & K_9[2] = y_9[10] \oplus C[2], \\
K_9[3] = y_9[15] \oplus C[3], & K_9[4] = y_9[4] \oplus C[4], & K_9[5] = y_9[9] \oplus C[5], \\
K_9[6] = y_9[14] \oplus C[6], & K_9[7] = y_9[3] \oplus C[7], & K_9[8] = y_9[8] \oplus C[8], \\
K_9[9] = y_9[13] \oplus C[9], & K_9[10] = y_9[2] \oplus C[10], & K_9[11] = y_9[7] \oplus C[11], \\
K_9[12] = y_9[12] \oplus C[12], & K_9[13] = y_9[1] \oplus C[13], & K_9[14] = y_9[6] \oplus C[14], \\
K_9[15] = y_9[11] \oplus C[15]. & &
\end{array}$$

Thus, placing them into Properties 3-(8), 3-(9), 3-(10) and 3-(11), we can obtain

$$\begin{aligned}
\widehat{K}_8[3] &\oplus 0x0b \otimes (y_9[8] \oplus y_9[4]) \oplus 0x0d \otimes (y_9[13] \oplus y_9[9]) \oplus \\
&0x09 \otimes (y_9[14] \oplus y_9[2]) \oplus 0x0e \otimes (y_9[3] \oplus y_9[7]) \\
&= 0x0b \otimes (C[8] \oplus C[4]) \oplus 0x0d \otimes (C[9] \oplus C[5]) \oplus \\
&0x09 \otimes (C[6] \oplus C[10]) \oplus 0x0e \otimes (C[7] \oplus C[11]), \\
\widehat{K}_8[6] &\oplus 0x0d \otimes (y_9[8] \oplus y_9[12]) \oplus 0x09 \otimes (y_9[13] \oplus y_9[1]) \oplus \\
&0x0e \otimes (y_9[2] \oplus y_9[6]) \oplus 0x0b \otimes (y_9[7] \oplus y_9[11]) \\
&= 0x0d \otimes (C[8] \oplus C[12]) \oplus 0x09 \otimes (C[9] \oplus C[13]) \oplus \\
&0x0e \otimes (C[10] \oplus C[14]) \oplus 0x0b \otimes (C[11] \oplus C[15]), \\
\widehat{K}_8[9] &\oplus 0x09 \otimes (y_9[0] \oplus y_9[12]) \oplus 0x0e \otimes (y_9[5] \oplus y_9[1]) \oplus \\
&0x0b \otimes (y_9[10] \oplus y_9[6]) \oplus 0x0d \otimes (y_9[15] \oplus y_9[11]) \\
&= \Theta_2 \oplus 0x09 \otimes (C[0] \oplus C[12]) \oplus 0x0e \otimes (C[1] \oplus C[13]) \oplus \\
&0x0b \otimes (C[2] \oplus C[14]) \oplus 0x0d \otimes (C[3] \oplus C[15]), \\
\widehat{K}_8[12] &\oplus 0x0e \otimes (y_9[0] \oplus y_9[4]) \oplus 0x0b \otimes (y_9[5] \oplus y_9[9]) \oplus \\
&0x0d \otimes (y_9[10] \oplus y_9[14]) \oplus 0x09 \otimes (y_9[15] \oplus y_9[3]) \\
&= \Theta_3 \oplus 0x0e \otimes (C[0] \oplus C[4]) \oplus 0x0b \otimes (C[1] \oplus C[5]) \oplus \\
&0x0d \otimes (C[2] \oplus C[6]) \oplus 0x09 \otimes (C[3] \oplus C[7]).
\end{aligned}$$

The generation of the $\mathcal{T}_4$ table produces the $(\widehat{K}_8[3,6,9,12], y_9)$ parameters on the left side of the equations, and the (Θ_2, Θ_3, C) parameters on the right side of the equations can be available during the online attack phase, and thus we make the index for $\mathcal{T}_4$. By this way, we can use the three additional one-byte key relations to further reduce memory complexity on the basis of Li et al.'s way. Note that there is no index byte from Eq. (4) in $\mathcal{T}_4$, because it is not possible to put the associated y_9 bytes into one side and put Θ_4 and the associated ciphertext bytes in the other side.

5.2 A 6-Round MitM Distinguisher and a 9-Round AES-192 Attack

We observe that the 5-round MitM distinguisher of Proposition 1 can be extended to a 6-round MitM distinguisher on AES-192. First, we have $z_7[13] = 0x09 \otimes w_7[12] \oplus 0x0e \otimes w_7[13] \oplus 0x0b \otimes w_7[14] \oplus 0x0d \otimes w_7[15]$ by the definition of the $\mathbf{M}^{-1}$ matrix, and $0x09 \otimes w_7[12] \oplus 0x0e \otimes w_7[13] \oplus 0x0b \otimes w_7[14] \oplus 0x0d \otimes w_7[15] = 0x09 \otimes (x_8[12] \oplus K_7[12]) \oplus 0x0e \otimes (x_8[13] \oplus K_7[13]) \oplus 0x0b \otimes (x_8[14] \oplus K_7[14]) \oplus 0x0d \otimes (x_8[15] \oplus K_7[15])$. Then, defining

$$\begin{aligned} e_{in} &= z_7[13], \\ e_{out} &= 0x09 \otimes x_8[12] \oplus 0x0e \otimes x_8[13] \oplus 0x0b \otimes x_8[14] \oplus 0x0d \otimes x_8[15], \end{aligned}$$

we have

$$e_{out} = e_{in} \oplus 0x09 \otimes K_7[12] \oplus 0x0e \otimes K_7[13] \oplus 0x0b \otimes K_7[14] \oplus 0x0d \otimes K_7[15].$$

Subsequently, we have the following 6-round distinguisher (refer also to Fig. 2) by computing e_{in}^i with $y_7^i[1]$ from the 5-round distinguisher of Proposition 1.

Proposition 2 (A 6-Round MitM Distinguisher on AES-192). *Encrypt the first 33 values $\{w_1^0, w_1^1, \cdots, w_1^{32}\}$ of a δ-set with byte (11) being active, through the 6-round AES-192 from the ARK operation of Round 1 to the ARK operation of Round 7. In case that a pair from the δ-set conforms to the 6-round truncated differential characteristic depicted in Fig. 2, the 256-bit ordered sequence $(e_{out}^1[1] \oplus e_{out}^0[1], e_{out}^2[1] \oplus e_{out}^0[1], \cdots, e_{out}^{32}[1] \oplus e_{out}^0[1])$ takes at most 2^{192} values (out of 2^{256} values theoretically).*

This 6-round distinguisher can be used to mount a MitM attack on 9-round AES-192, which is pretty similar to the 9-round AES-192 attack of Sect. 5.1, noting that $\Delta z_7[13]$ is equivalent to $\Delta x_8[12,13,14,15]$ and $\mathcal{T}_4$ should be modified to correspondingly store $(x_8[12,13,14,15], \Delta x_8[12,13,14,15])$ instead of $(\widehat{w}_7[13], \Delta z_7[13])$.

5.3 A Note

We note that another additional one-byte key relation Property 3-(13) (between the round keys of the precomputation phase and the round keys of the online phase) can be used to the 9-round attack of Sect. 5.1, but it does not produce a better result. We give this attack in the full version of this paper, where Property 3-(13) is used as an additional index to redefine the above $\mathcal{T}_4$, but this attack has the same memory complexity as but slightly larger data and time complexity than the 9-round attack of Sect. 5.1, although it is valid compared with exhaustive key search.

6 Conclusion

In this paper, we have described a few flaws in Li et al.'s 9-round AES-192 attacks, due to a wrong direction for the rotation operation of the AES-192 key schedule, have given a correct MitM distinguisher on 5-round AES-192, and have presented new MitM attacks on 9-round AES-192. Our 9-round AES-192 attacks correct and improve Li et al.'s 9-round AES-192 attacks. Particularly, we have demonstrated a trick for using more key relations between precomputational phase and online phase to further reduce memory complexity, which can potentially be used for MitM attacks on other block ciphers.

References

1. Biham, E., Shamir, A.: Differential Cryptanalysis of the Data Encryption Standard. Springer, New York (1993). https://doi.org/10.1007/978-1-4613-9314-6
2. Bogdanov, A., Khovratovich, D., Rechberger, C.: Biclique cryptanalysis of the full AES. In: Lee, D.H., Wang, X. (eds.) ASIACRYPT 2011. LNCS, vol. 7073, pp. 344–371. Springer, Heidelberg (2011). https://doi.org/10.1007/978-3-642-25385-0_19
3. Daemen, J., Rijmen, V.: The Design of Rijndael: AES–The Advanced Encryption Standard. Springer, Heidelberg (2002). https://doi.org/10.1007/978-3-662-04722-4
4. Daemen, J., Rijmen, V.: Understanding two-round differentials in AES. In: De Prisco, R., Yung, M. (eds.) SCN 2006. LNCS, vol. 4116, pp. 78–94. Springer, Heidelberg (2006). https://doi.org/10.1007/11832072_6
5. Demirci, H., Selçuk, A.A.: A Meet-in-the-middle attack on 8-round AES. In: Nyberg, K. (ed.) FSE 2008. LNCS, vol. 5086, pp. 116–126. Springer, Heidelberg (2008). https://doi.org/10.1007/978-3-540-71039-4_7
6. Derbez, P., Fouque, P.A.: Exhausting Demirci-Selçuk meet-in-the-middle attacks against reduced-round AES. In: Moriai, S. (ed.) FSE 2013. LNCS, vol. 8424, pp. 541–560. Springer, Heidelberg (2014). https://doi.org/10.1007/978-3-662-43933-3_28
7. Derbez, P., Fouque, P.A.: Automatic search of meet-in-the-middle and impossible differential attacks. In: Robshaw, M., Katz, J. (eds.) CRYPTO 2016. LNCS, vol. 9815, pp. 157–184. Springer, Heidelberg (2014). https://doi.org/10.1007/978-3-662-53008-5_6
8. Derbez, P., Fouque, P.A., Jean, J.: Improved key recovery attacks on reduced-round AES in the single-key setting. In: Johansson, T., Nguyen, P.Q. (eds.) EUROCRYPT 2013. LNCS, vol. 7881, pp. 371–387. Springer, Heidelberg (2013). https://doi.org/10.1007/978-3-642-38348-9_23

9. Diffie, W., Hellman, M.: Exhaustive cryptanalysis of the NBS data encryption standard. Computer **10**(6), 74–84 (1977)
10. Dunkelman, O., Keller, N., Shamir, A.: Improved single-key attacks on 8-round AES-192 and AES-256. In: Abe, M. (ed.) ASIACRYPT 2010. LNCS, vol. 6477, pp. 158–176. Springer, Heidelberg (2010). https://doi.org/10.1007/978-3-642-17373-8_10
11. Ferguson, N., et al.: Improved cryptanalysis of Rijndael. In: Schneier, B. (ed.) FSE 2000. LNCS, vol. 1978, pp. 213–230. Springer, Heidelberg (2001). https://doi.org/10.1007/3-540-44706-7_15
12. Gilbert, H., Minier, M.: A collision attack on 7 rounds of Rijndael. In: The Third Advanced Encryption Standard Candidate Conference, pp. 230–241. NIST (2000)
13. Gilbert, H., Peyrin, T.: Super-Sbox cryptanalysis: improved attacks for AES-like permutations. In: Hong, S., Iwata, T. (eds.) FSE 2010. LNCS, vol. 6147, pp. 365–383. Springer, Heidelberg (2010). https://doi.org/10.1007/978-3-642-13858-4_21
14. Knudsen, L.R.: Truncated and higher order differentials. In: Preneel, B. (ed.) FSE 1994. LNCS, vol. 1008, pp. 196–211. Springer, Heidelberg (1995). https://doi.org/10.1007/3-540-60590-8_16
15. Li, L., Jia, K., Wang, X.: Improved single-key attacks on 9-round AES-192/256. In: Cid, C., Rechberger, C. (eds.) FSE 2014. LNCS, vol. 8540, pp. 127–146. Springer, Heidelberg (2015). https://doi.org/10.1007/978-3-662-46706-0_7
16. Li, R., Jin, C.: Meet-in-the-middle attacks on 10-round AES-256. Des. Codes Cryptogr. **80**(3), 459–471 (2016). https://doi.org/10.1007/s10623-015-0113-3
17. Lu, J., Dunkelman, O., Keller, N., Kim, J.: New impossible differential attacks on AES. In: Chowdhury, D.R., Rijmen, V., Das, A. (eds.) INDOCRYPT 2008. LNCS, vol. 5365, pp. 279–293. Springer, Heidelberg (2008). https://doi.org/10.1007/978-3-540-89754-5_22
18. National Institute of Standards and Technology (NIST). Advanced Encryption Standard (AES), FIPS-197 (2001)
19. Wang, G., Zhu, C.: Single key recovery attacks on reduced AES-192 and Kalyna-128/256. Sci. China Inf. Sci. **60**, 099101:1-099101:3 (2017). https://doi.org/10.1007/s11432-016-0417-7
20. Wang, G., Zhu, C.: Single key recovery attacks on reduced AES-192 and Kalyna-128/256. Supplementary File

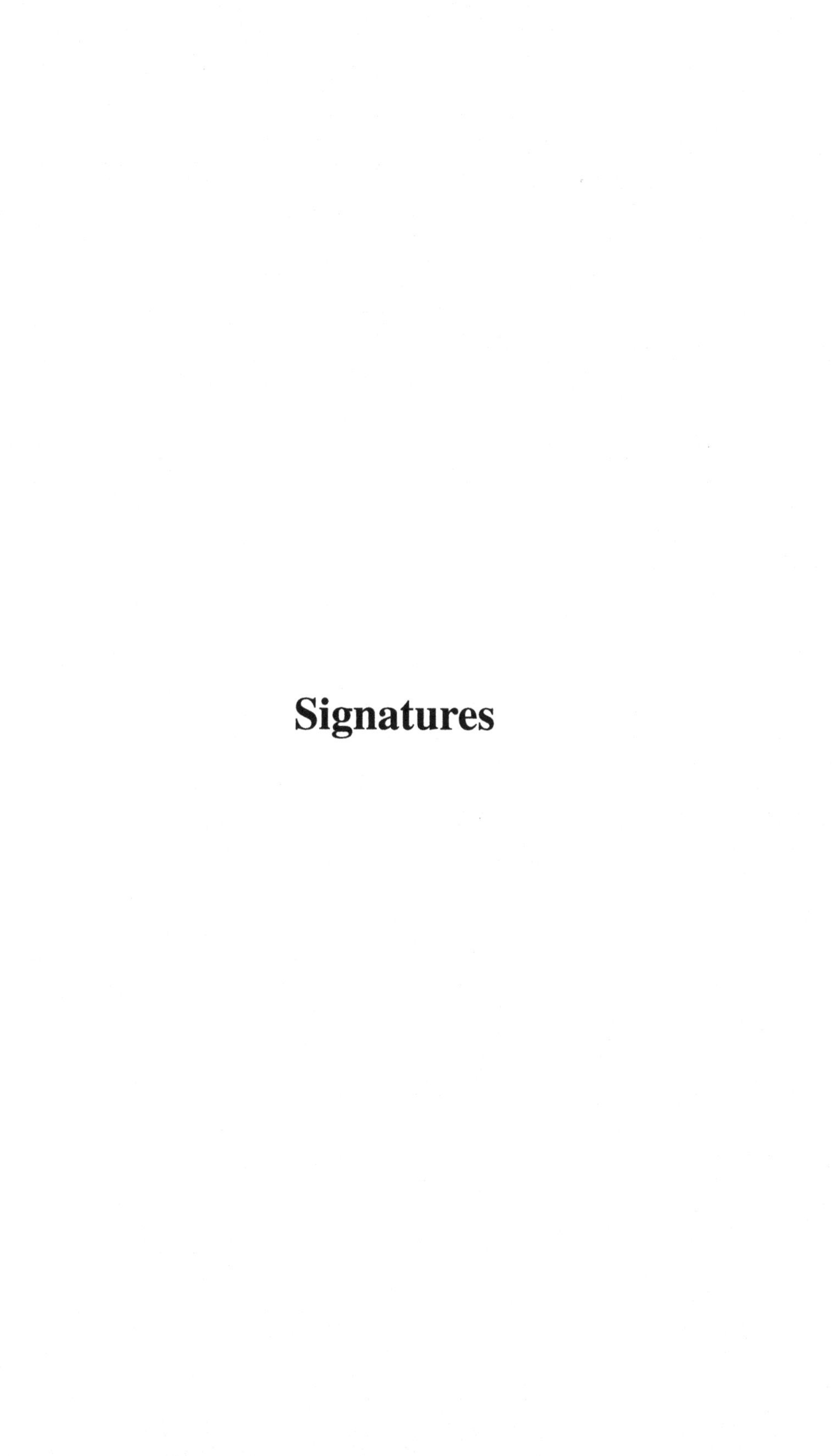

Signatures

Batch Signatures, Revisited

Carlos Aguilar-Melchor[1], Martin R. Albrecht[1], Thomas Bailleux[1], Nina Bindel[1(✉)], James Howe[1], Andreas Hülsing[1,2], David Joseph[1], and Marc Manzano[1]

[1] SandboxAQ, Palo Alto, CA, USA
{carlos.aguilar-melchor,martin.albrecht,thomas.bailleux,nina.bindel, james.howe,andreas.hulsing,david.joseph,marc.manzano}@sandboxaq.com
[2] Eindhoven University of Technology, Eindhoven, The Netherlands

Abstract. We revisit batch signatures (previously considered in a draft RFC and used in multiple recent works), where a single, potentially expensive, "inner" digital signature authenticates a Merkle tree constructed from many messages. We formalise a construction and prove its unforgeability and privacy properties.

We also show that batch signing allows us to scale slow signing algorithms, such as those recently selected for standardisation as part of NIST's post-quantum project, to high throughput, with a mild increase in latency and demonstrate the practical efficiency of batch signing in the context of TLS. For the example of Falcon-512 in TLS, we can increase the amount of connections per second by a factor 3.2, at the cost of an increase in the signature size by 14% and the median latency by 25%; both run on the same 30 core server. For SPHINCS$^+$-128, throughput improves by a factor 4.6, with a negligible impact on signature size and an 11% impact on median latency.

We also discuss applications where batch signatures allow us to increase throughput and to save bandwidth. For example, again for 16 Falcon-512 signatures, once one batch signature is available, the additional bandwidth for each of the remaining is only 82 bytes.

1 Introduction

The computational complexity of unkeyed and symmetric cryptography is known to be significantly lower than asymmetric cryptography. Indeed, hash functions, stream or block ciphers typically require between a few cycles [ADWF+10] to a few hundred cycles [GK12], whereas key establishment and digital signature primitives require between tens of thousands to hundreds of millions of cycles [BL18]. In situations where a substantial volume of signatures must be handled – e.g. a Hardware Security Module (HSM) renewing a large set of short-lived certificates or a load balancer terminating a large number of TLS connections per second – this may pose serious limitations on scaling these and related scenarios.

These challenges are amplified by upcoming public-key cryptography standards: In July 2022, the US National Institute of Standards and Technology (NIST) announced four algorithms for post-quantum cryptography

E. Oswald (Ed.): CT-RSA 2024, LNCS 14643, pp. 163–186, 2024.
https://doi.org/10.1007/978-3-031-58868-6_7

(PQC) standardisation. In particular, three digital signature algorithms – Dilithium [LDK+22], Falcon [PFH+22] and SPHINCS$^+$ [HBD+22] – were selected, and migration from current standards to these new algorithms is already underway [You22]. One of the key issues when considering migrating to PQC is that the computational costs of the new digital signature algorithms are significantly higher than those of ECDSA; the fastest currently-deployed primitive for signing. This severely impacts the ability of systems to scale and inhibits their migration to PQC, especially in higher-throughput settings.

For instance, at a 128-bit security level, using the standard SUPERCOP platform benchmarks on a Core i7 Tigerlake processor [BL18], ECDSA over an Edwards curve requires 85K cycles for signing. The equivalent Dilithium, Falcon and SPHINCS$^+$ signatures need 272K, 570K and 25M cycles, respectively (considering the fastest alternative among existing variants for each).[1] The performance gap between ECDSA and the three PQC alternatives is vast. Furthermore, there are good reasons to choose Falcon or SPHINCS$^+$ over Dilithium for certain scenarios, which increases the gap further: Falcon provides smaller signatures and verification key sizes which makes it a strong contender in networking applications and SPHINCS$^+$ relies on conservative security assumptions which are appropriate for long-term security.

In 2020 an RFC draft [Ben20] proposed *Batch Signing for TLS* to solve existing scalability challenges of classical digital signature standards in a high-throughput TLS setting. In this approach, one expensive "inner" signing operation signs the root of a Merkle tree constructed from a batch of messages. Then, the final signature for each message contains the sibling nodes of a message to recover the Merkle tree's root and the original "inner" signature. This represents a logarithmic increase in the signature size but asymptotically reduces the amortised cost to a few hash computations. The draft was not finalised and thus has now become a deprecated TLS working group document [Ben22]. While the proposal was motivated by classical signature standards and TLS, the approach can be generalised and used with any signature scheme, e.g. with one of the PQC schemes and in a myriad of additional settings.

Other recent works have considered using Merkle trees to reduce (amortised) signature sizes in certificates by signing them in batches and using the fact that they all share the same "inner" signature. A recent work [FHKS22] focuses on *stateful* signatures targeting such signature size reduction. Stateful signature schemes are capable of producing small signatures, which are ideal for use cases such as certificate authorities (CAs), but at the expense of a more involved design, with the critical need for state management. A *stateless* approach, in contrast, generalises more easily and allows for a more flexible design applicable to a plethora of use cases for increasing the throughput of signature schemes. A recent RFC draft [BOW23] proposes a stateless system to reduce certificate sizes by defining CAs that only sign certificates in batches and rely on a Certificate Transparency channel to deliver the large "inner" signatures.

These works highlight the increasing community interest in batch signatures.

[1] See also the discussion of Falcon's performance in Sect. 2.3.

1.1 Contributions

In this work, we study batch signatures and provide (i) a refinement of the construction from [Ben20] to reduce the size by removing the collision-resistance property from the requirements of the hash function used to build the Merkle tree, (ii) a formal treatment of the unforgeability and privacy of batch signatures, (iii) a description of several settings in which batch signatures can have a positive impact in terms of either throughput increase or bandwidth reduction and (iv) an empirical study into batch signatures for both classical and PQC schemes in the context of TLS and certificate signing.

In more detail, after some preliminaries in Sect. 2, we formally define batch signing and its security properties in Sect. 3. In particular, in addition to the usual unforgeability property, we also define batch privacy notions that essentially control the leakage of information due to signing in batches. We define two variants of batch privacy, with our construction achieving the weaker one. We then specify our batch signing scheme in Sect. 4, which is essentially a refined version of that in [Ben20]. The main difference is that we do not need to rely on collision resistance but instead on target collision resistance [BHK+19], allowing us to pick smaller parameters and thus reduce the signature size. The intuition here is roughly that the adversary has to commit to a set of images it will find a second preimage for before seeing the hash function. We prove the security properties of our construction in Sect. 5. We describe some realistic applications where batch signatures can provide significant improvements for throughput and bandwidth in Sect. 6. For the latter, the intuition is that the large "inner signature" can be cached and reused. Finally, we describe our implementation for TLS in Sect. 7.

1.2 Discussion

Latency. Overall, our performance study indicates that, while the amortised approach introduces a logarithmic overhead in signature sizes (cf. Table 1) and median signing latency (in some settings), it significantly reduces the CPU burden (cf. Table 2) allowing us to scale to a larger number of signatures per second compared with the plain approach using the same number of cores. The median latency increase is due to the additional waiting phase for batching. It applies in a setting where the number of requests is below the peak of what the 'plain' solution can handle. Once that threshold is reached, the approach discussed here indeed has lower latency per resource, by avoiding the queue incurred in the 'plain' version.

Size. The approach in this work can be seen as trading a small increase in signature size for increased throughput or computational efficiency. This might seem counter-intuitive or -productive when practitioners are chiefly concerned with the difficulty of handling post-quantum signature sizes, see e.g. [Wes21]. However, in many high-throughput applications size is not the chief concern. A

Table 1. Batch signature sizes for a targeted security level λ.

Scheme	λ	$\lvert\mathsf{vk}\rvert$	$\lvert\sigma\rvert$	N	$\lvert\mathsf{sig}\rvert$	$\lvert\mathsf{sig}_c\rvert$
ECDSA P256	128	64	64	32	180	98
Dilithium2	128	1312	2420	32	2536	98
Dilithium5	256	2592	4595	32	4823	194
Falcon-512	128	897	666	16	766	82
Falcon-1024	256	1793	1280	32	1508	194
Falcon-512-fpuemu	128	897	666	16	766	82
Falcon-1024-fpuemu	256	1793	1280	16	1476	162
SPHINCS$^+$-128f	128	32	17088	16	17188	82
SPHINCS$^+$-256f	256	64	49856	32	50084	194

All sizes, indicated by $|\cdot|$, are in bytes. Batch signature size is given in the column $|\mathsf{sig}|$, verification key size in $|\mathsf{vk}|$, "inner" signature size in $|\sigma|$; all for a batch of N messages. The compressed batch signature size, assuming the inner signature for multiple batch signatures is cached, is given in column $|\mathsf{sig}_c|$. We assume two bytes are used to encode N in sig; λ matches that of the inner signature scheme.
Signature sizes (or certificates) typically grow by fewer than one hundred bytes. This represents, for the algorithms considered (except ECDSA), at most ten percent when considering signatures and at most five percent when considering certificates (signatures + verification keys).

prime example is a typical website which is several orders of magnitude larger than a PQC signature. Web browsers can easily handle signatures of this size.

To give an illustrative example, a median website is about 2 MB in size [HTT23]. In contrast, the amortised signature size for Falcon-512 and $N = 16$ is 766 bytes, or 100 bytes larger than 'plain' Falcon-512. On the sender side, there is, too, an increase of 100B per connection on top of serving 2 MB+ of traffic per connection. In addition, sending these additional bytes also has a computing cost. In our example, signature sizes increase from 666 to 766, so transmission costs go up by 16%. In contrast, signing costs go down by 50%. While the cost per byte transmitted will vary depending on context, it is reasonable to assume that it would easily be dwarfed by the CPU cost savings.

Finally, we recall that for some applications we indeed get a bandwidth *reduction*, see Sect. 6.2.

2 Preliminaries

We write $x \leftarrow y$ for assigning y to x and $x \leftarrow\!\$\, \mathcal{D}$ for sampling x from some distribution $\mathcal{D}$. If $\mathcal{D}$ is a finite set, we assume the uniform distribution over this set. We write PPT for probabilistic polynomial time and BQP for bounded-error quantum polynomial time.

Table 2. Handshakes per second and latency for different percentiles in TLS using different signing algorithms.

Scheme and Instantiation		Handshakes Per Second	Latency (ms) med	p90	p99
ECDSA P256	Plain	39,000	1.2	1.3	1.5
	MT N=32, C=1	49,000	1.3	1.7	2.7
Dilithium2	Plain	29,000	1.6	1.8	2.1
	MT N=32, C=1	50,000	1.8	2.2	2.7
Dilithium5	Plain	25,000	1.9	2.2	2.4
	MT N=32, C=1	43,000	2.2	2.6	3.2
Falcon-512	Plain	28,000	1.1	1.3	1.5
	MT N=16, C=2	43,000	1.5	1.8	2.5
Falcon-1024	Plain	24,000	2.0	2.1	2.3
	MT N=32, C=2	43,000	2.2	2.5	3.3
Falcon-512 (fpemu)	Plain	5,000	5.1	5.2	6.0
	MT N=16, C=8	16,000	6.4	7.6	8.4
Falcon-1024 (fpemu)	Plain	2,600	9.9	10.0	11.0
	MT N=16, C=8	8,200	12.0	15.0	17.0
SPHINCS$^+$-128f	Plain	1,500	13.0	13.3	14.6
	MT N=16, C=16	7,000	14.5	16.5	21.0
SPHINCS$^+$-256f	Plain	750	33.7	34.3	38.3
	MT N=32, C=16	2,800	36.8	40.8	48.6

All experiments are run on a 30 core machine with HyperThreading disabled. The results are presented for a 'plain' multi-threaded implementation (pool of as many threads as CPU cores, with select/poll handling) and for the Merkle Tree (MT) approach with a limit N to the maximum size of a tree. The amount of cores used for signatures is fixed (by reserving cores explicitly) for the Merkle Tree approach and given as C. The 'plain' implementation may use all cores as needed.
The number of handshakes per second increases roughly by a factor of 1.5 for fast algorithms and multiplied by a factor between three and four for slow algorithms. Latency (99th percentile) is increased by roughly fifty percent (one millisecond for fast algorithms and up to six milliseconds for the slower ones).

2.1 Hash Functions

In this work we consider *tweakable* hash functions. These are keyed hash functions that take an additional input which can be thought of as a domain separator (while the key or public parameter serves as a separator between users). Tweakable hash functions allow us to tightly achieve target collision resistance even in multi-target settings where an adversary wins when they manage to attack one out of many targets.

Definition 1 (Tweakable Hash Function [BHK+19]**).** *Let $n, m \in \mathbb{N}$, let $\mathcal{P}$ be the public parameters space and $\mathcal{T}$ the tweak space. A* tweakable hash function *is a tuple of algorithms $\mathsf{H} = (\mathsf{KeyGen}, \mathsf{Eval})$ such that:*

KeyGen *The setup function takes the security parameter 1^λ and outputs a (possibly empty) public parameter p. We write $p \leftarrow \mathsf{KeyGen}(1^\lambda)$.*

Eval *The evaluation function takes public parameters p, a tweak t, an input $x \in \{0,1\}^m$ and returns a hash value h. We write $h \leftarrow \mathsf{Eval}(p, t, x)$ or simply $h \leftarrow \mathsf{H}(p, t, x)$. This is a deterministic function.*

In what follows, we will avoid relying on plain collision resistance but target collision resistance of tweakable hash functions.

Definition 2 (Target Collision Resistant Hash Function [BHK+19]**).** *An efficient tweakable hash function $\mathsf{H} = (\mathsf{KeyGen}, \mathsf{Eval})$ is called single-function multiple-targets target-collision resistant for distinct tweaks (SM-TCR) if the advantage $\mathsf{Adv}^{sm-tcr}_{\mathcal{A},\mathsf{H}}(k, \lambda)$ of any (PPT/ BQP) algorithms $\mathcal{A} = (\mathcal{A}_0, \mathcal{A}_1)$ that define up to k targets in the SM-TCR experiment defined in Fig. 1 is negligible with*

$$\mathsf{Adv}^{sm\text{-}tcr}_{\mathcal{A},\mathsf{H}}(k, \lambda) := \Pr\left[\text{SM-TCR}^{\mathcal{A}}_{\mathsf{H}}(k, \lambda) \Rightarrow 1\right].$$

$\text{SM-TCR}^{\mathcal{A}}_{\mathsf{H}}(k, \lambda)$

$P \leftarrow \mathsf{KeyGen}(1^\lambda)$
$S \leftarrow \mathcal{A}_0^{\mathsf{H}(P,\cdot,\cdot)}(1^\lambda)$
// $\mathcal{Q} = \{(t_0, \mu_0), \ldots, (t_{k-1}, \mu_{k-1})\}$ queries submitted to $\mathsf{H}(P, \cdot, \cdot)$
for $i, \ell \in \{0, \ldots, k-1\}, i \neq \ell$ **do**
  if $t_i = t_\ell$: **return** $\perp$
$(j, \mu) \leftarrow \mathcal{A}_1(1^\lambda, S, P, \mathcal{Q})$
return $0 \leq j < k \land \mu \neq \mu_j \land \mathsf{H}(P, t_j, \mu_j) = \mathsf{H}(P, t_j, \mu)$

Fig. 1. Single-function, Multi-Target Collision Resistance for distinct tweaks (SM-TCR).

We will also rely on one-time pseudrandomness to argue privacy.

Definition 3 (OT-PRF). *Let $n, m \in \mathbb{N}$, $\mathsf{F} : \{0,1\}^\lambda \times \{0,1\}^m \to \{0,1\}^n$ be a keyed function. We define*

$$\mathsf{Adv}^{\text{ot-prf}}_{\mathcal{A},\mathsf{F}}(\lambda) := \Pr[\text{OT-PRF}^{\mathcal{A}}_{\mathsf{F}}(\lambda) \Rightarrow 1]$$

for $\text{OT-PRF}^{\mathcal{A}}_{\mathsf{F}}(\lambda)$ *as in Fig. 2 and say* F *is an OT-PRF if no PPT/BQP adversary* $\mathcal{A}$ *has non-negligible advantage* $\mathsf{Adv}^{\text{ot-prf}}_{\mathcal{A},\mathsf{F}}(\lambda)$.

Commit	RoR(x)
$b \leftarrow\!\!\$\ \{0,1\}$	$k \leftarrow\!\!\$\ \{0,1\}^\lambda$
$b' \leftarrow \mathcal{A}^{\text{RoR}(\cdot)}()$	$y_0 \leftarrow \mathsf{F}(k, x)$
return $b = b'$	$y_1 \leftarrow\!\!\$\ \{0,1\}^n$
	return y_b

Fig. 2. One-time Pseudorandom Function (OT-PRF).

2.2 Digital Signatures

Definition 4 (Signature Scheme). *A signature scheme* S *consists of three PPT algorithms* ($\mathsf{KeyGen}, \mathsf{Sign}, \mathsf{Verify}$) *such that:*

KeyGen *The key generation algorithm is a randomised algorithm that takes as input a security parameter* 1^λ *and outputs a pair* $(\mathsf{vk}, \mathsf{sk})$, *the* verification key *and* signing key, *respectively. We write* $(\mathsf{vk}, \mathsf{sk}) \leftarrow \mathsf{KeyGen}(1^\lambda)$.

Sign *The signing algorithm takes as input a signing key* sk, *a message* μ *and outputs a signature* σ. *We write this as* $\sigma \leftarrow \mathsf{Sign}(\mathsf{sk}, \mu)$. *The signing algorithm may be randomised or deterministic. We may write* $\sigma \leftarrow \mathsf{Sign}(\mathsf{sk}, \mu; r)$ *to unearth the used randomness explicitly.*

Verify *The verification algorithm takes as input a verification key* vk, *a signature* σ *and a message* μ *and outputs a bit* b, *with* $b = 1$ *meaning the signature is valid and* $b = 0$ *meaning the signature is invalid.* Verify *is a deterministic algorithm. We write* $b \leftarrow \mathsf{Verify}(\mathsf{vk}, \sigma, \mu)$.

We require that except with negligible probability over $(\mathsf{vk}, \mathsf{sk}) \leftarrow \mathsf{KeyGen}(1^\lambda)$, *it holds that* $\mathsf{Verify}(\mathsf{vk}, \mathsf{Sign}(\mathsf{sk}, \mu), \mu) = 1$ *for all* μ.

We rely on the standard notion of existential unforgeability under chosen message attacks (EUF-CMA):

Definition 5 (EUF-CMA). *We define*

$$\mathsf{Adv}^{\text{euf-cma}}_{\mathcal{A},\mathsf{S}}(\lambda) := \Pr[\text{EUF-CMA}^{\mathcal{A}}_{\mathsf{S}}(\lambda) \Rightarrow 1]$$

for $\text{EUF-CMA}^{\mathcal{A}}_{\mathsf{S}}(\lambda)$ *as in Fig. 3 and say a signature scheme* S *is EUF-CMA secure if no PPT/BQP adversary* $\mathcal{A}$ *has non-negligible advantage* $\mathsf{Adv}^{\text{euf-cma}}_{\mathcal{A},\mathsf{S}}(\lambda)$.

$\text{EUF-CMA}_{\mathsf{S}}^{\mathcal{A}}(\lambda)$ / $\text{BEUF-CMA}_{\mathsf{S}}^{\mathcal{A}}(\lambda)$	$\text{SIGN}(\mu)$
$\mathcal{Q} \leftarrow \emptyset$	$\sigma \leftarrow \mathsf{Sign}(\mathsf{sk}, \mu)$
$\mathsf{vk}, \mathsf{sk} \leftarrow \mathsf{KeyGen}(1^\lambda)$	$\mathcal{Q} \leftarrow \mathcal{Q} \cup \{(\mu, \sigma)\}$
$(\mu^\star, \sigma^\star) \leftarrow \mathcal{A}^{\text{SIGN}}(\mathsf{vk})$ // EUF-CMA	**return** σ
$(\mu^\star, \sigma^\star) \leftarrow \mathcal{A}^{\text{BSIGN}}(\mathsf{vk})$ // BEUF-CMA	$\text{BSIGN}(\mathcal{M})$
return $(\mu^\star, \cdot) \notin \mathcal{Q} \wedge \mathsf{Verify}(\mathsf{vk}, \sigma^\star, \mu^\star) = 1$	$\mathcal{S} \leftarrow \mathsf{Sign}(\mathsf{sk}, \mathcal{M})$
	for $0 \le j < \lvert\mathcal{M}\rvert$ **do**
	$q_j \leftarrow (\mathcal{M}[j], \mathcal{S}[j])$
	$\mathcal{Q} \leftarrow \mathcal{Q} \cup \{q_j\}$
	return $\mathcal{S}$

Fig. 3. Existential Unforgeability under Chosen Message Attacks for Signatures (EUF-CMA) and Batch Signatures (BEUF-CMA).

Remark 1. In our construction, the signature scheme takes as inputs and outputs *batches* of messages and signatures, respectively. We formally define batch signature schemes and their security (BEUF-CMA) in Sect. 3.

2.3 Falcon Signature Scheme

Since our flagship demonstrator is the composition of our scheme with Falcon [PFH+20] (based on the GPV paradigm [GPV08]), we give a stylised description in Fig. 4, as this is sufficient for our purposes here. Let (TrapGen, SampD, SampPre) be PPT algorithms with the following syntax and properties [GPV08, MP12, GM18]:

- $(\boldsymbol{A}, \mathsf{td}) \leftarrow \mathsf{TrapGen}(1^\eta, 1^\ell, q, \mathcal{R}, \beta)$ takes dimensions $\eta, \ell \in \mathbb{N}$, a modulus $q \in \mathbb{N}$, a ring $\mathcal{R}$ and a norm bound $\beta \in \mathbb{R}$. It generates a matrix $\boldsymbol{A} \in \mathcal{R}_q^{\eta \times \ell}$ and a trapdoor td. For any $n \in \mathsf{poly}(\lambda)$ and $\ell \geq \mathsf{lhl}(\mathcal{R}, \eta, q, \beta)$, the distribution of $\boldsymbol{A}$ is within $\mathsf{negl}(\lambda)$ statistical distance to the uniform distribution on $\mathcal{R}_q^{\eta \times \ell}$.
- $\boldsymbol{u} \leftarrow \mathsf{SampD}(1^\eta, 1^\ell, \mathcal{R}, \beta')$ with $\ell \geq \mathsf{lhl}(\mathcal{R}, \eta, q, \beta)$ outputs an element in $\boldsymbol{u} \in \mathcal{R}^\ell$ with norm bound $\beta' \geq \beta$. We have that $\boldsymbol{v} := \boldsymbol{A} \cdot \boldsymbol{u} \bmod q$ is within $\mathsf{negl}(\lambda)$ statistical distance to the uniform distribution on $\mathcal{R}_q^\eta$.
- $\boldsymbol{u} \leftarrow \mathsf{SampPre}(\mathsf{td}, \boldsymbol{v}, \beta')$ with $\ell \geq \mathsf{lhl}(\mathcal{R}, \eta, q, \beta)$ takes a trapdoor td, a vector $\boldsymbol{v} \in \mathcal{R}_q^\eta$ and a norm bound $\beta' \geq \beta$. It samples $\boldsymbol{u} \in \mathcal{R}^\ell$ satisfying $\boldsymbol{A} \cdot \boldsymbol{u} \equiv \boldsymbol{v} \bmod q$ and $\|\boldsymbol{u}\| \leq \beta'$. Furthermore, $\boldsymbol{u}$ is within $\mathsf{negl}(\lambda)$ statistical distance to $\boldsymbol{u} \leftarrow \mathsf{SampD}(1^\eta, 1^\ell, \mathcal{R}, \beta')$ conditioned on $\boldsymbol{v} \equiv \boldsymbol{A} \cdot \boldsymbol{u} \bmod q$.

Assumption 1. *The Falcon signature scheme is EUF-CMA secure. In particular, no (quantum) adversary exists to forge messages with cost $\ll 2^{128}$ for Falcon-512 and no such adversary exists with cost $\ll 2^{256}$ for Falcon-1024.*

$\mathsf{KeyGen}(1^\lambda)$	$\mathsf{Sign}(\mu_j, \mathsf{sk}_i; r)$
$\boldsymbol{A}, \mathsf{td} \leftarrow \mathsf{TrapGen}(1^1, 1^2, q, \mathcal{R}, \beta)$	$\boldsymbol{y}_j \leftarrow \mathsf{SampPre}(\mathsf{td}, H(\mu_j, r), \beta')$
return $\mathsf{vk}_i = \boldsymbol{A}, \mathsf{sk}_i = \mathsf{td}$	**return** $\boldsymbol{y}$
$\mathsf{Verify}(\sigma_j, \mu_j, \mathsf{vk}_i)$	
return $\|\boldsymbol{y}_j\| \overset{?}{\leq} \beta' \wedge H(\mu_j) \overset{?}{\equiv} \boldsymbol{A} \cdot \boldsymbol{y}_j$	

Fig. 4. Falcon signatures [GPV08,PFH+22].

Performance. Consider Falcon-512 which minimises the signature size among the NIST selected post-quantum signature algorithms. An optimised implementation beats RSA-2048 signing by roughly a factor of five [BL18]. Critically, however, this optimised implementation relies on constant-time double-precision floating point arithmetic. This is not completely out of reach, as demonstrated by constant-time Falcon implementations [Por19] on several different CPUs, working around several CPU instructions' behaviours. However, the long-term reliability of this approach is less certain than for bit or integer operations. That is, future instructions or optimisations might prevent the desired constant-time behaviour. Furthermore, many CPUs to date simply lack fast constant-time double-precision arithmetic [HW22].

On systems where no sufficiently constant-time floating point unit is available or where floating-point arithmetic is avoided for the reasons mentioned above, floating-point arithmetic can be emulated (in constant time) at a hefty – approximately 20x – overhead [Por19].

3 Batch Signatures

We formally define batch signatures.

Definition 6 (Batch Signature Scheme). *A batch signature scheme* S *consists of three PPT algorithms* $(\mathsf{KeyGen}, \mathsf{BSign}, \mathsf{Verify})$ *such that:*

KeyGen *The key generation algorithm is a randomised algorithm that takes as input a security parameter* 1^λ *and outputs a pair* $(\mathsf{vk}, \mathsf{sk})$, *the* verification key *and* signing key, *respectively. We write* $(\mathsf{vk}, \mathsf{sk}) \leftarrow \mathsf{KeyGen}(1^\lambda)$.

BSign *The batch signing algorithm takes as input a signing key* sk, *a list of messages* $\mathcal{M} = \{\mu_i\}$ *and outputs a list of signatures* $\mathcal{S} = \{\mathsf{sig}_i\}$. *We write this as* $\mathcal{S} \leftarrow \mathsf{BSign}(\mathsf{sk}, \mathcal{M})$. *The signing algorithm may be randomised or deterministic. We may write* $\mathcal{S} \leftarrow \mathsf{BSign}(\mathsf{sk}, \mathcal{M}; r)$ *to unearth the used randomness explicitly.*

Verify *The verification algorithm takes as input a verification key* vk, *a signature* sig *and a message* μ *and outputs a bit* b, *with* $b = 1$ *meaning the signature is valid and* $b = 0$ *meaning the signature is invalid.* Verify *is a deterministic algorithm. We write* $b \leftarrow \mathsf{Verify}(\mathsf{vk}, \mathsf{sig}, \mu)$.

We require that except with negligible probability over $(\mathsf{vk}, \mathsf{sk}) \leftarrow \mathsf{KeyGen}(1^\lambda)$, *for all* $\mathcal{M} := \{\mu_i\}$ *and* $\mathcal{S} \leftarrow \mathsf{BSign}(\mathsf{sk}, \{\mu_i\})$ *it holds for all* $\mathsf{sig}_i \in \mathcal{S}$ *that* $\mathsf{Verify}(\mathsf{vk}, \mathsf{sig}_i, \mu_i) = 1$.

Definition 7 (EUF-CMA for Batch Signature Schemes). *We define*

$$\mathsf{Adv}^{\text{euf-cma}}_{\mathcal{A},\mathsf{S}}(\lambda) := \Pr[\text{BEUF-CMA}^{\mathcal{A}}_{\mathsf{S}}(\lambda) \Rightarrow 1]$$

for BEUF-CMA$^{\mathcal{A}}_{\mathsf{S}}(\lambda)$ *as in Fig. 3 and say that a batch signature scheme* S *is EUF-CMA secure if no PPT/BQP adversary* $\mathcal{A}$ *has non-negligible advantage* $\mathsf{Adv}^{\text{euf-cma}}_{\mathcal{A},\mathsf{S}}(\lambda)$.

The following proposition is immediate, by simply calling Sign for all $\mu_i \in \mathcal{M}$. We call this the *naïve construction.*

Proposition 1. *Every EUF-CMA secure signature scheme can be turned into an EUF-CMA secure batch signature scheme.*

We also define two privacy notions for batch signatures. These assert that no efficient adversary can distinguish whether signatures were signed in the same batch or not. A weak variant of privacy only guarantees that signatures from the same batch do not leak anything about a message for which no signature is made available.

BATCH-PRIV$^{\mathcal{A}}_{\mathsf{S}}(\lambda)$	SIGN($\mathcal{M}$)
$b \leftarrow\$ \{0,1\}$	**if** $b = 0$ **then**
$b^\star \leftarrow \mathcal{A}^{\text{SIGN}}(\mathsf{vk})$	**for** $\mu_i \in \mathcal{M}$ **do**
return $b^\star = b$	$\{\mathsf{sig}_i\} \leftarrow \mathsf{BSign}(\mathsf{sk}, \{\mu_i\})$
	$\mathcal{S} \leftarrow \{\mathsf{sig}_i\}_{0 \le i < \lvert\mathcal{M}\rvert}$
	else
	$\mathcal{S} \leftarrow \mathsf{BSign}(\mathsf{sk}, \mathcal{M})$
	return $\mathcal{S}$

wBATCH-PRIV$^{\mathcal{A}}_{\mathsf{S}}(\lambda)$	SIGN($\mathcal{M}, i, \{\mu_0, \mu_1\}$)
$b \leftarrow\$ \{0,1\}$	**if** $i \geq \lvert\mathcal{M}\rvert \vee i < 0$ **then return** $\bot$
$b^\star \leftarrow \mathcal{A}^{\text{SIGN}}(\mathsf{vk})$	$\mathcal{M}_i \leftarrow \mu_b$ // i-th message is μ_b
return $b^\star = b$	$\mathcal{S} \leftarrow \mathsf{BSign}(\mathsf{sk}, \mathcal{M})$
	$\mathcal{S}_i \leftarrow \bot$ // delete i-th signature
	return $\mathcal{S}$

Fig. 5. (Weak) Batch Privacy.

Definition 8 ((Weak) Batch Privacy). *We define*

$$\mathsf{Adv}_{\mathcal{A},\mathsf{S}}^{\text{batch-priv}}(\lambda) := \left|\Pr[\text{BATCH-PRIV}_{\mathsf{S}}^{\mathcal{A}}(\lambda) \Rightarrow 1] - 1/2\right|$$

and

$$\mathsf{Adv}_{\mathcal{A},\mathsf{S}}^{\text{wbatch-priv}}(\lambda) := \left|\Pr[\text{wBATCH-PRIV}_{\mathsf{S}}^{\mathcal{A}}(\lambda) \Rightarrow 1] - 1/2\right|$$

for the games defined in Fig. 5 and say a signature scheme S *has (weak) batch privacy if no PPT/BQP adversary* $\mathcal{A}$ *has non-negligible advantage* $\mathsf{Adv}_{\mathcal{A},\mathsf{S}}^{\text{(w)batch-priv}}(\lambda)$.

Our construction in Sect. 4 achieves wBATCH-PRIV but not BATCH-PRIV and thus establishes that there are schemes achieving the former but not the latter. Next, we establish that an adversary breaking wBATCH-PRIV can also break BATCH-PRIV.

Lemma 1. *Let* $\mathcal{A}$ *be an adversary against* wBATCH-PRIV *with* $\mathsf{Adv}_{\mathcal{A},\mathsf{S}}^{\text{wbatch-priv}}(\lambda)$. *Then there is an adversary* $\mathcal{B}$ *against* BATCH-PRIV *with advantage*

$$\mathsf{Adv}_{\mathcal{B},\mathsf{S}}^{\text{batch-priv}}(\lambda) \geq 1/2 \cdot \mathsf{Adv}_{\mathcal{A},\mathsf{S}}^{\text{wbatch-priv}}(\lambda).$$

Proof. To construct the adversary $\mathcal{B}$ against BATCH-PRIV, we use the provided BATCH-PRIV signing oracle to simulate the call to BSign that is expected by the wBATCH-PRIV adversary. For this, we sample a bit c to decide what set $\mathcal{M}$ to submit to the BATCH-PRIV signing oracle. When the adversary outputs $c^\star = c$ we output $b^\star = 1$, otherwise we output $b^\star = 0$.

To bound $\mathsf{Adv}_{\mathcal{B},\mathsf{S}}^{\text{batch-priv}}(\lambda)$ note that if $b = 0$ the signatures returned by the BATCH-PRIV signing oracle are independent of μ_0 and μ_1 by construction and thus the advantage of $\mathcal{A}$ is zero. If $b = 1$ then our signing oracle faithfully emulates the wBATCH-PRIV signing oracle. Thus,

$$\begin{aligned}
\mathsf{Adv}_{\mathcal{B},\mathsf{S}}^{\text{batch-priv}}(\lambda) &= \left|\Pr[\text{BATCH-PRIV}_{\mathsf{S}}^{\mathcal{B}}(\lambda) \Rightarrow 1] - 1/2\right| \\
&= 1/2 \cdot \left|\Pr[\text{wBATCH-PRIV}_{\mathsf{S}}^{\mathcal{A}}(\lambda) \Rightarrow 1 \mid b = 0] - 1/2\right| \\
&\quad +1/2 \cdot \left|\Pr[\text{wBATCH-PRIV}_{\mathsf{S}}^{\mathcal{A}}(\lambda) \Rightarrow 1 \mid b = 1] - 1/2\right| \\
&= 0 + 1/2 \cdot \left|\Pr[\text{wBATCH-PRIV}_{\mathsf{S}}^{\mathcal{A}}(\lambda) \Rightarrow 1 \mid b = 1] - 1/2\right| \\
&= 0 + 1/2 \cdot \mathsf{Adv}_{\mathcal{A},\mathsf{S}}^{\text{wbatch-priv}}(\lambda).
\end{aligned}$$

Finally, we note that BATCH-PRIV is achievable in the next proposition.

Proposition 2. *The naïve construction of batch signatures from the Falcon signature scheme is batch private.*

4 Construction

Our construction relies on a Merkle tree. When addressing nodes in a Merkle tree of height h with N leaves, we may label nodes and leaves in the tree by

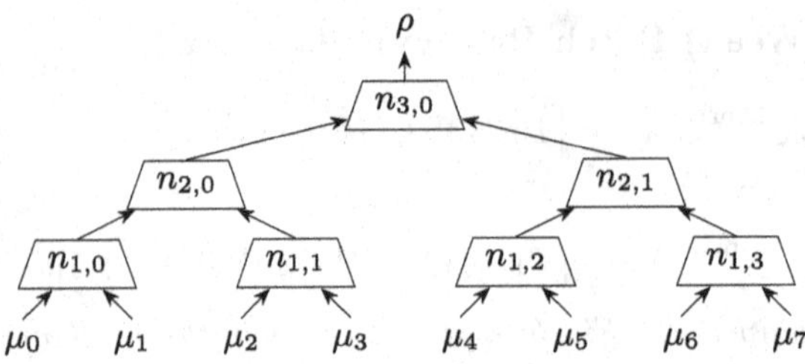

Fig. 6. A Merkle tree and addressing scheme.

their position: $n_{i,k}$ is the i-th node at height k, counting from left to right and from bottom upwards (i.e. leaves are on height 0 and the root is on height h). We illustrate this in Fig. 6.

Let $\mathsf{S} = (\mathsf{KeyGen}, \mathsf{Sign}, \mathsf{Verify})$ be a digital signature scheme as defined in Definition 4, let H be a tweakable hash function as defined in Definition 1. We define our batch signature scheme $\mathsf{BaS} = (\mathsf{KeyGen}, \mathsf{BSign}, \mathsf{Verify})$ with $\mathsf{KeyGen} := \mathsf{S.KeyGen}$ and BSign and Verify as in Algorithms 1 and 2, respectively.

Remark 2. For clarity we restrict our presentation to a fixed, power-of-two batch size N. To handle batches that do not satisfy this, we break down too long lists of messages into several batches of size at most N. To handle batches of size less than N we can either pad the tree by repeating leaves or use incomplete trees (see e.g. "L-trees" in [DOTV08]). Since this is standard in the literature, we omit the details here.

5 Security Proof

Theorem 1. *Let* $\mathsf{S} = (\mathsf{KeyGen}, \mathsf{Sign}, \mathsf{Verify})$ *be a digital signature scheme as in Definition 4,* H *be a tweakable hash function as in Definition 1. Let* $\mathsf{BaS} = (\mathsf{KeyGen}, \mathsf{BSign}, \mathsf{Verify})$ *be the batch signature scheme with* BSign *and* Verify *defined in Algorithms 1 and 2, respectively. If there exists a (classical or quantum) adversary* $\mathcal{A}$ *that breaks* BEUF-CMA *of* BaS *(see Definition 5) with* q_s *queries to the signing oracles, then it holds that*

$$\mathsf{Adv}^{\text{BEUF-CMA}}_{\mathsf{BaS},\mathcal{A}}(\lambda) \leq \mathsf{Adv}^{\text{EUF-CMA}}_{\mathsf{S},\mathcal{B}}(\lambda) + q_s \cdot \mathsf{Adv}^{\text{SM-TCR}}_{\mathsf{H},\mathcal{C}}(N, \lambda),$$

where $\mathcal{B}$ *makes* q_s *queries to its signing oracle.*

The idea of the proof is as follows. Assume adversary $\mathcal{A}$ forges a signature of BaS on some message. By definition of unforgeability this message has not been queried to the signing oracle. This enables us to distinguish two cases. Either the root (that is included in the signature) was part of a query response or not. If it has not been part of a response, we can extract a forgery for S. In the other case, there must be a collision somewhere in the hash tree which we can use to solve SM-TCR.

Algorithm 1. $\mathsf{BSign}(\mathsf{sk}, M = [\mu_0, \mu_1, \ldots, \mu_{N-1}])$ for $N = 2^n$

```
T ← [ ]
id ←$ {0,1}^λ                                         ▷ Tree identifier
for 0 ≤ i < N do                                      ▷ Generate N leaves
    r_i ←$ {0,1}^λ
    T[0, i] ← H(id, 0 | i, r_i | μ_i)
end for
h ← log_2 N
for 0 ≤ k < h do
    for 0 ≤ j < 2^{h-k-1} do                          ▷ Build tree
        left, right ← T[k, 2j], T[k, 2j + 1]
        ▷ id is public parameter, (1 | (k + 1) | j) is tweak
        T[k + 1, j] ← H(id, 1 | (k + 1) | j, left | right)
    end for
end for
root ← T[h, 0]
σ ← S.Sign(sk, id | root | N)
for 0 ≤ i < N do                                      ▷ Generate user signature
    path_i ← []
    for 0 ≤ k < log_2 N do
        j ← ⌊i/2^k⌋
        if j mod 2 = 0 then
            path_i[k] = T[k, j + 1]
        else
            path_i[k] = T[k, j − 1]
        end if
    end for
    sig_i ← (id, N, σ, i, r_i, path_i)
end for
return {sig_0, sig_1, ..., sig_{N-1}}
```

Proof. Let $\mathcal{A}$ be an adversary against BEUF-CMA of BaS. More concretely, assume that the adversary $\mathcal{A}$ gets the verification key vk, has access to a signing oracle and outputs a signature $\mathsf{sig}^\star := (\mathsf{id}^\star, N^\star, \sigma^\star, i^\star, r^\star, \mathsf{path}^\star)$ for a message $\mu^\star$ that has not been queried before, i.e. $(\mu^\star, \cdot) \notin \mathcal{Q}$. We proceed via a series of game hops. Throughout, we let Adv_i denote the advantage of $\mathcal{A}$ in Game_i. Also, we implicitly define root_i (and $\mathsf{root}^\star$) by sig_i (and $\mathsf{sig}^\star$) since they can be computed deterministically: it is the value that comes out of the authentication path evaluation in Verify, cf. up to Line 10 of Algorithm 2.

Game_0*:* BEUF-CMA *against* BaS. So,

$$\mathsf{Adv}_0 = \mathsf{Adv}^{\text{BEUF-CMA}}_{\mathsf{BaS},\mathcal{A}}.$$

Game_1*: Excluding* S*-forgeries.* Game_1 is identical to Game_0 except that it aborts if $(\cdot, (\mathsf{id}^\star, \mathsf{root}^\star, N^\star, \cdots)) \notin \mathcal{Q}$. Here, we use that $\mathsf{sig}^\star$ and sig_i implicitly define

Algorithm 2. $\mathsf{Verify}(\mathsf{vk}, \mu, \mathsf{sig} = (\mathsf{id}, N, \sigma, i, r, \mathsf{path}))$

```
h ← H(id, 0 | i, r | μ)
k ← 0
for 1 ≤ k < log_2 N do                              ▷ Construct root
    j ← ⌊i/2^k⌋
    if j mod 2 = 0 then
        h ← H(id, 1 | k | j, h | path[k])
    else
        h ← H(id, 1 | k | j, path[k] | h)
    end if
end for
return S.Verify(vk, id | h | N)
```

$\mathsf{root}^\star$ and root_i. In this case, $((\mathsf{id}^\star, \mathsf{root}^\star, N^\star), \sigma^\star)$ is an EUF-CMA forgery for S found by $\mathcal{A}$. In particular, if $\mathsf{Verify}(\mathsf{vk}, \mu^\star, \mathsf{sig}^\star) = 1$ it holds that

$$\mathsf{S.Verify}(\mathsf{vk}, \sigma^\star, (\mathsf{id}^\star, \mathsf{root}^\star, N^\star)) = 1.$$

To bound the distance between both games, we construct an algorithm $\mathcal{B}$ that breaks EUF-CMA of S using $\mathcal{A}$. Given vk, $\mathcal{B}$ runs $\mathcal{A}(\mathsf{vk})$. It implements the signing oracle for $\mathcal{A}$ following Algorithm 1 with the only difference that it asks its own S-signing oracle to sign $(\mathsf{id}, \mathsf{root}, N)$ in line 15. Hence, $\mathcal{B}$ makes the same number of signing queries $\mathcal{A}$ makes. Consider the event that Game_1 aborts but Game_0 does not. We can bound this probability by $\mathcal{B}$'s advantage $\mathsf{Adv}^{\text{EUF-CMA}}_{\mathsf{S},\mathcal{B}}$ with q_s many queries. So,

$$\mathsf{Adv}_0 - \mathsf{Adv}_1 \leq \mathsf{Adv}^{\text{EUF-CMA}}_{\mathsf{S},\mathcal{B}}.$$

Bounding Adv_1*: Forgery in the tree.* We now bound the probability that an adversary succeeds in Game_1. Note that if we did not abort in Game_1, we have that the id and root of the forgery $(\mathsf{id}^\star, \mathsf{root}^\star, N^\star)$ are identical to those of a tree that has been created during a signing query. Let this query be the j-th query $\mathcal{M}_j = \{\mu_0, \ldots, \mu_{N^\star-1}\}$ with response $\mathcal{S}_j$. Hence $(\mathsf{id}^\star, \mathsf{root}^\star, N^\star) = (\mathsf{id}_k, \mathsf{root}_k, N_k) \forall\, \mathsf{sig}_k \in \mathcal{S}_j$. Here, again, we implicitly define $\mathsf{root}^\star$ and root_k by $\mathsf{sig}^\star$ and sig_k. Also, given the fact that $\mu^\star, \mathsf{sig}^\star = (\mathsf{id}^\star, \sigma^\star, N^\star, i^\star, r_i^\star, \mathsf{path}_i^\star)$ is a forgery, by definition of BEUF-CMA, we must have that $\mu^\star \neq \mu_{i^\star}$. Running $\mathsf{Verify}(\mathsf{vk}, \mu^\star, \mathsf{sig}^\star)$ and $\mathsf{Verify}(\mathsf{vk}, \mu_{i^\star}, \mathsf{sig}_{i^\star})$ we note that this computes the same branch in two hash trees of same height and with identical roots but differing starting values. By the pigeonhole principle, this implies that there must be a collision in these paths which can be extracted.

Using the above observation we construct an adversary $\mathcal{C}$ against the SM-TCR security of H. At the beginning of the game, $\mathcal{C}$ guesses which signing query j the collision will occur in. To answer the j-th signing query, instead of sampling id (Line 2), $\mathcal{C}$ builds the tree using calls to its $\mathsf{H}(P, \cdot, \cdot)$ oracle (where P is chosen by the SM-TCR challenger, see Fig. 1). After finishing the tree, $\mathcal{C}$ requests P from the challenger before Line 15 and finishes Algorithm 1. Later, when the adversary $\mathcal{A}$ outputs a forgery $\mathsf{sig}^\star$ on $\mu^\star$, $\mathcal{C}$ extracts the collision using

Verify as outlined above. The algorithm submits the colliding value from the forgery as the solution in the SM-TCR$_{\mathsf{H}}^{\mathcal{A}}(\lambda)$ game.

We can bound the probability that $\mathcal{A}$ succeeds in Game_1 by $\mathcal{C}$'s advantage $\mathsf{Adv}_{\mathsf{H},\mathcal{C}}^{\text{SM-TCR}}(N,\lambda)$ and the probability of $\mathcal{C}$ guessing the right query j. So,

$$\mathsf{Adv}_1 \leq q_s \cdot \mathsf{Adv}_{\mathsf{H},\mathcal{C}}^{\text{SM-TCR}}(N,\lambda).$$

Combining both bounds confirms the claimed statement.

Remark 3. We note that our proof is not tight due to the factor q_s incurred from guessing the right query to play the SM-TCR game with. It is plausible that this factor of q_s can be removed by a more careful analysis of the required SM-TCR property. More precisely, we use a different public parameter id for each tree. For a good tweakable hash function, a query under public parameter id should not leak any information about the outcome using a different parameter $\mathsf{id}' \neq \mathsf{id}$. Hence, an adversary should intuitively not gain any advantage from targeting multiple instances of H at the same time, as long as they use different public parameters as we do. We leave an analysis of this property for follow-up work.

Theorem 2. *Let* $\mathsf{S} = (\mathsf{KeyGen}, \mathsf{Sign}, \mathsf{Verify})$ *be a digital signature scheme as in Definition 4,* H *be a tweakable hash function as in Definition 1. Let* $\mathsf{BaS} = (\mathsf{KeyGen}, \mathsf{BSign}, \mathsf{Verify})$ *be the batch signature scheme with* BSign *and* Verify *defined in Algorithms 1 and 2, respectively. If there exists a (classical or quantum) adversary* $\mathcal{A}$ *that breaks* wBATCH-PRIV *of* BaS *(see Definition 8), then it holds that*

$$\mathsf{Adv}_{\mathsf{BaS},\mathcal{A}}^{\text{wBATCH-PRIV}} \leq 2 \cdot \mathsf{Adv}_{\mathsf{F},\mathcal{B}}^{\text{OT-PRF}},$$

for $\mathsf{F}(k, (\mathsf{id}, i, x)) := \mathsf{H}(\mathsf{id},\ 0 \mid i,\ k \mid x)$.

Proof. On receipt of $\mathcal{M}$, we run the signing oracle as usual but call our RoR oracle with input (id, i, μ_b) in Line 5 of Algorithm 1. If the oracle returns random outputs (which happens with probability 1/2), the advantage of $\mathcal{A}$ is zero. Otherwise, if $\mathcal{A}$ returns the correct answer, this allows us to distinguish F from random, which is bounded by $\mathsf{Adv}_{\mathsf{F},\mathcal{B}}^{\text{OT-PRF}}$.

6 Applications

Batch signatures reduce the computational cost of signing by replacing one signature per message with fewer than two hashes per message and one signature per batch. We can thus make use of them to increase the throughput attainable at a given amount of computational power. In some applications, we can additionally reduce the amount of data that needs to be sent; namely, if a given entity (is aware that it) receives multiple signatures from the same batch. In this case, sending the signed root multiple times is redundant and we can asymptotically reduce the amount of received information to a few hashes per message.

In the following, we describe how to use batch signatures to reduce computational and communication costs in two operations: certificate generation (typically in an HSM) and transcript signature (typically in TLS). We then discuss two scenarios in which this can be particularly beneficial.

6.1 Computation

As noted, we will consider two scenarios: HSMs that generate a large set of short-lived certificates and server-side signing for TLS.

Hardware Security Modules. Generating a large set of certificates, for example when they are renewed for a group of entities, in general implies computing one signature per certificate and thus can represent a significant computational burden. Moreover, those signatures are in general computed on HSMs, which are significantly slower than traditional CPUs. For example, where a modern commodity CPU can sign tens of thousands of messages per second with ECDSA [BL18], some widely used enterprise-grade cloud HSMs can just sign a few hundred messages per second [Clo23]. Thus, e.g. short-lived certificates [TSH+12] can put significant stress on HSMs, especially when certificate renewal concerns a large set of devices or containers (e.g. an Envoy mesh network with 10K to 100K containers [Kle17]).

In such a setting, deploying a batch signing approach is quite straightforward. Interfacing with the HSM, an agent waits for a signal from the HSM indicating that it is ready to start a new signature. While waiting, the agent gathers incoming certificate requests that are hashed and builds a fixed size (e.g. of 32 leaves) Merkle tree. When the HSM signals "ready", the agent completes the Merkle tree with the appropriate number of zeroed leaves and sends it for signing to the HSM. In the opposite case, when the tree is full before the HSM is ready, the agent starts a new tree resulting in a queue of trees to be signed.

When the signature of the Merkle tree root is returned by the HSM, it is added to each certificate together with the sibling path associated with that request (see Line 26, Algorithm 1), resulting in the final certificate. Of course, this assumes that the certificate requester is able to verify batch signatures. Moreover, the CA generating the certificates using batch signatures needs to be updated accordingly. Naturally, this increases the throughput at which certificates can be signed by roughly a factor equal to the batch size, as we need only one signature per 32 certificates. For example, in the cloud HSM setting we would pass for ECDSA from hundreds to hundreds of thousands of signatures per second.

We expect that this effect will be more pronounced in a post-quantum setting where signing operations are much more expensive (as mentioned above). However, hard performance figures for post-quantum signatures on HSMs are not yet available, so we cannot give the likely throughput.

Transport Layer Security. Many of the recent TLS benchmarks (e.g. [SKD20]) show a significant performance penalty, especially on the computational and communication costs associated with signatures (generally done server-side) and the gap becomes much more apparent when considering packet loss [PST20]. This performance degradation in PQ TLS is incurred due to larger signature sizes and slower signing speeds. KEM sizes and performances while also worse are much closer to ECC in comparison. As a result, KEMTLS [SSW20] was

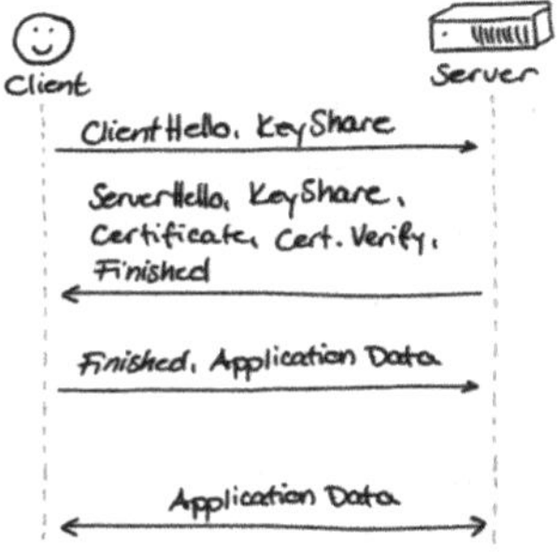

(a) High-level overview of TLS 1.3 1-RTT handshake. Certificate Verify contains the signature.

(b) High-level overview of KEMTLS handshake.

Fig. 7. TLS 1.3 and KEMTLS.

proposed to circumvent the use of (PQ) signatures for authentication in TLS. KEMTLS replaces static server authentication with a static KEM, so that only the involved KEM public keys need to be signed rather than the transcript. The results reported in [SSW20] show a reduction in the bandwidth required for the client and server communications, as well as reducing the computational costs on the server's CPU.

However, despite the performance virtues of KEMTLS, it requires a number of significant infrastructure changes in order for it to fully reach fruition. Specifically, in order for KEMTLS to be used in practice, it will rely on changes to (i) include KEM public keys into a public-key infrastructure (PKI) and (ii) TLS implementations to operate with different state machines on both client and server sides. These points inhibit the design of a KEMTLS standard and its uptake compared with "plain" PQ TLS. We illustrate the messages exchanged in TLS 1.3 and in KEMTLS in Figs. 7a and 7b.

A less invasive proposal is to use batch signing for server-side computations. As mentioned above, this approach goes back to [Ben20] and is explored in this work. As in Algorithm 1, a server can amortise its signature computation costs by adding each incoming client to a Merkle tree, building the tree, and returning the signed root to each client, in addition to some auxiliary information. This then reduces the number of "inner" signature computations required (by a factor equal to the batch size), which is the major contributing factor for the high-throughput improvements shown in Table 2. This significantly improves the performance of PQ TLS without any major changes to the PKI.

These improvements come at a few extra minor costs in TLS; these being a slight increase in the overall batch signature sizes (adding between 82 and 98 bytes, as shown in Table 1) compared to the non-batch version of the signature as well as a slight increase in latency (shown in Table 2) and computation for the client, which is due to the hash function calls when building the Merkle tree.

6.2 Communication

As noted previously, in [BOW23] a reduction in certificate sizes is proposed by a new type of CA which would exclusively sign a new type of batch oriented certificates. Such a CA would only be used together with a Certificate Transparency authority which changes the usual required flows for authentication. The benefits obtained in certificate size and verification/signature costs are significant. It also implies that the main criteria for being on a same batch are being signed by the same CA and being signed roughly at the same time.

In this section we consider what benefits we can obtain in a simpler setting, supposing just that a usual CA and its users can use multiple signing algorithms, one of them being a batch signature. In this case multiple certificates will be in the same batch when a client considers this beneficial. There are two flows in which we can expect bandwidth reduction for the entities with certificates belonging to the same signed batch.

First Flow: HSMs. The first flow is from the signing authority (again, typically, an HSM) to the entities corresponding to a same batch of signed certificates. Indeed, all the issued certificates have a signature that contains the same Merkle tree root signature but a different sibling path. Depending on the exact setting, it is then possible for the HSM to broadcast the root signature or the entire Merkle Tree and drop the information from the individual certificates that can be reconstructed from the broadcast.

Second Flow: TLS. The second flow is from the entities holding the certificates signed on the same batch to the entities receiving that certificate. This typically happens in TLS when the server sends their certificate to the client. In that setting, if the client is going to interact over the lifetime of the certificates with multiple servers from the same batch group, it can inform that the tree root signature is already known (for example in TLS with a variation to the TLS Cached Information Extension [ST16] that allows us to notify a server that some information is already known). The certificate can just contain the sibling path as the signature, leading to a bandwidth usage reduction (between 1 KB and 3 KB if using Falcon or Dilithium and up to 30 KB if using SPHINCS$^+$).

6.3 Use-Cases

We consider here two more fleshed-out examples of situations where forming batches is natural and can produce significant gains.

Fleet of Load Balancers. To reduce downtime (e.g. because of a Denial-of-Service attack, server maintenance, etc.) and to improve scalability (e.g. to efficiently (geographic) distribute requests under heavy network traffic) load balancers are essential for most of today's web applications. At the same time, they often act as a TLS termination proxy and as such decrypt, encrypt and sign

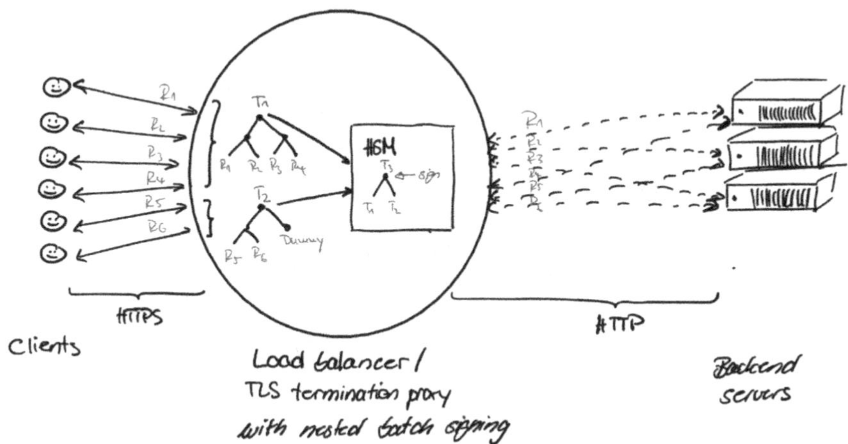

Fig. 8. Client–Load Balancer–Backend server connection with nested batch signatures.

the incoming and outgoing HTTPS traffic to offload cryptographic computations from back-end server(s), see Fig. 8. As a consequence, when cryptographic computations become more costly due to the transition to PQC, load balancers themselves may become a throughput bottle-neck. Batch signatures would significantly increase their workload capacity.

In this use-case, we consider a fleet of load balancers belonging to a large cloud provider that renew their certificates periodically (say, weekly). They form a natural group on the certificate renewal process and making a batch certificate signature request can significantly reduce the computational load on the associated HSMs, as described in Sect. 6.1, and the communications, as described at the beginning of this section. Most importantly, in such a setting, the fleet of load balancers would send full certificates only once per week and per user, and in all remaining connections load balancers will reduce the size of the certificates by 1 to 30 KB. From a user perspective, if major cloud providers use this system, a user will only have to download full sized certificates a few times per week (for connections served through cloud provider load balancers).

Instead of considering the bandwidth reduction, this can be seen as a usability question for schemes with large signatures such as SPHINCS$^+$. This algorithm relies on mild assumptions, and thus is a good candidate for CAs. Unfortunately, increasing certificate sizes to tens of kilobytes can be considered too steep of a requirement. Batch signing can solve this in the load balancer setting (and similar situations) as full certificates are only sent exceptionally.

mTLS Mesh. The second scenario is a large-scale container mesh network that renews the *mutual TLS* (mTLS) certificates in its Envoy instances. In this scenario, by considering all the Envoy instances as a single batch, there is no need to ever transmit the root signature between peers, as every peer has the root

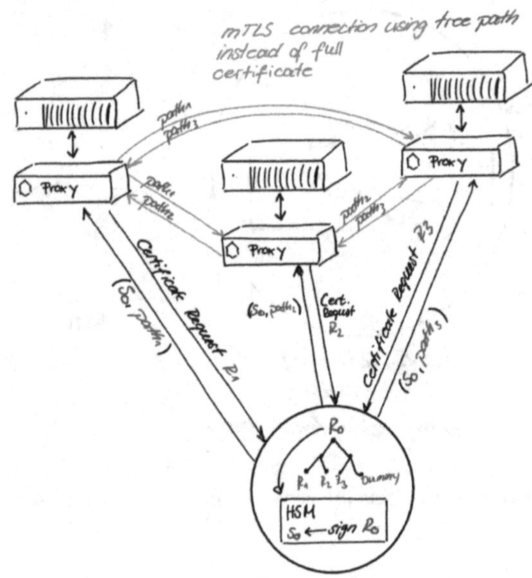

Fig. 9. Mesh network with envoys using nested signatures within mTLS.

signature in its own certificate (see Fig. 9). Of course, during the generation of the certificates we also benefit from the already described computational and communication reduction for the HSM which can be quite significant for mesh networks with thousands or tens of thousands of containers. The storage requirements for the whole set of mesh certificates (in cached key servers that are used throughout mesh networks) is also greatly reduced, e.g. for a ten thousand container mesh using SPHINCS$^+$ signatures it would be reduced from hundreds of megabytes to hundreds of kilobytes.

7 Implementation and Benchmark Setup

As a demonstrator for batch signatures we implement them for one of the most important use cases, TLS and set up a load balancer benchmark. Here we provide details on our implementation and on the benchmark setup.

7.1 Implementation Details

There are a number of components that make up the overall implementation for our proof-of-concept batch signing experiments in TLS. These allow us to estimate realistic conditions for secure network communications and thus accurately evaluate how effective our construction is under such conditions.

- `bsign_engine`: our Rust implementation of batch signing, which includes building the Merkle tree and batch signing functionalities. We also have a

benchmarking wrapper to produce results. This is the core component of our implementation. It is responsible for asynchronously gathering client requests into Merkle trees and signing the associated roots with a fixed number of signing threads.
- `openssl`: we use a patched version of OpenSSL 1.1.1, explained below.
- `tcpserver`: a TCP server, using `openssl` and `bsign_engine`, implemented from scratch.

We introduce two implementation-specific parameters, described below, which we use to tweak the performance of our implementation. This fine-tuning allows us to optimise performance based on a number of factors, most importantly what signature algorithm is used, the server specifications and the latency we are willing to accept.

1. **Merkle Tree Size.** This quantifies the amount of messages handled per batch signing transaction, which thus affects the latency and throughput of the server. Having a larger number of clients (messages as tree leaves) will reduce the average computation time per client, but at the same time will increase the size of the final signature (due to the longer path) and increase median and worst-case latency. We provide batch signature sizes in Table 1. We parametrise the Merkle tree using the number of leaves in the tree and commonly fix this to a power-of-two for efficiency reasons, e.g. `MT_size` $= 2^5$ which produces a (balanced) tree of height 5. However, this parameter may need to be adapted to fit other hardware or performance constraints.
2. **Signing Threads.** These are responsible for taking the ownership of a Merkle tree and for signing its root. When a signing thread is currently signing a Merkle tree root, it cannot handle the next tree. Thus, if the `bsign_engine` has a single signing thread, the worst observed latency will correspond to twice the time needed for a signature. By adding additional signing threads, the latency will get closer to the time needed for a signature. However, having too many signing threads may saturate the scheduling and may slow down the engine, or become sub-optimal at the very least. Inversely, if we reduce the number of signing threads we also limit the number of cores used for signatures. In Table 2, we choose the number of signing threads/cores as the smallest number that allows us to increase the number of handshakes significantly (with respect to the plain implementation) with a low latency increase.

OpenSSL Fork. We use the open-source Rust library `ring` [Smi23] for our ECDSA implementation as well as the open-source C library, `liboqs` [SM16],[2] for our implementations of post-quantum signatures. One reason for using this library in particular is because it has integration into OpenSSL 1.1.1[3] which we patch for our experiments to work with the `bsign_engine`. The patch modifies the state machine of OpenSSL to inject batch signing under certain conditions, but

[2] Commit `d5be452`, dated 28 April 2023.

[3] see https://openquantumsafe.org/applications/tls.html.

in such a way that it remains functional with classic TLS when these conditions are not met. More specifically, our patch adds a new structure – `BATCHTLS_CTX` – to the OpenSSL context – `SSL_CTX` – to track the context of the engine. We use environment variables for setting the parameters in `bsign_engine` for simplicity, as opposed to adding new APIs on top of `SSL_CTX`.

7.2 Benchmark Setup

We demonstrate the application of batch signatures for the TLS use case with the results for these shown in Table 2. For this setup we took between one and four client machines and a single server machine. Each of them uses a Google Cloud C2 instance which has an Intel 3.9 GHz Cascade Lake processor. The specific instance type we used was the `c2-standard-30`, which offers 30 (virtual) CPU threads, 120 GB memory and a (max) egress bandwidth of 32 Gbps. We disable hyper-threading in order to have more stable tests.

The results in Table 2 labelled as 'plain' are taken from a multi-threaded implementation (with a pool of as many threads as computer cores and with select/poll handling). For the batch signing results, we use a limit on the maximum size of the Merkle tree. The amount of cores used for signatures is estimated for the plain approach out of the computational cost of one signature and fixed (by reserving cores explicitly) for the batch signing approach.

The results in Table 2 provide both handshakes per second (essentially, throughput) and latency (for various percentiles). We kept Merkle tree sizes to either 16 or 32, since larger sizes incurred much higher latency costs. Indeed, for large trees the latency added is unrealistic, despite throughput being dramatically increased. Concretely, we aimed for a latency increase of no more than 20%. To measure expected latency, we distributed incoming signing requests uniformly which we consider to be a realistic assumption in, e.g., a web setting, where each client is independent.

Performance results are presented in Table 2 and discussed in the associated caption. In general, we see a throughput improvement in all the signature schemes we considered and without incurring a serious impact on latency.

As expected, the biggest improvements can be seen in the slower signing algorithms, such as Falcon (using FPU emulation), SPHINCS$^+$ and those schemes that target 256-bit security.

On the high throughput end of the benchmark, we observe that the signing times of Dilithium2 improves from being slower than ECDSA P256 to marginally faster with batch signing. Similarly, Falcon also benefits significantly and starts to compete with ECDSA P256 once batch signing is introduced.

References

[ADWF+10] Akdemir, K., et al.: Breakthrough AES Performance with Intel® AES New Instructions. Whitepaper, Intel (2010)

[Ben20] Benjamin, D.: Batch Signing for TLS. Internet-Draft draft-ietf-tls-batch-signing-00, Internet Engineering Task Force. January 2020. Work in Progress

[Ben22] Benjamin, D.: Private communication (2022)

[BHK+19] Bernstein, D.J., Hülsing, A., Kölbl, S., Niederhagen, R., Rijneveld, J., Schwabe, P.: The SPHINCS$^+$ signature framework. In: Cavallaro, L., Kinder, J., Wang, X., Katz, J (eds.), ACM CCS 2019, pp. 2129–2146. ACM Press, November 2019

[BL18] Bernstein, D.J., Lange, T.: SUPERCOP: system for unified performance evaluation related to cryptographic operations and primitives (2018). https://bench.cr.yp.to/supercop.html

[BOW23] Benjamin, D., O'Brien, D., Westerbaan, B.: Merkle Tree Certificates for TLS. Internet-Draft draft-davidben-tls-merkle-tree-certs-00, Internet Engineering Task Force, March 2023. Work in Progress

[Clo23] AWS CloudHSM. FAQS - Performance and capacity (2023). https://aws.amazon.com/cloudhsm/faqs/#Performance_and_capacity. Accessed 21 Feb 2023

[DOTV08] Dahmen, E., Okeya, K., Takagi, T., Vuillaume, C.: Digital signatures out of second-preimage resistant hash functions. In: Buchmann, J., Ding, J. (eds.) PQCrypto 2008. LNS, pp. 109–123. Springer, Heidelberg (2008). https://doi.org/10.1007/978-3-540-88403-3_8

[FHKS22] Fregly, A., Harvey, J., Kaliski, Jr., B.S., Sheth, S.: Merkle tree ladder mode: reducing the size impact of NIST PQC signature algorithms in practice. Cryptology ePrint Archive, Report 2022/1730 (2022). https://eprint.iacr.org/2022/1730

[GK12] Gueron, S., Krasnov, V.: Parallelizing message schedules to accelerate the computations of hash functions. J. Cryptogr. Eng. **2**(4), 241–253 (2012)

[GM18] Genise, N., Micciancio, D.: Faster Gaussian sampling for trapdoor lattices with arbitrary modulus. In: Nielsen, J., Rijmen, V. (eds.) EUROCRYPT 2018 Part I. LNCS, vol. 10820, pp. 174–203. Springer, Heidelberg (2018). https://doi.org/10.1007/978-3-319-78381-9_7

[GPV08] Gentry, C., Peikert, C., Vaikuntanathan, V.: Trapdoors for hard lattices and new cryptographic constructions. In: Ladner, R.E., Dwork, C. (eds.) 40th ACM STOC, pp. 197–206. ACM Press, May 2008

[HBD+22] Hülsing, A., et al.: SPHINCS$^+$. Technical report, National Institute of Standards and Technology (2022). https://csrc.nist.gov/Projects/post-quantum-cryptography/selected-algorithms-2022

[HTT23] HTTP Archive. Report: Page Weight (2023). https://httparchive.org/reports/page-weight. Accessed 21 July 2023

[HW22] Howe, J., Westerbaan, B.: Benchmarking and analysing the NIST PQC finalist lattice-based signature schemes on the ARM cortex M7. Cryptology ePrint Archive, Report 2022/405 (2022). https://eprint.iacr.org/2022/405

[Kle17] Klein, M.: Lyft's Envoy: Experiences Operating a Large Service Mesh. SREcon17 Americas (2017). https://www.usenix.org/sites/default/files/conference/protected-files/srecon17americas_slides_klein.pdf

[LDK+22] Lyubashevsky, V., et al.: CRYSTALS-DILITHIUM. Technical report, National Institute of Standards and Technology (2022)

[MP12] Micciancio, D., Peikert, C.: Trapdoors for lattices: Simpler, tighter, faster, smaller. In: Pointcheval, D., Johansson, T. (eds.) EUROCRYPT 2012. LNCS, vol. 7237, pp. 700–718. Springer, Heidelberg (2012). https://doi.org/10.1007/978-3-642-29011-4_41

[PFH+20] Prest, T., et al.: FALCON. Technical report, National Institute of Standards and Technology (2020). https://csrc.nist.gov/projects/post-quantum-cryptography/post-quantum-cryptography-standardization/round-3-submissions

[PFH+22] Prest, T., et al.: FALCON. Technical report, National Institute of Standards and Technology (2022)

[Por19] Pornin, T.: New efficient, constant-time implementations of Falcon. Cryptology ePrint Archive, Report 2019/893 (2019). https://eprint.iacr.org/2019/893

[PST20] Paquin, C., Stebila, D., Tamvada, G.: Benchmarking post-quantum cryptography in TLS. In: Ding, J., Tillich, J.-P. (eds.) PQCrypto 2020. LNCS, pp. 72–91. Springer, Heidelberg (2020). https://doi.org/10.1007/978-3-030-44223-1_5

[SKD20] Sikeridis, D., Kampanakis, P., Devetsikiotis, M.: Post-quantum authentication in TLS 1.3: a performance study. In: NDSS 2020. The Internet Society, February 2020

[SM16] Stebila, D., Mosca, M.: Post-quantum key exchange for the internet and the open quantum safe project. In: Avanzi, R., Heys, H.M. (eds.) SAC 2016. LNCS, vol. 10532, pp. 14–37. Springer, Heidelberg (2016). https://doi.org/10.1007/978-3-319-69453-5_2

[Smi23] Smith, B.: Crate ring (2023). https://github.com/briansmith/ring. Accessed 24 Feb 2023

[SSW20] Schwabe, P., Stebila, D., Wiggers, T.: Post-quantum TLS without handshake signatures. In: Ligatti, J., Ou, X., Katz, J., Vigna, G (eds.) ACM CCS 2020, pp. 1461–1480. ACM Press, November 2020

[ST16] Santesson, S., Tschofenig, H.: Transport Layer Security (TLS) Cached Information Extension. RFC 7924, July 2016

[TSH+12] Topalovic, E., Saeta, B., Huang, L.S., Jackson, C., Boneh, D.: Towards short-lived certificates. In: IEEE Oakland Web 2.0 Security and Privacy (W2SP) (2012)

[Wes21] Westerbaan, B.: Sizing up post-quantum signatures (2021). https://blog.cloudflare.com/sizing-up-post-quantum-signatures/. Accessed 21 July 23

[You22] Young, S.D.: National security memo on promoting United States leadership in quantum computing while mitigating risks to vulnerable cryptographic systems (NSM-10). Executive Office of the President, Office of Management and Budget, Washington, DC, USA (2022)

History-Free Sequential Aggregation of Hash-and-Sign Signatures

Alessio Meneghetti[1] and Edoardo Signorini[2,3](✉)

[1] University of Trento, Trento, Italy
alessio.meneghetti@unitn.it
[2] Telsy, Turin, Italy
edoardo.signorini@telsy.it
[3] Politecnico di Torino, Turin, Italy

Abstract. A sequential aggregate signature (SAS) scheme allows multiple users to sequentially combine their respective signatures in order to reduce communication costs. Historically, early proposals required the use of trapdoor permutation (e.g., RSA). In recent years, a number of attempts have been made to extend SAS schemes to post-quantum assumptions. Many post-quantum signatures have been proposed in the hash-and-sign paradigm, which requires the use of trapdoor functions and appears to be an ideal candidate for sequential aggregation attempts. However, the hardness in achieving post-quantum one-way permutations makes it difficult to obtain similarly general constructions. Direct attempts at generalizing permutation-based schemes have been proposed, but they either lack formal security or require additional properties on the trapdoor function, which are typically not available for multivariate or code-based functions. In this paper, we propose a (partial-signature) history-free SAS within the probabilistic hash-and-sign with retry paradigm, generalizing existing techniques to generic trapdoor functions. We prove the security of our scheme in the random oracle model and we instantiate our construction with three post-quantum schemes, comparing their compression capabilities. Finally, we discuss how direct extensions of permutation-based SAS schemes are not possible without additional properties, showing the lack of security of two existing multivariate schemes.

1 Introduction

An Aggregate Signature (AS) scheme allows n users to combine their individual signatures on separate messages to produce a single, directly verifiable aggregate signature. This approach aims to achieve shorter signature lengths compared to trivial concatenation of individual signatures. Aggregate signatures have interesting applications in various network scenarios with high communication costs, such as PKI certificate chains or secure routing protocols authentication. The concept of aggregate signatures was initially introduced in a seminal paper by Boneh, Gentry, Lynn, and Shacham [11]. They proposed a method that allows

E. Oswald (Ed.): CT-RSA 2024, LNCS 14643, pp. 187–223, 2024.
https://doi.org/10.1007/978-3-031-58868-6_8

any participant to aggregate signatures from distinct users using a public aggregation algorithm. Although this general aggregation approach is efficient and valuable, it is limited to the use of bilinear pairings. A restricted variant of aggregate signatures, known as Sequential Aggregated Signature (SAS), was introduced by Lysyanskaya, Micali, Reyzin, and Shacham [31]. In SAS schemes, signatures are aggregated in a specific sequence, starting from the so-far aggregated signature and possibly from the public key and message information of previous users. The sequential structure is still beneficial in many applications. Numerous works have been pursued in this direction, proposing constructions based on trapdoor permutations [13,23,31,32] or the use of bilinear pairings [4,21,30]. Additionally, it is possible to consider further aggregation variants such as the synchronous model [1,25], in which signers cannot produce more than one signature within a certain time interval, or the interactive model [5], in which signers participate in an interactive multi-round protocol to produce a signature.

Aggregate Signatures from Post-quantum Assumptions. In recent years, there has been a growing interest in post-quantum signatures, leading researchers to explore AS schemes in this field. Numerous Lattice-based schemes have been proposed, with generic solutions based on non-interactive arguments [2,18], results in the synchronous model [22] and sequential aggregations both in the Fiat-Shamir [12] and Hash-and-Sign paradigms [19,35]. Focusing on the latter, both [19,35] have extended previous trapdoor permutation-based approaches [23,32], but their security relies on the collision-resistance property of lattice trapdoor Preimage Sampleable Functions (PSF) [24]. These additional properties are not available for generic trapdoor functions employed, for instance, in multivariate-quadratic-based (MQ-based) or code-based signature schemes. Currently, SAS schemes based on these assumptions are very limited, with only two existing MQ-based schemes [15,20], which follow the construction of [31]. Unfortunately, both [15,20] lack formal security and there are instances of the underlying function for which they are insecure, as outlined below.

Our Contribution. In this work, we address the extension of permutation-based SAS schemes to generic trapdoor functions, making them applicable to a broader range of post-quantum signatures. In Sect. 3, we present a partial-signature history-free SAS scheme based on generic trapdoor functions. In a history-free SAS, introduced in [13], signers receive only the so-far aggregated signature without requiring previous users' public keys and messages. The partial-signature variant, initially presented in [16], reduces the amount of information the signer needs to receive from the previous one, but requires a final (public) aggregation step.

Our approach can be seen as a generalization of the work of Brogle, Goldberg, and Reyzin [13] for trapdoor permutations, adapting the encoding technique of [19,32] to include trapdoor functions beyond permutations. The main novelty of our work is the extension of the probabilistic hash-and-sign with retry paradigm, which is common in post-quantum signature constructions, to sequential aggregate signature schemes. As a result, we are able to reduce the security of our scheme to the one-wayness of the trapdoor function and to an additional notion of Preimage Sampling (PS) indistinguishability. While this further notion may appear restrictive in the choice of trapdoor functions, it turns out to be quite natural in security proofs of post-quantum hash-and-sign schemes, as recently shown in [28].

In Sect. 4, we apply our scheme to MQ-based signature schemes, specifically UOV [27] and MAYO [8], and the code-based scheme Wave [17]. For each scheme, we evaluate its compression capabilities and review its PS security so that it can be covered in our security proof.

Finally, in Sect. 5, we argue that the simpler approaches of [31,32] are not viable for generic trapdoor functions. As evidence, we show how two existing MQ-based aggregate signature schemes [15,20] are universally forgeable when instantiated with UOV and discuss their lack of provable security.

2 Notation and Preliminaries

For $n \in \mathbb{N}$, we denote by $[n]$ the set $\{1, \ldots, n\}$. For a finite set X, we write $|X|$ for the cardinality of X and $\text{len}(X)$ for the bit size of an element in X. By $x \leftarrow\!\!\$\ X$, we denote the sample of the element x from $U(X)$, the uniform distribution over X. For an algorithm A, we write $x \leftarrow A(y)$ to denote the assignment of x to the output of A on input y. We denote with $\mathcal{A}$ a (probabilistic) polynomial-time adversary. For an adversary $\mathcal{A}$ and a function F, we write $x \leftarrow \mathcal{A}^{\mathsf{OF}}$ the assignment of x of the output of $\mathcal{A}$ with oracle access to F. For two bit strings $x, y \in \{0,1\}^*$, we denote by $x \,\|\, y$ the bit string obtained by their concatenation. We write $\mathbb{F}_q$ for a finite field of q elements. We denote by $\mathbb{F}_q^{m \times n}$ the set of matrices over $\mathbb{F}_q$ with m rows and n columns. $\mathbf{I}_{n \times n}$ is the identity matrix of size n. $\mathbf{0}_{m \times n}$ is the $m \times n$ zero matrix and $\mathbf{0}_n$ is the zero vector in $\mathbb{F}_q^n$. In the remainder of this section, we introduce standard definitions and notions related to digital signature schemes based on trapdoor functions.

2.1 Trapdoor Functions

Definition 1. *A trapdoor function (TDF)* T *is a tuple of four algorithms* $(\mathsf{TrapGen}, \mathsf{F}, \mathsf{I}, \mathsf{SampDom})$*:*

- $\mathsf{TrapGen}(1^\lambda)$*: takes as input a security parameter* 1^λ *and generates an efficiently computable function* $\mathsf{F}\colon \mathcal{X} \to \mathcal{Y}$ *and a trapdoor* I *that allow to invert* F.
- $\mathsf{F}(x)$*: takes as input* $x \in \mathcal{X}$ *and outputs* $\mathsf{F}(x) \in \mathcal{Y}$.
- $\mathsf{I}(y)$*: takes as input* $y \in \mathcal{Y}$ *and outputs* $x \in \mathcal{X}$ *such that* $\mathsf{F}(x) = y$ *or it fails by returning* $\perp$.
- $\mathsf{SampDom}(\mathsf{F})$ *takes as input a function* $\mathsf{F}\colon \mathcal{X} \to \mathcal{Y}$ *and outputs* $x \in \mathcal{X}$.

We define the following notion of one-wayness (OW) for a trapdoor function.

Definition 2. *Let* $\mathsf{T} = (\mathsf{TrapGen}, \mathsf{F}, \mathsf{I}, \mathsf{SampDom})$ *be a TDF and let* $\mathcal{A}$ *be an adversary. We define the advantage of* $\mathcal{A}$ *playing the* OW *game against* T *as*

$$\mathsf{Adv}_{\mathsf{T}}^{\mathrm{ow}}(\mathcal{A}) = \Pr\left[\mathsf{F}(x) = y \;\middle|\; \begin{array}{c} (\mathsf{F}, \mathsf{I}) \leftarrow \mathsf{TrapGen}(1^\lambda) \\ y \leftarrow_{\$} \mathcal{Y} \\ x \leftarrow \mathcal{A}(\mathsf{F}, y) \end{array}\right]$$

Sometimes, the notion of one-wayness requires that the challenge is obtained as $\mathsf{F}(x)$ with x sampled following some distribution on $\mathcal{X}$. The use of uniformly random challenges appears necessary to prove the security of hash-and-sign schemes if the image via F of random input is not uniformly distributed in the codomain.

Definition 3 (Trapdoor Permutation (TDP)). *A TDF* $\mathsf{T} = (\mathsf{TrapGen}, \mathsf{F}, \mathsf{I}, \mathsf{SampDom})$ *is said to be a TDP if* F *and* I *are permutations.*

2.2 Digital Signatures

A digital signature scheme Sig is a tuple of three algorithms $(\mathsf{KGen}, \mathsf{Sign}, \mathsf{Vrfy})$:

- $\mathsf{KGen}(1^\lambda)$: takes as input a security parameter 1^λ and generates a key pair $(\mathsf{pk}, \mathsf{sk})$.
- $\mathsf{Sign}(\mathsf{sk}, m)$: takes as input a signing key sk and a message m and returns a signature σ.
- $\mathsf{Vrfy}(\mathsf{pk}, m, \sigma)$: takes as input a verification key pk, a message m and a signature σ and returns 1 for acceptance or 0 for rejection.

We define the standard notion of existential unforgeability against chosen-message attack (EUF-CMA).

Definition 4 (EUF-CMA security). *Let* O *be a random oracle, let* $\mathsf{Sig} = (\mathsf{KGen}, \mathsf{Sign}, \mathsf{Vrfy})$ *be a signature scheme, let* $\mathcal{A}$ *be an adversary. We define the advantage of* $\mathcal{A}$ *playing the* EUF-CMA *game against* Sig *in the random oracle model as:*

$$\mathsf{Adv}_{\mathsf{Sig}}^{\mathrm{euf\text{-}cma}}(\mathcal{A}) = \Pr\left[\begin{array}{c} \mathsf{Vrfy}(\mathsf{pk}, m, \sigma) = 1 \\ \mathsf{OSign}(\mathsf{sk}, \cdot) \text{ not queried on } m \end{array} \;\middle|\; \begin{array}{c} (\mathsf{pk}, \mathsf{sk}) \leftarrow \mathsf{KGen}(1^\lambda) \\ (m, \sigma) \leftarrow \mathcal{A}^{\mathsf{O}, \mathsf{OSign}(\mathsf{sk}, \cdot)}(\mathsf{pk}) \end{array}\right]$$

2.3 Hash-and-Sign Schemes

The (probabilistic) hash-and-sign (HaS) paradigm is a standard approach to building digital signature schemes in the random oracle model from a trapdoor function T and a hash function $\mathsf{H}\colon \{0,1\}^* \to \mathcal{Y}$. To sign a message m, a signer with secret key $\mathsf{sk} = \mathsf{I}$ applies the hash function, modeled as a random oracle, to the message $y \leftarrow \mathsf{H}(m)$ and computes its inverse $x \leftarrow \mathsf{I}(y)$ through the secret trapdoor. In some scenarios, the HaS paradigm requires using a random string r, which acts as a salt for the hash function, i.e., $y \leftarrow \mathsf{H}(m \parallel r)$. The resulting

Algorithm 1: Hash-and-sign with retry

$\mathsf{KGen}(1^\lambda)$:
- $(\mathsf{F}, \mathsf{I}) \leftarrow \mathsf{TrapGen}(1^\lambda)$
- **return** (F, I)

$\mathsf{Vrfy}(\mathsf{F}, m, (r, x))$:
- **return** $\mathsf{F}(x) = \mathsf{H}(r, m)$

$\mathsf{Sign}(\mathsf{I}, m)$:
- **repeat**
  - $r \leftarrow_{\$} \{0,1\}^\lambda$
  - $x \leftarrow \mathsf{I}(\mathsf{H}(r, m))$
- **until** $x \neq \perp$
- **return** (r, x)

Game 1: PS_b

- $(\mathsf{F}, \mathsf{I}) \leftarrow \mathsf{TrapGen}(1^\lambda)$
- $b^\star \leftarrow \mathcal{A}^{\mathsf{Sample}_b}(\mathsf{F})$
- **return** $b^\star \in \{0,1\}$

Sample_1:
- $r_i \leftarrow_{\$} \{0,1\}^\lambda$
- $x_i \leftarrow \mathsf{SampDom}(\mathsf{F})$
- **return** (r_i, x_i)

Sample_0:
- **repeat**
  - $r_i \leftarrow_{\$} \{0,1\}^\lambda$
  - $y_i \leftarrow_{\$} \mathcal{Y}$
  - $x_i \leftarrow \mathsf{I}(y_i)$
- **until** $x_i \neq \perp$
- **return** (r_i, x_i)

signature is the couple $\sigma = (x, r)$. A verifier uses the corresponding public key $\mathsf{pk} = \mathsf{F}$ to verify whether $\mathsf{F}(x) = \mathsf{H}(m \,\|\, r)$.

When T is a trapdoor permutation, this construction is known as Full Domain Hash, and the EUF-CMA security of the signature scheme can be proved from the one-wayness assumption of T [6]. For generic TDF, a black-box security proof is not known, and custom reductions are needed for different constructions. This becomes particularly significant in the post-quantum setting, where no constructions of one-way permutations are known. In order to achieve a secure signature scheme, it is possible to consider trapdoor functions with additional properties. For instance, Preimage Sampleable Functions (PSF) [24], which can be constructed from lattices [33], or Average Trapdoor PSF (ATPSF) [14], which can be constructed from code-based assumptions [17]. More generally, a slightly different paradigm, known as probabilistic hash-and-sign with retry (Algorithm 1), is used to prove the EUF-CMA security. With this approach, a random string r is sampled until a preimage for $\mathsf{H}(m \,\|\, r)$ is found. The security is based on the one-wayness of the trapdoor function and on the additional condition that the output of the signing algorithm (r, x) is indistinguishable from a couple (r', x') with $r' \leftarrow_{\$} \{0,1\}^\lambda$ and $x' \leftarrow_{\$} \mathsf{SampDom}(\mathsf{F})$. Ad-hoc versions of this paradigm are commonly employed for MQ-based signatures, and have been utilized to prove the security of Unbalanced Oil and Vinegar (UOV), Hidden-Field Equation (HFE) [34], and MAYO [8] signature schemes.

In this work, we build a partial-signature history-free sequential aggregate signature scheme HaS-HF-SAS within the probabilistic hash-and-sign with retry paradigm. The security of our scheme requires the indistinguishability condition on preimages, which we formalize by adopting the following notion from [28].

Definition 5 (Preimage Sampling [28]). *Let* $\mathsf{T} = (\mathsf{TrapGen}, \mathsf{F}, \mathsf{I}, \mathsf{SampDom})$ *be a TDF, let* $\mathcal{A}$ *be an adversary. We define the advantage of* $\mathcal{A}$ *playing the* PS *game (Game 1) against* T *as:*

$$\mathsf{Adv}_{\mathsf{T}}^{\mathsf{ps}}(\mathcal{A}) = |\Pr[\mathrm{PS}_0(\mathcal{A}) = 1] - \Pr[\mathrm{PS}_1(\mathcal{A}) = 1]|$$

Note that the OW notion of Definition 2 includes trapdoor functions for which the probability that a pre-image exists via F for a random element $y \in \mathcal{Y}$ is negligible. Such functions could not be used as a building block for hash-and-sign schemes, as even knowledge of the secret trapdoor would not allow the computation of a pre-image. Nevertheless, a non-negligible failure probability could impact the tightness of a security reduction from OW. In the security proof of our scheme, we explicitly consider this possibility by bounding the number of queries made to the random oracle during a signature attempt.

2.4 History-Free Sequential Aggregate Signature

History-Free Sequential Aggregate Signatures (HF-SAS) were first introduced in [13,21] as a variant of the original Full-History construction of [31] that does not require knowledge of previous messages and public keys in the aggregation step.

Definition 6 (HF-SAS). *A History-Free Sequential Aggregate Signature is a tuple of three algorithms* $(\mathsf{KGen}, \mathsf{AggSign}, \mathsf{AggVrfy})$*:*

- $\mathsf{KGen}(1^\lambda)$*: takes as input a security parameter* 1^λ *and generates a key pair* $(\mathsf{pk}, \mathsf{sk})$.
- $\mathsf{AggSign}(\mathsf{sk}_i, m_i, \Sigma_{i-1})$*: takes as input the secret key* sk_i *and the message* m_i *of the ith user and the previous aggregate signature* Σ_{i-1}. *Returns an aggregate signature* Σ_i.
- $\mathsf{AggVrfy}(L_n, \Sigma_n)$*: takes as input the full history* $L_n = (\mathsf{pk}_1, m_1), \ldots, (\mathsf{pk}_n, m_n)$ *of public key, message pairs and an aggregate signature* Σ_n. *Returns* 1 *if* Σ_n *is a valid aggregate signature and* 0 *otherwise.*

Every signer has a key pair $(\mathsf{pk}_i, \mathsf{sk}_i) \leftarrow \mathsf{KGen}(1^\lambda)$. The signature aggregation process is done iteratively: the first signer with keys $(\mathsf{pk}_1, \mathsf{sk}_1)$ generates a signature Σ_1 for message m_1 with $\Sigma_1 \leftarrow \mathsf{AggSign}(\mathsf{sk}_1, m_1, \varepsilon)$, where ε represents the empty string to indicate that this is the first signature in the sequence. The ith signer with keys $(\mathsf{pk}_i, \mathsf{sk}_i)$ receives an aggregate signature Σ_{i-1} from the $(i-1)$th signer and aggregate his signature on message m_i to obtain the aggregate signature $\Sigma_i \leftarrow \mathsf{AggSign}(\mathsf{sk}_i, m_i, \Sigma_{i-1})$. Note that the aggregation algorithm $\mathsf{AggSign}$ does not require the public keys and messages from the previous signers. Finally, the verifier can check the validity of the aggregate signature by running $\mathsf{AggVrfy}(L_n, \Sigma_n)$.

SAS schemes were originally introduced by [31] for generic trapdoor permutation with the FDH approach. The history-free variant of [13] still requires trapdoor permutation, while [21] relies on bilinear pairing. The main intuition behind the aggregation process in TDP schemes is to "embed" the previous

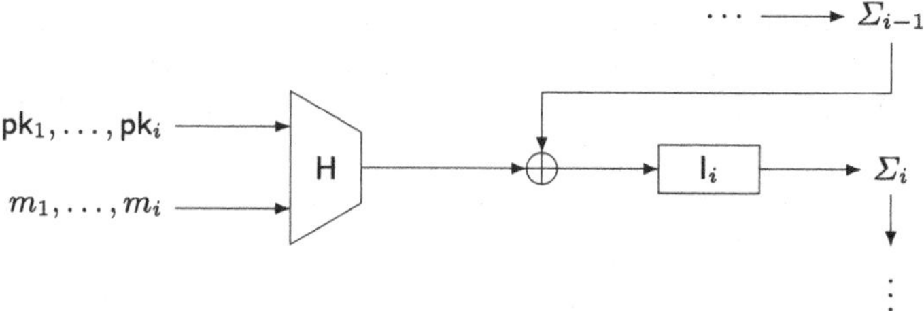

Fig. 1. High level description of SAS scheme from [31].

Game 2: strong PS-HF-UF-CMA$_\mathrm{S}$

$(\mathsf{pk}^\star, \mathsf{sk}^\star) \leftarrow \mathsf{KGen}(1^\lambda)$
$\mathcal{Q} \leftarrow \emptyset$
$(L_n, \bar{\Sigma}_n) \leftarrow \mathcal{A}^{\mathsf{O},\mathsf{OAggSign}}(\mathsf{pk}^\star)$
$(\mathsf{pk}_1, m_1), \ldots, (\mathsf{pk}_n, m_n) \leftarrow L_n$
if $\nexists i^\star : (\mathsf{pk}_{i^\star} = \mathsf{pk}^\star \wedge (m_{i^\star}, \varsigma_{i^\star}) \notin \mathcal{Q})$ **then**
    return $\perp$
return $\mathsf{AggVrfy}(L_n, \bar{\Sigma}_n)$

$\mathsf{OAggSign}(m, \varrho)$:
$(\varrho', \varsigma') \leftarrow \mathsf{AggSign}(\mathsf{sk}^\star, m, \varrho)$
$\mathcal{Q} \leftarrow \mathcal{Q} \cup \{(m, \varsigma')\}$
return ϱ', ς'

aggregate signature into the new message to be signed. This ensures that the aggregate signature can be retrieved during the verification process, as depicted in Fig. 1.

The main challenge in extending previous schemes to trapdoor functions that are not permutations lies in their lack of injectivity. This issue was addressed in [19] within the context of lattice-based signatures by employing an encoding technique derived from [32]. Subsequently, this idea was applied to MQ-based schemes instantiated with HFEv- [20] and UOV [15]. The proposed solution is to use a suitable encoding function, which splits the signature into two components. The first component can be injected into the codomain of the trapdoor function and subsequently made part of the computation of the aggregate signature, similar to the approach used in [31]. The second component is transmitted to the next signer and becomes part of the final aggregate signature. During the verification phase, this component is used to recover the partial aggregate signature through a corresponding decoding function. Notice that this method has a drawback in terms of the efficiency of the SAS scheme. In fact, storing part of the signature of each user without further aggregation causes a linear growth of the aggregate signature in the number of users. Therefore, it is currently unknown how to achieve sequential aggregate signatures of constant size in the post-quantum setting, where there are no one-way TDPs.

In the following, we define a slight modification of HF-SAS, as formalized in [12]. In this variant, the aggregation step requires only partial knowledge about the so-far aggregated signature. This description better captures the intuition behind the use of the encoding function and is better suited to our proposed scheme. During each aggregation step, the signer produces a partial signature information, which will be sent to the next signer, along with a complementary component. At the end of the aggregation sequence, an additional $\mathsf{Combine}$ step is performed, potentially by a third party. This step combines all the complementary information and the last signature of the sequence, resulting in the complete aggregated signature.

Definition 7 (PS-HF-SAS). *A Partial-Signature History-Free Sequential Aggregate Signature is a tuple of four algorithms* $(\mathsf{KGen}, \mathsf{AggSign}, \mathsf{AggVrfy}, \mathsf{Combine})$*:*

- KGen *and* $\mathsf{AggVrfy}$ *as described in Definition 6.*
- $\mathsf{AggSign}(\mathsf{sk}_i, m_i, \varrho_{i-1})$*: takes as input the secret key* sk_i *and the message* m_i *of the ith user and a partial description* ϱ_{i-1} *of the previous aggregate signature* Σ_{i-1}*. Computes an updated aggregate signature* Σ_i *and returns a partial description* ϱ_i *and some complementary information* ς_i*.*
- $\mathsf{Combine}(\varsigma_1, \ldots, \varsigma_{n-1}, \Sigma_n)$*: takes as input the complementary information* ς_i *of the first* $n-1$ *signatures and the full description of the last signature* Σ_n*. Returns the complete description of the aggregate signature* $\bar{\Sigma}_n$*.*

Below, we show the definition of partial-signature history-free unforgeability under adaptive chosen message (PS-HF-UF-CMA). In this model, the forger controls all signers' private keys except for at least one honest signer. The forger can choose the keys of the rogue signers and adaptively query an aggregate signature oracle. Finally, to win the experiment, the forger must produce a valid, non-trivial aggregate signature involving the public key of the honest signer. A stronger notion is also considered in [12], where the adversary may produce forgery on messages already queried to the signing oracle, provided that the complementary part of the corresponding signature is distinct from the oracle's response. We denote this variant as strong PS-HF-UF-CMA.

Definition 8 (PS-HF-UF-CMA **Security**). *Let* O *be a random oracle, let* $\mathsf{S} = (\mathsf{KGen}, \mathsf{AggSign}, \mathsf{AggVrfy}, \mathsf{Combine})$ *be a* PS-HF-SAS *scheme, let* $\mathcal{A}$ *be an adversary. We define the advantage of* $\mathcal{A}$ *playing the strong* PS-HF-UF-CMA *game (Game 2) against* S *as follows:*

$$\mathsf{Adv}_{\mathsf{S}}^{\text{ps-hf-uf-cma}}(\mathcal{A}) = \Pr[\text{PS-HF-UF-CMA}_{\mathsf{S}}(\mathcal{A}) = 1].$$

3 Sequential Aggregation of Hash-and-Sign Signatures

We present a PS-HF-SAS scheme following the probabilistic hash-and-sign with retry paradigm. The intuition behind our scheme closely follows the one of [13, 32]. We use a two-step hash procedure: first, the signature x_{i-1} of the previous signer and the message m_i are contracted to a short value h_i, and then expanded to the codomain of the trapdoor function. The value h_i can be aggregated and made available to the verifier, who can expand it before knowing x_{i-1}. In this way, Neven [32] showed that the verifier does not need to check the validity of

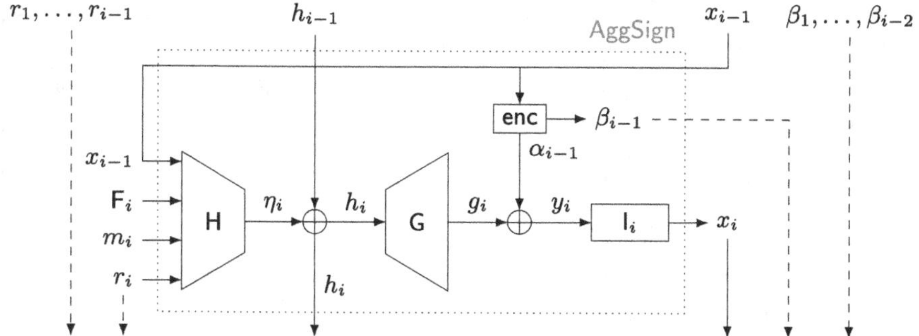

Fig. 2. High level description of our HaS-HF-SAS scheme. The dashed arrows in the output represent the complementary part of the signature.

the signers' public keys. When calculating the first hash, we also require the signer to concatenate a random salt r_i, which will later be part of the aggregate signature. In [13], the salt is introduced to prevent a chosen message attack in the history-free setting. In our scheme, the use of the salt descends from the probabilistic hash-and-sign paradigm and provides a solution to overcome the technical challenges of using trapdoor functions that are not permutations. As discussed later in Sect. 5, attempting to remove the random salt would make the construction insecure even in the full-history setting.

A high-level description of the scheme HaS-HF-SAS is shown in Fig. 2 while a detailed description is given in Algorithm 2. The properties of the underlying trapdoor function are as described in Sect. 2.1.

3.1 Security Proof

In the following, we prove the strong PS-HF-UF-CMA security of Algorithm 2.

Theorem 1. *Let* T *be a TDF. Let* $\mathcal{A}$ *be a strong* PS-HF-UF-CMA *adversary against the* HaS-HF-SAS *scheme on* T *in the random oracle model, which runs in time* t *and makes* $\mathsf{q_S}$ *signing queries,* $\mathsf{q_H}$ *queries to the random oracle* H *and* $\mathsf{q_G}$ *queries to the random oracle* G. *Then, there exist a* OW *adversary* $\mathcal{B}$ *against* T *that runs in time* $t + \mathcal{O}((\mathsf{q_H} + \mathsf{q_S} + 1) \cdot \mathsf{poly}(\mathrm{len}(\mathcal{X}), \mathrm{len}(\mathcal{Y})))$, *and a* PS *adversary* $\mathcal{D}$ *against* T *issuing* $\mathsf{q_S}$ *sampling queries that runs in time* $t + \mathcal{O}(\mathsf{q_S} \cdot \mathsf{poly}(\mathrm{len}(\mathcal{X}), \mathrm{len}(\mathcal{Y})))$, *such that*

$$\mathsf{Adv}^{\text{ps-hf-uf-cma}}_{\mathsf{HaS\text{-}HF\text{-}SAS}}(\mathcal{A}) \leq (\psi \mathsf{q_H}) \cdot \mathsf{Adv}^{\text{ow}}_{\mathsf{T}}(\mathcal{B}) + \mathsf{Adv}^{\text{ps}}_{\mathsf{T}}(\mathcal{D}) + \frac{(\mathsf{q_S} + \mathsf{q_H})(\mathsf{q}'_\mathsf{S} + \mathsf{q_H} + \mathsf{q_G})}{2^{2\lambda}} + \frac{\mathsf{q_S}(\mathsf{q}'_\mathsf{S} + \mathsf{q_H})}{2^{\lambda}} + \frac{\psi \mathsf{q}_\mathsf{H}^2}{2|\mathcal{Y}|} + \frac{(\psi \mathsf{q_H})^{\psi+1}|\mathcal{X}|}{(\psi+1)! \cdot |\mathcal{Y}|^{\psi+1}},$$

where $\psi \geq \lceil \mathrm{len}(\mathcal{X}) / \mathrm{len}(\mathcal{Y}) \rceil$, *and* q'_S *is a bound on the total number of queries to* H *in all the signing queries.*

Algorithm 2: HaS-HF-SAS

Let $h_0 = \varepsilon, x_0 = \varepsilon$. The random oracles are $\mathsf{H}: \{0,1\}^* \to \{0,1\}^{2\lambda}$ and $\mathsf{G}: \{0,1\}^{2\lambda} \to \mathcal{Y}$. The encoding function is $\mathsf{enc}: \mathcal{X} \to \mathcal{Y} \times \mathcal{X}'$ and the corresponding decoding function is $\mathsf{dec}: \mathcal{Y} \times \mathcal{X}' \to \mathcal{X}$ such that $\mathsf{dec}(\mathsf{enc}(x)) = x$. ϱ_i and ς_i are the partial description and the complementary information of the aggregate signature Σ_i, respectively.

$\mathsf{KGen}(1^\lambda)$:

- $(\mathsf{F}, \mathsf{I}) \leftarrow \mathsf{TrapGen}(1^\lambda)$
- **return** $\mathsf{pk} \leftarrow \mathsf{F}, \mathsf{sk} \leftarrow (\mathsf{F}, \mathsf{I})$

$\mathsf{AggSign}((\mathsf{F}_i, \mathsf{I}_i), m_i, \varrho_{i-1})$:

- $(h_{i-1}, x_{i-1}) \leftarrow \varrho_{i-1}$
- $(\alpha_{i-1}, \beta_{i-1}) \leftarrow \mathsf{enc}(x_{i-1})$
- **repeat**
  - $r_i \leftarrow_\$ \{0,1\}^\lambda$
  - $\eta_i \leftarrow \mathsf{H}(\mathsf{F}_i, m_i, r_i, x_{i-1})$
  - $h_i \leftarrow h_{i-1} \oplus \eta_i$
  - $g_i \leftarrow \mathsf{G}(h_i)$
  - $y_i \leftarrow g_i \oplus \alpha_{i-1}$
  - $x_i \leftarrow \mathsf{I}_i(y_i)$
- **until** $x_i \neq \perp$
- $\varrho_i \leftarrow (h_i, x_i)$
- $\varsigma_i \leftarrow (r_i, \beta_{i-1})$
- **return** ϱ_i, ς_i

$\mathsf{AggVrfy}(L_n, \bar{\Sigma}_n)$:

- $(\mathsf{F}_1, m_1), \ldots, (\mathsf{F}_n, m_n) \leftarrow L_n$
- $(\vec{r}_n, \vec{\beta}_{n-1}, h_n, x_n) \leftarrow \bar{\Sigma}_n$
- **for** $i \leftarrow n, \ldots, 2$ **do**
  - $y_i \leftarrow \mathsf{F}_i(x_i)$
  - $g_i \leftarrow \mathsf{G}(h_i)$
  - $\alpha_{i-1} \leftarrow g_i \oplus y_i$
  - $x_{i-1} \leftarrow \mathsf{dec}(\alpha_{i-1}, \beta_{i-1})$
  - $\eta_i \leftarrow \mathsf{H}(\mathsf{F}_i, m_i, r_i, x_{i-1})$
  - $h_{i-1} \leftarrow h_i \oplus \eta_i$
- **return** $h_1 = \mathsf{H}(\mathsf{F}_1, r_1, m_1, \varepsilon) \wedge \mathsf{F}_1(x_1) = \mathsf{G}(h_1)$

$\mathsf{Combine}(\varsigma_1, \ldots, \varsigma_{n-1}, \Sigma_n)$:

- $(r_i, \beta_{i-1}) \leftarrow \varsigma_i$
- $(r_n, \beta_{n-1}, h_n, x_n) \leftarrow \Sigma_n$
- $\vec{r}_n \leftarrow (r_1, \ldots, r_n)$
- $\vec{\beta}_{n-1} \leftarrow (\beta_1, \ldots, \beta_{n-1})$
- **return** $\bar{\Sigma}_n \leftarrow (\vec{r}_n, \vec{\beta}_{n-1}, h_n, x_n)$

Proof (sketch). We sketch the high-level idea of the proof; full details can be found in Appendix A.1. The complete reduction is described in Algorithm 3. We prove the reduction by showing that the strong PS-HF-UF-CMA game can be simulated by the OW adversary $\mathcal{B}$. First, we modify the PS-HF-UF-CMA game such that in $\mathsf{OAggSign}$ the salt r is chosen uniformly at random in $\{0,1\}^\lambda$ and the preimage is generated by $x \leftarrow \mathsf{SampDom}(\mathsf{F}^\star)$ instead of iterating until $\mathsf{I}^\star(y) \neq \perp$. The PS adversary $\mathcal{D}$ can simulate the two games by either playing PS_0 or PS_1 and the advantage in distinguishing the two games can therefore be estimated with $\mathsf{Adv}^{\mathrm{ps}}_{\mathsf{T}}(\mathcal{D})$. Once the preimages are produced by $x \leftarrow \mathsf{SampDom}(\mathsf{F}^\star)$ without retry, we can adapt the techniques for trapdoor permutations of [13] to complete the reduction. In particular, we will use a labeled tree HTree whose nodes will be populated by some of the queries to the random oracle H. The HTree is initialized with a root node with a single value $h_0 = \varepsilon$. Each subsequent node N_i is added following a query to the random oracle H with input $Q_i = (\mathsf{F}_i, m_i, r_i, x_{i-1})$ and will store the following values:

- a reference to its parent node N_{i-1};
- the query Q_i to the random oracle H;
- the hash response to the query $\eta_i \leftarrow \mathsf{H}(Q_i)$;

- the hash state $h_i \leftarrow h_{i-1} \oplus \eta_i$, where h_{i-1} is the hash state stored in the parent node N_{i-1};
- an additional value $y_i \leftarrow \mathsf{G}(h_i) \oplus \alpha_{i-1}$ (where α_{i-1} is computed from $\mathsf{enc}(x_{i-1})$) that will be used to establish if future nodes can be added as children of N_i.

A node N_i can be added as child of a node N_{i-1} if it satisfies the relation $\mathsf{F}_{i-1}(x_{i-1}) = y_{i-1}$, where F_{i-1} and y_{i-1} are stored in N_{i-1} while x_{i-1} is stored in N_i. This relationship establishes that the query Q_i can be properly used by the signer with key Fow_i to aggregate its signature on message m_i with previous signature x_{i-1}, produced by key Fow_{i-1} and hash state h_{i-1}, which in turn are stored in N_{i-1}. Whenever a query $Q_i = (\mathsf{F}_i, m_i, r_i, x_{i-1})$, with $x_{i-1} \neq \varepsilon$, satisfies this relation with a node N_{i-1} we say that Q_i can be *tethered* to N_{i-1}. If $x_{i-1} = \varepsilon$, then Q_i can always be tethered to the root of the HTree.

Eventually, when the adversary $\mathcal{A}$ outputs a valid aggregate signature $\bar{\Sigma}_n$ for the history $L_n = (\mathsf{pk}_1, m_1), \ldots, (\mathsf{pk}_n, m_n)$, the simulator takes $i^\star \in [n]$ such that $\mathsf{pk}_{i^\star} = \mathsf{pk}^\star$ and $(m_{i^\star}, \varsigma_{i^\star}) \notin \mathcal{Q}$ (the index $i^\star$ is guaranteed to exist when $\mathcal{A}$ is winning). It then recovers $x_{i^\star}$ by iterating the procedure of Lines 3 to 9 in AggVrfy for $n - i^\star$ steps. Then, the simulator checks if $x_{i^\star}$ is a preimage of a $y_{i^\star}$ in the HTree as a child of the node $N_{i^\star-1}$ storing $Q_{i^\star-1} = (\mathsf{pk}_{i^\star-1}, m_{i^\star-1}, r_{i^\star-1}, x_{i^\star-2})$, which is itself a child of the node $N_{i^\star-2}$, and so on until the node N_1. If this is not the case, the simulator aborts by raising $\mathsf{bad}_{\mathsf{teth}}$. Otherwise, the value $x_{i^\star}$ produced by the forgery will satisfy $\mathsf{F}^\star(x_{i^\star}) = y_{i^\star}$ for some $y_{i^\star}$ produced either on Line 19 or on Line 21 of H and stored in $N_{i^\star}$. With probability $1/(\psi \mathsf{q}_{\mathsf{H}})$, we have that $y_{i^\star}$ was produced on Line 21 of H and it is equal to $y^\star$. Therefore $\mathsf{F}^\star(x_{i^\star}) = y^\star$ and $\mathcal{B}$ wins his OW game by returning $x_{i^\star}$. □

4 Instantiation and Evaluation

In this section, we will provide some concrete applications of the HaS-HF-SAS of Sect. 3 to MQ-based and code-based HaS signature schemes. In particular, we analyze the compression capabilities of the scheme when instantiated with UOV, MAYO, and Wave. More details on the trapdoor functions and the application of Theorem 1 to these schemes are given in Appendix B. Our scheme could also be extended to lattice-based schemes, such as the NIST PQC selected algorithm Falcon [33], and generally with PSF-based signatures [24]. In particular, applying our construction would allow to achieve history-free aggregation over existing schemes[1]. However, we already noted how different design choices become feasible due to the additional properties of trapdoor PSF. Accordingly, a direct application would lead to unnecessary loss of efficiency. An analysis of how the HaS-HF-SAS scheme can be modified with PSF can be found in Appendix C.

The main measure of the efficiency of an aggregate signature scheme is the *compression rate*, i.e., the reduction in the length of the aggregate signature

[1] An attack on the, previously unique, history-free SAS of [35] was recently proposed in [12].

Algorithm 3: OW $\implies$ PS-HF-UF-CMA

$\mathcal{B}(\mathsf{F}^\star, y^\star)$:
$\mathcal{Q} \leftarrow \emptyset; c^\star \leftarrow_\$ [\mathsf{q_H}]; c \leftarrow 0$
$(L_n, \bar{\Sigma}_n) \leftarrow \mathcal{A}^{\mathsf{H},\mathsf{G},\mathsf{OAggSign}}(\mathsf{F}^\star)$
$(\mathsf{F}_1, m_1), \ldots, (\mathsf{F}_n, m_n) \leftarrow L_n$
if $\mathsf{AggVrfy}(L_n, \Sigma_n) \wedge \exists i^\star : (\mathsf{F}_{i^\star} = \mathsf{F}^\star \wedge m_{i^\star} \notin \mathcal{Q})$ **then**
  Recover $x_{i^\star}$ as in AggVrfy
  $\mathsf{NList} \leftarrow \mathsf{Lookup}(x_{i^\star})$
  if $\mathsf{NList} = \bot$ **then**
    raise $\mathsf{bad_{teth}}$
  for $N_{i^\star} \in \mathsf{NList}$ **do**
    Retrieve $y_{i^\star}$ from $N_{i^\star}$
    if $y_{i^\star} = y^\star$ **then**
      return $x_{i^\star}$
  raise $\mathsf{bad_{inv}}$

$\mathsf{OAggSign}(m, \varrho = (h, x))$:
$\mathcal{Q} \leftarrow \mathcal{Q} \cup \{m\}$
$(\alpha, \beta) \leftarrow \mathsf{enc}(x)$
$r \leftarrow_\$ \{0,1\}^\lambda$
if $\mathsf{HT}[\mathsf{F}^\star, m, r, x] \neq \bot$ **then**
  raise $\mathsf{bad_{hcol}}$
$\eta \leftarrow_\$ \{0,1\}^{2\lambda}$
$\mathsf{HT}[\mathsf{F}^\star, m, r, x] \leftarrow \eta$
$h' \leftarrow h \oplus \eta$
if $\mathsf{GT}[h'] \neq \bot$ **then**
  raise $\mathsf{bad_{gcol1}}$
$x' \leftarrow_\$ \mathcal{X}$
$y' \leftarrow \mathsf{F}^\star(x')$
$\mathsf{GT}[h'] \leftarrow y' \oplus \alpha$
return $(r, \beta), (h', x')$

$\mathsf{G}(h)$:
if $\mathsf{GT}[h] = \bot$ **then**
  $g \leftarrow_\$ \mathcal{Y}$
  $\mathsf{GT}[h] \leftarrow g$
return $\mathsf{GT}[h]$

$\mathsf{H}(\mathsf{F}, m, r, x)$:
$Q \leftarrow (\mathsf{F}, m, r, x)$
$c \leftarrow c + 1$
if $\mathsf{HT}[Q] = \bot$ **then**
  $\eta \leftarrow_\$ \{0,1\}^{2\lambda}$
  $\mathsf{HT}[Q] \leftarrow \eta$
  $\mathsf{NList} \leftarrow \mathsf{Lookup}(x)$
  if $\mathsf{F} = \mathsf{F}^\star \wedge c = c^\star$ **then**
    $i^\star \leftarrow_\$ [|\mathsf{NList}|]$
  for $i \in [|\mathsf{NList}|]$ **do**
    $N_i \leftarrow \mathsf{NList}[i]$
    $N_i' \leftarrow$ new node with parent N_i
    Retrieve h_i from N_i
    $h_i' \leftarrow h_i \oplus \eta$
    $(\alpha, \beta) \leftarrow \mathsf{enc}(x)$
    if $\mathsf{GT}[h_i'] \neq \bot$ **then**
      raise $\mathsf{bad_{gcol2}}$
    if $\mathsf{F} \neq \mathsf{F}^\star \vee c \neq c^\star \vee i \neq i^\star$ **then**
      $g_i' \leftarrow \mathsf{G}(h_i')$
      $y_i' \leftarrow g_i' \oplus \alpha$
    else
      $y_i' \leftarrow y_i^\star$
      $\mathsf{GT}[h_i'] \leftarrow y_i' \oplus \alpha$
    Populate node N_i' with Q, η, h_i', y_i'
return $\mathsf{HT}[Q]$

$\mathsf{Lookup}(x)$:
if $x = \varepsilon$ **then**
  return Root of HTree
$\mathsf{NList} \leftarrow \{N \in \mathsf{HTree} : (\mathsf{F}, y) \in N \wedge \mathsf{F}(x) = y\}$
if $|\mathsf{NList}| > \psi$ **then**
  raise $\mathsf{bad_{tcol}}$
else if $|\mathsf{NList}| = 0$ **then**
  return $\bot$
else
  return NList

$\bar{\Sigma}_N$ of N users compared to the trivial concatenation of N individual signatures σ. The compression rate of N signatures is defined as $\tau(N) = 1 - \frac{|\bar{\Sigma}_N|}{N \cdot |\sigma|}$. An HaS-HF-SAS signature of N users is the output of the Combine algorithm on $\varsigma_1, \ldots, \varsigma_{N-1}, \Sigma_N$ and is given by $\bar{\Sigma}_N = (\vec{r}_N, \vec{\beta}_{N-1}, h_N, x)$. An individual signature of a generic HaS scheme as described in Sect. 2.3 is given by $\sigma = (r, x)$. In the following, we assume that the aggregation scheme is applied to the signature scheme without further possible optimization, so that we have the same size for salts $|r| = \lambda$ and preimages $|x| = \text{len}(\mathcal{X})$, where $\text{len}(X)$ denotes the bit size of an element in X.

The compression rate is thus given by

$$\begin{aligned}\tau(N) &= 1 - \frac{N \cdot \lambda + (N-1) \cdot \text{len}(\mathcal{X}') + 2\lambda + \text{len}(\mathcal{X})}{N \cdot (\lambda + \text{len}(\mathcal{X}))} \\ &= 1 - \frac{N \cdot (\lambda + \text{len}(\mathcal{X}) - \text{len}(\mathcal{Y})) + 2\lambda + \text{len}(\mathcal{Y})}{N \cdot (\lambda + \text{len}(\mathcal{X}))} \\ &= \frac{\text{len}(\mathcal{Y})}{\lambda + \text{len}(\mathcal{X})} - \frac{2\lambda + \text{len}(\mathcal{Y})}{N \cdot (\lambda + \text{len}(\mathcal{X}))}.\end{aligned} \tag{1}$$

Notice that the aggregate signature is smaller than the trivial concatenation whenever $N > \frac{2\lambda}{\text{len}(\mathcal{Y})} + 1$, which for typical parameters is as soon as $N > 2$.

In [15,20], the size of an aggregate signature of N users is $N \cdot (\text{len}(\mathcal{X}) - \text{len}(\mathcal{Y})) + \text{len}(\mathcal{Y})$. Compared to our scheme, we have a small overhead of $(N+2)\lambda$ bytes due to the aggregated hash state and the random salts. However, as we will see in the next section, this increase in signature size is necessary to guarantee the security of the scheme.

UOV (Appendices B.2 and B.3). We consider the parameters proposed in [10] with respect to NIST security levels I, III, and V. For UOV, the domain $\mathcal{X}$ is given by $\mathbb{F}_q^n$ with elements of length $\text{len}(\mathcal{X}) = n\lceil \log_2 q \rceil$. The codomain $\mathcal{Y}$ is $\mathbb{F}_q^m$ with elements of length $\text{len}(\mathcal{Y}) = m\lceil \log_2 q \rceil$. Regardless of the security level, [10] use 128-bit salts. In our comparison, we consider salts of length $\lambda = 128, 192$ and 256 bits, respectively.

The size of a sequential aggregate signature instantiated with UOV is given by $|\bar{\Sigma}_N| = N \cdot (\lambda + (n-m)\lceil \log_2 q \rceil) + 2\lambda + m\lceil \log_2 q \rceil$ and the size of a single signature is given by $|\sigma| = n\lceil \log_2 q \rceil + \lambda$.

Concrete numbers for different security parameters and the number of signers are given in Table 1.

MAYO (Appendix B.4). We consider the parameters proposed in [9] with respect to NIST security levels I, III, and V. For MAYO, the domain $\mathcal{X}$ is given by $\mathbb{F}_q^{kn}$ with elements of length $\text{len}(\mathcal{X}) = kn\lceil \log_2 q \rceil$. The codomain $\mathcal{Y}$ is $\mathbb{F}_q^m$ with elements of length $\text{len}(\mathcal{Y}) = m\lceil \log_2 q \rceil$. In [9], the salt length $|r|$ is slightly longer than the security parameter for consistency with the security proof. In our comparison, we maintain this choice, adjusting the compression rate computation of Eq. (1).

The size of a sequential aggregate signature instantiated with MAYO is given by $|\bar{\Sigma}_N| = N \cdot (|r| + (kn - m)\lceil \log_2 q \rceil) + 2\lambda + m\lceil \log_2 q \rceil$ and the size of a single signature is given by $|\sigma| = kn\lceil \log_2 q \rceil + |r|$.

Concrete numbers for different security parameters and the number of signers are given in Table 2.

Wave (Appendix B.5). We consider the parameters proposed in [17] with respect to NIST security level I. Notice that this is not the same scheme later submitted to NIST's call for additional digital signatures. The submitted scheme incorporates an optimization derived from the Wavelet variant [3], which cannot be used during aggregation and for which only an asymptotically trivial compression rate can be obtained. For Wave, the domain $\mathcal{X}$ is given by $S_{w,n}$, the subset of $\mathbb{F}_q^n$ with vectors of hamming weight w, with elements of length $\text{len}(\mathcal{X}) = \lceil n \log_2 q \rceil$. The codomain $\mathcal{Y}$ is $\mathbb{F}_q^{n-k}$ with elements of length $\text{len}(\mathcal{Y}) = \lceil (n-k) \log_2 q \rceil$.

The size of a sequential aggregate signature instantiated with Wave is given by $|\bar{\Sigma}_N| = N \cdot (\lambda + \lceil k \log_2 q \rceil) + 2\lambda + \lceil (n-k) \log_2 q \rceil$ and the size of a single signature is given by $|\sigma| = \lceil n \log_2 q \rceil + \lambda$.

Concrete numbers for different security parameters and the number of signers are given in Table 3.

4.1 Single-Signature Optimizations

For proper evaluation of the efficiency of SAS, it is necessary to consider any optimizations of the single signature that cannot be used in aggregation. Ignoring possible optimizations can lead to an unfair comparison and an incorrect calculation of the compression rate.

In [12], Boudgoust and Takahashi observe that in the context of lattice-based signatures built on PSFs (e.g., Falcon) it is possible to reduce the size of signatures considerably by slightly modifying the verification process. However, the same variant is not applicable in the context of aggregate signatures. Similarly, as noted in the previous section, the optimization introduced by the Wavelet variant cannot be applied in the aggregation phase, causing a significant loss of efficiency.

More generally, any compression method applied to a single hash-and-sign signature can be employed in our construction, provided sufficient information exists in the signature to recover the message hash. To elaborate further, consider the generic hash-and-sign scheme outlined in Algorithm 1. Suppose that the Sign algorithm returns the pair $(r, C(x))$, where C is a compression algorithm on the preimage x. If, during the verification process, it is possible to recover $\mathsf{H}(r, m)$ from the public key F and $C(x)$, then the same optimization can be effectively employed within the $\mathsf{HaS\text{-}HF\text{-}SAS}$ scheme. In fact, the aggregation process of Algorithm 2 can be tweaked to aggregate part of the compressed preimage $C(x)$ without the need to modify the verification step further. However, the optimized versions of Falcon and Wave(let) do not conform to this description, as their

Table 1. Aggregate signature sizes and compression rates of HaS-HF-SAS scheme on UOV parameters from [10].

Parameter	ov-Ip	ov-Is	ov-III	ov-V
NIST SL	I	I	III	V
(n, m, q)	(112, 44, 256)	(160, 64, 16)	(184, 72, 256)	(244, 96, 256)
$N \cdot \lvert\sigma\rvert$ (bytes)	$128 \cdot N$	$96 \cdot N$	$208 \cdot N$	$276 \cdot N$
$\lvert\bar{\Sigma}_N\rvert$ (bytes)	$84 \cdot N + 76$	$64 \cdot N + 64$	$136 \cdot N + 120$	$180 \cdot N + 160$
$\tau(5)$	0.23	0.20	0.23	0.23
$\tau(20)$	0.31	0.30	0.32	0.32
$\tau(100)$	0.34	0.33	0.34	0.34
Asym. $\tau(N)$	0.34	0.33	0.35	0.35

Table 2. Aggregate signature sizes and compression rates of HaS-HF-SAS scheme on MAYO parameters from [9].

Parameter	MAYO_1	MAYO_2	MAYO_3	MAYO_5
NIST SL	I	I	III	V
(n, m, o, k, q)	(66, 64, 8, 9, 16)	(78, 64, 18, 4, 16)	(99, 96, 10, 11, 16)	(133, 128, 12, 12, 16)
$\lvert r\rvert$ (bytes)	24	24	32	40
$N \cdot \lvert\sigma\rvert$ (bytes)	$321 \cdot N$	$180 \cdot N$	$577 \cdot N$	$838 \cdot N$
$\lvert\bar{\Sigma}_N\rvert$ (bytes)	$289 \cdot N + 64$	$148 \cdot N + 64$	$529 \cdot N + 96$	$774 \cdot N + 128$
$\tau(5)$	0.06	0.11	0.05	0.05
$\tau(20)$	0.09	0.16	0.07	0.07
$\tau(100)$	0.10	0.17	0.08	0.07
Asym. $\tau(N)$	0.10	0.18	0.08	0.08

Table 3. Aggregate signature sizes and compression rates of HaS-HF-SAS scheme on Wave parameters from [17].

Parameter	128g
NIST SL	I
(n, k, w, q)	(8492, 5605, 7980, 3)
$N \cdot \lvert\sigma\rvert$ (bytes)	$1699 \cdot N$
$\lvert\bar{\Sigma}_N\rvert$ (bytes)	$1127 \cdot N + 604$
$\tau(5)$	0.27
$\tau(20)$	0.32
$\tau(100)$	0.33
Asym. $\tau(N)$	0.34

verification process does not enable the recovery of the message hash from the signature and the public key. Instead, the verification is based on a custom assertion involving the knowledge of F, $C(x)$, and $\mathsf{H}(r, m)$.

Game 3: FH-UF-CMA$_{\mathsf{S}'}$

$(\mathsf{pk}^\star, \mathsf{sk}^\star) \leftarrow \mathsf{KGen}(1^\lambda)$
$\mathcal{Q} \leftarrow \emptyset$
$(L_n, \Sigma_n) \leftarrow \mathcal{A}^{\mathsf{O},\mathsf{OAggSign}}(\mathsf{pk}^\star)$
$(\mathsf{pk}_1, m_1), \ldots, (\mathsf{pk}_n, m_n) \leftarrow L_n$
if $\nexists i^\star : (\mathsf{pk}_{i^\star} = \mathsf{pk}^\star \wedge (m_{i^\star}, L_{i^\star}) \notin \mathcal{Q})$ **then**
  return $\perp$
return $\mathsf{AggVrfy}(L_n, \Sigma_n)$

$\mathsf{OAggSign}(m_i,\ L_{i-1},\ \Sigma_{i-1})$:
if $\mathsf{AggVrfy}(L_{i-1}, \Sigma_{i-1}) = 0$ **then**
  return $\perp$
$\mathcal{Q} \leftarrow \mathcal{Q} \cup \{(L_{i-1}, m_i)\}$
$\Sigma_i \leftarrow \mathsf{AggSign}(\mathsf{sk}^\star, m_i, L_{i-1}, \Sigma_{i-1})$
return Σ_i

5 Security of Existing Multivariate SAS Schemes

In this section, we show a universal forgery for the sequential aggregate signature schemes of [15,20] when instantiated with the UOV signature scheme. Both schemes are based on the variant with encoding of [31] and require an alternative definition of SAS with the notion of *full-history*: at each aggregation step, the signer needs the so-far aggregated signature and the complete list of messages and public keys of previous signers. Moreover, knowledge of the full description of the aggregate signature is required, as the signer needs to check its validity before adding its own.

Definition 9 (FH-SAS). *A Full-History Sequential Aggregate Signature is a tuple of three algorithms* ($\mathsf{KGen}, \mathsf{AggSign}, \mathsf{AggVrfy}$)*:*

- $\mathsf{KGen}(1^\lambda)$ *as described in Definition 6.*
- $\mathsf{AggSign}(\mathsf{sk}_i, m_i, L_{i-1}, \Sigma_{i-1})$*: takes as input the secret key* sk_i *and the message* m_i *of the ith user, a list* $L_{i-1} = (\mathsf{pk}_1, m_1), \ldots, (\mathsf{pk}_{i-1}, m_{i-1})$ *of public keys, message pairs, and the previous aggregate signature* Σ_{i-1}*. If* $\mathsf{AggVrfy}(L_{i-1}, \Sigma_{i-1}) = 1$*, it returns an updated aggregate signature* Σ_i*.*
- $\mathsf{AggVrfy}(L_n, \Sigma_n)$*: takes as input the full history* $L_n = (\mathsf{pk}_1, m_1), \ldots, (\mathsf{pk}_n, m_n)$ *of public key, message pairs, and an aggregate signature* Σ_n*. Returns* 1 *if* Σ_n *is a valid aggregate signature and* 0 *otherwise.*

Below we show the definition of full-history unforgeability under adaptive chosen message (FH-UF-CMA). Compared to the notion of PS-HF-UF-CMA (Definition 8), the signing oracle $\mathsf{OAggSign}$ requires sending the list L_{i-1} of public keys and messages along with the aggregate signature Σ_{i-1} and returns the updated signature if and only if Σ_{i-1} is valid.

Definition 10 (FH-UF-CMA **Security**). *Let* O *be a random oracle, let* $\mathsf{S}' = (\mathsf{KGen}, \mathsf{AggSign}, \mathsf{AggVrfy})$ *be a* FH-SAS *scheme, let* $\mathcal{A}$ *be an adversary. We define the advantage of* $\mathcal{A}$ *playing the* FH-UF-CMA *game (Game 3) against* S' *as follows:*

$$\mathsf{Adv}_{\mathsf{S}'}^{\text{fh-uf-cma}}(\mathcal{A}) = \Pr[\text{FH-UF-CMA}_{\mathsf{S}'}(\mathcal{A}) = 1]\,.$$

Algorithm 4: Multivariate $\mathsf{FH\text{-}SAS_T}$

Let $\Sigma_0 = (\emptyset, \varepsilon)$.

$\mathsf{KGen}(1^\lambda)$:
- $(\mathsf{F}, \mathsf{I}) \leftarrow \mathsf{TrapGen}(1^\lambda)$
- **return** $\mathsf{pk} \leftarrow \mathsf{F}, \mathsf{sk} \leftarrow (\mathsf{F}, \mathsf{I})$

$\mathsf{AggVrfy}(L_n, \Sigma_n)$:
- $(\mathsf{F}_1, m_1), \ldots, (\mathsf{F}_n, m_n) \leftarrow L_n$
- $(\vec{\beta}_{n-1}, x_n) \leftarrow \Sigma_n$
- **for** $i \leftarrow n, \ldots, 2$ **do**
  - $L_i \leftarrow (\mathsf{F}_1, m_1), \ldots, (\mathsf{F}_i, m_i)$
  - $h_i \leftarrow \mathsf{H}(L_i)$
  - $\alpha_{i-1} \leftarrow \mathsf{F}_i(x_i) \oplus h_i$
  - $x_{i-1} \leftarrow \mathsf{dec}(\alpha_{i-1}, \beta_{i-1})$
- **return** $\mathsf{F}_1(x_1) = \mathsf{H}(\mathsf{F}_1, m_1)$

$\mathsf{AggSign}((\mathsf{F}_i, \mathsf{I}_i), m_i, L_{i-1}, \Sigma_{i-1})$:
- $(\vec{\beta}_{i-2}, x_{i-1}) \leftarrow \Sigma_{i-1}$
- **if** $\mathsf{AggVrfy}(L_{i-1}, \Sigma_{i-1}) = 0$ **then**
  - **return** $\perp$
- $L_i \leftarrow L_{i-1} \cup \{(\mathsf{F}_i, m_i)\}$
- $(\alpha_{i-1}, \beta_{i-1}) \leftarrow \mathsf{enc}(x_i)$
- $h_i \leftarrow \mathsf{H}(L_i)$
- $x_i \leftarrow \mathsf{I}_i(\alpha_{i-1} \oplus h_i)$
- $\vec{\beta}_{i-1} \leftarrow \vec{\beta}_{i-2} \cup \{\beta_{i-1}\}$
- **return** $\Sigma_i \leftarrow (\vec{\beta}_{i-1}, x_i)$

5.1 Multivariate FH-SAS

The FH-SAS schemes of [15,20] are instantiated with HFEv- and UOV, respectively, but no explicit use is made of unique features of these trapdoor functions. The description of Algorithm 4 refers to a generic multivariate trapdoor function T (as in Sect. 2.1) and is based on the construction of [20], which is slightly more general.

In Algorithm 4, the random oracle is $\mathsf{H}\colon \{0,1\}^* \to \mathcal{Y}$. The encoding function is $\mathsf{enc}\colon \mathcal{X} \to \mathcal{Y} \times \mathcal{X}'$ that splits an element x_i as $\mathsf{enc}(x_i) = (\alpha_i, \beta_i)$ and the corresponding decoding function is $\mathsf{dec}\colon \mathcal{Y} \times \mathcal{X}' \to \mathcal{X}$ such that $\mathsf{dec}(\mathsf{enc}(x)) = x$. To simplify the description we will also use the notation $\alpha(x_i) = \alpha_i$ and $\beta(x_i) = \beta_i$, where $\alpha(\cdot), \beta(\cdot)$ are implicitly defined by enc.

Both [20] and [15] provide a similar claim on the formal security of their sequential aggregate signature scheme. In the following, we are considering a generic multivariate trapdoor function since their choice does not influence the security claim.

Theorem 2 ([20]). *Let* T *be a multivariate trapdoor function. Let* $\mathcal{A}$ *be a* FH-UF-CMA *adversary against the* FH-SAS *scheme on* T *in the random oracle model, which makes* $\mathsf{q_S}$ *signing queries and* $\mathsf{q_H}$ *queries to the random oracle. Then, there exist a* OW *adversary* $\mathcal{B}$ *against* T *such that*

$$\mathsf{Adv}^{\text{fh-uf-cma}}_{\mathsf{FH\text{-}SAS_T}}(\mathcal{A}) \leq (\mathsf{q_S q_H} + 1) \cdot \mathsf{Adv}^{\text{ow}}_{\mathsf{T}}(\mathcal{B})$$

and the running time of $\mathcal{B}$ *is about that of* $\mathcal{A}$.

In [15], the authors omit the proof for their security claim, while in [20] the authors provide a sketch of the proof in which they state that almost all the steps of the security proof follow [31] with only some slight modifications taking into account the use of the encoding function.

In the next section, we show an explicit universal forgery on FH-SAS when instantiated with the UOV signature scheme. Then, in Sect. 5.3, we provide some insight into why the security proof of [31] cannot be applied to multivariate schemes and, more generally, to signature schemes based on trapdoor functions that are not permutations.

5.2 Description of the Forgery

We recall that in UOV, the trapdoor function is a multivariate quadratic map $\mathcal{P}\colon \mathbb{F}_q^n \to \mathbb{F}_q^m$ that vanishes on a secret linear subspace $O \subset \mathbb{F}_q^n$ of dimension m. A more in-depth description can be found in Appendix B.1.

In the following we are assuming that the encoding function $\mathsf{enc}(\boldsymbol{x})$ can be expressed via an appropriate affine map and, accordingly, $\alpha(\boldsymbol{x}) = R(\boldsymbol{x}) = \mathbf{A}\boldsymbol{x}+\boldsymbol{b}$, where $\mathbf{A} \in \mathbb{F}_q^{m\times n}, \boldsymbol{b} \in \mathbb{F}_q^m$. In [15,20], $\mathsf{enc}(\boldsymbol{x})$ is always the projection in the first m and the last $n-m$ components[2] of $\boldsymbol{x}$. This is a slight generalization that captures the intuition that there must be a corresponding efficient decoding function.

Lemma 1. *The multivariate* FH-SAS *scheme of Sect. 5.1, instantiated with UOV, is not* FH-UF-CMA.

Proof. Let $\mathsf{pk}_i = \mathcal{P}_i$ be the target public key and assume that the forger $\mathcal{F}$ knows a valid aggregate signature $\Sigma_i = (\boldsymbol{\beta}_1, \ldots, \boldsymbol{\beta}_{i-1}, \boldsymbol{x}_i)$ for a honest history $L_i = (\mathsf{pk}_1, m_1), \ldots, (\mathsf{pk}_i, m_i)$. This is a typical attack environment, much weaker than the notion of FH-UF-CMA that we introduced in Definition 10. Then, $\mathcal{F}$ select a message $m_i^\star$ on which it will produce a forged signature for the target user.

The forger $\mathcal{F}$ computes a forged signature by replacing the $(i-1)$th honest signer, as follows:

1. First, $\mathcal{F}$ appropriately generates a UOV key pair $(\mathsf{pk}_\mathcal{F}, \mathsf{sk}_\mathcal{F}) = (\mathcal{P}_\mathcal{F}, O_\mathcal{F})$ by randomly choosing an m-dimensional linear subspace $O_\mathcal{F} \subset \ker \mathbf{A}$ and use the same procedure of $\mathsf{TrapGen}_{\mathsf{uov}}$ (Algorithm 5) to sample $\mathcal{P}_\mathcal{F}$ that vanishes on $O_\mathcal{F}$.
2. Then, $\mathcal{F}$ arbitrarily chooses a message $m_\mathcal{F}$, computes a corresponding forged history $L^\star = L_{i-2} \cup \{(\mathsf{pk}_\mathcal{F}, m_\mathcal{F}), (\mathsf{pk}_i, m_i)\}$ and computes $\boldsymbol{\alpha}^\star \leftarrow \mathcal{P}_i(\boldsymbol{x}_i) \oplus \mathsf{H}(L^\star)$.
3. Finally, $\mathcal{F}$ finds a preimage $\boldsymbol{x}_\mathcal{F}$ under $\mathcal{P}_\mathcal{F}$ for $L_\mathcal{F} = L_{i-2} \cup \{(\mathsf{pk}_\mathcal{F}, m_\mathcal{F})\}$ such that
$$\mathcal{P}_\mathcal{F}(\boldsymbol{x}_\mathcal{F}) = \boldsymbol{\alpha}_{i-2} \oplus \mathsf{H}(L_\mathcal{F}) \qquad \text{and} \qquad \alpha(\boldsymbol{x}_\mathcal{F}) = \boldsymbol{\alpha}^\star. \tag{2}$$
Then $\Sigma^\star = (\boldsymbol{\beta}_1, \ldots, \boldsymbol{\beta}_{i-2}, \beta(\boldsymbol{x}_\mathcal{F}), \boldsymbol{x}_i)$ is a valid aggregate signature for the forged history $L^\star$.

[2] In this case we would have that $\alpha(\boldsymbol{x}) = \mathbf{A}\boldsymbol{x}$ with $\mathbf{A} = [\mathbf{I}_m \mid \mathbf{0}_{m,n-m}]$.

Finding a preimage $\boldsymbol{x}_{\mathcal{F}}$ that satisfies Eq. (2) is equivalent to finding partially fixed preimage for $\mathcal{P}_{\mathcal{F}}$ under the map R. In particular, the forger can use the appropriately generated secret key $O_{\mathcal{F}}$ to restrict the preimage search to an appropriate affine subspace and guarantee the condition $R(\boldsymbol{x}_{\mathcal{F}}) = \boldsymbol{\alpha}^{\star}$. The forger searches for a preimage of $\boldsymbol{t} = \boldsymbol{\alpha}_{i-2} \oplus \mathsf{H}(L_{\mathcal{F}})$ by using a procedure similar to the Sign procedure described in Algorithm 5: on Line 1, instead of randomly sampling the vectors $\boldsymbol{v}$ from $\mathbb{F}_q^n$, samples $\boldsymbol{v}$ from $\ker R'$, with $R'(\boldsymbol{x}) = \mathbf{A}\boldsymbol{x} + (\boldsymbol{b} - \boldsymbol{\alpha}^{\star})$. Then when a preimage $\boldsymbol{x}_{\mathcal{F}} \in \mathbb{F}_q^n$ of $\boldsymbol{t}$ is found, the forger would have $\boldsymbol{x}_{\mathcal{F}} \in \ker R'$, since $\boldsymbol{x}_{\mathcal{F}} = \boldsymbol{v} + \boldsymbol{o}$ with $\boldsymbol{v} \in \ker R'$ and $\boldsymbol{o} \in \ker \mathbf{A}$. Therefore $\alpha(\boldsymbol{x}_{\mathcal{F}}) = R(\boldsymbol{x}_{\mathcal{F}}) = \boldsymbol{\alpha}^{\star}$.

We then show that $\Sigma^{\star}$ passes the verification correctly for the forged history $L^{\star}$:

1. The verifier applies the first iteration of AggVrfy (Algorithm 4) to recover the previous signature $\boldsymbol{x}_{\mathcal{F}}$ from $\boldsymbol{x}_i$ as follows:
$$\alpha(\boldsymbol{x}_{\mathcal{F}}) \leftarrow \mathcal{P}_i(\boldsymbol{x}_i) \oplus \mathsf{H}(L^{\star}) = \alpha^{\star}, \qquad \boldsymbol{x}_{\mathcal{F}} \leftarrow \mathsf{dec}(\alpha(\boldsymbol{x}_{\mathcal{F}}), \beta(\boldsymbol{x}_{\mathcal{F}}))$$
2. Since $\boldsymbol{x}_{\mathcal{F}}$ is a preimage of $\boldsymbol{\alpha}_{i-2} \oplus \mathsf{H}(L_{\mathcal{F}})$, the verifier correctly obtains $\boldsymbol{x}_{i-2}$ proceeding in the iterations of AggVrfy:
$$\boldsymbol{\alpha}_{i-2} \leftarrow \mathcal{P}_{\mathcal{F}}(\boldsymbol{x}_{\mathcal{F}}) \oplus \mathsf{H}(L_{\mathcal{F}}), \qquad \boldsymbol{x}_{i-2} \leftarrow \mathsf{dec}(\boldsymbol{\alpha}_{i-2}, \boldsymbol{\beta}_{i-2}).$$
3. The $(i-2)$th signer was not tampered and, hence, the intermediate signature $\Sigma_{i-2} = (\boldsymbol{\beta}_1, \ldots, \boldsymbol{\beta}_{i-3}, \boldsymbol{x}_{i-2})$ can be correctly verified with AggVrfy on honest history L_{i-2}.

Therefore, the verifier determines the forged signature $\Sigma^{\star}$ as valid. □

5.3 Discussion

The previous forging procedure can be directly applied to constructions derived from [31] and instantiated via UOV, such as [15,20]. In particular, we have shown how the existential unforgeability claims of [15,20] are incorrect when the schemes are instantiated with UOV. The attack essentially involves finding a partially fixed preimage, following an adversarial key generation based on the public parameters of the aggregate signature scheme, specifically the encoding function. Although this attack may have applicability beyond UOV, it is not a universal forgery for generic trapdoor functions. However, this result aligns with the analysis of critical issues encountered when attempting to extend the security proof of [31] to generic trapdoor functions, as outlined in the following.

Programming the Random Oracle. In [31], the random oracle can be simulated to determine preimages for any permutation $\pi : \mathcal{X} \to \mathcal{X}$. This is typically achieved by sampling a uniformly random $x \leftarrow_{\$} \mathcal{X}$ and returning $\pi(x)$, which is uniformly distributed in $\mathcal{Y} = \mathcal{X}$. However, in the case of a generic trapdoor function, we cannot assume that the image of F is uniform. Consequently, to provide an accurate simulation, we must sample and return a uniformly random value in $\mathcal{Y}$.

Uniqueness of the Aggregate Signature. If we relax the previous condition and assume a uniformity property of the trapdoor functions[3] we may attempt to replicate the process described in [31] to answer the signing oracle. Indeed, on input $Q = (m^\star, L_{n-1}, \Sigma_{n-1})$ the simulator can use the knowledge of appropriate preimages for F_i to craft a valid aggregate signature on $L_{n-1} \cup \{(\mathsf{F}^\star, m^\star)\}$. However, we argue that this property alone is not sufficient for a correct simulation, which is instead based on the following fact of TDP-based constructions: for a fixed input $L_n = (\mathsf{F}_1, m_1), \ldots, (\mathsf{F}_n, m_n)$ there exists a unique aggregate signature on L_n. Otherwise, if the aggregate signature is not unique, the simulator would be unable to provide a valid response to the aggregate signature query. In fact, on input Q, the simulator would take the preimage $x^\star$ for $\mathsf{F}^\star$ on $\alpha(x_{n-1}) \oplus \mathsf{H}(L_n)$ associated to the random oracle query on input $L_n = L_{n-1} \cup \{(\mathsf{F}^\star, m^\star)\}$. But, without the knowledge that x_{n-1} is equal to the preimage computed by the adversary on input L_{n-1}, the aggregate signature produced by the simulator may not be properly verified, resulting in an invalid response.

Reduction to OW. Eventually, the adversary will produce a valid non-trivial aggregate signature Σ_n on input $L_n = (\mathsf{F}_1, m_1), \ldots, (\mathsf{F}_n, m_n)$, where we assume, for simplicity, that $\mathsf{F}_n = \mathsf{F}^\star$ is the target public key. Since the aggregate signature is correct, it follows that $\mathsf{F}^\star(x_n) = \alpha(x_{n-1}) \oplus \mathsf{H}(L_n) = y$. In the context of TDPs, [31] shows that y is equal to the target $y^\star$ of the OW game, with probability $(\mathsf{q_H} + \mathsf{q_S} + 1)^{-1}$.

When we consider generic TDFs, the previously mentioned approach is not valid, and it is necessary to modify the simulation of H by returning a fresh random value for each query. Moreover, we claim that in this setting it is not possible to correctly simulate the response to the oracles in order to obtain a preimage of $y^\star$. In fact, to obtain a valid preimage, the simulator would require $\mathsf{F}^\star(x_n) = \alpha(x_{n-1}) \oplus \mathsf{H}(L_n) = y^\star$ and therefore $\mathsf{H}(L_n) = y^\star \oplus \alpha(x_{n-1})$. It should then have been able to simulate the random oracle to return $y^\star \oplus \alpha(x_{n-1})$ when given the input L_n. However, it is not possible to provide this answer, as x_{n-1} is not part of the query input and is not uniquely determined.

Fixing the Forging Vulnerability. The main vulnerability of FH-SAS concerns the overall malleability of the aggregate signature. In the original scheme for TPDs, once the input $L_n = (\mathsf{F}_1, m_1), \ldots, (\mathsf{F}_n, m_n)$ is fixed, it was observed that there is a unique aggregate signature on messages $m_1, \ldots, m_n$ under public keys $\mathsf{F}_1, \ldots, \mathsf{F}_n$. Instead, in the extended version, uniqueness is lost due to the probabilistic nature of the inversion process. Consequently, it is always possible to construct two aggregate signatures on the same input, $\Sigma = (\beta_1, \ldots, \beta_{i-1}, x_n)$ and $\Sigma' = (\beta_1, \ldots, \beta_{i-1}, x_i')$, which differ only in the aggregation of the last signature. Furthermore, as shown in the forgery presented in Sect. 5.2, it is possible to have two aggregate signatures on the same input $\Sigma = (\beta_1, \ldots, \beta_{i-1}, x_i)$ and $\Sigma' = (\beta_1, \ldots, \beta_{i-1}', x_i)$ which differ only in the intermediate partial encodings. While the loss of uniqueness is unavoidable, it is possible to modify the

[3] For instance, this is the case for Trapdoor Preimage Sampleable Function [24].

scheme to prevent this additional form of malleability by making partial β encodings part of the random oracle input. We modify the aggregation step of $\mathsf{AggSign}((\mathsf{F}_i, \mathsf{I}_i), m_i, L_{i-1}, \Sigma_{i-1})$ (Algorithm 4): let $\Sigma_{i-1} = (\beta_1, \dots, \beta_{i-2}, x_{i-1})$ and compute

$$(\alpha_{i-1}, \beta_{i-1}) \leftarrow \mathsf{enc}(x_{i-1}), \qquad x_i \leftarrow \mathsf{I}_i(\alpha_{i-1} \oplus \mathsf{H}(L_i, \vec{\beta}_{i-1})),$$

where $L_i = L_{i-1} \cup \{(\mathsf{F}_i, m_i)\}$ and $\vec{\beta}_{i-1} = (\beta_1, \dots, \beta_{i-1})$.

Observe that now, once a new signature has been aggregated, it is no longer possible to modify the previous partial encodings while maintaining the validity of the aggregated signature. That is, if $\Sigma = (\beta_1, \dots, \beta_{i-1}, x_i)$ and $\Sigma' = (\beta_1, \dots, \beta'_{i-1}, x'_i)$ are valid aggregate signatures on the same input with $\beta_{i-1} \neq \beta'_{i-1}$, then $x_i \neq x'_i$. As a result, the forging procedure described in Sect. 5.2 is no longer applicable, as the adversary now needs to guess the partial encoding $\beta(x_{\mathcal{F}})$ of its own signature. However, in doing so $\beta(x_{\mathcal{F}})$ becomes fixed and $\alpha^\star$ is not under the adversary's direct control. Once $\alpha^\star$ is computed, the entire signature $x_{\mathcal{F}}$ is fixed, and with high probability, it is not a valid signature.

This minor modification addresses the vulnerability exploited by our attack. However, from a provable security perspective, this construction presents similar problems to the original attempt to generalize [31]. As a result, we are unable to provide a formal proof of security.

6 Conclusions

We proposed a partial-signature history-free sequential aggregate signature within the probabilistic hash-and-sign with retry paradigm, generalizing previous results to generic trapdoor functions. We proved the security of our scheme in the random oracle model, assuming only the one-wayness of the underlying TDF and an additional notion of indistinguishability on preimages. This additional property has been demonstrated for numerous post-quantum TDFs to achieve the security of the related signature schemes. This allowed us to easily instantiate our construction in Sect. 4 with the UOV, MAYO, and Wave schemes, for which we obtained a compression rate between 5% and 34%. We also pointed out in Sect. 5 how existing aggregation schemes for multivariate TDFs lack formal security and are insecure for some choices of the underlying function. Therefore, within our knowledge, ours is the first scheme that allows the aggregation of multivariate and code-based HaS signature schemes.

Acknowledgments. The authors would like to thank the anonymous reviewers of CT-RSA 2024 for their valuable feedback and suggestions. This publication was created with the co-financing of the European Union FSE-REACT-EU, PON Research and Innovation 2014–2020 DM1062/2021. The first author is a member of the INdAM Research Group GNSAGA. The second author is a member of CrypTO, the group of Cryptography and Number Theory of Politecnico di Torino. The first author acknowledges support from Ripple's University Blockchain Research Initiative.

A Missing Proofs

Lemma 2. *When a new node is added to the* HTree *as a result to a call to* H*, the additional value* y' *is chosen uniformly at random from* $\mathcal{Y}$.

Proof. When a new node is added to the HTree on Line 23 of H, there are two possibilities for the additional value y'. In both cases, y' is chosen uniformly at random from $\mathcal{Y}$ and is independent of the view of $\mathcal{A}$. In fact, whenever the query to H is not the special random guess $c^\star$ chosen by the simulator, we have $y' \leftarrow \mathsf{G}(h') \oplus \alpha$. Here, $\mathsf{G}(h')$ is guaranteed to be a fresh uniformly random value since, otherwise, H would abort on Line 16 and the node would not be added to the HTree. If, on the other hand, the query $c^\star$ was made to H, then we set $y' \leftarrow y^\star$ for one of the new nodes to be added. Since $c^\star$ was chosen randomly among all queries to H, the assignment of $y^\star$ is made independently of the view of $\mathcal{A}$ and previous interactions with H. □

Lemma 3. *For any* $k > \psi$ *functions* $\mathsf{F}_1, \dots, \mathsf{F}_k \colon \mathcal{X} \to \mathcal{Y}$ *and uniformly random* $y_1, \dots, y_k \in \mathcal{Y}$*, there exists* $x \in \mathcal{X}$ *such that* $\mathsf{F}_i(x) = y_i$*, for every* $i = 1, \dots, k$*, with probability at most* $|\mathcal{X}|/|\mathcal{Y}|^k$.

Proof. Let $S_y^{\mathsf{F}} = \{x \in \mathcal{X} : \mathsf{F}(x) = y\}$ be the set of preimages of y under F. For a random choice of y_1 it holds that $|S_{y_1}^{\mathsf{F}_1}| = \alpha$ for some $0 \le \alpha \le |\mathcal{X}|$. Then, there are at most α possible values for the tuple $(y_2, \dots, y_k)$, corresponding to $\{(\mathsf{F}_2(x), \dots, \mathsf{F}_k(x)) : x \in S_{y_1}^{\mathsf{F}_1}\}$, such that $\bigcap S_{y_i}^{\mathsf{F}_i} \neq \emptyset$. Since $y_2, \dots, y_k$ are uniformly chosen in $\mathcal{Y}$, the probability of a non-empty intersection is at most $\alpha|\mathcal{Y}|^{1-k}$. Therefore, the desired probability is bounded by varying over the possible values of α:

$$\sum_{\alpha=0}^{|\mathcal{X}|} \frac{\alpha}{|\mathcal{Y}|^{k-1}} \Pr_{y_1 \leftarrow_\$ \mathcal{Y}}\left[|S_{y_1}^{\mathsf{F}_1}| = \alpha\right] = \frac{1}{|\mathcal{Y}|^{k-1}} \sum_{\alpha=0}^{|\mathcal{X}|} \alpha \cdot \frac{|\{y_1 \in \mathcal{Y} : |S_{y_1}^{\mathsf{F}_1}| = \alpha\}|}{|\mathcal{Y}|} = \frac{|\mathcal{X}|}{|\mathcal{Y}|^k}.$$

□

Lemma 4. *If an input* Q *has not been entered in the* HTree *after being queried to* H*, the probability that it will ever become tethered to a node in* HTree *is at most* $\psi\mathsf{q}'/|\mathcal{Y}|$*, where* q' *is the number of queries made to* H *after* Q.

Proof. Suppose that $Q = (\mathsf{F}, m, r, x)$ was queried to H and was not added to the HTree, i.e. $\mathsf{Lookup}(x) = \perp$. Now suppose that a query $Q' = (\mathsf{F}', m', r', x')$ was subsequently sent to H and was added to HTree as part of a node N' with additional value y'. For Q to be tethered to N', it must hold that $\mathsf{F}'(x) = y'$. Following Lemma 2, when a new node is added to the HTree as a result to a call to H, the additional value y' is chosen uniformly at random from $\mathcal{Y}$. In particular, y' is random and independent of F' and x. Therefore, the probability of having $\mathsf{F}'(x) = y'$ is $|\mathcal{Y}|^{-1}$. Since there are at most q' queries to H after Q and each query can add at most ψ nodes to the HTree, the desired probability follows by the union bound. □

Game 4: Games for $\mathsf{OAggSign}(m, \varrho = (h, x))$

Game_0:

$(\alpha, \beta) \leftarrow \mathsf{enc}(x)$
repeat
  $r \leftarrow_{\$} \{0,1\}^\lambda$
  $\eta \leftarrow \mathsf{H}(\mathsf{F}^\star, m, r, x)$
  $h' \leftarrow h \oplus \eta$
  $g' \leftarrow \mathsf{G}(h')$
  $y' \leftarrow g' \oplus \alpha$
  $x' \leftarrow \mathsf{I}^\star(y')$
until $x' \neq \bot$
return $(r, \beta), (h', x')$

Game_1-Game_2:

$(\alpha, \beta) \leftarrow \mathsf{enc}(x)$
repeat
  $r \leftarrow_{\$} \{0,1\}^\lambda$
  if $\mathsf{HT}[\mathsf{F}^\star, m, r, x] \neq \bot$ **then**
    raise $\mathsf{bad}_{\mathsf{hcol}}$
  $\eta \leftarrow_{\$} \{0,1\}^{2\lambda}$
  $\mathsf{HT}[\mathsf{F}^\star, m, r, x] \leftarrow \eta$
  $h' \leftarrow h \oplus \eta$
  if $\mathsf{GT}[h'] \neq \bot$ **then**
    raise $\mathsf{bad}_{\mathsf{gcol1}}$
  $y' \leftarrow_{\$} \mathcal{Y}$
  $\mathsf{GT}[h'] \leftarrow y' \oplus \alpha$
  $x' \leftarrow \mathsf{I}^\star(y')$
until $x' \neq \bot$
return $(r, \beta), (h', x')$

Game_3-Game_5:

$(\alpha, \beta) \leftarrow \mathsf{enc}(x)$
$r \leftarrow_{\$} \{0,1\}^\lambda$
if $\mathsf{HT}[\mathsf{F}^\star, m, r, x] \neq \bot$ **then**
  raise $\mathsf{bad}_{\mathsf{hcol}}$
$\eta \leftarrow_{\$} \{0,1\}^{2\lambda}$
$\mathsf{HT}[\mathsf{F}^\star, m, r, x] \leftarrow \eta$
$h' \leftarrow h \oplus \eta$
if $\mathsf{GT}[h'] \neq \bot$ **then**
  raise $\mathsf{bad}_{\mathsf{gcol1}}$
$x' \leftarrow \mathsf{SampDom}(\mathsf{F}^\star)$
$y' \leftarrow \mathsf{F}^\star(x')$
$\mathsf{GT}[h'] \leftarrow y' \oplus \alpha$
return $(r, \beta), (h', x')$

A.1 Proof for strong PS-HF-UF-CMA security (Theorem 1)

Proof. We prove the reduction by presenting a sequence of hybrid games, modifying the strong PS-HF-UF-CMA game (Game 2) until it can be simulated by the OW adversary $\mathcal{B}$. In the following use the notation $\Pr[\mathsf{Game}_n(\mathcal{A}) = 1]$ to denote the probability that Game_n returns 1 when playing by $\mathcal{A}$. The game sequence Game_0-Game_3 for $\mathsf{OAggSign}$ is detailed in Game 4. The game sequence Game_3-Game_5 for H is detailed in Game 5.

Game_0 This is the original strong PS-HF-UF-CMA game against the $\mathsf{HaS\text{-}HF\text{-}SAS}$ scheme except that it uses programmable random oracles. At the start of the game, the challenger initializes two tables, HT for H and GT for G. When a query Q for H is received, if $\mathsf{HT}[Q] = \bot$ it uniformly samples $\eta \leftarrow_{\$} \{0,1\}^{2\lambda}$ and stores $\mathsf{HT}[Q] \leftarrow \eta$, finally it returns $\mathsf{HT}[Q]$ (similarly for G). It follows that $\Pr[\mathsf{Game}_0(\mathcal{A}) = 1] = \mathsf{Adv}^{\text{ps-hf-uf-cma}}_{\mathsf{HaS\text{-}HF\text{-}SAS}}(\mathcal{A})$.

Game_1 This game is identical to Game_0 except that $\mathsf{OAggSign}$ aborts by raising $\mathsf{bad}_{\mathsf{hcol}}$ if on query $(m, \varrho = (h, x))$ it samples a salt r such that the random oracle H was already queried at input $Q = (\mathsf{F}^\star, m, r, x)$, i.e. $\mathsf{HT}[Q] \neq \bot$. Otherwise it samples $\eta \leftarrow_{\$} \{0,1\}^{2\lambda}$ and programs $\mathsf{HT}[Q] \leftarrow \eta$. It follows that $|\Pr[\mathsf{Game}_0(\mathcal{A}) = 1] - \Pr[\mathsf{Game}_1(\mathcal{A}) = 1]| \leq \Pr[\mathsf{bad}_{\mathsf{hcol}}]$.

Game_2 This game is identical to Game_1 except that $\mathsf{OAggSign}$ aborts by raising $\mathsf{bad}_{\mathsf{gcol1}}$ if on query $(m, \varrho = (h, x))$, after sampling $\eta \leftarrow_{\$} \{0,1\}^{2\lambda}$ it computes $h' \leftarrow h \oplus \eta$ such that the random oracle G was already queried at input h', i.e. $\mathsf{GT}[h'] \neq \bot$. Otherwise it samples $y' \leftarrow_{\$} \mathcal{Y}$ and programs $\mathsf{GT}[h'] \leftarrow y' \oplus \alpha$. It follows that $|\Pr[\mathsf{Game}_1(\mathcal{A}) = 1] - \Pr[\mathsf{Game}_2(\mathcal{A}) = 1]| \leq \Pr[\mathsf{bad}_{\mathsf{gcol1}}]$.

Game_3 This game is identical to Game_2 except that $\mathsf{OAggSign}$ directly samples $r \leftarrow_\$ \{0,1\}^\lambda$, $x' \leftarrow \mathsf{SampDom}(\mathsf{F}^\star)$ and computes $y' \leftarrow \mathsf{F}^\star(x')$ instead of computing $x' \leftarrow \mathsf{I}^\star(y')$ after sampling $y' \leftarrow_\$ \mathcal{Y}$. The PS adversary $\mathcal{D}$ can simulate both Game_2 and Game_3, noticing that $y' = \mathsf{F}^\star(x')$ and programming G accordingly. More precisely, on receiving a query $Q = (m, \varrho = (h, x))$ for $\mathsf{OAggSign}$, $\mathcal{D}$ computes $(r, x') \leftarrow \mathsf{Sample}_b$ and programs $\mathsf{GT}[h'] \leftarrow \mathsf{F}^\star(x') \oplus \alpha$. Both Game_2 and Game_3 are equivalently modified by moving the programming step of H and G to the end of the $\mathsf{OAggSign}$. It now follows that when $\mathcal{D}$ is playing PS_0 its simulation coincides with Game_2, while when it is playing PS_1 it coincides with Game_3. Either way, $\mathcal{D}$ simulates the games with at most the same running time of $\mathcal{A}$ plus the time required for answering the queries to the sampling oracle. The latter takes $\mathcal{O}(\mathsf{poly}(\mathrm{len}(\mathcal{X}), \mathrm{len}(\mathcal{Y})))$ and is repeated at most $\mathsf{q_S}$ times. Finally, we have that $|\Pr[\mathsf{Game}_2(\mathcal{A}) = 1] - \Pr[\mathsf{Game}_3(\mathcal{A}) = 1]| \leq \mathsf{Adv}_{\mathsf{T}}^{\mathrm{ps}}(\mathcal{D})$.

Game_4 This game is identical to Game_3 except that the random oracle H is simulated as follows. At the start of the game, the challenger initializes a labeled tree HTree, as described at the beginning of the proof. When H receives a query $Q = (\mathsf{F}, m, r, x)$, if $\mathsf{HT}[Q] \neq \perp$ it returns it. Otherwise, it samples a uniformly random $\eta \leftarrow_\$ \{0,1\}^{2\lambda}$ and programs $\mathsf{HT}[Q] \leftarrow \eta$. Then, it checks if Q can be added as a child node of existing nodes in HTree. To determine whether this is the case, it uses the Lookup function (see Algorithm 3) on input x that checks if it can be tethered to existing nodes, i.e. there exists a node $N_i \in \mathsf{HTree}$ such that $\mathsf{F}_i(x) = y_i$. If Q can be tethered to more than ψ nodes, the game aborts by raising $\mathsf{bad_{tcol}}$. Otherwise, H add a new node N'_i with parent N_i for each node $N_i \in \mathsf{HTree}$ returned by $\mathsf{Lookup}(x)$. N'_i contains the original query Q, the hash response η, the hash state $h'_i \leftarrow h_i \oplus \eta$ (where h_i is stored in N_i) and an additional value $y'_i \leftarrow \mathsf{G}(h'_i) \oplus \alpha$ (where α is computed from $\mathsf{enc}(x)$) that will be used to check if a future node can be tethered via Lookup queries. It holds that $|\Pr[\mathsf{Game}_3(\mathcal{A}) = 1] - \Pr[\mathsf{Game}_4(\mathcal{A}) = 1]| \leq \Pr[\mathsf{bad_{tcol}}]$.

Game_5 This game is identical to Game_4 except that the random oracle H is simulated as follows. At the beginning of the game, the challenger uniformly chooses an index $c^\star \leftarrow_\$ [\mathsf{q_H}]$ among the queries to the random oracle H, initializes a counter $c \leftarrow 0$ and uniformly samples $y^\star \leftarrow_\$ \mathcal{Y}$. When H receives a query $Q = (\mathsf{F}, m, r, x)$ it increments $c \leftarrow c + 1$. Then, if $\mathsf{F} = \mathsf{F}^\star$ and $c = c^\star$ it samples a random index $i^\star$ from the number of nodes in NList. If, for any of the new nodes to be added, it computes $h'_i \leftarrow h_i \oplus \eta$ such that the random oracle G was already queried at input h'_i, i.e. $\mathsf{GT}[h'_i] \neq \perp$, it aborts by raising $\mathsf{bad_{gcol2}}$. Otherwise, if $\mathsf{F} = \mathsf{F}^\star$, $c = c^\star$ and $i = i^\star$, it sets $y'_i \leftarrow y^\star$ and programs $\mathsf{GT}[h'_i] \leftarrow y'_i \oplus \alpha$. It holds that $|\Pr[\mathsf{Game}_4(\mathcal{A}) = 1] - \Pr[\mathsf{Game}_5(\mathcal{A}) = 1]| \leq \Pr[\mathsf{bad_{gcol2}}]$.

Game 5: Games for $\mathsf{H}(\mathsf{F}, m, r, x)$

```
Game0-Game3:
Q ← (F, m, r, x)
if HT[Q] = ⊥ then
    η ←$ {0,1}^{2λ}
    HT[Q] ← η
return HT[Q]

Game4:
Q ← (F, m, r, x)
if HT[Q] = ⊥ then
    η ←$ {0,1}^{2λ}
    HT[Q] ← η
    NList ← Lookup(x)
    for i ∈ [|NList|] do
        N_i ← NList[i]
        N'_i ← new node with parent N_i
        Retrieve h_i from N_i
        h'_i ← h_i ⊕ η
        (α, β) ← enc(x)
        g'_i ← G(h'_i)
        y'_i ← g'_i ⊕ α
        N'_i ← (Q, η, h'_i, y'_i)
return HT[Q]

Game5:
Q ← (F, m, r, x)
c ← c + 1
if HT[Q] = ⊥ then
    η ←$ {0,1}^{2λ}
    HT[Q] ← η
    NList ← Lookup(x)
    if F = F* ∧ c = c* then
        i* ←$ [|NList|]
    for i ∈ [|NList|] do
        N_i ← NList[i]
        N'_i ← new node with parent N_i
        Retrieve h_i from N_i
        h'_i ← h_i ⊕ η
        (α, β) ← enc(x)
        if GT[h'_i] ≠ ⊥ then
            raise bad_gcol2
        if F ≠ F* ∨ c ≠ c* ∨ i ≠ i* then
            g'_i ← G(h'_i)
            y'_i ← g'_i ⊕ α
        else
            y'_i ← y*
            GT[h'_i] ← y'_i ⊕ α
        N'_i ← (Q, η, h'_i, y'_i)
return HT[Q]
```

If none of the bad events happen, $\mathcal{B}$ perfectly simulate Game_5 and we have that

$$\begin{aligned}\mathsf{Adv}^{\mathrm{ow}}_{\mathsf{T}}(\mathcal{B}) &= \frac{1}{\psi \mathsf{q}_{\mathsf{H}}} \Pr[\mathsf{Game}_5(\mathcal{A}) = 1] \\ &\geq \frac{1}{\psi \mathsf{q}_{\mathsf{H}}} (\mathsf{Adv}^{\mathrm{ps\text{-}hf\text{-}uf\text{-}cma}}_{\mathsf{HaS\text{-}HF\text{-}SAS}}(\mathcal{A}) - \Pr[\mathsf{bad}_{\mathsf{hcol}}] - \Pr[\mathsf{bad}_{\mathsf{gcol1}}] \\ &\qquad - \mathsf{Adv}^{\mathrm{ps}}_{\mathsf{T}}(\mathcal{D}) - \Pr[\mathsf{bad}_{\mathsf{tcol}}] - \Pr[\mathsf{bad}_{\mathsf{gcol2}}] - \Pr[\mathsf{bad}_{\mathsf{teth}}]).\end{aligned}$$

$\mathcal{B}$ can simulate Game_5 with at most the same running time of $\mathcal{A}$ plus the time required for running $\mathsf{AggVrfy}$ and answering the queries to the random oracles H, G, and to the signing oracle $\mathsf{OAggSign}$. These operations takes $\mathcal{O}(\mathsf{poly}(\mathrm{len}(\mathcal{X}), \mathrm{len}(\mathcal{Y})))$ and are repeated at most $\mathsf{q}_{\mathsf{H}} + \mathsf{q}_{\mathsf{S}} + 1$ times.

In the following, we bound the probability of each bad event happening.

Probability of $\mathsf{bad}_{\mathsf{hcol}}$ The event $\mathsf{bad}_{\mathsf{hcol}}$ occurs on Line 5 of $\mathsf{OAggSign}$ on input $(m, \varrho = (h, x))$ when it samples $r \leftarrow_{\$} \{0,1\}^{\lambda}$ such that a value for $Q =$

$(\mathsf{F}^\star, m, r, x)$ was already assigned in the HT. The table HT is populated by either $\mathsf{OAggSign}$ or H, so its entries are at most $\mathsf{q}'_\mathsf{S} + \mathsf{q}_\mathsf{H}$. The probability that a uniformly random r produces a collision with one of the entries is then at most $(\mathsf{q}'_\mathsf{S} + \mathsf{q}_\mathsf{H})2^{-\lambda}$. Since at most q_S are made to $\mathsf{OAggSign}$, then $\Pr[\mathsf{bad}_\mathsf{hcol}] \leq \mathsf{q}_\mathsf{S}(\mathsf{q}'_\mathsf{S} + \mathsf{q}_\mathsf{H})2^{-\lambda}$.

Probability of $\mathsf{bad}_\mathsf{gcol1}$ The event $\mathsf{bad}_\mathsf{gcol1}$ occurs on Line 10 of $\mathsf{OAggSign}$ on input $(m, \varrho = (h, x))$ when, after sampling $\eta \leftarrow\!\!\$\ \{0,1\}^{2\lambda}$, it computes $h' \leftarrow h \oplus \eta$ such that a value for h' was already assigned in the GT. The table GT is populated by either $\mathsf{OAggSign}$, H or G so its entries are at most $\mathsf{q}'_\mathsf{S} + \mathsf{q}_\mathsf{H} + \mathsf{q}_\mathsf{G}$. The probability that a uniformly random η produces a collision with one of the entries is then at most $(\mathsf{q}'_\mathsf{S} + \mathsf{q}_\mathsf{H} + \mathsf{q}_\mathsf{G})2^{-2\lambda}$. Since at most q_S are made to $\mathsf{OAggSign}$, then $\Pr[\mathsf{bad}_\mathsf{gcol1}] \leq \mathsf{q}_\mathsf{S}(\mathsf{q}'_\mathsf{S} + \mathsf{q}_\mathsf{H} + \mathsf{q}_\mathsf{G})2^{-2\lambda}$.

Probability of $\mathsf{bad}_\mathsf{tcol}$ The event $\mathsf{bad}_\mathsf{tcol}$ occurs on Line 5 of Lookup on input x when the HTree contains $k > \psi$ nodes $N_1, \ldots, N_k$ such that $\mathsf{F}_i(x) = y_i$ for $i = 1, \ldots, k$, where F_i, y_i are stored in their respective nodes N_i. The HTree is populated by the simulation of the random oracle H. There are at most q_H queries to H and each query contributes a maximum of ψ nodes to the tree. Consequently, the total number of nodes in HTree does not exceed $\psi\mathsf{q}_\mathsf{H}$. Therefore, we need to bound the probability that any $(\psi + 1)$-tuple of nodes produce a collision on x.

To conclude, we prove that for any $(\psi+1)$-tuple (possibly adversarially chosen) of functions $\mathsf{F}_i \colon \mathcal{X} \to \mathcal{Y}$ and uniformly random $y_i \in \mathcal{Y}$, there exists $x \in \mathcal{X}$ such that $\mathsf{F}_i(x) = y_i$, for any $i = 1, \ldots, \psi + 1$, with probability at most $|\mathcal{X}|/|\mathcal{Y}|^{\psi+1}$ (Lemma 3). Indeed, the adversary can issue $\psi+1$ queries to H with inputs any functions F_i to be stored in $\psi + 1$ nodes N_i in the HTree. However, from Lemma 2, we know that when a new node is added to the HTree on Line 23 of H, the value y'_i is chosen uniformly at random from $\mathcal{Y}$ and is independent of the view of $\mathcal{A}$. Therefore, the adversary would receive $\psi + 1$ random, independent values y_i.

Since the number of $(\psi + 1)$-tuple of nodes in the HTree are at most $(\psi\mathsf{q}_\mathsf{H})^{\psi+1}/(\psi + 1)!$, by the union bound, we obtain $\Pr[\mathsf{bad}_\mathsf{tcol}] \leq (\psi\mathsf{q}_\mathsf{H})^{\psi+1}|\mathcal{X}|/((\psi + 1)! \cdot |\mathcal{Y}|^{\psi+1})$.

Probability of $\mathsf{bad}_\mathsf{gcol2}$ The event $\mathsf{bad}_\mathsf{gcol2}$ occurs on Line 16 of H on input (F, m, r, x) when, after sampling $\eta \leftarrow\!\!\$\ \{0,1\}^{2\lambda}$ and retrieving h_{i-1} from the parent node N_{i-1}, it computes $h_i \leftarrow h_{i-1} \oplus \eta$ such that a value for h_i was already assigned in the GT. The same argument from the bound of $\Pr[\mathsf{bad}_\mathsf{gcol}]$ can be used to prove that $\Pr[\mathsf{bad}_\mathsf{gcol2}] \leq \mathsf{q}_\mathsf{H}(\mathsf{q}'_\mathsf{S} + \mathsf{q}_\mathsf{H} + \mathsf{q}_\mathsf{G})2^{-2\lambda}$.

Probability of $\mathsf{bad}_\mathsf{teth}$ The event $\mathsf{bad}_\mathsf{teth}$ occurs on Line 8 of the simulation of $\mathcal{B}$ when, after the adversary $\mathcal{A}$ outputs a valid aggregate signature $\bar{\Sigma}_n$ for the history $L_n = (\mathsf{pk}_1, m_1), \ldots, (\mathsf{pk}_n, m_n)$ the simulator recovers $x_{i^\star}$, with $i^\star \in [n]$ such that $\mathsf{pk}_{i^\star} = \mathsf{pk}^\star$ and $(m_{i^\star}, \varsigma_{i^\star}) \notin \mathcal{Q}$, but $x_{i^\star}$ cannot be tethered to any node in the HTree.

When $\mathsf{bad}_\mathsf{teth}$ happens, the aggregate signature $\bar{\Sigma}_n$ must be valid on L_n. In particular, the inputs $Q_1 = (\mathsf{F}_1, m_1, r_1, \varepsilon), Q_2 = (\mathsf{F}_2, m_2, r_2, x_1), \ldots, Q_{i^\star} = (\mathsf{F}_{i^\star}, m_{i^\star}, r_{i^\star}, x_{i^\star-1})$ have been queried to H in $\mathsf{OAggVrfy}$. Let $\eta_1, \ldots, \eta_{i^\star}$ be the outputs of these queries, so that $\mathsf{HT}[Q_j] = \eta_j$. Each of these entries has

been populated by H. In fact, the only exception could occur if $(m_{i^\star}, x_{i^\star-1})$ was queried to $\mathsf{OAggSign}$. Suppose (r, β) is the complementary part of the signature produced by the oracle as a response. Since the forgery is valid, the complementary part $\varsigma_{i^\star} = (r_{i^\star}, \beta_{i^\star-1})$ produced by $\mathcal{A}$ must be different from (r, β). However, both $\beta_{i^\star-i}$ and β must be the same partial encoding of $x_{i^\star-1}$, so that $r_{i^\star} \neq r$. Therefore, $x_{i^\star}$ must have been produced following a query to H with a fresh salt $r_{i^\star}$.
Each step of $\mathsf{OAggVrfy}$ also recovers a value $h_j \leftarrow h_{j+1} \oplus \eta_j$ which is the input of the G query. Since the aggregate signature is correct, we obtain that $h_1 = \eta_1$. Observe that since Q_1 was queried to H, it must be tethered to the root of HTree and was therefore inserted as a node of HTree with additional values $\eta_1, h_1 = \eta_1, y_1 = \mathsf{G}(h_1)$. Then, since $\mathsf{F}(x_1) = y_1$, the query Q_2 is tethered to N_1. Now we prove that either all $Q_1, \ldots, Q_{i^\star}$ are part of a path of nodes in HTree, or there exists an input Q_j that was queried to H, is tethered to a node in HTree and is not itself in a node of HTree. We proceed by induction on $j \leq i^\star$: we have already shown that Q_1 is in HTree; suppose that Q_j is in the HTree, then, since $\mathsf{F}_j(x_j) = y_j$, the query Q_{j+1} is tethered to Q_j and it may or may not be part of HTree. To conclude, we prove that if an input Q has not been entered in the HTree after being queried to H, the probability that it will ever become tethered to a node in HTree is at most $\psi \mathsf{q}'/|\mathcal{Y}|$, where q' is the number of queries made to H after Q (Lemma 4). Since there are at most q_H queries that add new nodes to HTree, we obtain, by the union bound, that $\Pr[\mathsf{bad}_{\mathsf{teth}}] \leq \psi \mathsf{q}_\mathsf{H}^2/(2|\mathcal{Y}|)$.

Combining the previous bound on bad events, we obtain the claimed estimate of $\mathsf{Adv}^{\mathsf{ps\text{-}hf\text{-}uf\text{-}cma}}_{\mathsf{HaS\text{-}HF\text{-}SAS}}(\mathcal{A})$. □

B Trapdoor Functions in Hash-and-Sign Signature Schemes

B.1 UOV Trapdoor Function

MQ-based trapdoor function consists of a multivariate quadratic map $\mathcal{P}\colon \mathbb{F}_q^n \longrightarrow \mathbb{F}_q^m$ together with a secret information that allows to efficiently find a preimage. For a random map $\mathcal{P}$, the problem of finding a preimage is called *Multivariate Quadratic (MQ) problem*. The MQ problem is NP-hard over a finite field. Moreover, it is believed to be hard on average if $n \sim m$, both classically and quantumly.

Both UOV and MAYO are based on the same trapdoor function. For the description of the trapdoor function we mainly use the formalism introduced by Beullens in [7].

The trapdoor secret information is a linear subspace $O \subset \mathbb{F}_q^n$ of dimension $\dim(O) = m$. The trapdoor public function is a homogeneous multivariate quadratic map $\mathcal{P}\colon \mathbb{F}_q^n \longrightarrow \mathbb{F}_q^m$ that vanishes on O. For key generation, an m-dimensional subspace $O \subset \mathbb{F}_q^n$ is randomly chosen, then a multivariate quadratic map $\mathcal{P}\colon \mathbb{F}_q^n \longrightarrow \mathbb{F}_q^m$ is randomly chosen such that it vanishes on O. Given a

Algorithm 5: UOV Signature Scheme

$\mathsf{TrapGen}_{\mathrm{uov}}(1^\lambda)$:
1: $O \leftarrow\$$ m-dimensional subspace of $\mathbb{F}_q^n$
2: $\mathcal{P} \leftarrow\$$ quadratic map $\mathbb{F}_q^n \rightarrow \mathbb{F}_q^m$ that vanishes on O
3: **return** $\mathsf{F}_{\mathrm{uov}} \leftarrow \mathcal{P}, \mathsf{I}_{\mathrm{uov}} \leftarrow (\mathcal{P}, O)$

$\mathsf{Sign}(\mathsf{I}_{\mathrm{uov}}, m)$:
1: $r \leftarrow\$ \{0,1\}^\lambda$
2: $\boldsymbol{\sigma} \leftarrow \mathsf{I}_{\mathrm{uov}}(\mathsf{H}(m, r))$
3: **return** $(r, \boldsymbol{\sigma})$

$\mathsf{I}_{\mathrm{uov}}(\boldsymbol{t})$:
1: **repeat**
2: $\quad \boldsymbol{v} \leftarrow\$ \mathbb{F}_q^n$
3: **until** $\{\boldsymbol{o} \in O \mid \mathcal{P}'(\boldsymbol{v}, \boldsymbol{o}) = \boldsymbol{t} - \mathcal{P}(\boldsymbol{v})\} \neq \emptyset$
4: $\boldsymbol{o} \leftarrow\$ \{\boldsymbol{o} \mid \mathcal{P}'(\boldsymbol{v}, \boldsymbol{o}) = \boldsymbol{t} - \mathcal{P}(\boldsymbol{v})\}$
5: $\boldsymbol{\sigma} \leftarrow \boldsymbol{v} + \boldsymbol{o}$
6: **return** $\boldsymbol{\sigma}$

target $\boldsymbol{t} \in \mathbb{F}_q^m$, the secret information O can be used to find a preimage $\boldsymbol{s} \in \mathbb{F}_q^n$, reducing the MQ problem to a linear system. For a map $\mathcal{P}$, we can define its *polar form* as $\mathcal{P}'(\boldsymbol{x}, \boldsymbol{y}) = \mathcal{P}(\boldsymbol{x} + \boldsymbol{y}) - \mathcal{P}(\boldsymbol{x}) - \mathcal{P}(\boldsymbol{y})$. It can be shown that the polar form of a multivariate quadratic map is a symmetric and bilinear map. Now, to find a preimage for $\boldsymbol{t}$, one randomly choose a vector $\boldsymbol{v} \in \mathbb{F}_q^n$ and solves $\mathcal{P}(\boldsymbol{v} + \boldsymbol{o}) = \boldsymbol{t}$ for $\boldsymbol{o} \in O$. Since

$$\boldsymbol{t} = \mathcal{P}(\boldsymbol{v} + \boldsymbol{o}) = \underbrace{\mathcal{P}(\boldsymbol{v})}_{\text{fixed}} + \underbrace{\mathcal{P}(\boldsymbol{o})}_{=0} + \underbrace{\mathcal{P}'(\boldsymbol{v}, \boldsymbol{o})}_{\text{linear in } \boldsymbol{o}},$$

the system reduce to the linear system $\mathcal{P}'(\boldsymbol{v}, \boldsymbol{o}) = \boldsymbol{t} - \mathcal{P}(\boldsymbol{v})$ of m equation and m variables $\boldsymbol{o}$. Notice that whenever the linear map $\mathcal{P}'(\boldsymbol{v}, \cdot)$ is non-singular[4], the system has a unique solution $\boldsymbol{o} \in O$ and the preimage is $\boldsymbol{s} = \boldsymbol{v} + \boldsymbol{o}$.

B.2 Original Unbalanced Oil and Vinegar

Let $\mathsf{T}_{\mathrm{uov}} = (\mathsf{TrapGen}_{\mathrm{uov}}, \mathsf{F}_{\mathrm{uov}}, \mathsf{I}_{\mathrm{uov}})$ be the TDF based on the description of the previous section. Unbalanced Oil and Vinegar (UOV) [27] is a HaS signature scheme based on $\mathsf{T}_{\mathrm{uov}}$. The key generation and the signing procedure with the trapdoor functions are shown in Algorithm 5.

In the original version of the UOV signature, the signer samples a random salt $r \leftarrow\$ \{0,1\}^\lambda$ and repeatedly samples $v \leftarrow\$ \mathbb{F}_q^n$ until there is a solution to the linear system $\mathcal{P}'(\boldsymbol{v}, \boldsymbol{o}) = \mathsf{H}(m, r) - \mathcal{P}(\boldsymbol{v})$. Notice that the UOV signature lies in the HaS *without* retry paradigm, therefore $\mathsf{q}_\mathsf{S}' = \mathsf{q}_\mathsf{S}$ holds in Theorem 1. On the other hand, the PS advantage term $\mathsf{Adv}^{\mathrm{ps}}_{\mathsf{T}_{\mathrm{uov}}}(\mathcal{D})$ cannot be omitted since signature simulation requires knowledge of the trapdoor function.

Corollary 1. *Let $\mathcal{A}$ be a strong* PS-HF-UF-CMA *adversary against the* HaS-HF-SAS *scheme on $\mathsf{T}_{\mathrm{uov}}$ in the random oracle model, which makes q_S signing queries, q_H queries to the random oracle* H *and q_G queries to the random*

[4] This happens with probability approximately $1 - 1/q$.

Algorithm 6: Provable UOV Signature Scheme

$\mathsf{TrapGen}_{\text{puov}}(1^\lambda)$:
1: $O \leftarrow\$$ o-dimensional subspace of $\mathbb{F}_q^n$
2: $\mathcal{P} \leftarrow\$$ quadratic map $\mathbb{F}_q^n \to \mathbb{F}_q^m$ that vanishes on O
3: **return** $\mathsf{F}_{\text{puov}} \leftarrow \mathcal{P}, \mathsf{I}_{\text{puov}} \leftarrow (\mathcal{P}, O)$

$\mathsf{I}^2_{\text{puov}}(\boldsymbol{v}, \boldsymbol{t})$:
1: **if** $\{\boldsymbol{o} \in O \mid \mathcal{P}'(\boldsymbol{v}, \boldsymbol{o}) = \boldsymbol{t} - \mathcal{P}(\boldsymbol{v})\} \neq \emptyset$ **then return** $\perp$
2: $\boldsymbol{o} \leftarrow\$ \{\boldsymbol{o} \mid \mathcal{P}'(\boldsymbol{v}, \boldsymbol{o}) = \boldsymbol{t} - \mathcal{P}(\boldsymbol{v})\}$
3: $\boldsymbol{\sigma} \leftarrow \boldsymbol{v} + \boldsymbol{o}$
4: **return** $\boldsymbol{\sigma}$

$\mathsf{I}^1_{\text{puov}}()$:
1: $\boldsymbol{v} \leftarrow\$ \mathbb{F}_q^n$
2: **return** $\boldsymbol{v}$

$\mathsf{Sign}(\mathsf{I}_{\text{puov}}, m)$:
1: $\boldsymbol{v} \leftarrow \mathsf{I}^1_{\text{puov}}()$
2: **repeat**
3: $\quad r \leftarrow\$ \{0,1\}^\lambda$
4: $\quad \boldsymbol{\sigma} \leftarrow \mathsf{I}^2_{\text{puov}}(\boldsymbol{v}, \mathsf{H}(m, r))$
5: **until** $\boldsymbol{\sigma} \neq \perp$
6: **return** $(r, \boldsymbol{\sigma})$

oracle G. *Then, there exist a* OW *adversary* $\mathcal{B}$ *against* T_{uov}, *and a* PS *adversary* $\mathcal{D}$ *against* T_{uov} *issuing* $\mathsf{q_S}$ *sampling queries, such that*

$$\mathsf{Adv}^{\text{ps-hf-uf-cma}}_{\text{HaS-HF-SAS}}(\mathcal{A}) \leq (\psi \mathsf{q_H}) \cdot \mathsf{Adv}^{\text{ow}}_{\mathsf{T}_{\text{uov}}}(\mathcal{B}) + \mathsf{Adv}^{\text{ps}}_{\mathsf{T}_{\text{uov}}}(\mathcal{D}) + \frac{(\mathsf{q_S} + \mathsf{q_H})(\mathsf{q_S} + \mathsf{q_H} + \mathsf{q_G})}{2^{2\lambda}} + \frac{\mathsf{q_S}(\mathsf{q_S} + \mathsf{q_H})}{2^\lambda} + \frac{\psi \mathsf{q_H^2}}{2|\mathcal{Y}|} + \frac{(\psi \mathsf{q_H})^{\psi+1}|\mathcal{X}|}{(\psi+1)! \cdot |\mathcal{Y}|^{\psi+1}},$$

where $\psi \geq \lceil \text{len}(\mathcal{X}) / \text{len}(\mathcal{Y}) \rceil$, *and the running time of* $\mathcal{B}$ *and* $\mathcal{D}$ *are about that of* $\mathcal{A}$.

The previous corollary can be applied to the UOV scheme [10] submitted to the NIST PQC Standardization of Additional Digital Signature. For typical parameters, n is chosen equal to $2.5m$. If we choose $\psi = 3$, the additive error terms in Corollary 1 are negligible for each parametrization in Table 1.

B.3 Provable Unbalanced Oil and Vinegar

By adopting the probabilistic HaS with retry paradigm, the UOV signature scheme can be proven EUF-CMA secure in the random oracle model [34]. To obtain uniform preimages over $\mathbb{F}_q^n$, the *provable* UOV (PUOV) signing procedure is slightly different from the generic one described in Algorithm 1. The signer starts by fixing a random $\boldsymbol{v} \leftarrow\$ \mathbb{F}_q^n$, then it repeatedly samples $r \leftarrow\$ \{0,1\}^\lambda$ until there is a solution to the linear system $\mathcal{P}'(\boldsymbol{v}, \boldsymbol{o}) = \mathsf{H}(m, r) - \mathcal{P}(\boldsymbol{v})$. Equivalently, the trapdoor I_{puov} can be split in two distinct functions $\mathsf{I}^1_{\text{puov}}$ and $\mathsf{I}^2_{\text{puov}}$. The former is invoked only once and randomly chooses $\boldsymbol{v} \leftarrow\$ \mathbb{F}_q^n$. The latter is part of the repeat loop and tries to find a preimage $\boldsymbol{s}$ of the corresponding linear system. The key generation and the signing procedure with the modified trapdoor functions are shown in Algorithm 6.

With this procedure, the authors of [34] proved that the preimages produced from $\mathsf{Sign}(\mathsf{I}_{\text{puov}}, \cdot)$ are indistinguishable from the output of $\mathsf{SampDom}(\mathsf{F}_{\text{puov}})$, so that in Theorem 1 we have $\mathsf{Adv}^{\text{ps}}_{\mathsf{T}_{\text{puov}}}(\mathcal{D}) = 0$.

Corollary 2. *Let $\mathcal{A}$ be a strong* PS-HF-UF-CMA *adversary against the* HaS-HF-SAS *scheme on* T_{puov} *in the random oracle model, which makes* $\mathsf{q_S}$ *signing queries,* $\mathsf{q_H}$ *queries to the random oracle* H *and* $\mathsf{q_G}$ *queries to the random oracle* G*. Then, there exist a* OW *adversary $\mathcal{B}$ against* T_{puov}*, such that*

$$\mathsf{Adv}^{\text{ps-hf-uf-cma}}_{\mathsf{HaS\text{-}HF\text{-}SAS}}(\mathcal{A}) \leq (\psi \mathsf{q_H}) \cdot \mathsf{Adv}^{\text{ow}}_{\mathsf{T}_{\text{puov}}}(\mathcal{B}) + \frac{(\mathsf{q_S} + \mathsf{q_H})(\mathsf{q'_S} + \mathsf{q_H} + \mathsf{q_G})}{2^{2\lambda}} + \frac{\mathsf{q_S}(\mathsf{q'_S} + \mathsf{q_H})}{2^{\lambda}} + \frac{\psi \mathsf{q_H^2}}{2|\mathcal{Y}|} + \frac{(\psi \mathsf{q_H})^{\psi+1}|\mathcal{X}|}{(\psi+1)! \cdot |\mathcal{Y}|^{\psi+1}},$$

where $\psi \geq \lceil \text{len}(\mathcal{X})/\text{len}(\mathcal{Y}) \rceil$, $\mathsf{q'_S}$ is a bound on the total number of queries to H *in all the signing queries, and the running time of $\mathcal{B}$ is about that of $\mathcal{A}$.*

Unlike Corollary 1, we cannot explicitly take $\mathsf{q'_S} = \mathsf{q_S}$, since in $\mathsf{I}^2_{\text{puov}}$ the probability of $\boldsymbol{\sigma} \neq \perp$ depends on the fixed value of $\boldsymbol{v}$ sampled in $\mathsf{I}^1_{\text{puov}}$. Depending on the concrete parameters of T_{puov}, we can give a meaningful bound on $\mathsf{q'_S}$ so that the probability of having a number of queries to H greater than $\mathsf{q'_S}$ is negligible. $\mathsf{I}^2_{\text{puov}}$ returns $\perp$ on input $(\boldsymbol{v}, \boldsymbol{t})$ if $\mathcal{P}'(\boldsymbol{v}, \cdot)$ does not have full rank and $\boldsymbol{t} - \mathcal{P}(\boldsymbol{v})$ does not belong to the image of $\mathcal{P}'(\boldsymbol{v}, \cdot)$. Let q_{ret} be a bound for the number of queries to H each signing query and let X_i be a random variable on the actual number of queries to H in the i-th query. Then

$$\Pr[X_i > \mathsf{q}_{ret}] = \sum_{j=1}^{m} \Pr[\text{rank}(\mathcal{P}'(\boldsymbol{v}, \cdot)) = j] \, (1 - q^{j-m})^{\mathsf{q}_{ret}}.$$

As done in [34], we can assume that for a random $\boldsymbol{v} \leftarrow\!\!\$\; \mathbb{F}_q^n$, $\mathcal{P}'(\boldsymbol{v}, \cdot)$ is distributed as a random $o \times m$ matrix. For $o \geq m$, the probability that a random $o \times m$ matrix over $\mathbb{F}_q$ has rank $1 \leq j \leq m$ is given in [29]:

$$q^{(j-m)(o-j)} \frac{\prod_{k=o-j+1}^{o}(1 - q^{-k}) \prod_{k=m-j+1}^{m}(1 - q^{-k})}{\prod_{k=1}^{j}(1 - q^{-k})}. \tag{3}$$

Then, if we choose q_{ret} such that $\mathsf{q_S} \Pr[X_i > \mathsf{q}_{ret}]$ is negligible, we can use $\mathsf{q'_S} = \mathsf{q}_{ret}\mathsf{q_S}$ in the bound of the corollary.

Corollary 2 can be applied to the PROV scheme [26] submitted to the NIST PQC Standardization of Additional Digital Signature. The parameters of PROV are selected so that the dimension of the trapdoor subspace is $o = m + \delta$. This choice significantly reduces the probability of Eq. (3) whenever $j < m$. For instance, with the parameters of PROV-I we have $\Pr[X_i > 1] \leq 2^{-72}$ and $\Pr[X_i > 2^{14}] \leq 2^{-160}$. Similarly to Original UOV, if we choose $\psi = 3$, the additive error terms in Corollary 2 are negligible for each parametrization in [26].

Algorithm 7: MAYO Signature Scheme

$\mathsf{TrapGen}_{\mathsf{mayo}}(1^\lambda)$:
1: $\mathbf{O} \leftarrow_\$ \mathbb{F}_q^{o\times(n-o)}$
2: $O \leftarrow \mathrm{RowSpace}(\mathbf{OI}_o)$
3: $\mathcal{P} \leftarrow_\$$ quadratic map $\mathbb{F}_q^n \rightarrow \mathbb{F}_q^m$ that vanishes on O
4: **return** $\mathsf{F}_{\mathsf{mayo}} \leftarrow \mathcal{P}, \mathsf{I}_{\mathsf{mayo}} \leftarrow (\mathcal{P}, \mathbf{O})$

$\mathsf{I}_{\mathsf{mayo}}(\boldsymbol{t})$:
1: $\mathcal{P}^*(\boldsymbol{x}_1,\ldots,\boldsymbol{x}_k) \leftarrow \sum_{i=1}^k \mathbf{E}_{i,i}\,\mathcal{P}(\boldsymbol{x}_i) + \sum_{1\le i<j\le k} \mathbf{E}_{i,j}\,\mathcal{P}'(\boldsymbol{x}_i,\boldsymbol{x}_j)$
2: $\boldsymbol{v}_1,\ldots,\boldsymbol{v}_k \leftarrow_\$ (\mathbb{F}_q^n \times \mathbf{0}_m)^k$
3: **if** $\mathcal{P}^*(\boldsymbol{v}_1+\boldsymbol{o}_1,\ldots,\boldsymbol{v}_k+\boldsymbol{o}_k)$ does not have full rank **then**
4: **return** $\perp$
5: $\boldsymbol{o}_1,\ldots,\boldsymbol{o}_k \leftarrow_\$ \{\boldsymbol{o}_1,\ldots,\boldsymbol{o}_k \in O \mid \mathcal{P}^*(\boldsymbol{v}_1+\boldsymbol{o}_1,\ldots,\boldsymbol{v}_k+\boldsymbol{o}_k) = \boldsymbol{t}\}$
6: $\boldsymbol{\sigma} \leftarrow (\boldsymbol{v}_1+\boldsymbol{o}_1,\ldots,\boldsymbol{v}_k+\boldsymbol{o}_k)$
7: **return** $\boldsymbol{\sigma}$

B.4 MAYO

MAYO [8] is a HaS signature scheme based on the UOV trapdoor function and employs a so-called *whipping* technique to use a smaller secret subspace O of dimension $\dim(O) = o < m$. Let $\mathsf{T}_{\mathsf{mayo}} = (\mathsf{TrapGen}_{\mathsf{mayo}}, \mathsf{F}_{\mathsf{mayo}}, \mathsf{I}_{\mathsf{mayo}})$ be the TDF of MAYO. The key generation process is the same as for UOV and produces a multivariate quadratic map $\mathcal{P}\colon \mathbb{F}_q^n \rightarrow \mathbb{F}_q^m$ that vanishes on O. In the signing procedure, $\mathcal{P}$ is deterministically transformed into a larger (whipped) map $\mathcal{P}^*\colon \mathbb{F}_q^{kn} \rightarrow \mathbb{F}_q^m$, for some $k > 1$, which vanishes on $O^k \subset \mathbb{F}_q^{kn}$ of dimension $ko \geq m$. In [8], the whipping transformation is obtained by choosing $k(k+1)/2$ random invertible matrices $\{\mathbf{E}_{i,j} \in \mathrm{GL}_m(\mathbb{F}_q)\}_{1\le i\le j\le k}$ and defining

$$\mathcal{P}^*(\boldsymbol{x}_1,\ldots,\boldsymbol{x}_k) = \sum_{i=1}^{k} \mathbf{E}_{i,i}\,\mathcal{P}(\boldsymbol{x}_i) + \sum_{1\le i<j\le k} \mathbf{E}_{i,j}\,\mathcal{P}'(\boldsymbol{x}_i,\boldsymbol{x}_j).$$

Similarly to UOV, to find a preimage for $\boldsymbol{t} \in \mathbb{F}_q^m$, we randomly choose $\boldsymbol{v}_1,\ldots,\boldsymbol{v}_k \in \mathbb{F}_q^{n-m} \times \mathbf{0}_m$. Then, $\mathcal{P}^*(\boldsymbol{v}_1+\boldsymbol{o}_1,\ldots,\boldsymbol{v}_k+\boldsymbol{o}_k) = \boldsymbol{t}$ is a system of m linear equation in $ko \geq m$ variables, so it will be solvable with high probability. The key generation and the preimage computation via $\mathsf{I}_{\mathsf{mayo}}$ are shown in Algorithm 7.

Instead of computing $\mathsf{Adv}^{\mathsf{ps}}_{\mathsf{T}_{\mathsf{mayo}}}(\mathcal{D})$, we can use the result of [8, Lemma 2] that bounds the probability B that $\mathcal{P}^*(\boldsymbol{v}_1+\boldsymbol{o}_1,\ldots,\boldsymbol{v}_k+\boldsymbol{o}_k)$ does not have full rank. It can be shown that if $\mathsf{I}_{\mathsf{mayo}}$ has never output $\perp$, then the preimages produced by $\mathsf{Sign}(\mathsf{I}_{\mathsf{mayo}},\cdot)$ are indistinguishable from $\mathsf{SampDom}(\mathsf{F}_{\mathsf{mayo}})$. Therefore, we can modify the proof of Theorem 1 by introducing a new intermediate game $\mathsf{Game}_{2\mathsf{b}}$. This game is identical to Game_2 except that $\mathsf{OAggSign}$ aborts if $\mathsf{I}_{\mathsf{mayo}}$ outputs $\perp$. Since there are at most $\mathsf{q_S}$ queries are made to $\mathsf{OAggSign}$, the probability that $\mathsf{Game}_{2\mathsf{b}}$ does not abort is at least $1 - \mathsf{q_S}\mathsf{B}$. It follows that $\Pr[\mathsf{Game}_2(\mathcal{A}) = 1] \le \frac{1}{1-\mathsf{q_S}\mathsf{B}} \Pr[\mathsf{Game}_{2\mathsf{b}}(\mathcal{A}) = 1]$. Now, when $\mathsf{Game}_{2\mathsf{b}}$ does not abort, the game is indistinguishable from Game_3, so that $\Pr[\mathsf{Game}_3(\mathcal{A}) = 1] = \Pr[\mathsf{Game}_{2\mathsf{b}}(\mathcal{A}) = 1]$. The remainder of the proof proceeds as the original. Finally, since MAYO now does not repeat any signature attempts, we can use $\mathsf{q}'_{\mathsf{S}} = \mathsf{q_S}$ in Theorem 1.

Algorithm 8: Wave Signature Scheme

$\mathsf{TrapGen}_{\mathrm{wave}}(1^\lambda)$:
1: $\mathbf{H}_{\mathsf{sk}} \in \mathbb{F}_q^{(n-k)\times n} \leftarrow\!\$$ generalized $(U, U+V)$-code
2: $\mathbf{S} \leftarrow\!\$ \mathrm{GL}_{n-k}(\mathbb{F}_q)$
3: $\mathbf{P} \leftarrow\!\$ n \times n$ permutation matrix
4: $\mathbf{H}_{\mathsf{pk}} \leftarrow \mathbf{S}\mathbf{H}_{\mathsf{sk}}\mathbf{P}$
5: **return** $\mathsf{F}_{\mathrm{mayo}} \leftarrow \mathbf{H}_{\mathsf{pk}}, \mathsf{I}_{\mathrm{mayo}} \leftarrow (\mathbf{H}_{\mathsf{sk}}, \mathbf{S}, \mathbf{P})$

$\mathsf{I}_{\mathrm{wave}}(\boldsymbol{y})$:
1: $\boldsymbol{e} \leftarrow D_{\mathbf{H}_{\mathsf{sk}}}(\boldsymbol{y}(\mathbf{S}^{-1})^\intercal)$
2: $\boldsymbol{x} \leftarrow \boldsymbol{e}\mathbf{P}$
3: **return** $\boldsymbol{x}$

Corollary 3. *Let $\mathcal{A}$ be a strong* PS-HF-UF-CMA *adversary against the* HaS-HF-SAS *scheme on $\mathsf{T}_{\mathrm{mayo}}$ in the random oracle model, which makes q_S signing queries, q_H queries to the random oracle* H *and q_G queries to the random oracle* G. *Then, there exist a* OW *adversary $\mathcal{B}$ against $\mathsf{T}_{\mathrm{mayo}}$, such that*

$$\begin{aligned}\mathsf{Adv}^{\text{ps-hf-uf-cma}}_{\mathsf{HaS\text{-}HF\text{-}SAS}}(\mathcal{A}) \leq & \frac{\psi \mathsf{q}_\mathsf{H}}{1-\mathsf{q}_\mathsf{S}\mathsf{B}} \cdot \mathsf{Adv}^{\mathrm{ow}}_{\mathsf{T}_{\mathrm{mayo}}}(\mathcal{B}) + \frac{(\mathsf{q}_\mathsf{S}+\mathsf{q}_\mathsf{H})(\mathsf{q}_\mathsf{S}+\mathsf{q}_\mathsf{H}+\mathsf{q}_\mathsf{G})}{2^{2\lambda}} \\ & + \frac{\mathsf{q}_\mathsf{S}(\mathsf{q}_\mathsf{S}+\mathsf{q}_\mathsf{H})}{2^\lambda} + \frac{\psi \mathsf{q}_\mathsf{H}^2}{2|\mathcal{Y}|} + \frac{(\psi \mathsf{q}_\mathsf{H})^{\psi+1}|\mathcal{X}|}{(\psi+1)! \cdot |\mathcal{Y}|^{\psi+1}},\end{aligned}$$

where $\psi \geq \lceil \mathrm{len}(\mathcal{X})/\mathrm{len}(\mathcal{Y}) \rceil$, and the running time of $\mathcal{B}$ is about that of $\mathcal{A}$.

The previous corollary can be applied to the MAYO scheme [9] submitted to the NIST PQC Standardization of Additional Digital Signature. In order to choose appropriate values for ψ, it is necessary to consider the whipped map $\mathcal{P}^* : \mathbb{F}_q^{kn} \to \mathbb{F}_q^m$, from which $\psi \geq \lceil kn/m \rceil$. If we consider the parameter sets in Table 2, we can choose ψ equal to $13, 7, 14$ and 14 for $\mathsf{MAYO}_1, \mathsf{MAYO}_2, \mathsf{MAYO}_3$ and MAYO_5 respectively, to obtain negligible additive terms in Corollary 3.

B.5 Wave

Wave [17] is a HaS signature scheme based on the family of the generalized $(U, U+V)$-codes. Let $\mathsf{T}_{\mathrm{wave}} = (\mathsf{TrapGen}_{\mathrm{wave}}, \mathsf{F}_{\mathrm{wave}}, \mathsf{I}_{\mathrm{wave}})$ be the TDF of Wave. The OW security of $\mathsf{F}_{\mathsf{Wave}}$ is based on the indistinguishability of $(U, U+V)$-codes from random codes and the Syndrome Decoding (SD) problem. The indistinguishability problem is NP-complete for large finite fields $\mathbb{F}_q$, while the SD problem is NP-hard for arbitrary finite fields. The trapdoor secret information is a random generalized $(U, U+V)$-code over $\mathbb{F}_q$ of length n and dimension $k = k_U + k_V$, described by its parity check matrix $\mathbf{H}_{\mathsf{sk}} \in \mathbb{F}_q^{(n-k)\times n}$, an invertible matrix $\mathbf{S} \in \mathbb{F}_q^{(n-k)\times(n-k)}$ and a permutation matrix $\mathbf{P} \in \mathbb{F}_q^{n\times n}$. Using the underlying structure of the $(U, U+V)$-code, an efficient decoding algorithm $D_{\mathbf{H}_{\mathsf{sk}}}$ is produced. The public function $\mathsf{F}_{\mathsf{Wave}}$ is obtained from the parity check matrix $\mathbf{H}_{\mathsf{pk}} = \mathbf{S}\mathbf{H}_{\mathsf{sk}}\mathbf{P}$. Let $S_{w,n}$ be the subset of vectors in $\mathbb{F}_q^n$

with Hamming weight w. The weight w is chosen such that the public function $\mathsf{F}_{\text{wave}}\colon \boldsymbol{e} \in S_{w,n} \mapsto \boldsymbol{e}\mathbf{H}_{\mathsf{pk}}^{\mathsf{T}} \in \mathbb{F}_q^{n-k}$ is a surjection. To find a preimage for $\boldsymbol{y} \in \mathbb{F}_q^{n-k}$, the signer uses the decoding algorithm $D_{\mathbf{H}_{\mathsf{sk}}}$ on $\boldsymbol{y}(\mathbf{S}^{-1})^{\mathsf{T}}$ to find $\boldsymbol{e} \in S_{w,n}$, and finally returns $\boldsymbol{e}\mathbf{P}$. The key generation and the preimage computation via I_{wave} are shown in Algorithm 8.

Wave can be described in the HaS *without* retry paradigm, therefore $\mathsf{q}_\mathsf{S}' = \mathsf{q}_\mathsf{S}$ holds in Theorem 1. In [14], T_{wave} is described in the context of ATPSF, a weaker notion of PSF where the uniformity property on preimages is required to hold only on average. In particular, for any $(\mathsf{F}, \mathsf{I}) \leftarrow \mathsf{TrapGen}_{\text{wave}}(1^\lambda)$, consider the statistical distance $\varepsilon_{\mathsf{F},\mathsf{I}} = \Delta(\mathsf{SampDom}(\mathsf{F}), \mathsf{I}(U(\mathcal{Y})))$. Then, it holds that $\mathbb{E}_{(\mathsf{F},\mathsf{I})}[\varepsilon_{\mathsf{F},\mathsf{I}}] \leq \varepsilon$, where ε is negligible in the security parameter λ. In Theorem 1 we can use this condition and [14, Prop. 1] to bound the distinguishing advantage on PS with ε, obtaining $\mathsf{Adv}^{\text{ps}}_{\mathsf{T}_{\text{wave}}}(\mathcal{D}) \leq \mathsf{q}_\mathsf{S}\varepsilon$.

Corollary 4. *Let $\mathcal{A}$ be a strong* PS-HF-UF-CMA *adversary against the* HaS-HF-SAS *scheme on T_{wave} in the random oracle model, which makes q_S signing queries, q_H queries to the random oracle* H *and q_G queries to the random oracle* G. *Then, there exist a* OW *adversary $\mathcal{B}$ against T_{wave}, such that*

$$\begin{aligned}\mathsf{Adv}^{\text{ps-hf-uf-cma}}_{\mathsf{HaS\text{-}HF\text{-}SAS}}(\mathcal{A}) \leq & (\psi \mathsf{q}_\mathsf{H}) \cdot \mathsf{Adv}^{\text{ow}}_{\mathsf{T}_{\text{wave}}}(\mathcal{B}) + \mathsf{q}_\mathsf{S}\varepsilon + \frac{(\mathsf{q}_\mathsf{S} + \mathsf{q}_\mathsf{H})(\mathsf{q}_\mathsf{S} + \mathsf{q}_\mathsf{H} + \mathsf{q}_\mathsf{G})}{2^{2\lambda}} \\ & + \frac{\mathsf{q}_\mathsf{S}(\mathsf{q}_\mathsf{S} + \mathsf{q}_\mathsf{H})}{2^\lambda} + \frac{\psi \mathsf{q}_\mathsf{H}^2}{2|\mathcal{Y}|} + \frac{(\psi \mathsf{q}_\mathsf{H})^{\psi+1}|\mathcal{X}|}{(\psi+1)! \cdot |\mathcal{Y}|^{\psi+1}},\end{aligned}$$

where $\psi \geq \lceil \text{len}(\mathcal{X})/\text{len}(\mathcal{Y}) \rceil$, and the running time of $\mathcal{B}$ is about that of $\mathcal{A}$.

In Corollary 4, we can choose $\psi = 3$ to have negligible additive error terms with respect to the parametrization of Table 3.

C PSF-Based Signatures

In Sect. 4, we briefly discussed the applicability of the HaS-HF-SAS scheme to Falcon [33] and PSF-based signatures. In general, lattice-based signatures within the GPV framework [24] require the use of PSF. In this section, we discuss how the construction of Sect. 3 can be modified in the presence of PSF.

Definition 11. *A TDF* $\mathsf{T} = (\mathsf{TrapGen}, \mathsf{F}, \mathsf{I}, \mathsf{SampDom})$ *is a Preimage Sampleable Function (PSF) if it satisfies the following properties:*

1. $y \leftarrow \mathsf{F}(\mathsf{SampDom}(\mathsf{F}))$ *is uniformly distributed over* $\mathcal{Y}$.
2. $x \leftarrow \mathsf{I}(y)$, *with* $y \leftarrow\!\!\$\ \mathcal{Y}$, *is distributed as* $x \leftarrow \mathsf{SampDom}(\mathsf{F})$ *conditioned on* $\mathsf{F}(x) = y$.
3. *For any* $y \in \mathcal{Y}$, $\mathsf{I}(y)$ *always returns* $x \in \mathcal{X}$ *such that* $\mathsf{F}(x) = y$.

   A collision-resistant PSF satisfies the following additional properties:

4. *For any* $y \in \mathcal{Y}$, *the conditional min-entropy of* $x \leftarrow \mathsf{SampDom}(\mathsf{F})$ *conditioned on* $\mathsf{F}(x) = y$ *is at least* $\omega(\log \lambda)$.
5. *For an adversary* $\mathcal{A}$, *the probability of* $\mathcal{A}(\mathsf{F})$ *returning two distinct* $x, x' \in \mathcal{X}$ *such that* $\mathsf{F}(x) = \mathsf{F}(x')$ *is negligible in* λ.

If we consider a PSF without collision resistance, we can apply Theorem 1 and observe that the distinguishing advantage of the PS adversary is 0. In fact, the PS notion of Definition 5 is a weaker condition for indistinguishability on preimages than property 2 of PSFs. Furthermore, following property 3, the signature associated with the PSF can be described in the HaS without retry paradigm. As a result, we can modify the proof of Theorem 1 by merging Game_2 and Game_3, without the need to introduce the PS adversary. Unfortunately, this would not change the tightness of the reduction.

Conversely, if we consider a collision-resistant PSF, we can further modify Theorem 1 to obtain a tighter reduction from collision resistance (CR) to PS-HF-UF-CMA. In the simulation of H in Algorithm 3, modify Line 21 by taking a random input $x' \leftarrow X$, assigning $y' \leftarrow F^{\star}(x')$ and programming the random oracle G on input h' with $y' \oplus \alpha$. Here the simulation of G is correct since, from property 1 of PSF, y' is uniformly distributed in $\mathcal{Y}$. After the adversary returns a forged aggregate signature, if none of the bad events happen, the value $x_{i^{\star}}$, from the forgery, and the value x', produced by H and stored in the HTree, constitute a collision for $F^{\star}$. When the reduction is performed from the OW game as in the original proof of Theorem 1, the OW adversary provides its challenge to the PS-HF-UF-CMA adversary in one of the q_{H} queries to the random oracle H. This results in a multiplicative loss of advantage by a factor q_{H}. However, when the reduction is performed as above, the CR adversary can prepare responses that will lead to a collision in each query to H involving the target public key. As a result, we get a tight reduction with only negligible losses from additive terms.

References

1. Ahn, J.H., Green, M., Hohenberger, S.: Synchronized aggregate signatures: new definitions, constructions and applications. In: Al-Shaer, E., Keromytis, A.D., Shmatikov, V. (eds.) ACM CCS 2010, pp. 473–484. ACM Press (2010). https://doi.org/10.1145/1866307.1866360
2. Albrecht, M.R., Cini, V., Lai, R.W.F., Malavolta, G., Thyagarajan, S.A.K.: Lattice-based SNARKs: publicly verifiable, preprocessing, and recursively composable - (extended abstract). In: Dodis, Y., Shrimpton, T. (eds.) CRYPTO 2022, Part II. LNCS, vol. 13508, pp. 102–132. Springer, Heidelberg (2022). https://doi.org/10.1007/978-3-031-15979-4_4
3. Banegas, G., Debris-Alazard, T., Nedeljković, M., Smith, B.: Wavelet: code-based postquantum signatures with fast verification on microcontrollers. Cryptology ePrint Archive, Report 2021/1432 (2021). https://eprint.iacr.org/2021/1432
4. Bellare, M., Namprempre, C., Neven, G.: Unrestricted aggregate signatures. In: Arge, L., Cachin, C., Jurdziński, T., Tarlecki, A. (eds.) ICALP 2007. LNCS, vol. 4596, pp. 411–422. Springer, Heidelberg (2007). https://doi.org/10.1007/978-3-540-73420-8_37

5. Bellare, M., Neven, G.: Multi-signatures in the plain public-key model and a general forking lemma. In: Juels, A., Wright, R.N., De Capitani di Vimercati, S. (eds.) ACM CCS 2006, pp. 390–399. ACM Press (2006). https://doi.org/10.1145/1180405.1180453
6. Bellare, M., Rogaway, P.: Random oracles are practical: a paradigm for designing efficient protocols. In: Denning, D.E., Pyle, R., Ganesan, R., Sandhu, R.S., Ashby, V. (eds.) ACM CCS 1993, pp. 62–73. ACM Press (1993). https://doi.org/10.1145/168588.168596
7. Beullens, W.: Improved cryptanalysis of UOV and rainbow. In: Canteaut, A., Standaert, F.-X. (eds.) EUROCRYPT 2021, Part I. LNCS, vol. 12696, pp. 348–373. Springer, Cham (2021). https://doi.org/10.1007/978-3-030-77870-5_13
8. Beullens, W.: MAYO: practical post-quantum signatures from oil-and-vinegar maps. In: AlTawy, R., Hülsing, A. (eds.) SAC 2021. LNCS, vol. 13203, pp. 355–376. Springer, Cham (2022). https://doi.org/10.1007/978-3-030-99277-4_17
9. Beullens, W., Campos, F., Celi, S., Hess, B., Kannwischer, M.J.: MAYO. Technical report, National Institute of Standards and Technology (2023). https://csrc.nist.gov/Projects/pqc-dig-sig/round-1-additional-signatures
10. Beullens, W., et al.: UOV—Unbalanced Oil and Vinegar. Technical report, National Institute of Standards and Technology (2023). https://csrc.nist.gov/Projects/pqc-dig-sig/round-1-additional-signatures
11. Boneh, D., Gentry, C., Lynn, B., Shacham, H.: Aggregate and verifiably encrypted signatures from bilinear maps. In: Biham, E. (ed.) EUROCRYPT 2003. LNCS, vol. 2656, pp. 416–432. Springer, Heidelberg (2003). https://doi.org/10.1007/3-540-39200-9_26
12. Boudgoust, K., Takahashi, A.: Sequential half-aggregation of lattice-based signatures. Cryptology ePrint Archive, Report 2023/159 (2023). https://eprint.iacr.org/2023/159
13. Brogle, K., Goldberg, S., Reyzin, L.: Sequential aggregate signatures with lazy verification from trapdoor permutations. In: Wang, X., Sako, K. (eds.) ASIACRYPT 2012. LNCS, vol. 7658, pp. 644–662. Springer, Heidelberg (2012). https://doi.org/10.1007/978-3-642-34961-4_39
14. Chailloux, A., Debris-Alazard, T.: Tight and optimal reductions for signatures based on average trapdoor preimage sampleable functions and applications to code-based signatures. In: Kiayias, A., Kohlweiss, M., Wallden, P., Zikas, V. (eds.) PKC 2020, Part II. LNCS, vol. 12111, pp. 453–479. Springer, Cham (2020). https://doi.org/10.1007/978-3-030-45388-6_16
15. Chen, J., Ling, J., Ning, J., Peng, Z., Tan, Y.: MQ aggregate signature schemes with exact security based on UOV signature. In: Liu, Z., Yung, M. (eds.) Inscrypt 2019. LNCS, vol. 12020, pp. 443–451. Springer, Cham (2020). https://doi.org/10.1007/978-3-030-42921-8_26
16. Chen, Y., Zhao, Y.: Half-aggregation of Schnorr signatures with tight reductions. In: Atluri, V., Di Pietro, R., Jensen, C.D., Meng, W. (eds.) ESORICS 2022, Part II. LNCS, vol. 13555, pp. 385–404. Springer, Heidelberg (2022). https://doi.org/10.1007/978-3-031-17146-8_19
17. Debris-Alazard, T., Sendrier, N., Tillich, J.-P.: Wave: a new family of trapdoor one-way preimage sampleable functions based on codes. In: Galbraith, S.D., Moriai, S. (eds.) ASIACRYPT 2019, Part I. LNCS, vol. 11921, pp. 21–51. Springer, Cham (2019). https://doi.org/10.1007/978-3-030-34578-5_2
18. Devadas, L., Goyal, R., Kalai, Y., Vaikuntanathan, V.: Rate-1 non-interactive arguments for batch-NP and applications. In: 63rd FOCS, pp. 1057–1068. IEEE Computer Society Press (2022). https://doi.org/10.1109/FOCS54457.2022.00103

19. El Bansarkhani, R., Buchmann, J.: Towards lattice based aggregate signatures. In: Pointcheval, D., Vergnaud, D. (eds.) AFRICACRYPT 2014. LNCS, vol. 8469, pp. 336–355. Springer, Cham (2014). https://doi.org/10.1007/978-3-319-06734-6_21
20. El Bansarkhani, R., Mohamed, M.S.E., Petzoldt, A.: MQSAS - a multivariate sequential aggregate signature scheme. In: Bishop, M., Nascimento, A.C.A. (eds.) ISC 2016. LNCS, vol. 9866, pp. 426–439. Springer, Cham (2016). https://doi.org/10.1007/978-3-319-45871-7_25
21. Fischlin, M., Lehmann, A., Schröder, D.: History-free sequential aggregate signatures. In: Visconti, I., De Prisco, R. (eds.) SCN 2012. LNCS, vol. 7485, pp. 113–130. Springer, Heidelberg (2012). https://doi.org/10.1007/978-3-642-32928-9_7
22. Fleischhacker, N., Simkin, M., Zhang, Z.: Squirrel: efficient synchronized multi-signatures from lattices. In: Yin, H., Stavrou, A., Cremers, C., Shi, E. (eds.) ACM CCS 2022, pp. 1109–1123. ACM Press (2022). https://doi.org/10.1145/3548606.3560655
23. Gentry, C., O'Neill, A., Reyzin, L.: A unified framework for trapdoor-permutation-based sequential aggregate signatures. In: Abdalla, M., Dahab, R. (eds.) PKC 2018, Part II. LNCS, vol. 10770, pp. 34–57. Springer, Cham (2018). https://doi.org/10.1007/978-3-319-76581-5_2
24. Gentry, C., Peikert, C., Vaikuntanathan, V.: Trapdoors for hard lattices and new cryptographic constructions. In: Ladner, R.E., Dwork, C. (eds.) 40th ACM STOC, pp. 197–206. ACM Press (2008). https://doi.org/10.1145/1374376.1374407
25. Gentry, C., Ramzan, Z.: Identity-based aggregate signatures. In: Yung, M., Dodis, Y., Kiayias, A., Malkin, T. (eds.) PKC 2006. LNCS, vol. 3958, pp. 257–273. Springer, Heidelberg (2006). https://doi.org/10.1007/11745853_17
26. Goubin, L., et al.: PROV—PRovable unbalanced Oil and Vinegar. Technical report, National Institute of Standards and Technology (2023). https://csrc.nist.gov/Projects/pqc-dig-sig/round-1-additional-signatures
27. Kipnis, A., Patarin, J., Goubin, L.: Unbalanced oil and vinegar signature schemes. In: Stern, J. (ed.) EUROCRYPT 1999. LNCS, vol. 1592, pp. 206–222. Springer, Heidelberg (1999). https://doi.org/10.1007/3-540-48910-X_15
28. Kosuge, H., Xagawa, K.: Probabilistic hash-and-sign with retry in the quantum random oracle model. Cryptology ePrint Archive, Report 2022/1359 (2022). https://eprint.iacr.org/2022/1359
29. Levitskaya, A.: Systems of random equations over finite algebraic structures. Cybern. Syst. Anal. **41**, 67–93 (2005)
30. Lu, S., Ostrovsky, R., Sahai, A., Shacham, H., Waters, B.: Sequential aggregate signatures and multisignatures without random oracles. In: Vaudenay, S. (ed.) EUROCRYPT 2006. LNCS, vol. 4004, pp. 465–485. Springer, Heidelberg (2006). https://doi.org/10.1007/11761679_28
31. Lysyanskaya, A., Micali, S., Reyzin, L., Shacham, H.: Sequential aggregate signatures from trapdoor permutations. In: Cachin, C., Camenisch, J.L. (eds.) EUROCRYPT 2004. LNCS, vol. 3027, pp. 74–90. Springer, Heidelberg (2004). https://doi.org/10.1007/978-3-540-24676-3_5
32. Neven, G.: Efficient sequential aggregate signed data. In: Smart, N. (ed.) EUROCRYPT 2008. LNCS, vol. 4965, pp. 52–69. Springer, Heidelberg (2008). https://doi.org/10.1007/978-3-540-78967-3_4
33. Prest, T., et al.: FALCON. Technical report, National Institute of Standards and Technology (2022). https://csrc.nist.gov/Projects/post-quantum-cryptography/selected-algorithms-2022

34. Sakumoto, K., Shirai, T., Hiwatari, H.: On provable security of UOV and HFE signature schemes against chosen-message attack. In: Yang, B.-Y. (ed.) PQCrypto 2011. LNCS, vol. 7071, pp. 68–82. Springer, Heidelberg (2011). https://doi.org/10.1007/978-3-642-25405-5_5
35. Wang, Z., Wu, Q.: A practical lattice-based sequential aggregate signature. In: Steinfeld, R., Yuen, T.H. (eds.) ProvSec 2019. LNCS, vol. 11821, pp. 94–109. Springer, Cham (2019). https://doi.org/10.1007/978-3-030-31919-9_6

Attribute-Based Signatures with Advanced Delegation, and Tracing

Cécile Delerablée[1], Lénaïck Gouriou[1(✉)], and David Pointcheval[2]

[1] Leanear, Paris, France
lg@leanear.io
[2] DIENS, École normale supérieure, CNRS, Inria, PSL University, Paris, France

Abstract. Attribute-based cryptography allows fine-grained control on the use of the private key. In particular, attribute-based signature (ABS) specifies the capabilities of the signer, which can only sign messages associated to a policy that is authorized by his set of attributes. Furthermore, we can expect signature to not leak any information about the identity of the signer. ABS is a useful tool for identity-preserving authentication process which requires granular access-control, and can furthermore be enhanced with additional properties, for example delegation where users are able to manage a set of keys derived from their original one.

In this paper, we address delegation of signing keys. Our first delegation works for any subset of the original attributes, which is the intuitive approach of delegation. Furthermore, we also provide another kind of delegation where the delegator can choose a policy at delegation time to produce keys that can sign any message under this specific policy. This last approach to delegation is a direct application of a new version of the *indexing* technique, which was first introduced by Okamoto and Takashima in order to prove adaptive security in ABS and its counterpart for encryption, ABE. On top of that, we prove that our scheme is compatible with a well studied feature of ABS, traceability, by using an approach based on Linearly-Homomorphic signatures. All our schemes also guarantee the anonymity of the real signer.

The unforgeability of our schemes is proven using the SXDH assumption, and our constructions use the Dual Pairing Vector Spaces (DPVS) framework developed by Okamoto and Takashima, which has been widely used for all kind of attribute and functional cryptography mechanisms.

1 Introduction

Digital signatures have key applications into emerging technologies like smart contracts, e-signatures, and authentication to online services. All of them require some kind of signature from the user, that must be verified by another party.

Furthermore, some applications are reliant on the anonymity granted to its participants, like e-vote and anonymous auctions. It can be because of mandatory data privacy regulations (US Data Privacy Laws, Europe's GDPR), or because it provides a concurrential advantage, as users are concerned about their privacy. Hence, these applications should only enforce verifications that are strictly

E. Oswald (Ed.): CT-RSA 2024, LNCS 14643, pp. 224–248, 2024.
https://doi.org/10.1007/978-3-031-58868-6_9

necessary, like verifying the legitimacy of a signer to sign a contract or access a service, without revealing the identity of the signer.

As mentioned in CT-RSA 2021 [2], blockchain applications like cryptocurrencies must also ensure accountability and identity management to follow regulatory requirements (*Know Your Customer/Anti-Money Laundering*), as well as public verifiability to keep their users' trust. Therefore, suitable primitives should allow to reconcile these regulations and principles with anonymity. This can be achieved through tracing, which also prevents abuse and makes signers accountable. This crosses out fully anonymous primitives like ring signatures [21].

One could use solutions based on group signatures [1], where a designated tracer can remove the anonymity of a signer, but they unfortunately lack expressivity. Indeed, they can only express membership of a group of potential signers, and not more complex policies, based on boolean expressions. This is not enough for the many applications we have mentioned, where we need to verify precise but varied statements and conditionals.

Attribute-based signatures (ABS), introduced in [17], combine anonymity, expressivity and traceability. It allows users to sign a message for a policy that is validated with a set of attributes. ABS are appropriate for situations where high-granularity of the policy is required: management of rights for members of a team, industrial contracts, financial operations, and blockchain operations.

The expressivity and granularity of ABS can be pushed even further with delegation, where users can create sub-keys with restricted rights from their original keys. This technique grants users the capacity to manage access rights on a case-by-case basis, without the need to refer to an authority for approval.

Applications of delegation can be found in project management and team management. Since delegated keys can be tailored by the delegator depending on its needs, they can include restricted timeframes of validity, scope perimeters, and authorizations of specific sets of actions. This can be useful to integrate temporary members in an existing team, or allow cooperation between members of two different teams in a secure way. Another application is the management of many devices by a single user. In this scenario, a user is in possession of many devices, and he wishes to configure them following common security practices like the least privilege principle. Thanks to delegation, this can be done dynamically on a device-per-device basis, without referring to an authority.

These possibilities make delegation a promising feature for ABS, as it furthers the granularity needed to manage modern applications (both from a security and a functionality standpoint), while maintaining the anonymity and traceability required by different regulations.

Related Work. Attribute-Based Signature was introduced by Maji *et al.* [17], as the signature version of Attribute-Based Encryption (ABE) [11]. They define what one can expect as unforgeability for ABS: one is unable to produce a convincing signature for any policy he wouldn't satisfy. Unforgeability can be *adaptive*, where the adversary can choose the challenge policy at the moment it outputs the forgery, or *selective*, a weaker version where the adversary must choose the challenge policy at the beginning of the game. They also introduce privacy (or anonymity) for ABS, where any verifier does not learn anything on the identity nor the attributes of the signer when seeing a signature, except that the signature is valid or not, with respect to the claimed policy.

Our constructions are based on Okamoto and Takashima's [18] original work in the Dual-Pairing Vector Space (DPVS) framework, which is still the basis for their recent work for signatures [3]. The DPVS allows to prove adaptive unforgeability in ABS and adaptive security in its ABE counterpart [18,19]. Most of their previous works are based on the DLIN assumption or variants. Along with Attrapadung *et al.*, they focused on the expressivity of the policy [23].

A common feature for ABS is tracing [5,10] where a dedicated tracing authority can remove the anonymity of signatures for accountability. The most common approach for traceability in the litterature is the one proposed by Ghadafi *et al.* [7], where a designated tracer with a secret tracing key can produce a proof of identity of the signer, which is verifiable by any third party with a public verification key. It relies on attaching an encryption of the identity of the signer to signatures, along with a NIZK proof that the identity is the one used to sign. The tracer simply own the secret key to decrypt any identity when tracing a signature, and can produce NIZK proof of the identity to any verifying third-party to prove tracing was done correctly.

Another functionality which has not received much attention in ABS is the delegation functionality. A work from [16] proposes proxy signature with a warrant for ABS, which works as a delegation of pre-set policies. Their work is in a restricted setting, where policies are a subset cover of attributes, and their construction is selectively secure and doesn't consider anonymity.

A recent line of work from Manulis *et al.* [6,9] explores a Hierarchical ABS with a focus on the management of intermediate authorities, where the delegation keeps track of the delegation path containing all the authorities that participated in the creation of someone's key. While this allows delegation via intermediate authorities, the tracing of the delegation path makes the size of keys and signatures linear in the number of attributes *and* the length of the delegation path. This additional cost cannot be avoided as their delegation and tracing are intermingled. Since delegation cannot be separated from tracing in their construction, this also means that delegation cannot be done without the NIZK that is used for tracing.

Contributions. In this paper, we propose and prove an ABS construction with two different types of delegation: delegation of attributes and delegation of policies. A depiction of these functionalities is given in Fig. 1. This construction is existentially unforgeable, as well as perfectly anonymous, under the following two standard assumptions: the SXDH assumption in the standard model, and the collision-resistance of some hash functions.

We also present a new version of indexing for DPVS, that builds on the one introduced by [19]. We then show as an application that this new version of indexing can be used to separate the commitment between message and policy with a hash function in our signature scheme, which is the core component of our delegation of policies.

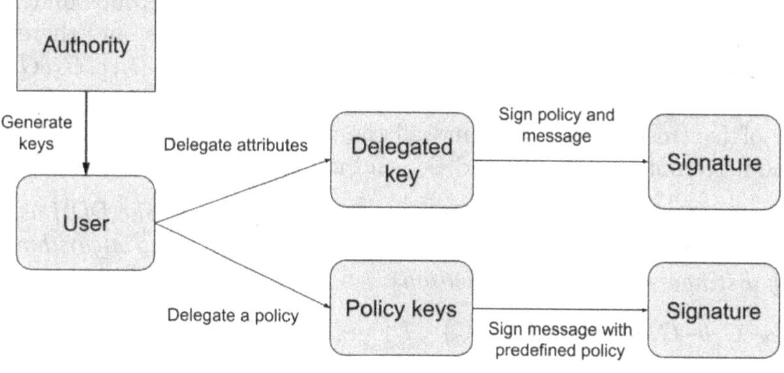

Fig. 1. Two types of delegation: attributes and policies.

Finally, we present a construction for ABS with traceability, which is compatible with our first construction with delegation. It is existentially unforgeable under the SXDH assumption in the standard model, and the collision-resistance of some hash functions. It is also computationally anonymous under these same assumptions, and the perfect zero-knowledge of the Square Diffie-Hellman problem [12] in the Random Oracle Model (ROM). The traceability stands in the ROM, and relies on the security of a Linearly-Homomorphic signature scheme, the simulation-extractability of some non-interactive zero-knowledge proof (NIZK) and the soundness of some other NIZK. We exploit the scheme from [12], whose security is proven in the generic bilinear group model.

The keys and signatures of both our schemes are linear in the number of attributes involved, with performances comparable to [18]. See Fig. 2.

Feature	[18]	[9]	Ours
Unforge. assumpt.	DLIN	q-type, SXDH, GGM	SXDH
Delegation	×	✓	✓
Traceability	×	Delegation path	Original delegator
Trace. assumpt.	×	×	GGM, ROM
Signature size	$\mathbb{G}_2 : 9t + 11$	$\mathbb{G}_1 : 6(2\ell - 1)t + 24$ $\mathbb{G}_2 : 4(2.5\ell - 1)t + 17$	$\mathbb{G}_2 : 10t + 14$

Fig. 2. Comparison with Related Work. t is the number of attributes used in a signature, and ℓ is the height of the delegation hierarchy.

2 Preliminaries

Our constructions will heavily use the Dual Pairing Vector Spaces (DPVS), proposed for efficient schemes with adaptive security [13,19], in the same vein as

Dual System Encryption (DSE) [14,25], in either prime-order groups under the DLIN assumption or pairings on composite-order elliptic curves, and thereafter on the SXDH assumption in a pairing-friendly setting $(\mathbb{G}_1, \mathbb{G}_2, \mathbb{G}_t, e, G_1, G_2, q)$, with a bilinear map e from $\mathbb{G}_1 \times \mathbb{G}_2$ into $\mathbb{G}_t$, where G_1 (respectively G_2) is a generator of $\mathbb{G}_1$ (respectively $\mathbb{G}_2$), and all the groups are of prime order q. We will use additive notation for $\mathbb{G}_1$ and $\mathbb{G}_2$, and multiplicative notation in $\mathbb{G}_t$.

Definition 1 (Decisional Diffie-Hellman Assumption). *The DDH assumption in $\mathbb{G}$, of prime order q with generator G, states that no algorithm can efficiently distinguish the two distributions*

$$\mathcal{D}_0 = \{(a \cdot G, b \cdot G, ab \cdot G), a, b \stackrel{\$}{\leftarrow} \mathbb{Z}_q\} \quad \mathcal{D}_1 = \{(a \cdot G, b \cdot G, c \cdot G), a, b, c \stackrel{\$}{\leftarrow} \mathbb{Z}_q\}$$

And we will denote by $\mathsf{Adv}^{\mathsf{ddh}}_{\mathbb{G}}(T)$ the best advantage an algorithm can get in distinguishing the two distributions within time bounded by T. Eventually, we will make the following more general Symmetric eXternal Diffie-Hellman (SXDH) Assumption which makes the DDH assumptions in both $\mathbb{G}_1$ and $\mathbb{G}_2$. Then, we define $\mathsf{Adv}^{\mathsf{sxdh}}(T) = \max\{\mathsf{Adv}^{\mathsf{ddh}}_{\mathbb{G}_1}(T), \mathsf{Adv}^{\mathsf{ddh}}_{\mathbb{G}_2}(T)\}$.

2.1 Dual Pairing Vector Spaces

We will use the framework from [4] which uses a lower number of bases than the original framework from Okamoto and Takashima [18]. One could also consider the more recent framework from Datta *et al.* [3] for a lower number of bases, but it also implies a higher number of specific sub-problems for the proof, which makes it less modular for the security proof.

To define Dual Pairing Vector Spaces (DPVS) under the SXDH assumption, we consider the additional law between an element $X \in \mathbb{G}_1^n$ and $Y \in \mathbb{G}_2^n$: $X \times Y \stackrel{\mathsf{def}}{=} \prod_i e(X_i, Y_i)$. If $X = (X_i)_i = \vec{x} \cdot G_1 \in \mathbb{G}_1^n$ and $Y = (Y_i)_i = \vec{y} \cdot G_2 \in \mathbb{G}_2^n$: $(\vec{x} \cdot G_1) \times (\vec{y} \cdot G_2) = X \times Y = \prod_i e(X_i, Y_i) = g_t^{\langle \vec{x}, \vec{y} \rangle}$, where $g_t = e(G_1, G_2)$ and $\langle \vec{x}, \vec{y} \rangle$ is the inner product between vectors $\vec{x}$ and $\vec{y}$.

From any basis $\mathcal{B} = (\vec{b}_i)_i$ of $\mathbb{Z}_q^n$, we can define the basis $\mathbb{B} = (\mathbf{b}_i)_i$ of $\mathbb{G}_1^n$, where $\mathbf{b}_i = \vec{b}_i \cdot G_1$. This allows us to note $(a_1, \ldots, a_n)_{\mathbb{B}} = \sum_i a_i \cdot \mathbf{b}_i$.

Such a basis $\mathcal{B}$ is equivalent to a random invertible matrix $B \stackrel{\$}{\leftarrow} \mathrm{GL}_n(\mathbb{Z}_q)$, the matrix with $\vec{b}_i$ as its i-th row. If we additionally use $\mathbb{B}^* = (\mathbf{b}_i^*)_i$, the basis of $\mathbb{G}_2^n$ associated to the matrix $B' = (B^{-1})^\top$, as $B \cdot B'^\top = I_n$,

$$\mathbf{b}_i \times \mathbf{b}_j^* = (\vec{b}_i \cdot G_1) \times (\vec{b}'_j \cdot G_2) = g_t^{\langle \vec{b}_i, \vec{b}'_j \rangle} = g_t^{\delta_{i,j}},$$

where $\delta_{i,j} = 1$ if $i = j$ and $\delta_{i,j} = 0$ otherwise, for $i, j \in \{1, \ldots, n\}$: $\mathbb{B}$ and $\mathbb{B}^*$ are called *Dual Orthogonal Bases*. A pairing-friendly setting with such dual orthogonal bases $\mathbb{B}$ and $\mathbb{B}^*$ of size n is called a *Dual Pairing Vector Space*.

2.2 Change of Basis

The security games will heavily rely on indistinguishable change of basis. We recap the indistinguishable modifications on *random* dual orthogonal bases $\mathbb{B}$

and $\mathbb{B}^*$, under the DDH assumption in $\mathbb{G}_1$ (can also be applied in $\mathbb{G}_2$), proven in [4]. We illustrate these theorems in the full version.

SubSpace-Ind Property, on $(\mathbb{B}, \mathbb{B}^*)_{1,2}$**:** from the view of $\mathbb{B}$ and $\mathbb{B}^* \backslash \{\mathbf{b}_2^*\}$, and any vector $(y_1, y_2, \ldots, y_n)_{\mathbb{B}^*}$, for chosen $y_2, \ldots, y_n \in \mathbb{Z}_q$, but unknown random $y_1 \xleftarrow{\$} \mathbb{Z}_q$, one cannot distinguish the vectors $(x_1, x_2', x_3, \ldots, x_n)_{\mathbb{B}}$ and $(x_1, x_2, x_3, \ldots, x_n)_{\mathbb{B}}$, for chosen $x_2', x_2, \ldots, x_n \in \mathbb{Z}_q$, but unknown random $x_1 \xleftarrow{\$} \mathbb{Z}_q$.

Swap-Ind Property, on $(\mathbb{B}, \mathbb{B}^*)_{1,2,3}$**:** from the view of $\mathbb{B}$ and $\mathbb{B}^* \backslash \{\mathbf{b}_1^*, \mathbf{b}_2^*\}$, and any vector $(y_1, y_1, y_3, \ldots, y_n)_{\mathbb{B}^*}$, for chosen $y_1, y_3, \ldots, y_n \in \mathbb{Z}_q$, one cannot distinguish the vectors $(x_1, 0, x_3, x_4, \ldots, x_n)_{\mathbb{B}}$ and $(0, x_1, x_3, x_4, \ldots, x_n)_{\mathbb{B}}$, for chosen $x_1, x_4, \ldots, x_n \in \mathbb{Z}_q$, but unknown random $x_3 \xleftarrow{\$} \mathbb{Z}_q$.

Index-Ind Property, on $(\mathbb{B}, \mathbb{B}^*)_{1,2,3}$**:** from the view of $\mathbb{B}$ and $\mathbb{B}^* \backslash \{\mathbf{b}_3^*\}$, and any vector $(\pi \cdot (t, -1), y_3, \ldots, y_n)_{\mathbb{B}^*}$, for chosen $y_3, \ldots, y_n \in \mathbb{Z}_q$, but unknown random $\pi \xleftarrow{\$} \mathbb{Z}_q$, and for any chosen $p \neq t \in \mathbb{Z}_q$, one cannot distinguish the vectors $(\sigma \cdot (1, p), x_3, x_4, \ldots, x_n)_{\mathbb{B}}$ and $(\sigma \cdot (1, p), x_3', x_4, \ldots, x_n)_{\mathbb{B}}$, for chosen $x_3', x_3, x_4, \ldots, x_n \in \mathbb{Z}_q$, but unknown random $\sigma \xleftarrow{\$} \mathbb{Z}_q$.

We also present a new version of Index-Ind in dimension 3 (instead of 2). The proof is presented in the full version.

Theorem 2 (Index-Ind Property). *In* $(\mathbb{B}, \mathbb{B}^*)$ *of dimension 6, from the view of* $(\mathbf{b}_1, \mathbf{b}_2, \mathbf{b}_3, \mathbf{b}_1^*, \mathbf{b}_2^*, \mathbf{b}_3^*, \mathbf{b}_4^*)$*, and any vector* $\mathbf{u} = (\pi \cdot (x + \rho x', -1, -\rho), \beta, 0, 0)_{\mathbb{B}}$*, for chosen* $x, x', \beta \in \mathbb{Z}_q$*, but unknown random* $\pi, \rho \xleftarrow{\$} \mathbb{Z}_q$*, and for any chosen* $(y, y') \neq (x, x') \in \mathbb{Z}_q^2$*, one cannot distinguish the vectors* $\mathbf{v}_0^* = (\sigma \cdot (1, y, y'), 0, 0, 0)_{\mathbb{B}^*}$ *and* $\mathbf{v}_1^* = (\sigma \cdot (1, y, y'), \alpha, 0, 0)_{\mathbb{B}^*}$*, for chosen* $\alpha \in \mathbb{Z}_q$*, but unknown random* $\sigma \xleftarrow{\$} \mathbb{Z}_q$*, with an advantage better than* $4 \times \mathsf{Adv}_{\mathbb{G}_2}^{\mathsf{ddh}}(t) + 2 \times \mathsf{Adv}_{\mathbb{G}_1}^{\mathsf{ddh}}(t)$.

An important application of this theorem for our construction is that we can now have independent commitment for the message and for the policy, contrary to [18]. In their construction, the message m and the policy $\mathcal{T}$ are commited together inside a single call of a hash function $\mathcal{H}$, which can then be used as part of an indexing in dimension 2, where $\mathcal{H}(m, \mathcal{T})$ plays the role of p in the 2-Dimension property. A direct application of the 3-Dimensional Indexing allows to decorrelate $\mathcal{H}(m, \mathcal{T})$ into $\mathcal{H}(m)$ and $\mathcal{H}(\mathcal{T})$, which can then be used to build the new delegation functionalities that we present in our construction.

2.3 Attribute-Based Signature

Standard ABS Definition. Attribute-Based Signatures (ABS) have been formalized in [17], with attributes in the keys and policies in the signatures:

$\mathsf{Setup}(1^\kappa)$. From the security parameter κ, the algorithm defines all the global parameters PK and the master secret key MK;

$\mathsf{KeyGen}(\mathsf{MK}, \mathsf{id}, \Gamma)$. For a master secret key MK, an identity id and a list of attributes Γ, the algorithm outputs a private key $\mathsf{SK}_{\mathsf{id},\Gamma}$ specific to the user id and the set of attributes Γ;

$\mathsf{Sig}(\mathsf{SK}_{\mathsf{id},\Gamma}, m, \mathcal{T})$. For a private key $\mathsf{SK}_{\mathsf{id},\Gamma}$, on a set of attributes Γ, a message m and a policy $\mathcal{T}$ satisfied by Γ, the algorithm outputs a signature σ;

$\mathsf{Verif}(\mathsf{PK}, m, \mathcal{T}, \sigma)$. Given the public parameters PK, a signature σ for a message m under a policy $\mathcal{T}$, the algorithm outputs 1 for accept or 0 for reject.

For correctness, the Verif algorithm should output 1 with overwhelming probability on $(\sigma, m, \mathcal{T})$ if σ has been generated on m and $\mathcal{T}$, with a private key $\mathsf{SK}_{\mathsf{id},\Gamma}$ that has been generated from the KeyGen algorithm associated on a set Γ that satisfies $\mathcal{T}$. We will note $\mathcal{T}(\Gamma) = 1$ when $\mathcal{T}$ is satisfied by Γ, and $\mathcal{T}(\Gamma) = 0$ otherwise.

ABS with Delegation. We now consider two different kinds of delegation. The first one is to delegate a subset of attributes from a key, which is the usual approach to delegation where keys are a set of attributes. The other one is to choose a policy which can be validated by the delegator key, and create a new delegated key that is commited to this policy. The new delegated key can sign any new message under the commited policy. We will prove that both these delegations are fully compatible with anonymity.

For ABS with delegation, in addition to the initial definition of an ABS, we also consider delegation algorithms, with an additional signing algorithm:

$\mathsf{Delegate\text{-}Attributes}(\mathsf{SK}_{\mathsf{id},\Gamma}, \bar{\mathsf{id}}, \Gamma')$. From $\mathsf{SK}_{\mathsf{id},\Gamma}$, and for a subset $\Gamma' \subset \Gamma$, one can derive a signing key $\mathsf{SK}_{\bar{\mathsf{id}},\Gamma'}$ for a user $\bar{\mathsf{id}}$.

$\mathsf{Delegate\text{-}Policy}(\mathsf{SK}_{\mathsf{id},\Gamma}, \bar{\mathsf{id}}, \mathcal{T})$. For a private key $\mathsf{SK}_{\mathsf{id},\Gamma}$ on a set of attributes Γ and a policy $\mathcal{T}$ satisfied by Γ, the algorithm outputs a policy key $\mathsf{SK}_{\bar{\mathsf{id}},\mathcal{T}}$;

$\mathsf{DelegateSig}(\mathsf{SK}_{\mathsf{id},\mathcal{T}}, m)$. For a delegated key $\mathsf{SK}_{\mathsf{id},\mathcal{T}}$ on a policy $\mathcal{T}$ and a message m, the algorithm outputs a signature σ;

The delegated keys from the first algorithm can be used in a similar way as a fresh key. For this reason, when we refer to a key in the following, it can be from either KeyGen or Delegate-Attributes without distinction, except if specified otherwise. It thus allows hierarchical delegation of attributes. On the other hand, policy delegation provides different keys, hence another signing algorithm, which is why we'll refer to them as *policy keys*.

For the correctness, we add that the Verif algorithm should output 1 with overwhelming probability on $(\sigma, m, \mathcal{T})$ even if σ has been generated on m with a policy key $\mathsf{SK}_{\bar{\mathsf{id}},\mathcal{T}}$. In both cases, we note $\bar{\mathsf{id}}$ the new full identity associated to the keys, which could be formed for example by concatenation: $\bar{\mathsf{id}} = \mathsf{id}||\mathsf{id}'$, for some id', and even possibly a longer chain, as only delegated attributes under the exact same chain might be combined as a new key.

2.4 Security Model

As for any signature scheme, with ABS, one should not be able to produce a valid signature under a policy $\mathcal{T}$ if one does not own the appropriate attributes to fulfill it. However, we also account for the nature of delegated keys: One should not be able to produce a valid signature under a policy $\mathcal{T}$ if one does not own the appropriate attributes or the delegated key for unforgeability.

In particular, for the delegation of attributes, we consider that the adversary will have access to delegated keys via the ODelegateAttributes oracle, which he can use on keys previously queried via either OKeyGen or ODelegateAttributes. Regarding the policy delegation, we add two additional oracles: ODelegatePolicy to generate a policy key from a previous OKeyGen or ODelegateAttributes query, and ODelegateSig to obtain a signature from a policy key ODelegatePolicy that has already been queried. None of the keys are actually revealed to the adversary, unless he queries specifically for them via OGet, to model the real information learnt by the adversary. Indeed, some keys can be generated, but only as source of delegations, and only delegated keys will be known to the adversary, in case the adversary is just a delegatee.

Definition 3 (Existential Unforgeability). *EUF for ABS with delegation is defined by the following game between the adversary and a challenger:*

Initialize: *The challenger runs the* Setup *algorithm of ABS and gives the public parameters* PK *to the adversary;*

Oracles: *The following oracles can be called in any order and any number of times:*

- OKeyGen(id, Γ): *to model* KeyGen*-queries for any identity* id *and any set of attributes* Γ *of its choice, and gets back the index* k *of the key;*
- ODelegateAttributes$(k, \bar{\mathsf{id}}, \Gamma')$: *to model* Delegate-Attributes*-queries for identity* $\bar{\mathsf{id}}$ *and any subset of attributes* $\Gamma' \subset \Gamma$*, for the* k*-indexed generated key from* Γ*. It generates the signing key but only outputs the index* k' *of the new key;*
- ODelegatePolicy$(k, \bar{\mathsf{id}}, \mathcal{T})$: *to model* Delegate-Policy*-queries for identity* $\bar{\mathsf{id}}$ *and any policy* $\mathcal{T}$*, from the* k*-indexed generated key for* Γ *so that* $\mathcal{T}(\Gamma) = 1$*. It generates the new policy key but only outputs the index* k' *of the new policy key;*
- OGet(k): *the adversary obtains the* k*-indexed key generated by one of the above oracles;*
- OSig$(\mathsf{id}, m, \mathcal{T}, k)$: *to model* Sig*-queries under any policy* $\mathcal{T}$ *of its choice for a message* m*, for the identity* id*, and a key index* k*. It generates and outputs the signature;*
- ODelegateSig$(\bar{\mathsf{id}}, m, \mathcal{T}, k)$: *to model* DelegateSig*-queries for any message* m*, for identity* $\bar{\mathsf{id}}$*, policy* $\mathcal{T}$*, and key index* k*. It generates and outputs the signature.*

Finalize(b'): *The adversary outputs a forgery* $(m', \mathcal{T}', \sigma')$*. If for some attribute set* Γ *corresponding to a key asked to the* OGet *oracle,* $\mathcal{T}'(\Gamma) = 1$*, or if the adversary queried* OSig *or* ODelegateSig *on* $(m', \mathcal{T}')$*, or if the adversary queries* ODelegatePolicy *on* $\mathcal{T}'$*, one outputs* 0*. Otherwise one outputs* Verif$(\mathsf{PK}, m', \mathcal{T}', \sigma')$.

The advantage $\mathsf{Adv}^{\mathsf{del\text{-}euf}}(\mathcal{A})$ *of an adversary* $\mathcal{A}$ *in this game is defined as the probability to output* 1.

As usual, the Finalize-step excludes trivial attacks, where the adversary owns a key able to generate an acceptable signature or just forwards a query asked to the signing oracle.

Another security notion that should also be satisfied by an ABS scheme, even more so with delegation, is that a signature generated for a given policy should be independent of the user, and signatures generated by fresh keys or delegated keys should be indistinguishable. We refer to this property as anonymity, as in [17]. Our definition requires to examine six different distributions, to take into account the possibility of delegation:

Definition 4 (Anonymity). *An ABS with delegation scheme is said anonymous if, for any* $(\mathsf{PK}, \mathsf{MK}) \xleftarrow{\$} \mathsf{Setup}$, *any message* m, *any identities* $\mathsf{id}_0, \mathsf{id}_1$, *any attribute sets* Γ_0, Γ_1, *any signing keys* $\mathsf{SK}_0 \xleftarrow{\$} \mathsf{KeyGen}(\mathsf{MK}, \mathsf{id}_0, \Gamma_0)$, $\mathsf{SK}_1 \xleftarrow{\$} \mathsf{KeyGen}(\mathsf{MK}, \mathsf{id}_1, \Gamma_1)$, *any delegated keys* $\mathsf{SK}'_0 \xleftarrow{\$} \mathsf{Delegate\text{-}Attributes}(\mathsf{SK}_0, \mathsf{id}'_0, \Gamma'_0)$, $\mathsf{SK}'_1 \xleftarrow{\$} \mathsf{Delegate\text{-}Attributes}(\mathsf{SK}_1, \mathsf{id}'_1, \Gamma'_1)$, *for* $\Gamma'_0 \subset \Gamma_0$ *and* $\Gamma'_1 \subset \Gamma_1$, *any policy keys* $\widetilde{\mathsf{SK}'}_0 \xleftarrow{\$} \mathsf{Delegate\text{-}Policy}(\mathsf{SK}_0, \mathcal{T})$, $\widetilde{\mathsf{SK}'}_1 \xleftarrow{\$} \mathsf{Delegate\text{-}Policy}(\mathsf{SK}_1, \mathcal{T})$, *for any policy* $\mathcal{T}$ *satisfied by both* Γ'_0 *and* Γ'_1, *the six distributions of the signatures generated by* $\mathsf{Sig}(\mathsf{SK}_0, m, \mathcal{T})$, $\mathsf{Sig}(\mathsf{SK}'_0, m, \mathcal{T})$, $\mathsf{DelegateSig}(\widetilde{\mathsf{SK}'}_0, m)$, $\mathsf{Sig}(\mathsf{SK}_1, m, \mathcal{T})$, $\mathsf{Sig}(\mathsf{SK}'_1, m, \mathcal{T})$, $\mathsf{DelegateSig}(\widetilde{\mathsf{SK}'}_1, m)$ *are indistinguishable.*

Indistinguishability can be perfect, statistical or computational, which leads to perfect, statistical or computational anonymity.

Whereas perfect anonymity excludes traceability, computational anonymity may allow the existence of a trapdoor leading to traceability. We will propose both in the following.

2.5 Policies and Access-Trees

We use the same approach as [11] by defining a policy on attributes in $\mathcal{U}$: we will consider a policy as an access-tree $\mathcal{T}$ with only AND and OR gates instead of more general threshold gates (an AND-gate being an n-out-of-n gate, whereas an OR-gate is a 1-out-of-n gate). Nevertheless, access-trees with only AND and OR gates are as expressive as access-trees with threshold gates.

Access-trees have a similar structure to boolean expressions, which are commonly used in applicative security. This makes the access-tree approach easily compatible with existing security infrastructures that already rely on such expressions for their policy.

Definition of Access-Trees. We only recall the important notations of access-trees, and refer the reader to [4] for a full definition of access-trees. We also introduce the additional notion of dual trees, that will be used to prove the correctness and anonymity our signatures.

An access-tree $\mathcal{T}$ is a rooted labeled tree from the root ρ, with internal nodes associated to AND and OR gates and leaves associated to attributes. For each leaf $\lambda \in \mathcal{L}$, $A(\lambda) \in \mathcal{U}$ is an attribute, and any internal node $\nu \in \mathcal{N}$ is labeled with a gate $G(\nu) \in \{\mathsf{AND}, \mathsf{OR}\}$ as an AND or an OR gate to be satisfied among the children in $\mathsf{children}(\nu)$.

Satisfying an Access-Tree. On a given list $\Gamma \subseteq \mathcal{U}$ of attributes, each leaf $\lambda \in \mathcal{L}$ is either satisfied (considered or set to True), if $A(\lambda) \in \Gamma$, or not (ignored or set to False) otherwise. We will denote $\mathcal{L}_\Gamma$ the restriction of $\mathcal{L}$ to the satisfied leaves in the tree $\mathcal{T}$ (corresponding to an attribute in Γ). Then, for each internal node ν, one checks whether all children (AND-gate) or at least one of the children (OR-gate) are satisfied, from the attributes associated to the leaves, and then ν is itself satisfied or not. We then denote $\mathcal{T}(\Gamma) = 1$ when the access-tree $\mathcal{T}$ is satisfied by the set of attributes Γ.

Evaluation Pruned Trees. We consider an access-tree $\mathcal{T}$ with leaves $\mathcal{L}$ and a set Γ of attributes so that $\mathcal{T}(\Gamma) = 1$. A Γ-evaluation tree $\mathcal{T}' \subset \mathcal{T}$ is a pruned version of $\mathcal{T}$, where one children only is kept for OR-gate nodes, down to the leaves, so that $\mathcal{T}'(\Gamma) = 1$. Basically, we keep a skeleton with only necessary True leaves to evaluate the internal nodes up to the root. We will denote $\mathsf{EPT}(\mathcal{T}, \Gamma)$ the set of all the evaluation pruned trees of $\mathcal{T}$ with respect to Γ. $\mathsf{EPT}(\mathcal{T}, \Gamma)$ is non-empty if and only if $\mathcal{T}(\Gamma) = 1$.

Labelings of a Tree. We define the labeling of a tree, which can be seen as a linear secret sharing among the leaves of the tree.

Definition 5 (Random y-Labeling). *A random y-labeling Λ_y of an access-tree $\mathcal{T}$, for any $y \in \mathbb{Z}_p$, is the probabilistic algorithm $\Lambda_y(\mathcal{T})$ that sets $a_\rho \leftarrow y$ for the root, and then in a top-down manner starting from the root, set a_ν for each internal node ν : if ν is an AND-node with n children, a random n-out-of-n sharing of a_ν is associated to each children* i.e., *random values are associated to a_κ for all $\kappa \in \mathsf{children}(\nu)$, such that the sum is equal to a_ν in $\mathbb{Z}_p$; if ν is an OR-gate, each children is associated to the value a_ν.*

Algorithm $\Lambda_y(\mathcal{T})$ outputs $\Lambda_y = (a_\lambda)_{\lambda \in \mathcal{L}}$, for all the leaves $\lambda \in \mathcal{L}$ of the tree $\mathcal{T}$. Random labelings have several properties: the sum of a y-labeling and a random z-labeling is a random $(y + z)$-labeling of $\mathcal{T}$. And multiplying all the labels of a y-labeling by a constant c leads to a cy-labeling. Furthermore, because of the recursive definition of labelings, one can see that, given a labeling (a_λ) on $\mathcal{T}$, we can extract a a_ν-labeling for any subtree of $\mathcal{T}$, rooted at node ν, which coincides with $\mathcal{T}$ on all values a_λ for leaves of the subtree.

Evaluation of a Labeled Tree. As noted above, labels on leaves are a linear secret sharing of the root that allows reconstruction of the secret if and only if the policy is satisfied: for a set Γ that satisfies $\mathcal{T}$ and a labeling Λ_y of $\mathcal{T}$ for a random y, given only $(a_\lambda)_{\lambda \in \mathcal{L}_\Gamma}$, one can reconstruct $y = a_\rho$. Indeed, as $\mathcal{T}(\Gamma) = 1$, we use an evaluation pruned tree $\mathcal{T}' \in \mathsf{EPT}(\mathcal{T}, \Gamma)$. Then, in a bottom-up way, starting from the leaves, one can compute the labels of all the internal nodes, up to the root.

Dual-Trees. For our construction, we will use another type of tree, called the *dual-tree* $\mathcal{T}^*$ of $\mathcal{T}$: this is the exact same tree as $\mathcal{T}$, except that all OR gates in $\mathcal{T}$ become AND gates in $\mathcal{T}^*$, and conversely all AND gates in $\mathcal{T}$ become OR gates in $\mathcal{T}^*$. We note that the structure of $\mathcal{T}$ and $\mathcal{T}^*$ is identical, in particular all leaves are present on both trees, thus we will abuse notations and consider $\mathcal{L}_\mathcal{T} = \mathcal{L}_{\mathcal{T}^*}$ when there is no ambiguity.

Dual-trees will be crucial in our constructions. They will allow the signer to share enough information to the verifier for the verification of the signature, to prove correctness. At the same time, it prevents revealing anything about the validity of the access-tree other than the signer could sign it with its attributes, to ensure anonymity. This is formalized in the two next propositions, proven in the full version.

Proposition 6. *If $(a_\lambda)_\lambda$ is an a_0-labeling of $\mathcal{T}$, and $(b_\lambda)_\lambda$ is a b_0-labeling of its dual tree $\mathcal{T}^*$, then $\sum_{\lambda\in\mathcal{L}} a_\lambda b_\lambda = a_0 b_0$.*

This stems from the fact that there is always an OR-gate (from either $\mathcal{T}$ or $\mathcal{T}'$) which creates a common factor when recursively evaluating the product at each node on both trees (Illustration on Fig. 3).

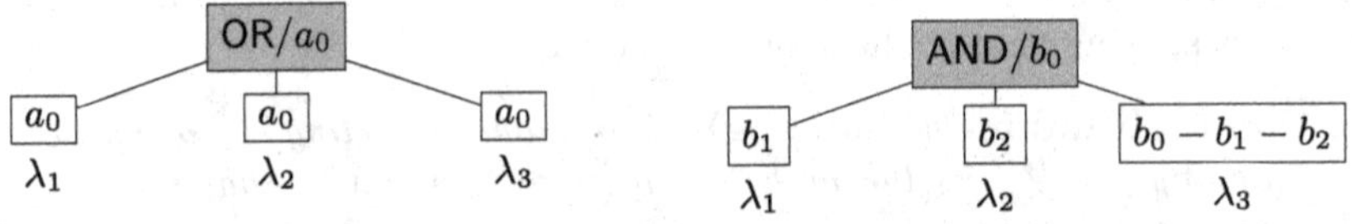

Fig. 3. A trivial access-tree with an OR-gate (left) and its dual tree with an AND-gate (right). Each tree has a random labeling for a_0 or b_0. One can see that $\sum_{\lambda\in\mathcal{L}} a_\lambda b_\lambda = a_0 b_1 + a_0 b_2 + a_0(b_0 - b_1 - b_2) = a_0 b_0$. This generalizes to any number of children for a gate, and to any access-tree by recursion from bottom to top.

Proposition 7. *Let $\mathcal{T}$ be an access-tree and Γ a set of attributes so that $\mathcal{T}(\Gamma) = 1$. Then, for any Evaluation Pruned Tree $\mathcal{T}' \in \mathsf{EPT}(\mathcal{T}, \Gamma)$, there is a 1-labeling $(b_\lambda)_\lambda$ of the dual $\mathcal{T}^*$ which verifies: $b_\lambda = 1$ for all $\lambda \in \mathcal{L}_{\mathcal{T}'}$ and $b_\lambda = 0$ for all $\lambda \notin \mathcal{L}_{\mathcal{T}'}$.*

If a tree $\mathcal{T}$ is satisfied by a set of attributes, we can associate the value 1 to the leaves of the satisfied attributes in the tree (which defines the pruned tree $\mathcal{T}' \subset \mathcal{T}$), and this association is effectively a 1-labeling of the dual-tree $\mathcal{T}'^* \subset \mathcal{T}^*$, but also a 1-labeling of the dual-tree $\mathcal{T}^*$. As this is a 1-labeling of $\mathcal{T}^*$, but specific to $\mathcal{T}'$, we can then randomize it for anonymity, with a 0-labeling of $\mathcal{T}^*$, through the linearity of labelings on $\mathcal{T}^*$, while maintaining correctness (Illustration on Fig. 4).

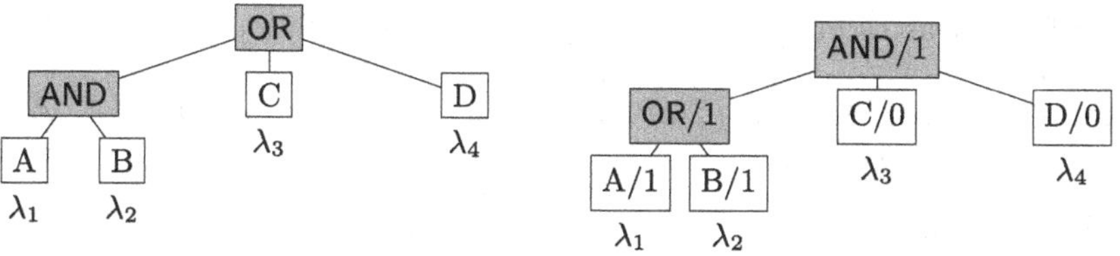

Fig. 4. An access-tree fulfilled by the set $\{A, B\}$ (left). One can extract a 1-labeling from its dual-tree (right) which has values 1 on leaves $\{A, B\}$ and 0 on all other leaves.

3 ABS with Attribute and Policy Delegation

In this section, we describe a Delegatable ABS scheme with perfect anonymity, and an unbounded universe of attributes. The basic idea is to derive the scheme from a KP-ABE, where signatures can be seen as a decryption key associated to a policy, and the verification algorithm tries to decrypt a ciphertext on a set of attributes. If decryption works, the signature is valid, otherwise the signature is invalid. To enable delegations of attributes and policies, we separate the commitment to the message and the policy in the signing process, which is a critical difference from the [20] construction.

3.1 Description of Our ABS Scheme

In our ABS, users can delegate subset of attributes with Delegate-Attributes, or pre-signed policies with Delegate-Policy. Then, they can sign using Sig with keys generated from either KeyGen or Delegate-Attributes, using any attributes they want. Alternatively, they can sign using DelegateSig with keys generated from Delegate-Policy, on a pre-chosen access-tree included in the keys.

To simplify reading, we also detail the distribution of vectors of each element, which will be enough to make the security proof afterwards. 0^k denotes k zero components in a vector.

$\mathsf{Setup}(1^\kappa)$. The algorithm chooses three random dual orthogonal bases, in a pairing-friendly setting $\mathcal{PG} = (\mathbb{G}_1, \mathbb{G}_2, \mathbb{G}_t, e, G_1, G_2, q)$:

$$\mathbb{B} = (\mathbf{b}_1, \ldots, \mathbf{b}_4) \qquad \mathbb{D} = (\mathbf{d}_1, \ldots, \mathbf{d}_{10}) \qquad \mathbb{H} = (\mathbf{h}_1, \ldots, \mathbf{h}_8)$$
$$\mathbb{B}^* = (\mathbf{b}_1^*, \ldots, \mathbf{b}_4^*) \qquad \mathbb{D}^* = (\mathbf{d}_1^*, \ldots, \mathbf{d}_{10}^*) \qquad \mathbb{H}^* = (\mathbf{h}_1^*, \ldots, \mathbf{h}_8^*).$$

It picks two full-domain hash functions $\mathcal{H}$ and $\mathcal{H}'$ onto $\mathbb{Z}_q$. It sets the public parameters $\mathsf{PK} = \{\mathcal{PG}, \mathcal{H}, \mathcal{H}', (\mathbf{b}_1, \mathbf{b}_3), (\mathbf{b}_2^*), (\mathbf{d}_1, \mathbf{d}_2, \mathbf{d}_3, \mathbf{d}_5), (\mathbf{d}_1^*, \mathbf{d}_2^*, \mathbf{d}_3^*, \mathbf{d}_4^*), (\mathbf{h}_1, \mathbf{h}_2, \mathbf{h}_3, \mathbf{h}_5), (\mathbf{h}_4^*)\}$, and master secret key $\mathsf{MK} = \{(\mathbf{b}_1^*), (\mathbf{h}_1^*, \mathbf{h}_2^*, \mathbf{h}_3^*)\}$.

$\mathsf{KeyGen}(\mathsf{MK}, \mathsf{id}, \Gamma)$. A random scalar $\delta_{\mathsf{id}} \stackrel{\$}{\leftarrow} \mathbb{Z}_q^*$ is associated to id, to define

$$\mathbf{k}_0^* = (\delta_{\mathsf{id}}, \phi_0, 0^2)_{\mathbb{B}^*} \qquad \mathbf{k}_t^* = (\delta_{\mathsf{id}}, \pi_t(1,t), \phi_t, 0^6)_{\mathbb{D}^*}$$
$$\mathbf{r}_1^* = (\delta_{\mathsf{id}}, 0, 0, \psi_1, 0^4)_{\mathbb{H}^*} \quad \mathbf{r}_2^* = (0, \delta_{\mathsf{id}}, 0, \psi_2, 0^4)_{\mathbb{H}^*} \quad \mathbf{r}_3^* = (0, 0, \delta_{\mathsf{id}}, \psi_3, 0^4)_{\mathbb{H}^*}$$

for all attributes $t \in \Gamma$, with $\phi_0, \psi_1, \psi_2, \psi_3, (\phi_t)_t, (\pi_t)_t \stackrel{\$}{\leftarrow} \mathbb{Z}_q^*$ for each t. The signing key $\mathsf{SK}_{\mathsf{id},\Gamma}$ is then set $(\mathbf{k}_0^*, (\mathbf{k}_t^*)_{t\in\Gamma}, \mathbf{r}_1^*, \mathbf{r}_2^*, \mathbf{r}_3^*)$. It can be computed later for new attributes t, for id, with extra $\mathbf{k}_t^*$, using the same δ_{id}, specific to user id.

$\mathsf{Delegate\text{-}Attributes}(\mathsf{SK}_{\mathsf{id},\Gamma}, \bar{\mathsf{id}}, \Gamma')$. Pick random $\alpha_{\bar{\mathsf{id}}}, \phi_0', (\phi_t')_t, \psi_1', \psi_2', \psi_3' \xleftarrow{\$} \mathbb{Z}_q$ for $t \in \Gamma' \subset \Gamma$, and compute

$$\bar{\mathbf{k}}_0^* = \alpha_{\bar{\mathsf{id}}} \cdot \mathbf{k}_0^* + \phi_0' \cdot \mathbf{b}_2^* \quad \bar{\mathbf{k}}_t^* = \alpha_{\bar{\mathsf{id}}} \cdot \mathbf{k}_t^* + \phi_t' \cdot \mathbf{d}_4^*$$
$$\bar{\mathbf{r}}_1^* = \alpha_{\bar{\mathsf{id}}} \cdot \mathbf{r}_1^* + \psi_1' \cdot \mathbf{h}_4^* \quad \bar{\mathbf{r}}_2^* = \alpha_{\bar{\mathsf{id}}} \cdot \mathbf{r}_2^* + \psi_2' \cdot \mathbf{h}_4^* \quad \bar{\mathbf{r}}_3^* = \alpha_{\bar{\mathsf{id}}} \cdot \mathbf{r}_3^* + \psi_3' \cdot \mathbf{h}_4^*$$

The delegated signing key $\mathsf{SK}_{\bar{\mathsf{id}},\Gamma'}$ is then set as $(\bar{\mathbf{k}}_0^*, (\bar{\mathbf{k}}_t^*)_{t\in\Gamma'}, \bar{\mathbf{r}}_1^*, \bar{\mathbf{r}}_2^*, \bar{\mathbf{r}}_3^*)$. More delegations can be provided with additional $\bar{\mathbf{k}}_t^*$ for $\bar{\mathsf{id}}$ from id using the same $\alpha_{\bar{\mathsf{id}}}$, specific to the attribute-delegation from id to $\bar{\mathsf{id}}$.
This results in the vectors, with $\alpha_{\bar{\mathsf{id}}}, \phi_0, \phi_0', (\phi_t)_t, (\phi_t')_t, (\pi_t)_t, \psi_1, \psi_1', \psi_2, \psi_2', \psi_3, \psi_3' \xleftarrow{\$} \mathbb{Z}_q$

$$\bar{\mathbf{k}}_0^* = (\alpha_{\bar{\mathsf{id}}}\delta_{\mathsf{id}}, \alpha_{\bar{\mathsf{id}}}\phi_0 + \phi_0', 0^2)_{\mathbb{B}^*} \qquad \bar{\mathbf{k}}_t^* = (\alpha_{\bar{\mathsf{id}}}\delta_{\mathsf{id}}, \alpha_{\bar{\mathsf{id}}}\pi_t(1,t), \alpha_{\bar{\mathsf{id}}}\phi_t + \phi_t', 0^6)_{\mathbb{D}^*}$$
$$\bar{\mathbf{r}}_1^* = (\alpha_{\bar{\mathsf{id}}}\delta_{\mathsf{id}}, 0, 0, \alpha_{\bar{\mathsf{id}}}\psi_1 + \psi_1', 0^4)_{\mathbb{H}^*}$$
$$\bar{\mathbf{r}}_2^* = (0, \alpha_{\bar{\mathsf{id}}}\delta_{\mathsf{id}}, 0, \alpha_{\bar{\mathsf{id}}}\psi_2 + \psi_2', 0^4)_{\mathbb{H}^*} \quad \bar{\mathbf{r}}_3^* = (0, 0, \alpha_{\bar{\mathsf{id}}}\delta_{\mathsf{id}}, \alpha_{\bar{\mathsf{id}}}\psi_3 + \psi_3', 0^4)_{\mathbb{H}^*}$$

which follow the same distributions as, with $\delta_{\bar{\mathsf{id}}}, (\pi_t)_t, \phi_0, (\phi_t)_t, \psi_1, \psi_2, \psi_3 \xleftarrow{\$} \mathbb{Z}_q^*$

$$\bar{\mathbf{k}}_0^* = (\delta_{\bar{\mathsf{id}}}, \phi_0, 0^2)_{\mathbb{B}^*} \qquad \bar{\mathbf{k}}_t^* = (\delta_{\bar{\mathsf{id}}}, \pi_t(1,t), \phi_t, 0^6)_{\mathbb{D}^*} \qquad \forall t \in \Gamma$$
$$\bar{\mathbf{r}}_1^* = (\delta_{\bar{\mathsf{id}}}, 0, 0, \psi_1, 0^4)_{\mathbb{H}^*}$$
$$\bar{\mathbf{r}}_2^* = (0, \delta_{\bar{\mathsf{id}}}, 0, \psi_2, 0^4)_{\mathbb{H}^*} \qquad \bar{\mathbf{r}}_3^* = (0, 0, \delta_{\bar{\mathsf{id}}}, \psi_3, 0^4)_{\mathbb{H}^*}$$

$\mathsf{Sig}(\mathsf{SK}_{\mathsf{id},\Gamma}, m, \mathcal{T})$. Let $\mathcal{T}' \in \mathsf{EPT}(\mathcal{T}, \Gamma)$ be an Evaluation Pruned Tree, scalars $\nu, \xi, \zeta, (\omega_\lambda)_\lambda, (q_\lambda)_\lambda \xleftarrow{\$} \mathbb{Z}_q^*$, and $(\alpha_\lambda)_\lambda$ the 1-labeling of the dual $\mathcal{T}^*$ specific to $\mathcal{T}'$ (see Proposition 7), where $\alpha_\lambda = 1$ if $\lambda \in \mathcal{L}_{\mathcal{T}'}$, else $\alpha_\lambda = 0$. This is possible as $\mathcal{T}(\Gamma) = 1$. Compute $(\beta_\lambda)_\lambda$ to be a random 0-labeling of the dual $\mathcal{T}^*$ associated to $\mathcal{T}$.
Eventually, set, for $H = \mathcal{H}(\mathcal{T}), H' = \mathcal{H}'(m)$:

$$U^* = \xi \mathbf{k}_0^* + \zeta \mathbf{b}_2^* \qquad S_\lambda^* = \alpha_\lambda \xi \cdot \mathbf{k}_{t_\lambda}^* + \beta_\lambda \cdot \mathbf{d}_1^* + \omega_\lambda \cdot (\mathbf{d}_2^* + t_\lambda \cdot \mathbf{d}_3^*) + q_\lambda \cdot \mathbf{d}_4^*$$
$$V^* = \xi(\mathbf{r}_1^* + H \cdot \mathbf{r}_2^* + H' \cdot \mathbf{r}_3^*) + \nu \cdot \mathbf{h}_4^*$$

for all the leaves λ, where t_λ is the associated attribute of λ. The signature is thus $\sigma = (U^*, V^*, (S_\lambda^*)_\lambda)$.
This results in the vectors, with $\delta_{\mathsf{id}}, \nu, \xi, \zeta, (\omega_\lambda)_\lambda, (q_\lambda)_\lambda, \phi_0, \psi_1, \psi_2, \psi_3, (\phi_{t_\lambda})_\lambda, (\pi_{t_\lambda})_{t_\lambda} \xleftarrow{\$} \mathbb{Z}_q^*$

$$U^* = (\xi\delta_{\mathsf{id}}, \xi\phi_0 + \zeta, 0^2)_{\mathbb{B}^*}$$
$$S_\lambda^* = (\alpha_\lambda\xi\delta_{\mathsf{id}} + \beta_\lambda, (\alpha_\lambda\xi\pi_{t_\lambda} + \omega_\lambda)(1, t_\lambda), \alpha_\lambda\xi\phi_{t_\lambda} + q_\lambda, 0^6)_{\mathbb{D}^*}$$
$$V^* = (\xi\delta_{\mathsf{id}} \cdot (1, H, H'), \xi(\psi_1 + \psi_2 H + \psi_3 H') + \nu, 0^4)_{\mathbb{H}^*}$$

which follow the same distributions as, with $\delta, \nu, \zeta, (\omega_\lambda)_\lambda, (q_\lambda)_\lambda \xleftarrow{\$} \mathbb{Z}_q^*$, and $(\beta_\lambda)_\lambda$ a random 0-labeling of $\mathcal{T}^*$,

$$U^* = (\delta, \zeta, 0^2)_{\mathbb{B}^*} \qquad S^*_\lambda = (\alpha_\lambda \delta + \beta_\lambda, \omega_\lambda(1, t_\lambda), q_\lambda, 0^6)_{\mathbb{D}^*}$$
$$V^* = (\delta \cdot (1, H, H'), \nu, 0^4)_{\mathbb{H}^*}$$

Delegate-Policy($\mathsf{SK}_{\mathsf{id},\Gamma}, \bar{\mathsf{id}}, \mathcal{T}$). Let $\mathcal{T}' \in \mathsf{EPT}(\mathcal{T}, \Gamma)$ be an Evaluation Pruned Tree, scalars $\nu, \xi, \zeta, \psi'_3, (\omega_\lambda)_\lambda, (q_\lambda)_\lambda \overset{\$}{\leftarrow} \mathbb{Z}_q^*$, and $(\alpha_\lambda)_\lambda$ the 1-labeling of $\mathcal{T}^*$ specific to $\mathcal{T}'$ (see Proposition 7), where $\alpha_\lambda = 1$ if $\lambda \in \mathcal{L}_{\mathcal{T}'}$, else $\alpha_\lambda = 0$. This is possible as $\mathcal{T}(\Gamma) = 1$. Then, compute $(\beta_\lambda)_\lambda$ to be a random 0-labeling of the dual $\mathcal{T}^*$ associated to $\mathcal{T}$.
Eventually, set for $H = \mathcal{H}(\mathcal{T})$:

$$U^* = \xi \mathbf{k}_0^* + \zeta \mathbf{b}_2^* \qquad S^*_\lambda = \alpha_\lambda \xi \cdot \mathbf{k}^*_{t_\lambda} + \beta_\lambda \mathbf{d}_1^* + \omega_\lambda(\mathbf{d}_2^* + t_\lambda \cdot \mathbf{d}_3^*) + q_\lambda \cdot \mathbf{d}_4^*$$
$$\mathbf{r}'^*_3 = \xi \mathbf{r}_3^* + \psi'_3 \mathbf{h}_4^* \qquad V^* = \xi(\mathbf{r}_1^* + H \cdot \mathbf{r}_2^*) + \nu \cdot \mathbf{h}_4^*$$

for all the leaves λ, where t_λ is the associated attribute of λ. The delegated key is thus $\mathsf{SK}_{\bar{\mathsf{id}},\mathcal{T}} = (U^*, V^*, \mathbf{r}'^*_3, (S^*_\lambda)_\lambda)$.
This results in the vectors, with $\delta_{\mathsf{id}}, \nu, \xi, \zeta, (\omega_\lambda)_\lambda, (q_\lambda)_\lambda, \phi_0, \psi_1, \psi_2, (\phi_{t_\lambda})_\lambda, (\pi_{t_\lambda})_{t_\lambda} \overset{\$}{\leftarrow} \mathbb{Z}_q^*$

$$\begin{aligned}
U^* &= (\xi \delta_{\mathsf{id}}, \xi \phi_0 + \zeta, 0^2)_{\mathbb{B}^*}\\
S^*_\lambda &= (\alpha_\lambda \xi \delta_{\mathsf{id}} + \beta_\lambda, (\alpha_\lambda \xi \pi_{t_\lambda} + \omega_\lambda)(1, t_\lambda), \alpha_\lambda \xi \phi_{t_\lambda} + q_\lambda, 0^6)_{\mathbb{D}^*}\\
V^* &= (\xi \delta_{\mathsf{id}} \cdot (1, H, 0), \xi(\psi_1 + \psi_2 H) + \nu, 0^4)_{\mathbb{H}^*}\\
\mathbf{r}'^*_3 &= (0, 0, \xi \delta_{\mathsf{id}}, \xi \psi_3 + \psi'_3, 0^4)_{\mathbb{H}^*}
\end{aligned}$$

which follow the same distributions as, with $\delta_{\mathsf{id}}, \nu, \zeta, (\omega_\lambda)_\lambda, (q_\lambda)_\lambda, \psi'_3 \overset{\$}{\leftarrow} \mathbb{Z}_q^*$, and $(\beta_\lambda)_\lambda$ a random 0-labeling of $\mathcal{T}^*$

$$U_i^* = (\delta_{\mathsf{id}}, \zeta, 0^2)_{\mathbb{B}^*} \qquad S^*_\lambda = (\alpha_\lambda \delta_{\mathsf{id}} + \beta_\lambda, \omega_\lambda(1, t_\lambda), q_\lambda, 0^6)_{\mathbb{D}^*}$$
$$V^* = (\delta_{\mathsf{id}} \cdot (1, H, 0), \nu, 0^4)_{\mathbb{H}^*} \qquad \mathbf{r}'^*_3 = (\delta_{\mathsf{id}} \cdot (0, 0, 1), \psi'_3, 0^4)_{\mathbb{H}^*}$$

DelegateSig($\mathsf{SK}_{\mathsf{id},\mathcal{T}}, m$). Let $\mathcal{T}' \in \mathsf{EPT}(\mathcal{T}, \Gamma)$ be an Evaluation Pruned Tree, $\nu, \xi, \zeta, (\omega'_\lambda)_\lambda, (q'_\lambda)_\lambda \overset{\$}{\leftarrow} \mathbb{Z}_q^*$, $(\beta'_\lambda)_\lambda$ a random 0-labeling of $\mathcal{T}^*$. Set, for $H' = \mathcal{H}'(m)$:

$$U'^* = \xi U^* + \zeta \mathbf{b}_2^* \qquad S'^*_\lambda = \xi \cdot S^*_\lambda + \beta'_\lambda \mathbf{d}_1^* + \omega'_\lambda(\mathbf{d}_2^* + t_\lambda \cdot \mathbf{d}_3^*) + q'_\lambda \cdot \mathbf{d}_4^*$$
$$V'^* = \xi(V^* + H' \cdot \mathbf{r}'^*_3) + \nu \cdot \mathbf{h}_4^*$$

for all the leaves λ, where t_λ is the associated attribute of λ. The signature is thus $\sigma = (U'^*, V'^*, (S'^*_\lambda)_\lambda)$.
This results in the vectors, with $\delta_{\mathsf{id}}, \nu, \nu', \xi, \zeta, \zeta', (\omega_\lambda)_\lambda, (\omega'_\lambda)_\lambda, (q_\lambda)_\lambda, (q'_\lambda)_\lambda \overset{\$}{\leftarrow} \mathbb{Z}_q^*$, and $(\alpha_\lambda)_\lambda$ the 1-labeling of $\mathcal{T}^*$,

$$\begin{aligned}
U'^* &= (\xi \delta_{\mathsf{id}}, \xi \zeta + \zeta', 0^2)_{\mathbb{B}^*}\\
S'^*_\lambda &= (\xi(\alpha_\lambda \delta_{\mathsf{id}} + \beta_\lambda) + \beta'_\lambda, (\alpha_\lambda \xi \omega_\lambda + \omega'_\lambda)(1, t_\lambda), \alpha_\lambda \xi q_\lambda + q'_\lambda, 0^6)_{\mathbb{D}^*}\\
V'^* &= (\xi \delta_{\mathsf{id}} \cdot (1, H, H'), \xi \nu + \nu', 0^4)_{\mathbb{H}^*}
\end{aligned}$$

which follow the same distributions as, with $\delta_{\mathsf{id}}, \nu, \zeta, (\omega_\lambda)_\lambda, (q_\lambda)_\lambda \overset{\$}{\leftarrow} \mathbb{Z}_q^*$, $(\beta_\lambda)_\lambda$ a random 0-labeling of $\mathcal{T}^*$, and $H = \mathcal{H}(\mathcal{T})$

$$U'^* = (\delta_{\mathsf{id}}, \zeta, 0^2)_{\mathbb{B}^*} \qquad S'^*_\lambda = (\alpha_\lambda \delta_{\mathsf{id}} + \beta_\lambda, \omega_\lambda(1, t_\lambda), q_\lambda, 0^6)_{\mathbb{D}^*}$$
$$V'^* = (\delta_{\mathsf{id}} \cdot (1, H, H'), \nu, 0^4)_{\mathbb{H}^*}$$

$\mathsf{Verif}(\mathsf{PK}, m, \mathcal{T}, \sigma)$. Let $\kappa, \kappa_0, (\kappa_\lambda)_\lambda, s, s_0, \theta, \theta', (\theta_\lambda)_\lambda \xleftarrow{\$} \mathbb{Z}_q$. Let $(s_\lambda)_\lambda$ be a random s_0-labeling of $\mathcal{T}$, then set, for $\bar{H} = \mathcal{H}(\mathcal{T}), \bar{H}' = \mathcal{H}'(m)$:

$$u = (-s_0 - s, 0, \kappa_0, 0)_{\mathbb{B}} \qquad c_\lambda = (s_\lambda, \theta_\lambda(t_\lambda, -1), 0, \kappa_\lambda, 0^5)_{\mathbb{D}}$$
$$v = (s + \theta \bar{H} + \theta' \bar{H}', -\theta, -\theta', 0, \kappa, 0^3)_{\mathbb{H}}$$

If $e(\mathbf{b}_1, U^*) \neq 1_{\mathbb{G}_t} \wedge e(u, U^*) \cdot e(v, V^*) \cdot \prod e(c_\lambda, S^*_\lambda) = 1_{\mathbb{G}_t}$, accept and output 1, else reject and output 0.

One can note that, as usual with Dual Pairing Vectors Spaces, some basis vectors are kept hidden to real-life players, as they will only be used in the security proofs: $(\mathbf{b}_2, \mathbf{b}_4)$, $(\mathbf{b}^*_3, \mathbf{b}^*_4)$, $(\mathbf{d}_4, \mathbf{d}_6, \mathbf{d}_7, \mathbf{d}_8, \mathbf{d}_9, \mathbf{d}_{10})$, $(\mathbf{d}^*_5, \mathbf{d}^*_6, \mathbf{d}^*_7, \mathbf{d}^*_8, \mathbf{d}^*_9, \mathbf{d}^*_{10})$, $(\mathbf{h}_4, \mathbf{h}_6, \mathbf{h}_7, \mathbf{h}_8)$, and $(\mathbf{h}^*_5, \mathbf{h}^*_6, \mathbf{h}^*_7, \mathbf{h}^*_8)$.

Correctness. Let $(U^*, V^*, (S^*_\lambda)_\lambda)$ be a signature generated by Sig with a key $\mathsf{SK}_{\mathsf{id},\Gamma}$, or by $\mathsf{DelegateSig}$ with a key $\mathsf{SK}_{\mathsf{id},\mathcal{T}}$, for an access-tree $\mathcal{T}$ and attributes Γ so that $\mathcal{T}(\Gamma) = 1$. Let $(u, v, (c_\lambda)_\lambda)$ the verification vectors generated by Verif for the same access-tree. We note $\mathcal{T}' \in \mathsf{EPT}(\mathcal{T}, \Gamma)$ the Evaluation Pruned Tree used during signature.

We remind from Proposition 6 that $\sum_{\lambda \in \mathcal{L}} s_\lambda \alpha_\lambda = s_0$ and $\sum_{\lambda \in \mathcal{L}} s_\lambda \beta_\lambda = 0$, as we have labelings of $\mathcal{T}$ and $\mathcal{T}^*$. We have $\sum_{\lambda \in \mathcal{L}} s_\lambda(\alpha_\lambda \delta_{\mathsf{id}} + \beta_\lambda) = s_0(\delta_{\mathsf{id}} + 0) = s_0 \delta_{\mathsf{id}}$. The first check $e(\mathbf{b}_1, U^*) = g_t^{\delta_{\mathsf{id}}} \neq 1_{\mathbb{G}_t}$ is to make sure $\delta_{\mathsf{id}} \neq 0$, and thus that $\xi \neq 0$ during the signing process. For the second verification:

$$\prod e(c_\lambda, S^*_\lambda) = g_t^{\sum_{\lambda \in \mathcal{L}} s_\lambda(\alpha_\lambda \delta_{\mathsf{id}} + \beta_\lambda)} = g_t^{s_0 \delta_{\mathsf{id}}} \tag{1}$$
$$e(u, U^*) \cdot e(v, V^*) = g_t^{\delta_{\mathsf{id}} \cdot (-s_0 - s)} \cdot g_t^{\delta_{\mathsf{id}} s} = g_t^{-\delta_{\mathsf{id}} s_0} \tag{2}$$

This leads to an accept if the signature was properly generated, with the same t_λ in the S^*_λ's and c_λ's, such that the vectors $(1, t_\lambda)$ and $(t_\lambda, -1)$ are orthogonal in Eq. (1), and $(H, H') = (\bar{H}, \bar{H})$ so that $(1, H)$ and $(\bar{H}, -1)$, as well as $(1, H')$ and $(\bar{H}', -1)$ are orthogonal, to guarantee that for random θ and θ', $(1, H, H')$ and $(\theta \bar{H} + \theta' \bar{H}', -\theta, -\theta')$ are orthogonal in Eq. (2).

Issuing New Attributes to an Existing Key. We propose a way for the Central Authority, as well as any delegator, to compute new attributes for an existing signing key without having to recompute the full key.

The main insight of our technique is that all keys possess a random δ_{id} (which can be of the form $\alpha_{\mathsf{id}} \delta_{\mathsf{id}}$ after any number of delegation), specific to the current id considered, that binds every part of the key together. Thus, we use a Pseudo-Random Function on the entry id to generate these δ_{id}.

The key of the PRF used by each agent (the Central Authority, and any delegator) shall be unique and secret, as the knowledge of δ_{id} is enough to generate new attributes arbitrarily for any existing signing key.

3.2 Security Results

About the above ABS with delegation, one can claim the unforgeability and the perfect anonymity, as defined in Sect. 2.4.

Theorem 8 (Existential Unforgeability). *The ABS scheme with delegation described in Sect. 3.1 is existentially unforgeable under the collision-resistance of the hash functions $\mathcal{H}, \mathcal{H}'$ and the SXDH assumption.*

Theorem 9 (Perfect Anonymity). *The ABS scheme with delegation described in Sect. 3.1 is perfectly anonymous.*

4 Sketches of the Security Proofs

We provide here some sketches of the proofs. Full proofs are detailed in the full version.

4.1 Perfect Anonymity

Proof. Let us define an alternative signing algorithm AltSig, that uses the master secret key instead of an individual signing key. We will first show that this alternative signature algorithm produces signatures indistinguishable from the ones created by an ABS without delegation. Then, we show that the distribution of signatures generated by delegated keys, whether via delegation of attributes or delegation of policies, is the same as the distribution of signatures made by keys in an ABS without delegation. This will show that the distribution of all the possible signatures made with our scheme is the same.

Let us begin with AltSig:

$\mathsf{AltSig}(\mathsf{MK}, m, \mathcal{T})$. With random scalars $\delta', \zeta, \nu, (q_\lambda)_\lambda, (\gamma_\lambda)_\lambda \stackrel{\$}{\leftarrow} \mathbb{Z}_q$, and $(\beta'_\lambda)_\lambda$ a random δ'-labeling of $\mathcal{T}^*$, set, for $H = \mathcal{H}(\mathcal{T})$ and $H' = \mathcal{H}'(m)$:

$$U^* = (\delta', \zeta, 0^2)_{\mathbb{B}^*} \quad S^*_\lambda = (\beta'_\lambda, \gamma_\lambda(1, t_\lambda), q_\lambda, 0^6)_{\mathbb{D}^*} \quad V^* = (\delta' \cdot (1, H, H'), \nu, 0^4)_{\mathbb{H}^*}$$

We claim that this is the same distribution as a real signature generated by a signing key $\mathsf{SK}_{\mathsf{id},\Gamma}$ from the KeyGen algorithm (which is detailed in the full version), except for two elements that we now discuss.

First, the random $(\gamma_\lambda)_\lambda$ from the second component of S^*_λ follows the same random uniform distribution as $(\alpha_\lambda \xi \pi_\lambda + \omega_\lambda)_\lambda$.

Second, the random δ'-labeling $(\beta'_\lambda)_\lambda$ of $\mathcal{T}^*$ replaces $(\alpha_\lambda \delta' + \beta_\lambda)_\lambda$, where (α_λ) is the 1-labeling of $\mathcal{T}^*$ specific to the Evaluation Pruned Tree associated to Γ, and (β_λ) a random 0-labeling of $\mathcal{T}^*$. As already noted, from the linearity of the labelings on $\mathcal{T}^*$, the linear combination is a random $1 \cdot \delta' + 0$-labeling of $\mathcal{T}^*$, as $(\beta'_\lambda)_\lambda$ is. We stress that adding a random 0-labeling of $\mathcal{T}^*$, which only depends on the policy $\mathcal{T}$, completely hides the initial labeling that was specific to Γ, and thus to the verifier.

Finally, we prove that the distribution of signatures made using delegation is the same as the one from AltSig. This is shown in the full version, as we instantiate the first game for our EUF proof.

As an additional note for the incoming EUF proof, we note that, should it be necessary, AltSig would also be able to return the value $\mathbf{r}_3^* = \delta' \cdot \mathbf{h}_3^*$, which will be useful to simulate answer to ODelegatePolicy queries, and output $\mathbf{r}_3^*$.

4.2 Existential Unforgeability

Proof. The proof is done in two parts. First, we show that if the adversary is only allowed access to oracles OKeyGen and OSig, then the scheme is EUF. This is effectively considering an adversary without delegation. Then, we show that we can simulate all the other oracles (ODelegateAttributes, ODelegatePolicy, ODelegateSig) using only the OKeyGen and OSig oracles.

$\mathbf{G}_0$ Initialization of the EUF security game
For the (at most) K different id's and S different indices i's.

$$
\begin{array}{rl}
\mathbf{k}_{\mathsf{id},0}^* = & (\ \delta_{\mathsf{id}}\quad \phi_{\mathsf{id},0}\quad 0\quad 0\ )_{\mathbb{B}^*}\\
U_i^* = & (\ \delta_i\quad \zeta_i\quad 0\quad 0\ )_{\mathbb{B}^*}\\
u = & (\ -s_0 - s\quad 0\quad \kappa_0\quad 0\ )_{\mathbb{B}}\\
\hline
\mathbf{r}_{\mathsf{id},1}^* = & (\ \delta_{\mathsf{id}}\quad 0\quad 0\quad \psi_{\mathsf{id},1}\quad 0\quad 0\quad 0\quad 0\ )_{\mathbb{H}^*}\\
\mathbf{r}_{\mathsf{id},2}^* = & (\ 0\quad \delta_{\mathsf{id}}\quad 0\quad \psi_{\mathsf{id},2}\quad 0\quad 0\quad 0\quad 0\ )_{\mathbb{H}^*}\\
\mathbf{r}_{\mathsf{id},3}^* = & (\ 0\quad 0\quad \delta_{\mathsf{id}}\quad \psi_{\mathsf{id},3}\quad 0\quad 0\quad 0\quad 0\ )_{\mathbb{H}^*}\\
V_i^* = & (\ \delta_i\quad \delta_i H_i\quad \delta_i H_i'\quad \nu_i\quad 0\quad 0\quad 0\quad 0\ )_{\mathbb{H}^*}\\
v = & (\ s+\theta\bar{H}+\theta'\bar{H}'\quad -\theta\quad -\theta'\quad 0\quad \kappa\quad 0\quad 0\quad 0\ )_{\mathbb{H}}\\
\hline
\mathbf{k}_{\mathsf{id},t}^* = & (\ \delta_{\mathsf{id}}\quad \pi_{\mathsf{id},t}\quad \pi_{\mathsf{id},t}t\quad \phi_{\mathsf{id},t}\quad 0\quad 0\quad 0\quad 0\quad 0\quad 0\ )_{\mathbb{D}^*}\\
S_{i,\lambda}^* = & (\ \beta_{i,\lambda}'\quad \gamma_{i,\lambda}\quad \gamma_{i,\lambda}t_\lambda\quad q_{i,\lambda}\quad 0\quad 0\quad 0\quad 0\quad 0\quad 0\ )_{\mathbb{D}^*}\\
c_\lambda = & (\ s_\lambda\quad \theta_\lambda t_\lambda,\quad -\theta_\lambda\quad 0\quad \kappa_\lambda\quad 0\quad 0\quad 0\quad 0\quad 0\ )_{\mathbb{D}}
\end{array}
$$

$\mathbf{G}_1$ r_λ is a r_0-labeling, ω is random
SubSpace-Ind on $(\mathbb{B},\mathbb{B}^*)_{3,4}$, $(\mathbb{D},\mathbb{D}^*)_{5,6}$ and $(\mathbb{H},\mathbb{H}^*)_{4,5}$

$$
\begin{array}{rl}
u = & (\ -s_0 - s\quad 0\quad \kappa_0\quad -r_0\ )_{\mathbb{B}}\\
v = & (\ s+\theta\bar{H}+\theta'\bar{H}'\quad -\theta\quad -\theta'\quad 0\quad \kappa\quad \omega\quad 0\quad 0\ )_{\mathbb{H}}\\
c_\lambda = & (\ s_\lambda\quad \theta_\lambda t_\lambda\quad -\theta_\lambda\quad 0\quad \kappa_\lambda\quad r_\lambda\quad 0\quad 0\quad 0\quad 0\ )_{\mathbb{D}}
\end{array}
$$

$\mathbf{G}_2$ δ_{id}'' all random: Hybrid sub-sequence (see the full version)

$$
\begin{array}{rl}
\mathbf{k}_{\mathsf{id},0}^* = & (\ \delta_{\mathsf{id}}\quad \phi_{\mathsf{id},0}\quad 0\quad \delta_{\mathsf{id}}''\ )_{\mathbb{B}^*}\\
\mathbf{k}_{\mathsf{id},t}^* = & (\ \delta_{\mathsf{id}}\quad \pi_{\mathsf{id},t}\quad \pi_{\mathsf{id},t}t\quad \phi_{\mathsf{id},t}\quad 0\quad 0\quad 0\quad 0\quad 0\quad 0\ )_{\mathbb{D}^*}
\end{array}
$$

$\mathbf{G}_3$ r_0' random: Formal change of basis on $(\mathbb{B},\mathbb{B}^*)_4$

$$
u = (\ -s_0 - s\quad 0\quad \kappa_0\quad r_0'\ )_{\mathbb{B}}
$$

$\mathbf{G}_4$ ρ_i, τ_i all random: Hybrid sub-sequence (see the full version)

$$
\begin{array}{rl}
U_i^* = & (\ \delta_i\quad \zeta_i\quad 0\quad \rho_i\ )_{\mathbb{B}^*}\\
V_i^* = & (\ \delta_i\quad \delta_i H_i\quad \delta_i H_i'\quad \nu_i\quad 0\quad \tau_i\quad 0\quad 0\ )_{\mathbb{H}}
\end{array}
$$

$\mathbf{G}_5$ s' random : Formal change of basis on $(\mathbb{B},\mathbb{B}^*)_{4,1}$

$$
u = (\ s'\quad 0\quad \kappa_0\quad r_0'\ )_{\mathbb{B}}
$$

Fig. 5. Sequence of Games for Unforgeability. Grey rectangles indicate the values changed in each game

Proof Without Delegation. For this proof, thanks to the (perfect) indistinguishability of the Sig and AltSig outputs from the Anonymity of the scheme, we will first replace the simulation of the signing oracle by the AltSig procedure.

We will use the index id for all the KeyGen queries/answers, and we assume the number of KeyGen queries bounded by K. We use the index i for all the Sig queries/answers, and we assume the number of Sig queries bounded by S. We will also use t to denote the attributes, and we assume the number of attributes involved in a security game bounded by T.

The verification done by the challenger (on the candidate forgery output by the adversary) uses a pair $(m, \mathcal{T})$ that is different from any pair that appeared in the signing queries, hence with $\bar{H} = \mathcal{H}(\mathcal{T})$ and $\bar{H}' = \mathcal{H}'(m)$, but $(\bar{H}, \bar{H}') \neq (H_i, H'_i)$ for all i, under the collision-resistance of $\mathcal{H}$ and $\mathcal{H}'$, as for any pair $(m_i, \mathcal{T}_i)$ at least $m \neq m_i$ or $\mathcal{T} \neq \mathcal{T}_i$. Then, the proof follows the sequence of games presented on Fig. 5, to show, as proven in the full version, that

$$\begin{aligned}\mathsf{Adv}_0 - \mathsf{Adv}_5 \leq (6KT + 2S + 2) \times \mathsf{Adv}^{\mathsf{ddh}}_{\mathbb{G}_1}(t) + (4T^2K + 6K + 4S) \times \mathsf{Adv}^{\mathsf{ddh}}_{\mathbb{G}_2}(t) \\ + S/q + \mathsf{Adv}^{\mathsf{coll}}_{\mathcal{H}}(t) + \mathsf{Adv}^{\mathsf{coll}}_{\mathcal{H}'}(t).\end{aligned}$$

We now deal with the final game $\mathbf{G}_5$ and consider a signature $(U^*, V^*, (S^*_\lambda)_\lambda)$ generated by the adversary. If $e(\mathbf{b}_1, U^*) = 1_{\mathbb{G}_t}$, then the verification fails, by definition of Verif. Hence, the first component of U^* must be non-zero, in the basis $\mathbb{B}^*$. We now consider the value $e(u, U^*) \cdot e(v, V^*) \cdot \prod e(c_\lambda, S^*_\lambda)$. Since the coefficient s' of $\mathbf{b}_1$ in u is uniform and independent from all other values, then $e(u, U^*)$ is uniform and independent from all other pairings in the Verif algorithm. This implies $e(u, U^*) \cdot e(v, V^*) \cdot \prod e(c_\lambda, S^*_\lambda) \neq 1_{\mathbb{G}_t}$ except with probability $1/q$: $\mathsf{Adv}_5 \leq 1/q$. As a consequence,

$$\begin{aligned}\mathsf{Adv}^{\mathsf{euf}} = \mathsf{Adv}_0 \leq (6KT + 2S + 2) \times \mathsf{Adv}^{\mathsf{ddh}}_{\mathbb{G}_1}(t) + (4T^2K + 6K + 4S) \times \mathsf{Adv}^{\mathsf{ddh}}_{\mathbb{G}_2}(t) \\ + (S + 1)/q + \mathsf{Adv}^{\mathsf{coll}}_{\mathcal{H}}(t) + \mathsf{Adv}^{\mathsf{coll}}_{\mathcal{H}'}(t).\end{aligned}$$

Proof with Delegation. We reduce the EUF proof for our ABS with delegation to the proof without delegation. To do this, we simulate the oracles for delegated keys: keys from ODelegateAttributes can be simulated with OKeyGen, and signatures from ODelegateSig and policy keys from ODelegatePolicy can be simulated with AltSig.

Once we have shown these simulations, we are in a similar game as $\mathbf{G}_0$ for the Existential Unforgeability proof in the case without delegation. The sequence of games can continue the same way, with thus the same security bounds.

5 ABS with Traceability

In usual ABS definitions, and as shown in our construction, one usually expects perfect anonymity. But one could also require traceability of the signer, as in group signatures [1], with an opener able to trace back the signer, and even prove the correct opening.

We propose such a construction, where tracers can be held accountable by a designated Tracing Authority. The traceability we propose does not ensure non-frameability from the Central Authority [7], but it does ensure the traditional traceability property, which guarantees that malicious signers cannot deceive the designated tracer.

The way we design traceability make it compatible with our construction with delegation, from Sect. 3. This would result in a scheme where delegation of any signing key is possible, and where a Tracing Authority can trace any signature. However, we underline that a scheme that combines both our delegation and tracing can only trace back to the original delegator of the signing key that was used to produce the signature that is being tracked.

A more fine-grained solution for tracing delegated keys and path of delegations can be found in [9], but it comes at the cost of a scheme whose signatures' sizes are linear in both the number of attributes used and the length of the delegation path.

5.1 Traceable ABS

This extends the initial definition of an ABS, with the algorithms Setup (with additional tracing key TK and verification key VK), KeyGen, Sig, and Verif, we also consider the Trace and Judge algorithms:

Trace(TK, $m, \mathcal{T}, \sigma$). Given the tracing key TK and a valid signature σ on $(m, \mathcal{T})$, the algorithm outputs the identity id of the signer together with a proof π, both set to $\perp$ in case of failure.

Judge(VK, m, σ, id, π). Given the verification key VK, a signature σ for a message m, and a proof π that user id generated $(m, \mathcal{T}, \sigma)$, the algorithm outputs 1 if π is valid or 0 else.

Correctness, unforgeability and anonymity are the same as for a regular ABS (see definitions from [18]), except that anonymity cannot be perfect, but computational. We also ask for any valid signature to be traced back to its signer, with a convincing proof π, either for a judge or anybody when VK is public.

Definition 10 (Traceability). *Traceability for ABS is defined by the following game between the adversary and a challenger:*

Initialize: *The challenger runs the* Setup *algorithm of ABS and gives the public parameters* PK *to the adversary;*

Oracles: *The following oracles can be called in any order and any number of times.*

- OKeyGen(id, Γ): *to model* KeyGen*-queries for any identity* id *and any set of attributes Γ of its choice, and the adversary gets back the key* $\mathsf{SK}_{\mathsf{id},\Gamma}$*;*
- OSig(id, $m, \mathcal{T}$): *to model* Sig*-queries for any identity* id *and under any policy $\mathcal{T}$ of its choice for a message m, and the adversary gets the signature σ;*

Finalize(b'): *The adversary outputs a signature $(m', \mathcal{T}', \sigma')$. One asks* (id, π) = Trace(TK, σ'). *If one of the following is true (non-legitimate attack)*

- *$(m', \mathcal{T}')$ has been queried to the* OSig*-oracle;*
- id *has been queried to the* OKeyGen*-oracle with Γ such that $\mathcal{T}'(\Gamma) = 1$ and* $\mathsf{Judge}(\mathsf{VK}, m', \sigma', \mathsf{id}, \pi) = 1$*;*

then output 0, otherwise output $\mathsf{Verif}(\mathsf{PK}, m', \mathcal{T}', \sigma')$.

The success $\mathsf{Adv}^{\mathsf{trace}}(\mathcal{A})$ *of an adversary $\mathcal{A}$ against traceability is the probability to have 1 as output in this game.*

More precisely, we consider the adversary wins the traceability game if it manages to mislead the tracing procedure: by making it either fail or output an honest user (whose key has not been asked to the key-oracle), or by making the result of the tracing impossible to prove.

We will add the restriction that the adversary can only corrupt disjoint sets of identities between any key-query and any other signing-query. We will call it the *distinct-user setting.*

One-Time Linearly-Homomorphic Signature. We will rely on a (One-Time) Linearly-Homomorphic Signature (OT-LH) [15]. An OT-LH scheme is a signature scheme where one can produce a valid signature out of any linear combination of valid signatures, provided he knows those other signatures. In other words, one can produce a valid signature σ of $\sum_i \alpha_i m_i$, provided he knows valid signatures σ_i of the messages m_i.

Another OT-LH scheme is proposed in [12] which has been proven in the generic group model, with an extractor that provides the coefficients in the linear combination of the initial messages for the new signed message. From this paper, we will also use the following theorem, that states the intractability of the Linear-Square problem:

Theorem 11 (Linear-Square Problem). *Given n Square Diffie-Hellman tuples $(g_i, a_i = g_i^{w_i}, b_i = a_i^{w_i})$, together with w_i, for random $g_i \stackrel{\$}{\leftarrow} \mathbb{G}^*$ and $w_i \stackrel{\$}{\leftarrow} \mathbb{Z}_q^*$, outputting $(\alpha_i)_{i=1,\ldots,n}$ such that $(G = \prod g_i^{\alpha_i}, A = \prod a_i^{\alpha_i}, B = \prod b_i^{\alpha_i})$ is a valid Square Diffie-Hellman, with at least two non-zero coefficients α_i, is computationally hard under the Discrete Logarithm assumption.*

5.2 Construction of Traceable ABS

We consider any OT-LH scheme $(\mathsf{KeyGen}', \mathsf{Sig}', \mathsf{DerivSign}', \mathsf{Verif}')$ in $\mathbb{G}_2^n$. We will also use a non-interactive zero-knowledge proof of knowledge (NIZKPoK-SqDH, VERIF-SqDH) of the witness w for a Square Diffie-Hellman tuple $(h_t, h_t^w, h_t^{w^2})$ in $\mathbb{G}_t$ and a non-interactive zero-knowledge proof (NIZKPoK-DH, VERIF-DH) of Diffie-Hellman tuple $(g_t, g_t^w, g_t^\delta, g_t^{\delta w})$ in $\mathbb{G}_t$. For both proofs, one can simply use Schnorr-like proofs [24] with the Fiat-Shamir paradigm [8]. They are well-known to provide simulation-soundness [22]. We now detail our construction, with access-trees for policies, where we just complete the signing key $\mathbf{k}_0^*$ with a square Diffie-Hellman tuple where one can identify the signer, if and only if the scalar w_{id} is known. The public value $g_t^{w_{\mathsf{id}}}$ associated to user id will then be enough to verify the tracing, without revealing w_{id}:

$\mathsf{Setup}(1^\kappa)$. The algorithm chooses three random dual orthogonal bases, in a pairing-friendly setting $\mathcal{PG} = (\mathbb{G}_1, \mathbb{G}_2, \mathbb{G}_t, e, G_1, G_2, q)$:

$$\mathbb{B} = (\mathbf{b}_1, \ldots, \mathbf{b}_6) \qquad \mathbb{D} = (\mathbf{d}_1, \ldots, \mathbf{d}_{10}) \qquad \mathbb{H} = (\mathbf{h}_1, \ldots, \mathbf{h}_8)$$
$$\mathbb{B}^* = (\mathbf{b}_1^*, \ldots, \mathbf{b}_6^*) \qquad \mathbb{D}^* = (\mathbf{d}_1^*, \ldots, \mathbf{d}_{10}^*) \qquad \mathbb{H}^* = (\mathbf{h}_1^*, \ldots, \mathbf{h}_8^*).$$

It also chooses two full-domain hash function $\mathcal{H}$ and $\mathcal{H}'$ onto $\mathbb{Z}_q$. The algorithm calls the OT-LH signature algorithm $\mathsf{KeyGen}'(1^\kappa, 6)$, for vectors in $\mathbb{G}_2^6$, and gets back the keys sk and vk. It also gets $\Sigma_2 = \mathsf{Sig}'(\mathsf{sk}, \mathbf{b}_2^*)$, and sets the public parameters as $\mathsf{PK} = \{\mathcal{PG}, \mathcal{H}, (\mathbf{b}_1, \mathbf{b}_3, \mathbf{b}_5, \mathbf{b}_6), (\mathbf{b}_2^*, \Sigma_2), (\mathbf{d}_1, \mathbf{d}_2, \mathbf{d}_3, \mathbf{d}_5), (\mathbf{d}_1^*, \mathbf{d}_2^*, \mathbf{d}_3^*, \mathbf{d}_4^*), (\mathbf{h}_1, \mathbf{h}_2, \mathbf{h}_3, \mathbf{h}_5), (\mathbf{h}_4^*), \mathsf{vk}\}$, and the master secret key is set as $\mathsf{MK} = \{(\mathbf{b}_1^*, \mathbf{b}_5^*, \mathbf{b}_6^*), (\mathbf{h}_1^*, \mathbf{h}_2^*, \mathbf{h}_3^*), \mathsf{sk}\}$. Finally, the tracing key TK and the verification key VK are initialized as empty sets.

$\mathsf{KeyGen}(\mathsf{MK}, \mathsf{id}, \Gamma)$. Random scalars $\delta_{\mathsf{id}}, w_{\mathsf{id}} \stackrel{\$}{\leftarrow} \mathbb{Z}_q^*$ are associated to id, with

$$\mathbf{k}_0^* = \delta_{\mathsf{id}} \cdot \mathbf{b}_1^* + \phi_0 \cdot \mathbf{b}_2^* + \delta_{\mathsf{id}} \cdot w_{\mathsf{id}} \cdot \mathbf{b}_5^* + \delta_{\mathsf{id}} \cdot w_{\mathsf{id}}^2 \cdot \mathbf{b}_6^*$$
$$\mathbf{k}_t^* = \delta_{\mathsf{id}} \cdot \mathbf{d}_1^* + \pi_t \cdot (\mathbf{d}_2^* + t \cdot \mathbf{d}_3^*) + \phi_t \cdot \mathbf{d}_4^*$$
$$\mathbf{r}_1^* = \delta_{\mathsf{id}} \cdot \mathbf{h}_1^* + \psi_1 \cdot \mathbf{h}_4^* \quad \mathbf{r}_2^* = \delta_{\mathsf{id}} \cdot \mathbf{h}_2^* + \psi_2 \cdot \mathbf{h}_4^* \quad \mathbf{r}_3^* = \delta_{\mathsf{id}} \cdot \mathbf{h}_3^* + \psi_3 \cdot \mathbf{h}_4^*$$

for all attributes $t \in \Gamma$, with $\phi_0, (\phi_t)_t, (\pi_t)_t \stackrel{\$}{\leftarrow} \mathbb{Z}_q^*$ for each t. The algorithm calls for $\Sigma_{\mathsf{id}} = \mathsf{Sig}'(\mathsf{sk}, \mathbf{k}_0^*)$. The signing key $\mathsf{SK}_{\mathsf{id},\Gamma}$ is set as $(w_{\mathsf{id}}, \mathbf{k}_0^*, \Sigma_{\mathsf{id}}, (\mathbf{k}_t^*)_{t\in\Gamma}, \mathbf{r}_1^*, \mathbf{r}_2^*, \mathbf{r}_3^*)$, for id. It can be computed later for new attributes, but only by using the same δ_{id}. The pair $(\mathsf{id}, w_{\mathsf{id}})$ is appended to TK, and $(\mathsf{id}, g_t^{w_{\mathsf{id}}})$ is appended to VK.

$\mathsf{Sig}(\mathsf{SK}_{\mathsf{id},\Gamma}, m, \mathcal{T})$. Let $\mathcal{T}' \in \mathsf{EPT}(\mathcal{T}, \Gamma)$ be an Evaluation Pruned Tree, $\nu, \xi, \zeta \stackrel{\$}{\leftarrow} \mathbb{Z}_q^*$. Compute the following 1-labeling of the dual tree $\mathcal{T}^*$: for each leaf λ, choose $\alpha_\lambda = 1$ if $\lambda \in \mathcal{L}_{\mathcal{T}'}$, else $\alpha_\lambda = 0$. Then, choose a random 0-labeling (β_λ) of $\mathcal{T}^*$, and $(q_\lambda)_\lambda, (\omega_\lambda)_\lambda$ random scalars, and set, for $H = \mathcal{H}(\mathcal{T}), H' = \mathcal{H}'(m)$:

$$U^* = \xi \mathbf{k}_0^* + \zeta \mathbf{b}_2^* \qquad S_\lambda^* = \alpha_\lambda \xi \cdot \mathbf{k}_{t_\lambda}^* + \beta_\lambda \mathbf{d}_1^* + \omega_\lambda (\mathbf{d}_2^* + t_\lambda \cdot \mathbf{d}_3^*) + q_\lambda \cdot \mathbf{d}_4^*$$
$$V^* = \xi(\mathbf{r}_1^* + H \cdot \mathbf{r}_2^* + H' \cdot \mathbf{r}_3^*) + \nu \cdot \mathbf{h}_4^*$$

for all the leaves λ, where t_λ is the associated attribute of λ. From the linearly-homomorphic property, one can compute a signature on $U^* \in \mathbb{G}_2^6$:

$$\Sigma = \mathsf{DerivSign}'(\mathsf{vk}, ((\xi, \mathbf{k}_0^*, \Sigma_{\mathsf{id}}), (\zeta, \mathbf{b}_2^*, \Sigma_2))$$

Eventually, using w_{id}, one can generate the proof of Square Diffie-Hellman tuple $\Pi = \mathsf{NIZKPoK\text{-}SqDH}(w_{\mathsf{id}}, (e(\mathbf{b}_1, U^*), e(\mathbf{b}_5, U^*), e(\mathbf{b}_6, U^*)))$, as this tuple is equal to $(h_t, h_t^{w_{\mathsf{id}}}, h_t^{w_{\mathsf{id}}^2})$, for some $h_t \in \mathbb{G}_t$. The final signature consists of the tuple $\sigma = (U^*, V^*, (S_\lambda^*)_\lambda), \Sigma, \Pi)$.

$\mathsf{Verif}(\mathsf{PK}, m, \mathcal{T}, \sigma)$. Let $\kappa, \kappa_0, (\kappa_\lambda)_\lambda, s, s_0, \theta, \theta'(\theta_\lambda)_\lambda \stackrel{\$}{\leftarrow} \mathbb{Z}_q$. Let $(s_\lambda)_\lambda$ be a random s_0-labeling of $\mathcal{T}$, then set, for $\bar{H} = \mathcal{H}(\mathcal{T}), \bar{H}' = \mathcal{H}'(\mathcal{T})$:

$$u = -(s_0 + s) \cdot \mathbf{b}_1 + \kappa_0 \cdot \mathbf{b}_3 \qquad c_\lambda = s_\lambda \cdot \mathbf{d}_1 + \theta_\lambda t_\lambda \cdot \mathbf{d}_2 - \theta_\lambda \cdot \mathbf{d}_3 + \kappa_\lambda \cdot \mathbf{d}_5$$
$$v = (s + \theta \bar{H} + \theta' \bar{H}') \cdot \mathbf{h}_1 - \theta \cdot \mathbf{h}_2 - \theta' \cdot \mathbf{h}_3 + \kappa \cdot \mathbf{h}_5$$

Accept if $e(\mathbf{b}_1, U^*) \neq 1_{\mathbb{G}_t}$ and $e(u, U^*) \cdot e(v, V^*) \cdot \prod e(c_\lambda, S^*_\lambda) = 1_{\mathbb{G}_t}$, but also if $\mathsf{Verif}'(\mathsf{vk}, U^*, \Sigma) = 1$ and $\mathsf{VERIF\text{-}SqDH}((e(\mathbf{b}_1, U^*), e(\mathbf{b}_5, U^*), e(\mathbf{b}_6, U^*)), \Pi) = 1$, otherwise reject.

$\mathsf{Trace}(\mathsf{TK}, \sigma')$. Compute $B_1 = e(\mathbf{b}_1, U^*)$ and $B_2 = e(\mathbf{b}_5, U^*)$. Then, for $(\mathsf{id}, w_{\mathsf{id}}) \in \mathsf{TK}$, check until $B_1^{w_{\mathsf{id}}} = B_2$. When the equality holds then generate the proof $\pi = \mathsf{NIZKPoK\text{-}DH}(g_t, g_t^{w_{\mathsf{id}}}, e(\mathbf{b}_1, U^*), e(\mathbf{b}_5, U^*))$ and output (id, π). Otherwise output $\perp$.

$\mathsf{Judge}(\mathsf{VK}, m, \sigma', \mathsf{id}, \pi)$. Extract $g_t^{w_{\mathsf{id}}}$ corresponding to id from VK and output $\mathsf{VERIF\text{-}DH}((g_t, g_t^{w_{\mathsf{id}}}, e(\mathbf{b}_1, U^*), e(\mathbf{b}_5, U^*)), \pi)$.

As VK can be a public list, anybody can run the Judge algorithm. This means that anyone can know the current number of users in the system.

5.3 Correctness

This construction is a slight variation of the previous ABS scheme. Thus the correctness directly ensues from the correctness of the scheme formerly presented in Sect. 3, the correctness and linear-homomorphic property of the $\mathsf{OT\text{-}LH}$ scheme, and the completeness of both the zero-knowledge proof.

5.4 Security Results

Since the verification process is even more restrictive than in the previous scheme, one can claim the same unforgeability result:

Theorem 12 (Existential Unforgeability). *The* ABS *scheme described in Sect. 5.2 is existentially unforgeable under the collision-resistance of the hash functions $\mathcal{H}, \mathcal{H}'$ and the* SXDH *assumption.*

Because of the additional elements in the signature (which are useful for tracing), the signature is no longer perfectly anonymous, but still computationally anonymous:

Theorem 13 (Computational Anonymity). *The* ABS *scheme described in Sect. 5.2 is computationally anonymous, when w_0 and w_1, in* SK_0 *and* SK_1*, are unknown, under the Decisional Square Diffie-Hellman assumption in $\mathbb{G}_2$, and the perfect zero-knowledge of the* NIZKPoK-SqDH *in the ROM.*

Proof. The additional elements are the Square Diffie-Hellman tuple in the 1-st, 5-th, and 6-th components of $U^* = (\delta', \phi'_0, 0, 0, \delta' \cdot w_{\mathsf{id}}, \delta' \cdot w_{\mathsf{id}}^2)_{\mathbb{B}^*}$, the signature Σ, and the proof Π.

The Square Diffie-Hellman tuple in U^* can be generated from a Square Diffie-Hellman tuple $(\delta' G_2, w \cdot \delta' G_2, w^2 \cdot \delta' G_2) \in \mathbb{G}_2^3$. Under the Decisional Square Diffie-Hellman assumption in $\mathbb{G}_2$, this tuple is indistinguishable from a random tuple in $\mathbb{G}_2^3$. This makes U^* generated from w_0 or w_1 indistinguishable when those scalars are unknown. Since Σ is a signature of U^* that is itself indistinguishable for w_0 and w_1, Σ is also indistinguishable for w_0 and w_1. Eventually, Π being a zero-knowledge proof on the above tuple, it can be simulated without knowing the witness. It thus does not leak any additional information.

Finally, we state the traceability result. The proof is postponed to the full version.

Theorem 14 (Traceability). *The* ABS *scheme described in Sect. 5.2 is traceable in the ROM according to the Definition 10, in the distinct-user setting, under the security of the* OT-LH *signature scheme, the intractability of the Linear-Square problem, the simulation-extractability of the* NIZKPoK-SqDH*, and the soundness of the* NIZKPoK-DH.

References

1. Chaum, D., van Heyst, E.: Group signatures. In: Davies, D.W. (ed.) EUROCRYPT 1991. LNCS, vol. 547, pp. 257–265. Springer, Heidelberg (1991). https://doi.org/10.1007/3-540-46416-6_22
2. Damgård, I., Ganesh, C., Khoshakhlagh, H., Orlandi, C., Siniscalchi, L.: Balancing privacy and accountability in blockchain identity management. In: Paterson, K.G. (ed.) CT-RSA 2021. LNCS, vol. 12704, pp. 552–576. Springer, Cham (2021). https://doi.org/10.1007/978-3-030-75539-3_23
3. Datta, P., Okamoto, T., Takashima, K.: Efficient attribute-based signatures for unbounded arithmetic branching programs. In: Lin, D., Sako, K. (eds.) PKC 2019. LNCS, vol. 11442, pp. 127–158. Springer, Cham (2019). https://doi.org/10.1007/978-3-030-17253-4_5
4. Delerablée, C., Gouriou, L., Pointcheval, D.: Key-policy ABE with switchable attributes. In: Galdi, C., Jarecki, S. (eds.) SCN 2022. LNCS, vol. 13409, pp. 147–171. Springer, Cham (2022). https://doi.org/10.1007/978-3-031-14791-3_7, https://eprint.iacr.org/2021/867
5. Ding, S., Zhao, Y., Liu, Y.: Efficient traceable attribute-based signature. In: 2014 IEEE 13th International Conference on Trust, Security and Privacy in Computing and Communications, pp. 582–589 (2014). https://doi.org/10.1109/TrustCom.2014.74
6. Drăgan, C.-C., Gardham, D., Manulis, M.: Hierarchical attribute-based signatures. In: Camenisch, J., Papadimitratos, P. (eds.) CANS 2018. LNCS, vol. 11124, pp. 213–234. Springer, Cham (2018). https://doi.org/10.1007/978-3-030-00434-7_11
7. El Kaafarani, A., Ghadafi, E., Khader, D.: Decentralized traceable attribute-based signatures. In: Benaloh, J. (ed.) CT-RSA 2014. LNCS, vol. 8366, pp. 327–348. Springer, Cham (2014). https://doi.org/10.1007/978-3-319-04852-9_17
8. Fiat, A., Shamir, A.: How to prove yourself: practical solutions to identification and signature problems. In: Odlyzko, A.M. (ed.) CRYPTO 1986. LNCS, vol. 263, pp. 186–194. Springer, Heidelberg (1987). https://doi.org/10.1007/3-540-47721-7_12
9. Gardham, D., Manulis, M.: Hierarchical attribute-based signatures: short keys and optimal signature length. In: Deng, R.H., Gauthier-Umaña, V., Ochoa, M., Yung, M. (eds.) ACNS 2019. LNCS, vol. 11464, pp. 89–109. Springer, Cham (2019). https://doi.org/10.1007/978-3-030-21568-2_5
10. Ghadafi, E.: Stronger security notions for decentralized traceable attribute-based signatures and more efficient constructions. In: Nyberg, K. (ed.) CT-RSA 2015. LNCS, vol. 9048, pp. 391–409. Springer, Cham (2015). https://doi.org/10.1007/978-3-319-16715-2_21

11. Goyal, V., Pandey, O., Sahai, A., Waters, B.: Attribute-based encryption for fine-grained access control of encrypted data. In: Juels, A., Wright, R.N., De Capitani di Vimercati, S. (eds.) ACM CCS 2006, pp. 89–98. ACM Press (2006). https://doi.org/10.1145/1180405.1180418. Available as Cryptology ePrint Archive Report 2006/309
12. Hébant, C., Phan, D.H., Pointcheval, D.: Linearly-homomorphic signatures and scalable mix-nets. In: Kiayias, A., Kohlweiss, M., Wallden, P., Zikas, V. (eds.) PKC 2020, Part II. LNCS, vol. 12111, pp. 597–627. Springer, Cham (2020). https://doi.org/10.1007/978-3-030-45388-6_21
13. Lewko, A., Okamoto, T., Sahai, A., Takashima, K., Waters, B.: Fully secure functional encryption: attribute-based encryption and (hierarchical) inner product encryption. In: Gilbert, H. (ed.) EUROCRYPT 2010. LNCS, vol. 6110, pp. 62–91. Springer, Heidelberg (2010). https://doi.org/10.1007/978-3-642-13190-5_4
14. Lewko, A., Waters, B.: New techniques for dual system encryption and fully secure HIBE with short ciphertexts. In: Micciancio, D. (ed.) TCC 2010. LNCS, vol. 5978, pp. 455–479. Springer, Heidelberg (2010). https://doi.org/10.1007/978-3-642-11799-2_27
15. Libert, B., Peters, T., Joye, M., Yung, M.: Linearly homomorphic structure-preserving signatures and their applications. In: Canetti, R., Garay, J.A. (eds.) CRYPTO 2013, Part II. LNCS, vol. 8043, pp. 289–307. Springer, Heidelberg (2013). https://doi.org/10.1007/978-3-642-40084-1_17
16. Liu, W., Mu, Y., Yang, G.: Attribute-based signing right delegation. In: Au, M.H., Carminati, B., Kuo, C.-C.J. (eds.) NSS 2014. LNCS, vol. 8792, pp. 323–334. Springer, Cham (2014). https://doi.org/10.1007/978-3-319-11698-3_25
17. Maji, H.K., Prabhakaran, M., Rosulek, M.: Attribute-based signatures. In: Kiayias, A. (ed.) CT-RSA 2011. LNCS, vol. 6558, pp. 376–392. Springer, Heidelberg (2011). https://doi.org/10.1007/978-3-642-19074-2_24
18. Okamoto, T., Takashima, K.: Efficient attribute-based signatures for non-monotone predicates in the standard model. In: Catalano, D., Fazio, N., Gennaro, R., Nicolosi, A. (eds.) PKC 2011. LNCS, vol. 6571, pp. 35–52. Springer, Heidelberg (2011). https://doi.org/10.1007/978-3-642-19379-8_3
19. Okamoto, T., Takashima, K.: Fully secure unbounded inner-product and attribute-based encryption. In: Wang, X., Sako, K. (eds.) ASIACRYPT 2012. LNCS, vol. 7658, pp. 349–366. Springer, Heidelberg (2012). https://doi.org/10.1007/978-3-642-34961-4_22
20. Okamoto, T., Takashima, K.: Decentralized attribute-based signatures. In: Kurosawa, K., Hanaoka, G. (eds.) PKC 2013. LNCS, vol. 7778, pp. 125–142. Springer, Heidelberg (2013). https://doi.org/10.1007/978-3-642-36362-7_9
21. Rivest, R.L., Shamir, A., Tauman, Y.: How to leak a secret. In: Boyd, C. (ed.) ASIACRYPT 2001. LNCS, vol. 2248, pp. 552–565. Springer, Heidelberg (2001). https://doi.org/10.1007/3-540-45682-1_32
22. Sahai, A.: Non-malleable non-interactive zero knowledge and adaptive chosen-ciphertext security. In: 40th FOCS, pp. 543–553. IEEE Computer Society Press (1999). https://doi.org/10.1109/SFFCS.1999.814628
23. Sakai, Y., Katsumata, S., Attrapadung, N., Hanaoka, G.: Attribute-based signatures for unbounded languages from standard assumptions. In: Peyrin, T., Galbraith, S. (eds.) ASIACRYPT 2018. LNCS, vol. 11273, pp. 493–522. Springer, Cham (2018). https://doi.org/10.1007/978-3-030-03329-3_17

24. Schnorr, C.P.: Factoring integers and computing discrete logarithms via diophantine approximation. In: Davies, D.W. (ed.) EUROCRYPT 1991. LNCS, vol. 547, pp. 281–293. Springer, Heidelberg (1991). https://doi.org/10.1007/3-540-46416-6_24
25. Waters, B.: Dual system encryption: realizing fully secure IBE and HIBE under simple assumptions. In: Halevi, S. (ed.) CRYPTO 2009. LNCS, vol. 5677, pp. 619–636. Springer, Heidelberg (2009). https://doi.org/10.1007/978-3-642-03356-8_36

Lattice-Based Threshold, Accountable, and Private Signature

Yingfei Yan[1], Yongjun Zhao[2], Wen Gao[3](✉), and Baocang Wang[1]

[1] State Key Laboratory of Integrated Service Networks, Xidian University, Xi'an, China
yanxi@stu.xidian.edu.cn, bcwang@xidian.edu.cn
[2] Shanghai, China
yongjunzhao@ieee.org
[3] School of Cyberspace Security, Xi'an University of Posts and Telecommunications, Xi'an, China
gaowen@xupt.edu.cn

Abstract. Recently, Boneh and Komlo (CRYPTO 2022) initiated the study of threshold, accountable, and private signature (TAPS) schemes. Classical threshold signature schemes are either fully private or fully accountable. At a high level, a fully private threshold signature reveals no information about the signing parties, while the signers of a fully accountable threshold signature can be easily traced because their identities are revealed directly in the signature. TAPS opens up a brand new opportunity to enjoy the two seemingly contradicting features at the same time and therefore has great potential to be applicable in emerging blockchain applications. Unfortunately, the only TAPS to date are based on classical cryptographic assumptions that do not hold against quantum computers.

In this paper, we propose the first TAPS from lattice-based assumptions, which remain hard against quantum algorithms. Our main building blocks are a new lattice-based t-out-of-N proof of knowledge that employs a recent framework by Lyubashevsky et al. (CRYPTO 2022) and a lattice-based accountable threshold signature, which may be of independent interest. Using these building blocks, we provide a compact construction of lattice-based TAPS with asymptotically optimal signature size. Instantiating the scheme with our suggested parameters, the signature size is 42.34 KB for $N = 32$.

Keywords: lattice · threshold signature · accountability · privacy · proof of knowledge

1 Introduction

A t-out-of-N threshold signature scheme [18] divides the ability to generate signatures to N parties to better tolerate failure or key compromise. In threshold signature schemes, a valid signature can be generated only when at least t parties holding the partial signing keys agree to participate in a signing protocol.

Y. Zhao—IEEE Member.

E. Oswald (Ed.): CT-RSA 2024, LNCS 14643, pp. 249–274, 2024.
https://doi.org/10.1007/978-3-031-58868-6_10

Traditionally, threshold signatures are either *fully private* or *fully accountable*. The signatures generated in a fully private threshold signature [8,26,45] scheme reveal no information about the signing parties, while the signatures generated in a fully accountable threshold signature [3,10,39,42] reveal the identities of all the signing parties (and hence are trivially traceable). These two security flavors of threshold signatures find different application scenarios. A fully private threshold signature can be used by the board of directors in a company to sign important documents while hiding the internal structure and the identities of the signers. A fully accountable threshold signature, on the other hand, can be used in financial applications in which the accountability of all participating parties is a must for regulatory purposes.

Although the two security notions seem to be inherently contradictory, the recent emergence of blockchain applications often requires both features simultaneously. Consider the case where an organization has deposited some digital assets to a public blockchain under the constraint that the asset can be transferred away only when a sufficient number of shareholders endorse the transaction. For financial security purposes, the signatures need to be accountable but the organization also needs to protect the privacy of the shareholders. Given this realistic demand, Boneh and Komlo [9] initiated the study of *threshold accountable private signatures* (TAPS) that enjoy the best features of both. They formalized its security definition and proposed a practical Schnorr-based construction.

While the Schnorr-based TAPS construction is efficient, it is based on a classical complexity assumption (*e.g.*, DDH), and will therefore be insecure in the post-quantum era. Given such a challenge, designing TAPS schemes based on post-quantum secure hardness assumptions is a pressing research problem.

1.1 Our Contributions

We propose a *lattice-based* TAPS scheme based on the hardness of the Module Short Integer Solution (MSIS) problem and the Module Learning With Errors (MLWE) problem. Our design follows the modular design of the Diffie-Hellman-based TAPS construction (BK22) [9]. However, as not all building blocks have an existing lattice-based construction, we independently construct some from lattices during the course, ensuring compatibility.

Specifically, we introduce a lattice-based accountable threshold signature (ATS) and a lattice-based t-out-of-n zero-knowledge argument. To the best of our knowledge, these are the first instances of ATS and the zero-knowledge argument in the literature, and they may hold independent interest.

In Table 1, we present a performance comparison of our TAPS with other recent group or threshold signature schemes. Note that as observed by Boneh and Komol [9], the $O(N)$ signature size is *optimal* for TAPS schemes concealing the threshold value t. To further demonstrate the practical efficiency, we provide parameter recommendations for our scheme across different group sizes and threshold values. Table 3 displays the signature sizes under the chosen parameters. For example, for $t = 8$, $N = 32$, the resulting signature is about 42.34 KB, aligning with recent lattice-based privacy-preserving signatures [14].

Table 1. Comparison with Other Recent (Threshold) Group/Ring Signature Schemes. (TRS stands for threshold ring signature)

Schemes	Sig. size	Asymptotic	Assumptions
TAPS: BK22 [9]	–	$O(N)$	DL
Group Sig: LN22 [34]	17.4 KB ($N \approx 2^{11}$)	$O(N)$	MSIS, MLWE, NTRU
Group Sig: LNP22 [35]	92 KB	$O(\log N)$	MSIS, MLWE
TRS: CLR+10 [13]	45 MB ($n = 100$)	$O(N)$	SIS
This paper	113.54 KB ($N = 2^{11}$)	$O(N)$	MSIS, MLWE

1.2 Technical Overview

Our construction still follows the design blueprint of BK22 construction [9], which is built from an underlying (Diffie-Hellman-based) ATS scheme, ElGamal encryption, and non-interactive zero-knowledge proofs (Sigma protocol or Bulletproof). At a high level, our main idea is to carefully select compatible lattice-based alternatives for each submodule to glue them together organically. This process is not as straightforward as expected, as there is no immediately applicable lattice-based t-out-of-n zero-knowledge proof in literature. As a result, we construct one using the framework from [35]. Along the way, we also make several twists and optimizations to the underlying building blocks.

Accountable Threshold Signature. We use an accountable threshold signature (ATS) scheme based on a threshold version of the lattice-based n-out-of-n signature (multi-signature) MS_2 from [17], where the verification algorithm only verifies t instead of n partial signatures. Each party i holds a secret signing key share $\mathbf{x}_i \in \mathcal{R}_q^{\ell+k}$ with small coefficients and a public matrix $\bar{\mathbf{A}} = [\mathbf{A}|\mathbf{I}] \in \mathcal{R}_q^{k\times(\ell+k)}$. The public verification key is $(\mathbf{A}, \mathbf{t})$, where $\mathbf{t} = \bar{\mathbf{A}}\mathbf{x}$. The partial signature is generated following the "Fiat-Shamir with aborts" paradigm [19,21,33]. Concretely, the signer computes the following:

1. Compute $\mathbf{w} := \mathbf{A}\mathbf{y}$ by sampling a random short vector $\mathbf{y}$;
2. Commit to $\mathbf{w}$ by using the randomness $\mathbf{r}$ and send *com* to the combiner;
3. After obtaining the challenge c, compute $\mathbf{z} := c\mathbf{x} + \mathbf{y}$ with rejection sampling and send out $\mathbf{z}, \mathbf{r}$.

Notably, we use a(n) (additively homomorphic) commitment scheme in Step 2 to deal with the leakage from the "Fiat-Shamir with abort" paradigm. If abort occurs after sending $\mathbf{w}$ directly, the combiner will learn about the abort, in which situation the scheme cannot be proven secure [25]. Thus, We send the commitment of $\mathbf{w}$ instead and open it only if the rejection sampling is successful; otherwise, $\mathbf{w}$ remains secret to the public. The final signature is the summation of the outputs above from the contributing signers.

Constructing TAPS. To construct a TAPS from ATS, we aim to protect the privacy of the signers' identity without compromising the accountability of ATS.

Our lattice-based TAPS scheme closely follows the construction in [9]. At a high-level, the TAPS signature (ct, π) is computed in the following way:

1. The signers and combiner generate an ATS signature σ';
2. The combiner encrypts σ' into ct under the tracer's public key;
3. The combiner generates a proof π that the decryption of ct is a valid ATS signature σ'.

Importantly, we only encrypt parts of the ATS signature related to the signers' identities and the threshold t, optimizing the TAPS scheme for compactness and efficiency, as not all parts of the signature contain the signer's identity.

Our construction involves the following lattice-based primitives: (1) an ATS described above; (2) a verifiable encryption for encrypting the signers' identities and providing proof of knowledge of the plaintext; (3) a symmetric encryption scheme for encrypting the threshold t; (4) a digital signature connecting different modules; and (5) a NIZK argument for overall unforgeability.

After obtaining the ATS signatures from the signers, the combiner constructs a binary indicator string $\vec{v}$ of length N based on the identity of the contributing signers, *i.e.*, $\vec{v}[i] = 1$ if and only if the signer i contributed an ATS signature. To hide the identities of the signers, we encrypt $\vec{v}$ using verifiable encryption (VE). We further design a non-interactive zero-knowledge proof below to bind the VE ciphertext and the ATS signature together.

While the above design framework seems to be complete and sound, there is still a final caveat: the ATS signature $\sigma' = (com, \mathbf{z}, \mathbf{r})$ may leak information about the threshold t. This is because the distributions of the partial signatures $\mathbf{z}_i$ and $\mathbf{r}_i$ are public and the combined signature is a sum of the partial signatures. As a result, the verifier can obtain the threshold t by observing the distributions of $\mathbf{z}$ and $\mathbf{r}$. To prevent such leakage, our TAPS signature only outputs com, uniformly distributed over $\mathcal{R}_q$, while $\mathbf{z}$ and $\mathbf{r}$ are replaced by their commitments, accompanied by a proof of correct opening.

The Underlying Proofs. We now turn to the non-interactive zero-knowledge argument used in our TAPS, which can be converted easily into a lattice-based t-out-of-N argument by adding the signers' private signing key shares $\mathbf{x}$ into the witness. This proof establishes the well-formedness of the ciphertexts $\mathsf{ct}_{\mathsf{se}}$ and $\mathsf{ct}_{\mathsf{pe}}$ of symmetric key encryption (SKE) and VE and ensures the validity of the ATS signature σ'. Specifically, we turn these relations into linear or quadratic equations and apply the framework in [35] to prove them.

For the ATS signature, the verification algorithm computes $\mathbf{w} = \bar{\mathbf{A}}\mathbf{z} - \sum_{j \in S} c_j \mathbf{t}_j$ and checks if $\mathsf{Open}(\mathsf{ck}, com, \mathbf{w}, \mathbf{r}) = 1$. To bind $\mathbf{w}$ with the signers' identities, we embed the indicator vector $\vec{v}$ into the set of public keys $(\mathbf{t}_1, \ldots, \mathbf{t}_N)$, resulting in an alternative equation $\mathbf{w}' = \bar{\mathbf{A}}\mathbf{z}' - \sum_{j \in [N]} c_j \mathbf{t}_j v_j$. As mentioned above, we encrypt $\vec{v}$ by a lattice-based verifiable encryption scheme [35]. In this way, we also prove $\vec{v} \in \{0,1\}^N$ when providing the proof of well-formedness of VE ciphertext, *i.e.*, is binary.

Because encrypting $\vec{v}$ bit-by-bit is rather costly, we encode it to a binary vector $\mathbf{u} \in \mathcal{R}_q^{N/d}$ over the polynomial ring over $\mathcal{R}_q$ by coefficient padding, denoted by $\mathbf{B}_v$, to achieve a speed-up of $1/d$ in both proof size and ciphertext size.

However, the compressed polynomial vector $\mathbf{u}$ cannot directly replace $\vec{v}$ in the above equation concerning $\mathbf{w}$, as the dimensions do not match. Note that the padding from $\vec{v}$ to $\mathbf{u}$ is invertible, we can therefore obtain the vector $\vec{v}$ by using the inverse transform, denoted by $\mathbf{B}_v^{-1}$, *i.e.*, $\mathbf{v} = \mathbf{B}_v^{-1}\mathbf{u}$. Because $\mathbf{v}$ is a constant polynomial vector for $\vec{v}$, over $\mathcal{R}_q$ rather than a binary vector over $\mathbb{Z}$, it can be used in the later proof.

By putting $\mathbf{u}$ into the expression of $\mathbf{w}$, we obtain $\bar{\mathbf{A}}\mathbf{z} - \mathbf{T}\mathbf{B}_v^{-1}\mathbf{u} = \mathbf{w}$, where $\mathbf{T} = (c_1\mathbf{t}_1, \ldots, c_N\mathbf{t}_N)$. Here we need to emphasize that $\mathbf{w}$ and $\mathbf{z}$ are private, otherwise, the verifier may know the signers' identities by $\mathbf{T}\vec{v} := \bar{\mathbf{A}}\mathbf{z} - \mathbf{w}$.

To hide the threshold value t, we use the symmetric key encryption [23] based on the LWE problem to encrypt it in the setup phase and publish it as part of the public parameter. Finally, to prove that the number of contributing signers satisfies the threshold value, we add a final zero-knowledge proof to show that the inner-product $\langle \vec{v}, \vec{v} \rangle$ equals the decryption of the LWE ciphertext, namely t.

1.3 Related Works

Ring Signatures. A ring signature scheme [44] is an anonymous variant of normal digital signatures. In a ring signature, a signer is allowed to generate a signature in the name of a ring that includes themselves. Recently, several lattice-based ring signatures [22,34,38] applying *one-out-of-many proofs* have been proposed with compact signature size and excellent efficiency. Because ring signatures offer full anonymity, (*i.e.*, anyone in the ring can generate a signature and no one can trace the signature back), signature abuse is an immediate concern. A threshold ring signature [11,27,41] is the t-out-of-n threshold version which needs at least t ring members to generate a valid signature cooperatively, but they do not offer accountability.

Group Signatures. Similar to ring signatures, group signatures scheme [15] allow a group member to sign messages in the name of a *group* anonymously, but unlike ring signatures, the group is managed by a trusted group manager. The group manager has the power to reveal the signer's identity if needed. In the past two decades, many researchers focused on post-quantum group signatures [2,7,24,28,29,31,35,36]. A threshold type of group signature scheme was proposed by Camenisch *et al.*, [12] recently to decrease the power of the group manager. It offers a different functionality than TAPS, which enforces a quorum of the signers of minimum size to participate in the signing process.

Threshold Signatures. Previous threshold signatures provide either full privacy or accountability for the signing quorum, but none of them can offer both. To solve the above issue, Boneh and Komlo proposed the notion of TAPS (Threshold, Accountable, and Private Signature) [9] and provided a concrete construction based on discrete logarithm assumptions. However, their construction is facing the threat of quantum computers. Recently, Damgard *et al.*, [17] proposed an n-out-of-n and multi-signature scheme, which can be viewed as a special case of the general (t, n)-threshold signatures. Our TAPS is also built on lattices, which is one of the most promising quantum-resistant primitives so far and offers richer security guarantees like accountability.

2 Preliminaries

2.1 Notations

Let $\mathbb{Z}_p$ be the ring of integers modulo p and then $\vec{v} \in \mathbb{Z}_q^m$ be a vector over $\mathbb{Z}_q$. All vectors are column vectors by default. We denote by $\vec{v}\|\vec{u}$ the concatenation of vectors $\vec{v}$ and $\vec{u}$. For a finite set S, let $|S|$ be the order of set S. We write $x \leftarrow S$ when the element x is sampled uniformly at random from the set S. Similarly, we write $x \leftarrow D$ when x is sampled according to the distribution D. For an integer N, we denote by $[N]$ the set $\{1, ..., N\}$. We write $\|\cdot\|_1$ and $\|\cdot\|$ for the 1-norm and 2-norm of a vector, respectively.

2.2 Cyclotomic Rings

Let d be a power of two and p be a positive integer. We denote by $\mathcal{R}$ and $\mathcal{R}_p$ the rings $\mathbb{Z}[X]/(X^d+1)$ and $\mathbb{Z}_p[X]/(X^d+1)$, respectively. We write lower-case letters for elements in $\mathcal{R}$ or $\mathcal{R}_p$ and bold lower-case (resp. upper-case, *e.g.*, $\mathbf{A}$) letters for vectors (resp. matrices) with entries in $\mathcal{R}$ or $\mathcal{R}_p$. For a vector $\vec{u} = (u_0, ..., u_{m-1})$ over $\mathbb{Z}_q$, $\mathbf{u}$ is a vector over $\mathcal{R}_q$ whose constant coefficients are $u_0, ..., u_{m-1}$.

The ring $\mathcal{R}$ has a group of automorphisms $\mathsf{Aut}(\mathcal{R})$ that is isomorphic to $\mathbb{Z}_{2d}^\times$. Let $\sigma \in \mathsf{Aut}(\mathcal{R})$ be an element defined by $\sigma(X) = X^{-1}$. For a vector $\mathbf{m} \in \mathcal{R}^k$, we denote $\sigma(\mathbf{m}) := (\sigma(m_1), ..., \sigma(m_k))$. For vectors $\mathbf{u}, \mathbf{v}$, we write $\langle \mathbf{u}, \mathbf{v} \rangle \in \mathbb{Z}$ for the inner product of their coefficient vectors. We recall the challenge space in [35]. Fix $\eta > 0$ and a power-of-two k, then the challenge space is: $\mathcal{C} = \left\{c \in \mathcal{S}_\kappa : \sigma(c) = c, \sqrt[2k]{\|c^{2k}\|_1} \leqslant \eta\right\}$, where $\mathcal{S}_\kappa = \{x \in \mathcal{R}_q : \|x\|_\infty \leqslant \kappa\}$.

We define a map $\mathsf{T} : \mathbb{Z}^{kd} \times \mathbb{Z}^{kd} \to \mathcal{R}$ and introduce Lemma 1 as follows. Given two input vectors $\vec{a} = (a_0, ..., a_{kd-1})$ and $\vec{b} = (b_0, ..., b_{kd-1})$, it outputs:

$$\mathsf{T}(\vec{a}, \vec{b}) := \sum_{i=0}^{k-1} \sigma\left(\sum_{j=0}^{d-1} a_{id+j} X^j\right) \cdot \left(\sum_{j=0}^{d-1} b_{id+j} X^j\right) \in \mathcal{R} \tag{1}$$

Lemma 1 ([35]). *Let* T *be a map defined above,* $\vec{a}, \vec{b} \in \mathbb{Z}^{kd}$. *The constant coefficient of* $\mathsf{T}(\vec{a}, \vec{b})$ *equals to* $\left\langle \vec{a}, \vec{b} \right\rangle$.

2.3 Module-SIS and Module-LWE Problems

The security of our protocols relies on two lattice problems, Module-LWE (MLWE) and Module-SIS (MSIS) [30].

Definition 1 ($\mathsf{MSIS}_{\kappa,m,B}$). *Let* $\kappa, m > 0$ *be integers and* B *be a real number with* $0 < B < q$. *Given* $\mathbf{A} \leftarrow \mathcal{R}_q^{\kappa \times m}$, *the Module-SIS problem is defined to find a short solution* $\mathbf{z} \in \mathcal{R}_q^m$ *such that* $\mathbf{Az} = \mathbf{0}$ *and* $0 < \|\mathbf{z}\| \leqslant B$.

Definition 2 ($\mathsf{MLWE}_{m,\lambda,\chi}$). *Let* $m, \lambda > 0$ *be integers and* λ *be an error distribution over* $\mathcal{R}$. *The module-LWE problem is defined to distinguish the given arbitrary many samples between the following two distributions: (1)* $(\mathbf{A}, \mathbf{As} + \mathbf{e})$ *for* $\mathbf{A} \leftarrow \mathcal{R}_q^{m \times \lambda}$, *a secret* $\mathbf{s} \leftarrow \chi^\lambda$ *and an error* $\mathbf{e} \leftarrow \chi^m$, *and (2)* $\mathbf{A}, \mathbf{b} \leftarrow \mathcal{R}_q^{m \times \lambda} \times \mathcal{R}_q^m$.

We also provide the definition of Extended Module-LWE problem [37].

Definition 3 (Extended $\mathsf{MLWE}_{m,\lambda,\chi,\mathcal{C},\mathsf{s}}$). *Let $m, \lambda > 0$ be integers, λ be an error distribution over $\mathcal{R}_q$, $\mathcal{C} \subseteq \mathcal{R}_q$ be a challenge space and a real number σ be the standard deviation. The Extended* MLWE *problem is to distinguish the given arbitrary many samples between the following two distributions:*
1. $(\mathbf{B}, \mathbf{Br}, c, \mathbf{z}, \mathsf{sign}(\langle \mathbf{z}, c\mathbf{r}\rangle))$ for $\mathbf{B} \leftarrow \mathcal{R}_q^{m\times(m+\lambda)}$, a secret $\mathbf{r} \leftarrow \chi^{m+\lambda}$, $\mathbf{z} \leftarrow D_{\mathsf{s}}^{(m+\lambda)d}$, and $c \leftarrow \mathcal{C}$;
2. $(\mathbf{B}, \mathbf{u}, c, \mathbf{z}, \mathsf{sign}(\langle \mathbf{z}, c\mathbf{r}\rangle))$ for $\mathbf{B} \leftarrow \mathcal{R}_q^{m\times(m+\lambda)}$, $\mathbf{u} \leftarrow \mathcal{R}_q^m$, $\mathbf{z} \leftarrow D_{\mathsf{s}}^{(m+\lambda)d}$, and $c \leftarrow \mathcal{C}$, where $\mathsf{sign}(a) = 1$ for $a \geqslant 0$ and 0 otherwise.

2.4 Rejection Sampling

In lattice-based zero-knowledge proofs, the prover needs to output a proof $\vec{z}$ whose distribution is independent of the secret randomness $\vec{r}$ so that $\vec{z}$ does not leak any information about $\vec{r}$. Concretely, the prover commits to a mask vector $\vec{y}$ with $\vec{w} = A\vec{y}$. After receiving the challenge value c from the verifier, the prover computes $\vec{z} = \vec{y} + c\vec{r}$, where $\vec{r}$ is the opening. To ensure the security of $\vec{r}$, we use the rejection sampling technique [32,33] and reject some $\vec{z}$ that might leak the distribution of $\vec{r}$. We recall the following lemma in previous work [33].

Lemma 2 (Rejection Sampling). *Let $V \subseteq \mathcal{R}^\ell$ be a set of polynomials with the norm at most T and $\rho : V \to [0,1]$ be a probability distribution. Set the standard deviation $\mathsf{s} = \gamma T$. Define the rejection sampling algorithm as follows.*

> $\mathsf{Rej}(\vec{z}, \vec{v}, \mathsf{s})$: *Sample $u \leftarrow [0,1)$. If $u > \frac{1}{M}\cdot \exp\left(\frac{-2\langle \vec{z},\vec{v}\rangle + \|\vec{v}\|^2}{2\mathsf{s}^2}\right)$, return 1(*reject*), otherwise, return 0 (*accept*).*

The following statement holds:

Set $M = \exp\left(\frac{14}{\gamma} + \frac{1}{2\gamma^2}\right)$. Sample $\mathbf{v} \leftarrow \rho$ and $\mathbf{y} \leftarrow D_{\mathsf{s}}^l$, compute $\mathbf{z} = \mathbf{y} + \mathbf{v}$ and run $b \leftarrow \mathsf{Rej}(\vec{z}, \vec{v}, \mathsf{s})$. Then,

1) the probability that $b = 0$ is at least $\frac{1-2^{-128}}{M}$;
2) the distribution of accepted $(\mathbf{v}, \mathbf{z})$ and the distribution $\rho \times D_{\mathsf{s}}^\ell$ are statistical close within a distance of 2^{-128}.

In the later discussion of completeness, we need the following useful lemma [4].

Lemma 3 (Tail Bound). *Let $\mathbf{z} \leftarrow D_{\mathsf{s}}^m$, then $\Pr[\|\mathbf{z}\| > \tau \mathsf{s}\sqrt{md}] < \left(te^{\frac{1-t^2}{2}}\right)^{md}$.*

2.5 Commitment Schemes

We recall the ABDLOP commitment scheme [35], which is a combination of Ajtai commitment [1] and BDLOP commitment [5]. It works as follows:

- $\mathsf{Setup}(1^\lambda) \to \mathsf{cpp}$: The algorithm takes the security parameter 1^λ as input and outputs the public parameters $\mathsf{cpp} = (q, n_1, m_1, m_2, n_2, D_{\mathsf{s}})$.

- $\mathsf{CGen}(\mathsf{cpp}) \to \mathsf{ck}$: The algorithm takes the public parameters cpp as input and outputs the commitment key ck. In detail, it samples the matrices $\mathbf{A}_1 \leftarrow \mathcal{R}_q^{n_1 \times m_1}, \mathbf{A}_2 \leftarrow \mathcal{R}_q^{n_1 \times m_2}, \mathbf{B} \leftarrow \mathcal{R}_q^{n_2 \times m_2}$ uniformly at random and outputs the commitment key $\mathsf{ck} := (\mathbf{A}_1, \mathbf{A}_2, \mathbf{B})$.
- $\mathsf{Com}(\mathsf{ck}, (\mathbf{m}_1, \mathbf{m}_2), \mathbf{r}) \to com$: The algorithm takes the commitment key ck, the commitment messages $\mathbf{m}_1 \in \mathcal{R}_q^{m_1}, \mathbf{m}_2 \in \mathcal{R}_q^{n_2}$, and the randomness $\mathbf{r} \leftarrow D_{\mathsf{s}}^{m_2}$ as inputs and outputs a commitment com. The algorithm computes

$$com := \begin{bmatrix} \mathbf{t}_A \\ \mathbf{t}_B \end{bmatrix} = \begin{bmatrix} \mathbf{A}_1 \\ \mathbf{0} \end{bmatrix} \mathbf{m}_1 + \begin{bmatrix} \mathbf{A}_2 \\ \mathbf{B} \end{bmatrix} \mathbf{r} + \begin{bmatrix} \mathbf{0} \\ \mathbf{m}_2 \end{bmatrix}$$

- $\mathsf{Open}(\mathsf{ck}, com, (\mathbf{m}_1, \mathbf{m}_2), \mathbf{r}) \to b$: It outputs $b = 1$ iff.

$$com = \begin{bmatrix} \mathbf{A}_1 \\ \mathbf{0} \end{bmatrix} \mathbf{m}_1 + \begin{bmatrix} \mathbf{A}_2 \\ \mathbf{B} \end{bmatrix} \mathbf{r} + \begin{bmatrix} \mathbf{0} \\ \mathbf{m}_2 \end{bmatrix},$$

  otherwise, it outputs $b = 0$.

The following lemmas show the ABDLOP commitment is computationally binding and computationally hiding.

Lemma 4 *[35, Lemma 3.1]. The* ABDLOP *commitment is computationally binding under the assumption that* $\mathsf{MSIS}_{n_1, m_1+m_2, B}$ *is hard for the bound* $B = 4\eta\sqrt{B_1^2 + B_2^2}$, *where* $\|c\mathbf{m}_1\| \leqslant B_1, \|c\mathbf{r}\| \leqslant B_2$.

Lemma 5. *The* ABDLOP *commitment scheme is computationally hiding under the assumption that* $\mathsf{MLWE}_{n_1+n_2, m_2, \mathsf{s}}$ *is hard.*

In addition, we introduce three algorithms to convert the above scheme into a trapdoor commitment. The security follows the literature [17].

- $\mathsf{TCGen}(\mathsf{cpp}) \to (\mathsf{tck}, \mathsf{td})$: This algorithm takes the public parameters cpp as input and outputs the commitment key tck and a trapdoor td as follows.
  1. Sample the matrices $\mathbf{A}_1 \leftarrow \mathcal{R}_q^{n_1 \times m_1}$ and $\mathbf{A} \leftarrow \mathcal{R}_q^{(n_1+n_2) \times m_2}$ uniformly at random.
  2. Sample $\mathbf{R} \leftarrow D_{\mathsf{s}}^{(n_1+n_2) \times m_2}$ and compute $\hat{\mathbf{A}} = [\mathbf{A} | \mathbf{G} - \mathbf{A}\mathbf{R}]$.
  3. Set $[\mathbf{A}_2^\top | \mathbf{B}^\top]^\top := \hat{\mathbf{A}}^\top$, return $\mathsf{tck} := (\mathbf{A}_1, \mathbf{A}_2, \mathbf{B})$ and $\mathsf{td} := \mathbf{R}$.
- $\mathsf{TCom}(\mathsf{td}) \to com$: This algorithm returns a uniformly random commitment $com := (\mathbf{t}_A, \mathbf{t}_B) \leftarrow \mathcal{R}_q^{n_1+n_2}$.
- $\mathsf{Eqv}(com, \mathsf{tck}, \mathsf{td}, \mathbf{m}_1, \mathbf{m}_2) \to \mathbf{r}$: This algorithm returns an equivocal opening $\mathbf{r}$ by applying the preimage sampling of [40]. Namely, Sample a short vector $\mathbf{r} \in D_{\mathsf{s}}^{m_2}$ such that

$$\begin{bmatrix} \mathbf{A}_2 \\ \mathbf{B} \end{bmatrix} \mathbf{r} = \begin{bmatrix} \mathbf{t}_A \\ \mathbf{t}_B \end{bmatrix} - \begin{bmatrix} \mathbf{A}_1 \\ \mathbf{0} \end{bmatrix} \mathbf{m}_1 - \begin{bmatrix} \mathbf{0} \\ \mathbf{m}_2 \end{bmatrix}.$$

2.6 TAPS

We focus on threshold accountable private signature (TAPS) [9] that provides anonymity, privacy, and unforgeability at the same time.

Definition 4. *A private and accountable threshold signature* $\mathsf{TAPS} = (\mathsf{KGen}, \mathsf{Sign}, \mathsf{Combine}, \mathsf{Vf}, \mathsf{Trace})$ *scheme consists of the following five algorithms:*

- $\mathsf{KGen}(1^\lambda, N, \mathsf{t}) \rightarrow (\mathsf{pk}, \mathsf{pk_t}, (\mathsf{sk}_1, \ldots, \mathsf{sk}_N), \mathsf{sk_c}, \mathsf{sk_t})$: *a probabilistic algorithm that takes inputs a security parameter* 1^λ, *the number of parties* N *and threshold* t. *It outputs a master public key* pk, *a set of private keys* $\{\mathsf{sk}_i\}_{i\in[N]}$, *a combiner secret key* $\mathsf{sk_c}$, *a tracing public/secret key pair* $(\mathsf{pk_t}, \mathsf{sk_t})$.
- $\mathsf{Sign}(\mathsf{sk}_i, m, S) \rightarrow \delta_i$: *a probabilistic algorithm executed by* one signer *that takes input a message, a signing key* sk_i *and optionally a signing quorum* S. *It outputs a signature "share"* δ_i.
- $\mathsf{Combine}(\mathsf{pk_t}, \mathsf{sk_c}, m, S, \{\delta_i\}_{i\in S}) \rightarrow \sigma$: *a probabilistic algorithm that takes as inputs the tracing public key* $\mathsf{pk_t}$, *the combiner's secret key, a message* m, *a description of the signing quorum* S *where* $|S| \leq \mathsf{t}$, *and at least* t *valid signature shares over* m *by members of* S. *If the output is valid, the algorithm outputs a* TAPS *signature* σ *over* m.
- $\mathsf{Vf}(\mathsf{pk}, m, \sigma) \rightarrow \{0, 1\}$: *a deterministic algorithm that verifies the signature* z *on a message* m *with respect to the public key* pk.
- $\mathsf{Trace}(\mathsf{sk_t}, m, \sigma) \rightarrow \{C/\mathsf{fail}\}$: *a deterministic algorithm that takes as inputs the tracer's secret key* $\mathsf{sk_t}$, *a message* m *and a signature* σ. *It outputs a set* $C \subseteq [N]$, *where* $|C| \leqslant \mathsf{t}$, *or a special symbol* fail.

For correctness, we require that for all allowable $1 \leq \mathsf{t} \leq N$, *for all* t*-size sets* $S \subseteq [N]$, *all* $m \in \mathcal{M}$, *and for* $(\mathsf{pk}, (\mathsf{sk}_1, \ldots, \mathsf{sk}_N), \mathsf{sk_c}, \mathsf{sk_t}) \rightarrow \mathsf{KGen}(1^\lambda, N, \mathsf{t})$ *the following two conditions hold:*

$$\Pr[\mathsf{Vf}(\mathsf{pk}, m, \mathsf{Combine}(\mathsf{pk_t}, \mathsf{sk_c}, m, S, \{\mathsf{Sign}(\mathsf{sk}_i, m, S)\}_{i\in S})) = 1] = 1$$

$$\Pr[\mathsf{Trace}(\mathsf{sk_t}, m, \mathsf{Combine}(\mathsf{pk_t}, \mathsf{sk_c}, m, S, \{\mathsf{Sign}(\mathsf{sk}_i, m, S)\}_{i\in S})) = S] = 1$$

As for security, Boneh and Komlo [9] formalized two security notions for TAPS: (1) *Existential Unforgeability under a Chosen Message Attack with Traceability* and (2) *Privacy*. As for privacy, there are two types: *privacy against the public* and *privacy against signers.*

Unforgeability and Accountability. Let $\mathsf{Adv}_{\mathcal{A}}^{\mathrm{forg}}(\lambda)$ be the probability that adversary $\mathcal{A}$ wins the game of Fig. 1 against the TAPS scheme $\mathcal{S}$.

Definition 5 (Unforgeability and Accountability). *A TAPS scheme is* unforgeable and accountable *if for all probabilistic polynomial time adversaries* $\mathcal{A} = (\mathcal{A}_0, \mathcal{A}_1)$, *the function* $\mathsf{Adv}_{\mathcal{A}}^{\mathrm{forg}}(\lambda)$ *is a negligible function of* λ.

Privacy. Following [9], the threshold t is private from the public in Fig. 2. This is captured by having the challenger pick one of the two threshold values (t_0 and

Unforgeability and accountability game: $(N, \mathsf{t}, C, state) \leftarrow \mathcal{A}_0(1^\lambda)$, where $\mathsf{t} \in [N]$ and $C \subseteq [N]$ // $\mathcal{A}_0$ chooses corrupted users C. $(\mathsf{pk}, \{\mathsf{sk}_1, ..., \mathsf{sk}_N\}, \mathsf{sk}_\mathsf{c}, \mathsf{pk}_\mathsf{t}) \leftarrow \mathsf{KGen}(1^\lambda, N, \mathsf{t})$. $(m^*, \sigma^*) \leftarrow \mathcal{A}_1^{\mathcal{O}(\cdot,\cdot)}(\mathsf{pk}, \{\mathsf{sk}_i\}_{i \in C}, \mathsf{sk}_\mathsf{c}, \mathsf{sk}_\mathsf{t}, st)$, where $\mathcal{O}(S_j, m_j)$ returns the signature shares: $\{\mathsf{Sign}(\mathsf{sk}_i, m_j, S_j)\}_{i \in S_j}$	Winning condition: Let $(S_1, m_1), (S_2, m_2), \cdots$ be $\mathcal{A}_1$'s queries to $\mathcal{O}(\cdot,\cdot)$. Let $S' \leftarrow \bigcup S_j$ be the union of the signing quorums over all oracle queries $\mathcal{O}(S_j, m')$. If no such queries, set $S' := \varnothing$. Let $S_t := \mathsf{Trace}(\mathsf{sk}_\mathsf{t}, m^*, \sigma^*)$. Output 1 if $\mathsf{Vf}(\mathsf{pk}, m^*, \sigma^*) = 1$ and either $S_t \not\subseteq (S \cup S')$ or $S_t = \mathsf{fail}$.

Fig. 1. Unforgeability and accountability game.

Privacy against the public game (priv1): Sample $b \leftarrow \{0, 1\}$. $(N, \mathsf{t}_0, \mathsf{t}_1, S_0, S_1, st) \leftarrow \mathcal{A}_0(1^\lambda)$, where $\mathsf{t}_1, \mathsf{t}_2 \in [N]$. $(\mathsf{pk}, \{\mathsf{sk}_1, ..., \mathsf{sk}_N\}, \mathsf{sk}_\mathsf{c}, \mathsf{sk}_\mathsf{t}) \leftarrow \mathsf{KGen}(1^\lambda, N, \mathsf{t}_b)$. $b' \leftarrow \mathcal{A}_1^{\mathcal{O}_1(\cdot,\cdot,\cdot),\mathcal{O}_2(\cdot,\cdot)}(\mathsf{pk}, st)$. Output $(b \stackrel{?}{=} b')$.	$\mathcal{O}_1(S_0, S_1, m)$ returns: $\sigma \leftarrow \mathsf{Combine}(\mathsf{sk}_\mathsf{c}, m, S_b, \{\delta_i\}_{i \in S_b})$. for $S_0, S_1 \subseteq [N]$ with $\vert S_0\vert = \mathsf{t}_0, \vert S_1\vert = \mathsf{t}_1$. $\mathcal{O}_2(m, \sigma)$ returns $\mathsf{Trace}(\mathsf{sk}_\mathsf{t}, m, \sigma)$. Restriction: if z is obtained from a query $\mathcal{O}_1(\cdot, \cdot, m)$, then $\mathcal{O}_2$ is never queried at (m, σ).

Fig. 2. Privacy against the public game.

Privacy against signers game (priv2): Sample $b \leftarrow \{0, 1\}$. $(N, \mathsf{t}, S_0, S_1, st) \leftarrow \mathcal{A}_0(1^\lambda)$, where $\mathsf{t} \in [N]$. $(\mathsf{pk}, \{\mathsf{sk}_1, ..., \mathsf{sk}_N\}, \mathsf{sk}_\mathsf{c}, \mathsf{sk}_\mathsf{t}) \leftarrow \mathsf{KGen}(1^\lambda, N, \mathsf{t})$. $b' \leftarrow \mathcal{A}_1^{\mathcal{O}_1(\cdot,\cdot,\cdot),\mathcal{O}_2(\cdot,\cdot)}(\mathsf{pk}, \{\mathsf{sk}_i\}_{i \in [N]}, st)$. Output $(b \stackrel{?}{=} b')$.	$\mathcal{O}_1(S_0, S_1, m)$ returns: $z \leftarrow \mathsf{Combine}(\mathsf{sk}_\mathsf{c}, m, S_b, \{\delta_i\}_{i \in S_b})$ for $S_0, S_1 \subseteq [N]$ with $\vert S_0\vert = \vert S_1\vert = \mathsf{t}$. $\mathcal{O}_2(m, z)$ returns $\mathsf{Trace}(\mathsf{sk}_\mathsf{t}, m, \sigma)$. Restriction: if z is obtained from a query $\mathcal{O}_1(\cdot, \cdot, m)$, then $\mathcal{O}_2$ is never queried at (m, σ).

Fig. 3. Privacy against signers game.

t_1) that the adversary have chosen. The adversary needs to guess which value was chosen by the challenger.

Let W, W' be the event that the game in Fig. 2 and Fig. 3 outputs 1, respectively. The advantage that adversary $\mathcal{A}$ breaks the TAPS scheme are

$$\mathsf{Adv}_{\mathcal{A}}^{\mathrm{priv1}}(\lambda) = |2\Pr[W] - 1| \text{ and } \mathsf{Adv}_{\mathcal{A}}^{\mathrm{priv2}}(\lambda) = |2\Pr[W'] - 1|.$$

Definition 6 (Privacy). *A TAPS scheme is* private *if for all probabilistic polynomial time adversaries* $\mathcal{A} = (\mathcal{A}_0, \mathcal{A}_1)$, $\mathsf{Adv}_{\mathcal{A}}^{priv1}(\lambda)$ *and* $\mathsf{Adv}_{\mathcal{A}}^{priv2}(\lambda)$ *are both negligible in* λ.

3 Lattice-Based TAPS

We now describe our lattice-based TAPS construction outlined in Sect. 1.2. We will first introduce the necessary building blocks from lattice: symmetric encryption, verifiable encryption, and accountable threshold signature schemes.

3.1 Building Blocks

Symmetric Encryption Scheme from LWE [23]**.** The symmetric encryption SKE from [23] is defined as follows.

- $\mathsf{KGen}(1^\lambda)$: The algorithm outputs a secret key $\mathsf{sk}_{\mathsf{se}} := \vec{s}_{\mathsf{se}} \leftarrow \mathcal{S}_1^{K_1}$.
- $\mathsf{Enc}(\mathsf{sk}_{\mathsf{se}}, m)$: On inputs the secret key $\mathsf{sk}_{\mathsf{se}}$ and the message $m \in \mathbb{Z}_p^{M_1}$ with binary coefficients, the algorithm samples $C_{\mathsf{se}} \leftarrow \mathbb{Z}_p^{M_1 \times K_1}$ and $\vec{e}_{\mathsf{se}} \leftarrow \mathcal{S}_1^{M_1}$ and outputs $\mathsf{ct}_{\mathsf{se}} = (C_{\mathsf{se}}, C_{\mathsf{se}}\vec{s}_{\mathsf{se}} + \vec{e}_{\mathsf{se}} + \lfloor \frac{p}{2} \rceil m)$.
- $\mathsf{Dec}(\mathsf{sk}_{\mathsf{se}}, \mathsf{ct}_{\mathsf{se}})$: On inputs the secret key $\mathsf{sk}_{\mathsf{se}}$ and the ciphertext $\mathsf{ct} = (C_{\mathsf{se}}, \vec{b}_{\mathsf{se}})$, the algorithm computes $m' := \vec{b}_{\mathsf{se}} - C_{\mathsf{se}}\vec{s}_{\mathsf{se}}$. Then it decodes the message m in the following way: if the i-th coordinate of m' is close to $p/2$, then the i-th coordinate of m is 1; otherwise, i-th coordinate of m is 0.

Verifiable Encryption. Using verifiable encryption, a prover who has a message m can produce a ciphertext $\mathsf{ct} = \mathsf{Enc}(\mathsf{pk}, m)$ and a zero-knowledge proof of knowledge π_{ct} showing that he knows the value of $\mathsf{Dec}(\mathsf{sk}, \mathsf{ct})$. This is equivalent to proving that ct is a correctly formed ciphertext along with proving the knowledge of m that was used to construct it.

We recall the verifiable encryption scheme VE proposed in [35], which is based on Regev's public-key encryption scheme [43]. The scheme works as follows:

- $\mathsf{KGen}(1^\lambda)$:
  1. Sample $\mathbf{C}_{\mathsf{pe}} \leftarrow \mathcal{R}_p^{M_2 \times K_2}$ and $\mathbf{s}_{\mathsf{pe}} \leftarrow \mathcal{S}_\nu^{M_2}, \mathbf{e} \leftarrow \mathcal{S}_\nu^{K_2}$.
  2. Compute $\mathbf{b}_{\mathsf{pe}} := \mathbf{s}_{\mathsf{pe}}^\top \mathbf{C}_{\mathsf{pe}} + \mathbf{e}$.
  3. Output $\mathsf{pk}_{\mathsf{pe}} := (\mathbf{C}_{\mathsf{pe}}, \mathbf{b}_{\mathsf{pe}})$ and $\mathsf{sk}_{\mathsf{pe}} := \mathbf{s}_{\mathsf{pe}}$.
- $\mathsf{Enc}(\mathsf{pk}_{\mathsf{pe}}, m)$:
  1. Sample a randomness $\mathbf{r} \leftarrow \xi^{K_2}$.
  2. Compute the ciphertext $\mathsf{ct}_{\mathsf{pe}} := (\mathbf{d}_0, d_1)$ as follows:

$$\begin{bmatrix} \mathbf{d}_0 \\ d_1 \end{bmatrix} := \begin{bmatrix} \mathbf{C}_{\mathsf{pe}} \\ \mathbf{b}_{\mathsf{pe}}^T \end{bmatrix} \mathbf{r} + \begin{bmatrix} \mathbf{0} \\ \lfloor \frac{p}{2} \rceil m \end{bmatrix} \tag{2}$$

  3. Generate a proof π_{ct} for relation R_{ct} and output $(\mathsf{ct}_{\mathsf{pe}}, \pi_{\mathsf{ct}})$.
- $\mathsf{Dec}(\mathsf{sk}_{\mathsf{pe}}, \mathsf{ct}_{\mathsf{pe}})$:
  1. Compute $m' := d_1 - \langle \mathbf{d}_0, \mathbf{s}_{\mathsf{pe}} \rangle$.
  2. Decode m according to m' and outputs m.
- $\mathsf{Vf}(\mathsf{pk}_{\mathsf{pe}}, \mathsf{ct}_{\mathsf{pe}}, \pi_{\mathsf{ct}})$: Return 1 if the proof π_{ct} verifies; otherwise return 0. The relation R_{ct} of π_{ct} will be described below immediately.

To encrypt a binary message $m \in \mathcal{R}_q$, the encryption algorithm samples a random vector $\mathbf{r} \leftarrow \xi^{K_2}$, where ξ is a distribution over $\mathcal{R}$ such that $\|\mathbf{r}\| > B$ happens only with small possibility for $\mathbf{r} \leftarrow \xi^{K_2}$, and computes $\mathsf{ct_{pe}}$ according to Eq. (2) over $\mathcal{R}_q := \mathbb{Z}_p[X]/(X^d+1)$ and $\|\mathbf{r}\| \leqslant B$. Therefore, we define a relation $\mathsf{R_{ct}}$ for the above ciphertext as:

$$\mathsf{R_{ct}} = \left\{ (\mathsf{pk_{pe}}, \mathsf{ct_{pe}}); (\mathbf{r}, m) : \begin{array}{c} \begin{bmatrix} \mathbf{d}_0 \\ d_1 \end{bmatrix} = \begin{bmatrix} \mathbf{C_{pe}} \\ \mathbf{b}_{\mathsf{pe}}^T \end{bmatrix} \mathbf{r} + \begin{bmatrix} \mathbf{0} \\ \lfloor \frac{p}{2} \rceil m \end{bmatrix}, \\ \vec{m} \in \{0,1\}^d, \|\mathbf{r}\| \leqslant B. \end{array} \right\}$$

Embedding into Polynomials. In our scheme, we need to encrypt message $\vec{v} = (v_1, ..., v_N) \in \mathbb{Z}^N$ and prove that the resultant ciphertext is well-formed. To reduce the number of ciphertexts, we encode $\vec{v}$ into a polynomial vector $\mathbf{u} \in \mathcal{R}_q^{\mathsf{b}}$ by coefficient padding, where $\mathsf{b} = N/d$. For simplicity, we suppose N is divisible by d; otherwise, we can pad 0 s for vector $\vec{v}$.

To confirm $\mathbf{u}$ is an encoding vector of $\vec{v}$, we use the following matrices:

$$\mathbf{B}_v = (1, X, \cdots, X^{d-1}) \otimes \mathbf{I}_b, \mathbf{B}_v^{-1} = (1, -X^{d-1}, \cdots, -X)^\top \otimes \mathbf{I}_b.$$

So we have $\mathbf{u}_t = \mathbf{B}_v \vec{v}$. Similarly, for a binary polynomial vector over $\mathcal{R}_q$, we can decode it to a binary vector with $\mathbf{B}_v^{-1}$. Although the resulting vector $\mathbf{v} := \mathbf{B}_v^{-1}\mathbf{u}$ is over $\mathcal{R}_q$ with only binary constant terms, it suffices to complete the well-formedness proof in Sect. 4.

3.2 An Accountable Threshold Signature

In this section, we give a lattice-based accountable threshold signature (ATS) scheme from an N-out-of-N signature (multi-signature) [17]. It works as follows:

- $\mathsf{Setup}(1^\lambda)$: Output $\mathsf{pp} := (q_1, d, N, \mathsf{t}, k, \ell, x, D_\mathsf{s}, \mathsf{H}_0, \mathsf{H}_1, B, B_t)$.
- $\mathsf{KGen}(\mathsf{pp})$: On input the public parameter pp, it outputs the key pairs.
  1. Sample $\mathbf{A} \leftarrow \mathcal{R}_{q_1}^{k\times\ell}$ uniformly at random and set $\bar{\mathbf{A}} := [\mathbf{A}|\mathbf{I}_k]$.
  2. Sample a secret key share $\mathbf{x}_i \leftarrow \mathcal{S}_x^{\ell+k}$ and compute a public key share $\mathbf{t}_i := \bar{\mathbf{A}}\mathbf{x}_i$.
  3. Send out the key pair $(\mathsf{sk}_i, \mathsf{pk_{at}}) = (\mathbf{x}_i, (\mathbf{A}, \mathbf{t}_1, \dots, \mathbf{t}_N))$ to each party i.
- $\mathsf{Sign}(\mathsf{sk}_i, \mathsf{pk_{at}}, m)$:
  1. Compute the first message as follows:
     (a) Sample $\mathbf{y}_i \leftarrow D_\mathsf{s}^{\ell+k}$ and compute $\mathbf{w}_i := \bar{\mathbf{A}}\mathbf{y}_i$.
     (b) Generate the commitment key $\mathsf{ck} := \mathsf{H}_1(m, \mathsf{pk_{at}})$ for message m, and sample a randomness $\mathbf{r}_i \leftarrow D_\mathsf{s}^{m_2}$.
     (c) Compute commitment $com_i := \mathsf{Com}(\mathsf{ck}, \mathbf{w}_i, \mathbf{r}_i)$.
     (d) Send com_i to the combiner.
  2. Upon receiving com_j for all $j \in S$, the combiner computes $com := \sum_{j\in S} com_j$ and sends it to signer i. Then, the signature share is generated as follows:
     (a) Generate a challenge $c_i := \mathsf{H}_0(\mathbf{t}_i, com, m, \mathsf{pk_{at}})$.

(b) Compute a signature share $\mathbf{z}_i := c_i\mathbf{x}_i + \mathbf{y}_i$. If $\mathsf{Rej}(\mathbf{z}_i, c_i\mathbf{x}, \mathsf{s})$, send out *abort*; otherwise, send out $\delta_i = (\mathbf{z}_i, \mathbf{r}_i)$.

- $\mathsf{Combine}(\mathsf{pk}_{\mathsf{at}}, m, S, \{\delta_j\}_{j\in S})$: On inputs the public key $\mathsf{pk}_{\mathsf{at}}$, the message m, the signers set S and the partial signatures $\{\delta_j\}_{j\in S}$, this algorithm combines the signatures as follows:
  1. For each $j \in S$, compute the challenge $c_j := \mathsf{H}_0(\mathbf{t}_j, com, m, \mathsf{pk}_{\mathsf{at}})$, reconstruct $\mathbf{w}_j := \bar{\mathbf{A}}\mathbf{z}_j - c_j\mathbf{t}_j$ and verify if $\|\mathbf{z}_j\| \leqslant B, \mathsf{Open}(\mathsf{ck}, com_j, \mathbf{w}_j, \mathbf{r}_j) = 1$, otherwise, output *abort*.
  2. Compute $\mathbf{z} := \sum_{j\in S} \mathbf{z}_j$ and $\mathbf{r} := \sum_{j\in S} \mathbf{r}_j$, and output $\sigma := (com, \mathbf{z}, \mathbf{r}, S)$.
- $\mathsf{Vf}(\mathsf{pk}_{\mathsf{at}}, m, S, \sigma)$: On inputs a signature $\sigma = (com, \mathbf{z}, \mathbf{r}, S)$, a message m, the public key $\mathsf{pk}_{\mathsf{at}}$ and the signers set S, output a bit b as follows:
  1. Output $b = 0$ if $|S| \neq t$.
  2. For each $j \in S$, derive the challenge $c_j := \mathsf{H}(\mathbf{t}_j, com, m, \mathsf{pk}_{\mathsf{at}})$ and reconstruct $\mathbf{w} := \bar{\mathbf{A}}\mathbf{z} - \sum_j c_j\mathbf{t}_j$.
  3. Output $b = 1$, if $\|\mathbf{z}\| \leqslant B_t, \mathsf{Open}(\mathsf{ck}, com, \mathbf{w}, \mathbf{r}) = 1$, otherwise, output $b = 0$.
- $\mathsf{Trace}(\mathsf{pk}_{\mathsf{at}}, m, \sigma)$: Run $\mathsf{Vf}(\mathsf{pk}_{\mathsf{at}}, m, \sigma)$ and output S if σ is valid; otherwise, output fail.

Lemma 6. *The above ATS is secure (unforgeable and accountable), assuming that the commitment scheme is hiding and binding and* $\mathsf{MSIS}_{k,\ell+1,\beta}$ *and* $\mathsf{MLWE}_{k,\ell,S_x}$ *are hard, where* $\beta = 2\sqrt{B_t^2 + (\eta d)^2}$.

We omit the proof since it naturally follows the proof of unforgeability in [17].

3.3 Our Lattice-Based TAPS Scheme

With such an ATS scheme, we now describe our lattice-based TAPS scheme, using a digital signature scheme $\mathsf{SIG} = (\mathsf{KGen}, \mathsf{Sign}, \mathsf{Vf})$, a symmetric encryption scheme $\mathsf{SKE} = (\mathsf{KGen}, \mathsf{Enc}, \mathsf{Dec})$ and a verifiable encryption scheme $\mathsf{VE} = (\mathsf{KGen}, \mathsf{Enc}, \mathsf{Dec})$ (which are all instantiated via lattice-based constructions above).

- $\mathsf{KGen}(1^\lambda, N, \mathsf{t})$: On inputs the secure parameter λ, the number of parties N and the threshold t, the algorithm works as follows:
  1. Run $\mathsf{ATS.KGen}(1^\lambda)$ and obtain key pairs $(\mathsf{pk}_{\mathsf{at}}, \mathsf{sk}_1, \ldots, \mathsf{sk}_N)$.
  2. Run $\mathsf{SKE.KGen}(1^\lambda)$ to obtain the secret key $\mathsf{sk}_{\mathsf{se}}$ and encrypt t with $\mathsf{ct}_{\mathsf{se}} := \mathsf{SKE.Enc}(\mathsf{sk}_{\mathsf{se}}, \mathsf{t})$.
  3. Run $\mathsf{VE.KGen}(1^\lambda)$ to obtain the encryption key pairs $(\mathsf{pk}_{\mathsf{pe}}, \mathsf{sk}_{\mathsf{pe}})$.
  4. Run $\mathsf{SIG.KGen}(1^\lambda)$ to obtain the key pairs $(\mathsf{pk}_{\mathsf{sig}}, \mathsf{sk}_{\mathsf{sig}})$.
  5. Output the public key $\mathsf{pk} := (\mathsf{pk}_{\mathsf{at}}, \mathsf{pk}_{\mathsf{pe}}, \mathsf{pk}_{\mathsf{sig}}, \mathsf{ct}_{\mathsf{se}})$, the combiner's secret key $\mathsf{sk}_{\mathsf{c}} := (\mathsf{sk}_{\mathsf{sig}}, \mathsf{t}, \mathsf{sk}_{\mathsf{se}})$, the tracing secret key $\mathsf{sk}_{\mathsf{t}} := (\mathsf{sk}_{\mathsf{pe}}, \mathsf{t})$ and the signers' secret key $(\mathsf{sk}_1, \ldots, \mathsf{sk}_N)$.
- $\mathsf{Sign}(\mathsf{sk}_i, m, S)$: The signing algorithm invokes $\mathsf{ATS.Sign}(\mathsf{sk}_i, m)$ and outputs $\delta_i' = (com_i', \mathbf{z}_i', \mathbf{r}_i')$ for all $i \in S$.

- $\mathsf{Combine}(\mathsf{sk_c}, m, S, \{\delta_i\}_{i\in S})$: On inputs the combiner's secret key $\mathsf{sk_c}$, the message m, the signers set S and the partial signatures $\{\delta_i'\}_{i\in S}$, the algorithm does the following:
  1. Run $\mathsf{ATS.Combine}$ and obtain $\sigma' = (com', \mathbf{z}', \mathbf{r}')$.
  2. Set $\vec{v} = (v_1, \ldots, v_N) \in \{0,1\}^N$, such that $v_i = 1$ iff. $i \in S$.
  3. Encrypt $\vec{v}$ and obtain the ciphertext $\mathsf{ct_{pe}} := \mathsf{VE.Enc}(\mathsf{pk_{pe}}, \vec{v})$.
  4. Generate a zero-knowledge argument π for relation R_s.
  5. $tg := \mathsf{SIG.Sign}(\mathsf{sk_{sig}}, (m, com', \mathsf{ct_{pe}}, \pi))$.
  6. Output the signature $\sigma := (com', \mathsf{ct_{pe}}, \pi, tg)$.
- $\mathsf{Vf}(\mathsf{pk}, m, \sigma)$: Parse $\sigma := (com', \mathsf{ct_{pe}}, \pi, tg)$, $\mathsf{pk} := (\mathsf{pk_{at}}, \mathsf{pk_{pe}}, \mathsf{pk_{sig}}, \mathsf{ct_{se}})$. Output $b = 1$ iff. the following conditions are satisfied.
  1. $\mathsf{SIG.Vf}(\mathsf{pk_{sig}}, (m, com', \mathsf{ct_{pe}}, \pi), tg) = 1$.
  2. π is valid for the relation R_s.
- $\mathsf{Trace}(\mathsf{pk}, \mathsf{sk_t}, m, \sigma)$: On inputs the public key pk, the tracing key $\mathsf{sk_t}$, the message m and the signature σ, the algorithm works as follows:
  1. Abort if $\mathsf{Vf}(\mathsf{pk}, m, \sigma) = 0$.
  2. Parse $\sigma := (com', \mathsf{ct_{pe}}, \pi, tg)$ and decrypt $\mathsf{ct_{pe}}$ to obtain $\vec{v} := \mathsf{VE.Dec}(\mathsf{sk_{pe}})$.
  3. Output a set $S \subset [N]$ such that $v_i = 1$ iff. $i \in S$. If S does not exist, output fail.

We describe the relation R_s used in $\mathsf{TAPS.Combine}$ as follows and instantiate the proof in Sect. 4.

$$\mathsf{R}_s = \left\{ \begin{array}{l} ((\mathsf{pk_{at}}, \mathsf{pk_{pe}}, \mathsf{pk_{sig}}, \mathsf{ct_{se}}), m, com', \mathsf{ct_{pe}}); \\ (\mathsf{t}, \mathsf{sk_{se}}, \vec{v}, \sigma') \end{array} : \begin{array}{l} \mathsf{ATS.Vf}(\mathsf{pk_{at}}, m, \sigma') = 1 \\ \mathsf{ct_{pe}} = \mathsf{VE.Enc}(\mathsf{pk_{pe}}, \vec{v}), \\ \vec{v} \in \{0,1\}^N, \\ \mathsf{ct}_{se} = \mathsf{SKE.Enc}(\mathsf{sk_{se}}, \mathsf{t}) \end{array} \right\} \quad (3)$$

Security. The security of our TAPS scheme is based on the following lemmas.

Lemma 7 (Unforgeable and Accountable). *The scheme* TAPS *in Sect. 3.3 is* unforgeable and accountable, *assuming that the accountable threshold signature scheme* ATS *is secure, and the non-interactive argument for relation* R_s *is extractable.*

Proof (sketch). Suppose there exists an adversary that breaks the *unforgeable and accountable* game. The adversary is required to output a valid signature after interactions with the challenger. We can rewind the adversary to obtain the witness of the NIZK argument, which includes the threshold t, the signers' identities, and a valid ATS signature. Hence, this adversary either breaks the unforgeability of the underlying ATS, or the soundness of NIZK.

Lemma 8 (Private against the Public). *The scheme* TAPS *in Sect. 3.3 is* private against the public, *assuming that the accountable threshold signature scheme* ATS *is secure, the non-interactive argument for relation* R_s *is zero-knowledge, and the signature scheme* SIG *is strongly unforgeable.*

Proof (sketch). We need to show that this signature scheme is private against the public. Namely, the signature produced by ATS.Combine will not leak the threshold t and the identities of the signers (*e.g.*, the vector $\vec{v}$). In the security reduction, we gradually replace the zero-knowledge proof with the simulator's answer, the encryption key with a random string, and the ciphertext of the VE with a random ciphertext. In the end, the challenge signature will no longer contain the above secret information. Therefore, we conclude that the signature scheme is private against the public.

Lemma 9 (Private against Signers). *The scheme* TAPS *in Sect. 3.3 is* private against signers, *assuming that the accountable threshold signature scheme* ATS *is secure, the non-interactive argument for relation* R_s *is zero-knowledge, and the signature scheme* SIG *is strongly unforgeable.*

Note that the partial signature δ will not reveal the signer's information. We omit the proof of Lemma 9 as it is mostly the same as the proof of privacy against the public.

4 The Underlying Zero-Knowledge Argument

In this section, we discuss the underlying zero-knowledge argument used in the TAPS scheme of Sect. 3.3.

4.1 Basic Relation

As shown in the basic relation R_s (Eq. (3)), we prove the following items:

- ATS signature σ' is verified: $\mathsf{ATS.Vf}(\mathsf{pk}_{\mathsf{at}}, m, \sigma') = 1$.
- $\mathsf{ct}_{\mathsf{pe}}$ is correctly computed: $\mathsf{ct}_{\mathsf{pe}} = \mathsf{VE.Enc}(\mathsf{pk}_{\mathsf{pe}}, \vec{v})$.
- $\vec{v}$ is the expression of the set S: $\vec{v} \in \{0,1\}^N$.
- $\mathsf{ct}_{\mathsf{se}}$ hides the threshold value t: $\mathsf{ct}_{\mathsf{se}} = \mathsf{SKE.Enc}(\mathsf{sk}_{\mathsf{se}}, \mathsf{t})$.

To prove that the ATS signature $\sigma' = (com, \mathbf{z}', \mathbf{r}')$ can be verified, we have the expression: $|\vec{v}| = \mathsf{t}, \mathbf{z}' \leqslant B_t, \mathbf{w}' = \bar{\mathbf{A}}\mathbf{z}' - \sum_{j\in S} c_j \mathbf{t}_j$ and $\mathsf{Open}(\mathsf{ck}', com', \mathbf{w}', \mathbf{r}') = 1$, where $c_j = \mathsf{H}_0(\mathbf{t}_j, com, m, \mathsf{pk}_{\mathsf{at}})$ and $\mathsf{ck}' = \mathsf{H}_1(m, \mathsf{pk}_{\mathsf{at}})$ is public.

As we want to keep the signers' identities private, we should make full use of the vector $\vec{v}$ to hide the partial keys and the signers' set S. Therefore, we convert $\mathbf{w}' = \bar{\mathbf{A}}\mathbf{z}' - \sum_{j\in S} c_j \mathbf{t}_j$ to

$$\mathbf{w}' = \bar{\mathbf{A}}\mathbf{z}' - \sum_{j\in[N]} c_j \mathbf{t}_j v_j. \tag{4}$$

Since com' reveals nothing about the signing keys or the threshold, we set it as public information. Proving the opening of com' is equivalent to proving:

$$com' = \begin{bmatrix} \mathbf{t}'_A \\ \mathbf{t}'_B \end{bmatrix} = \begin{bmatrix} \mathbf{A}'_2 \\ \mathbf{B}' \end{bmatrix} \mathbf{r}' + \begin{bmatrix} \mathbf{0} \\ \mathbf{w}' \end{bmatrix} \text{ and } \|\mathbf{r}'\| < B_r \tag{5}$$

hold for private vectors $\mathbf{r}' \in \mathcal{R}_q^{m_2'}$ and $\mathbf{w}' \in \mathcal{R}_q^k$, where $(\mathbf{A}_2', \mathbf{B}') = \mathsf{ck}' \in \mathcal{R}_q^{n_1' \times m_2'} \times \mathcal{R}_q^{k \times m_2'}$. By setting B_r and B_t independently, We can hide the threshold t from $\mathbf{r}$ and $\mathbf{z}$.

For the encryptions, we omit the knowledge proof for $\mathsf{ct_{pe}}$ as the verifiable encryption covers it. The ciphertext $\mathsf{ct_{se}}$ can be written as $\vec{b}_{\mathsf{se}} \approx C_{\mathsf{se}}\vec{s}_{\mathsf{se}} + \vec{e}_{\mathsf{se}} + \lfloor \frac{p}{2} \rceil \mathsf{t_{bin}}$, where $\mathsf{t_{bin}} \in \mathbb{Z}_p^{\log t}$ is the binary representation of the threshold value t. Namely, we have $\mathsf{t} = \mathbf{g} \cdot \mathsf{t_{bin}}$ for the gadget vector $\mathbf{g} = [1\ 2\ \cdots\ 2^{2\log t}]$.

After the above discussion, we rewrite the relation R_s as follows,

$$\mathsf{R}_1 = \left\{ \begin{array}{l} ((\mathbf{A}, \mathbf{t}_1, \ldots, \mathbf{t}_N), \mathsf{pk_{pe}}, B_t, \\ B_r, (C_{\mathsf{se}}, \vec{b}_{\mathsf{se}}), m, \mathsf{ct_{pe}}, com'); \\ (\mathsf{t}, \mathsf{t_{bin}}, \vec{s}_{\mathsf{se}}, \vec{v}, \mathbf{z}', \mathbf{r}', \mathbf{w}') \end{array} : \begin{array}{l} \|\vec{v}\|_1 = \mathsf{t},\ \vec{v} \in \{0,1\}^N,\ \|\mathbf{z}'\| \leqslant B_t, \\ \mathbf{w}' = \bar{\mathbf{A}}\mathbf{z}' - \sum_{j \in [N]} c_j \mathbf{t}_j v_j, \\ \mathsf{Open}(\mathsf{ck}', com', \mathbf{w}', \mathbf{r}') = 1,\ \|\mathbf{r}'\| < B_r, \\ \mathsf{ct_{pe}} = \mathsf{VE.Enc}(\mathsf{pk}_{pe}, \vec{v}), \\ \vec{b}_{\mathsf{se}} \approx C_{\mathsf{se}}\vec{s}_{\mathsf{se}} + \lfloor p/2 \rceil \mathsf{t_{bin}},\ \mathsf{t} = \mathbf{g} \cdot \mathsf{t_{bin}} \end{array} \right\}.$$

4.2 Instantiating the Proofs

In this section, we present the proof for relation R_1. Our approach involves committing to the secret vectors and proving an opening of the ABDLOP commitment. To facilitate this, we split R_1 into several linear or quadratic relations. This decomposition allows us to leverage the framework presented in [35] as building blocks. The complete protocol is detailed in Fig. 4.

Commit to Secrets. Denote $\mathbf{R} = (\mathbf{r}_1\|\ldots\|\mathbf{r}_b)$ to be the randomness used in $\mathsf{ct_{pe}}$. The secrets in R_1 include $(\mathsf{t}, \mathsf{t_{bin}}, \vec{s}_{\mathsf{se}}, \vec{v}, \mathbf{R}, \mathbf{z}', \mathbf{r}', \mathbf{w}')$. As we mentioned in Sect. 3.1, we encode $\vec{v}$ to a polynomial vector $\mathbf{u} \in \mathcal{R}_q^b$, and same $\mathbf{s}_{\mathsf{se}}$ for $\vec{s}_{\mathsf{se}}$. Recall that $\mathbf{r}'$ and $\mathbf{w}'$ is committed in com'. Now we can set the short message $\mathbf{m}_1 := (\mathbf{s}_{\mathsf{se}}\|\mathsf{t_{bin}}\|\mathbf{R}\|\mathbf{u}\|\mathbf{z}')$ and obtain the following equation by applying ABDLOP commitment:

$$\begin{bmatrix} t_A \\ t_B \end{bmatrix} = \begin{bmatrix} \mathbf{A}_1 \\ \mathbf{0} \end{bmatrix} \mathbf{m}_1 + \begin{bmatrix} \mathbf{A}_2 \\ \mathbf{b}^\top \end{bmatrix} \mathbf{r} + \begin{bmatrix} \mathbf{0} \\ \mathsf{t} \end{bmatrix}.$$

Linear Relations. We start from Eq. (4). Recall that using $\mathbf{B}_v^{-1}$, $\mathbf{u}$ can be decoded to a polynomial vector $\mathbf{v}$ of length N. We have

$$\bar{\mathbf{A}}\mathbf{z}' - \mathbf{T}\mathbf{B}_v^{-1}\mathbf{u} = \mathbf{w} \tag{6}$$

where $\mathbf{T} = (c_1\mathbf{t}_1, \ldots, c_N\mathbf{t}_N)$. Besides, the equation between the commitment com' and the witness $(\mathbf{r}', \mathbf{w}')$ (as shown in Eq. (5)), and the equation: $\mathsf{t} = \mathbf{g} \cdot \mathsf{t_{bin}}$ are linear relations.

Quadratic Relations. We show that $\vec{v} \in \{0,1\}^N$ and $|\vec{v}| = \mathsf{t}$ can be converted to quadratic relations.

Lemma 10 [35]. *Let* $\mathsf{n} \in \mathbb{N}$ *and* $\vec{a} \in \mathbb{Z}^{\mathsf{n}}$. *If* $\langle \vec{a}, \vec{a} - \mathbf{1}_{\mathsf{n}} \rangle = 0$, *then* $\vec{a} \in \{0,1\}^{\mathsf{n}}$.

Using the above lemma, we obtain $\langle \vec{v}, \vec{v} - \mathbf{1}_N \rangle = 0$ for $\vec{v} \in \{0,1\}^N$. Then we can use the quadratic function as defined in Eq. (1), Namely, the constant coefficient of $F_1 = \mathsf{T}(\mathbf{u}, \mathbf{u} - \mathbf{1}_\mathsf{b})$ equals to 0.

We next discuss about the relation $\|\vec{v}\|_1 = \mathsf{t}$, *i.e.*, the constant coefficient of $\langle \mathbf{u} - \mathbf{1}_\mathsf{b}, \mathbf{u} - \mathbf{1}_\mathsf{b} \rangle$ is t. According to the commitment $t_B = \langle \mathbf{b}, \mathbf{r} \rangle + \mathsf{t}$, we can define the function $F_2(\mathbf{u}, \mathbf{b}, \mathbf{r}) = \mathsf{T}(\mathbf{u} - \mathbf{1}_\mathsf{b}, \mathbf{u} - \mathbf{1}_\mathsf{b}) + \mathsf{T}(\mathbf{b}, \mathbf{r}) - t_B$ and prove its constant coefficient is 0. As t is an integer, *i.e.*, all the coefficients are zeros except for the constant term, we additionally prove that $\langle X^i, \mathsf{t} \rangle = 0$ for $i = 1, \ldots, d-1$. It can be done by defining functions: $\forall 1 \leqslant i \leqslant d-1, G_i(\mathsf{t}) = \mathsf{T}(X^i, \mathsf{t})$.

Shortness in Euclidean Norm. From R_1 we see that $\|\mathbf{z}'\| \leqslant B_t$ and $\|\mathbf{r}'\| < B_r$, where $<$ means that we accept some "slack".

For $\|\mathbf{z}'\| \leqslant B_t$, we apply the technique in [35]. The strategy is to append an additional secret integer x such that $x = B_t^2 - \langle \mathbf{z}', \mathbf{z}' \rangle$ and $x \leqslant B_t^2$. By writing the integer x in binary representation, we can obtain the following relations:

$$\vec{x} \in \{0,1\}^d, \ \langle \mathbf{z}', \mathbf{z}' \rangle + [1 \ 2 \ \cdots \ 2^{2 \log B_t} \ 0 \ \cdots \ 0]\vec{x} = B_t^2 \mod q,$$
$$\vec{x} \text{ is small such that the above holds over } \mathbb{Z}.$$

Similarly, $\vec{x} \in \{0,1\}^d$ is equivalent to the inner-product relation: $\langle \vec{x}, \mathbf{1}_d - \vec{x} \rangle = 0 \bmod q$. The latter is the quadratic relation defined by the following function:

$$F_3(\mathbf{z}', \vec{x}) = \mathsf{T}(\mathbf{z}', \mathbf{z}') + \mathsf{T}(\vec{\rho}, \vec{x}) - B_t^2, \tag{7}$$

where $\vec{\rho} = [1 \ 2 \ \cdots \ 2^{2 \log B_t} \ 0 \ \cdots \ 0] \in \mathbb{Z}_q^d$. The approximate shortness is proved by using rejection sampling and verifying the result is short, which we apply directly in the later protocol (Fig. 4). The well-formedness of the ciphertexts can also be converted to the shortness. As for $\mathsf{ct}_{\mathsf{se}}$, we have

$$\left\| [C_{\mathsf{se}} | I] \begin{bmatrix} \vec{s}_\mathsf{s} \\ \mathsf{t}_{\mathsf{bin}} \end{bmatrix} - \vec{b}_{\mathsf{se}} \right\| \leqslant B_{\mathsf{se}}.$$

Similar to Eq. (7), we define functions F_4 and $\{H_j\}_{j \in [\mathsf{b}]}$ for $\mathsf{ct}_{\mathsf{se}}$ and $\mathsf{ct}_{\mathsf{pe}}$, respectively. Besides, we denote $\mathbf{x}$ to be the concatenation of the additional secrets $\vec{x}$ and define $\mathbf{m}_1 := (\mathbf{m}_1 \| \mathbf{x})$.

Putting All Together. Now we have a few quadratic functions of which we want to prove the constant coefficients are zeros. As shown in [35], we can linear-combine the above equations into one by asking challenges $\gamma_1, \gamma_2, \cdots \leftarrow \mathbb{Z}_q$ and sending $h := g + \sum_{j=1}^{4} \gamma_j F_j + \sum_{j=1}^{d-1} \gamma_{j+4} G_j + \sum_{j=1}^{\mathsf{b}} \gamma_{j+d+3} H_j$, where g is a polynomial with a vanishing constant coefficient used to mask the functions F, G and H. To achieve one-shot soundness, the above computation can be repeated λ times in parallel. Hence, we compute for $i \in [\lambda]$:

$$h_i := g_i + \sum_{j=1}^{4} \gamma_{i,j} F_j + \sum_{j=1}^{d-1} \gamma_{i,j+4} G_j + \sum_{j=1}^{\mathsf{b}} \gamma_{i,j+d+3} H_j. \tag{8}$$

To prove $\mathbf{h} = (h_1, \ldots, h_\lambda)$ is well-formed, the prover instead proves

$$0 = \sum_{i=1}^{\lambda} \mu_i \left(g_i + \sum_{j=1}^{4} \gamma_{i,j} F_j + \sum_{j=1}^{d-1} \gamma_{i,j+4} G_j + \sum_{j=1}^{\mathsf{b}} \gamma_{i,j+d+3} H_j - h_i \right). \quad (9)$$

Let us define: $\mathbf{m}_1 := (\mathsf{s}_{\mathsf{se}} \| \mathsf{t}_{\mathsf{bin}} \| \mathbf{R} \| \mathbf{u} \| \mathbf{z}' \| \mathbf{x}), \mathbf{m}_2 := (\mathbf{w}' \| \mathsf{t} \| \mathbf{w} \| \mathbf{y}_3 \| \mathbf{g})$, $\mathbf{m} := (\mathbf{m}_1 \| \sigma(\mathbf{m}_1) \| \mathbf{m}_2 \| \sigma(\mathbf{m}_2))$, $\mathbf{B} := \begin{bmatrix} \mathbf{B}_y \\ \mathbf{B}_g \end{bmatrix}$, $\mathbf{y} := (\mathbf{y}_1 \| \sigma(\mathbf{y}_1) \| - \mathbf{B}'\mathbf{y}' \| - \sigma(\mathbf{B}'\mathbf{y}') \| - \mathbf{B}\mathbf{y}_2 \| - \sigma(\mathbf{B}\mathbf{y}_2))$, where $\mathbf{w}, \mathbf{y}_1, \mathbf{y}_2, \mathbf{y}_3, \mathbf{y}'$ are used to mask the secrets, $\mathbf{B}_y, \mathbf{B}_g$ are public matrices served as commitment keys.

Now we can combine Eq. (9) and the linear relations: Eq. (6), *com* and $\mathsf{t} = \mathbf{g} \cdot \mathsf{t}_{\mathsf{bin}}$ to obtain a general expression: $\mathbf{m}^\top \mathbf{D}_2 \mathbf{m} + \mathbf{d}_1^\top \mathbf{m} + d_0 = 0$, where $\mathbf{D}_2, \mathbf{d}_1$ and d_0 are the public information.

Security. We discuss the security of the protocol shown in Fig. 4.

Theorem 1. *Let $\gamma_1, \gamma_2, \gamma_3, \gamma > 0$, and $\lambda, \nu \in \mathbb{N}$. Define χ to be a uniform distribution on $\mathcal{S}_\eta$. Fix $\mathsf{s}_1 = \gamma_1 \eta \sqrt{B_1}, \mathsf{s}_2 = \gamma_2 \eta \sqrt{m_2 d}$, $\mathsf{s}_3 = \gamma_3 \omega \sqrt{B_1^2 + B_r^2}$, $\mathsf{s}' = \gamma \eta \sqrt{B_r}$ and $m_1 = N/d(K_2+2)+k+\ell+4$, where B_1 is the maximum norm of $\mathbf{m}_1$. Protocol Π satisfies the following properties:*

For completeness, if $m_1, m_2, m' \geqslant 640/d$, then the honest prover $\mathcal{P}$ convinces the honest verifier $\mathcal{V}$ with probability $\frac{1}{\prod_{i=1}^{3} \exp\left(\frac{14}{\gamma_i} + \frac{1}{2\gamma_i^2}\right) \cdot \exp\left(\frac{14}{\gamma'} + \frac{1}{2\gamma'^2}\right)}$.

The protocol Π is zero-knowledge, assuming that Extended-$\mathsf{MLWE}_{n_1+\lambda+2, m_2, \chi, \mathcal{C}, \mathsf{s}_2}$ and Extended-$\mathsf{MLWE}_{n_1'+k, m_2', \chi, \mathcal{C}, \mathsf{s}'}$ are hard, and Π is extractable, assuming that $\mathsf{MSIS}_{n_1, m_1+m_2, B}$ and $\mathsf{MSIS}_{n_1', m_1', B'}$ are hard.

Completeness. By Lemma 2, the probability that Rej does not abort is at least

$$\frac{1}{\prod_{i=1}^{3} \exp\left(\frac{14}{\gamma_i} + \frac{1}{2\gamma_i^2}\right) \cdot \exp\left(\frac{14}{\gamma} + \frac{1}{2\gamma^2}\right)}.$$

Moreover, by Lemma 3, for $\tau = \sqrt{2}$, and the assumption $m_1, m_2, m' \geqslant 640/d$, the probability that $\|\mathbf{z}_1\| \leqslant \mathsf{s}_1 \sqrt{2 m_1 d}$, $\|\mathbf{z}_2\| \leqslant \mathsf{s}_2 \sqrt{2 m_2 d}$ and $\|\mathbf{z}_3\| \leqslant \mathsf{s}' \sqrt{2 m' d}$ is overwhelming *i.e.*, greater than $1 - 2^{-140}$. The remaining equations hold based on the discussion in Sect. 4.2.

Knowledge Soundness. We discuss the intuition of extractibility. Assume there is a PPT adversary $\mathcal{P}^*$ that has the ability to forge the proof π, then we can construct an extractor $\mathcal{E}$ that either extracts the witness w satisfying the statement x or breaks $\mathsf{MSIS}_{n_1, m_1+m_2, B}$ for $B = 8\eta \sqrt{2\mathsf{s}_1^2 m_1 d + 2\mathsf{s}_2^2 m_2 d}$ and $\mathsf{MSIS}_{n_1', m_1', B'}$ for $B' = 8\eta \mathsf{s}' \sqrt{2 m_1' d}$.

$\mathcal{E}$ runs as follows. Upon receiving the first valid forge $\pi^{(0)} = (\mathbf{t}_A', \mathbf{t}_B', \mathbf{t}_A, t_B, \mathbf{t}_y, \mathbf{t}_g, \mathbf{w}, \mathbf{v}, \vec{z}^{(0)}, \mathbf{h}^{(0)}, t_g^{(0)}, v^{(0)}, \mathbf{z}_1^{(0)}, \mathbf{z}_2^{(0)}, \mathbf{z}_3^{(0)})$ under the challenge

Public information:

$\mathbf{A}_1 \in \mathcal{R}_q^{n_1 \times m_1}, \mathbf{A}_2 \in \mathcal{R}_q^{n_1 \times m_2}, \mathbf{B}_g \in \mathcal{R}_q^{\lambda \times m}, \mathbf{b}_g, \mathbf{b} \in \mathcal{R}_q^{m}, \mathbf{A}'_2 \in \mathcal{R}_q^{n'_1 \times m'_2}, \mathbf{B}' \in \mathcal{R}_q^{k \times m'_2}$,
$\mathbf{m}^\top \mathbf{D}_2 \mathbf{m} + \mathbf{d}_1^\top \mathbf{m} + d_0 = 0$.
Commitments: $com = (\mathbf{t}_A \| t_B)$, and $com' = (\mathbf{t}'_A \| \mathbf{t}'_B)$ as defined in Equ.(5).

Prover		Verifier
Sample $\mathbf{r} \in \chi^{m_2}$ and compute:		
$\begin{bmatrix} \mathbf{t}_A \\ t_B \end{bmatrix} = \begin{bmatrix} \mathbf{A}_1 \\ \mathbf{0} \end{bmatrix} \mathbf{m}_1 + \begin{bmatrix} \mathbf{A}_2 \\ \mathbf{b}^\top \end{bmatrix} \mathbf{r} + \begin{bmatrix} \mathbf{0} \\ \mathbf{t} \end{bmatrix}$.		
$\mathbf{y}_1 \leftarrow D_{\mathsf{s}_1}^{m_1}, \mathbf{y}_2 \leftarrow D_{\mathsf{s}_2}^{m_2}, \mathbf{y}_3 \leftarrow D_{\mathsf{s}_3}^{256/d}$.		
$\mathbf{y}' \leftarrow D_{\mathsf{s}'}^{m'_2}$, $\mathbf{g} \leftarrow \{x \in \mathcal{R}_q : x_0 = 0\}^\lambda$.		
$\mathbf{w} := \mathbf{A}_1\mathbf{y}_1 + \mathbf{A}_2\mathbf{y}_2$, $\mathbf{v} := \mathbf{A}'_2\mathbf{y}'$.		
$\mathbf{t}_y := \mathbf{B}_y\mathbf{r} + \mathbf{y}_3$, $\mathbf{t}_g := \mathbf{B}_g\mathbf{r} + \mathbf{g}$.	$\xrightarrow{\mathbf{t}_A, t_B, \mathbf{t}_y, \mathbf{t}_g, \mathbf{w}, \mathbf{v}}$	
	$\xleftarrow{R}$	$R \leftarrow \{0,1\}^{256 \times (m_1 + m'_2)}$
$\vec{z} = \vec{y_3} + R \begin{bmatrix} \vec{m}_1 \\ \vec{r}' \end{bmatrix}$.		
If $\mathsf{Rej}(\vec{z}, R\vec{m}_1, \mathsf{s}_3)$, $\vec{z} := \perp$.	$\xrightarrow{\vec{z}}$	
	$\xleftarrow{\Gamma}$	If $\vec{z} \neq \perp$, $\Gamma \leftarrow \mathbb{Z}_q^{\lambda \times (d+\mathsf{b}+3)}$
For $i \in [\lambda]$, computes h_i as in Equ.(8).		
	$\xrightarrow{h_1, \ldots, h_\lambda}$	
	$\xleftarrow{\mu_1, \ldots, \mu_\lambda}$	$\mu_1, \ldots, \mu_\lambda \leftarrow \mathcal{R}_q$.
Compute $\mathbf{D}_2, \mathbf{d}_1, d_0$, $\mathbf{B}$ and $\mathbf{y}$.		
$g := \mathbf{m}^\top \mathbf{D}_2 \mathbf{y} + \mathbf{y}^\top \mathbf{D}_2 \mathbf{m} + \mathbf{d}_1^\top \mathbf{y}$.		
$t_g := \mathbf{b}_g^\top \mathbf{r} + g$, $v := \mathbf{y}^\top \mathbf{D}_2 \mathbf{y} + \mathbf{b}^\top \mathbf{y}_2$.	$\xrightarrow{t_g, v}$	
	$\xleftarrow{c}$	$c \leftarrow \mathcal{C}$
$\mathbf{z}_1 := c\mathbf{m}_1 + \mathbf{y}_1$, $\mathbf{z}_2 := c\mathbf{r} + \mathbf{y}_2$,		
$\mathbf{z}_3 := c\mathbf{r}' + \mathbf{y}'$		
If $\mathsf{Rej}(\mathbf{z}_1, c\mathbf{m}_1, \mathsf{s}_1)$ or $\mathsf{Rej}(\mathbf{z}_2, c\mathbf{r}, \mathsf{s}_2)$		
or $\mathsf{Rej}(\mathbf{z}_3, c\mathbf{r}', \mathsf{s}')$, then $\mathbf{z}_1, \mathbf{z}_2, \mathbf{z}_3 := \perp$.	$\xrightarrow{\mathbf{z}_1, \mathbf{z}_2, \mathbf{z}_3}$	Run verification Vf.

Verification Vf:
If $\vec{z} = \perp$ or $\mathbf{z}_i = \perp$, for $i = 1, 2, 3$, return 0.
$\mathbf{z} := (\mathbf{z}_1 \| \sigma(\mathbf{z}_1) \| (c\mathbf{t}'_B - \mathbf{B}\mathbf{z}_3) \| \sigma(c\mathbf{t}'_B - \mathbf{B}\mathbf{z}_3) \| (c\mathbf{t}_B - \mathbf{B}\mathbf{z}_2) \| \sigma(c\mathbf{t}_B - \mathbf{B}\mathbf{z}_2))$.
Accept iff.:

1. $\|\mathbf{z}_1\| \leqslant \mathsf{s}_1\sqrt{2m_1 d}$, $\|\mathbf{z}_2\| \leqslant \mathsf{s}_2\sqrt{2m_2 d}$, $\|\vec{z}\| \leqslant 1.7\sqrt{256}\mathsf{s}_3$, $\|\mathbf{z}_3\| \leqslant \mathsf{s}'\sqrt{2m' d}$,
2. $\mathbf{z}^\top \mathbf{D}_2 \mathbf{z} + c\mathbf{d}_1^\top \mathbf{z} + c^2 d_0 - (ct - \mathbf{b}^\top \mathbf{z}_2) = v$,
3. $\mathbf{A}_1\mathbf{z}_1 + \mathbf{A}_2\mathbf{z}_2 = \mathbf{w} + c\mathbf{t}_A$, $\mathbf{A}'_2\mathbf{z}_3 = \mathbf{v} + c\mathbf{t}'_A$,
4. const. coeff. of $h_1, \ldots, h_\lambda$ are 0s.

Fig. 4. Commit-and-prove protocol Π for relation R_1

value $c^{(0)}$, $\mathcal{E}$ samples challenges to rewind $\mathcal{P}^*$ and obtains another accepted forge $\pi^{(1)} = (\mathbf{t}'_A, \mathbf{t}'_B, \mathbf{t}_A, t_B, \mathbf{t}_y, \mathbf{t}_g, \mathbf{w}, \mathbf{v}, \vec{z}^{(1)}, \mathbf{h}^{(1)}, t^{(1)}, v^{(1)}, \mathbf{z}_1^{(1)}, \mathbf{z}_2^{(1)}, \mathbf{z}_3^{(1)})$.

Define $\bar{c} := c^{(1)} - c^{(0)}$, $\bar{\mathbf{m}}_1 = \frac{\mathbf{z}^{(1)} - \mathbf{z}^{(0)}}{c^{(1)} - c^{(0)}}$, $\bar{\mathbf{r}} = \frac{\mathbf{z}_2^{(1)} - \mathbf{z}_2^{(0)}}{c^{(1)} - c^{(0)}}$, $\bar{\mathbf{r}}' = \frac{\mathbf{z}_3^{(1)} - \mathbf{z}_3^{(0)}}{c^{(1)} - c^{(0)}}$. As both forges are verified, we have $\bar{\mathbf{m}}_1 \leqslant 2\mathsf{s}_1\sqrt{2m_1 d}$, $\bar{\mathbf{r}} \leqslant 2\mathsf{s}_2\sqrt{2m_2 d}$ and $\bar{\mathbf{r}}' \leqslant 2\mathsf{s}'\sqrt{2m' d}$. Further, we have $\mathbf{A}_1\bar{\mathbf{m}}_1 + \mathbf{A}_2\bar{\mathbf{r}} = \mathbf{t}_A$ and $\mathbf{A}_2\bar{\mathbf{r}}' = \mathbf{t}'_A$. We extract $\bar{\mathrm{t}}, \bar{\mathbf{y}_3}, \bar{\mathbf{g}}, \bar{g}, \mathbf{w}'$ by

$$\begin{bmatrix} \bar{\mathbf{t}} \\ \bar{\mathbf{y}}_3 \\ \bar{\mathbf{g}} \end{bmatrix} = \begin{bmatrix} t_B \\ \mathbf{t}_y \\ \mathbf{t}_g \end{bmatrix} - \begin{bmatrix} \mathbf{b} \\ \mathbf{B}_y \\ \mathbf{B}_g \end{bmatrix} \bar{\mathbf{r}}, \text{and } \bar{\mathbf{w}}' = \mathbf{t}'_B - \mathbf{B}'\bar{\mathbf{r}}'.$$

Let $\bar{\mathbf{y}}_1 := \mathbf{z}^{(1)} - c^{(1)}\bar{\mathbf{m}}_1 = \mathbf{z}^{(0)} - c^{(0)}\bar{\mathbf{m}}_1$, $\bar{\mathbf{y}}_2 := \mathbf{z}_2^{(1)} - c^{(1)}\bar{\mathbf{r}} = \mathbf{z}^{(0)} - c^{(0)}\bar{\mathbf{r}}$ and $\bar{\mathbf{y}}' := \mathbf{z}_2^{(1)} - c^{(1)}\bar{\mathbf{r}}' = \mathbf{z}^{(0)} - c^{(0)}\bar{\mathbf{r}}'$. We can extract $\bar{\mathbf{y}}, \bar{\mathbf{m}}, \bar{g}, \bar{z}$ and $\bar{v}$ accordingly.

Now the extractor extracts another tuple $(\tilde{\mathbf{m}}_1, \tilde{\mathbf{r}}, \tilde{\mathbf{r}}', \tilde{c})$ by rewinding $\mathcal{P}^*$. If $(\tilde{\mathbf{m}}_1, \tilde{\mathbf{r}}, \tilde{\mathbf{r}}') \neq (\bar{\mathbf{m}}_1, \bar{\mathbf{r}}, \bar{\mathbf{r}}')$, we have $\mathbf{A}_1\bar{\mathbf{m}}_1 + \mathbf{A}_2\bar{\mathbf{r}} = \mathbf{t}_A = \mathbf{A}_1\tilde{\mathbf{m}}_1 + \mathbf{A}_2\tilde{\mathbf{r}}$ and $\mathbf{A}'_2\bar{\mathbf{r}}' = \mathbf{t}'_A = \mathbf{A}'_2\tilde{\mathbf{r}}'$, which break the binding of the commitments. In this way $\mathcal{E}$ can extract MSIS solutions $(\bar{c}\tilde{\mathbf{z}}_1 - \tilde{c}\bar{\mathbf{z}}_1, \bar{c}\tilde{\mathbf{z}}_2 - \tilde{c}\bar{\mathbf{z}}_2) \leqslant 8\eta\sqrt{2\mathsf{s}_1^2 m_1 d + 2\mathsf{s}_2^2 m_2 d}$ and $(\bar{c}\tilde{\mathbf{z}}' - \tilde{c}\bar{\mathbf{z}}') \leqslant 8\eta\mathsf{s}'\sqrt{2m'd}$ for the matrix $[\mathbf{A}_1\ \mathbf{A}_2] \in \mathcal{R}_q^{n_1\times(m_1+m_2)}$ and $\mathbf{A}'_1 \in \mathcal{R}_q^{n'_1\times m'_1}$.

Simulatability. We discuss the sketch of simulatability. Our goal is to show that: there exists a simulator $\mathcal{S}$ (without access to private information) that can output simulated commitments $(\mathbf{t}_A, \mathbf{t}_B)$ and $(\mathbf{t}'_A, \mathbf{t}'_B)$, along with a non-aborting transcript of the protocol between the prover $\mathcal{P}$ and the verifier $\mathcal{V}$. For every $\mathcal{A}$, $\mathcal{S}$ has an advantage ε in distinguishing the simulated transcript from the real transcript. Whenever the prover $\mathcal{P}$ does not abort, there exists another algorithm $\mathcal{A}'$ that has advantage ε in distinguishing *Extended*-$\mathsf{MLWE}_{n_1+256/d+\lambda+2,m_2,\chi,\mathcal{C},\mathsf{s}_2}$ and *Extended*-$\mathsf{MLWE}_{n'_1+k,m'_2,\chi,\mathcal{C},\mathsf{s}'}$, using almost the same running time.

$\mathcal{S}$ runs as follows. Firstly, $\mathcal{S}$ samples the challenge $c \leftarrow \mathcal{C}$ and $\mathbf{z}_1 \leftarrow D_{\mathsf{s}_1}^{m_1}, \mathbf{z}_2 \leftarrow D_{\mathsf{s}_2}^{m_2}, \mathbf{z}_3 \leftarrow D_{\mathsf{s}'}^{m'_1}$ and sets $\mathbf{z}_i :=\perp$ according to rejection sampling lemma. Then, it defines $\mathbf{w} = \mathbf{A}_1\mathbf{z}_1 + \mathbf{A}_2\mathbf{z}_2 - c\mathbf{t}_A$, and $\mathbf{v} = \mathbf{A}'_2\mathbf{z}_3 - c\mathbf{t}'_A$. Further, $\mathcal{S}$ computes $\mathbf{z}$ and $v = \mathbf{z}^\top\mathbf{D}_2\mathbf{z} + c\mathbf{d}_1^\top\mathbf{z} + c^2 d_0 - (ct - \mathbf{b}^\top\mathbf{z}_2)$. As for the commitment, $\mathcal{S}$ samples $\mathbf{u} \leftarrow \mathcal{R}_q^{n_1+256/d+\lambda+2}, \mathbf{u}' \leftarrow \mathcal{R}_q^{n'_1+k}$ and computes

$$\begin{bmatrix} \mathbf{t}_A \\ t_B \\ \mathbf{t}_y \\ \mathbf{t}_g \\ t_g \end{bmatrix} = \mathbf{u} + \begin{bmatrix} \mathbf{A}_1\mathbf{m}_1 \\ \mathbf{t} \\ \mathbf{y}_3 \\ \mathbf{g} \\ g \end{bmatrix}, \text{and } \begin{bmatrix} \mathbf{t}'_A \\ \mathbf{t}'_B \end{bmatrix} = \mathbf{u}' + \begin{bmatrix} 0 \\ \mathbf{w}' \end{bmatrix},$$

which are equivalent to sample $\mathbf{t}_A, t_B, \mathbf{t}_y, \mathbf{t}_g, t_g \leftarrow \mathcal{R}_q^{n_1+256/d+\lambda+2}$ and $\mathbf{t}'_A, \mathbf{t}'_B \leftarrow \mathcal{R}_q^{n'_1+k}$ uniformly at random. If the adversary $\mathcal{A}$ can distinguish the above commitments from the real ones, $\mathcal{S}$ can distinguish *Extended*-$\mathsf{MLWE}_{n_1+256/d+\lambda+2,m_2,\chi,\mathcal{C},\mathsf{s}_2}$ and *Extended*-$\mathsf{MLWE}_{n'_1+k,m'_2,\chi,\mathcal{C},\mathsf{s}'}$ by calling $\mathcal{A}$ as a subroutine. At last, $\mathcal{S}$ samples $\vec{z} \leftarrow D_{\mathsf{s}_3}^{256}$ and sets $\vec{z} :=\perp$ according to rejection sampling. So far, the simulator $\mathcal{S}$ simulates the transcript of the protocol.

4.3 The Underlying t-out-of-N Proof in Our Construction

We discuss briefly how to achieve a t-out-of-N membership proof by applying [35], where a prover proves the knowledge of t signing keys without leaking the corresponding identities. This proof is implicit in our construction described above: the following basic relation is similar to the proof in Sect. 4.2 except removing the ciphertext, as in a standard t-out-of-N membership proof, we do not hide the threshold value t.

$$\mathsf{R}_{\mathsf{t},N} = \left\{ \begin{array}{l} ((\mathbf{A}, \mathbf{t}_1, \ldots, \mathbf{t}_N), \mathsf{t}) \\ (\{\mathbf{x}_j\}_{j\in S}, S, \vec{v}) \end{array} : \begin{array}{c} \|\vec{v}\|_1 = \mathsf{t},\ \vec{v} \in \{0,1\}^N, \\ \sum_{j\in[S]} \mathbf{A}\mathbf{x}_j = \sum_{j\in[N]} \mathbf{t}_j v_j \end{array} \right\}.$$

According to the above discussion, we write $\sum_{j\in[S]} \mathbf{A}\mathbf{x}_j = \sum_{j\in[N]} \mathbf{t}_j v_j$ as the linear relation: $\sum_{j\in[S]} \mathbf{A}\mathbf{x}_j - \mathbf{T}'\mathbf{B}_{\vec{v}}^{-1}\mathbf{u} = 0$, where $\mathbf{T}' = [\mathbf{t}_1, \ldots, \mathbf{t}_N]$ is public.

5 Parameters and Sizes

Parameters. We select the parameters to ensure that (1) the security of hard problems, such as MSIS or MLWE, hold in each primitive; (2) the soundness and zero-knowledge properties of the proof hold. For the MSIS or MLWE problem, our approach includes choosing the modulus, determining dimensions, and selecting standard deviations of Gaussian distributions. For the proof, it is important to guarantee security and a sufficiently large challenge space for a negligible soundness error. Our concrete parameters target more than 128-bit security [20].

Specifically, we choose the parallel repetition time $\lambda = 12$, the degree of polynomials $d = 128$ and the modulus q such that $q^{-\lambda}$ and $q^{-d/2}$ are negligible, *i.e.*, less than 2^{-128}. We set the encryption modulus p_i and dimensions M_i, K_i to ensure the security of symmetric key encryption (SKE) and verifiable encryption (VE). For SKE, we set $p_1 = 3313$ and $M_1 = 128, K_1 = 512$. For VE, we choose $p_2 = 3313$ and $M_2 = 4, K_2 = 6$, similar to Kyber512. Here we set that p_2 and q_1 divide q such that we do not need to do an approximate range proof(*e.g.*, $q = 660061 \times 3313 \times 251 \approx 2^{39}$).

Now, we determine the rejection sampling constants for the ATS signatures and the zero-knowledge proof. For efficiency, we set the repetition time to be 8. There are 4 (resp. t) rejection sampling algorithms in the protocol Π_{R_1} (resp. the ATS signature scheme). In the zero-knowledge proof, like [35], we apply bimodal rejection sampling [19] and thus the repetition rate in Π_{R_1} is at least

$$2\exp\left(\frac{14}{\gamma_1} + \frac{1}{2\gamma_1^2} + \frac{1}{2\gamma_2^2} + \frac{1}{2\gamma_3^2} + \frac{1}{2\gamma^2}\right).$$

Concerning the ATS signature, the repetition rate is at least $2\exp\left(\frac{14\mathsf{t}}{\gamma_s} + \frac{\mathsf{t}}{2\gamma_s^2}\right)$. We set γ_s for different t. Consequently, as the threshold value t increases, to maintain the same repetition rate and security, γ_s should also increase accordingly. This adjustment increases the ATS system modulus q_1 or the dimensions k and ℓ. The detailed parameters for the TAPS scheme are provided in Table 2.

Table 2. Parameters for ATS, SKE, PKE, and the proof system under different t.

ATS			SKE			Proof Parameters					Differ from t		
q_1	ℓ	k	p_1	M_1	K_1	d	η	n_1	m_2	n_1'	t	$\lvert\mathbf{x}\rvert_\infty$	γ_s
660061	6	5	3313	128	768	128	27	11	10	4	4	12	39
PKE				Proof Parameters							8	4	78
p_2	M_2	K_2	ν	m_1'	m_2'	λ	γ_1	γ_2	γ_3	γ	16	2	155
3313	4	6	3	6	5	12	9.1	6	6	9	–		

Table 3. Signature sizes under different threshold value t and number of parties N.

(t, N)	$(4, 2^5)$	$(8, 2^9)$	$(16, 2^{10})$	$(16, 2^{11})$
Modulus, q	$\approx 2^{39}$	$\approx 2^{41}$	$\approx 2^{43}$	$\approx 2^{44}$
Sig. Size (in KB)	42.34	57.03	76.13	113.54

Signature Size. The signature consists of a commitment com', a ciphertext $\mathsf{ct}_{\mathsf{pe}}$, a proof π, and a digital signature tg. The commitment com' is a length $n_1' + k$ vector over $\mathcal{R}_q$ that takes $(n_1' + k)d\lceil \log q \rceil$ bits. The ciphertext $\mathsf{ct}_{\mathsf{pe}}$ consists of b vectors of length M_2+1 over $\mathcal{R}_p$ and takes $N(M_2+1)\lceil \log p \rceil$ bits. We instantiate the digital signature as Dilithium and the signature size refers to [21]. As for the proof Π, we follow the general strategy provided in [35] to calculate its size.

We present the signature size for various N equals to 2^5, 2^9, 2^{10} and 2^{11} in Table 3. The size is comparable with other privacy-preserving signatures [14].

6 Conclusion and Future Work

We construct the first lattice-based TAPS scheme. Our construction employs the recent compact techniques from [35] and hence the signature size is small enough for practical applications such as Bitcoin multi-sig transactions and other privacy-preserving protocols. Along the way, we build the first lattice-based t-out-of-N membership proof and the first lattice-based ATS, which may also be of independent interest. For future work, we outline the following directions:

Bulletproof. In [9], the authors used bulletproof to optimize the proof size. However, in this paper, the lattice-based proof is linear in the size of the witness. This linearity arises from the fact that, in verifiable encryption (VE), the proof of knowledge is linear in the length of the plaintext, i.e., N.

Note that a recent paper, titled *LaBRADOR* [6], introduces a sublinear proof system for Rank-1 Constraint Systems (R1CS) from lattice-based cryptography. We believe that by applying its techniques, it may be possible to achieve sublinear proof sizes in the context of TAPS.

Beyond Static Unforgeability. Recently, Crites *et al.*, [16] proposed a Schnorr threshold signature with a stronger security notion that allows the adversary to adaptively corrupt parties and learn their state. We believe that it would also be an interesting and practical research question to generalize TAPS or the underlying ATS signatures to adaptive security in post-quantum settings.

Acknowledgements. We thank Baishun Sun and Ziyu Li for their help (in parameter selection). We are grateful for the feedback and suggestions from CT-RSA shepherd and anonymous reviewers. This work is supported by the National Natural Science Foundation of China (Grant No. 62002288, 62272362) and the National Key R&D Program of China (Grant No. 2023YFB4403500).

References

1. Ajtai, M.: Generating hard instances of lattice problems (extended abstract). In: ACM Symposium on the Theory of Computing (1996)
2. Alamélou, Q., Blazy, O., Cauchie, S., Gaborit, P.: A code-based group signature scheme. Des. Codes Cryptogr. **82**(1–2), 469–493 (2017)
3. Bagherzandi, A., Cheon, J.H., Jarecki, S.: Multisignatures secure under the discrete logarithm assumption and a generalized forking lemma. In: ACM CCS (2008)
4. Banaszczyk, W.: New bounds in some transference theorems in the geometry of numbers. Math. Ann. **296**, 625–635 (1993)
5. Baum, C., Damgård, I., Lyubashevsky, V., Oechsner, S., Peikert, C.: More efficient commitments from structured lattice assumptions. In: Catalano, D., De Prisco, R. (eds.) SCN 2018. LNSC, vol. 11035, pp. 368–385. Springer, Cham (2018). https://doi.org/10.1007/978-3-319-98113-0_20
6. Beullens, W., Seiler, G.: LaBRADOR: compact proofs for R1CS from module-SIS. In: Handschuh, H., Lysyanskaya, A. (eds.) CRYPTO 2023. LNCS, vol. 14085, pp. 518–548. Springer, Cham (2023). https://doi.org/10.1007/978-3-031-38554-4_17
7. Blazy, O., Gaborit, P., Mac, D.T.: A rank metric code-based group signature scheme. In: Wachter-Zeh, A., Bartz, H., Liva, G. (eds.) CBCrypto 2021. LNCS, vol. 13150, pp. 1–21. Springer, Cham (2021). https://doi.org/10.1007/978-3-030-98365-9_1
8. Boldyreva, A.: Threshold signatures, multisignatures and blind signatures based on the gap-Diffie-Hellman-group signature scheme. In: Desmedt, Y.G. (ed.) PKC 2003. LNCS, vol. 2567, pp. 31–46. Springer, Heidelberg (2003). https://doi.org/10.1007/3-540-36288-6_3
9. Boneh, D., Komlo, C.: Threshold signatures with private accountability. In: Dodis, Y., Shrimpton, T. (eds.) CRYPTO 2022. LNCS, vol. 13510, pp. 551–581. Springer, Cham (2022). https://doi.org/10.1007/978-3-031-15985-5_19
10. Boneh, D., Lynn, B., Shacham, H.: Short signatures from the Weil Pairing. In: Boyd, C. (ed.) ASIACRYPT 2001. LNCS, vol. 2248, pp. 514–532. Springer, Heidelberg (2001). https://doi.org/10.1007/3-540-45682-1_30
11. Bresson, E., Stern, J., Szydlo, M.: Threshold ring signatures and applications to ad-hoc groups. In: Yung, M. (ed.) CRYPTO 2002. LNCS, vol. 2442, pp. 465–480. Springer, Heidelberg (2002). https://doi.org/10.1007/3-540-45708-9_30
12. Camenisch, J., Drijvers, M., Lehmann, A., Neven, G., Towa, P.: Short threshold dynamic group signatures. In: Galdi, C., Kolesnikov, V. (eds.) SCN 2020. LNCS, vol. 12238, pp. 401–423. Springer, Cham (2020). https://doi.org/10.1007/978-3-030-57990-6_20

13. Cayrel, P.L., Lindner, R., Rückert, M., Silva, R.: A lattice-based threshold ring signature scheme. In: Abdalla, M., Barreto, P.S.L.M. (eds.) LATINCRYPT 2010. LNCS, vol. 6212, pp. 255–272. Springer, Heidelberg (2010). https://doi.org/10.1007/978-3-642-14712-8_16
14. Chator, A., Green, M., Tiwari, P.R.: SoK: privacy-preserving signatures. IACR Cryptology ePrint Archive (2023)
15. Chaum, D., van Heyst, E.: Group signatures. In: Davies, D.W. (ed.) EUROCRYPT 1991. LNCS, vol. 547, pp. 257–265. Springer, Heidelberg (1991). https://doi.org/10.1007/3-540-46416-6_22
16. Crites, E., Komlo, C., Maller, M.: Fully adaptive schnorr threshold signatures. In: Handschuh, H., Lysyanskaya, A. (eds.) CRYPTO 2023. LNCS, vol. 14081, pp. 678–709. Springer, Cham (2023). https://doi.org/10.1007/978-3-031-38557-5_22
17. Damgård, I., Orlandi, C., Takahashi, A., Tibouchi, M.: Two-round n-out-of-n and multi-signatures and trapdoor commitment from lattices. J. Cryptol. **35**, 14 (2022)
18. Desmedt, Y.: Threshold cryptography. Eur. Trans. Telecommun. **5**(4), 449–458 (1994)
19. Ducas, L., Durmus, A., Lepoint, T., Lyubashevsky, V.: Lattice signatures and bimodal Gaussians. In: Canetti, R., Garay, J.A. (eds.) CRYPTO 2013. LNCS, vol. 8042, pp. 40–56. Springer, Heidelberg (2013). https://doi.org/10.1007/978-3-642-40041-4_3
20. Ducas, L., Espitau, T., Postlethwaite, E.W.: Finding short integer solutions when the modulus is small. In: Handschuh, H., Lysyanskaya, A. (eds.) CRYPTO 2023. LNCS, vol. 14083, pp. 150–176. Springer, Cham (2023). https://doi.org/10.1007/978-3-031-38548-3_6
21. Ducas, L., et al.: CRYSTALs-Dilithium: a lattice-based digital signature scheme. IACR Trans. Cryptogr. Hardw. Embed. Syst. **2018**(1), 238–268 (2018)
22. Esgin, M.F., Steinfeld, R., Sakzad, A., Liu, J.K., Liu, D.: Short lattice-based one-out-of-many proofs and applications to ring signatures. In: Deng, R.H., Gauthier-Umaña, V., Ochoa, M., Yung, M. (eds.) ACNS 2019. LNCS, vol. 11464, pp. 67–88. Springer, Cham (2019). https://doi.org/10.1007/978-3-030-21568-2_4
23. Goldwasser, S., Kalai, Y.T., Peikert, C., Vaikuntanathan, V.: Robustness of the learning with errors assumption. In: Innovations in Computer Science - ICS 2010 (2010)
24. Gordon, S.D., Katz, J., Vaikuntanathan, V.: A group signature scheme from lattice assumptions. IACR Cryptology ePrint Archive (2011)
25. Kiltz, E., Lyubashevsky, V., Schaffner, C.: A concrete treatment of Fiat-Shamir signatures in the quantum random-oracle model. In: Nielsen, J.B., Rijmen, V. (eds.) EUROCRYPT 2018. LNCS, vol. 10822, pp. 552–586. Springer, Cham (2018). https://doi.org/10.1007/978-3-319-78372-7_18
26. Komlo, C., Goldberg, I.: FROST: flexible round-optimized schnorr threshold signatures. In: Dunkelman, O., Jacobson, Jr., M.J., O'Flynn, C. (eds.) SAC 2020. LNCS, vol. 12804, pp. 34–65. Springer, Cham (2021). https://doi.org/10.1007/978-3-030-81652-0_2
27. Krenn, S., Slamanig, D., Striecks, C.: Logarithmic-size (linkable) threshold ring signatures in the plain model. In: Hanaoka, G., Shikata, J., Watanabe, Y. (eds.) PKC 2022. LNCS, vol. 13178, pp. 437–467. Springer, Cham (2022). https://doi.org/10.1007/978-3-030-97131-1_15
28. Laguillaumie, F., Langlois, A., Libert, B., Stehlé, D.: Lattice-based group signatures with logarithmic signature size. In: Sako, K., Sarkar, P. (eds.) ASIACRYPT 2013. LNCS, vol. 8270, pp. 41–61. Springer, Heidelberg (2013). https://doi.org/10.1007/978-3-642-42045-0_3

29. Langlois, A., Ling, S., Nguyen, K., Wang, H.: Lattice-based group signature scheme with verifier-local revocation. In: Krawczyk, H. (ed.) PKC 2014. LNCS, vol. 8383, pp. 345–361. Springer, Heidelberg (2014). https://doi.org/10.1007/978-3-642-54631-0_20
30. Langlois, A., Stehlé, D.: Worst-case to average-case reductions for module lattices. Des. Codes Cryptogr. **75**(3), 565–599 (2015)
31. Libert, B., Ling, S., Mouhartem, F., Nguyen, K., Wang, H.: Signature schemes with efficient protocols and dynamic group signatures from lattice assumptions. In: Cheon, J.H., Takagi, T. (eds.) ASIACRYPT 2016. LNCS, vol. 10032, pp. 373–403. Springer, Heidelberg (2016). https://doi.org/10.1007/978-3-662-53890-6_13
32. Lyubashevsky, V.: Fiat-Shamir with aborts: applications to lattice and factoring-based signatures. In: Matsui, M. (ed.) ASIACRYPT 2009. LNCS, vol. 5912, pp. 598–616. Springer, Heidelberg (2009). https://doi.org/10.1007/978-3-642-10366-7_35
33. Lyubashevsky, V.: Lattice signatures without trapdoors. In: Pointcheval, D., Johansson, T. (eds.) EUROCRYPT 2012. LNCS, vol. 7237, pp. 738–755. Springer, Heidelberg (2012). https://doi.org/10.1007/978-3-642-29011-4_43
34. Lyubashevsky, V., Nguyen, N.K.: BLOOM: bimodal lattice one-out-of-many proofs and applications. In: Agrawal, S., Lin, D. (eds.) ASIACRYPT 2022. LNCS, vol. 13794, pp. 95–125. Springer, Cham (2022). https://doi.org/10.1007/978-3-031-22972-5_4
35. Lyubashevsky, V., Nguyen, N.K., Plançon, M.: Lattice-based zero-knowledge proofs and applications: shorter, simpler, and more general. In: Dodis, Y., Shrimpton, T. (eds.) CRYPTO 2022. LNCS, vol. 13508, pp. 71–101. Springer, Cham (2022). https://doi.org/10.1007/978-3-031-15979-4_3
36. Lyubashevsky, V., Nguyen, N.K., Plancon, M., Seiler, G.: Shorter lattice-based group signatures via "almost free" encryption and other optimizations. In: Tibouchi, M., Wang, H. (eds.) ASIACRYPT 2021. LNCS, vol. 13093, pp. 218–248. Springer, Cham (2021). https://doi.org/10.1007/978-3-030-92068-5_8
37. Lyubashevsky, V., Nguyen, N.K., Seiler, G.: Shorter lattice-based zero-knowledge proofs via one-time commitments. In: Garay, J.A. (ed.) PKC 2021. LNCS, vol. 12710, pp. 215–241. Springer, Cham (2021). https://doi.org/10.1007/978-3-030-75245-3_9
38. Lyubashevsky, V., Nguyen, N.K., Seiler, G.: SMILE: set membership from ideal lattices with applications to ring signatures and confidential transactions. In: Malkin, T., Peikert, C. (eds.) CRYPTO 2021. LNCS, vol. 12826, pp. 611–640. Springer, Cham (2021). https://doi.org/10.1007/978-3-030-84245-1_21
39. Micali, S., Ohta, K., Reyzin, L.: Accountable-subgroup multisignatures: extended abstract. In: ACM CCS (2001)
40. Micciancio, D., Peikert, C.: Trapdoors for lattices: simpler, tighter, faster, smaller. In: Pointcheval, D., Johansson, T. (eds.) EUROCRYPT 2012. LNCS, vol. 7237, pp. 700–718. Springer, Heidelberg (2012). https://doi.org/10.1007/978-3-642-29011-4_41
41. Munch-Hansen, A., Orlandi, C., Yakoubov, S.: Stronger notions and a more efficient construction of threshold ring signatures. In: Longa, P., Ràfols, C. (eds.) LATINCRYPT 2021. LNCS, vol. 12912, pp. 363–381. Springer, Cham (2021). https://doi.org/10.1007/978-3-030-88238-9_18
42. Nick, J., Ruffing, T., Seurin, Y.: MuSig2: simple two-round schnorr multi-signatures. In: Malkin, T., Peikert, C. (eds.) CRYPTO 2021. LNCS, vol. 12825, pp. 189–221. Springer, Cham (2021). https://doi.org/10.1007/978-3-030-84242-0_8

43. Regev, O.: On lattices, learning with errors, random linear codes, and cryptography. J. ACM **56**(6), 1–40 (2009)
44. Rivest, R.L., Shamir, A., Tauman, Y.: How to leak a secret. In: Boyd, C. (ed.) ASIACRYPT 2001. LNCS, vol. 2248, pp. 552–565. Springer, Heidelberg (2001). https://doi.org/10.1007/3-540-45682-1_32
45. Shoup, V.: Practical threshold signatures. In: Preneel, B. (ed.) EUROCRYPT 2000. LNCS, vol. 1807, pp. 207–220. Springer, Heidelberg (2000). https://doi.org/10.1007/3-540-45539-6_15

Homomorphic Encryption

TFHE Public-Key Encryption Revisited

Marc Joye(✉)

Zama, Paris, France
marc@zama.ai

Abstract. Fully homomorphic encryption allows directly processing encrypted data without having to decrypt it. The result of the computation is encrypted, typically under the same key. This unique feature offers a strong form of privacy. A service provider can so provide the same service but without ever seeing the user's data. Examples of application include [privacy-preserving] preventive medicine, facial recognition or voice assistants. Fully homomorphic encryption can also be used to solve the privacy issues of the blockchain.

This paper introduces a public-key variant of fully homomorphic encryption scheme TFHE. The output ciphertexts are of LWE type and compatible with TFHE. Interestingly, the public key is much shorter and the resulting ciphertexts are less noisy. The security of the scheme holds under the standard RLWE assumption. Several variations and extensions are also described. The proposed scheme has been integrated in fhEVM, a protocol enabling developers to create encrypted on-chain smart contracts.

Keywords: Fully homomorphic encryption (FHE) · Public-key encryption · Learning with errors (LWE) · Ring LWE (RLWE) · TFHE cryptosystem

1 Introduction

TFHE and its variants (e.g., [4,6]) are natively *private-key* fully homomorphic encryption schemes. The same key is used to encrypt or to decrypt messages. As already demonstrated in [8, § 6.1] (see also [3,12]), certain private-key homomorphic encryption schemes can be turned into a public-key encryption scheme by providing encryptions of zero. A more general result by Rothblum is provided in [17].

FROM PRIVATE-KEY TO PUBLIC-KEY ENCRYPTION. If $[\![\cdot]\!]_{\mathsf{sk}}$ denotes a probabilistic [private-key] homomorphic encryption algorithm, the public encryption key consists of z encryptions of 0; i.e., $\mathsf{pk} = \big(a_1 \leftarrow [\![0]\!]_{\mathsf{sk}}, \dots, a_z \leftarrow [\![0]\!]_{\mathsf{sk}}\big)$. Let $\boxplus$ denote the ciphertext addition. The public-key encryption of a plaintext m then proceeds as follows:

- Draw a random bit-string $(r_1, \dots, r_z) \xleftarrow{\$} \{0,1\}^z$;
- Compute a randomized encryption of zero as $S \leftarrow \boxplus_{i=1}^{z} r_i\, a_i$;

E. Oswald (Ed.): CT-RSA 2024, LNCS 14643, pp. 277–291, 2024.
https://doi.org/10.1007/978-3-031-58868-6_11

- Compute a trivial[1] encryption of m and get $M \leftarrow [\![m]\!]_{\mathsf{sk}}$;
- Output the ciphertext $C \leftarrow S \boxplus M$.

Noting that $C = [\![m]\!]_{\mathsf{sk}}$, the ciphertext C can be decrypted using the private key sk.

APPLICATION TO TFHE. In the case of TFHE [4] (see also [10]), the private decryption key is an n-bit string $\boldsymbol{s} = (s_1, \ldots, s_n)$. Let two positive integers q and t with $t < q$. With the previous construction, the matching public encryption key is

$$\{(\boldsymbol{a}_i, b_i) \in (\mathbb{Z}/q\mathbb{Z})^n \times \mathbb{Z}/q\mathbb{Z}\}_{1 \le i \le z}$$

where

$$\begin{cases} \boldsymbol{a}_i \xleftarrow{\$} (\mathbb{Z}/q\mathbb{Z})^n \\ b_i \leftarrow e_i + \sum_{j=1}^{n} (\boldsymbol{a}_i)_j\, s_j \pmod{q} \end{cases};$$

e_i denotes an independent noise error term (typically drawn from a Gaussian distribution centered around 0) for security reasons and $(\boldsymbol{a}_i)_j$ denotes the j-th component of vector $\boldsymbol{a}_i$. The encryption of a plaintext $m \in \mathbb{Z}/t\mathbb{Z}$ is given by $\mathbf{c} = (\boldsymbol{a}, b) \in (\mathbb{Z}/q\mathbb{Z})^{n+1}$ with

$$\boldsymbol{a} = \sum_{i=1}^{z} r_i\, \boldsymbol{a}_i \quad \text{and} \quad b = \sum_{i=1}^{z} r_i\, b_i + \Delta m$$

where $\Delta = q/t$. This assumes that t divides q. If not, an option is for example to define $\Delta = \lfloor q/t \rfloor$ (flooring), $\Delta = \lceil q/t \rceil$ (ceiling), or $\Delta = \lceil q/t \rfloor$ (rounding). An example of plaintexts encoded using the flooring function is given in [15, Sect. 5] for $t = 2$. Observe that $(\mathbf{0}, \Delta m) \in (\mathbb{Z}/q\mathbb{Z})^{n+1}$ is a trivial encryption of m.

Remark 1. Using matrix notation with vectors as column matrices, if we view the public key as the pair $\mathsf{pk} = (\mathbf{A}, \boldsymbol{b})$ with

$$\mathbf{A} = \begin{pmatrix} (\boldsymbol{a}_1)_1 & \cdots & (\boldsymbol{a}_z)_1 \\ \vdots & & \vdots \\ (\boldsymbol{a}_1)_n & \cdots & (\boldsymbol{a}_z)_n \end{pmatrix} \in (\mathbb{Z}/q\mathbb{Z})^{n \times z} \quad \text{and} \quad \boldsymbol{b} = \begin{pmatrix} b_1 \\ \vdots \\ b_z \end{pmatrix} \in (\mathbb{Z}/q\mathbb{Z})^z$$

where $\boldsymbol{b} = \mathbf{A}^{\intercal} \boldsymbol{s} + \boldsymbol{e}$, then ciphertext $\mathbf{c}$ can be expressed as $\mathbf{c} = (\boldsymbol{a}, b)$ with $\boldsymbol{a} = \mathbf{A}\, \boldsymbol{r}$ and $b = \boldsymbol{b}^{\intercal} \boldsymbol{r} + \Delta m$ where $\boldsymbol{r} = \begin{pmatrix} r_1 & \ldots & r_z \end{pmatrix}^{\intercal} \in (\mathbb{Z}/q\mathbb{Z})^z$.

The decryption of a ciphertext $\mathbf{c} = (a_1, \ldots, a_n, b) \in (\mathbb{Z}/q\mathbb{Z})^{n+1}$ proceeds in two steps. The first step is to recover the corresponding phase defined as

$$\phi_{\boldsymbol{s}}(\mathbf{c}) = b - \sum_{j=1}^{n} a_j\, s_j \bmod q$$

[1] A "trivial" encryption is an (insecure) encryption that can be obtained without the knowledge of the private key. The so-obtained ciphertext decrypts to the input plaintext.

which represents a noisy value of plaintext m. Indeed, it turns out from the definition that $\phi_s(\boldsymbol{c}) = \Delta m + \mathrm{Err}(\boldsymbol{c})$. The second step is to remove the noise $\mathrm{Err}(\boldsymbol{c})$ to get Δm and, in turn, m.

Remark 2. The above description makes use of the ring $\mathbb{Z}/q\mathbb{Z}$. TFHE and the likes can similarly be defined over the discretized torus $\mathbb{T}_q = \frac{1}{q}\mathbb{Z}/\mathbb{Z}$.

PARAMETER SELECTION. In order to have a sufficient security margin, the leftover hash lemma teaches that the value of z should verify

$$z = (n+1)\,|q|_2 + \kappa\,;$$

the additional term κ, where κ is the security parameter, accounts for the corresponding subset-sum problems. $|\cdot|_2$ denotes the binary length.

PERFORMANCE ANALYSIS. For a random variable X, its expectation is denoted by $\mathbb{E}[X]$ and its variance by $\mathrm{Var}(X)$; see Appendix A. Assuming that the noise e_i $(1 \leq i \leq n)$ is Gaussian, centered around zero and that its variance is bounded by the same threshold $\sigma^2 = \mathrm{Var}(e_i)$, the noise variance in an output ciphertext—where $\boldsymbol{r} \xleftarrow{\$} \{0,1\}^z$—is of $\frac{1}{2} z\,\sigma^2$. In the worst case, $\boldsymbol{r} = (1,1,\ldots,1)$ and $\mathrm{Var}(\mathrm{Err}(\boldsymbol{c})) = z\,\sigma^2$.

Proof. Let $\boldsymbol{c}$ denote the output ciphertext. It is easy to check that $\phi_s(\boldsymbol{c}) = \sum_{i=1}^{z} r_i\, e_i + \Delta m$ and thus $\mathrm{Err}(\boldsymbol{c}) = \sum_{i=1}^{z} r_i\, e_i$. Noting that for a uniform bit b in $\{0,1\}$, $\mathbb{E}[b] = 1/2$ and $\mathrm{Var}(b) = 1/4$, it follows that $\mathrm{Var}(\mathrm{Err}(\boldsymbol{c})) = \sum_{i=1}^{z} \mathrm{Var}(r_i\, e_i) = \sum_{i=1}^{z} \big(\frac{1}{4}\,\sigma^2 + \frac{1}{4}\,0 + \sigma^2\,(\frac{1}{2})^2\big) = z\,\frac{1}{2}\,\sigma^2$. If $\boldsymbol{r} = (1,1,\ldots,1)$ then $\mathrm{Var}(\mathrm{Err}(\boldsymbol{c})) = \sum_{i=1}^{z} \mathrm{Var}(e_i) = z\,\sigma^2$. □

Further, assuming for more efficiency that the masks $\boldsymbol{a}_i$ are derived from a random seed $\vartheta \in \{0,1\}^\kappa$ where κ is the security parameter, the size of the public encryption key is of

$$\kappa + \big((n+1)|q|_2 + \kappa\big)\,|q|_2$$

bits.

As an illustration, at the 128-bit security level, with parameters $n = 1024$, $q = 2^{64}$ and $\sigma = 2^{-25}q = 2^{39}$,[2] it follows that $z = 65728 \approx 2^{16}$. This leads to an increase of the noise variance in an output ciphertext by an expected factor of 2^{15}. With $\sigma = 2^{39}$, the standard deviation of the noise in an output ciphertext is of $2^{46.5}$. It also results that the public encryption key takes 4206720 bits, that is, about 526 kB.

OUR CONTRIBUTIONS. The noise increase and, more importantly, the large size of the public key can be prohibitive for certain applications. In this paper, we replace the normal public-key encryption methodology for TFHE via a methodology which goes via ring LWE. This significantly reduces the size of the associated public key. While broadly applicable, the technique is essentially tailored for TFHE for two main reasons:

[2] Parameters were obtained from the Lattice Estimator available at https://github.com/malb/lattice-estimator.

- The output format of the public-key encrypted messages is of the LWE type, exactly as in TFHE. In particular, the bootstrapping applies in the same way.
- The security of the resulting scheme relies on the RLWE assumption. This assumption is already required for the bootstrapping in TFHE and its programmable version [5].

This is achieved by astutely convoluting vectors in the key generation and for the associated encryption. The decryption process remains unchanged. We present an abstract version of our basic scheme that allows for more flexibility in the parameter selection and efficiency trade-offs. Furthermore, we describe efficient packing techniques when multiple plaintexts need to be encrypted. Again, the output format is of LWE type.

Outline of the Paper. The rest of this paper is organized as follows. The next section introduces a specialized convolution operator and builds therefrom an efficient public-key FHE scheme. It establishes its semantic security under the RLWE assumption and analyzes its performance. This basic scheme is then abstracted and generalized Sect. 3. The generalized construction offers more flexibility in the parameter selection. Several variants are also presented. Section 4 studies the case of multiple plaintexts. It describes how sharing the randomness allows for more compact ciphertexts. The corresponding conversion to regular LWE ciphertexts is also presented. Finally, Sect. 5 concludes the paper.

2 Smaller Public Keys, Less Noisy Ciphertexts

It is useful to introduce a new vector operator. The *reverse negative wrapped convolution* of two vectors $\boldsymbol{u} = (u_1, \ldots, u_n), \boldsymbol{v} = (v_1, \ldots, v_n) \in \mathbb{Z}^n$ is the vector $\boldsymbol{w} = \boldsymbol{u} \circledast \boldsymbol{v} = (\boldsymbol{u} \circledast_1 \boldsymbol{v}, \ldots, \boldsymbol{u} \circledast_n \boldsymbol{v}) \in \mathbb{Z}^n$ defined by

$$w_i = \boldsymbol{u} \circledast_i \boldsymbol{v} = \sum_{j=1}^{i} u_j \, v_{n+j-i} - \sum_{j=i+1}^{n} u_j \, v_{j-i} .$$

For example, over $\mathbb{Z}$, $(1,2,3,4) \circledast (5,6,7,8)$ is the vector $(-48,-16,24,70)$.

Remark 3. For a vector $\boldsymbol{v} \in \mathbb{Z}^n$, $\overleftarrow{\boldsymbol{v}}$ denotes vector $\boldsymbol{v}$ in reverse order; i.e., if $\boldsymbol{v} = (v_1, \ldots, v_n)$ then $\overleftarrow{\boldsymbol{v}} = (v_n, \ldots, v_1)$. The above convolution bears its name from the classical negative wrapped convolution (a.k.a. skew circular convolution or negacyclic convolution) defined by $\boldsymbol{w} = \boldsymbol{u} * \boldsymbol{v}$ where $w_i = \sum_{j=1}^{i} u_j \, v_{i+1-j} - \sum_{j=i+1}^{n} u_j \, v_{n+1+i-j}$. Indeed, it turns out that $\boldsymbol{u} \circledast \boldsymbol{v} = \boldsymbol{u} * \overleftarrow{\boldsymbol{v}}$.

The main properties of the reverse negative wrapped convolution are captured by the next lemma.

Lemma 1. *Given three vectors $\boldsymbol{t}, \boldsymbol{u}, \boldsymbol{v} \in \mathbb{Z}^n$, it holds that*

1. $\boldsymbol{u} \circledast \boldsymbol{v} = \overleftarrow{\boldsymbol{v}} \circledast \overleftarrow{\boldsymbol{u}}$;

2. $\boldsymbol{u} \circledast_n \boldsymbol{v} = \langle \boldsymbol{u}, \boldsymbol{v} \rangle$;
3. $\langle \boldsymbol{t} \circledast \boldsymbol{u}, \boldsymbol{v} \rangle = \langle \boldsymbol{t} \circledast \boldsymbol{v}, \boldsymbol{u} \rangle$.

Proof. The first property is immediate. Since $*$ is commutative, it follows that $\boldsymbol{u} \circledast \boldsymbol{v} = \boldsymbol{u} * \overleftarrow{\boldsymbol{v}} = \overleftarrow{\boldsymbol{v}} * \boldsymbol{u} = \overleftarrow{\boldsymbol{v}} \circledast \overleftarrow{\boldsymbol{u}}$.

Now, write $\boldsymbol{t} = (t_1, \ldots, t_n)$, $\boldsymbol{u} = (u_1, \ldots, u_n)$, and $\boldsymbol{v} = (v_1, \ldots, v_n)$. From the definition, denoting $[\text{pred}] = 1$ if some predicate pred is true and $[\text{pred}] = 0$ otherwise, we can express $\boldsymbol{u} \circledast_i \boldsymbol{v}$ compactly as

$$\sum_{j=1}^{n} (-1)^{[j>i]} \, u_j \, v_{[j \le i]n + j - i}.$$

Plugging $i = n$, we so get $\boldsymbol{u} \circledast_n \boldsymbol{v} = \sum_{j=1}^{n} u_j \, v_j = \langle \boldsymbol{u}, \boldsymbol{v} \rangle$.

Likewise, we also get

$$\begin{aligned}
\langle \boldsymbol{t} \circledast \boldsymbol{u}, \boldsymbol{v} \rangle &= \sum_{i=1}^{n} \Big(\sum\nolimits_{j=1}^{n} (-1)^{[j>i]} \, t_j \, u_{[j \le i]n+j-i} \Big) \, v_i \\
&= \sum_{j=1}^{n} t_j \Big(\sum\nolimits_{i=1}^{n} (-1)^{[i<j]} \, u_{[i \ge j]n+j-i} \, v_i \Big) \\
&= \sum_{j=1}^{n} t_j \Big(-\sum\nolimits_{i=1}^{j-1} u_{j-i} \, v_i + \sum\nolimits_{i=j}^{n} u_{n+j-i} \, v_i \Big) \\
&= \sum_{j=1}^{n} t_j \Big(-\sum\nolimits_{i=1}^{j-1} v_{j-i} \, u_i + \sum\nolimits_{i=j}^{n} v_{n+j-i} \, u_i \Big) \\
&= \langle \boldsymbol{t} \circledast \boldsymbol{v}, \boldsymbol{u} \rangle
\end{aligned}$$

by symmetry. □

2.1 Description

Equipped with the $\circledast$ operator, we can now present a public-key cryptosystem. Interestingly, the encryption algorithm outputs regular LWE-type ciphertexts [15]. As a consequence, the original decryption algorithm is unchanged.

A public-key LWE-type scheme

KeyGen(1^κ) On input security parameter κ, define an integer $n = 2^\eta$ for some $\eta > 0$, select positive integers t and q with $t \mid q$, let $\Delta = q/t$, and define two discretized error distributions $\hat{\chi}_1$ and $\hat{\chi}_2$ over $\mathbb{Z}$.
Sample uniformly at random a vector $\boldsymbol{s} = (s_1, \ldots, s_n) \xleftarrow{\$} \{0,1\}^n$.
Using $\boldsymbol{s}$, select uniformly at random a vector $\mathfrak{a} \xleftarrow{\$} (\mathbb{Z}/q\mathbb{Z})^n$ and form the vector $\mathfrak{b} = \mathfrak{a} \circledast \boldsymbol{s} + \boldsymbol{e} \in (\mathbb{Z}/q\mathbb{Z})^n$ with $\boldsymbol{e} \leftarrow \hat{\chi}_1{}^n$.

The plaintext space is $\mathcal{M} = \{0, 1, \ldots, t-1\}$. The public parameters are $\mathsf{pp} = \{n, \hat{\chi}_1, \hat{\chi}_2, t, q, \Delta\}$, the public key is $\mathsf{pk} = (\mathfrak{a}, \mathfrak{b})$, and the private key is $\mathsf{sk} = \boldsymbol{s}$.

$\mathsf{Encrypt}_{\mathsf{pk}}(m)$ The public-key encryption of a plaintext $m \in \mathcal{M}$ is given by $\boldsymbol{c} = (\boldsymbol{a}, b) \in (\mathbb{Z}/q\mathbb{Z})^{n+1}$ with

$$\begin{cases} \boldsymbol{a} = \mathfrak{a} \circledast \boldsymbol{r} + \boldsymbol{e}_1 \\ b = \langle \mathfrak{b}, \boldsymbol{r} \rangle + \Delta m + e_2 \end{cases}$$

for a random vector $\boldsymbol{r} \xleftarrow{\$} \{0,1\}^n$, and where $\boldsymbol{e}_1 \leftarrow \hat{\chi}_1{}^n$ and $e_2 \leftarrow \hat{\chi}_2$.

$\mathsf{Decrypt}_{\mathsf{sk}}(\boldsymbol{c})$ To decrypt $\boldsymbol{c} = (\boldsymbol{a}, b)$, using secret decryption key $\boldsymbol{s}$, return

$$\lceil (\mu^* \bmod q)/\Delta \rfloor \bmod t$$

where $\mu^* = b - \langle \boldsymbol{a}, \boldsymbol{s} \rangle$.

2.2 Correctness

Let $\boldsymbol{c} = (\boldsymbol{a}, b) \leftarrow \mathsf{Encrypt}_{\mathsf{pk}}(m)$. Then, by Lemma 1, we have $b - \langle \boldsymbol{a}, \boldsymbol{s} \rangle = \langle \mathfrak{a} \circledast \boldsymbol{s} + \boldsymbol{e}, \boldsymbol{r} \rangle + \Delta m + e_2 - \langle \mathfrak{a} \circledast \boldsymbol{r} + \boldsymbol{e}_1, \boldsymbol{s} \rangle = \Delta m + e_2 + \langle \boldsymbol{e}, \boldsymbol{r} \rangle - \langle \boldsymbol{e}_1, \boldsymbol{s} \rangle + \langle \mathfrak{a} \circledast \boldsymbol{s}, \boldsymbol{r} \rangle - \langle \mathfrak{a} \circledast \boldsymbol{r}, \boldsymbol{s} \rangle = \Delta m + E$ where $E = e_2 + \langle \boldsymbol{e}, \boldsymbol{r} \rangle - \langle \boldsymbol{e}_1, \boldsymbol{s} \rangle$. Decryption correctness thus requires that $|E| < \Delta/2$.

2.3 Security

We state the semantic security [9] of the proposed cryptosystem under the RLWE assumption [12] in $\mathbb{Z}_{n,q}[X] := (\mathbb{Z}/q\mathbb{Z})[X]/(X^n + 1)$.

Definition 1 (RLWE Assumption). *Given a security parameter κ, let $n, q \in \mathbb{N}$ with n a power of 2 and let $\mathscr{s} \xleftarrow{\$} \mathbb{B}[X]/(X^n + 1)$ where $\mathbb{B} = \{0,1\}$. Let also $\hat{\chi}$ be an error distribution over $\mathbb{Z}[X]/(X^n + 1)$; namely, over polynomials of $\mathbb{Z}[X]/(X^n + 1)$ with coefficients drawn according to $\hat{\chi}$. The* ring learning with errors (RLWE) problem *is to distinguish samples chosen according to the following distributions:*

$$\mathrm{dist}_0(1^\kappa) = \{(\mathscr{a}, \mathscr{b}) \mid \mathscr{a} \xleftarrow{\$} \mathbb{Z}_{n,q}[X], \mathscr{b} \xleftarrow{\$} \mathbb{Z}_{n,q}[X]\}$$

and

$$\mathrm{dist}_1(1^\kappa) = \{(\mathscr{a}, \mathscr{b}) \mid \mathscr{a} \xleftarrow{\$} \mathbb{Z}_{n,q}[X], \mathscr{b} = \mathscr{a}\,\mathscr{s} + \mathscr{e} \in \mathbb{Z}_{n,q}[X], \mathscr{e} \leftarrow \hat{\chi}\}.$$

The RLWE assumption *posits that for all probabilistic polynomial-time algorithms $\mathcal{R}$, the advantage*

$$\left|\Pr\left[\mathcal{R}(\mathscr{a}, \mathscr{b}) = 1 \mid (\mathscr{a}, \mathscr{b}) \xleftarrow{\$} \mathrm{dist}_0(1^\kappa)\right] - \Pr\left[\mathcal{R}(\mathscr{a}, \mathscr{b}) = 1 \mid (\mathscr{a}, \mathscr{b}) \xleftarrow{\$} \mathrm{dist}_1(1^\kappa)\right]\right|$$

is negligible in κ.

We identify polynomials in $\mathbb{Z}_{n,q}[X]$ with their coefficient vectors in $(\mathbb{Z}/q\mathbb{Z})^n$, and conversely. A vector $\boldsymbol{u} = (u_1, \ldots, u_n) \in (\mathbb{Z}/q\mathbb{Z})^n$ corresponds to polynomial $\mathcal{u} = \sum_{i=0}^{n-1} u_{j+1} X^j \in \mathbb{Z}_{n,q}[X]$; the correspondence is written $\boldsymbol{u} \cong \mathcal{u}$.

The next lemma relates the corresponding operations.

Lemma 2. *Let* $\boldsymbol{u} = (u_1, \ldots, u_n)$ *and* $\boldsymbol{v} = (v_1, \ldots, v_n) \in (\mathbb{Z}/q\mathbb{Z})^n$. *Let also* $\mathcal{u} = \sum_{j=0}^{n-1} u_{j+1} X^j$ *and* $\mathcal{v} = \sum_{j=0}^{n-1} v_{j+1} X^j \in \mathbb{Z}_{n,q}[X]$. *Then*

$$\boldsymbol{u} \circledast \overleftarrow{\boldsymbol{v}} = \boldsymbol{v} \circledast \overleftarrow{\boldsymbol{u}} \cong \mathcal{u} \cdot \mathcal{v}.$$

Proof. From Remark 3, if $*$ denotes the negative wrapped convolution, it turns out that $\boldsymbol{w} = (w_1, \ldots, w_n) := \boldsymbol{u} \circledast \overleftarrow{\boldsymbol{v}} = \boldsymbol{u} * \boldsymbol{v}$ with $w_i = \sum_{j=1}^{i} u_j \, v_{i+1-j} - \sum_{j=i+1}^{n} u_j \, v_{n+1+i-j}$. Now looking at the corresponding polynomials $\mathcal{u}$ and $\mathcal{v}$, it is easily seen that their multiplication in $\mathbb{Z}_{n,q}[X] = (\mathbb{Z}/q\mathbb{Z})[X](X^n + 1)$ yields polynomial $\mathcal{w} = \sum_{j=0}^{n-1} w_{j+1} X^j$. Hence, we have $\boldsymbol{w} \cong \mathcal{w}$ or, equivalently, $\boldsymbol{u} \circledast \overleftarrow{\boldsymbol{v}} \cong \mathcal{u} \cdot \mathcal{v}$. The equality $\boldsymbol{u} \circledast \overleftarrow{\boldsymbol{v}} = \boldsymbol{v} \circledast \overleftarrow{\boldsymbol{u}}$ follows from Lemma 1. □

Back to the encryption scheme, it is instructive to observe that the public key $\mathsf{pk} = (\mathfrak{a}, \mathfrak{b} = \mathfrak{a} \circledast \boldsymbol{s} + \boldsymbol{e})$ corresponds to a (polynomial) RLWE sample under secret key $\sum_{j=0}^{n-1} s_{n-j} X^j \cong \overleftarrow{\boldsymbol{s}} = (s_n, \ldots, s_1)$. Under the RLWE assumption, the public key as output by the key generation algorithm is therefore pseudo-random; i.e., indistinguishable from uniform. Regarding a ciphertext $\boldsymbol{c} = (\boldsymbol{a}, b)$ with $\boldsymbol{a} = \mathfrak{a} \circledast \boldsymbol{r} + \boldsymbol{e}_1$ and $b = \langle \mathfrak{b}, \boldsymbol{r} \rangle + \Delta\, m + e_2$, consider the vector $\boldsymbol{b} := \mathfrak{b} \circledast \boldsymbol{r} + \boldsymbol{e_2}$ for some $\boldsymbol{e_2} \in \hat{\chi}_2{}^n$ such that $(\boldsymbol{e_2})_n = e_2$. Again, it is worth noting that the pairs $(\mathfrak{a}, \boldsymbol{a} = \mathfrak{a} \circledast \boldsymbol{r} + \boldsymbol{e}_1)$ and $(\mathfrak{b}, \boldsymbol{b} = \mathfrak{b} \circledast \boldsymbol{r} + \boldsymbol{e_2})$ correspond respectively to two (polynomial) RLWE samples under 'secret key' $\sum_{j=0}^{n-1} r_{n-j} X^j \cong \overleftarrow{\boldsymbol{r}}$ and thus appear to be pseudo-random. The same is true for $\langle \mathfrak{b}, \boldsymbol{r} \rangle + e_2$ since, from Lemma 1, this turns out to be the nth component of vector $\mathfrak{b} \circledast \boldsymbol{r} + \boldsymbol{e_2}$: $\langle \mathfrak{b}, \boldsymbol{r} \rangle + e_2 = \mathfrak{b} \circledast_n \boldsymbol{r} + (\boldsymbol{e_2})_n$. It is also important that the randomness can be re-used in multiple ciphertexts provided they are all encrypted under different keys. This follows from [2]. Indeed, when the randomness is given explicitly in a ciphertext, it is readily verified that the "reproducibility" criterion [1, Definition 9.3] is satisfied.

The semantic security under the RLWE assumption now follows by a series of hybrid games where the different RLWE samples are successively replaced with uniform samples.

2.4 Performance

The public key expands to $2n\,|q|_2$ bits. If the component $\mathfrak{a}$ of the public key is generated from a random seed, the public key only requires $n\,|q|_2 + \kappa$ bits for its storage or transmission. With the example parameters of Sect. 1, this amounts to 65664 bits, or about 8.2 kB.

Suppose $\hat{\chi}_i = \mathcal{N}(0, {\sigma_i}^2)$ for $i \in \{1, 2\}$. For a ciphertext $\boldsymbol{c}$ output by the encryption algorithm, from Sect. 2.2, the noise variance satisfies $\mathrm{Var}(\mathrm{Err}(\boldsymbol{c})) = \mathrm{Var}(e_2 + \langle \boldsymbol{e}, \boldsymbol{r} \rangle - \langle \boldsymbol{e}_1, \boldsymbol{s} \rangle) = \mathrm{Var}(e_2) + \sum_{j=1}^{n} \mathrm{Var}((\boldsymbol{e})_i\, r_i) + \sum_{j=1}^{n} \mathrm{Var}((\boldsymbol{e}_1)_j\, s_j) =$

$\sigma_2{}^2 + 2n\big(\sigma_1{}^2\,\frac{1}{4} + \sigma_1{}^2\,(\frac{1}{2})^2 + \frac{1}{4}\,0\big) = \sigma_2{}^2 + n\,\sigma_1{}^2$. Again, with the example parameters of Sect. 1, for $\sigma_1{}^2 = \sigma_2{}^2$, this translates in an increase of $n+1 \approx 2^{10}$ in the noise variance. With $\sigma_1 = \sigma_2 = 2^{39}$, the standard deviation of the noise in an output ciphertext is of 2^{44}. Larger values for ciphertext modulus q lead to larger gains compared to the direct approach using encryptions of 0 for the public key (Sect. 1).

3 Generalization

3.1 General Construction

Let $\mathscr{p}$ be a monic (irreducible) polynomial of degree n. Let also $\mathfrak{R}$ and $\mathfrak{R}_q$ denote the polynomial rings $\mathbb{Z}[X]/(\mathscr{p}(X))$ and $\mathfrak{R}/(q) = (\mathbb{Z}/q\mathbb{Z})[X]/(\mathscr{p}(X))$, respectively. A polynomial $\mathscr{a} \in \mathfrak{R}$ (resp. $\mathscr{a} \in \mathfrak{R}_q$) of degree less than n and given by $\mathscr{a}(X) = \sum_{i=0}^{n-1} a_i\,X^i$ with $a_i \in \mathbb{Z}$ (resp. $a_i \in \mathbb{Z}/q\mathbb{Z}$) can be identified with its coefficient vector $\boldsymbol{a} := (a_0, a_1, \dots, a_{n-1}) \in \mathbb{Z}^n$ (resp. $\in (\mathbb{Z}/q\mathbb{Z})^n$). Over $\mathfrak{R}_q$, we let Υ_q denote the corresponding coefficient-embedding map

$$\Upsilon_q \colon \mathfrak{R}_q \xrightarrow{\sim} (\mathbb{Z}/q\mathbb{Z})^n, \mathscr{a} = \textstyle\sum_{i=0}^{n-1} a_i\,X^i \longmapsto \Upsilon_q(\mathscr{a}) = (a_0, a_1, \dots, a_{n-1}).$$

This one-to-one correspondence defines the convolution $*$ between two vectors in $(\mathbb{Z}/q\mathbb{Z})^n$. Given $\boldsymbol{a}, \boldsymbol{b} \in (\mathbb{Z}/q\mathbb{Z})^n$, their convolution is defined as

$$\boldsymbol{a} * \boldsymbol{b} = \Upsilon_q\big(\Upsilon_q{}^{-1}(\boldsymbol{a}) \cdot \Upsilon_q{}^{-1}(\boldsymbol{b})\big) \in (\mathbb{Z}/q\mathbb{Z})^n$$

where $\cdot$ denote the polynomial multiplication in $\mathfrak{R}_q$.

Interestingly, the convolution operator allows expressing an RLWE ciphertext with vectors. One advantage of RLWE-type encryption is that it comes with an efficient public-key variant. For example, adapting [7, Sect. 3.2] following [13] (see also [12]), an RLWE public-key encryption scheme can be abstracted as follows. The key generation draws at random a small secret key $\mathscr{s} \in \mathfrak{R}$ and forms the matching public key $(\mathscr{A}, \mathscr{B}) \in (\mathfrak{R}_q)^2$ where $\mathscr{A}$ is a random polynomial in $\mathfrak{R}_q$ and $\mathscr{B} = \mathscr{A} \cdot \mathscr{s} + \mathscr{e}$ for a small random noise error $\mathscr{e} \in \mathfrak{R}$. Let $t \mid q$ and $\Delta = q/t$. The public-key encryption of a plaintext $\mathscr{m} := \mathscr{m}(X) = \sum_{i=0}^{n-1} m_i\,X^i \in \mathfrak{R}_t$ is given by the pair of polynomials $(\mathscr{a}, \mathscr{b}) \in (\mathfrak{R}_q)^2$ with

$$\begin{cases} \mathscr{a} = \mathscr{A} \cdot \mathscr{r} + \mathscr{e}_1 \\ \mathscr{b} = \mathscr{B} \cdot \mathscr{r} + \Delta\,\mathscr{m} + \mathscr{e}_2 \end{cases}$$

for some small random polynomial $\mathscr{r} \in \mathfrak{R}$ and small random noise errors $\mathscr{e}_1, \mathscr{e}_2 \in \mathfrak{R}$. The decryption of ciphertext $(\mathscr{a}, \mathscr{b})$, using secret key $\mathscr{s}$, proceeds in two steps: (i) compute in $\mathfrak{R}_q$ the phase $\mathscr{b} - \mathscr{a} \cdot \mathscr{s} = \Delta\,\mathscr{m} + \mathscr{E}$ with $\mathscr{E} := \mathscr{e} \cdot \mathscr{r} + \mathscr{e}_2 - \mathscr{e}_1 \cdot \mathscr{s} \in \mathfrak{R}$, and (ii) remove $\mathscr{E}$ to get $\Delta\,\mathscr{m}$ and, in turn, $\mathscr{m} \in \mathfrak{R}_t$.

Using the convolution operator as defined above, we get the corresponding formulation using vectors. The secret key is a small vector $\boldsymbol{s} \in \mathbb{Z}^n$ and the public key is a pair of vectors $(\boldsymbol{A}, \boldsymbol{B})$ where $\boldsymbol{A}$ is a random vector in $(\mathbb{Z}/q\mathbb{Z})^n$ and

$\boldsymbol{B} = \boldsymbol{A} * \boldsymbol{s} + \boldsymbol{e} \pmod{q}$ for some small random vector $\boldsymbol{e} \in \mathbb{Z}^n$. Then encryption of a plaintext $\boldsymbol{m}$ seen as a vector in $(\mathbb{Z}/t\mathbb{Z})^n$ is given by the pair of vectors $(\boldsymbol{a}, \boldsymbol{b})$ in $(\mathbb{Z}/q\mathbb{Z})^n$ where

$$\begin{cases} \boldsymbol{a} = \boldsymbol{A} * \boldsymbol{r} + \boldsymbol{e_1} \\ \boldsymbol{b} = \boldsymbol{B} * \boldsymbol{r} + \Delta\, \boldsymbol{m} + \boldsymbol{e_2} \end{cases} \tag{1}$$

for some small random vector $\boldsymbol{r} \in \mathbb{Z}^n$ and small random noise errors $\boldsymbol{e_1}, \boldsymbol{e_2} \in \mathbb{Z}^n$. Next, given ciphertext $(\boldsymbol{a}, \boldsymbol{b})$, plaintext $\boldsymbol{m}$ can be recovered using secret key $\boldsymbol{s}$ from the phase $\boldsymbol{b} - \boldsymbol{a} * \boldsymbol{s} = \Delta\, \boldsymbol{m} + \boldsymbol{E} \pmod{q}$ where $\boldsymbol{E} := \boldsymbol{e} * \boldsymbol{r} + \boldsymbol{e_2} - \boldsymbol{e_1} * \boldsymbol{s} \in \mathbb{Z}^n$.

Three important observations are in order:

1. If b_i (resp. m_i) denotes the i-th component of vector $\boldsymbol{b}$ (resp. $\boldsymbol{m}$) in (1) then the pair $(\boldsymbol{a}, b_i)$ is an LWE-type encryption of message $m_i \in \mathbb{Z}/t\mathbb{Z}$ provided that
$$b_i - \langle \boldsymbol{a}, \boldsymbol{s} \rangle = \Delta\, m_i + (\text{small noise}).$$
In particular, we have
$$\begin{aligned} b_i - \langle \boldsymbol{a}, \boldsymbol{s} \rangle &= (\boldsymbol{B} * \boldsymbol{r})_i + \Delta\, m_i + (\boldsymbol{e_2})_i - \langle \boldsymbol{A} * \boldsymbol{r} + \boldsymbol{e_1}, \boldsymbol{s} \rangle \\ &= \big((\boldsymbol{A} * \boldsymbol{s} + \boldsymbol{e}) * \boldsymbol{r}\big)_i + \Delta\, m_i + (\boldsymbol{e_2})_i - \langle \boldsymbol{A} * \boldsymbol{r} + \boldsymbol{e_1}, \boldsymbol{s} \rangle \\ &= \Delta\, m_i + (\boldsymbol{A} * \boldsymbol{s} * \boldsymbol{r})_i - \langle \boldsymbol{A} * \boldsymbol{r}, \boldsymbol{s} \rangle \\ &\qquad + (\boldsymbol{e} * \boldsymbol{r})_i + (\boldsymbol{e_2})_i - \langle \boldsymbol{e_1}, \boldsymbol{s} \rangle . \end{aligned}$$
As a consequence, if the condition
$$(\boldsymbol{A} * \boldsymbol{s} * \boldsymbol{r})_i \approx \langle \boldsymbol{A} * \boldsymbol{r}, \boldsymbol{s} \rangle \tag{2}$$
is satisfied, one ends up with an LWE-type ciphertext for plaintext $m_i \in \mathbb{Z}/t\mathbb{Z}$.
2. If the public key is replaced with $(\boldsymbol{A}, \boldsymbol{B} = \boldsymbol{A} * \varphi_1(\boldsymbol{s}) + \boldsymbol{e}) \in (\mathbb{Z}/q\mathbb{Z})^n \times (\mathbb{Z}/q\mathbb{Z})^n$ for some (bijective) map $\varphi_1 \colon (\mathbb{Z}/q\mathbb{Z})^n \to (\mathbb{Z}/q\mathbb{Z})^n$ then Condition (2) relaxes to
$$(\boldsymbol{A} * \varphi_1(\boldsymbol{s}) * \boldsymbol{r})_i \approx \langle \boldsymbol{A} * \boldsymbol{r}, \boldsymbol{s} \rangle . \tag{3}$$
3. Further, the above encryption scheme is unchanged if vector $\boldsymbol{r}$ is replaced with vector $\varphi_2(\boldsymbol{r})$ for some (bijective) map $\varphi_2 \colon (\mathbb{Z}/q\mathbb{Z})^n \to (\mathbb{Z}/q\mathbb{Z})^n$. In particular, taking $\varphi_2 = \varphi_1$ and letting $\boldsymbol{u} \circledast \boldsymbol{v} = \boldsymbol{u} * \varphi_1(\boldsymbol{v})$, Condition (3) can be written as
$$(\boldsymbol{A} \circledast \boldsymbol{s} \circledast \boldsymbol{r})_i = (\boldsymbol{A} \circledast \boldsymbol{r} \circledast \boldsymbol{s})_i \approx \langle \boldsymbol{A} \circledast \boldsymbol{r}, \boldsymbol{s} \rangle . \tag{4}$$

We argue that one can find a map φ_1 such that Condition (4) is strictly verified. Define $\boldsymbol{C} = \boldsymbol{A} \circledast \boldsymbol{r} = (C_1, \dots, C_n)$ and write $\varphi_1(\boldsymbol{s}) = (s'_1, \dots, s'_n)$. Then

$$\begin{aligned} &(\boldsymbol{C} \circledast \boldsymbol{s})_i := (\boldsymbol{C} * \varphi_1(\boldsymbol{s}))_i = \langle \boldsymbol{C}, \boldsymbol{s} \rangle \iff \\ &\quad \Big(\Upsilon_q\Big(\big(\textstyle\sum_{j=1}^n C_j\, X^{j-1}\big) \cdot \big(\sum_{j=1}^n s'_j\, X^{j-1}\big)\Big)\Big)_i = \sum_{j=1}^n C_j\, s_j \pmod{q}. \end{aligned} \tag{5}$$

The left-hand side of the last equation can be rewritten as

$$\sum_{j=1}^{n} C_j \left(\sum_{k=1}^{n} \alpha_{j,k}\, s'_k\right) \tag{6}$$

for some $\alpha_{j,k} \in \mathbb{Z}/q\mathbb{Z}$ given by the multiplication $\cdot$ in $\mathfrak{R}_q$. Equating each multiplier of C_j yields a system of n equations, $\sum_{k=1}^{n} \alpha_{j,k}\, s'_k = s_j$ (for $1 \le j \le n$), from which values for $s'_1, \dots, s'_n$ can be derived and, in turn, map φ_1.

This leads to the following public-key encryption scheme. For security and efficiency reasons, we restrict quotient polynomial $\mathfrak{p}(X)$ to cyclotomic polynomials $\Phi_M(X)$. We so have $\mathfrak{R}_q = (\mathbb{Z}/q\mathbb{Z})[X]/(\Phi_M(X))$ with $n = \deg(\Phi_M)$. The multiplication in $\mathfrak{R}_q$ is denoted by $\cdot$ and the corresponding convolution in $(\mathbb{Z}/q\mathbb{Z})^n$ by $*$. The 'specialized' convolution operator in $(\mathbb{Z}/q\mathbb{Z})^n$ is denoted by $\circledast$. For any two vectors $\boldsymbol{u}, \boldsymbol{v} \in (\mathbb{Z}/q\mathbb{Z})^n$, we define $\boldsymbol{u} \circledast \boldsymbol{v} = \boldsymbol{u} * \varphi_1(\boldsymbol{v})$. With this corresponding definition of φ_1, it holds by construction that $\boldsymbol{u} \circledast_i \boldsymbol{v} = \langle \boldsymbol{u}, \boldsymbol{v} \rangle$; see Eq. (5).

A public-key LWE-type scheme (General case)

KeyGen(1^κ) On input security parameter κ, define an integer $n = \phi(M)$ for some integer M and where ϕ denotes Euler's totient function, select positive integers t and q with $t \mid q$, let $\Delta = q/t$, and define two discretized error distributions $\hat{\chi}_1$ and $\hat{\chi}_2$ over $\mathbb{Z}$.
Sample uniformly at random a vector $\boldsymbol{s} = (s_1, \dots, s_n) \xleftarrow{\$} \{0,1\}^n$. Using $\boldsymbol{s}$, select uniformly at random a vector $\mathfrak{a} \xleftarrow{\$} (\mathbb{Z}/q\mathbb{Z})^n$ and form the vector $\mathfrak{b} = \mathfrak{a} \circledast \boldsymbol{s} + \boldsymbol{e} \in (\mathbb{Z}/q\mathbb{Z})^n$ with $\boldsymbol{e} \leftarrow \hat{\chi}_1{}^n$.
The plaintext space is $\mathcal{M} = \{0, 1, \dots, t-1\}$. The public parameters are $\mathsf{pp} = \{n, \hat{\chi}_1, \hat{\chi}_2, t, q, \Delta\}$, the public key is $\mathsf{pk} = (\mathfrak{a}, \mathfrak{b})$, and the private key is $\mathsf{sk} = \boldsymbol{s}$.

Encrypt$_{\mathsf{pk}}(m)$ The public-key encryption of a plaintext $m \in \mathcal{M}$ is given by $\boldsymbol{c} = (\boldsymbol{a}, b) \in (\mathbb{Z}/q\mathbb{Z})^{n+1}$ with

$$\begin{cases} \boldsymbol{a} = \mathfrak{a} \circledast \boldsymbol{r} + \boldsymbol{e}_1 \\ b = \langle \mathfrak{b}, \boldsymbol{r} \rangle + \Delta\, m + e_2 \end{cases}$$

for a random vector $\boldsymbol{r} \xleftarrow{\$} \{0,1\}^n$, and where $\boldsymbol{e}_1 \leftarrow \hat{\chi}_1{}^n$ and $e_2 \leftarrow \hat{\chi}_2$.

Decrypt$_{\mathsf{sk}}(\boldsymbol{c})$ To decrypt $\boldsymbol{c} = (\boldsymbol{a}, b)$, using secret decryption key $\boldsymbol{s}$, return

$$\lceil (\mu^* \bmod q)/\Delta \rfloor \bmod t$$

where $\mu^* = b - \langle \boldsymbol{a}, \boldsymbol{s} \rangle$.

3.2 Basic Scheme

Applied to the basic scheme given in Sect. 2, this corresponds to $M = 2^{\eta+1}$, $\mathfrak{p}(X) = X^n + 1$ with $n = 2^\eta$ and, letting $\boldsymbol{s} = (s_1, \dots, s_n)$, $\varphi_1(\boldsymbol{s}) = (s_n, \dots, s_1)$. Indeed, for $i = n$ and $\mathfrak{p}(X) = X^n + 1$, left-hand side of Eq. (5) becomes

$$\left(\Upsilon_q\left(\left(\sum_{j=1}^n C_j X^{j-1}\right)\cdot\left(\sum_{j=1}^n s'_j X^{j-1}\right)\right)\right)_n = \sum_{j=1}^n C_j\, s'_{n+1-j}$$

that is, comparing with Eq. (6),

$$(\alpha_{j,k})_{\substack{1\le j\le n\\1\le k\le n}} = \begin{pmatrix} 0\,0\ldots 0\,1\\ 0\,0\ldots 1\,0\\ \vdots\;\vdots\;\iddots\;\vdots\\ 0\,1\ldots 0\,0\\ 1\,0\ldots 0\,0\end{pmatrix}.$$

Equating each multiplier of C_j with those of $\sum_{j=1}^n C_j\, s_j$ yields $s'_{n+1-j} = s_j$ or, equivalently, $(s'_1,\ldots,s'_n) = (s_n,\ldots,s_1)$; and thus $\varphi_1(\boldsymbol{s}) = (s_n,\ldots,s_1)$.

The map φ_1 in the basic scheme of Sect. 2 is obtained by selecting $i = n$; namely, $\varphi_1(\boldsymbol{s}) = (s_n,\ldots,s_1)$. However, another vector convolution operator that is 'compatible' with the multiplication in $\mathfrak{R}_q = \mathbb{Z}_{n,q}[X] := (\mathbb{Z}/q\mathbb{Z})/(X^n+1)$ can be used. An alternative therefore consists in choosing another value for i. For a general value for $i \ne n$, the vector $\boldsymbol{s} = (s_1,\ldots,s_n)$ is mapped to

$$\begin{aligned}\varphi_1(\boldsymbol{s}) &= (s_i,\ldots,s_1,-s_n,\ldots,-s_{i+1})\\ &= \left((-1)^{[j>i]}\, s_{1+(i-j \bmod n)}\right)_{1\le j\le n}.\end{aligned}$$

For example, for $i = n-1$, we get $\varphi_1(\boldsymbol{s}) = (s_{n-1},\ldots,s_1,-s_n)$. The matching specialized convolution operator is defined as $\boldsymbol{u} \circledast \boldsymbol{v} = \boldsymbol{u} * \varphi_1(\boldsymbol{v})$ for any two vectors $\boldsymbol{u}$ and $\boldsymbol{v}$, where $*$ denotes the classical negative wrapped convolution operator.

3.3 Higher-Order Convolutions and More

The general construction presents the advantage that the condition n being a power of two can be relaxed. For quotient polynomial $\mathfrak{p}(X) = \Phi_M(X)$, the corresponding value for n is given by the Euler's totient function of M. For example, if $M = 3^w$ then $n = 2\cdot 3^{w-1} = 2M/3$ and $\mathfrak{p}(X) = X^n + X^{n/2} + 1$. For $i = n$, $*$ corresponds to the multiplication in $(\mathbb{Z}/q\mathbb{Z})[X]/(X^n + X^{n/2} + 1)$ and

$$\begin{aligned}\varphi_1(\boldsymbol{s}) &= \big(s_n + s_{n/2}, s_{n-1} + s_{n/2-1},\ldots,s_{n-(n/2-1)} + s_{n/2-(n/2-1)},\\ &\qquad s_{n/2}, s_{n/2} - 1,\ldots,s_{n/2-(n/2-1)}\big)\\ &= \left(s_{n+1-j} + [j\le n/2]\, s_{1+(n/2-j \bmod n)}\right)_{1\le j\le n}.\end{aligned}$$

Again, by construction, letting $\boldsymbol{u} \circledast \boldsymbol{v} = \boldsymbol{u} * \varphi_1(\boldsymbol{v})$, it holds that $\boldsymbol{u} \circledast_n \boldsymbol{v} = \langle \boldsymbol{u}, \boldsymbol{v}\rangle$ for any two vectors $\boldsymbol{u}$ and $\boldsymbol{v}$. The process generalizes to any cyclotomic Φ_M.

The general construction can also be extended to the general case of an irreducible polynomial $\mathfrak{p}$. The hardness of the corresponding (R)LWE-like assumptions is studied in [16] and [14]. A potential drawback of moving away from cyclotomics is a loss of efficiency. We refer the reader to [11] for an adaptation of the (programmable) bootstrapping to quotient polynomials beyond power-of-two cyclotomics.

3.4 Variants

There are a number of possible variants. Instead of selecting $t \mid q$, plaintext modulus t can be more generally chosen as an arbitrary positive integer $< q$. In this case, a plaintext m is for example encrypted as $\boldsymbol{c} = (\boldsymbol{a}, b)$ with $\boldsymbol{a} = \mathfrak{a} \circledast \boldsymbol{r} + \boldsymbol{e}_1$ and $b = \langle \mathfrak{b}, \boldsymbol{r} \rangle + \lfloor q/t \rceil\, m + e_2$; see Sect. 1.

Another variant is to select private key $\boldsymbol{s}$ and/or randomizer $\boldsymbol{r}$ at random in e.g. $\{-1, 0, 1\}^n$, or in any small subset of $\mathbb{Z}/q\mathbb{Z}$.

4 Encrypting Multiple Plaintexts

When multiple plaintexts need to be encrypted, the natural way is to encrypt them individually. For Z plaintexts this requires $Z \cdot (n+1)\,|q|_2$ bits for the corresponding ciphertexts. We show in this section how to only make use of $(\lceil Z/n \rceil\, n + Z)\,|q|_2$ bits. This saves

$$(Z - \lceil Z/n \rceil) \cdot n\,|q|_2$$

bits.

Given an LWE dimension n and a convolution operator $*$ operating on n-dimensional vectors, fix an integer $i \in \{1, \ldots, n\}$. This integer i defines a map φ_1 and, in turn, the matching specialized convolution operator $\circledast$ as $\boldsymbol{u} \circledast \boldsymbol{v} = \boldsymbol{u} * \varphi_1(\boldsymbol{v})$ for any two n-dimensional vectors $\boldsymbol{u}$ and $\boldsymbol{v}$. As detailed in the previous sections, this operator $\circledast$ gives rise to a public-key encryption scheme. With the previous notations, a plaintext m is encrypted under public key $(\mathfrak{a}, \mathfrak{b}) \in (\mathbb{Z}/q\mathbb{Z})^{2n}$ as

$$\begin{cases} \boldsymbol{a} = \mathfrak{a} \circledast \boldsymbol{r} + \boldsymbol{e}_1 \\ b = \langle \mathfrak{b}, \boldsymbol{r} \rangle + \Delta\, m + e_2 \end{cases}$$

for some $\boldsymbol{r} \xleftarrow{\$} \{0,1\}^n$, $\boldsymbol{e}_1 \leftarrow \hat{\chi}_1{}^n$, and $e_2 \leftarrow \hat{\chi}_2$. Part $\boldsymbol{a}$ is called the mask of the ciphertext and part b is called the body of the ciphertext.

When Z plaintexts, $m_1, \ldots, m_Z$, need to be encrypted, they are first put in $\lceil Z/n \rceil$ bins so that each bin contains at most n plaintexts. Next, for each bin:

1. A fresh mask $\boldsymbol{a}$ is generated from a fresh randomizer $\boldsymbol{r} \xleftarrow{\$} \{0,1\}^n$ and a fresh noise vector $\boldsymbol{e}_1 \leftarrow \hat{\chi}_1{}^n$ as $\boldsymbol{a} \leftarrow \mathfrak{a} \circledast \boldsymbol{r} + \boldsymbol{e}_1$;
2. The first plaintext, say m_1, is encrypted as above; namely, by adding the body $b := b_1 \leftarrow \langle \mathfrak{b}, \boldsymbol{r} \rangle + \Delta\, m_1 + e_{2,1}$ for a fresh random noise $e_{2,1} \leftarrow \hat{\chi}_2$;
3. The remaining plaintexts in the bin (if any), say $m_2, \ldots, m_L$ for some $L \le n$, are represented by pairs of the form

$$\{(\boldsymbol{a}, b_\ell)\}_{2 \le \ell \le L}$$

where $\boldsymbol{a}$ is the mask generated in 1. and

$$b_\ell \leftarrow (\mathfrak{b} \circledast \boldsymbol{r})_{j_\ell} + \Delta\, m_\ell + e_{2,\ell} \quad (\text{for } 2 \le \ell \le L)$$

for a fresh random noise $e_{2,\ell} \leftarrow \hat{\chi}_2$ and distinct indexes $j_\ell \in \{1, \ldots, n\} \setminus \{i\}$. (Note that, by construction, $(\mathfrak{b} \circledast \boldsymbol{r})_i = \langle \mathfrak{b}, \boldsymbol{r} \rangle$.)

Ciphertext $(\boldsymbol{a}, b_1)$ is an LWE-type ciphertext but ciphertexts in $\{(\boldsymbol{a}, b_\ell)\}_{2\le\ell\le L}$ are not. To turn them into LWE-type ciphertexts the common mask $\boldsymbol{a}$ needs first to be converted into the corresponding mask $\Psi_{j_\ell}(\boldsymbol{a})$ to get the LWE-type ciphertext $(\Psi_{j_\ell}(\boldsymbol{a}), b_{j_\ell})$ for some map $\Psi_{j_\ell} \colon (\mathbb{Z}/q\mathbb{Z})^n \to (\mathbb{Z}/q\mathbb{Z})^n$. There is always such a map. For instance, map Ψ_{j_ℓ} can be chosen as a linear map satisfying

$$(\boldsymbol{C} \circledast \boldsymbol{s})_{j_\ell} \approx \langle \Psi_{j_\ell}(\boldsymbol{C}), \boldsymbol{s}\rangle$$

for any vector $\boldsymbol{C} = (C_1, \dots, C_n)$. An expression for ψ_{j_ℓ} can be obtained in a way similar to what is done to derive map φ_1; see Sect. 3.

For example, for $i = n$ and n a power of two as in Sect. 2.1, for a vector $\boldsymbol{x} = (x_1, \dots, x_n)$, we can define

$$\Psi_{j_\ell}(\boldsymbol{x}) = \left((-1)^{[k\le n-j_\ell]}\, x_{1+(k+j_\ell-1 \bmod n)}\right)_{1\le k\le n}.$$

For such a choice for Ψ_{j_ℓ}, it can be verified that $(\Psi_{j_\ell}(\boldsymbol{a}), b_{j_\ell})$ is an LWE-type ciphertext encrypting plaintext m_ℓ; that is, that

$$b_{j_\ell} - \langle \Psi_{j_\ell}(\boldsymbol{a}), \boldsymbol{s}\rangle = \Delta\, m_\ell + (\text{small noise}).$$

This choice of the map Ψ_{j_ℓ} therefore ensures correct decryption. It is also interesting to observe that when $i = n$, replacing j_ℓ by i yields $\Psi_i(\boldsymbol{x}) = (x_k)_{1\le k\le n} = (x_1, \dots, x_n)$; namely, Ψ_i is the identity map.

5 Conclusion

This paper introduced a public-key variant of TFHE with ciphertexts as LWE samples. The scheme significantly improves the public-key size and lowers the noise in the resulting ciphertexts, departing from the direct approach defining as public key a set of encryptions of 0 (typically, of the order of 2^{16} LWE samples). The security of the scheme is shown to hold under the standard RLWE assumption. Generalizations and extensions of the basic construction are presented and discussed. A packing technique to get a compressed representation of multiple ciphertexts and companion conversion to their standard LWE representation are described. The proposed public-key FHE scheme has recently been integrated in the private smart-contract protocol fhEVM.

A Variance and Covariance

The variance captures how much a randomly drawn variable is spread out from the average value. Formally, the variance of a random variable X is defined as

$$\operatorname{Var}(X) = \mathbb{E}\left[(X - \mathbb{E}[X])^2\right]$$

or, equivalently, as $\operatorname{Var}(X) = \mathbb{E}[X^2] - \mathbb{E}[X]^2$.

COMPOSITION FORMULAS. For two *independent* variables X_1 and X_2, the expectation and variance of their sum and of their product satisfy

$$\begin{cases} \mathbb{E}[X_1 + X_2] = \mathbb{E}[X_1] + \mathbb{E}[X_2] \\ \mathrm{Var}(X_1 + X_2) = \mathrm{Var}(X_1) + \mathrm{Var}(X_2) \end{cases}$$

and

$$\begin{cases} \mathbb{E}[X_1\, X_2] = \mathbb{E}[X_1]\,\mathbb{E}[X_2] \\ \mathrm{Var}(X_1\, X_2) = \mathrm{Var}(X_1)\mathrm{Var}(X_2) + \mathrm{Var}(X_1)\,\mathbb{E}[X_2]^2 + \mathrm{Var}(X_2)\,\mathbb{E}[X_1]^2 \end{cases}.$$

The covariance indicates the joint variability of two random variables X_1 and X_2; it is written $\mathrm{Cov}(X_1, X_2)$. In particular, the covariance is zero when X_1 and X_2 are independent.

For correlated random variables X_1 and X_2, the composition formulas generalize to

$$\begin{cases} \mathbb{E}[X_1 + X_2] = \mathbb{E}[X_1] + \mathbb{E}[X_2] \\ \mathrm{Var}(X_1 + X_2) = \mathrm{Var}(X_1) + \mathrm{Var}(X_2) + 2\mathrm{Cov}(X_1, X_2) \end{cases}$$

and

$$\begin{cases} \mathbb{E}[X_1\, X_2] = \mathbb{E}[X_1]\,\mathbb{E}[X_2] + \mathrm{Cov}(X_1, X_2) \\ \mathrm{Var}(X_1\, X_2) = \mathrm{Cov}({X_1}^2, {X_2}^2) \\ \qquad\qquad + (\mathrm{Var}(X_1) + \mathbb{E}[X_1]^2))\,(\mathrm{Var}(X_2) + \mathbb{E}[X_2]^2) \\ \qquad\qquad - (\mathrm{Cov}(X_1, X_2) + \mathbb{E}[X_1]\,\mathbb{E}[X_2])^2 \end{cases}.$$

References

1. Bellare, M., Boldyreva, A., Kurosawa, K., Staddon, J.: Multi-recipient encryption schemes: how to save on bandwidth and computation without sacrificing security. IEEE Trans. Inf. Theory **53**(11), 3927–3943 (2007). https://doi.org/10.1109/TIT.2007.907471
2. Bellare, M., Boldyreva, A., Staddon, J.: Randomness re-use in multi-recipient encryption schemeas. In: Desmedt, Y.G. (ed.) PKC 2003. LNCS, vol. 2567, pp. 85–99. Springer, Heidelberg (2003). https://doi.org/10.1007/3-540-36288-6_7
3. Brakerski, Z., Vaikuntanathan, V.: Efficient fully homomorphic encryption from (standard) LWE. In: Ostrovsky, R. (ed.) 52nd Annual Symposium on Foundations of Computer Science, pp. 97–106. IEEE Computer Society Press (2011). https://doi.org/10.1109/FOCS.2011.12
4. Chillotti, I., Gama, N., Georgieva, M., Izabachène, M.: TFHE: fast fully homomorphic encryption over the torus. J. Cryptol. **33**(1), 34–91 (2020). https://doi.org/10.1007/s00145-019-09319-x
5. Chillotti, I., Joye, M., Paillier, P.: Programmable bootstrapping enables efficient homomorphic inference of deep neural networks. In: Dolev, S., Margalit, O., Pinkas, B., Schwarzmann, A. (eds.) CSCML 2021. LNCS, vol. 12716, pp. 1–19. Springer, Cham (2021). https://doi.org/10.1007/978-3-030-78086-9_1

6. Ducas, L., Micciancio, D.: FHEW: bootstrapping homomorphic encryption in less than a second. In: Oswald, E., Fischlin, M. (eds.) EUROCRYPT 2015. LNCS, vol. 9056, pp. 617–640. Springer, Heidelberg (2015). https://doi.org/10.1007/978-3-662-46800-5_24
7. Fan, J., Vercauteren, F.: Somewhat practical fully homomorphic encryption. Cryptology ePrint Archive, Report 2012/144 (2012). https://eprint.iacr.org/2012/144
8. Gentry, C., Peikert, C., Vaikuntanathan, V.: Trapdoors for hard lattices and new cryptographic constructions. In: Ladner, R.E., Dwork, C. (eds.) 40th Annual ACM Symposium on Theory of Computing, pp. 197–206. ACM Press (2008). https://doi.org/10.1145/1374376.1374407
9. Goldwasser, S., Micali, S.: Probabilistic encryption. J. Comput. Syst. Sci. **28**(2), 270–299 (1984)
10. Joye, M.: SoK: Fully homomorphic encryption over the [discretized] torus. IACR Trans. Cryptograph. Hardw. Embed. Syst. **2022**(4), 661–692 (2022). https://doi.org/10.46586/tches.v2022.i4.661-692
11. Joye, M., Walter, M.: Liberating TFHE: Programmable bootstrapping with general quotient polynomials. In: Brenner, M., Costache, A., Rohloff, K. (eds.) Proceedings of the 10th Workshop on Encrypted Computing & Applied Homomorphic Cryptography (WAHC 2022), pp. 1–11. ACM Press (2022). https://doi.org/10.1145/3560827.3563376
12. Lyubashevsky, V., Peikert, C., Regev, O.: On ideal lattices and learning with errors over rings. In: Gilbert, H. (ed.) EUROCRYPT 2010. LNCS, vol. 6110, pp. 1–23. Springer, Heidelberg (2010). https://doi.org/10.1007/978-3-642-13190-5_1
13. Lyubashevsky, V., Peikert, C., Regev, O.: On ideal lattices and learning with errors over rings. J. ACM **6**(43), 1–35 (2013). https://doi.org/10.1145/2535925
14. Peikert, C., Pepin, Z.: Algebraically structured LWE, revisited. In: Hofheinz, D., Rosen, A. (eds.) TCC 2019. LNCS, vol. 11891, pp. 1–23. Springer, Cham (2019). https://doi.org/10.1007/978-3-030-36030-6_1
15. Regev, O.: On lattices, learning with errors, random linear codes, and cryptography. In: Gabow, H.N., Fagin, R. (eds.) 37th Annual ACM Symposium on Theory of Computing, pp. 84–93. ACM Press (2005). https://doi.org/10.1145/1060590.1060603
16. Rosca, M., Stehlé, D., Wallet, A.: On the ring-LWE and polynomial-LWE problems. In: Nielsen, J.B., Rijmen, V. (eds.) EUROCRYPT 2018. LNCS, vol. 10820, pp. 146–173. Springer, Cham (2018). https://doi.org/10.1007/978-3-319-78381-9_6
17. Rothblum, R.: Homomorphic encryption: from private-key to public-key. In: Ishai, Y. (ed.) TCC 2011. LNCS, vol. 6597, pp. 219–234. Springer, Heidelberg (2011). https://doi.org/10.1007/978-3-642-19571-6_14

Differential Privacy for Free? Harnessing the Noise in Approximate Homomorphic Encryption

Tabitha Ogilvie(✉)

Intel Labs, London, UK
tabitha.l.ogilvie@gmail.com

Abstract. Homomorphic Encryption (HE) is a type of cryptography that allows computing on encrypted data, enabling computation on sensitive data to be outsourced securely. Many popular HE schemes rely on noise for their security. On the other hand, Differential Privacy (DP) seeks to guarantee the privacy of data subjects by obscuring any one individual's contribution to an output. Many mechanisms for achieving DP involve adding appropriate noise. In this work, we investigate the extent to which the noise native to Homomorphic Encryption can provide Differential Privacy "for free".

We identify the dependence of HE noise on the underlying data as a critical barrier to privacy, and derive new results on the Differential Privacy under this constraint. We apply these ideas to a proof of concept HE application, ridge regression training using gradient descent, and are able to achieve privacy budgets of $\varepsilon \approx 2$ after 50 iterations.

Keywords: Differential Privacy · Homomorphic Encryption · Machine Learning

1 Introduction

Homomorphic Encryption (HE) is a technology which allows computing on encrypted data without knowing the decryption key. Efficient and secure Homomorphic Encryption has the potential to make many standard scenarios private, including outsourced computation, database queries, machine learning inference, and many more. On the other hand, Differential Privacy is a technique for ensuring the privacy of each data contributor while outputting some statistic or function or a database. At a high level, the goal of both technologies is the same – *keep the data secret*.

Standard techniques for achieving this secrecy are also superficially similar between the two technologies: namely, both introduce noise. Many popular HE schemes [6,7,14,16,26] use the Learning with Errors (LWE) [55] or Ring Learning with Errors (RLWE) [46] problem, which involve adding noise during encryption for security. Differential Privacy (DP) is also achieved by adding noise, but in this context the noise serves to obscure the contribution of any one individual [2, 9,24,25].

E. Oswald (Ed.): CT-RSA 2024, LNCS 14643, pp. 292–315, 2024.
https://doi.org/10.1007/978-3-031-58868-6_12

In this work, we investigate the following question: *does the noise in Homomorphic Encryption give Differential Privacy "for free"?*

At first glance, this may seem unlikely for several reasons. Firstly, as noise is only introduced in HE as part of encryption, standard schemes will remove the noise during decryption. Secondly, to formally quantify Differential Privacy guarantees, we must be able to specify how the noise is distributed, and not just an upper bound, which is the typical output of an HE noise analysis. Lastly, as we only introduce noise in HE for security, and do not want it to corrupt the result of our computation, typically the noise is small relative to the message, and so cannot be sufficient to guarantee privacy.

However, there are contexts where none of these difficulties apply. For the first, the CKKS, or HEAAN, scheme [14] departs from traditional constructions in that noise is *not* removed during decryption, and is retained in the least significant bits of the final output. For this reason, it is sometimes called "Approximate Homomorphic Encryption". For the second, a recent work [19] analyzed noise growth when computing over CKKS, and argues that the noise can be modelled as normally distributed throughout the course of an algorithm. For the final challenge, we make the following observation: when evaluating a very complex or deep algorithm using CKKS, noise can start to overwhelm the message, becoming as large as is required to guarantee privacy. It is this intuition, of noise growing over the course of an application, which we explore in the case study in this paper.

We therefore have HE applications where noise is never removed, grows over the course of an algorithm, and is normally distributed, which suggests these HE applications can achieve DP without further processing; in other words, for free. We just need the noise to grow large enough to mask the contribution of any one individual.

But there is an additional complication. If we examine the results of [19], we find the variance after a multiplication depends on the messages being multiplied. In other words, changing the entries in a database will not only change the "true" output of the algorithm, but the variance of the noise we will add to it. We derive novel results on the impact this has on Differential Privacy, and find that, at least for our case study, this message dependent variance is more important than noise growth in preventing us from achieving Differential Privacy for free.

Building on this result, we are able to formally quantify the Differential Privacy of our case study, and show that, for the proposed parameters, we can achieve privacy budgets of $\varepsilon \approx 2$ without post-processing. In contexts where this is an acceptable level of privacy, we therefore find that Homomorphic Encryption gives Differential Privacy for free.

Our work also establishes another important connection between Differential Privacy and approximate Homomorphic Encryption: these two technologies are not composable. In fact, if we evaluate an algorithm using approximate Homomorphic Encryption, the parameters we use to make the result differentially private will be different than if we had evaluated that same algorithm in the clear.

This is because the message dependent variance creates an additional privacy leakage which must be masked.

1.1 Contributions

In this work, we identify a connection between noise in Homomorphic Encryption and Differential Privacy, and explore this correspondence when Homomorphic Encryption noise is treated as a database dependent output perturbation. We present novel results on the Differential Privacy guarantees of adding database dependent noise in both the one- and multi-dimensional case. We believe this is the first time database dependent noise has been analyzed in the Differential Privacy literature, and may be of independent interest.

We explore these results with a proof of concept case study from the HE literature: ridge regression training using gradient descent [50]. Two factors constrain the choice of case study. Firstly, we require the noise growth analysis from [19], which does not extend to powers beyond the square, so any polynomial evaluation must be at most quadratic[1]; quadratic circuits are however not required in general, and in principle our techniques extend to higher degrees. Secondly, we are guided by the intuition that the noise growth over high depth algorithms is what will guarantee privacy, and so require an application of high multiplicative complexity. In the HE literature, the only application we are aware of that meets both of these criteria is the ridge regression training introduced in [50]. For this case study, we provide a blueprint for how to derive all parameters relevant to Differential Privacy, and present findings on noise growth, message dependence, and finally privacy.

1.2 Related Work

Homomorphic Encryption. Since Gentry's breakthrough construction of a fully homomorphic encryption (FHE) scheme based on lattices [29], many schemes have been proposed following similar principles [6,14,16,23,30].

Due to its ability to handle approximate real numbers, CKKS has been applied to various Machine Learning problems, including ridge and logistic regression training [40,41,50], neural network inference [4,10,36], federated learning [48], and decision tree training [3].

In this work, we will restrict our attention to CKKS as originally presented [14]. However, there have been many works improving and extending the functionality of CKKS, including a Residue Number System (RNS) variant [12].

Differential Privacy. For an in depth overview of the core concepts and literature for differentially private machine learning, we refer to [34]. There, the authors give a helpful representation of the different stages in an algorithm where

[1] More practical use cases might include [40,41], which use degree 3, 5, or 7 approximations to the sigmoid function.

we can add noise to achieve Differential Privacy, which we have reproduced in Algorithm 1. The inclusion of "Input Perturbation" is our own. We present relevant works following this taxonomy, cataloguing output, gradient, objective, and input perturbations.

Algorithm 1. Mechanisms for Achieving Differential Privacy in Machine Learning Training (based on Algorithm 1 of [34]).

```
Input: Data X
Output: A result β
β ← 0
#1 Input perturbation: add noise to data, X ← X + e.
#2 Objective perturbation: add noise to the loss function, J(β, X) ← J(β, X) + e.
for t = 1, ..., T do
    #3 Gradient perturbation: add noise to the gradient updates,
    ∇J(β, X) ← ∇J(β, X) + e.
    β ← β − α∇J(β, X)
end for
#4 Output perturbation: add noise to the final result β ← β + e
return β
```

Output perturbation methods involve analyzing how much the algorithm's output can change from one database to another, and adding enough noise to mask this difference. This technique is pursued when the training algorithm uses a finite number of updates in [61,62], and the algorithm outputs a global minimum in [9,35,45].

For deep learning tasks, when loss functions may be non-convex or non-smooth, it can be difficult to quantify and bound how sensitive the training algorithm is to a single data point in general. Instead, perturbing gradients during training serves to obscure the contribution, and so preserve the privacy, of any one individual each iteration, and then a composition theorem may be used to find the total privacy loss over the course of the algorithm. This approach is adopted in many works, including [2,35,51,56,57].

Objective perturbations broadly fall into two categories. The first seeks to ensure the objective function itself can be released without compromising privacy, while the second seeks to ensure that the minimizer of the objective function can be released without compromising privacy. In other words, the first approach achieves Differential Privacy before training begins, while the second achieves Differential Privacy for the returned value only. The first approach is also called a "Functional Mechanism", and is explored in [22,63], while for the second we refer to [9,33,38].

Input perturbation is the least established of these methods in the context of Machine Learning. The authors of [27] use the terminology to refer to perturbing each data contributor's contribution to the loss function coefficients, and so in our framework is better categorized as an objective perturbation. In [28], the authors achieve a differentially private chi-squared test by perturbing each of the frequencies at the outset, so that we have differential privacy before the algorithm starts. In [37,58], the authors observe that input perturbations in turn perturb the gradients, and so argue that it is sufficient to lower bound this induced perturbation with a known threshold from the gradient perturbation literature. However, this reasoning fails to consider that the width of this induced perturbation will depend on the data itself for almost all loss functions, and so constitutes an additional leakage which needs to be analyzed.

DP and HE. The authors of [52] use both HE and DP in their work, training models homomorphically and then adding a perturbation after decryption to give differential privacy. The protocol proposed in [54] processes sensitive queries homomorphically, and then adds an optional perturbation to achieve Differential Privacy, depending on the clearance of the user. In [59], a two-party protocol is constructed where the input data is differentially private while the output is calculated homomorphically.

Differential Privacy is also combined with Homomorphic Encryption in [44], where DP is used as a tool to harden the security of CKKS in certain security models [43]. Here, the authors' goal is to give privacy to the HE noise itself. Our security model is weaker than that in these works, where in particular, we require that the cryptography adversary and the Differential Privacy adversary do not collude. More details are given in Sect. 5. Future work may wish to examine whether the modification to the CKKS scheme proposed in these works is sufficient to give privacy when the cryptography adversary and Differential Privacy are combined. As an additional observation, we remark that the issues the authors of [44] identify in Section 5, which considers Dynamic Error Estimation, seem analogous to the message dependent variance problem we identify in this work.

1.3 Paper Outline

In Sect. 2 we give the necessary background material. In Sect. 3 we present a formal analysis of the Differential Privacy guarantees of algorithms evaluated homomorphically. In Sect. 4 we apply our results to Ridge Regression to provide a proof of concept analysis, including experimental outcomes in Sect. 4.2. We describe our security model in Sect. 5. We conclude and outline future research directions in Sects. 6 and 7. Omitted details and proofs are provided in the full version of this paper.

2 Background

2.1 Basic Notation

We will use $\log(\cdot)$, for the base-2 logarithm, and $\ln(\cdot)$ for the natural logarithm. For a vector v, we will write v_j to denote the jth component of v, and $||v||$ to denote the 2-norm. For a polynomial m, we will write $||m||$ to denote the 2-norm of the vector of its coefficients. If the coefficients are modulo q, we consider their absolute value to be their representative in $[-q/2, q/2]$. We use $v \leftarrow D$ to denote sampling v according to the distribution D, and $N(\mu, \Sigma)$ for the multivariate Gaussian distribution with mean $\mu \in \mathbb{R}^d$ and covariance matrix $\Sigma \in \mathbb{R}^{d \times d}$. We extend this notation to the 1-dimensional case, where we will use $N(\mu, \sigma^2)$ for the univariate Gaussian with mean μ and variance σ^2. We will write $\chi_d^2(\nu)$ for the non-central chi-squared distribution with d degrees of freedom and non-centrality parameter ν. In more detail, if we have for $X_i \sim N(\mu_i, 1)$ for $i = 1, ..., d$ then $Y = \sum_{i=1}^d X_i^2$ has distribution $\chi_d^2(\nu)$, where $\nu = \sum_{i=1}^d \mu_i^2$.

We will use the following standard tail bound for Gaussian distributions.

Lemma 1. *Let $X \sim \mathcal{N}(0, \rho^2)$. Then for any $t > 0$ we have*

$$\Pr[X > t] \leq \frac{\rho}{\sqrt{2\pi}t} \exp\left(\frac{-t^2}{2\rho^2}\right).$$

Rearranging for t gives the following corollary.

Corollary 1. *Let $X \sim \mathcal{N}(0, \rho^2)$. Then if $t > 0$ and*

$$\ln(t/\rho) + t^2/2\rho^2 > \ln\left(\sqrt{\frac{2}{\pi}}\frac{1}{\delta}\right)$$

we have $\Pr[X > t] < \delta/2$.

As we will need to quote results from two literatures, which frequently use the same symbol for different concepts, we additionally provide a table of the notation we follow in this paper in Sect. 2.6.

2.2 CKKS

Our work focuses on the CKKS scheme [14]. Typically, HE schemes [6,26,30,46] maintain a strict separation between message bits and noise bits, enabling the noise bits to be efficiently removed during decryption. On the other hand, the authors of CKKS argue that in some contexts this is unnecessary, and it is sufficient to allow the noise to interact with the lower bits of the message, controlling the noise growth via a Rescale() procedure. This relaxation is compared to floating point precision errors, which are tolerable in some contexts. This relaxation also enables efficiently encrypting and homomorphically processing high precision real numbers.

For our purposes, we will only need to consider a few key features of the CKKS scheme: CKKS is parametrised by a power of 2 polynomial modulus N, as well as a (typically power of 2) precision parameter Δ. The scheme has *message space* given by $\mathbb{C}^{N/2}$, where $\mathbb{C}$ is the set of complex numbers, and *plaintext space* given by the ring $\mathbb{Z}[X]/(X^N + 1)$. Data is *encoded* from the native message space into the plaintext space before encryption. For a more comprehensive exploration of the CKKS scheme, we refer to [5,11,14,39,53]

The approximate nature of CKKS requires additional security considerations in many scenarios, which should be taken into consideration whenever deploying CKKS based solutions. Further details can be found in [13,43,44].

CKKS Noise Growth. Understanding and bounding noise growth is critical to applications of HE. A typical approach[2] [8,20] involves arguing that "fresh" sources of noise are normally distributed, and so uses a Gaussian tail bound to give a high probability bound B, which can be used to bound the noise in decrypted results. Together with the triangle inequality, this gives high probability bounds for the noise resulting from homomorphic computation. For example, if we add two ciphertexts with noise bounds B_1 and B_2 respectively, we can bound the noise of the resulting ciphertext by $B_1 + B_2$.

A different approach is explored in [19,21,49], where it is argued that, due to the Central Limit Theorem, noise remains Gaussian throughout the entire computation. This approach generates much tighter noise bounds. For example, in [19], the authors show that if we multiply encryptions of plaintexts m_1 and m_2 with noise variances σ_1^2 and σ_2^2 respectively, the resulting ciphertext has Gaussian noise in the ring with variance

$$\sigma^2 = N\sigma_1^2\sigma_2^2 + \sigma_1^2 \,||m_2||_2^2 + \sigma_2^2 \,||m_1||_2^2 .$$

In order to translate a variance σ^2 in the plaintext space to a variance ρ^2 in $\mathbb{R}^{N/2}$, we have to understand the impact of decoding on a Gaussian distribution. As shown in [19], and observed in other contexts [47,53], if we restrict ourselves to real messages, we have that the noise in the message space is also normally distributed, with variance $\rho^2 = \frac{N}{2\Delta^2}\sigma^2$, where Δ is the decoding scale factor. We give full details of how to update the ring variance after various homomorphic operations in the appendices to the full version of this paper, using the analysis of [19].

2.3 Differential Privacy

We draw extensively from [24,34]. Differential Privacy seeks to formally quantify and minimise the extent to which an algorithm's output depends on the input of any one individual to the dataset. To this end, we will say two databases $\mathcal{D}$ and $\mathcal{D}'$ are *neighboring* or *adjacent* if they differ on at most one row. We define Differential Privacy as follows:

Definition 1 ((ε, δ)-Differential Privacy). *A randomized algorithm $\mathcal{M}$ with domain $\mathbb{N}^{|\mathcal{X}|}$ is (ε, δ) differentially private if for all $\mathcal{S} \subseteq \text{Range}(\mathcal{M})$ and for all neighboring databases $\mathcal{D}$ and $\mathcal{D}'$,*

$$\Pr[\mathcal{M}(\mathcal{D}) \in \mathcal{S}] \leqslant \exp(\varepsilon) \Pr[\mathcal{M}(\mathcal{D}') \in \mathcal{S}] + \delta,$$

where the probability is over the randomness of $\mathcal{M}$.

[2] For TFHE and related schemes [16,17], a so-called "average case", or variance tracking, approach is more common – see for example [15,18,42].

We can interpret this as any outcome $\mathcal{S}$ does not become much more or less likely by modifying a single entry, except with a small tolerance probability δ. There are various alternative notions of Differential Privacy in the literature: we refer to [34] for an overview.

Observe that the algorithm $\mathcal{M}$ can take many forms, from individual database entries, to summary statistics, to the outcome of a machine learning training algorithm with training set $\mathcal{D}$, and in each case the Differential Privacy considerations will be different. It will be necessary to understand the extent to which an algorithm can be influenced by a single entry, which is captured in the following definition.

Definition 2 (l_p Sensitivity). *The l_p sensitivity of an algorithm $f : \mathbb{N}^{|\mathcal{X}|} \to \mathbb{R}^k$ is:*

$$\delta_f^{(p)} = \max_{\substack{\mathcal{D},\mathcal{D}' \in \mathbb{N}^{|\mathcal{X}|} \\ adjacent}} ||f(\mathcal{D}) - f(\mathcal{D}')||_p$$

In this work we will only consider $p = 2$, and so will omit the (p)-superscript.

Frequently Differential Privacy is achieved via adding random noise. One such method is the *Gaussian Mechanism*, defined as follows.

Definition 3 (Gaussian Mechanism). *The Gaussian Mechanism with parameter ρ^2 adds zero-mean Gaussian noise with variance ρ^2 to each of the d coordinates of an algorithm's output.*

The relationship between (ε, δ)-Differential Privacy, sensitivity, and the Gaussian Mechanism is a standard result in the literature, but we will defer it's presentation to Sect. 3, in order to properly motivate our own analysis.

Finally, we repeat the *post-processing* principle, which guarantees that if an algorithm is (ε, δ)-differentially private, any further data-independent computation preserves this privacy.

Proposition 1 (Proposition 2.1 of [24]). *Let $\mathcal{M} : \mathbb{N}^{|\mathcal{X}|} \to R$ be a randomized algorithm that is (ε, δ)-differentially private. Let $f : R \to R'$ be an arbitrary mapping. Then $f \circ \mathcal{M} : \mathbb{N}^{|\mathcal{X}|} \to R'$ is (ε, δ)-differentially private.*

The parameter ε is sometimes referred to as a *privacy budget*, and an acceptable value will depend on the context. Indeed, in [34], it is observed that for simpler applications, a privacy budget in the range $(0, 1)$ is sufficient to have a performant algorithm. On the other hand, for more complex learning tasks, a typical privacy budget can be around 10. As observed by the authors of [34] however, in standard applications, the privacy implications of budgets this high may be unacceptable. Indeed, if $\varepsilon = 10$, an outcome can go from almost impossible to almost certain by changing just one value in the dataset, completely compromising the privacy of the individual added.

2.4 Update Rules

In the analysis of sensitivity for our case study, we will use the terminology and notation of [61] and [31] for clarity, namely *update rules*. An update rule is simply a function $G : \Omega \to \Omega$ for some arbitrary set Ω. For gradient descent, $\Omega = \mathbb{R}^d$, and we would have an update rule of the following form

$$G(\beta) = \beta - \alpha \nabla J(\beta, \mathcal{D}).$$

where J is our cost function, ∇J its derivative, and α the learning rate. In particular, the update rule G *depends on the database.* The authors of [31,61] use this terminology to analyze, respectively, the stability and differential privacy of Permutation Based Stochastic Gradient Descent (PSGD). PSGD differs from Gradient Descent in that it only uses one randomly selected training example per update.

If we have an iterative procedure with updates $G_1, G_2, ..., G_T$, and a fixed starting point $\beta^{(0)}$, the full algorithm is therefore equivalent to the composition $G_T \circ G_{T-1} \circ ... \circ G_1$ applied to $\beta^{(0)}$.

2.5 Ridge Regression Case Study

We will explore our results with an application to ridge regression training using gradient descent. This algorithm was originally implemented using CKKS in [50].

As an additional assumption, we will assume databases satisfy each $|y_i|, |x_{ij}| \leq 1$ which can be achieved via normalization.

Ridge regression takes n entries $x_i \in \mathbb{R}^d$ with n labels y_i, and seeks weights $\beta_1, \beta_2, ...\beta_d$ such that[3]:

$$y_i \approx \beta_1 x_{i1} + \beta_2 x_{i2} + ... + \beta_d x_{id}$$

for each i. Ridge regression additionally seeks to prevent overfitting by penalising large values of β_j with $l2$ regularisation. The cost function for ridge regression is of the form:

$$J(\beta, \mathcal{D}) = \frac{1}{2}\lambda ||\beta||^2 + \frac{1}{2n}\sum_{i=1}^{n}(y_i - \beta \cdot x_i)^2, \tag{1}$$

where the parameter λ is the *regularization parameter*, and determines the degree of penalization of large coefficients. We will sometimes omit the second argument $\mathcal{D}$.

We will be considering minimising (1) using gradient descent. We will initialize $\beta = 0$, and then iteratively update the parameters via

$$\beta \leftarrow \beta - \alpha \nabla J(\beta), \tag{2}$$

where α is the *learning rate*, which possibly changes from iteration to iteration. Differentiating our cost function, this is equivalent to updating each weight via

$$\beta_j \leftarrow (1 - \lambda\alpha)\beta_j + \frac{\alpha}{n}\sum_{i=1}^{n} x_{ij}\,(y_i - \beta \cdot x_i) \tag{3}$$

[3] In this work, for simplicity we do not train a constant weight β_0.

Without additional restrictions, the unbounded gradients of the cost function make it impossible to bound the sensitivity of ridge regression parameters after a fixed number of updates. We therefore assume the following additional heuristic.

Heuristic 2.51. *The learning rate is such that $J(\beta, \mathcal{D})$ decreases each iteration.*

Observe that such a learning rate can be chosen whenever the cost function is Lipschitz continuous, which is not the case here. In our experiments, we will use a decaying learning rate, which perhaps makes this heuristic more reasonable. For our case study, as a consequence, we will only be able to claim differential privacy over the subset of databases for which this heuristic holds. If the heuristic fails, it may be possible to distinguish which database was used during training.

From the heuristic, we can derive the following[4].

Lemma 2. *Assuming Heuristic 2.51, at each iteration we have that β satisfies $||\beta||_2 \leq \frac{1}{\sqrt{\lambda}}$.*

Proof. As the cost decreases each iteration, letting $\beta^{(k)}$ be the output of the kth update, so that $\beta^{(0)} = 0$, and recalling each $|y_i| \leq 1$,

$$J(\beta^{(k)}, \mathcal{D}) \leq J(\beta^{(0)}, \mathcal{D}) = \frac{1}{2n}\sum_{i=1}^{n} y_i^2 \leq \frac{1}{2},$$

while on the other hand

$$\lambda \left|\left|\beta^{(k)}\right|\right|_2^2 \leq \lambda \left|\left|\beta^{(k)}\right|\right|_2^2 + \frac{1}{n}\sum_{i=1}^{n}(y_i - \beta^{(k)} \cdot x_i)^2 = 2J(\beta^{(k)}, \mathcal{D}),$$

so we can conclude $\left|\left|\beta^{(k)}\right|\right|_2^2 \leq 1/\lambda$.

2.6 Notation Key

We present a guide to the notation we will use throughout this paper (Table 1).

As we are unifying concepts from various fields, some of these depart from standard notation. Most prominently, in Differential Privacy, it is typical to use Δ to denote sensitivity, whereas in CKKS, this symbol is used for the precision parameter. For the noise analysis, we consistently use σ^2 for noise variances in the plaintext space (ring), and ρ^2 for the variance of error over the reals.

3 Differential Privacy Analysis

Let us now consider how best to analyze the Differential Privacy guarantees of an algorithm evaluated homomorphically using the CKKS scheme. Let us first note that, since all intermediary stages are encrypted, it is sufficient to consider

[4] This bound applies unconditionally to the *minimum* of the cost function – see [45]. However, in our case study we will only evaluate a fixed number of iterations of gradient descent, and so cannot assume we converge to the minimum.

Table 1. A guide to the notation we follow in this paper.

HE	N	polynomial modulus
	Δ	precision parameter
	ct.X	a ciphertext encrypting X
	σ_X^2	ring variance when calculating X homomorphically
	ρ_X^2	real variance when calculating X homomorphically
DP	ε	privacy budget
	δ	failure probability
	δ_f	sensitivity of the function f
Database	n	number of database rows
	d	number of database columns
	x_{ij}	feature j of ith entry
	y_i	label of ith entry
ML	β	vector of model weights
	λ	regularization coefficient
	α	learning rate

the privacy of the final output. Secondly, we can use the results in [19] to argue that the final output follows a normal distribution of the following form

$$\beta + N(0, \rho^2) \tag{4}$$

where β is the "true" output of the algorithm. Thus an initial approach may attempt to ensure ρ is large enough to mask the difference $\beta - \beta'$ over adjacent databases. For this approach, we have the following classical result on the privacy guarantee of the Gaussian Mechanism [24,38].

Theorem 1. *Let $\varepsilon \in (0,1)$ be arbitrary. For $c^2 > 2\ln(1.25/\delta)$, the Gaussian Mechanism is (ε, δ)-differentially private whenever $\rho \geq c\delta_f/\varepsilon$, where δ_f is the sensitivity.*

Therefore, if we bound $||\beta - \beta'||$ at iteration k by δ_k, and have the variance at iteration k is (at least) ρ^2, then if we have $\rho^2 > 2\ln(1.25/\delta)\delta_k^2/\varepsilon^2$ it may seem we can argue we have (ε, δ) Differential Privacy at the kth iteration. We present experimental results for this approach applied to our case study in Sect. 4.2.

However, let us look more closely at how we update the variance after a multiplication. If we multiply encryptions of plaintexts m_1 and m_2 with ring noise variances σ_1^2 and σ_2^2 respectively, the resulting encryption has ring noise with variance:

$$N\sigma_1^2\sigma_2^2 + \sigma_1^2 \left|\left|m_2\right|\right|^2 + \sigma_2^2 \left|\left|m_1\right|\right|^2 . \tag{5}$$

Therefore, the variance of an algorithm's output when evaluated homomorphically using CKKS *is dependent on the input data.* Therefore, our situation is more accurately modelled as outputs from the distribution

$$\beta_{\mathcal{D}} + N\left(0, \rho_{\mathcal{D}}^2\right) \tag{6}$$

where mean *and* variance depend on the underlying database. We therefore need to properly quantify the impact of this additional database dependency on Differential Privacy. This is accomplished in the one dimensional case by the following theorem.

Theorem 2. *Suppose we use a Gaussian mechanism with variance $\rho_{\mathcal{D}}^2$ dependent on the underlying database. Then the resulting mechanism is (ε, δ) differential private if $D = 2\ln\left(\sqrt{\frac{2}{\pi}\frac{1}{\delta}}\right) > 1$ and*

$$\varepsilon > T^2 K\sqrt{D} + \frac{1}{2}T^2K^2 + \frac{1}{2}(T^2-1)D + \ln T$$

where $\max \frac{\rho_{\mathcal{D}}}{\rho_{\mathcal{D}'}} \leq T$, $\max \frac{|\beta_{\mathcal{D}} - \beta_{\mathcal{D}'}|}{\rho_{\mathcal{D}}} \leq K$, where the maximums are taken over adjacent databases.

Proof. The proof is given in Appendix B of the extended version of this paper.

Remark 1. In the case $T = 1$, we might hope to recover the standard Gaussian Mechanism inequality, since this corresponds to the variance having no message dependence. And indeed, if we let $T = 1$, we have $\varepsilon > K\sqrt{D} + \frac{1}{2}K^2 = O\left(\sqrt{\ln(\frac{1}{\delta})}\delta_f/\rho\right)$, which is asymptotically the same as in the standard case.

In the multidimensional case, we instead prove the following.

Theorem 3. *Suppose we use the following Gaussian mechanism: for a database $\mathcal{D}$, we provide a sample from the distribution $N(\beta_{\mathcal{D}}, \Sigma_{\mathcal{D}})$, where $\beta_{\mathcal{D}} \in \mathbb{R}^d$, and $\Sigma_{\mathcal{D}}$ is a diagonal matrix with diagonal entries $\rho_{\mathcal{D},1}, ..., \rho_{\mathcal{D},d}$ which are dependent on the database $\mathcal{D}$. This mechanism is (ε, δ) differentially private if*

$$\varepsilon > \sqrt{(\frac{1}{2}d(T^2-1) + T^4K^2)D} + \frac{1}{2}T^2K^2 + \frac{1}{2}(T^2-1)(D+d) + d\ln T$$

where $D = 2\ln\frac{1}{\delta}$, $\max \frac{\rho_{\mathcal{D},i}}{\rho_{\mathcal{D}',i}} \leq T$ for all i, and

$$\max \left|\left|\left(\frac{\beta_{\mathcal{D},1} - \beta_{\mathcal{D}',1}}{\rho_{\mathcal{D},1}}, ..., \frac{\beta_{\mathcal{D},d} - \beta'_{\mathcal{D}',d}}{\rho_{\mathcal{D},d}}\right)\right|\right| \leq K,$$

where maximums are taken over adjacent databases $\mathcal{D}$ and $\mathcal{D}'$.

Proof. The proof is given in Appendix B of the extended version of this paper.

Remark 2. We again have that the asymptotic behaviour when $T = 1$ is equal to that in the classical case. However, when $d = 1$ the multivariate ε is strictly larger than in the univariate case. This may be an artefact of our proof technique, and in particular that the tail bound we use for a noncentral chi-squared distribution is strictly looser than the tail bound we use for a Gaussian distribution.

The full version of this theorem provides the opportunity to treat different components of the algorithm output differently. This may be valuable if, for example, we want to release the evaluation of different functions which have distinct sensitivities or variance growth. For our case study we will not take advantage of this flexibility, and so give the following corollary for the homogeneous case.

Corollary 2. *The mechanism from Theorem 3 is* (ε, δ) *differentially private whenever*

$$\varepsilon > \sqrt{(\frac{1}{2}d(T^2-1)+T^4K^2)D} + \frac{1}{2}T^2K^2 + \frac{1}{2}(T^2-1)(D+d) + d\ln T,$$

where $D = 2\ln\frac{1}{\delta}$, $\max\frac{\rho_{\mathcal{D},i}}{\rho_{\mathcal{D}',i}} \leq T$ *for all* i *and* $\delta_f/\rho \leq K$*, where* δ_f *is the sensitivity and we have* $\rho_{\mathcal{D},i} \geq \rho$ *for all* i *and all databases* $\mathcal{D}$*.*

4 Case Study

Now that we have an analysis of the privacy guarantees of an abstract homomorphic algorithm, we make these ideas concrete by analysing ridge regression, and provide a "recipe" for how to use these ideas for other applications. As we are pursuing a gradient descent approach, we will be investigating the differential privacy guarantees after k iterations.

Looking at Corollary 2 and Theorem 1, we must analyze the following quantities:

- *Sensitivity.* Written δ_f, a bound on $||\beta - \beta'||$ at iteration k where β and β' are produced by neighboring databases. We provide a novel analysis in Sect. 4.1.
- *Noise Variance.* Written $\rho_{\mathcal{D},i}$, we must understand the variance of the noise on each β_i in the message space. We give an analysis including upper and lower bounds, in the appendices of the full version of this paper. We believe this is the first "average case" analysis of the noise growth across a full CKKS algorithm. For the lower bounds, we introduce a density parameter c which corresponds to a lower bound on relevant message magnitudes.
- *Message Dependence.* Written T, we must bound the ratio of variances produced by neighboring databases.

We make essential use of the heuristics derived in [19], which to the best of our knowledge represents the state of the art for average case analysis of CKKS, and argue that deriving additional average case heuristics is beyond the scope of this work. We use the noise analysis for textbook CKKS, and restrict our attention to the non-SIMD case, as this is not treated by the authors of [19].

4.1 Sensitivity

To bound the difference $||\beta - \beta'||$, we will use a corollary to the following lemma.

Lemma 3. *Fix an arbitrary sequence of updates $G_1, ..., G_T : \Omega \to \Omega$ and another sequence $G'_1, ..., G'_T : \Omega \to \Omega$. Let $\beta_0 = \beta'_0$ be a fixed starting point in Ω and define $\delta_t = ||\beta_t - \beta'_t||$ where β_t, β'_t are defined recursively through*

$$\beta_t = G_t(\beta_{t-1}), \quad \beta'_k = G'_t(\beta'_{t-1})$$

Let $\mathcal{B} = \{\beta_0, ..., \beta_T, \beta'_0, ..., \beta'_T\}$ be the "update set". Then, if $\sup_{x\in\mathcal{B}} ||G_t(x) - G'_t(x)|| \le \eta_t$ and either G_t or G'_t is L_t-Lipschitz, we have $\delta_t \le \eta_t + L_t\delta_{t-1}$.

Proof. See Appendix C of the extended version.

Corollary 3. *Let δ_k be the sensitivity of the kth ridge regression update as described in Sect. 2.5. Then we have the recurrence relation*

$$\delta_0 = 0, \quad \delta_1 = \frac{2\alpha\sqrt{d}}{n}, \quad \delta_k \le \frac{2\alpha}{n}\left(\sqrt{d} + \frac{d}{\sqrt{\lambda}}\right) + (|1-\lambda| + \alpha d)\delta_{k-1}.$$

Proof. See Appendix C of the extended version.

4.2 Experiments

We now explore the Differential Privacy of our case study experimentally by simulating the noise growth with the heuristics. Since we see in [50] that this algorithm exhibits very slow convergence, we do not report on the accuracy of derived models – we will be exclusively interested in the privacy properties. Our primary goal in this section is to use this case study to explore the theory developed in Sect. 3.

Between the database, algorithm, HE, and DP parameters, we will not be able to explore the impact of all choices on Differential Privacy, and fix many throughout. For the database, we set $n = 4096$ and $d = 10$, while for the regression we let $\lambda = 1$, and use a dynamic learning rate $\alpha = 1/i$ at iteration i. On the privacy side, we fix the failure tolerance as $\delta = 1/n = 1/4096$. For the homomorphic encryption, we will fix all but the precision parameter Δ – for the other parameters, we let $N = 2^{16}$, set χ as the discrete Gaussian with standard deviation 3.2, and let S be the uniform ternary distribution, so that the hamming weights of both s and v are well approximated by $\frac{2}{3}N$. For the keyswitching, we assume the auxiliary modulus has the same size as the top level modulus, or $Q_L = P$, as was the case in the original CKKS implementation [32]. We also implicitly assume the final modulus is large enough that neither plaintext nor noise have a wrap-around.

We first examine how variance grows as we compute more and more iterations for a fixed precision. This is done in Fig. 1a, where we plot the variance lower

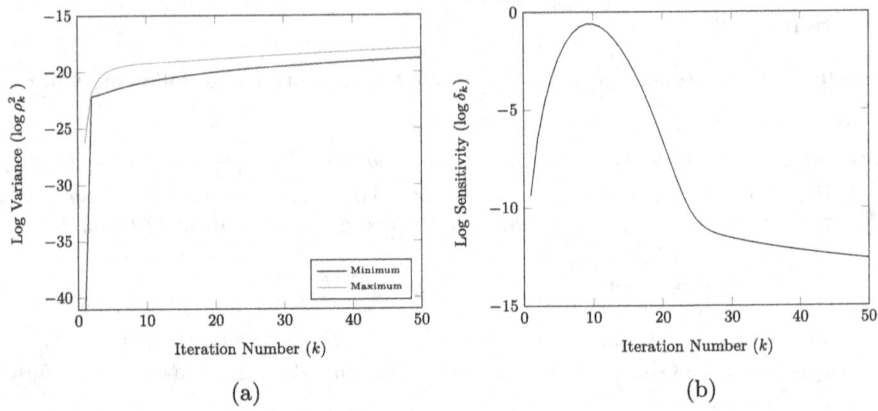

Fig. 1. (a) Variance Growth with Iteration. $\log \Delta = 25$. (b) Sensitivity Growth with Iteration.

and upper bound against the iteration number. From this graph, we observe that, as expected, the variance grows with iteration number in both "best" and "worst" case for this value of Δ. We also observe that for these parameters the maximum and minimum values of the variance have a difference of around 1 bit by iteration 50.

We additionally show how sensitivity changes with iteration in Fig. 1b. Due to our parameter choices, in particular the decay of the learning rate α, we have that sensitivity increases at first, and then decreases. This shape is echoed in many of the following figures, as many quantities are dependent on sensitivity.

"Variance Only" Approach. Let us now investigate how much Differential Privacy we might expect if we only look at the variance, i.e., if we treat this as a standard Gaussian Mechanism. In more detail, we calculate a lower bound on the variance ρ^2, and use Theorem 1 to calculate the ε for which we have (ε, δ) privacy. The results are displayed in Fig. 2a. These values for the precision parameter may appear quite low, with $\log \Delta$ in the range 30 to 40 being more common. However, this graph does suggest that a small parameter relaxation can give Differential Privacy, with all parameter sets reaching a privacy leakage less than 1 by iteration 30. As we might expect, we also find that, for this approach, the privacy leakage increases with $\log \Delta$. This corresponds to higher precision Δ giving smaller noise.

To give an additional insight into the relationship between Δ and privacy in this model, we plot $\log \Delta$ against the number of iterations required to achieve (ε, δ) privacy for a variety of privacy budgets ε in Fig. 2b. Lines cutting off correspond to not being able to stay within the privacy budget for a given $\log \Delta$ within 100 iterations.

Full Approach. Modelling Homomorphic Encryption noise as a simple Gaussian Mechanism suggests we can be cautiously optimistic about achieving Differ-

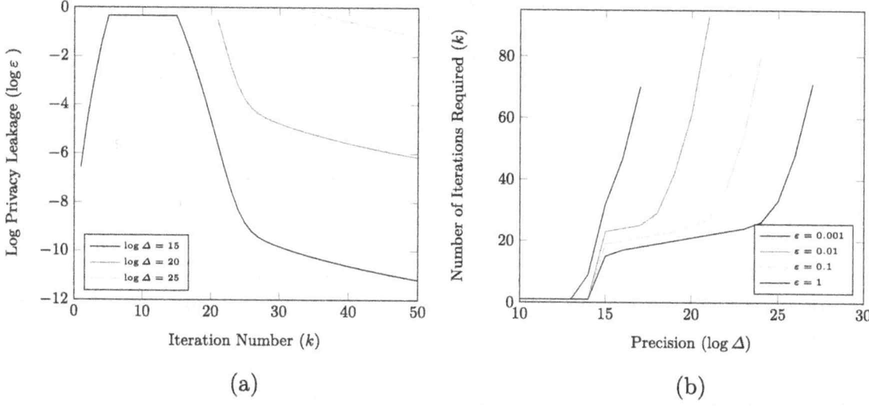

Fig. 2. (a) ε Growth with Iteration for Varying Δ in the Variance Only Model. (b) Number of Iterations for (ε, δ) Privacy as a Function of Δ and ε in the Variance Only Model.

ential Privacy with only a small relaxation of the precision parameter. However, to accurately capture the situation we must consider the impact of message dependence. We plot how this varies over many iterations in Fig. 3a. We first note that perhaps surprisingly, message dependence for this case study decreases with iteration, getting very close to the "no message dependence" by iteration 50 for $\log \Delta = 20$ and 25. We also have that the lines for $\log \Delta = 20$ and 25 almost coincide completely. Another key observation is that message dependence decreases as $\log \Delta$ increases.

Lastly, we look at the full privacy leakage of this case study. We plot the privacy budget of each iteration, for a range of $\log \Delta$, following Corollary 2. We

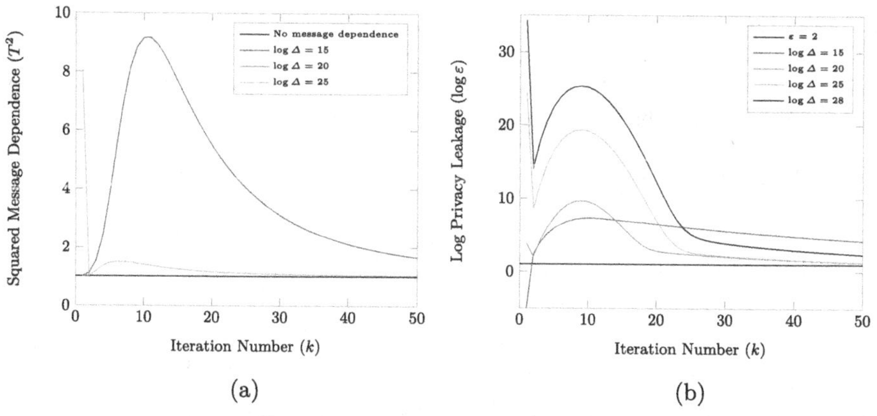

Fig. 3. (a) Message Dependence Change with Iteration. (b) Change in Log Privacy Leakage with Iteration.

find the privacy leakage is much worse than we might expect, given the small leakage in the "variance only" approach (Fig. 2a) and the low message dependence for later iterations (Fig. 3a). In fact, for these parameters, ε never falls below 2.

Interestingly, we find the opposite relationship between Δ and privacy than was observed when only considering the variance – namely, past a certain number of iterations, higher Δ gives better privacy. This is because message dependence (T) dominates the sensitivity to variance ratio ($\delta_f/\rho \leq K$) in the calculation of ε.

We find that for this case study, privacy leakage falls as we perform more iterations. This observation contrasts with findings in the differential privacy literature, where early stopping is used to reduce privacy leakage [60,64].

We also probed our privacy budget formula ε to determine exactly which term(s) dominate, at least for this case study. We found that the $\frac{1}{2}dD(T^2-1)$ inside the square root has a large impact on the privacy leakage in later iterations. Interestingly, this term is not present in our result for the one dimensional case (Theorem 2), implying algorithms with one dimensional outputs may be able to achieve stronger privacy guarantees.

To understand the privacy-accuracy trade off, we can use the $6\sqrt{V}$ tail bound which is standard in HE noise analysis to give a worst case error on each coefficient of the output. We compute that for $\log \Delta = 25$, our heuristics give an error of at most -6 bits.

The number of iterations we suggest to give good privacy guarantees is much higher than that of the existing implementation. Indeed, the authors of [50] perform only 9 iterations at 40 bit precision, and 13 iterations at 30 bit precision. However, our simplified algorithm actually has lower depth consumption[5]. We could therefore evaluate k iterations of this algorithm consuming a bit length of $(k+1) \cdot \log \Delta$.

5 Relationship to IND-CPA^{D} Security

In combining Homomorphic Encryption with Differential Privacy, we are implicitly considering two adversaries: one against the security of the encryption scheme, and one against the Differential Privacy of the input data. Let us clarify what each adversary has access to during a standard "left or right" game.

Encryption Adversary $\mathcal{A}_E$	DP Adversary $\mathcal{A}_{DP}$
	$(\mathcal{D}_0, \mathcal{D}_1) \leftarrow \mathcal{A}_{DP}$
$\mathsf{ct}.\mathcal{D} \leftarrow \mathsf{Encrypt}(\mathcal{D}_b)$	
$\mathsf{ct}.\beta \leftarrow \mathsf{Eval}(\mathsf{ct}.\mathcal{D}, C)$	
	$\beta \leftarrow \mathsf{Decrypt}(\mathsf{ct}.\beta)$

[5] Indeed, high precision constants are used, requiring an additional rescale, as well as multiplying by 1-hot masks to compensate for the feature by feature encoding. By contrast, our method uses 1 level in precomputation of M_{jk}, Y_j, and then one multiplication per iteration.

where $\mathcal{D}_0$ and $\mathcal{D}_1$ are adjacent databases. The goal of both adversaries is to determine the bit b.

Observe that if these adversaries collude, then the CKKS scheme is vulnerable to the key recovery attack exhibited in [43], so that this stronger adversary can simply decrypt the ciphertext $\mathsf{ct}.\mathcal{D}$ and determine the bit b. In more detail, if the ciphertext is given by $(a, b) = (a, m - as + e)$, and we give the adversary access to the decryption of this ciphertext, the adversary can compute

$$b - \mathsf{Decrypt}((a, b)) = (m - as + e) - (m + e) = -as,$$

giving a full key recovery by multiplying by $-a^{-1}$.

To achieve security against this combined adversary, we must at least have security in the $\mathsf{IND\text{-}CPA^D}$ game introduced in [43]. In fact, our adversary may be stronger than in this game as it is not limited to decryptions for which the true value coincides on the right and left.

To achieve $\mathsf{IND\text{-}CPA^D}$ security, it was proposed in [44] to post process decryption results by adding noise from a discrete Gaussian with standard deviation

$$\sigma = \sqrt{12\tau}2^{s/2}B,$$

where τ is the number of calls the adversary can make to the decryption oracle, s is the desired bit security in the $\mathsf{IND\text{-}CPA^D}$ game, and B is a bound on the noise in the decryption result[6] If we limit the adversary to 1 query and target 30 bits of security, as in [1], we lose an additional 15 bits of precision compared to the model where we have two non-colluding adversaries.

6 Conclusion

In this work, we investigated the extent to which the noise growth in homomorphic encryption can provide differential privacy to the output. We identify that the major challenge is that the noise growth is dependent on the input messages, and so forms an additional privacy leakage. To this end, we derive new results on the differential privacy guarantees when adding message dependent noise. Using a case study, we find that a small relaxation of the precision parameter is enough to give reasonable privacy guarantees when we do not consider message dependence, achieving privacy budgets of $\varepsilon < 0.5$ within 50 iterations. However, when we properly account for message dependence, the privacy leakage is much higher, and we find that message dependence dominates noise growth, leading to noise budgets of $\varepsilon \approx 2$ after 50 iterations.

An unexpected consequence of our analysis is that this kind of approximate homomorphic encryption is not *composable* with differential privacy. In more detail, if we evaluate a function f using approximate HE, it is not sufficient to postprocess the result with a DP mechanism tuned to f only. To achieve Differential Privacy in this setting, we must also quantify the additional privacy leakage coming from the homomorphic evaluation noise itself, and apply results like Theorems 2 and 3.

[6] We use the formula from [1] as we bound noise in the canonical embedding.

7 Further Work

Further Noise Analysis. We were limited in our case study by the state of the art in average case, or variance tracking, analysis for CKKS. In particular, to investigate the privacy guarantees of more practical algorithms, we would need to develop heuristics for degrees beyond squaring, and polynomial evaluations more generally. We would also need to understand the impact of packing and packing techniques on slotwise variance growth.

From Heuristic to Guarantee. While heuristic results may be sufficient when developing functionality, the burden of proof is higher when we want to use these results to argue for privacy. Independence assumptions are commonplace; in this paper for example, we assumed independence between the noise of certain ciphertexts and implicitly between keyswitching keys. More generally in the RLWE setting, it is common to assume independence between the noise on each coefficient, and discrete distributions are approximated with continuous ones. Without understanding either the validity of these assumptions, or their impact on privacy, it is premature to make claims on the Differential Privacy of applications "in the wild".

Alternative Applications and Schemes. As a major challenge identified in our work is message dependent noise growth, future work may seek encodings and algorithms which minimize this factor, in order to take advantage of Differential Privacy "for free". In particular, we note that message dependence is not present until the first multiplication – if an algorithm begins with many additions, it may be possible to argue that differential privacy has already been achieved before message dependence becomes an issue, and then argue privacy via post processing. Alternatively, schemes such as TFHE do not appear to suffer from the same message dependence, so that relaxing the exactness requirements may result in differentially private outputs.

Beyond Output Perturbation. In this work, we only looked into whether the final noise was sufficient to give differential privacy. In short, we modelled the homomorphic noise as behaving like an output perturbation. However, noise is added to the data during encryption, and so could alternatively be characterized as an input perturbation. Indeed, in some contexts which have very sensitive message spaces, it may be possible that the noise added during encryption means that differential privacy is already achieved at this stage, and then argue by post processing that any output must also be differentially private. It may also be possible to draw from known results on objective and gradient perturbation, since any noise added to the data will perturb the objective as well as any gradient.

DP "At a Discount". We have explored Differential Privacy "for free" – i.e., without making modifications to the algorithm or scheme. Future work could investigate whether hybrid solutions can achieve better Differential Privacy guarantees, while still harnessing the noise in approximate HE. For example, it may be possible to introduce independent noise which is less than would be required in a pure DP solution, but compensates for the message dependence present in a pure HE solution.

Acknowledgements. We thank Fernando Virdia for his invaluable suggestions and discussions in the development of this work, including detailed comments on an early draft of this paper.

References

1. Openfhe noise flooding. https://github.com/openfheorg/openfhe-development/blob/main/src/pke/examples/CKKS_NOISE_FLOODING.md. Accessed 21 Jan 2024
2. Abadi, M., et al.: Deep learning with differential privacy. In: Proceedings of the 2016 ACM SIGSAC Conference on Computer and Communications Security, pp. 308–318 (2016)
3. Akavia, A., Leibovich, M., Resheff, Y.S., Ron, R., Shahar, M., Vald, M.: Privacy-preserving decision trees training and prediction. ACM Trans. Priv. Secur. **25**(3), 1–30 (2022)
4. Boemer, F., Cammarota, R., Demmler, D., Schneider, T., Yalame, H.: MP2ML: a mixed-protocol machine learning framework for private inference. In: Proceedings of the 15th International Conference on Availability, Reliability and Security, pp. 1–10 (2020)
5. Bossuat, J.P., Troncoso-Pastoriza, J., Hubaux, J.P.: Bootstrapping for approximate homomorphic encryption with negligible failure-probability by using sparse-secret encapsulation. In: Ateniese, G., Venturi, D. (eds.) ACNS 2022. LNCS, vol. 13269, pp. 521–541. Springer, Cham (2022). https://doi.org/10.1007/978-3-031-09234-3_26
6. Brakerski, Z., Gentry, C., Vaikuntanathan, V.: (Leveled) fully homomorphic encryption without bootstrapping. ACM Trans. Comput. Theory (TOCT) **6**(3), 1–36 (2014)
7. Brakerski, Z., Vaikuntanathan, V.: Efficient fully homomorphic encryption from (standard) LWE. SIAM J. Comput. **43**(2), 831–871 (2014)
8. Castryck, W., Iliashenko, I., Vercauteren, F.: On error distributions in ring-based LWE. LMS J. Comput. Math. **19**(A), 130–145 (2016). https://doi.org/10.1112/S1461157016000280
9. Chaudhuri, K., Monteleoni, C., Sarwate, A.D.: Differentially private empirical risk minimization. J. Mach. Learn. Res. **12**(29), 1069–1109 (2011). http://jmlr.org/papers/v12/chaudhuri11a.html
10. Chen, H., Dai, W., Kim, M., Song, Y.: Efficient multi-key homomorphic encryption with packed ciphertexts with application to oblivious neural network inference. In: Proceedings of the 2019 ACM SIGSAC Conference on Computer and Communications Security, pp. 395–412 (2019)

11. Cheon, J.H., Han, K., Kim, A., Kim, M., Song, Y.: Bootstrapping for approximate homomorphic encryption. In: Nielsen, J.B., Rijmen, V. (eds.) EUROCRYPT 2018. LNCS, vol. 10820, pp. 360–384. Springer, Cham (2018). https://doi.org/10.1007/978-3-319-78381-9_14
12. Cheon, J.H., Han, K., Kim, A., Kim, M., Song, Y.: A full RNS variant of approximate homomorphic encryption. In: Cid, C., Jacobson, M., Jr. (eds.) SAC 2018. LNCS, vol. 11349, pp. 347–368. Springer, Cham (2019). https://doi.org/10.1007/978-3-030-10970-7_16
13. Cheon, J.H., Hong, S., Kim, D.: Remark on the security of CKKS scheme in practice. Cryptology ePrint Archive (2020)
14. Cheon, J.H., Kim, A., Kim, M., Song, Y.: Homomorphic encryption for arithmetic of approximate numbers. In: Takagi, T., Peyrin, T. (eds.) ASIACRYPT 2017. LNCS, vol. 10624, pp. 409–437. Springer, Cham (2017). https://doi.org/10.1007/978-3-319-70694-8_15
15. Chillotti, I., Gama, N., Georgieva, M., Izabachène, M.: Faster packed homomorphic operations and efficient circuit bootstrapping for TFHE. In: Takagi, T., Peyrin, T. (eds.) ASIACRYPT 2017. LNCS, vol. 10624, pp. 377–408. Springer, Cham (2017). https://doi.org/10.1007/978-3-319-70694-8_14
16. Chillotti, I., Gama, N., Georgieva, M., Izabachène, M.: TFHE: fast fully homomorphic encryption over the torus. J. Cryptol. **33**(1), 34–91 (2020)
17. Chillotti, I., Joye, M., Ligier, D., Orfila, J.B., Tap, S.: CONCRETE: concrete operates on ciphertexts rapidly by extending TFHE. In: WAHC 2020-8th Workshop on Encrypted Computing & Applied Homomorphic Cryptography (2020)
18. Chillotti, I., Ligier, D., Orfila, J.-B., Tap, S.: Improved programmable bootstrapping with larger precision and efficient arithmetic circuits for TFHE. In: Tibouchi, M., Wang, H. (eds.) ASIACRYPT 2021. LNCS, vol. 13092, pp. 670–699. Springer, Cham (2021). https://doi.org/10.1007/978-3-030-92078-4_23
19. Costache, A., Curtis, B.R., Hales, E., Murphy, S., Ogilvie, T., Player, R.: On the precision loss in approximate homomorphic encryption. In: Carlet, C., Kalikinkar Mandal, V.R. (eds.) SAC 2023. LNCS, vol. 14201, pp. 325–345. Springer, Cham (2023). https://doi.org/10.1007/978-3-031-53368-6_16
20. Costache, A., Laine, K., Player, R.: Evaluating the effectiveness of heuristic worst-case noise analysis in FHE. In: Chen, L., Li, N., Liang, K., Schneider, S. (eds.) ESORICS 2020. LNCS, vol. 12309, pp. 546–565. Springer, Cham (2020). https://doi.org/10.1007/978-3-030-59013-0_27
21. Costache, A., Nürnberger, L., Player, R.: Optimisations and tradeoffs for HElib. In: Rosulek, M. (ed.) CT-RSA 2023. LNCS, vol. 13871, pp. 29–53. Springer, Cham (2023). https://doi.org/10.1007/978-3-031-30872-7_2
22. Ding, J., Zhang, X., Li, X., Wang, J., Yu, R., Pan, M.: Differentially private and fair classification via calibrated functional mechanism. In: Proceedings of the AAAI Conference on Artificial Intelligence, vol. 34, pp. 622–629 (2020)
23. Ducas, L., Micciancio, D.: FHEW: bootstrapping homomorphic encryption in less than a second. In: Oswald, E., Fischlin, M. (eds.) EUROCRYPT 2015. LNCS, vol. 9056, pp. 617–640. Springer, Heidelberg (2015). https://doi.org/10.1007/978-3-662-46800-5_24
24. Dwork, C., Roth, A., et al.: The algorithmic foundations of differential privacy. Found. Trends® Theor. Comput. Sci. **9**(3–4), 211–407 (2014)
25. Dwork, C., Rothblum, G.N., Vadhan, S.: Boosting and differential privacy. In: 2010 IEEE 51st Annual Symposium on Foundations of Computer Science, pp. 51–60. IEEE (2010)

26. Fan, J., Vercauteren, F.: Somewhat practical fully homomorphic encryption. Cryptology ePrint Archive (2012)
27. Fukuchi, K., Tran, Q.K., Sakuma, J.: Differentially private empirical risk minimization with input perturbation. In: Yamamoto, A., Kida, T., Uno, T., Kuboyama, T. (eds.) DS 2017. LNCS (LNAI), vol. 10558, pp. 82–90. Springer, Cham (2017). https://doi.org/10.1007/978-3-319-67786-6_6
28. Gaboardi, M., Lim, H., Rogers, R., Vadhan, S.: Differentially private chi-squared hypothesis testing: goodness of fit and independence testing. In: International Conference on Machine Learning, pp. 2111–2120. PMLR (2016)
29. Gentry, C.: Fully homomorphic encryption using ideal lattices. In: Proceedings of the Forty-First Annual ACM Symposium on Theory of Computing, STOC 2009, pp. 169–178. Association for Computing Machinery, New York (2009). https://doi.org/10.1145/1536414.1536440
30. Gentry, C., Sahai, A., Waters, B.: Homomorphic encryption from learning with errors: conceptually-simpler, asymptotically-faster, attribute-based. In: Canetti, R., Garay, J.A. (eds.) CRYPTO 2013. LNCS, vol. 8042, pp. 75–92. Springer, Heidelberg (2013). https://doi.org/10.1007/978-3-642-40041-4_5
31. Hardt, M., Recht, B., Singer, Y.: Train faster, generalize better: stability of stochastic gradient descent. In: Proceedings of the 33rd International Conference on International Conference on Machine Learning, ICML 2016, vol. 48, pp. 1225–1234. JMLR.org (2016)
32. Heaan v1.0. Online (2018). https://github.com/snucrypto/HEAAN/releases/tag/1.0
33. Jain, P., Thakurta, A.: Differentially private learning with kernels. In: Dasgupta, S., McAllester, D. (eds.) Proceedings of the 30th International Conference on Machine Learning. Proceedings of Machine Learning Research, Atlanta, Georgia, USA, vol. 28, pp. 118–126. PMLR (2013). https://proceedings.mlr.press/v28/jain13.html
34. Jayaraman, B., Evans, D.: Evaluating differentially private machine learning in practice. In: 28th USENIX Security Symposium (USENIX Security 2019), Santa Clara, CA, pp. 1895–1912. USENIX Association (2019). https://www.usenix.org/conference/usenixsecurity19/presentation/jayaraman
35. Jayaraman, B., Wang, L., Evans, D., Gu, Q.: Distributed learning without distress: privacy-preserving empirical risk minimization. In: Bengio, S., Wallach, H., Larochelle, H., Grauman, K., Cesa-Bianchi, N., Garnett, R. (eds.) Advances in Neural Information Processing Systems, vol. 31. Curran Associates, Inc. (2018). https://proceedings.neurips.cc/paper/2018/file/7221e5c8ec6b08ef6d3f9ff3ce6eb1d1-Paper.pdf
36. Jiang, X., Kim, M., Lauter, K., Song, Y.: Secure outsourced matrix computation and application to neural networks. In: Proceedings of the 2018 ACM SIGSAC Conference on Computer and Communications Security, pp. 1209–1222 (2018)
37. Kang, Y., Liu, Y., Niu, B., Tong, X., Zhang, L., Wang, W.: Input perturbation: a new paradigm between central and local differential privacy (2020). https://doi.org/10.48550/ARXIV.2002.08570. https://arxiv.org/abs/2002.08570
38. Kifer, D., Smith, A., Thakurta, A.: Private convex empirical risk minimization and high-dimensional regression. In: Mannor, S., Srebro, N., Williamson, R.C. (eds.) Proceedings of the 25th Annual Conference on Learning Theory. Proceedings of Machine Learning Research, Edinburgh, Scotland, vol. 23, pp. 25.1–25.40. PMLR (2012). https://proceedings.mlr.press/v23/kifer12.html

39. Kim, A., Papadimitriou, A., Polyakov, Y.: Approximate homomorphic encryption with reduced approximation error. In: Galbraith, S.D. (ed.) CT-RSA 2022. LNCS, vol. 13161, pp. 120–144. Springer, Cham (2022). https://doi.org/10.1007/978-3-030-95312-6_6
40. Kim, A., Song, Y., Kim, M., Lee, K., Cheon, J.H.: Logistic regression model training based on the approximate homomorphic encryption. BMC Med. Genomics **11**(4), 23–31 (2018)
41. Kim, M., Song, Y., Wang, S., Xia, Y., Jiang, X., et al.: Secure logistic regression based on homomorphic encryption: design and evaluation. JMIR Med. Inform. **6**(2), e8805 (2018)
42. Klemsa, J.: Setting up efficient TFHE parameters for multivalue plaintexts and multiple additions. Cryptology ePrint Archive (2021)
43. Li, B., Micciancio, D.: On the security of homomorphic encryption on approximate numbers. In: Canteaut, A., Standaert, F.-X. (eds.) EUROCRYPT 2021. LNCS, vol. 12696, pp. 648–677. Springer, Cham (2021). https://doi.org/10.1007/978-3-030-77870-5_23
44. Li, B., Micciancio, D., Schultz, M., Sorrell, J.: Securing approximate homomorphic encryption using differential privacy. In: Dodis, Y., Shrimpton, T. (eds.) CRYPTO 2022. LNCS, vol. 13507, pp. 560–589. Springer, Cham (2022). https://doi.org/10.1007/978-3-031-15802-5_20
45. Ligett, K., Neel, S., Roth, A., Waggoner, B., Wu, Z.S.: Accuracy first: selecting a differential privacy level for accuracy-constrained ERM. In: Proceedings of the 31st International Conference on Neural Information Processing Systems, NIPS 2017, Red Hook, NY, USA, pp. 2563–2573. Curran Associates Inc. (2017)
46. Lyubashevsky, V., Peikert, C., Regev, O.: On ideal lattices and learning with errors over rings. J. ACM (JACM) **60**(6), 1–35 (2013)
47. Lyubashevsky, V., Peikert, C., Regev, O.: A toolkit for ring-LWE cryptography. In: Johansson, T., Nguyen, P.Q. (eds.) EUROCRYPT 2013. LNCS, vol. 7881, pp. 35–54. Springer, Heidelberg (2013). https://doi.org/10.1007/978-3-642-38348-9_3
48. Ma, J., Naas, S.A., Sigg, S., Lyu, X.: Privacy-preserving federated learning based on multi-key homomorphic encryption. Int. J. Intell. Syst. **37**(9), 5880–5901 (2022)
49. Murphy, S., Player, R.: A central limit framework for ring-LWE decryption. Cryptology ePrint Archive (2019)
50. Ogilvie, T., Player, R., Rowell, J.: Improved privacy-preserving training using fixed-hessian minimisation. In: Brenner, M., Lepoint, T. (eds.) Proceedings of the 8th Workshop on Encrypted Computing and Applied Homomorphic Cryptography (WAHC 2020) (2020). https://doi.org/10.25835/0072999
51. Papernot, N., Abadi, M., Erlingsson, U., Goodfellow, I., Talwar, K.: Semi-supervised knowledge transfer for deep learning from private training data. arXiv preprint arXiv:1610.05755 (2016)
52. Phong, L.T., Aono, Y., Hayashi, T., Wang, L., Moriai, S.: Privacy-preserving deep learning via additively homomorphic encryption. IEEE Trans. Inf. Forensics Secur. **13**(5), 1333–1345 (2018). https://doi.org/10.1109/TIFS.2017.2787987
53. Polyakov, Y., Rohloff, K., Ryan, G.W.: Palisade lattice cryptography library user manual (2017)
54. Raisaro, J.L., et al.: Protecting privacy and security of genomic data in i2b2 with homomorphic encryption and differential privacy. IEEE/ACM Trans. Comput. Biol. Bioinf. **15**(5), 1413–1426 (2018). https://doi.org/10.1109/TCBB.2018.2854782
55. Regev, O.: On lattices, learning with errors, random linear codes, and cryptography. J. ACM **56**(6), 1–40 (2009). https://doi.org/10.1145/1568318.1568324

56. Shokri, R., Shmatikov, V.: Privacy-preserving deep learning. In: Proceedings of the 22nd ACM SIGSAC Conference on Computer and Communications Security, pp. 1310–1321 (2015)
57. Song, S., Chaudhuri, K., Sarwate, A.D.: Stochastic gradient descent with differentially private updates. In: 2013 IEEE Global Conference on Signal and Information Processing, pp. 245–248. IEEE (2013)
58. Tang, P., Wang, W., Gu, X., Lou, J., Xiong, L., Li, M.: Two birds, one stone: achieving both differential privacy and certified robustness for pre-trained classifiers via input perturbation (2021)
59. Tang, X., Zhu, L., Shen, M., Du, X.: When homomorphic cryptosystem meets differential privacy: training machine learning classifier with privacy protection. arXiv preprint arXiv:1812.02292 (2018)
60. Triastcyn, A., Faltings, B.: Federated learning with Bayesian differential privacy. In: 2019 IEEE International Conference on Big Data (Big Data), pp. 2587–2596. IEEE (2019)
61. Wu, X., Li, F., Kumar, A., Chaudhuri, K., Jha, S., Naughton, J.: Bolt-on differential privacy for scalable stochastic gradient descent-based analytics. In: Proceedings of the 2017 ACM International Conference on Management of Data, SIGMOD 2017, pp. 1307–1322. Association for Computing Machinery, New York (2017). https://doi.org/10.1145/3035918.3064047
62. Zhang, J., Zheng, K., Mou, W., Wang, L.: Efficient private ERM for smooth objectives. In: Proceedings of the 26th International Joint Conference on Artificial Intelligence, IJCAI 2017, pp. 3922–3928. AAAI Press (2017)
63. Zhang, J., Zhang, Z., Xiao, X., Yang, Y., Winslett, M.: Functional mechanism: regression analysis under differential privacy. Proc. VLDB Endow. **5**(11), 1364–1375 (2012). https://doi.org/10.14778/2350229.2350253
64. Zhang, T., Zhu, T., Gao, K., Zhou, W., Philip, S.Y.: Balancing learning model privacy, fairness, and accuracy with early stopping criteria. IEEE Trans. Neural Netw. Learn. Syst. **34**(9), 5557–5569 (2021)

Identity-Based Encryption

Identity-Based Encryption from LWE with More Compact Master Public Key

Parhat Abla[1,2(✉)]

[1] School of Software, South China Normal University, Guangzhou, China
parhat@scnu.edu.cn

[2] Research Station in Mathematics, South China Normal University, Guangzhou, China

Abstract. This paper presents an adaptively secure identity-based encryption (IBE) scheme from Learning With Errors (LWE) in the standard model. Compared to the previous LWE-based most compact construction of Yamada (CRYPTO17), one of the distinguishing properties of our IBE scheme is that the master public key size of our IBE scheme is significantly smaller, and our design is explicitly given, and thus all the IBE parameters can be instantiated.

To achieve this, we design a more compact homomorphic equality test algorithm over LWE problems, which is significantly better than the previous bit-wise comparison of Yamada (CRYPTO17) and Katsumata (ASIACRYPT17). We show that our homomorphic equality test algorithms can pack a super-constant number of GSW-type bit encodings and thus may find other improvements in other LWE-based crypto schemes.

Keywords: IBE · Equality Test · LWE

1 Introduction

Identity-Based Encryption (IBE) is a generalization of the concept of Public Key Encryption (PKE), where the public keys in an IBE are derived from the recipient's identity rather than the predetermined public key. The concept of IBE was introduced by Shamir [31] without concrete construction. However, the first construction is given by Boneh and Franklin [12] from the Weil pairing.

There are two types of security models for an IBE scheme: security in the standard model and security in the random oracle model (ROM). The later security notion assumes the existence of a heuristic cryptographic primitive-random oracle—whereas the former notion does not. The work of [15] demonstrates that there exists a crypto-scheme that is insecure if the RO is replaced with any concrete instantiation. There are a series of works on constructing IBE schemes from classic assumptions both in the standard model [9,10,17–19,33,34] and in the RO [11,22].

E. Oswald (Ed.): CT-RSA 2024, LNCS 14643, pp. 319–353, 2024.
https://doi.org/10.1007/978-3-031-58868-6_13

The other security notions for an IBE scheme are selective security and adaptive security. The former requires that the challenge identity be given to the challenger at the outset of the security game, while in the latter case, the adversary can output the challenge identity at any stage of the game (before, after, or during the key extraction queries). It is not hard to see that adaptive security is the most common notion, and thus we focus on the adaptive security of IBE schemes in this paper.

All of the above IBE schemes are constructed from the classic computationally hard assumptions, which are not secure if a general quantum computer is available [32]. Fortunately, we have many candidates from different assumptions; among them, the lattice-based schemes are more plausible than others because of their simplicity, efficiency, and plentiful, prolific cryptosystems. The first lattice-based IBE is presented in [20], yet their construction is in the RO. The first LWE-based IBE in the standard model is presented in [2,16]. The adaptively secure scheme of [2] has large master public keys (contains λ public matrices[1] in $\mathbb{Z}_q^{n\times m}$), and thus not even close to practical. Although there is a sequence of high-level works [1,7,25,26,35–37] on improving the space efficiency (mostly on master public keys, denoted as mpk) of lattice-based IBEs. Yet they all have some shortcomings, which we will elaborate on next.

In this paper, we focus on the adaptively secure LWE-based IBE in the standard model. Below, we show some shortcomings of previous works and the contribution of this paper.

1.1 Challenges and Our Contributions

As our main focus in this paper is to design a more compact, adaptively secure IBE scheme based on LWE assumptions, we only present the related works and current challenges below.

Challenges. Since the first adaptively secure LWE-based IBE constructions of [2,16], a series of works [1,7,26,35–37] have tried to reduce the number of matrices (ring vectors) in the mpk. Among them, the best compact IBE design is given by Abla et al. [1], and the mpk of their IBE scheme contains $\omega(1)$ ring vectors[2]. Yet their scheme makes elegant use of the structure of the rings, and it does not appear to be adaptable to the case of plain LWE. Currently, the LWE-based best compact design of adaptively secure IBE is from the work of Yamada [36], yet it still has the following shortcomings:

- Although one of the IBE schemes presented in [36] showed the existence of an LWE-based adaptively secure IBE scheme whose master public key contains $\omega(\log(n))$ matrices, due to the IBE construction using the Barrington's theorem [8], the construction is implicit. Since the work of [36] also presented an explicit design of the IBE scheme that contains $\omega(\log^2(n))$ matrices in

[1] λ denotes the security parameter of the IBE scheme. q is the modulus of the IBE scheme, n, m are two integers such that $m \geq n \cdot \log(q)$.

[2] $\omega(1)$: An asymptotic notation that represents a super-constant number.

the master public key, there has been no substantial improvement on this research line, making it a huge challenge to improve.

Thus, there is a natural question:

Can we ***explicitly*** *construct an LWE-based adaptively secure IBE scheme in the standard model that contains significantly fewer matrices than $\omega(\log(n))$ in the master public key?*

Our Contributions. Motivated by the above challenges, we construct an adaptively secure, more compact LWE-based IBE scheme in the standard model. In order to achieve this, we design LWE-based homomorphic equality test algorithms. Then we use our LWE-based equality test function to design a new, more compact partition function. Finally, we utilize our partition function to construct an LWE-based IBE scheme. Our main contributions to this paper are as follows:

- We design a more compact LWE-based homomorphic equality test algorithm: Given a GSW type of encoding, we construct public evaluation algorithms that can make homomorphic equality tests for the integers in the set of integers $\{0, 1, \cdots, \lceil \log / \log\log(n) \rceil\}$. Our construction significantly improves the previous bit-wise comparison technique of [25,36]. Furthermore, benefiting from our design, we can pack $\omega(1)$ homomorphic GSW type encodings (of bits) into one encoding, which significantly improves lattice-based ABE and others without any modification to the main structure of the scheme.
- We design an adaptively secure, more compact IBE scheme over LWE problems: Our IBE scheme has two advantages over the current most compact LWE-based design of [36]:(1) Our construction is explicit, and thus we can compute the LWE hardness parameter $\frac{1}{\alpha}$ while the construction of [36] is implicit design, and thus the LWE hardness parameter can't be explicitly computed; (2) The master public key of our IBE scheme contains $\omega\left(\frac{\log(n)}{\log\log(n)}\right)$ matrices, which is noticeably better than that of [36] (whose master public key contains $\omega(\log(n))$ matrices.

In Table 1, we compare our IBE scheme with previous adaptively secure partition-based *typical* construction (in the standard model) on the number of matrices in the mpk, number of vectors in ciphertexts, and LWE parameter $\frac{1}{\alpha}$, where the smaller the LWE parameter $\frac{1}{\alpha}$, the harder the corresponding LWE problem. Since the (almost) tightly constructed lattice-based IBEs [14,27] suffer from large public key sizes (need super-poly modulus or large number of matrices in public keys), we don't list them in Table 1. We also note that the recent work of [24] also constructed an adaptively secure IBE scheme from LWE in the standard model with the master public key containing $\omega(\log(\lambda))$ matrices. However, their construction and the security analysis of the IBE scheme rely on the so-called near collision-resistant hash function, and it is not known if this kind of hash function can be constructed from LWE or any variants of LWE. So, we didn't list it in Table 1.

Table 1. Comparison with Adaptively Secure LWE-based IBE Schemes.

Scheme	# of matrices/ring vectors in mpk	# of vectors in ct/sk$_{\mathsf{id}}$	LWE Param $\frac{1}{\alpha}$	Remarks
[2]	$O(\lambda)$	$O(1)$	$\tilde{O}(n^{3.5})$	
[26]	$O(\lambda^{1/\mu})^{\dagger}$	$O(1)$	$O(n^{0.5+2\mu})$	Ring-based
[7]	$O(\lambda^{1/\mu})^{\dagger}$	$O(1)$	$O(n^{0.5+2\mu})$	
[37]	$O(\log(Q))$	$O(1)$	$O(Q^2 n^{6.5})$	Q-bounded
[36] I + [25]	$\omega(\log^2(\lambda))$	$O(1)$	$\tilde{O}(n^{5.5})$	
[36] II	$\omega(\log(\lambda))$	$O(1)$	$\mathsf{poly}(n)^*$	Barrington's theorem
[1] A	$\omega(\log(\lambda))$	$O(1)$	$O(n^{4.5+\frac{4}{\kappa}})^{\dagger\dagger}$	Ring-based
[1] B	$\omega(1)$	$O(1)$	$\tilde{O}(n^{7.5+\frac{4}{\kappa}})$	Ring-based
Ours	$\omega(\frac{\log(\lambda)}{\log\log(\lambda)})$	$O(1)$	$\tilde{O}(\lambda^{8.5})^{\ddagger}$	

Notations: $\mathsf{mpk}, \mathsf{ct}, \mathsf{sk}_{\mathsf{id}}$ denotes the master public key, ciphertext, and secret key of identity id. α, λ and n denotes R-DLWE parameter, security parameter and the ring dimension.

($\ddagger$) This value can be reduced to $\tilde{O}(n^{4.5})$ if we consider our IBE scheme in the crs model as in [1] A.

$*$ $\mathsf{poly}(n)$ denotes some fixed but large polynomial. It is hard to determine an explicit bound for comparison due to the implicit construction of the work.

$\dagger$ $\mu \in \mathbb{N}$ is a constant that can be chosen arbitrarily. Since the reduction cost is exponential in μ, this value is typically set very small (e.g., $\mu = 2$ or 3).

$\dagger\dagger$ $\kappa \geq 1$ can be any constant that satisfies $n^{\frac{1}{\kappa}} > 3 + \kappa$, e.g., 2 or 4, depending on how we set parameters of the underlying error correcting code.

Note that we can significantly improve the space efficiency of previous homomorphic evaluations for the predicate functions [25] (e.g., bit-fixing predicates, subset conjunction predicates, range conjunction predicates) by straightforward application of our homomorphic equality test functions.

1.2 Overview of Our Techniques

In this section, we provide an overview of our high-level design approaches.

More Compact Homomorphic Equality Testing

Recap of Previous Approaches. For an integer d, let $[\mathsf{d}]$ denotes the integer set $\{1, \cdots, \mathsf{d}\}$, then for a index $j \in [\mathsf{d}]$, the equality test function for an input $\alpha \in [\mathsf{d}]$ is defined as

$$\mathsf{Equal}_j(\alpha) = \begin{cases} 1 & if \;\; \alpha = j \\ 0 & if \;\; \alpha \neq j \end{cases}.$$

To homomorphically evaluate the above equality test function, the work of [25, 36] used the bitwise expression of $\alpha \in [\mathsf{d}]$, and thus the homomorphic evaluation algorithm needs $\lceil \log(\mathsf{d}) \rceil$ GSW type encodings. Recently, Abla et al. [1] observed that 1 GSW type encoding is sufficient for doing a homomorphic equality test over the set $[n]$ if considering a quotient ring $\mathbb{Z}_q[x]/(x^n+1)$. Note that in the ring setting $R_q := \mathbb{Z}_q[x]/(x^n+1)$, to encode an integer $\alpha \in [n]$, the work of [1] used a simple but powerful GSW type encoding trick that encoded the exponent x^α instead of the integer α, that is $\mathsf{Encode}(\alpha) := \mathsf{A} \cdot R + x^\alpha \cdot \mathsf{G}_b$, where A is a random matrix over $\mathbb{Z}_q^{n\times m}$, R is a small entry matrix, and G_b is the gadget matrix [28]. Hence, to test if $\alpha \stackrel{?}{=} j$, it needs to test if $x^{\alpha-j} \stackrel{?}{=} 1$. They observe that $x^{2n}=1$ and the value of $m^{-1}\cdot\sum_{i=0}^{2n-1}\left(x^{\alpha-j}\right)^i = 1$ if $\alpha = j$ and it equals to 0 otherwise.

Challenges. Although the bitwise comparison of [25,36] is more intuitive and flexible, it needs more GSW-type encodings (integer matrices) to do a homomorphic equality test. On the other hand, the ring setting can accomplish a more compact homomorphic equality test, yet it heavily depends on the meticulous design of the rings. Thus, it's a huge challenge to port the method of [1] into the non-ring setting or design more compact homomorphic equality test algorithms that are significantly better than those of [25,36].

Our Techniques. We observe that the equality test procedure can be regarded as an interpolation at d distinct points. From the Lagrange interpolation theorem, we know that for d distinct input points $x_1,\cdots x_{\mathsf{d}} \in [\mathsf{d}] = \{1,2,\cdots \mathsf{d}\}$ and the corresponding output set $y_1,\cdots y_{\mathsf{d}} \in \{0,1\}$, there is a unique integer coefficient polynomial P of degree $\mathsf{d}-1$ such that $P(x_i)=y_i$. Inspired by the construction idea of Lagrange interpolation, we observe that if we define the function $P_j(x)$ as follows:

$$P_j(x) = \frac{\prod\limits_{i=1,i\neq j}^{\mathsf{d}} (x-i)}{\prod\limits_{i=1,i\neq j}^{\mathsf{d}} (j-i)},$$

then we have $P_j(\alpha)=1$ if $j=\alpha$ and $P_j(x)=0$ otherwise. Therefore, the function $P_j(*)$ is a desired analytic expression of the equality test function Equal_j.

However, there comes a crux: the homomorphic evaluation of $P_j(*)$ for the function domain d results in a factor of d^{d} in the modulus. Therefore, the blow-up factor d^{d} leads to a super-poly modulus if d is as large as $\omega(\log(n))$. We observe that if set $\mathsf{d} = O\left(\frac{\log(n)}{\log\log(n)}\right)$, then the blow-up factor d^{d} can be bounded by some polynomial in n. Thus, we can pack more bits, which is significantly more compact than that of [25,36].

IBE from LWE

Recap of Previous Approaches. As the previous works [2,36] implicitly pointed out, the construction of the so-called partition function (or *admissible hash*) and its homomorphic evaluation are key for designing a lattice-based adaptively secure IBE in the standard model. Recall that, for the key extraction identities $\mathsf{id}_1, \cdots, \mathsf{id}_Q$ and the challenge identity id^*, the partition function $F_K : \mathsf{ID} \to \{0,1\}$ for some key K should have the partition property that $\bigwedge_{i=1}^{Q} F_K(\mathsf{id}_i) = 1 \wedge F_K(\mathsf{id}^*) = 0$ holds with noticeable probability, where the probability is taken over the randomness of the function key.

Previously, the LWE-based most compact design was given in [36]. In the work of [36], the partition function is defined as $F_K(\mathsf{id}) := \alpha \cdot \mathsf{id} + \beta \mod \rho$, where $K = (\alpha, \beta, \rho) \in \mathbb{Z}^3$ and each of α, β, ρ contains at most $\omega(\log(\lambda))$ bits. From Barrington's theorem, the above partition function can be implemented by a depth $O(\log(\lambda))$ circuit. Given $\omega(\log(n))$ GSW type encodings, the homomorphic evaluation of them leads to polynomial moduli. Note that the circuit of the above partition function depends on the input identity, and thus it's hard to explicitly evaluate the quality of this homomorphic evaluation algorithm.

Challenges. Although the partition function in [36] is very simple, its homomorphic evaluation process is implicit, and thus it is impossible to present concrete parameters of the corresponding IBE scheme. Therefore, making the partition function of [36] explicit or design an LWE-based, more compact partition function than above becomes a great challenge in this research line.

Our Techniques. For some prime p, and an integer L, let $\mathsf{ECC} : \mathsf{ID} \to \mathbb{Z}_p^{\mathsf{L}}$ be an error-correction code [1], then our partition function indexed by $K := (\boldsymbol{\alpha}, \boldsymbol{\beta})$ for some integer $t = \omega(1)$ is defined as

$$F_{\boldsymbol{\alpha},\boldsymbol{\beta}}(\mathsf{id}) := \sum_{i=1}^{t} (\mathsf{ECC}(\mathsf{id})[\boldsymbol{\alpha}_i] - \boldsymbol{\beta}_i)^2 ,$$

where $\boldsymbol{\alpha}_i$ ($\boldsymbol{\beta}_i$) is the i-th element of $\boldsymbol{\alpha}$ ($\boldsymbol{\beta}$), and $\mathsf{ECC}(\mathsf{id})[\boldsymbol{\alpha}_i]$ is the $\boldsymbol{\alpha}_i$-th entry of $\mathsf{ECC}(\mathsf{id})$. The partition property of this function is presented in Sect. 4.

To homomorphically evaluate our partition function, we note that

$$F_{\boldsymbol{\alpha},\boldsymbol{\beta}}(\mathsf{id}) := \sum_{i=1}^{t} \left(\underbrace{\sum_{j=1}^{\mathsf{L}} \mathsf{Equal}_j(\boldsymbol{\alpha}_i) \cdot \mathsf{ECC}(\mathsf{id})[j]}_{= \begin{cases} \mathsf{ECC}(\mathsf{id})[\alpha_i] & if\ j = \alpha_i \\ 0 & otherwise \end{cases}} - \boldsymbol{\beta}_i \right)^2 ,$$

where we use the fact that $\alpha_i \in [\mathsf{L}]$. Observe that, given the GSW type encodings of $\mathsf{Equal}_j(\alpha_i)$ and $\boldsymbol{\beta}_i$ for all $i \in [t], j \in [\mathsf{L}]$, we can explicitly present a homomorphic evaluation algorithm for our partition function. Note that, given the GSW type encodings of $\{\boldsymbol{\alpha}_i\}_{i \in [t]}$, encodings of $\mathsf{Equal}_j(\alpha_i)$ can be computed via our LWE-based equality testing technique presented in the previous section. Thus, we have explicit homomorphic evaluation algorithms for our partition function. More details can be found in the next sections.

2 Preliminaries

Notations. We use $[k]$ to denote the index set $\{1, 2, \cdots, k\}$. We use lower-case bold letters to denote the vectors (e.g., a) and upper-case bold letters to denote the matrices (e.g., A). For a probability distribution χ, we use $x \leftarrow \mathcal{X}$ to denote that x is sampled from the distribution $\mathcal{X}$. For a set S, $x \xleftarrow{\$} S$ denotes that x is uniformly sampled from the set S. The 2-norm of a vector a is denoted by $\|\mathsf{a}\|$. For a square matrix T, we use $\|\mathsf{T}\|_{\mathsf{GS}}$ to denote the longest column of Gram-Schmidt orthogonalization of T and use $s_1(\mathsf{T})$ to denote the largest spectral norm of T. The function $\mathsf{negl}(\cdot)$ denotes the negligible function, that is, for any constant c, there is an λ_0 such that for all $\lambda > \lambda_0$ we have $\mathsf{negl}(\lambda) < \frac{1}{\lambda^c}$. We define the statistical distance between two random variables $\mathcal{X}$ and $\mathcal{Y}$ over the support Ω as $\Delta(X, Y) := \sum s \in \Omega|\Pr[X = s] - \Pr[Y = s]|$. For two probability distributions $\mathcal{P}$ and $\mathcal{Q}$, we say $\mathcal{P}$ is statistically close to $\mathcal{Q}$ if $\Delta(\mathcal{P}, \mathcal{Q}) \leq \mathsf{negl}(\lambda)$.

Definition 2.1 (Relative Distance). *Let $\mathbb{F}$ be some finite field and $\mathsf{L} \in \mathbb{N}$, $\mathcal{D}$ be some input domain, and $\mathsf{ECC} : \mathcal{D} \to \mathbb{F}^{\mathsf{L}}$ be some encoding, where the output vector is indexed by $[1, \ldots, \mathsf{L}]$. Define the relative distance of* ECC, *denoted* d, *as*

$$\mathsf{d} := \min \left\{ \Pr_{i \xleftarrow{\$} [1,\ldots,\mathsf{L}]} \left[\mathsf{ECC}(\mathsf{a})[i] \neq \mathsf{ECC}(\mathsf{b})[i] \right] \middle| \mathsf{a} \neq \mathsf{b}, \mathsf{a}, \mathsf{b} \in \mathcal{D} \right\}$$

2.1 Identity Based Encryption

Definition 2.2. *An* IBE *scheme consists of 4 algorithms* (Setup, KeyGen, Enc, Dec) *as follows:*

$\mathsf{Setup}(\lambda) \to (\mathsf{mpk}, \mathsf{msk})$: *On input of the security parameter λ, it outputs the master public key* mpk *and master secret key* msk.

$\mathsf{KeyGen}(\mathsf{msk}, \mathsf{mpk}, \mathsf{id}) \to \mathsf{sk}_{\mathsf{id}}$: *On input of the master key pair* (mpk, msk) *and an identity* id, *it outputs the secret key* $\mathsf{sk}_{\mathsf{id}}$ *for the corresponding identity* id.

$\mathsf{Enc}(\mathsf{mpk}, \mathsf{id}, \mu) \to \mathsf{ct}$: *On input the master public key* mpk, *an identity* id *and a message μ, it outputs the ciphertext* ct *of the message μ under the identity* id.

$\mathsf{Dec}(\mathsf{mpk}, \mathsf{ct}, \mathsf{sk}_{\mathsf{id}}) \to \mu/\perp$: *On input of the master public key* mpk, *ciphertext* ct *and the secret key* $\mathsf{sk}_{\mathsf{id}}$ *of identity* id, *it outputs a message μ if* ct *is the encryption of μ under the identity* id, *and outputs $\perp$ otherwise.*

Correctness. We say an IBE scheme Π_{IBE} is δ-correct if for the security parameter λ, identity $\mathsf{id} \in \mathsf{ID}$, and any message μ, the following holds:

$$\Pr \left[\mu' \neq \mu \middle| \begin{array}{rl} (\mathsf{mpk}, \mathsf{msk}) & \leftarrow \mathsf{Setup}(\lambda); \\ \mathsf{sk}_{\mathsf{id}} & \leftarrow \mathsf{KeyGen}(\mathsf{msk}, \mathsf{mpk}, \mathsf{id}); \\ \mathsf{ct} & \leftarrow \mathsf{Enc}(\mathsf{mpk}, \mathsf{id}, \mu); \\ \mu' & \leftarrow \mathsf{Dec}(\mathsf{mpk}, \mathsf{ct}, \mathsf{sk}_{\mathsf{id}}) \end{array} \right] < \delta,$$

where the probability is taken over the randomness of the algorithms Setup, KeyGen, and the encryption algorithm Enc. If the value of δ is negligible in the security parameter λ, then we simply call the IBE scheme correct.

Adaptive Security. The adaptive security of an IPE scheme is described by the following experiment $\mathsf{EXPT}^{\mathsf{ID\text{-}CPA}}_{\mathcal{A},\pi}(\lambda)$ between a challenger and an adversary $\mathcal{A}$ as follows:

$\mathsf{EXPT}^{\mathsf{ID\text{-}CPA}}_{\mathcal{A},\mathsf{IBE}}(\lambda) \to \{0,1\}$:

Setup: At the beginning of the game, the challenger runs $\mathsf{Setup}(\lambda)$ to obtain the master key pair $(\mathsf{mpk}, \mathsf{msk})$, and then it sends the public master key mpk to the adversary $\mathcal{A}$.

Phase 1: The adversary may adaptively make secret key queries for the identities in ID. Receiving an identity $\mathsf{id} \in \mathsf{ID}$ as a key query from the adversary, the challenger runs $\mathsf{KeyGen}(\mathsf{msk}, \mathsf{mpkid})$ to get a secret key $\mathsf{sk_{id}}$ for the identity id and sends it to the adversary.

Chall: After finishing Phase 1, the adversary sends out two equal-length messages μ_0, μ_1 and an identity $\mathsf{id}^* \in \mathsf{ID}$, which was never made a secret key query in previous Phase 1, to the challenger as its challenge. The challenger chooses a random bit $b \in \{0,1\}$, obtains challenge ciphertext ct^* by encrypting μ_b under the challenge identity id^*, and then sends ct^* to the adversary.

Phase 2: After the challenge query, the adversary $\mathcal{A}$ continues to make an adaptive secret key query for any identity $\mathsf{id} \neq \mathsf{id}^*$. The challenger responds as in Phase 1.

Guess: After all, the adversary outputs a guess of b. The experiment outputs 1 if $b = b'$, and 0 otherwise.

Definition 2.3. *We say an* IBE *scheme achieves adaptive security under a chosen message security attack (simply, adaptive security) if for any probabilistic polynomial time (PPT) adversary* $\mathcal{A}$ *and the experiment* $\mathsf{EXPT}^{\mathsf{ID\text{-}CPA}}_{\mathcal{A},\mathsf{IBE}}(\lambda)$ *defined above, the following holds:*

$$\left| \Pr\left[\mathsf{EXPT}^{\mathsf{ID\text{-}CPA}}_{\mathcal{A},\mathsf{IBE}}(\lambda) \to 1\right] - \frac{1}{2} \right| \leq \mathsf{negl}(\lambda),$$

where $\mathsf{negl}(\lambda)$ *is the negligible function in security parameter* λ.

Partition Function and Its Properties

In this section, we will recall the definition of the partition function [36] which is also known as a balanced admissible hash function [23], vital to the security proof of partition-based IBE schemes. We observe that, instead of outputting a binary value (true or false), the invertibility in $\mathbb{Z}_q$ is sufficient for the security proof of LWE lattice-based IBE schemes. Thus, we add a subtle modification and generalize the definition of the partition function in [36]. Due to the space limit, we postpone definitions and related results to Appendix A.1.

2.2 Lattices, Gaussian and LWE

Lattices. For a full-rank matrix $\mathsf{B} = [\mathsf{b}_1, \cdots, \mathsf{b}_n] \in \mathbb{Z}^{m \times n}$, the lattice defined by B is the set $\Lambda = L(\mathsf{B}) := \{\mathsf{B} \cdot \mathsf{c} = \sum_{i=1}^{n} c_i \cdot \mathsf{b}_i | \mathsf{c} = (c_1, \cdots, c_n) \in \mathbb{Z}^n\}$. In this paper, we focus on so-called q-ary integer lattices for some prime integer q. For the positive integers n, m, q, a matrix $\mathsf{A} \in \mathbb{Z}_q^{n \times m}$ defines the following two types of full-rank m-dimensional q-ary lattices:

$$\Lambda^{\perp}(\mathsf{A}) := \{\mathsf{e} | \mathsf{A}^{\top} \cdot \mathsf{e} = 0 \mod q\},$$
$$\Lambda(\mathsf{A}) := \{\mathsf{e} | \exists \mathsf{z} \in \mathbb{Z}_q^n \ s.t., \mathsf{A} \cdot \mathsf{z} = \mathsf{e} \mod q\}$$

For any vector $\mathsf{u} \in \mathbb{Z}_q^m$, the "shifted" lattice $\Lambda_{\mathsf{u}}^{\perp}(\mathsf{A})$ is defined as $\Lambda_{\mathsf{u}}^{\perp}(\mathsf{A}) := \{\mathsf{e} | \mathsf{A}^{\top} \cdot \mathsf{e} = \mathsf{u} \mod q\}$.

Gaussians. The n-dimensional gaussian function with parameter $s > 0$ is defined as $\rho_s(x) := \exp(-\pi \frac{\|\mathsf{x}\|^2}{s^2})$. For any n-dimensional vector c, the shifted gaussian $\rho_{s,\mathsf{c}} := \exp(-\pi \frac{\|\mathsf{x}-\mathsf{c}\|^2}{s^2})$ The distribution function of the spherical continuous Gaussian D_s over $\mathbb{R}^n$ is proportional to ρ_s.

Gaussian distributions have Pythagorean additivity, that is, for any two independent Gaussian variables X_1 and X_2 with parameters s_1, s_2, respectively, the sum $X_1 + X_2$ is a Gaussian distribution with parameter $\sqrt{s_1^2 + s_2^2}$. In particular, if X is the Gaussian variable with parameter s, then for any $c \in \mathbb{R}^+$, cX is a Gaussian with parameter $s\sqrt{c}$. Similarly, we define discrete gaussian over a lattice Λ with parameter s, denoted $D_{\Lambda,s}(\mathsf{x})$, as $D_{\Lambda,s}(\mathsf{x}) := \frac{\rho_s(\mathsf{x})}{\rho_s(\Lambda)}$.

We recall the definition of the smoothing parameter of a lattice and its upper bound as follows:

Definition 2.4 ([29]). *For any n-dimensional lattice Λ and positive real $\epsilon > 0$, the smoothing parameter $\eta_\epsilon(\Lambda)$ is the smallest real $s > 0$ such that $\rho_{1/s}(\Lambda^* \backslash \{0\}) \leq \epsilon$, where Λ^* is the dual lattice of Λ.*

Lemma 2.5 (Lemma 3.1 of [20]**).** *For any n-dimensional lattice Λ with basis B and real $\epsilon_s > 0$, we have $\eta_{\epsilon_s}(\Lambda) \leq \|\mathsf{B}\|_{\mathsf{GS}} \cdot \sqrt{\log(2n(1 + 1/\epsilon_s))/\pi}$. Then, for any $\omega(\sqrt{\log(n)})$ function, there is a negligible $\epsilon_s(n)$ for which $\eta_{\epsilon_s}(\Lambda) \leq \|\mathsf{B}\|_{\mathsf{GS}} \cdot \omega(\sqrt{\log(n)})$*

The following lemma shows the tail-bound property of the Gaussian distribution over a lattice.

Lemma 2.6 ([3,20,28])**.** *For any n-dimensional lattice, center $\mathsf{c} \in \mathbb{R}^n$, positive $\epsilon > 0$, and $s \geq 2\eta_\epsilon$, and for every $\mathsf{x} \in \Lambda$, we have*

$$\Pr_{\mathsf{v} \leftarrow D_{\Lambda,s,\mathsf{c}}}\left[\|\mathsf{v} - \mathsf{c}\| \geq s\sqrt{n}\right] \leq \frac{1+\epsilon}{1-\epsilon} 2^{-n}.$$

In particular, for $\epsilon < 1/3$, the min-entropy of $D_{\Lambda,s,\mathsf{c}}$ is at least $n - 1$.

An important tool in lattice-based cryptography is the leftover hash lemma. If we let $\log_\rho(1) := 1$, then we have the following results from a more general leftover hash lemma:

Lemma 2.7 ([2,36]). *Let q be an odd prime, m be some integer such that $m \geq \frac{(n+1)\log(q)+\omega(\log(n))}{\log(\rho)}$, for a random matrix $\mathsf{R} \leftarrow [-\rho, \rho]^{m\times m}$ and $\mathsf{A}, \mathsf{A}' \leftarrow \mathbb{Z}_q^{n\times m}$, we have*

$$\Delta\Big((\mathsf{A}, \mathsf{A}'), (\mathsf{A}, \mathsf{A}\cdot\mathsf{R}) \Big) \leq 2^{-\omega(\log(n))}$$

LWE. The LWE problem was first introduced in [30]. Let χ be some distribution, then the LWE distribution is defined as follows:

Definition 2.8. *The D-$\mathsf{LWE}_{n,p,q,\chi}$ distribution is the distribution of the pair $(\mathsf{A}, \mathsf{b}) \in \mathbb{Z}_q^{n\times m} \times \mathbb{Z}_q^m$, where A is a uniform matrix over $\mathbb{Z}_q^{n\times m}$ and $\mathsf{b} = \mathsf{A}\cdot\mathsf{s} + \mathsf{e}$ for some uniform $\mathsf{s} \leftarrow \mathbb{Z}_q^n$ and an error $\mathsf{e} \leftarrow \chi$.*

We recall the D-$\mathsf{LWE}_{n,p,q,\chi}$ problem via the above D-$\mathsf{LWE}_{n,p,q,\chi}$ distribution as follows:

Definition 2.9. *Given a pair $(\mathsf{A}, \mathsf{b}) \in \mathbb{Z}_q^{n\times m} \times \mathbb{Z}_q^m$ for the random matrix $\mathsf{A} \leftarrow \mathbb{Z}_q^{n\times m}$, the D-$\mathsf{LWE}_{n,p,q,\chi}$ problem asks to distinguish if the pair is from the D-$\mathsf{LWE}_{n,p,q,\chi}$ distribution or the uniform distribution over $\mathbb{Z}_q^{n\times m} \times \mathbb{Z}_q^m$.*

In this paper, we use the following hardness result of LWE problems from [30].

Theorem 2.10 ([30]). *If there exists an efficient, possibly quantum, algorithm for solving the D-$\mathsf{LWE}_{n,p,q,D_{\mathbb{Z}_q^m,\sigma}}$ problem for $\sigma > 2\sqrt{n}$ then there is an efficient quantum algorithm for approximating the SIVP and GapSVP problems to within $\tilde{O}(q\cdot n/\sigma)$ factors in the 2-norm, in the worst case*

The following re-randomization lemma from [26] plays an important role in the security proof of our IBE scheme.

Lemma 2.11 (Noise Rerandomization [26]). *Let q, ℓ, m be positive integers and r a positive real satisfying $r > \max\{\eta_{\epsilon_s}(\mathbb{Z}^m), \eta_{\epsilon_s}(\mathbb{Z}^\ell)\}$. Let $\mathsf{b} \in \mathbb{Z}_q^m$ be arbitrary and x chosen from $D_{\mathbb{Z}^m,r}$. Then for any $\mathsf{V} \in \mathbb{Z}^{m\times\ell}$ and positive real $\sigma > \mathsf{s}_1(\mathsf{V})$, there exists a PPT algorithm $\mathsf{ReRand}(\mathsf{V}, \mathsf{b}+\mathsf{x}, r, \sigma)$ that outputs $\mathsf{b}'^{\top} = \mathsf{b}^{\top}\mathsf{V} + \mathsf{x}'^{\top} \in \mathbb{Z}_q^\ell$ where the statistical distance of the discrete Gaussian $D_{\mathbb{Z}^\ell,2r\sigma}$ and the distribution of x' is within $8\epsilon_s$.*

Lemma 2.12 ([28]). *Let $matX \in \mathbb{R}^{n\times m}$ be a δ-subgaussian random matrix with parameter s. There exists a universal constant $C > 0$ such that for any $t \geq 0$, we have*

$$\Pr_{\mathsf{X}\leftarrow D_s}\left[s_1(\mathsf{X}) \leq C\cdot s\cdot(\sqrt{m}+\sqrt{n}+t)\right] \geq 1 - 2\cdot\exp(\delta)\cdot\exp(-\pi t^2).$$

2.3 Lattice Trapdoors

For positive integers b and $k > k' \geq \lceil\log_b(q)\rceil$, let $\mathsf{g}_b^{\top} = [1|b|b^2|...|b^{k'}|0] \in \mathbb{Z}^k$ be the gadget vector, then the gadget matrix G_b is defined as $\mathsf{G}_b := \mathsf{I}\otimes\mathsf{g}_b$. As stated in the work of [28], this gadget matrix has a public trapdoor $\mathsf{T}_{\mathsf{G}_b}$ with small norm, i.e., $\|\mathsf{T}_{\mathsf{G}_b}\| \leq \sqrt{b^2+1}$. Next, we present several useful sampling algorithms from the work of [4,6,13,28].

Lemma 2.13 ([13]). *Let n, m be integers and q be a prime modulus. Let ρ be positive integers satisfying $\rho < \frac{1}{2}\sqrt{q/n}$, and define $\log_1(\cdot) := \log_2(\cdot)$. There are efficient algorithms such that:*

- $\mathsf{TrapGen}(n, m, \rho, b, q) \to (\mathsf{A}, \mathsf{T_A})$ ([28], Lemma 5.3): *A randomized algorithm that, when $m = \Theta(n \log(q))$, outputs a full-rank matrix $\mathsf{A} \in \mathbb{Z}_q^{n\times m}$ and a basis $\mathsf{T_A} \in \mathbb{Z}_q^{m\times m}$ for $\Lambda_q^\top(\mathsf{A})$ such that A is statistically close to uniform and $\|\mathsf{T_A}\|_{\mathsf{GS}} = O\left(b\rho\sqrt{n \log_\rho(q)}\right)$.*
- $\mathsf{SampleLeft}(\mathsf{A}, \mathsf{B}, \mathsf{T_A}, \mathsf{u}, \sigma) \to \mathsf{e}$ ([16]): *A randomized algorithm that, on input a full-rank matrix $\mathsf{A} \in \mathbb{Z}_q^{n\times m}$, a matrix $\mathsf{B} \in \mathbb{Z}_q^{n\times m}$, a basis $\mathsf{T_A} \in \mathbb{Z}_q^{m\times m}$ for $\Lambda_q^\top(\mathsf{A})$, an element $u \in R_q$, and a Gaussian parameter $\sigma > \|\mathsf{T_A}\|_{\mathsf{GS}} \cdot \omega(\sqrt{\log(n)})$, outputs a vector $\mathsf{e} \in \mathbb{Z}_q^{2m}$ sampled from a distribution that is statistically close to $D_{\Lambda_{\mathsf{u}}^\perp([\mathsf{A}^\top|\mathsf{B}^\top]),\sigma}$, i.e., $[\mathsf{A}^\top|\mathsf{B}^\top]\cdot \mathsf{e} = \mathsf{u}$.*
- $\mathsf{SampleRight}(\mathsf{A}, \mathsf{R}, \mathsf{u}, y, \mathsf{G}_b, \mathsf{T}_{\mathsf{G}_b}, \sigma) \to \mathsf{e}$ *where* $\mathsf{B} = \mathsf{AR} + y \cdot \mathsf{G}_b$ ([2]): *A randomized algorithm that, on input full-rank matrices $\mathsf{A}, \mathsf{G}_b \in \mathbb{Z}_q^{n\times m}$, elements $y \in R^*, u \in R$, a matrix $\mathsf{R} \in [-\rho, \rho]^{m\times m}$, a basis $\mathsf{T}_{\mathsf{G}_b} \in \mathbb{Z}_q^{m\times m}$ for the lattice $\Lambda^\perp(\mathsf{G}_b)$, and a Gaussian parameter $\sigma > s_1(\mathsf{R}) \cdot \|\mathsf{T}_{\mathsf{G}_b}\|_{\mathsf{GS}} \cdot \omega(\sqrt{\log(n)})$, outputs a vector $\mathsf{e} \in \mathbb{Z}_q^{2m}$ sampled from a distribution which is statistically close to $D_{\Lambda_{\mathsf{u}}^\perp([\mathsf{A}^\top|\mathsf{B}^\top]),\sigma}$, i.e., $[\mathsf{A}^\top|\mathsf{B}^\top]\cdot \mathsf{e} = \mathsf{u}$.*
- ([28]) *Let $m \geq n \cdot \lceil \log_b(q) \rceil$. There is a publicly known matrix $\mathsf{T}_{\mathsf{G}_b}$ such that $\mathsf{T}_{\mathsf{G}_b}$ is a basis for the lattice $\Lambda^\perp(\mathsf{G}_b^\top)$ and $\|\mathsf{T}_{\mathsf{G}_b}\|_{\mathsf{GS}} \leq \sqrt{b^2+1}$. Furthermore, there exists a deterministic polynomial time algorithm G_b^{-1} which takes input a matrix $\mathsf{A} \in \mathbb{Z}_q^{n\times m}$ and outputs $\mathsf{R} = \mathsf{G}_b^{-1}(\mathsf{A})$ such that $\mathsf{R} \in [-b, b]^{m\times m}$, $\mathsf{G}_b \cdot \mathsf{R} = \mathsf{A}$, and $s_1(\mathsf{R}) \leq mb$. Similarly, there exists a randomized polynomial time algorithm $\widehat{\mathsf{G}_b}^{-1}$ which takes input a matrix $\mathsf{A} \in \mathbb{Z}_q^{n\times m}$ and outputs $\mathsf{R} \leftarrow \widehat{\mathsf{G}_b}^{-1}(\mathsf{A}^\top)$ such that $\mathsf{G}_b \cdot \mathsf{R} = \mathsf{A}$. Each coefficient in any entry of R follows a sub-Gaussian centered 0 with parameter $O(1)$, implying $s_1(\mathsf{R}) \leq \tilde{O}(b\sqrt{m})$ with an overwhelming probability.*

2.4 Homomorphic Computations

Here, we present some homomorphic encoding techniques and homomorphic evaluations that are associated with adaptively secure lattice-based IBE.

Homomorphic Encoding. In our design of the IBE scheme, we use the GSW-type [5,13,21] homomorphic encodings. For an integer α, we define its encoding as

$$\mathsf{Encode}(\alpha) := \mathsf{A} \cdot \mathsf{R} + \alpha \cdot \mathsf{G}_b,$$

where the matrix $\mathsf{A} \in \mathbb{Z}_q^{n\times m}$ and R is a small norm integer matrix, and G_b is the gadget matrix presented in the previous section. It is not hard to see the homomorphic additivity and multiplicativity of this GSW-type ([5,13,21]) homomorphic encoding. For a function $f : \mathbb{Z}_\mathsf{d} \to \mathbb{Z}_q$, we can obtain the encoding of the function value $f(\alpha)$ if given the encoding of α.

Homomorphic Evaluation. Next, we present the notion of δ-expanding, which quantitatively reflects the quality of a homomorphic evaluation process. The smaller the δ is, the better the homomorphic evaluation. We add a subtle modification to the definition of δ-expanding from the previous definitions [1,7]. The specific definition is as follows:

Definition 2.14. *For an integer $k > 0$, let $f : \mathcal{X}^k \to \mathcal{Y}$ be a function, and $\{\mathsf{A}_i\}_{i\in[k]}$ be matrices over $\mathbb{Z}_q^{n\times m}$, then the description of deterministic algorithms* $(\mathsf{PubEval}, \mathsf{TrapEval})$ *is as follows:*

$\mathsf{PubEval}\left(\{\mathsf{A}_i\}_{i\in[k]}, f\right) \to \mathsf{A}_f \in \mathbb{Z}_q^{n\times m}$: *On input a encoding matrix $\{\mathsf{A}_i\}_{i\in[k]}$ and a function f, it outputs a matrix $\mathsf{A}_f \in \mathbb{Z}_q^{n\times m}$.*

$\mathsf{TrapEval}\left(\{x_i\}_{i\in[k]}, \{\mathsf{R}_i\}_{i\in[k]}, f, \{\mathsf{A}_i\}_{i\in[k]}\right) \to \mathsf{R}_f$: *On input the encoding matrices $\{\mathsf{A}_i\}_{i\in[k]}$, trapdoor information $\{\mathsf{R}_i\}_{i\in[k]}$, an element $\mathsf{x} \in \mathcal{X}^k$, and the function f, this trapdoor evaluation algorithm outputs a matrix $\mathsf{R}_f \in \mathbb{Z}_q^{n\times m}$*

Let $\mathsf{A}_i = \mathsf{A}\cdot\mathsf{R}_i + x_i\cdot\mathsf{G}_b$ for all $i \in [k]$, then the correctness and δ-expanding of $(\mathsf{PubEval}, \mathsf{TrapEval})$ *are defined as follows:*

Correctness: *We say the deterministic algorithms* $(\mathsf{PubEval}, \mathsf{TrapEval})$ *are correct to homomorphically evaluate the function f if*

$$\mathsf{A}_f = \mathsf{A}\cdot\mathsf{R}_f + f(\mathsf{x})\cdot\mathsf{G}_b$$

δ-expanding: *We say the deterministic algorithms* $(\mathsf{PubEval}, \mathsf{TrapEval})$ *are δ-expanding if*

$$\|\mathsf{R}_f\| \le \delta\cdot\max_{i\in[k]}\{\|\mathsf{R}_i\|\}.$$

where the matrices $\mathsf{R}_f := \mathsf{TrapEval}\left(\{x_i\}_{i\in[k]}, \{\mathsf{R}_i\}_{i\in[k]}, f, \{\mathsf{A}_i\}_{i\in[k]}\right)$ and $\mathsf{A}_f := \mathsf{PubEval}\left(\{\mathsf{A}_i\}_{i\in[k]}, f\right)$.

3 Semi-homomorphic Equality Testing

In this section, we present a new and more compact LWE-based semi-homomorphic equality testing algorithm and its homomorphic evaluation quality. Thereafter, use our first construction to show semi-homomorphic equality testing algorithms for larger ranges.

3.1 The Construction

In this paper, we focus on equality testing functions defined as follows:

Definition 3.1. *Let η be a positive integer, then the equality testing function $\mathsf{Equal}_j(\star)$ indexed by $j \in [\eta]$ is defined as:*

$$\mathsf{Equal}_j(x) = \begin{cases} 0 & j \neq x \\ 1 & j = x \end{cases}.$$

Now we show our construction of a semi-homomorphic evaluation of the equality testing function. Given the GSW type encoding $\mathsf{A} \cdot \mathsf{R} + x \cdot \mathsf{G}_b$ of an input x, to homomorphically evaluate the equality testing function, we need to explore alternative circuits or expressions that have the same functionality as the equality test function. As discussed in the introduction, we use the idea of Lagrange interpolation. More precisely, we use the analytic expression of equality testing function that $\mathsf{Equal}_j(x) := P_j(x) = \prod_{i=1, i \neq j}^{\eta} (x-i) \cdot \left(\prod_{i=1, i \neq j}^{\eta} (j-i) \right)^{-1}$, and our construction of semi-homomorphic evaluation algorithms ($\mathsf{PubEval}, \mathsf{TrapEval}$) for $P_j(\star)$ is as follows.

Construction 3.2. *Given the function index $j \in [\eta]$ and a GSW type encoding of B_x of $x \in [\eta]$, the semi-homomorphic evaluation algorithms* ($\mathsf{PubEval}, \mathsf{TrapEval}$) *for* $\mathsf{Equal}_j(\star) = P_j(\star)$ *are described as follows.*

$\mathsf{PubEval}(\mathsf{B}_x, j) \to \mathsf{B}_\eta$:

1 Computes $p^j := \left(\prod_{i=1, i \neq j}^{\eta} (j-i) \right)^{-1} \mod q$.

2 For $i = 1$ to η compute $\bar{\mathsf{B}}_i$ recursively as:

$$\mathsf{B}_i = \begin{cases} \bar{\mathsf{B}}_x - i \cdot \mathsf{G}_b & i \neq j \\ G & i = j \end{cases}.$$

3 For $i = 1$ to η compute B'_i recursively as:

$$\mathsf{B}'_i = \begin{cases} \bar{\mathsf{B}}_i \cdot \mathsf{G}_b^{-1}\left(\mathsf{B}'_{i-1}\right) & i \neq j \\ \bar{\mathsf{B}}_1 & i = 1 \end{cases}.$$

4 Compute $\mathsf{B}_\eta := \mathsf{B}'_\eta \cdot \mathsf{G}_b^{-1}\left(p^j \cdot \mathsf{G}_b\right)$ *and output it.*

$\mathsf{TrapEval}(\mathsf{R}_x, j, \mathsf{B}_x) \to \mathsf{R}_\eta$:

1 Computes $\mathsf{R}_{p^j} := 0$.

2 For $i = 1$ to η compute $\bar{\mathsf{R}}_i$ recursively as:

$$\bar{\mathsf{R}}_i = \begin{cases} \mathsf{R}_x & i \neq j \\ 0 & i = j \end{cases}.$$

3 For $i = 1$ to η compute R'_i recursively as:

$$\mathsf{R}'_i = \begin{cases} \bar{\mathsf{R}}_i \cdot \mathsf{G}_b^{-1}\left(\mathsf{B}'_{i-1}\right) + \mathsf{R}'_{i-1} \cdot (x-i) & i \neq j \\ \bar{\mathsf{R}}_1 & i = 1 \end{cases}.$$

4 Compute $\mathsf{R}_\eta := \mathsf{R}'_\eta \cdot \mathsf{G}_b^{-1}\left(p^j \cdot \mathsf{G}_b\right)$ *and output it.*

Below, we show the correctness and the expanding factor of the above algorithms, respectively.

Correctness. Here we show the correctness of the above deterministic homomorphic evaluation algorithms.

Theorem 3.3. *The deterministic algorithms* (PubEval, TrapEval) *presented in Construction 3.2 are correct to homomorphically evaluate the function $P_j(x)$.*

Proof. To show the correctness of (PubEval, TrapEval), we need to show that

$$\mathsf{PubEval}\left(\mathsf{B}_x = \mathsf{A} \cdot \mathsf{R}_x + x \cdot \mathsf{G}_b, j\right) = \mathsf{A}_\eta = \mathsf{A} \cdot \mathsf{R}_\eta + P_j(x) \cdot \mathsf{G}_b.$$

Note that if $\mathsf{B}_x = \mathsf{A} \cdot \mathsf{R}_x + x \cdot \mathsf{G}_b$, then from the second step of algorithm PubEval, we know that $\mathsf{B}_i = \mathsf{A} \cdot \mathsf{R}_x + (x - i) \cdot \mathsf{G}_b$. In addition, from the step 3 of PubEval, we have that

$$\begin{aligned}
\mathsf{B}'_\eta &= \mathsf{A} \cdot \mathsf{R}_\eta \cdot \mathsf{G}_b^{-1}\left(\mathsf{B}'_{\eta-1}\right) + \cdot (x - \eta) \cdot \mathsf{B}'_{\eta-1} \\
&= \mathsf{A} \cdot \mathsf{R}_\eta \cdot \mathsf{G}_b^{-1}\left(\mathsf{B}'_{\eta-1}\right) + (x - \eta) \cdot \left(\mathsf{A} \cdot \mathsf{R}'_{\eta-1} + \prod_{i=1, i \neq j}^{\eta-1} (x - i) \cdot \mathsf{G}_b\right) \\
&= \mathsf{A} \cdot \underbrace{\left(\mathsf{R}_\eta \cdot \mathsf{G}_b^{-1}\left(\mathsf{B}'_{\eta-1}\right) + (x - \eta) \cdot \mathsf{R}'_{\eta-1}\right)}_{=\mathsf{R}'_\eta} + \prod_{i=1, i \neq j}^{\eta} (x - i) \cdot \mathsf{G}_b.
\end{aligned}$$

Furthermore, from step 4 of PubEval, we have that

$$\begin{aligned}
\mathsf{B}_\eta &= \left(\mathsf{A} \cdot \mathsf{R}'_\eta + \prod_{i=1, i \neq j}^{\eta} (x - i) \cdot \mathsf{G}_b\right) \cdot \mathsf{G}_b^{-1}\left(p^j \cdot \mathsf{G}_b\right) \\
&= \mathsf{A} \cdot \underbrace{\mathsf{R}'_\eta \cdot \mathsf{G}_b^{-1}\left(p^j \cdot \mathsf{G}_b\right)}_{=\mathsf{R}_\eta := \mathsf{TrapEval}(\mathsf{R}_x, j, \mathsf{B}_x)} + \underbrace{\prod_{i=1, i \neq j}^{\eta} (x - i) \cdot \left(\prod_{i=1, i \neq j}^{\eta} (j - i)\right)^{-1}}_{=: P_j(x)} \cdot \mathsf{G}_b \\
&= \mathsf{A} \cdot \mathsf{R}_\eta + P_j(x) \cdot \mathsf{G}_b.
\end{aligned}$$

This completes the proof of the theorem. □

Quality. Note that the quality of homomorphic evaluation algorithms significantly impacts the efficiency and security of the corresponding cryptosystems. The following theorem shows the quality of (PubEval, TrapEval) via the expanding factor. Due to the space limit, we postpone the proof of the following theorem to Appendix B.1.

Theorem 3.4. *The homomorphic evaluation algorithms* (PubEval, TrapEval) *presented in Construction 3.2 are $\eta^\eta \cdot n(kb)^2$-expanding.*

Note that if we let $\eta = \frac{\log(n)}{\log\log(n)}$, then we have that $\eta^\eta \leq n$. Therefore, from Theorem 3.4, we have the following corollary.

Corollary 3.5. *There exists a LWE-based homomorphic evaluation algorithm* (PubEval, TrapEval) *for the function class $\{\mathsf{Equal}_j(\star)\}_{j \in [\eta]}$ that are $O((nkb)^2)$-expanding.*

3.2 Homomorphic Equality Testing for Larger Ranges

In the above section, from the Construction 3.2, we know that the homomorphic evaluation algorithms (PubEval, TrapEval) have poly-expanding factor if the equality testing domain is $[\frac{\log(n)}{\log\log(n)}]$. Although it is asymptotically more compact than that of the previous construction of [25,36], for larger domains (i.e., compared with the set $[n]$ which was studied in the recent work of [1]) it results in an exponential expanding factor, which significantly impacts the security of lattice-based cryptosystems. In this section, we show how to perform semi-homomorphically equality testing over the set $[n]$ given $O(\log(n)/\log\log(n))$ GSW type of encodings.

Design Idea. Note that for any element $\alpha \in [n]$, we need $\lceil \log(n) \rceil$ bits to represent it. From this bit representation, we have that $\alpha = i$ for some $i \in [n]$ if each bit of i is equal to α. This idea was used in the previous cryptographic construction of [25,36]. Benefiting from the more compactness of our semi-homomorphic evaluation construction from the above section, we can improve the homomorphic equality testing of [25,36] significantly as follows.

Notations. For an integer $\alpha \in [\mathsf{d}]$, we use η-adic representation of α that $\alpha = \alpha_1\alpha_2\cdots\alpha_\xi$, where $\xi = \lceil \log_\eta(\mathsf{d}) \rceil$ and $\alpha_i \in [\eta]$ for $i \in [\xi]$.

Construction 3.6. *Given the function index $j \in [\mathsf{d}]$ with the η-adic representation $j = j_1 j_2 \cdots j_\xi$ and the GSW-type encodings $\mathsf{B}_1, \mathsf{B}_2, \cdots \mathsf{B}_\xi$ of $x_1, x_2 \cdots x_\xi \in [\eta]$, the semi-homomorphic evaluation algorithms ($\mathsf{PubEval}_n$, $\mathsf{TrapEval}_n$) for the equality test function $\mathsf{Equal}_j(\star)$ are described as follows:*

$\mathsf{PubEval}_n\left(\{\mathsf{B}_i\}_{i\in[\xi]}, j = \{j_i\}_{i\in[\xi]}\right) \to \mathsf{B}_\mathsf{d}$:

1. *For i=1 to ξ compute B'_i as $\mathsf{B}'_i = \mathsf{PubEval}\left(\mathsf{B}_i, j_i\right)$.*
2. *For i=1 to ξ recursively compute B''_i as follows*

$$\mathsf{B}''_i = \begin{cases} \mathsf{B}'_i \cdot \mathsf{G}_b^{-1}\left(\mathsf{B}''_{i-1}\right) & i \geq 2 \\ \mathsf{B}'_1 & i = 1 \end{cases}$$

Then let $\mathsf{B}_\mathsf{d} := \mathsf{B}''_\xi$ and output it.

$\mathsf{TrapEval}_n\left(\{\mathsf{R}_i\}_{i\in[\xi]}, j = \{j_i\}_{i\in[\xi]}, \{\mathsf{B}_i\}_{i\in[\xi]}\right) \to \mathsf{R}_\mathsf{d}$:

1. *For i=1 to ξ compute R'_i as $\mathsf{R}'_i = \mathsf{PubEval}\left(\mathsf{R}_i, j_i, \mathsf{B}_i\right)$.*
2. *For i=1 to ξ recursively compute R''_i as follows*

$$\mathsf{R}''_i = \begin{cases} \mathsf{R}'_i \cdot \mathsf{G}_b^{-1}\left(\mathsf{B}''_{i-1}\right) + \left(j_i \stackrel{?}{=} x_i\right) \cdot \mathsf{R}''_{i-1} & i \geq 2 \\ \mathsf{R}'_1 & i = 1 \end{cases}$$

Then let $\mathsf{R}_\mathsf{d} := \mathsf{R}''_\xi$ and output it.

Below, we show the correctness and quality of the above deterministic homomorphic evaluation algorithms via the expanding factor.

Correctness and Quality. Below, we use correctness and the homomorphic evaluation quality of $(\mathsf{PubEval}, \mathsf{TrapEval})$ for the function class $\{\mathsf{Equal}_j(\star)\}_{j\in[\eta]}$ to show the correctness and the quality of the homomorphic evaluation algorithms $(\mathsf{PubEval_d}, \mathsf{TrapEval_d})$ for the function class $\{\mathsf{Equal}_j(\star)\}_{j\in[\mathsf{d}]}$. Due to the space limit, we postponed the proof of the following theorems to Appendix B.2 and Appendix B.3.

Theorem 3.7. *The deterministic algorithms* $(\mathsf{PubEval_d}, \mathsf{TrapEval_d})$ *presented in Construction 3.6 are correct to homomorphically evaluate the function class* $\{\mathsf{Equal}_j(\star)\}_{j\in[\mathsf{d}]}$ *if the determinixtic algorithms* $(\mathsf{PubEval}, \mathsf{TrapEval})$ *are correct to homomorphically evaluate the function class* $\{\mathsf{Equal}_j(\star)\}_{j\in[\eta]}$.

Theorem 3.8. *The homomorphic evaluation algorithms* $(\mathsf{PubEval_d}, \mathsf{TrapEval_d})$ *for the function class* $\{\mathsf{Equal}_j(\star)\}_{j\in[\mathsf{d}]}$ *presented in Construction 3.6 are* $\xi(nkb)\cdot\delta$*-expanding if the homomorphic evaluation algorithms* $(\mathsf{PubEval}, \mathsf{TrapEval})$ *for the function class* $\{\mathsf{Equal}_j(\star)\}_{j\in[\eta]}$ *are* δ*-expanding.*

Note that if let $\eta = O(\log(n)/\log\log(n))$, then $\xi \le O(\log(n)/\log\log(n))$, and thus combining Corollary 3.5 and above Theorem 3.8, we have the following corollary.

Corollary 3.9. *There are LWE-based homomorphic evaluation algorithm pair* $(\mathsf{PubEval_d}, \mathsf{TrapEval_d})$ *that are* $O(\log(n)/\log\log(n)\cdot(nkb)^2)$*-expanding for the function class* $\{\mathsf{Equal}_j(\star)\}_{j\in[\mathsf{d}]}$ *for some* $\mathsf{d} = \mathsf{poly}(n)$.

4 Partition Function

In this section, we describe our design of the partition function and then show its homomorphic evaluation and the quality of the homomorphic evaluation process.

4.1 Design of Partition Function

Here, we show our new design of the partitioning function. The key of the partition function is $K := (\boldsymbol{\alpha}, \boldsymbol{\beta}) \in \mathsf{L}^t \times \mathbb{Z}_p^t$ for some super constant integer t. Note that the ECC parameter L can be set as large as $O(n^c)$ for some constant c. The concrete construction is as follows.

Definition 4.1. *Let* $t = \omega(1)$ *be a positive integer,* $\mathsf{ECC} : \mathbb{Z}_p^{\hat{\ell}} \to \mathbb{Z}_p^{\mathsf{L}}$ *be an error correcting code with relative distance* d*,* q *be some prime modulus such that* $q > t\cdot p^2$*, and the key space* $\mathcal{K} := [\mathsf{L}]^t \times [p]^t$*, then for a key* $K = (\boldsymbol{\alpha}, \boldsymbol{\beta}) \in \mathcal{K}$*, we define the function* $F_K : \mathbb{Z}_p^{\hat{\ell}} \to \mathbb{Z}_q$ *as follows:*

$$F_K(\mathsf{x}) := \sum_{i=1}^{t} (\mathsf{ECC}(\mathsf{x})[\alpha_i] - \beta_i)^2$$

It is not hard to see from the above definition of $F_K(*)$ that we have the following result.

Lemma 4.2. *For any function key $K = (\boldsymbol{\alpha}, \boldsymbol{\beta}) \in \mathcal{K}$, the function $F_K(*)$ given in the Definition 4.1 has the following two properties:*

1 *For any input $\mathsf{x} \in \mathbb{Z}_p^{\hat{\ell}}$ such that $\wedge_{i=1}^t \mathsf{ECC}(\mathsf{x})[\alpha_i] = \boldsymbol{\beta}_i$, we have $F_K(\mathsf{x}) = 0$.*

2 *For any input $\mathsf{x} \in \mathbb{Z}_p^{\hat{\ell}}$, if there is an index $i \in [t]$ such that $\mathsf{ECC}(\mathsf{x})[\alpha_i] \neq \boldsymbol{\beta}_i$, then we have $F_K(\mathsf{x})$ is invertible in $\mathbb{Z}_q$, that is, $F_K(\mathsf{x}) \in \mathbb{Z}_q^*$.*

The following theorem shows that the partition property A.1 of the above function. To make the presentation of the proof of the theorem clear, we make a simple modification on the ECC that we set the index set of ECC as $\{0\} \cup [\mathsf{L}]$ (instead of $[\mathsf{L}]$ as in the above definition). That is, the index of the output of ECC is started with zero. Furthermore, we set $\mathsf{ECC}(x) = 0$ for any input $x \in \mathbb{Z}_p^{\hat{\ell}}$. Due to the space limit, we postpone the proof of the following theorem to Appendix C.1.

Theorem 4.3. *The function $F_{\alpha,\beta}$ described in Definition 4.1 is a partition function.*

4.2 Homomorphic Evaluation of Partition Function

Here in this section, we show the deterministic homomorphic evaluation algorithms ($\mathsf{PubEval}_{\mathsf{IBE}}, \mathsf{TrapEval}_{\mathsf{IBE}}$) of our partitioning function and the efficiency of them. The concrete construction is as follows.

Construction 4.4. *Given the function indexes $\boldsymbol{\alpha} = (\boldsymbol{\alpha}_1, \cdots, \boldsymbol{\alpha}_t) \in [\eta]^t$ with the η-adic representation of each element α_i as $\alpha_i = (\alpha_{i,1}, \cdots, \alpha_{i,\xi})$, $\boldsymbol{\beta} = (\boldsymbol{\beta}_i, \cdots, \boldsymbol{\beta}_t) \in [\eta]^t$ and matrices $\mathsf{A}_{1,1}, \cdots \mathsf{A}_{t,\xi}$ and $\mathsf{B}_1, \mathsf{B}_2, \cdots \mathsf{B}_t$, then the semi-homomorphic evaluation algorithms ($\mathsf{PubEval}_{\mathsf{IBE}}, \mathsf{TrapEval}_{\mathsf{IBE}}$) for the partition function $F_{\alpha,\beta}(\star)$ is described as follows.*

$\mathsf{PubEval}_{\mathsf{IBE}}\left(\{\mathsf{A}_{i,j}\}_{i\in[t],j\in[\xi]}, \{\mathsf{B}_i\}_{i\in[t]}, x\right)$:

1 For $i = 1$ to t compute followings:

$$\mathsf{A}_i := \sum_{k=1}^{\mathsf{L}} \mathsf{PubEval}_{\mathsf{L}}\left(\{\mathsf{A}_{i,j}\}_{j\in[\xi]}, \mathsf{Equal}_k\right) \cdot \mathsf{G}_b^{-1}\left(\mathsf{ECC}(x)[k] \cdot \mathsf{G}_b\right)$$

2 Compute A_x as follow and output it.

$$\mathsf{A}_x := \sum_{i=1}^{t} (\mathsf{A}_i - \mathsf{B}_i) \cdot \mathsf{G}_b^{-1}\left(\mathsf{A}_i - \mathsf{B}_i\right)$$

$\mathsf{TrapEval}_{\mathsf{IBE}}\left(\{\alpha_{i,j}, \mathsf{R}_{i,j}^A\}_{i\in[t],j\in[\xi]}, \{\beta_i, \mathsf{R}_i^B\}_{i\in[t]}, x, \{\mathsf{A}_{i,j}\}_{i\in[t],j\in[\xi]}, \{\mathsf{B}_i\}_{i\in[t]}\right)$:

1 For $i = 1$ to t compute followings:

$$\mathsf{R}_i := \sum_{j=1}^{\mathsf{L}} \mathsf{TrapEval}_{\mathsf{L}}\left(\{\alpha_{i,j}, \mathsf{R}_{i,j}^A\}_{j\in[\xi]}, \mathsf{Equal}_j\right) \cdot \mathsf{G}_b^{-1}\left(\mathsf{ECC}(x)[j] \cdot \mathsf{G}_b\right)$$

2 Compute R_x *as follow and output it.*

$$\mathsf{R}_x := \sum_{i=1}^{t} \left(\left(\mathsf{R}_i - \mathsf{R}_i^B\right) \cdot \mathsf{G}_b^{-1}\left(\mathsf{A}_i - \mathsf{B}_i\right) + \left(\mathsf{ECC}(x)[\alpha_i] - \beta_i\right)\left(\mathsf{R}_i - \mathsf{R}_i^B\right) \right)$$

Below, we show the correctness and quality of the above homomorphic evaluation algorithms for our partition function.

Correctness. Let $\mathsf{ECC} : \mathbb{Z}_p^{\hat{\ell}} \to \mathbb{Z}_p^{\mathsf{L}}$ be an error correcting code with relative distance d. The following theorem shows the correctness of the above deterministic algorithms $(\mathsf{PubEval}_{\mathsf{IBE}}, \mathsf{TrapEval}_{\mathsf{IBE}})$.

Theorem 4.5. *The homomorphic evaluation algorithms* $(\mathsf{PubEval}_{\mathsf{IBE}}, \mathsf{TrapEval}_{\mathsf{IBE}})$ *presented in Construction 4.4 are correct to homomorphically evaluate the partition function class* $\{F_{\boldsymbol{\alpha},\boldsymbol{\beta}}(\star)\}_{(\boldsymbol{\alpha},\boldsymbol{\beta})\in[\mathsf{L}]^t\times[p]^t}$ *if the deterministic algorithm tuple* $(\mathsf{PubEval}_{\mathsf{L}}, \mathsf{TrapEval}_{\mathsf{L}})$ *is correct to homomorphically evaluate the function class* $\{\mathsf{Equal}_j(\star)\}_{j\in[\mathsf{L}]}$.

Proof. We show this theorem by analyzing each step of $(\mathsf{PubEval}_{\mathsf{IBE}}, \mathsf{TrapEval}_{\mathsf{IBE}})$ in Construction 4.4. Since $\mathsf{A}_{i,j} = \mathsf{A} \cdot \mathsf{R}_{i,j} + \alpha_{i,j} \cdot \mathsf{G}_b$ for all $i \in [t], j \in [\xi]$, and $\mathsf{B}_i = \mathsf{A} \cdot \mathsf{R}_i + \beta_i \cdot \mathsf{G}_b$ for all $i \in [t]$, we have followings for each step.

Step 1: Since the deterministic algorithms $(\mathsf{PubEval}_{\mathsf{L}}, \mathsf{TrapEval}_{\mathsf{L}})$ are correct to homomorphically evaluate the function class $\{\mathsf{Equal}_j(\star)\}_{j\in[\mathsf{L}]}$, thus we have

$$\begin{aligned}\mathsf{A}_i &= \sum_{k=1}^{\mathsf{L}} \left(\mathsf{A} \cdot \mathsf{R}_{i,k}^{\mathsf{L}} + \left(\alpha_i \stackrel{?}{=} k\right) \cdot \mathsf{G}_b\right) \cdot \mathsf{G}_b^{-1}\left(\mathsf{ECC}(x)[k] \cdot \mathsf{G}_b\right) \\ &= \mathsf{A} \cdot \underbrace{\left(\sum_{i=1}^{\mathsf{L}} \mathsf{R}_{i,k}^{\mathsf{L}} \cdot \mathsf{G}_b^{-1}\left(\mathsf{ECC}(x)[k] \cdot \mathsf{G}_b\right)\right)}_{:=\mathsf{R}_i} + \underbrace{\sum_{i=1}^{\mathsf{L}} \left(\alpha_i \stackrel{?}{=} k\right) \cdot \mathsf{ECC}(x)[k]}_{:=\mathsf{ECC}(x)[\boldsymbol{\alpha}_i]} \cdot \mathsf{G}_b \\ &= \mathsf{A} \cdot \mathsf{R}_i + \mathsf{ECC}(x)[\boldsymbol{\alpha}_i] \cdot \mathsf{G}_b,\end{aligned}$$

where $\mathsf{R}_{i,k}^{\mathsf{L}} = \mathsf{TrapEval}_{\mathsf{L}}\left(\{\alpha_{i,j}, \mathsf{R}_{i,j}^A\}_{j\in[\xi]}, \mathsf{Equal}_j\right)$;

Step 2: From the description of step 2 in $\mathsf{PubEval}_{\mathsf{IBE}}$ and $\mathsf{TrapEval}_{\mathsf{IBE}}$, we have that

$$\begin{aligned}\mathsf{A}_x &= \sum_{i=1}^{t} \left(\mathsf{A} \cdot \left(\mathsf{R}_i - \mathsf{R}_i^B\right) + \left(\mathsf{ECC}(x)[\boldsymbol{\alpha}_i] - \boldsymbol{\beta}_i\right) \cdot \mathsf{G}_b\right) \cdot \mathsf{G}_b^{-1}\left(\mathsf{A}_i - \mathsf{B}_i\right) \\ &= \mathsf{A} \cdot \underbrace{\left(\sum_{i=1}^{t} \left(\mathsf{R}_i - \mathsf{R}_i^B\right) \cdot \mathsf{G}_b^{-1}\left(\mathsf{A}_i - \mathsf{B}_i\right) + \left(\mathsf{R}_i - \mathsf{R}_i^B\right) \cdot \left(\mathsf{ECC}(x)[\boldsymbol{\alpha}_i] - \boldsymbol{\beta}_i\right)\right)}_{:=\mathsf{R}_x} \\ &\quad + \underbrace{\sum_{i=1}^{t} \left(\mathsf{ECC}(x)[\boldsymbol{\alpha}_i] - \boldsymbol{\beta}_i\right)^2}_{:=F_{\boldsymbol{\alpha},\boldsymbol{\beta}}(x)} \cdot \mathsf{G}_b = \mathsf{A} \cdot \mathsf{R}_x + F_{\boldsymbol{\alpha},\boldsymbol{\beta}}(x) \cdot \mathsf{G}_b\end{aligned}$$

This completes the proof of theorem. □

Quality. As we discussed in the introduction, the partition function and its homomorphic evaluation are vital for the security and efficiency of the adaptively secure IBE schemes. The following theorem shows the expanding factor of homomorphic evaluation algorithms ($\mathsf{PubEval}_\mathsf{L}, \mathsf{TrapEval}_\mathsf{L}$) presented in Construction 4.4.

Theorem 4.6. *The homomorphic evaluation algorithms* ($\mathsf{PubEval}_\mathsf{IBE}$, $\mathsf{TrapEval}_\mathsf{IBE}$) *presented in Construction 4.4 are* $2t \cdot (nkb + p)\delta$*-expanding for the partition function class* $\{F_{\alpha,\beta}(\star)\}_{\alpha\in[\mathsf{L}]^t,\beta\in[p]^t}$ *if the homomorphic evaluation algorithms* ($\mathsf{PubEval}_\mathsf{L}, \mathsf{TrapEval}_\mathsf{L}$) *for the function class* $\{\mathsf{Equal}_j(\star)\}_{j\in[\mathsf{L}]}$ *are* δ*-expanding.*

Proof. From the description of $\mathsf{TrapEval}_\mathsf{IBE}$ and the definition of ECC, we know that

$$\begin{aligned}\|\mathsf{R}_x\| &\leq t \cdot (\| (\mathsf{R}_i - \mathsf{R}_i^B) \cdot nkb\| + p \cdot (\mathsf{R}_i - \mathsf{R}_i^B)) \\ &\leq t \cdot (nkb + p) \cdot 2\delta \cdot \max_{i\in[t],j\in[\xi]} \{\|\mathsf{R}_{i,j}\|, \|\mathsf{R}_i^B\|\}\end{aligned}$$

where the first inequality is from Lemma 2.13; the second inequality is from the theorem assumption that the algorithms ($\mathsf{PubEval}_\mathsf{L}, \mathsf{TrapEval}_\mathsf{L}$) are δ-expanding. From the definition of δ-expanding, the theorem follows. □

If let the ECC parameter $p \leq O(nkb)$, then combining the above Theorem 4.6 and Corollary 3.9, we have the following corollary.

Corollary 4.7. *There is* $O(t \cdot \log(n)/\log\log(n) \cdot (nkb)^3)$*-expanding homomorphic evaluation algorithms* ($\mathsf{PubEval}_\mathsf{IBE}, \mathsf{TrapEval}_\mathsf{IBE}$) *respect to the function class* $\{F_{\alpha,\beta}(\star)\}_{\alpha\in[\mathsf{L}]^t,\beta\in[p]^t}$ *defined in Construction 4.4.*

5 Our IBE Scheme

In this section, we show our construction of an LWE-based IBE scheme. Then, we show the correctness and security analysis of our scheme.

5.1 The Construction

Let ID be the identity space of the scheme; the homomorphic evaluation algorithms ($\mathsf{PubEval}_\mathsf{IBE}, \mathsf{TrapEval}_\mathsf{IBE}$) are the deterministic algorithms as described in Construction 4.4; let $t, \xi \in \mathbb{Z}$ be some integers that we will determine in the next section; then our IBE scheme is described as follows:

Construction 5.1.

$\mathsf{Setup}(1^\lambda) \to (\mathsf{msk}, \mathsf{mpk})$: *On input of the security parameter* λ*, it first sets the system parameters* $n, m, q, \rho, \sigma_0, \sigma_1, \sigma$ *and then runs as follows:*

- *It runs* $\mathsf{TrapGen}(n, m, \rho, q)$ *to get* $(\mathsf{A} \in \mathbb{Z}_q^{n\times m}, \mathsf{T}_\mathsf{A} \in \mathbb{Z}_q^{m\times m})$.

- *Chooses random matrices* $\mathsf{A}_{1,1}, \mathsf{A}_{1,1}, \cdots \mathsf{A}_{t,\xi}$ *and* $\mathsf{B}_1, \mathsf{B}_2, \cdots \mathsf{B}_t$ *from* $\mathbb{Z}_q^{n\times m}$, *and selects a random vector* u *over* $\mathbb{Z}_q^n$.
- *It outputs the master secret key* $\mathsf{msk} = (\mathsf{T_a})$ *and the master public key* $\mathsf{mpk} = (\mathsf{A}, \{\mathsf{A}_{i,j}\}_{i\in[t],j\in[\xi]}, \{\mathsf{B}_i\}_{i\in[t]}, \mathsf{u})$.

$\mathsf{KeyGen}(\mathsf{msk}, \mathsf{mpk}, \mathsf{id}) \rightarrow (\mathsf{sk_{id}})$: *On input the master pair* (msk, mpk) *and an identity* $\mathsf{id} \in \mathsf{ID}$, *it runs the following:*
- *Computes* $\mathsf{A_{id}} = \mathsf{PubEval_{IBE}}\left(\{\mathsf{A}_{i,j}\}_{i\in[t],j\in[\xi]}, \{\mathsf{B}_i\}_{i\in[t]}, \mathsf{id}\right)$.
- *It runs* $\mathsf{SampleLeft}(\mathsf{A}, \mathsf{A_{id}}, \mathsf{T_A}, \mathsf{u}, \sigma)$ *to obtain a vector* $\mathsf{e} \in \mathbb{Z}_q^{2m}$ *such that* $[\mathsf{A}|\mathsf{A_{id}}]\cdot \mathsf{e} = \mathsf{u}$.
- *Outputs* $sk_{\mathsf{id}} = \mathsf{e}$ *as a secret key for the identity* id.

$\mathsf{Enc}(\mathsf{mpk}, \mathsf{id}, \mu) \rightarrow \mathsf{ct} = (c_0, c_1)$: *On input of the master key* mpk, *an identity* $\mathsf{id} \in \mathsf{ID}$, *and a message* $\mu \in \mathbb{Z}_2$, *it runs as follows:*
- *Computes* $\mathsf{A_{id}} = \mathsf{PubEval_{IBE}}\left(\{\mathsf{A}_{i,j}\}_{i\in[t],j\in[\xi]}, \{\mathsf{B}_i\}_{i\in[t]}, \mathsf{id}\right)$.
- *Samples a random vector* $\mathsf{s} \xleftarrow{\$} \mathbb{Z}_q$, *Gaussian vectors* $\mathsf{e}_1, \mathsf{e}_2 \leftarrow D_{\mathbb{Z}_q^m,\sigma_1}$, *and a Gaussian error* $e_0 \leftarrow D_{\mathbb{Z}_q,\sigma_0}$.
- *Computes* $c_0 = \mathsf{u}^\top \cdot \mathsf{s} + e_0 + \lceil \frac{q}{2} \rceil \cdot \mu$, *and* $\mathsf{c}_1 = \begin{bmatrix} \mathsf{A}^\top \\ \mathsf{A}_{\mathsf{id}}^\top \end{bmatrix} \cdot \mathsf{s} + \begin{bmatrix} \mathsf{e}_1 \\ \mathsf{e}_2 \end{bmatrix}$.
- *Outputs* $\mathsf{ct} = (c_0, \mathsf{c}_1)$ *as a ciphertext of* μ.

$\mathsf{Dec}(\mathsf{sk_{id}}, \mathsf{ct}) \rightarrow \mu$: *On input the secret key* $\mathsf{sk_{id}} = \mathsf{e}$ *and the ciphertext* $\mathsf{ct} = (c_0, \mathsf{c}_1) \in \mathbb{Z}_q \times \mathbb{Z}_q^{2m}$, *it runs as follows:*
- *Computes* $\mu' = \left\lceil \frac{2}{q}\left(c_0 - \mathsf{e}^\top \cdot \mathsf{c}_1\right) \right\rfloor \mod 2$.
- *Outputs* μ' *as the decrypted message of* ct.

5.2 Correctness and Security

The following theorem shows the correctness of our IBE scheme, corresponding proof is given in the full version of this paper.

Theorem 5.2. *For the parameters* n, m, *modulus* q, *and Gaussian parameters* $\sigma, \sigma_0, \sigma_1$ *such that* $q \geq O\left(\omega(\log(n))\sigma_0 + \sigma\sigma_1 \cdot \omega(\log(n)) \cdot \sqrt{2m}\right)$, *the* IBE *scheme presented in Construction 5.1 is correct.*

The following theorem shows the adaptive security of our IBE scheme, and refer to the full version for the corresponding proof.

Theorem 5.3. *The* IBE *scheme described in Construction 5.1 achieves adaptive security if the underlying problem* $D\text{-}\mathsf{LWE}_{n,m+1,q,\sigma_0}$ *is hard.*

6 Parameters

In this section, we show constraints on parameters and present asymptotic parameterization, from which we can easily see the parameter-related advantages of our schemes over the previous LWE-based IBE designs [2,36]. Before presenting our asymptotic parameterization, we recall the parameters related to our schemes presented in Construction 5.1 as follows:

System parameters: λ denotes the security parameter; Q denotes the upper bound on the number of key extractions in the IBE scheme that an adversary can query; ℓ denotes the length of identity.

D-LWE parameters: n, m denotes the dimension of master public key matrices; q denotes the modulus; and σ_0 denotes the Gaussian parameter related to the LWE error distribution.

ECC parameters: L denotes the block length of ECC; d denotes the relative distance of ECC; and p denotes the alphabet size of the codewords.

Lattice parameters: b denotes the base of G_b; ρ denotes the element range of trapdoor matrices in TrapGen; σ denotes the Gaussian parameter of SampleLeft; σ_1 denotes the gaussian parameter used in the encryption procedure to generate c_1;

Others: t denotes the dimension of partition key vectors $(\boldsymbol{\alpha}, \boldsymbol{\beta})$; η denotes the range of compact equality testing function with polynomial expanding factor;ξ denotes the η-adic length of each element of α.

Due to the space limit, the parameter constraints of our IBE scheme are presented in Appendix E.1.

6.1 Asymptotic Parameterization

Now, we asymptotically determine other parameters in terms of the security parameters λ and n. In order to do this, we consider two type settings for ρ and b, as shown in Table 2. Note that Type I is common in the literature, yet we consider that Type II may have a smaller matrix dimension.

Table 2. Asymptotic parameterization of our IBE scheme.

Parameters	TypeI : $\rho = 1, b = 2$	TypeII : $\rho = b = n^{\nu^*}$
ℓ	$O(\lambda)$	$O(\lambda)$
Q	$\mathsf{poly}(n)$	$\mathsf{poly}(n)$
n	$\Theta(\lambda)$	$\Theta(\lambda)$
m	$O(\lambda \log(\lambda))$	$O(\lambda \log(sep))$
q	$\tilde{O}(\lambda^9)$	$\tilde{O}(\lambda^9 b^7)$
σ_0	$\tilde{O}(\sqrt{\lambda})$	$\tilde{O}(\sqrt{\lambda})$
σ	$\tilde{O}(\lambda^4)$	$\tilde{O}(\lambda^4 b^4)$
σ_1	$\tilde{O}(\lambda^{4.5})$	$\tilde{O}(\lambda^{4.5} b^3)$
L	$O\left(\lambda^{1+\frac{2}{\kappa}}\right)^{\dagger}$	$O\left(\lambda^{1+\frac{2}{\kappa}}\right)$
d	$1 - O\left(\lambda^{-\frac{1}{\kappa}}\right)$	$1 - O\left(\lambda^{-\frac{1}{\kappa}}\right)$
p	$O\left(\lambda^{\frac{1}{\kappa}}\right)$	$O\left(\lambda^{\frac{1}{\kappa}}\right)$
η	$O(\log(\lambda)/\log\log(\lambda))$	$O(\log(\lambda)/\log\log(\lambda))$
ξ	$O(\log(\lambda)/\log\log\log(\lambda))$	$O(\log(\lambda)/\log\log\log(\lambda))$
t	$\omega(1)$	$\omega(1)$

(*) $\nu > 0$ is any positive real.

(†) $\kappa > 1$ can be any constant that satisfies $n^{\frac{1}{\kappa}} > 3+\kappa$, depending on how we set parameters of the underlying error correcting code.

Note that the proportion $1/\alpha = q/\sigma$ directly reflects the hardness of D-LWE problems. It is common in the literature to use $\frac{1}{\alpha}$ to reflect the quality of the reduction. Thus, from the parameterizations in Table 2, we have the following result for the IBE scheme in Construction 5.1.

Corollary 6.1. *If there exists a polynomial time adversary $\mathcal{A}$ who breaks the* IBE *scheme in Construction 5.1 with the parameters as in Table 2 (TypeI) with noticeable probability, then there is a polynomial time algorithm* $\mathsf{Sim}_{D\text{-LWE}}$ *who breaks the* $D\text{-LWE}_{n,m+1,q,\sigma_0}$ *problem for* $\frac{1}{\alpha} = \frac{q}{\sigma_0} = \tilde{O}\left(\lambda^{8.5}\right)$.

A Supplementary Materials for Section 2

A.1 Definition of Partition Function and Related Results

Definition A.1 (Partition Function [36]). *Let* $\mathbf{F} = \{\mathbf{F}_\lambda : \mathcal{K}_\lambda \times \mathcal{X}_\lambda \to R_2\}$ *be an ensemble of function family, we say that* $\mathbf{F}$ *is a partition function, if there exists an efficient algorithm* $\mathsf{PrtSmp}(1^\lambda)$*, which takes as input polynomial bounded* $Q = Q(\lambda) \in \mathbb{N}$ *and noticeable* $\epsilon = \epsilon(\lambda) \in (0, 1/2]$ *and outputs* K *such that:*

- *There exists* $\lambda_0 \in N$ *such that*

$$\Pr\left[K \in \mathcal{K}_\lambda : K \xleftarrow{\$} \mathsf{PrtSmp}(1^\lambda, Q(\lambda), \epsilon(\lambda))\right] = 1$$

  for all $\lambda > \lambda_0$*, where* λ_0 *may depend on* $Q(\lambda)$ *and* $\epsilon(\lambda)$.
- *For* $\lambda > \lambda_0$*, there exists* $\gamma_{\max}(\lambda)$ *and* $\gamma_{\min}(\lambda)$ *that depends on* $Q(\lambda)$ *and* $\epsilon(\lambda)$ *such that for all* $X^{(1)}, \cdots, X^{(Q)}, X^* \in \mathcal{X}_\lambda$ *with* $X^* \notin \{X^{(1)}, \cdots, X^{(Q)}\}$

$$\gamma_{\max}(\lambda) \geq \Pr\left[\mathbf{F}\left(X^{(1)}\right) \in R_q^*, \cdots, \mathbf{F}\left(X^{(Q)}\right) \in R_q^* \wedge \mathbf{F}\left(X^*\right) = 0\right] \geq \gamma_{\min}(\lambda)$$

  holds and the function $\tau(\lambda)$ *defined as*

$$\tau(\lambda) := \gamma_{\min} \cdot \epsilon(\lambda) - \frac{\gamma_{\max}(\lambda) - \gamma_{\min}(\lambda)}{2}$$

  is noticeable. The probability is taken over the randomness of the function key $K \xleftarrow{\$} \mathsf{PrtSmp}(1^\lambda, Q(\lambda), \epsilon(\lambda))$.

We call K *the partition key and* $\tau(\lambda)$ *the quality of the partition function.*

The proof of the following lemma can be found in the paper of [2,26].

Lemma A.2 (Lemma 8 in [26]). *Let us consider an IBE scheme and an adversary A that breaks the adaptively-anonymous security (resp. Pseudorandomness) with advantage* λ*. Let the identity space (resp. input space) be* X *and consider a map* γ *that maps a sequence of elements in* X *to a value in [0,1]. We consider the following experiment. We first execute the security game for* $\mathcal{A}$*. Let*

X^* be the challenge identity (resp. challenge input) and $X_1, \cdots, X_Q$ be the identities (resp. inputs) for which key extraction queries (resp. evaluation queries) were made. We denote $\mathbb{X} = (X^*, X_1, \cdots, X_Q)$. At the end of the game, we set coin′ $\in \{0,1\}$ as $\hat{b} = b'$ with probability $\gamma(\mathbb{X})$ and $\hat{b} \leftarrow \{0,1\}$ with probability $1 - \gamma(\mathbb{X})$. Then, the following holds

$$\left|\Pr[\hat{b} == b] - \frac{1}{2}\right| \geq \gamma_{\min} \cdot \epsilon - \frac{\gamma_{\max} - \gamma_{\min}}{2}$$

where $\gamma_{\max}$ and $\gamma_{\min}$ are the maximum and the minimum of $\gamma(\mathbb{X})$ taken over all possible $\mathbb{X}$, respectively.

B Supplementary Materials for Section 3

B.1 Proof of Theorem 3.4

Proof. From the description of Construction 3.2, we have that

$$\|\mathsf{R}_\eta\| \leq \|\mathsf{R}'_\eta \cdot \mathsf{G}_b^{-1}\left(p^j \cdot \mathsf{G}_b\right)\| \leq \|\mathsf{R}'_\eta\| \cdot kb$$

Thus to prove the theorem, showing $\|\mathsf{R}'_\eta\| \leq \eta^\eta \cdot (nkb) \cdot \|\mathsf{R}_x\|$ is sufficient, and we show it by induction. Namely, we prove $\|\mathsf{R}'_{j^*}\| \leq \eta^{j^*} \cdot (nkb) \cdot \|\mathsf{R}_x\|$ for all $\eta \geq j^* \geq 1$ below. Furthermore, by taking $j^* := \eta$, we have that $\|\mathsf{R}'_\eta\| \leq \eta^\eta \cdot (nkb) \cdot \|\mathsf{R}_x\|$, and the theorem follows.

For the basis step that when $j^* = 1$, we have $\|\mathsf{R}'_1\| \leq \|\mathsf{R}_x\| \leq \eta^1 \cdot (nkb) \cdot \|\mathsf{R}_x\|$. For the induction step, assume that $\|\mathsf{R}'_{j^*}\| \leq \eta^{j^*} \cdot (nkb) \cdot \|\mathsf{R}_x\|$ holds for some $\eta > j^* > 1$, then we need to prove that $\|\mathsf{R}'_{j^*+1}\| \leq \eta^{j^*+1} \cdot (nkb) \cdot \|\mathsf{R}_x\|$. Note that we have followings for $\|\mathsf{R}'_{j^*+1}\|$.

$$\begin{aligned}
\|\mathsf{R}'_{j^*+1}\| &\leq \|\mathsf{R}_{j^*+1}\| \cdot nkb + \|\mathsf{R}'_{j^*}\| \cdot |(x - j^* - 1)| \\
&\leq \|\mathsf{R}_x\| \cdot nkb + |(x - j^* - 1)| \cdot \eta^{j^*} \cdot (nkb) \cdot \|\mathsf{R}_x\| \\
&\leq \|\mathsf{R}_x\| \cdot nkb \left(|(x - j^* - 1)| \cdot \eta^{j^*} + 1\right) \\
&\leq \|\mathsf{R}_x\| \cdot nkb \cdot \eta^{j^*+1},
\end{aligned}$$

where the first inequality is from the description of step 2 of algorithm $\mathsf{TrapEval}$; the second inequality is from the induction assumption; the third and last inequality is from a simple rearranging the terms and from the fact that $|x - j - 1| + 1 \leq \eta$. This is the case, since $x \in [\eta]$ and $1 < j < \eta$, we have that $|x - j - 1| \leq \eta - 1$ and thus $\eta - |x - j - 1| \leq \eta$. Therefore, from the induction, we have that $\|\mathsf{R}'_{j^*}\| \leq \eta^{j^*} \cdot (nkb) \cdot \|\mathsf{R}_x\|$ for all $\eta \geq j^* \geq 1$ below □

B.2 Proof of Theorem 3.7

Proof. If $\mathsf{B}_{x_i} = \mathsf{A} \cdot \mathsf{R}_{x_i} + x_i \cdot \mathsf{G}_b$ for all $i \in [\xi]$, then from the description of step 1 of $\mathsf{PubEval_d}$ and $\mathsf{TrapEval_d}$, we have that

$$\mathsf{B}'_i = \mathsf{A} \cdot \mathsf{R}'_i + \left(j_i \stackrel{?}{=} x_i\right) \cdot \mathsf{G}_b,$$

where we use the theorem assumption that deterministic algorithms (PubEval, TrapEval) are correct to homomorphically evaluate the function class $\{\mathsf{Equal}_j(\star)\}_{j\in[\eta]}$, and $\left(j_i \stackrel{?}{=} x_i\right)$ is 1 if $j_i = x_i$ and is zero otherwise. From the second step of algorithm PubEval, we know that

$$\begin{aligned}
\mathsf{B_d} &= \mathsf{B'_d} \cdot \mathsf{G}_b^{-1}\left(\mathsf{B''_{d-1}}\right) = \left(\mathsf{A}\cdot\mathsf{R}'_\xi + \left(j_\xi \stackrel{?}{=} x_\xi\right)\cdot \mathsf{G}_b\right)\cdot \mathsf{G}_b^{-1}\left(\mathsf{B}''_{\xi-1}\right) \\
&= \mathsf{A}\cdot \underbrace{\left(\mathsf{R}'_\xi \cdot \mathsf{G}_b^{-1}\left(\mathsf{B}''_{\xi-1}\right) + \left(j_\xi \stackrel{?}{=} x_\xi\right)\cdot \mathsf{R}''_{\xi-1}\right)}_{=\mathsf{R_d}} + \underbrace{\prod_{i=1}^{\xi}\left(j_i \stackrel{?}{=} x_i\right)}_{=\mathsf{Equal}_j(x)} \cdot \mathsf{G}_b \\
&= \mathsf{A}\cdot\mathsf{R_d} + \mathsf{Equal}_j(x)\cdot \mathsf{G}_b
\end{aligned}$$

Therefore, the correctness follows. □

B.3 Proof of Theorem 3.8

Proof. From the description of Construction 3.6, we know that showing $\|\mathsf{R}''_\xi\| \le \xi\cdot(nkb)\cdot\delta\cdot\max_{i\in[\xi]}\|\mathsf{R}_{x_i}\|$ is sufficient to show the theorem. We show it by induction.

For the basis step that when $j^* = 1$, we have

$$\|\mathsf{R}''_1\| \le \|\mathsf{R}'_1\| \le \delta\cdot\max_{i\in[\xi]}\|\mathsf{R}_{x_i}\|,$$

where the second inequality is from theorem assumption that (PubEval, TrapEval) are δ-expanding, that is $\|\mathsf{R}'_i\| \le \delta\cdot\max_{i\in[\xi]}\|\mathsf{R}_{x_i}\|$ for all $i\in[\xi]$.

For the induction step, assume that $\|\mathsf{R}''_{i^*}\| \le i^*\cdot(nkb)\cdot\delta\cdot\max_{i\in[\xi]}\|\mathsf{R}_{x_i}\|$ holds for some $\xi > i^* > 1$, then we need to prove that $\|\mathsf{R}''_{i^*+1}\| \le (i^*+1)\cdot(nkb)\cdot\delta\cdot\max_{i\in[\xi]}\|\mathsf{R}_{x_i}\|$. Note that we have followings for $\|\mathsf{R}''_{i^*+1}\|$.

$$\begin{aligned}
\|\mathsf{R}''_{i^*+1}\| &\le \|\mathsf{R}'_{i^*+1}\|\cdot nkb + \left(j_{i^*} \stackrel{?}{=} x_{i^*}\right)\|\mathsf{R}''_{i^*}\| \\
&\le nkb\cdot\delta\cdot\max_{i\in[\xi]}\|\mathsf{R}_{x_i}\| + i^*\cdot(nkb)\cdot\delta\cdot\max_{i\in[\xi]}\|\mathsf{R}_{x_i}\| \\
&\le (i^*+1)\cdot nkb\cdot\delta\cdot\max_{i\in[\xi]}\|\mathsf{R}_{x_i}\|
\end{aligned}$$

where the first inequality is from the description of step 2 of algorithm $\mathsf{TrapEval_d}$ and triangle inequality of the 2-norm; the second inequality is from the induction assumption and the theorem assumption; the last inequality is from a simple amplifying the first term. Furthermore, by taking $i^* := \xi$, we have that $\|\mathsf{R}''_\xi\| \le \xi\cdot(nkb)\cdot\delta\cdot\max_{i\in[\xi]}\|\mathsf{R}_{x_i}\|$, and thus this completes the proof of the theorem. □

C Supplementary Materials for Section 4

C.1 Proof of Theorem 4.3

Proof. To show the theorem, we need to define an algorithm PrtSmp and show it equipped two properties of partition function in Definition A.1. First, our definition of PrtSmp as follows:

$\mathsf{PrtSmp}\left(1^\lambda, Q(\lambda), \epsilon(\lambda)\right) \rightarrow K$: Let $t' := \lceil \log_{1-\mathsf{d}}(\frac{3Q}{\epsilon}) \rceil$, then randomly sample a vector $\boldsymbol{\alpha}' \leftarrow [\mathsf{L}]^{t'}$ and a vector $\boldsymbol{\beta}' \in [p]^{t'}$. Then we pad zeros to each of $\boldsymbol{\alpha}', \boldsymbol{\beta}$ to get the vectors $\boldsymbol{\alpha}$ and $\boldsymbol{\beta}$ such that each has length t. Finally, outputs $K = (\boldsymbol{\alpha}, \boldsymbol{\beta})$.

Note that above algorithm PrtSmp has the first property of partition function (Definition A.1). Since Q is polynomially bounded and ϵ is noticeable, when $t = \omega(1)$, we have that $\frac{3Q}{\epsilon}$ is polynomially bounded, and thus we have that t' is constant. Furthermore, due to the setting that $t = \omega(1)$, for large enough λ, we have that $t' < t$, thus $K = (\boldsymbol{\alpha}, \boldsymbol{\beta}) \in \mathcal{K} = [\mathsf{L}]^t \times [p]^t$.

Next we show the partition property of PrtSmp. If let γ be the partition probability that

$$\gamma = \gamma(X^{(1)}, X^{(2)}, \cdots, X^{(Q)}, X^*) := \Pr_K\left[\bigwedge_{i=1}^{Q} F_K\left(X^{(i)}\right) \in \mathbb{Z}_q^* \wedge F_K\left(X^*\right) = 0\right],$$

then we have

$$\begin{aligned}\gamma &= \Pr_K\left[\bigwedge_{i=1}^{Q} F_K\left(X^{(i)}\right) \in \mathbb{Z}_q^* | F_K\left(X^*\right) = 0\right] \cdot \Pr_K\left[F_K\left(X^*\right) = 0\right] \\ &= \left(1 - \Pr_K\left[\exists j \in [Q], s.t., F_K\left(X^{(j)}\right) \notin \mathbb{Z}_q^* | F_K\left(X^*\right) = 0\right]\right) \cdot \Pr_K\left[F_K\left(X^*\right) = 0\right].\end{aligned}$$

To show PrtSmp has second property of Definition A.1, we first show (1) $\gamma_{\max} = \frac{1}{p^{t'}}$ is an upper bound of γ, and (2) $\gamma_{\min} = \left(1 - (1-\mathsf{d})^{t'}\right) \cdot \gamma_{\max}$ is a lower bound of γ.

First we show property (1). Note that we have

$$\begin{aligned}\gamma &\leq \Pr_{\boldsymbol{\alpha},\boldsymbol{\beta}}\left[F_{\boldsymbol{\alpha},\boldsymbol{\beta}}(X^*) = 0\right] = \Pr_{\boldsymbol{\alpha},\boldsymbol{\beta}}\left[\bigwedge_{i=1}^{t} (\mathsf{ECC}(X^*)[\alpha_i] - \beta_i = 0)\right] \\ &= \prod_{i=1}^{t} \Pr_{\boldsymbol{\alpha},\boldsymbol{\beta}}\left[(\mathsf{ECC}(X^*)[\alpha_i] = \beta_i)\right] = \underbrace{\left(\frac{1}{p}\right)^{t'}}_{:=\gamma_{\max}},\end{aligned}$$

where the first equality is from the fact the sum of quadratic terms is zero iff each quadratic term is zero; the second equality is from the fact that each entry of $\boldsymbol{\alpha}$ and $\boldsymbol{\beta}$ are independent; the last equality is from the randomness of β_i in $\mathbb{Z}_p$.

Next we show property (2). Since the modulus q is prime, we know that $F_K(X^{(j)})$ is invertible in $\mathbb{Z}_q$ if it is non-zero. Therefore, we have

$$\begin{aligned}\gamma &= \left(1 - \Pr_K\left[\exists j \in [Q], s.t., F_K\left(X^{(j)}\right) = 0 | F_K(X^*) = 0\right]\right) \cdot \gamma_{\max} \\ &\geq \left(1 - Q \cdot \Pr_K\left[F_K\left(X^{(j)}\right) = 0 | F_K(X^*) = 0\right]\right) \cdot \gamma_{\max} \\ &= \underbrace{\left(1 - Q \cdot \Pr_K\left[F_K\left(X^{(j)}\right) = F_K(X^*)\right]\right) \cdot \gamma_{\max}}_{:=\gamma_{\min}}\end{aligned}$$

Note that for any two distinct $x_1 \neq x_2$, we have

$$\begin{aligned}\Pr_{\alpha,\beta}\left[\underset{\alpha,\beta}{F}(x_1)=0 | \underset{\alpha,\beta}{F}(x_2)=0\right] &= \Pr_{\alpha,\beta}\left[\bigwedge_{i=1}^{t}(\mathsf{ECC}(x_1)[\alpha_i] = \beta_i) \mid \bigwedge_{i=1}^{t}(\mathsf{ECC}(x_2)[\alpha_i] = \beta_i)\right] \\ &= \prod_{i=1}^{t} \Pr_{\alpha,\beta}\left[\mathsf{ECC}(x_1)[\alpha_i] = \beta_i | \mathsf{ECC}(x_2)[\alpha_i] = \beta_i\right] \\ &= \prod_{i=1}^{t} \Pr_{\alpha,\beta}\left[\mathsf{ECC}(x_1)[\alpha_i] = \mathsf{ECC}(x_2)[\alpha_i]\right] = (1 - \mathsf{d})^{t'},\end{aligned}$$

where the first equality is from the fact the sum of quadratic terms is zero iff each quadratic term is zero; the second equality is from the fact that each entry of $\boldsymbol{\alpha}$ and $\boldsymbol{\beta}$ are independent; the third and last equalities are from a simple substitution, randomness of $\boldsymbol{\alpha}$ and the relative distance of ECC. Therefore, we have

$$\gamma_{\min} = \left(1 - Q \cdot (1 - \mathsf{d})^{t'}\right) \cdot \gamma_{\max}$$

Next we show that $\tau(\lambda) = \gamma_{\min} \cdot \epsilon - \frac{\gamma_{\max} - \gamma_{\min}}{2}$ is noticeable. From above results, we have that

$$\begin{aligned}\tau &= \left(1 - Q \cdot (1 - \mathsf{d})^{t'}\right) \cdot \gamma_{\max} \cdot \epsilon - Q \cdot (1 - \mathsf{d})^{t'} \cdot \gamma_{\max} && (1) \\ &\geq \frac{1}{2} \cdot \gamma_{\max} \cdot \epsilon - \frac{\epsilon}{6} \cdot \gamma_{\max} && (2) \\ &\geq \frac{1}{3} \cdot \gamma_{\max} \cdot \epsilon && (3)\end{aligned}$$

where the inequalities are from the setting of t'. Since ϵ is noticeable and Q is polynomially bounded, we have that t' is some constant from the definition of t', therefore $\gamma_{\max} = 1/p^{t'}$ is noticeable, and thus $\tau(\lambda)$ is noticeable. This completes the proof. $\square$

D Supplementary Materials for Section 5

D.1 Proof of Theorem 5.2

Proof. From the description of the decryption algorithm, we know that

$$c_0 - \mathsf{e} \cdot \mathsf{c}_1 = \mathsf{u}^\top \cdot \mathsf{s} + e_0 + \left\lceil \frac{q}{2} \right\rceil \cdot \mu - \mathsf{e}^\top \cdot \left(\begin{bmatrix} \mathsf{A} \\ \mathsf{A}_{\mathsf{id}} \end{bmatrix} \cdot \mathsf{s} - \begin{bmatrix} \mathsf{e}_1 \\ \mathsf{e}_2 \end{bmatrix} \right)$$
$$= \left\lceil \frac{q}{2} \right\rceil \cdot \mu + e_0 - \mathsf{e}^\top \cdot \begin{bmatrix} \mathsf{e}_1 \\ \mathsf{e}_2 \end{bmatrix}$$

Note that e_0 is sampled from the Gaussian distribution $D_{\mathbb{Z}_q,\sigma_0}$, thus from the Gaussian tail bound (Lemma 2.6), we have that $\mathsf{Pr}[\|e_0\|_\infty \leq \omega(\log(n)) \cdot \sigma_0] \leq \mathsf{negl}(\lambda)$. Furthermore, we have followings:

$$\left\| \mathsf{e}^\top \cdot \begin{bmatrix} \mathsf{e}_1 \\ \mathsf{e}_2 \end{bmatrix} \right\|_\infty \leq \max_{j \in [n]} \|\mathsf{e}^\top\| \cdot \left\| \begin{bmatrix} \mathsf{e}_1 \\ \mathsf{e}_2 \end{bmatrix}_j \right\|_\infty$$
$$\leq \sqrt{2m}\sigma \cdot \omega(\log(n)) \cdot \sigma_1,$$

where the last inequality holds except with negligible probability by Lemma 2.6. Thus from the above results, we have that

$$\mathsf{Pr}\left[\left\| e_0 - \mathsf{e}^\top \cdot \begin{bmatrix} \mathsf{e}_1 \\ \mathsf{e}_2 \end{bmatrix} \right\|_\infty \leq \omega(\log(n))\sigma_0 + \sigma\sigma_1 \cdot \omega(\log(n)) \cdot \sqrt{2m} \right] \leq \mathsf{negl}(\lambda).$$

Thus, from the description of the decryption algorithm, it decrypts correctly except with negligible probability, and thus the IBE scheme is correct. □

D.2 Proof of Theorem 5.3

Proof. To show the theorem, we prove that if there is an adversary $\mathcal{A}$ who breaks the IBE scheme in the Construction 5.1 in polynomial running time with noticeable probability ϵ via making an polynomially bounded number, say Q, of key extraction queries for Q identities, then there is an algorithm $\mathsf{Sim}_{D\text{-}\mathsf{LWE}}$ which invokes $\mathcal{A}$ to solve the D-$\mathsf{LWE}_{n,k+1,q,\sigma_0}$ problem with noticeable probability in polynomial time as well. This contradicts to the theorem assumption that D-$\mathsf{LWE}_{n,m+1,q,\sigma_0}$ is hard, and thus the theorem follows. Before presenting the concrete description of $\mathsf{Sim}_{D\text{-}\mathsf{LWE}}$, we first define and analysis follows hybrid games, from which the design idea of $\mathsf{Sim}_{D\text{-}\mathsf{LWE}}$ can be easily seen. The hybrid games are defined as follows.

Game_0: This is the original adaptive IBE security game between the adversary $\mathcal{A}$ and the challenger Chall.

Game_1: In this game, we change the Game_0 so that the challenger Chall procedure an conditional abort at the end of the game. Namely, this game is identical to the Game_0 except that at the end of the game, the challenger runs $\mathsf{PrtSmp}(1^\lambda, t_{\mathcal{A}}, \epsilon) \rightarrow K = (\boldsymbol{\alpha}, \boldsymbol{\beta})$ and *abort* the game if the following condition holds;

$$\bigwedge_{i=1}^{Q} \left(F_K\left(id^i\right) \in \mathbb{Z}_q^*\right) \bigwedge F_K\left(id^*\right) = 0,$$

where $\mathsf{id}^1, \cdots, \mathsf{id}^Q$ are the identities for which $\mathcal{A}$ has made key extraction queries, and id^* is the challenge identity.

Game_2: In this game, we change the way that the matrices $\{\mathsf{A}_{i,j}\}_{i\in[t],j\in[\xi]}$, $\{\mathsf{B}_i\}_{i\in[t]}$ are generated. Here, instead of sampling them uniformly over $\mathbb{Z}_q^{n\times m}$, the challenger first samples $\{\mathsf{R}_{i,j}\}_{i\in[t],j\in[\xi]}, \{\mathsf{R}_i^B\}_{i\in[t]} \leftarrow \mathbb{Z}_{[-\rho,\rho]}^{m\times m}$, and sets

$$\mathsf{A}_{i,j} := \mathsf{A}^\top \cdot \mathsf{R}_{i,j} + \boldsymbol{\alpha}_{i,j} \cdot \mathsf{G}_b, \text{ for } i \in [t], j \in [\xi]$$
$$\mathsf{B}_i := \mathsf{A}^\top \cdot \mathsf{R}_i^B + \boldsymbol{\beta}_i \cdot \mathsf{G}_b,, \text{ for } i \in [t],$$

where $\boldsymbol{\alpha}_{i,j}$ is the j-th η-adic representation of $\boldsymbol{\alpha}$.

Game_3: This game is the same as Game_2 except that we change way of generating public matrix A and the key extraction procedure. Here, the challenger samples $\mathsf{A} \xleftarrow{\$} \mathbb{Z}_q^{n\times m}$ uniformly instead of generating it with trapdoor by running the trapdoor generating algorithm $\mathsf{TrapGen}$. To extract a secret key for an identity id, the challenger first computes

$$\mathsf{R}_{\mathsf{id}} = \mathsf{TrapEval}_{\mathsf{IBE}}\left(\{\mathsf{R}_{i,j}\}_{i\in[t],j\in[\xi]}, \{\mathsf{R}_i^B\}_{i\in[t]}, \boldsymbol{\alpha}, \boldsymbol{\beta}, \mathsf{id}\right).$$

Then sample a vector $\mathsf{e}_{\mathsf{id}} \in \mathbb{Z}_q^{2m}$ by running $\mathsf{SampleRight}$ as

$$\mathsf{e}_{\mathsf{id}} = \mathsf{SampleRight}\left(\mathsf{A}, \mathsf{R}_{\mathsf{id}}, \mathsf{u}, F_{\alpha,\beta}(\mathsf{id}), \mathsf{G}_b, \mathsf{T}_{\mathsf{G}_b}, \sigma\right).$$

Finally, the challenger outputs e_{id} as a corresponding key for the identity id.

Game_4: In this game, we change the way that the challenge ciphertext $\mathsf{ct}^* = (c_0^*, \mathsf{c}_1^*)$ is generated. Here, the challenger first selects $\mathsf{s} \xleftarrow{\$} \mathbb{Z}_q^n$ and $\mathsf{x} \leftarrow D_{\mathbb{Z}_q^m,\sigma_0}$, and compute $\mathsf{v} = \mathsf{A} \cdot \mathsf{s} + \mathsf{x}$. Then the challenger samples $e_0 \leftarrow D_{\mathbb{Z}_q^m,\sigma_0}$, and generates the challenge ciphertext as follows:

$$c_0^* = \mathsf{u} \cdot \mathsf{s} + e_0 + \left\lceil \frac{q}{2} \right\rceil \cdot \mu, \ , \ \mathsf{c}_1^* = \mathsf{ReRand}\left([I_m|\mathsf{R}_{\mathsf{id}^*}]^\top, \mathsf{v}, \sigma_0, \frac{\sigma_1}{2\sigma_0}\right),$$

where I_m is the identity matrix.

Game_5: In this game, we change the way that the challenge ciphertext $\mathsf{ct}^* = (c_0^*, \mathsf{c}_1^*)$ is generated. Here, instead of masking the message with LWE samples, the challenger masks the message with uniformly random samples. Formally, the challenger first samples $u_0 \leftarrow \mathbb{Z}_q$, $\mathsf{v}' \leftarrow \mathbb{Z}_q^m$ and $\mathsf{x} \leftarrow D_{\mathbb{Z}_q^m,\sigma_0}$, then set $\mathsf{v} = \mathsf{v}' + x$ and compute the challenger ciphertext as follows:

$$c_0^* = u_0 + \left\lceil \frac{q}{2} \right\rceil \cdot \mu, \ , \ \mathsf{c}_1^* = \mathsf{ReRand}\left([I_m|\mathsf{R}_{\mathsf{id}^*}]^\top, \mathsf{v}, \sigma_0, \frac{\sigma_1}{2\sigma_0}\right),$$

For $i \in \{0,1,2,3,4,5\}$, let E_1 be the event that the adversary $\mathcal{A}$ wins in Game_i, and let abort be the event that challenger aborts in Game_1. From the above assumption, we have that $\Pr[E_0] = \epsilon$. Additionally, from the description of Game_5, it is easy to see that c_0 is independent of c_1, and from the uniformity of u_0, the advantage of any adversary in Game_5 is exactly 0, that is $\Pr[E_5] = 0$. Due to the space limit, we postpone the proof of following lemmas to Appendix D.3 to Appendix D.7.

Lemma D.1. $\Pr[E_1]$ *is noticeable if* ϵ *is noticeable.*

Lemma D.2. $|\Pr[E_2] - \Pr[E_1]| \leq \mathsf{negl}(\lambda)$

Lemma D.3. $|\Pr[E_3] - \Pr[E_2]| \leq \mathsf{negl}(\lambda)$

Lemma D.4. $|\Pr[E_4] - \Pr[E_3]| \leq \mathsf{negl}(\lambda)$

Lemma D.5. $|\Pr[E_5] - \Pr[E_4]| \leq \mathsf{negl}(\lambda)$ *if the* $D\text{-}\mathsf{LWE}_{n,m+1,q,\sigma_0}$ *problem is hard.*

Put All Together. Combining the above results, we have

$$\begin{aligned}\Pr[E_5] &= \sum_{i=1}^{4} (\Pr[E_{i+1}] - \Pr[E_i]) + \Pr[E_1] \geq \Pr[E_1] - \sum_{i=1}^{4} |(\Pr[E_{i+1}] - \Pr[E_i])| \\ &\geq \Pr[E_1] - \mathsf{negl}(\lambda) \geq \epsilon \cdot \frac{1}{p^{t'}} - \mathsf{negl}(\lambda),\end{aligned}$$

where $t' = \lceil \log_{1-\mathsf{d}}(\frac{3Q}{\epsilon}) \rceil$. Since ϵ is noticeable and Q is polynomially bounded, the value $p^{t'}$ is polynomially bounded, and thus $\Pr[E_5]$ is noticeable. Which is contradicts to the fact that $\Pr[E_5] = 0$. This completes the proof of Theorem 5.3. □

D.3 Proof of Lemma D.1

Proof. Since the $\mathcal{A}$'s advantage ϵ is noticeable and the running time $T_{\mathcal{A}}$ is polynomially bounded, the Lemma A.2 and the second property of the partition function implies that

$$\Pr[E_1] \geq \gamma_{\min} \cdot \epsilon - \frac{1}{2}(\gamma_{\max} - \gamma_{\min}) \geq \epsilon \cdot \frac{1}{3p^{t'}},$$

where $t' = \lceil \log_{1-\mathsf{d}}(\frac{3Q}{\epsilon}) \rceil$. Since ϵ is noticeable and Q is polynomially bounded, thus $p^{t'}$ is polynomially bounded, and thus the probability $\Pr[E_1]$ is noticeable. This completes the proof of Lemma D.1. □

D.4 Proof of Lemma D.2

Proof. Recall that the difference between the Game_1 and Game_2 is the way that they generate the public matrices $\{\mathsf{A}_{i,j}\}_{i\in[t],j\in[\xi]}$ and $\{\mathsf{B}_i\}_{i\in[t]}$. Namely, the two games generate the public ring vectors as follows:

$$\mathsf{Game}_1 : \begin{cases} \mathsf{A}_{i,j} & \xleftarrow{\$} \mathbb{Z}_q^{n\times m}, \text{ for } i \in [t], j \in [\xi] \\ \mathsf{B}_i & \xleftarrow{\$} \mathbb{Z}_q^{n\times m}, \text{ for } i \in [t], \end{cases}$$

$$\mathsf{Game}_2 : \begin{cases} \mathsf{A}_{i,j} & := \mathsf{A}^\top \cdot \mathsf{R}_{i,j} + \boldsymbol{\alpha}_{i,j} \cdot \mathsf{G}_b, \text{ for } i \in [t], j \in [\xi] \\ \mathsf{B}_i & := \mathsf{A}^\top \cdot \mathsf{R}_i^B + \boldsymbol{\beta}_i \cdot \mathsf{G}_b, , \text{ for } i \in [t], \end{cases}$$

where $\mathsf{R}_{i,j}, \mathsf{R}_i^B \leftarrow \mathbb{Z}_{-\rho,\rho}^{m\times m}$. Thus, Lemma 2.7 shows that the difference between the above two games is negligible. This completes the proof of Lemma D.2. □

D.5 Proof of Lemma D.3

Proof. Note that, in Game_3, the challenger changed the way of generating the public matrix A and the key extraction procedure. So, to show this lemma, it suffices to show that (1) the difference between the generating processes of A is negligible, and (2) the difference between the key extraction procedures is negligible. Thus, applying the probability union bound, we complete the proof of this lemma.

Now we show the statement (1): Note that public matrix A is sampled uniformly from the $\mathbb{Z}_q^{n\times m}$ in Game_3 instead of by running $\mathsf{TrapGen}$ as in Game_2. From the first property of Lemma 2.13, the difference between the two cases is negligible in security parameter λ.

Next we show the statement (2):Note that in Game_2, the challenger uses the trapdoor information of A to extract the identity key by running $\mathsf{SampleLeft}$ algorithm of Lemma 2.13. However, in Game_3, the challenger has no trapdoor information about the matrix A, yet it can use R_{id} to generate the corresponding secret identity key by running the $\mathsf{SampleRight}$ algorithm of Lemma 2.13. The second and third property of Lemma 2.13 shows that the outputs of above two sampling algorithms are statistically close to $D_{[\mathsf{A}^\top|\mathsf{A}_{\mathsf{id}}^\top],\mathsf{u},\sigma}$. Thus the difference between the above two procedures of generating identity keys is negligible. □

D.6 Proof of Lemma D.4

Proof. Note that the only difference between the Game_3 and Game_4 is the way the challenger generates the challenge ciphertext $\mathsf{ct} = (\mathsf{c}_0, \mathsf{c}_1)$. In Game_3, the challenge ciphertext is generated by the encryption algorithm, while in $game_4$, c_0 is generated by the same way as in Game_3, yet $\mathsf{c}_1 = \mathsf{ReRand}\left([I_m|\mathsf{R}_{\mathsf{id}^*}, \mathsf{v}, \sigma_0, \frac{\sigma}{2\sigma_0}]\right)$. From Lemma 2.11, we have that the difference between the above two games is negligible. □

D.7 Proof of Lemma D.5

Proof. To show this lemma, we construct a simulation algorithm $\mathsf{Sim}_{D\text{-}\mathsf{LWE}}$ (which is desired in Theorem 5.3) which tries to solve the D-LWE problem by invoking an algorithm $\mathcal{B}$ who tries to distinguish Game_4 and Game_5 . The description if $\mathsf{Sim}_{D\text{-}\mathsf{LWE}}$ is as follows:

$\mathsf{Sim}_{D\text{-}\mathsf{LWE}}\left((\mathsf{A}^\top|\mathsf{u}),(\mathsf{b}^\top,b_0)\right)\rightarrow\{0,1\}$:

On input the $D\text{-}\mathsf{LWE}_{n,m+1,q,\sigma_0}$ challenge samples $\left([\mathsf{A}\top|\mathsf{u}],[\mathsf{b}^\top,b_0]\right)$, algorithm $\mathsf{Sim}_{D\text{-}\mathsf{LWE}}$ simulates the Game_4 for $\mathcal{B}$ except the challenge ciphertext respond. It first lets A as the part of the master public key of IBE scheme, and generates the matrices $\{\mathsf{A}_{i,j}\}_{i\in[t],j\in[\xi]}$ and $\{\mathsf{B}_i\}_{i\in[t]}$ as in Game_4, and let $\mathsf{mpk}=\left(\mathsf{A},\{\mathsf{A}_{i,j}\}_{i\in[t],j\in[\xi]},\{\mathsf{B}_i\}_{i\in[t]},\mathsf{u}\right)$ as the master public key of the IBE scheme. The identity key extraction procedure is the same as in Game_4, yet it generates the challenge ciphertext as follows:

$$c_0^*=b_0+\left\lceil\frac{q}{2}\right\rceil\cdot\mu\ ,\ \mathsf{c}_1^*=\mathsf{ReRand}\left(\left[I_m|\mathsf{R}_{\mathsf{id}^*}\right],\mathsf{b},\sigma_0,\frac{\sigma}{2\sigma_0}\right).$$

If the algorithm $\mathcal{B}$ outputs 1, meaning that the simulated game is Game_4, then the algorithm $\mathsf{Sim}_{D\text{-}\mathsf{LWE}}$ outputs 1 implies the challenge samples are from $\mathsf{Sim}_{D\text{-}\mathsf{LWE}}$ distribution. If $\mathcal{B}$ outputs 0, meaning that the simulated game is Game_5, then the algorithm $\mathsf{Sim}_{D\text{-}\mathsf{LWE}}$ outputs 0 implies the challenge samples are from uniform distribution.

It is not hard to see that if the given challenge samples $\left([\mathsf{A}\top|\mathsf{u}],\mathsf{b}^\top,b_0\right)$ are from D-LWE distribution, then the algorithm $\mathsf{Sim}_{D\text{-}\mathsf{LWE}}$ exactly simulates the Game_4; if the given challenge samples are from uniform distribution, then the algorithm $\mathsf{Sim}_{D\text{-}\mathsf{LWE}}$ exactly simulates the Game_5. Thus the advantage of the simulation algorithm $\mathsf{Sim}_{D\text{-}\mathsf{LWE}}$ is exactly the advantage of the distinguishing advantage of $\mathcal{B}$. From the hardness assumption of D-LWE problem, the advantage of $\mathsf{Sim}_{D\text{-}\mathsf{LWE}}$ is negligible, and thus the distinguishing advantage of any algorithm $\mathcal{B}$ is negligible. This completes the proof of Lemma D.5 □

E Supplementary Materials for Section 6

E.1 Parameters for Our IBE Scheme

Parameter Constraints. Here we present the parameter constraints which ensure our IBE in Construction 5.1 reaches the correctness and the adaptive security. To meet the corresponding requirements, the parameters should satisfy the following constraints:

- For the requirements of $\mathsf{TrapGen}$ algorithm and gadget vector G_b, we need

$$m\geq\frac{(n+1)\log(q)+\omega(\log(n))}{\log(\rho)},$$
$$m\geq n\cdot\lceil\log_\rho(q)\rceil$$

- To ensure the Lemma 4.2 to hold, we need
$$q > t \cdot p^2$$
- To ensure the existence of such t' in the definition of PrtSmp in Theorem 4.3, we need to set t' such that
$$t' = \log_{1-\mathsf{d}}\left(\frac{3Q}{\epsilon}\right),$$
where Q is the number key queries and λ is the advantage of the adversary.
- To ensure the hardness of D-LWE problem, we need σ_0 satisfies the condition of the reduction in Lemma 2.10, that is
$$\sigma_0 \geq 2\sqrt{n}.$$
- To meet the requirement of ReRand algorithm, we set
$$\sigma_0 \geq \omega\left(\sqrt{\log(n)}\right) \text{ and } \sigma_1 \geq 2\sigma_0 \cdot \sqrt{s_1^2(\mathsf{R}_{\mathsf{id}^*}) + 1}.$$
- To meet the requirement of $\mathsf{SampleLeft}$ algorithm in Lemma 2.13, we need
$$\sigma > \|\mathsf{rot}(\mathsf{T_A})\|_{\mathsf{GS}} \cdot \omega\left(\sqrt{\log(n)}\right)$$
where $\|\mathsf{rot}(\mathsf{T_A})\|_{\mathsf{GS}} < O\left(b\rho\sqrt{n\log_\rho(q)}\right)$.
- To meet the requirement of $\mathsf{SampleRight}$ algorithm in Lemma 2.13, we need
$$\sigma > s_1(\mathsf{R_{id}}) \cdot \|\mathsf{rot}(\mathsf{T}_{\mathsf{G}_b})\|_{\mathsf{GS}} \cdot \omega\left(\sqrt{\log(n)}\right),$$
where $s_1(\mathsf{R_{id}})$ satisfies following
$$s_1(\mathsf{R_{id}}) < \tilde{O}\left(t \cdot (mb + p) \cdot \xi \cdot (mb)^3\right) \cdot \|\mathsf{R}\|,$$
Additionally, $\|\mathsf{R}\| \leq C \cdot s \cdot (\sqrt{m} + \sqrt{n} + t)$ with probability $2e^{-\pi t^2}$ for some $t > 0$, and $\|\mathsf{rot}(\mathsf{T}_{\mathsf{g}_b})\|_{\mathsf{GS}} \leq \sqrt{b^2 + 1}$.
- For the correctness of our IBE scheme, we need the modulus q satisfy
$$q \geq O\left(\omega(\log(n)) \cdot \sigma_0 + \sigma\sigma_1 \cdot \omega(\log(n)) \cdot \sqrt{2m}\right)$$
to achieve overwhelming correctness.

References

1. Abla, P., Liu, F.-H., Wang, H., Wang, Z.: Ring-based identity based encryption – asymptotically shorter MPK and tighter security. In: Nissim, K., Waters, B. (eds.) TCC 2021, Part III. LNCS, vol. 13044, pp. 157–187. Springer, Cham (2021). https://doi.org/10.1007/978-3-030-90456-2_6

2. Agrawal, S., Boneh, D., Boyen, X.: Efficient lattice (H)IBE in the standard model. In: Gilbert, H. (ed.) EUROCRYPT 2010. LNCS, vol. 6110, pp. 553–572. Springer, Heidelberg (2010). https://doi.org/10.1007/978-3-642-13190-5_28
3. Agrawal, S., Gentry, C., Halevi, S., Sahai, A.: Discrete Gaussian leftover hash lemma over infinite domains. In: Sako, K., Sarkar, P. (eds.) ASIACRYPT 2013, Part I. LNCS, vol. 8269, pp. 97–116. Springer, Heidelberg (2013). https://doi.org/10.1007/978-3-642-42033-7_6
4. Ajtai, M.: Generating hard instances of the short basis problem. In: Wiedermann, J., van Emde Boas, P., Nielsen, M. (eds.) ICALP 1999. LNCS, vol. 1644, pp. 1–9. Springer, Heidelberg (1999). https://doi.org/10.1007/3-540-48523-6_1
5. Alperin-Sheriff, J., Peikert, C.: Faster bootstrapping with polynomial error. In: Garay, J.A., Gennaro, R. (eds.) CRYPTO 2014, Part I. LNCS, vol. 8616, pp. 297–314. Springer, Heidelberg (2014). https://doi.org/10.1007/978-3-662-44371-2_17
6. Alwen, J., Peikert, C.: Generating shorter bases for hard random lattices. In: Albers, S., Marion, J. (eds.) 26th International Symposium on Theoretical Aspects of Computer Science, STACS 2009, Freiburg, Germany, 26–28 February 2009, Proceedings. LIPIcs, vol. 3, pp. 75–86. Schloss Dagstuhl - Leibniz-Zentrum für Informatik, Germany (2009)
7. Apon, D., Fan, X., Liu, F.: Vector encoding over lattices and its applications. IACR Cryptology ePrint Archive, p. 455 (2017)
8. Barrington, D.A.M.: Bounded-width polynomial-size branching programs recognize exactly those languages in NC^1. J. Comput. Syst. Sci. **38**(1), 150–164 (1989)
9. Bellare, M., Ristenpart, T.: Simulation without the artificial abort: simplified proof and improved concrete security for waters' IBE scheme. In: Joux, A. (ed.) EUROCRYPT 2009. LNCS, vol. 5479, pp. 407–424. Springer, Heidelberg (2009). https://doi.org/10.1007/978-3-642-01001-9_24
10. Boneh, D., Boyen, X.: Secure identity based encryption without random oracles. In: Franklin, M. (ed.) CRYPTO 2004. LNCS, vol. 3152, pp. 443–459. Springer, Heidelberg (2004). https://doi.org/10.1007/978-3-540-28628-8_27
11. Boneh, D., Boyen, X., Goh, E.-J.: Hierarchical identity based encryption with constant size ciphertext. In: Cramer, R. (ed.) EUROCRYPT 2005. LNCS, vol. 3494, pp. 440–456. Springer, Heidelberg (2005). https://doi.org/10.1007/11426639_26
12. Boneh, D., Franklin, M.: Identity-based encryption from the Weil pairing. In: Kilian, J. (ed.) CRYPTO 2001. LNCS, vol. 2139, pp. 213–229. Springer, Heidelberg (2001). https://doi.org/10.1007/3-540-44647-8_13
13. Boneh, D., et al.: Fully key-homomorphic encryption, arithmetic circuit ABE and compact garbled circuits. In: Nguyen, P.Q., Oswald, E. (eds.) EUROCRYPT 2014. LNCS, vol. 8441, pp. 533–556. Springer, Heidelberg (2014). https://doi.org/10.1007/978-3-642-55220-5_30
14. Boyen, X., Li, Q.: Towards tightly secure lattice short signature and Id-based encryption. In: Cheon, J.H., Takagi, T. (eds.) ASIACRYPT 2016, Part II. LNCS, vol. 10032, pp. 404–434. Springer, Heidelberg (2016). https://doi.org/10.1007/978-3-662-53890-6_14
15. Canetti, R., Goldreich, O., Halevi, S.: The random oracle methodology, revisited (preliminary version). In: 30th ACM STOC, pp. 209–218. ACM Press (1998)
16. Cash, D., Hofheinz, D., Kiltz, E., Peikert, C.: Bonsai trees, or how to delegate a lattice basis. In: Gilbert, H. (ed.) EUROCRYPT 2010. LNCS, vol. 6110, pp. 523–552. Springer, Heidelberg (2010). https://doi.org/10.1007/978-3-642-13190-5_27
17. Döttling, N., Garg, S.: From selective IBE to full IBE and selective HIBE. In: Kalai, Y., Reyzin, L. (eds.) TCC 2017, Part I. LNCS, vol. 10677, pp. 372–408. Springer, Cham (2017). https://doi.org/10.1007/978-3-319-70500-2_13

18. Döttling, N., Garg, S.: Identity-based encryption from the Diffie-Hellman assumption. In: Katz, J., Shacham, H. (eds.) CRYPTO 2017, Part I. LNCS, vol. 10401, pp. 537–569. Springer, Cham (2017). https://doi.org/10.1007/978-3-319-63688-7_18
19. Gentry, C.: Practical identity-based encryption without random oracles. In: Vaudenay, S. (ed.) EUROCRYPT 2006. LNCS, vol. 4004, pp. 445–464. Springer, Heidelberg (2006). https://doi.org/10.1007/11761679_27
20. Gentry, C., Peikert, C., Vaikuntanathan, V.: Trapdoors for hard lattices and new cryptographic constructions. In: Ladner, R.E., Dwork, C. (eds.) 40th ACM STOC, pp. 197–206. ACM Press (2008)
21. Gentry, C., Sahai, A., Waters, B.: Homomorphic encryption from learning with errors: conceptually-simpler, asymptotically-faster, attribute-based. In: Canetti, R., Garay, J.A. (eds.) CRYPTO 2013, Part I. LNCS, vol. 8042, pp. 75–92. Springer, Heidelberg (2013). https://doi.org/10.1007/978-3-642-40041-4_5
22. Gentry, C., Silverberg, A.: Hierarchical ID-based cryptography. In: Zheng, Y. (ed.) ASIACRYPT 2002. LNCS, vol. 2501, pp. 548–566. Springer, Heidelberg (2002). https://doi.org/10.1007/3-540-36178-2_34
23. Jager, T.: Verifiable random functions from weaker assumptions. In: Dodis, Y., Nielsen, J.B. (eds.) TCC 2015, Part II. LNCS, vol. 9015, pp. 121–143. Springer, Heidelberg (2015). https://doi.org/10.1007/978-3-662-46497-7_5
24. Jager, T., Kurek, R., Niehues, D.: Efficient adaptively-secure IB-KEMs and VRFs via near-collision resistance. In: Garay, J.A. (ed.) PKC 2021, Part I. LNCS, vol. 12710, pp. 596–626. Springer, Cham (2021). https://doi.org/10.1007/978-3-030-75245-3_22
25. Katsumata, S.: On the untapped potential of encoding predicates by arithmetic circuits and their applications. In: Takagi, T., Peyrin, T. (eds.) ASIACRYPT 2017, Part III. LNCS, vol. 10626, pp. 95–125. Springer, Cham (2017). https://doi.org/10.1007/978-3-319-70700-6_4
26. Katsumata, S., Yamada, S.: Partitioning via non-linear polynomial functions: more compact IBEs from ideal lattices and bilinear maps. In: Cheon, J.H., Takagi, T. (eds.) ASIACRYPT 2016, Part II. LNCS, vol. 10032, pp. 682–712. Springer, Heidelberg (2016). https://doi.org/10.1007/978-3-662-53890-6_23
27. Lai, Q., Liu, F.-H., Wang, Z.: Almost tight security in lattices with polynomial moduli – PRF, IBE, all-but-many LTF, and more. In: Kiayias, A., Kohlweiss, M., Wallden, P., Zikas, V. (eds.) PKC 2020, Part I. LNCS, vol. 12110, pp. 652–681. Springer, Cham (2020). https://doi.org/10.1007/978-3-030-45374-9_22
28. Micciancio, D., Peikert, C.: Trapdoors for lattices: simpler, tighter, faster, smaller. In: Pointcheval, D., Johansson, T. (eds.) EUROCRYPT 2012. LNCS, vol. 7237, pp. 700–718. Springer, Heidelberg (2012). https://doi.org/10.1007/978-3-642-29011-4_41
29. Micciancio, D., Regev, O.: Worst-case to average-case reductions based on Gaussian measures. In: 45th FOCS, pp. 372–381. IEEE Computer Society Press (2004)
30. Regev, O.: On lattices, learning with errors, random linear codes, and cryptography. In: Gabow, H.N., Fagin, R. (eds.) 37th ACM STOC, pp. 84–93. ACM Press (2005)
31. Shamir, A.: Identity-based cryptosystems and signature schemes. In: Blakley, G.R., Chaum, D. (eds.) CRYPTO 1984. LNCS, vol. 196, pp. 47–53. Springer, Heidelberg (1985). https://doi.org/10.1007/3-540-39568-7_5
32. Shor, P.W.: Algorithms for quantum computation: discrete logarithms and factoring. In: 35th FOCS, pp. 124–134. IEEE Computer Society Press (1994)

33. Waters, B.: Dual system encryption: realizing fully secure IBE and HIBE under simple assumptions. In: Halevi, S. (ed.) CRYPTO 2009. LNCS, vol. 5677, pp. 619–636. Springer, Heidelberg (2009). https://doi.org/10.1007/978-3-642-03356-8_36
34. Boneh, D., Boyen, X.: Efficient selective-ID secure identity-based encryption without random oracles. In: Cachin, C., Camenisch, J.L. (eds.) EUROCRYPT 2004. LNCS, vol. 3027, pp. 223–238. Springer, Heidelberg (2004). https://doi.org/10.1007/978-3-540-24676-3_14
35. Yamada, S.: Adaptively secure identity-based encryption from lattices with asymptotically shorter public parameters. In: Fischlin, M., Coron, J.-S. (eds.) EUROCRYPT 2016, Part II. LNCS, vol. 9666, pp. 32–62. Springer, Heidelberg (2016). https://doi.org/10.1007/978-3-662-49896-5_2
36. Yamada, S.: Asymptotically compact adaptively secure lattice IBEs and verifiable random functions via generalized partitioning techniques. In: Katz, J., Shacham, H. (eds.) CRYPTO 2017, Part III. LNCS, vol. 10403, pp. 161–193. Springer, Cham (2017). https://doi.org/10.1007/978-3-319-63697-9_6
37. Zhang, J., Chen, Yu., Zhang, Z.: Programmable hash functions from lattices: short signatures and IBEs with small key sizes. In: Robshaw, M., Katz, J. (eds.) CRYPTO 2016, Part III. LNCS, vol. 9816, pp. 303–332. Springer, Heidelberg (2016). https://doi.org/10.1007/978-3-662-53015-3_11

Towards Compact Identity-Based Encryption on Ideal Lattices

Huiwen Jia[1,2], Yupu Hu[3], Chunming Tang[1,2(✉)], and Lin Wang[4]

[1] School of Mathematics and Information Science, Key Laboratory of Information Security, Guangzhou University, Guangzhou, China
ctang@gzhu.edu.cn

[2] Guangzhou Center for Applied Mathematics, Guangzhou University, Guangzhou, China

[3] State Key Laboratory of Integrated Services Networks, Xidian University, Xi'an, Shaanxi, China

[4] Science and Technology on Communication Security Laboratory, Chengdu 610041, China

Abstract. Basic encryption and signature on lattices have comparable efficiency to their classical counterparts in terms of speed and key size. However, Identity-based Encryption (IBE) on lattices is much less efficient in terms of compactness, even when instantiated on ideal lattices and in the Random Oracle Model (ROM). This is because the underlying preimage sampling algorithm used to extract the users' secret keys requires huge public parameters. In this work, we specify a compact IBE instantiation for practical use by introducing various optimizations. Specifically, we first propose a modified gadget that offers a tradeoff between security and compactness, making it more suitable for the instantiation of practical IBEs. Then, by incorporating our gadget and the non-spherical Gaussian technique, we provide an efficient preimage sampling algorithm, based on which, we give a specification of a compact IBE on ideal lattice. Finally, two parameter sets and a proof-of-concept implementation are presented. Given the importance of the preimage sampling algorithm in lattice-based cryptography, we believe that our technique can also be applied to the practical instantiation of other advanced cryptographic schemes.

1 Introduction

Identity-Based Encryption. Identity-based encryption (IBE), introduced by Shamir in [56], is considered as a viable alternative to the classical public key encryption, which requires a dedicated infrastructure. Indeed, an IBE scheme avoids a certificate repository by deriving a user's public key from its identity, and the associated private key is extracted by a trusted authority using a master secret key. This simplifies the key generation and distribution in a multi-user system and is particularly attractive in resource constrained environments. The first IBE schemes, based on bilinear maps and on quadratic residue assumptions

E. Oswald (Ed.): CT-RSA 2024, LNCS 14643, pp. 354–378, 2024.
https://doi.org/10.1007/978-3-031-58868-6_14

respectively, appeared in [11,18], followed by improvements from various perspectives [7,10,19,40,43,58]. However, these traditional constructions are vulnerable to quantum attacks due to Shor's algorithm [57].

Lattice-Based Cryptography. Lattice-based cryptography is seen as a desirable alternative to the traditional number theoretic cryptography, due to its presumed security against quantum computers, algorithmic simplicity, and versatility for constructing various advanced schemes. For the basic encryption and signature, lattice-based constructions are the most practically efficient among post-quantum cryptosystems. In July 2022, NIST announced the first four post-quantum algorithms to be standardized, and three of them are lattice-based: Kyber [55] for public key encryption/KEM; Dilithium [45] and Falcon [53] for digital signature. These algorithms have an efficiency comparable to their classical counterparts.

When it comes to lattice-based IBE, however, this is far from the case. Even when instantiated on ideal lattice and in the Random Oracle Model (ROM), lattice-based IBE schemes still suffer from inefficiencies, particularly in terms of key size. The reason for this is the low efficiency of the associated *preimage sampling algorithm*, which essentially forms the backbone of the user key extraction procedure in lattice-based IBE schemes. In fact, the preimage sampling algorithm plays a central role in a large fraction of the advanced lattice-based cryptosystems.

Preimage Sampling. At the heart of many lattice-based schemes is what is known as Ajtai's function $f_{\mathbf{A}}(\mathbf{x}) = \mathbf{A}\mathbf{x} \bmod Q$, where $\mathbf{A} \in \mathbb{Z}_Q^{n \times m}$ is a short and fat random matrix. Ajtai's function actually defines the inhomogeneous short integer solution (ISIS) problem, which is believed to be hard [3,30,48] for appropriate parameters. Given a lattice trapdoor for $\mathbf{A}$, one can efficiently compute a short preimage. However, some early proposals [31,34] based on lattice trapdoor were broken by statistical attacks [22,50,60], since the preimages leak information from the trapdoor.

Towards the proper use of lattice trapdoors, the preimage sampling algorithm was first formalized by Gentry, Peikert and Vaikuntanathan [30], which samples preimages from a given lattice coset with a specific Gaussian distribution. Since then, it has become an essential building block in most advanced cryptographic applications. From an implementation perspective, however, the algorithm itself is inherently sequential and inefficient. In 2010, Peikert [51] proposed the convolution technique and made the sampling procedure parallelizable, at the cost of a moderate increase in the Gaussian parameter of the preimages, which yields some security loss. In the past decade, preimage sampling has been further improved by a batch of follow-up works [15,20,23–25,47,52,61], with the emphasis on the practical instantiations of the hash-and-sign signatures [30], the simplest application of the preimage sampling algorithm. Basically, these instantiations can be classified into two families: *NTRU trapdoor based* and *gadget based.*

1. NTRU trapdoor based. In 2014, Ducas, Lybashevsky and Prest [21] presented the first practical instantiation over NTRU lattices of the sampler in [30], by exploiting a nearly optimal NTRU trapdoor. This scheme was further developed as Falcon [53] by integrating the fast Fourier sampler [23]. Falcon offers good performance in terms of time and space, but its signing and key generation are rather complex. Espitau et al. proposed a simplified variant of Falcon, called Mitaka [24], which uses the hybrid sampler [52] for easier implementation at the cost of a moderate security loss. Recently, Espitau et al. [25] have further optimized Falcon and Mitaka by sampling the preimage from an ellipsoidal discrete Gaussian distribution.

2. Gadget based. The gadget based preimage sampling was invented by Micciancio and Peikert in [47]. Following the idea of [51], the sampling procedure of the Micciancio-Peikert framework is decomposed into offline and online phases. The online sampling boils down to the sampling over the lattice $\Lambda_Q^{\perp}(\mathbf{g}) = \{\mathbf{z} \mid \langle \mathbf{g}, \mathbf{z}\rangle = 0 \bmod Q\}$ where $\mathbf{g} = (1, b, \cdots, b^{k-1})$ is called a *gadget* vector. As shown in [47], sampling over the gadget lattice $\Lambda_Q^{\perp}(\mathbf{g})$ is easy and fast, and the key generation is quiet simple, which offers significant advantages in terms of implementation. In addition, the gadget based framework turns out to be extremely versatile for the construction of advanced primitives [13,32,33]. However, the gadget based constructions suffer from rather large key sizes. To improve the practicality, Chen, Genise and Mukherjee introduced the notion of approximate trapdoor [15] and proposed to use truncated gadget $\mathbf{f} = (b^l, \cdots, b^{k-1})$ for trapdoor construction. While the improvement is substantial, the size of the gadget-based scheme is still much larger than desired. Recently, Yu, Jia and Wang developed a compact gadget framework in which the gadget used is a square matrix, instead of the short and fat one used in [15,47]. This further reduces the key size.

Lattice-Based IBE. The first lattice-based IBE scheme was proposed in [30] in the ROM under the LWE and SIS assumptions (GPV-IBE), by using the preimage sampling algorithm devised therein. Subsequently, considerable research related to lattice-based IBE has been conducted from different perspectives, such as weakening the assumptions by removing the random oracle [1,5,41,59], and additional security properties [2,12,14]. These constructions demonstrate, on the theoretical side, the versatility of the preimage sampling algorithm for the construction of lattice-based IBE.

On the practical side, the first (proof-of-concept) implementation of IBE with practical parameters was instantiated on the NTRU lattice [21], and its performance was later improved by a number of software optimizations in [46]. As for implementations on ideal lattices, in 2018, Bert et al. [9] mixed the IBE scheme [1] in the standard model on the Ring-SIS/LWE assumptions with the efficient trapdoor of Peikert and Micciancio [47] and provided an efficient implementation. Later, Bert et al. [8] implemented preimage sampling algorithms on module lattices, relying on the works of [28,47], and several instantiations on module lattice based schemes were presented, including the IBE in the standard model [1]. The above two implementations of IBE schemes instantiated on ideal lattice are mainly aimed at demonstrating the time efficiency of the preimage sampling, ignoring the huge key size. For example, if we choose a parameter set in [9], the master public key is more than 325 KB for 41-bit security in the classical core-SVP model [4].

Challenges for Compact Lattice-Based IBE in Practice. Currently, the state of the art in terms of efficiency is still the GPV-IBE instantiated on structured lattices. Recall that in the GPV-IBE, the fat matrix $\mathbf{A} \in \mathbb{Z}_Q^{n\times m}$ and its associated trapdoor $\mathbf{T}$ represent the master public key and the master secret key respectively. Given any identity $id \in \{0,1\}^*$, the trusted authority extracts a sk_{id} for user id by using $\mathbf{T}$. Specifically, id is first hashed to some $\mathbf{u} \in \mathbb{Z}_Q^n$, then a short vector $\mathbf{x}$ following the discrete Gaussian distribution is output as the corresponding sk_{id} by invoking a preimage sampling algorithm, i.e., $\mathbf{x} \sim D_{\mathbb{Z}^m,\sigma}$ conditioned on $\mathbf{Ax} = \mathbf{u} \bmod Q$. On input a bit $\mu \in \{0,1\}$, the encryption algorithm uses the Dual-Regev scheme [30], which first samples $\mathbf{s} \leftarrow \chi_s^n, \mathbf{e} \leftarrow \chi_e^m, e \leftarrow \chi_e$ from some distributions χ_s, χ_e, then computes $\mathbf{c} = \mathbf{s}^t \cdot \mathbf{A} + \mathbf{e}^t \bmod Q$ and $c = \mathbf{s}^t \cdot \mathbf{u} + e + \lfloor \frac{Q}{2} \rceil \cdot \mu \bmod Q$, and finally outputs $ct = (\mathbf{c}, c)$ as the ciphertext. Using its secret key $\mathbf{x}$, the decryption algorithm computes $z = c - \mathbf{c} \cdot \mathbf{x} = e - \mathbf{e}^t \cdot \mathbf{x} + \lfloor \frac{Q}{2} \rceil \cdot \mu \bmod Q$ and outputs 0 if z is closer to 0 than to $\lfloor \frac{Q}{2} \rceil$; otherwise it outputs 1.

Note that the correctness requires that the absolute value of the error term, dominated by $\mathbf{e}^t \cdot \mathbf{x}$, should be less than $\lfloor \frac{Q}{4} \rceil$. Typically, the distribution χ_e is the centered binomial distribution with an appropriate parameter, say η, to hide the plaintext μ under the LWE assumption. Roughly, according to the central limit theorem, $\mathbf{e}^t \cdot \mathbf{x}$ follows a distribution that is very close to a discrete Gaussian distribution with a standard deviation of $\sigma\sqrt{m} \cdot \sqrt{\frac{\eta}{2}}$ and an expectation of 0. Consequently, the decryption failure rate for a single-bit encryption can be approximated by the Gaussian error function as $\delta \approx 1 - \mathsf{erf}\left(\frac{\lfloor Q/4 \rceil}{\sigma\sqrt{m}\cdot\sqrt{\eta}}\right)$. Note that $\sigma\sqrt{m}$ is the expected ℓ_2-norm of the preimage $\mathbf{x}$. This implies that for a reasonable decryption failure rate, the ratio $\frac{Q}{\sigma\sqrt{m}}$ should be greater than $c \cdot 4\sqrt{\eta}$ for some constant c. For instance, having $c = 3$ (i.e. the ratio $\frac{Q}{\sigma\sqrt{m}} = 12 \cdot \sqrt{\eta}$) leads to a decryption failure rate of about $1 - \mathsf{erf}(3) \approx 2^{-15.5}$, which can be reduced small enough by Error Correction Codes (ECC). For current preimage samplers, however, the best achievable ratio $\frac{Q}{\sigma\sqrt{m}}$ is far less than desired. As an illustration, recall that Falcon [53] uses the GPV sampler [30] and is instantiated on the most compact NTRU lattice, which means that the the standard deviation σ and the lattice dimension m are simultaneously the smallest. Even in this case, the ratio is $\frac{Q}{\sigma\sqrt{m}} \approx 2.3$, which cannot guarantee the correctness of the decryption algorithm when used directly in IBE. This explains why the GPV-IBE based on the NTRU lattice uses very large parameters [46]. The situation becomes even worse when the GPV-IBE is instantiated on ideal lattices.

Our Contributions. In this work, we present an efficient instantiation of the GPV-IBE [30] on ideal lattice, called SRNSG, by incorporating various optimizations, with the emphasis on compactness. More specifically, the contributions of this paper are summarized as follows.

1. Preimage sampling for IBE on ideal lattices. As for preimage sampling on ideal lattices, the state of the art is the compact gadget in [61] *combined with* the non-spherical Gaussian in [38], which gives the most efficient hash-and-sign signature on ideal lattice. However, this may not be the best choice for IBE to balance security and key sizes. In this work, we present an adapted compact lattice gadget, which can be seen as a combination of [15] and [61]. This brings more flexibility in parameter selection and therefore may be more suitable for advanced lattice-based constructions. Besides, we incorporate the non-spherical Gaussian [38] into our preimage sampler to reduce the size of the users' secret keys.

2. Practical instantiation of GPV-IBE. By plugging our preimage sampler into the GPV-IBE [30], we obtain a compact IBE based on ideal lattice, named SRNSG. Like LAC [44], a candidate in the NIST proposals of round 2, to save the bandwidth as much as possible, we use a smaller modulus Q, together with the BCH code in the decryption algorithm to address the problem of increasing the decryption failure rate caused by using a smaller Q.

3. Proof-of-concept implementation. Finally, we provide new parameter sets and give a proof-of-concept implementation of SRNSG to demonstrate its efficiency. The performance is summarized in Table 1.

Table 1. Summarized performance of SRNSG

Security level	NIST-1	NIST-5
mpk size (in bytes)	4896	10272
ct size (in bytes)	8510	16638
Extract (in cycles)	4,364,517	9,999,207
Enc (in cycles)	1,029,074	2,329,433
Security C/Q	133/121	294/267

Rode Map. We begin with preliminary materials in Sect. 2, followed by our improved preimage sampling in Sect. 3. Then we present the instantiated GPV-IBE by using our new sampler in Sect. 4. In Sect. 5, the concrete security analysis are presented. Besides, we provide new parameter sets and the performance of the implementation. Finally, we draw a conclusion in Sect. 6.

2 Preliminary

Let $\mathbb{R}$, $\mathbb{Z}$ and $\mathbb{N}$ denote the set of real numbers, integers and natural numbers respectively. For positive integer q, let $\mathbb{Z}_q = \{-\lfloor q/2 \rfloor, -\lfloor q/2 \rfloor + 1, \cdots, q - \lfloor q/2 \rfloor - 1\}$ denotes the quotient ring $\mathbb{Z}/(q\mathbb{Z})$. For $a \in \mathbb{Z}$, let $(a \bmod q)$ be the unique integer $a' \in \mathbb{Z}_q$ such that $a = a' \bmod q$. For a real-valued function f and a countable set S, we write $f(S) = \sum_{x \in S} f(x)$ assuming this sum is absolutely convergent.

2.1 Linear Algebra and Lattices

A vector is denoted by a bold lower case letter, e.g. $\mathbf{x} = (x_1, \ldots, x_n)$, and in column form. The concatenation of $\mathbf{x}_1, \mathbf{x}_2$ is denoted by $(\mathbf{x}_1, \mathbf{x}_2)$. Let $\langle \mathbf{x}, \mathbf{y} \rangle$ be the inner product of $\mathbf{x}, \mathbf{y} \in \mathbb{R}$ and $\|\mathbf{x}\| = \sqrt{\langle \mathbf{x}, \mathbf{x} \rangle}$ be the ℓ_2 norm of $\mathbf{x}$. A matrix is denoted by a bold upper case letter, e.g. $\mathbf{A} = [\mathbf{a}_1 \mid \cdots \mid \mathbf{a}_n]$, where $\mathbf{a}_i$ denotes the ith column of $\mathbf{A}$. Let $\widetilde{\mathbf{A}} = [\widetilde{\mathbf{a}_1} \mid \cdots \mid \widetilde{\mathbf{a}_n}]$ denote the Gram-Schmidt orthogonalization of $\mathbf{A}$. Let $\otimes$ denote the tensor product. Let $\mathbf{A} \oplus \mathbf{B}$ denote the block diagonal concatenation of $\mathbf{A}$ and $\mathbf{B}$. The largest singular value of $\mathbf{A}$ is denoted by $s_1(\mathbf{A}) = \max_{\mathbf{x} \neq \mathbf{0}} \frac{\|\mathbf{A}\mathbf{x}\|}{\|\mathbf{x}\|}$. Let $\mathbf{A}^t$ be the transpose of $\mathbf{A}$.

We write $\Sigma \succ 0$, when a symmetric matrix $\Sigma \in \mathbb{R}^{m \times m}$ is positive definite, i.e. $\mathbf{x}^t \Sigma \mathbf{x} > 0$ for all nonzero $\mathbf{x} \in \mathbb{R}^m$. We write $\Sigma_1 \succ \Sigma_2$ if $\Sigma_1 - \Sigma_2 \succ 0$. For any scalar s, we write $\Sigma \succ s$ if $\Sigma - s \cdot \mathbf{I} \succ 0$. If $\Sigma = \mathbf{B}\mathbf{B}^t$, we call $\mathbf{B}$ a square root of Σ. We use $\sqrt{\Sigma}$ to denote any square root of Σ when the context permits it.

Given $\mathbf{B} = [\mathbf{b}_1 \mid \cdots \mid \mathbf{b}_n] \in \mathbb{R}^{m \times n}$ with all $\mathbf{b}_i$'s linearly independent, the lattice generated by $\mathbf{B}$ is $\Lambda(\mathbf{B}) = \{\mathbf{B}\mathbf{z} \mid \mathbf{z} \in \mathbb{Z}^n\}$. The dimension of $\Lambda(\mathbf{B})$ is n and $\mathbf{B}$ is called a basis. Let $\Lambda^* = \{\mathbf{y} \in \mathrm{span}(\Lambda) \mid \langle \mathbf{x}, \mathbf{y} \rangle \in \mathbb{Z}, \forall \mathbf{x} \in \Lambda\}$ be the dual lattice of Λ.

In lattice-based cryptography, the q-ary lattice is of special interest and defined by some $\mathbf{A} \in \mathbb{Z}_q^{n \times m}$ as:

$$\Lambda_q^{\perp}(\mathbf{A}) = \{\mathbf{x} \in \mathbb{Z}^m : \mathbf{A}\mathbf{x} = \mathbf{0} \mod q\}.$$

The dimension of $\Lambda_q^{\perp}(\mathbf{A})$ is m and $(q \cdot \mathbb{Z})^m \subseteq \Lambda_q^{\perp} \subseteq \mathbb{Z}^m$. For any $\mathbf{u} \in \mathbb{Z}_q^n$ and $\mathbf{x} \in \mathbb{Z}^m$ such that $\mathbf{A} \cdot \mathbf{x} = \mathbf{u} \bmod q$, the "shifted lattice" is the set

$$\Lambda_{\mathbf{u}}^{\perp}(\mathbf{A}) = \{\mathbf{z} \in \mathbb{Z}^m : \mathbf{A} \cdot \mathbf{z} = \mathbf{u} \mod q\} = \Lambda_q^{\perp}(\mathbf{A}) + \mathbf{x}.$$

2.2 Gaussians

The Gaussian function $\rho : \mathbb{R}^m \to (0, 1]$ is defined as $\rho(\mathbf{x}) = \exp(-\pi \cdot \langle \mathbf{x}, \mathbf{x} \rangle)$. Applying a linear transformation given by an invertible matrix $\mathbf{B}$ yields

$$\rho_{\mathbf{B}}(\mathbf{x}) = \rho(\mathbf{B}^{-1}\mathbf{x}) = \exp(-\pi \cdot \mathbf{x}^t \Sigma^{-1} \mathbf{x}),$$

where $\Sigma = \mathbf{B}\mathbf{B}^t$. For any $\mathbf{c} \in \mathrm{span}(\mathbf{B})$, the shifted $\rho_{\sqrt{\Sigma}}$ with center $\mathbf{c}$ is defined as $\rho_{\sqrt{\Sigma}, \mathbf{c}}(\mathbf{x}) = \rho_{\sqrt{\Sigma}}(\mathbf{x} - \mathbf{c})$. Normalizing $\rho_{\sqrt{\Sigma}, \mathbf{c}}$, we obtain the continuous Gaussian distribution $D_{\sqrt{\Sigma},\mathbf{c}}$. Restricting the support of the distribution to the lattice Λ, we get the discrete Gaussian distribution $D_{\Lambda,\sqrt{\Sigma},\mathbf{c}}$. Formally, for any $\mathbf{x} \in \Lambda$,

$$D_{\Lambda,\sqrt{\Sigma},\mathbf{c}}(\mathbf{x}) = \frac{\rho_{\sqrt{\Sigma},\mathbf{c}}(\mathbf{x})}{\rho_{\sqrt{\Sigma},\mathbf{c}}(\Lambda)}.$$

Let $\eta_\epsilon(\Lambda) = \min\{s > 0 \mid \rho(s \cdot \Lambda^*) \leq 1 + \epsilon\}$ be the smoothing parameter with respect to a lattice Λ and $\epsilon \in (0,1)$. We write $\sqrt{\Sigma} \geq \eta_\epsilon(\Lambda)$, if $\rho_{\sqrt{\Sigma^{-1}}}(\Lambda^*) \leq 1+\epsilon$. We also use $\eta'_\epsilon(\Lambda) = \eta_\epsilon(\Lambda)/\sqrt{2\pi}$ to denote the scaled smoothing parameter.

Let $D^+_{\mathbb{Z},r}$ be the half integer Gaussian defined by $\rho_r(x)/\rho_r(\mathbb{N})$ for any $x \in \mathbb{N}$. We denote $\mathcal{N}_k(\mathbf{c}, \mathbf{\Sigma})$ as the k-dimensional normal distribution with center $\mathbf{c}$ and covariance $\mathbf{\Sigma}$. If $\mathbf{c} = \mathbf{0}$ and $\mathbf{\Sigma} = \mathbf{I}$, we write $\mathcal{N}_k(\mathbf{c}, \mathbf{\Sigma})$ as $\mathcal{N}_k$.

Lemma 1 ([30]). *Let Λ be an m-dimensional lattice with a basis $\mathbf{B}$, then $\eta_\epsilon(\Lambda) \leq \max_i \|\widetilde{\mathbf{b}}_i\| \cdot \sqrt{\log(2m(1+1/\epsilon))/\pi}$, where $\widetilde{\mathbf{b}}_i$ is the i-th vector of $\widetilde{\mathbf{B}}$.*

Lemma 2 ([48]). *Let Λ be a lattice, $\mathbf{c} \in \mathrm{span}(\Lambda)$. Then for any $\epsilon \in (0, \frac{1}{2})$ and $s \geq \eta_\epsilon(\Lambda)$, $\rho_s(\Lambda + \mathbf{c}) \in [\frac{1-\epsilon}{1+\epsilon}, 1]\rho_s(\Lambda)$.*

Theorem 1 ([29]). *For any $\epsilon \in [0,1)$ defining $\bar{\epsilon} = 2\epsilon/(1-\epsilon)$, a matrix $\mathbf{S}$ of full column rank, a lattice coset $A = \Lambda + \mathbf{a} \subset \mathrm{span}(\mathbf{S})$, and a matrix $\mathbf{T}$ such that $\ker(\mathbf{T})$ is a Λ-subspace and $\eta_\epsilon(\Lambda \cap \ker(\mathbf{T})) \leq \mathbf{S}$, we have*

$$\mathbf{T} \cdot D_{A,\mathbf{S}} \approx_{\bar{\epsilon}} D_{\mathbf{T}A,\mathbf{TS}}.$$

2.3 Cyclotomics

Let $\mathbb{Z}^*_m$ be the set of the $d = \varphi(m)$ integers invertible modulo m. Let ζ_m be the m-th primitive root of 1 and $\Phi_m(X) = \sum_{i\in\mathbb{Z}^*_m}(X - \zeta^i_m) \in \mathbb{Z}[X]$ be the m-th cyclotomic polynomial. We denote by $\mathcal{R} = \mathbb{Z}[\zeta_m] \simeq \mathbb{Z}[X]/(\Phi_m(X))$ the cyclotomic ring of conductor m and by $\mathcal{K} = \mathbb{Q}[\zeta_m] \simeq \mathbb{Q}[X]/(\Phi_m(X))$ the corresponding cyclotomic field. Let $\mathcal{K}_\mathbb{R} = \mathcal{K} \otimes \mathbb{R} = \mathbb{R}[\zeta_m] \simeq \mathbb{R}[X]/(\Phi_m(X))$. In this paper, we focus on the case of power-of-two conductor, i.e. $m = 2^t$ for some $t \in \mathbb{Z}$.

Any $f \in \mathcal{K}$ can be uniquely written as $f = \sum_{i=0}^{d-1} f_i\zeta^i_m$ with $f_i \in \mathbb{Q}$. We call $(f)_c = (f_0, \cdots, f_{d-1}) \in \mathbb{Q}^d$ the coefficient embedding (or coefficient vector) of f. The element of $f \in \mathcal{K}$ can also be identified with the matrix form $\mathcal{M}(f) = [(f)_c \mid (\zeta_m f)_c \mid (\zeta^{d-1}_m f)_c] \in \mathbb{Q}^{d\times d}$.

There are d embeddings of $\mathcal{K}$ fixing over $\mathbb{Q}$. Concretely, for $i \in \mathbb{Z}^*_m$, the embedding σ_i is defined by $\sigma_i(\zeta_m) = \zeta^i_m$. These d embeddings are the singular values of $\mathcal{M}(f)$. The canonical embedding of $f \in \mathcal{K}$ is $\sigma(f) = (\sigma_i(f))_{i\in\mathbb{Z}^*_m} \in \mathcal{K}^d$. The conjugate of f is denoted by f^*.

2.4 Identity-Based Encryption

- $\mathsf{Setup}(1^\lambda)$: on input the security parameter 1^λ, output the master public key and master secret key pair (mpk, msk).

- $\mathsf{Extract}(msk, id)$: given msk and a user identity $id \in \{0,1\}^*$, output a secret key sk_{id} for that identity.
- $\mathsf{Enc}(mpk, id, \mu)$: on input mpk, id and a plaintext μ, output a ciphertext ct.
- $\mathsf{Dec}(sk_{id}, ct)$: given sk_{id} and ct, output a plaintext μ.

The correctness condition is that for all identities id, Dec correctly decrypts a ciphertext encrypted to id, given the sk_{id} produced by $\mathsf{Extract}$.

3 A New Preimage Sampler

In this section, we present our preimage sampler by incorporating a new gadget and the non-spherical Gaussian. This new sampler offers more flexibility in parameter selection to balance security and key sizes, therefore it may be used for advanced applications as well.

3.1 A Modified Gadget Sampler

In this subsection we give a modified gadget that is more suitable for practicalisation of advanced cryptographic schemes. Notice that compared with [15,47], the most compact gadget, proposed by Yu, Jia and Wang [61], uses a square matrix as the gadget, instead of a fat one. This extreme compactness [61] induces a relatively large error term in the preimage, which may increase the decryption failure rate when used in IBE. We present a modified gadget, seen as a combination of [15] and [61], which offers a tradeoff between key sizes and security. We begin with the description of our gadget, followed by proving the simulatability of the gadget sampler, which is a crucial property in the security proof.

Our gadget works with a composite modulus $Q = pq$ where p, q are positive integers, as in [61]. Instead of using the square matrix $p{\cdot}\mathbf{I}$ as the gadget, we choose the gadget as in [15,47], but the semi-random sampling technique [61] is retained. In more detail, let b be a small integer, $w = \lceil \log_b q \rceil$ and let $\mathbf{g} = (1, b, \ldots, b^{w-1}) \in \mathbb{Z}^w$. Given a target $t \in \mathbb{Z}_Q$, our sampler outputs some $\mathbf{z} = (z_0, \ldots, z_{w-1}) \in \mathbb{Z}^w$ following discrete Gaussian such that $\langle \mathbf{f}, \mathbf{z} \rangle = t - e \mod Q$ for some small e, where $\mathbf{f} = p \cdot \mathbf{g}$ is the gadget vector in our sampler. We note the bijection $\tau : \mathbb{Z}_Q \mapsto \mathbb{Z}_p \times \mathbb{Z}_q$ defined by $\tau(t) = (t_p, t_q)$ such that $t = pt_q + t_p$. The main idea of our algorithm is to deterministically treat the remainder t_p as the approximation error e as in [61], then sample $\mathbf{z}$ over the coset $\Lambda_{t_q}^{\perp}(\mathbf{g}^t)$ as in [15,47]. A formal description is given in Algorithm 1.

It is straightforward to define $\mathsf{ApproxGadget}(\mathbf{t}, r, p, q)$ for $\mathbf{t} \in \mathbb{Z}_Q^n$ by independently calling Algorithm 1 on each entry of $\mathbf{t}$. The correctness of Algorithm 1 is shown in Lemma 3.

Lemma 3. *Algorithm 1 is correct. More precisely, let $p, q > 0$ be integers, $Q = pq$, $r > 0$ and $t \in \mathbb{Z}_Q$ such that $\tau(t) = (t_p, t_q)$. Then* $\mathsf{ApproxGadget}(t, r, p, q)$ *outputs $\mathbf{z}$ such that $\mathbf{z} \sim D_{\Lambda_{t_q}^{\perp}(\mathbf{g}^t), r}$ and $\langle \mathbf{f}, \mathbf{z} \rangle = t - t_p \mod Q$.*

Algorithm 1: ApproxGadget(t, r, p, q)

Require: a target $t \in \mathbb{Z}_Q$, a positive real $r > 0$ and integers $p, q > 0$ with $Q = pq$
Ensure: a vector $\mathbf{z} \sim D_{\mathbb{Z}^w,r}$ conditioned on $\langle \mathbf{f}, \mathbf{z} \rangle = t - e \bmod Q$ for some $e \in \mathbb{Z}_p$.
1: $(t_p, t_q) \leftarrow \tau(t)$
2: sample $\mathbf{z} \leftarrow D_{\Lambda_{t_q}^{\perp}(\mathbf{g}^t),r}$
3: **return** $\mathbf{z}$

Proof. In Algorithm 1, $\mathbf{z}$ is sampled from $D_{\Lambda_{t_q}^{\perp}(\mathbf{g}^t),r}$, with q being the modulus, hence $\langle \mathbf{g}, \mathbf{z} \rangle = t_q \bmod q$, that is, $p(\langle \mathbf{g}, \mathbf{z} \rangle - t_q) = 0 \bmod Q$. Immediately, we have $\langle \mathbf{f}, \mathbf{z} \rangle = t - t_p \bmod Q$. On the other hand, for any $\mathbf{z} \in \mathbb{Z}^w$, the error $e \in \mathbb{Z}_p$ satisfying $\langle \mathbf{f}, \mathbf{z} \rangle = t - e \bmod Q$ is unique, i.e. $e = t_p$. Then $\langle \mathbf{f}, \mathbf{z} \rangle = t - t_p \bmod Q$ holds if and only if $\mathbf{z} \in \Lambda_{t_q}^{\perp}(\mathbf{g}^t)$. Therefore, the distribution of $\mathbf{z}$ is exactly $D_{\mathbb{Z}^w,r}$ conditioned on $\langle \mathbf{f}, \mathbf{z} \rangle = t - t_p \bmod Q$ for some $e \in \mathbb{Z}_p$.

Remark 1. In step 2 of Algorithm 1, we can sample $\mathbf{z} \leftarrow D_{\Lambda_{t_q}^{\perp}(\mathbf{g}^t),r}$ by using the techniques in [28,30,37,47,62]. In SRNSG the parameter q is a power of b, i.e., $q = b^w$, therefore we can sample $\mathbf{z}$ with great ease as in [47].

We now prove that for uniformly random target $t \in \mathbb{Z}_Q$, the preimage and error distributions of ApproxGadget(t, r, p, q) can be simulated.

Lemma 4. *Let $p, q > 0$ be integers, $Q = pq$, $r \geq \eta_\epsilon(\Lambda_q^{\perp}(\mathbf{g}^t))$ with some negligible $\epsilon > 0$. Then the following two distributions are statistically close.*

1. *First sample $t \leftarrow U(\mathbb{Z}_Q)$, then sample $\mathbf{z} \leftarrow$ ApproxGadget(t, r, p, q), compute $e = t \bmod p$, output $(\mathbf{z}, t, e)$;*
2. *First sample $e \leftarrow U(\mathbb{Z}_p)$, then sample $\mathbf{z} \leftarrow D_{\mathbb{Z}^w,r}$, compute $t = e + \langle \mathbf{f}, \mathbf{z} \rangle \bmod Q$, output $(\mathbf{z}, t, e)$.*

Proof. The supports of two distributions are identical as follows:

$$\{(\mathbf{z}, t, e) \in \mathbb{Z}^w \times \mathbb{Z}_Q \times \mathbb{Z}_p \mid t = e + pz \bmod Q\}.$$

Distribution 1 outputs $(\mathbf{z}, t, e)$ with probability $P_1[(\mathbf{z}, t, e)] = \frac{1}{Q} \cdot P_1[\mathbf{z} \mid t] = \frac{1}{pq} \cdot \frac{\rho_r(\mathbf{z})}{\rho_r(\Lambda_{t_q}^{\perp}(\mathbf{g}^t))}$, and Distribution 2 with $P_2[(\mathbf{z}, t, e)] = \frac{1}{p} P_2[\mathbf{z} \mid e] = \frac{1}{p} \frac{\rho_r(\mathbf{z})}{\rho_r(\mathbb{Z}^w)}$. Since $r \geq \eta_\epsilon(\Lambda_q^{\perp}(\mathbf{g}^t))$ and $\rho_r(\mathbb{Z}^w) = \sum_{i \in \mathbb{Z}_q} \rho_r(\Lambda_i^{\perp}(\mathbf{g}^t))$, Lemma 2 shows $\rho_r(\Lambda_{t_q}^{\perp}(\mathbf{g}^t)) \in [\frac{1-\epsilon}{1+\epsilon}, \frac{1+\epsilon}{1-\epsilon}] \frac{\rho_r(\mathbb{Z}^w)}{q}$. Hence $P_1[(z, t, e)] \in [\frac{1-\epsilon}{1+\epsilon}, \frac{1+\epsilon}{1-\epsilon}] \cdot P_2[(z, t, e)]$ and we complete the proof.

3.2 Our Improved Preimage Sampler

In this subsection, we describe a new preimage sampler based on the aforementioned gadget, together with the non-spherical Gaussian [38]. Let $\Gamma = (n, m, p, q, Q, \chi)$ denote the global parameters where $Q = pq$ and χ is the distribution of secrets. Let $\mathbf{A} \in \mathbb{Z}_Q^{n \times m}$ be a matrix such that $m > n$. Our approximate trapdoor for $\mathbf{A}$ is defined as a matrix $\mathbf{T} \in \mathbb{Z}^{m\times n}$ such that $\mathbf{A}\cdot\mathbf{T} = \mathbf{F} = \mathbf{I}_n \otimes \mathbf{f} \bmod Q$, where $\mathbf{f} = p\cdot\mathbf{g} = p\cdot(1, b, \ldots, b^{w-1})$ is the gadget vector. The quality of the trapdoor is measured by its largest singular value $s_1(\mathbf{T})$. Similar to [15,47], our trapdoor can be instantiated in statistical mode or computational mode, for higher efficiency, we only consider the computational mode in this work.

Let $\Sigma = \sigma_1^2\cdot\mathbf{I}_{2n}\oplus\sigma_2^2\cdot\mathbf{I}_{wn}$ and $\Sigma_\mathbf{p} = \Sigma - r^2\cdot\mathbf{T}\cdot\mathbf{T}^t$. Algorithm 2 illustrates the preimage sampling algorithm by using the aforementioned approximate gadget trapdoor and the non-spherical technique in [38]. At a high level, the sampling procedure follows the same manner with [15,47] and uses the gadget sampler as "black-box". The output $\mathbf{x}$ satisfies

$$\mathbf{Ax} = \mathbf{Fz} + \mathbf{Ap} = \mathbf{v} - \mathbf{e} + \mathbf{Ap} = \mathbf{u} - \mathbf{e} \bmod Q.$$

Thus the approximation error $\mathbf{e}$ in Algorithm 2 is exactly the one in Algorithm 1, i.e., for uniformly random $\mathbf{u}$, the error $\mathbf{e}$ is uniformly random over $\mathbb{Z}_p^n$.

Algorithm 2: $\mathsf{ApproxPreSamp}(\mathbf{A}, \mathbf{T}, \mathbf{u}, r, \Sigma)$

Require: $(\mathbf{A}, \mathbf{T}) \in \mathbb{Z}_Q^{n\times m}\times\mathbb{Z}^{m\times wn}$ such that $\mathbf{AT} = \mathbf{F} \bmod Q$, a vector $\mathbf{u}\in\mathbb{Z}_Q^n$, $r \geq \eta_\epsilon(\Lambda_q^\perp(\mathbf{g}^t))$ and Σ such that $\Sigma_\mathbf{p} \succ \mathbf{0}$

Ensure: an approximate preimage $\mathbf{x}$ of $\mathbf{u}$ for $\mathbf{A}$.

1: $\mathbf{p} \leftarrow D_{\mathbb{Z}^m,\sqrt{\Sigma_\mathbf{p}}}$
2: $\mathbf{v} = \mathbf{u} - \mathbf{Ap} \bmod Q$
3: $\mathbf{z} \leftarrow \mathsf{ApproxGadget}(\mathbf{v}, r, p, q)$
4: **return** $\mathbf{x} = \mathbf{p} + \mathbf{Tz}$

Let $\mathbf{L} = [\mathbf{I}_m \mid \mathbf{T}]$. The next lemma characterizes the distribution of the linear transformation on the concatenation of $\mathbf{p} \leftarrow D_{\mathbb{Z}^m,\sqrt{\Sigma_\mathbf{p}}}$ and $\mathbf{z} \leftarrow D_{\mathbb{Z}^n,r}$, which represents the convolution step, i.e.,

$$\mathbf{x} = \mathbf{p} + \mathbf{Tz} = \mathbf{L}\cdot(\mathbf{p}, \mathbf{z}).$$

Lemma 5 ([38], adapted). *Let $\Sigma = \sigma_1^2\cdot\mathbf{I}_{2n}\oplus\sigma_2^2\cdot\mathbf{I}_{wn}$. For $\sigma_1^2 \geq (r^2 + \bar{r}^2)\cdot(s_1(\mathbf{T}))^2 + 2r^2 + 4\bar{r}^2$ and any σ_2^2 such that $\Sigma_\mathbf{p} \geq \bar{r}^2$, the distribution $\mathbf{L}\cdot D_{\mathbb{Z}^{m+wn},\sqrt{\Sigma_\mathbf{p}\oplus r^2\cdot\mathbf{I}_{wn}}}$ is statistically close to $D_{\mathbb{Z}^m,\sqrt{\Sigma}}$.*

Now we are ready to present the main theorem to state that the preimage and error distributions are simulatable without knowing the trapdoor, for uniformly random target $\mathbf{u}$, as in [15]. The proof follows that in [15,38], but is slightly simpler, as we only use Theorem 1 once instead of twice.

Theorem 2. *Let $(\mathbf{A}, \mathbf{T})$ be a matrix-approximate trapdoor pair, $\mathbf{B} = \left[\begin{smallmatrix}\mathbf{T}\\-\mathbf{I}_n\end{smallmatrix}\right]$ and (r, Σ) such that $\sqrt{\Sigma_\mathbf{p}\oplus r^2\mathbf{I}_n} \geq \eta_\epsilon(\mathcal{L}(\mathbf{B}))$. Denote by $\mathbf{A}^{-1}(\cdot)$ the shorthand of*

$\mathsf{ApproxPreSamp}(\mathbf{A}, \mathbf{T}, \cdot, r, \Sigma)$. *Then the following two distributions are statistically indistinguishable:*

$$\{(\mathbf{A}, \mathbf{x}, \mathbf{u}, \mathbf{e}) : \mathbf{u} \leftarrow U(\mathbb{Z}_Q^n),\ \mathbf{x} \leftarrow \mathbf{A}^{-1}(\mathbf{u}),\ \mathbf{e} = \mathbf{u} - \mathbf{A}\mathbf{x} \bmod Q\}$$
$$\{(\mathbf{A}, \mathbf{x}, \mathbf{u}, \mathbf{e}) : \mathbf{x} \leftarrow D_{\mathbb{Z}^m, \sqrt{\Sigma}},\ \mathbf{e} \leftarrow U(\mathbb{Z}_p^n),\ \mathbf{u} = \mathbf{A}\mathbf{x} + \mathbf{e} \bmod Q\}$$

Proof. Let

- $\mathbf{p} \leftarrow D_{\mathbb{Z}^m, \sqrt{\Sigma_\mathbf{p}}}$ be a perturbation,
- $\mathbf{u} \in \mathbb{Z}_Q^n$ be the input target,
- $\mathbf{v} = \mathbf{u} - \mathbf{A}\mathbf{p} \bmod Q$ be the target of the algorithm $\mathsf{ApproxGadget}(\mathbf{v}, r, p, q)$.

Real distribution: The real distribution of $(\mathbf{A}, \mathbf{x}, \mathbf{u}, \mathbf{e})$ is

$$\mathbf{A}, \mathbf{u} \leftarrow U(\mathbb{Z}_Q^n), \mathbf{p} \leftarrow D_{\mathbb{Z}^m, \sqrt{\Sigma_\mathbf{p}}}, \mathbf{v} = \mathbf{u} - \mathbf{A}\mathbf{p},$$
$$\mathbf{z} \leftarrow \mathsf{ApproxGadget}(\mathbf{v}, r, p, q), \mathbf{x} = \mathbf{p} + \mathbf{T}\mathbf{z}, \mathbf{e} = \mathbf{u} - \mathbf{A}\mathbf{x}.$$

Hybrid 1: Instead of sampling $\mathbf{u} \leftarrow U(\mathbb{Z}_Q^n)$, we sample $\mathbf{v} \leftarrow U(\mathbb{Z}_Q^n)$ and $\mathbf{p} \leftarrow D_{\mathbb{Z}^m, \sqrt{\Sigma_\mathbf{p}}}$, and compute $\mathbf{u} = \mathbf{v} + \mathbf{A}\mathbf{p}$. We keep $(\mathbf{z}, \mathbf{e}, \mathbf{x})$ unchanged. Clearly, the real distribution and Hybrid 1 are the same.

Hybrid 2: Instead of sampling $\mathbf{v}, \mathbf{z}$ and computing $\mathbf{e}$ as in Hybrid 1, we sample $\mathbf{z} \leftarrow D_{\mathbb{Z}^{wn}, r}$ and $\mathbf{e} \leftarrow U(\mathbb{Z}_p^n)$, and compute $\mathbf{v} = \mathbf{e} + \mathbf{F}\mathbf{z}$. All other terms $(\mathbf{p}, \mathbf{x}, \mathbf{u})$ remain unchanged. By Lemma 4, Hybrid 1 and Hybrid 2 are statistically close.

Hybrid 3: Instead of sampling $\mathbf{p}, \mathbf{z}$ and compute $\mathbf{x} = \mathbf{p} + \mathbf{T}\mathbf{z}$ in Hybrid 2, we sample directly $\mathbf{x} \leftarrow D_{\mathbb{Z}^m, s}$ and compute $\mathbf{u} = \mathbf{A}\mathbf{x} + \mathbf{e}$. Note that in Hybrid 2,

$$\mathbf{u} = \mathbf{v} + \mathbf{A}\mathbf{p} = \mathbf{e} + p\mathbf{z} + \mathbf{A}\mathbf{p} = \mathbf{e} + \mathbf{A}(\mathbf{p} + \mathbf{T}\mathbf{z}) = \mathbf{A}\mathbf{x} + \mathbf{e} \bmod Q$$

and $\mathbf{x} = \mathbf{p} + \mathbf{T}\mathbf{z}$ follows the distribution $[\mathbf{I}_m \mid \mathbf{T}] \cdot D_{\mathbb{Z}^{m+n}, \sqrt{\Sigma_\mathbf{p} \oplus r^2 \mathbf{I}_n}}$. By Lemma 5, Hybrid 3 and Hybrid 2 are statistically close. This completes the proof.

4 Specification of the Optimized IBE

This section gives a complete specification of the SRNSG IBE algorithm. We first summarize the parameters and notations in Table 2. For ease of notation, we treat the each element $f \in \mathcal{K}$ and its matrix form $\mathcal{M}(f)$ as identical.

4.1 Setup

SRNSG uses the RLWE-style key pair. Its master secret key is $\mathbf{R} \leftarrow \chi_n^{2 \times w}$ and the master public key is essentially $(a, \mathbf{b} = \mathbf{f} - [1, a] \cdot \mathbf{R} \bmod Q)$, where $\mathbf{f}$ is the gadget. A formal description of the key generation is given in Algorithm 3.

The element $a \in \mathcal{R}_Q$ is generated by an ideal extendable-output function XOF with a 32-byte seed seed_a. For compactness, it is stored as seed_a.

Table 2. Description of parameters and notations.

	Description
l_m	message length, $l_m = 256$
l_s	seed length, $l_s = 256$
l_v	codeword length $l_v = 511$
l_t	ECC codeword distance
(p, q)	gadget parameters
Q	global modulus, $Q = pq$
b	a small integer as the log base
w	dimension of gadget vector $\mathbf{f}$, $w = \lceil \log_b q \rceil$
n	a power of 2 integer
$\mathcal{R}$	$\mathbb{Z}[X]/(X^n + 1)$
$\mathcal{R}_Q$	$\mathcal{R}/(Q \cdot \mathcal{R})$
χ	centered binomial distribution with parameter 1/2, i.e., $\{-1 : \frac{1}{8}, 0 : \frac{3}{4}, 1 : \frac{1}{8}\}$
χ_n	centered binomial distribution over $\mathcal{R}$ with parameter 1/2
Q_s	upper bound of extraction query number, $Q_s = 2^{30}$
ϵ	closeness parameter, $\epsilon = 1/\sqrt{Q_s \cdot 256}$
$\bar{r}$	base Gaussian parameter $\bar{r} = \eta_\epsilon\left(\mathbb{Z}^{(2+w)\cdot 2048}\right)$
r	gadget Gaussian parameter $r = b\bar{r}$ by Lemma 1
σ_1, σ_2	standard deviation of the preimage
$\mathbf{\Sigma}$	covariance matrix of the preimage, $\mathbf{\Sigma} = \sigma_1^2 \cdot \mathbf{I} \oplus \sigma_2^2 \cdot \mathbf{I}$
$\mathbf{f}$	gadget vector $\mathbf{f} = p \cdot [1, b, \ldots, b^{w-1}] \in \mathcal{R}^w$
$\mathbf{R}$	secret matrix $\mathbf{R} \leftarrow \chi_n^{2\times w}$
$(a, \mathbf{b})$	public elements $a \leftarrow U(\mathcal{R})$, $\mathbf{b} = \mathbf{f} - [1,\ a] \cdot \mathbf{R} \bmod Q$
$\mathbf{\Sigma_p}$	perturbation covariance $\mathbf{\Sigma_p} = \mathbf{\Sigma} - r^2 \cdot \left[\begin{smallmatrix}\mathbf{R}\\ \mathbf{I}\end{smallmatrix}\right] \cdot [\mathbf{R}^t\ \mathbf{I}] = \left[\begin{smallmatrix}\sigma_1^2\cdot\mathbf{I} - r^2\mathbf{R}\mathbf{R}^t & -r^2\mathbf{R}\\ -r^2\mathbf{R}^t & (\sigma_2^2 - r^2)\cdot\mathbf{I}\end{smallmatrix}\right] \succ \bar{r}^2$
$\mathbf{\Sigma}_2$	the Schur complement of $(\sigma_2^2 - r^2) \cdot \mathbf{I}$ in $\mathbf{\Sigma_p}$, i.e., $\mathbf{\Sigma}_2 = \sigma_1^2 \cdot \mathbf{I} - \frac{\sigma_2^2 \cdot r^2}{\sigma_2^2 - r^2}\mathbf{R}\mathbf{R}^t = \left[\begin{smallmatrix}a & b\\ b^* & d\end{smallmatrix}\right]$
$\mathbf{C}$	$\mathbf{C} = \left[\begin{smallmatrix}a - bd^{-1}b^* & b\\ & d\end{smallmatrix}\right]$

In step 3 to step 5 of Algorithm 3, we need to sample the trapdoor $\mathbf{R}$ such that $\mathbf{\Sigma_p} - \bar{r}^2 \cdot \mathbf{I}$ is positive definite. This can be realized by: (1) checking the positive definiteness of the Schur complements of sub-matrices in $\mathbf{\Sigma_p}$ recursively; then (2) checking the definiteness of ring elements in $\mathcal{K}$. In more detail, since $\sigma_2 > r$ in our parameters, we need to check the positive definiteness of the Schur complement $\mathbf{\Sigma}_2$ of $(\sigma_2^2 - r^2) \cdot \mathbf{I}$, which in turn follows this procedure and boils down to check the positive definiteness of field elements in $\mathcal{K}_\mathbb{R}$. To this end, we simply compute their canonical embedding respectively, then check whether each element is positive or not.

In step 7, the element $a - bd^{-1}b^*$ in $\mathbf{C}$ is the Schur complement of d in $\mathbf{\Sigma}_2$. We include the triangular matrix $\mathbf{C}$ as a part of the secret key to simplify the key extraction procedure.

Algorithm 3: Setup

Require: None
Ensure: $(mpk,\ msk)$
1: $\mathsf{seed}_a \leftarrow \{0,1\}^{l_s}$, $a \leftarrow \mathsf{XOF}(\mathsf{seed}_a)$ ▷ $a \in \mathcal{R}_Q$
2: **repeat**
3: $\quad \mathbf{R} \leftarrow \chi_n^{2\times w}$ ▷ $\mathbf{R} \in \mathcal{R}^{2\times w}$
4: $\quad \mathbf{\Sigma_p} = \begin{bmatrix} \sigma_1^2 \cdot \mathbf{I} & \\ & \sigma_2^2 \cdot \mathbf{I} \end{bmatrix} - r^2 \cdot \begin{bmatrix} \mathbf{R} \\ \mathbf{I} \end{bmatrix} \cdot [\mathbf{R}^t\ \mathbf{I}]$
5: **until** $\mathbf{\Sigma_p} \succ \bar{r}^2$
6: Let $\mathbf{\Sigma}_2 = \sigma_1^2 \cdot \mathbf{I} - \frac{r^2}{r^2 - \bar{r}^2}\mathbf{R}\mathbf{R}^t = \begin{bmatrix} a & b \\ b^* & d \end{bmatrix}$
7: $\mathbf{C} = \begin{bmatrix} a - bd^{-1}b^* & b \\ & d \end{bmatrix}$ ▷ $\mathbf{C} \in \mathcal{K}_{\mathbb{R}}^{2\times 2}$
8: $\mathbf{f} = p \cdot [1,\ b, \ldots,\ b^{w-1}]$ ▷ $\mathbf{f} \in \mathcal{R}^{1\times w}$
9: $\mathbf{b} = \mathbf{f} - [1,\ a] \cdot \mathbf{R} \bmod Q$ ▷ $\mathbf{b} \in \mathcal{R}^{1\times w}$
10: **return** $(mpk = (\mathsf{seed}_a, \mathbf{b}),\ msk = (\mathbf{R}, \mathbf{C}))$

4.2 Extract Users' Secret Keys

On input a user's $id \in \{0,1\}^*$, the extracting procedure shown in Algorithm 4 produces a short preimage $\mathbf{y} = (y_0, \ldots, y_{w+1}) \in \mathcal{R}^{2+w}$ such that $[1, a, \mathbf{b}] \cdot \mathbf{y} = \mathsf{H}(id) - e \bmod Q$ for some small $e \in \mathcal{R}$. This procedure consists of two phases: offline and online, following the idea of [47,51]. In the offline phase, it samples an integer perturbation vector $\mathbf{p}$ from $D_{\mathcal{R}^{2+w},\mathbf{\Sigma_p}}$. Then in the online phase, it produces an approximate preimage using the semi-random sampling technique [61], as shown in the previous section. The output secret key for each user is essentially $(\mathbf{y}_1, \ldots, \mathbf{y}_{w+1})$. For compactness, we use some encoding technique, like [25], to compress $(\mathbf{y}_1, \ldots, \mathbf{y}_{w+1})$.

Algorithm 4: Extract

Require: $msk,\ id \in \{0,1\}^*$
Ensure: sk_{id}
Offline phase:
1: $\mathbf{p} \leftarrow \mathsf{SampleP}(msk)$ ▷ $\mathbf{p} \in \mathcal{R}^{2+w}$
2: $a \leftarrow \mathsf{XOF}(\mathsf{seed}_a)$
3: $u = H(id)$ ▷ $u \in \mathcal{R}_Q$
4: $v = u - [1, a, \mathbf{b}] \cdot \mathbf{p} \bmod Q$ ▷ $v \in \mathcal{R}_Q$
Online phase:
5: $\mathbf{x} \leftarrow \mathsf{SampleGadgetF}(v)$ ▷ $\mathbf{f} \cdot \mathbf{x} \approx v \bmod Q$
6: $\mathbf{y} = \mathbf{p} + \begin{bmatrix} \mathbf{R} \\ \mathbf{I} \end{bmatrix} \cdot \mathbf{x}$ ▷ $\mathbf{y} = (y_0, y_1, \ldots, y_{w+1}),\ [1, a, \mathbf{b}] \cdot \mathbf{y} \approx u \bmod Q$
7: **return** $sk_{id} = (y_1, \cdots, y_{w+1})$ ▷ $[a, \mathbf{b}] \cdot sk_{id} \approx u - y_0 \bmod Q$

The perturbation sampling algorithm is implemented with Peikert's Gaussian convolution technique [51] at the ring level, together with Genise and Micciancio's technique [28] that samples perturbation $\mathbf{p}$ by gradually updating the center and the covariance matrix using the Schur complement. In more detail, SampleP proceeds as follows. First, it samples $\mathbf{p}' = (p_2, \ldots, p_{w+1}) \in \mathcal{R}^w$ with variance $\sigma_2^2 - r^2$. Then by [28], it samples $(p_0, p_1) \in \mathcal{R}^2$ with covariance $\mathbf{\Sigma}_2 = \sigma_1^2 \cdot \mathbf{I} - \frac{\sigma_2^2 \cdot r^2}{\sigma_2^2 - r^2}\mathbf{R}\mathbf{R}^t = \left[\begin{smallmatrix} a & b \\ b^* & d \end{smallmatrix}\right]$ and center $\mathbf{c} = -\frac{r^2}{\sigma_2^2 - r^2} \cdot \mathbf{R} \cdot \mathbf{p}' = (c_0, c_1)$. To achieve this, it continues the above recursive procedure, i.e., 1. sample p_1 with covariance d and center c_1; 2. sample p_0 with updated covariance $a - bd^{-1}b^*$ and center $c_0 + (p_1 - c_1)bd^{-1}$. Notice that the above procedure can be adapted recursively to sampling over $\mathcal{R}$ by exploiting the tower structures of $\mathcal{R}$ and $\mathcal{K}$, as shown in [28]. However, to avoid sampling over $\mathbb{Z}$ with large and varying variance, which has great impact on time efficiency and side-channel security, we use Peikert's Gaussian convolution technique [51] at the ring level to keep efficiency. That is, given covariance $d \in \mathcal{K}_{\mathbb{R}}$ and center $c \in \mathcal{K}_{\mathbb{R}}$, it first samples a continuous Gaussian vector y of covariance $d - \bar{r}^2$, which can be done by applying the linear transformation defined by the Gram root of $d - \bar{r}^2$. Then it rounds the real coefficients of $y + c$ to some near integer by the integer Gaussian sampler SampleZ (Algorithm 7). The detailed algorithm is shown in Algorithm 5.

Algorithm 5: SampleP

Require: msk
Ensure: $\mathbf{p} \sim D_{\mathcal{R}^{2+w}, \sqrt{\mathbf{\Sigma_p}}}$
1: $\mathbf{p}' \leftarrow D_{\mathbb{Z}^{w \cdot n}, \sqrt{\sigma_2^2 - r^2}}$ ▷ $\mathbf{p}' \sim D_{\mathcal{R}^w, \sqrt{\sigma_2^2 - r^2}}$
2: $\mathbf{c} = (c_0, c_1) = -\frac{r^2}{\sigma_2^2 - r^2} \cdot \mathbf{R} \cdot \mathbf{p}'$ ▷ $\mathbf{c} \in \mathcal{K}_{\mathbb{R}}^2$
3: $\mathbf{\Sigma}_2 = \sigma_1^2 \cdot \mathbf{I} - \frac{\sigma_2^2 \cdot r^2}{\sigma_2^2 - r^2}\mathbf{R}\mathbf{R}^t = \left[\begin{smallmatrix} a & b \\ b^* & d \end{smallmatrix}\right]$
4: $p_1 \leftarrow$ SampleFz(d, c_1)
5: $p_0 \leftarrow$ SampleFz$(a - bd^{-1}b^*, c_0 + (p_1 - c_1)bd^{-1})$
6: **return** $\mathbf{p} = (p_0, p_1, \mathbf{p}')$

Algorithm 6 is simply a ring variant of Peikert's sampler [51]. In step 3 we abuse the notation and it means that each coefficient c'_i of c' is used as input of SampleZ, i.e., n independent parallel invocations of Algorithm 7.

Algorithm 6: SampleFz

1: **Require:** a covariance d and a center c ▷ $d, c \in \mathcal{K}_{\mathbb{R}}$
Ensure: $z \leftarrow D_{\mathcal{R}, d, c}$
1: $y \leftarrow \mathcal{N}_n$
2: $c' = c + \sqrt{d - \bar{r}^2} \cdot y$ ▷ $c' = c'_0 + c'_1 \cdot X + \cdots + c'_{n-1} \cdot X^{n-1} \in \mathcal{K}_{\mathbb{R}}$
3: $z \leftarrow$ SampleZ(c') ▷ $z \in \mathcal{R}$
4: **return** z

Algorithm 7 shows the sampler for $D_{\mathbb{Z}, \bar{r}, c}$ with arbitrary center $c \in \mathbb{R}$, which is adapted from [36,53]. It samples some fixed Gaussian using table-based approach (Algorithm 8) followed by a rejection sampling to make the output correct.

Algorithm 7: SampleZ

Require: a center c
Ensure: $z \leftarrow D_{\mathbb{Z},\bar{r},c}$
1: $d \leftarrow c - \lfloor c \rceil$
2: $z^{+} \leftarrow$ BaseSample()
3: $b \leftarrow U(\{0,1\})$
4: $z \leftarrow b + (2b-1)z^{+}$
5: $x \leftarrow \frac{(z-d)^2-(z^{+})^2}{2\bar{r}^2}$
6: $r \leftarrow U(\{0,1,\ldots,2^{64}-1\})$
7: **if** $r > \exp(x)$ **then**
8: restart
9: **end if**
10: **return** $z + \lfloor c \rceil$

In step 4 of Algorithm 8, RCDT means the reverse cumulative distribution table with size 13, similar to that in Falcon [53], according to which one can sample a non-negative integer efficiently.

Algorithm 9 consists mainly of n parallel approximate gadget sampling and outputs a vector $\mathbf{x} \in \mathcal{R}^w$ such that $\mathbf{x}$ is an approximate image under the gadget $\mathbf{f} \in \mathcal{R}^w$. This is a concrete specification of our gadget sampler presented in Section III. Notice that in step 4, $\mathbf{z}_i$'s form a w-by-n matrix and each row of the matrix is converted naturally to a ring element by the coefficient embedding.

Given a target $u \in \mathbb{Z}_Q$, Algorithm 10 samples an approximate $\mathbf{z}$ such that $\langle p \cdot \mathbf{g}, \mathbf{z} \rangle = u - e \mod Q$ for some small $e \in \mathbb{Z}_p$, where $\mathbf{g} = (1, b, \ldots, b^{w-1}) \in \mathbb{Z}^w$. In step 1, the approximate error e is generated deterministically [61], and the remaining steps follow the highly optimized gadget sampler (for modulus q being power-of-b) in [47], which consists of sampling and shift operations over

Algorithm 8: BaseSample

Require: None
Ensure: $z^{+} \leftarrow D^{+}_{\mathbb{Z},\bar{r}}$
1: $u \leftarrow U(\{0,1\}^{72})$
2: $z^{+} \leftarrow 0$;
3: **for** $i = 0, \ldots, 12$ **do**
4: $z^{+} \leftarrow z^{+} + [\![u < \mathrm{RCDT}[i]]\!]$
5: **end for**
6: **return** z^{+}

Algorithm 9: SampleGadgetF

Require: $v \in \mathcal{R}_Q$ ▷ $v(X) = v_0 + v_1 X + \cdots + v_{n-1} X^{n-1}$
Ensure: $\mathbf{x} \in \mathcal{R}^w$
for $i = 0$ to $n-1$ **do**
  $\mathbf{z}_i \leftarrow \mathsf{ApproxGadget}(v_i)$ ▷ $\mathbf{z}_i \in \mathbb{Z}^w$
end for
$[\mathbf{z}_0, \ldots, \mathbf{z}_{n-1}] \Rightarrow (x_0, \ldots, x_{w-1}) = \mathbf{x} \in \mathcal{R}^w$
return $\mathbf{x}$ ▷ $\mathbf{f} \cdot \mathbf{x} \approx v \bmod Q$

integers. Notice that step 3 can be accomplished by calling Algorithm 7: $z_i \leftarrow b \cdot \mathsf{SampleZ}(-v/b) + v$.

Algorithm 10: ApproxGadget

Require: $u \in \mathbb{Z}_Q$
Ensure: $\mathbf{z} \in \mathbb{Z}^w$ ▷ $\langle p \cdot \mathbf{g}, \mathbf{z} \rangle \approx u \mod Q$
1: $e = u \bmod p,\ v = (u - e)/p$
2: **for** $i = 0$ to $w - 1$ **do**
3:   $z_i \leftarrow D_{b\mathbb{Z}+v,r}$
4:   $v = \frac{v - z_i}{b}$
5: **end for**
6: **return** $\mathbf{z} = (z_1, \ldots, z_w)$

4.3 Encryption

On input mpk, id and a message $\mu \in \{0,1\}^{l_m}$, the encryption procedure use the Dual-Regev encryption scheme [30]. The subroutine ECCEnc converts the message μ into a codeword $\hat{\mu}$.

Algorithm 11: Enc

Require: mpk, id, μ
Ensure: ct
$a \leftarrow \mathsf{XOF}(\mathsf{seed}_a)$ ▷ $a \in \mathcal{R}_Q$
$u = H(id)$ ▷ $u \in \mathcal{R}_Q$
$\hat{\mu} = \mathsf{ECCEnc}(\mu)$ ▷ $\hat{\mu} \in \{0,1\}^{l_v}$
$s \leftarrow \chi_n, \mathbf{e} \leftarrow \chi_n^{1+w}, e \leftarrow \mathbb{Z}^{l_v}$ ▷ $s \in \mathcal{R},\ e \in \mathbb{Z}^{l_v}$
$\mathbf{c} = s \cdot [a, \mathbf{b}] + \mathbf{e} \bmod Q$ ▷ $\mathbf{c} \in \mathcal{R}_Q^{1 \times (1+w)}$
$c = (s \cdot u)_{l_v} + e + \frac{Q}{2} \cdot \hat{\mu} \bmod Q$ ▷ $c \in \mathbb{Z}_Q^{l_v}$
return $ct = (\mathbf{c},\ c)$

4.4 Decryption

On input sk_{id}, ct, the decryption procedure first recovers the corresponding $\hat{\mu}$, then uses the subroutine ECCDec to decode it.

Algorithm 12: Dec

Require: sk_{id}, ct
Ensure: μ
$\widetilde{\mu} = c - (\mathbf{c} \cdot sk_{id})_{l_v}$
for $i = 0$ to $l_v - 1$ **do**
    if $\frac{Q}{4} \leq \widetilde{\mu}_i < \frac{3Q}{4}$ **then**
        $\hat{\mu}_i = 1$
    else
        $\hat{\mu}_i = 0$
    end if
end for
$\mu = \mathsf{ECCDec}(\hat{\mu})$
return μ

4.5 Recommended Parameters

We specify three sets of parameter for the toy, NIST-1, NIST-5 security levels respectively in Table 3.

5 Security and Performance

5.1 Security

We consider the cost of known lattice attacks and the estimation of concrete security following the core-SVP methodology [4]. We summarize the security estimation in Table 4.

Table 3. Recommended parameters.

Security level	toy	NIST-1	NIST-5
Polynomial degree n	512	1024	2048
Modulus Q	98304	393216	1048576
Gadget parameters (p, q)	$(1536, 2^6)$	$(1536, 2^8)$	$(2^{12}, 2^8)$
Log base b	8	16	16
Gadget dimension w	2	2	2
Standard deviation σ_1	291.9	820.4	1159.9
Standard deviation σ_2	65.8	249.2	261.6
ℓ_2-norm of sk_{id}	14422.8	42967.3	96752.1
ECC codeword distance l_t	33	33	33
Single bit error rate	$2^{-11.3}$	$2^{-17.7}$	$2^{-21.9}$
Decryption error rate	$2^{-88.3}$	$2^{-196.8}$	$2^{-268.1}$
mpk size (in bytes)	2208	4896	10272
sk_{id} size (in bytes)	1696	4096	8320
ct size (in bytes)	4350	8510	16638

Table 4. The concrete security are estimated as the core-SVP hardness of known attacks.

Security level	toy	NIST-1	NIST-5
BKZ blocksize for primal attack	206	458	**1008**
Classical core-SVP security	60	133	**294**
Quantum core-SVP security	54	121	**267**
BKZ blocksize for dual attack	204	**458**	**1012**
Classical core-SVP security	**59**	**133**	295
Quantum core-SVP security	**54**	**121**	268

5.2 Performance

We provide a proof-of-concept implementation for x86 64 platform, written in standard C for both parameter sets. In this section, we report its performance.

The implementation is complied by gcc 8.3.0 and runs on Deepin 20.9. Table 5 shows the performance of our implementations on a single core of Intel Core i7-10710U @ 1.1 GHz with 8 GB RAM.

5.3 Comparison

We do not compare the implementations of IBE based on ideal lattice in [9] and [8], as the different security models would make the comparison irrelevant. In contrast, in Table 6, we compare with the implementation based on NTRU lattice in [46], which is the instantiation of the GPV-IBE as well. Notice that

Table 5. Performance of SRNSG. Numbers are the median cycle measured over 1,000 executions.

Security level	toy	NIST-1	NIST-5
Setup	3,095,820	7,136,414	4,812,673
Extract	2,152,345	4,364,517	9,999,207
Enc	496,206	1,029,074	2,329,433
Dec	353,271	689,747	1,624,520

for a fair comparison, we re-estimate the security for their parameters in the core-SVP model.

Table 6. Comparison of SRNSG with [46]. Sizes are in bytes. Note that here we only consider trapdoor size in the msk and omit the auxiliary matrix $\mathbf{C}$ in SRNSG or the Falcon tree in [46].

Security level	toy	NIST-1	NIST-5
SRNSG Security C/Q	59/54	133/121	294/267
[46] Security C/Q	43/39	122/111	—
SRNSG mpk size	2208	4896	10272
[46] mpk size	1472	2944	—
SRNSG msk size	512	1024	2048
[46] msk size	2208	4160	—
SRNSG sk_{id} size	1696	4096	8320
[46] sk_{id} size	872	1744	—
SRNSG ct size	3808	7904	16000
[46] size	1728	3584	—

As shown in Table 6, generally, the NTRU-based instantiation is more compact than SRNSG. For the NIST-I security level, while SRNSG has higher security level and much smaller msk size, the sizes of mpk, sk_{id} and ct are about 2 times the sizes of that in [46]. This is an inherent gap, as the dimension of the underlying SIS problems instance is 2 times the dimension of that in [46]. The higher dimension increases the sizes, although SRNSG uses smaller modulus.

However, it is worthy to note that SRNSG removes the NTRU assumption and its concrete security relies essentially on the Ring LWE assumption. This is an attractive feature especially for more powerful applications with overstretched parameters. Besides, SRNSG has significant advantages from the implementation standpoint: (1) SRNSG has very compact msk and avoids the notoriously complex NTRU trapdoor generation; (2) the offline phase of the extraction procedure in SRNSG can be more conveniently implemented without floating-point numbers [20]; (3) the base samplings of the online phase of the extraction procedure in SRNSG are in the form $D_{b\mathbb{Z}+z,r}$ for $z \in \mathbb{Z}$, which is beneficial for further optimization and side-channel protections. Finally, SRNSG can be more conveniently adapted to the unstructured setting, thanks to the absence of costly matrix inversions in the key generation.

6 Conclusion

We present the first instantiation of GPV-IBE on ideal lattices towards practical use. The main technique is a new preimage sampler, which integrates a modified gadget sampler that is more suitable for practicalisation of advanced cryptographic schemes, and the non-spherical Gaussian technique [38]. Besides, we provide two parameter sets and a proof-of-concept implementation. Thanks to the gadget structure, the key extraction procedure is easy and fast, which makes SRNSG an attractive post-quantum IBE for constrained environments. Given the importance of the preimage sampling algorithm in lattice-based cryptography, we believe that our technique can also be applied in the practicalisation of other advanced cryptographic schemes.

6.1 Future Works

To support more flexible parameter choices, we can use the cyclotomic ring of 3-smooth conductor $m = 2^{\ell} \cdot 3^{k}$, instead of power-of-2 conductors. Alternatively, we may adapt the ring structure to the module setting, at the cost of increasing the master public key size.

It is worthy to implement our algorithms fully over integers by the techniques of [20] in the key extraction procedure, and [17] in the encryption and decryption algorithms, which supports NTT multiplication for our NTT-unfriendly modulus Q. We leave the optimized implementation as future works.

From the perspective of cryptographic functionality, we focus more on the basic IBE itself in this work. Actually, by using the FSXY [26] and FO [27,35,39] transformations, we can get efficient identity-based key exchange protocol in the CK^{+} model and the identity-based KEM against the chosen ciphertext attack in the (Quantum) ROM.

Acknowledgements. We would like to thank the anonymous reviewers for helpful comments and suggestions. This work is supported by the National Key Research and Development Program of China (Grant No. 2021YFB3100200), the National Natural Science Foundation of China (Grant No. 12171114), the Guangzhou Science and Technology Plan Project (Grant No. 2024A04J3272).

References

1. Agrawal, S., Boneh, D., Boyen, X.: Efficient lattice (H)IBE in the standard model. In: Gilbert, H. (ed.) Advances in Cryptology - EUROCRYPT 2010. Lecture Notes in Computer Science, vol. 6110, pp. 553–572. Springer, Berlin (2010). https://doi.org/10.1007/978-3-642-13190-5_28

2. Agrawal, S., Boneh, D., Boyen, X.: Lattice basis delegation in fixed dimension and shorter-ciphertext hierarchical IBE. In: Rabin, T. (ed.) Advances in Cryptology - CRYPTO 2010. Lecture Notes in Computer Science, vol. 6223, pp. 98–115. Springer, Berlin (2010). https://doi.org/10.1007/978-3-642-14623-7_6
3. Ajtai, M.: Generating hard instances of lattice problems. In: Proceedings of the Twenty-Eighth Annual ACM Symposium on Theory of Computing, pp. 99–108 (1996)
4. Alkim, E., Ducas, L., Pöppelmann, T., Schwabe, P.: Post-quantum key exchange-a new hope. In: USENIX Security 2016, pp. 327–343 (2016)
5. Apon, D., Fan, X., Liu, F.H.: Compact identity based encryption from LWE. Cryptology ePrint Archive, Report 2016/125 (2016)
6. Becker, A., Ducas, L., Gama, N., Laarhoven, T.: New directions in nearest neighbor searching with applications to lattice sieving. In: SODA 2016, pp. 10–24 (2016)
7. Bellare, M., Waters, B., Yilek, S.: Identity-based encryption secure against selective opening attack. In: Ishai, Y. (ed.) Theory of Cryptography. Lecture Notes in Computer Science, vol. 6597, pp. 235–252. Springer, Berlin (2011). https://doi.org/10.1007/978-3-642-19571-6_15
8. Bert, P., Eberhart, G., Prabel, L., Roux-Langlois, A., Sabt, M.: Implementation of lattice trapdoors on modules and applications. In: Cheon, J.H., Tillich, J.P. (eds.) Post-Quantum Cryptography. Lecture Notes in Computer Science(), vol. 12841, pp. 195–214. Springer, Cham (2021). https://doi.org/10.1007/978-3-030-81293-5_11
9. Bert, P., Fouque, P.A., Roux-Langlois, A., Sabt, M.: Practical implementation of Ring-SIS/LWE based signature and IBE. In: Lange, T., Steinwandt, R. (eds.) Post-Quantum Cryptography. Lecture Notes in Computer Science(), vol. 10786, pp. 271–291. Springer, Cham (2018). https://doi.org/10.1007/978-3-319-79063-3_13
10. Boldyreva, A., Goyal, V., Kumar, V.: Identity-based encryption with efficient revocation. In: ACM CCS 2008, pp. 417–426 (2008)
11. Boneh, D., Franklin, M.: Identity-based encryption from the Weil pairing. In: Kilian, J. (ed.) Advances in Cryptology - CRYPTO 2001. Lecture Notes in Computer Science, vol. 2139, pp. 213–229. Springer, Berlin (2001). https://doi.org/10.1007/3-540-44647-8_13
12. Brakerski, Z., Lombardi, A., Segev, G., Vaikuntanathan, V.: Anonymous IBE, leakage resilience and circular security from new assumptions. In: Nielsen, J., Rijmen, V. (eds.) Advances in Cryptology - EUROCRYPT 2018. Lecture Notes in Computer Science(), vol. 10820, pp. 535–564. Springer, Cham (2018). https://doi.org/10.1007/978-3-319-78381-9_20
13. Brakerski, Z., Vaikuntanathan, V., Wee, H., Wichs, D.: Obfuscating conjunctions under entropic ring LWE. In: ITCS 2016, pp. 147–156 (2016)
14. Cash, D., Hofheinz, D., Kiltz, E., Peikert, C.: Bonsai trees, or how to delegate a lattice basis. In: Gilbert, H. (ed.) Advances in Cryptology - EUROCRYPT 2010. Lecture Notes in Computer Science, vol. 6110, pp. 523–552. Springer, Berlin (2010). https://doi.org/10.1007/978-3-642-13190-5_27
15. Chen, Y., Genise, N., Mukherjee, P.: Approximate trapdoors for lattices and smaller hash-and-sign signatures. In: Galbraith, S., Moriai, S. (eds.) Advances in Cryptology - ASIACRYPT 2019. Lecture Notes in Computer Science(), vol. 11923, pp. 3–32. Springer, Cham (2019). https://doi.org/10.1007/978-3-030-34618-8_1
16. Chen, Y., Nguyen, P.Q.: BKZ 2.0: better lattice security estimates. In: Lee, D.H., Wang, X. (eds.) Advances in Cryptology - ASIACRYPT 2011. Lecture Notes in Computer Science, vol. 7073, pp. 1–20. Springer, Berlin (2011). https://doi.org/10.1007/978-3-642-25385-0_1

17. Chung, C.M.M., et al.: NTT multiplication for NTT-unfriendly rings: new speed records for saber and NTRU on Cortex-M4 and AVX2. IACR Trans. CHES 2021 (2), 159–188 (2021)
18. Cocks, C.: An identity based encryption scheme based on quadratic residues. In: Honary, B. (ed.) Cryptography and Coding. Lecture Notes in Computer Science, vol. 2260, pp. 360–363. Springer, Berlin (2001). https://doi.org/10.1007/3-540-45325-3_32
19. Döttling, N., Garg, S.: Identity-based encryption from the Diffie-Hellman assumption. In: Katz, J., Shacham, H. (eds.) Advances in Cryptology - CRYPTO 2017. Lecture Notes in Computer Science(), vol. 10401, pp. 537–569. Springer, Cham (2017). https://doi.org/10.1007/978-3-319-63688-7_18
20. Ducas, L., Galbraith, S., Prest, T., Yu, Y.: Integral matrix gram root and lattice gaussian sampling without floats. In: Canteaut, A., Ishai, Y. (eds.) Advances in Cryptology - EUROCRYPT 2020. Lecture Notes in Computer Science(), vol. 12106, pp. 608–637. Springer, Cham (2020). https://doi.org/10.1007/978-3-030-45724-2_21
21. Ducas, L., Lyubashevsky, V., Prest, T.: Efficient identity-based encryption over NTRU lattices. In: Sarkar, P., Iwata, T. (eds.) Advances in Cryptology - ASIACRYPT 2014. Lecture Notes in Computer Science, vol. 8874, pp. 22–41. Springer, Berlin (2014). https://doi.org/10.1007/978-3-662-45608-8_2
22. Ducas, L., Nguyen, P.Q.: Learning a zonotope and more: cryptanalysis of NTRUSign countermeasures. In: Wang, X., Sako, K. (eds.) Advances in Cryptology - ASIACRYPT 2012. Lecture Notes in Computer Science, vol. 7658, pp. 433–450. Springer, Berlin (2012). https://doi.org/10.1007/978-3-642-34961-4_27
23. Ducas, L., Prest, T.: Fast fourier orthogonalization. In: ISSAC 2016, pp. 191–198 (2016)
24. Espitau, T., et al.: MITAKA: a simpler, parallelizable, maskable variant of FALCON. In: Dunkelman, O., Dziembowski, S. (eds.) Advances in Cryptology - EUROCRYPT 2022. Lecture Notes in Computer Science, vol. 13277, pp. 222–253. Springer, Cham (2022). https://doi.org/10.1007/978-3-031-07082-2_9
25. Espitau, T., Tibouchi, M., Wallet, A., Yang, Yu.: Shorter hash-and-sign lattice-based signatures. In: Dodis, Y., Shrimpton, T. (eds.) Advances in Cryptology - CRYPTO 2022. Lecture Notes in Computer Science, vol. 13508, pp. 245–275. Springer, Cham (2022). https://doi.org/10.1007/978-3-031-15979-4_9
26. Fujioka, A., Suzuki, K., Xagawa, K., Yoneyama, K.: Strongly secure authenticated key exchange from factoring, codes, and lattices. In: Fischlin, M., Buchmann, J., Manulis, M. (eds.) Public Key Cryptography - PKC 2012. Lecture Notes in Computer Science, vol. 7293, pp. 467–484. Springer, Berlin (2012). https://doi.org/10.1007/978-3-642-30057-8_28
27. Fujisaki, E., Okamoto, T.: How to enhance the security of public-key encryption at minimum cost. In: Public Key Cryptography. Lecture Notes in Computer Science, vol. 1560, pp. 53–68. Springer, Berlin (1999). https://doi.org/10.1007/3-540-49162-7_5
28. Genise, N., Micciancio, D.: Faster gaussian sampling for trapdoor lattices with arbitrary modulus. In: Nielsen, J., Rijmen, V. (eds.) Advances in Cryptology - EUROCRYPT 2018. Lecture Notes in Computer Science(), vol. 10820, pp. 174–203. Springer, Cham (2018). https://doi.org/10.1007/978-3-319-78381-9_7
29. Genise, N., Micciancio, D., Peikert, C., Walter, M.: Improved discrete gaussian and subgaussian analysis for lattice cryptography. In: Kiayias, A., Kohlweiss, M., Wallden, P., Zikas, V. (eds.) Public-Key Cryptography - PKC 2020. Lecture Notes

in Computer Science(), vol. 12110, pp. 623–651. Springer, Cham (2020). https://doi.org/10.1007/978-3-030-45374-9_21
30. Gentry, C., Peikert, C., Vaikuntanathan, V.: Trapdoors for hard lattices and new cryptographic constructions. In: STOC 2008, pp. 197–206 (2008)
31. Goldreich, O., Goldwasser, S., Halevi, S.: Public-key cryptosystems from lattice reduction problems. In: Kaliski, B.S. (ed.) Advances in Cryptology - CRYPTO 1997. Lecture Notes in Computer Science, vol. 1294, pp. 112–131. Springer, Berlin (1997). https://doi.org/10.1007/BFb0052231
32. Gorbunov, S., Vaikuntanathan, V., Wee, H.: Attribute-based encryption for circuits. In: STOC 2013, pp. 545–554 (2013)
33. Gorbunov, S., Vaikuntanathan, V., Wee, H.: Predicate encryption for circuits from LWE. In: Gennaro, R., Robshaw, M. (eds.) Advances in Cryptology - CRYPTO 2015. Lecture Notes in Computer Science(), vol. 9216, pp. 503–523. Springer, Berlin (2015). https://doi.org/10.1007/978-3-662-48000-7_25
34. Hoffstein, J., Howgrave-Graham, N., Pipher, J., Silverman, J.H., Whyte, W.: NTRUSIGN: digital signatures using the NTRU lattice. In: Joye, M. (ed.) Topics in Cryptology- CT-RSA 2003. Lecture Notes in Computer Science, vol. 2612, pp. 122–140. Springer, Berlin (2003). https://doi.org/10.1007/3-540-36563-x_9
35. Hofheinz, D., Hövelmanns, K., Kiltz, E.: A modular analysis of the Fujisaki-Okamoto transformation. In: Kalai, Y., Reyzin, L. (eds.) Theory of Cryptography. Lecture Notes in Computer Science(), vol. 10677, pp. 341–371. Springer, Cham (2017). https://doi.org/10.1007/978-3-319-70500-2_12
36. Howe, J., Prest, T., Ricosset, T., Rossi, M.: Isochronous gaussian sampling: from inception to implementation. In: Ding, J., Tillich, J.P. (eds.) Post-Quantum Cryptography. Lecture Notes in Computer Science(), vol. 12100, pp. 53–71. Springer, Cham (2020). https://doi.org/10.1007/978-3-030-44223-1_4
37. Hu, Y., Jia, H.: A new gaussian sampling for trapdoor lattices with arbitrary modulus. Des. Codes Cryptogr. **87**, 2553–2570 (2019)
38. Jia, H., Hu, Y., Tang, C.: Lattice-based hash-and-sign signatures using approximate trapdoor, revisited. IET Inf. Secur. **16**(1), 41–50 (2022)
39. Jiang, H., Zhang, Z., Chen, L., Wang, H., Ma, Z.: IND-CCA-secure key encapsulation mechanism in the quantum random oracle model, revisited. In: Shacham, H., Boldyreva, A. (eds.) Advances in Cryptology - CRYPTO 2018. Lecture Notes in Computer Science(), vol. 10993, pp. 96–125. Springer, Cham. (2018). https://doi.org/10.1007/978-3-319-96878-0_4
40. Jutla, C.S., Roy, A.: Shorter quasi-adaptive NIZK proofs for linear subspaces. In: Sako, K., Sarkar, P. (eds.) Advances in Cryptology - ASIACRYPT 2013. Lecture Notes in Computer Science, vol. 8269, pp. 1–20. Springer, Berlin (2013). https://doi.org/10.1007/978-3-642-42033-7_1
41. Katsumata, S., Yamada, S.: Partitioning via non-linear polynomial functions: more compact IBEs from ideal lattices and bilinear maps. In: Cheon, J., Takagi, T. (eds.) Advances in Cryptology - ASIACRYPT 2016. Lecture Notes in Computer Science(), vol. 10032, pp. 682–712. Springer, Berlin (2016). https://doi.org/10.1007/978-3-662-53890-6_23
42. Laarhoven, T.: Search problems in cryptography. PhD thesis, PhD thesis, Eindhoven University of Technology, 2016 (2016)
43. Lewko, A.: Tools for simulating features of composite order bilinear groups in the prime order setting. In: Pointcheval, D., Johansson, T. (eds.) Advances in Cryptology - EUROCRYPT 2012. Lecture Notes in Computer Science, vol. 7237, pp. 318–335. Springer, Berlin (2012). https://doi.org/10.1007/978-3-642-29011-4_20

44. Lu, X., et al.: LAC: practical Ring-LWE based public-key encryption with byte-level modulus. Cryptology ePrint Archive, Paper 2018/1009 (2018)
45. Lyubashevsky, V., et al.: Dilithium: submission to the NIST's post-quantum cryptography standardization process (2022)
46. McCarthy, S., Smyth, N., O'Sullivan, E.: A practical implementation of identity-based encryption over NTRU lattices. In: O'Neill, M. (ed.) Cryptography and Coding. Lecture Notes in Computer Science(), vol. 10655, pp. 227–246. Springer, Cham (2017). https://doi.org/10.1007/978-3-319-71045-7_12
47. Micciancio, D., Peikert, C.: Trapdoors for lattices: simpler, tighter, faster, smaller. In: Pointcheval, D., Johansson, T. (eds.) Advances in Cryptology - EUROCRYPT 2012. Lecture Notes in Computer Science, vol. 7237, pp. 700–718. Springer, Berlin (2012). https://doi.org/10.1007/978-3-642-29011-4_41
48. DMicciancio, D., Regev, O.: Worst-case to average-case reductions based on gaussian measures. SIAM J. Comput., 372–381 (2004)
49. Micciancio, D., Walter, M.: Practical, predictable lattice basis reduction. In: Fischlin, M., Coron, J.S. (eds.) Advances in Cryptology - EUROCRYPT 2016. Lecture Notes in Computer Science(), vol. 9665, pp. 820–849. Springer, Berlin (2016). https://doi.org/10.1007/978-3-662-49890-3_31
50. Nguyen, P.Q., Regev, O.: Learning a parallelepiped: cryptanalysis of GGH and NTRU signatures. In: Vaudenay, S. (ed.) Advances in Cryptology - EUROCRYPT 2006. Lecture Notes in Computer Science, vol. 4004, pp. 271–288. Springer, Berlin (2006). https://doi.org/10.1007/11761679_17
51. Peikert, C.: An efficient and parallel Gaussian sampler for lattices. In: Rabin, T. (ed.) Advances in Cryptology - CRYPTO 2010. Lecture Notes in Computer Science, vol. 6223, pp. 80–97. Springer, Berlin (2010). https://doi.org/10.1007/978-3-642-14623-7_5
52. Prest, T.: Gaussian sampling in lattice-based cryptography. PhD thesis, PhD thesis, École Normale Supérieure Paris (2015)
53. Prest, T., et al.: Falcon: submission to the NIST's post-quantum cryptography standardization process (2022)
54. Schnorr, C.-P., Euchner, M.: Lattice basis reduction: improved practical algorithms and solving subset sum problems. Math. Program. **66**, 181–199 (1994)
55. Schwabe, P., et al.: Kyber: submission to the NIST's post-quantum cryptography standardization process (2020)
56. Shamir, A.: Identity-based cryptosystems and signature schemes. In: Blakley, G.R., Chaum, D. (eds.) Advances in Cryptology. Lecture Notes in Computer Science, vol. 196, pp. 47–53. Springer, Berlin (1984). https://doi.org/10.1007/3-540-39568-7_5
57. Shor, P.W.: Polynomial-time algorithms for prime factorization and discrete logarithms on a quantum computer. SIAM Rev. **41**(2), 303–332 (1999)
58. Waters, B.: Dual system encryption: Realizing fully secure IBE and HIBE under simple assumptions. In: Halevi, S. (ed.) Advances in Cryptology - CRYPTO 2009. Lecture Notes in Computer Science, vol. 5677, pp. 619–636. Springer, Berlin (2009). https://doi.org/10.1007/978-3-642-03356-8_36
59. Yamada, S.: Adaptively secure identity-based encryption from lattices with asymptotically shorter public parameters. In: Fischlin, M., Coron, J.S. (eds.) Advances in Cryptology - EUROCRYPT 2016. Lecture Notes in Computer Science(), vol. 9666, pp. 32–62. Springer, Berlin (2016). https://doi.org/10.1007/978-3-662-49896-5_2
60. Yang, Yu., Ducas, L.: Learning strikes again: the case of the DRS signature scheme. In: Peyrin, T., Galbraith, S. (eds.) Advances in Cryptology - ASIACRYPT 2018. Lecture Notes in Computer Science(), vol. 11273, pp. 525–543. Springer, Cham (2018). https://doi.org/10.1007/978-3-030-03329-3_18

61. Yu, Y., Jia, H., Wang, X.: Compact lattice gadget and its applications to hash-and-sign signatures. In: Handschuh, H., Lysyanskaya, A. (eds.) Advances in Cryptology - CRYPTO 2023. Lecture Notes in Computer Science, vol. 14085, pp. 390–420. Springer, Cham (2023). https://doi.org/10.1007/978-3-031-38554-4_13
62. Zhang, S., Yang, Yu.: Towards a simpler lattice gadget toolkit. In: Hanaoka, G., Shikata, J., Watanabe, Y. (eds.) Public-Key Cryptography - PKC 2022. Lecture Notes in Computer Science(), vol. 13177, pp. 498–520. Springer, Cham (2022). https://doi.org/10.1007/978-3-030-97121-2_18

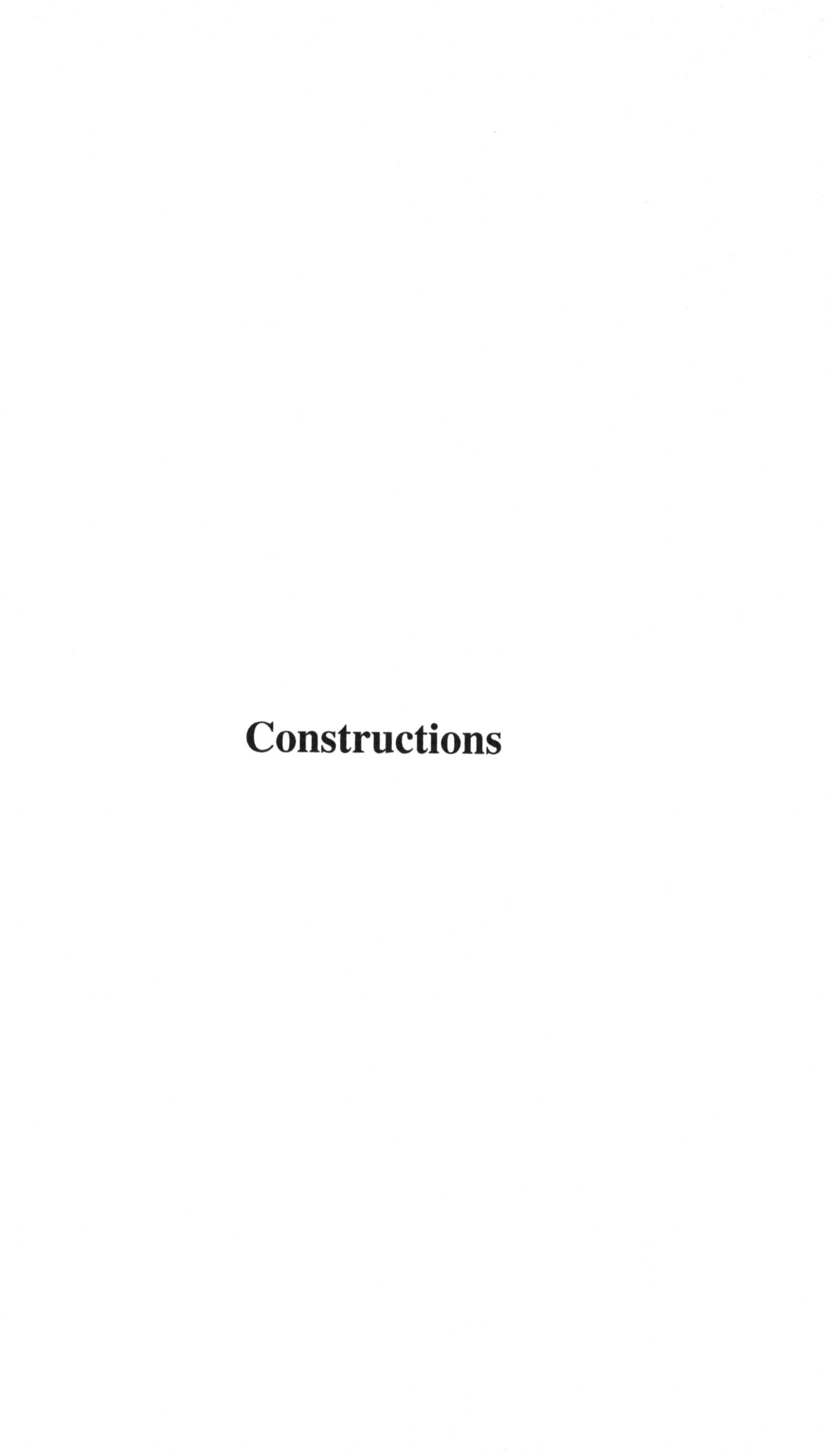

Constructions

ASCON MAC, PRF, and Short-Input PRF

Lightweight, Fast, and Efficient Pseudorandom Functions

Christoph Dobraunig[1], Maria Eichlseder[2], Florian Mendel[3], and Martin Schläffer[3(✉)]

[1] Intel Labs, Hillsboro, USA
christoph.dobraunig@intel.com
[2] Graz University of Technology, Graz, Austria
maria.eichlseder@iaik.tugraz.at
[3] Infineon Technologies AG, Neubiberg, Germany
{florian.mendel,martin.schlaeffer}@infineon.com

Abstract. In 2023, NIST has selected ASCON as the new standard for lightweight cryptography. The ASCON v1.2 family provides authenticated encryption, hash functions, and extendable output functions, all using the same ASCON permutation. The main use case of ASCON is to provide efficient cryptographic primitives for resource-constraint devices. While additional primitives can be built on top of the existing ASCON functions, dedicated schemes are often more efficient. In this paper, we enrich the functionality of ASCON by providing efficient Pseudorandom Functions (PRFs), Message Authentication Codes (MACs), and a fast short-input PRF for messages up to 128 bits.

Keywords: Permutation-based cryptography · Pseudorandom function · Message authentication code · Ascon

1 Introduction

The ASCON family of authenticated encryption schemes [DEMS14] was first published in the beginning of 2014 as a submission to the CAESAR competition [CAE14]. After 5 years of public scrutiny, the authenticated encryption schemes ASCON-128 and ASCON-128a (v1.2) [DEMS16] were recommended as the first choice for lightweight applications in the final portfolio of CAESAR for resource-constrained environments. Subsequently, the cipher suite ASCON (v1.2) [DEMS21b, DEMS21a], containing authenticated encryption as well as hashing functionality, has been submitted to the NIST lightweight cryptography (LWC) competition [Nat18]. After another 4 years in a public competition, ASCON has been selected in 2023 to form the new NIST lightweight cryptography standard [NIS23].

ASCON's permutation also serves as a basis of ISAP [DEM+20, DEM+21], an authenticated encryption scheme designed to provide enhanced robustness against side-channel and fault attacks on algorithmic level. ISAP was a finalist in the NIST LWC standardization process. In these contexts, the cryptanalytic

E. Oswald (Ed.): CT-RSA 2024, LNCS 14643, pp. 381–403, 2024.
https://doi.org/10.1007/978-3-031-58868-6_15

security and implementation properties of the Ascon permutation have been analyzed very thoroughly.

The Ascon schemes offer a full symmetric cipher suite satisfying most needs in a typical communication protocol. They can help protect authenticity and confidentiality in a keyed setting as well as integrity in an unkeyed setting. However, many applications can still profit from more efficient tailored solutions that only cover either authenticity, or confidentiality [MSP+23]. Especially MACs have traditionally been built using underlying symmetric primitives, like block ciphers or hash functions, which often results in inferior performance.

To address these needs, we define two lightweight and efficient pseudorandom functions (PRFs) in this paper; Ascon-PRF and Ascon-PRFshort. The function Ascon-PRF processes inputs of arbitrary length and produces outputs of arbitrary length. In particular, Ascon-PRF adapts the full-keyed sponge (FKS) mode [BDPV07,BDPV12,MRV15,DMV17] using a rate of 256 bits during absorption and a rate of 128 bits in the squeezing phase. In contrast, Ascon-PRFshort operates only on short inputs ($\leq$128 bits) producing outputs of short length ($\leq$128 bits).

PRFs are very versatile building blocks allowing to instantiate various cryptographic functionalities. For example, Ascon-PRF is an efficient and versatile choice for general-purpose lightweight message authentication. We define the corresponding message authentication code (MAC) Ascon-MAC based on Ascon-PRF, which produced a fixed 128-bit tag. Other use-cases of PRFs are, e.g., stream ciphers or to instantiate SIV [RS06].

Ascon-PRFshort excels whenever short data needs to be authenticated, e.g., the authentication of pointers, in challenge-response protocols, or key derivation functions (KDFs) that derive symmetric keys of entities from a master key. Since Ascon-PRFshort can very efficiently map a 128-bit input to a 128-bit output, it can potentially be used in modes of operation, which are commonly instantiated with pseudorandom permutations (block ciphers), but would work as well with a PRF.

For all proposed designs, we provide a security analysis based on the properties of the permutation and the used modes of operation. We also present a performance evaluation to show the efficiency on different software platforms.

Outline. In Sect. 2, we specify the new modes of operation and its parameters. In Sect. 3, we recall the definition of the Ascon permutation to complete the specification. In Sect. 4, we provide the design rationale for the new designs together with security claims and performance results on different software platforms. Finally, in Sect. 5 we provide preliminary cryptanalysis results of the new modes based on existing related work on Ascon.

2 Specification

In this section, we introduce the state layout and notation for our functions and specify the PRFs and the MAC. Note that these specifications are based on Ascon v1.2 while the final Ascon NIST standard may be slightly adapted (e.g. using a different endianness).

2.1 State and Notation

Our algorithms operate on a 320-bit state S which is updated using the a-round permutation p^a. The state S is divided into an outer part and an inner part, whose size is different for the absorbing and squeezing phase.

For the description and application of the round transformations (Sect. 3), the 320-bit state S is split into five 64-bit words x_i, as follows:

$$S = x_0 \,\|\, x_1 \,\|\, x_2 \,\|\, x_3 \,\|\, x_4.$$

Whenever S needs to be interpreted as a byte-array (or bitstring) used in the sponge interface, the array starts with the most significant byte (or bit) of x_0 as byte 0 and ends with the least significant byte (or bit) of x_4 as byte 39. Table 1 lists the notation.

Table 1. Notation used for ASCON's interface, mode, and permutation

K	Secret key K of k bits
M, T	Input message M, output tag T (in blocks M_i, T_i)
S	The 320-bit state S of the sponge construction
p, p^a	Permutation p^aconsisting of a update rounds p
$x \in \{0,1\}^k$	Bitstring x of length k (variable if $k = *$)
0^k	Bitstring of k bits (variable length if $k = *$), all 0
$\|x\|$	Length of the bitstring x in bits
$\lfloor x \rfloor_k$	Bitstring x truncated to the first (most significant) k bits
$\lceil x \rceil^k$	Bitstring x truncated to the last (least significant) k bits
$x \,\|\, y$	Concatenation of bitstrings x and y
$x \oplus y$	XOR of bitstrings x and y
$x \bmod y$	Remainder in integer division of x by y
$\lceil x \rceil$	Ceiling function, smallest integer larger than x
p_C, p_S, p_L	Constant-addition, substitution and linear layer of $p = p_L \circ p_S \circ p_C$
$x_0, \ldots, x_4$	The five 64-bit words of the state S
$x_{0,i}, \ldots, x_{4,i}$	Bit i, $0 \leq i < 64$, of words $x_0, \ldots, x_4$, with $x_{\cdot,0}$ the rightmost bit (LSB)
$x \oplus y$	Bitwise XOR of 64-bit words or bits x and y
$x \odot y$	Bitwise AND of 64-bit words or bits x and y (denoted xy in the ANF)
$x \ggg i$	Right-rotation (circular shift) by i bits of 64-bit word x

2.2 Algorithms

Pseudorandom Functions. ASCON-PRF is parameterized by the key length of k bits, output rate of r_o bits, internal round number a, and maximum output length of $0 < t < 2^{32}$ bits (or $t = 0$ for unlimited output). The algorithm $\mathcal{G}_{k,r_o,a,t}$

takes as its input a secret key K with k bits, input data M of arbitrary length, and a requested output length $\ell \leq t$. It returns an output T of size ℓ bits:

$$\mathcal{G}_{k,r_o,a,t}(K, M, \ell) = T.$$

ASCON-PRFSHORT is parameterized by the key length k bits, input length $m \leq 128$ bits, internal round number a, and output size $t \leq 128$ bits. The algorithm $\mathcal{F}_{k,m,a,t}$ takes as its input a secret key K with k bits and some input data M of m bits. It produces an output T of size t bits:

$$\mathcal{F}_{k,m,a,t}(K, M) = T.$$

Message Authentication. ASCON-MAC is parameterized by the key length k bits, output rate r_o, internal round number a, and tag length t. It specifies an authentication algorithm $\mathcal{A}_{k,r_o,a,t}$ and a verification algorithm $\mathcal{V}_{k,r_o,a,t}$, both calling $\mathcal{G}_{k,r_o,a,t}$. The authentication algorithm $\mathcal{A}_{k,r_o,a,t}$ takes as its input a secret key K with k bits and a message M of arbitrary length. It produces a tag T of length t as its output:

$$\mathcal{A}_{k,r_o,a,t}(K, M) = T.$$

The verification procedure $\mathcal{V}_{k,r_o,a,t}$ takes as input the key K, message M and tag T, and outputs either pass if the verification of the tag is correct or fail if it fails:

$$\mathcal{V}_{k,r_o,a,t}(K, M, T) \in \{\mathsf{pass}, \mathsf{fail}\}.$$

2.3 Recommended Parameter Sets

Table 2 lists our recommended instances for all PRFs and MACs and specifies their parameters. The relevant parameters include the key size k, message input size limit m, input rate (block size) r_i, tag output size limit t, output rate (block size) r_o, and the number of rounds a for the permutation p^a.

Table 2. Parameters for recommended **Pseudorandom Functions (PRF)** and **Message Authentication Codes (MAC)**. Unlimited input/output lengths ('unlim.') are implicitly limited by the security claim to $\leq 2^{64}$ blocks.

Name	Algorithms	Bit size of					Rounds
		key k	data m	block r_i	output t	block r_o	p^a
ASCON-MAC	$\mathcal{A}, \mathcal{V}_{128,128,12,128}$	128	unlim.	256	128	128	12
ASCON-PRF	$\mathcal{G}_{128,128,12,0}$	128	unlim.	256	unlim.	128	12
ASCON-PRFSHORT	$\mathcal{F}_{128,*,12,*}$	128	$\leq$128	128	$\leq$128	128	12

2.4 Arbitrary-Length Pseudorandom Functions

The mode of operation of ASCON-PRF is based on full-state keyed sponge modes [BDPV07] such as the DonkeySponge [BDPV12] mode. The PRF is illustrated in Fig. 1 and specified in Algorithm 1.

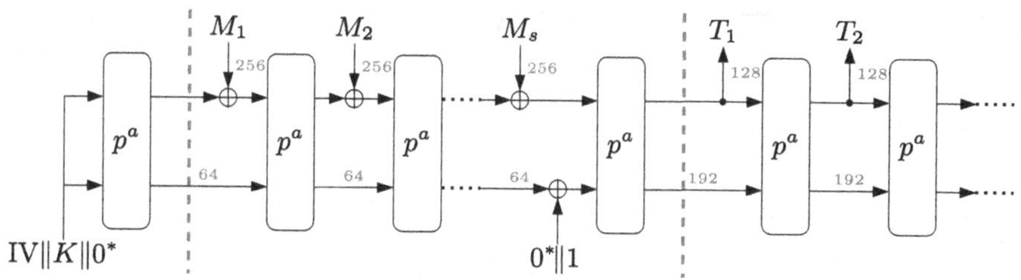

Fig. 1. Pseudorandom Function $\mathcal{G}_{k,r_o,a,t}$ with output length ℓ ($\ell \leq t$ or $t = 0$).

Initialization. The 320-bit initial state of ASCON-PRF is formed by the secret key K of k bits and an IV specifying the algorithm. The 64-bit IV of ASCON-PRF specifies the algorithm parameters in a similar format as for ASCON, including k and the rate r_o each written as an 8-bit integer, round number a encoded as an 8-bit integer as $2^7 + a = (1\|0^7) \oplus a = 80 \oplus a$, followed by a zero byte and the maximum output bitsize t as a 32-bit integer, or $t = 0$ for arbitrarily long output:

$$\mathrm{IV}_{k,r_o,a,t} \leftarrow k \,\|\, r_o \,\|((1\|0^7) \oplus a) \,\|\, 0^8 \,\|\, t$$
$$S \leftarrow \mathrm{IV}_{k,r_o,a,t} \,\|\, K \,\|\, 0^{256-k}$$

In the initialization, the a-round permutation p^a is applied to the initial state:

$$S \leftarrow p^a(S)$$

Absorb Message. The PRF processes the padded message M in blocks of r_i bits. The padding process appends a single 1 and the smallest number of 0 s to M such that the length of the padded message is a multiple of r_i bits. The resulting padded message is split into s blocks $M_1 \| \dots \| M_s$ of $r_i = 256$ bits:

$$M_1, \dots, M_s \leftarrow r_i\text{-bit blocks of } M \,\|\, 1 \,\|\, 0^{r_i - 1 - (|M| \bmod r_i)}$$

The message blocks M_i with $i = 1, \dots, s-1$ are processed as follows. Each block M_i is XORed to the state S, followed by an application of the a-round permutation p^a to S. For the last message block M_s, a single 1 is xored to the state in addition to the message block followed by an application of the a-round permutation p^a to S:

$$S \leftarrow \begin{cases} p^a(S \oplus (M_i \,\|\, 0^{320-r_i})) & \text{if } 1 \leq i \leq s-1 \\ p^a(S \oplus (M_i \,\|\, 0^{320-r_i}) \oplus (0^{319} \,\|\, 1)) & \text{if } i = s \end{cases}$$

Algorithm 1. Pseudorandom function $\mathcal{G}_{k,r_o,a,t}$ specified for ASCON-PRF with key size $k = 128$, output rate $r_o = 128$ bits, rounds $a = 12$, and any given output size limit $t < 2^{32}$ (or $t = 0$ for unlimited output). Only $\ell \leq t$ bits of output are actually produced and returned.

Pseudorandom Function $\mathcal{G}_{k,r_o,a,t}(K, M, \ell) = T$

Input: key $K \in \{0,1\}^k$,
  input $M \in \{0,1\}^*$,
  output bitsize $\ell \leq t$ or ℓ arbitrary if $t = 0$
Output: output $T \in \{0,1\}^\ell$

Initialization
  $S \leftarrow p^a(\mathrm{IV}_{k,r_o,a,t} \,\|\, K \,\|\, 0^{256-k})$
Absorbing
  $M_1 \ldots M_s \leftarrow r_i$-bit blocks of $M \| 1 \| 0^*$
  for $i = 1, \ldots, s-1$ **do**
    $S \leftarrow p^a(S \oplus (M_i \,\|\, 0^{320-r_i}))$
  $S \leftarrow p^a(S \oplus (M_i \,\|\, 0^{320-r_i}) \oplus (0^{319} \,\|\, 1))$
Squeezing
  $u = \lceil \ell / r_o \rceil$
  for $i = 1, \ldots, u-1$ **do**
    $T_i \leftarrow \lfloor S \rfloor_{r_o}$
    $S \leftarrow p^a(S)$
  $T_u \leftarrow \lfloor S \rfloor_{r_o}$
  return $\lfloor T_1 \,\|\, \ldots \,\|\, T_u \rfloor_\ell$

Squeeze Tag. Then the output is extracted from the state in r_o-bit blocks T_i until the requested output length $\ell \leq t$ (or ℓ arbitrary if $t = 0$) is completed after $u = \lceil \ell / r_o \rceil$ blocks. After each extraction (except the last one), the internal state S is transformed by the a-round permutation p^a:

$$\begin{aligned} T_i &\leftarrow \lfloor S \rfloor_{r_o} \\ S &\leftarrow p^a(S), \qquad 1 \leq i \leq u = \lceil t / r_o \rceil \end{aligned}$$

The last output block T_u is truncated to $\ell \bmod r_o$ bits and $\lfloor T_1 \,\|\, \ldots \,\|\, T_u \rfloor_\ell$ is returned.

2.5 Message Authentication

ASCON-MAC calls the PRF $\mathcal{G}_{k,r_o,a,t}$ as specified in Algorithm 2. For verification, it checks if the transmitted tag T matches the computed tag T^*.

Algorithm 2. Authentication and verification procedures $\mathcal{A}_{k,r_o,a,t}(K, M, T)$, $\mathcal{V}_{k,r_o,a,t}(K, M, T)$ specified for ASCON-MAC with the same parameters as the PRF $\mathcal{G}_{k,r_o,a,t}$ in 1, but fixing $t = 128$.

Authentication $\mathcal{A}_{k,r_o,a,t}(K, M)$	Verification $\mathcal{V}_{k,r_o,a,t}(K, M, T)$
Input: key $K \in \{0,1\}^k$, message $M \in \{0,1\}^*$	**Input:** key $K \in \{0,1\}^k$, message $M \in \{0,1\}^*$, tag $T \in \{0,1\}^t$
Output: tag $T \in \{0,1\}^t$	**Output:** pass or fail
$T \leftarrow \mathcal{G}_{k,r_o,a,t}(K, M, t)$ **return** T	$T^* \leftarrow \mathcal{G}_{k,r_o,a,t}(K, M, t)$ **if** $T = T^*$ **return** pass **else return** fail

2.6 Short-Input Pseudorandom Functions

ASCON-PRFSHORT uses a single permutation call p^a and resembles the initialization of ASCON-128 with a different IV and the nonce replaced by a single message block M of length $m \leq 128$ bits. The PRF is illustrated in Fig. 2 and specified in Algorithm 3.

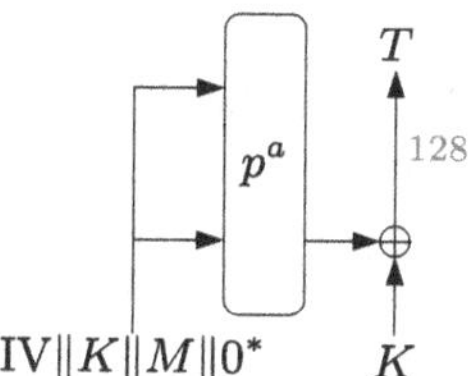

Fig. 2. PRF $\mathcal{F}_{k,m,a,t}$ for short inputs

As shown in Algorithm 3, the 320-bit input to p^a is formed by an IV specifying the algorithm, the secret key K of k bits, and the message M of m bits. The 64-bit IV of $\mathcal{F}_{k,m,a,t}$ includes the key bitsize k, the bitsize of the input block m, and the bitsize of the output block t, each written as an 8-bit integer, and the round number a encoded as an 8-bit integer as $2^6 + a = (0\|1\|0^6) \oplus a = 40 \oplus a$:

$$\text{IV}_{k,m,a,t} \leftarrow k \,\|\, m \,\|((0\|1\|0^6) \oplus a) \,\|\, t \,\|\, 0^{32}$$

This IV is concatenated with the secret key K and the message M. Note that no padding is applied to M and hence, $\mathcal{F}_{k,m,a,t}$ only accepts M matching the length m. The permutation p^a is applied to this state:

$$S \leftarrow p^a(\text{IV}_{k,m,a,t} \,\|\, K \,\|\, M \,\|\, 0^{256-k-m})$$

Algorithm 3. Short-input PRF $\mathcal{F}_{k,m,a,t}(K, M) = T$ specified for ASCON-PRFSHORT with keysize $k = 128$ and $a = 12$ rounds. In an implementation, $m \leq 128$ and $t \leq 128$ can be inputs (instead of parameters).

Pseudorandom function $\mathcal{F}_{k,m,a,t}(K, M) = T$

Input: key $K \in \{0,1\}^k$,
input $M \in \{0,1\}^m$
Output: output $T \in \{0,1\}^t$

$S \leftarrow p^a(\mathrm{IV}_{k,m,a,t} \| K \| M \| 0^{256-k-m})$
$T \leftarrow \lceil S \rceil^t \oplus \lceil K \rceil^t$
return T

The XOR of the last t bits of the state with the key K are then extracted as the tag T, similarly to the authenticated encryption schemes:

$$T \leftarrow \lceil S \rceil^t \oplus \lceil K \rceil^t$$

3 Permutation

The main component of the PRFs is the 320-bit permutation p^a specified for ASCON (v1.2). We recite the specification of the permutations [DEMS21a] here for the sake of completeness. The permutation iteratively applies an SPN-based round transformation p for a rounds that in turn consists of three steps p_C, p_S, p_L:

$$p = p_L \circ p_S \circ p_C.$$

For the description and application of the round transformations, the 320-bit state S is split into five 64-bit words x_i as follows: $S = x_0 \| x_1 \| x_2 \| x_3 \| x_4$ (see Fig. 3).

3.1 Addition of Constants

The step p_C adds a round constant c_r to word x_2 of the state S in round i (see Fig. 3a), where we use $r = i$ for p^a (see Table 3):

$$x_2 \leftarrow x_2 \oplus c_r.$$

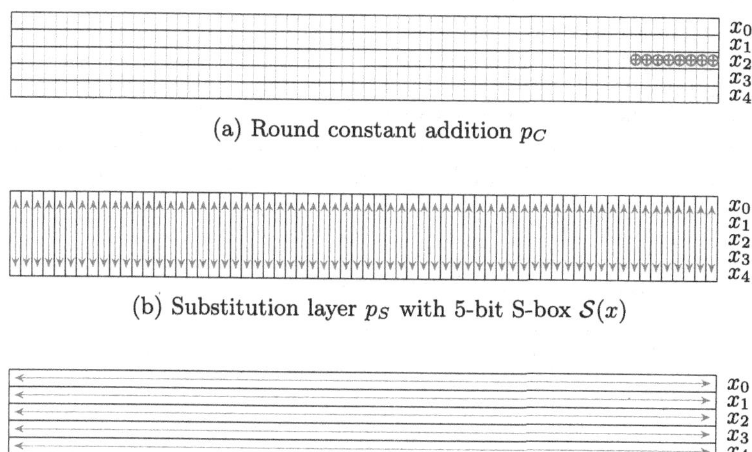

(a) Round constant addition p_C

(b) Substitution layer p_S with 5-bit S-box $\mathcal{S}(x)$

(c) Linear layer with 64-bit diffusion functions $\Sigma_i(x_i)$

Fig. 3. The five 64-bit words of the 320-bit state S and operations $p_L \circ p_S \circ p_C$.

Table 3. The round constants c_r used in each round i of p^a.

p^{12}	Constant c_r	p^{12}	Constant c_r
0	00000000000000f0	6	0000000000000096
1	00000000000000e1	7	0000000000000087
2	00000000000000d2	8	0000000000000078
3	00000000000000c3	9	0000000000000069
4	00000000000000b4	10	000000000000005a
5	00000000000000a5	11	000000000000004b

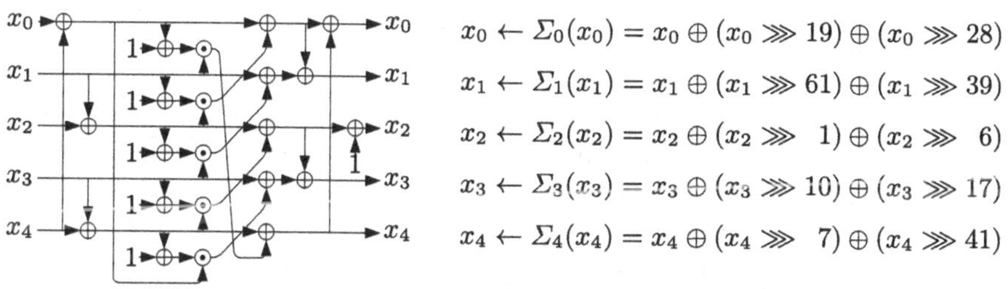

$x_0 \leftarrow \Sigma_0(x_0) = x_0 \oplus (x_0 \ggg 19) \oplus (x_0 \ggg 28)$
$x_1 \leftarrow \Sigma_1(x_1) = x_1 \oplus (x_1 \ggg 61) \oplus (x_1 \ggg 39)$
$x_2 \leftarrow \Sigma_2(x_2) = x_2 \oplus (x_2 \ggg 1) \oplus (x_2 \ggg 6)$
$x_3 \leftarrow \Sigma_3(x_3) = x_3 \oplus (x_3 \ggg 10) \oplus (x_3 \ggg 17)$
$x_4 \leftarrow \Sigma_4(x_4) = x_4 \oplus (x_4 \ggg 7) \oplus (x_4 \ggg 41)$

(a) Ascon's 5-bit S-box $\mathcal{S}(x)$ (b) Ascon's linear layer with 64-bit functions $\Sigma_i(x_i)$

Fig. 4. Ascon's substitution layer and linear diffusion layer.

3.2 Substitution Layer

The step p_S updates the state S with 64 parallel applications of the 5-bit S-box $\mathcal{S}(x)$ to each bit-slice of the five words $x_0, \ldots, x_4$ (Fig. 3b). The operations specified in Fig. 4a are performed bitsliced on the entire 64-bit words. For reference, the lookup table of $\mathcal{S}$ is given in Table 4, where x_0 is the MSB and x_4 the LSB.

Table 4. ASCON's 5-bit S-box $\mathcal{S}$ as a lookup table.

x	0	1	2	3	4	5	6	7	8	9	a	b	c	d	e	f	10	11	12	13	14	15	16	17	18	19	1a	1b	1c	1d	1e	1f
$\mathcal{S}(x)$	4	b	1f	14	1a	15	9	2	1b	5	8	12	1d	3	6	1c	1e	13	7	e	0	d	11	18	10	c	1	19	16	a	f	17

3.3 Linear Diffusion Layer

The linear diffusion layer p_L provides diffusion within each 64-bit word x_i (Fig. 3c). It applies a linear function $\Sigma_i(x_i)$ defined in Fig. 4b to each word x_i:

$$x_i \leftarrow \Sigma_i(x_i), \quad 0 \leq i \leq 4.$$

4 Design Rationale

While PRF and MAC functions can be generated from AEAD and hash functions, more efficient schemes based on the ASCON permutation can be constructed. Our proposed schemes are designed to provide a security level of 128 bits. The schemes follow the design strategy of previous ASCON v1.2 functions to maximize reusability.

4.1 ASCON-PRF

One major difference of ASCON-PRF compared to ASCON-128 and ASCON-128a is the missing keyed initialization and finalization. Not using a keyed initialization and finalization means that ASCON-PRF lacks the robustness of ASCON-128 and ASCON-128a in the case of a side-channel adversary or state recovery. We sacrificed this robustness in favor of throughput for ASCON-PRF. Due to the (almost) full-state absorption, ASCON-PRF cannot obtain the same robustness properties as ASCON-128 and ASCON-128a. If robustness is preferred, one can still use ASCON-128 or ASCON-128a instead.

An obvious difference of our construction compared to a sponge with full-state absorption [MRV15] is that we just do an almost full-state absorption. The reason for this is that it allows us to introduce domain separation between the phases of absorb and squeeze. This context switch allows us to get better security properties when increasing the rate r_o during squeezing to 128 bits. A formal security analysis of this effect is given by Bart Mennink [Men23].

4.2 ASCON-PRFSHORT

We decided to add a PRF called ASCON-PRFSHORT, where the input and output can be a maximum of 128 bits, because we see many use-cases that can profit from a dedicated lightweight PRF. Examples are key derivation functions or pointer authentication. ASCON-PRFSHORT is designed to follow the layout of ASCON-128's initialization.

4.3 Security Claim

ASCON-PRF, ASCON-PRFSHORT, and ASCON-MAC are designed to help provide 128-bit security against key recovery, and $\min(128, t)$-bit security against distinguishers and guessing T for a random key and newly queried M, all obeying the data limit of 2^{64} per key. Although the number of message blocks processed and the number of blocks output by the algorithms is limited to a total of 2^{64} blocks per key, we consider this as more than sufficient for lightweight applications in practice.

It is beneficial that a system or protocol implementing the MAC algorithms monitors and, if necessary, limits the number of tag verification failures per key. After reaching this limit, the verification rejects all tags. In applications that use a session key, for instance TLS, this limit might be small in practice, sometimes even one.

We emphasize that we do not require ideal properties for the permutation p^a. Non-random properties of the permutations p^a are known and are unlikely to affect the claimed security properties of the algorithm.

4.4 Performance

The main performance improvements of ASCON-PRF and ASCON-MAC is related to the larger input rate r_i of 256 bits, compared to the 64-bit rate of ASCON-128, ASCON-HASH and ASCON-XOF. ASCON-PRF, ASCON-MAC, ASCON-HASH and ASCON-XOF all have the same number of 12 rounds in the absorption phase, while ASCON-128 has 6 rounds in the absorption phase. Hence, absorption for ASCON-PRF and ASCON-MAC can be up to 2× faster than ASCON-128 or up to 4× faster than a KMAC based on ASCON-HASH in the ideal case.

During squeezing, the output rate r_o of ASCON-PRF and ASCON-MAC is reduced to 128 bits. Therefore, performance is typically halved compared to the absorption phase for long messages. For ASCON-128a and ASCON-HASHA we get slightly different numbers due to the different round numbers and rates. Compared to ASCON-128a, ASCON-PRF is about 1.3× faster.

The performance advantage of ASCON-PRFSHORT comes from the fact that only a single permutation call to p^a is used, while ASCON-128 requires at least two calls to p^a for a 128-bit message.

In Table 5, a preliminary software performance overview of ASCON-PRF, ASCON-PRFSHORT, and ASCON-MAC is given, in comparison with ASCON-128a, ASCON-128, ASCON-HASHA, and ASCON-HASH. These results show that

Table 5. Software performance in cycles per byte of Ascon-PRFshort, Ascon-PRF and Ascon-MAC compared to Ascon-128a, Ascon-128, Ascon-Hasha, and Ascon-Hash for different message lengths (in bytes).

(a) Ascon-PRFshort

Message Length	1	8	16
Intel® Core™ i5-6300U	185	23	12
ARM1176JZF-S (ARMv6)	1057	132	69

(b) Ascon-PRF and Ascon-MAC

Message Length	1	8	16	32	64	1536	long
Intel® Core™ i5-6300U	369	46	24	18	11.7	6.4	6.3
ARM1176JZF-S (ARMv6)	1769	223	117	85	57.5	31.9	31.6

(c) Ascon-128a

Message Length	1	8	16	32	64	1536	long
Intel® Core™ i5-6300U	365	47	31	19	13.5	8.0	7.8
ARM1176JZF-S (ARMv6)	1908	235	156	99	70.4	43.0	42.9

(d) Ascon-128

Message Length	1	8	16	32	64	1536	long
Intel® Core™ i5-6300U	367	58	35	23	17.6	11.9	11.4
ARM1176JZF-S (ARMv6)	1921	277	167	112	83.7	57.2	56.8

(e) Ascon-Hasha and Ascon-Xofa

Message Length	1	8	16	32	64	1536	long
Intel® Core™ i5-6300U	550	83	49	33	23.7	15.6	15.5
ARM1176JZF-S (ARMv6)	2390	356	211	138	100.7	65.7	65.3

(f) Ascon-Hash and Ascon-Xof

Message Length	1	8	16	32	64	1536	long
Intel® Core™ i5-6300U	747	114	69	46	34.2	23.2	23.1
ARM1176JZF-S (ARMv6)	3051	462	277	184	137.3	92.6	92.2

a dedicated Ascon-MAC can be more than 3 times faster than a KMAC alternative using Ascon-Hash or Ascon-Xof. More Ascon implementations and performance benchmarks can be found at: https://github.com/ascon/ascon-c.

5 Relation to Existing Cryptanalysis

Ascon and its permutation have been the subject of extensive cryptanalysis efforts by the community. In this section, we provide a preliminary discussion of how the existing results relate to Ascon-PRF, Ascon-PRFshort, and Ascon-MAC. We focus on results that are applicable in the specified modes of operation and omit pure permutation distinguishers that are not relevant in this setting, such as non-random permutation properties like inside-out zero-sum [HPTY23] or zero-sum partition [DEMS15] distinguishers. For a detailed overview of existing analysis of Ascon, including the isolated permutation, we refer to [DEMS21a] and [DEMS22].

5.1 Ascon-PRF and Ascon-MAC

Initialization. As outlined in the paper describing the DonkeySponge [BDPV12], the purpose of the initialization is to diffuse the key, so that every state-bit after the initialization depends in a complex manner on the secret key K. For all permutation calls of Ascon-PRF and Ascon-MAC, we use the permutation p^a with 12 rounds as also used in the initialization of the authenticated encryption schemes Ascon-128 and Ascon-128a [DEMS16]. Full diffusion is reached after 4 rounds.

The initialization of Ascon-PRF and Ascon-MAC is invertible, unlike the doubly keyed initialization of the authenticated encryption schemes Ascon-128 and Ascon-128a. While the authenticated encryption schemes maintain resilience under misuse attacks that lead to state recovery during data processing (e.g., side-channel attacks), this is not the case for the more efficient schemes Ascon-PRF and Ascon-MAC. In applications where such robustness properties are desired for the authentication scheme, we recommend to use Ascon-128 or Ascon-128a and absorb the message as associated data.

Absorbing. In order to withstand attacks, it should be hard for an adversary to find pairs of messages M, M' that lead to the same internal state without knowing the secret key. Such a collision would allow the adversary to forge the output for M' after querying M. Additionally, an adversary could attempt to recover (parts of) the internal state by testing whether collisions occur in a conditional differential approach, and then invert the initialization to recover the key.

To prevent both of these, the permutation p^a should have good differential properties. Recent work by Erlacher et al. [EME22] and El Hirch et al. [EMMD22] provides provable bounds for linear and differential characteristics of the Ascon permutation. More specifically, any characteristic for the 6-round

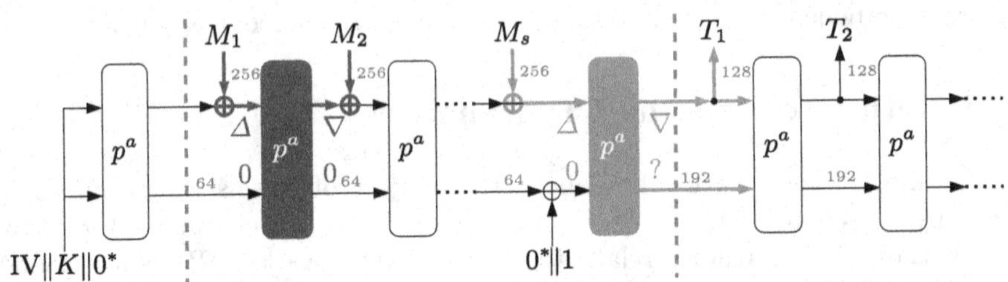

(a) Forgery (■) or MAC forgery (■) via differential cryptanalysis

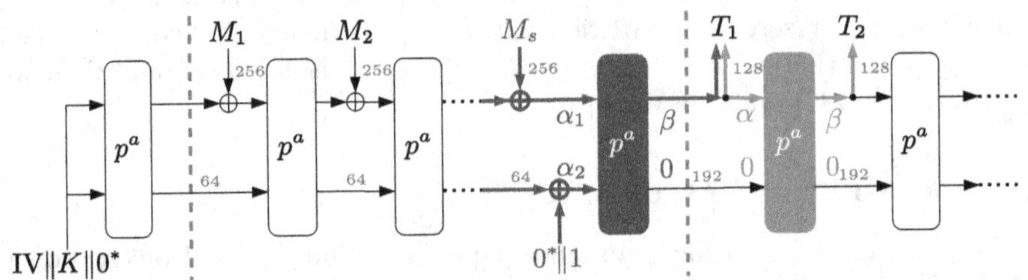

(b) State recovery (■) or PRF distinguisher (■) via linear cryptanalysis

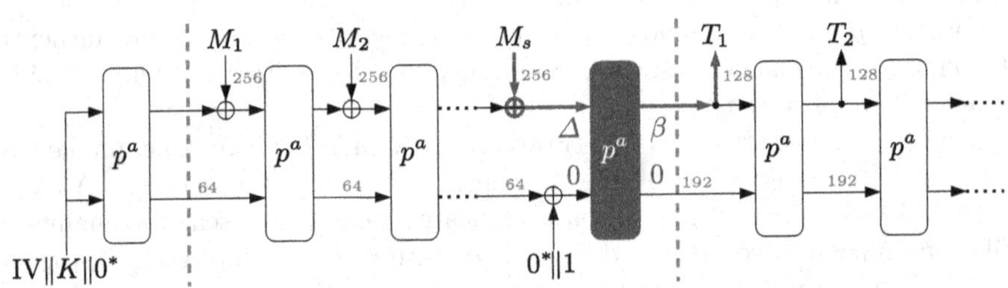

(c) Distinguisher (■) via differential-linear cryptanalysis

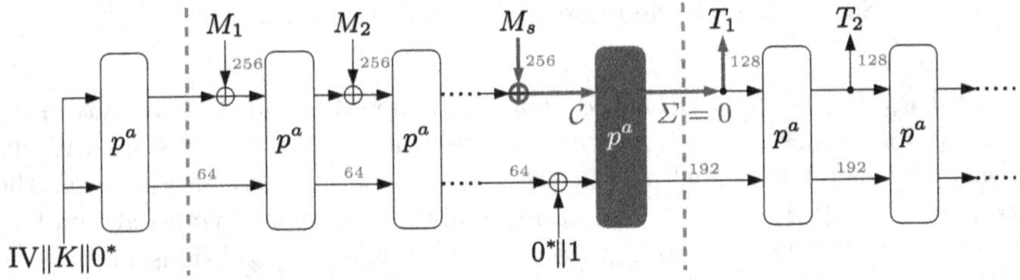

(d) Distinguisher or MAC forgery (■) via integral cryptanalysis

Fig. 5. Cryptanalysis approaches for ASCON-PRF and ASCON-MAC

Table 6. A 4-round truncated differential characteristic $(\Delta, 0) \to (\nabla, 0)$ with 44 active S-boxes during absorbing.

r	x_i	Differences	Differences and conditions (binary)	$\#\mathcal{S}$
0	x_0	0000000000040000	-0---0-----0--00--0--00-00--------0---00-00-0x--00--0-0-0----0--	23
	x_1	441326c02368ca84	-x---x-----x--xx--x--xx-xx--------x---xx-xx-x1--xx--x-x-x----x--	
	x_2	0000000000000000	-x---x-----x--xx--x--xx-xx--------x---xx-xx-x1--xx--x-x-x----x--	
	x_3	441326c0236cca84	-x---x-----x--xx--x--xx-xx--------x---xx-xx-xx--xx--x-x-x----x--	
	x_4	0000000000000000	-0---0-----0--00--0--00-00--------0---00-00-00--00--0-0-0----0--	
1	x_0	8040000000040000	x--------x-----------------------------------x------------------	3
	x_1	0000000000000000	1--------1-----------------------------------1------------------	
	x_2	0000000000000000	1--------1-----------------------------------1------------------	
	x_3	8040000000040000	x--------x-----------------------------------x------------------	
	x_4	0000000000000000	0--------0-----------------------------------0------------------	
2	x_0	0000100004040000	-------------------x-----------------x-------x------------------	3
	x_1	0000000000000000	-------------------0-----------------0-------0------------------	
	x_2	0000000000000000	--	
	x_3	0000000000000000	--	
	x_4	0000000000000000	--	
3	x_0	c040100006050080	xx-------x---------x-----------------xx------x-x--------x-------	15
	x_1	0008980024240020	00-------0--x---x--xx-------------x--x0---x--x-0--------0-x-----	
	x_2	0000000000000000	------------0---0--00-------------0--0----0--0------------0-----	
	x_3	0000000000000000	------------1---0--11-------------0--0----0--0------------0-----	
	x_4	0000000000000000	-------------------1-----------------0-------0------------------	
4	x_0	0000000400040040	-----------------------------x---------------x-----------x------	
	x_1	c2040200328d8496	xx----x----------x-x--x----------xxx--x-x-x-x--xx----x--x----xx-	
	x_2	????????????????	??	
	x_3	????????????????	??	
	x_4	????????????????	??	

Ascon permutation has at least 54 differentially active S-boxes [EME22] and differential probability less than 2^{-128} [EMMD22]. Characteristics for the full 12-round permutation p^a have at least 108 active S-boxes [EME22] and differential probability less than 2^{-256} [EMMD22]. Hence, collisions during absorption for a secret key are very unlikely, even more so within the data limit of 2^{64} blocks.

Moreover, these bounds are likely not tight, particularly for constrained differentials $(\Delta, 0) \to (\nabla, 0)$ with zero difference in the $(320 - r_i)$-bit inner part (see Fig. 5a). Not all characteristics can be transformed to be consistent with these constraints: For each S-box transition in the first round, out of 32 possible S-box output differences, 23 are easy to transform, i.e., at least one of its optimal input differences is of the form ????0 and is thus compatible. For the remaining 9 output differences, all optimal input differences are of the form ????1, but there is a suitable difference which only decreases the probability by a factor of 2. For the S-box transitions in the last round, out of 32 possible S-box input differences, 28 are easy to transform, while 4 have no compatible output difference of the form ????0 at all. We used a heuristic search tool similar to the one used in the analysis of SHA-2 [MNS11, MNS13, EMS14] to find compatible characteristics. In Table 9, we provide a characteristic for 4 rounds with 44 active S-boxes and one for 5 rounds with 72 active S-boxes.

Switch Between Absorbing and Squeezing. With the last message block, an attacker can potentially manipulate a constant incoming state and observe the

Table 7. A 3-round linear characteristic $(\alpha_1, \alpha_2) \rightarrow (\beta, 0)$ with 13 active S-boxes and bias 2^{-16} between absorbing and squeezing.

r	x_i	Masks	Masks (binary)	$\#\mathcal{S}$
	x_0	0000220000000000	------------------x---x---	
	x_1	0000800240020401	----------------x-------------x--x------------x------x---------x	
0	x_2	0000800240820401	----------------x-------------x--x------x-----x------x---------x	9
	x_3	0000220000000000	------------------x---x---	
	x_4	0000000000000000	--	
	x_0	0000000000000000	--	
	x_1	0000000000000000	--	
1	x_2	0000000000000000	--	3
	x_3	0000000040800001	---------------------------------x------x----------------------x	
	x_4	0000000040800001	---------------------------------x------x----------------------x	
	x_0	0000000000000000	--	
	x_1	0000000000000000	--	
2	x_2	0000000000000000	--	1
	x_3	0000000000000000	--	
	x_4	0000000000800000	--x-----------------------	
	x_0	6925b76d24c9125b	-xx-x--x--x--x-xx-xx-xxx-xx-xx-x--x--x--xx--x--x---x--x--x-xx-xx	
	x_1	443dd4b48f9974dc	-x---x----xxxx-xxx-x-x--x-xx-x--x---xxxxx--xx--x-xxx-x--xx-xxx--	
3	x_2	0000000000000000	--	
	x_3	0000000000000000	--	
	x_4	0000000000000000	--	

effects of this manipulation on the first output block after an application of the permutation p^a. This is a similar scenario as we have during the initialization of the authenticated encryption schemes Ascon-128 and Ascon-128a (with empty associated data).

The attacks penetrating the highest number of rounds in case of the authenticated encryption schemes are 7 out of 12 in the case of algebraic attacks [LZWW17, LDW17, RHSS21, RS21] followed by differential-linear attacks on up to 5 out of 12 rounds [DEMS15, Tez20]. Here, the setting is slightly more difficult for the attacker, who cannot exploit known or freely controllable variables as in the IV and nonce, but only differentially influence the state. On the other hand, the attacker can differentially control a larger part of the state. The adversary can use such an integral or differential-linear distinguisher to distinguish the output stream, to facilitate forgery attacks on the first output block T_1, or to help recover the state after absorbing some fixed message $(M_1, \ldots, M_{s-1})$ and thus derive the key K. We expect that a similar number of rounds can also be attacked in the case of Ascon-PRF and Ascon-MAC.

An adversary could also increase the success probability of forgery attempts on the first output block T_1 or recover the internal state with the help of a high-probability (truncated) differential distinguisher $(\Delta, 0) \rightarrow (\nabla, *)$ or a high-correlation linear distinguisher $(\alpha_1, \alpha_2) \rightarrow (\beta, 0)$. Based on the available bounds [EMMD22] and cryptanalytic results, we expect that these techniques are less efficient than integral attacks. The truncated differential characteristic in Table 6 yields a forgery attack on Ascon-MAC with p^a reduced to 4 rounds: When considering the truncated transition probability in the last round, the differential probability of the truncated characteristic is 2^{-112}. We provide suitable linear characteristics for 3 rounds in Table 7, as well as for 4 and 5 rounds in Table 10.

These characteristics were obtained by using a heuristic search tool similar to the one used in [DEM15]. Since all characteristics are rotationally invariant, the 3-round characteristic with bias 2^{-16} in Table 7 can be rotated to obtain 64 similar characteristics. These could be used to distinguish the output stream based on a set of messages where only the last message block M_s varies, or to minimally improve the success probability of forging the first output block T_1. Overall, we expect that 12 rounds provide a comfortable security margin.

Table 8. A 3-round linear characteristic $(\alpha, 0) \to (\beta, 0)$ with 47 active S-boxes and bias 2^{-81} during squeezing.

r	x_i	Masks	Masks (binary)	$\#\mathcal{S}$
0	x_0	0cc60086530a1c53	----xx--xx---xx---------x----xx--x-x--xx----x-x----xxx---x-x--xx	29
	x_1	a0201a0000000020	x-x-------x--------xx-x-------------------------------------x-----	
	x_2	0000000000000000	--	
	x_3	0000000000000000	--	
	x_4	0000000000000000	--	
1	x_0	0422100203400821	-----x----x---x----x---------x-------xx-x---------x-----x----x	14
	x_1	0420000202400834	-----x----x--------------------x-------x--x---------x-----xx-x--	
	x_2	0022000201000811	----------x---x----------------x-------x------------x------x---x	
	x_3	0820100201000001	----x-----x--------x----------x-------x---------------------x	
	x_4	0000000000000000	--	
2	x_0	0402000002000020	-----x--------x-----------------------x-------------------x-----	4
	x_1	0000000002000020	--------------------------------------x-------------------x-----	
	x_2	0400000000000000	-----x--	
	x_3	0402000000000000	-----x--------x---	
	x_4	0000000000000000	--	
3	x_0	72dbb16fda762deb	-xxx--x-xx-xx-xx-xxx-xx---x-xx-xxxxxx-xx-x--xxx-xx---x-xx-xxxx-x-xx	
	x_1	9ffe260e3a5807c5	x--xxxxxxxxxxxx---x--xx-----xxx---xxx-x--x-xx---------xxxxx---x-x	
	x_2	0000000000000000	--	
	x_3	0000000000000000	--	
	x_4	0000000000000000	--	

Squeezing. One relevant attack vector during squeezing is linear cryptanalysis, which could be used to detect a bias in the output blocks. For this, the attacker needs good linear approximations for constrained masks $(\alpha, 0) \to (\beta, 0)$ with no active bits in the $320 - r_o$-bit inner part. Due to the smaller output rate $r_o = 128$, these characteristics are quite constrained. We used a heuristic search tool to find such constrained characteristics and provide results for 3 rounds in Table 8, as well as for 4 and 5 rounds in Table 11. Even this 3-round characteristic already has 47 active S-boxes. Based on the available bounds [EMMD22] and results, the 12-round permutation p^a should provide a very high security margin.

5.2 ASCON-PRFSHORT

ASCON-PRFSHORT is very similar to the initialization of ASCON-128a followed by the first block of encryption in the absence of associated data. The main difference is that a different part of the state is returned: in ASCON-128a, the adversary receives the first two words of the state; in ASCON-PRFSHORT, the output instead covers the last two words of the state and is additionally

Table 9. Differential characteristics for constrained differentials $(\Delta, 0) \rightarrow (\nabla, 0)$

(a) 4-round characteristic with 44 active S-boxes ($\# \mathcal{S}$)

r	x_i	Differences	Differences and conditions (binary)	$\# \mathcal{S}$
0	x_0	0000000000040000	-0---0-----0--00--0--00-00--------0---00-00-0x--00--0-0-0----0--	23
	x_1	441326c02368ca84	-x---x-----x--xx--x--xx-xx--------x---xx-xx-x1--xx--x-x-x----x--	
	x_2	0000000000000000	-x---x-----x--xx--x--xx-xx--------x---xx-xx-x1--xx--x-x-x----x--	
	x_3	441326c0236cca84	-x---x-----x--xx--x--xx-xx--------x---xx-xx-xx--xx--x-x-x----x--	
	x_4	0000000000000000	-0---0-----0--00--0--00-00--------0---00-00-00--00--0-0-0----0--	
1	x_0	8040000000040000	x--------x-----------------------------------x------------------	3
	x_1	0000000000000000	1--------1-----------------------------------1------------------	
	x_2	0000000000000000	1--------1-----------------------------------1------------------	
	x_3	8040000000040000	x--------x-----------------------------------x------------------	
	x_4	0000000000000000	0--------0-----------------------------------0------------------	
2	x_0	0000100004040000	-------------------x-----------------x-------x------------------	3
	x_1	0000000000000000	-------------------0-----------------0-------0------------------	
	x_2	0000000000000000	--	
	x_3	0000000000000000	--	
	x_4	0000000000000000	--	
3	x_0	c040100006050080	xx-------x---------x-----------------xx------x-x--------x-------	15
	x_1	0008980024240020	00-------0--x---x--xx-------------x--x0---x--x-0--------0-x-----	
	x_2	0000000000000000	------------0---0--00-------------0--0----0--0------------0-----	
	x_3	0000000000000000	------------1---0--11-------------0--0----0--0------------0-----	
	x_4	0000000000000000	-------------------1-----------------0-------0------------------	
4	x_0	0000000400040040	-----------------------------x---------------x-----------x------	
	x_1	c2040200328d8496	xx----x----------x-x--x----------xxx--x-x-x-x--xx----x--x----xx-	
	x_2	800cf66036a69030	x-----------xx--xxxx-xx--xx-------xx-xx-x-x--xx-x--x------xx----	
	x_3	4808aa2664281830	-x--x-------x---x-x-x-x---x--xx--xx--x----x-x------xx-----xx----	
	x_4	0000000000000000	--	

(b) 5-round characteristic with 72 active S-boxes ($\# \mathcal{S}$)

r	x_i	Differences	Differences and conditions (binary)	$\# \mathcal{S}$
0	x_0	0100000000000000	-------x--	5
	x_1	8100000001400004	x------x-------------------------------x-x-------------------x--	
	x_2	8000000001400004	x------1-------------------------------x-x-------------------x--	
	x_3	0100000000000000	-------x--	
	x_4	0000000000000000	-------1--	
1	x_0	0000000000000000	1---0--0--------0---------------------01-0----0--------------1--	9
	x_1	0900800002420000	0---x--x--------x---------------------x0-x----x--------------0--	
	x_2	0000000000000000	----0--0--------0---------------------0--0----0-----------------	
	x_3	0000000000000000	1---0--0--------0---------------------01-0----0--------------1--	
	x_4	8900800003420004	x---x--x--------x---------------------xx-x----x--------------x--	
2	x_0	0000000000000000	1----------0--00--1--------------------1-------------1---0---1--	10
	x_1	8002000000000020	x----------0--x0--0--------------------1-------------1---1x--1--	
	x_2	0000000000000000	1-------------1---0-----	
	x_3	0000000000000000	0----------1--00--1--------------------1-------------1---11--1--	
	x_4	8013200001000444	x----------x--xx--x--------------------x-------------x---x---x--	
3	x_0	1088c44001000464	0--x0---x--1x---xx---x1--x--1---1------x------------1x--1xx0-x--	23
	x_1	8088200880000020	x--1----x--0x--101x--10-----x---x------0------------00--01x1-0--	
	x_2	8001840000000030	x--1----0---0--xx11--x------0---0------------------------0xx----	
	x_3	9801444880000060	x--xx---0--00--x1x0--x1--x--x---x-------------------1---1xx0----	
	x_4	0011024000000890	0--10---1--x0--x10---0x--x--1---1-------------------x---x00x----	
4	x_0	0806805081044454	1--1x---1----xx-x--------x-x---0x00----x-----x---x---x---x-x-x--	25
	x_1	9096901161004810	x--x0---x--x-xx0x--x----1--x---x0xx----x---------x--x0---1-x-0--	
	x_2	1897109000000000	0--xx---x--x-xxx1--x----x--x---1-00----1---------1--1----0-1----	
	x_3	9883005120044040	x--xx---x-----xx0-------0x-x---x-1x----1-----x---x--1----x-0----	
	x_4	0801004040040000	1--1x---1-----1x0--------x-0---0-x0----1-----x---1-------0-0----	
5	x_0	198a464040003448	---xx--xx---x-x--x---xx--x-------x----------------xx-x---x--x---	
	x_1	2122100e48020344	--x----x--x---x----x--------xxx--x--x---------x-------xx-x---x--	
	x_2	54a04ea2d4021c38	-x-x-x--x-x------x--xxx-x-x---x-xx-x-x--------x----xxx----xxx---	
	x_3	940140c0a0400842	x--x-x---------x-x------xx------x-x------x----------x----x----x-	
	x_4	0000000000000000	----1-----------------------------0-----------------------------	

Table 10. Linear characteristics for $(\alpha_1, \alpha_2) \to (\beta, 0)$

(a) 4-round characteristic with $\#\mathcal{S} = 44$ active S-boxes and bias 2^{-75}

r	x_i	Masks	Masks (binary)	$\#\mathcal{S}$
	x_0	d000044000900009	xx-x-----------------x---x--------------x--x----------------x--x	
	x_1	0000000021000230	----------------------------------x----x--------------x---xx----	
0	x_2	0000000021000230	----------------------------------x----x--------------x---xx----	14
	x_3	0000000000000000	--	
	x_4	5000044000100000	-x-x-----------------x---x-----------------x--------------------	
	x_0	0000000000000000	--	
	x_1	8000000000800008	x---------------------------------------x-------------------x---	
1	x_2	8000000000800008	x---------------------------------------x-------------------x---	3
	x_3	0000000000000000	--	
	x_4	0000000000000000	--	
	x_0	0000000000000000	--	
	x_1	0000000000000000	--	
2	x_2	80000000000218a7	x---x----xx---x-x--xxx	9
	x_3	0000000000000000	--	
	x_4	0000000000000000	--	
	x_0	0200000020100806	------x---------------------------x------x--------x----------xx-	
	x_1	0000000000000000	--	
3	x_2	8000000000000802	x---x---------x-	18
	x_3	0000000000000000	--	
	x_4	c881031100040045	xx--x---x------x------xx---x---x-------------x-----------x---x-x	
	x_0	27b583bf0cce6dd4	--x--xxxx-xx-x-xx-----xxx-xxxxxx----xx--xx--xxx--xx-xx-xxx-x-x--	
	x_1	40db8037ba8483e6	-x------xx-xx-xxx---------xx-xxxx-xxx-x-x----x--x-----xxxxx--xx-	
4	x_2	0000000000000000	--	
	x_3	0000000000000000	--	
	x_4	0000000000000000	--	

(b) 5-round characteristic with $\#\mathcal{S} = 78$ active S-boxes and bias 2^{-136}

r	x_i	Differences	Differences and conditions (binary)	$\#\mathcal{S}$
	x_0	2800008480120201	--x-x-------------------x----x--x----------x--x-------x---------x	
	x_1	0000010804200042	-----------------------x----x---------x----x---------------x----x-	
0	x_2	0000010804200042	-----------------------x----x---------x----x---------------x----x-	15
	x_3	0000000000000000	--	
	x_4	2800008080020200	--x-x-------------------x-------x-------------x-------x---------	
	x_0	0000000000000000	--	
	x_1	0000000400100001	-----------------------------x----------x----------------------x	
1	x_2	0000000400100001	-----------------------------x----------x----------------------x	3
	x_3	0000000000000000	--	
	x_4	0000000000000000	--	
	x_0	0000000000000000	--	
	x_1	0000000000000000	--	
2	x_2	0000000000000000	--	3
	x_3	0000000000020401	--x------x---------x	
	x_4	0000000000000000	--	
	x_0	6d5b69224494d848	-xx-xx-x-x-xx-xx-xx-x--x--x---x--x---x--x--x-x--xx-xx----x--x---	
	x_1	0000000000000000	--	
3	x_2	0000000000000000	--	28
	x_3	0000000000000001	---x	
	x_4	0000000000000000	--	
	x_0	48c94331c1c24239	-x--x---xx--x--x-x----xx--xx---xxx-----xxx----x--x----x---xxx--x	
	x_1	2009201000008008	--x---------x--x--x--------x---------------------x-----------x---	
4	x_2	28c16331c0024801	--x-x---xx-----x-xx---xx--xx---xxx------------x--x--x----------x	29
	x_3	2040002040000000	--x------x----------------x------x------------------------------	
	x_4	2000204000008810	--x---------------x-------x----------------------x---x------x----	
	x_0	b90a3b90d45fa1c1	x-xxx--x----x-x---xxx-xxx--x----xx-x-x---x-xxxxxx-x----xxx-----x	
	x_1	82f23012ad744a2a	x-----x-xxxx--x---xx-------x--x-x-x-xx-x-xxx-x---x--x-x---x-x-x-	
5	x_2	0000000000000000	--	
	x_3	0000000000000000	--	
	x_4	0000000000000000	--	

Table 11. Linear characteristics for $(\alpha, 0) \rightarrow (\beta, 0)$

(a) 4-round characteristic with $\#\mathcal{S} = 68$ active S-boxes and bias 2^{-105}

r	x_i	Masks	Masks (binary)	$\#\mathcal{S}$
0	x_0	741d408c41873d05	-xxx-x-----xxx-x-x------x---xx---x-----xx----xxx--xxxx-x-----x-x	40
	x_1	00609d063064008b	---------xx-----x--xxx-x-----xx---xx-----xx--x----------x---x-xx	
	x_2	0000000000000000	--	
	x_3	0000000000000000	--	
	x_4	0000000000000000	--	
1	x_0	0200c80220811808	------x---------xx--x---------x---x-----x------x---xx-------x---	22
	x_1	0462c00000010c0b	-----x---xx---x-xx-----------------------------x----xx------x-xx	
	x_2	0463400220811402	-----x---xx---xx-x------------x---x-----x------x---x-x--------x-	
	x_3	0240880600001803	------x--x------x---x--------xx--------------------xx---------xx	
	x_4	000000162000084b	---------------------------x-xx---x-----------------x----x--x-xx	
2	x_0	0001000020000000	---------------x------------------x-----------------------------	5
	x_1	0001001000000040	---------------x-----------x-----------------------------x------	
	x_2	0001000000000000	---------------x--	
	x_3	0201001000000040	------x--------x-----------x-----------------------------x------	
	x_4	0200001020000040	------x--------------------x------x----------------------x------	
3	x_0	0000000020000000	----------------------------------x-----------------------------	1
	x_1	0000000000000000	--	
	x_2	0000000000000000	--	
	x_3	0000000000000000	--	
	x_4	0000000020000000	----------------------------------x-----------------------------	
4	x_0	0000000000000000	--	
	x_1	0f752d23e65d3711	----xxxx-xxx-x-x--x-xx-x--x---xxxxx--xx--x-xxx-x--xx-xxx---x---x	
	x_2	0000000000000000	--	
	x_3	0000000000000000	--	
	x_4	0000000000000000	--	

(b) 5-round characteristic with $\#\mathcal{S} = 93$ active S-boxes and bias 2^{-145}

r	x_i	Differences	Differences and conditions (binary)	$\#\mathcal{S}$
0	x_0	57dc09af5052a314	-x-x-xxxxx-xxx------x--xx-x-xxxx-x-x-----x-x--x-x-x---xx---x-x--	44
	x_1	24212a480309d822	--x--x----x----x--x-x-x--x--x---------xx----x--xxx-xx-----x---x-	
	x_2	0000000000000000	--	
	x_3	0000000000000000	--	
	x_4	0000000000000000	--	
1	x_0	254182a618460120	--x--x-x-x-----xx-----x-x-x--xx----xx----x---xx--------x--x-----	36
	x_1	21688230f8094962	--x----x-xx-x---x-----x---xx----xxxxx-------x--x-x--x--x-xx---x-	
	x_2	046b8232f1474943	-----x---xx-x-xxx-----x---xx--x-xxxx---x-x---xxx-x--x--x-x----xx	
	x_3	21408232304c0022	--x----x-x------x-----x---xx--x---xx-----x--xx------------x---x-	
	x_4	256392b2e0484de0	--x--x-x-xx---xxx--x--x-x-xx--x-xxx------x--x----x--xx-xxxx-----	
2	x_0	0000000040000001	---------------------------------x-----------------------------x	9
	x_1	0000800240020401	----------------x-------------x--x------------x------x---------x	
	x_2	0000800240820401	----------------x-------------x--x------x-----x------x---------x	
	x_3	0000220000020001	------------------x---x-----------------------x----------------x	
	x_4	0000220000020001	------------------x---x-----------------------x----------------x	
3	x_0	0000000000000000	--	3
	x_1	0000000000000000	--	
	x_2	0000000000000000	--	
	x_3	0000000040800001	---------------------------------x------x----------------------x	
	x_4	0000000040800001	---------------------------------x------x----------------------x	
4	x_0	0000000000000000	--	1
	x_1	0000000000000000	--	
	x_2	0000000000000000	--	
	x_3	0000000000000000	--	
	x_4	0000000000800000	--x-----------------------	
5	x_0	6925b76d24c9125b	-xx-x--x--x--x-xx-xx-xxx-xx-xx-x--x--x--xx--x--x---x--x--x-xx-xx	
	x_1	443dd4b48f9974dc	-x---x----xxxx-xxx-x-x--x-xx-x--x---xxxxx--xx--x-xxx-x--xx-xxx--	
	x_2	0000000000000000	--	
	x_3	0000000000000000	--	
	x_4	0000000000000000	--	

masked with the key. Additionally, the constant IV is different, which only has a very minor impact on the applicable attacks. Hence, we expect that similar attacks that target the initialization of Ascon and work for up to 7 out of 12 rounds [LZWW17,LDW17,RHSS21,RS21] also apply in the case of Ascon-PRFshort. In particular, this includes different variations of cube attacks for key recovery. Rohit et al. [RHSS21] proposed key recovery attacks on 7-round Ascon-128a with a time complexity of 2^{123} that respect the data limit of 2^{64} blocks per key, as well as distinguishing attacks based on 60-dimensional cubes with a time complexity of 2^{60}. While this attack details depends on the specific constant IV and the position of the output bits, it is likely that comparable attacks are possible for Ascon-PRFshort. For example, based on [RHSS21, Table 3], the complexity of the distinguisher can be reduced from 2^{60} to 2^{59} when using state word X_4 instead of X_0 or X_1. In a weak-key setting, the data complexity can be decreased further [RS21].

6 Conclusion

In this paper, we complement the existing functionality of the Ascon cipher suite with the fast and efficient pseudo-random functions Ascon-PRF and Ascon-PRFshort. PRFs are very versatile building blocks allowing to instantiate various cryptographic functionalities. We think that this additional functionality can be very useful in practice.

Ascon-PRF can be used to instantiate, e.g., schemes providing authentication or confidentiality. Examples are general-purpose lightweight and efficient message authentication, stream ciphers or to instantiate SIV. Ascon-PRFshort excels whenever short data needs to be authenticated, e.g., the authentication of pointers, in challenge-response protocols, or key derivation functions (KDFs). Since Ascon-PRFshort efficiently maps 128-bit inputs to 128-bit outputs, it may even be used as a PRF in some block cipher modes.

Acknowledgments. The authors would like to thank all researchers contributing to the design, analysis, and implementation of Ascon. In particular, we want to thank Hannes Gross and Robert Primas for all their support and various implementations of Ascon. Furthermore, we want to thank Bart Mennink for giving feedback on this document.

References

[BDPV07] Bertoni, G., Daemen, J., Peeters, M., Van Assche, G.: Sponge functions. In: Ecrypt Hash Workshop 2007 (2007). http://sponge.noekeon.org/SpongeFunctions.pdf

[BDPV12] Bertoni, G., Daemen, J., Peeters, M., Van Assche, G.: Permutation-based encryption, authentication and authenticated encryption. In: DIAC 2012 (2012)

[CAE14] CAESAR committee. CAESAR: Competition for authenticated encryption: security, applicability, and robustness (2014). https://competitions.cr.yp.to/caesar-submissions.html

[DEM15] Dobraunig, C., Eichlseder, M., Mendel, F.: Heuristic tool for linear cryptanalysis with applications to CAESAR candidates. In: Iwata, T., Cheon, J.H. (eds.) ASIACRYPT 2015. LNCS, vol. 9453, pp. 490–509. Springer, Heidelberg (2015). https://doi.org/10.1007/978-3-662-48800-3_20

[DEM+20] Dobraunig, C., et al.: Isap v2.0. IACR Trans. Symmetric Cryptol. **2020**(S1), 390–416 (2020). https://doi.org/10.13154/tosc.v2020.iS1.390-416

[DEM+21] Dobraunig, C., et al.: Isap v2.0 (submission to NIST). Finalist of NIST lightweight cryptography standardization process (2021). https://csrc.nist.gov/Projects/Lightweight-Cryptography/

[DEMS14] Dobraunig, C., Eichlseder, M., Mendel, F., Schläffer, M.: Ascon v1. Submission to the CAESAR competition (2014). https://ascon.iaik.tugraz.at

[DEMS15] Dobraunig, C., Eichlseder, M., Mendel, F., Schläffer, M.: Cryptanalysis of Ascon. In: Nyberg, K. (ed.) CT-RSA 2015. LNCS, vol. 9048, pp. 371–387. Springer, Cham (2015). https://doi.org/10.1007/978-3-319-16715-2_20. arXiv:2015/030

[DEMS16] Dobraunig, C., Eichlseder, M., Mendel, F., Schläffer, M.: Ascon v1.2. Submission to Round 3 of the CAESAR competition (2016). https://ascon.iaik.tugraz.at

[DEMS21a] Dobraunig, C., Eichlseder, M., Mendel, F., Schläffer, M.: Ascon v1.2: lightweight authenticated encryption and hashing. J. Cryptol. **34**(3), 33 (2021). https://doi.org/10.1007/s00145-021-09398-9

[DEMS21b] Dobraunig, C., Eichlseder, M., Mendel, F., Schläffer, M.: Ascon v1.2 (Submission to NIST). Finalist of NIST lightweight cryptography standardization process (2021). https://csrc.nist.gov/Projects/Lightweight-Cryptography/

[DEMS22] Dobraunig, C., Eichlseder, M., Mendel, F., Schläffer, M.: Status update on Ascon v1.2. Technical report (2022). https://csrc.nist.gov/csrc/media/Projects/lightweight-cryptography/documents/finalist-round/status-updates/ascon-update.pdf

[DMV17] Daemen, J., Mennink, B., Van Assche, G.: Full-state keyed duplex with built-in multi-user support. In: Takagi, T., Peyrin, T. (eds.) ASIACRYPT 2017. LNCS, vol. 10625, pp. 606–637. Springer, Cham (2017). https://doi.org/10.1007/978-3-319-70697-9_21. arXiv:2017/498

[EME22] Erlacher, J., Mendel, F., Eichlseder, M.: Bounds for the security of Ascon against differential and linear cryptanalysis. IACR Trans. Symmetric Cryptol. **2022**(1), 64–87 (2022). https://doi.org/10.46586/tosc.v2022.i1.64-87

[EMMD22] El Hirch, S., Mella, S., Mehrdad, A., Daemen, J.: Improved differential and linear trail bounds for ASCON. IACR Trans. Symmetric Cryptol. **2022**(4), 145–178 (2022). https://doi.org/10.46586/tosc.v2022.i4.145-178. arXiv:2022/1377

[EMS14] Eichlseder, M., Mendel, F., Schläffer, M.: Branching heuristics in differential collision search with applications to SHA-512. In: Cid, C., Rechberger, C. (eds.) FSE 2014. LNCS, vol. 8540, pp. 473–488. Springer, Heidelberg (2015). https://doi.org/10.1007/978-3-662-46706-0_24

[HPTY23] Hu, K., Peyrin, T., Tan, Q.Q., Yap, T.: Revisiting higher-order differential-linear attacks from an algebraic perspective. In: Guo, J., Steinfeld, R. (eds.) ASIACRYPT 2023. LNCS, vol. 14440, pp. 405–435. Springer, Singapore (2023). https://doi.org/10.1007/978-981-99-8727-6_14

[LDW17] Li, Z., Dong, X., Wang, X.: Conditional cube attack on round-reduced ASCON. IACR Trans. Symmetric Cryptol. **2017**(1), 175–202 (2017). https://doi.org/10.13154/tosc.v2017.i1.175-202. arXiv:2017/160

[LZWW17] Li, Y., Zhang, G., Wang, W., Wang, M.: Cryptanalysis of round-reduced ASCON. Sci. China Inf. Sci. **60**(3), 38102 (2017). https://doi.org/10.1007/s11432-016-0283-3

[Men23] Mennink, B.: Understanding the duplex and its security. IACR Trans. Symmetric Cryptol. **2023**(2), 1–46 (2023). https://doi.org/10.46586/tosc.v2023.i2.1-46

[MNS11] Mendel, F., Nad, T., Schläffer, M.: Finding SHA-2 characteristics: searching through a minefield of contradictions. In: Lee, D.H., Wang, X. (eds.) ASIACRYPT 2011. LNCS, vol. 7073, pp. 288–307. Springer, Heidelberg (2011). https://doi.org/10.1007/978-3-642-25385-0_16

[MNS13] Mendel, F., Nad, T., Schläffer, M.: Improving local collisions: new attacks on reduced SHA-256. In: Johansson, T., Nguyen, P.Q. (eds.) EUROCRYPT 2013. LNCS, vol. 7881, pp. 262–278. Springer, Heidelberg (2013). https://doi.org/10.1007/978-3-642-38348-9_16

[MRV15] Mennink, B., Reyhanitabar, R., Vizár, D.: Security of full-state keyed sponge and duplex: applications to authenticated encryption. In: Iwata, T., Cheon, J.H. (eds.) ASIACRYPT 2015. LNCS, vol. 9453, pp. 465–489. Springer, Heidelberg (2015). https://doi.org/10.1007/978-3-662-48800-3_19

[MSP+23] Mattsson, J.P., Selander, G., Paavolainen, S., Karakoç, F., Tiloca, M., Moskowitz, R.: Proposals for standardization of the Ascon family. In: Sixth Lightweight Cryptography Workshop (2023). https://csrc.nist.gov/csrc/media/Events/2023/lightweight-cryptography-workshop-2023/documents/accepted-papers/03-proposals-for-standardization-of-ascon-family.pdf

[Nat18] National Institute of Standards and Technology. Submission requirements and evaluation criteria for the lightweight cryptography standardization process (2018). https://csrc.nist.gov/CSRC/media/Projects/Lightweight-Cryptography/documents/final-lwc-submission-requirements-august2018.pdf

[NIS23] NIST Lightweight Cryptography Team. Lightweight cryptography standardization process: NIST selects Ascon (2023). https://csrc.nist.gov/News/2023/lightweight-cryptography-nist-selects-ascon

[RHSS21] Rohit, R., Hu, K., Sarkar, S., Sun, S.: Misuse-free key-recovery and distinguishing attacks on 7-round Ascon. IACR Trans. Symmetric Cryptol. **2021**(1), 130–155 (2021). https://doi.org/10.46586/tosc.v2021.i1.130-155

[RS06] Rogaway, P., Shrimpton, T.: A provable-security treatment of the key-wrap problem. In: Vaudenay, S. (ed.) EUROCRYPT 2006. LNCS, vol. 4004, pp. 373–390. Springer, Heidelberg (2006). https://doi.org/10.1007/11761679_23

[RS21] Rohit, R., Sarkar, S.: Diving deep into the weak keys of round reduced Ascon. IACR Trans. Symmetric Cryptol. **2021**(4), 74–99 (2021). https://doi.org/10.46586/tosc.v2021.i4.74-99

[Tez20] Tezcan, C.: Analysis of Ascon, DryGASCON, and Shamash permutations. Int. J. Inf. Secur. Sci. **9**(3), 172–187 (2020). arXiv:2020/1458

Interactive Oracle Arguments in the QROM and Applications to Succinct Verification of Quantum Computation

Islam Faisal(✉)

Boston University, Boston, MA, USA
islam@bu.edu

Abstract. This work is motivated by the following question: can an untrusted quantum server convince a classical verifier of the answer to an efficient quantum computation using only polylogarithmic communication? We show how to achieve this in the quantum random oracle model (QROM), after a non-succinct instance-independent setup phase.

We introduce and formalize the notion of post-quantum interactive oracle arguments for languages in QMA, a generalization of interactive oracle proofs (Ben-Sasson–Chiesa–Spooner). We then show how to compile any non-adaptive public-coin interactive oracle argument (with private setup) into a succinct argument (with setup) in the QROM.

To conditionally answer our motivating question via this framework under the post-quantum hardness assumption of LWE, we show that the ZX local Hamiltonian problem with at least inverse-polylogarithmic relative promise gap has an interactive oracle argument with instance-independent setup, which we can then compile.

Assuming a variant of the quantum PCP conjecture that we introduce called the *weak ZX quantum PCP conjecture*, we obtain a succinct argument for QMA (and consequently the verification of quantum computation) in the QROM (with non-succinct instance-independent setup) which makes only black-box use of the underlying cryptographic primitives.

Keywords: succinct arguments · interactive oracle proofs · delegation of quantum computation · quantum random oracle model · QROM · BQP · QMA

1 Introduction

This work is motivated by the following use case which is desirable in a world where quantum computers reach larger scales but are only available in controlled facilities or laboratories.

The author was partially supported by the National Science Foundation (NSF) grants CCF-1947889 and CNS-1414119. Thanks to Mark Bun and Nicholas Spooner for their mentorship and help with refining and revising this project.

E. Oswald (Ed.): CT-RSA 2024, LNCS 14643, pp. 404–429, 2024.
https://doi.org/10.1007/978-3-031-58868-6_16

Real World Application: Alice owns only classical devices (e.g. laptop and/or tablet) and a classical internet connection. She wants to delegate some efficient quantum-computational tasks to a quantum server (Merlin) in a remote location. How can she make sure that the quantum server performed the intended tasks using only a *succinct* amount of classical internet communication?

Under some assumptions, we show how this can be achieved after a non-succinct initial setup phase that does not depend on the subsequent tasks to be delegated. In particular, we show the following result.

Informal Theorem 1 (Informal Statement of Theorem 4). *If a variant of the quantum PCP conjecture (Conjecture 1) is true as well as the post-quantum hardness of LWE, then there exists a classical-verifier succinct-communication argument with non-succinct setup in the QROM for* QMA *(and consequently for the verification of quantum computation).*

The general topic of delegating quantum computation has been studied for a while (for a non-exhaustive list of works, see for example [3,13,16,22,23,31, 35,41]). In early work, the verifier was modeled as a (possibly weaker) quantum device (e.g. [16]). Mahadev's breakthrough [30,31] enabled classical verification of quantum computation under the post-quantum hardness assumption of Learning with Errors (LWE). This opened the door to further subsequent developments in the topic of classical verification of quantum computation (e.g. [3,38]). In particular, the question of succinct verification of quantum computation has been studied in these works [6,7,12,13,25,40]. We discuss how they differ from our work in Sect. 1.1.

We will now go from our motivating question to the more general problem of deciding whether a local Hamiltonian has a low-energy groundstate. The details of the reduction from verification of quantum computation to the local Hamiltonian problem can be found in [22] where the standard Feynman-Kitaev *circuit-to-Hamiltonian* reduction is used. As alluded to in some papers such as [10,22], one can obtain ZX[1] Hamiltonians from the Kitaev construction by using a suitable universal gate set[2].

This circuit-to-Hamiltonian reduction is analogous to the *circuit-to-SAT* reduction, the hallmark of the Cook-Levin proof [18,29] of NP-completeness of the SAT problem. The original Feynman-Kitaev reduction goes from decision quantum circuits to *local Hamiltonians* of the following form:

$$H = H_{\text{in}} + H_{\text{out}} + H_{\text{prop}} + H_{\text{clock}}. \tag{1}$$

[1] The Pauli X, Z matrices are $X = \begin{pmatrix} 0 & 1 \\ 1 & 0 \end{pmatrix}, Z = \begin{pmatrix} 1 & 0 \\ 0 & -1 \end{pmatrix}$ and they are used frequently in physics and quantum computation.

[2] Consider, for example, the universal gate set $G = \{H, X, \text{CCNOT}\}$. Note that $H = \frac{1}{\sqrt{2}}(X+Z)$ and $\text{CCNOT} = I - \frac{1}{4}(I-Z_1)(I-Z_2)(I-X_3)$. G is a universal gate set with real matrices and can be used to obtain propagation Hamiltonians whose Pauli decomposition has the real Pauli matrices X and Z.

The purpose of this Hamiltonian is to "detect" any "violation" or deviation from the prescribed circuit. The terms inside each component in this Hamiltonian act as "validators" for the following conditions:

- H_{in} checks that the input is indeed the input that Alice intended to work with,
- H_{out} checks that the output of the decision circuit is 0 (or 1),
- H_{prop} checks that the circuit was computed by honestly going gate-by-gate from the input to the output as intended, and
- H_{clock} checks the encoding of the *clock register*. The clock register "affixes" a timestamp to the system state at each step in the progression of the computation from the input (start time) to the output (end time).

The Hamiltonians of the Feynman-Kitaev construction and inspired extensions thereof are known as *k-local Hamiltonians* because each component of the above $(H_{\text{in}}, H_{\text{out}}, H_{\text{prop}}, H_{\text{clock}})$ is the sum of terms such that each term needs to measure at most k qubits to be able to perform the needed checks. This concept of *locality* is analogous to the *arity* of constraints in *constraint satisfaction problems (CSPs)*.

For the quantum server to convince Alice that it indeed performed the requested computation, it prepares[3] a quantum state known as the *history state* that describes the execution history of such computation. An honest history state should not be marked as a "violator" by the Hamiltonian H corresponding to that computation (this property is known as *completeness*). Additionally, the Hamiltonian H should mark any dishonest state as a violator (this property is known as *soundness*). The measure of such violation is known as the *energy* of a quantum state $|\psi\rangle$ with respect to the Hamiltonian H (written as $\langle\psi| H |\psi\rangle$). The quantum states that have *low energy* (i.e. low violation measure) are called *ground states* of the Hamiltonian. The lowest energy level that such quantum states attain is known as the *ground energy* of the Hamiltonian.

A classical-verifier protocol for the ZX local-Hamiltonian problem has been given in [3] by iterating on a long sequence of works starting by Kitaev in 1999 and culminating in the recent works of [17,22,31,33,34,38]. We modify the protocol to eliminate redundant communication. Then we identify the modified protocol as an instance of an *interactive oracle argument*, a concept that we define by generalizing interactive oracle proofs [9].

Post-quantum interactive oracle arguments - which we define in this paper - are interactive protocols for yes/no promise problems where yes instances are defined by a quantum-witness relation. In this class of protocols, prover messages are modeled as *oracles* that can be query-accessed by the verifier. Our main technical contribution (Informal Theorem 2) shows that interactive oracle arguments with succinct query complexity can be compiled into succinct-communication arguments.

---

[3] It is known how to efficiently prepare such history state for an efficient quantum computation, but we do not include the details here.

Informal Theorem 2 (Informal Statement of Corollary 1). *Any public-coin non-adaptive interactive oracle argument (with setup) with succinct (i.e. at most polylogarithmic) query complexity can be compiled into a succinct-communication argument (with setup) in the quantum random oracle model (QROM).*

Informal Theorem 2 is the bridge that will get us to Informal Theorem 1. However, we need a starting protocol with succinct query complexity to compile using the framework of Informal Theorem 2. We obtain this by modifying [3]'s classical-verifier protocol for the ZX local Hamiltonian problem by eliminating some redundant communication. The modified protocol will have succinct query complexity when the promise gap of the local Hamiltonian is at least inverse-polylogarithmic. The result of compilation using Informal Theorem 2 can be summarized as follows.

Informal Theorem 3. *For any constant k and any relative promise gap that is at least inverse-polylogarithmic, the ZX k-local Hamiltonian problem has a classical-verifier succinct-communication argument system with non-succinct setup in the quantum random oracle model and under the post-quantum hardness assumption of LWE.*

In the quantum realm, *Quantum Merlin Arthur* (QMA) [28] refers to the quantum analogue of the complexity class MA. QMA is the class of languages where a prover, Merlin, can convince a quantum verifier, Arthur, of a true proposition by sending a polynomially-sized quantum witness state (instead of a polynomially-sized classical proof string). However, sending any polynomially-sized quantum witness state trying to convince Arthur about false propositions is doomed to fail. Both cases are within some error probabilities. The local Hamiltonian problem is QMA-complete when the promise gap is inverse-polynomial [26].

Hoping for a quantum analogue of the celebrated classical PCP Theorem [4,5], the quantum PCP conjecture [2] states that the local Hamiltonian problem remains QMA-complete when the promise gap is constant. For Informal Theorem 3 to apply to QMA (and obtain Informal Theorem 1), it suffices that the ZX local Hamiltonian problem be QMA-complete with at least inverse-polylogarithmic gap. We call this condition the *weak ZX quantum PCP conjecture.*

Conjecture 1. *There exists a constant k such that the ZX k-local Hamiltonian problem with a promise gap that is at least inverse-polylogarithmic is* QMA*-complete.*

The qualifier "weak" here is to indicate that it is enough to amplify the gap to be inverse-polylogarithmic. When it is amplified to a constant, we call the conjecture the ZX quantum PCP conjecture.

Conjecture 2. *There exists a constant k such that the ZX k-local Hamiltonian problem with a constant relative promise gap is* QMA*-complete.*

One can see that Conjecture 2 implies Conjecture 1 because a constant promise gap is one that is at least inverse-polylogarithmic. However, the exact relationship between either of these modified conjectures and the standard quantum PCP conjecture is unknown to us and we pose as an open problem.

Open Question 1. *Does the standard quantum PCP conjecture imply the (weak) ZX quantum PCP conjecture?*

We strongly conjecture a positive answer to that question because as mentioned earlier a proper choice of a universal gate set can lead to real Hamiltonians whose Pauli decomposition has the real Pauli matrices X and Z.

1.1 Recent Related Works

Below we discuss the most relevant recent works. In the extended version of this paper [21], we discuss more recent works [7,12,13,40]. While most of the recent works address the motivating problem of succinct verification of quantum computation, our work addresses also the general problem of compiling classical-verifier interactive oracle arguments into succinct arguments in the QROM. The succinct verification of quantum computation is a motivation and application of that compilation framework, but may not be the only application.

- **Succinct classical verification of quantum computation** [6]: Their work achieves succinct arguments for QMA (both succinct communication and succinct verification) in the standard model assuming the post-quantum security of indistinguishability obfuscation (iO) and Learning with Errors (LWE). A key contribution of that work is showing how to replace the non-succinct setup phase of the Mahadev protocol with succinct key generation based on iO. As a result, in the interactive setting, they obtain a 12-message succinct argument for QMA in the standard model, which can be reduced to 8 messages assuming post-quantum FHE; the latter protocol can be made non-interactive in the QROM.
  Our work achieves a 5-message[4] (excluding 1 offline message setup) argument in the QROM with non-succinct instance-independent setup without using FHE, but assuming a variant of the quantum PCP conjecture and LWE.
  Our protocol resembles practical succinct arguments for NP that compile PCPs and are used in real-world applications today. This makes it easier to implement in practice if a constructive proof of the (weak) ZX quantum PCP conjecture is discovered. We expect that the succinct key generation technique in [6] can also be applied to our protocol, which would remove the non-succinct setup at the cost of assuming and using post-quantum iO.
  Furthermore, our work more importantly addresses the general problem of compiling interactive oracle arguments into succinct arguments. The succinct verification of quantum computation is a motivation and application of this compilation framework, but may not be the only application.

[4] We conjecture that it is possible to reduce the number of messages to 3 in our work. More details are provided in the extended version of this paper [21].

- **Quantum-computational soundness of the Kilian transformation:** The soundness of the Kilian transformation from classical probabilistically checkable proofs (PCPs) against quantum polynomial-time cheating devices had been recently formally established in a line of works [14,15]. [15] proved its soundness when the hash function is modeled via the QROM. Later, [14] showed its soundness in the standard model when the hash function family is any *collapsing* (see [37]) hash function family. Families of such functions exist under the LWE assumption [36]. In our work, the input to the Kilian transformation is not a classical PCP, but rather a quantum PCP that was transformed into a classical-verifier interactive oracle protocol using Mahadev's verifiable measurement protocol. [15] proves the soundness of SNARGs based on IOPs with round-by-round soundness in the QROM. However, in our work we do not assume any special soundness properties about the IOArgs except for standard computational soundness.
- **Online extractability in the quantum random oracle model** [19,20]: We make use of the online extractability framework of [20] to prove the online extraction of Merkle trees (see Theorem 1) which is implicit in their follow-up work [19] that appeared while we were working on this paper. We kept the explicit theorem statement needed for our work and proved it in the extended version [21] because the statement in our paper as well as the notation and exposition fit better with the rest of the manuscript.
- **Commitment to quantum states** [25]: [25] announced a construction of quantum Merkle trees from quantum-cryptographic assumptions (implied by one-way functions) in the standard model, and proved that the proposed succinct argument of [12] is secure with this instantiation (against cheating provers). This protocol is public coin and relies on very weak cryptographic assumptions, but requires quantum communication like [12] while our work focuses on classical verifiers with only classical communication.

1.2 Outline

The rest of this paper is organized as follows. Section 2 reviews important background topics and preliminaries. Section 3 introduces the notion of interactive oracle arguments and proves the soundness of the compilation framework which compiles any interactive oracle argument with succinct query complexity into a succinct argument. Section 4 uses the framework of Sect. 3 to build a succinct argument for QMA under Conjecture 1 and the hardness of LWE in the QROM. Section 5 concludes the paper.

Extended Version: In an extended version of this paper [21], we give an exposition of how to build Protocol 1 modularly. There, we generalize the proofs of [3] to work with any constant locality k and any promise gap function γ and provide extended details on all the building blocks of the protocol. We also give a detailed proof of Theorem 1 in the extended version [21].

2 Background and Prior Work

2.1 Mathematical Preliminaries

We recall some of the definitions and facts frequently used later in the paper. Let p and q be two classical probability distributions on a finite sample space Ω. The *total variation distance* between p and q is

$$d_{\mathrm{TV}}(p,q) = \frac{1}{2}\sum_{x\in\Omega}|p(x)-q(x)| = \max_{A\subseteq\Omega}|p(A)-q(A)|.$$

A generalization of the total variation distance is the *trace distance*. To define it, let's first define the *trace norm (Schatten 1-norm)* of a matrix ρ as: $\left\|\rho\right\|_1 = \mathrm{tr}(\sqrt{\rho\rho^\dagger})$. Recall that for a density matrix ρ, it holds that $\rho = \rho^\dagger$. The trace distance between two quantum states represented by their density matrices ρ and σ is:

$$\delta(\rho,\sigma) = \left\|\rho-\sigma\right\|_{\mathrm{tr}} = \frac{1}{2}\left\|\rho-\sigma\right\|_1 = \frac{1}{2}\mathrm{tr}(\sqrt{(\rho-\sigma)^2}) = \max_P \mathrm{tr}(P(\rho-\sigma))$$

where P ranges over projectors. We now state some helpful propositions about the trace distance.

Proposition 1. *The trace distance between two pure quantum states can be bounded as follows:*

$$\delta(|\psi\rangle\langle\psi|, |\phi\rangle\langle\phi|) = \left\||\psi\rangle\langle\psi| - |\phi\rangle\langle\phi|\right\|_{\mathrm{tr}} \leq \left\||\psi\rangle - |\phi\rangle\right\|.$$

The *commutator* of two operators is given by: $[A,B] := AB - BA$. Notice that $[A,B] = -[B,A]$ and that $[A,B]^\dagger = B^\dagger A^\dagger - A^\dagger B^\dagger = [B^\dagger, A^\dagger]$. We say that two operators A, B *commute* if their commutator is 0 i.e. $[A,B] = [B,A] = 0$ and we say that they ϵ*-almost commute* if $\left\|[A,B]\right\| = \left\|[B,A]\right\| \leq \epsilon$. If A, B are two linear operators that ϵ-almost commute, the following proposition tells us that ϵ also bounds the $\|\cdot\|$-distance between an output quantum state resulting from applying A then B on an input state and the output state had we applied B then A instead on the same input.

Proposition 2 (ϵ-almost commutativity). *If A, B are two linear operators that ϵ-almost commute, the following statements hold:*

1. *for a pure quantum state $|\psi\rangle$, it holds that (note that $\left\||\psi\rangle\right\| = 1$):*

$$\left\|AB|\psi\rangle - BA|\psi\rangle\right\| = \left\|[A,B]|\psi\rangle\right\| \leq \left\|[A,B]\right\| \cdot \left\||\psi\rangle\right\| \leq \epsilon. \tag{2}$$

2. *for a (mixed) quantum state represented by the density matrix $\rho = \sum_i p_i |\psi_i\rangle\langle\psi_i|$, it holds that:*

$$\delta(AB\rho B^\dagger A^\dagger, BA\rho A^\dagger B^\dagger) \leq \epsilon. \tag{3}$$

2.2 Merkle Trees

A classical[5] *Merkle tree* [32] of depth d is a binary tree used to commit to a sequence of blocks of data (called *leaves*) $\pi = (\pi_j)_{j \in [2^d]}$ using a cryptographic hash function $h : \mathcal{X} \to \{0,1\}^\lambda$. The *root* of the Merkle tree represents a *digest* of the blocks of the data at its leaves. For a leaf node at index $j \in [2^d]$, its *authentication path* can be used to verify its authenticity with respect to a root rt. Figure 1 illustrates a Merkle tree of depth $d = 3$ to commit to a sequence of leaves $\pi = (\pi_1, \ldots, \pi_8)$.

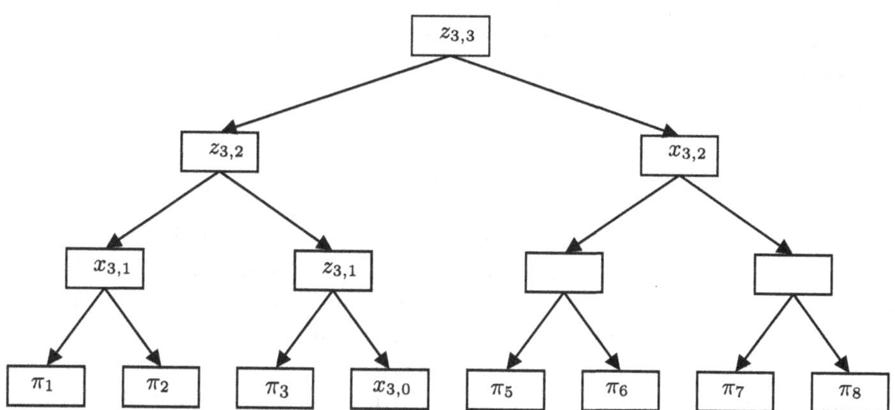

Fig. 1. This figure illustrates a Merkle tree of depth $d = 3$ to commit to $2^3 = 8$ leaves with the root $rt = z_{3,3}$. The intermediate nodes for the authentication path of π_3 are marked with the notation used in this paper. Notice that $z_{3,0} = \pi_3$ and $x_{3,0} = \pi_4$ and $rt = z_{3,3}$ in a valid authentication path.

For notational convenience, let $z_{j,0} = \pi_j$. We will use the notation $h(x, x')$ to indicate applying the hash function to the proper concatenation of x and x' (respecting which is left/right child). Define $h_{j,\ell} := h(x_{j,\ell}, z_{j,\ell-1})$ where $h_{j,0} := \pi_j$. The authentication path consists of the hash values at levels $0 \leq \ell \leq d$ as follows: $\mathsf{ap}_j = (x_{j,\ell}, z_{j,\ell})_{0 \leq \ell \leq d}$. An authentication path ap_j is *valid* if and only if $z_{j,d} = rt$ and $h_{j,\ell} = z_{j,\ell}$ for all $0 \leq \ell \leq d$. Let Q be a set of indices for some leaves. At each level ℓ (from 0 to d), we define the following sequence Z_ℓ which corresponds to the hash values at this level needed to verify all authentication paths: $Z_{Q,\ell} = (z_{j,\ell})_{j \in Q}$. We will use $\widehat{Z_{Q,\ell}}$ to denote the augmented sequence created from $Z_{Q,\ell}$ by ordering these intermediate Merkle tree nodes from left to right and replacing any missing nodes with $\perp$. When Q is clear in the context, we write $Z_{Q,\ell}$ as Z_ℓ and $\widehat{Z_{Q,\ell}}$ as $\widehat{Z_\ell}$ for brevity. Similarly, we define: $X_{Q,\ell} = (x_{j,\ell})_{j \in Q}$

[5] In this paper we will only work with classical Merkle trees where the data are classical strings and the (honest) algorithms are executed on classical devices. However, their security is established against a cheating quantum device in the quantum random oracle model.

and $\widehat{X_{Q,\ell}}$ as well as their shorted notations X_ℓ and $\widehat{X_\ell}$ respectively when Q is clear in the context. The suite of Merkle tree algorithms used in this paper are as follows:

- $\textsc{Commit}^h(\pi_1, \ldots, \pi_{2^d})$: returns the root of the Merkle tree rt and all intermediate nodes,
- $\textsc{Valid}^h(rt, j, \mathsf{ap}_j)$: returns true if and only if the given authentication path ap_j for the j-th leaf is valid against the root rt by using the hash function h,
- $\textsc{Consistent}(Q, \{\mathsf{ap}_j\}_{j \in Q})$: returns true if and only if the authentication paths for leaves at indices $Q \subseteq [2^d]$ are well-formed and *consistent* at the common intermediate nodes[6], and
- $\textsc{Verify}^h(rt, Q, \mathsf{ap}_{j \in Q})$: validates a batch of authentication paths and returns true if and only if both $\textsc{Consistent}(Q, \mathsf{ap}_{j \in Q})$ and $\forall j \in Q$: $\textsc{Valid}^h\left(rt, j, \mathsf{ap}_j\right)$ are true.

2.3 Merkle Trees in the Quantum Random Oracle Model (QROM)

The *random oracle* [8] models a concrete cryptographic hash function $H : \mathcal{X} \to \mathcal{Y}$ as an external random oracle RO that answers queries randomly the first time they are submitted and consistently whenever they are resubmitted. Precisely, the random oracle is a uniformly random function from $\mathcal{X}$ to $\mathcal{Y}$. The quantum random oracle [11] is a unitary oracle $U_H : |x\rangle |y\rangle \mapsto |x\rangle |y \oplus H(x)\rangle$ defined with an underlying uniformly random function H. The query is submitted in the x register and an answer $H(x)$ is returned by XORing such answer with the content of the y register.

Since the introduction of the QROM, different techniques and applications were introduced, most notably the *compressed oracle* technique due to Zhandry [39]. Building on the success of this line of work, [20] introduced a framework for *online extractability* in the quantum random oracle model. Online extraction means that the extraction happens (i) *on-the-fly* during the algorithm's execution, and (ii) in a *straightline* which means that no rewinding of the algorithm calling the random oracle is needed. The framework in [20] encapsulates many of the inner workings that needed to be handled extensively before. Their framework offers an *extractable* random oracle simulator $\mathcal{S}$ which has an internal database state and two query interfaces (which are operators):

1. $\mathcal{S}$.RO-query: the quantum random oracle unitary, and
2. $\mathcal{S}.E$-query: a classical extraction query that applies a measurement to the simulator state.

We will use the following result about the online extraction of Merkle trees which is implicit in a follow-up work by [19], but we also provide a detailed

[6] This is equivalent to sending each overlapping intermediate node once instead of sending it multiple times inside possibly overlapping paths for each leaf. However, for easier notation and exposition, we send the authentication paths for each leaf and require this consistency condition when verifying a batch of authentication paths.

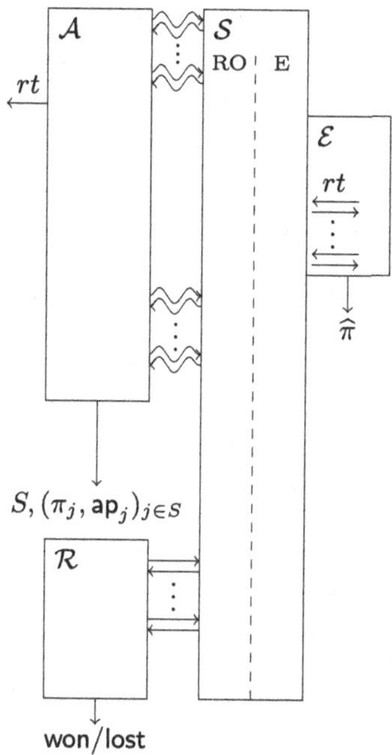

Fig. 2. This figure illustrates the game G_1 referenced in Theorem 1. $\mathcal{A}$ wins if $S \subseteq [2^d]$, $|S| = r$, and $\text{VERIFY}^{\text{RO}}(rt, S, \mathsf{ap}_{j \in S})$, but $\exists j \in S : \pi_j \neq \widehat{\pi}_j$. The "snaked" arrowed lines represent *quantum* queries and responses thereof, while the straight arrowed lines represent *classical* queries and responses thereof. The referee $\mathcal{R}$ consists of two main procedures: (1) verifying the authentication paths which needs to interact with the $\mathcal{S}$.RO interface, and (2) comparing the output of the adversary and the extractor which does not interact with $\mathcal{S}$.

discussion and a proof of it in the extended version of this paper [21] which was written prior to the publication of [19]. The theorem bounds the probability of winning a game $G_1(\lambda, d, r, q)$ illustrated in Fig. 2 where a quantum adversary $\mathcal{A}$ interacts with only the RO interface while a classical honest extraction algorithm $\mathcal{E}$ only (classically) interacts with the E interface of the simulated random oracle. The adversary announces a classical value rt which is *supposedly* the root of a Merkle tree of depth d and they win if they can later *"fake"* at least one of r leaves. Faking a leaf here means giving a leaf value that can be authenticated against the prior commitment, but different from that output by extraction. A referee algorithm $\mathcal{R}$ determines whether the adversary won by validating the authentication paths against the root rt then comparing the adversary's leaves against the leaves given by the extraction algorithm.

Theorem 1. *For the game G_1 defined in Fig. 2 by the universal referee and extractor algorithms described earlier such that $\lambda = \omega(d)$, $q \leq \text{poly}(2^d)$, and any quantum adversary $\mathcal{A} = (\mathcal{A}_1, \mathcal{A}_2)$ where $\mathcal{A}_1$ makes q_1 queries to the random* *oracle, then $\mathcal{A}_1$ announces a value rt, followed by $\mathcal{A}_2$ making q_2 queries to the random oracle such that $q_1 + q_2 \leq q$, then $\mathcal{A}_2$ outputs a classical string, it holds that:*

$$\Pr[\mathcal{A} \text{ wins } G_1(\lambda, d, r, q)] \leq \text{negl}(\lambda).$$

2.4 The Local Hamiltonian Problem

Definition 1 (Local Hamiltonian Problem (n, k, γ)-LH**).** *The k-local Hamiltonian problem notated as (n, k, γ)-LH is a decision promise problem where the input is a classical binary string $x = (H, a, b)$ and the output is (yes/no) deciding whether the input is a yes/no instance under the promise such that:*

- *H is a k-local Hamiltonian $H = \sum_{s=1}^{S} H_s$ on a total of n qubits where $S = \text{poly}(n)$ and each H_s is a Hermitian matrix with a bounded operator norm $||H_s|| \leq 1$ and its entries are specified by $\text{poly}(n)$ bits and H_s is non-identity on at most k qubits,*
- *a and b are two numbers represented with $\text{poly}(n)$ bits such that $a < b$; the gap $\Gamma = b - a$ is called the* ***absolute promise gap*** *and $\gamma = \Gamma/S$ is called the* ***relative promise gap****,*
- *for yes-instances, there exists an n-qubit quantum state $|\psi\rangle$ such that $\langle\psi| H |\psi\rangle \leq a$ (i.e. energy of the state w.r.t. H is at most a),*
- *for no-instances, for every n-qubit quantum state $|\psi\rangle$, it holds that $\langle\psi| H |\psi\rangle \geq b$ (i.e. energy of the state w.r.t. H is at least b), and*
- *it is promised that any instance will be either a yes or no instance.*

This problem is called the ZX k-local Hamiltonian problem and we notate it as (n, k, γ)-LH-ZX when each H_s is a constant-scaled tensor product of n matrices from the set of 2×2 matrices $\{\mathbb{1}, X, Z\}$ such that at most k of the matrices in each product are non-identity.

This problem is QMA-complete when the promise gap is at least inverse polynomial i.e. $\gamma \geq 1/\text{poly}(n)$. The k-LH problem remaining QMA-hard even when this promise gap is constant i.e. $\gamma \geq \alpha$ for some constant α is known as the *quantum PCP conjecture* (qPCP for brevity), which is still unsettled to date. [1] showed that the qPCP statement is equivalent to obtaining PCPs for QMA where quantum reductions[7] are used to prove that the proof verification version implies the gap amplification version.

[7] It is an open question whether they are equivalent under classical reductions. In fact, the proof checking formulation itself could end up being more specific than that provided in [1] which was the reason why it was not straightforward to prove the equivalence under classical reductions. For the details of the quantum reduction, we refer the reader to the proof of Theorem 5.5. in [24].

2.5 Classical-Verifier Argument for ZX Local Hamiltonians

We will now describe Protocol 1 culminated in [3] which is a quantum-prover classical-verifier argument system with an instance-independent setup phase. The protocol can be parallel-repeated to obtain negligible completeness and soundness errors. In the extended version [21] of this paper, we give detailed exposition and proofs of completeness and soundness and explain the modular construction of this protocol while generalizing the locality to any constant k and the promise gap to any function. We give below a summarized description of the protocol.

Protocol 1 [3] uses Mahadev's verifiable measurement protocol [30,31] to make the verifier of a protocol for local Hamiltonian verification [22,33,34] classical instead of quantum. In an earlier version [22,33,34] of Protocol 1, the choice of measurements (X or Z) depended on the choice of the Hamiltonian term. This is because a particular Hamiltonian term may act by X on a qubit while another term could act by Z on the same qubit. This poses a challenge when using Mahadev's verifiable measurement because the first step of Mahadev's protocol samples keys that depend on the basis choice. [3] got around this issue by randomly sampling a basis for each qubit. When the time comes to select a Hamiltonian term, the verifier first checks whether this selected term is consistent with the randomly selected bases on the affected qubits.

In the first round of Protocol 1, the verifier generates a set of private trapdoors and corresponding public keys (a trapdoor/key for each qubit in the witness state) to initiate the Mahadev protocol. The prover then sends a commitment for the witness state - they allegedly have - using the received public keys. The verifier then sends a challenge bit (0/1) that dictates certain measurements to be done by the prover. The prover measures accordingly and sends the measurement outcomes. We have two cases as follows:

1. If the verifier sent 0 as the challenge bit, a Mahadev *"test round"* (TestCheck) is executed whose purpose is making sure that the prover "did not change their mind" after the commitment.
2. If the verifier sent 1 as the challenge bit, a Mahadev *"Hadamard round"* (HadRound) is executed to extract the measurements needed to execute the verification procedure on the Hamiltonian term.

The protocol is executed multiple times in parallel using multiple copies of the witness state.

Protocol 1 (Protocol 4 in [3]; Quantum-Prover Classical-Verifier Argument System for ZX local Hamiltonians with Instance-Independent Setup).

Parties: *Quantum polynomial-time prover $\mathcal{P}$ & classical probabilistic polynomial-time verifier $\mathcal{V}$.*

Parameters: *1. n: number of qubits.*

2. r, m: number of repetitions in the LH verification and Mahadev protocols respectively.

3. λ: a security parameter $\geq n$.

Setup: *1. $\mathcal{V}$ samples uniformly random bases $h \in \{0,1\}^{nrm}$.*
2. $\mathcal{V}$ runs Mahadev's key generation algorithm $(pk, sk) \leftarrow \mathsf{Gen}(1^\lambda, h)$. 3. $\mathcal{V}$ sends the public keys pk to $\mathcal{P}$, but maintains sk secretly[8].

Inputs: ***Inputs to both parties:*** *$x = (H = \sum_{s=1}^{S} d_s H_s, a, b)$ i.e. instance of the (n, k, γ)-LH-ZX.*
Input to honest prover on yes instances: *$|\Psi\rangle = |\psi\rangle^{\otimes rm}$ (i.e. rm copies of $|\psi\rangle$ the ground state of the Hamiltonian H). This state is in the register W. For each $i \in [m], \ell \in [r], j \in [n]$, we use $W_{i\ell j}$ to denote the corresponding qubit.*

Round $\mathcal{P}_1$: *For each $W_{i\ell j}$, the prover prepares the "commitment" state (see the extended version [21] for the details; we use here F to denote f or g depending on the uniformly chosen basis):*

$$\frac{1}{\sqrt{|\mathcal{X}|}} \sum_{x \in \mathcal{X}} \sum_{b \in \{0,1\}} \phi_b |b\rangle_{W_{i\ell j}} |x\rangle_{X_{i\ell j}} |F_{pk_{i\ell j}}(b, x)\rangle_{Y_{i\ell j}}.$$

$\mathcal{P}$ measures each register $Y_{i\ell j}$ in the standard basis & sends the outcomes $y = (y_{i\ell j})$ to $\mathcal{V}$.

Round $\mathcal{V}_2$: *$\mathcal{V}$ samples challenge bits $c_1, \ldots, c_m \leftarrow \{0,1\}$ and sends $c = (c_1, \ldots, c_m)$ to $\mathcal{P}$. 0 or 1 means asking the prover to engage in test or Hadamard rounds (respectively) of the Mahadev protocol.*

Round $\mathcal{P}_2$: *For each $i \in [m], \ell \in [r], j \in [n]$,*
1. *If $c_i = 0$, $\mathcal{P}$ performs a standard basis measurement and gets $u_{i\ell j} = (w_{i\ell j}, x_{i\ell j})$.*
2. *If $c_i = 1$, $\mathcal{P}$ performs a Hadamard basis measurement and gets $u_{i\ell j} = (w_{i\ell j}, x_{i\ell j})$.*

$\mathcal{P}$ sends $u = (u_{i\ell j})$ to $\mathcal{V}$.

$\mathcal{V}$'s Verdict: *For each $i \in [m]$,*
1. *If $c_i = 0$, $\mathcal{V}$ sets $v_i := \bigwedge_{\ell, j} \mathsf{TestCheck}(sk_{i\ell j}, u_{i\ell j}, y_{i\ell j})$.*
2. *If $c_i = 1$, $\mathcal{V}$ records the set $A_i \subseteq [r]$ (the subset of copies consistent with the random bases choice). For each $\ell \in A_i$:*
   (a) *Run the Hadamard round for each $j \in [n]$:*

   $$(z_{i\ell j}, e_{i\ell j}) := \mathsf{HadRound}(sk_{i\ell j}, u_{i\ell j}, y_{i\ell j}, h_{i\ell j}).$$

   If it rejects (i.e. $z_{i\ell j} = 0$ for some j), set $v_{i\ell} = 0$; otherwise enter the next step.
   (b) *Sample a Hamiltonian term $s_{i\ell} \leftarrow \pi$ where the distribution π is given by:*

   $$\pi(s) = \frac{|d_s|}{\sum_s |d_s|}.$$

[8] Later, we will use the term "public-coin protocols with private setup" to highlight this again.

Denote by $\mathcal{S}(i,\ell)$ the set of indices of the qubits acted upon by non-identity Pauli observables.

Set $v_{i\ell} := \frac{1}{2}\left(1 - \mathrm{SGN}(d_{s_{i\ell}}) \cdot \prod_{j\in\mathcal{S}(i,\ell)} e_{i\ell j}\right)$ (i.e. set to 1 iff the measurement has the opposite sign of the coefficient of the selected term).

Then, $\mathcal{V}$ sets $v_i = 1$ iff:

$$\sum_{\ell\in A_i} v_{i\ell} \geq \frac{(c+s)}{2} \cdot |A_i| = \frac{\left(2 - (b-a)/\sum_s |d_s|\right)}{4} \cdot |A_i|$$

where[9]*:*

$$c := \frac{1}{2} - \frac{a}{2\sum_s |d_s|} \quad \text{and} \quad s := \frac{1}{2} - \frac{b}{2\sum_s |d_s|}.$$

Finally, $\mathcal{V}$ accepts iff $v := \bigwedge_{i=1}^{m} v_i$ evaluates to 1 (i.e. v_i is 1 for each parallel repetition $i \in [m]$).

3 Succinct Communication from Interactive Oracle Arguments

3.1 Defining Interactive Oracle Arguments

We now formalize the notion of *quantum-computationally sound classical-verifier interactive oracle proofs* for quantum-witness relations (which for brevity we also call IOArgs for *interactive oracle arguments*) by generalizing interactive oracle proofs (IOPs) in [9]. In particular, we introduce IOArgs with a pre-processing (setup) phase where the verifier sends a message to the prover that does not depend on the input instance but only on an upper bound on the instance size n. Since this step does not need the input and can happen temporally before the execution of the protocol on a particular input, we do not account for its cost when analyzing succinctness of the protocol's communication.

Definition 2 (Interactive Oracle Arguments with Setup; Generalizing Interactive Oracle Proofs in [9]). *Let $p(n)$ be a polynomial and $\mathcal{R}$ be a relation: $\mathcal{R} \subseteq \bigcup_{n=0}^{\infty} \{0,1\}^n \times \mathcal{H}_{p(n)}$ where $\mathcal{H}_{p(n)}$ is the Hilbert space of $p(n)$-qubit pure quantum states. Consider a promise problem $A = (A_{yes}, A_{no})$ where $A_{yes} \cap A_{no} = \emptyset$ and $A_{yes} := \{x \mid \exists |\psi\rangle : (x, |\psi\rangle) \in \mathcal{R}\}$. We say that A has a quantum-computationally sound classical-verifier interactive oracle proof system with setup with the following parameters (notated as $A \in \mathrm{IOARG}_{c,s}[t(n), \ell(n), r(n), q(n)]$):*

- *round complexity $t(n)$: number of prover oracle messages in the protocol,*

[9] Please refer to the extended version of this paper [21] for full details on the choice of these thresholds as well as the Test and Hadamard round of the Mahadev protocol.

- *total length of all prover messages:* $\ell(n)$,
- *randomness complexity* $r(n)$*: total number of random bits used by the verifier,*
- *query complexity* $q(n)$*: number of queries by the verifier to the prover's oracle messages,*
- *completeness* $c(n)$*, and soundness* $s(n)$

if there is an interactive protocol between:

Parties: *1.* $\mathcal{P}^{|\psi\rangle}$*: a quantum* poly$(n)$*-time algorithm (when the input* x *is a yes instance, an honest prover will receive a state* $|\psi\rangle$ *such that* $(x, |\psi\rangle) \in \mathcal{R}$*), and*
2. $\mathcal{V} = (\mathcal{V}_0, \ldots, \mathcal{V}_{t(n)})$*: a classical probabilistic* poly(n)*-time algorithm using* $r(n)$ *random bits. The verifier's sub-algorithm* $\mathcal{V}_0 = \text{SETUP}(1^n)$ *is an optional setup phase that only depends on the input length*[10] *but not the input itself while the other sub-algorithms* $\mathcal{V}_1, \ldots, \mathcal{V}_{t(n)}$ *depend on the input* x*.*

Setup: *The protocol starts with an optional setup phase run by the verifier* $(p_0, v_0) \leftarrow \text{SETUP}(1^n)$*. The verifier sends* p_0 *to the prover and* ***keeps***[11] v_0*.*

Interaction: *For any round* $i \in [t(n)]$*, the following interaction takes place:*

1. *The prover sends an oracle message* $p_i = \mathcal{P}(x, p_0, p_1, \ldots, p_{i-1}, v_1, \ldots, v_{i-1})$*.*
2. *If* $i < t(n)$*, the verifier samples randomness* $\$_i$ *and outputs a message* $v_i = \mathcal{V}(x, v_0, v_1, \ldots v_{i-1}; \$_i)$*.*

Verdict: *At the end of the protocol, the verifier samples randomness* $\$_{t(n)}$ *and chooses* $q(n)$ *locations* $Q = (Q_1, \ldots, Q_{t(n)})$ *to access from previous prover oracle messages* $p_1, \ldots, p_k$*. Finally, the verifier runs a predicate*

$$\text{VERDICT}(x, p_{1|Q_1}, \ldots, p_{t(n)|Q_{t(n)}}, v_0, v_1, \ldots, v_{t(n)-1}; \$_{t(n)})$$

to output a decision (accept/reject).

Completeness: *If* x *is a yes-instance, with* $|x| = n$*, then for an honest prover* $\mathcal{P}$ *receiving a quantum state* $|\psi\rangle$ *such that* $(x, |\psi\rangle) \in \mathcal{R}$*:* $\Pr[\langle \mathcal{P}, \mathcal{V}\rangle \text{ accepts } x] \geq c(n)$*.*

Soundness: *If* x *is a no-instance, with* $|x| = n$*, then for any quantum polynomial-time interactive algorithm* $\widetilde{\mathcal{P}}$*:* $\Pr[\langle \widetilde{\mathcal{P}}, \mathcal{V}\rangle \text{ accepts } x] \leq s(n)$*.*

We say that an IOArg is ***public-coin with private setup*** *if the verifier sends the randomness they generate to the prover*[12] *(except for the randomness used in the setup step). In our definition, the queries of the IOArg are* ***non-adaptive*** *in the sense that one query does not depend on the answer to another. In this paper, we work with non-adaptive public-coin IOArgs with private setup.*

---

10 In most useful interactive oracle arguments including the argument system for the local Hamiltonian problem discussed in this paper, we do not have to know the input length exactly, but it suffices to know an upper bound.

11 Keeping the randomness used in the setup enables the verifier to store information such as secret keys and/or trapdoors without revealing them to the prover.

12 or its oracle messages.

3.2 Succinct Communication by Applying the Kilian Transformation

We now show how to apply the standard Kilian transformation [27] to compile any non-adaptive public-coin IOArg with private setup and succinct query complexity into a succinct-communication argument. To prove the soundness of the compiled protocol, we will use the online extraction of Merkle trees in the quantum random oracle model formalized earlier in Theorem 1.

Protocol 2 (Succinct-communication argument from non-adaptive public-coin IOArg with private setup and succinct query complexity).

Model: RO : $\mathcal{X} \to \{0,1\}^\lambda$ *is a quantum random oracle which could be called in superposition.*

Promise Problem: $A \in \text{IOARG}_{c,s}[t(n), \ell(n), r(n), q(n)]$ *with an underlying relation* $\mathcal{R}$ *where* $q(n) = \widetilde{O}(\lambda)$.

Parties: *Quantum poly-time prover* $\mathcal{P}$ *& classical probabilistic poly-time verifier* $\mathcal{V}$.

Setup: *The verifier runs* $(p_0, v_0) \leftarrow \text{SETUP}(1^n)$ *from the underlying IOArg, keeps* v_0*, and sends* p_0 *to the prover.*

Inputs: ***To both parties:*** x *where* $|x| = n$ *&* x *is a yes/no instance of the promise problem* A.

To the prover: *The setup message* p_0 *received during the setup. An honest prover will also receive a state* $|\psi\rangle$ *on yes-instances* x *such that* $(x, |\psi\rangle) \in \mathcal{R}$.

Round $\mathcal{P}_i$: *The prover computes the message* p_i *according to the underlying IOArg. The prover then uses* $\text{COMMIT}^{\text{RO}}$ *to compute a Merkle tree root* rt_i *for the message* p_i *and sends* rt_i *to the verifier.*

Round $\mathcal{V}_i$: *If* $i < t(n)$*: according to the underlying IOArg the verifier samples randomness* $\$_i$ *and sends the message* v_i.

If $i = t(n)$*: According to the underlying IOArg, the verifier samples randomness* $\$_{t(n)}$ *and determines the* $q(n)$ *locations* $Q = (Q_1, \ldots, Q_{t(n)})$ *to access from the previous prover oracle messages* $p_1, \ldots, p_{t(n)}$ *that were supposedly committed with the roots* $rt_1, \ldots, rt_{t(n)}$ *respectively. The verifier sends these indices* Q *to the prover.*

Round $\mathcal{P}_{t+1}$: *The prover sends the* $q(n)$ *bits at locations* Q *along with authentication paths to the verifier i.e. they send the sequence* $\left((\pi_{i,j}, \mathsf{ap}_{i,j})_{j \in Q_i}\right)_{1 \le i \le t(n)}$ *where* $\mathsf{ap}_{i,j}$ *means the authentication path of the* j*th location with respect to the root* rt_i *of the* i*th Merkle tree.*

Verdict: *For each* $i = 1 \ldots t(n)$*, the verifier verifies the authentication paths with access to the random oracle* RO *and using the predicate* VERIFY *defined in Sect. 2.2. Precisely, in the* i*th iteration, the verifier performs this verification by calling* $\text{VERIFY}^{\text{RO}}\left(rt_i, Q_i, (\mathsf{ap}_{i,j})_{j \in Q_i}\right)$. *It rejects if this predicate rejects. Otherwise, the verifier outputs the output of:*

$$\text{VERDICT}(x, \pi_{1|Q_1}, \ldots, \pi_{t|Q_t}, v_0, v_1, \ldots, v_{t-1}; \$_{t(n)})$$

where VERDICT *is the verdict predicate of the underlying IOArg and* $\pi_{i|Q_i}$ *are the locations received from the prover during the round* $\mathcal{P}_{t(n)+1}$.

3.3 Completeness of Protocol 2

Theorem 2 (Completeness of Protocol 2). *For a promise problem $A \in \text{IOARG}_{c,s}[t(n), \ell(n), r(n), q(n)]$ such that $c(n)$ is the completeness of the IOArg, Protocol 2 built on that IOArg also has completeness $c(n)$.*

Proof. This follows by the idempotence property of the RO interface (see Theorem 4.3. in [20] or the extended version [21] of our paper). When the verifier $\mathcal{V}$ of Protocol 2 makes the queries to the random oracle to verify the authentication paths, they will be consistent with the classical queries that the honest prover made while generating the Merkle tree commitments. Let x be a yes instance, and $|\psi\rangle$ be the quantum state given to the honest prover $\mathcal{P}$. For brevity, let $\pi_{|Q} = (\pi_{1|Q_1}, \ldots, \pi_{t|Q_t})$ be the locations sent by $\mathcal{P}$ and $V_{\text{IOARG}}^{\pi_{|Q}}(x)$ denote the output of the IOArg verifier for the same randomness choices of $\mathcal{V}$. Then, we can compute the acceptance probability as follows:

$$\begin{aligned}
\Pr[\langle \mathcal{P}, \mathcal{V}\rangle \text{ accepts } x] &= \Pr_{\pi_{|Q} \leftarrow \mathcal{P}|\psi\rangle}[V_{\text{IOARG}}^{\pi_{|Q}}(x) \text{ accepts and } \forall i \leq t \ \text{VERIFY}^{\text{RO}}(rt_i, Q_i, (\mathsf{ap}_{i,j})_{j \in Q_i})] \\
&= \Pr_{\pi_{|Q} \leftarrow \mathcal{P}|\psi\rangle}[V_{\text{IOARG}}^{\pi_{|Q}}(x) \text{ accepts }] \qquad \text{by idempotence} \\
&= \Pr[\langle \mathcal{P}_{\text{IOARG}}^{|\psi\rangle}, \mathcal{V}_{\text{IOARG}}\rangle \text{ accepts } x].
\end{aligned}$$

□

3.4 Soundness of Protocol 2

Theorem 3 (Computational Soundness of Protocol 2). *Consider a promise problem A with an interactive oracle argument i.e. $A \in \text{IOARG}_{c,s}[t(n), \ell(n), r(n), q(n)]$. Let Protocol 2 be built on top of this IOArg in the quantum random oracle model with $\lambda = \omega(\log(\ell(n)))$. Let x be an instance of A with $n = |x|$. If a (possibly cheating) quantum prover $\mathcal{P}$ running in polynomial time $T_{\mathcal{P}}(n) = \text{poly}(n)$ and access to RO can make an honest verifier $\mathcal{V}$ in such protocol accept x with probability $\geq \delta(n)$, then there exists a polynomial-time (quantum) IOArg prover $\widetilde{P}_{\text{IOARG}}(x)$ that can make an honest IOArg verifier accept x with probability $\geq \delta(n) - \text{negl}(\lambda)$.*

Proof of Theorem 3. Consider a quantum polynomial-time prover $\mathcal{P}$ in Protocol 2 running in $T_{\mathcal{P}}(n)$ time that makes the honest verifier $\mathcal{V}$ accept on an instance x with probability $\geq \delta(n)$ where $n = |x|$. According to the protocol description, this prover $\mathcal{P}$ can be decomposed into the quantum channels $(\mathcal{P}_1, \ldots, \mathcal{P}_k, \mathcal{P}_{k+1})$ where $\mathcal{P}_i$ makes h_i queries to RO such that $\sum_{1 \leq i \leq t(n)+1} h_i \leq T_{\mathcal{P}}(n)$. Furthermore, notice that the honest verifier can be decomposed into the classical algorithms $(\mathcal{V}_1, \ldots, \mathcal{V}_{t(n)}, \mathcal{V}_{\mathcal{R}}, \mathcal{V}_{\text{IOARG}})$ such that:

- $\mathcal{V}_i$ is basically a relay interface connected to the incoming messages from the IOArg verifier $\widetilde{\mathcal{V}}$ (in particular $\mathcal{V}_{t(n)}$ is where the verifier sends the challenged locations),

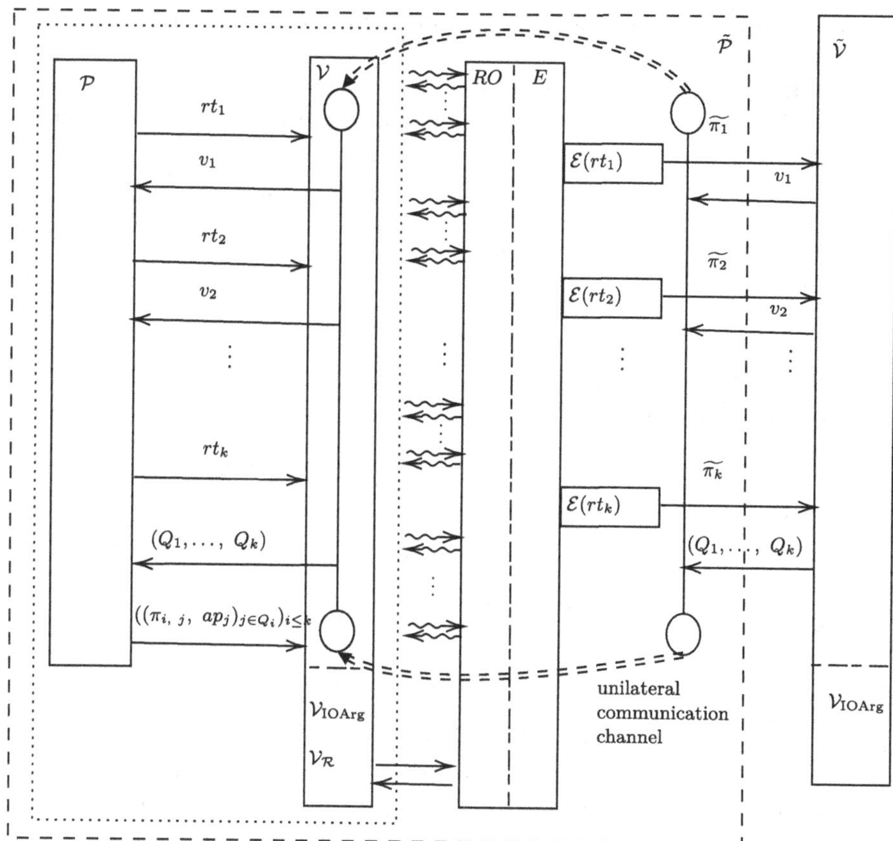

Fig. 3. This figure illustrates the reduction from the succinct argument interaction $\langle \mathcal{P}, \mathcal{V} \rangle$ to a polynomial-time IOArg prover $\widetilde{\mathcal{P}}$ interacting with the honest IOArg verifier $\widetilde{\mathcal{V}}$. The prover is split into two parts: one that interacts with the E interface and one that interacts with the RO interface. Communication goes unilaterally from the former to the latter. The unilateral communication is indicated by a line with two circles at its ends. This IOArg prover can make the IOArg verifier accept the instance x with probability $\geq \delta(n) - \text{negl}(\lambda)$.

- $\mathcal{V}_{\mathcal{R}}$ is the predicate that verifies the authentication paths of the claimed nodes, and
- $\mathcal{V}_{\text{IOArg}}$ is the verdict algorithm of the underlying IOArg.

As illustrated in Fig. 3, we construct a (quantum) polynomial-time IOArg prover $\widetilde{\mathcal{P}}$ (in the quantum random oracle). This prover is a quantum polynomial-time interactive algorithm described by the following sequence of sub-algorithms: $\widetilde{\mathcal{P}} = \left(\widetilde{\mathcal{P}}_1, \ldots, \widetilde{\mathcal{P}}_{t(n)}\right)$. Each $\widetilde{\mathcal{P}}_i$ performs the following in order:

1. it executes $\mathcal{P}_i$ which is the corresponding action of the prover $\mathcal{P}$ in the ith round, then
2. it calls the extractor $\mathcal{E}$ with access to the $\mathcal{S}$.E interface of the simulated oracle. It will then send the extracted string $\widetilde{\pi}_i$ to the verifier $\widetilde{\mathcal{V}}$ in the form of an oracle message.

Given the description of the constructed prover $\widetilde{\mathcal{P}}$, we bound $\eta := \Pr_{\substack{rt_i \leftarrow \mathcal{P}_i(x) \\ \widetilde{\pi}_i \leftarrow \mathcal{E}(rt_i) \\ \$ \xleftarrow{\$} \{0,1\}^{r(n)}}} [\langle \mathcal{P}, \mathcal{V} \rangle \text{ accepts } x]$

$$\begin{aligned}
\eta &= \Pr[\langle \mathcal{P}, \mathcal{V} \rangle \text{ accepts } x \text{ and } \forall i \, \pi_{i|Q_i} = \widetilde{\pi}_{i|Q_i}] \\
&\quad + \Pr[\langle \mathcal{P}, \mathcal{V} \rangle \text{ accepts } x \text{ and } \exists i \, \pi_{i|Q_i} \neq \widetilde{\pi}_{|Q_i}] \qquad \text{(law of total probability)} \\
&= \Pr[\mathcal{V}^{\pi|Q}_{\text{IOARG}}(x) \text{ accepts, } \mathcal{V}_{\mathcal{R}} \text{ accepts, and } \forall i \, \pi_{i|Q_i} = \widetilde{\pi}_{i|Q_i}] \\
&\quad + \Pr[\mathcal{V}^{\pi|Q}_{\text{IOARG}}(x) \text{ accepts, } \mathcal{V}_{\mathcal{R}} \text{ accepts, and } \exists i \, \pi_{i|Q_i} \neq \widetilde{\pi}_{i|Q_i}] \\
&\leq \Pr[\mathcal{V}^{\widetilde{\pi}|Q}_{\text{IOARG}}(x) \text{ accepts }] + \Pr[\mathcal{V}_{\mathcal{R}} \text{ accepts and } \exists i \, \pi_{i|Q_i} \neq \widetilde{\pi}_{i|Q_i}].
\end{aligned}$$

If $\Pr[\mathcal{V}_{\mathcal{R}}$ accepts and $\exists i \, \pi_{i|Q_i} \neq \widetilde{\pi}_{i|Q_i}] \leq \text{negl}(\lambda)$, we can conclude that:

$$\Pr[\mathcal{V}^{\widetilde{\pi}|Q}_{\text{IOARG}}(x) \text{ accepts }] \geq \Pr[\langle \mathcal{P}, \mathcal{V} \rangle \text{ accepts } x] - \text{negl}(\lambda) \geq \delta(n) - \text{negl}(\lambda). \quad (4)$$

Now, it remains to show that $\Pr[\mathcal{V}_{\mathcal{R}}$ accepts and $\exists i \, \pi_{|Q_i} \neq \widetilde{\pi}_{|Q_i}] \leq \text{negl}(\lambda)$ which we will prove by applying Theorem 1. To do that, we notice that for each round i, we can build an adversary $\mathcal{A}^{(i)} = (\mathcal{A}_1^{(i)}, \mathcal{A}_2^{(i)})$ where $\mathcal{A}_1^{(i)} = (\mathcal{P}_1, \mathcal{V}_1, \ldots, \mathcal{P}_{i-1}, \mathcal{V}_{i-1}, \mathcal{P}_i)$ and $\mathcal{A}_2^{(i)} = (\mathcal{V}_i, \mathcal{P}_{i+1}, \mathcal{V}_{i+1}, \ldots, \mathcal{P}_{t(n)})$ that already matches the syntax of an adversary for game $G_1\,(\lambda(n), \log(\ell_i(n)), q_i(n), h(n))$ with the game parameters properly set via the parameters of the underlying IOArg (Definition 2). Indeed, we have $h(n) \leq \text{poly}(\ell_i(n))$ since $h(n) = \text{poly}(n)$ and $\ell_i(n) \leq \text{poly}(n)$. We also have $q_i(n) \leq \ell_i(n)$. Therefore, for any adversary $\mathcal{A}$ making at most $h(n)$ queries, we have:

$$\Pr[\mathcal{A} \text{ wins } G_1] \leq \text{negl}(\lambda). \quad (5)$$

Let $\mathcal{I}$ be the final state at the end of the interaction in Fig. 3. Let $\mathcal{I}'$ be obtained by moving the extractors $\mathcal{E}(rt_1), \ldots, \mathcal{E}(rt_{i-1})$ past the extractor $\mathcal{E}(rt_i)$ while preserving their order. Notice that all the queries made to RO are independent of these E calls. Also, each of these extractors' chain of E-queries is independent of the queries of $\mathcal{E}(rt_i)$. Also, notice that because we are working with non-adaptive IOArgs in this paper, the behavior of $\widetilde{\mathcal{V}}$ does not depend on these calls. There are $i - 1 \leq t(n)$ extractors that we will move past at most $h(n)$ queries. Each jth extractor makes $\ell_j(n) - 1 \leq \ell(n)$ queries. Therefore, we conclude by Property (2c) of Theorem 4.3 in [20] that:

$$\delta(\mathcal{I}, \mathcal{I}') \leq h(n) \cdot t(n) \cdot \ell(n) \cdot 8 \cdot \sqrt{2^{1-\lambda}}. \quad (6)$$

Therefore, we have:

$$\begin{aligned}
&\Pr[\mathcal{V}_{\mathcal{R}} \text{ accepts, and } \exists i\, \pi_{iQ_i} \neq \widetilde{\pi}_{iQ_i} \text{ in interaction } \mathcal{I}] \\
&\leq \Pr[\mathcal{V}_{\mathcal{R}} \text{ accepts, and } \exists i\, \pi_{iQ_i} \neq \widetilde{\pi}_{iQ_i} \text{ in interaction } \mathcal{I}'] + \delta(\mathcal{I}, \mathcal{I}') \\
&\leq \Pr[\mathcal{A} \text{ wins } G_1\,(\lambda(n), \log(\ell_i(n)), q_i(n), h(n))] + 8 \cdot t(n) \cdot h(n) \cdot \ell(n)\sqrt{2^{1-\lambda}} && \text{Inequality (6)} \\
&\leq \mathrm{negl}(\lambda) + \mathrm{poly}(\ell(n))\sqrt{2^{1-\lambda}} && \text{Theorem 1} \\
&\leq \mathrm{negl}(\lambda) && \text{since } \lambda = \omega(\log(\ell(n))).
\end{aligned}$$

Finally, we need to verify that $\widetilde{\mathcal{P}}$ runs in $\mathrm{poly}(n)$ time as long as the underlying argument prover $\mathcal{P}$ runs in polynomial time. This is true because each of $\mathcal{P}_i$, $\mathcal{E}(rt_i)$, $\mathcal{V}_i$ run in polynomial time. Furthermore, by Theorem 4.3 in [20] the simulator $\mathcal{S}$ runs in time $T_{\mathcal{S}} = O\left(q_{\mathrm{RO}} \cdot q_E + q_{\mathrm{RO}}^2\right)$ where q_E and q_{RO} are the number of queries to $\mathcal{S}$.RO and $\mathcal{S}.E$ respectively. The number of queries for either type is at most $\mathrm{poly}(n)$ because they are made by the underlying polynomial time algorithms. □

3.5 Communication Complexity of Protocol 2

We analyze Protocol 2's communication complexity (excluding the setup message) provided that the underlying IOArg is parameterized as $\mathrm{IOA{\small RG}}_{c,s}[t(n), \ell(n), r(n), q(n)]$. In the ith round, the prover sends a Merkle tree root which is in the range of the random oracle and therefore has length λ. The verifier sends then the message v_i which has $r_i(n)$ bits. For $t(n)$ rounds, a total of $\lambda \cdot t(n) + r(n)$ is sent so far by both the prover and verifier excluding the setup. The verifier at the end sends the $q(n)$ locations needed where each location is expressed by $\log(\ell(n))$ where $\log(\ell(n)) = O(\log(n))$ because $\ell(n) \leq \mathrm{poly}(n)$. This means that a total of $O(q(n) \cdot \log(n))$ bits are sent by the verifier for this purpose. Finally, the prover sends the requested leaves and their authentication paths. Each authentication path is represented by $O(\log(\ell(n)) \cdot \lambda) = O(\log(n) \cdot \lambda)$ bits. Therefore, the prover sends a total of $O(q(n) \cdot \log(n) \cdot \lambda)$ bits in this round. Therefore, the total communication cost in this protocol is $O\left(\lambda \cdot (t(n) + q(n) \cdot \log(n)) + r(n)\right)$ classical bits. The resulting protocol is succinct when $q(n) = O(\mathrm{poly}(\log(n))) = \tilde{O}(1)$, $r(n) = \tilde{O}(1)$, $t(n) = \tilde{O}(1)$, and $\ell(n) = \mathrm{poly}(n)$. We can now summarize the results of this section in the following corollary.

Corollary 1 (Succinct-Communication Arguments from IOArgs). *In the quantum random oracle model with* $\mathrm{RO} : \mathcal{X} \to \{0,1\}^\lambda$ *and* $\lambda = \omega(\log(n))$*: Protocol 2 built for a promise problem* $A \in \mathrm{IOA{\small RG}}_{c,s}[\widetilde{O}(1), \mathrm{poly}(n), \widetilde{O}(1), \widetilde{O}(1)]$ *is a succinct-communication argument with (possibly non-succinct) setup with completeness* c *and soundness* $s - \mathrm{negl}(\lambda)$.

4 Classical-Verifier Succinct-Communication Argument for ZX Local Hamiltonians

4.1 Eliminating Redundancy in [3]'s Classical-Verifier Argument

Protocol 3 is a modified version of Protocol 1. When executing the Mahadev verifiable measurement test/Hadamard rounds in the protocol, we only verify the measurements for the qubits that would have been necessary to run the LH verification. Precisely, the difference here is that - even in Mahadev's test round - the index j ranges over the set $\mathcal{S}(i,\ell)$ which is the set of qubit indices affected by non-identity observables in the Hamiltonian term $s_{i\ell}$ instead of ranging over $[n]$ (i.e. all qubits).

Protocol 3 (Modified version of Protocol 1 after eliminating redundancy).

Parties, Inputs, Setup: *Same as in Protocol 1.*
Rounds $\mathcal{P}_1, \mathcal{V}_2, \mathcal{P}_2$: *Same as in Protocol 1.*
$\mathcal{V}$**'s Verdict** *For each* $i \in [m], \ell \in [r]$: $\mathcal{V}$ *samples a Hamiltonian term* $s_{i\ell} \leftarrow \pi$ *where the distribution* π *is given by:*

$$\pi(s) = \frac{|d_s|}{\sum_s |d_s|}.$$

Denote by $\mathcal{S}(i,\ell)$ *the set of indices of the qubits acted upon by non-identity Pauli observables.*

Also, let $A_i \subseteq [r]$ *be the subset of copies consistent with the random bases choice.*

For each $i \in [m]$*:*

1. *If* $c_i = 0$ *(test round), set* $v_i := \bigwedge_{\ell \in A_i,\ j \in \mathcal{S}(i,\ell)} \mathsf{TestCheck}(sk_{i\ell j}, u_{i\ell j}, y_{i\ell j})$.
2. *If* $c_i = 1$ *(Hadamard round), for each* $\ell \in A_i$*:*
   (a) *Run the Hadamard round for each* $j \in \mathcal{S}(i,\ell)$*:*

$$(z_{i\ell j}, e_{i\ell j}) := \mathsf{HadRound}(sk_{i\ell j}, u_{i\ell j}, y_{i\ell j}, h_{i\ell j}).$$

   If it rejects (i.e. $z_{i\ell j} = 0$ *for some* j*), set* $v_{i\ell} = 0$*; otherwise enter the next step.*
   (b) *Set* $v_{i\ell} := \frac{1}{2}\left(1 - \mathrm{SGN}(d_{s_{i\ell}}) \cdot \prod_{j \in \mathcal{S}(i,\ell)} e_{i\ell j}\right)$ *(i.e. set to 1 iff the measurement has the opposite sign of the coefficient of the selected term).*

Then, as in Protocol 1: $\mathcal{V}$ *sets* $v_i = 1$ *iff:*

$$\sum_{\ell \in A_i} v_{i\ell} \geq \frac{(c+s)}{2} \cdot |A_i| = \frac{\left(2 - (b-a)/\sum_s |d_s|\right)}{4} \cdot |A_i|$$

where:

$$c := \frac{1}{2} - \frac{a}{2\sum_s |d_s|} \quad \text{and} \quad s := \frac{1}{2} - \frac{b}{2\sum_s |d_s|}.$$

Finally, as in Protocol 1, $\mathcal{V}$ accepts iff $v := \bigwedge_{i=1}^{m} v_i$ evaluates to 1 (i.e. v_i is 1 for each parallel repetition $i \in [m]$).

In the extended version of this paper [21], we follow [3]'s proof of the soundness of Protocol 1 to show how the soundness of this modified protocol still holds even when we only verify the Mahadev measurements for the qubits affected by the selected local Hamiltonian term. We outline a corollary to that result below.

Corollary 2 (Mirror of Theorem 4.6. in [3]). *Under the LWE assumption, for every constant k, Protocol 3 with $r = \omega(\frac{\log(n)}{\gamma^2})$ and $m = \omega(\log(n))$ has negligible completeness and soundness errors.*

4.2 Compiling Towards Succinct Communication

Since only a number of selected locations are read from each prover message, we can rewrite Protocol 3 as an IOArg by modeling the prover messages as message oracles instead of message strings. As a result, we get Protocol 4 which is a two-round public-coin non-adaptive interactive oracle argument with a private setup. Specifically, the verifier's choices with the exception of key-generation - which happens in setup - are revealed to the prover (or its message oracles). Note that the setup phase is non-succinct because the verifier needs to send a key for each qubit. The verifier sends a total of m (the number of parallel repetitions of the Mahadev protocol) classical bits in the first round. The verifier needs to query $k \cdot r \cdot m$ locations from each prover oracle. Corollary 2 still directly applies to this protocol because it is exactly the same as Protocol 3 from the point of view of both the prover and verifier. When γ is at least inverse polylogarithmic, one can take $r = \omega(\log n/\gamma^2)$ to obtain negligible completeness and soundness errors in Protocol 4 as well as polylogarithmic query complexity. We can then apply Corollary 1 to conclude with Corollary 3.

Protocol 4 (Interactive Oracle Argument with Preprocessing for ZX Local Hamiltonians).
Parties, Inputs, Setup: *Same as in Protocol 3.*

Round $\mathcal{P}_1$: *$\mathcal{P}$ follows the steps of Protocol 3 (as described in Protocol 1) and sends an oracle $\mathcal{O}_y$ that represents the measurement outcomes on the commitment qubits.*
Round $\mathcal{V}_1$: *$\mathcal{V}$ samples $c_1, \ldots, c_m \leftarrow \{0, 1\}$ and sends $c = (c_1, \ldots, c_m)$ to $\mathcal{P}$.*
Round $\mathcal{P}_2$: *$\mathcal{P}$ follows the steps of Protocol 3 and sends an oracle $\mathcal{O}_u$ to $\mathcal{V}$ that represents the measurement outcomes of measuring the pre-image and committed qubit registers.*
Round $\mathcal{V}_2$: *$\mathcal{V}$ samples terms $s_1, \ldots, s_{rm} \leftarrow \pi$ and queries their corresponding indices from the oracles $\mathcal{O}_y$ and $\mathcal{O}_u$.*
$\mathcal{V}$'s Verdict: *$\mathcal{V}$ executes and returns the output of the verdict round of Protocol 3.*

Corollary 3. *Under the post-quantum hardness of LWE and for any natural number n, there exists a classical-verifier succinct-communication argument system with instance-independent setup and negligible completeness and soundness* *errors for instances of size at most n of the (n, k, γ)-LH-ZX problem with at least inverse-polylogarithmic relative promise gap in the quantum random oracle model with* $\mathrm{RO} : \mathcal{X} \to \{0,1\}^\lambda$ *and any* $\lambda = \omega(\log(n))$.

4.3 ZX Quantum PCP Conjecture and Consequences to QMA

We now formally state the *weak ZX quantum PCP conjecture (Conjecture 3)* which was defined informally in Informal Conjecture 1.

Conjecture 3 (Weak ZX Quantum PCP Conjecture). *There exist a constant k and a function $f(n) = \widetilde{O}(1)$ such that the (n, k, γ)-LH-ZX problem with relative promise gap $\gamma(n) = 1/f(n)$ is* QMA*-hard.*

The (weak) ZX quantum PCP conjecture (Conjecture 3) and Corollary 3 imply the existence of succinct-communication arguments with setup for QMA under the LWE assumption in the QROM which can be stated as follows.

Theorem 4. *If the Weak ZX Quantum PCP Conjecture (Conjecture 3) is true as well as the post-quantum hardness of LWE, then for any promise problem $A \in$* QMA *and any natural number n, there exists a succinct-communication argument system with setup for all instances of A of size at most n in the quantum random oracle model with* $\mathrm{RO} : \mathcal{X} \to \{0,1\}^\lambda$ *and any* $\lambda = \omega(\log(n))$.

While we could not prove that Conjecture 3 is implied by the standard quantum PCP conjecture, we conjecture that this would be possible via a gap-preserving reduction. The tools to prove an implication like that may come to light when more progress is made towards settling the standard quantum PCP conjecture. Actually, it might be the case that a long-awaited proof of the quantum PCP conjecture would be established via the QMA-hardness of ZX local Hamiltonians.

5 Conclusion

We formalized the notion of post-quantum interactive oracle arguments (with setup). Given that formalism, we proved the soundness of a framework to compile any public-coin non-adaptive interactive oracle argument (with private setup) into a succinct-communication argument (with possibly non-succinct setup). Our soundness proof utilized the online extraction of Merkle trees in the quantum random oracle model. We stated the (weak) ZX quantum PCP conjectures as variants of the standard quantum PCP conjectures. In the QROM, either of these conjectures is sufficient to imply the existence of succinct-communication classical-verifier arguments with non-succinct setup for QMA under the LWE assumptions (and consequently a protocol for succinct-communication classical verification of quantum computation with non-succinct setup).

Acknowledgements. The author was partially supported by NSF grants CCF-1947889 and CNS-1414119. Thanks to Mark Bun and Nicholas Spooner for their mentorship and help with refining and revising this project. Thanks - in alphabetical order

- to Adam Smith, Alex Bredariol Grilo, Alex Lombardi, Anand Natarajan, Andrea Coladangelo, Anurag Anshu, Assaf Kfoury, Azer Bestavros, Chris Laumann, Fermi Ma, Ibrahim Faisal, James Bartusek, Jiayu Zhang, Leo Reyzin, Ludmila Glinskih, Luowen Qian, Mayank Varia, Muhammad Faisal, Nadya Voronova, Nathan Ju, Ran Canetti, Sam Gunn, Steve Homer, Thomas Vidick, Urmila Mahadev, and others for their time listening to ideas, helpful discussions, and explanations. I specially thank Thomas Vidick for his online lectures that spurred my interest in this research topic as well as his continued support. Thanks to [3,20] for making the LaTeX sources of their papers accessible which helped in typesetting this paper. Thanks to UCLA's Institute for Pure and Applied Mathematics (IPAM) for the support received to participate in the Graduate Summer School on Post-quantum and Quantum Cryptography where I discussed this work with other participants. Thanks to the reviewers of this paper for helping with iterating and refining it.

References

1. Aharonov, D., Arad, I., Landau, Z., Vazirani, U.: The detectability lemma and quantum gap amplification. In: Proceedings of the 41st Annual ACM Symposium on Symposium on Theory of Computing, STOC 2009 (2009). https://doi.org/10.1145/1536414.1536472
2. Aharonov, D., Arad, I., Vidick, T.: The Quantum PCP Conjecture (2013)
3. Alagic, G., Childs, A.M., Grilo, A.B., Hung, S.: Non-interactive classical verification of quantum computation. In: Pass, R., Pietrzak, K. (eds.) TCC 2020, Part III. LNCS, vol. 12552, pp. 153–180. Springer, Cham (2020). https://doi.org/10.1007/978-3-030-64381-2_6
4. Arora, S., Lund, C., Motwani, R., Sudan, M., Szegedy, M.: Proof verification and the hardness of approximation problems. J. ACM **45**(3), 501–555 (1998). https://doi.org/10.1145/278298.278306
5. Arora, S., Safra, S.: Probabilistic checking of proofs: a new characterization of NP. J. ACM **45**(1), 70–122 (1998). https://doi.org/10.1145/273865.273901
6. Bartusek, J., et al.: Succinct classical verification of quantum computation. In: Dodis, Y., Shrimpton, T. (eds.) CRYPTO 2022, Part II. LNCS, vol. 13508, pp. 195–211. Springer, Cham (2022). https://doi.org/10.1007/978-3-031-15979-4_7
7. Bartusek, J., Malavolta, G.: Indistinguishability obfuscation of null quantum circuits and applications. In: Braverman, M. (ed.) 13th Innovations in Theoretical Computer Science Conference, ITCS 2022, Berkeley, CA, USA, 31 January–3 February 2022. LIPIcs, vol. 215, pp. 15:1–15:13. Schloss Dagstuhl - Leibniz-Zentrum für Informatik (2022). https://doi.org/10.4230/LIPIcs.ITCS.2022.15
8. Bellare, M., Rogaway, P.: Random oracles are practical: a paradigm for designing efficient protocols. In: Proceedings of the 1st ACM Conference on Computer and Communications Security, CCS 1993, pp. 62–73. Association for Computing Machinery, New York (1993). https://doi.org/10.1145/168588.168596
9. Ben-Sasson, E., Chiesa, A., Spooner, N.: Interactive oracle proofs. In: Hirt, M., Smith, A. (eds.) Theory of Cryptography, pp. 31–60. Springer, Heidelberg (2016). https://doi.org/10.1007/978-3-662-53644-5_2
10. Biamonte, J.D., Love, P.J.: Realizable Hamiltonians for universal adiabatic quantum computers. Phys. Rev. A **78**(1) (2008). https://doi.org/10.1103/physreva.78.012352
11. Boneh, D., Dagdelen, Ö., Fischlin, M., Lehmann, A., Schaffner, C., Zhandry, M.: Random oracles in a quantum world. In: Lee, D.H., Wang, X. (eds.) ASIACRYPT

2011. LNCS, vol. 7073, pp. 41–69. Springer, Cham (2011). https://doi.org/10.1007/978-3-642-25385-0_3
12. Chen, L., Movassagh, R.: Quantum Merkle trees (2021). https://doi.org/10.48550/ARXIV.2112.14317
13. Chia, N., Chung, K., Yamakawa, T.: Classical verification of quantum computations with efficient verifier. In: Pass, R., Pietrzak, K. (eds.) TCC 2020, Part III. LNCS, vol. 12552, pp. 181–206. Springer, Cham (2020). https://doi.org/10.1007/978-3-030-64381-2_7
14. Chiesa, A., Ma, F., Spooner, N., Zhandry, M.: Post-quantum succinct arguments: breaking the quantum rewinding barrier. In: 62nd IEEE Annual Symposium on Foundations of Computer Science, FOCS 2021, Denver, CO, USA, 7–10 February 2022, pp. 49–58. IEEE (2021). https://doi.org/10.1109/FOCS52979.2021.00014
15. Chiesa, A., Manohar, P., Spooner, N.: Succinct arguments in the quantum random oracle model. In: Hofheinz, D., Rosen, A. (eds.) TCC 2019, Part II. LNCS, vol. 11892, pp. 1–29. Springer, Cham (2019). https://doi.org/10.1007/978-3-030-36033-7_1
16. Childs, A.M.: Secure assisted quantum computation. Quantum Inf. Comput. **5**(6), 456–466 (2005). https://doi.org/10.26421/QIC5.6-4
17. Coladangelo, A., Vidick, T., Zhang, T.: Non-interactive zero-knowledge arguments for QMA, with preprocessing. In: Micciancio, D., Ristenpart, T. (eds.) CRYPTO 2020, Part III. LNCS, vol. 12172, pp. 799–828. Springer, Cham (2020). https://doi.org/10.1007/978-3-030-56877-1_28
18. Cook, S.A.: The complexity of theorem-proving procedures. In: Proceedings of the Third Annual ACM Symposium on Theory of Computing, STOC 1971, pp. 151–158. Association for Computing Machinery, New York (1971). https://doi.org/10.1145/800157.805047
19. Don, J., Fehr, S., Majenz, C., Schaffner, C.: Efficient NIZKs and signatures from commit-and-open protocols in the QROM. In: Dodis, Y., Shrimpton, T. (eds.) CRYPTO 2022, Part II. LNCS, vol. 13508, pp. 729–757. Springer, Cham (2022). https://doi.org/10.1007/978-3-031-15979-4_25
20. Don, J., Fehr, S., Majenz, C., Schaffner, C.: Online-extractability in the quantum random-oracle model. In: Dunkelman, O., Dziembowski, S. (eds.) EUROCRYPT 2022, Part III. LNCS, vol. 13277, pp. 677–706. Springer, Cham (2022). https://doi.org/10.1007/978-3-031-07082-2_24
21. Faisal, I.: Interactive oracle arguments in the QROM and applications to succinct verification of quantum computation. Cryptology ePrint Archive, Paper 2023/421 (2023). https://eprint.iacr.org/2023/421
22. Fitzsimons, J., Hajdušek, M., Morimae, T.: Post hoc verification of quantum computation. Phys. Rev. Lett. **120**(4) (2018)
23. Gheorghiu, A., Kapourniotis, T., Kashefi, E.: Verification of quantum computation: an overview of existing approaches. Theory Comput. Syst. **63**(4), 715–808 (2018). https://doi.org/10.1007/s00224-018-9872-3
24. Grilo, A.B.: Quantum proofs, the local Hamiltonian problem and applications. (Preuves quantiques, le problème des Hamiltoniens locaux et applications). Ph.D. thesis, Sorbonne Paris Cité, France (2018). https://tel.archives-ouvertes.fr/tel-02152364
25. Gunn, S., Ju, N., Ma, F., Zhandry, M.: Commitments to quantum states. Cryptology ePrint Archive, Paper 2022/1358 (2022). https://eprint.iacr.org/2022/1358
26. Kempe, J., Kitaev, A., Regev, O.: The complexity of the local Hamiltonian problem. SIAM J. Comput. **35**(5), 1070–1097 (2006). https://doi.org/10.1137/s0097539704445226

27. Kilian, J.: A note on efficient zero-knowledge proofs and arguments (extended abstract). In: Proceedings of the Twenty-Fourth Annual ACM Symposium on Theory of Computing, STOC 1992, pp. 723–732. Association for Computing Machinery, New York (1992). https://doi.org/10.1145/129712.129782
28. Kitaev, A.: Quantum NP (1999). Talk at AQIP'99: Second Workshop on Algorithms in Quantum Information Processing
29. Levin, L.A.: Universal sequential search problems. Problemy peredachi informatsii **9**(3), 115–116 (1973)
30. Mahadev, U.: Classical homomorphic encryption for quantum circuits. In: Thorup, M. (ed.) 59th IEEE Annual Symposium on Foundations of Computer Science, FOCS 2018, Paris, France, 7–9 October 2018, pp. 332–338. IEEE Computer Society (2018). https://doi.org/10.1109/FOCS.2018.00039
31. Mahadev, U.: Classical verification of quantum computations. In: 59th IEEE Annual Symposium on Foundations of Computer Science, FOCS 2018, Paris, France, 7–9 October 2018, pp. 259–267 (2018). https://doi.org/10.1109/FOCS.2018.00033
32. Merkle, R.C.: A digital signature based on a conventional encryption function. In: Pomerance, C. (ed.) CRYPTO 1987. LNCS, vol. 293, pp. 369–378. Springer, Heidelberg (1988). https://doi.org/10.1007/3-540-48184-2_32
33. Morimae, T., Fitzsimons, J.F.: Post hoc verification with a single prover. arXiv preprint arXiv:1603.06046 (2016)
34. Morimae, T., Nagaj, D., Schuch, N.: Quantum proofs can be verified using only single-qubit measurements. Phys. Rev. A **93**(2) (2016). https://doi.org/10.1103/physreva.93.022326
35. Takeuchi, Y., Morimae, T., Tani, S.: Sumcheck-based delegation of quantum computing to rational server. Theor. Comput. Sci. **924**, 46–67 (2022). https://doi.org/10.1016/j.tcs.2022.04.016. https://www.sciencedirect.com/science/article/pii/S0304397522002250
36. Unruh, D.: Collapse-binding quantum commitments without random oracles. In: Cheon, J.H., Takagi, T. (eds.) ASIACRYPT 2016, Part II. LNCS, vol. 10032, pp. 166–195. Springer, Cham (2016). https://doi.org/10.1007/978-3-662-53890-6_6
37. Unruh, D.: Computationally binding quantum commitments. In: Fischlin, M., Coron, J. (eds.) EUROCRYPT 2016, Part II. LNCS, vol. 9666, pp. 497–527. Springer, Cham (2016). https://doi.org/10.1007/978-3-662-49896-5_18
38. Vidick, T., Zhang, T.: Classical zero-knowledge arguments for quantum computations. IACR Cryptology ePrint Archive **2019**, 194 (2019). https://eprint.iacr.org/2019/194
39. Zhandry, M.: How to record quantum queries, and applications to quantum indifferentiability. In: Boldyreva, A., Micciancio, D. (eds.) CRYPTO 2019, Part II. LNCS, vol. 11693, pp. 239–268. Springer, Cham (2019). https://doi.org/10.1007/978-3-030-26951-7_9
40. Zhang, J.: Succinct blind quantum computation using a random oracle. In: Khuller, S., Williams, V.V. (eds.) STOC 2021: 53rd Annual ACM SIGACT Symposium on Theory of Computing, Virtual Event, Italy, 21–25 June 2021, pp. 1370–1383. ACM (2021). https://doi.org/10.1145/3406325.3451082
41. Zhang, J.: Classical verification of quantum computations in linear time. In: 63rd IEEE Annual Symposium on Foundations of Computer Science, FOCS 2022, Denver, CO, USA, 31 October–3 November 2022, pp. 46–57. IEEE (2022). https://doi.org/10.1109/FOCS54457.2022.00012

Threshold Signatures and Fault Attacks

SoK: Parameterization of Fault Adversary Models Connecting Theory and Practice

Dilara Toprakhisar[1(✉)], Svetla Nikova[1], and Ventzislav Nikov[2]

[1] COSIC, KU Leuven, Leuven, Belgium
{dilara.toprakhisar,svetla.nikova}@esat.kuleuven.be
[2] NXP Semiconductors, Leuven, Belgium

Abstract. Since the first fault attack by Boneh *et al.* in 1997, various physical fault injection mechanisms have been explored to induce errors in electronic systems. Subsequent fault analysis methods of these errors have been studied, and successfully used to attack many cryptographic implementations. This poses a significant challenge to the secure implementation of cryptographic algorithms. To address this, numerous countermeasures have been proposed. Nevertheless, these countermeasures are primarily designed to protect against the particular assumptions made by the fault analysis methods. These assumptions, however, encompass only a limited range of the capabilities inherent to physical fault injection mechanisms.

In this paper, we narrow our focus to fault attacks and countermeasures specific to ASICs, and introduce a novel parameterized fault adversary model capturing an adversary's control over an ASIC. We systematically map (a) the physical fault injection mechanisms, (b) adversary models assumed in fault analysis, and (c) adversary models used to design countermeasures into our introduced model. This model forms the basis for our comprehensive exploration that covers a broad spectrum of fault attacks and countermeasures within symmetric key cryptography as a comprehensive survey. Furthermore, our investigation highlights a notable misalignment among the adversary models assumed in countermeasures, fault attacks, and the intrinsic capabilities of the physical fault injection mechanisms. Through this study, we emphasize the need to reevaluate existing fault adversary models, and advocate for the development of a unified model.

Keywords: Adversarial Models · Fault Attacks · Fault Countermeasures

1 Introduction

The first fault attack by Boneh *et al.* [10] initiated a new research area focused on the malicious injection of faults and their mathematical analyses to attack cryptographic implementations. This seminal milestone also instigated the development of countermeasures to mitigate these attacks. Instead of targeting the

E. Oswald (Ed.): CT-RSA 2024, LNCS 14643, pp. 433–459, 2024.
https://doi.org/10.1007/978-3-031-58868-6_17

cryptanalytic properties of the algorithms, these attacks exploit implementation vulnerabilities caused by errors. Unlike passive implementation attacks that solely observe the target device's behavior, fault attacks actively disturb computations through physical means, such as clock/voltage glitches [2,4], electromagnetic waves [39], and laser injection [54]. The attacker then observes the device's reaction to the injected faults. Along with the discovered physical fault injection mechanisms, several fault analysis methods analyzing the injected faults have been proposed, including Differential Fault Analysis (DFA) [8], Statistical Ineffective Fault Attacks (SIFA) [19,21], and others. The combination of injecting faults through physical fault injection mechanisms and the subsequent fault analyses has proven successful in real-world scenarios. In parallel to these attacks, numerous countermeasures have been proposed to protect against them. These countermeasures often employ some kind of redundancy (*i.e.*, time, area, or information) to achieve error detection or correction. Besides fault attacks, the emergence of combined attacks that exploit both side-channel and fault vulnerabilities simultaneously necessitates more sophisticated countermeasures capable of mitigating these attacks. In the context of fault attacks, the term *adversarial model* pertains to defining an adversary performing fault injection through physical fault injection mechanisms. Fault analysis methods, as the second step in a fault attack, rely on certain assumptions regarding the injected fault(s). These assumptions formulate an adversary who carries out the fault injection step, ensuring that the faults align with the assumptions. These assumptions encompass factors such as the fault location on the target device and how they alter the target variables. Similarly, countermeasures rely on analogous assumptions to describe the adversary they aim to protect against.

Physical fault injection mechanisms can execute various fault injection scenarios with varying fault locations, number of faults, and so on, which are then exploited by different fault analysis methods. However, as we will show, the proposed fault analysis methods leverage only a fraction of the capabilities offered by these fault injection mechanisms, with each method exploiting specific properties of the errors resulting from the fault injections. Consequently, the divergence among fault analysis methods, each based on different adversarial models and objectives, complicates the comprehensive assessment of the security of cryptographic implementations. Countermeasures proposed in response to this variety of fault analysis methods are, however, tailored to address specific fault analysis methods and adversarial models (*e.g.*, DFA and/or SIFA). Unfortunately, they often fall short of harnessing the capabilities of physical fault injection mechanisms. Recognizing the diverse capabilities of the physical mechanisms, it is crucial to establish more realistic assumptions for countermeasures. This is essential, as fault adversaries possess the potential to exploit a broader spectrum of fault scenarios than previously assumed within the context of fault attacks. Illustratively, Bartkewitz *et al.* [6] demonstrate that an adversary model, typically thought to be challenging to achieve in real-world scenarios, is, in fact, more feasible than previously believed. This finding raises questions about the effectiveness of certain countermeasures.

Inherently protecting against a larger spectrum of adversary models necessitates the development of a consolidated parameterized adversary model encompassing various fault adversary models prevalent in practical contexts. Such a comprehensive model should be capable of accommodating the diverse fault adversary models reflecting the capabilities of physical injection mechanisms. Moreover, it will facilitate a systematic exploration of fault attacks and countermeasures. Such a unified model will enable the designing of countermeasures based on adversaries having a broader and more realistic spectrum of capabilities. Moreover, this approach can contribute to reducing the complexity and the cost of the designed countermeasures by providing a comprehensive and systematic framework to address different physical fault injection mechanisms and adversary models. The literature contains several studies such as [5,31] and [45] that analyze the theoretical exploitation of injected faults, or formulate a fault adversary model using a range of parameters. However, they often neglect some aspects of a physical adversary, thus failing to provide a comprehensive understanding of how theoretical assumptions (*i.e.*, fault analysis methods and countermeasures) align with practical scenarios. In this work, we establish a novel parameterized fault adversary model comprehensively capturing an adversary's control span on an ASIC, with the goal of assessing the alignment of theoretical assumptions with practical realities. To achieve this objective, we introduce some notions to differentiate between the assumptions inherent in fault analysis methods, countermeasures, and the actual capabilities of a physical adversary. Specifically, we employ the term *physical adversary model* to characterize an adversary physically injecting faults; *analytical adversary model* to characterize an adversary assumed in fault analysis methods; and *mitigative adversary model* to characterize an adversary assumed in countermeasures.

Contributions. In this paper, we investigate the assumptions inherent to fault analysis methods and countermeasures, and discuss their alignment with real-world scenarios. To facilitate this investigation, we first propose a novel parameterized fault adversary model, providing a comprehensive characterization of different factors that a physical fault adversary can control specifically on ASICs. Our model accommodates various adversary capabilities through its comprehensive set of parameters. Then, we employ the introduced parameterized adversary model to describe the impacts of physical fault injection mechanisms on ASICs. We conduct a comparative analysis, presenting both similarities and differences in their respective capabilities, thus offering a comprehensive perspective on real-world feasibility. After describing the capabilities a physical fault adversary can possess in practice, we first present a survey of several fault and combined analysis methods on the *ASIC implementations of symmetric ciphers*, and the countermeasures proposed to mitigate them. We map the analytical adversary models of the presented attacks, and the mitigative adversary models of the countermeasures into the parameterized adversary model. These mappings reveal a discrepancy between the analytical adversary models, mitigative adversary models, and the physical adversary models accommodating the physical fault injection mechanisms. Through this analysis, we reveal certain limitations and challenges of the existing countermeasures against physical fault injection mechanisms. Building upon the mismatch of the different adversarial models and reality, we discuss the shortcomings of the existing analytical adversary models which highlights the need for a unified fault adversary model. In essence, we stress the need to reassess the assumptions underlying the mitigative adversary model, accounting for the broad range of capabilities of the physical fault injection mechanisms. Then, we pose an open question to define a unified adversary model that can be used as a more accurate representation of the fault adversaries and enable researchers to develop more effective countermeasures against fault attacks. We provide suggestions on what such a unified model should contain.

Outline. In Sect. 2, we discuss the widely used physical fault injection mechanisms and their impacts on ASICs. Then, in Sect. 3, we introduce a novel parameterized fault adversary model, and in Sect. 4, we describe the physical fault adversaries using the introduced model. Then, we present a survey of existing fault and combined analysis methods in Sect. 5, and countermeasures in Sect. 6 together with the mappings of the respective analytical and mitigative fault models into the parameterized model. Finally, in Sect. 7, we discuss our findings.

2 Preliminaries

In this section, we describe the physical fault injection mechanisms that are used to inject faults to an ASIC as the first step to attack the implementations of symmetric key algorithms. Additionally, we present the notations that serve as the foundation for our parameterized fault adversary model.

2.1 The Attack Surface: Circuit Model

The attack surface is assumed to be a digital circuit that is formed of gates and wires, where the gates are composed of combinational Boolean logic gates and memory gates. A combinational gate computes its output as a Boolean function of the present inputs. Unlike combinational gates, a memory gate is a clock-synchronized gate where the output depends on the previous input in addition to the present input. In other words, memory gates (*i.e.*, registers), store Boolean variables being dependent on the clock. The digital circuit takes an input, has an internal state, and produces an output where the state corresponds to the secret data stored in the registers. Note that we focus on ASICs and deliberately exclude FPGAs and CPUs since they would necessitate considering also other types of memories such as RAM, ROM, Non-Volatile, etc.

2.2 Physical Fault Injection Mechanisms

In this section, we introduce the most common physical fault injection mechanisms altering the execution of an ASIC: clock glitches [2,36], underpowering and voltage glitches [4,58], EM-fault injections [22,37–39], and laser fault injections [16,50,54]. While not delving into the technical details, our focus is solely on elucidating the physical effects of the fault injection mechanisms on ASICs. The efficacy of the mechanisms described in this section has been validated through successful fault attacks against the ASIC implementations of symmetric key algorithms. Among them, non-invasive clock/voltage glitches stand as cost-effective yet powerful methods to inject faults on a global scale on the whole IC. On the other hand, laser fault injection has the highest locality which in turn provides greater precision. Between these two extremes, EM-fault injection impacts the circuits in a particular area chosen by the adversary.

Clock Glitches. In synchronous ICs the data is processed by combinational logic blocks separated by memory gates (*i.e.*, D flip-flop registers) sharing the same clock as illustrated in Fig. 1. The raising clock edges trigger the registers to latch the data, and in between, the intermediate combinational logic block operates on the data. Once the rising edge of the clock arrives, the signal traveling through the combinational logic block achieves stability. The time taken for the signal to travel through the combinational logic block is called the propagation delay. The set-up time of the register (*i.e.*, the minimum time period the data should remain present at the register before being latched ($t_{\text{set-up}}$)), the maximal propagation delay (*i.e.*, critical path (t_{critical})), the clock skew (δ), and the register delay ($t_{\text{reg'}}$) define the (maximum) clock period T_{clk} of the circuit:

$$T_{\text{clk}} + \delta = t_{\text{critical}} + t_{\text{reg'}} + t_{\text{set-up}}.$$

The propagation delay of computations is susceptible to variations in temperature and power supply voltage. These fluctuations can potentially interrupt the normal functioning of the circuit. Therefore, in order to ensure a reliable circuit operation, the clock period is taken to be greater than T_{clk}.

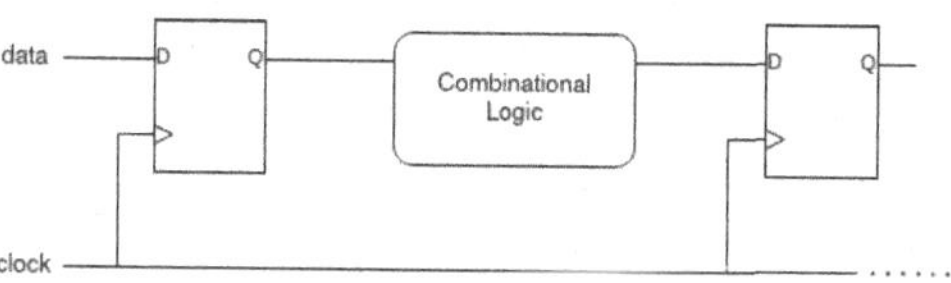

Fig. 1. A synchronously operating IC.

An attacker can alter the external reference clock from which the internal clock of an IC is derived. Such alterations to the external reference clock can allow an attacker to decrease the clock period ($T_{\text{clk'}}$). As $T_{\text{clk'}}$ approaches to t_{critical}, one starts to observe faulty results as the altered clock period prevents the completion of the combinational logic and therefore, the arrival of the correct data at the register on time. As a result, faulty input gets latched in the register. Naturally, decreasing the clock period potentially affects the logical paths that have a propagation delay greater than ($T_{\text{clk'}} - t_{\text{reg'}} - t_{\text{set-up}} + \delta$). Therefore, an attacker lacks direct control over the specific location of the injected fault. In fact, clock glitching can potentially affect the undesired components, leading to undesired faulty outputs. Nevertheless, Ning *et al.* [36] states that the first faulty bit is theoretically located on the critical path characterized by the longest delay. As the fault intensity increases, more bit failures are likely to happen.

Underpowering and Voltage Glitches. ICs are designed to operate properly within a specified voltage supply range, and any deviation from this specified range may produce faulty outputs. In essence, underpowering and voltage glitches affect the ICs in a similar way to the clock glitches. However, rather than changing the clock period, the decreased supply voltage leads to an increase in the critical path. This is due to the fact the variation in supply voltage amplifies the propagation delay of the gates. Consequently, similar to clock glitches, correct data might not arrive at the register on time. Likewise, undesired components may be affected which will then potentially produce undesired faulty outputs. In addition to manipulating the power supply voltage, an attacker can also alter the critical path through a ground input to the IC.

EM-Fault Injection. An EM-fault injection directly affects the input and control signals of D flip-flops. In fact, if the fault injection is performed just before the arrival of the rising edge of the clock, then a faulty sampling occurs at the D flip-flop as noted by previous studies [37,38]. As stated by Dumont *et al.* [22], EM-fault injection does not disrupt the interconnect wires.

This technique induces a voltage swing in the IC between the power and ground grid. The falling edge of the swing causes the potential of the clock and input signals to go down. Consequently, the rising edge of the swing triggers the circuit to recover its original state, *i.e.*, all signals start to recover the correct state. However, this causes a race between the clock and input signals [22]. If the clock signal recovers its correct state first, then the register stores a value dictated by the fault injection. The stored faulty value is related to the polarity created by the EM-fault injection; while a positive swing is more likely to cause the register to store 1, a negative swing is more likely to cause the register to store 0. The effectiveness of the injected fault is, therefore, determined by the polarity and the previously stored value in the register. Note that the EM affects all registers in the neighborhood and the attacker does not have precise control over this.

Laser Fault Injection. The target of the laser fault injection is the transistor layer of an IC. Through a focused laser beam, it produces electron hole pairs in the target area, which in turn might cause a high current drift, ultimately changing the output of a gate. Once the current drift collapses, the output switches back to its original value.

It has been shown that both memory and combinational gates are susceptible to laser fault injection [16,50] which can manifest in the effect of bit-level output flipping, outputting 1 or outputting 0, or changing the type of the combinational gate. Moreover, the target area of the laser fault injection ranges from a single gate to multiple (but limited) number of gates [6].

2.3 Modeling the Faults in the Circuit

In this section, we describe the terminology to model the injected faults. In ICs, various fault models can be used to describe the effects of the injected faults. We consider a set and reset faults that correspond to faulting a binary variable to get the logical values 1 and 0, respectively. A bit-flip fault corresponds to faulting a binary variable to get the complementary logical value.

In this work, we model the injected faults as manipulations at the gates excluding the wires, which includes set, reset, and bit-flip faults to any combinational logic or memory gates. Thus, faulting a gate is equivalent to altering its output. In principle, a faulty gate returns a faulty output for at least one input combination. We note that, in addition to the common combinational Boolean logic gates like AND, XOR, NOT, etc., digital circuits may also contain other types of combinational gates that are considered as part of the wire at an algorithmic level. One example of such gates is buffers, which are primarily used to regenerate the input. However, they can also be used to increase the propagation delay in the wire. While these buffers are not important at the functional algorithmic level, they become essential when modeling faults in the circuit since faults can be injected in them in the same way to the Boolean logic gates. *Therefore, we argue that such gates have to be part of the functional algorithmic level description of circuits when one considers fault adversaries.*

Beyond manipulating an injected fault at the gate level, a fault attack involves several additional factors in practice. We outline these factors in Sect. 3 by introducing the parameters that characterize the behavior of an adversary performing a fault injection.

3 Parameterized Fault Injection Adversary Model

In this section, we introduce our parameterized adversary model that encapsulates the control span a fault injection adversary can exert on an IC. This model encompasses the parameters such an adversary can actively control using a physical fault injection mechanism, namely: the number of fault injection events (n), fault location (l), fault timing (t), number of affected bits (b), duration of the injected fault (d), targeted type of gates (g), and fault type (p). Through these parameters, we can accurately represent an adversary by capturing the full control span of them on an IC in the event of a fault injection. We describe the parameters and summarize them in Table 1.

As noted in Sect. 1, the literature contains several studies that modeled a fault injection adversary using a range of parameters. We stress that the primary objective of our parameterized model is to precisely define a physical adversary. This allows us to question the alignment between analytical and mitigative adversary models, and the actual capabilities that an adversary can leverage through the physical fault injection mechanisms. For instance, Karaklajić *et al.* [31] characterized a fault adversary by encompassing the ability to control the fault location, time, effect, the number of affected bits, and the fault duration. However, this model overlooks some aspects such as the number of fault injection events and the targeted gate types. Likewise, Richter-Brockmann *et al.* [45] proposed a parameterized adversary model that captures an adversary through the number of affected bits, fault type, and fault location. Notably, this model is anticipated to have a better congruence with the models assumed in fault analysis methods. Thereby, it finds greater alignment with theoretical assessments rather than physical fault adversaries. This, in turn, prompts the central inquiry of this paper: To what degree do the analytical and mitigative adversary models align with practical scenarios? Given this context, our proposed parameterized adversary model emerges as a more holistic representation of a physical adversary with its comprehensive integration of parameters. Consequentially, our model stands as a bridge between analytical, mitigative and physical fault adversaries offering a framework to understand and counteract the fault injection vulnerabilities arising in practice.

Number of Fault Injection Events (n). This parameter defines the number of fault injection events an adversary performs during a specified time window (*e.g.*, the encryption/decryption operation, or a cycle). In particular, this parameter proves valuable, for instance, when describing an adversary injecting identical faults into replicated paths, or injecting faults at distinct cycles to circumvent some countermeasures. Note that we define the following parameters for each fault injection event.

Fault Location (l). This parameter defines the capabilities of an adversary over the location of an injected fault. Specifically, an adversary can have a *precise*, *loose*, or *no control* over the fault location. Having precise control implies that the adversary is able to inject a fault to a specific gate or cluster of a few gates, *i.e.*, can alter the specific bit(s). This level of control requires an adversary to have a high degree of knowledge of the implementation details. In contrast, having loose control implies that the adversary is able to target a specific (bigger) cluster of gates but has no/partial control over the location of the faulted bit(s). This level of control, being less precise, still requires some knowledge about the implementation. Lastly, having no control implies that the adversary is not able to target a specific gate, thereby precluding any direct control over the location of the faulted bit(s). Note that, the ability of an adversary to control the fault location highly depends on the fault injection setup. Hence, the model aims to capture various levels of control that an adversary possesses through different physical fault injection mechanisms.

Fault Timing (t). This parameter defines the capabilities of an adversary over the timing of the injected fault. Similar to fault location, an adversary can have a *precise, loose*, or *no control* over the fault timing. Having precise control over the timing implies that the adversary is able to inject a fault at a specific time (*i.e.*, in a specific clock cycle, an operation). Having loose control over timing implies that an adversary is able to target a set of operations or clock cycles. Lastly, no control implies that the adversary is not able to inject a fault at a specific time or period.

Number of Affected Bits (b). This parameter defines the number of bits affected by a fault injection. It is noteworthy that this parameter does not necessarily correspond to the number of observable faults in the circuit. That is, with time (*i.e.*, number of cycles) an injected fault might propagate to multiple locations as the erroneous value is subsequently used as input to other gates, or get ineffective. Moreover, a fault might have an ineffective effect on the target, *i.e.*, causing no change in the value.

Duration of the Injected Fault (d). This parameter defines the effectiveness period of an injected fault. The duration of an injected fault can be either *transient*, *persistent*, or *destructive*. A transient fault is effective for a limited period of time until the correct value is recovered again (*i.e.*, self-recoverable). This period varies depending on the time required to recover the original state and can be a fraction of a cycle, or multiple cycles. A persistent fault is effective as long as the fault injection finishes and the target variable is explicitly overwritten, implying duration of multiple cycles. A destructive fault damages the physical layer, *e.g.*, a fault in logic or memory that cannot be reversed, or the value of the target variable cannot be read anymore.

Targeted Gate Type (g). This parameter defines the type of the targeted gates in the circuit by a fault injection: combinational gates only, memory gates only, or both.

Fault Type (p). This parameter defines the manifestation of the fault on the output(s) of the targeted gate(s). The fault type can be set, reset, flip, random, or custom. Set, reset, and flip faults refer to setting, resetting, and flipping the output of the targeted gate. Random fault refers to a fault that has an unpredictable outcome on the output of the targeted gate. Custom fault is used to define an adversary that is able to modify the mapping function of the targeted gate implements, which requires the strongest capabilities. Note that, in our parameterized adversary model, we deviate from the often used notation of *stuck-at 1/0* as also done by Richter-Brockmann *et al.* [45]. This is because stuck-at 0/1 faults are equivalent to reset/set faults for longer transient or persistent fault duration, and can thus be described by two fault parameters (*i.e.*, d and p).

In the next sections, we apply the parameterized fault adversary model to the physical fault injection mechanisms, and analytical and mitigative adversary models.

4 Parameterization of Physical Fault Injection Mechanisms

This section maps the capabilities of the physical fault injection mechanisms into the parameterized adversary model. All the described fault injection mechanisms impact the physical layer of the target device. However, they exhibit distinct characteristics leading to diverse fault scenarios in an IC. Clock/voltage glitching, for instance, affects the longest critical path, and depending on the timing of the glitch (hence, the physical layout and the state of the circuit), more

Table 1. The parameters defining the parameterized adversary model

Parameters	Description
Number of Fault Injection Events (n)	The number of physical fault injections performed in a specified time window
Fault Location (l)	**Precise:** Specific gate(s) **Loose:** Specific cluster of gates, no/partial control on which gates are affected **No control:** Random location
Fault Timing (t)	**Precise:** Specific clock cycle/operation **Loose:** Set of clock cycles/operations **No control:** Random timing
Number of Affected Bits (b)	The number of affected bits by the fault injection
Duration of the Injected Fault (d)	**Transient:** Limited, self-recoverable **Persistent:** Limited, needs to be explicitly overwritten **Destructive:** Irreversible
Targeted Gate Type (g)	**Combinational** gates only **Memory** gates only **Both**
Fault Type (p)	**Set:** Faulting to 1 **Reset:** Faulting to 0 **Random:** Random outcome **Flip:** Flipping the value **Custom:** Attacker specified gate modification

than one path might be affected. Therefore, while clock/voltage glitching does not require an expensive setup, it lacks precision in targeting a particular part of the IC. That is, a clock/voltage glitching adversary encounters constraints in terms of governing a precise fault location, in comparison to EM- and laser fault injection adversaries. On the other hand, EM-fault injection exhibits a higher spatial resolution compared to clock/voltage glitching, impacting all memory gates within the focus area of the setup. This distinction sets it apart from laser fault injection retaining the ability to selectively target individual gate(s).

Additionally, the number of gates faulted by clock/voltage glitching is random as it depends on the processed data and the underlying circuit at the targeted time. Nonetheless, if a circuit at the targeted time has a data path notably deeper than the others regarding the logic gates, the fault is inclined to occur within this data path, imposing a constraint on the number of gates affected by the fault. In contrast, EM- and laser fault injection exhibit heightened precision, as they allow for finer control over the specific target area on the IC. Notably, laser fault injection can target a fixed number of gates, thereby enhancing its precision beyond that of EM-fault injection. Another differentiating feature is that voltage glitching is incapable of performing multiple fault injection events within a single cycle (still can affect multiple bits). On the other hand, clock glitching, EM- and laser fault injection have the potential to perform multiple fault injection events within a single cycle. Additionally, the duration of fault injection can vary between these mechanisms. While EM- and laser fault injection can induce prolonged faults that last much longer than a single cycle [22], this is not the case for clock/voltage glitching which exhibit limitations in this regard. Moreover, with the exception of voltage glitching, all the aforementioned techniques can be executed within a fraction of a cycle.

We summarize the capabilities of the physical fault injection mechanisms in Table 2. Subsequently, in the next chapter, we parameterize the analytical adversary models of several fault/combined analysis methods discussed in the literature. Through this analysis, we illustrate the extent to which these analytical adversary models leverage the capabilities of the physical fault injection mechanisms.

Table 2. Physical fault injection mechanisms described as an adversary model

Fault Mechanism/Parameters	Clock	Voltage	EM	Laser
(n) shots (per cycle)	Several	One	Several	Several
(l) location	Loose		Loose	Precise
(t) time	Precise		Precise	Precise
(b) bits	Random		Random	Several
(d) duration	Transient		Transient/ Destructive	Transient/ Persistent/ Destructive
(g) gates	Combinational		Memory	Both
(p) type	Random		Random	Custom

5 Parameterization of Analytical Adversary Models of Fault and Combined Analysis Methods

In this section, we revisit the analytical adversary models assumed in the most widely recognized fault and combined analysis methods in the literature. For each method, we map the analytical adversary model into our parameterized adversary model. We emphasize the necessity for a standardized adversary model by pointing out that the assumed models are not well-defined. A commonly agreed adversary model is crucial, not only for describing the fault adversaries of the fault/combined analysis methods but also for designing unified countermeasures against them. From this section on, we only consider the methods utilizing transient faults. Throughout the section, we denote the word length of the target implementations with w.

Note that, the literature often defines *the order of the fault attack* (t) as the total number of bits/variables altered during a cycle or the encryption/decryption operation, which is actually a function of parameters b and n. We will come back to the fault attack order and discuss it in Sect. 7.

Faults are often referred to as *effective* when the error propagates to the cipher output (*i.e.*, ciphertext is incorrect); or *ineffective* when the error propagation stops before reaching the cipher output (*i.e.*, ciphertext is correct). A method based on effective faults is DFA. However, two types of ineffective faults should be distinguished: faults that do not modify the intermediate value (*e.g.*, IFA), and faults that modify the intermediate value (*e.g.*, SIFA). It is easy to protect against IFA by using masking, while protection against SIFA is more challenging.

5.1 Fault Analysis Methods

In this section, we parameterize the analytical adversary models of the methods utilizing only fault injection mechanisms (versus combined analysis methods in Sect. 5.2), and list them in Table 3.

Differential Fault Analysis (DFA). DFA [8] exploits the differential information between correct and faulty ciphertexts obtained by injecting a fault to a state element during the last few rounds. Then, by analyzing the differential equations derived from both faulty and correct ciphertexts, it becomes possible to retrieve the last round key. Initially proposed on DES, DFA has also been applied to other algorithms such as AES [27]. We describe the analytical adversary model as follows:

(n) shots: One	(l) location: Loose	(t) time: Precise	(b) bits: Up to w
(d) duration: Transient	(g) gates: Both	(p) type: Any	

We note other methods that have the same exploit mechanism assuming the same analytical adversary model. For example, Algebraic Fault Attacks (AFA) [17] form algebraic equations and use an SAT solver afterward, Impossible Differential Fault Attacks (IDFA) [7] exploit the zero differentials rather than the high probability ones, and Linear Fault Analysis (LFA) [33] exploit the linear characteristics for some consecutive rounds.

Collision Fault Attack (CFA). CFA [9] combines the principles of DFA and collision attacks, using the collision information that is obtained when faulty and non-faulty encryptions have the same output. Then, the analysis of the collision information and the injected fault reveals information about the intermediate state. We describe the analytical adversary model as follows:

(n) shots: One	(l) location: Precise	(t) time: Precise	(b) bits: One
(d) duration: Transient	(g) gates: Memory	(p) type: Flip	

Fault Sensitivity Analysis (FSA). FSA [32] observes the data dependency of the fault occurrence as the intensity of the fault injection mechanism increases. The intensity of the fault injection mechanism could be controlled through adjustments in power supply reduction or clock period elongation. FSA assumes that the attacker begins fault injection at an intensity level that results in the correct ciphertext. They gradually increase the intensity until the fault injection has a nonzero success rate, and eventually, a success rate of one. The attacker uses this fault sensitivity information to recover secret information as it depends on the secret data. The analytical adversary model is described as follows:

(n) shots: One	(l) location: Loose	(t) time: Precise	(b) bits: Up to w
(d) duration: Transient	(g) gates: Comb	(p) type: Random	

We note the extension of FSA, Collision FSA [35], that extends FSA with correlation enhanced collision side-channel attacks, and Differential Fault Intensity Analysis (DFIA) [26] that uses fault intensity and faulty output in the statistical analysis, assume the same analytical adversary model.

Safe Error Attack (SEA), Ineffective Fault Analysis (IFA). SEA [57] was initially proposed for RSA targeting the right-to-left exponentiation, but has been shown to be applicable to other algorithms. Essentially, SEA exploits *safe errors* that do not alter the output revealing information about the path executed by the algorithm, thereby revealing some secret information. In this context, IFA [14] applied to symmetric key algorithms shares a common approach with SEA by not altering the output. Whereas SEA reveals algorithm specific information by actually modifying the intermediate values, IFA reveals information about the targeted variable by not modifying the intermediate value. That is, if an attacker receives a correct output, it indicates that the injected fault did not modify the targeted variable. Here, the attacker needs to know the type of the injected fault as it reveals the value of the faulted variable. We describe the analytical adversary model assumed in IFA as follows:

(n) shots: One	(l) location: Precise	(t) time: Precise	(b) bits: Up to w
(d) duration: Transient	(g) gates: Both	(p) type: Set, reset, custom	

Given the parameters of the analytical adversary model, the attack can be carried out by a laser fault injection as the method calls for a strong adversary which can inject a known fault.

Statistical Fault Attacks (SFA). SFA [25] was originally proposed for AES introducing a bias to an intermediate variable through fault injection. In essence, due to the introduced bias, the statistical distribution of the targeted variable obtained from the faulty ciphertexts is non-uniform, which can be exploited by the attacker to perform key recovery.

SFA is performed via clock glitching and laser fault injection by Dobraunig *et al.* [20]. However, it is also possible to carry out the attack via EM-fault injection or voltage glitching as the analysis method does not call for strong assumptions on the fault. The analytical adversary model can be described as follows:

(n) shots: One	(l) location: Loose	(t) time: Precise	(b) bits: Up to w
(d) duration: Transient	(g) gates: Both	(p) type: Any	

Statistical Ineffective Fault Attacks (SIFA). Similar to SFA, SIFA [19,21] also exploits the bias introduced to the target variable by the fault injection. However, SIFA analyses the statistical distribution of the targeted variable obtained from the correct ciphertexts.

We categorize SIFA in two: SIFA-1 [21] and SIFA-2 [19] as in [49]. SIFA-1 assumes a fault is injected to a state variable, or to a linear operation. On the other hand, SIFA-2 assumes a fault is injected to non-linear operations like an S-box. SIFA-2 stands as a more powerful method as masking with detection countermeasures do not protect against it, whereas they protect against SIFA-1. All fault types except bit-flip and random faults can result in SIFA-1. On the contrary, SIFA-2 can only be performed via a bit-flip and a random fault. The attack is performed via clock/voltage glitches, however, it is possible to carry out the attack via EM and laser fault injections. The analytical adversary model can be described as follows:

(n) shots: One	(l) location: Loose	(t) time: Precise	(b) bits: Up to w
(d) duration: Transient	(g) gates: Both	(p) type: SIFA-1 - Set, reset, custom SIFA-2 - Bit flip, random	

We note that Fault Intensity Map Analysis (FIMA) [40] generalizes FSA, DFIA, and SIFA by employing biased fault injections with varying intensities. FIMA assumes the same analytical adversary model as SIFA-1 and -2.

Fault Template Attacks (FTA). FTA [48] exploits the dependency of the fault activation and propagation on the secret data. Although the analysis is similar to SIFA, FTA does not require the correct/faulty outputs, but only the knowledge of the output being faulty or not. Moreover, while SIFA is demonstrated only in the last rounds, FTA extends the analysis to the middle rounds. FTA builds a fault pattern for different fault locations collected from different cipher executions depending on whether the fault is effective or not, which happens at the offline phase to characterize the circuit. Then, in the online phase, the templates are matched to the execution that is being analyzed.

The authors perform the attack via EM-fault injection assuming the following analytical adversary model:

(n) shots: One	(l) location: Precise	(t) time: Precise	(b) bits: One
(d) duration: Transient	(g) gates: Both	(p) type: Set, reset, bit flip	

Fault Correlation Analysis (FCA). FCA [55] investigates the relation between side-channel analysis and fault injection. The probability of a fault occurring is dependent on the data being processed, and the operation being performed, thereby, it is hypothesized to be correlated to the power consumption. The main idea of FCA is to turn the observed faults into a probability at a given time and to repeat this at different points in time to get probability traces, which are equivalent to power traces. These traces are then exploited with a standard side-channel analysis. The analytical adversary model can be described as follows:

(n) shots: One	(l) location: Loose	(t) time: Precise	(b) bits: Up to w
(d) duration: Transient	(g) gates: Both	(p) type: Random	

Statistical Effective Fault Attacks (SEFA). Similar to SIFA, SEFA [56] exploits the non-uniformity of the distribution of an intermediate value. While SIFA utilizes ineffective ciphertexts, SEFA utilizes non-faulty ciphertexts corresponding to effective faults. Thus, SEFA requires less number of ciphertexts to do a key-recovery attack. In general, SEFA exhibits better performance than SIFA in the presence of fault injection setup noise.

Similar to SIFA, the attack is performed via clock/voltage glitches by the authors using the same analytical adversarial model, described as follows:

(n) shots: One	(l) location: Loose	(t) time: Precise	(b) bits: Up to w
(d) duration: Transient	(g) gates: Both	(p) type: Any	

5.2 Combined Analysis Methods

In this section, we parameterize the analytical adversary models of the methods utilizing both fault injection and side-channels in a combined setting, and list them in Table 3.

Passive and Active Combined Attacks (PACA). PACA [3], originally proposed for RSA, combines passive and active analysis. It exploits the fault countermeasures reacting at the end of the execution by recovering the secret via classical power analysis before the countermeasure takes effect. Clavier *et al.* [15] applied this analysis concept to a masked AES implementation, which we consider in this section. The analysis assumes a fault that sets the output of an XOR operation to zero (or a constant value) which is injected to the first key addition before the first round. Then, using the differentials obtained from correct and faulty ciphertexts, and the power curves of the random values used in masking, the attacker performs a key recovery. We describe the analytical adversary model as follows:

(n) shots: One	(l) location: Precise	(t) time: Precise	(b) bits: Up to w
(d) duration: Transient	(g) gates: Comb	(p) type: Set, reset, custom	

A Combined Analysis on a Protected AES. This analysis [46] targets a fault analysis resistant and masked AES implementation by combining DFA and Correlation Power Analysis (CPA) [12]. The idea is to utilize fault injection to affect the last but one round of the key scheduling algorithm to fault the last two round keys. However, as the faulty ciphertexts are being suppressed due to fault detection/correction, side-channel information is instead used to collect the corresponding information for these faulty ciphertexts. Then, the analysis follows the round key retrieving strategy of DFA, through the differential equations. We describe the analytical adversary model as follows:

(n) shots: One	(l) location: Loose	(t) time: Precise	(b) bits: Up to w
(d) duration: Transient	(g) gates: Both	(p) type: Any	

SCA-Enhanced Fault Template Attacks (SCA-FTA). SCA-FTA [47] enhances FTA using side-channel leakage in the presence of faults, and building the templates using the leakage information from the detection and correction operations. SCA-FTA exploits the observations of the S-box output differentials in the presence of faults that leak information about the S-box inputs. The analysis works similarly to FTA. However, it uses the side-channel leakage from the error-handling logic to build the templates rather than the knowledge of the effectiveness of the fault. The analysis assumes the same analytical adversary model used in FTA:

(n) shots: One	(l) location: Precise	(t) time: Precise	(b) bits: One
(d) duration: Transient	(g) gates: Both	(p) type: Set, reset, bit flip	

Table 3. Mapping of the adversary models of the presented fault/combined attacks where S, R, BF, C and RM refer to set, reset, bit flip, custom and random, respectively.

Parameters/Attacks	(n) *shots*	(l) location	(t) time	(b) bits	(d) duration	(g) gates	(p) type
DFA [8]	One	Loose	Precise	Up to w	Transient	Both	Any
CFA [9]	One	Precise	Precise	One	Transient	Mem.	BF
FSA [32]	One	Loose	Precise	Up to w	Transient	Comb.	Random
IFA [14]	One	Precise	Precise	Up to w	Transient	Both	S,R,C
SFA [25]	One	Loose	Precise	Up to w	Transient	Both	Any
SIFA1 [21]	One	Loose	Precise	Up to w	Transient	Both	S,R,C
SIFA2 [19]							BF,RM
FTA [48]	One	Precise	Precise	One	Transient	Both	S,R,BF
FCA [55]	One	Loose	Precise	Up to w	Transient	Both	RM
SEFA [56]	One	Loose	Precise	Up to w	Transient	Both	Any
PACA [3]	One	Precise	Precise	Up to w	Transient	Comb.	S,R,C
Roche *et al.* [46]	One	Loose	Precise	Up to w	Transient	Both	Any
SCA-FTA [47]	One	Precise	Precise	One	Transient	Both	S,R,BF

6 Parameterization of Mitigative Adversaries Assumed in Countermeasures

In this section, we revisit the mitigative adversary models assumed in several countermeasures. To provide a comprehensive evaluation, we map the mitigative adversary models used in each countermeasure into our parameterized adversary model. We stress that the mitigative adversary models assumed in these countermeasures are not always precisely defined, which is partially due to the lack of a standardized adversary model. Furthermore, many of these countermeasures are designed to protect against specific fault analysis methods, rather than physical fault injection mechanisms that an adversary may utilize. This makes it more challenging to provide complete protection against all known analysis methods as each method may need to be addressed individually. We list a summary of the parameters used to describe the mitigative adversary models assumed in the countermeasures in Table 4.

ParTI. ParTI [51] assumes an adversary possessing both SCA and faulting capabilities. Its design predates the introduction of SIFA, and at the time it was designed, it was secure against all known fault attacks. However, despite not being explicitly designed to protect against SIFA, ParTI offers protection against SIFA-1-like attacks. It employs threshold implementations (TI) combined with error detection using linear codes. More specifically, ParTI makes use of a systematic code in which the prediction functions are also masked to secure against SCA and all the listed fault attacks exploiting effective faults and ineffective faults with the exception of SIFA-2-like attacks. We describe the mitigative adversary model assumed by the authors using the parameters as follows:

(n) shots: Up to k	(l) location: Any	(t) time: Any	(b) bits: Up to t
(d) duration: Transient	(g) gates: Both	(p) type: Any	

We note that the countermeasure proposed by Richter-Brockmann *et al.* [44] extends the approach combining TI and linear codes by dynamically changing the applied (non-systematic) linear codes as a hiding technique, offering higher-order side-channel security. Taking a different approach, RS-Mask [41] extends TI with random space masking.

CAPA. CAPA [43] provides provable security against higher-order SCA, higher-order fault attacks, and combined attacks by leveraging the principles of the MPC protocol SPDZ. Unlike the common SCA and analytical adversary models that assume the t-probing model [30], and faulting up to a limited number of gates, CAPA adopts a unique approach in its mitigative adversary model: *The Tile Probe and Fault Model.* This model assumes that the chip is partitioned into tiles connected by wires having their own combinational and control logic, and PRNGs. Additionally, each tile processes at most one share of an intermediate variable. Unlike the standard models, the Tile Probe and Fault Model allows an attacker to probe t tiles (out of $t+1$ tiles) with all their possessed intermediate values, making it more robust than the t-probing wire model. Similarly, the model allows an attacker to inject a random fault to any variable possessed by any of the tiles. It also allows an attacker to inject a non-stochastic fault to any variable possessed by up to t tiles. The first type of faults can be injected using clock glitches while the second type requires a laser fault injection.

Despite being designed prior to the introduction of SIFA, CAPA provides comprehensive security against all the listed effective and ineffective fault attacks, including SIFA-2. It is worth noting that at the time of SIFA publication, it was the only provable secure countermeasure that existed and was secure against SIFA-2. We formulate the mitigative adversary model assumed by the authors (*i.e.*, the Tile Probe and Fault Model) using the parameters as follows:

(n) shots: Stochastic any, else up to k (l) location: Any (t) time: Any
(b) bits: Stochastic any, else up to t
(d) duration: Transient (g) gates: Both (p) type: Any

M&M. M&M [34] protects against fault attacks by ensuring data integrity using information-theoretic MAC tags extending any SCA-secure masking scheme. The design of M&M was inspired by the principles of CAPA. However, unlike CAPA, M&M assumes a simplified mitigative adversary model that operates on wires and gates rather than tiles, while still distinguishing between the two types of adversaries. Besides providing security against SCA due to the underlying masking scheme, M&M provides generic order security against all the listed attacks, explicitly excluding SIFA-2-like attacks. M&M infects the output if a fault is detected. We describe the mitigative adversary model using the parameters as follows:

(n) shots: Stochastic any, else up to k (l) location: Any (t) time: Any
(b) bits: Stochastic any, else up to t
(d) duration: Transient (g) gates: Both (p) type: Any

We note that Hirata *et al.* [29] extends M&M to resist certain specific SIFA-2 attacks caused by clock glitches. Unlike M&M, it employs a detection mechanism instead of infection.

Transform-and-Encode (TaE). TaE [49] was designed based on two strategies, namely *transform* and *encode*. The transform strategy aims to randomize the state such that injected faults at the state do not cause biased distributions. This strategy particularly protects against SIFA-1, where masking is a potential candidate. Therefore, it can be implemented using any SCA secure masking scheme, providing protection against both SCA and SIFA-1-like attacks. The encode strategy utilizes error correction techniques to protect against SIFA-2-like attacks. In this manner, TaE provides protection against all the listed fault attacks utilizing effective and ineffective faults. We describe the mitigative adversary model using the parameters as follows:

(n) shots: Up to k (l) location: Any (t) time: Any (b) bits: Up to t
(d) duration: Transient (g) gates: Both (p) type: Any

We note that DOMREP [28] uses a similar approach as TaE combining domain-oriented masking and repetition codes, and the countermeasure by Breier *et al.* [11] uses error correction codes at gate level.

Impeccable Circuits (ImC) I, II, III. ImC schemes are based on linear codes: ImC I [1] utilizes error detection, ImC II [52] utilizes error correction, and ImC III [42] utilizes both error detection and correction. To handle fault propagation, the authors proposed using additional error check/correction points and forced independence. The forced independence property requires that no gate is shared between any two component circuits, where each component circuit computes a single output bit. However, these properties come with increased area overhead.

ImC I was specifically designed to secure against effective faults. ImC II utilizes error correction, which in turn protects against both effective and ineffective faults. The authors report that ImC II has no significant performance benefits when compared to majority voting, which led the authors to design ImC III combining error detection and correction. Specifically, ImC III corrects faults as long as the number of faulty bits is below a threshold, otherwise, it detects the fault if the number of faulty bits is again below another threshold depending on the used linear code.

ImC schemes are not SCA secure by their nature, however, hardware Boolean masking schemes can be easily implemented as the linear codes do not increase the algebraic degree of the construction. ImC I, II, and III share the common mitigative adversary model that allows to fault up to t bits in a *single* clock cycle of the entire operation (*i.e.*, a univariate adversary model), or at *multiple* clock cycles (*i.e.*, a multivariate adversary model). We describe the model as follows:

(n) shots: Up to k (l) location: Any (t) time: Any (b) bits: Up to t
(d) duration: Transient (g) gates: Both (p) type: Any

Permutations and Fine-Grained Fault Detection. Daemen *et al.* [18] proposed two strategies aimed at thwarting SIFA-1 and -2. The first technique is to use permutations as the building blocks. The second technique is to use a fine-grained fault detection mechanism that can detect faults before they become ineffective later in the circuit.

The authors have a slightly different approach to describe their mitigative adversary model. Injected faults are abstracted at the basic circuit level (*i.e.*, non-complete permutations) which do not depend on any secrets as the basic circuits are non-complete. Then, a single fault is defined as faulting a single basic circuit, which modifies the circuit such that it returns an incorrect output for at least one input combination. We describe the mitigative adversary model using the parameters as follows:

(n) shots: One	(l) location: Any	(t) time: Any	(b) bits: Up to t
(d) duration: Transient	(g) gates: Both	(p) type: Any	

We note that FRIET [53], a duplex-based authenticated encryption scheme, provides first order SIFA protection using the countermeasures introduced in [18].

Combined Private Circuits (CPC). Combined Private Circuits [23] applies the core ideas behind Probe-Isolating Non-Interference (PINI) [13] to both fault and combined security. The authors propose an attack against CINI-MINIS [24], and new (fixed) composable gadgets. The proposed gadgets rely on both masking and spacial replication (*i.e.*, error correction via majority voting). We describe the mitigative adversary model as follows:

(n) shots: Up to k	(l) location: Any	(t) time: Any	(b) bits: Up to t
(d) duration: Transient	(g) gates: Both	(p) type: Any	

Table 4. Mapping the adversary models of the presented countermeasures to the parameterized model

Parameters/Attacks	(n) shots	(l) location	(t) time	(b) bits	(d) duration	(g) gates	(p) type
ParTI [51]	Up to k	Any	Any	Up to t	Transient	Both	Any
CAPA [43]	Any RM Up to k	Any	Any	Any RM Up to t	Transient	Both	Any
M&M [34]	Any RM Up to k	Any	Any	Any RM Up to t	Transient	Both	Any
TaE [49]	Up to k	Any	Any	Up to t	Transient	Both	Any
ImC [1,42,52]	Up to k	Any	Any	Up to t	Transient	Both	Any
Permutations [18]	One	Any	Any	Up to t	Transient	Both	Any
CPC [23]	Up to k	Any	Any	Up to t	Transient	Both	Any

7 Discussion

Our work presents a parameterized adversary model into which we mapped the physical adversary models reflecting the capabilities of physical fault injection mechanisms, and the existing analytical and mitigative adversary models. Through these three mappings, our parameterized adversary model facilitates a comprehensive evaluation of the extent to which analytical and mitigative adversary models correspond to real-world scenarios.

We start our analysis with the following findings, based on Table 2. Upon mapping the physical fault injection mechanisms into the parameterized adversary model, it becomes evident that these mechanisms exhibit a notable degree of precision, either in terms of time or both time and location. Moreover, this mapping highlights their considerable power, enabling attackers to inject as many faults as desired. In light of these features, we can categorize these mechanisms into two groups: (i) high precision with relatively small target areas, and (ii) low precision with relatively large target areas, or more precisely:

i) The first group of physical fault injection mechanisms empowers attackers with the capacity to precisely target specific gates with the desired fault types. However, their target location on ASIC is confined to a few gates, and once the location is selected at the beginning of the encryption, it remains fixed. Despite this limitation, the attacker can still perform several fault injection events within a cycle, and keep the injection active over several cycles. Laser fault injection is an example of such an injection mechanism.
ii) The second group of physical fault injection mechanisms, while lacking such precision, targets larger areas, affecting more adjacent gates than those originally intended. Although such an attacker can simultaneously affect multiple gates, they have limited control over the resulting faulty values. Additionally, similar to the first group, the target location of the mechanism is static once chosen at the beginning of the encryption. Nonetheless, the attacker is capable of performing multiple fault injection events within a cycle, and keeping the injection active over several cycles. Clock and voltage glitches, as well as EM-fault injection, exemplify such injection mechanisms possessing these features.

We note that this categorization also matches well with the different fault types (p) of the methods, namely the second group can introduce only random faults to the intermediate value, while the first group can introduce all possible fault types. Both groups share the common characteristic of being capable of having only a few fixed target locations (non-adaptively), since too many lasers or EM-probes cannot simultaneously inject faults. Most importantly, both groups have the capability to inject faults as many times as desired and thus fault as many bits as desired.

In summary, *two types of adversaries can be distinguished: the first one injects only a few (upper bounded) but precise faults; whereas the second one injects many (unlimited) but random faults.*

However, as Table 3 indicates, fault and combined analysis methods do not fully utilize the capabilities of physical fault injection mechanisms, demanding only a fraction of them for a successful analysis. Specifically, these methods exploit a single injection over the entire encryption process, only when the limited number of bits have been faulted. To the best of our knowledge, there have been no proposed fault analysis methods requiring multiple fault injections (for ASIC implementations).

Table 4 shows that the mitigative adversary models tend to align better with the analytical adversary models rather than the capabilities of the physical fault injection mechanisms. The classical analytical adversary model is assuming *precise but a limited number of faults, i.e., bounded order of attack. In other words, it is assumed that an attacker can fault only a limited number (up to t) of bits/variables within a cycle or during the encryption process, and that they can always introduce precise faults. However, two exceptions to this trend are CAPA and M&M, which consider also attackers injecting many but random faults.*

We note that the mitigative adversary models' assumption that the order of attack is bounded is not always correct, as we have shown the physical injection mechanisms exhibit no such limitations. Moreover, whenever the attacker can introduce an unbounded number of faults they are no longer capable of being precise on the type of the faults. *Due to this discrepancy between the classical analytical adversary models and the physical reality, proposed countermeasures may provide only limited protection against physical fault injection mechanisms, despite their provable security within a more restricted mitigative adversary model.*

Conversely, the mitigative adversary models allow the attacker to target up to l locations and sometimes to be adaptive, while practical scenarios limit the injection to a few fixed positions. As such, the countermeasures may be considered *over-designed* with respect to the actual capabilities of the physical fault injection mechanisms.

This discussion leads us to the conclusion that in contrast to side-channel attacks, fault attacks do not have a known limitation regarding the number of fault injection events as well as the number of bits being faulted due to the capabilities of the physical fault injection mechanisms. SCA is known to be constrained by the noise level in the power/EM traces, which limits the order of the attack. However, for fault attacks, an attacker can inject several faults in a single clock cycle, potentially targeting a few locations based on the specific implementation and the fault setup, and hence the attacker can go beyond the order of attack chosen by the countermeasure.

We finish this overview by posing several open questions. We strongly believe that a more comprehensive and unified fault/combined adversary model must be established. The parameterized adversarial model presented in this work represents the first step towards such a model. We suggested two such sub-models, noting that more characteristics for them can be specified. The next step would aim to design improved countermeasures that are provably secure in this unified model. The error-correction and error-detection mechanisms used in countermeasures are typically limited in their capacity to handle a large number of faults. Thus, a mechanism is required that can provide finer granularity before the errors accumulate to an excessive extent. However, it remains an open question whether such a mechanism is achievable even if the fault propagation is inherently limited by design and given the capabilities of the fault injection mechanisms which can fault multiple bits at a single location. In addition, since all fault injection mechanisms have precise timing and duration control, time redundancy as a countermeasure seems to be more vulnerable than spatial redundancy. Probing the error propagation framework [23] matches well the classical mitigative adversary. However, when the number of faults is unbounded and they can happen on "any" location/value injecting a random value, the investigation of the propagations might become infeasible. A modification or extension of such a framework will be required. All those open questions we leave as future work.

Acknowledgements. This work was supported by CyberSecurity Research Flanders with reference number VR20192203.

References

1. Aghaie, A., Moradi, A., Rasoolzadeh, S., Shahmirzadi, A.R., Schellenberg, F., Schneider, T.: Impeccable circuits. IEEE Trans. Comput. **69**(3), 361–376 (2020). https://doi.org/10.1109/TC.2019.2948617
2. Agoyan, M., Dutertre, J., Naccache, D., Robisson, B., Tria, A.: When clocks fail: on critical paths and clock faults. In: Gollmann, D., Lanet, J., Iguchi-Cartigny, J. (eds.) CARDIS 2010. LNCS, vol. 6035, pp. 182–193. Springer, Heidelberg (2010). https://doi.org/10.1007/978-3-642-12510-2_13
3. Amiel, F., Villegas, K., Feix, B., Marcel, L.: Passive and active combined attacks: Combining fault attacks and side channel analysis. In: Breveglieri, L., Gueron, S., Koren, I., Naccache, D., Seifert, J. (eds.) Fourth International Workshop on Fault Diagnosis and Tolerance in Cryptography, 2007, FDTC 2007, Vienna, Austria, 10 September 2007, pp. 92–102. IEEE Computer Society (2007). https://doi.org/10.1109/FDTC.2007.4318989
4. Aumüller, C., Bier, P., Fischer, W., Hofreiter, P., Seifert, J.: Fault attacks on RSA with CRT: concrete results and practical countermeasures. In: Jr., B.S.K., Koç, Ç.K., Paar, C. (eds.) CHES 2002. LNCS, vol. 2523, pp. 260–275. Springer, Heidelberg (2002). https://doi.org/10.1007/3-540-36400-5_20
5. Bar-El, H., Choukri, H., Naccache, D., Tunstall, M., Whelan, C.: The sorcerer's apprentice guide to fault attacks. Proc. IEEE **94**(2), 370–382 (2006). https://doi.org/10.1109/JPROC.2005.862424
6. Bartkewitz, T., Bettendorf, S., Moos, T., Moradi, A., Schellenberg, F.: Beware of insufficient redundancy an experimental evaluation of code-based FI countermeasures. IACR Trans. Cryptogr. Hardw. Embed. Syst. **2022**(3), 438–462 (2022). https://doi.org/10.46586/tches.v2022.i3.438-462
7. Biham, E., Granboulan, L., Nguyen, P.Q.: Impossible fault analysis of RC4 and differential fault analysis of RC4. In: Gilbert, H., Handschuh, H. (eds.) FSE 2005. LNCS, vol. 3557, pp. 359–367. Springer, Heidelberg (2005). https://doi.org/10.1007/11502760_24
8. Biham, E., Shamir, A.: Differential fault analysis of secret key cryptosystems. In: Jr., B.S.K. (ed.) CRYPTO 1997. LNCS, vol. 1294, pp. 513–525. Springer, Heidelberg (1997). https://doi.org/10.1007/BFb0052259, https://doi.org/10.1007/BFb0052259
9. Blömer, J., Krummel, V.: Fault based collision attacks on AES. In: Breveglieri, L., Koren, I., Naccache, D., Seifert, J.P. (eds.) FDTC 2006. LNCS, vol. 4236, pp. 106–120. Springer, Heidelberg (2006). https://doi.org/10.1007/11889700_11

10. Boneh, D., DeMillo, R.A., Lipton, R.J.: On the importance of checking cryptographic protocols for faults (extended abstract). In: Fumy, W. (ed.) EUROCRYPT 1997. LNCS, vol. 1233, pp. 37–51. Springer, Heidelberg (1997). https://doi.org/10.1007/3-540-69053-0_4
11. Breier, J., Khairallah, M., Hou, X., Liu, Y.: A countermeasure against statistical ineffective fault analysis. IEEE Trans. Circuits Syst. **67-II**(12), 3322–3326 (2020). https://doi.org/10.1109/TCSII.2020.2989184
12. Brier, E., Clavier, C., Olivier, F.: Correlation power analysis with a leakage model. In: Joye, M., Quisquater, J. (eds.) CHES 2004. LNCS, vol. 3156, pp. 16–29. Springer, Heidelberg (2004). https://doi.org/10.1007/978-3-540-28632-5_2
13. Cassiers, G., Standaert, F.: Trivially and efficiently composing masked gadgets with probe isolating non-interference. IEEE Trans. Inf. Forensics Secur. **15**, 2542–2555 (2020). https://doi.org/10.1109/TIFS.2020.2971153
14. Clavier, C.: Secret external encodings do not prevent transient fault analysis. In: Paillier, P., Verbauwhede, I. (eds.) CHES 2007. LNCS, vol. 4727, pp. 181–194. Springer, Heidelberg (2007). https://doi.org/10.1007/978-3-540-74735-2_13
15. Clavier, C., Feix, B., Gagnerot, G., Roussellet, M.: Passive and active combined attacks on AES combining fault attacks and side channel analysis. In: 2010 Workshop on Fault Diagnosis and Tolerance in Cryptography, pp. 10–19 (2010). https://doi.org/10.1109/FDTC.2010.17
16. Courbon, F., Loubet-Moundi, P., Fournier, J.J.A., Tria, A.: Adjusting laser injections for fully controlled faults. In: Prouff, E. (ed.) COSADE 2014. LNCS, vol. 8622, pp. 229–242. Springer, Heidelberg (2014). https://doi.org/10.1007/978-3-319-10175-0_16
17. Courtois, N.T., Ware, D., Jackson, K.M.: Fault-algebraic attacks on inner rounds of des. In: The eSmart 2010 European Smart Card Security Conference (2010)
18. Daemen, J., Dobraunig, C., Eichlseder, M., Groß, H., Mendel, F., Primas, R.: Protecting against statistical ineffective fault attacks. IACR Trans. Cryptogr. Hardw. Embed. Syst. **2020**(3), 508–543 (2020). https://doi.org/10.13154/tches.v2020.i3.508-543
19. Dobraunig, C., Eichlseder, M., Groß, H., Mangard, S., Mendel, F., Primas, R.: Statistical ineffective fault attacks on masked AES with fault countermeasures. In: Peyrin, T., Galbraith, S.D. (eds.) ASIACRYPT 2018, Part II. LNCS, vol. 11273, pp. 315–342. Springer, Heidelberg (2018). https://doi.org/10.1007/978-3-030-03329-3_11
20. Dobraunig, C., Eichlseder, M., Korak, T., Lomné, V., Mendel, F.: Statistical fault attacks on nonce-based authenticated encryption schemes. In: Cheon, J.H., Takagi, T. (eds.) ASIACRYPT 2016, Part I. LNCS, vol. 10031, pp. 369–395. Springer, Heidelberg (2016). https://doi.org/10.1007/978-3-662-53887-6_14
21. Dobraunig, C., Eichlseder, M., Korak, T., Mangard, S., Mendel, F., Primas, R.: Sifa: exploiting ineffective fault inductions on symmetric cryptography. Trans. Cryptogr. Hardw. Embed. Syst. **2018**, 547–572 (2018). https://doi.org/10.13154/tches.v2018.i3.547-572
22. Dumont, M., Lisart, M., Maurine, P.: Electromagnetic fault injection: how faults occur. In: 2019 Workshop on Fault Diagnosis and Tolerance in Cryptography, FDTC 2019, Atlanta, GA, USA, 24 August 2019, pp. 9–16. IEEE (2019). https://doi.org/10.1109/FDTC.2019.00010
23. Feldtkeller, J., et al.: Combined private circuits - combined security refurbished, p. 1341 (2023). https://eprint.iacr.org/2023/1341

24. Feldtkeller, J., Richter-Brockmann, J., Sasdrich, P., Güneysu, T.: CINI MINIS: domain isolation for fault and combined security. In: Yin, H., Stavrou, A., Cremers, C., Shi, E. (eds.) Proceedings of the 2022 ACM SIGSAC Conference on Computer and Communications Security, CCS 2022, Los Angeles, CA, USA, 7–11 November 2022, pp. 1023–1036. ACM (2022). https://doi.org/10.1145/3548606.3560614
25. Fuhr, T., Jaulmes, É., Lomné, V., Thillard, A.: Fault attacks on AES with faulty ciphertexts only. In: Fischer, W., Schmidt, J. (eds.) 2013 Workshop on Fault Diagnosis and Tolerance in Cryptography, Los Alamitos, CA, USA, 20 August 2013, pp. 108–118. IEEE Computer Society (2013). https://doi.org/10.1109/FDTC.2013.18
26. Ghalaty, N.F., Yuce, B., Taha, M.M.I., Schaumont, P.: Differential fault intensity analysis. In: Tria, A., Choi, D. (eds.) 2014 Workshop on Fault Diagnosis and Tolerance in Cryptography, FDTC 2014, Busan, South Korea, 23 September 2014, pp. 49–58. IEEE Computer Society (2014). https://doi.org/10.1109/FDTC.2014.15
27. Giraud, C.: DFA on AES. In: Dobbertin, H., Rijmen, V., Sowa, A. (eds.) AES 2024, vol. 3373, pp. 27–41. Springer, Heidelberg (2005). https://doi.org/10.1007/11506447_4
28. Gruber, M., et al.: Domrep-an orthogonal countermeasure for arbitrary order side-channel and fault attack protection. IEEE Trans. Inf. Forensics Secur. **16**, 4321–4335 (2021). https://doi.org/10.1109/TIFS.2021.3089875
29. Hirata, H., et al.: All you need is fault: zero-value attacks on AES and a new λ-detection m&m. IACR Cryptol. ePrint Arch., p. 1129 (2023). https://eprint.iacr.org/2023/1129
30. Ishai, Y., Sahai, A., Wagner, D.A.: Private circuits: securing hardware against probing attacks. In: Boneh, D. (ed.) CRYPTO 2003. LNCS, vol. 2729, pp. 463–481. Springer, Heidelberg (2003). https://doi.org/10.1007/978-3-540-45146-4_27
31. Karaklajic, D., Schmidt, J., Verbauwhede, I.: Hardware designer's guide to fault attacks. IEEE Trans. Very Large Scale Integr. Syst. **21**(12), 2295–2306 (2013). https://doi.org/10.1109/TVLSI.2012.2231707
32. Li, Y., Sakiyama, K., Gomisawa, S., Fukunaga, T., Takahashi, J., Ohta, K.: Fault sensitivity analysis. In: Mangard, S., Standaert, F.X. (eds.) CHES 2010. LNCS, vol. 6225, pp. 320–334. Springer, Heidelberg (2010). https://doi.org/10.1007/978-3-642-15031-9_22
33. Liu, Z., Gu, D., Liu, Y., Li, W.: Linear fault analysis of block ciphers. In: Bao, F., Samarati, P., Zhou, J. (eds.) ACNS 2012. LNCS, vol. 7341, pp. 241–256. Springer, Heidelberg (2012). https://doi.org/10.1007/978-3-642-31284-7_15
34. Meyer, L.D., Arribas, V., Nikova, S., Nikov, V., Rijmen, V.: M&m: masks and macs against physical attacks. IACR Trans. Cryptogr. Hardw. Embed. Syst. **2019**(1), 25–50 (2019). https://doi.org/10.13154/tches.v2019.i1.25-50
35. Moradi, A., Mischke, O., Paar, C., Li, Y., Ohta, K., Sakiyama, K.: On the power of fault sensitivity analysis and collision side-channel attacks in a combined setting. In: Preneel, B., Takagi, T. (eds.) CHES 2011. LNCS, vol. 6917, pp. 292–311. Springer, Heidelberg (2011). https://doi.org/10.1007/978-3-642-23951-9_20
36. Ning, B., Liu, Q.: Modeling and efficiency analysis of clock glitch fault injection attack. In: Asian Hardware Oriented Security and Trust Symposium, AsianHOST 2018, Hong Kong, China, 17–18 December 2018, pp. 13–18. IEEE (2018). https://doi.org/10.1109/AsianHOST.2018.8607175
37. Ordas, S., Guillaume-Sage, L., Maurine, P.: EM injection: Fault model and locality. In: Homma, N., Lomné, V. (eds.) 2015 Workshop on Fault Diagnosis and Tolerance in Cryptography, FDTC 2015, Saint Malo, France, 13 September 2015, pp. 3–13. IEEE Computer Society (2015). https://doi.org/10.1109/FDTC.2015.9

38. Ordas, S., Guillaume-Sage, L., Maurine, P.: Electromagnetic fault injection: the curse of flip-flops. J. Cryptogr. Eng. **7**(3), 183–197 (2017). https://doi.org/10.1007/s13389-016-0128-3
39. Quisquater, J.J., Samyde, D.: Eddy current for magnetic analysis with active sensor. In: Proceedings of ESmart 2002 (2002)
40. Ramezanpour, K., Ampadu, P., Diehl, W.: FIMA: fault intensity map analysis. In: Polian, I., Stöttinger, M. (eds.) COSADE 2019. LNCS, vol. 11421, pp. 63–79. Springer, Heidelberg (2019). https://doi.org/10.1007/978-3-030-16350-1_5
41. Ramezanpour, K., Ampadu, P., Diehl, W.: Rs-mask: random space masking as an integrated countermeasure against power and fault analysis. In: 2020 IEEE International Symposium on Hardware Oriented Security and Trust, HOST 2020, San Jose, CA, USA, 7–11 December 2020, pp. 176–187. IEEE (2020). https://doi.org/10.1109/HOST45689.2020.9300266
42. Rasoolzadeh, S., Shahmirzadi, A.R., Moradi, A.: Impeccable circuits III. In: IEEE International Test Conference, ITC 2021, Anaheim, CA, USA, 10–15 October 2021, pp. 163–169. IEEE (2021). https://doi.org/10.1109/ITC50571.2021.00024
43. Reparaz, O., Meyer, L.D., Bilgin, B., Arribas, V., Nikova, S., Nikov, V., Smart, N.P.: CAPA: the spirit of beaver against physical attacks. In: Shacham, H., Boldyreva, A. (eds.) CRYPTO 2018, Part I. LNCS, vol. 10991, pp. 121–151. Springer, Heidelberg (2018). https://doi.org/10.1007/978-3-319-96884-1_5
44. Richter-Brockmann, J., Güneysu, T.: Improved side-channel resistance by dynamic fault-injection countermeasures. In: 31st IEEE International Conference on Application-specific Systems, Architectures and Processors , ASAP 2020, Manchester, United Kingdom, 6–8 July 2020, pp. 117–124. IEEE (2020). https://doi.org/10.1109/ASAP49362.2020.00029
45. Richter-Brockmann, J., Sasdrich, P., Güneysu, T.: Revisiting fault adversary models - hardware faults in theory and practice. IEEE Trans. Comput. **72**(2), 572–585 (2023). https://doi.org/10.1109/TC.2022.3164259
46. Roche, T., Lomné, V., Khalfallah, K.: Combined fault and side-channel attack on protected implementations of AES. In: Prouff, E. (ed.) -CARDIS 2011. LNCS, vol. 7079, pp. 65–83. Springer, Heidelberg (2011). https://doi.org/10.1007/978-3-642-27257-8_5
47. Saha, S., Bag, A., Jap, D., Mukhopadhyay, D., Bhasin, S.: Divided we stand, united we fall: Security analysis of some SCA+SIFA countermeasures against sca-enhanced fault template attacks. In: Tibouchi, M., Wang, H. (eds.) ASIACRYPT 2021, Part II. LNCS, vol. 13091, pp. 62–94. Springer, Heidelberg (2021). https://doi.org/10.1007/978-3-030-92075-3_3
48. Saha, S., Bag, A., Roy, D.B., Patranabis, S., Mukhopadhyay, D.: Fault template attacks on block ciphers exploiting fault propagation. In: Canteaut, A., Ishai, Y. (eds.) EUROCRYPT 2020, Part I. LNCS, vol. 12105, pp. 612–643. Springer, Heidelberg (2020). https://doi.org/10.1007/978-3-030-45721-1_22
49. Saha, S., Jap, D., Roy, D.B., Chakraborti, A., Bhasin, S., Mukhopadhyay, D.: Transform-and-encode: A countermeasure framework for statistical ineffective fault attacks on block ciphers. IACR Cryptol. ePrint Arch., p. 545 (2019). https://eprint.iacr.org/2019/545
50. Schellenberg, F., Finkeldey, M., Gerhardt, N., Hofmann, M., Moradi, A., Paar, C.: Large laser spots and fault sensitivity analysis. In: Robinson, W.H., Bhunia, S., Kastner, R. (eds.) 2016 IEEE International Symposium on Hardware Oriented Security and Trust, HOST 2016, McLean, VA, USA, 3–5 May 2016, pp. 203–208. IEEE Computer Society (2016). https://doi.org/10.1109/HST.2016.7495583

51. Schneider, T., Moradi, A., Güneysu, T.: Parti - towards combined hardware countermeasures against side-channel and fault-injection attacks. In: Robshaw, M., Katz, J. (eds.) CRYPTO 2016, Part II. LNCS, vol. 9815, pp. 302–332. Springer, Heidelberg (2016). https://doi.org/10.1007/978-3-662-53008-5_11
52. Shahmirzadi, A.R., Rasoolzadeh, S., Moradi, A.: Impeccable circuits II. In: 57th ACM/IEEE Design Automation Conference, DAC 2020, San Francisco, CA, USA, 20–24 July 2020, pp. 1–6. IEEE (2020). https://doi.org/10.1109/DAC18072.2020.9218615
53. Simon, T., et al.: Friet: an authenticated encryption scheme with built-in fault detection. In: Canteaut, A., Ishai, Y. (eds.) EUROCRYPT 2020, Part I. LNCS, vol. 12105, pp. 581–611. Springer, Heidelberg (2020). https://doi.org/10.1007/978-3-030-45721-1_21
54. Skorobogatov, S.P., Anderson, R.J.: Optical fault induction attacks. In: Jr., B.S.K., Koç, Ç.K., Paar, C. (eds.) CHES 2002. LNCS, vol. 2523, pp. 2–12. Springer, Heidelberg (2002). https://doi.org/10.1007/3-540-36400-5_2
55. Spruyt, A., Milburn, A., Chmielewski, L.: Fault injection as an oscilloscope: fault correlation analysis. IACR Trans. Cryptogr. Hardw. Embed. Syst. **2021**(1), 192–216 (2021). https://doi.org/10.46586/tches.v2021.i1.192-216
56. Vafaei, N., Zarei, S., Bagheri, N., Eichlseder, M., Primas, R., Soleimany, H.: Statistical effective fault attacks: the other side of the coin. IEEE Trans. Inf. Forensics Secur. **17**, 1855–1867 (2022). https://doi.org/10.1109/TIFS.2022.3172634
57. Yen, S., Joye, M.: Checking before output may not be enough against fault-based cryptanalysis. IEEE Trans. Comput. **49**(9), 967–970 (2000). https://doi.org/10.1109/12.869328
58. Zussa, L., Dutertre, J., Clédière, J., Tria, A.: Power supply glitch induced faults on FPGA: an in-depth analysis of the injection mechanism. In: 2013 IEEE 19th International On-Line Testing Symposium (IOLTS), Chania, Crete, Greece, 8–10 July 2013, pp. 110–115. IEEE (2013). https://doi.org/10.1109/IOLTS.2013.6604060

Cutting the GRASS: Threshold GRoup Action Signature Schemes

Michele Battagliola[1], Giacomo Borin[4,5](✉), Alessio Meneghetti[1], and Edoardo Persichetti[2,3]

[1] Università di Trento, Trento, Italy
{michele.battagliola,alessio.meneghetti}@unitn.it
[2] Florida Atlantic University, Boca Raton, USA
epersichetti@fau.edu
[3] Sapienza University, Rome, Italy
[4] IBM Research, Zurich, Rüschlikon, Switzerland
giacomo.borin@ibm.com
[5] University of Zurich, Zürich, Switzerland

Abstract. Group actions are fundamental mathematical tools, with a long history of use in cryptography. Indeed, the action of finite groups at the basis of the discrete logarithm problem is behind a very large portion of modern cryptographic systems. With the advent of post-quantum cryptography, however, other group actions, such as isogeny-based ones, received interest from the cryptographic community, attracted by the possibility of translating old discrete logarithm-based functionalities.

Usually, research focuses on abelian group actions; however in this work we show that isomorphism problems which stem from non-abelian cryptographic group actions can be viable building blocks for threshold signature schemes. In particular, we construct a full N-out-of-N threshold signature scheme, and discuss the efficiency issues arising from extending it to the generic T-out-of-N case. To give a practical outlook on our constructions, we instantiate them with two different flavors of code-based cryptographic group actions, respectively at the basis of the LESS and MEDS signature schemes, two of NIST's candidates in the recent call for post-quantum standardization.

1 Introduction

With the threat of quantum computers looming ever closer, the community has stirred to produce alternative cryptographic solutions, that will be resistant to attackers equipped with such technology. Indeed, considering the timeline expected to design, standardize, implement and deliver such solutions, initiatives such as NIST's [55] are definitely timely. To be sure, NIST's standardization effort can be considered a first step, with more to follow. For instance, while the first standards are about to be drafted, covering key encapsulation and signatures, the situation with the latter is considered not fully satisfactory, to the point that NIST launched an "on-ramp" process to standardize new signature designs [56]. Furthermore, there is a scarcity of threshold-friendly schemes

E. Oswald (Ed.): CT-RSA 2024, LNCS 14643, pp. 460–489, 2024.
https://doi.org/10.1007/978-3-031-58868-6_18

among the current solutions, which is prompting more research in this area, and will lead to its own standardization process [24].

Code-based cryptography, which makes use of problems and techniques coming from coding theory, is the second largest area within the post-quantum realm, capable of offering interesting solutions, particularly in the context of key establishment. Indeed, all three candidates in NIST's 4th round of standardization are code-based [2,4,5], with two of them expected to be added to the current list of standards (which, for KEMs, includes only Kyber [58]). On the other hand, this area has historically struggled to produce efficient signature schemes: as a litmus test, none of those presented to NIST in 2017 made it past the first round. This steered the community towards experimenting with different paradigms, such as, for instance MPC-in-the-head [39,40,48].

The work of LESS [19], which started in 2020 and continued with various follow-ups [7–9], uses a different approach, stepping away from the traditional decoding problem, and focusing instead on the difficulty of finding an *isometry* between two linear codes. In fact, the security of LESS relies solely on the well-known *code equivalence problem.* This idea was recently extended [29] to the class of *matrix codes*, which are measured in the rank metric, and yields the parallel notion of *matrix equivalence.* Interestingly, the action of isometries on the respective types of codes can be formulated as a (non-commutative) group action, which gives a new perspective on the field, and opens the way to other constructions beyond plain signatures. Indeed, the use of group actions in cryptography dates back all the way to Diffie and Hellman, and has found new vigor as a post-quantum method, thanks to the recent developments on isogenies [18,26].

Non commutativity of code-based group actions has advantages from a security viewpoint since it prevents quantum attacks on commutative group actions like Kuperberg's algorithm for the dihedral hidden subgroup problem [50]. However this clearly reduce the possible cryptographic primitives based on them, for example we cannot build a Diffie-Hellmann like key exchange or use Linear Secret Sharing.

1.1 Related Work

A (T, N)-threshold digital signature scheme is a protocol designed to distribute the right to sign messages to any subset of at least T out of N key owners, with the restriction that none of the N players can repudiate a valid signature. A key point in most threshold digital signature schemes is compatibility with existing schemes: even though the key generation and signing algorithms are multi-party protocols (MPC), in fact, the verification algorithm is identical to that of an existing signature scheme, usually referred to as the "centralized" scheme.

In 1996, a first $(T+1, 2T+1)$-threshold digital signature scheme was proposed [44]. A few years later, the same authors discuss the security of distributed key generation for the case of schemes based on the Discrete Logarithm Problem [45,46]. Since 2001, several authors started working first on two-party variants of digital signatures [53,54] and then on ECDSA [36,51]. The first general (T, N)-threshold scheme was proposed in 2016 [43], improved first in 2017 [21], and then again in 2018 [42]. In 2019, the work of [36] has been generalized by the same authors to the multi-party case [37]. While the signing algorithm requires the participation of at least T players to take part in a multi-party protocol, the key generation algorithm requires the involvement of a Trusted Authority or the active participation of all N players. This requirement has been relaxed in a recent $(2, 3)$ threshold ECDSA version [14], where the key generation algorithm involves only 2 out the 3 parties.

As noted in [23], a challenging task in designing a threshold version of the EdDSA signature scheme is the distribution among the parties of the deterministic nonce generation, a task that can be carried out either with MPC techniques or with zero-knowledge proofs (ZKP). Following the latter approach, the work presented in [14] has successively been extended to a $(2, 3)$-threshold EdDSA instantiation [13]. In [22], the authors propose instead an MPC-based threshold scheme for HashEdDSA. In the latter, T is bounded to be less than $\frac{N}{2} + 1$. Finally, in 2022, a variant of [13] suitable for Schnorr signatures has been proposed [11] and then generalized to a ZKP-based (T, N)-threshold Schnorr digital signature scheme whose key generation algorithm does not involve any trusted party [12].

Recently, driven by both the NIST call for Post-Quantum Standardization [55] and the call for Multi-Party Threshold Schemes [24], many researchers have started to wonder whether it could be possible to design post-quantum versions of threshold digital signature schemes. Since most of the existing literature for threshold schemes focuses on trapdoors that rely on the difficulty of the Discrete Logarithm Problem, new methods have to be investigated, likely starting with tools already utilized to design plain signatures, such as lattices, codes, multivariate equations etc. In [31], the (round 2) proposals of the standardization process were analyzed in order to determine ways to define threshold variants, eventually identifying multivariate schemes as the most suitable starting point, with schemes based on the Unbalanced Oil and Vinegar (UOV) framework being the most promising. Even though, from a theoretical point of view, it appears to be indeed possible to obtain a threshold version of UOV by exploiting MPC protocols using Linear Secret Sharing Schemes (LSSS), this approach remains, at the present time, only theoretical.

Notably, threshold signature schemes for cryptographic cyclic group actions have been already discussed in 2020 and applied to isogeny-based schemes [35], where they proposed a way to apply a group actions in a threshold like way by using the classical Shamir Secret sharing on a group action induced by a cyclic group. They showed how to apply this for an El Gamal like encryption schemes and a signature based on Σ-protocols proving their simulatability, however this schemes are only secure in the honest-but-curious model and miss a distributed key generation mechanisms. In [32] they showed a way to combine the use of zero-knowledge proofs and replicated secret sharing to obtain a secure threshold signature scheme from isogeny assumptions. The work is an important step for the research and can be extended to more general group actions, but the main drawbacks are the number of shares necessary to implement replicated secret sharing and the important slow down caused by the additional ZKPs required.

In [16] they showed how to define a distributed key generation algorithm by using a new primitive called *piecewise verifiable proofs*; proving their security in the quantum random oracle model. All previous techniques are then incorporated in [25] to have actively secure attributed based encryption and signature schemes, in which threshold signature are a particular case.

1.2 Our Contribution

In this work, we investigate constructions for post-quantum threshold signature schemes, using cryptographic group actions as the main building block. However, our goal is to take a step back, and keep requirements to a minimum, without needing additional properties such as, for instance, commutativity. This will allow our frameworks to be instantiated with a wider variety of candidates, such as the aforementioned code-based signature schemes.

A Full Threshold Scheme. As a first contribution, we present a construction for a "full" (N, N)-threshold signature scheme with a distributed key generation mechanism. The core idea is to split both the secret key and the ephemeral map as a product of N group elements, i.e. as $g = g_1 \cdots g_N$, so that thanks to this shared knowledge the users are able to prove the knowledge of secret the key. We then prove its security via a reduction to the original centralized signature[1] without relying on additional ZKPs during the signature phase, but instead relying on a securely generated salt. The details of the construction, as well as the security proof, are given in Sect. 3.

Bootstrapping Using Replicated Secret Sharing. Our second contribution is the (T, N) version of scheme. Since we cannot assume any properties on the groups (except the security of the group actions), our construction is quite inefficient in terms of memory required. This is because we need to distribute multiple keys to each user. We illustrate this by presenting some performance figures in the selected scenario, namely, the code-based setting. Nevertheless, our construction remains practical for certain use cases, especially for low values of T and N, or whenever T and N are very close.

1.3 Outline

We begin in Sect. 2, where we provide all the necessary preliminary definitions and notions used in the paper. Then, in Sect. 3 we present the full threshold version of the signature, together with a security proof. In Sect. 4 we show how to construct a possible solution to obtain a general (T, N)-version, adapting the previous framework as well as its proof. To provide a practical outlook, we present a concrete instantiation of both protocols, in Sect. 5, utilizing the code equivalence group actions at the basis of the LESS and MEDS signature schemes. We conclude in Sect. 6.

[1] This is a generic signature scheme that is simply an abstraction, but has appeared in literature when instantiated in various works, such as LESS [8] and MEDS [29].

2 Preliminaries

We begin by laying down our notation. Throughout the paper we will denote with capital letters objects such as sets and groups, and with lowercase letters their elements. We will use instead boldface letters to denote vectors and matrices. We indicate by $\mathbb{F}_q$ the finite field of cardinality q, and by $\mathbb{F}_q^{k \times n}$ the set of $k \times n$ matrices with entries in $\mathbb{F}_q$; when $k = 1$, we write simply $\mathbb{F}_q^n$, which denotes the corresponding vector space over $\mathbb{F}_q$. Due to space constraints, we omit standard notions from coding theory; these are included, for completeness, in Appendix A.

2.1 Cryptographic Group Actions

A *group action* is a well-known object in mathematics. It can be described as a function, as shown below, where X is a set and G a group.

$$\begin{aligned} \star : G \times X &\to X \\ (g, x) &\mapsto g \star x \end{aligned}$$

A group action's only requirement is to be *compatible* with the group; using multiplicative notation for G, and denoting with e its identity element, this means that for all $x \in X$ we have $e \star x = x$ and that moreover for all $g, h \in G$, it holds that $h \star (g \star x) = (h \cdot g) \star x$. The orbit of a set element is the set $\mathcal{O}(x) := \{g \star x \mid g \in G\}$. A group action is also said to be:

- *Transitive*, if for every $x, y \in X$, there exists $g \in G$ such that $y = g \star x$;
- *Faithful*, if there does not exist a $g \in G$ such that $x = g \star x$ for all $x \in X$, other than the identity;
- *Free*, if an element $g \in G$ is equal to identity whenever there exists an $x \in X$ such that $x = g \star x$;
- *Regular*, if it is free and transitive.

The adjective *cryptographic* is added to indicate that the group action in question has additional properties that are relevant to cryptography. For instance, a cryptographic group action should be *one-way*, i.e. given randomly chosen $x, y \in X$, it should be hard to find $g \in G$ such that $g \star x = y$ (if such a g exists). Indeed, the problem of finding such an element is known as the *vectorization* problem, or sometimes *Group Action Inverse Problem (GAIP)*.

Problem 1 (GAIP). *Given x and y in X, compute an element $g \in G$ such that $y = g \star x$.*

A related problem asks to compute the action of the product of two group elements, given the result of the individual actions on a fixed element. This is known as the *parallelization* problem, and it corresponds to, essentially, the computational version of the Diffie-Hellman problem, formulated for generic group actions. A definition is given next.

Problem 2 (cGADH). *Given x, $g \star x$ and $h \star x$, for $g, h \in G$, compute $(g \cdot h) \star x$.*

In fact, the analogy to the case of discrete logarithms is easily drawn, once one realizes that this is simply the group action given by the exponentiation map on finite cyclic groups. Then GAIP corresponds to DLP and cGADH to the CDH problem. Observe that GAIP is related to the one-wayness of the group action while the cGAGH is linked to its pseudorandomness, in fact requiring the hardness of the decisional version is implied by the following stronger definition:

Definition 1. *A group action is 2-weakly pseudorandom if no probabilistic polynomial time algorithm that given* $(x, g \star x)$ *can distinguish with non negligible probability between* (x_1, y) *and* $(x_1, g \star x_1)$ *with* $x, x_1, y \xleftarrow{\$} X$ *and* $g \xleftarrow{\$} G$.

Note that Definition 1 is a weaker assumption than the classical weak pseudorandomness from [3, Definition 3.6]. This new assumption is required since it was recently shown that many cryptographic group actions do not achieve the weakly pseudorandomness property, as per [33].

It is possible to obtain a signature scheme from cryptographic group actions, in full generality; a description is given in Appendix B. A quick overview of code-based group actions can also be found in the appendix, namely, in Appendix C.

2.2 Threshold Signatures

We briefly summarize here the relevant notions for threshold signature schemes. In a nutshell, a (T, N)-threshold signature is a multi-party protocol that allows any T parties out of a total of N to compute a signature that may be verified against a common public key. We assume that each user has access to a secure, reliable and authenticated private channel with each of the other users, without worrying about specific design and peculiarities of the channel.

Usually, threshold signature protocols involve a key-generation protocol that constructs the key pair $(\mathsf{sk}, \mathsf{pk})$ as well as shares of the private key sk_i, and a multiparty signature protocol Thre.Sign, such that any set of T parties who agree on a common message m is able to compute a signature, which is verifiable against the public key via the procedure Verify. KeyGen can be executed by a trusted party or by the N parties alone collaborating. In this "decentralized" case, the parties get access to the additional exchanged information.

Often, threshold signature protocols are obtained by adapting "plain" signature schemes, which are then referred to as "centralized", for obvious reasons. In this case, a common requested property is that signatures produced by the threshold protocol are indistinguishable from signatures produced by the centralized one. We refer as the *view* of a user as the probability distribution on the transcripts of all the data available to him during the execution of the multi-party protocol.

The main security property for threshold signature schemes is *Existential Unforgeability under Chosen Message Attacks (EUF-CMA)*:

Definition 2. *A threshold digital signature is secure in the EUF-CMA if for any probabilistic polynomial-time adversary* Evl *that is allowed to:*

1. *Corrupt* $T-1$ *out of* N *users;*
2. *Query a key generation oracle for the* $T-1$ *corrupted users shares and the public key* pk*. In the decentralized case it gets access also to the corrupted users view of* KeyGen *during the shared execution;*
3. *Perform a polynomial number of adaptive queries to a signing oracle that on chosen messages* m_i *obtaining the view of* Thre.Sign*;*

it is not able to obtain a valid signature on a non queried message, i.e.

$$Adv^{\mathsf{Evl}}_{CMA} = \mathbb{P}\left[\mathsf{DS.Verify}(\mathsf{pk}, \mathsf{m}^*, \sigma^*) = 1 \,\middle|\, \begin{matrix} \mathsf{m}^*, \sigma^* \leftarrow \mathsf{Evl}\,, \\ \mathsf{m}^* \neq \mathsf{m}_i \; \forall i\;. \end{matrix}\right] \leqslant \mathsf{negl}(\lambda) \quad (1)$$

Informally, the idea is that less than T views cannot be combined to obtain a valid signature.

3 The Full Scheme

We start our analysis with the *full threshold* cases, in which all the users are required to produce a signature (i.e. $T = N$).

Decentralized Key Generation Algorithm. The goal of this protocol is to produce a common public key $y = g \star x$ with $g = g_1 \cdot \ldots \cdot g_N$, where each party holds one g_i, in the same way of [10,32]. To do so the users sequentially apply a previously committed random group element to the origin x and add the non-interactive Zero-Knowledge proof from [32] (see it also in Fig. 4, in the appendix) to show the freshness of the group element. The resulting protocol is shown in Algorithm 1. At line 5, the Zero-Knowledge Proof is sent and tested by the other parties; the protocol is trusted by all of them if and only if all the ZKPs are valid. The main difference with [32] is that our scheme is specialized for non-abelian group actions and we are able to prove the security with only one ZKP per user, compared to the two required by [32].

Algorithm 1. KeyGen

Require: $x \in X$ origin.
Ensure: Public key $y = g \star x$, each participant holds g_i such that $\prod g_i = g$.
1: Each participant P_i chooses $g_i \in G$ and publishes $x_i' = g_i \star x$.
2: Set $x_0 = x$.
3: **for** $i = 1$ to N **do**
4: $\quad P_i$ computes $x_i = g_i \star x_{i-1}$
5: $\quad P_i$ publishes a ZKP as in Figure 4 proving $x_i' = \tilde{g}_i \star x \wedge x_i = \tilde{g}_i \star x_{i-1}$.
6: $\quad P_i$ sends x_i to P_{i+1} (if $i < N$)
7: **return** $y = x_N$. The private key of P_i is g_i.

A relevant limitation, for the proposed protocol, is that each user P_i needs to receive the set element x_{i-1} by P_{i-1} before starting its computations. Thus, as explained in [35], it is necessary to adopt a *sequential round-robin* communication structure that makes it impossible to parallelize the algorithm; this results in a slowing of the execution time. Moreover, the users need to agree on a precise execution order at the start.

Signing Algorithm. The signing protocol generalizes the one presented in [32,35] for non-abelian group actions, by computing the commitment and response phase of the protocol in Fig. 3 in a multiparty setting.

In the commitment phase, each user P_i receives x^j_{i-1}, computes $x^j_i = \tilde{g}^j_i \star x^j_{i-1}$ for random $\tilde{g}_i$ and outputs it. During the response phase (lines 17,18) P_i get u^j_{i-1} and outputs $u^j_i = \tilde{g}^j_i u^j_{i-1} g_i^{-\mathsf{ch}_j}$. In line 19 for the challenge $\mathsf{ch}_j = 0$ the parties verify that $\tilde{x}^j_i = u^j_i \star x$, while in the other case they check $\tilde{x}^j_i = u^j_i \star x_i$. The idea of this multiparty protocol is illustrated in Fig. 1.

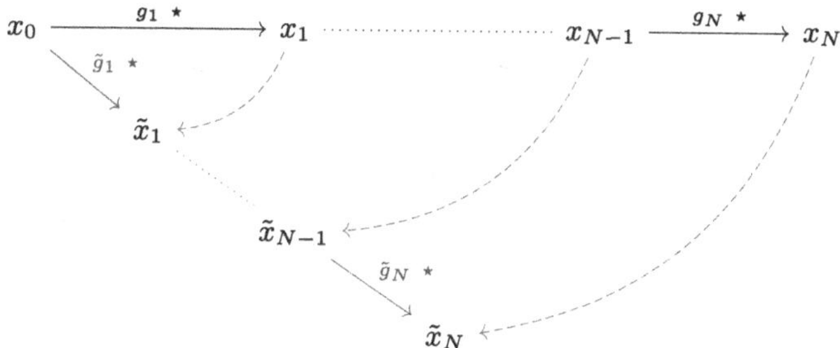

Fig. 1. Scheme representing the idea behind the protocol in Algorithm 2. In blue are the ephemeral group elements revealed on $\mathsf{ch} = 0$, while in red the map reconstructed for $\mathsf{ch} = 1$. (Color figure online)

A detailed description of the algorithm is given in Algorithm 2. We also include the verification algorithm Algorithm 3, which is the same as the centralized one, for completeness.

A key feature of Algorithm 2, with respect to the previous literature, is the use of secure salt during the challenge evaluation (line 11), a technique used also in [27]. The salt is crucial to reduce the number of ZKPs in the signing protocol while maintaining security in the presence of malicious users. Indeed, without the salt verification, the scheme can be attacked by a *malicious* adversary opening several concurrent sessions. Intuitively, suppose that the adversary is in control of the N-th user and wants to sign the message m for the public key $y = g \star x$, knowing only g_N. He can proceed in the following way:

1. The adversary starts λ signing sessions for any messages m_1, ..., m_λ.
2. For every session s, he receives by P_{N-1} $x^1_{N-1}, \dots, x^\lambda_{N-1}$. At this point he evaluates $x^1_N = \tilde{g}^1_N \star x^1_{N-1}$ for each session s as described in the protocol. Let us call this element $\hat{x}^s$ for each session.

Algorithm 2. Thre.Sign

Require: $x \in X$, security parameter λ, hash function H, public key $(x, y = g \star x)$, secure commitment scheme COM. The party P_i knows the (multiplicative) share g_i of $g = g_1 \cdots g_N$.

Ensure: A valid signature for the message m under the public key (x, y).

P_1 set $x_0^j = x$ for all $j = 1$ to λ ▷ Shared commitment generation phase
for $i = 1$ to N **do**
    Each party pick salt_i uniformly random and sends $\mathsf{COM}(\mathsf{salt}_i)$
for $i = 1$ to N **do**
    If $i > 1$ P_i receives x_{i-1}^j from P_{i-1} for all $j = 1$ to λ
    for $j = 1$ to λ **do**
        P_i chooses $\tilde{g}_i^j \in G$ and computes $x_i^j = \tilde{g}_i^j \star x_{i-1}^j$
        P_i outputs x_i^j;
Set $x^j = x_N^j$ for all $j = 1$ to λ. Party N broadcasts all x^j to all players.
Each party publishes salt_i and checks the consistency of the received data with the initial commitment.
$\mathsf{salt} = \sum_i \mathsf{salt}_i$
Compute $\mathsf{ch} = \mathsf{H}(x^1 \| \ldots \| x^\lambda \| \mathsf{salt} \| \mathsf{m})$ ▷ Non-iterative challenges evaluation
P_1 set $u_0^j = e$ for all $j = 1$ to λ ▷ Shared response generation phase
for $i = 1$ to N **do**
    If $i > 1$ P_i receives u_{i-1}^j from P_{i-1} for all $j = 1, \ldots, \lambda$
    for $j = 1$ to λ **do**
        P_i computes $u_i^j = \tilde{g}_i^j u_{i-1}^j g_i^{-\mathsf{ch}_j}$
        P_i outputs u_i^j
        All users verify u_i^j is valid;
$\mathsf{resp}_j = u_N^j$ for all $j = 1$ to λ
$\mathsf{sig} = \mathsf{ch} \| \mathsf{salt} \| \mathsf{rsp}_1 \| \ldots \| \mathsf{rsp}_\lambda$

3. He evaluates the challenge $\mathsf{ch} = \mathsf{H}(\hat{x}^1 \| \ldots \| \hat{x}^\lambda \| \mathsf{m})$.
4. For each session s, the adversary then evaluates $x_N^2, \ldots, x_N^{\lambda-1}$ legitimately, then chooses $\tilde{g}_N^\lambda$ so that the first bit of $\mathsf{H}(x_N^1 \| \ldots \| x_N^\lambda \| \mathsf{m}_i)$ is equal to the s-th bit of ch. This would not be possible if we had a secure salt.
5. Finally, the adversary closes all the concurrent sessions obtaining, for the session s, the response u_{N-1}^1 received from P_{N-1}, which is used to evaluate rsp_1. This can be used to answer ch_s and obtain a valid signature $\mathsf{ch} \| \hat{\mathsf{rsp}}_1 \| \ldots \| \hat{\mathsf{rsp}}_\lambda$.

Algorithm 3. Verify

Require: $x \in X$, security parameter λ, hash function H, public key $(x, y = g \star x)$.
Ensure: Accept if the signature for the message m is valid under the public key (x, y).

1: Parse $\mathsf{ch}, \mathsf{salt}, \mathsf{rsp}_1, \ldots, \mathsf{rsp}_\lambda$ from sig
2: **for** $j = 1$ to λ **do**
3:     **if** $\mathsf{ch}_j = 0$ **then**
4:         set $\hat{x}^j = \mathsf{rsp}_j \star x$
5:     **else**
6:         set $\hat{x}^j = \mathsf{rsp}_j \star y$
7: Accept if $\mathsf{ch} = \mathsf{H}(\hat{x}^1 \| \ldots \| \hat{x}^\lambda \| \mathsf{salt} \| \mathsf{m})$

3.1 Security Proof

Theorem 1. *For a 2-weakly pseudorandom free group action (Definition 1), if the centralized signature is unforgeable in the quantum random oracle model, then the full-threshold signature scheme composed by* KeyGen, Thre.Sign *(Algorithms 1 and 2) and the verification* Verify *is EUF-CMA secure in the quantum random oracle model.*

Lemma 1. *For a 2-weakly pseudorandom free group action (Definition 1), the protocol* KeyGen *can be simulated in the quantum random oracle model in polynomial time so that any probabilistic polynomial-time adversary is convinced that the public key is any fixed pair $x, y \in X$.*

The main idea of the proof is to use the ZKPs to recover their secret shares and simulate a view of the protocol. Unlike [32], here we only have one ZKP for any user, thus we rely in rewinding the tape to change the set element sent in line 6. This proof works in the quantum random oracle model since the protocol in Fig. 4 is a non-interactive zero-knowledge quantum proof of knowledge in the quantum random oracle for a free group action [16, Theorem 1] .

Algorithm 4. Sim.KeyGen (Simulation of KeyGen)

Require: $x, y \in X$, a non corrupted user P_{i_0}.

1: Send to Evl a random x'_{i_0} generated from x (as normal);
2: Checks all the ZKP for $i < i_0$ (as normal);
3: Send to Evl a random x_{i_0};
4: Send a ZKP for x_{i_0} and x'_{i_0}.
5: Continue the protocol and estranct g_i from the ZKPs for all $i > i_0$;
6: Rewind the tape of the adversary up to the same state as in line 3;
7: Send $x_{i_0} = (g_{i_0+1}^{-1} \cdots g_N^{-1}) \star y$;
8: Simulate again ZKP for x_{i_0} and x'_{i_0}.
9: The protocol is executed normally leading to x, y as public key.

Proof of Lemma 1. Algorithm 4 shows the simulation strategy for a probabilistic polynomial-timeadversary Evl. We now need to prove that the simulation terminates in expected polynomial time, it is indistinguishable from a real execution, and outputs y.

The simulation terminates in polynomial time with non-negligible probability if also Evl is a probabilistic polynomial-time algorithm; in fact we have to carry over:

- one rewind of Evl in line 6;
- at most $N-1$ extractions of secrets from the ZKPs, that can be carried over in polynomial time using the Forking Lemma [15] on the single ZKP. The probability for the adversary to fake the ZKP where a share does not exists is negligible, assuming the one-wayness of the group action.

Note that the rewinding can be performed since the adversary has already committed to the values g_i before the rewinding phase. In addition, thanks to the ZKPs, these group elements must exist, and the adversary is forced to apply them on $x_{i_0} = (g_{i_0+1}^{-1} \cdots g_N^{-1}) \star y$, so that the output of the simulation is the public key x, y as desired.

To send the crafted element x_{i_0} and simulate the ZKPs in lines 7 and 8, we need the 2-weakly pseudorandom property (Definition 1). This is because a common group element g_{i_0} such that $x'_{i_0} = g_{i_0} \star x \wedge x_{i_0} = g_{i_0} \star x_{i_0-1}$ does not exist anymore. The simulation can be carried over in the quatum random oracle since the protocol in Fig. 4 is a non-interactive zero-knowledge quantum proof of knowledge (see Proposition 3). □

The proof of Theorem 1 follows the game-based argument proposed in [47, Theorem 3]. The key idea is to reduce the security of the full threshold signature to the security of the centralized one. We need 3 games (Algorithm 5), and we need to reprogram the random oracle, thanks to [47, Proposition 1].

Proof Theorem 1. Consider a probabilistic polynomial-time adversary Evl that make up to q_s sign queries and q_h quantum call to the random oracle H. By in Lemma 1 we can simulate the KeyGen on any public key x, y, so we will not discuss it here again.

Consider the games from Algorithm 5. Since the protocol Thre.Sign and KeyGen are executed in multiparty, if by any reason the protocol is aborted because of Evl misbehaviour, the game ends and returns 0.

Game G_0. This game is the same one played for the EUF-CMA security in Definition 2, thus $\mathbb{P}[G_0^{\mathsf{Evl}} \to 1] = \mathsf{Adv}_{CMA}^{\mathsf{Evl}}$ by definition.

Game G_1. In this game nothing is changed but we set ch at random and we reprogram the random oracle. We can observe that any statistical difference between the games can be used to build a distinguisher for the reprogramming of the oracle; in particular we can adapt the distinguisher from the proof of [47, Theorem 3]. In total, we reprogram the oracle q_s times (one for every signature) and Evl performs q_h quantum calls. Moreover, note that $x^1, \ldots, x^\lambda$, m are (at least partially) controlled by the adversary, while salt is randomly sampled thanks to the initial commitments and the secure aggregation. Thus, by [47, Proposition 1] we have:

$$|\mathbb{P}[G_0^{\mathsf{Evl}} \to 1] - \mathbb{P}[G_1^{\mathsf{Evl}} \to 1]| \leqslant \frac{3g_s}{2^{1+\lambda}}\sqrt{q_h} \tag{2}$$

Game G_2. First of all, note that during the computation of the response, it is possible to check whether the received u_i^j is correct or not, if the user $i+1$ saved all the x_i during the key generation step. We exploit this property in our simulation. Indeed, to simulate a signature, the simulator first acts honestly and follows the protocol. Upon receiving all the responses u_i^j of $P_1, ..., P_{i_0-1}$, it checks the correctness of all of them. If they are all correct, it rewinds the adversary up until receiving $\tilde{x}_{i_0-1}$ and chooses $\tilde{x}_{i_0}$ according to challenge ch_j (Fig. 2 shows schematically of how the simulation strategy works). In particular:

- linking $\tilde{x}_{i_0-1}$ and $\tilde{x}_{i_0}$ on challenge $\mathsf{ch}_j = 0$;
- linking x_{i_0} and $\tilde{x}_{i_0}$ on challenge $\mathsf{ch}_j = 1$;

The idea is that every time the adversary acts honestly until P_{i_0}, the simulator produces an indistinguishable transcript that will not be rejected during the response computation. When, instead, the adversary sends something wrong before P_{i_0}, the simulation is perfect. Indeed, even if P_{i_0} is not able to answer to the challenge, the error spotted allows for an early abort and the simulation is indistinguishable.

We have shown that G_2 simulates the multiparty signature protocol Thre.Sign, thus we need to bound the distance between the two last games. We are able to prove that the two views have the same distribution, implying null game distance.

If the simulator spots an error and aborts, the simulation is correct and indistinguishable from the real execution, since P_{i_0} followed the protocol normally. If the simulator rewind the adversary, then the view is given by salt_{i_0}, $x_{i_0}^j$, $\tilde{g}_{i_0}^j$ for all $j = 1, ..., \lambda$. The salt and the group elements are uniformly distributed both in the signature and in the simulation, so they are indistinguishable even for an unbounded adversary. Also for j with $\mathsf{ch}_j = 0$ the set elements $x_{i_0}^j$ are indistinguishable since the simulator is just following the protocol Thre.Sign.

For j with $\mathsf{ch}_j = 1$ we consider the tuples $(\tilde{x}_{i_0-1}^j, \tilde{x}_{i_0}^j)$ with $\tilde{x}_{i_0}^j = \tilde{g}_{i_0}^j \star \tilde{x}_{i_0-1}^j$ in the honest execution and $\tilde{x}_{i_0}^j = \tilde{g}_{i_0}^j \star x_{i_0}$ in the simulated ones.

We have rewound Evl, so we know that $\tilde{x}_{i_0-1}^j = u_{i_0-1}^j \star x_{i_0-1} \in \mathcal{O}(x_{i_0-1}) = \mathcal{O}(x)$. Since the group action is free, there exists a unique $\tilde{h}$ with $\tilde{x}_{i_0}^j = \tilde{h} \star \tilde{x}_{i_0-1}^j$. The element $\tilde{h}$ has the same distribution as $\tilde{g}_{i_0}^j$ thanks to the uniqueness of the solution; it follows that these pairs are again indistinguishable.

Finally, we observe that game G_2 is executed entirely without the use of the secret share g_{i_0}, thanks to the simulation, and so succeeding in the game implies being able to forge a signature for the centralized scheme in the quantum random oracle. Since we assumed quantum unforgebility for the centralized signature,

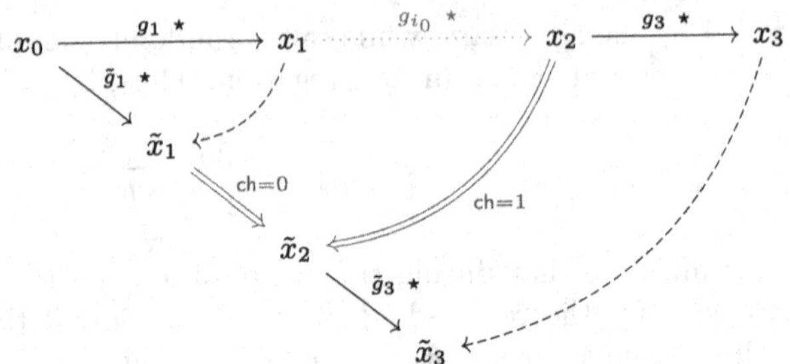

Fig. 2. Example of simulation for $N = 3$ and $i_0 = 2$, in red the missing link, while in blue the elements used to generate x_{i_0} and to answer the challenge. (Color figure online)

this probability is negligible. Combining all the game distances we prove the desired reduction by the resulting equivalence:

$$\mathsf{Adv}^{\mathsf{EvI}}_{CMA} \leqslant \frac{3g_s}{2^{1+\lambda}}\sqrt{q_h} + \mathsf{negl}(\lambda)\ .$$

□

4 Threshold via Replicated Secret Sharing

In this section, we explain how to modify the full threshold scheme, to obtain a T-out-of-N scheme, via replicated secret sharing[2] [49]. Our approach was first proposed in [32].

Definition 3. *A* monotone access structure $\mathcal{A}$ *for the parties* $\mathcal{P} := \{P_1, .., P_N\}$ *is a family of subsets* $S \subset \mathcal{P}$ *that are authorized (to sign a message) such that given any* $S \in \mathcal{A}$ *and* $S' \supset S$ *then* $S' \in \mathcal{A}$*. To each access structure we can associate a family of unqualified sets* $\mathcal{U}$ *that satisfies that for all* $S \in \mathcal{A}$, $U \in \mathcal{U}$ *then* $S \cap U = \emptyset$*. For all the section we will define the unqualified sets in the canonical way as* $\mathcal{U} = 2^{\mathcal{P}} \setminus \mathcal{A}$*.*

If we want to share a secret s in a group G for a monotone access structure $\mathcal{A}$, we need to consider the family $\mathcal{U}^+$ of the maximal unqualified set with respect to inclusion and define $\mathcal{I}$ as the family of complements for $\mathcal{U}^+$, i.e.

$$\mathcal{I} := \{I \in \mathcal{A} \mid \forall U \in \mathcal{U}\, .\, U \supseteq \mathcal{P} \setminus I \implies U = \mathcal{P} \setminus I\}\, .$$

Having fixed $M = \#\mathcal{I}$, we sort the elements in $\mathcal{I}$ as $I_1, I_2, ...$ and for each $l \in \{1, ..., M\}$ we define the shares s_l so that $s = s_1 \cdots s_M$; each party P_i is then given access to s_l if and only if $I_l \ni i$. This leads to the following (already known) result.

[2] Unfortunately, while standard linear secret sharing would be more efficient, it is difficult to use in a non-abelian setting.

Algorithm 5. Threshold Signature Simulation

procedure GAMES $G_0 - G_1 - G_2$
    Evl chose at least a non corrupted user P_{i_0};
    Execute KeyGen with Evl;
    $\mathsf{m}^*, \sigma^* \leftarrow \mathsf{Evl}^{\mathsf{Sign},|\mathsf{H}\rangle}$;
    return $\mathsf{Verify}((x, y), \sigma^*, \mathsf{m}^*) \wedge \mathsf{m}^* \notin S_M$.

procedure $\mathsf{Sign}(\mathsf{m})$
    $S_M \leftarrow S_M \cup \{\mathsf{m}\}$;
    Run $\mathsf{Thre.Sign}(\mathsf{m}, g_{i_0})$ up to line 11; ▷ $G_0 - G_1$
    $\mathsf{ch} \leftarrow \mathsf{H}(x^1 \| ... \| x^\lambda \| \mathsf{salt} \| \mathsf{m})$; ▷ G_0
    Get $\mathsf{ch} \xleftarrow{\$} \{0, 1\}^\lambda$; ▷ G_1
    $\mathsf{H} \leftarrow \mathsf{H}^{(x^1 \| ... \| x^\lambda \| \mathsf{salt} \| \mathsf{m}) \mapsto \mathsf{ch}}$; ▷ G_1
    Run $\mathsf{Thre.Sign}(\mathsf{m}, g_{i_0})$ to the end; ▷ $G_0 - G_1$
    Run $\mathsf{Sim.Thre.Sign}(\mathsf{m})$; ▷ G_2
    return $\mathsf{salt}_{i_0}, \tilde{x}^j_{i_0}, u^j_{i_0}$ for all j.

procedure $\mathrm{SIM}.\mathsf{Thre.Sign}(\mathsf{m}, g_i$ for $i \neq i_0)$
    Run $\mathsf{Thre.Sign}(\mathsf{m}, g_{i_0})$ until line 15.
    Check all the $u^j_{i_0-1}$ received.
    if At least one $u^j_{i_0-1}$ is not correct **then**:
        return 0 ▷ Abortion in Thre.Sign
    else
        Rewind Evl to line 4 after having received $x^j_{i_0-1}$
        for $j = 1, ..., \lambda$ **do**
            Get $\tilde{g}^j_{i_0} \leftarrow G$;
            Set $\tilde{g}^j_{i_0} \leftarrow \tilde{g}^j_{i_0} \cdot (g_N \cdots g_{i_0+1})^{-\mathsf{ch}_j}$;
            if $\mathsf{ch}_j = 0$ **then**
                output $x^j_{i_0} = \tilde{g}^j_{i_0} \star x^j_{i_0-1}$;
            else
                output $x^j_{i_0} = \tilde{g}^j_{i_0} \star y$;
        After receiving x^j_N, open salt_{i_0};
        if salt_i are correct **then**
            compute $\mathsf{salt} = \sum_i \mathsf{salt}_i$;
        else return 0 ▷ Abortion in Thre.Sign
        $\mathsf{H} \leftarrow \mathsf{H}^{(x^1 \| ... \| x^\lambda \| \mathsf{salt} \| \mathsf{m}) \mapsto \mathsf{ch}}$;
        Output $u^j_{i_0} = \tilde{g}^j_{i_0}$ for all j;

Proposition 1. *Any authorized subset $J \in \mathcal{A}$ of users can get the secret s, whilst any non-authorized set $A \in \mathcal{U}$ of users cannot retrieve at least one share.*

Proof. We prove that it is possible to recover the share by proving that any share s_I for $I \in \mathcal{I}$ is known by at least one user in J. In fact, suppose that there exists $I \in \mathcal{I}$ so that no user in J has access to it. This means that $I \not\ni P_i$ for all $P_i \in J$, so we have $I \cap J = \emptyset$. This implies that $S \subseteq I^c$. Since $\mathcal{A}$ is monotone, we have $I^c \in \mathcal{A}$, but I^c lies also in $\mathcal{U}^+$ (because of the definition of $\mathcal{I}$), so $I^c \in \mathcal{A} \cap \mathcal{U}$, which is impossible due to Definition 3.

For any $A \in \mathcal{U}$, we know that there exists a maximal element $B \in \mathcal{U}^+$ such that $B \supseteq A$. This implies $B^c \subseteq A^c$ and $B^c \cap A = \emptyset$. In addition, we have that $B^c \in \mathcal{I}$ by definition, but no $P_i \in A$ can have access to s_{B^c} since otherwise there would be an intersection. □

By using this proposition, the parties in the authorized set J can recover the secret just by agreeing on which one of them should be the one sharing each share, i.e. by agreeing on a turn function $\tau(J, i)$ such that $\tau(J, i) \in I_i$ (i.e. $P_{\tau(J,i)}$ knows I_i).

For the T-out-of-N scheme, the authorized sets are the ones having cardinality at least T. In this way, $\mathcal{U}^+$ are all the subsets with at most $T-1$ element, $\mathcal{I}$ the ones of cardinality $N-T+1$ and $M = \#\mathcal{I} = \binom{N}{T-1}$. The final protocol is depicted in Algorithm 6.

Algorithm 6. $\mathsf{Thre.Sign}_{T,N}$

Require: $x \in X$, a security parameter λ, a hash function H, a public key $(x, y = g \star x)$, a secure commitment scheme COM, a set J of T parties and the turn function τ. Observe that the party P_i knows all the (multiplicative) shares g_{I_j} of $g = g_{I_1} \cdots g_{I_N}$ so that $I_j \ni i$.

Ensure: A valid signature for the message m under the public key (x, y).

for $t \in J$ **do**
  P_t pick salt_t uniformly random and sends $\mathsf{COM}(\mathsf{salt}_t)$
$P_{\tau(J,1)}$ set $x_0^j = x$ for all $j = 1$ to λ ▷ Shared commitment generation phase
for $i = 1$ to M **do**
  If $i > 1$ $P_{\tau(J,i)}$ receives x_{i-1}^j from $P_{\tau(J,i-1)}$ for all $j = 1$ to λ
  for $j = 1$ to λ **do**
    $P_{\tau(J,i)}$ chooses $\tilde{g}_i^j \in G$ and computes $x_i^j = \tilde{g}_i^j \star x_{i-1}^j$
    P_i outputs x_i^j
Set $x^j = x_N^j$ for all $j = 1$ to λ. Party $\tau(J, N)$ broadcast all x^j to all players.
Each party publish salt_t and checks the consistency of the received data with the initial commitment.
$\mathsf{salt} = \sum_t \mathsf{salt}_t$
Compute $\mathsf{ch} = \mathsf{H}(x^1 \| ... \| x^\lambda \| \mathsf{salt} \| \mathsf{m})$ ▷ Non-iterative challenges evaluation
$P_{\tau(J,1)}$ set $u_0^j = e$ for all $j = 1$ to λ ▷ Shared response generation phase
for $i = 1$ to M **do**
  If $i > 1$ $P_{\tau(J,i)}$ receives u_{i-1}^j from $P_{\tau(J,i-1)}$ for all $j = 1, ..., \lambda$
  for $j = 1$ to λ **do**
    $P_{\tau(J,i)}$ computes $u_i^j = \tilde{g}_i^j u_{i-1}^j g_i^{-\mathsf{ch}_j}$
    $P_{\tau(J,i)}$ outputs u_i^j
    All users verify u_i^j is valid;
$\mathsf{resp}_j = u_N^j$ for all $j = 1$ to λ
$\mathsf{sig} = \mathsf{ch} \| \mathsf{salt} \| \mathsf{rsp}_1 \| ... \| \mathsf{rsp}_\lambda$

Distributed Key Generation. The distributed key generation protocol in Algorithm 1 can be used also in this threshold case. The central point is that during the generation each share g_i is known to several users, so to apply it on x_{i-1} they can:

1. jointly generate a shard of it and then combine the shard, essentially repeating a protocol similar to the key generation;
2. delegate one of the users that should know a share to apply it; said user can then share it with the others.

We prefer the second option since it has a lower latency for the non-abelian case, but still achieves the same security, assuming that all the users take part to at least one generation round, thanks to the zero-knowledge proofs.

The signature algorithm is also performed in the same way as the full threshold scheme, using the turn function τ to determine which party sends which messages at each round. The proof of security for this scheme is practically equal to the full threshold one: in fact, one can imagine that, after an initial phase to see who has the required shares, the scheme is essentially an (M, M)-threshold scheme.

Theorem 2. *For a 2-weakly pseudorandom free group action, if the centralized signature is unforgeable in the quantum random oracle model, then the (T, N)-threshold signature scheme composed by* KeyGen*,* $\mathsf{Thre.Sign}_{T,N}$ *adjoined with replicated secret sharing and the verification* Verify *is EUF-CMA secure in the quantum random oracle model.*

Sketch. The proof is very similar to that of the full threshold case (Theorem 1). First of all, note that, since the adversary controls at most $T-1$ players, there must be at least a set $I_{\mathsf{ho}} \in \mathcal{I}$ composed only by honest players on which the adversary has no control, as showed in the proof of Proposition 1. Thus we just use the strategies from Algorithm 4 and Algorithm 5 using as non corrupted user $P_{\tau(J,\mathsf{ho})}$. □

Usability of Replicated Secret Sharing. The main drawback of replicated secret sharing is that the number of shares grows proportionally to the cardinality of $\mathcal{U}^+$, which is usually exponential in the number of parties. In particular, in the threshold case, there are $\binom{N}{T-1}$ shares in total, and each party needs to save $\binom{N}{T}$ shares. Since the group is non-abelian, the number of rounds cannot be reduced and is equal to the total number of shares.

All of this means that the scheme is practical only in certain scenarios; for example, for $T = N$ (full threshold) or N small. For the case $T = N - 1$ and $N > 3$, the size of the shares is already linear in N and the rounds are quadratic in N. Nevertheless, we would like to point out that for the most used combinations of (T, N) such as $(2, 3)$ or $(3, 5)$, the number of shares (and rounds) is manageable and the protocol maintains an acceptable level of efficiency.

5 Concrete Instantiations

In this section, we show how several optimizations used in literature for generic group actions can also be used for this multiparty protocol. We will then present concrete instantiations of our protocols, based on the LESS and MEDS signature schemes [8,29], and discuss tailored optimizations. We will denote by ξ the bit-weight of an element of X, and γ to denote that of an element of G.

5.1 Multi-bit Challenges

Multi-bit challenges are a way to reduce the computational time at the price of bigger keys and are widely used in signature design (e.g. [34]). In a nutshell, the optimization consists of replacing the binary challenge space of the verifier with one of cardinality $r > 1$, where each challenge value corresponds to a different public key. Note that the case $r = 2$ corresponds to the original protocol. In this way, it is possible to amplify soundness, at the cost of an increase in public key size. Security is then based on a new problem:

Problem 3 (mGAIP: Multiple Group Action Inverse Problem). *Given a collection $x_0, \dots, x_{r-1}$ in X, find, if any, an element $g \in G$ and two different indices $j \neq j'$ such that $x_{j'} = g \star x_j$.*

It is folklore that this problem is equivalent to the one-wayness of the group action, e.g. see Theorem 3 from [8]. We can then consider $r - 1$ public keys $x_1, \dots, x_{r-1}$ generated from the initial element x_0 by $r - 1$ shared keys $g^{(1)}, \dots, g^{(r-1)}$ (with the notation $g^{(0)} = e$). At this point the challenge is generated as an integer $\mathsf{ch} \in \{0, \dots, r-1\}$, thus to evaluate the response (line 17) P_i computes $u_i^j = \tilde{g}_i^j u_{i-1}^j (g_i^{(\mathsf{ch}_j)})^{-1}$. As mentioned above, the soundness error is reduced to r^{-1}, thus in the signing algorithm we only need to execute $\lceil \frac{\lambda}{\log_2(r)} \rceil$ rounds, reducing both signature size and computational cost, but increasing the public key size.

5.2 Fixed-Weight Challenges

Another possible optimization is to use fixed-weight challenge strings, as shown for instance in [8,17]. Indeed, while $\mathsf{ch} = 1$ requires to send a group element, in the case $\mathsf{ch} = 0$ the Prover can simply send the PRNG seed used to generate the random group element $\tilde{g}$. This consists usually of only λ bits, thus is usually much shorter than a group element. To exploit this, we can use a hash function H that returns a vector of fixed weight ω and length t.

To avoid a security loss we need to have a *preimage security* (the difficulty of guessing in the challenge space) of still λ bits, thus t, ω are such that: $\binom{t}{\omega} \geqslant 2^\lambda$. In this way, for carefully selected parameters, we can obtain shorter signature size at the price of an higher number of rounds.

To further reduce the signature size, it is possible to send multiple seeds at the same time by using a *seed tree*. This primitive uses a secret master seed to generate t seeds recursively exploiting a binary structure: each parent node is used to generate two child nodes via a PRNG. When a subset of $t-\omega$ seeds is requested for the signature, we only need to send the appropriate nodes, reducing the space required for the seeds from $\lambda(t-\omega)$ to a value bounded above by $\lambda N_{\mathsf{seeds}}$, where

$$N_{\mathsf{seeds}} = 2^{\lceil \log(\omega) \rceil} + \omega(\lceil \log(t) \rceil - \lceil \log(\omega) \rceil - 1) ,$$

as shown in [29,48]. In [27], the author noted that, to avoid collisions attacks, a fresh salt should be used in combination of the seed tree structure. Since salt_i is already needed to achieve the security of the threshold construction, the parties could use it also for the PRNG call.

Applying this optimization to a threshold signature is not straightforward and requires particular parameters to be used. Indeed, the parties can not share a single seed used for the generation of the ephemeral map $\tilde{g}$, but have to share $M = \binom{N}{T-1}$ of them. Thus, if the challenge bit is 0, the parties need to send all the M bits, and the total communication cost becomes $M \cdot \lambda$. So, for this strategy to make sense, we need $M\lambda$ to be smaller than the weight of the group element. Moreover, in some applications, it can be desirable to not disclose the parameters T and N, and thus the fixed-weight challenge should not be used.

5.3 Scheme Parameters

When the two approaches are combined, the final signature weight result is $(N_{\mathsf{seeds}}M + 2)\lambda + \omega\gamma + t$ with t the number of rounds ($\#\mathsf{rounds}$) satisfying

$$\binom{t}{\omega}(r-1)^{\omega} \geqslant 2^{\lambda} .$$

In our signing algorithm, for each of the $\binom{N}{T-1}$ iteration of the for loop over $1, ..., M$, each user needs to send the following quantities to the next user:

- $\#\mathsf{rounds} \cdot \xi$ bits for the commitment phase,
- $\#\mathsf{rounds} \cdot \gamma + 2\lambda$ bits in general and $(N_{\mathsf{seeds}}M + 2)\lambda + \omega\gamma$ when using fixed-weight challenges.

At this point, we can see specific choices for LESS and MEDS. In our analysis, we choose the public parameters that satisfy the requirement of 128 bits of classical security and at least 64 bits of quantum security, and evaluate ξ and γ accordingly. We include here the data for the original signature schemes, as well as parameters that we found in order to optimize the sum $|\mathsf{pk}| + |\sigma|$ for the cases $(2, 3)$, $(3, 5)$ and the case without fixed-weight challenges to hide T and N.

Instantiations with LESS. From [6] we have taken the secure balanced LESS parameters for the NIST Security Category 1 $n = 252, k = 126$ (length and dimension of the code), $q = 127$ (the field size). We obtain that the size of a single code in systematic form is given by $(n-k)k\lceil \log_2(q) \rceil$ bits, so $\xi = 13.7\mathsf{KiB}$. Instead, to send a monomial map, we can use the IS-LEP technique from [57].

This recent optimization requires the use of a new canonical representation of the generator matrices via information sets. In this way, the equality can be verified using only the monomial map, truncated on the preimage of the information set, thus nearly halving the communication cost to $k(\lceil \log_2(q-1) \rceil + \lceil \log_2(n) \rceil)$ bits for each group element. This optimization (and any other possible new optimization based leveraging modified canonical forms, such as [30]) can be used also for the threshold protocol since:

- for the commitment phase, the last user can simply commit using the modified canonical form, then store the additional information received (the information set used);
- for the response phase, when the monomial map $g^{-1}\tilde{g}$ is recovered, it can be truncated again by the last user by using the additional information from the commitment.

For the cases in which fixed-weight cannot be used, we simply send all the truncated monomial maps. In this case, we can cut the signature size without enlarging too much the public key, by decreasing the code dimension to $k = 50$. Clearly, this requires to increase the code length up to $n = 440$ for $q = 127$ leading to a public key size of 17.1KiB and truncated monomial map size of 100B. Numbers are reported in Table 1, where we report, in the last column, also the total amount of exchanged data.

Table 1. Parameters for the threshold version of LESS

Case	Variant	t	ω	|pk| (KiB)	|sig| (KiB)	Exc. (MiB)
centralized	Fixed	247	30	13.7	8.4	-
(2,3)	Fixed	333	26	13.7	10.59	13.30
(3,5)	Fixed	333	26	13.7	21.09	44.43
(N,T)	$[440, 50]_{127}$	-	-	16.68	12.55	$\binom{N}{T-1}2.19$

Instantiations with MEDS. From [28] we have taken the secure parameters for the matrix code equivalence problem: $n = m = k = 14$ (matrix sizes and dimension of the code), $q = 4093$ (the field size). Thus we obtain that the size of a single code in systematic form is given by $(nm - k)k\lceil \log_2(q) \rceil$ bits, so $\xi = 3.84$KiB. Observe that in the distributed key generation case we cannot use the public key compression mechanism from [29, Section 5]. A group element is instead composed by two invertible matrices, so it has size $(n^2 + m^2)\lceil \log_2(q) \rceil$ bits and we have $\gamma = 588$B.

Numbers are reported in Table 2; as above, in the last column we report the total amount of exchanged data.

Table 2. Parameters for the threshold version of MEDS

Case	Variant	t	ω	r	|pk| (KiB)	|sig| (KiB)	Exc. (MiB)
MEDS-13220	F+M	192	20	5	13.2	13.0	-
(2,3)	F+M	291	19	4	11.26	14.49	3.24
(3,5)	F+M	113	22	6	18.76	20.80	4.34
(*,*)	M	-	-	8	26.24	24.74	$\binom{N}{T-1}0.182$
[28, Section 8]	M	-	-	3	7.50	3.37	$\binom{N}{T-1}0.342$

To reduce signature size, another compression technique for group elements is proposed in [28, Section 8], and we briefly recall it here. Consider two equivalent $[m \times n, k]$ matrix codes $\mathcal{C}$, $\mathcal{C}' = \mathbf{A}\mathcal{C}\mathbf{B}$; the core idea is that, using two pairs of independent codewords $(\mathbf{C}_i, \mathbf{C}'_i) \in \mathcal{C} \times \mathcal{C}'$ satisfying $\mathbf{A}\mathbf{C}_i\mathbf{B} = \mathbf{C}'_i$ for $i = 1, 2$, the two invertible matrices $\mathbf{A}, \mathbf{B}$ can be recovered in polynomial time just by solving the system:

$$\begin{cases} \mathbf{A}\mathbf{C}_1 = \mathbf{C}'_1\mathbf{B}^{-1} \\ \mathbf{A}\mathbf{C}_2 = \mathbf{C}'_2\mathbf{B}^{-1} \end{cases} . \tag{3}$$

Note that this is the same process used for key compression in [28, Section 3.2]. To see how it is implemented for the MEDS signature, it is enough to see [28, Section 8]; in here, instead, we propose a slightly less efficient version which is however more suitable for the multiparty calculations (in which the last user modifies its execution).

- **Commitment**: the last user generates via a public seed a full-rank matrix $\mathbf{R} \in \mathbb{F}_q^{2\times mn}$, i.e. random independent codewords, and takes two random codewords in the code received by the previous user. Finally he solves Eq. (3) to get $\tilde{\mathbf{A}}_M, \tilde{\mathbf{B}}_M$ and evaluate the final code as usual.
- **Response**: At the end of the response phase, the last user has access (for each round) to $\tilde{\mathbf{A}}, \tilde{\mathbf{B}}$ such that $\mathrm{SF}(\mathbf{G}_{\mathsf{ch}}(\tilde{\mathbf{A}}^\top \otimes \tilde{\mathbf{B}})) = \tilde{\mathbf{G}}$, thus from $\mathbf{R}$ he can find the two associated codewords that can be used to recover the group element as $\mathbf{R}(\tilde{\mathbf{A}}^\top \otimes \tilde{\mathbf{B}})^{-1}$. Since these codewords are in the code $\mathcal{C}_{\mathsf{ch}}$, they can be represented as linear combinations of the $\mathbf{G}_{\mathsf{ch}}$ rows, i.e. as a $2 \times k$ matrix $\mathbf{M}$ such that
$$\mathbf{R}(\tilde{\mathbf{A}}^\top \otimes \tilde{\mathbf{B}})^{-1} = \mathbf{M}\mathbf{G}_{\mathsf{ch}} .$$
From $\mathbf{M}$, the verifier can recover the group element as explained in [28, Section 8]; thus, the communication cost per round is cut down to $2k\lceil \log_2(q)\rceil$ bits.

Remark 1. Unlike the original optimization, in this case we do not know the change-of-basis matrix used in the public key, implying that:

- there are additional linear systems to be solved since we need to invert $(\tilde{\mathbf{A}}^\top \otimes \tilde{\mathbf{B}})$ and find $\mathbf{M}$;

- in the case $\mathsf{ch} = 0$, we cannot save space by sending only the seed used to sample the codewords. To be precise, we could send it together with the seeds used for the previous ephemeral elements, but in most cases it would not save space since seeds and $2 \times k$ matrices have comparable sizes.

5.4 Latency

Because of the *sequential round-robin* structure each party must wait for the previous one results to start its execution, both during the commitment and the response phase, thus increasing the latency of the protocol. Usually the most expensive computation is the group action evaluation, so we can estimate the latency per round as t group actions for the commitment phase and t group actions for the response, since each of the users (in particular the one responsible to publish u_i^j) verify the previous user responses. Thus, we have $2Mt$group actions, where M is the number of shares equal to $\binom{N}{T-1}$ while t is the number of repetitions for the basic identification protocol. Note that these are already much less then the group actions estimated for Sashimi in Sect. 4.1 [32].

The latency can be lowered by observing that, if several consecutive rounds are assigned to the same user, the required group actions can be reduced to only one by previously multiplying the group elements, both during commitment and verification phase. For example, in the 2-out of-N case where for each user misses only one of the secret shares, we can always chose the turn function τ so that the rounds can be divided in two consecutive series assigned to the two parties, thus compressing the latency to just $4t$ group actions per user. An estimate and comparison of the latency for the different protocols can be seen in Table 3.

Table 3. Comparison of the estimated latency for the 2-out of-N case for Sashimi (from [32]) and the threshold version of LESS and MEDS proposed in this work. We assumed a latency per group actions of 0.21 ms for LESS [6] and 0.24 ms for MEDS [28].

Per party:	Sashimi	T-LESS	T-MEDS
# gr. actions	55377	1332	1164
time	283 s	279 ms	230 ms

6 Conclusions

We introduced a threshold signature scheme based on the Group Action Inverse Problem that is agnostic about which particular group action is used, and works without any further hypotheses. Our schemes are similar to well-known abelian group action threshold schemes such as the one presented in [25,32,35], and share the strictly sequential round-robin communication sequence. Unfortunately, this structure seems to be unavoidable due to the inherent properties of group action computation.

Additionally, we were able to prove the security of the key generation algorithm using fewer ZKPs than in [32]. Differently from [25,35], we use the jointly generated salt to reduce the security of the scheme to that of the centralized one without relying on intensive use of ZKPs, cutting by a lot communication cost and overhead computations.

When instantiated, our proposed schemes benefit from optimizations in use, eventually adapted to the multiparty scenario, and are practical for several real-world instances, such as $(2,3)$ or $(3,5)$ sharing, but cannot be used for arbitrary (T,N) since the number of shares required grows as a binomial coefficient.

Acknowledgement. This publication was created with the co-financing of the European Union FSE-REACT-EU, PON Research and Innovation 2014-2020 DM1062/2021. The authors acknowledge support from Ripple's University Blockchain Research Initiative. The first author acknowledges support from TIM S.p.A. through the Ph.D. scholarship. The second author acknowledges support from Telsy S.p.A. and De Componendis Cifris through the M.Sc. scholarship and Collegio Clesio. The third author is a member of the INdAM Research Group GNSAGA. The fourth author acknowledges support from NSF through grant 1906360 and NSA through grant H98230-22-1-0328.

All the authors would like to thank Giuseppe D'Alconzo and Leonardo Errati for their comments and suggestions.

The core of this work is contained also in the second author's M.Sc. thesis.

A Coding Theory Notions

A linear code $\mathcal{C}$ is a vector subspace $\mathcal{C} \subseteq \mathbb{F}_q^n$ of dimension k, and it is usually referred to as an $[n,k]$ linear code. It follows that a basis for $\mathcal{C}$ is given by a set of k linearly independent vectors in $\mathbb{F}_q^n$. When these vectors are put as rows of a matrix $\mathbf{G}$, this is known as a *generator matrix* for the code, as it can generate each vector of $\mathcal{C}$ (i.e. a *codeword*) as a linear combination of its rows. Note that such a generator is not unique, and any invertible $k \times k$ matrix $\mathbf{S}$ yields another generator via a change of basis; however, it is always possible to utilize a "standard" form simply performing a Gaussian elimination on the left-hand side. This is usually called *systematic* if the result is the identity matrix (i.e. if the leftmost $k \times k$ block is invertible); we denote this by SF.

Linear codes are traditionally measured with the Hamming metric, which associates a *weight* to each codeword by simply counting the number of its non-zero entries. It follows, then, that an *isometry* (i.e. a map preserving the weight) is given by any $n \times n$ permutation matrix $\mathbf{P}$ acting on each word, or indeed, on the columns of $\mathbf{G}$ (since every codeword can be generated as a linear combination of the rows of $\mathbf{G}$). Moreover, it is possible to generalize this notion by adding some non-zero scaling factors from $\mathbb{F}_q$ to each column. Such a matrix is commonly known as a *monomial* matrix, and we denote it by $\mathbf{Q}$; it can be seen as a product $\boldsymbol{D} \cdot \mathbf{P}$ between a permutation matrix and a diagonal matrix with non-zero components.

The notion of linear codes can be generalized to the case where each codeword is a matrix, instead of a vector; more precisely, $m \times n$ matrices over $\mathbb{F}_q$. We talk then about $[m \times n, k]$ *matrix code*, which can be seen as a k-dimensional subspace $\mathcal{C}$ of $\mathbb{F}_q^{m \times n}$. These objects are usually measured with a different metric, known as *rank* metric, where the weight of each codeword corresponds to its rank as a matrix. In this case, then, isometries are maps which preserve the rank of a matrix, and are thus identified by two non-singular matrices $\mathbf{A} \in \mathrm{GL}_m$ and $\mathbf{B} \in \mathrm{GL}_n$ acting respectively on the left and on the right of each codeword, by multiplication.

In both of the metrics defined above, we are able to formulate a notion of *equivalence* in the same way, by saying that two codes are equivalent if they are connected by an isometry. In other words, with a slight abuse of notation, we say that two linear codes $\mathcal{C}$ and $\mathcal{C}'$ are *linearly equivalent* if $\mathcal{C}' = \mathcal{C}\mathbf{Q}$, and two matrix codes $\mathcal{C}$ and $\mathcal{C}'$ are *matrix equivalent* if $\mathcal{C}' = \mathbf{A}\mathcal{C}\mathbf{B}$. Note that the notion of *permutation equivalence* is just a special case of linear equivalence (with the diagonal matrix $\boldsymbol{D}$ being the identity matrix), yet is often treated separately for a variety of reasons of both historical and practical nature (for instance, certain solvers behave quite differently).

B Signatures from Generic Group Actions

We summarize here briefly how to design a signature scheme from generic group actions. To begin, we formulate the Sigma protocol described in Fig. 3.

Public Data : Group G acting on X via $\star$, element $x \in X$ and hash function H.
Private Key : Group element g with $g_i \in G$.
Public Key : $y = g \star x$.

PROVER		**VERIFIER**
Get $\tilde{g} \xleftarrow{\$} G$, send $\mathsf{com} = \mathsf{H}(\tilde{g} \star x)$	$\xrightarrow{\mathsf{com}}$	
	$\xleftarrow{\mathsf{ch}}$	$\mathsf{ch} \xleftarrow{\$} \{0,1\}$.
If $\mathsf{ch} = 0$ then $\mathsf{rsp} \leftarrow \tilde{g}$.	$\xrightarrow{\mathsf{rsp}}$	Accept if $\mathsf{H}(\mathsf{rsp} \star x) = \mathsf{com}$.
If $\mathsf{ch} = 1$ then $\mathsf{rsp} \leftarrow \tilde{g}g^{-1}$.		Accept if $\mathsf{H}(\mathsf{rsp} \star y) = \mathsf{com}$.

Fig. 3. Identification protocol for the knowledge of the private key.

The protocol above intuitively provides a soundness error of 1/2; it is in fact trivial to prove that an adversary who could solve answer both challenges simultaneuosly, would be able to recover a solution to GAIP. It is then necessary to amplify soundness, in order to reach the desired authentication level. This is accomplished, in the simplest way, by parallel repetition; in practice, several optimizations can be applied, as we will see in Sect. 5, without impacting security. At this point, a signature scheme can be obtained using the Fiat-Shamir transformation [41], which guarantees EUF-CMA security in the (Quantum) Random Oracle Model. The next result is intentionally a little vague, since it is well-known in literature, and we do not want to overly expand this section.

Proofs tailored to the specific instantiations can be found, for example, in [8,34]. For further discussions on Fiat-Shamir, and its security in the ROM and QROM, we point instead the reader to [1,38,41,52].

Proposition 2. *Let* I *be the identification protocol described above, and* $\mathbf{S}$ *be the signature scheme obtained by iterating* I *and then applying Fiat-Shamir. Then* $\mathbf{S}$ *is existentially unforgeable against chosen-message attacks, based on the hardness of GAIP.*

Note that the protocol does not require any specific property from the group action in use, except those connected to efficient sampling and computation. Indeed, even though the action could in principle be non-transitive, as is the case for code-based group actions, the construction makes it so that we operate on a single orbit (i.e. it is transitive by design in this specific use case). It is however advisable to utilize a free group action, since this could have an impact on the difficulty of GAIP.

C Code-Based Group Actions

We now present the group action associated to code equivalence, according to the definitions given in the previous sections. First, consider the set $X \subseteq \mathbb{F}_q^{k\times n}$ of all full-rank $k \times n$ matrices, i.e. the set of generator matrices of $[n, k]$-linear codes. We then set $G = \mathsf{M}_n$, by which we denote the group of monomial matrices. Note that this group is isomorphic to $(\mathbb{F}_q^*)^n \rtimes \mathsf{S}_n$ if we decompose each monomial matrix $\mathbf{Q} \in \mathsf{M}_n$ into a product $\boldsymbol{D} \cdot \mathbf{P}$. The group operation can be then seen simply as multiplication, and the group action is given by

$$\begin{aligned} \star : G \times X &\to X \\ (\mathbf{G}, \mathbf{Q}) &\to \mathrm{SF}(\mathbf{GQ}) \end{aligned}$$

It is easy to see that the action is well-formed, with the identity element being $\mathbf{I}_n$, and compatible with respect to (right) multiplication.

Remark 2. The definition above considers a standardized choice of representative by utilizing the systematic form SF. This simplifies the definition and makes sure to avoid cases where multiple generators for the same code could be chosen. Indeed, since the systematic form uniquely identifies linear codes, this allows us to see our group action as effectively acting on linear codes, rather than on their representatives (generator matrices).

The case of matrix code equivalence can be framed analogously. In this case, the set X is formed by the k-dimensional matrix codes of size $m \times n$ over some base field $\mathbb{F}_q$; similarly to linear codes, matrix codes can be represented via generator matrices $\mathbf{G} \in \mathbb{F}_q^{k\times mn}$. Then, the action of the group $G = \mathrm{GL}_m \times \mathrm{GL}_n$ on this set can be described compactly as follows:

$$\begin{aligned} \star : G \times X &\to X \\ ((\mathbf{A}, \mathbf{B}), \mathbf{G}) &\to \mathrm{SF}(\mathbf{G}(\mathbf{A}^\top \otimes \mathbf{B})) \end{aligned}$$

Note that this is equivalent to applying the matrices **A** and **B** to each codeword **C** in the matrix code as **ACB**; indeed this is often the most convenient notation.

Note that, in both cases, the action is not commutative and in general neither transitive nor free. It is however possible to restrict the set X to a single well-chosen orbit to make the group action both transitive and free. In fact, picking any orbit generated from some starting code ensures transitivity, and the group action is free if the chosen code has a trivial automorphism group, where trivial means up to scalars in $\mathbb{F}_q$. The non-commutativity is both a positive and negative feature: although it limits the cryptographical design possibilities, e.g. key exchange becomes hard, it prevents quantum attacks to which commutative cryptographic group actions are vulnerable, such as Kuperberg's algorithm for the dihedral Hidden Subgroup Problem [50].

The vectorization problems for the code-based group actions are well-known problems in coding theory. We report them below.

Problem 4 (Linear Equivalence (LEP)). *Given two k-dimensional linear codes* $\mathcal{C}, \mathcal{C}' \subseteq \mathbb{F}_q^n$, *find, if any,* $\mathbf{Q} \in M_n$ *such that* $\mathcal{C}' = \mathcal{C}\mathbf{Q}$.

We have not defined explicitly here the *Permutation Equivalence Problem (PEP)*, since we will not use it directly; this can be seen as just a special case of LEP, where the monomial matrix **Q** is a permutation.

Problem 5 (Matrix Code Equivalence (MCE)). *Given two k-dimensional matrix codes* $\mathcal{C}, \mathcal{C}'$, *find, if any,* $\mathbf{A} \in \mathrm{GL}_m, \mathbf{B} \in \mathrm{GL}_n$ *such that* $\mathcal{C}' = \mathbf{A}\mathcal{C}\mathbf{B}$.

Note that both of the above problems are traditionally formulated as decisional problems. Extensive discussion of their hardness is given, for instance, in [9,29].

D Zero-Knowledge Proof for Action Equality

In the Distributed Key Generation given in Algorithm 1, we need a proof for the knowledge of a set element g_i such that the following relation holds:

$$y_i = g_i \star x \wedge x_i = g_i \star x_{i-1} \, .$$

The protocol presented below is a straightforward generalization of the one presented in Sect. 3.1 of [32], for a general group action.

Public Data : $x_a, x_b \in X$ and hash function H.		
Private Key : Group element $g \in G$.		
Public Key : $y_a = g \star x_a$ and $y_b = g \star x_b$.		
PROVER		**VERIFIER**
Choose $\tilde{g} \xleftarrow{\$} G$ and set: $\tilde{x}_a = \tilde{g} \star x_a$, $\tilde{x}_b = \tilde{g} \star x_b$. Set com $= \mathsf{H}(\tilde{x}_a \| \tilde{x}_b)$.	$\xrightarrow{\mathsf{com}}$	
	$\xleftarrow{\mathsf{ch}}$	ch $\xleftarrow{\$} \{0,1\}$.
If ch $= 0$ then rsp $= \tilde{g}$.	$\xrightarrow{\mathsf{rsp}}$	Accept if $\mathsf{H}(\mathsf{rsp} \star x_a \| \mathsf{rsp} \star x_b) =$ com.
If ch $= 1$ then rsp $= \tilde{g}g^{-1}$.		Accept if $\mathsf{H}(\mathsf{rsp} \star y_a \| \mathsf{rsp} \star y_b) =$ com.

Fig. 4. One round of the identification protocol prove that the Private Key is used for the calculation.

For completeness we report here the proof of security for the non interactive version of the protocol, contained in [32] and [16].

Proposition 3. *The protocol in Fig. 4 can be rendered to a non interactive computationally zero-knowledge quantum proof of knowledge for a free 2-weakly pseudorandom group actions in the QROM.*

Proof. First we prove that the underlying protocol is complete, sound and computationally zero-knowledge. The completeness is straightforward. We need to prove soundness and zero knowledge.

- **Soundness:** suppose that the Prover is able to answer both the challenges with u_0 and u_1, by the collision resistance of the hash function at this point we would retrieve g as $u_1^{-1}u_0$ against the one wayness of the group action (thus also against 2-weakly pseudorandomness) and having that the public keys are generated by the same group elements.
- **Zero Knowledge:** to simulate the protocol without knowing the secret g and for any pairs of elements (x_a, y_a), (x_b, y_b) the Prover flips a coin c. If $c = 0$, the Prover follows the protocol normally and is able to answer the challenge if $b = 0$. If $c = 1$, it computes $\bar{x}_a = \bar{g}y_a$ and $\bar{x}_b = \bar{g}y_b$ and sends them in place of $\tilde{x}_a$ and $\tilde{x}_b$. In this way it is able to answer to the challenge $b = 1$. Thus, if $c = b$ the prover can convince the verifier, otherwise it rewind the verifier and try again. Since at every iteration the prover has probability $\frac{1}{2}$ of guessing the correct c the simulation ends in expected polynomial time. Note that this transcript is indistinguishable from the honestly-obtained one, because a distinguisher between the honestly generated transcripts and the simulated one can be used to distinguish pairs $(\bar{x}, g \star \bar{a})$ from random ones, against the 2-weakly pseudorandomness.

For the quantum resistance we can observe that since the automorphisms are all trivial the sigma protocol has perfect unique responses (see [20, Lemma 1]) then by [38, Theorem 25] the protocol is a quantum proof of knowledge. Then the protocol has completeness, high min entropy[3] and HVZK and is zero-knowledge against quantum adversaries thanks to [59]. □

References

1. Abdalla, M., An, J.H., Bellare, M., Namprempre, C.: From identification to signatures via the Fiat-Shamir transform: minimizing assumptions for security and forward-security. In: Knudsen, L.R. (ed.) EUROCRYPT 2002. LNCS, vol. 2332, pp. 418–433. Springer, Heidelberg (2002). https://doi.org/10.1007/3-540-46035-7_28
2. Aguilar Melchor, C., et al.: HQC. NIST PQC Submission (2020)
3. Alamati, N., De Feo, L., Montgomery, H., Patranabis, S.: Cryptographic group actions and applications. In: Moriai, S., Wang, H. (eds.) ASIACRYPT 2020. LNCS, vol. 12492, pp. 411–439. Springer, Cham (2020). https://doi.org/10.1007/978-3-030-64834-3_14
4. Albrecht, M.R., et al.: Classic McEliece. NIST PQC Submission (2020)
5. Aragon, N., et al.: BIKE. NIST PQC Submission (2020)
6. Baldi, M., et al.: Matrix equivalence digital signature (2023). https://www.less-project.com/LESS-2023-08-18.pdf. Accessed 15 Sept 2023
7. Barenghi, A., Biasse, J.-F., Ngo, T., Persichetti, E., Santini, P.: Advanced signature functionalities from the code equivalence problem. Cryptology ePrint Archive, Paper 2022/710 (2022). https://eprint.iacr.org/2022/710
8. Barenghi, A., Biasse, J.-F., Persichetti, E., Santini, P.: LESS-FM: fine-tuning signatures from the code equivalence problem. In: Cheon, J.H., Tillich, J.P. (eds.) PQCrypto 2021. LNCS, vol. 12841, pp. 23–43. Springer, Cham (2021). https://doi.org/10.1007/978-3-030-81293-5_2
9. Barenghi, A., Biasse, J.-F., Persichetti, E., Santini, P.: On the computational hardness of the code equivalence problem in cryptography. Adv. Math. Commun. **17**(1), 23–55 (2023)
10. Basso, A., et al.: Supersingular curves you can trust. In: Hazay, C., Stam, M. (eds.) EUROCRYPT 2023. LNCS, vol. 14005, pp. 405–437. Springer, Cham (2023). https://doi.org/10.1007/978-3-031-30617-4_14
11. Battagliola, M., Galli, A., Longo, R., Meneghetti, A.: A provably-unforgeable threshold schnorr signature with an offline recovery party. In: DLT2022 at Itasec 2022, CEUR Workshop Proceedings (2022)
12. Battagliola, M., Longo, R., Meneghetti, A.: Extensible decentralized secret sharing and application to schnorr signatures (2022). https://eprint.iacr.org/2022/1551
13. Battagliola, M., Longo, R., Meneghetti, A., Sala, M.: A provably-unforgeable threshold EdDSA with an offline recovery party (2020). https://arxiv.org/abs/2009.01631
14. Battagliola, M., Longo, R., Meneghetti, A., Sala, M.: Threshold ECDSA with an offline recovery party. Mediterr. J. Math. **19**(4) (2022)
15. Bellare, M., Neven, G.: Multi-signatures in the plain public-key model and a general forking lemma. In: Proceedings of the 13th ACM Conference on Computer and Communications Security, CCS 2006, pp. 390–399. Association for Computing Machinery, New York (2006)

[3] i.e. the probability of guessing the commitment is negligible.

16. Beullens, W., Disson, L., Pedersen, R., Vercauteren, F.: CSI-RAShi: distributed key generation for CSIDH. In: Cheon, J.H., Tillich, J.P. (eds.) PQCrypto 2021. LNCS, vol. 12841, pp. 257–276. Springer, Cham (2021). https://doi.org/10.1007/978-3-030-81293-5_14
17. Beullens, W., Katsumata, S., Pintore, F.: Calamari and Falafl: logarithmic (linkable) ring signatures from isogenies and lattices. Cryptology ePrint Archive, Paper 2020/646 (2020). https://eprint.iacr.org/2020/646
18. Beullens, W., Kleinjung, T., Vercauteren, F.: CSI-FiSh: efficient isogeny based signatures through class group computations. In: Galbraith, S., Moriai, S. (eds.) ASIACRYPT 2019. LNCS, vol. 11921, pp. 227–247. Springer, Cham (2019). https://doi.org/10.1007/978-3-030-34578-5_9
19. Biasse, J.-F., Micheli, G., Persichetti, E., Santini, P.: Less is more: code-based signatures without syndromes. In: Nitaj, A., Youssef, A. (eds.) AFRICACRYPT 2020. LNCS, vol. 12174, pp. 45–65. Springer, Cham (2020). https://doi.org/10.1007/978-3-030-51938-4_3
20. Bläser, M., et al.: On digital signatures based on isomorphism problems: qrom security, ring signatures, and applications. Cryptology ePrint Archive (2022)
21. Boneh, D., Gennaro, R., Goldfeder, S.: Using level-1 homomorphic encryption to improve threshold DSA signatures for bitcoin wallet security. In: Lange, T., Dunkelman, O. (eds.) LATINCRYPT 2017. LNCS, vol. 11368, pp. 352–377. Springer, Cham (2017). https://doi.org/10.1007/978-3-030-25283-0_19
22. Bonte, C., Smart, N.P., Tanguy, T.: Thresholdizing hasheddsa: MPC to the rescue. Int. J. Inf. Secur. **20**, 879–894 (2021)
23. Brandão, L.T.A.N., Davidson, M.: Notes on threshold eddsa/schnorr signatures. Accessed 01 May 2023
24. Brandão, L.T.A.N., Davidson, M., Vassilev, A.: NIST roadmap toward criteria for threshold schemes for cryptographic primitives. Accessed 27 Aug 2020
25. Campos, F., Muth, P.: On actively secure fine-grained access structures from isogeny assumptions. In: Cheon, J.H., Johansson, T. (eds.) PQCrypto 2022. LNCS, vol. 13512, pp. 375–398. Springer, Cham (2022). https://doi.org/10.1007/978-3-031-17234-2_18
26. Castryck, W., Lange, T., Martindale, C., Panny, L., Renes, J.: CSIDH: an efficient post-quantum commutative group action. In: Peyrin, T., Galbraith, S. (eds.) ASIACRYPT 2018. LNCS, vol. 11274, pp. 395–427. Springer, Cham (2018). https://doi.org/10.1007/978-3-030-03332-3_15
27. Chailloux, A.: On the (in) security of optimized stern-like signature schemes. In: WCC (2022)
28. Chou, T., et al.: Matrix equivalence digital signature (2023). https://meds-pqc.org/spec/MEDS-2023-05-31.pdf. Accessed 12 Sept 2023
29. Chou, T., Niederhagen, R., Persichetti, E., Randrianarisoa, T.H., Reijnders, K., Samardjiska, S., Trimoska, M.: Take your meds: digital signatures from matrix code equivalence. In: El Mrabet, N., De Feo, L., Duquesne, S. (eds.) AFRICACRYPT 2023. LNCS, vol. 14064, pp. 28–52. Springer, Cham (2023). https://doi.org/10.1007/978-3-031-37679-5_2
30. Chou, T., Persichetti, E., Santini, P.: On linear equivalence, canonical forms, and digital signatures (2023). https://tungchou.github.io/papers/leq.pdf. Accessed 20 Sept 2023
31. Cozzo, D., Smart, N.P.: Sharing the LUOV: threshold post-quantum signatures. In: Albrecht, M. (ed.) IMACC 2019. LNCS, vol. 11929, pp. 128–153. Springer, Cham (2019). https://doi.org/10.1007/978-3-030-35199-1_7

32. Cozzo, D., Smart, N.P.: Sashimi: cutting up CSI-FiSh secret keys to produce an actively secure distributed signing protocol. In: Ding, J., Tillich, J.-P. (eds.) PQCrypto 2020. LNCS, vol. 12100, pp. 169–186. Springer, Cham (2020). https://doi.org/10.1007/978-3-030-44223-1_10
33. D'Alconzo, G., Scala, A.J.D.: Representations of group actions and their applications in cryptography. Cryptology ePrint Archive, Paper 2023/1247 (2023)
34. De Feo, L., Galbraith, S.D.: SeaSign: compact isogeny signatures from class group actions. In: Ishai, Y., Rijmen, V. (eds.) EUROCRYPT 2019. LNCS, vol. 11478, pp. 759–789. Springer, Cham (2019). https://doi.org/10.1007/978-3-030-17659-4_26
35. De Feo, L., Meyer, M.: Threshold schemes from isogeny assumptions. In: Kiayias, A., Kohlweiss, M., Wallden, P., Zikas, V. (eds.) PKC 2020. LNCS, vol. 12111, pp. 187–212. Springer, Cham (2020). https://doi.org/10.1007/978-3-030-45388-6_7
36. Doerner, J., Kondi, Y., Lee, E., Shelat, A.: Secure two-party threshold ECDSA from ECDSA assumptions. In: 2018 IEEE Symposium on Security and Privacy (SP), pp. 980–997. IEEE (2018)
37. Doerner, J., Kondi, Y., Lee, E., Shelat, A.: Threshold ECDSA from ECDSA assumptions: the multiparty case. In: 2019 IEEE Symposium on Security and Privacy (SP), pp. 1051–1066. IEEE (2019)
38. Don, J., Fehr, S., Majenz, C., Schaffner, C.: Security of the Fiat-Shamir transformation in the quantum random-oracle model. In: Boldyreva, A., Micciancio, D. (eds.) CRYPTO 2019. LNCS, vol. 11693. Springer, Cham (2019). https://doi.org/10.1007/978-3-030-26951-7_13
39. Feneuil, T., Joux, A., Rivain, M.: Syndrome decoding in the head: shorter signatures from zero-knowledge proofs. In: Dodis, Y., Shrimpton, T. (eds.) CRYPTO 2022. LNCS, vol. 13508, pp. 541–572. Springer, Cham (2022). https://doi.org/10.1007/978-3-031-15979-4_19
40. Feneuil, T., Joux, A., Rivain, M.: Shared permutation for syndrome decoding: new zero-knowledge protocol and code-based signature. Des. Codes Crypt. **91**(2), 563–608 (2023)
41. Fiat, A., Shamir, A.: How to prove yourself: practical solutions to identification and signature problems. In: Odlyzko, A.M. (ed.) CRYPTO 1986. LNCS, vol. 263. Springer, Heidelberg (1987). https://doi.org/10.1007/3-540-47721-7_12
42. Gennaro, R., Goldfeder, S.: Fast multiparty threshold ECDSA with fast trustless setup. In: Proceedings of the 2018 ACM SIGSAC Conference on Computer and Communications Security, pp. 1179–1194 (2018)
43. Gennaro, R., Goldfeder, S., Narayanan, A.: Threshold-optimal DSA/ECDSA signatures and an application to bitcoin wallet security. In: Manulis, M., Sadeghi, A.R., Schneider, S. (eds.) ACNS 2016. LNCS, vol. 9696, pp. 156–174. Springer, Cham (2016). https://doi.org/10.1007/978-3-319-39555-5_9
44. Gennaro, R., Jarecki, S., Krawczyk, H., Rabin, T.: Robust threshold DSS signatures. In: Maurer, U. (ed.) EUROCRYPT 1996. LNCS, vol. 1070, pp. 354–371. Springer, Heidelberg (1996). https://doi.org/10.1007/3-540-68339-9_31
45. Gennaro, R., Jarecki, S., Krawczyk, H., Rabin, T.: Secure distributed key generation for discrete-log based cryptosystems. In: Stern, J. (ed.) EUROCRYPT 1999. LNCS, vol. 1592. Springer, Heidelberg (1999). https://doi.org/10.1007/3-540-48910-X_21
46. Gennaro, R., Jarecki, S., Krawczyk, H., Rabin, T.: Secure distributed key generation for discrete-log based cryptosystems. J. Cryptol. **20**, 51–83 (2007)
47. Grilo, A.B., Hövelmanns, K., Hülsing, A., Majenz, C.: Tight adaptive reprogramming in the QROM. In: Tibouchi, M., Wang, H. (eds.) ASIACRYPT 2021. LNCS, vol. 13090. Springer, Cham (2021). https://doi.org/10.1007/978-3-030-92062-3_22

48. Gueron, S., Persichetti, E., Santini, P.: Designing a practical code-based signature scheme from zero-knowledge proofs with trusted setup. Cryptography **6**(1), 5 (2022)
49. Ito, M., Saito, A., Nishizeki, T.: Secret sharing scheme realizing general access structure. Electron. Commun. Japan **72**(9), 56–64 (1989)
50. Kuperberg, G.: Another subexponential-time quantum algorithm for the dihedral hidden subgroup problem. In: Severini, S., Brandão, F.G.S.L. (eds.) TQC 2013. LIPIcs, vol. 22. Schloss Dagstuhl (2013)
51. Lindell, Y.: Fast secure two-party ECDSA signing. In: Katz, J., Shacham, H. (eds.) CRYPTO 2017. LNCS, vol. 10402. Springer, Cham (2017). https://doi.org/10.1007/978-3-319-63715-0_21
52. Liu, Q., Zhandry, M.: Revisiting post-quantum Fiat-Shamir. In: Boldyreva, A., Micciancio, D. (eds.) CRYPTO 2019. LNCS, vol. 11693, pp. 326–355. Springer, Cham (2019). https://doi.org/10.1007/978-3-030-26951-7_12
53. MacKenzie, P., Reiter, M.K.: Two-party generation of DSA signatures. In: Kilian, J. (ed.) CRYPTO 2001. LNCS, vol. 2139, pp. 137–154. Springer, Heidelberg (2001). https://doi.org/10.1007/3-540-44647-8_8
54. MacKenzie, P., Reiter, M.K.: Two-party generation of DSA signatures. Int. J. Inf. Secur. (2004)
55. NIST. Post-Quantum Cryptography Standardization (2017). https://csrc.nist.gov/Projects/Post-Quantum-Cryptography
56. NIST. Call for Additional Digital Signature Schemes for the Post-Quantum Cryptography Standardization Process (2023). https://csrc.nist.gov/projects/pqc-dig-sig/standardization/call-for-proposals
57. Persichetti, E., Santini, P.: A new formulation of the linear equivalence problem and shorter less signatures. Cryptology ePrint Archive (2023)
58. Schwabe, P., et al.: CRYSTALS-KYBER. NIST PQC Submission (2020)
59. Unruh, D.: Post-quantum security of Fiat-Shamir. In: Takagi, T., Peyrin, T. (eds.) ASIACRYPT 2017. LNCS, vol. 10624, pp. 65–95. Springer, Cham (2017). https://doi.org/10.1007/978-3-319-70694-8_3

Author Index

A
Abla, Parhat 319
Aguilar-Melchor, Carlos 163
Albrecht, Martin R. 163

B
Bailleux, Thomas 163
Battagliola, Michele 460
Bindel, Nina 163
Blazy, Olivier 3
Borin, Giacomo 460

D
Delerablée, Cécile 224
Dobraunig, Christoph 381

E
Eichlseder, Maria 381

F
Faisal, Islam 404
Ferreira, Loïc 25

G
Gao, Wen 249
Gouriou, Lénaïck 224

H
Howe, James 163
Hu, Yupu 354
Hülsing, Andreas 163

J
Jia, Huiwen 354
Joseph, David 163
Joye, Marc 277

L
Li, Chao 78
Li, Yingxin 78
Liu, Guoqiang 78
Lu, Jiqiang 136

M
Manzano, Marc 163
Mendel, Florian 381
Meneghetti, Alessio 187, 460
Mukherjee, Sayantan 3

N
Naito, Yusuke 51, 112
Nikov, Ventzislav 433
Nikova, Svetla 433

O
Ogilvie, Tabitha 292

P
Persichetti, Edoardo 460
Pointcheval, David 224

S
Sasaki, Yu 112
Schläffer, Martin 381
Shi, Jiali 78
Signorini, Edoardo 187
Sugawara, Takeshi 112

T
Tang, Chunming 354
Toprakhisar, Dilara 433

W
Wang, Baocang 249
Wang, Lin 354

Y
Yan, Yingfei 249

Z
Zhao, Yongjun 249
Zhou, Wenchang 136

E. Oswald (Ed.): CT-RSA 2024, LNCS 14643, p. 491, 2024.
https://doi.org/10.1007/978-3-031-58868-6

Author Index

Printed in the United States
by Baker & Taylor Publisher Services